TEXT, CASES AND M
ON CONTRACT

This clear and highly accessible volume, presented in a coherent structure, provides full coverage of the topics commonly found in the contract law syllabus, alongside up-to-date illustrative case examples and stimulating commentary.

Written by leading authors in the field, this book takes account of a variety of theoretical perspectives, including economic, relational and empirical conceptions of the law. A meticulous and insightful commentary is provided throughout, illuminating complex areas of law and promoting more detailed analysis of important issues.

Composed of one-quarter authors' commentaries and three-quarters cases and materials, including academic articles and extracts from books and Law Commission papers, this book facilitates the development of personal study skills and encourages readers to engage with the leading academic commentaries in the area (extracts are included from the Principles of European Contract Law to create a solid foundation for comparative analysis). Clearly signposted chapter introductions (with short table of contents to aid navigation) highlight the salient features under discussion and learning support is provided in a regularly updated companion website. Additional reading collected at the end of each chapter guides further study and independent research.

The range of material covered and the straightforward style makes this book an invaluable resource for all undergraduate students of contract law.

Richard Stone is Professor of Law at the University of Lincoln.

Ralph Cunnington is Lecturer in Law at the University of Birmingham.

TEXT, CASES AND MATERIALS ON CONTRACT LAW

Richard Stone and Ralph Cunnington

Routledge·Cavendish
Taylor & Francis Group
LONDON AND NEW YORK

First published 2007 by Routledge-Cavendish
2 Park Square, Milton Park, Abingdon, Oxon OX14 4RN

Simultaneously published in the USA and Canada
by Routledge-Cavendish
270 Madison Ave, New York, NY 10016

Routledge-Cavendish is an imprint of the Taylor & Francis Group, an informa business

© 2007 Richard Stone and Ralph Cunnington

Typeset in Garamond Three and Helvetica Neue by
RefineCatch Limited, Bungay, Suffolk
Printed and bound in Great Britain by
MPG Books Ltd, Bodmin, Cornwall

British Library Cataloguing in Publication Data
A catalogue record for this book is available from the British Library

Library of Congress Cataloging in Publication Data
A catalog record for this book has been requested

ISBN10: 1–85941–913–5
ISBN13: 978–1–85941–913–7

OUTLINE CONT[ENTS]

OUTLINE CONTENTS

DETAILED CONTENTS

PREFACE

Contract law often elicits a mixed response from students. Some find it boring; others struggle with its complexity; still others find it challenging and rewarding. Our intention in writing this book is to enable our readers to experience the satisfaction of falling into that latter category.

The book has four main aims. First and foremost the book seeks to provide a clear, accessible, and yet detailed exposition of English contract law. Complex ideas are explained and hard cases are unpacked. Secondly, it aims to encourage readers to adopt a critical approach to understanding the law. The book contains numerous academic articles, extracts from books and law reform papers. It is hoped that these will challenge the more discerning readers to question the current conceptions of the law and to develop new ideas and lines of argument for themselves. Thirdly, the book adopts a comparative analysis, taking into account the law in other common law jurisdictions and under the various international instruments, such as the Principles of European Contract Law and the UNIDROIT Principles of International Commercial Contracts. Finally, the book encourages readers to consider possible paths for law reform.

The book is composed of one-quarter authors' commentaries and three-quarters cases and materials. The commentary is sufficiently detailed to enable the reader to dip in and out of the cases and materials. It is hoped that the integration of these primary and secondary sources will help to deepen the reader's understanding of the law. We have aimed to keep the extracts from judgments as short as possible. On occasion, however, large extracts have been included in the belief that these provide the best exposition of the current law. The book is suitable for use alongside *The Modern Law of Contract*, 7th edn, 2007. Structurally the books are very similar, being designed to supplement one another, although either book can be used independently. Each chapter begins with a short table of contents and a clearly signposted introduction, highlighting the salient points under discussion. Additional learning support is provided by a regularly updated companion website which can be accessed at www.routledgecavendish.com/textbooks/9781859419137.

The authors would like to thank a number of people who have assisted with the preparation of this text. We are indebted to our students at the University of Birmingham and the University of Lincoln who have provided us with numerous opportunities to further develop our understanding and ability to explain the complexities of contract law. Your thoughtful questions and puzzled looks were not in vain. Thanks are also due to Kate Brookson-Morris, Emma Cunnington, Tanya Corrigan, Steven Cammiss and Djakhongir Saidov. We are extremely grateful to Routledge-Cavendish and in particular Constance Sutherland for all their patience, encouragement and assistance in the preparation of this book. Most of all we would like to thank our wives, Maggie and Anna, and the rest of our families who have been a constant support during the writing process. The book is dedicated to Sophie Cunnington who was born three months prior to the completion of the manuscript.

The law is stated, as far as possible, as it stood on 1 February 2007.

Richard Stone
Elston, Newark

Ralph Cunnington
Birmingham

ACKNOWLEDGEMENTS

Chapter 1 – Introduction

Pluto Press for permission to reproduce extracts from Wightman, J, *Contract: A Critical Commentary* (1996). Pluto Press: pp 48–51.

Oxford University Press for permission to reproduce extracts from Brownsword, R, *Contract Law. Themes for the twenty-first century* (2000). Butterworths and Oxford University Press: pp 1–2; 5–8; 36–40.

Hart Publishing for permission to reproduce extracts from Burrows, A, *Understanding the Law of Obligations* (1998). Hart Publishing: pp 3–5.

Cambridge University Press and Hugh Collins (© 2003) for permission to reproduce extracts from Collins, H, *The Law of Contract* (2003). 4th edn. LexisNexis/Butterworths: pp 8–9.

Professor Ian R Macneil and Northwestern University Law Review for permission to reproduce extracts from Macneil, IR, 'Contracts: adjustments of long-term economic relations under classical, neo-classical and relational contract law' (1978). 72 *Northwestern University Law Review*: 854–60.

Professor Anthony Kronman, Judge Richard Posner and Aspen Law and Business for permission to reproduce extracts from Kronman, A and Posner, R, *The Economics of Contract Law* (1979). Little, Brown: pp 1–3.

Sweet & Maxwell for permission to reproduce extracts from Adams, J and Brownsword, R, *Understanding Contract Law* (2004) 4th edn. Sweet & Maxwell: pp 36–44.

Sweet & Maxwell for permission to reproduce extracts from Yates, D, *Exclusion Clauses in Contracts* (1982) 2nd edn. Sweet & Maxwell: pp 18–33.

Hart Publishing for permission to reproduce extracts from McKendrick, E, *Harmonisation of European Contract Law: The State We Are In* (2006). Hart Publishing: pp 7–13.

Chapter 2 – Forming the Agreement

Sweet & Maxwell for permission to reproduce extracts from Howarth, W, 'The meaning of objectivity in contract' (1984). 100 *Law Quarterly Review*: 265–66; 279–81.

Cambridge University Press and Hugh Collins (© 2003) for permission to reproduce extracts from Collins, H, *The Law of Contract* (2003) 4th edn. LexisNexis/Butterworths: pp 4; 171–73.

Journal of Legal Studies for permission to reproduce extracts from Simpson, AWB, 'Quackery and Contract Law: The Case of the Carbolic Smoke Ball' © University of Chicago (1985). 14 *Journal of Legal Studies*: 345, 375–79

Blackwell Publishing for permission to reproduce extracts from Miller, CJ, 'Felthouse v Bindley Re-visited' (1972). 35 *Modern Law Review*: 489–end.

Oxford University Press for permission to reproduce extracts from Gardner, S, 'Trashing with Trollope: a deconstruction of the postal rules' (1992). 170 *Oxford Journal of Legal Studies*: 178–184.

Chapter 3 – Tests of Enforceability

Oxford University Press for permission to reproduce extracts from Atiyah, PS, *Essays on Contract* (2000). Oxford University Press: pp 182–83; 191–92; 226–40.

Sweet & Maxwell for permission to reproduce extracts from Treitel, GH, *The Law of Contract* (2003) 11th edn. Sweet & Maxwell: pp 70–71.

Blackwell Publishing for permission to reproduce extracts from Luther, P, 'Campbell, Espinasse and the sailors: text and comment in the common law' (1999). 19 *Legal Studies*: 525–28; 550–51.

Ohio State University Press for permission to reproduce extracts from Gilmore, G, *The Death of Contract* (1974). Ohio State University Press: pp 24–30.

Oxford University Press for permission to reproduce extracts from Denning, A, *The Discipline of Law* (1979). Butterworths: pp 200–205.

Informa law for permission to reproduce extracts from Halson, R, 'The Offensive Limits of Promissory Estoppel' (1999). 256 *Lloyd's Maritime and Commercial Law Quarterly*: 258–61.

Chapter 4 – Intention to Create Legal Relations

Cambridge University Press and Hugh Collins (© 2003) for permission to reproduce extracts from Collins, H, *The Law of Contract* (2003) 4th edn. LexisNexis/Butterworths: pp 104–105.

Professor Sir Bob Hepple for permission to reproduce extracts from Bob Hepple, 'Intention to create legal relations' (1970). 122 *The Cambridge Law Journal*: 127–37.

Chapter 5 – Privity

Cambridge University Press for permission to reproduce extracts from Harris, D, Campbell, D and Halson, R, *Remedies in Contract and Tort* (2002). © Cambridge University Press: pp 80–81.

Oxford University Press for permission to reproduce extracts from Smith, S., *Atiyah's Introduction to the Law of Contract* (2006) 6th edn. Oxford University Press: pp 348–50.

Chapter 7 – The Contents of the Contract

HMSO for permission to reproduce extracts from The Law Commission, 'The contract: the parole law of evidence rule', Report no 154 (1986). para 2.7. Reproduced under the terms of PSI Licence C2007000258.

Oxford University Press for permission to reproduce extracts from Kramer, A, 'Common sense principles of contract interpretation (and how we've been using them all along)' Copyright © 2003 University of Chicago (2003). 23 *Oxford Journal of Legal Studies*: 173; 177–179; 184–186; 188–190.

Cambridge University Press and Hugh Collins (© 2003) for permission to reproduce extracts from Collins, H, *The Law of Contract* (2003) 4th edn, LexisNexis/Butterworths: p 240.

Sydney Law Review for permission to reproduce extracts from Bryan, M and Ellinghaus, F, 'Fault lines in the law of obligations: Roxborough v Rothmans of Pall Mall Australia Ltd' (2000). 22 *Sydney Law Review*: 636; 645; 647.

The Cambridge Law Journal and Adam Kramer for permission to reproduce extracts from Kramer, A, 'Implication in fact as an instance of contractual interpretation' (2004). 63 *Cambridge Law Journal*: 384; 395–402.

Sweet & Maxwell for permission to reproduce extracts from Lord Steyn, 'Contract Law: Fulfilling the Reasonable Expectations of Honest Men' (1997). 113 *Law Quarterly Review*: 433; 441–42.

Chapter 8 – Clauses Excluding or limiting Liability

HMSO for permission to reproduce extracts from Law Commission, Report No 69, *Second Report on Exemption Clauses in Contracts* (1975). para 11. Reproduced under the terms of PSI Licence C2007000258.

Sweet & Maxwell for permission to reproduce extracts from Coote, B, *Exception Clauses* (1964). Sweet & Maxwell: pp 10–11; 17–18.

Tottel Publishing Ltd. for permission to reproduce extracts from MacDonald, E, *Exemption Clauses and Unfair Terms* (2006) 2nd edn. Tottel Publishing: pp 105–108; 227.

Blackwell Publishing for permission to reproduce extracts from Dean, M, 'Defining Unfair Terms in Consumer Contracts – Crystal Ball Gazing? *Director General of Fair Trading v First National Bank plc*' (2002). 65 *Modern Law Review*: 773; 776–77.

Blackwell Publishing for permission to reproduce extracts from Bright, S, 'Winning the Battle Against Unfair Terms' (2000). 20 *Legal Studies*: 331–33; 338.

HMSO for permission to reproduce extracts from The Law Commission, *Unfair Terms in Contracts* (2005). Law Com No 292, Scot Law Com, No 199, Cm 6464, para 1.14 and Summary – paras 1–21. Reproduced under the terms of PSI Licence C2007000258.

Chapter 9 – Misrepresentation

Sweet & Maxwell for permission to reproduce extracts from Treitel, GH, *The Law of Contract* (2003) 11th edn. Sweet & Maxwell: p 344.

Sweet & Maxwell for permission to reproduce extracts from Hooley, R, 'Damages and the Misrepresentation Act 1967' (1991). 107 *Law Quarterly Review*: 547; 549–51.

Sweet & Maxwell for permission to reproduce extracts from Peel, E, 'Reasonable exemption clauses' (2001). 117 *Law Quarterly Review*: 545; 549.

Chapter 10 – Mistake

Sweet & Maxwell for permission to reproduce extracts from Smith, JC 'Contracts: mistake, frustration and implied terms' (1944). 110 *Law Quarterly Review*: 400.

Cambridge University Press and Hugh Collins (© 2003) for permission to reproduce extracts from Collins, H, *The Law of Contract* (2003) 4th edn, LexisNexis/Butterworths: p 125.

Professor John Spencer © and The Cambridge Law Journal for permission to reproduce extracts from Spencer, JR, 'Signature Consent and the Rule in L'Estrange v Graucob' (1973). 32 *The Cambridge Law Journal*: 104, 108–10; 112–14.

Blackwell Publishing for permission to reproduce extracts from Hare, C, 'Identity Mistakes: A Missed Opportunity' (2004). 67 *Modern Law Review*: 993; 1006.

Sweet & Maxwell for permission to reproduce extracts from MacMillan, C, 'How Temptation Led to Mistake: an Explanation of Bell v Lever Bros Ltd' (2003). 119 *Law Quarterly Review*: 625.

Professor JD McCamus and Canadian Business Law Journal for permission to reproduce extracts from McCamus, JD, 'Mistaken Assumptions in Equity: Sound Doctrine or Chimera?' (2004). 40 *Canadian Business Law Journal*: 46; 75–76; 81–82.

Sweet & Maxwell for permission to reproduce extracts from Reynolds, FMB, 'Reconsider the Contract Textbook' (2003). 199 *Law Quarterly Review*: 117; 179.

Chapter 11 – Duress

The Cambridge Law Journal and Professor Stephen Smith for permission to reproduce extracts from Smith, S, 'Contracting under pressure: a theory of duress' (1997). 343 *Cambridge Law Journal*: 371–73.

Blackwell Publishing for permission to reproduce extracts from Lanham, D, 'Duress and void contracts' (1966). 29 *Modern Law Review*: 615; 617–20.

The Cambridge Law Journal and The Hon. Mr Justice Beatson for permission to reproduce extracts from Beatson, J, 'Duress as a vitiating factor in contract' (1974). 97 *The Cambridge Law Journal*: 106–108.

Sweet & Maxwell for permission to reproduce extracts from Enonchong, N, *Duress, Undue Influence and Unconscionable Dealing* (2006). Sweet & Maxwell: pp 25–6; 40–41.

Chapter 12 – Undue Influence

Sweet & Maxwell for permission to reproduce extracts from Enonchong, N, *Duress, Undue Influence and Unconscionable Dealing* (2006). Sweet & Maxwell: pp 82–3.

Oxford University Press for permission to reproduce extracts from Birks, P and Chin, NY, 'On the nature of undue influence' in Beatson, J and Friedmann, D, (eds), *Good Faith and Fault in Contract Law* (1995). Clarendon Press: pp 63–4; 95.

Sweet & Maxwell for permission to reproduce extracts from Ferguson, P, 'Partial rescission for misrepresentation rejected' (1995). 111 *Law Quarterly Review*: 555; 556–58.

Blackwell Publishing for permission to reproduce extracts from Waddams, S, 'Unconscionability in contracts' (1976). 39 *Modern Law Review*: 369; 390–93.

Journal of Legal Studies and Professor Eric Posner for permission to reproduce extracts from Posner, E, 'Contract law in the welfare state: a defence of usury laws, the unconscionability doctrine, and related limitations on the freedom to contract'

Copyright © The University of Chicago (1995). 24 *Journal of Legal Studies*: 283; 285–87.

Kluwer Law International, Professor Ole Lando and Professor Hugh Beale for permission to reproduce extracts from Lando, O and Beale, H, *Principles of European Contract Law Parts I and II* (2000). Kluwer Law International: pp 262–63.

Chapter 13 – Illegality

Oxford University Press for permission to reproduce extracts from Atiyah, P, *An Introduction to the Law of Contract* (1995) 5th edn. Clarendon Press: pp 342–44.

Informa law for permission to reproduce extracts from Enonchong, N, *Illegal Transactions* (1998). Lloyd's of London Press: pp 15–17.

The Cambridge Law Journal for permission to reproduce extracts from Hamson, CJ, 'Illegal Contracts and Limited Interests' (1949). 10 *Cambridge Law Journal*: 249–59.

Sweet & Maxwell for permission to reproduce extracts from Treitel, GH, *The Law of Contract* (2003) 11th edn. Sweet & Maxwell: p 489.

HMSO for permission to reproduce extracts from Consultation Paper No 154, *Illegal Transactions: The Effect of Illegality on Contracts and Trusts* (1999). 1.18–1.21. Reproduced under the terms of PSI Licence C2007000258.

Blackwell Publishing for permission to reproduce extracts from Buckley, RA, 'Illegal transactions: chaos or discretion?' (2000). 20 *Legal Studies*: 155; 179–80.

Chapter 14 – Contracts in Restraint of Trade

Oxford University Press for permission to reproduce extracts from Smith, S, 'Reconstructing Restraint of Trade' (1995). 15 *Oxford Journal of Legal Studies*: 565; 570; 594–95; 584–85.

Sweet & Maxwell for permission to reproduce extracts from Heydon, JD, 'The Frontiers of the Restraint of Trade Doctrine' (1969). 85 *Law Quarterly Review*: 229; 250–51.

Chapter 15 – Frustration

Oxford University Press for permission to reproduce extracts from McKendrick, E, 'The regulation of long term contracts in English Law', Chapter 12 in Beatson, J and Friedmann, D (eds), *Good Faith and Fault in Contract Law* (1995). Oxford University Press: pp 326–27.

Sweet & Maxwell for permission to reproduce extracts from Beale, H (ed), *Chitty on Contracts* (2004) 29th edn. Sweet & Maxwell: para 23–018.

Sweet & Maxwell for permission to reproduce extracts from Haycroft, AM and Waksman, DM, 'Frustration and Restitution' (1984). 207 *Journal of Business Law*: 225.

Professor John Carter and Dr Gregory Tolhurst for permission to reproduce extracts from Carter, JW and Tolhurst, G, 'Gigs N' Restitution: Frustration and the Statutory Adjustment of Payments and Expenses (1996). 10 *Journal of Contract Law*: 264.

Sweet & Maxwell for permission to reproduce extracts from Treitel, GH, *The Law of Contract* (2003) 11th edn. Sweet & Maxwell: p 915.

Informa law for permission to reproduce extracts from McKendrick, E, 'The Consequences of Frustration – The Law Reform (Frustrated Contracts) Act 1943' in *Force Majeure and Frustration of Contract* (1995) 2nd edn. Lloyd's of London Press: pp 238; 243.

Cambridge University Press for permission to reproduce extracts from Harris, D, Campbell, D and Halson, R, *Remedies in Contract and Tort* (2002) 2nd edn. Butterworths: p 253.

The Cambridge Law Journal, Professor Andrew Stewart and Professor John Carter for permission to reproduce extracts from Stewart, A, and Carter, JW, 'Frustrated contracts and statutory adjustment: the case for a reappraisal' (1992). 66 *The Cambridge Law Journal*: 109–10.

Oxford University Press for permission to reproduce extracts from McKendrick, E, 'Frustration, Restitution and Loss Apportionment' in Burrows, A (ed), *Essays on the Law of Restitution* (1991). Clarendon Press: pp 168–69.

Sweet & Maxwell for permission to reproduce extracts from Treitel, GH, *Frustration and Force Majeure* (2004) 2nd edn. Sweet & Maxwell: Para 2–025; Para 16–016; Para 7–014; Para 14–024.

Chapter 16 – Discharge by Performance or Breach

Sweet & Maxwell for permission to reproduce extracts from Dockray, M, 'Cutter v Powell: a trip outside the text' (2001). 117 *Law Quarterly Review*: 664; 673.

HMSO for permission to reproduce extracts from The Law Commission, *Pecuniary Restitution on Breach of Contract* (1983). Report no 121, para 2.37. Reproduced under the terms of PSI Licence C2007000258.

Kluwer Law International, Professor Ole Lando and Professor Hugh Beale for permission to reproduce extracts from Lando, O and Beale, H, *Principles of European Contract Law Parts I and II* (2000). Kluwer Law International: pp 262–324.

Sweet & Maxwell for permission to reproduce extracts from Treitel, GH, ' "Conditions" and "Conditions Precedent" ' (1990). 106 *Law Quarterly Review*: 185.

Sweet & Maxwell for permission to reproduce extracts from Treitel, GH, *The Law of Contract* (2003) 11th edn. Sweet & Maxwell: pp 796–97.

Sweet & Maxwell for permission to reproduce extracts from Reynolds, FMB, 'Discharge of contract by breach' (1981). 97 *Law Quarterly Review*: 541; 548.

Chapter 17 – Remedies

The Yale Law Journal Company and William S. Hein Company for permission to reproduce extracts from Fuller, L and Purdue, W Jr, 'The reliance interest in contract damages' (1936). 46 *Yale Law Journal*: 52–62.

Oxford University Press for permission to reproduce extracts from Atiyah, P, 'Contracts, promises and the law of obligations' in Atiyah, P, *Essays in Contract* (1986). Clarendon: pp 29–33; 39–43.

Sweet & Maxwell for permission to reproduce extracts from Friedmann, D, 'The performance interest in contract damages' (1995). 111 *Law Quarterly Review*: 628–38; 646–51; 654.

The Oxford University Commonwealth Law Journal for permission to reproduce extracts from McKendrick, E, 'The common law at work: the saga of Alfred McAlpine Construction Ltd v Panatown Ltd' (2003). 145 *Oxford University Commonwealth Law Journal*: 167–68

Blackwell Publishing for permission to reproduce extracts from Ogus, A, 'Damages for pre-contract expenditure' (1972). 35 *Modern Law Review*: 423; 424.

Cambridge University Press for permission to reproduce extracts from Harris, D, Campbell, D and Halson, R, *Remedies in Contract and Tort* (2002) 2nd edn. Butterworths: pp 131; 139–42.

Professor David McLauchlan for permission to reproduce extracts from McLauchlan, D, 'Reliance Damages for Breach of Contract' to be printed in (2007) *New Zealand Law Review*.

HMSO for permission to reproduce extracts from The Law Commission, *Contributory Negligence as a Defence in Contract,* Law Com No 219 (1993). para 4.7. Reproduced under the terms of PSI Licence C2007000258.

Journal of Legal Studies and Richard Danzig for permission to reproduce extracts from Danzig, R, 'Hadley v Baxendale: a study in the industrialization of the law' © The University of Chicago (1975). 4 *Journal of Legal Studies*: 249; 270–80.

Oxford University Press for permission to reproduce extracts from Burrows, A, *Remedies for Torts and Breach of Contract* (2004) 3rd edn. Oxford University Press: p 90.

Sweet & Maxwell for permission to reproduce extracts from Bridge, M, 'Mitigation of damages in contract and the meaning of avoidable loss' (1989). 105 *Law Quarterly Review*: 398–99; 413–14.

Northumbria Law Press at Northumbria University for permission to reproduce extracts from Cunnington, R, 'Rock, restitution and disgorgement' (2004). 46 *Journal of Obligations and Remedies*: 47–50.

Blackwell Publishing for permission to reproduce extracts from Cunnington, R, 'Should Punitive Damages be part of the judicial arsenal in contract cases?' (2006). 26 *Legal Studies*: 369; 385–89.

The Yale Law Journal Company and William S Hein Company for permission to reproduce extracts from Schwartz, A, 'The Case for Specific Performance' (1979). 89 *Yale Law Journal*: 271–306.

Chapter 18 – Unjust Enrichment

Cambridge University Press for permission to reproduce extracts from Waddams, S, *Dimensions of Private Law* (2003). Cambridge University Press: pp 165–66.

Oxford University Press for permission to reproduce extracts from Burrows, A, *The Law of Restitution* (2002) 2nd edn. Oxford University Press: p 373.

Informa law for permission to reproduce extracts from Cunnington, R, 'Failure of Basis' (2004). 234 *Lloyd's Maritime and Commercial Law Quarterly*: 244–47.

TABLE OF CASES

TABLE OF STATUTES

INTRODUCTION

CONTENTS

1.1 INTRODUCTION

This chapter considers issues relating to identifying the nature and scope of the English law of contract. It discusses, first, the 'classical' law of contract – the origins of this analysis of contract doctrine are to be found in the nineteenth century. It is based on the concept of freedom of contract, and the idea that the typical contract involves a 'one-off' exchange of promises between two parties. This leads on to consideration of the subject matter of contract law, for example, whether contracts are in fact about enforcing promises, or regulating markets, or facilitating exchanges, and the implications of each analysis. As a contrast to the 'classical' analysis, an alternative approach based on the distinction between 'discrete' and 'relational' contracts is discussed. This explores the challenges to the idea that the typical contract is a one-off discrete event, and considers the extent to which contracts involve continuing relationships between the parties.

Some techniques for analysing contracts are then reviewed, examining the extent to which 'doctrinal' analysis can be supplemented or replaced by analyses based on economics or sociology. Finally, there is a short section on international influences, based around current discussion of proposals for a European contract law.

1.2 THE CLASSICAL LAW OF CONTRACT

It is generally agreed that during the latter part of the nineteenth century various writers about contract law, including in particular textbooks writers, such as Anson (whose *Law of Contract,* written for students was first published in 1879), produced analyses and rationalisations of the case law that have become to be termed the 'classical law of contract'. The process is described by Wightman.

> **Wightman, J, *Contract: A Critical Commentary*, 1996, London: Pluto Press, pp 48–51**
>
> **The Invention of Classical Contract**
> An engagement with history is a necessary part of any critical understanding of contract. Compared with other legal subjects, the traditional study of contract is one of the least touched by historical analysis, yet is in much need of it. In some subjects a short history is indispensable to orientate the modern appearance of the subject, perhaps most clearly in the case of land law where the structure of law and equity can only be understood chronologically. In the case of contract there is no introductory story or origin myth – we just plunge straight in. Why? Partly because the underlying ideas of contract are more immediately available as a matter of common sense. Also, the structure of contract rules and principles is sufficiently abstract, coherent, and self referential (rather like the rules of chess) for it to be able to stand plausibly on its own without reference to the context – both legal and social – out of which it grew. This appearance of autonomy both reinforces the normative appeal of agreement and consent as the foundational principles of liability and deprives the traditional understanding of the law of any perspective which can introduce competing grounds of obligation. In this sense contract law conceals its history and it is one of the tasks of a critical understanding to penetrate that smooth deflecting surface.
>
> Historical understanding can also demystify the apparent solidity and seeming inevitability of the shape of the modern law by displaying it as the product of a process of development. Tracing the emergence of the mature form can help to recover the sense of open endedness with which earlier generations of lawyers encountered the law, and this in itself can act as an antidote to the closure of the possibilities of change which the slow speed of change in general contract doctrine can exert.
>
> History is also indispensable in any appraisal of transformation theories of contract. The modern understanding of the law of contract has been enormously influenced by relatively recent work on the eighteenth- and nineteenth-century history of contract.

Until the 1970s, the study of contract was divided between those concerned with the modern law and a relatively small group of scholars interested in the evolution of the early precursors of contract before the industrial revolution. Where contract law of the eighteenth and nineteenth centuries was addressed it was usually ahistorically as a part of the modern law which happened to reach further back.

This changed in the 1970s principally as a result of the work of Horwitz, Simpson and Atiyah. They treated the eighteenth and nineteenth centuries as a period of rapid change rather than as the repository of case law the main function of which was to be fitted where possible into modern expository accounts of the law. The switch from regarding the nineteenth century as present to regarding it as history relaxed the presumption of determinacy embodied in the expository tradition and that period of contract history was looked at afresh. In the process, a kind of received wisdom emerged about the flourishing of a particular conception of contract law – classical contract law – by the middle of the nineteenth century, albeit neighboured by controversy over what preceded it and what followed; some scholars saw transformation more easily than others. Classical contract was therefore invented in two senses: it was the nineteenth-century intellectual product of the judges and treatise writers, but it was only identified as such by the invention of the construct of the 'classical law' in the 1970s. As we shall see, the emergence of the modern construct was a vehicle both for the criticism of the model of contractual obligation it embodied, and for the attribution to it of greater intellectual coherence than before.

The first step in unravelling the history of contract is to look more closely at the idea of classical contract law which has so dominated modern perceptions of the history: we will consider the broad contours of this dominant view before turning to probe the story in more depth.

THE IDEA OF A CLASSICAL LAW OF CONTRACT

A number of modern writers on contract have made the transformation of contract law in the nineteenth century the linchpin of their account. The version of contract dubbed the classical law or classical model is seen as the mature form which emerged out of the less structured pre classical clutter of cases infused by a conception of substantive fairness, and which was followed by fragmentation at the hands of the regulatory state of the twentieth century. Although I will be strongly disputing its meaning and importance, there can be no denying the influence of the classical law in shaping broad perceptions of the development of the law of contract. We will examine the idea of the classical law in more detail by focusing on three dimensions: its content, the values on which it was based, and the type of transactions where its normative appeal was most plausible.

The leading feature which distinguished the classical law from what went before was the generality of the scope of its rules. By the third quarter of the nineteenth century the law of contract was regarded as consisting of rules which were not only general in form but also applied to most actual contracts. Before the emergence of the classical law there was no sense that the multifarious relations which became later analysed as contracts were instances within the general category of contract: rules were more situation specific with little attempt to develop an overall theory of liability.

It was a necessary property of the generality of the rules that they were abstract. They were addressed to individuals in general (offeror, seller, etc) rather than to individuals standing in specific social relationships to others. As Lawrence Friedman (1967) put it:

> Pure contract doctrine is blind to details of subject matter and person. It does not ask who buys and sells, and what is bought and sold . . . [c]ontract law is an abstraction – what is left when all particularities of person and subject matter are removed. (p 7)

Generality and abstractness were ushered in by the spread of the governing idea that both the terms of the contract and its quality of being legally binding was grounded in an exercise of the parties' wills – the 'will theory' of contract. Although the subjectivity of the will theory in its pure form was fairly soon attenuated by emphasising the appearance rather than the reality of consent, its legacy endured in the idea that a contract was formed by the agreement of the parties. A bare agreement – conceptualised as an exchange of promises – came to be seen as a sufficient basis of enforceability, without the necessity for any payment, performance or acts in reliance. This model of contract came to be seen as typical, with the result that all manner of situations were standardly analysed as bilateral executory contracts: bilateral because both parties were bound at once, and executory because the obligations arose before anything was done.

The second dimension of the classical law was the broad moral and political values on which it drew for its justification. At the root was the idea that the only legal obligations imposed on individuals were those not to harm others, which chiefly meant, as far as the civil law was concerned, duties not to interfere with another's property or person. Beyond this, legal obligation could only be incurred by the individual's act of will in agreeing or consenting to be bound. Thus the will theory not only provided the content of contract doctrine with a justification but also connected it with prevailing ideological conceptions of relationships between individuals within a society increasingly penetrated by market relations.

A corollary of the individualistic basis of the classical law was freedom of contract, so that parties were free not only to decide whether to incur consensual obligations at all, but also to determine the extent and content of such obligations. The role of the court was that of neutral referee or umpire, responsible only for enforcing the parties' agreement and not imposing duties which were not agreed nor removing those which had been agreed.

Where it was necessary to go beyond the parties' wills and derive the content of obligation from norms of behaviour, then the norms adopted tended to assume a robust attitude to a person's ability to look after their own interests and would permit advantage to be taken of poor business sense. This was particularly evident in relation to the development of the objective theory of agreement which attended to the appearance of agreement where subjective agreement was not total.

The values which underpinned the classical law were at their most persuasive when applied to something like the following idealised picture of the making of a contract:

- the parties are dealing at arm's length (that is, on a commercial basis without any other connection);
- they are of equal bargaining power (that is, they have similar wealth, knowledge and negotiating skill);
- they negotiate each term of the contract so that the terms are all the product of their deliberation;
- the contract terms provide clearly for all eventualities;
- the parties only come together for one contract (there is no continuing relationship).

Although the classical law could be most plausibly applied to these circumstances, its importance lay in the way it reached out beyond these circumstances and became the default body of rules to apply across a wide range of social relations which came to be regarded as more or less contractual.

The concept of freedom of contract is central to this analysis of contract law. As Brownsword has pointed out, however, freedom of contract has several aspects.

Brownsword, R, *Contract Law: Themes for the 21ˢᵗ Century*, 2000, London: Butterworths, pp 36–40

2.5 As we move on to look more carefully at the idea of freedom of contract, it is helpful to distinguish between freedom of contract in a broad sense and freedom of contract in a narrow sense. In a broad sense, freedom of contract embraces three related ideas: freedom to contract (or party freedom), freedom of contract (or term freedom), and sanctity of contract. In a narrow sense, freedom of contract (term freedom) emphasises that the law should recognise the importance of respecting the parties' own choices and preferences as expressed in the kinds of transactions they enter upon and the particular terms to which they agree. It follows that freedom of contract in the narrow sense argues for a minimalist (ie, light regulatory) approach both to the categories of transaction that are treated as illegal and to the kinds of terms that are black-listed as void and unenforceable.

2.6 According to Lord Devlin, it is axiomatic within the classical view that free dealing is fair dealing. Thus, in *Printing and Numerical Registering Co v Sampson*, Sir George Jessel MR famously said:

[I]f there is one thing which more than another public policy requires it is that men of full age and competent understanding shall have the utmost liberty of contracting, and that their contracts when entered into freely and voluntarily shall be held sacred and shall be enforced by Courts of justice. Therefore, you have this paramount public policy to consider—that you are not lightly to interfere with this freedom of contract.

Sir George's remarks suggest that respect for freedom of contract involves two related forms of legislative and judicial restraint. First, freedom of contract enjoins that the parties shall have 'the utmost liberty of contracting', in the sense that they are left free to set their own terms. It follows that legislatures and courts should be slow to limit the kinds of transactions, or the kinds of terms, that the parties can agree upon within the domain of contract. An over-restrictive approach disallows options that should be available to the parties and, to this extent, illegitimately trims the parties' autonomy. Secondly, freedom of contract enjoins that the parties' freely-made agreements shall be enforced by the courts. Courts might be tempted to release parties from hard bargains, but where agreements have been freely made such a temptation must be resisted: even well-meaning paternalism betrays a lack of respect for a person's autonomy. To mark these two aspects of freedom of contract (in the broad sense), we can call the first form of restraint the ideal of 'term freedom' (that is, freedom of contract in the narrow sense) and the second the ideal of 'sanctity of contract'.

2.7 Absolute term freedom implies a licence to write contracts with any content, that is, an absence of legal restriction upon the kinds of bargains, or the types of contractual provision that the parties can agree upon. A legal system guided by the ideal of term freedom will limit such a licence only where it has good reason. Of course, what constitutes 'a good reason' will depend upon the background philosophy of the particular legal order. Thus, if a legal system is guided by utilitarian (or by wealth maximising) thinking, countervailing good reasons will involve disutilities (or wealth losses) occasioned by term freedom; whereas, in a legal system that is guided by an individual rights-led morality, the right of freedom of contract will be abridged only where more important rights are at stake.

Bearing in mind the important caveat that different views can be taken about what constitutes a good reason for limiting term freedom, we can say that, in principle, arguments for a restriction upon term freedom might be based on one or more of the following four grounds: (i) that the terms (or the general purpose of the contract) are harmful to the interests of third parties (e g, where the purpose of an agreement is to kill an innocent third party); (ii) that the terms (or the general purpose of the contract) are harmful to the public interest (e g, where the purpose of an agreement is to evade liability under a justifiable tax regime); (iii) that the transaction is harmful to the interests of one of the contracting parties (e g, a sale at undervalue, a usury agreement, or a contract of enslavement might be seen as falling into this category); and (iv) that the transaction is harmful to the interests of both the contracting parties (e g, some might argue that gaming and wagering agreements, or contracts for sexual favours fall into this category). In some instances, of course, the arguments against term freedom overlap. For example, it might be argued that the parties' freedom to make surrogacy contracts should be restricted on a variety of grounds—that such agreements are harmful to third parties (the surrogate children), to the broader public interest (by commodifying reproduction), to the surrogate mother (whose dignity is violated), and to the commissioning parents (who might find themselves exploited).

In this light, it is interesting to look back at the basis of the (unsuccessful) argument for restriction on term freedom in *Printing and Numerical Registering Co v Sampson*. The agreement in that case was one in which an inventor assigned a patent to a company. Under the agreement, the vendor undertook to enter into a covenant with the company for the assignment of any future patents acquired (in the United Kingdom and various other places) in relation to the particular invention in question (or any similar invention). The vendor subsequently argued that this undertaking was contrary to the public interest in that it discouraged both inventors and the bringing forward of inventions into the public domain. The Master of the Rolls, however, was unconvinced. In his opinion, it was perfectly reasonable for the company to contract for this covenant; there was no compelling evidence of damage to the public interest; and this was no more than a case of the vendor trying to escape from the consequences of a sound commercial bargain. Suppose, though, the vendor of the patent had been in a weak bargaining position as a result of which the agreement struck was unreasonably one-sided in favour of the company. Would Sir George have appealed so strongly to the principle of freedom of contract? In fact, he probably would. For, in *Bennet v Bennet*, he upheld a moneylending agreement entered into at rates of 60 per cent, saying that borrowers can agree to pay 100 per cent if they so choose, that '[t]here is no reason why a man should not be a fool', and that the law does not prevent men from being fools. Term freedom, therefore, countenances the possibility that parties—at any rate, as Sir George put it, 'men of full age and competent understanding'—should be given the utmost liberty to make improvident and foolish contracts.

2.8 Closely related to the ideal of term freedom, is the ideal of sanctity of contract. Whereas term freedom sets up a presumption against unnecessary restrictions on the kinds of agreements that parties can make, sanctity of contract emphasises that parties are to be held to the agreements that they have freely made. This general idea can be deployed in more than one context. Most obviously, it applies in the context of hard cases and improvident contracts. In a legal system that subscribes to the principle of sanctity of contract, there will be no jurisdiction to grant paternalistic relief where a party is simply trying to avoid the consequences of a bargain that is now regretted. Accordingly, in *Printing and Numerical Registering Co v Sampson*, if the court had felt that the company had contracted for a greater protection than it really needed, and if the contract had subsequently worked a significant hardship upon the vendor-inventor, then sanctity of contract would treat such considerations as irrelevant—contracts, as Sir George said, are sacred; and the justification for their enforcement originates in free agreement, not in some calculus of sympathy and antipathy in relation to the parties. In addition to this obvious application, sanctity of contract can have a bearing on the renegotiation or variation of contracts. In this context, sanctity of contract does not preclude a party waiving the right to hold a fellow contractor to the agreed terms of the bargain, but it does encourage courts to take a hard look at renegotiated agreements apparently showing benefit to just one side—particularly a hard look at whether the renegotiation was free and fully consensual.

Where the express terms of a freely agreed bargain quite clearly cover a disputed situation, an appeal to the ideal of sanctity of contract is relatively straightforward (although, of course, not uncontroversial). However, where the express terms of the contract either (i) do not clearly apply or (ii) make no provision for the disputed situation (which has not been anticipated), then an appeal to sanctity of contract is more problematic. In the former case, arguably, an appeal to sanctity of contract is premature: until the meaning of the express provisions has been settled, it is surely unhelpful to invoke the rhetoric of enforcing the bargain according to its terms. In the latter case, because an appeal to sanctity of contract no longer seems to rest on respect for the parties' autonomous decision-making (because, in the absence of express contractual provision, there is apparently no relevant decision), it might be thought to have no application. The position, however, is not quite so clear-cut.

2.10 The third element of freedom of contract (in the broad sense), it will be recalled, is party freedom. This is the right to choose one's contracting partners which, in practice, means the right to refuse to deal with a particular person. It is, of course, axiomatic within the general idea of freedom of contract that there is a threshold freedom to decline an offer (even an offer that, in practice, no rational person would refuse). However, party freedom constitutes a licence to discriminate against a particular person or particular types of person by excluding such persons from one's contracting activities for whatever reason or whim one likes. This is not to say that those who actually make offers may then pick and choose amongst acceptors who are eligible relative to the scope of the offer: if the offer is open to everyone, anyone may accept; if the offer is open to any member of a particular class, anyone within that class may accept; if the offer is open to all save for a particular restriction, anyone not excluded by that restriction may accept, and so on. However, what party freedom does mean is that offerors may restrict their offers in the first place (by specifying who is and who is not eligible to accept); that offerees may decline to accept offers because they do not want to deal with particular offerors; and that, in both cases, the grounds that offerors and offerees have for so doing are not subject to legal regulation or judicial scrutiny.

Does the paradigm of the contract, which is discrete, based on promises and in relation to which the obligations of the parties are determined by free negotiation, fit with the reality of modern contract law? The answer is that it does so for a limited range of contracts, but there are many that will not fall within its scope. It is often the case, for example, that there is no equality of bargaining power between the parties, so that the idea of a freely negotiated agreement is unrealistic. This is most obviously the case where one party is a consumer and the other a large corporation. But similar imbalances can occur between large and small companies. In the commercial world, moreover, the totally discrete contractual exchange is by no means typical. Many contracts will be made between businesses that are in a continuing commercial relationship and planning to trade with each other for some time. The classical theory cannot easily deal with such situations. In addition, there is increasing statutory intervention into the area of contract law, often influenced by law emerging from the European Union (EU). Such regulation will often take a different approach to that which would have been expected under the common law.

It is nevertheless the case that the English courts, as will be seen from many of the extracts in later chapters, still tend to rely on the language of the classical doctrine when analysing contractual situations. This can be the case even where that approach does not fit comfortably with the facts before the court. There is therefore a tension arising from the fact that the courts are using a nineteenth-century analysis (which even at the time may well have been artificial), to deal with problems that arise in a twenty-first-century context. The following chapters will use the classical doctrine as a framework for exploring the case law, but will draw attention as appropriate to the difficulties that this can cause, and to alternative analyses that have been proposed.

▌1.3 THE SUBJECT MATTER OF CONTRACT LAW

There are differing views as to what contract law is 'about', or what its purpose is.

Burrows, A, *Understanding the Law of Obligations*, 1998, Oxford: Hart Publishing, pp 3–5

2. CONTRACT

The law of contract is concerned with binding promises. It looks at what constitutes a binding promise and how such a promise is made; at the remedies for breach of such a promise; and at who is entitled to those remedies.

It has been a traditionally accepted feature of English law that only bargain promises—that is, promises supported by consideration—are binding. Gratuitous promises, apart from promises made by deed and those enforceable through proprietary or promissory estoppel, are not binding. But even if a bargain promise has been made and accepted it may still not be binding for various reasons. For example, it may not be sufficiently certain; or it may be a social or domestic promise where it is presumed that the promisor does not intend to create legal relations; or it may have been induced by the promisee's misrepresentation or duress or undue influence; or the promisor may have made a mistake; or there may have been such a change of events subsequent to the making of the promise that the notion of 'frustration' is brought into play; or the plaintiff may have broken his own promise in such a serious way as to make the defendant's promise, performance of which was conditional upon performance of the plaintiff's own promise, no longer binding. A number of these factors which render a promise that would otherwise be binding, non-binding, can be coherently linked by saying that a promise is not binding if it is unfair to the promisor to hold him or her to it. Using this notion of fairness, the expansion of invalidating factors that has taken place during the twentieth century, such as the widening of the doctrines of mistake and duress, and the passing of statutes such as the Unfair Contract Terms Act 1977, is readily explicable as reflecting the different view of fairness that holds sway today than in the past. That is, the laissez-faire/ freedom of contract view of fairness is today tempered by a paternalistic/protection of the weak view of fairness.

The remedies for breach of a binding promise are (almost always) concerned to fulfil the expectations engendered by that promise. This is most clearly shown by the remedy of specific performance where the defendant is ordered to carry out the promise made to the plaintiff. Although the courts have become more willing to grant specific performance, the general position remains that it is a secondary remedy available only where damages are inadequate. However, the normal method of assessing damages for the breach of a binding promise is also concerned to fulfil the plaintiff's expectations. This was made clear by Parke B in *Robinson v Harman*. He said, 'The rule of common law is that, where a party sustains a loss by reason of a breach of contract, he is, so far as money can do it to be placed in the same situation, with respect to damages, as if the contract had been performed.'

Traditionally, under the doctrine of 'privity of contract', only a party to the contract (that is, the promisee) can enforce it. A third-party beneficiary has no such entitlement. Although there are exceptions to the privity doctrine, it still basically holds sway. Whether that will still be so at the millennium is open to debate, particularly given the Law Commission's recent recommendations for legislative reform of the doctrine.

It is important to add that the notion of 'promise' that is being used, when one refers to the law of contract being concerned with binding promises, is a wide one. One can define a promise, in a wide sense, as 'a statement or action by which the speaker or actor appears to accept an obligation to another (or others) to do or not to do something.' So a promise may be made by an oral statement, by writing, or by conduct. Conduct constituting a promise will be context-specific but it may include, for example, a hand-shake, or a nod-of-the-head, or the delivery of requested goods (where, by delivery, one may be taken to have accepted an obligation to provide a certain quality or quantity of goods), or conduct encouraging another to perform services (where, by the encouragement, one may be taken to have accepted an obligation to pay for the services).

Although many would agree that promises are central to the idea of 'contract', there are difficulties with this, as pointed out by Brownsword.

Brownsword, R, *Contract Law: Themes for the 21ˢᵗ Century*, 2000, London: Butterworths, pp 5–8

Promise as a necessary condition

1.6 What is the problem with viewing the giving of a promise as a necessary condition for the existence of a contract? Surely, there cannot be a contract without the giving of a promise. Is it not precisely non-performance or defective performance of a promise that the innocent party will cite in an action for breach?

1.7 To see how one kind of reservation unfolds, we can consider any typical market-place transaction, any contract for the sale or supply of goods or services. Without doubt, many transactions of this kind exemplify not only contract as promise but also agreement and exchange. In a large-scale construction contract, for example, there is an agreement (however understood) that certain building work will be carried out for a certain price; there is an exchange (no one is making a gift); and the client's promise to pay is reciprocated by the contractor's promise to carry out the work. Alongside such tailored transactions, however, there is a myriad of routine transactions where commerce is conducted on a taken-for-granted basis. Suppose, for example, that the aforementioned construction contract is for a garage and self-service petrol station. When the garage has been built and is functioning, agreements to carry out repair work for customers may well resemble the tailored transacting of the construction project itself. However, motorists who call in at the garage simply to fill up their petrol tanks may well participate in a transaction that is so routine that nothing is actually said between the parties. Similarly, customers who purchase items from the garage self-service shop may complete the transaction by tendering the appropriate money—and, again, neither party to the transaction will necessarily give an express promise, the exchange will simply be made. In other words, in routine everyday transactions, an exchange will often take place in a setting where promising is implicit rather than explicit.

1.8 If the only reservation about the necessity of a promise (in a promise-based definition) were that promises are sometimes implicit rather than explicit—that, for example, in routine consumer transactions the purchaser implicitly promises to pay for the goods and services at the advertised prices—this would give rise to no real difficulty. However, the legal backcloth presupposed by routine consumer transactions gives such a reservation a fresh twist. To a large extent, the law supplies the content for standard everyday transactions by writing in various types of implied terms, some of which are strictly non-negotiable. Although these implied terms do take the form of a promise, it would be a distortion to treat them as implicit promises in the sense that we have been using that term thus far. Rather, given widespread ignorance amongst contractors about the details of these implied term regimes, it would be more accurate to say that promises of this kind are attributed (or imputed) to the parties. Nevertheless, so long as a promise-based definition allows for attributed (or imputed) promises, it can cover this difficulty.

1.9 A further obstacle to treating promise as a necessary condition for contract might be thought to arise where the law shifts into a remedial gear, constructing contracts *ex post facto* in order to facilitate some form of relief or redress. For example, in cases such as *The Eurymedon* where, in the context of the carriage of goods by sea, a contract was constructed between the owners of the goods (who contracted with the carriers) and the stevedores (who were sub-contracted by the carriers), the parties did not realise that they were entering into a transaction with one another, let alone that they were issuing promises to one another. To be sure, we might defend a promise-based definition by insisting that even such *ex post facto* rationalisation eventually returns to the idea of a promise. In other words, whether we reason forwards from promise to contract to remedy, or backwards from remedy to contract to promise, contract is essentially, and necessarily, about enforceable promises. Such a robust defence, however, might be thought to miss an opportunity to draw out the sophisticated way in which contract law is used to protect the expectations of those who are involved in transactions.

1.10 For instance, in *Blackpool and Fylde Aero Club Ltd v Blackpool Borough Council*, the defendants, who owned and managed Blackpool airport, raised revenue by granting concessions to operators to use it. The plaintiff club was granted the concession in 1975, 1978 and 1980. Shortly before the plaintiff's last (1980) concession was due to expire, the council sent an invitation to the plaintiff to tender for the new concession to the club. The council also sent invitations to six other parties. The invitations stated *inter alia* that tenders received after 12 noon on 17 March 1983 would not be considered. The plaintiff's tender was put in the Town Hall letter box at 11 am on 17 March, but the box was not emptied as it was supposed to be. As a result, the plaintiff's letter was incorrectly recorded as having been received late, and it was not considered when the relevant committee met to award the concession. The plaintiff sued alleging a breach of warranty on the part of the defendants to the effect that, if the tender were received by the deadline, it would be considered along with the others. The Court of Appeal unanimously upheld the decision of the court at first instance that the defendants were liable for a breach of contract.

Amongst the arguments presented on behalf of the defendants, it was contended that a contract should not be implied merely because it was reasonable to do so; and that there was a distinction between reasonable expectation and contractual obligation. Responding to these arguments, Bingham LJ observed:

> [W]hat if, in a situation such as the present, the council had opened and thereupon accepted the first tender received, even though the deadline had not expired and other invitees had not responded? Or if the council had considered

and accepted a tender admittedly received well after the deadline? Counsel answered that although by so acting the council might breach its own standing orders, and might fairly be accused of discreditable conduct, it would not be in breach of any legal obligation because at that stage there would be none to breach. This is a conclusion I cannot accept, and if it were accepted there would in my view be an unacceptable discrepancy between the law of contract and the confident assumptions of commercial parties . . . [W]here, as here, tenders are solicited from selected parties all of them known to the invitor, and where a local authority's invitation prescribes a clear, orderly and familiar procedure . . . the invitee is in my judgment protected at least to this extent: if he submits a conforming tender before the deadline he is entitled, *not as a matter of mere expectation but of contractual right*, to be sure that his tender will after the deadline be opened and considered in conjunction with all other conforming tenders or at least that his tender will be considered if others are.

These remarks might seem to gloss over a number of potentially important distinctions, in particular between intentional and unintentional violation of the principles of good tendering practice, and between holding the council contractually bound to consider all conforming tenders, as opposed to holding the council so bound *only if any tenders were considered*. However, for Bingham LJ's purposes, such nice points were largely immaterial: the critical question was simply whether tenderers reasonably assumed that the council would observe certain ground rules in dealing with the tenders; if they did, then an appropriate contractual relationship would be implied in line with their expectations.

1.11 Taking stock of these remarks, we cannot define a contract in a way that presupposes the giving of an express promise. If contract is to be defined in terms of promises, we must allow for express, implicit, and imputed promises. We must also allow, however, for promises constructed *ex post facto*; and the thought prompted by cases such as *Blackpool* and *The Eurymedon* is that, if a promise is necessary to give form to a contract, reasonable expectation is perhaps the key to contractual substance.

An alternative approach is suggested by Collins:

Collins, H, *Law of Contract*, 2003 pp 8–9

We need to construct a new conception of the law of contract. It should provide a system of thought that illuminates present concerns of government, and that helps to analyse issues within an intellectual framework which has a place for all the relevant rules and doctrines. It should also provide a key for an interpretation of law's past, which simultaneously reconstructs the law and enables further transformations to take place.

The place to start no doubt, as did the Victorians before us, is with a desire to understand the market order. We still require legal systems of thought for interpreting, analysing, and guiding events and relations in the marketplace. The difference between our enterprise and theirs springs not from the site of the inquiry, but rather from the alteration in both the market order itself, and the nature of political and moral justifications for its legal regulation.

During the twentieth century, the state intervened to devise new principles to govern the operation and outcomes of the market. With respect to outcomes, the evidence is incontrovertible. Instead of permitting the distribution of wealth to be determined by voluntary choices to enter market transactions, the social security system which relieves poverty and all the other dimensions of the Welfare State, funded largely through progressive taxation, clearly affect the eventual outcomes of the distribution of wealth. What seems to be less generally perceived is that at the same time similar ideals of social justice have justified the channelling and regulation of market transactions. The purpose of these limits upon the exercise of voluntary choices lies in the realization of a compatible scheme of social justice. The persistence of traditional descriptions of the law of contract no doubt contributes to this failure to perceive how the ground rules for the establishment of obligations in economic relations have been substantially altered in order that they may fit better with contemporary ideals of social justice.

How, therefore, should we conceive the law of contract today? It comprises those rules, standards, and doctrines which serve to channel, control, and regulate the social practices which we can loosely describe as market transactions. This branch of the law certainly facilitates the growth of the social practice of making economic transactions, especially those transactions where performance is not instantaneous; but it also sets limits to the exercise of voluntary choice. By emphasizing how modern ideals of social justice channel market transactions into approved patterns, this conception of contract removes the assumption that the law provides an open-ended facility for making binding commitments. Although some flexibility persists, especially with regard to the price, this freedom should be regarded as a privilege granted on stringent conditions, rather than a general licence to enter contractual obligations of one's choice.

Related to this is the concept of a contract as a mechanism for facilitating exchanges – generally of goods or services provided for payment. 'Contract' is a device that can be used by those who want to clothe an exchange with legal enforceability. By constructing their transaction in a way that the courts will recognise as 'contractual', they ensure that if anything goes wrong, legal remedies will be available. The agreement will also have the effect of allocating risks between the parties – deciding who is to bear the loss in the event of problems.

There are some problems with this analysis, however. In particular it does not explain how the transfer of property by 'deed', which the courts treat as a type of contract, does not need to involve an exchange in order to be enforceable. Brownsword suggests that it may not be feasible to find one single definition which will work.

Brownsword, R, *Contract Law: Themes for the 21st Century*, 2000, London: Butterworths, pp 1–2

1.1 A contract, it seems, is one of those phenomena that is relatively easy to recognise but difficult to define. On the one hand, to state some truisms, one of the functions of the law of contract is to discriminate between those transactions that are enforceable as contracts and those that are not. Doctrine lays down the constituents of a contract (agreement, consideration, certainty, intention and, in exceptional cases, written formality) as well as stipulating the conditions of enforceability (the absence of fraud, coercion, illegal purpose and so on). There will be cases where, for one reason or another, doctrine is uncertain in its application. However, for the most part, lawyers will expect to recognise a 'contract', as specified by the law of contract, when they see one. On the other hand, whilst we might hope to construct a definition of a 'contract' around the shared idea of an enforceable transaction, there is little agreement about how this is best articulated. Some definitions might centre on the idea of an enforceable agreement; others might be anchored to the concept of an enforceable promise (or set of promises); and others might emphasise that contracts are essentially exchanges, or perhaps bargained-for exchanges. Which definition, if any, is correct?

As with any question of definition, it is important to be clear about what kind of defining statement is at issue. Broadly speaking, definitions are either stipulative, prescriptive, or reportive. Whereas a stipulative definition specifies (in the definer's own lexicon) a particular meaning for a word (or a concept), and a prescriptive definition purports to lay down for others such a meaning, a reportive definition (as we might expect to find in a dictionary) purports to describe usage (in a particular place at a particular time by a particular group) of a particular word (or concept). When we ask for a general definition of a 'contract', we are not asking for a stipulation; we are not interested in a particular definer's idiosyncratic usage of the term. Nor are we asking for a prescription as to the usage of this term; in a sense, the law of contract already so prescribes. Rather, we are asking for an account that captures the employment of the idea within the law of contract and, thus, the exercise is akin to that of reportive definition. It follows that any proffered general definition will be deficient if it does not fit the various transactions that the law of contract picks out as 'contracts'.

A report that aspires to capture usage of a particular term (such as the term 'contract' as used in the law) might attempt to do so in the form of an essential definition (in which one or more elements are identified as the necessary and sufficient conditions for correct usage) or in the form of a cluster concept (in which several elements are identified with the usage, but where no single set of these elements can be combined to represent the necessary and sufficient conditions for correct usage). Insofar as the puzzle about defining a contract is approached as an exercise in essential (reportive) definition, a proffered definition will fail if the given condition, or conditions (agreement, exchange, promise, or whatever) is or are not strictly necessary (ie, if a contract can exist without meeting such conditions); and, equally, it will fail if the given condition, or conditions, is/are not sufficient (ie, if, despite meeting such conditions, a transaction fails to be recognised as a contract). Insofar as the puzzle is approached as an exercise in non-essential cluster concept definition, the challenge is less demanding.

1.3.1 VOLUNTARY TRANSACTIONS

It appears to be a characteristic of a contractual exchange that it is at some level 'voluntary'. Although in practice there may be little choice as to whether to make certain contracts (for example, to buy the necessities of life), or the terms on which contracts are made, some element of freedom must exist. It has been held, for example, that if a transaction is entirely regulated by statute, then it cannot be regarded as contractual.

Norweb plc v Dixon **[1995] 3 All ER 952 (CA)**

Facts: D claimed to have been harassed as a debtor by Norweb plc – an offence under the Administration of Justice Act 1970. The magistrates convicted Norweb, and it appealed.

Held: The relationship between Norweb and D was not contractual, as it was entirely regulated by statute.

Dyson J:

'. . . *Conclusion on the contract point*
I deal first with the general question whether an agreement for the supply of electricity between a tariff customer and a public electricity supplier (i.e. not a special agreement within the meaning of section 22) is a contract. There are many examples of cases where the law to some extent restricts the freedom of parties to enter into a relationship, but where the relationship that results is a contract. Mrs. Cover gave some good examples, although I do not consider that her point about section 65 of the Housing Act 1985 is apt. A further good example is that it is unlawful to refuse a person employment "because he is, or is not, a member of a trade union:" section 1(1)(a) of the Employment Act 1990. In all these cases, a relationship which results from some degree of legal compulsion is nevertheless regarded as contractual, because the parties still have considerable freedom to regulate its incidents.
    But there are other cases in which a relationship created by legal compulsion is clearly not contractual. Thus a person whose property is compulsorily acquired against

his will does not make a contract with the acquiring authority, even though he receives compensation: see *Sovmots Investments Ltd. v Secretary of State for the Environment* [1977] Q.B. 411, 443. In *Pfizer Corporation v Ministry of Health* [1965] A.C. 512 the House of Lords held that a patient to whom medicines are supplied under the National Health Service does not make a contract to buy them either from the chemist or the Minister of Health even if he pays a subscription charge. The transaction is sui generis, the creation of statute and not a sale pursuant to a contract. Lord Reid said, at pp. 535–536:

> "I shall consider the case on the footing that a patient is not entitled to demand the drug unless he tenders 2s. The appellants' argument is that when the patient pays 2s. and gets the drug there is a sale of the drug to him by the hospital or the chemist and that 2s. is the price. If that were right, the appellants say that section 46 does not authorise the department or its servants or agents to sell or vend, it only authorises them to make, use or exercise the invention. But in my opinion there is no sale in this case. Sale is a consensual contract requiring agreement, express or implied. In the present case there appears to me to be no need for any agreement. The patient has a statutory right to demand the drug on payment of 2s. The hospital has a statutory obligation to supply it on such payment. And if the prescription is presented to a chemist he appears to be bound by his contract with the appropriate authority to supply the drug on receipt of such payment. There is no need for any agreement between the patient and either the hospital or the chemist, and there is certainly no room for bargaining. Moreover the 2s. is not in any true sense the price: the drug may cost much more and the chemist has a right under his contract with the authority to receive the balance from them. It appears to me that any resemblance between this transaction and a true sale is only superficial. I would therefore decide against the appellants on this point."

The issue in this case is: which side of the line does the relationship between a tariff customer and a public electricity supplier fall? In my judgment, the legal compulsion as to both the creation of the relationship and the fixing of its terms is inconsistent with the existence of a contract. As regards the creation of the relationship, the supplier is obliged by section 16(1) of the Act of 1989 to supply if requested to do so. The exceptions from the duty to supply provided in section 17 are very limited in scope. Mrs. Cover submits that section 17(2)(c) gives the supplier what she calls a "discretion" not to supply. That is not so. A supplier is excused from supplying if (the burden being on him) it is not reasonable in all the circumstances for him to be required to do so. What is reasonable is a question of fact to be established objectively. Discretion does not come into play. Thus, save in certain narrowly defined circumstances, if a consumer requests the supply of electricity, the supplier is obliged to supply.

As for the terms of the supply, Mrs. Cover submits that there is scope for what she calls "bargaining". I cannot agree. The tariff is fixed by the supplier: section 18. The supplier can require the consumer to defray any expenses reasonably incurred in supplying any electric line or plant (section 19), and to give reasonable security: section 20(1). The supplier can also impose additional terms of supply: section 21. The consumer has no bargaining power in relation to these matters. It seems to me that the principal terms are imposed on the consumer by the supplier not as a result of any bargaining, but by the supplier exercising the power conferred on it by the Act of 1989.

The words of section 22 of the Act of 1989 provide further support for the view that there is no contract. That section refers to a special agreement "for the supply on such terms as may be specified in the agreement". What is contemplated is a negotiated agreement to meet the particular requirements of a consumer. Section 22(3) states that the rights and liabilities of the parties to the special agreement shall be those arising under the agreement, and not those provided for by sections 16 to 21 of the Act. Thus a clear distinction is drawn as to the source of the rights and liabilities between (i) supplies under special agreements which are governed by the terms of those agreements and (ii) supplies to tariff customers which are governed by the Act of 1989. This provides clear confirmation that the rights and liabilities as between tariff customers and their public electricity suppliers are governed by statute and not by contract.

The justices were of the opinion that, if there was no contract between the parties, there would be no basis in law for the supplier to recover debts owed to it. In my view, they were mistaken. Paragraph 1(1) of Schedule 6 gives the supplier the power to recover any charges due to it. There is, therefore, no need to have recourse to contract.

I have already mentioned *Willmore v South Eastern Electricity Board* [1957] 2 Lloyd's Rep. 375. In that case, electricity was supplied by the defendant electricity board to the plaintiffs. It was alleged by the plaintiffs that the defendant was in breach of its contract to supply adequate current. The claim was put on the basis of breach of a term of the supply agreement, and in the alternative breach of a collateral warranty. Dealing with the first point, Glyn-Jones J. said, at p. 380:

> "I am unable to accept Mr. Lawson's arguments based upon the language of the application form. It seems to me significant that the supply for which the consumer applies is expressed to be 'subject to the conditions imposed by statute, order or regulation with respect to supplies of electricity by the board'. I have come to the conclusion that Mr. Jukes is right and that I ought to treat the supply of electricity by the board not as the acceptance of an offer by the plaintiffs to take and pay for a supply, so as to create a contract, but as given in pursuance of the board's statutory duty to give a supply to any consumer who, being entitled, demands it."

Mrs. Cover submits that that authority is distinguishable since the statutory obligation to supply electricity was different from that under consideration in the present case. That is, of course, true, but our attention was not drawn to any provisions of the Electricity Act 1947 which are materially different from the provisions of the Act of 1989. In my view, that case was correctly decided.

I now turn to consider Mrs. Cover's submission that the appellants' supply to the respondent was subject to a special agreement. Section 40(1) of the Act of 1970 is concerned with "money claimed . . . as a debt due under a contract". In my view, the offence does not require proof of the existence and terms of a contract which has in fact been concluded between the consumer and supplier, any more than it requires proof that the debt is in fact due. What is required is proof that the supplier has made demands for payment of a debt which he claims to be due under a contract which he claims to exist. It cannot have been intended that it should be an offence to claim a non-existent debt under a contract which in fact exists, but not an offence to claim a debt under a fictitious contract. It seems to me, therefore, that what the justices should have considered was the relationship that the appellants *claimed* to constitute a special agreement. The justices' findings, however, simply do not support any special agreement within the meaning of section 22 of the Act of 1989, let alone a special agreement in the terms for which Mrs. Cover contends. Indeed, the justices were of the opinion that the contract arose simply because the appellants had provided the respondent with the supply in return for which he had agreed to pay. Accordingly, I reject her argument on this point.

It must follow that there was no contract between the appellants and the respondent, nor was the debt claimed under a contract. That is because, in the absence of any findings to support a special agreement, the relationship between the appellants and the respondent (both actual and claimed) could only be that of public electricity supplier/tariff customer. For the reasons already given, in my view such a relationship is not founded in contract.

A similar view was taken in a subsequent case concerned with the relationship between foster parents and the local authority from whom they agreed to accept children for fostering.

W v Essex County Council [1999] Fam 90 (CA)

Facts: The plaintiffs, signed an agreement with the council, the first defendants, to become foster parents, after receiving assurances that no sexual abuser would be placed with them. A 15-year-old boy, was placed with them following a false representation by the council's social worker that the boy was not a sexual abuser. A month after the placement the plaintiffs discovered that G had during that period sexually abused their children, then aged between seven and 12 years. The plaintiffs sued the council for, inter alia, breach of contract and the mental distress thereby caused. The judge struck out the contractual claim. The parents appealed.

Held: The relationship between the plaintiffs and the council was not contractual.

Stuart-Smith, LJ:

. . . .The claim in contract

'**47.** On 15 October 1992 the parents signed a written document entitled "Specialist Foster Carer Agreement Supplementary to Form DSS 91 and the Code of Practice" ("the Specialist Foster Carer Agreement"). This document is expressed to be "between the council and . . ." There then follows a blank space, which is obviously intended to include the parents named. No one has been able to identify Form DSS 91. The plaintiffs alleged in the statement of claim that this agreement, together with a number of other documents, including an unsigned "Adolescent Foster Carer Agreement", which on its first page has the names and address of the parents, and a "Specialist Foster Carer Agreement Code of Practice", constitute a legally binding contract between the parents and the council. The Code of Practice begins with the statement that it:

> "is not legally binding or enforceable in law. It is designated [sic] to act as a guideline for both staff and carers with a view to ensuring the professional discretion is clearly defined and correctly exercised".

There is a further reference in paragraph 9.1 of the Code of Practice, in which attention is drawn to the need to observe certain statutory requirements, to the fact that it is not legally binding.

48. Paragraph 3 of the Specialist Foster Carer Agreement provides that the parents had the "right to decline any placement of a child or young person, provided such rejection was not made unreasonably". Paragraph 6.4 of the Code of Practice provides that "the social worker will ensure the foster carer will be fully informed about the child's background of any problem relating to that background legal, developmental or practical in writing". The plaintiffs allege that this paragraph constituted an express term of the contract and that the council were in breach of it. Alternatively they allege that there was an implied term of the contract that the defendants would inform the plaintiffs of any knowledge or suspicion of the child being a sexual abuser and in support of the implied term they rely on the conversation and assurances to the effect that the foster child would not be a sexual abuser.

49. The judge held that the Code of Practice was not intended to be legally enforceable. He held that the Specialist Foster Carer Agreement was a legally enforceable agreement but that the alleged term was not to be implied. The plaintiffs appeal against the judge's conclusion as to the express or implied term. The defendants cross-appeal against his conclusion that the Specialist Foster Care Agreement was a legally binding agreement.

50. There are, in my judgment, a number of reasons why the plaintiffs' claim in contract must fail. First, although the Specialist Foster Carer Agreement had a number of features which one would expect to find in a contract, such as the payment of an allowance and expenses, provisions as to national insurance, termination and restriction on receiving a legacy or engaging in other gainful employment and other matters to which the judge referred [1997] 2 F.L.R. 535, 565e–f, I do not accept that this makes the agreement a contract in the circumstances of this case. A contract is essentially an agreement that is freely entered into on terms that are freely negotiated. If there is a statutory obligation to enter into a form of agreement the terms of which are laid down, at any rate in their most important respects, there is no contract: see *Norweb Plc v Dixon* [1995] 1 W.L.R. 636, 643f.

51. In *S v Walsall Metropolitan Borough Council* [1985] 1 W.L.R. 1150 the question was whether foster parents were the agents of the defendant council who had placed the child in care. Oliver L.J., with whose judgment Balcombe L.J. agreed, reviewed the statutory provisions which are similar to those relevant in this case. He said, at p 1154f, that the statute and the regulations "provide a statutory code and they underline the fact that the whole of this area is covered by a complicated and detailed statutory scheme." and later he said, at p 1155e, that the "relationship between the child and the local authority, and indeed between the child and the foster parents, is one which is regulated . . . simply and solely by the provisions of the statutory scheme". It is true that he does not include the relationship between the foster parents and the council as being so regulated; but it must, in my judgment, follow. The contents of the agreement are strictly laid down in the regulations and cannot be varied. The remuneration is set by the statutory scheme and cannot be freely negotiated.

52. Furthermore, I am very doubtful whether the judge was right to consider the Specialist Foster Carer Agreement separate from the Code of Practice, which specifically stated that it is not to be legally binding. The plaintiffs had pleaded that this document formed part of the agreement, and if that is correct it shows that the agreement, whatever it was, was not to be regarded as a legally binding contract. Even if I am wrong in the conclusion I have reached in paragraph 50, I would agree with the judge that paragraph 6.4 of the Code cannot be relied upon as an express term of the contract in view of the express disclaimer to which I have referred.

53. Furthermore, even if the Specialist Foster Carer Agreement was a contract I agree with the judge that it is not necessary to imply the pleaded term. It is not necessary to do so in order to give business efficacy to the contract, nor does it represent the obvious and unexpressed intention of both parties. Indeed, as I have already pointed out, it seems to me to be in conflict with the provision in the Guidance that the information to be given was that which the council considered necessary. Furthermore, the same public policy reasons for granting immunity in tort apply equally in contract: see *Rondel v Worsley* [1969] 1 A.C. 191 and *Saif Ali v Sydney Mitchell & Co* [1980] A.C. 198, where it was held that a solicitor acting as an advocate under contract enjoys the same immunity as a barrister, who is not in a contractual relationship.

54. Finally, even if there was such an implied term it would not in my judgment avail the parties. So far as the parents are concerned I do not consider that the psychiatric shock which they suffered on learning that the children had been abused would have been within the reasonable contemplation of the parties. So far as the children are concerned there should be no privity of contract to enable them to sue. The judge expressed the view obiter that this would not have presented a problem because the strike-out procedure is not appropriate in a developing state of the law. But there is nothing novel or developing about the law relating to privity of contract.'

1.4 DISCRETE AND RELATIONAL TRANSACTIONS

As we have seen, the classical law of contract tends to assume that the typical contract is one that is a 'one-off' event – in other words a 'discrete' transaction. This has been challenged over the past 30 years by a number of commentators, the most prominent of whom has been Professor Ian Macneil. His view is that contracts are 'relational' – by which he means, first, that contracts always exist in a social and economic context, and second, that many contracts are not isolated transactions between the parties, but part of a continuing relationship. It is the second type of 'relationality' that has attracted the most attention, particularly in the context of applying contractual principles to commercial transactions. Many such contracts are expected to last for a period of time, during which the relationship between the parties, or the surrounding circumstances, may change. The classical law has difficulty dealing with this, because it assumes that all aspects of the contract have been agreed when it is first formed. All that the courts need to do is to discover what the parties intended at that point, and this will then answer all questions that may in future arise in relation to their agreement. This process is what Macneil calls 'presentiation'. It has difficulty dealing with attempts to modify the contract while it is in progress, either because of a changed relationship between the parties, or because of changed external circumstances. A relational approach to contracts can cope with such issues much more flexibly. The following extract from one of Macneil's many articles on this topic gives an idea of his approach.

Macneil, IR, 'Contracts: adjustments of long-term economic relations under classical, neo-classical and relational contract law' (1978) 72 *Northwestern UL Rev* 854

Contracts: Adjustment of Long-Term Economic Relations Under Classical, Neoclassical, and Relational Contract Law

Introduction

This article concerns the constant clash in modern economic structures between the need for stability and the need to respond to change.

The range of the conflict is, of course, immense. This article is aimed at but one segment of the problem: that centered around contractual ways of organizing production and distribution of goods and services. It focuses initially on the relation between classical and neoclassical contract law and the organization of production and distribution in flexible patterns that stress discrete transactional characteristics. It then treats the changes in planning and dispute resolution techniques required where the need for flexibility and change exceeds the dispute-resolving capabilities of a system of neoclassical law.

Variations of the following four questions form the core of the article:

1. How is flexibility planned into economic relations and what is the legal response to such planning?
2. How is conflict between specific planning and needs to adapt to subsequent change in circumstances treated?
3. How are contractual relations preserved when conflicts arise?
4. How are economic activities terminated when they have outlived their usefulness?

The first section focuses on these issues in a system dominated by discrete transactions, the second on a system with substantial infusions of relational patterns. The third section deals with highly relational patterns, where the first three questions tend to merge, and contains a separate discussion of the fourth question.

Discrete Transactions: Classical Contract Law

The Nature of Discrete Transactions

A *truly* discrete exchange transaction would be entirely separate not only from all other present relations but from all past and future relations as well. In short, it could occur, if at all, only between total strangers, brought together by chance (not by any common social structure, since that link constitutes at least the rudiments of a relation outside the transaction). Moreover, each party would have to be completely sure of never again seeing or having anything else to do with the other. Such an event could involve only a barter of goods, since even money available to one and acceptable to the other postulates some kind of common social structure. Moreover, everything must happen quickly lest the parties should develop some kind of a relation impacting on the transaction so as to deprive it of discreteness. For example, bargaining about quantities or other aspects of the transaction can erode discreteness, as certainly does any effort to project the transaction into the future through promises.

The characteristics of entirely discrete transactions, if they could occur at all deprive them of any utility as social tools of production and distribution of scarce goods and services. That fact by no means, however, renders the construct useless as a tool of economic or legal analysis, because some discreteness is present in all exchange transactions and relations. One must simply not forget that great modification is required before the model can represent a reasonably accurate picture of actual economic life. (Unfortunately, this kind of forgetfulness is an endemic problem in both economics and law.) When so modified, the construct will no longer represent an entirely discrete transaction, but will retain substantial discreteness while nevertheless remaining relatively realistic.

We do find in real life many quite discrete transactions: little personal involvement of the parties, communications largely or entirely linguistic and limited to the subject matter of transaction, the subjects of exchange consisting of an easily monetized commodity and money, little or no social (Blau 1964) or secondary exchange, (Parsons and Smelser, 1956) and no significant past relations nor likely future relations. For example, a cash purchase of gasoline at a station on the New Jersey Turnpike by someone rarely traveling the road is such a quite discrete transaction. Such quite discrete transactions are no rarity in modern technological societies. They have been and continue to be an extremely productive economic technique both to achieve distribution of goods and to encourage their production.

Thus far we have dealt only with present exchanges of existing goods. Such exchanges can, however, play but a limited role in advanced economies. Advanced economies require greater specialization of effort and more planning than can be efficiently achieved by present exchanges through discrete transactions; they require the projection of exchange into the future through planning of various kinds, that is, planning permitting and fostering the necessary degree of specialization of effort. The introduction of this key factor of futurity gives rise to the question: what happens to discreteness when exchanges are projected into the future?

The answer is that a massive erosion of discreteness occurs. This is obvious when projection of exchange into the future occurs within structures such as the family, corporations, collective bargaining, and employment, structures obviously relational in nature. Similarly obvious are various relational ways of organizing and controlling markets, for example, the guilds of the feudal era or the planning described by Professor Galbraith in *The New Industrial State* (1985, ch. 3). But this erosion of discreteness occurs even when the projection is by direct and fairly simple promise and where the subject of exchange, if transferred immediately, would permit high levels of discreteness.

Discreteness is lost even in the simple promise situation, because a basis for trust must exist if the promise is to be of any value. Trust in turn presupposes some kind of a relation between the parties. Whether it is that created by a shared morality, by prior experience, by the availability of legal sanction, or whatever, trust depends upon some kind of mutual relation into which the transaction is integrated. And integration into a relation is the antithesis of discreteness. (Lowry 1976)

In spite of the great leap away from pure discreteness occurring when exchange is projected into the future, promises themselves inherently create or maintain at least a certain minimum of discreteness. A promise presupposes that the promisor's individual will can affect the future at least partially free of the communal will, thus separating the individual from the rest of his society. Such separation is an element of discreteness. Promise also stresses the separateness of the promisor and the promisee, another element of discreteness. Moreover, some specificity and measured reciprocity is essential to an exchange of promises—no one in his right mind promises the world. This, again, results in an irreducible level of discreteness.

The foregoing can be seen in the following definition of contract promise: present communication of a commitment to future engagment in a specified reciprocal measured exchange. Thus, the partially discrete nature of promise permits the retention of a great deal of discreteness in transactions where promise projects exchange into the future. Where no massive relational elements counterbalance this discreteness (as they do, for example, in the case of collective bargaining), sense is served by speaking of the contract as discrete, even though the contract is inevitably less discrete than would be an equivalent present exchange.

The combination of exchange with promise has been one of the most powerful social tools ever developed for the production of goods and services. Moreover, discreteness in transactions so projected has its own special virtues. Just as a system of discrete transactions for exchanging present goods may be an effective way to conduct business free of all sorts of extraneous social baggage, so too may discrete transaction contracts serve this function. With this background we can now turn to the questions set out above as they relate to a system of discrete transactions.

Adjustment and Termination of Economic Relations in a System of Discrete Transactions

An economic and legal system dominated by discrete transactions deals with the conflict between various needs for stability and needs for flexibility in ways described below. (The treatment following deals both with present exchanges of existing goods and with forward contracts where exchange is projected into the future. But the latter are assumed to be of a fairly discrete nature, *e.g.* a contract for 100 tons of iron at a fixed price, delivery in one month.)

Planning Flexibility into Economic Relations—Within itself, a discrete transaction is rigid, there being no intention to achieve internal flexibility. Planning for flexibility must, therefore, be achieved outside the confines of the transaction. Consider, for example, a nineteenth century manufacturer of stoves who needs iron to be cast into stove parts but does not know how many stoves he can sell. The required flexibility has to be achieved, in a pattern of discrete transactions, by keeping each iron purchase contract small in amount, thereby permitting adjustments of quantity up or down each time a contract is entered. Thus, the needed flexibility comes from the opportunity to enter or to refrain from entering the market for iron. This market is external to the transaction rather than within it. The epitome of this kind of flexibility is the purchasing of needs for immediate delivery, rather than using any kind of a forward contract for future delivery. Such flexibility is reduced by use of forward contracts; the larger and longer they are, the greater is the reduction.

Dealing with Conflict between Specific Planning and Needs to Adapt to Change Arising Thereafter.—Only rarely in a discrete transaction will the items contracted for become useless before the forward contract is performed or become of such lessened value that the buyer either will not want them or will want them in greatly changed form. To put this another way, only rarely will there be *within* the transaction a serious conflict between specific planning and changed needs. To return to the stove manufacturer as an example, seldom will the demand for iron stoves drop so much that the manufacturer comes to regret that he contracted for as much iron as he did.

The discrete transaction technique does not, however, produce a paradise of stability for economic activity; the conflict between specific planning and the need to adapt to change arising thereafter still remains. In those relatively rare cases of difficulties arising while the contract remains unperformed, the conflict exists but is resolved entirely in favor of the specific planning and against the party desiring flexibility. Moreover, outside the discrete transaction, planning must go on; *e.g.* the seller earlier built an iron smelter in order to sell in the iron market to organizations like the stove manufacturer. Except to the modest extent that the iron producer can shift the risks to the stove manufacturer and other buyers by forward contracts, the risks of change remain with the iron producer. If the demand for iron decreases greatly, the capital invested in building the iron smelter may be largely or entirely lost. Thus, in an economy built on discrete transactions, the risks of change remain but in large measure are not shifted by the transactions. When they are shifted they are shifted totally; *e.g.* the stove manufacturer bears all those risks to the extent of the quantity for which he contracted. In effect, the contract system does not provide planning for changes; it leaves that to the internal planning of each firm.

Preserving Relations When Conflicts Arise—Where the mode of operation is a series of discrete transactions, no significant relations exist to be preserved when conflicts arise. Inside the discrete transaction all that remains is a dispute. Outside the discrete transaction no relation (other than legal rights arising out of the dispute) exists to be preserved. Thus, all that remains is a dispute to be settled or otherwise resolved. The existence of the market that the discrete transactional system presupposes eliminates the necessity for economic relations between the firms to continue in spite of the disputes. That market, rather than continued relations between these particular parties, will supply their future needs.

Terminating Economic Activities Outliving Their Usefulness—This economic need is simply a particular aspect of the need for planning flexibility into economic relations, the ultimate example of which is to scrap the specific planning altogether. If sheet steel becomes the only technologically sensible substance with which to make stoves, then the stove manufacturer simply makes no more contracts to buy iron. The iron manufacturer continues to produce iron if remaining markets make it worthwhile, or he shifts his production facilities to their next most valuable use. In extreme cases that may mean selling the facilities for scrap or even their abandonment.

. . .

Classical Contract Law and Discrete Transactions

Any contract law system necessarily must implement certain norms. It must permit and encourage participation in exchange, promote reciprocity, reinforce role patterns appropriate to particular kinds of exchange relations, provide limited freedom for exercise of choice, effectuate planning, and harmonize the internal and external matrixes of particular contracts. A contract law system reinforcing discrete contract transactions, however, must add two further goals: enhancing discreteness and enhancing presentiation.

Presentiation is a way of looking at things in which a person perceives the effect of the future on the present. It is a recognition that the course of the future is so unalterably bound by present conditions that the future has been brought effectively into the present so that it may be dealt with just as if it were in fact the present. Thus, the presentiation of a transaction involves restricting its expected future effects to those defined in the present, *i.e.* at the inception of the transaction. No eternal distinctions prevent treating the contract norm of enhancing presentiation as simply an aspect of the norm of enhancing discreteness. It is, however, such an important aspect of the projection of exchange into the future in discrete contracts—to say nothing of microeconomic theory—that separate treatment aids analysis significantly.

A classical contract law system implements these two norms in a number of ways. To implement discreteness, classical law initially treats as irrelevant the identity of the parties to the transaction. Secondly, it transactionizes or commodifies as much as possible the subject matter of contracts, *e.g.* it turns employment into a short-term commodity by interpreting employment contracts without express terms of duration as terminable at will. Thirdly, it limits strictly the sources to be considered in establishing the substantive content of the transaction. For example, formal communication (*e.g.* writings) controls informal communication (*e.g.* oral statements); linguistic communication controls nonlinguistic communication; and communicated circumstances (to the limited extent that any circumstances outside of 'agreements' are taken into account at all) control noncommunicated circumstances (*e.g.* status). Fourthly, only limited contract remedies are available, so that should the initial presentiation fail to materialize because of nonperformance, the consequences are relatively predictable from the beginning and are not openended, as they would be, for example, if damages for unforeseeable or psychic losses were allowed. Fifthly, classical contract law draws clear lines between being in and not being in a transaction; *e.g.* rigorous and precise rules of offer and acceptance prevail with no half-way houses where only some contract interests are protected or where losses are shared. Finally, the introduction of third parties into the relation is discouraged since multiple poles of interest tend to create discreteness-destroying relations.

Since discreteness enhances the possibility and likelihood of presentiation, all of the foregoing implementations of discreteness by the classical law also tend to enhance presentiation. Other classical law techniques, however, are even more precisely focused on presentiation. (Macneil 1975b, 592–94). The first of these is the equation of the legal effect of a transaction with the promises creating it. This characteristic of classical contract law is commonly explained in terms of freedom of contract, providing maximum scope to the exercise of choice. Nevertheless, a vital consequence of the use of the technique is presentiation of the transaction. Closely related to the first technique is the second: supplying a precise, predictable body of law to deal with all aspects of the transaction not encompassed by the promises. In theory, if not practice, this enables the parties to know exactly what the future holds, no matter what happens to disrupt performance. Finally, stress on expectation remedies, whether specific performance or damages measured by the value of performance, tends to bring the future into the present, since all risks, including market risks, are thereby transferred at the time the 'deal is made.'

In summary, classical contract law very closely parallels the discrete transactional patterns described in the preceding section. Such a legal system, superimposed on economic patterns of such a nature, constitutes the stereotype of interfirm (or firm and consumer or firm and employee) contracting of the laissez faire era.

Summary

A system of discrete transactions and its corresponding classical contract law provides for flexibility and change through the market outside the transactions, rather than within them. This enables the system to work while the transactions themselves remain highly discrete and presentiated, characteristics preserved and enhanced by classical contract law.

A system of more relational contract and its corresponding neoclassical contract law remains theoretically structured on the discrete and classical models, but involves significant changes. Such contracts, being more complex and of greater duration than discrete transactions, become dysfunctional if too rigid, thereby preventing the high level of presentiation of the discrete transaction. Thus, flexibility, often a great deal of it, needs to be planned into such contracts, or gaps need to be left in the planning to be added as needed. The neoclassical system responds to this by a range of techniques. These run from some open evasion of its primary theoretical commitment to complete presentiation through initial consent on to the more common techniques of stretching consent far beyond its actual bounds and by fictions to squeeze later changes within an initial consent framework.

Somewhere along the line of increasing duration and complexity, trying to force changes into a pattern of original consent becomes both too difficult and too unrewarding to justify the effort, and the contractual relation escapes the bounds of the neoclassical system. That system is replaced by very different adjustment processes of an ongoing-administrative kind in which discreteness and presentiation become merely two of the factors of decision, not the theoretical touchstones. Moreover, the substantive relation of change to the status quo has now altered from what happens in some kind of a market external to the contract to what can be achieved through the political and social processes of the relation, internal and external. This includes internal and external dispute-resolution structures. At this point, the relation has become a minisociety with a vast array of norms beyond the norms centered on exchange and its immediate processes.

1.5 DIFFERENT APPROACHES TO ANALYSING CONTRACT

Traditionally, the English approach to the analysis of contract law has been to look at the cases and statutes and to argue about what principles can be derived from those sources, whether those principles are coherent and consistent, and whether there are other principles that would serve the law's purpose better, in other words – 'doctrinal analysis'. Other approaches are, of course, possible, and are increasingly used in academic writing about contract law (though only to a limited extent in judicial consideration of contract problems). These tend to draw on the social sciences as a means of interpreting contracts – in particular economics, sociology and politics.

1.5.1 ECONOMIC ANALYSIS

Since contracts are largely concerned with the exchange of goods and services for money, it is not surprising that attempts have been made to use economic theories as a basis for analysing them. Much of the work in this area has originated in the US, and the approach taken by Kronman and Posner indicates the nature of the type of analysis, based on an acceptance of free market economics, which has resulted.

Kronman, A and Posner, R, *The Economics of Contract Law*, 1979, Boston: Little Brown, pp 1–3

The law of contracts regulates, among other kinds of transactions, the purchase and sale of goods (including real estate) and services. Since buying and selling—and related transactions, such as leasing and borrowing, which are also governed by contract law—are quintessentially economic activities, it would seem that economics should have something useful to say to students of contract law. For example, economics may be able to tell us why people make contracts and how contract law can facilitate the operation of markets. And to the extent that contract doctrines reflect judicial efforts, whether deliberate or unconscious, to achieve efficiency, economics may help toward an understanding of the meaning of the doctrines and their appropriate limits.

. . .

The fundamental economic principle with which we begin is that if voluntary exchanges are permitted—if, in other words, a market is allowed to operate—resources will gravitate toward their most valuable uses. If *A* owns a good that is worth only $100 to him but $150 to *B*, both will be made better off by an exchange of *A*'s good for *B*'s money at any price between $100 and $150; and if they realize this, they will make the exchange. By making both of them better off, the exchange will also increase the wealth of the society (of which they are members), assuming the exchange does not

---

reduce the welfare of nonparties more than it increases *A*'s and *B*'s welfare. Before the exchange—which, let us say, takes place at a price of $125—*A* had a good worth $100 to him and *B* had $125 in cash, a total of $225. After the exchange, *A* has $125 in cash and *B* has a good worth $150 to him, a total of $275. The exchange has increased the wealth of society by $50 (ignoring, as we have done, any possible third-party effects).

The principle is the same whether we are speaking of the purchase of a string of pearls, a lawyer's time, a machine for making shoes, or an ingot of aluminum. The existence of a market—a locus of opportunities for mutually advantageous exchanges—facilitates the allocation of the good or service in question to the use in which it is most valuable, thereby maximizing the wealth of society.

This conclusion may be questioned on various grounds. For example, it may be argued that since 'value' in this analysis is measured by willingness to pay, which in turn is affected by the distribution of income and wealth (one cannot offer to buy a good without having money or the means to obtain it), the maximization of value cannot be regarded as an uncontroversially proper goal for society to pursue. An introductory chapter is not the place to explore the philosophical basis of the economist's concept of value. For our purposes it is enough that the reader understand the technical meaning of the concept. The reader (assisted by some of the selections in this book) can then decide whether there is any 'value,' in an ultimate social sense, to the *economic* concept of value which the system of free exchanges promotes.

The principle that voluntary exchange should be freely permitted in order to maximize value is frequently summarized in the concept (or slogan) of 'freedom of contract.' This is something of a misnomer, for the concept of *contract* typically plays an insignificant role in elucidations and critiques of the principle of voluntary exchange. Many value-maximizing exchanges occur without contracts, or with contracts so rudimentary or transitory as to have little interest for economists studying the phenomenon of voluntary exchange. If *A* buys the Chicago Tribune from *B*, a news vendor, paying 20¢ for it on the spot, this is a value-maximizing exchange; but it would be pretentious to speak of a contract between *A* and *B*, though technically there is one (if a section of the paper is missing, *A* can probably rescind the contract and get his 20¢ back). One can talk about the principle or system of voluntary exchange for quite some time before it becomes necessary to consider the role of contracts and contract law in facilitating the process.

In the newspaper example, the exchange is virtually (though not completely) instantaneous; and this provides a clue to the role of contracts in the process of voluntary exchange. It is true that, although money and good cross at the same moment, the actual *use* of the good—the reading of the newspaper—occurs after the exchange and takes some time; so really the process of exchange is not complete until the paper has been opened and inspected. Only then can the buyer be satisfied that he got what he paid for (that no pages are missing or illegible, etc.). Still, the time required to complete the exchange in the newspaper example is quite short. Where the time is long, contracts and contract law become important.

Suppose that *A* promises to build a house for *B*, construction to take six months to complete and B to pay either periodically or on completion. With construction so time-consuming, there is a significant likelihood that something will occur to frustrate the exchange—insolvency, changes in the price of inputs, labor troubles, etc. Nor is A's performance complete when construction of the house is finished. A durable good like a house by definition yields services to the purchaser over a period of time, a long one in the case of a house; and it is these services rather than the physical structure itself that the purchaser is hoping to acquire. If the house wears out long before the purchaser reasonably believed it would, the exchange will be effectively thwarted long after nominal completion of performance by the promisor.

Economists have pointed out that the cost of an undertaking tends to be inversely related to the time allowed for completion. Stated differently, it is costly to accelerate completion of a time-consuming task. It would also be costly to make goods less durable in order to compress the period in which the full exchange of the goods could be completed. These observations suggest that a system of contract rights, and not merely one of property rights, may be necessary to minimize the costs of production in a market system.

1.5.2 SOCIOPOLITICAL ANALYSIS

Any analysis of the law of contract will be based on political assumptions. The classical law of contract is underpinned by a belief in the freedom of contract, which is a political viewpoint. Very often these assumptions are implicit. Some writers bring their political standpoint to the forefront of their analysis, whether it be capitalist, Marxist, socialist, etc.

One example is the work of Collins, as indicated in the extract reproduced above at pp 13–14.

Another interesting approach, which is useful in analysing many specific areas of contract law is that expounded by Adams and Brownsword. They identify four particular ideologies that may compete or conflict in considering the application of the law to contractual problems. These are formalism, realism, consumer-welfarism, and market-individualism. They are explained and described in the following extract.

Adams, J and Brownsword, R, *Understanding Contract Law*, 2004,
4th edn, London: Sweet & Maxwell, pp 36–44

JUDGES AND THE RULE-BOOK: AN INTERPRETIVE FRAMEWORK
In this section we introduce a theoretical framework which we will employ in Part II as a tool for analysis of material in the contract rule-book. Our purpose at this point is merely to develop this framework sufficiently for readers to be able to follow our

discussion in Part II. As that discussion proceeds, the theoretical framework and its implications should move more clearly into focus. We therefore postpone a more comprehensive analysis until Chapter 8.

Our first step in constructing the theoretical framework is to think about how judges might proceed where they are called upon to interpret and apply the rule-book. In principle, we suggest, judges may approach their task from two different starting points. According to one approach, let us call it the 'formalist' approach, judges will see their role in terms of unpacking the materials in the rule-book. Crucially, the rule-book will be treated as decisive even where the results are for some reason hard on one party. By contrast, according to the alternative approach, which we can call the 'realist' approach, judges will proceed in a result-orientated fashion, irrespective of the dictates of the rule-book.

We can indicate the significance of these rival approaches if we imagine that a second case had arisen out of Esso's World Cup coins promotion, but with the following facts (which, incidentally, are far removed from the actual facts, which we will recall raised an issue of revenue law). Suppose that Alf, having chased half-way across London, found an Esso garage having a coin showing the head of his favourite England player, and suppose that, having purchased the required amount of petrol, Alf was told that he could not have the coin. Now, suppose that Alf sued Esso for breach of contract, arguing that he had a single contract for the sale of the petrol plus the coin. Guided by the *Esso* decision (where it will be recalled the single contract analysis was rejected by the majority of the Law Lords), a judge following the formalist approach would reject Alf's claim—irrespective of the hardship worked on Alf. By contrast, a judge following the realist approach, sensitive to the result of Alf's case, might well reason that Esso should not be able to get away with such sharp practice, and that Alf must win. This being so, Alf would be allowed to succeed either on his single contract analysis or on a collateral contract analysis (this being easy to square with *Esso* itself).

Now, before we continue, we must enter two clarifying reservations against our distinction between the formalist and realist approaches. First, the distinction is exceedingly stark. The implication of our presentation is that any judge who nods in the direction of the rule-book must be categorised as adopting a formalist approach whilst any judge who shows an interest in results must be pigeonholed as following a realist approach. Plainly, however, this suffers from the sort of distortion which we would instantly recognise if we were to describe everyone living in Britain as 'northerners' or 'southerners'. To do justice to the complexity of judicial reasoning, we would have to construct categories lying between the formalist and realist poles (allowing, for example, for a result-orientated approach which holds only where some degree of fit with the rule-book is possible, or a rule-book approach which becomes result-orientated where the materials in the rule-book fail to settle the point *cf.* Adams and Brownsword, 2003). For our purposes, however, which are a matter of roughly getting our bearings, our crude distinction between formalist and realist approaches will suffice.

Secondly, judicial reasoning has been the focus of a wealth of jurisprudential writing (most recently see Dworkin, 1986). The terms 'formalism' and 'realism' enjoy some currency in this literature; indeed, some would argue that they are so overworked that they are no longer useful labels. The point, however, is that they are labels in common employment and it is difficult to think of satisfactory alternatives. The reader must however be aware of the particular way in which we use these labels. When we use 'formalism' and 'realism' (and similarly when, later on in this chapter, we use the labels 'market-individualism', 'consumer-welfarism' and 'ideology') we use these terms *stipulatively*: that is, they mean in this book what we say they mean, not what anyone else says they mean. We use these approaches as *descriptive* models of how judges *do* decide cases, not as *prescriptive* models recommending how judges *ought* to decide cases. To be sure, the models could be used either descriptively or prescriptively, but in this book, at least, they are employed primarily as a descriptive resource (see, further, Chapter 10, especially pp 250–251).

The formalist and realist approaches are 'ideal-typical' in the sense that we can conceive of them without either inspecting judicial practice or supposing that they will be fully instantiated therein (*cf.* Chapter 10). If we focus on the realist approach, however, it will be appreciated that we could conceive, in principle, of any number of criteria to serve as the measure of fitness of particular results. In our contention, however, two realist philosophies dominate contractual thinking in practice. These are what we shall term 'market-individualism' and 'consumer-welfarism'.

Market-individualism has two limbs, a market philosophy and an individualistic philosophy. The market philosophy sees the function of the law of contract as the facilitation of competitive exchange. This demands clear contractual ground rules, transactional security, and the accommodation of commercial practice. The individualistic side of market-individualism enshrines the landmark principles of 'freedom of contract' and 'sanctity of contract', the essential thrust of which is to give the parties the maximum licence in setting their own terms, and to hold parties to their freely made bargains. One particularly important entailment of market-individualism is that judges should offer no succour to parties who are simply trying to escape from a bad bargain, for the sum total of freely negotiated bargains is the good of society as a whole in that it results in an economically efficient use of resources.

The tenets of consumer-welfarism cannot be stated so crisply. In the most abstract terms, consumer-welfarism stands for reasonableness and fairness in contracting. More concretely, this is reflected in a policy of consumer-protection and a pot-pourri of specific principles. For example, consumer-welfarism holds that contracting parties should not mislead one another, that they should act in good faith, that a stronger party should not exploit the weakness of another's bargaining position, that no party should profit from his own wrong or be unjustly enriched, that remedies should be proportionate to the breach, that contracting parties who are at fault should not be able to dodge their responsibilities, and so on. Crucially, consumer-welfarism subscribes to the paternalistic principle that contractors who enter into bad bargains may be relieved from their obligations where justice so requires. To this extent, and at the price of some oversimplification, consumer-welfarism may be said to treat justice as more important than freedom (and vice versa for market-individualism). We can illustrate the potential opposition between the market-individualist and consumer-welfarist philosophies by considering a much debated modern case—*L. Schuler AG v Wickman Machine Tool Sales Ltd* (1974).

In *Schuler*, the parties had a distributorship agreement under which Wickman had sole selling rights in respect of panel presses manufactured by Schuler. Clause 7(b) of the agreement (specifically designated as a 'condition' of the contract) placed Wickman under an obligation to send one of its representatives to visit the six largest UK motor manufacturers at least once a week to solicit orders. Wickman being guilty of a number of failures under cl. 7(b), the question was whether Schuler were entitled to terminate the agreement. The nub of Schuler's argument was that, by designating cl. 7(b) a 'condition', they had indicated that any breach of the visiting obligation—even a single breach, and even a breach occasioning no apparent loss—entitled them to withdraw from the contract if they so wished.

The arbitrator, the majority of the Court of Appeal, and the majority of the House of Lords found in favour of Wickman; but Mocatta J. (hearing the appeal from the arbitrator's decision), Stephenson L.J. (dissenting in the Court of Appeal), and Lord Wilberforce (dissenting in the House of Lords) ruled in favour of Schuler. Superficially, the case was all about the technical meaning of the label 'condition', but the policy considerations underlying this debate surfaced dramatically in the House of Lords. The majority of their Lordships could not accept the proposition that Schuler should, in principle, be able to put an end to the contract as soon as Wickman, in breach of cl. 7(b), failed to make one visit. This was, for them, altogether too much, and they condemned such a suggestion as 'unreasonable' (Lord Reid at p.251), and 'utterly fantastic' (Lord Morris at pp 255–6), and as 'productive of absurd results' (Lord Simon at p 265), and 'grotesque consequences' (Lord Kilbrandon at p 272). By contrast, Lord Wilberforce delivered a forceful dissent saying:

> '. . . to call the clause arbitrary, capricious or fantastic, or to introduce as a test of its validity the ubiquitous reasonable man (I do not know whether he is English or German) is to assume, contrary to the evidence, that both parties to this contract adopted a standard of easygoing tolerance rather than one of aggressive, insistent punctuality and efficiency. This is not an assumption I am prepared to make, nor do I think myself entitled to impose the former standard upon the parties if their words indicate, as they plainly do, the latter.' (p 263)

Therefore, Wickman won, but not without Lord Wilberforce's strong dissent. What are we to make of such a sharp difference of judicial opinion?

Pretty clearly, Lord Wilberforce thought it right to defer to the commercial standards and expectations of the parties as plainly expressed in their contract. For him, the intentions of the contracting parties were paramount, at least within the bounds of public policy. It simply was not for judges to rewrite commercial agreements. Freedom of contract (*cf.* Chapter 8, p 192) was the ruling principle, market-individualism the underlying philosophy.

Ranged against Lord Wilberforce's position were the views of the four majority members of the House. One interpretation of the majority position is that their Lordships actually shared Lord Wilberforce's principle of freedom of contract but thought that, on the evidence, the parties had not intended to give Schuler the right to terminate the contract simply on the strength of a single breach of the visiting obligation. A more plausible interpretation, however, is that the majority acted on a different principle. Central to their thinking was the idea that it is appropriate for judges to relieve parties from contracts the effects of which as things have turned out are particularly oppressive. Seen from this perspective, it is perfectly legitimate for judges to impose their standards upon the contracting parties where this is necessary to preserve reasonableness in contracting. Such, of course, is the philosophy of consumer-welfarism.

Our two ideal-typical judicial approaches (formalism and realism) can be combined with our two contractual philosophies (market-individualism and consumer-welfarism) to yield the interpretive framework shown opposite.

Although each of the four elements contributing to this theoretical framework represents an essential ideological thread, it is important to underline the distinction between, on the one hand, formalism and realism as *general* ideologies of adjudication and, on the other hand, market-individualism and consumer-welfarism as area-*specific* ideologies. As general ideologies, formalism and realism constitute distinctive views about (or attitudes towards) the judicial role—views about how adjudication ought to be, and is, approached. Such ideologies are not specifically concerned with the judicial role in contract cases; in principle, they represent approaches to adjudication in any area of law, whether statute-based or case-based (see further Adams and Brownsword, 2003). Market-individualism and consumer-welfarism, however, are concerned specifically with contract law—not with criminal law, or property law, or family law, or any other branch of law. At one level, these are the ideologies that underlie much of contract doctrine; at another level, these are the ideologies that feed specifically into the adjudication of contract cases. Once we put together the general ideologies of adjudication with the specific ideologies of contract, we produce the more complex interpretive framework (as shown below) in which there is a synthesis of the general and the contract-specific ideologies. Moreover, each synthesis represents a new ideology, a distinctive cluster of ideas, values, and attitudes capable of shaping and directing the judicial approach to particular contract cases (*cf.* Chapter 10).

	Formalism	Realism
Market-Individualism	Rule-book approach (rules in rule-book reflecting market-individualism)	Result-orientated approach (guided by market-individualism)
Consumer-Welfarism	Rule-book approach (rules in rule-book reflecting consumer-welfarism)	Result-orientated approach (guided by consumer-welfarism)

Once again we must pause to avoid misunderstanding. Our theoretical framework is constituted by the concepts of 'formalism', 'realism', 'market-individualism', and 'consumer-welfarism', each of which is presented as an 'ideology'. Readers who have previously encountered some of these terms may be thinking that a framework so constituted is an eclectic mess. For instance, it may be thought that we mismatch formalism and realism because American writers tend to use the former term prescriptively and the latter descriptively; that our sketch of market-individualism is a perverse distortion of welfare-maximising economic theory, or of utilitarianism, to which neither Adam Smith nor Jeremy Bentham would ever have subscribed; and that our brief description of the concept of ideology betrays a breathtaking ignorance of Marxism. Should we not, therefore, go back to the drawing board? On the contrary, as we pointed out above, we are employing this terminology *stipulatively*. The correct usage of these terms is not written in tablets of stone (far from it), and it is simply irrelevant how anyone else, even Great Men, would employ them. For the purposes of this book, the terms mean what we stipulatively say they mean—and we say what we mean at an introductory level in this chapter, and comprehensively in Chapter 8.

Our discussion in the next part of the book is guided by our theoretical framework. The implications of this are twofold. First, we relate the materials in the rule-book to the ideologies of market-individualism and consumer-welfarism, our thesis being that these two philosophies constitute important ideological underpinnings of substantive contract doctrine, though they are not necessarily the only underpinnings. Secondly, we relate particular judicial decisions to the ideologies within our framework. Our thesis here is that our theoretical framework yields three basic approaches in contract cases, represented by the formalist, market-individualist-realist (hereafter 'market-individualist'), and consumer-welfarist-realist (hereafter 'consumer-welfarist') ideologies. It is our contention that judicial decisions in contract would be better understood if they were described against the backcloth of this triangular ideological contest (*i.e.* formalist v market-individualist v consumer-welfarist). The overall pattern of our thinking is represented in the figure below.

Some final cautions are in order. First, and very importantly, the triangular ideological contest represents a field of tensions within which judges operate. In any particular case, the tensions will be resolved in favour of one of the approaches. Now, it is sometimes convenient to talk about 'formalist', 'market-individualist' or 'consumer-welfarist' in relation to the predilections of judges, rather than in relation to approaches they may adopt in particular cases. Our intention should not be misunderstood, however. We do not imply that all judges can be rigidly categorised as belonging to one or other ideological school bearing these labels. No doubt some judges are more consistent than others in following a particular approach, but the extent to which judges are consistent in this respect is a matter for investigation. Thus, whenever we use locutions such as 'formalist judge(s)' or simply 'formalist(s)', this important reservation should be recalled. Secondly, it would be a mistake to suppose that the market-individualist and consumer-welfarist approaches are irrelevant to the rule-book. Although judges adopting a realist approach of either sort by definition (ours) do not rely on the rule-book, their decisions nevertheless feed back into the rule-book. Thirdly, we have so far given only an outline specification of the ideologies within our theoretical framework. If it is not already evident, readers will see in due course that each of the ideologies embraces a cluster of ideas. Therefore, when we state that a judge in a particular case has followed, say, the formalist approach, we do not necessarily mean that he has followed all aspects of that particular ideology, merely some part or parts of it. Finally, by drawing our stark distinction between formalism and realism, by reducing judicial reasoning in contract cases to three basic approaches, and by packing into each ideology a whole cluster of ideas, we invite the charge that we caricature the judicial process. Our intention certainly is not to lampoon the judiciary. On the contrary, our thesis is that judges are inescapably caught in a web of tensions, of which we highlight three, and which they in good faith endeavour to resolve according to their own lights. If this involves simplification on our part, it is simplification which we hope is justified in the interests of stimulating the reader's thought and gaining some appreciation of the larger picture of contract.

1.5.3 EMPIRICAL RESEARCH

One way of analysing contract law is to look at the way in which it works, or does not work, in practice. Do those who make contracts actually use the law to assist them to make 'better' bargains, or to provide solutions when problems arise? This involves empirical research. Relatively little of such work appears in the academic commentaries of contract, but one example is given here, drawn from the work of Yates on exclusion clauses.

Yates, D, *Exclusion Clauses in Contracts*, 1982, 2nd edn, London: Sweet & Maxwell, pp 18–33

A relatively small amount of empirical research has been carried out into the attitude of businessmen towards contractual procedures in their conduct of business affairs. In the U.S.A. Professor Macaulay carried out research among 48 companies and six law firms in Wisconsin. He described contract as involving 'two distinct elements: (a) rational planning of the transaction with careful provision for as many future contingencies as can be foreseen, and (b) the existence or use of actual or potential legal sanctions to induce performance of the exchange or to compensate for non-performance.' It is interesting that these two elements approximately correspond with Summers' private arranging and grievance remedial techniques. Macaulay identified four types of issue which might be planned for—description of the primary obligations, contingencies, defective performances and legal sanctions. Exclusion clauses, of course, may be key devices in planning for all of these. Macaulay concluded that while many business exchanges will involve a high degree of planning about each category, equally many at least 'reflect no planning or only a minimal amount of it, especially concerning legal sanctions and the effect of defective performance.' He found very little use was made of 'contractual practices' in the later adjustment of relationships, though there was some evidence of tacit reliance on contractual rights. Very little use was made of formal dispute-settlement procedures available through the courts.

The most important published research on the attitudes of British businessmen to the use of contractual practices is that carried out by Beale and Dugdale in Bristol during 1973 and 1974. Their conclusions were not dissimilar to Macaulay's. Businessmen tended to eschew contractual remedies as being too inflexible, and lawyers as being unsympathetic to the problems of businessmen. There was a similar reluctance to use the law in planning operations generally, save that if the risk justified it, there might be some careful planning, hard bargaining and detailed legal drafting.

The presence of an exclusion clause indicates either the presence of a risk which one party wishes to transfer to the other, or it indicates a very precise attempt to define the obligations the promisor is undertaking. There is a third possibility, in that the clause is intended to have simply a cosmetic effect, *i.e.* it is inserted by a party who is indifferent to the clause's efficiacy at law, but who believes that its presence has a threatening or deterrent effect upon performance. Whenever a clause is used, however, and whatever its function, it indicates a high level of planning at some stage in the drafting process, and a close regard for the private arranging technique, at least in relation to certain parts of the legal framework for agreement.

An attempt has therefore been made, by means of questions directed towards businessmen, to ascertain first, when exclusion clauses will be drafted into agreements and why, and second, the circumstances in which they are relied upon during the grievance remedy procedures. For this purpose a survey was conducted during the years 1974–1976 among three groups of business operations in the south west and north west regions of England, using Bristol and Manchester as bases. Fifty-one firms cooperated in the survey, 31 being light or heavy mechanical or civil engineering firms, 12 being finance companies and eight being insurance companies or Lloyd's brokers. Fourteen of the firms who were prepared to answer questions about their practices had their own legal departments. There was quite a significant difference in the attitude of non-lawyer businessmen towards lawyers in those firms with legal departments and those without. As one might expect, those firms who had their own 'in-house' lawyers had a far greater trust of a lawyer's ability to understand business problems, although as one executive in the aero-engine industry said: 'We trust our lawyers to get us out of a jam, but we don't trust them not to get us into one.' Curiously, in the engineering industry particularly, lawyers seemed to be consulted at a much earlier stage in discussions on company policy in those firms without their own legal departments than in those with 'in-house' lawyers. For example, one light engineering company, worried about possible patent infringement, consulted outside lawyers with a view to devising distribution contracts that might relieve them of liability in the event of unintentional infringement, even before the product had completed the design stage. An engine manufacturer with its own legal department, on the other hand, stated that they would not seek the advice of their legal colleagues until the engine reached production stage, and not necessarily then unless one of the lawyers raised it. The general and rather innocent view was that designers and engineers who worked for such large companies had to be trusted not to infringe patents.

The explanation of these differing attitudes to 'in-house' or outside law firms is probably as much to do with the nature of the company and its size as anything else. In-house lawyers tend to be fairly senior in the management hierarchy. They are likely to be known personally to managers who make the major executive decisions, they are viewed more as colleagues than as legal advisors, and that is almost certainly the major reason why greater trust is reposed in them as against outside firms. It is unlikely that judgments of legal competence enter very much into the assessment and, in any event, any such judgments are likely to be distorted by feelings of loyalty and attachment to the common employer. On the other hand, only large business enterprises (or insurance companies, who need not necessarily be large ones) can afford to maintain their own legal departments. In large firms the work is much more compartmentalised. Decisions are reached at departmental level and the development of a product tends to pass through several well-defined stages or departments, with little overlap between them. Interestingly, in those large firms that excluded their legal departments until a late stage in the process, marketing departments were also excluded: design, or research and development departments were given a much longer exclusive contact with the product. In smaller firms such departmentalisation tended not to occur. Often the managing director was personally and directly involved from an early stage, and he insisted upon early consultation with professional advisors, both financial and legal.

The types of businesses dealt with by the firms consulted fell into two very distinct groups. First were those businesses who dealt mainly with other businessmen and whose contracts were geared to what one might term 'commercial' operations, and secondly were those, mainly financial institutions, who dealt with the general public and whose operations were in the consumer market.

1. Commercial operators

Exclusion clauses, as opposed to limitation clauses, were not commonly found in the commercial agreements (some of which were in 'standard form') examined. Those that did occur (leaving aside excepted perils clauses in insurance contracts, see *post*) tended to be drafted in such a way as to prevent liability arising on the part of a supplier as a result of specified causes perceived as being beyond his control, the most common being delay caused by strikes, the non-availability of materials and government action (this last almost certainly written in as a result of the 3-day week in 1974).

More common were limitation clauses and procedural clauses such as arbitration provisions. Some firms limited liability in their contracts of supply to a particular sum, usually a multiplier of the contract price. This device was justified on the ground that it was regarded as commercially unacceptable in many cases to incur liability in respect of consequential loss. This seemed to be a particularly strongly felt view among component manufacturers. Many of the light engineering firms were involved in making components, each part of a relatively small value, under sub-contract. The price paid per component manufactured (often on a 'royalty only' basis) was considered so small, in relation to the risks likely to be incurred if the manufacturer undertook liability for consequential losses, that it was thought to be not only prudent, but reasonable, to limit liability to a multiplier of the contract price. The alternative of insurance had been considered by some firms but, where profit margins were small and risks possibly high, (the shearing of a vital bolt or breaking of a steel cable could involve massive liability for consequential losses) the expensive premiums frequently demanded were regarded as an unjustifiable expense if the head contractor or manufacturer of the finished article or structure was prepared to take the risk upon himself.

Where liquidated damages clauses were used, some firms thought these figures to be a genuine attempt to pre-estimate damages, although eight engineering firms expressed the view that the figures specified (usually varying amounts of the contract sum), were unlikely to bear much relation to the likely loss sustained, for the reasons given above. All those firms, however, felt that the commercial sense of such clauses was so obvious that their insertion would be likely to discourage litigation on an individual claim unless business relations between the parties had otherwise broken down. Many senior managers thought that litigation upon such matters as limitation clauses was likely to arise when lawyers had been called in to reinforce complaints that had started, not as arguments about the contract terms, but about other matters such as erratic supplies, poor after-sales service or bad marketing.

Very common in contracts for the sale or supply of goods were various limitations as to time. These took the form either of time limits on a party's right to go to arbitration or limits on the time within which claims must be made or notified. Exceptions designed to exclude liability in respect of express conditions or warranties of the contract were very rare and found in specially negotiated agreements rather than in standard forms.

Where they were found, they were justified on the ground that businessmen, on occasion, wish to put declarations of intent in their contracts, so that both parties have a clear idea of the aims and purposes of the business relationship, without those declarations attracting legal liability. For example, a civil engineering contract for the construction of a bridge contained general statements concerning the desire, on the part of the local authority, that the bridge be acceptable on environmental grounds, although the contract also contained a clause that the contractors were *only* to be liable on the express undertakings contained in the schedules, which contained terms as to time, payment, labour force, construction specifications and so on. Some firms, notably those with their own legal departments, confessed to having spent much time in attempting to draft clauses that it was hoped would exclude various of the terms implied by the Sale of Goods Act 1893 (now 1979). Section 12 proved a particular obstacle here although, because of its possible utility in litigation arising from patent infringement, it was the provision that often exercised lawyers' minds the most in manufacturing firms. Various devices were adopted to make the clauses appear 'reasonable,' the most common being differential prices (putting a higher price on the supply of goods or services if the supplier carried all risks) or an offer to supply on alternative standard terms (such as those of the Federation of Associations of Specialists and Sub-contractors). None of the firms approached used contract documents that expressly excluded either the right to reject or rescind or the right to damages altogether, although some firms did so by implication in that they *only* undertook to repair or replace defective goods.

Several reasons were advanced for incorporating exclusion clauses into contracts. The first has already been mentioned in the context of sub-contracted component manufacture, and that was the desire to exclude or reduce liability for consequential loss. This reason was advanced by other manufacturers and suppliers also. Since most of the specially negotiated contracts appeared to involve large, complex items such as expensive electronic medical equipment, engineering production equipment, bridges, buses, aircraft and such like, there was always the risk of a manufacturing or installation defect causing considerable consequential loss. In this area, and in contrast to the sub-contractors, rather than be his own insurer the manufacturer or constructor would take out extensive insurance cover. In many cases, therefore, such exclusion or limitation clauses as were found in these specially negotiated contracts would be there solely to pass on those risks which the insurance company had refused to cover at all, or would only cover with very high premium payments that were commercially unacceptable. One insurance company had a firm rule that it would only offer cover to contractors where the contract price exceeded one million pounds, if it had a right of veto on the contractual terms. Aside from these large, complex engineering and related contracts, however, most businesses appeared to insure against surprisingly few risks. Loss by fire and theft, damage by flood and sprinkler valves, loss through explosion and similar disasters causing destruction or damage, loss or damage in transit and occasionally loss as a result of failure to meet delivery dates. Very few insured against loss of production as a result of deliberate 'in-house' sabotage. In most other respects, small enterprise manufacturers appeared to be their own insurers. No one seemed prepared to admit however, that, aside from the problem of consequential loss, this was a factor that influenced the decision as to whether a specially drafted contract should be commissioned from the legal department or the firm's solicitors, although it is hard to accept that it was not.

The desire to avoid court proceedings in the event of dispute was also a reason advanced for using exemption, especially limitation clauses which, it was often felt, gave each party a clearer indication of where they stood. The desire to avoid litigation in the courts also explained the insertion of arbitration clauses, time limit clauses and 'contingency' clauses. Distrust of lawyers' and more especially judges' ability to understand the businessman's problems was very marked.

Another reason frequently advanced was simply 'because everyone else does it.' This is not quite as mindless as it at first sounds. A very large number of contracts in the engineering industry (electrical, mechanical and civil) are conducted by means of forms containing standard conditions of sale or purchase. The forms have the terms such as the description of the goods, the price, delivery dates, terms of payment, etc. on the front, while the terms providing for adjustment, specification variation, contingencies and exclusions would be on the back. The buyer would frequently order in accordance with his conditions and the seller would acknowledge with his printed conditions. The exact correspondence between offer and acceptance was often difficult to determine and its significance clearly escaped many of the businessmen consulted. Where lawyers had been involved in the drafting of these forms (which was by no means always the case) some attempt was made to achieve uniformity between suppliers' forms and those of their more important customers. Firms who did not make use of the services of a lawyer in drafting their 'back of order' terms either drafted their own without legal assistance (25 per cent, of the sample of engineering firms) or used standard conditions such as those of the Royal Institute of British Architects, the Joint Contracts Tribunal, the Institution of Civil Engineers, the Institution of Mechanical Engineers, the Institution of Electrical Engineers and the Association of Consulting Engineers. All the insurance companies and finance houses received substantial legal assistance in drafting their terms. Comprehensive exclusions designed to provide protection should one's client find himself the victim of the other party's terms as a result of losing the 'battle of the forms' were sometimes, therefore, adopted by insurance companies who had only agreed to provide cover if the contract were conducted by the client on *his* terms. This problem is discussed in greater detail in Chapter 2.

Both standard form and specially drafted contracts contained numerous devices that were not actually exclusion clauses in the conventional sense, but were clearly designed to achieve the same result. Contracts might provide that a representative of the other side could attend pre-delivery inspections and tests and sometimes, notably with engines and complex electrical apparatus, was asked to sign an acceptance note or an acknowledgement that the goods complied, in construction and performance, with specification. Contracts would also contain indemnity clauses, often with an associated obligation imposed upon the indemnifier to insure against the risks to be indemnified (see Clause 26 of the British Steel Corporation's General Conditions of Contract). Buyers would sometimes provide in their conditions that the last instalment of the purchase price may be withheld until the machine was operating satisfactorily in the buyer's own plant. Indeed, the use of stipulations as to payment (operating either on the obligation to pay the price or as a penalty) appeared to be relied upon by many businessmen as being more efficacious than any exclusions or genuine liquidated damages clauses. The insistence, for example, of cash with order or, on the buyer's part, no payment without satisfactory performance, seems like a clear attempt at self-regulation, obviating the need to seek the lawyer's services at all in grievance procedures.

2. Consumer agreements

In the consumer field all those companies questioned, both finance companies and insurance companies, used standard-form agreements. Contracts were never specially negotiated, although occasionally forms seemed to be accepted from clients or customers with individual clauses or questions struck out. Where this was done the firms concerned seemed to think that it made no difference to the terms of the agreement. One finance company said that applicants frequently strike out or incorrectly complete some part of the proposal form which later forms the basis of the contract between customer and finance company. In the view of the company this made no difference, since by then the customer had been made aware of the terms upon which the company was prepared to contract. It is almost certain that the company's confidence in this matter was misplaced. Most proposal forms were sent in by the retail dealer or broker, already completed by the prospective client. After vetting the proposal, it would either be accepted or rejected by the company. The client was usually notified of acceptance by the statutorily required despatch of the second, executed copy of the agreement. The offer, then, came from the proposer, not the company, and if the proposal contains deleted or incomplete clauses, and the form is accepted in this state by the company, then a binding contract on those terms comes into effect.

Most exclusions found in finance companies' standard form documents related to exclusion of liability for misrepresentation—an attempt was frequently made to circumvent section 3 of the Misrepresentation Act 1967, by requiring agreement to a clause stating that the customer had not relied upon any statements made to him (but see Chapter 3, *post*). Any express agency between dealer and finance company was refuted in the standard form, and express conditions and warranties were excluded. Some attempts were still being made to exclude implied terms, notwithstanding that such exclusions were void and, indeed, are now also sometimes criminal (see Chapter 3, *post*). The warranty of title was nearly always limited to such title as the company might have. Hire-purchase forms usually contained a provision entitling the company to terminate the agreement for breach of any undertaking given by the hirer and there was also frequently a provision excluding liability for personal injuries or consequential loss. Many of these exclusions, if not void at the time of the survey, would now be void under the Unfair Contract Terms Act 1977.

It was also common for hire-purchase agreements used by the finance companies to contain clauses in which the hirer acknowledged and agreed a certain set of facts, such as that the finance company as owner has complied with its obligations and liabilities (*e.g.* that the goods are in good condition and suitable for the purpose for which they are required) or that the requirements of the Hire Purchase Act 1965 (at the time of the survey, no part of the Consumer Credit Act 1974 was in force) had been complied with. These would include declarations that the cash price was stated to the intending hirer before the agreement was entered into, that the clause excluding the statutory condition as to fitness was brought to the notice of the hirer and its effect made clear to him and so on. Again, many of these clauses would not be enforceable if litigated (see Chapter 3, *post*). Most agreements also contained provisions permitting the company to rescind the agreement should there be any misstatement by the hirer, and provisions requiring indemnity of the company by the customer or client for any loss sustained consequent upon the agreement.

Most of the companies consulted were not particularly sanguine about the enforceability of the exclusion clauses in their agreements. While they would, as a matter of policy, always be relied upon, their insertion seemed to be largely a question of psychology. One representative of a finance company stated that the presence of exclusions is more likely to secure compliance with the agreement, and far more likely to secure payment before the court hearings should the debt turn bad, since it left the customer with the (frequently erroneous) view that he had few enforceable contractual rights against the finance company. All the companies would enter bad debts on one of the two major credit reference agency lists and would pursue defaulters rigorously, as a matter of policy, through the courts. The first stage would usually be a letter from a solicitor (where there was an 'in-house' lawyer) or a standard default letter from the collections department where there was not, followed by the repossession of the goods if possible and/or county court proceedings.

Most finance companies were prepared to admit, under pressure, that several of the retailers with whom they dealt did not always observe scrupulous standards of fair dealing. One 'in-house' lawyer reported that the exclusion clauses in his company's agreements were there as much to protect the company against unscrupulous or incompetent retail outlets as to shield the company from customer complaints originating in the finance company's own offices. The reducing chances of these clauses being upheld in litigation, as increasingly fierce attacks upon them are launched both by the legislature and the judiciary, has resulted in some finance companies turning away from the traditional hire-purchase agreement, sacrificing real security for the flexibility of personal loans or budget accounts. All the finance companies consulted were, however, certain that these new devices were of relatively short-lived efficacy since, being mostly debtor-creditor-supplier agreements within the Consumer Credit Act 1974, s. 12, the lender becomes liable for the retailer's breaches of contract and misrepresentations under section 75 of that Act even though the goods are purchased by the borrower from the retailer direct and not from the finance company. Most finance companies said that they would continue to use exclusion clauses in their agreements, simply because they assisted in persuading the borrower to take his obligations seriously, but no one doubted the impact that recent legislation had on the consumer credit field. Most of the companies reported turning to alternative forms of risk allocation and the insurance companies reported a large increase in bad debt insurance from the smaller finance companies. Where repossession of the goods is difficult or impossible, and where the risk of defects can no longer be passed to the hirer, passing them back to the retailer under recourse agreements or obtaining appropriate insurance cover offer the only other solutions.

3. Conclusions

It seemed to all those enterprises questioned that detailed contract planning (though not necessarily specially negotiated contracts) had an important place in commercial practice. However, in the non-consumer context, such planning is, generally speaking, aimed at producing commercially efficacious and legally enforceable contracts. It is by no means clear that this is the case in the consumer field. There the contract may have been equally carefully planned (at least, the 'original' of the standard form will have been) yet the legal enforceability of many of the terms will be almost irrelevant. The contract will be planned to have the greatest psychological impact on the average borrower, who will generally not be legally represented, will not be highly educated or well-off, and will be intimidated by being faced with the contractual document. In this case efficacy is achieved through non-enforcement.

Perhaps because of what many will see as these less than wholly laudable reasons for recourse to planned exclusions and standard forms, those businesses consulted who dealt directly with the general public were less willing to discuss their justifications for adopting particular contractual practices than were those operating wholly in the commercial field. In the case of those large businesses questioned that operated from more than one factory or office, for instance, the use of standard form contracts was readily justified because they achieved a uniformity of dealing with all customers in accordance with a policy decided upon by head office. Certain issues could then be removed from future negotiation and branch managers and sales staff could not make concessions to customers by altering back-of-order terms without first consulting a departmental head. Also, businesses tended to feel that detailed planning and negotiation of contract terms was worth the time and cost in those cases where significant claims were likely to arise if something went wrong. The degree of injury in a case of default was especially significant and this factor, of course, cut both ways. For example, an airline or bus company is subject to claims from the survivors and dependants of those injured in an accident. Therefore, in buying aeroplanes or buses from the airframe manufacturers or coachbuilders, the airlines or bus companies insist upon carefully defined and legally enforceable obligations. But an aircraft or bus will usually be designed to operate with one and only one particular type of engine, so the aero or bus engine manufacturer has a virtual monopoly, at least so far as that particular design of aircraft or vehicle is concerned. What started as a buyers' market, therefore, with the airline or bus company, finishes with a sellers' market with the engine.

Although the need to preserve harmonious long-term business relations may operate as a counterweight to this apparent market imbalance, one does find aero and bus engine manufacturers imposing quite rigorous exclusions of liability for consequential loss which the airframe manufacturer or coachbuilder cannot pass on to the airline or bus company. The intermediate risks must therefore be carried by insurance if it is not to be borne by the manufacturers themselves, who are unable to pass the risk on down the chain.

In the normal way, however, insurance was used rather less than expected. Commercial operators who were their own insurers tended, as one might expect, to use exclusion clauses far more than those who had full insurance cover or who operated in the consumer market. They also, consequently, tended to make use of specially drafted and negotiated contracts where large sums of money were involved. So far as legal sanctions or the threat of them were concerned, these were more readily resorted to by the consumer operator than the non-consumer. Although businesses operating in the consumer market perhaps had less prospect of recovering, *e.g.* bad debts from customers, in that the general consumer is less likely to possess the means to meet judgment should he lose than the business or commercial litigant, nevertheless the finance companies did not feel that frequent litigation was likely to do much harm to their businesses. Their trade did not appear to suffer according to how many county court actions they were involved in. Managers and lawyers in the commercial market, on the other hand, took the totally opposite view. Good-will was vital and a company that became known for resorting to the courts too frequently to settle disputes was likely to be avoided by potential customers. A litigious reputation soon turned a business into a commercial pariah. There seemed to be less fear of and aversion to arbitration proceedings, for then the matter could be dealt with by someone who, while frequently still a lawyer, was felt to have expertise in the general areas of business covered by the firms in dispute. There was, however, a general reluctance to entrust the resolution of disputes to lawyers *qua* outside, disinterested professionals (as opposed to lawyer-businessmen), or to the courts, since generally speaking, in commercial terms, the costs were thought to outweigh the gains.

Such empirical research as there is tends to support the conclusions arrived at by Yates – that is that the law of contract is of much less importance to business people than lawyers would like to think. See, for example, Macaulay 1963, Beale and Dugdale 1975, Lewis 1982.

1.6 EUROPEAN CONTRACT LAW

There are three developments which should be noted in relation to the European influence on English contract law. First, there are certain areas of contract law that are now the subject of directives emanating from the EU. Examples included regulations dealing with distance selling, electronic contracts and unfair contract terms. The provisions of these regulations are noted at the appropriate point in subsequent chapters. Second, there is the work of the Lando Commission, which has produced a set of 'Principles of European Contract Law'. These are not binding in any legal system, but are available for adoption by parties, or indeed governments. They attempt to bring together principles derived from the common law and from the European code-based systems of contract, to provide a standard that could be applicable across the whole of Europe.

The third development is the move by the EU to put forward a European Contract Code. This suggestion, which has been under consideration for some time, has begun to be taken forward in the last couple of years. The current developments are described in the next extract.

> **McKendrick, E, 'Harmonisation of European Contract Law: The State We Are In', 2006, Ch 2 in Vogenauer, S and Weatherill, S, *The Harmonisation of European Contract Law*, Oxford: Hart Publishing, pp 7–13**
>
> The next major stage in the development of a harmonised European contract law can be said to be the work done on the Principles of European Contract Law (PECL). The PECL were prepared by scholars drawn from the Member States of the European Community under the chairmanship of Professor Ole Lando (hence the frequent description of the group working on the Principles as 'the Lando Commission'). The PECL were published in three phases: Part I was published in 1995, Parts I and II in 2000, and Part III in 2003. The work of those responsible for drafting the PECL was very much influenced by the work of those who had gone before them. Thus the significance of the CISG can be seen at numerous points in the Principles, even though the Principles frequently go beyond the solutions prescribed in the CISG—and, in this way, the members of the Lando Commission made the best use of the opportunity to learn from the problems and gaps that had become apparent in the final text of the CISG. Further, the fact that the members of the Lando Commission were not aiming to produce a legally binding text gave them greater latitude in developing novel or 'best' solutions to some old and some new problems in the law of contract. The work on PECL was also influenced, at least in part, by the UNIDROIT Principles of International Commercial Contracts. These were first published in 1994, and were thus available to members of the Lando Commission when they were preparing the early drafts of their text. However, the Lando Commission quickly began to catch up on the work of UNIDROIT and, indeed, Part III of PECL was produced before the second edition of the UNIDROIT Principles made its appearance in 2004. It would perhaps be fair to say that, latterly, the two Principles operated in tandem (or even in competition with one another), and that the learning experience was not necessarily a one-way process (with PECL always drawing on the experience of UNIDROIT).

As has been noted, the PECL is a very different type of instrument from the CISG in that the Principles were not drafted as, nor were they intended to be, a legally binding set of rules. Professors Lando and Beale, in their editorial introduction to *Principles of European Contract Law: Parts I and II*, set out a number of purposes for which the Principles are designed. First, they state that the Principles may form a foundation for European legislation, including a possible first step in the work of preparing a future European Code of Contracts. Secondly, the Principles are stated to be suitable for express adoption by contracting parties, who can declare that their contract is to be governed by the PECL. However, the ability of contracting parties to incorporate the PECL into their contract in this way is limited by Article 3 of the Rome Convention on the Law Applicable to Contractual Obligations. While contracting parties are free to incorporate the Principles as a set of contract terms, they cannot incorporate them into the contract as the applicable law, at least in the context of litigation in national courts. Article 3 requires the parties to choose the law of a country as the applicable law, so that any choice of the Principles can only take effect subject to the national law that is found to be applicable to the contract, applying the usual conflict of law rules. Thirdly, Lando and Beale state that the Principles are a 'modern formulation of a *lex mercatoria*' (in other words, they can be applied by arbitrators in the case where a contract is stated to be governed by 'general principles of law' or 'the *lex mercatoria*'). Fourthly, they are a model for judicial and legislative development of the law of contract. Finally, they may form the basis for the harmonisation of contract law among the Member States of the European Union. Lando and Beale conclude:

> [T]he Principles have both immediate and longer-term objectives. They are available for immediate use by parties making contracts, by courts and arbitrators in deciding contract disputes and by legislators in drafting contract rules whether at the European or the national level. Their longer-term objective is to help bring about the harmonisation of general contract law within the European Union.

Thus far, no mention has been made of the impact of European community law on the development of a European contract law. This omission must now be rectified. Community law has had an impact on national contract law, although it is probably fair to say that its intervention has been rather episodic or selective to date. However, its role is steadily increasing. The principal examples of the contribution of community law to the development of a harmonised contract law take the form of the various Directives which have been introduced over the last twenty years. These Directives cover subjects such as doorstep selling, self-employed commercial agents, package travel, unfair terms in consumer contracts, timeshares, sale of consumer goods and associated guarantees, and late payment in commercial transactions.

A more expansive role for the EU has been signalled in recent years. On 13 July 2001 the European Commission issued a Communication on European Contract Law to the European Parliament and the Council. The purpose of the Communication was to broaden the debate on the creation of a European contract law by encouraging contributions from consumers, businesses, professional organisations, public admin-istrations and institutions, the academic world and all interested parties. The Commission was concerned about possible obstacles to cross-border trade within the internal market caused by the differences between the various national contract laws in Europe and sought to ascertain the extent to which differences between national laws created difficulties for commercial parties. The Communication discussed options for the future of contract law in the EC and set out a non-exhaustive list of four options to stimulate discussion:

— *Option I: no EC action*, leaving interest groups and others to advise on cross-border trade and solve problems encountered in it;

— *Option II: promote the development of common contract law principles leading to more convergence of national laws*, encouraging the development of non-binding restatements of principles;

— *Option III: improve the quality of legislation already in place*, concentrating attention on reviewing existing Directives, modernising, extending and simplify-ing them so as to produce a more rational and coherent set of laws; and

— *Option IV: adopt new comprehensive legislation at EC level*. This could take the form of a Directive, a Regulation or a Recommendation, and could range from an optional set of rules to be incorporated by the parties to rules that apply unless excluded or even to a mandatory code. The level of harmonisation that would be effected would depend very much on the form and extent of the model chosen.

Following the publication of the Communication, the Commission received contribu-tions from some 180 stakeholders, the largest number coming from the academic and business communities, with a considerable number from governments and legal practitioners. In addition, the European Council, the European Parliament and the Economic and Social Committee each produced responses to the Communication. This interest of the Community Institutions and stakeholders shows the importance of the debate launched by the Communication. Of the four options put forward, the majority of contributors rejected Option I on the grounds that it was unrealistic and inadequate, and that it failed to give sufficient protection to weaker parties. By con-trast, Option II attracted more favourable comment, although a number of respondents saw this as merely a step on the way to a new legal instrument at the community level (Option IV). Option III seemed to be the most favoured solution, receiving support from governments, business, consumer organisations, legal practitioners and academic lawyers. Opinions varied on Option IV. Some respondents saw a uniform and com-prehensive European civil code as the best solution to the problems identified, whereas others were strongly opposed to the creation of a civil code.

In 2003 the Commission produced a further communication in the form of an Action Plan. In this document the Commission identified various areas in which problems may undermine the proper functioning of the internal market and the uniform application of community law. It noted support for Option II and that the 'overwhelming majority' of respondents supported Option III, and therefore proposed to continue a broad strategy of sector-specific legislation as well as non-regulatory measures. Steps to promote standard EU-wide cross-border contract terms were launched immediately.

However, the central plank of the Action Plan was more ambitious and consisted of a plan to produce a Common Frame of Reference (CFR). The CFR was to consist of a delineation of fundamental principles of European contract law (such as the principle of freedom of contract), definitions of legal terms (the examples given were 'contract' and 'damage') and possibly model rules. The CFR was intended for use when existing legislation was being reviewed and new legislation drawn up so as to improve consistency in community legislation; it was also hoped that the CFR would be taken into account in the drafting of national legislation and so further encourage the convergence of contract legal rules throughout Europe. Finally, it was hoped that the CFR would provide the foundation for the development of an optional instrument, should that option be pursued. Over 120 responses to the Action Plan were received and published on the website, again from a wide range of stakeholders. There was some scepticism about the efficacy and desirability of measures intended to increase the use of EU-wide standard contract terms. With regard to the CFR, there was broad support, although perhaps some confusion as to what exactly it entailed.

On 11 October 2004 the Commission issued a further Communication on a European contract law and the revision of the *acquis*: The Way Forward. In this document the Commission stated that it would 'pursue the elaboration of the CFR.' It is clear that the CFR will play a crucial role in the development of a European contract law. At present, the Commission considers that 'the CFR would be a non-binding instrument,' although it acknowledges that this is an issue on which divergent views have been expressed and which it may be necessary to re-visit. The main role of the CFR will lie, at least initially, in the improvement of the existing *acquis*. To this end, there will be a review of eight consumer Directives in order to determine whether the Directives meet the Commission's consumer protection and internal market goals. But the CFR will not be confined to the present and future *acquis*: a more extensive role for the CFR is envisaged. Thus it is suggested that the CFR could: (i) be taken into account by national legislators 'when transposing EU directives in the area of contract law into national legislation'; (ii) be used in arbitration to 'find unbiased and balanced solutions to resolve conflicts arising between contractual parties'; (iii) be developed 'into a body of standard contract terms to be made available to legal practitioners'; and (iv) 'inspire the European Court of Justice when interpreting the *acquis* on contract law.' The preparation of the CFR will be undertaken, at least initially, by a group of researchers who will be expected to deliver a final report to the Commission in 2007. This research

> will aim to identify best solutions, taking into account national contract laws (both case law and established practice), the EC *acquis* and relevant international instruments, particularly the UN Convention on Contracts for the International Sale of Goods.

The proposed structure of the CFR bears a remarkable resemblance to the structure of the Principles of European Contract Law (although the Communication does not expressly acknowledge this) with the addition of chapters on sales contracts and insurance contracts. A number of workshops have been held in Brussels at which drafts prepared by the researchers have been considered by stakeholder experts. Once the report prepared by the researchers has been received by the Commission, it will consider the report and subject it to a 'practicability test on the basis of concrete examples of the anticipated uses of the CFR,' and will consult with a wide range of interested parties. It is hoped that the adoption of the CFR will take place in 2009, when it will be published in the Official Journal of the European Union and reviewed as necessary.

The Communication of 11 October 2004 also deals with the promotion of the use of EU-wide standard terms and conditions, but there is little here that is new. The Commission stated that it would 'host a website' on which market participants could exchange information about EU-wide standard terms and conditions which they were currently using or planning to develop. However, the Commission has since changed its mind and decided that it is not appropriate to host such a website, largely because of the costs involved in setting up and maintaining such a site and its likely limited utility. In particular, the Commission pointed out that standard terms and conditions tend to be drafted for a specific sector, have a limited life-span and, if they were to be held out as enforceable terms in all European jurisdictions, would have to satisfy the 'most restrictive national law' (and a standard term which was drafted in order to comply with the most restrictive national law would be of limited utility to traders who enter into transactions in Europe but not in the jurisdiction which happens to have the most restrictive national law).

Finally, the Communication of 11 October 2004 raises the more difficult issue of 'an optional instrument in European contract law.' Here the Commission states that it intends 'to continue this process in parallel with the work on developing the CFR.' But the message which emerges from this section of the document is ambiguous. On the one hand, the document states that 'it is premature to speculate about the possible outcome of this reflection,' but on the other hand it states that

> it is neither the Commission's intention to propose a 'European Civil Code' which would harmonise contract laws of Member States, nor should the reflections be seen as in any way calling into question the current approaches to promoting free circulation on the basis of flexible and efficient solutions.

Nevertheless, the linkage of the optional instrument to the progress of the CFR suggests that it would be premature to dismiss the possibility of a European civil code at some time in the medium to long term. Quite what will emerge from this process is hard to predict, but the CFR may (together with the Principles of European Contract Law) turn out to be one of the first significant steps on a road that will end with a European code of contract law.

1.7 ADDITIONAL READING

Beale, H and Dugdale, T, 'Contracts between businessmen' (1975) 2 Brit J Law & Society 45.

Campbell, D (ed), *The Relational Theory of Contrac: Selected Works of Ian Macneil*, 2001, London: Sweet & Maxwell.

Campbell, C, Collins, H and Wightman, J (eds), *Implicit Dimensions of Contract*, 2003, Oxford: Hart Publishing.

Collins, H, *Regulating Contracts*, 1999, Oxford: OUP.

Gilmore, G, *The Death of Contract*, 1974, Columbus: Ohio State University Press.

Macaulay, S, 'Non-contractual relations in business' (1963) 28 Am Sociological Rev 35.

Mulcahy, L and Wheeler, S, *Feminist Perspectives on Contract* Law, 2005, London: Glasshouse Press.

Robertson, A (ed), *The Law of Obligations: Connections and Boundaries*, 2004, London: UCL Press.

Smith, S, *Atiyah's Introduction to the Law of Contract*, 2006, 6th edn, Oxford: Clarendon Press.

Smith, S, *Contract Theory*, 2004, Oxford: Clarendon Press.

CHAPTER 2

FORMING THE AGREEMENT

CONTENTS	

█ 2.1 INTRODUCTION

'Agreement' is central to the English law of contract. In most cases that are adjudicated the courts regard themselves as giving effect to an agreement reached between the parties. The question of whether such an agreement has been formed is therefore a crucial one. The agreement must also be intended to be legally binding. This aspect is considered in detail in Chapter 3. The focus in this chapter is on the mechanisms that the courts use to decide whether an agreement has been reached. The topics that are covered include, first, formalities. To what extent does English law use formal mechanisms to decide whether an agreement has been reached? Generally this will happen where a 'deed' is used, or where a statute requires formality in relation to a particular type of contract. The more general approach is, however, simply to look for informal evidence of agreement. In other words, courts decide whether an agreement has been reached by taking an 'objective' approach, looking at what the parties have said or done as indicators of their state of mind. The identification of a matching offer and acceptance is the most common way for the courts to find that an agreement has been made. An offer must be distinguished from an invitation to treat, and an acceptance from a counter-offer. The time and place of acceptance can cause problems when parties are contracting at a distance. Special rules apply to posted acceptances, as opposed to those communicated by telephone or electronically. The chapter concludes by considering the ways in which an offer is revoked, and when will it lapse if not accepted.

2.2 FORMING AN AGREEMENT

There are a number of possibilities as to the way in which it could be decided if the parties have reached an agreement. The courts could look for formal signs (for example, a signed written document), or particular forms of words, or simply any extrinsic evidence of an intention to make an agreement – a 'meeting of the minds'. As will be seen, English law makes use of a variety of approaches. It is important to note from the outset, however, that formality is by no means an essential require-ment for most contracts. Many everyday contracts – for example, purchases from a shop – are made purely orally, and with no documentation in writing. It is possible for very large contracts, involving substantial sums of money, to be made in such an informal way, though in practice most large organisations will want to contract on the basis of terms that are set out in writing. It is only in a relatively small number of situations that English law actually imposes on the parties a requirement of formal-ity, and will hold the agreement unenforceable unless it follows these requirements.

2.2.1 FORMALITIES

One way of conclusively demonstrating an agreement is to put it into the form of a 'deed'. The requirements for a valid deed are set out in the Law of Property (Miscellaneous Provisions) Act 1989:

1. – *Deeds and their execution*

(1)   Any rule of law which –

    (a)   restricts the substances on which a deed may be written;

    (b)   requires a seal for the valid execution of an instrument as a deed by an individual; or

    (c)   requires authority by one person to another to deliver an instrument as a deed on his behalf to be given by deed,

    is abolished.

(2)   An instrument shall not be a deed unless –

    (a)   it makes it clear on its face that it is intended to be a deed by the person making it or, as the case may be, by the parties to it (whether by describing itself as a deed or expressing itself to be executed or signed as a deed or otherwise); and

    (b)   it is validly executed as a deed

        (i)   by that person or a person authorised to execute it in the name or on behalf of that person, or

    (ii) by one or more of those parties or a person authorised to execute it in the name or on behalf of one or more of those parties.

(2A) For the purposes of subsection (2)(a) above, an instrument shall not be taken to make it clear on its face that it is intended to be a deed merely because it is executed under seal.

(3) An instrument is validly executed as a deed by an individual if, and only if –

    (a) it is signed –

        (i) by him in the presence of a witness who attests the signature; or

        (ii) at his direction and in his presence and the presence of two witnesses who each attest the signature; and

    (b) it is delivered as a deed.

(4) In subsections (2) and (3) above 'sign', in relation to an instrument, includes

    (a) an individual signing the name of the person or party on whose behalf he executes the instrument; and

    (b) making one's mark on the instrument,

and 'signature' is to be construed accordingly.

(4A) Subsection (3) above applies in the case of an instrument executed by an individual in the name or on behalf of another person whether or not that person is also an individual.

Any contract can be put into a deed. The only situation, however, in which a deed must be used to give a contract full effect is in a relation to a lease of land for more than three years, as required by ss 52 and 54(2) of the Law of Property Act 1925.

Other contracts dealing with interests in land do not have to be in the form of a deed, but must be in writing, by virtue of s 2(1) of the Law of Property (Miscellaneous Provisions) Act 1989:

s 2 *Contracts for sale etc. of land to be made by signed writing*

(1) A contract for the sale or other disposition of an interest in land can only be made in writing and only by incorporating all the terms which the parties have expressly agreed in one document or, where contracts are exchanged, in each.

(2) The terms may be incorporated in a document either by being set out in it or by reference to some other document.

(3) The document incorporating the terms or, where contracts are exchanged, one of the documents incorporating them (but not necessarily the same one) must be signed by or on behalf of each party to the contract. . . .

(5) This section does not apply in relation to –

    (a) a contract to grant such a lease as is mentioned in section 54(2) of the Law of Property Act 1925 (short leases);

    (b) a contract made in the course of a public auction; . . .

(7) Nothing in this section shall apply in relation to contracts made before this section comes into force.

(8) Section 40 of the Law of Property Act 1925 (which is superseded by this section) shall cease to have effect.

There are also requirements of writing in relation to certain consumer credit agreements, by virtue of the Consumer Credit Act 1974.

CONSUMER CREDIT ACT 1974

s 61 Signing of agreement

(1) A regulated agreement is not properly executed unless –

    (a) a document in the prescribed form itself containing all the prescribed terms and conforming to regulations under section 60(1) is signed in the prescribed manner both by the debtor or hirer and by or on behalf of the creditor or owner, and

    (b) the document embodies all the terms of the agreement, other than implied terms, and

    (c) the document is, when presented or sent to the debtor or hirer for signature, in such a state that all its terms are readily legible.

Finally, one of the oldest statutes still in force in relation to English contract law, the Statute of Frauds 1677, imposes a requirement of writing in relation to an agreement to guarantee a third-party's debts:

'no action shall be brought . . . whereby to charge the defendant upon any special promise to answer for the debt, default or miscarriages of another person. . . unless the agreement upon which such action shall be brought, or some memorandum or note thereof, shall be in writing, and signed by the party to be charged therewith, or some other person thereunto by him lawfully authorised.'

The continuing practical importance of this provision was confirmed by the following decision of the House of Lords:

Actionstrength Ltd v International Glass Engineering [2003] 2 All ER 615

Facts: The claimant had a contract to supply labour with the first defendant. Concerns about late payment led, according to the claimant, to an agreement with the second defendant as a result of which the claimant continued with the work, in return for the second defendant promising, if necessary, to pay the claimant directly out of money owed by the second defendant to the first defendant. This agreement was oral. The claimant subsequently tried to sue the second defendant on its promise. The second defendant denied that any promise had been made, but argued that in any case the agreement was a guarantee falling within s. 4 of the Statute of Frauds 1677, and was therefore not enforceable, because it was not in writing. The claimant alleged that by persuading the claimant to carry on with the work, the second defendant was estopped from relying on the Statute. The trial judge held, on an preliminary issue, that the claimant might be able to succeed. The Court of Appeal held that the agreement was a guarantee, and that the second defendant could not be estopped from relying on the Statute of Frauds.

Held: The House of Lords confirmed the decision of the Court of Appeal.

Lord Hoffmann: . . .

'**15.** This is a fairly common dispute over who said what; in the ordinary way it would have been resolved by a judge hearing the witnesses and deciding which of them he believed. But St-Gobain [the second defendant] says that a hearing is unnecessary because, even if Actionstrength's [the claimant's] version were to be accepted, the promise would be unenforceable by virtue of section 4 of the Statute of Frauds 1677 . . .

16. So St-Gobain applied for summary judgment on the ground that the action had no real prospect of success (CPR r 24.2). The application was refused by Mitting J on the ground that it was arguable that St-Gobain's promise was not 'to answer for the debt . . . of another person' and therefore outside the statute. But the Court of Appeal held that it plainly was and this finding has not been challenged in your Lordships' House. Instead, Mr McGhee for Actionstrength submits that St-Gobain should not be allowed to rely on the Statute because, on the facts as alleged, and which must for present purposes be assumed to be true, it would be unconscionable for St-Gobain not to keep its promise.

17. This argument received short shrift in the Court of Appeal. Simon Brown LJ said [2002] 1 WLR 566, 576–577 that it was "quite hopeless" and dismissed it in one paragraph. The other members of the court had nothing to add.

18. If one assumes that a judge would find that Actionstrength's version of events was right, to hold the promise unenforceable would certainly appear unfair. Actionstrength would have supplied Inglen with services which were indirectly for the benefit of St-Gobain, because they enabled Inglen to perform the main contract, in reliance on St-Gobain's promise to pay for them. Morally, there would be no excuse for St-Gobain not keeping its promise. On the other hand, if one assumes that a judge would find that St-Gobain's version was right, the Statute enables it to dispose summarily of proceedings which should never have been brought.

19. In an application for summary judgment such as this, which is in the nature of a demurrer, one has to assume that Actionstrength's version is true. And that naturally inclines one to try to find some way in which the putative injustice can be avoided. It is, however, important to bear in mind that the purpose of the Statute was precisely to avoid the need to decide which side was telling the truth about whether or not an oral promise had been made and exactly what had been promised. Parliament decided that there had been too many cases in which the wrong side had been believed. Hence the title, "An Act for prevention of frauds and perjuries". It is quite true, as Mr McGhee said, that the system of civil procedure in 1677 was not very well adapted to discovering the truth. For one thing, the parties to the action were not competent witnesses. But the question of whether the Act should be preserved in its application to guarantees was considered in 1953 by the Law Reform Committee (First Report, Statute of Frauds and Section 4 of the Sale of Goods Act 1893 (Cmd 8809)) and the recommendation of a very strong committee was to keep it.

20. The terms of the Statute therefore show that Parliament, although obviously conscious that it would allow some people to break their promises, thought that this injustice was outweighed by the need to protect people from being held liable on the basis of oral utterances which were ill-considered, ambiguous or completely fictitious. This means that while normally one would approach the construction of a statute on the basis that Parliament was unlikely to have intended to cause injustice by allowing people to break promises which had been relied upon, no such assumption can be made about the Statute. Although the scope of the Statute must be tested on the assumption that the facts alleged by Actionstrength are true, it must not be construed in a way which would undermine its purpose.

21. It its original form, section 4 of the 1677 Act also applied to sales of land . . .

22. Very soon after the Statute of 1677, the courts introduced the doctrine of part performance to restrict its application to sales of land. It was held that a contract, initially unenforceable because of the statute, could become enforceable by virtue of acts which the plaintiff did afterwards. The doctrine was justified by a combination to two reasons. The first was a form of estoppel; as Lord Reid said in *Steadman v Steadman* [1976] AC 536, 540:

> "If one party to an agreement stands by and lets the other party incur expense or prejudice his position on the faith of the agreement being valid he will not then be allowed to turn round and assert that the agreement is unenforceable."

. . .

25. What Mr McGhee submits in this case is that the estoppel principle which partly underpins the doctrine of part performance is wide enough to be applied to contracts of guarantee. On the facts presently alleged, it is also the case that, in Lord Reid's words, St-Gobain stood by and let Actionstrength prejudice its position, by extending credit to Inglen, on the faith of the guarantee being valid. There is authority for saying that estoppel is a principle of broad, not to say protean, application: see, for example *Taylors Fashions Ltd v Liverpool Victoria Trustees Co Ltd (Note)* [1982] QB 133. Although he cited no case in any jurisdiction in which estoppel had been applied to avoid the application of the Statute to a guarantee, Mr McGhee says that there is no argument of principle against it.

26. The difficulty which faces this submission is that while the nature of a sale of land is such that the contract and part performance can co-exist in their respective domains, no such co-existence is possible between the Statute and the estoppel for which Mr McGhee contends. It is in the nature of a contract of guarantee that the party seeking to enforce it will always have performed first. Unless he has advanced credit or forborne from withdrawing credit, there will be no guaranteed debt for which he can sue. It will always be the case that the creditor will have acted to his prejudice on the faith of the guarantor's promise. To admit an estoppel on these grounds would be to repeal the Statute.

. . .

29. It is not necessary to consider whether circumstances may arise in which a guarantor may be estopped from relying upon the Statute. It is sufficient that in my opinion the estoppel which Actionstrength seeks to rely upon in this case would be inconsistent with the provisions of the Statute. I would therefore dismiss the appeal.'

2.2.2 THE OBJECTIVE APPROACH TO AGREEMENT

Where the courts are relying on finding an agreement in fact between the parties, rather than any formal requirement, it is obvious that they cannot actually know what is in the parties' minds. The approach must be 'objective', based on what was said and done at the time of the alleged agreement. This does not answer all questions, however, since there are different types of 'objectivity'.

Howarth, W 'The meaning of objectivity in contract' (1984) 100 LQR 265, pp 265–266, 279–281

1. Introduction
A 'general if not universal principle of our law of contract' is that English law adopts an objective test of agreement in matters of contract formation. Indeed, given the overwhelming consensus regarding the need for objectivity in judging contract formation it might be thought that a plea for greater precision in this area can only be regarded as quibbling. Objectivity having been given the universal endorsement of academics and practitioners alike, one might be forgiven for thinking that little in the law of contract could be more certain. What is not so clear however, is the precise *meaning* that should be given to the undisputed requirement of objectivity. A closer examination of the concept of objectivity in this paper will attempt to draw out the different senses in which that concept is capable of being understood and highlight the range of crucially difficult issues which appeals to objectivity commonly neglect.

In order to appreciate the difficulties left unsolved by general appeals to objectivity it is necessary to look at the different perspectives on a situation where contract formation is in contention, and to see the differences between viewpoints which may be claimed to be in some sense 'objective'. Consider the following situation. P (the promisee) enters into an apparent agreement with D (the promisor). P believes (subjectively) that the agreement has been concluded on terms A. D believes (subjectively) that the terms of the contract are B (where A and B are materially different in some contentious respect). The reasonable man taking an objective view of the situation from the position of P would conclude that the terms of the contract were C, but placed in the position of D he would conclude that they were E (where, once again, C and E are different in point of substance and different to either A or B). Finally, if the objective observer were to be placed 'above' the parties in a position where he could take an over-view of the proceedings which was independent of either a reasonable P or a reasonable D, he might conclude that the terms of the contract were actually F (again different to the other conclusions). Doubtless actual cases would never raise all of these complications from a single set of facts, but nonetheless the discrepancies of perspective that are illustrated remain logical possibilities, the existence of any two of which may raise problems for objectivity. Although in most situations the first two perspectives postulated (*i.e.* promisee subjectivity and promisor subjectivity) can be discounted, there remain three 'objective' options: promisor objectivity, promisee objectivity and detached objectivity. Choosing a preferable version of objectivity from amongst these three presents no small problem of evaluation. None can be initially ruled out as a non-starter on ground of logical incoherence since each is equally objective within its own frame of reference. The important preference lies simply in the choice of perspective which is adopted. On this question of perspective . . . the problem is compounded by the fact that each of the possibilities seems to enjoy an amount at least, of persuasive support.

5. Conclusion

Having outlined the possibilities and seen that none are necessarily wrong or even internally inconsistent, a choice between these mutually incompatible versions of objectivity remains to be made. The final question that must be asked is, on what ground must preference be based? The answer to this type of inquiry must ultimately fall back upon the higher objectives behind a theory of the law of contract, and the balance of competing purposes which that body of law is designed to achieve. Here the existence of disparity amongst legal values according to the social, economic and political systems in which they arise has been convincingly argued. The remaining task is to relate the versions of objectivity which have been outlined to the polarity between liberal-abstentionist and corporate-interventionist models of legal regulation in modern societies.

On the liberal model the function of a law regarding objectivity in contract formation is to give effect to the intention of the parties and enforce *their* agreements, rather than the court imposing agreement upon them 'from above'. Having started from the premise that objectivity is necessary however, the laissez-faire theorist would wish to limit its effect to a minimum, and it is consistent with this position to adopt either promisor objectivity or promisee objectivity. Both of these perspectives provide a rationale for resolving disputes between the subjective views actually held by the parties whilst doing the minimum damage to the ideal of freedom of contract. They place the greatest possible restraint upon judges (to prevent them 'making agreements' for the parties) which is compatible with the use of objectivity to resolve this kind of dispute. The dilemma confronting the abstentionist however is that he has no reason for preference between the two alternatives open to him. The choice between taking the perspective of a reasonable promisor or a reasonable promisee is a choice between equal degrees of abstention, or put the other way around, equally respectful positions regarding the agreement made by the parties. It is perhaps for this reason that the liberal theory and practice of the law of contract in the courts has, it is suggested, never reached a clearly articulated resolution between these two positions.

On the other side of things, detached objectivity appears to provide greater scope to the judiciary to rule against the actual intentions of the parties on the ground that an objective overview may differ from the actual or reasonable perspective that either the promisor or promisee might have of the situation. The position holds greater scope for judicial intervention and the imposition of agreements upon parties contrary to their intentions. Clearly this is a consequence which has ostensibly been resisted by the courts who with some notable exceptions, have often reaffirmed their reluctance to do more than give effect to what the parties themselves have agreed. The principal judicial line is the stricter abstentionist test for contract formation and, rather than venture beyond this, the judicial tendency has been to find extra-contractual remedies for worthy plaintiffs. Nonetheless the position of detached objectivity and concomitant judicial interventionalism is not without academic support. Atiyah, in his *Introduction to the Law of Contract*, includes a chapter entitled 'Contracts made by the Courts', which provides a number of illustrations of cases where courts have imposed agreements upon the parties in circumstances where they regarded it as just to do so. If his contention that, 'the law of contract has nearly always had room for cases of this character', or alternatively, that the law of contract is presently developing in that direction, is correct, then it would seem that detached objectivity is, or may become, the better theoretical perspective to describe the way that judges approach difficult problems of contract formation.

The dilemma is a compound one. If the courts wish to cling to the liberal values which they have so often espoused in the past then they must clarify what rule of law follows from those values and in so doing choose between two equally acceptable (if imperfect) alternatives: the perspective of the reasonable promisor *or* the perspective of the reasonable promisee. Otherwise the admission must be made that objectivity may involve the imposition of contractual relations upon the parties independently of what either might reasonably be understood to have intended. This is arguably a new departure from previously announced practice but, as we have seen, a departure for which there may be both good reasons of principle and a line of authoritative support as rational as any other open to the courts. What is certain however, and it is hoped that this paper has shown, is that an appeal to objectivity without clarification is to place a cloak over a range of crucial problems in contract formation which lurk underneath the plausibly precise term 'objective', and, in a body of law in principle knowable to all, ought to be articulated and resolved rather than concealed from view.

2.2.3 THE EXTERNAL SIGNS OF AGREEMENT

Where the courts are trying to decide whether the behaviour of the parties, viewed objectively, indicates that they intended to make a contract, they will look primarily for evidence of a matching 'offer' and 'acceptance'.

2.2.4 OFFER

An 'offer' is an indication of a firm intention to contract on specified terms. It must be distinguished from a mere invitation to enter into negotiations. The difficulty in drawing this distinction is indicated in a number of cases.

Gibson v Manchester City Council [1979] 1 All ER 972 (HL)

Facts: Mr Gibson had been in correspondence with Manchester City Council about the possible purchase of his council house. The Council changed from Conservative to Labour control and the sale of council houses was stopped. Mr Gibson alleged that he already had a binding contract, based on his correspondence with the Council, for the purchase of his house. The trial judge and Court of Appeal held in favour of Mr Gibson. The Council appealed to the House of Lords.

Held: The House of Lords held that the Council had not made a definite offer to sell the house to Mr Gibson – its communications had not got past the stage of the 'invitation to treat'.

Lord Diplock:
'My Lords, this is an action for specific performance of what is claimed to be a contract for the sale of land. The only question in the appeal is of a kind with which the courts are very familiar. It is whether in the correspondence between the parties there can be found a legally enforceable contract for the sale by the Manchester Corporation to Mr Gibson of the dwelling-house of which he was the occupying tenant at the relevant time in 1971. That question is one that, in my view, can be answered by applying to the particular documents relied on by Mr Gibson as constituting the contract, well settled, indeed elementary, principles of English law. This being so, it is not the sort of case in which leave would have been likely to be granted to appeal to your Lordships' House, but for the fact that it is a test case. The two documents principally relied on by

Mr Gibson were in standard forms used by the council in dealing with applications from tenants of council houses to purchase the freehold of their homes under a scheme that had been adopted by the council during a period when it was under Conservative Party control. Political control passed to the Labour Party as a result of the local government elections held in May 1971. The scheme was then abandoned. It was decided that no more council houses should be sold to any tenant with whom a legally binding contract of sale had not already been concluded. At the date of this decision there were a considerable number of tenants, running into hundreds, whose applications to purchase the houses which they occupied had reached substantially the same stage as that of Mr Gibson. The two documents in the same standard form as those on which he principally relies had passed between each one of them and the council. So their rights too are likely to depend on the result of this appeal . . .

In the Manchester County Court where the action started, the case was pleaded in the conventional way. The particulars of claim alleged an offer in writing by the council to sell the freehold interest in the house to Mr Gibson at a price of £2,180 and an acceptance in writing of that offer by Mr Gibson. The judge (his Honour Judge Bailey) followed the same conventional approach to the question that fell to be decided. He looked to see whether there was an offer of sale and an acceptance. He held that, on their true construction, the documents relied on as such in the particulars of claim did amount to an offer and an acceptance respectively and so constituted a legally enforceable contract. He ordered specific performance of an open contract for the sale to Mr Gibson of the freehold interest in the house at the price of £2,180.

The council's appeal against this judgment was dismissed by the majority of the Court of Appeal (Lord Denning MR and Ormrod LJ); Geoffrey Lane LJ dissented. Lord Denning MR rejected what I have described as the conventional approach of looking to see whether on the true construction of the documents relied on there can be discerned an offer and acceptance. One ought, he said, to "look at the correspondence as a whole and at the conduct of the parties and see therefrom whether the parties have come to an agreement on everything that was material". This approach . . . led him however to the conclusion that there should be imported into the agreement to be specifically performed additional conditions, against use except as a private dwelling-house and against advertising and a restriction not to sell or lease the property for five years. These are conditions which would not be implied by law in an open contract for the sale of land. The reason for so varying the county court judge's order was that clauses in these terms were included in the standard form of "Agreement for Sale of a Council House" which, as appears from the earlier case of *Storer* v *Manchester City Council* [1974] 3 All ER 824, was entered into by the council and council tenants whose applications to purchase the freehold of their council house reached the stage at which contracts were exchanged. There was, however, no reference to this standard form of agreement in any of the documents said to constitute the contract relied on in the instant case, nor was there any evidence that Mr Gibson had knowledge of its terms at or before the time that the alleged contract was concluded.

Ormrod LJ, who agreed with Lord Denning MR, adopted a similar approach but he did also deal briefly with the construction of the document relied on by Mr Gibson as an unconditional offer of sale by the council. On this he came to the same conclusion as the county court judge.

Geoffrey Lane LJ in a dissenting judgment, which for my part I find convincing, adopted the conventional approach. He found that on the true construction of the documents relied on as constituting the contract, there never was an offer by the council acceptance of which by Mr Gibson was capable in law of constituting a legally enforceable contract. It was but a step in the negotiations for a contract which, owing to the change in the political complexion of the council, never reached fruition.

My Lords, there may be certain types of contract, though I think they are exceptional, which do not fit easily into the normal analysis of a contract as being constituted by offer and acceptance; but a contract alleged to have been made by an exchange of correspondence between the parties in which the successive communications other than the first are in reply to one another is not one of these. I can see no reason in the instant case for departing from the conventional approach of looking at the handful of documents relied on as constituting the contract sued on and seeing whether on their true construction there is to be found in them a contractual offer by the council to sell the house to Mr Gibson and an acceptance of that offer by Mr Gibson. I venture to think that it was by departing from this conventional approach that the majority of the Court of Appeal was led into error.

The genesis of the relevant negotiations in the instant case is a form filled in by Mr Gibson on 28th November 1970 enquiring what would be the price of buying his council house at 174 Charlestown Road, Blackley, and expressing his interest in obtaining a mortgage from the council. The form was a detachable part of a brochure which had been circulated by the council to tenants who had previously expressed an interest in buying their houses. It contained details of a new scheme for selling council houses that had been recently adopted by the council. The scheme provided for a sale at market value less a discount dependent on the length of time the purchaser had been a council tenant. This, in the case of Mr Gibson, would have amounted to 20%. The scheme also provided for the provision by the council of advances on mortgage which might amount to as much as the whole of the purchase price.

As a result of that enquiry Mr Gibson's house was inspected by the council's valuer and on 10th February 1971 the letter which is relied on by Mr Gibson as the offer by the council to sell the house to him was sent from the city treasurer's department. It was in the following terms:

> Dear Sir,
> 'Purchase of Council House
> 'Your Reference Number 82463 03
> I refer to your request for details of the cost of buying your Council house. *The Corporation may be prepared to sell the house to you at the purchase price of £2,725 less 20% = £2,180 (freehold).*

Maximum mortgage the Corporation may grant: £2,177 repayable over 20 years.
Annual fire insurance premium: £2.45
Monthly Repayment charge calculated by:—
(i) flat rate repayment method: £19.02

If you wish to pay off some of the purchase price at the start and therefore require a mortgage for less than the amount quoted above, the monthly instalment will change; in these circumstances, I will supply new figures on request. The above repayment figures apply so long as the interest rate charged on home loans is 8%. The interest rate will be subject to variation by the Corporation after giving not less than three months' written notice, and if it changes, there will be an adjustment to the monthly instalment payable. This letter should not be regarded as firm offer of a mortgage.

If you would like to make formal application to buy your Council house, please complete the enclosed application form and return it to me as soon as possible.
Yours faithfully,
(Sgd) H. R. Page
City Treasurer
Mr Robert Gibson.

My Lords, the words I have italicised seem to me, as they seemed to Geoffrey Lane LJ, to make it quite impossible to construe this letter as a contractual offer capable of being converted into a legally enforceable open contract for the sale of land by Mr Gibson's written acceptance of it. The words "may be prepared to sell" are fatal to this; so is the invitation, not, be it noted, to accept the offer, but "to make formal application to buy" on the enclosed application form. It is, to quote Geoffrey Lane LJ, a letter setting out the financial terms on which it may be the council would be prepared to consider a sale and purchase in due course.

Both Ormrod LJ and the county court judge, in reaching the conclusion that this letter was a firm offer to sell the freehold interest in the house for £2,180, attached importance to the fact that the second paragraph, dealing with the financial details of the mortgage of which Mr Gibson had asked for particulars, stated expressly, "This letter should not be regarded as a firm offer of a mortgage". The necessary implication from this, it is suggested, is that the first paragraph of the letter *is* to be regarded as a firm offer to sell despite the fact that this is plainly inconsistent with the express language of that paragraph. My Lords, with great respect, this surely must be fallacious. If the final sentence had been omitted the wording of the second paragraph, unlike that of the first, with its use of the indicative mood in such expressions as "the interest rate *will* change", might have been understood by council tenants to whom it was addressed as indicating a firm offer of a mortgage of the amount and on the terms for repayment stated if the council were prepared to sell the house at the stated price. But, whether or not this be the explanation of the presence of the last sentence in the second paragraph, it cannot possibly affect the plain meaning of the words used in the first paragraph.

Mr Gibson did fill in the application form enclosed with this letter. It was in three sections: section A headed "Application to buy a council house", section B "Application for a loan to buy a council house", and section C "Certificate to be completed by all applicants". He left blank the space for the purchase price in section A and sent the form to the council on 5th March 1971 with a covering letter in which he requested the council either to undertake at their own expense to carry out repairs to the tarmac path forming part of the premises or to make a deduction from the purchase price to cover the cost of repairs. The letter also intimated that Mr Gibson would like to make a down payment of £500 towards the purchase price instead of borrowing the whole amount on mortgage. In reply to the request made in this letter the council, by letter of 12th March 1971, said that the condition of the property had been taken into consideration in fixing the purchase price and that repairs to the tarmac by the council could not be authorised at this stage. This letter was acknowledged by Mr Gibson by his letter to the council of 18th March 1971 in which he asked the council to "carry on with the purchase as per my application already in your possession".

My Lords, the application form and letter of 18th March 1971 were relied on by Mr Gibson as an unconditional acceptance of the council's offer to sell the house; but this cannot be so unless there was a contractual offer by the council available for acceptance, and, for the reason already given I am of opinion that there was none. It is unnecessary to consider whether the application form and Mr Gibson's letters of 5th and 18th March 1971 are capable of amounting to a contractual offer by him to purchase the freehold interest in the house at a price of £2,180 on the terms of an open contract, for there is no suggestion that, even if it were, it was ever accepted by the council. Nor would it ever have been even if there had been no change in the political control of the council, as the policy of the council before the change required the incorporation in all agreements for sale of council houses to tenants of the conditions referred by Lord Denning MR in his judgment and other conditions inconsistent with an open contract.

I therefore feel compelled to allow the appeal. One can sympathise with Mr Gibson's disappointment on finding that his expectations that he would be able to buy his council house at 20% below its market value in the autumn of 1970 cannot be realised. Whether one thinks this makes it a hard case perhaps depends on the political views that one holds about council housing policy. But hard cases offer a strong temptation to let them have their proverbial consequences. It is a temptation that the judicial mind must be vigilant to resist.'

Lords Edmund-Davies, Russell, Fraser and Keith concurred.

Following the decision in *Gibson*, the courts have generally adopted the 'offer and acceptance' approach to deciding whether an agreement has been reached. Lord Diplock does, however, recognise that there are 'exceptional' cases that need a different analysis. He does not specify what these may be, but we shall later in this chapter see some examples where the 'offer and acceptance' approach has been stretched or departed from.

2.2.4.1 Shop sales

Does the display of the goods on a shelf in a supermarket or a shop window indicate that the goods are being 'offered' for sale? In everyday speech we would generally say so, but the law takes a different view, as is shown in the following:

Pharmaceutical Society of Great Britain v Boots Cash Chemists [1953] 1 QB 401

Facts: This case involved a criminal prosecution of Boots for selling certain medicines without the supervision of a pharmacist, contrary to the Pharmacy and Poisons Act 1933. The drugs were selected by the customer from the shelf, and then paid for at a cash desk, where a pharmacist was able to supervise. The question was whether offer and acceptance (and therefore the contract between the customer and the shop) took place when the goods were selected, or when they were paid for at the till. At trial, the Lord Chief Justice held that the latter was the case, so that no offence was committed. The prosecutor appealed.

Held: The Court of Appeal held that the display of goods did not constitute an offer. The contract was made at the cash desk, where there was supervision by a pharmacist, and so met the requirements of the Pharmacy and Poisons Act 1933.

Somervell LJ:
'This is an appeal from a decision of the Lord Chief Justice on an agreed statement of facts, raising a question under section 18(1)(a)(iii) of the Pharmacy and Poisons Act 1933. The plaintiffs are the Pharmaceutical Society, incorporated by Royal charter. One of their duties is to take all reasonable steps to enforce the provisions of the Act. The provision in question is contained in section 18. [His Lordship read the section and stated the facts, and continued:] It is not disputed that in a chemist's shop where this self-service system does not prevail a customer may go in and ask a young woman assistant, who will not herself be a registered pharmacist, for one of these articles on the list, and the transaction may be completed and the article paid for, although the registered pharmacist, who will no doubt be on the premises, will not know anything himself of the transaction, unless the assistant serving the customer, or the customer, requires to put a question to him. It is right that I should emphasize, as did the Lord Chief Justice, that these are not dangerous drugs. They are substances which contain very small proportions of poison, and I imagine that many of them are the type of drug which has a warning as to what doses are to be taken. They are drugs which can be obtained, under the law, without a doctor's prescription. The point taken by the plaintiffs is this: it is said that the purchase is complete if and when a customer going round the shelves takes an article and puts it in the receptacle which he or she is carrying, and that therefore, if that is right, when the customer comes to the pay desk, having completed the tour of the premises, the registered pharmacist, if so minded, has no power to say: "This drug ought not to be sold to this customer". Whether and in what

---

circumstances he would have that power we need not inquire, but one can, of course, see that there is a difference if supervision can only be exercised at a time when the contract is completed.

I agree with the Lord Chief Justice in everything that he said, but I will put the matter shortly in my own words. Whether the view contended for by the plaintiffs is a right view depends on what are the legal implications of this layout – the invitation to the customer. Is a contract to be regarded as being completed when the article is put into the receptacle, or is this to be regarded as a more organized way of doing what is done already in many types of shops – and a bookseller is perhaps the best example – namely, enabling customers to have free access to what is in the shop, to look at the different articles, and then, ultimately, having got the ones which they wish to buy, to come up to the assistant saying "I want this"? The assistant in 999 times out of 1,000 says "That is all right", and the money passes and the transaction is completed. I agree with what the Lord Chief Justice has said, and with the reasons which he has given for his conclusion, that in the case of an ordinary shop, although goods are displayed and it is intended that customers should go and choose what they want, the contract is not completed until the customer having indicated the articles which he needs, the shop-keeper, or someone on his behalf, accepts that offer. Then the contract is completed. I can see no reason at all, that being clearly the normal position, for drawing any different implication as a result of this layout.

The Lord Chief Justice, I think, expressed one of the most formidable difficulties in the way of the plaintiffs' contention when he pointed out that, if the plaintiffs are right, once an article has been placed in the receptacle the customer himself is bound and would have no right, without paying for the first article, to substitute an article which he saw later of a similar kind and which he perhaps preferred. I can see no reason for implying from this self-service arrangement any implication other than that which the Lord Chief Justice found in it, namely, that it is a convenient method of enabling customers to see what there is and choose, and possibly put back and substitute, articles which they wish to have, and then to go up to the cashier and offer to buy what they have so far chosen. On that conclusion the case fails, because it is admitted that there was supervision in the sense required by the Act and at the appropriate moment of time. For these reasons, in my opinion, the appeal should be dismissed.'

Birkett and Romer LJJ concurred.

Collins, H, *The Law of Contract*, 2003, 4th edn, London: Butterworths, pp 171–173

Instrumentalism

Even where the traditional rules of offer and acceptance are applied, it is apparent . . . that the facts do not conveniently label themselves as 'offers' and 'acceptances'. On the contrary, a hidden element of discretion permits the courts to label the facts with the terminology of offer and acceptance, whenever they believe it is fair and reasonable to impose contractual liability.

Consider, for example, the purchase of goods in a self-service store. At what point is an agreement completed by an acceptance? Does the customer accept the offer when he or she places the goods in the wire basket? Or does acceptance take place when the customers present the goods to the assistant at the cash register? Alternatively, we can even argue that the assistant accepts the offer to buy by ringing up the prices of the goods on the cash register. Or is that merely an offer, accepted by the customer by the presentation of the right amount of money? Since each interpretation is plausible, a court must make a discretionary choice between them, concealing the real grounds for the decision by the formalist reasoning of offer and acceptance. In this brief section we cannot hope to identify all the relevant considerations which a court takes into account. Instead we will illustrate the surprising variety of such considerations in order to reveal the complexity of the issues.

The variety of potentially relevant considerations emerges with a brief review of conflicting decisions from different jurisdictions concerning the moment of formation of a contract of sale in a self-service store. Sometimes the courts desire to make the moment of responsibility as late as possible, in order to avoid making the customer liable to pay for the goods before he or she has had a chance to inspect them and compare the price between different brands. Courts encourage this consumer circum-spection by holding that the customer forms the contract by presenting the goods at the cash register. In contrast, in other cases courts insist that the parties enter a contract when the customer places the goods in the wire basket, if for instance this result strengthens the legal position of a customer injured by a bottle exploding as it is placed in the basket. The relative advantage to a customer of being allowed a contractual claim against the shopkeeper for personal injuries depends upon the state of the law of tort governing the liability of owners of premises towards those injured upon them, so courts in different jurisdictions react in the light of the background law applicable to personal injuries.

Another reason for deferring the moment of acceptance emerges in cases involving charges of shoplifting. If the customer completes the contract when he or she removes goods from the shelf, the shoplifter could defend himself or herself against a charge of theft by arguing that he or she had purchased the goods before taking them from the store. Of course, the shoplifter would in these circumstances be liable to pay the price of the goods, and might also be guilty of another criminal offence involving fraud. But the shoplifter would avoid liability for theft if the contract is formed by taking the goods from the shelf, for logically one cannot steal goods which belong to oneself as a result of a contractual purchase. For this reason, the court is likely to defer the moment of formation of the contract until the goods have been paid for.

These conflicting considerations which influence the determination of the moment of contractual responsibility in a simple case of supermarket purchases explain why courts reach such different results. They also illustrate how difficult it is to anticipate all the relevant considerations. Further complications are introduced in the leading

English case, which illustrates how special statutory provisions give added legal significance to a particular result. In *Pharmaceutical Society of Great Britain v Boots Cash Chemists*, the self-service store was required to demonstrate that it satisfied a statutory requirement that all sales of certain non-prescription drugs should be made under the supervision of a registered pharmacist. The store argued that it complied with the statute by posting a pharmacist in the vicinity of the cash register, as opposed to stationing one near all the display shelves. The Court of Appeal facilitated the development of self-service pharmacies, and incidentally reduced the need for registered pharmacists whose professional body had commenced the action, by concluding that customers made contracts of sale at the cash register and therefore the store complied with the law. The reason given by the court for its decision was simply one of permitting customers to inspect the goods and change their minds in the shop. But one wonders also how impressed the court was by the desire of the pharmacists to retain their restrictive practices, although this consideration was not explicitly acknowledged.

The *Boots'* case deals with the position where the goods are on display inside the shop. What about the display of goods in a shop window? If, for example, goods are displayed at a particular price, is this an offer that a customer can accept simply by going into the shop and asking for the goods? This issue has also been addressed in criminal cases, a good example of which is *Fisher v Bell*.

Fisher v Bell [1961] 1 QB 394 Divisional Court

Facts: A shopkeeper displayed a 'flick-knife' in his shop window. He was charged with offering the knife for sale, contrary to s 1 of the Restriction of Offensive Weapons Act 1959. The justices dismissed the charge, and the prosecutor appealed.

Held: The word 'offer' was not defined in the statute, and so had to be interpreted in accordance with its meaning in the law of contract. On that basis, the shopkeeper was not making an offer by displaying the knife, and so had not committed the offence.

Lord Parker, CJ:

'The sole question is whether the exhibition of that knife in the window with the ticket constituted an offer for sale within the statute. I confess that I think most lay people and, indeed, I myself when I first read the papers, would be inclined to the view that to say that if a knife was displayed in a window like that with a price attached to it was not offering it for sale was just nonsense. In ordinary language it is there inviting people to buy it, and it is for sale; but any statute must of course be looked at in the light of the general law of the country. Parliament in its wisdom in passing an Act must be taken to know the general law. It is perfectly clear that according to the ordinary law of contract the display of an article with a price on it in a shop window is merely an invitation to treat. It is in no sense an offer for sale the acceptance of which constitutes a contract.

That is clearly the general law of the country. Not only is that so, but it is to be observed that in many statutes and orders which prohibit selling and offering for sale of goods it is very common when it is so desired to insert the words "offering or exposing for sale", "exposing for sale" being clearly words which would cover the display of goods in a shop window. Not only that, but it appears that under several statutes – we have been referred in particular to the Prices of Goods Act, 1939, and the Goods and Services (Price Control) Act, 1941 – Parliament, when it desires to enlarge the ordinary meaning of those words, includes a definition section enlarging the ordinary meaning of "offer for sale" to cover other matters including, be it observed, exposure of goods for sale with the price attached.

In those circumstances I am driven to the conclusion, though I confess reluctantly, that no offence was here committed. At first sight it sounds absurd that knives of this sort cannot be manufactured, sold, hired, lent, or given, but apparently they can be displayed in shop windows; but even if this – and I am by no means saying it is – is a casus omissus it is not for this court to supply the omission. I am mindful of the strong words of Lord Simonds in *Magor and St. Mellons Rural District Council v Newport Corporation* [1952] A.C. 189; [1951] 2 All E.R. 839, H.L. In that case one of the Lords Justices in the Court of Appeal had, in effect, said that the court having discovered the supposed intention of Parliament must proceed to fill in the gaps – what the Legislature has not written the court must write – and in answer to that contention Lord Simonds in his speech said: "It appears to me to be a naked usurpation of the legislative function under the thin disguise of interpretation." '

These cases mean that, as far as the law of contract is concerned, a shopkeeper who displays goods at a particular price is not bound by that price, but may tell a customer who asks to buy that the goods are in fact more expensive. This situation raises possibilities of business sellers taking advantage of consumer buyers, and has been addressed by providing criminal penalties for businesses that display misleading prices. The main relevant offence is to be found in s 20 of the Consumer Protection Act 1987. Local Trading Standards Officers, rather than individuals, will normally enforce this. This does not, however, directly affect the position in the law of contract, under which the shop owner has the freedom to decide whether or not to sell at the price indicated. Nor does the statute provide compensation for a disappointed customer – the outcome of a successful prosecution is likely to be a fine imposed on the shop owner, which is paid to the court rather than the customer.

CONSUMER PROTECTION ACT 1987

s 20 *Offence of giving misleading indication*

(1) Subject to the following provisions of this Part, a person shall be guilty of an offence if, in the course of any business of his, he gives (by any means whatever) to any

consumers an indication which is misleading as to the price at which any goods, services, accommodation or facilities are available (whether generally or from particular persons).

(2) Subject as aforesaid, a person shall be guilty of an offence if–

(a) in the course of any business of his, he has given an indication to any consumers which, after it was given, has become misleading as mentioned in subsection (1) above; and

(b) some or all of those consumers might reasonably be expected to rely on the indication at a time after it has become misleading; and

(c) he fails to take all such steps as are reasonable to prevent those consumers from relying on the indication . . .

(4) A person guilty of an offence under subsection (1) or (2) above shall be liable –

(a) on conviction on indictment, to a fine;

(b) on summary conviction, to a fine not exceeding the statutory maximum.

2.2.4.2 Advertisements

If a person advertises goods for sale in a newspaper, or on a notice board, or on the internet, does that constitute an offer? Can a person who wants to buy the goods accept, and form a binding contract simply by replying?

This issue was considered in relation to newspaper advertisements in another criminal case, *Partridge v Crittenden*.

Partridge v Crittenden [1968] 2 All ER 421 (QB)

Facts: The defendant had placed an advertisement in a periodical, 'Cage and Aviary Birds' indicating that he had bramblefinches for sale at 25s each. In no place was there any direct use of the words 'offers for sale'. In answer to the advertisement, T. wrote, enclosing a cheque for 25s, and asked that a hen be sent to him. The defendant was convicted of unlawfully offering for sale a bramblefinch, contrary to section 6 (1) of the Protection of Birds Act, 1954. The defendant appealed.

Held: The appeal was allowed, because the advertisement was an invitation to treat, not an offer for sale.

Ashworth J:

'. . . the real point of substance in this case arose from the words "offer for sale", and it is to be noted in s 6 of the Act of 1954 that the operative words are "any person sells, offers for sale or has in his possession for sale". For some reason which counsel for the respondent has not been able to explain, those responsible for the prosecution in this case chose, out of the trio of possible offences, the one which could not succeed. There was a sale here, in my view, because Mr Thompson sent his cheque and the bird was sent in reply; and a completed sale. On the evidence there was also a plain case of the appellant having in possession for sale this particular bird; but they chose to prosecute him for offering for sale, and they relied on the advertisement. A similar point arose before this court in 1960 dealing, it is true, with a different statute but with the same words, that is *Fisher v Bell* [1960] 3 All ER 731 . . .

The words are the same here "offer for sale", and in my judgment the law of the country is equally plain as it was in regard to articles in a shop window, namely that the insertion of an advertisement in the form adopted here under the title "Classified Advertisements" is simply an invitation to treat. That is really sufficient to dispose of this case . . .'

Lord-Parker CJ:

'I agree and with less reluctance than in *Fisher v Bell*, to which Ashworth J has referred, and the case of *Mella v Monahan* [1961] Crim LR 175. I say "with less reluctance" because I think that when one is dealing with advertisements and circulars, unless they indeed come from manufacturers, there is business sense in their being construed as invitations to treat and not offers for sale. In a very different context Lord Herschell in *Grainger & Son v Gough* (*Surveyor of Taxes*) [1896] AC 325, said this in dealing with a price-list:

> The transmission of such a price-list does not amount to an offer to supply an unlimited quantity of the wine described at the price named, so that as soon as an order is given there is a binding contract to supply that quantity. If it were so, the merchant might find himself involved in any number of contractual obligations to supply wine of a particular description which he would be quite unable to carry out, his stock of wine of that description being necessarily limited.

It seems to me accordingly that not only is that the law, but common sense supports it.'

Generally speaking, therefore, advertisements will not constitute offers. This is likely to be true of internet advertisements, though there is no reported case law on the point. Note, however, that some businesses that sell via the internet specify that the contract will not come into existence until the goods are despatched to the customer. This illustrates the important point that it is generally acceptable for the person who puts forward an advertisement to make clear the basis on which any contract will be made. The courts will normally give effect to this. It is only where there is no specific statement that the court will fall back on the general rules relating to what constitutes an "offer".

The position is similar where it is a service that is being advertised, as is shown by *Harris v Nickerson*.

Harris v Nickerson (1872–3) LR 8 QB 286

Facts: An auction was advertised, at which certain office furniture was to be sold. The plaintiff travelled to the auction for the express purpose of bidding for the office furniture. This was, however, withdrawn from the sale. The plaintiff sued the auctioneer for breach of contract, claiming his wasted expenses in attending the auction. The trial judge held for the plaintiff. The defendant auctioneer appealed.

Held: The advertisement of the auction did not constitute an offer capable of becoming a contract.

Blackburn J:

'I am of opinion that the judge was wrong. The facts were that the defendant advertised bonâ fide that certain things would be sold by auction on the days named, and on the third day a certain class of things, viz., office furniture, without any previous notice of their withdrawal, were not put up. The plaintiff says, inasmuch as I confided in the defendant's advertisement, and came down to the auction to buy the furniture (which it is found as a fact he was commissioned to buy) and have had no opportunity of buying, I am entitled to recover damages from the defendant, on the ground that the advertisement amounted to a contract by the defendant with anybody that should act upon it, that all the things advertised would be actually put up for sale, and that he would have an opportunity of bidding for them and buying. This is certainly a startling proposition, and would be excessively inconvenient if carried out. It amounts to saying that any one who advertises a sale by publishing an advertisement becomes responsible to everybody who attends the sale for his cab hire or travelling expenses . . . [U]nless every declaration of intention to do a thing creates a binding contract with these who act upon it, and in all cases after advertising a sale the auctioneer must give notice of any articles that are withdrawn, or be liable to an action, we cannot hold the defendant liable.'

Quain, J:

'I am of the same opinion. To uphold the judge's decision it is necessary to go to the extent of saying that when an auctioneer issues an advertisement of the sale of goods, if he withdraws any part of them without notice, the persons attending may all maintain actions against him. In the present case, it is to be observed that the plaintiff bought some other lots; but it is said he had a commission to buy the furniture, either the whole or in part, and that therefore he has a right of action against the defendant. Such a proposition seems to be destitute of all authority; and it would be introducing an extremely inconvenient rule of law to say that an auctioneer is bound to give notice of the withdrawal or to be held liable to everybody attending the sale.'

Archibald J, agreed.

The court noted, however, that the position might be different if the auction was advertised as being 'without reserve'. This is considered further at 2.2.6.2. The fact, however, that there are certain limited situations where an advertisement may constitute an offer is illustrated by the famous case of *Carlill v Carbolic Smoke Ball Company*.

Carlill v Carbolic Smoke Ball Co. [1893] 1 QB 256 (CA)

Facts: During a flu epidemic, the Carbolic Small Ball Company published an advertisement which offered £100 to any person who caught influenza after using its smoke ball. Mrs Carlill used the smoke ball, but caught influenza. She sued for the £100.

Held: The advertisement was an offer 'to the world'. A customer who accepted by using the smoke ball was entitled to recover £100 if he or she then caught influenza.

Lindley LJ:
'The first observation I will make is that we are not dealing with any inference of fact. We are dealing with an express promise to pay £100 in certain events. Read the advertisement how you will, and twist it about as you will, here is a distinct promise expressed in language which is perfectly unmistakable – "£100 reward will be paid by the Carbolic Smoke Ball Company to any person who contracts the influenza after having used the ball three times daily for two weeks according to the printed directions supplied with each ball".

We must first consider whether this was intended to be a promise at all, or whether it was a mere puff which meant nothing. Was it a mere puff? My answer to that question is No, and I base my answer upon this passage: "£1000 is deposited with the Alliance Bank, shewing our sincerity in the matter". Now, for what was that money deposited or that statement made except to negative the suggestion that this was a mere puff and meant nothing at all? The deposit is called in aid by the advertiser as proof of his sincerity in the matter – that is, the sincerity of his promise to pay this £100 in the event which he has specified. I say this for the purpose of giving point to the observation that we are not inferring a promise; there is the promise, as plain as words can make it.

Then it is contended that it is not binding. In the first place, it is said that it is not made with anybody in particular. Now that point is common to the words of this advertisement and to the words of all other advertisements offering rewards. They are offers to anybody who performs the conditions named in the advertisement, and anybody who does perform the condition accepts the offer. In point of law this advertisement is an offer to pay £100 to anybody who will perform these conditions, and the performance of the conditions is the acceptance of the offer. That rests upon a string of authorities, the earliest of which is *Williams v Carwardine* (1833) 4 B & Ad 621, which has been followed by many other decisions upon advertisements offering rewards.

But then it is said, "Supposing that the performance of the conditions is an acceptance of the offer, that acceptance ought to have been notified". Unquestionably, as a general proposition, when an offer is made, it is necessary in order to make a binding contract, not only that it should be accepted, but that the acceptance should be notified. But is that so in cases of this kind? I apprehend that they are an exception to that rule, or, if not an exception, they are open to the observation that the notification of the acceptance need not precede the performance. This offer is a continuing offer. It was never revoked, and if notice of acceptance is required – which I doubt very much, for I rather think the true view is that which was expressed and explained by Lord Blackburn in the case of *Brogden v Metropolitan Ry. Co.* (1877) 2 App Cas 666 – if notice of acceptance is required, the person who makes the offer gets the notice of acceptance contemporaneously with his notice of the performance of the condition. If he gets notice of the acceptance before his offer is revoked, that in principle is all you want. I, however, think that the true view, in a case of this kind, is that the person who makes the offer shews by his language and from the nature of the transaction that he does not expect and does not require notice of the acceptance apart from notice of the performance.

We, therefore, find here all the elements which are necessary to form a binding contract enforceable in point of law . . .'

The approach taken in *Carlill* will also be taken where what is being advertised is a 'reward' – for example, for the return of lost property, or information leading to the conviction of an offender. These 'unilateral' contracts, which depend on someone choosing to do something in order to 'earn' a payment are distinguished from straightforward advertisements promoting goods, or indicating the terms on which they are available for purchase, which are likely to be treated as 'mere puffs', or at most as 'invitations to treat'.

In relation to *Carlill's* case itself, Collins has pointed out some features of the case, which might mean that we should be surprised that the court treated it as involving a 'contract':

Collins, Hugh, *The Law of Contract*, 2003, 4th edn, London: Butterworths, p 4

The amusing circumstances of the cases should not obscure the surprising extent to which the court was prepared to conceive social relations in terms of contracts. The parties to the alleged contract had never met or communicated with each other directly. Nor had they exchanged goods, money or services between themselves. The law of contract is used by the court as an instrument for discouraging misleading and extravagant claims in advertising and for deterring the marketing of unproven, and perhaps dangerous, pharmaceuticals. The court protects the gullible and confused consumer by interpreting the events in the form of a contractual relationship giving rise to reciprocal obligations. In so doing it ignores alternative interpretations of these events, such as the idea that the misleading advertisement might constitute a civil wrong in itself, or that consumers who are ignorant of the properties of goods put on the market should be protected from any harmful consequences.

Simpson, AWB, 'Quackery and Contract Law: the case of the Carbolic Smoke Ball' (1985) 14 *J Leg St* 345, pp 375–379

The Smoke Ball and Contractual Theory

For lawyers, and particularly for law students, *Carlill v Carbolic Smoke Ball Co* rapidly achieved the status of a leading case, a status which it has retained perhaps more securely in England than in the United States. Part of its success derived from the comic and slightly mysterious object involved, but there were two reasons of a legal character that suggest that it deserves its place in the firmament. The first, which is not always fully appreciated, is historical; it was the vehicle whereby a new legal doctrine was introduced into the law of contract. The second is that the decision could be used by expositors of the law of contract to illustrate the arcane mysteries surrounding the conception of a unilateral or one-sided contract.

So far as the first point is concerned, the so-called will theory of contract supposed that all contractual obligations were the product of the joint wills of the contracting parties, embodied in their agreement. The function of law courts, according to this theory, was merely that of faithfully carrying into effect the wishes of the parties to the contract. Further reflection on the implications of this theory, which had powerful support in nineteenth-century thought, suggested that it must necessarily follow that a court should not enforce an agreement unless it was the will of the parties that it should be legally enforced. They might indeed have agreed to do something, for example go on a picnic, but be unwilling to have this agreement legally enforced. There must, it was said, be a joint intention to create legal relations before an agreement should have any legal consequences. The principal exponent of this dogma was the German jurist Savigny, and some English contract writers, in particular Sir Frederick Pollock, had incorporated this notion into their accounts of the law without being able to cite any case in which the doctrine had been laid down as law. It could be used to explain certain old cases in which the courts had held there to be no contract, cases in reality decided in sublime ignorance of the theories of Savigny and some long predating his birth. But in legal dogmatics this retrospective reinterpretation is a normal practice, as it is in theological reasoning, which so resembles legal reasoning. But until Mrs. Carlill brought her action there was no case which had clearly recognized the requirement of an intention to create legal relations; her case did. It was indeed explicitly argued in this trial by Asquith that 'the advertisement was a mere representation of what the advertisers intended to do in a certain event. The defendants did not by issuing it mean to impose upon themselves any obligations enforceable by law.' In all probability he took the idea from one of the text writers. This argument was firmly rejected by the trial judge, who relied in particular on the fact that the advertisement had stated that £1,000 had been deposited in the Alliance Bank 'showing our sincerity in the matter'. This, he argued, 'could only have been inserted with the object of leading those who read it to believe that the defendants were serious in their proposal'. In the Court of Appeal the same view was taken. Thus Lord Justice Lindley, early in his opinion said: 'We must first consider whether this was intended to be a promise at all, or whether it was a mere puff which meant nothing. Was it a mere puff? My answer to that question is No, and I base my answer on this passage: "£1000 is deposited with the Alliance Bank, shewing our sincerity in the matter." '

The fact that the judges found it necessary to make this point entailed their acceptance of the idea that without an intention to create legal relations there could be no actionable contract. In fact in the argument before the Court of Appeal little was made of the point, though Mr. Terrell did argue that the promise was too *vague* to be actionable, adding: 'It is like the case in which the man intended to induce a person to marry his daughter', a reference to *Weeks v Tybald* (1605). The 'vagueness' point was picked up by other counsel engaged in the case. But Lindley's opinion was so framed as to enable the case to be used as an authority for the view that Savigny's doctrine was part of English law.

As for the second point, most contracts that concern the courts involve two-sided agreements, two-sided in the sense that the parties enter into reciprocal obligations to each other. A typical example is a sale of goods, where the seller has to deliver the goods and the buyer to pay for them. The doctrines of nineteenth-century contract law were adapted to such bilateral contracts, but the law also somewhat uneasily recognized that there could be contracts in which only one party was ever under any obligation to the other. The standard example was a published promise to pay a reward for information on the recovery of lost property: £10 to anyone who finds and returns my dog. In such a case obviously nobody is obligated to search for the dog, but if they do so successfully, they are entitled to the reward. Such contracts seem odd in another way; there is a promise, but no agreement, for the parties never even meet until the reward is claimed. Promises of rewards, made to the world at large, will not involve an indefinite number of claims—there is only one reward offered—and the courts will uphold the claimant's right to the reward although he has never communicated any acceptance of the promise. Classified as 'unilateral' contracts, such arrangements presented special problems of analysis to contract theorists, whose standard doctrines had not been evolved to fit them. Thus it was by 1892 orthodox to say that all contracts were formed by the exchange of an offer and an acceptance, but it was by no means easy to see how this could be true of unilateral contracts, where there was, to the eyes of common sense, no acceptance needed.

The analytical problems arose in a particularly acute form in the smoke ball case. Thus it seemed very peculiar to say there had been any sort of agreement between Mrs. Carlill and the company, which did not even know of her existence until January 20, when her husband wrote to them to complain. There were indeed earlier cases permitting the recovery of advertised rewards; the leading case here was *Williams v Cawardine*, where a reward of £20 had been promised by handbill for information leading to the conviction of the murderer of Walter Cawardine, and Williams, who gave such information, successfully sued to recover the reward. But this was long before the more modern doctrines had become so firmly embodied in legal thinking, and in any event the case was quite distinguishable. It concerned a reward, whereas Mrs. Carlill was seeking compensation. There could be at most only a few claimants for this, but there is no limit on the number of those who may catch influenza. Furthermore, the Carbolic Smoke Ball Company had had no chance to check the validity of claims, of which there could be an indefinite number; much was made of this point in the argument. But the judges were not impressed with these difficulties, and their attitude was no doubt influenced by the view that the defendants were rogues. They fit their decision into the structure of the law by boldly declaring that the performance of the conditions was the acceptance, thus fictitiously extending the concept of acceptance to cover the facts. And, since 1893, law students have been introduced to the mysteries of the unilateral contract through the vehicle of *Carlill v Carbolic Smoke Ball Co* and taught to repeat, as a sort of magical incantation of contract law, that in the case of unilateral contracts performance of the act specified in the offer constitutes acceptance, and need not be communicated to the offeror.

Lord Justice Bowen's analysis of the facts places the moment of acceptance as the moment when Mrs. Carlill completed the three-week period of use stipulated by the directions for use. This was not the only possible view. In argument Finlay attributed the one-sniff theory to his opponents: 'According to the plaintiff, having taken one sniff at the ball, the defendant would not be at liberty to withdraw from the contract— (laughter)—because she had altered her position by sniffing.' But Dickens did not agree that this was his view, though he is reported as saying that 'Here the contract arose when the plaintiff began to sniff the ball': he thought that the contract only became binding on the defendants on completion of the course. A difficulty with Bowen and Dickens's view is that it leads to the conclusion that the offer could be withdrawn up to the moment of the last sniff, although the act of reliance by Mrs. Carlill took place earlier than this—either when she bought the ball or when she started to use it. This apparently unjust result has encouraged the further complexity of supposing there to be two contracts involved—a contract to pay the £100 if the complete course fails, and a second promise not to revoke the promise to pay the £100 once the purchaser of the ball starts the course of treatment. Other complexities somewhat inadequately dealt with in the case centered on the scope of the promise. Did it cover influenza contracted at any date in the future, or within the period of the epidemic, or while the ball was being used, or within a reasonable time thereafter? The court settled for the last possibility. And did the offer apply to any user—even one who had stolen the ball? But the judges were clearly not impressed with these problems—the defendants had not behaved as gentlemen, and that was essentially that.

Modern consumer law, which overlaps but is not coterminous with contract law, adopts more direct approaches to controlling misleading advertising and selling, through legislation such as the Trade Descriptions Act 1968 and the Consumer Protection Act 1987, which we have already noted in relation to misleading prices (see, above, p 71). If the facts of *Carlill v Carbolic Smoke Ball Company* were to occur today, it is by no means certain that it would be treated as a case on the law of contract.

2.2.5 UNILATERAL AND BILATERAL CONTRACTS

The contract in *Carlill v Carbolic Smoke Ball Company* was of a particular type, generally referred to as a 'unilateral contract'. They are also sometimes known as 'if' contracts, in that they can always be expressed in the form of one party (A) saying to the other (B) – 'If you act in a certain way, then I promise to do something for you'; for example, 'If you buy my smoke ball and, having used it, catch influenza, I promise I will pay you £100'. In this type of contract, B, the person doing the action, has not made any promise to A. B is under no obligation to do the suggested act. If he or she does decide to do it, however, A will be bound by his or her promise. That is why the agreement is 'unilateral'. Under a bilateral contract both parties have obligations as soon as the contract is made.

Offers made 'to the world', as in *Carlill*, will generally be 'unilateral', but it is quite possible to have a unilateral contract where the offer is made to a particular person, as in, for example, *Daulia v Four Millbank Nominees* [1978] 2 All ER 557.

Daulia v Four Millbank Nominees [1978] 2 All ER 557

Facts: The parties were negotiating over the sale of some properties. The seller promised the buyer, that if the buyer produced a signed contract plus a banker's draft by 10 am the next morning, the seller would go through with the contract. When the buyer complied with this requirement, the seller refused to go ahead.

Held: The Court of Appeal held in favour of the seller because of the lack of writing in relation to what was in effect a contract for the sale of land, but indicated that otherwise there would have been a unilateral contract.

Goff, LJ:

'Was there a concluded unilateral contract by the first defendants to enter into a contract for sale on the agreed terms? The concept of a unilateral or "if contract" is somewhat anomalous, because it is clear that, at all events until the offeree starts to perform the condition, there is no contract at all, but merely an offer which the offeror is free to revoke.

   Doubts have been expressed whether the offeror becomes bound so soon as the offeree starts to perform or satisfy the condition, or only when he has fully done so. In my judgment, however, we are not concerned in this case with any such problem, because in my view the plaintiffs had fully performed or satisfied the condition when they presented themselves at the time and place appointed with a banker's draft for the deposit, and their part of the written contract for sale duly engrossed and signed and there tendered the same, which I understand to mean proffered it for exchange. Actual exchange, which never took place, would not in my view have been part of the satisfaction of the condition but something additional which was inherently necessary to be done by the plaintiffs to enable, not to bind the first defendants to perform the unilateral contract.

Accordingly in my judgment, the answer to the first question must be in the affirmative.'

Buckley and Orr LJJ concurred.

2.2.6 SOME SPECIAL SITUATIONS

2.2.6.1 Tenders

Generally, where a firm 'puts work out to tender' it is inviting interested parties to offer to do the work. The invitation may be made to selected parties, or to the world. In either case it will constitute an 'invitation to treat' and any responses received will be 'offers'. In some situations, however, the invitation itself may involve a subsidiary obligation, in the form of a unilateral contract, which can have contractual force. If, for example, the invitation to tender indicates that the work will go to the lowest bidder, then the responder who puts in the lowest bid will be entitled to insist that the other party contracts with it. The situation can be compared to that which applies to auctions, as discussed in the next section.

Even where the invitation to tender contains no commitment to accept the lowest bid, there may be other implicit obligations, as shown by *Blackpool and Fylde Aero Club Ltd v Blackpool Borough Council* [1990] 3 All ER 25.

Blackpool and Fylde Aero Club Ltd v Blackpool Borough Council [1990] 3 All ER 25

Facts: A council invited tenders for the operation of an airfield for pleasure flights. Tenders had to be submitted in a particular form by a particular date. The plaintiffs submitted their tender in accordance with these instructions, but it was overlooked, and not considered with the other tenders.

Held: The Court of Appeal upheld the trial judge's decision that the defendants were in breach of an implicit obligation to give proper consideration to all bids that had been submitted in the correct form.

Bingham LJ:

'. . . The council own and manage Blackpool Airport. For purposes of raising revenue they have made it a practice to grant a concession to an air operator to operate pleasure flights from the airport, no doubt largely for the entertainment of holiday-makers. The club, one of whose directors was and is a Mr. Bateson, tendered for and were granted this concession in 1975 and again in 1978 and again in 1980. In 1983 the

---

most recently granted concession was due to expire. The council accordingly prepared an invitation to tender. This was sent to the club and to six other parties, all of
them in one way or another connected with the airport. [The document set out the
terms for the operation of the concession which was being offered]

There then followed provision, with blank spaces to be filled in by the tenderer, for
alternative offers for different sizes of aircraft and for the naming of willing sureties. The
invitation then continued:

> "This form of tender, fully completed and enclosed in the envelope provided
> endorsed 'Tender for pleasure flying concession' and not bearing any name or
> mark indicating the identity of the sender, is to be received by
> THE TOWN CLERK
> P.O. Box 11
> Town Hall
> Blackpool FY1 1NS
> not later than 12 o'clock noon on Thursday 17th March 1983.
> 'Please note the attached notice in red' "

"The attached notice in red" was an extract from the council's standing orders in these
terms:

> "Important Notice
> The council's standing orders with respect to contracts include the following
> provisions: 1. Tenders shall be submitted in a plain, sealed envelope bearing the
> words 'Tender . . . (followed by the subject to which it relates) . . . .' and shall not
> bear any name or mark indicating the identity of the sender, and 2. No tender
> which is received after the last date and time specified shall be admitted for
> consideration. STRICT COMPLIANCE WITH THESE STANDING ORDERS IS
> REQUESTED
> [Signature]
> Town Clerk."

The envelope provided to the selected tenderers was printed and addressed to the
town clerk at the post office box number given in the invitation. The envelopes also
bore the printed words "tender for" and "due in" to which the council's employees
had added in manuscript "Pleasure Flying Concession" and "12 noon Thursday 17
March 1983."

Only three of the selected tenderers responded to the council's invitation. One put in a
low bid for the lighter size of aircraft only. The second, Red Rose Helicopters Ltd.,
submitted a larger bid, also for the lighter size of aircraft. Mr. Bateson for the club filled
in the form of tender, submitting a bid substantially larger, on its face, than the others,
for the lighter size of aircraft, and also submitting a bid for the heavier size. He put it in
the envelope provided by the council, took it to the town hall and posted it in the town
hall letter box at about 11 a.m. on Thursday 17 March. This was about an hour before

the advertised deadline expired. The town clerk's staff were supposed to empty the letter box each day at 12 o'clock. They failed to do so. The club's tender accordingly remained in the letter box until the next morning, 18 March, when the letter box was next opened. The envelope was then taken out and date-stamped 18 March 1983 by the town clerk's department. At some time thereafter the word "late" was written on the envelope, because that is what the club's tender was mistakenly thought to be.

On 29 March 1983 the chairman of the council's relevant committee considered which tender to accept. The club's tender had been recorded as being late, and was in accordance with the council's standing orders excluded from consideration when the chairman made his decision. He accordingly made his choice between the two tenders believed to be in time, recommending acceptance of Red Rose Helicopters' tender, no doubt because it was bigger.

An indication that its tender was accepted was given to Red Rose Helicopters. The town clerk wrote to the club to say that their tender was not received until 18 March and was therefore received too late for consideration. Mr. Bateson replied that the club's tender had been delivered to the town hall before the deadline. "You will appreciate", he wrote, "that this matter is of some considerable importance to our company." The council evidently made inquiries and established that the club's tender had been received in time.

[Nevertheless, after initially declaring the tendering process invalid, the Council decided that it was legally bound to the contract made with Red Rose Helicopters.]

The contractual argument hinges on paragraph 4 of the club's amended statement of claim in which it was alleged that the council

> "warranted that if a tender was returned to the town hall, Blackpool before noon on Thursday 17 March 1983 the same would be considered along with other tenders duly returned when the decision to grant the concession was made."

Mr. Shorrock for the club declined to put the contractual term contended for in any other way, save that he accepted that "when" might with advantage be read as "when or if". It was for breach of this warranty that damages in contract were claimed.

Mr. Bateson was the only witness called. His examination in chief included this passage:

> "(Q) . . . when you submitted your tenders before noon on 17 March, did you believe or not that the tender would be considered along with others that had been submitted?
> (A) We were under no doubt that it would be considered as other tenders had been considered in previous years.
> (Q) If you had known or thought that a tender submitted by you would not have been considered, would you have bothered to tender in the first place? (A) It would have been very questionable whether to bother to tender, but we would probably have pursued the matter beforehand."

Mr. Bateson was not cross-examined.

The judge resolved the contractual issue in favour of the club, holding that an express request for a tender might in appropriate circumstances give rise to an implied obligation to perform the service of considering that tender. Here, the council's stipulation that tenders received after the deadline would not be admitted for consideration gave rise to a contractual obligation, on acceptance by submission of a timely tender, that such tenders would be admitted for consideration. . . .

I found great force in the submissions made by Mr. Toulson [for the Council] and agree with much of what he said. Indeed, for much of the hearing I was of opinion that the judge's decision, although fully in accord with the merits as I see them, could not be sustained in principle. But I am in the end persuaded that Mr. Toulson's argument proves too much. During the hearing the questions were raised: what if, in a situation such as the present, the council had opened and thereupon accepted the first tender received, even though the deadline had not expired and other invitees had not yet responded? Or if the council had considered and accepted a tender admittedly received well after the deadline? Mr. Toulson answered that although by so acting the council might breach its own standing orders, and might fairly be accused of discreditable conduct, it would not be in breach of any legal obligation because at that stage there would be none to breach. This is a conclusion I cannot accept. And if it were accepted there would in my view be an unacceptable discrepancy between the law of contract and the confident assumptions of commercial parties, both tenderers (as reflected in the evidence of Mr. Bateson) and invitors (as reflected in the immediate reaction of the council when the mishap came to light).

A tendering procedure of this kind is, in many respects, heavily weighted in favour of the invitor. He can invite tenders from as many or as few parties as he chooses. He need not tell any of them who else, or how many others, he has invited. The invitee may often, although not here, be put to considerable labour and expense in preparing a tender, ordinarily without recompense if he is unsuccessful. The invitation to tender may itself, in a complex case, although again not here, involve time and expense to prepare, but the invitor does not commit himself to proceed with the project, whatever it is; he need not accept the highest tender; he need not accept any tender; he need not give reasons to justify his acceptance or rejection of any tender received. The risk to which the tenderer is exposed does not end with the risk that his tender may not be the highest or, as the case may be, lowest. But where, as here, tenders are solicited from selected parties all of them known to the invitor, and where a local authority's invitation prescribes a clear, orderly and familiar procedure – draft contract conditions available for inspection and plainly not open to negotiation, a prescribed common form of tender, the supply of envelopes designed to preserve the absolute anonymity of tenderers and clearly to identify the tender in question, and an absolute deadline – the invitee is in my judgment protected at least to this extent: if he submits a conforming tender before the deadline he is entitled, not as a matter of mere expectation but of contractual right, to be sure that his tender will after the deadline be opened and considered in conjunction with all other conforming tenders or at least that his tender will be considered if others are. Had the club, before tendering, inquired of the council whether it could rely on any timely and conforming tender being considered along with others, I feel quite sure that the answer would have been "of course". The law would, I think, be defective if it did not give effect to that.

It is of course true that the invitation to tender does not explicitly state that the council will consider timely and conforming tenders. That is why one is concerned with implication. But the council do not either say that they do not bind themselves to do so, and in the context a reasonable invitee would understand the invitation to be saying, quite clearly, that if he submitted a timely and conforming tender it would be considered, at least if any other such tender were considered.

I readily accept that contracts are not to be lightly implied. . . . In all the circumstances of this case, and I say nothing about any other, I have no doubt that the parties did intend to create contractual relations to the limited extent contended for. Since it has never been the law that a person is only entitled to enforce his contractual rights in a reasonable way (*White and Carter (Councils) Ltd v McGregor* [1962] A.C. 413, 430A, *per* Lord Reid), Mr. Shorrock was in my view right to contend for no more than a contractual duty to consider. I think it plain that the council's invitation to tender was, to this limited extent, an offer, and the club's submission of a timely and conforming tender an acceptance . . .

I accordingly agree with the judge's conclusion on the contractual issue, essentially for the reasons which he more briefly gave . . .

I would accordingly dismiss the appeal. The practical consequences of deciding the contractual issue on liability in the club's favour must, if necessary, be decided hereafter.'

2.2.6.2 Auctions

The general rule at a 'live' auction is that offers are made by the bidders. The acceptance is made by the auctioneer, signalled by the fall of the hammer.

SALE OF GOODS ACT 1979, s 57

(1) Where goods are put up for sale by auction in lots, each lot is prima facie deemed to be the subject of a separate contract of sale.

(2) A sale by auction is complete when the auctioneer announces its completion by the fall of the hammer, or in other customary manner; and until the announcement is made any bidder may retract his bid.

An advertisement that an auction is going to take place, or that specific goods will be included in it, is not in itself to be treated as an offer. This was the result of the decision in *Harris v Nickerson* (1873) LR 8 QB 286. What is the position, however, if the auction of one or more items is advertised as being 'without reserve'? That is, the auctioneer is indicating that the there is no minimum bid requirement, and that the highest bid, however low it may be, will be accepted. This was considered first in *Warlow v Harrison* (1859) 1 E & E 309. The court indicated that it considered the auctioneer to be bound by such an indication, but had to decide against the plaintiff because the case had not been pleaded correctly. The situation has been reconsidered much more recently in *Barry v Heathcote Ball & Co (Commercial Auctions) Ltd* [2001] 1 All ER 944.

Barry v Heathcote Ball & Co (Commercial Auctions) Ltd [2001] 1 All ER 944

Facts: An auction was held by the defendant on 25 June 1997. One of the lots for sale consisted of two engine analysers, the list price of which was over £14,000 each. The claimant had seen the machines and had been told that they were to be sold without reserve. At the auction the claimant bid £200 for each machine. The auctioneer refused to accept this bid, and withdrew the machines. The claimant sued, and was awarded damages of £27,600 for breach of contract.

Held: The Court of Appeal held that the statement that the auction was to be without reserve constituted a promise that if the claimant made the highest bid, it would be accepted. It upheld the trial judge's decision.

Sir Murray Stuart-Smith:

'. . . The claimant runs a car tuning business. He saw the machines being delivered to the auction house on 20 June. He returned on the viewing day and spoke to Mr Cross [the auctioneer] who said that they would be sold at noon on 25 June without reserve. The claimant decided they would be useful in his business and decided to bid for them.

   The claimant attended the auction house for a few minutes before noon. When it came to the lots in question Mr Cross said that the machines were to be "sold that day" on behalf of the VAT office, that each was worth £14,000, "ready to plug in and away you go". He tried to obtain a bid of £5,000 to start with; there was no bid; he tried £3,000; still no response. He then asked what bids there were for the machines, and the claimant bid £200 for each. No other bid was made. In fact Mr Cross had received a bid from his son-in-law for £400 each; but he made no mention of this.

   Mr Cross then withdrew the machines from the sale. His explanation was:

> "I could not see how I could sell for as little as this, even though it was without reserve. I think I am justified in not selling at an auction without reserve if I think I could get more in some other way later. I did not take up [the offer of] £400. I thought they were worth more."

He told those present that he was not prepared to sell the machines for £200. They were sold a few days later for £1,500 (£750 each) after advertisement in a magazine.

   The claimant claimed damages on the basis that he was the highest bidder. The particulars of the damage claimed was the difference between the value of the machines, said to be £28,000 and the bid of £400.

The judge held that it would be the general and reasonable expectation of persons attending at an auction sale without reserve that the highest bidder would and should be entitled to the lot for which he bids. Such an outcome was in his view fair and logical. As a matter of law he held that there was a collateral contract between the auctioneer and the highest bidder which was accepted when the bid was made. In so doing he followed the view of the majority of the Court of Exchequer Chamber in *Warlow v Harrison* (1859) 1 E & E 309, [1843–60] All ER Rep 620 . . .

Mr Moran on behalf of the defendant criticises this conclusion on a number of grounds. First he submits that the holding of an auction without reserve does not amount to a promise on the part of the auctioneer to sell the lots to the highest bidder. There are no express words to the effect, merely a statement of fact that the vendor has not placed a reserve on the lot. Such an intention, he submits, is inconsistent with two principles of law, namely that the auctioneer's request for bids is not an offer which can be accepted by the highest bidder (see *Payne v Cave* (1789) 3 Term Rep 148, [1775–1802] All ER Rep 492) and that there is no completed contract of sale until the auctioneer's hammer falls and the bidder may withdraw his bid up until that time (Sale of Goods Act 1979, s 57(2) which reflects the common law). There should be no need to imply such a promise into a statement that the sale is without reserve, because there may be other valid reasons why the auctioneer should be entitled to withdraw the lot, for example if he suspected an illegal ring or that the vendor had not title to sell.

Secondly Mr Moran submits that there is no consideration for the auctioneer's promise. He submits that the bid itself cannot amount to consideration because the bidder has not promised to do anything, he can withdraw the bid until it is accepted and the sale completed by the fall of the hammer. At most the bid represents a discretionary promise, which amounts to illusory consideration, for example promising to do something 'if I feel like it'. The bid only had real benefit to the auctioneer at the moment the sale is completed by the fall of the hammer. Furthermore the suggestion that consideration is provided because the auctioneer has the opportunity to accept the bid or to obtain a higher bid as the bidding is driven up depends upon the bid not being withdrawn . . .

These submissions were forcefully and attractively argued by Mr Moran. The authorities, such as they were, do not speak with one voice. The starting point is s 57 of the 1979 Act, which re-enacted the Sale of Goods Act 1893, itself in this section a codification of the common law. I have already referred to the effect of sub-s(2). Subsections (3) and (4) are also important. They provide:

> "(3) A sale by auction may be notified to be subject to a reserve or upset price, and a right to bid may also be reserved expressly by or on behalf of the seller.
>
> (4) Where a sale by auction is not notified to be subject to a right to bid by or on behalf of the seller, it is not lawful for the seller to bid himself or to employ any persons to bid at the sale, or for the auctioneer knowingly to take any bid from the seller or any such person."

Although the 1979 Act does not expressly deal with sales by auction without reserve, the auctioneer is the agent of the vendor and unless sub-s(4) has been complied with, it is not lawful for him to make a bid. Yet withdrawing the lot from the sale because it has not reached the level which the auctioneer considers appropriate is tantamount to bidding on behalf of the seller. The highest bid cannot be rejected simply because it is not high enough.

The judge based his decision on the reasoning of the majority of the Court of Exchequer Chamber in *Warlow v Harrison* [1859] 1 E & E 309, [1843–60] All ER Rep 620. The sale was of "the three following horses, the property of a gentleman, without reserve". The plaintiff bid 60 guineas for one of the horses; another person, who was in fact the owner, immediately bid 61 guineas. The plaintiff, having been informed that the bid was from the owner declined to bid higher, and claimed he was entitled to the horse. He sued the auctioneer; he based his claim on a plea that the auctioneer was his agent to complete the contract on his behalf. On that plea the plaintiff succeeded at first instance; but the verdict was set aside in the Court of Queen's Bench. The plaintiff appealed. Although the Court of Exchequer Chamber upheld the decision on the case as pleaded, all five members of the court held that if the pleadings were appropriately amended, the plaintiff would be entitled to succeed on a retrial. Martin B gave the judgment of the majority consisting of himself, Byles J and Watson B. He said:

"Upon the facts of the case, it seems to us that the plaintiff is entitled to recover. In a sale by auction there are three parties, viz. the owner of the property to be sold, the auctioneer, and the portion of the public who attend to bid, which of course includes the highest bidder. In this, as in most cases of sales by auction, the owner's name was not disclosed: he was a concealed principal. The name of the auctioneers, of whom the defendant was one, alone was published; and the sale was announced by them to be 'without reserve'. This, according to all the cases both at law and equity, means that neither the vendor nor any person on his behalf shall bid at the auction, and that the property shall be sold to the highest bidder, whether the sum bid be equivalent to the real value or not; *Thornett v Haines* (1846) 15 M & W 367, 153 ER 892). We cannot distinguish the case of an auctioneer putting up property for sale upon such a condition from the case of the loser of property offering a reward, or that of a railway company publishing a time table stating the times when, and the places to which, the trains run. It has been decided that the person giving the information advertised for, or a passenger taking a ticket, may sue as upon a contract with him; *Denton v Great Northern Railway Company* ((1856) 5 E & B 860, 119 ER 701). Upon the same principle, it seems to us that the highest bona fide bidder at an auction may sue the auctioneer who puts the property up for sale upon such a condition pledges himself that the sale shall be without reserve; or, in other words, contracts that it shall be so; and that this contract is made with the highest bona fide bidder; and, in case of a breach of it, that he has a right of action against the auctioneer."
(See (1859) 1 E&E 309 at 316–17, [1843–60] All ER Rep 620 at 622.). . . .

So far as textbook writers are concerned both *Chitty on Contracts* (28th edn, 1999) para 2–010 and *Benjamin on Sale of Goods* (5th edn, 1997) para 2–005 adopt the view expressed by the majority of the court in *Warlow*'s case.

As to consideration, in my judgment there is consideration both in the form of detriment to the bidder, since this bid can be accepted unless and until it is withdrawn, and benefit to the auctioneer as the bidding is driven up. Moreover attendance at the sale is likely to be increased if it is known that there is no reserve . . .

For these reasons I would uphold the judge's decision on liability.'

Sir Murray Stuart-Smith also upheld the judge's approach to the award of damages. Pill LJ concurred.

Some 'auctions' do not take place on the basis of bidders competing against each other, and responding to each other, but by means of sealed bids. Another issue that can arise in this type of sale is whether a bid, which refers to others, is valid. If one bidder says in a sealed bid: 'I will pay £5 more than the next highest bid', can this be accepted? The situation was considered by the House of Lords in *Harvela Investments v Royal Trust of Canada* [1986] 1 AC 207.

Harvela Investments Ltd v Royal Trust Co. of Canada (CI) Ltd [1985] 2 All ER 966 (HL)

Facts: The sellers invited H and L to make offers to buy some shares. The offers were to be in the form of sealed bids. The sellers indicated that they would accept the highest bid. H offered $2,175,000. L offered $2,100,000 or 'C$101,000 in excess of any other which you may receive . . .' When the bids were disclosed, both parties claimed to be entitled to the shares. The trial judge held for H. The Court of Appeal held for L.

Held: The form in which the invitation to bid was expressed ruled out referential bids. This was not an 'auction' in the true sense, where bidders compete with knowledge of the other bidders' bids, but a 'fixed bidding sale', which ruled out referential bids. H was entitled to the shares, as the only valid bid submitted by L was for $2,100,000.

Lord Templeman:

'On 15 September 1981 the invitation [to bid for the shares] was dispatched to Harvela and Sir Leonard [who had both submitted previous offers to buy them]. The full terms of the invitation, as subsequently amended, were as follows:

We have before us two similar offers but subject to differing terms and conditions and value. Accordingly we invite you to submit to the Royal Trust Company of Canada (C.I.) Limited the registered holder of the shares referred to below any revised offer which you may wish to make by sealed tender or confidential telex to be submitted to our London solicitors, Messrs. Bischoff and Co., City Wall

House, 79/83 Chiswell Street, London EC1 by 3 p.m. London time Wednesday 16 September 1981. Attention J. Jowitt who has undertaken not to disclose any details of any revised offer to any party before that time . . . Tenders are to be submitted on the following terms:— 1. That tenders are a single offer for all shares held by us. 2. That payment of the agreed purchase price shall be within 30 days of 16th September 1981. (The date of actual payment hereafter called the 'closing date'). 3. Payment shall be in full on the closing date without any deduction. 4. The closing shall take place at Messrs Bischoffs' office payment being by banker's draft payable at sight drawn on the head office of a London clearing bank in Canadian dollars. 5. In the event that closing shall not take place within 30 days other than by reason of any delay on our part interest shall be payable by the purchaser on the full purchase price at a rate higher by 4 per cent than the Bank of Montreal prime rate from time to time for Canadian dollar loans. We hereby agree subject to acceptance by us of any offer made by you . . . C) We confirm that if any offer made by you is the highest offer received by us we bind ourselves to accept such offer provided that such offer complies with the terms of this telex . . .

Before the invitation expired Harvela and Sir Leonard made the offers which resulted in this litigation, namely by Harvela $2,175,000 and by Sir Leonard $2,100,000 "or C$101,000 in excess of any other offer which you may receive which is expressed as a fixed monetary amount, whichever is the higher".

Where a vendor undertakes to sell to the highest bidder the vendor may conduct the sale by auction or by fixed bidding. In an auction sale each bidder may adjust his bid by reference to rival bids. In an auction sale the purchaser pays more than any other bidder is prepared to pay to secure the property. The purchaser does not necessarily pay as much as the purchaser was prepared to pay to secure the property. In an auction a purchaser who is prepared to pay $2.5m to secure a property will be able to purchase for $2.2m if no other bidder is prepared to offer as much as $2.2m.

In a fixed bidding sale a bidder may not adjust his bid. Each bidder specifies a fixed amount which he hopes will be sufficient, but not more than sufficient, to exceed any other bid. The purchaser in a fixed bidding sale does not necessarily pay as much as the purchaser was prepared to pay to secure the property. But any bidder who speci-fies less than his best price knowingly takes a risk of being outbid. In a fixed bidding sale a purchaser who is prepared to pay $2.5m to secure the property may be able to purchase for $2.2m if the purchaser offers $2.2m and no other bidder offers as much as $2.2m. But if a bidder prepared to pay $2.5m only offers $2.2m he will run the risk of losing the property and will be mortified to lose the property if another bidder offers $2.3m. Where there are two bidders with ample resources, each determined to secure the property and to prevent the other bidder from acquiring the property, the stronger will prevail in the fixed bidding sale and may pay more than in an auction which is decided not by the strength of the stronger but by the weakness of the weaker of the two bidders. On the other hand, an open auction provides the stimulus of perceived bidding and compels each bidder, except the purchaser, to bid up to his maximum.

Thus auction sales and fixed bidding sales are liable to affect vendors and purchasers in different ways and to produce different results. The first question raised by this appeal, therefore, is whether Harvela and Sir Leonard were invited to participate in a fixed bidding sale, which only invited fixed bids, or were invited to participate in an auction sale, which enabled the bid of each bidder to be adjusted by reference to the other bid. A vendor chooses between a fixed bidding sale and an auction sale. A bidder can only choose to participate in the sale or to abstain from the sale. The ascertainment of the choice of the vendors in the present case between a fixed bidding sale and an auction sale by means of referential bids depends on the presumed intention of the vendors. That presumed intention must be deduced from the terms of the invitation read as a whole. The invitation contains three provisions which are only consistent with the presumed intention to create a fixed bidding sale and which are inconsistent with any presumed intention to create an auction sale by means of referential bids.

By the first significant provision, the vendors undertook to accept the highest offer; this shows that the vendors were anxious to ensure that a sale should result from the invitation. By the second provision, the vendors extended the same invitation to Harvela and Sir Leonard; this shows that the vendors were desirous that each of them, Harvela and Sir Leonard, and nobody else, should be given an equal opportunity to purchase the shares. By the third provision, the vendors insisted that offers must be confidential and must remain confidential until the time specified by the vendors for the submission of offers had elapsed; this shows that the vendors were desirous of provoking from Sir Leonard an offer of the best price he was prepared to pay in ignorance of the bid made by Harvela and equally provoking from Harvela the best price they were prepared to pay in ignorance of the bid made by Sir Leonard.

A fixed bidding sale met all the requirements of the vendors deducible from the terms of the invitation. A fixed bidding sale was bound to result in a sale of shares save in the unlikely event of both Harvela and Sir Leonard failing to respond to the invitation. A fixed bidding sale gave an equal opportunity to Harvela and Sir Leonard to acquire the shares. A fixed bidding sale provoked the best price, or at any rate something approximate to the best price, which the purchaser was prepared to pay to secure the shares and to ensure that the rival bidder did not acquire the shares. On the other hand, if the invitation is construed so as to create an auction sale by means of referential bids, the requirements of the vendors deducible from the terms of the invitation could not be met.

First, if referential bids were permissible, there was a danger, far from negligible, that the sale might be abortive and the shares remain unsold. The shares would only be sold if at least one bidder submitted a fixed bid and the other bidder based his referential offer on that fixed bid. In the events which happened Harvela put forward a fixed bid of $2,175,000 and Sir Leonard made a referential bid of $101,000 more than Harvela's fixed bid, thus enabling Sir Leonard's referential bid to be quantified at $2,276,000. But if Sir Leonard's referential bid had not been expressed to be based on Harvela's fixed bid, or if Harvela had not made a fixed bid but only a referential bid, then Sir Leonard's bid could not have been quantified. Similarly, if Harvela had made a referential bid not expressed to be tied to Sir Leonard's fixed bid, or if Sir Leonard had not made a fixed bid but only a referential bid, then Harvela's bid could not have been quantified. The sale would have been abortive although both bidders were anxious to purchase and submitted offers.

Second, if referential bids were permissible, there was also a possibility, which in fact occurred, that one bidder would never have an opportunity to buy. In the present case Harvela, by putting forward a fixed bid, could never succeed in buying the shares although the invitation had been extended to them. Harvela's only part in the sale was unwittingly to determine the price at which Sir Leonard was entitled and bound to purchase the shares. Harvela could not win and Sir Leonard could not lose. There was nothing in the invitation to warn Harvela that they must submit a referential bid if they wished to make sure of being able to compete with Sir Leonard. There was nothing in the invitation which indicated to Sir Leonard that he was entitled to submit a referential bid. But no one has argued that the invitation did not invite fixed bids; indeed, Sir Leonard submitted a fixed bid, albeit as an unsuccessful alternative to his referential bid.

Third, if referential bids were permissible, the vendors' object of provoking the best price that Harvela and Sir Leonard were each prepared to offer in ignorance of the rival bid was frustrated. Harvela put forward the fixed bid of $2,175,000 which represented the amount which Harvela hoped would exceed Sir Leonard's bid and which, because Harvela was bidding in ignorance of Sir Leonard's bid, must be or approximate to the best price which Harvela was prepared to pay to secure the shares and to ensure that Sir Leonard did not acquire the shares. Sir Leonard did not put forward his best price; Sir Leonard put forward his worst price, $2,100,000, but declared that he would pay $101,000 more than Harvela. Sir Leonard could have achieved the same purpose by offering five dollars or one dollar more than Harvela. If Sir Leonard had appreciated that he was taking part in a fixed bidding sale, then, judging by his minimum fixed bid of $2,100,000 and his unlimited referential bid, he might have been prepared to offer as his best price more than the sum of $2,276,000 which he now claims to be the purchase price of the shares. We shall never know because Sir Leonard did not reveal his best price.

Finally, if referential bids were permissible by implication, without express provision in the invitation for that purpose, and without any indication in the invitation of the nature of the referential bids which would be acceptable, the results could have been bizarre. In the present case Sir Leonard bid $2,100,000 or $101,000 in excess of Harvela's fixed bid. If Harvela had bid $2,000,000 or one dollar more than Sir Leonard's fixed bid then Sir Leonard would have become the purchaser with his referential bid of $2,101,000 as against Harvela's referential bid of $2,100,001. But if Harvela had offered $1,900,000 or one dollar more than Sir Leonard's fixed bid then Harvela would have been the purchaser at their referential bid of $2,100,001 as against Sir Leonard's referential bid of $2,001,000. Sir Leonard's bid in the second example is the same as his bid in the first example but he loses. Harvela's bid in the second example is lower than Harvela's bid in the first example but Harvela wins. The vendors are worse off by $999 in the second example.

It would have been possible for the vendors to conduct an auction sale through the medium of confidential referential bids but only by making express provision in the invitation for the purpose. It would not have been sufficient for the invitation expressly to authorise 'referential bids' without more. For such an authorisation would have rendered the result of the sale uncertain and random in view of the illustrations and examples I have already given. It would have been necessary for the invitation to require each bidder who made a referential bid to specify a maximum sum he was prepared to bid. That requirement would ensure that the sale was not abortive and that both bidders had a genuine chance of winning. A maximum bid requirement would ensure a sale at a price in excess of the maximum bid of the unsuccessful bidder, but it would not necessarily procure a sale at the maximum price of the successful bidder. The sale would in effect be an auction sale and produce the consequences of an auction sale because the vendors would have made express provision for bids to be adjusted and finalised by reference to the maximum bid of the unsuccessful bidder. But without such express provisions the invitation is not consistent with an auction sale.

To constitute a fixed bidding sale all that was necessary was that the vendors should invite confidential offers and should undertake to accept the highest offer. Such was the form of the invitation. It follows that the invitation on its true construction created a fixed bidding sale and that Sir Leonard was not entitled to submit and the vendors were not entitled to accept a referential bid. . . .

The vendors were bound to accept Harvela's offer.'

Lords Fraser, Diplock, Edmund Davies and Templeman concurred.

2.2.7 ACCEPTANCE

Once it is clear that an offer has been made, then a contract can be formed simply by the other party indicating its acceptance. The acceptance must match the offer exactly, however. If it attempts to modify the offer, or introduce new terms, it will not be an 'acceptance' but a 'counter-offer'. Moreover, once a counter-offer is made, this also constitutes a rejection of the original offer, which is no longer available for acceptance. The application of these rules is exemplified by the following case:

Hyde v Wrench (1840) 3 Beav 334 (Rolls Court)

Facts: The defendant offered to sell a farm to the plaintiff for £1,000. The plaintiff offered £900, which was rejected. The plaintiff then purported to accept the offer to sell at £1,000. The defendant refused to go through with the transaction and the plaintiff sued for specific performance of the contract.

Held: The counter-offer of £900 in effect destroyed the original offer to sell at £1,000, and it was no longer open for acceptance.

Lord Langdale MR:
'Under the circumstances stated in this bill, I think there exists no valid binding contract between the parties for the purchase of the property. The defendant offered to sell it for £1,000, and if that had been at once unconditionally accepted, there would undoubtedly have been a perfect binding contract; instead of that, the plaintiff made an offer of his own, to purchase the property for £950, and he thereby rejected the offer previously made by the defendant. I think that it was not afterwards competent for him to revive the proposal of the defendant, by tendering an acceptance of it; and that, therefore, there exists no obligation of any sort between the parties; the demurrer must be allowed.

A response to an offer may in some circumstances be neither a counter-offer nor an acceptance. The offeree may simply want clarification on a particular point, without intending to accept or reject the offer. Such a 'request for information' will leave the offer open for later acceptance, and has no legal significance as far as the formation of the contract is concerned. This is illustrated by the following decision:

Stevenson v McLean (1880) 5 QBD 346 (QB)

Facts: Following negotiations over the sale of a quantity of iron, a firm offer to sell at a particular price was made, with the offer to be held open for a specified period. The offeree inquired about delivery. The seller did not respond, but sold the iron elsewhere. The offeree, not knowing of this, sought to accept the offer to sell, within the original time limit. When the offeree discovered that the iron had been sold elsewhere, he brought an action for breach of contract.

Held: The inquiry about delivery was not a counter-offer, but simply a request for information. The original offer therefore remained open for acceptance.

Lush J:
'. . . The plaintiffs are makers of iron and iron merchants at Middlesborough. The defendant being possessed of warrants for iron, which he had originally bought off the plaintiffs, wrote on the 24th of September to the plaintiffs from London, where he carries on his business: "I see that No. 3 has been sold for immediate delivery at 39s., which means a higher price for warrants. Could you get me an offer for the whole or part of my warrants? I have 3,800 tons, and the brands you know."

On the 26th one of the plaintiffs wrote from Liverpool: "Your letter has followed me here. The pig iron trade is at present very excited, and it is difficult to decide whether prices will be maintained or fall as suddenly as they have advanced. Sales are being made freely for forward delivery chiefly, but not in warrants. It may, however, be found advisable to sell the warrants as maker's iron. I would recommend you to fix your price, and if you will write me your limit to Middlesborough, I shall probably be able to wire you something definite on Monday." This letter was crossed by a letter written on the same day by the clerk of one Fossick, the defendant's broker in London, and which was in these terms:

> Referring to R. A. McLean's letter to you re warrants, I have seen him again to-day, and he considers 39s. too low for same. At 40s. he says he would consider an offer. However, I shall be obliged by your kindly wiring me, if possible, your best offer for all or part of the warrants he has to dispose of.

On the 27th (Saturday) the plaintiffs sent to Fossick the following telegram:

> Cannot make an offer today; warrants rather easier. Several sellers think might get 39s. 6d. if you could wire firm offer subject reply Tuesday noon.

In answer to this Fossick wrote on the same day: "Your telegram duly to hand re warrants. I have seen Mr McLean, but he is not inclined to make a firm offer. I do not think he is likely to sell at 39s.6d., but will probably prefer to wait. Please let me know immediately you get any likely offer."

On the same day the defendant, who had then received the Liverpool letter of the 26th, wrote himself to the plaintiffs as follows:

> Mr Fossick's clerk shewed me a telegram from him yesterday mentioning 39s. for No. 3 as present price, 40s. for forward delivery. I instructed the clerk to wire you that I would now sell for 40s., nett cash, open till Monday.

No such telegram was sent by Fossick's clerk.

The plaintiffs were thus on the 28th (Sunday) in possession of both letters, the one from Fossick stating that the defendant was not inclined to make a firm offer; and the other from the defendant himself, to the effect that he would sell for 40s., nett cash, and would hold it open all Monday. This it was admitted must have been the meaning of "open till Monday".

On the Monday morning, at 9.42, the plaintiffs telegraphed to the defendant: "Please wire whether you would accept forty for delivery over two months, or if not, longest limit you would give".

> This telegram was received at the office at Moorgate at 10.1 a.m., as an inquiry, expecting an answer for his guidance, and this, I think, is the sense in which the defendant ought to have regarded it.

It is apparent throughout the correspondence, that the plaintiffs did not contemplate buying the iron on speculation, but that their acceptance of the defendant's offer depended on their finding someone to take the warrants off their hands. All parties knew that the market was in an unsettled state, and that no one could predict at the early hour when the telegram was sent how the prices would range during the day. It was reasonable that, under these circumstances, they should desire to know before business began whether they were to be at liberty in case of need to make any and what concession as to the time or times of delivery, which would be the time or times of payment, or whether the defendant was determined to adhere to the terms of his letter; and it was highly unreasonable that the plaintiffs should have intended to close the negotiation while it was uncertain whether they could find a buyer or not, having the whole of the business hours of the day to look for one. Then, again, the form of the telegram is one of inquiry. It is not "I offer forty for delivery over two months", which would have likened the case to *Hyde v Wrench* (1840) 3 Bear 334, where one party offered his estate for £1000, and the other answered by offering £950. Lord Langdale, in that case, held that after the £950 had been refused, the party offering it could not, by then agreeing to the original proposal, claim the estate, for the negotiation was at an end by the refusal of his counter proposal. Here there is no counter proposal. The words are, "Please wire whether you would accept forty for delivery over two months, or, if not, the longest limit you would give". There is nothing specific by way of offer or rejection, but a mere inquiry, which should have been answered and not treated as a rejection of the offer. This ground of objection therefore fails.'

2.2.7.1 Battle of the forms

Where two businesses are negotiating over contract, they may well both have a set of standard terms that they will prefer to use. Some aspects of these terms may well be in conflict. If this is the case, and is not resolved prior to the performance of the agreement, the courts may be left with having to decide whether there was ever a contract between the parties and, if so, what its terms were. If there was no matching offer and acceptance, the outcome ought to be that there was no contract; the courts are reluctant to come to such a conclusion, however, particularly where an agreement has been performed. At times they may be able to find an oral agreement that did not refer to any of the documentation (as in *Hertford Foods Ltd v Lidl UK GmbH*, CA, 20 June 2001); alternatively, they may try to find that there was in fact a matching offer and acceptance, despite initial appearances to the contrary. This may well be said to be what happened in the next case.

Butler Machine Tool Co v Ex-Cell-O Corporation [1979] 1 All ER 965 (CA)

Facts: The case concerned an alleged contract for the sale of a machine. The seller's standard terms included a price variation clause; the buyer's standard terms had no such clause. The final relevant communication was from the seller to the buyer. The seller returned a slip acknowledging the buyer's terms, but also included a letter indicating that their own terms should prevail. The trial judge held that the contract was made on the seller's terms.

Held: The acknowledgement slip was the crucial document. This indicated that the contract was made on the buyer's terms.

Lord Denning MR:

'This case is a "battle of forms". The suppliers of a machine, Butler Machine Tool Co. Ltd ("the sellers"), on 23rd May 1969 quoted a price for a machine tool of £75,535. Delivery was to be given in ten months. On the back of the quotation there were terms and conditions. One of them was a price variation clause. It provided for an increase in the price if there was an increase in the costs and so forth. The machine tool was not delivered until November 1970. By that time costs had increased so much that the sellers claimed an additional sum of £2,892 as due to them under the price variation clause.

The buyers, Ex-Cell-O Corpn, rejected the excess charge. They relied on their own terms and conditions. They said: "We did not accept the sellers' quotation as it was. We gave an order for the self-same machine at the self-same price, but on the back of our order we had our own terms and conditions. Our terms and conditions did not contain any price variation clause".

The judge held that the price variation clause in the sellers' form continued through the whole dealing and so the sellers were entitled to rely on it. He was clearly influenced by a passage in the 24th edition of Anson's *Law of Contract*, of which the editor is Professor Guest; and also by a passage in Treitel's *The Law of Contract*. The judge said that the sellers did all that was necessary and reasonable to bring the price variation clause to the notice of the buyers. He thought that the buyers would not "browse over the conditions" of the sellers, and then, by printed words in their (the buyers') document, trap the sellers into a fixed price contract.

> I am afraid that I cannot agree with the suggestion that the buyers "trapped" the sellers in any way. Neither party called any oral evidence before the judge. The case was decided on the documents alone. I propose therefore to go through them.

On 23rd May 1969 the sellers offered to deliver one "Butler" double column plano-miller for the total price of £75,535, "Delivery: 10 months (Subject to confirmation at time of ordering) Other terms and conditions are on the reverse of this quotation". On the back there were 16 conditions in small print starting with this general condition:

> All orders are accepted only upon and subject to the terms set out in our quotation and the following conditions. These terms and conditions shall prevail over any terms and conditions in the Buyer's order.

Clause 3 was the price variation clause. It said:

> . . . Prices are based on present day costs of manufacture and design and having regard to the delivery quoted and uncertainty as to the cost of labour,

materials etc., during the period of manufacture, we regret that we have no alternative but to make it a condition of acceptance of order that goods will be charged at prices ruling upon date of delivery.

The buyers, Ex-Cell-O, replied on 27th May 1969 giving an order in these words: "Please supply on terms and conditions as below and overleaf". Below there was a list of the goods ordered, but there were differences from the quotation of the sellers in these respects: (i) there was an additional item for the cost of installation, £3,100; (ii) there was a different delivery date; instead of 10 months, it was 10 to 11 months. Overleaf there were different terms as to the cost of carriage, in that it was to be paid to the delivery address of the buyers; whereas the sellers' terms were ex warehouse. There were different terms as to the right to cancel for late delivery. The buyers in their conditions reserved the right to cancel if delivery was not made by the agreed date, whereas the sellers in their conditions said that cancellation of order due to late delivery would not be accepted.

On the foot of the buyers' order there was a tear-off slip:

Acknowledgement: Please sign and return to Ex-Cell-O Corp. (England) Ltd. We accept your order on the Terms and Conditions stated thereon – and undertake to deliver by . . . Date . . . Signed . . .

In that slip the delivery date and signature were left blank ready to be filled in by the sellers.

On 5th June 1969 the sellers wrote this letter to the buyers:

We have pleasure in acknowledging receipt of your official order dated 27th May covering the supply of one "Butler" Double Column Plano-Miller . . . This is being entered in accordance with our revised quotation of 23rd May for delivery in 10/ 11 months, ie March/April, 1970. We return herewith, duly completed, your acknowledgement of order form.

They enclosed the acknowledgment form duly filled in with the delivery date, March/ April 1970, and signed by the Butler Machine Tool Co. Ltd.

No doubt a contract was then concluded. But on what terms? The sellers rely on their general conditions and on their last letter which said "in accordance with our revised quotation of 23rd May" (which had on the back the price variation clause). The buyers rely on the acknowledgment signed by the sellers which accepted the buyers' order "on the terms and conditions stated thereon" (which did not include a price variation clause).

If those documents are analysed in our traditional method, the result would seem to me to be this: the quotation of 23rd May 1969 was an offer by the sellers to the buyers containing the terms and conditions on the back. The order of 27th May 1969 pur- ported to be an acceptance of that offer in that it was for the same machine at the same price, but it contained such additions as to cost of installation, date of delivery and so forth, that it was in law a rejection of the offer and constituted a counter-offer. That is clear from *Hyde v Wrench* (1840) 3 Bear 334. As Megaw J said in *Trollope & Colls Ltd v Atomic Power Construction Ltd* [1962] 3 All ER 1035: ". . . the counter-offer kills the original offer". The letter of the sellers of 5th June 1969 was an acceptance of that counter-offer, as is shown by the acknowledgment which the sellers signed and returned to the buyers. The reference to the quotation of 23rd May 1969 referred only to the price and identity of the machine.

To go on with the facts of the case. The important thing is that the sellers did not keep the contractual date of delivery which was March/April 1970. The machine was ready about September 1970 but by that time the buyers' production schedule had to be rearranged as they could not accept delivery until November 1970. Meanwhile the sellers had invoked the price increase clause. They sought to charge the buyers an increase due to the rise in costs between 27th May 1969 (when the order was given) and 1st April 1970 (when the machine ought to have been delivered). It came to £2,892. The buyers rejected the claim. The judge held that the sellers were entitled to the sum of £2,892 under the price variation clause. He did not apply the traditional method of analysis by way of offer and counter-offer. He said that in the quotation of 23rd May 1969 "one finds the price variation clause appearing under a most emphatic heading stating that it is a term or condition that is to prevail". So he held that it did prevail.

I have much sympathy with the judge's approach to this case. In many of these cases our traditional analysis of offer, counter-offer, rejection, acceptance and so forth is out-of-date. This was observed by Lord Wilberforce in *New Zealand Shipping Co Ltd v AM Satterthwaite* [1974] 1 All ER 1015. The better way is to look at all the documents passing between the parties and glean from them, or from the conduct of the parties, whether they have reached agreement on all material points, even though there may be differences between the forms and conditions printed on the back of them. As Lord Cairns LC said in *Brogden v Metropolitan Railway* (1877) 2 App Cas 666:

> . . . there may be a *consensus* between the parties far short of a complete mode of expressing it, and that *consensus* may be discovered from letters or from other documents of an imperfect and incomplete description.

Applying this guide, it will be found that in most cases when there is a "battle of forms" there is a contract as soon as the last of the forms is sent and received without objection being taken to it. That is well observed in Benjamin on Sale. The difficulty is to decide which form, or which part of which form, is a term or condition of the contract. In some cases the battle is won by the man who fires the last shot. He is the man who puts forward the latest term and conditions: and, if they are not objected to by the other party, he may be taken to have agreed to them. Such was *British Road Services Ltd v Arthur V Crutchley & Co. Ltd* [1968] 1 All ER 811 per Lord Pearson; and the illustration given by Professor Guest in Anson's *Law of Contract* where he says that "the terms of the contract consist of the terms of the offer subject to the modifications contained in the acceptance". That may however go too far. In some cases, however, the battle is won by the man who gets the blow in first. If he offers to sell at a named price on the terms and conditions stated on the back and the buyer orders the goods purporting to accept the offer on an order form with his own different terms and conditions on the back, then, if the difference is so material that it would affect the price, the buyer ought not to be allowed to take advantage of the difference unless he draws it specifically to the attention of the seller. There are yet other cases where the battle depends on the shots fired on both sides. There is a concluded contract but the forms vary. The terms and conditions of both parties are to be construed together. If they can be reconciled so as to give a harmonious result, all well and good. If differences are irreconcilable, so that they are mutually contradictory, then the conflicting terms may have to be scrapped and replaced by a reasonable implication.

In the present case the judge thought that the sellers in their original quotation got their blow in first; especially by the provision that "These terms and conditions shall prevail over any terms and conditions in the Buyer's order". It was so emphatic that the price variation clause continued through all the subsequent dealings and that the buyer must be taken to have agreed to it. I can understand that point of view. But I think that the documents have to be considered as a whole. And, as a matter of construction, I think the acknowledgment of 5th June 1969 is the decisive document. It makes it clear that the contract was on the buyers' terms and not the sellers' terms: and the buyers' terms did not include a price variation clause.

I would therefore allow the appeal and enter judgment for the buyers.'

Lawton and Bridge LJJ concurred.

On rare occasions the courts have been prepared to recognise that contract can be made without it being possible to identify a clear offer and acceptance – but as Lord Diplock put it in *Gibson v Manchester City Council* (above, p 62):

My Lords, there may be certain types of contract, though I think they are exceptional, which do not fit easily into the normal analysis of a contract as being constituted by offer and acceptance; but a contract alleged to have been made by an exchange of correspondence between the parties in which the successive communications other than the first are in reply to one another is not one of these.

A similar, if perhaps slightly broader, view was expressed by Lord Wilberforce, in an often-quoted passage from *New Zealand Shipping Co v Satterthwaite, The Eurymedon* [1975] AC 154 (the facts of which can be found below, at p 308). Discussing the commercial relationship that existed in that case, and whether it had given rise to a contract, he commented (p 167):

It is only the precise analysis of this complex of relations into the classical offer and acceptance, with identifiable consideration, that seems to present difficulty, but this same difficulty exists in many situations of daily life, e.g., sales at auction; supermarket purchases; boarding an omnibus; purchasing a train ticket; tenders for the supply of goods; offers of rewards; acceptance by post; warranties of authority by agents; manufacturers' guarantees; gratuitous bailments; bankers' commercial credits. These are all examples which show that English law, having committed itself to a rather technical and schematic doctrine of contract, in application takes a practical approach, often at the cost of forcing the facts to fit uneasily into the marked slots of offer, acceptance and consideration.

An example of a judge being prepared to find a contract without a clear offer and acceptance is the judgment of Steyn J in *Trentham Ltd v Archital Luxfer* [1993] 1 Lloyd's Rep 25. He expressed the view that in relation to a fully executed contract it was possible for a contract to come into existence during performance, even if it cannot be precisely analysed in terms of offer and acceptance (pp 29–30). Very often, however, in this situation it will be possible for the court to find acceptance through conduct, as indeed the trial judge had in *Trentham's* case.

2.2.7.2 Acceptance by conduct

It is not necessary for acceptance to take the form of words – spoken or written – as long as it is communicated to the other party. This can be done by conduct – for example, by starting to perform the contract. This issue was explored in *Brogden v Metropolitan Railway Company* (1876–77) LR 2 App Cas 666.

Brogden v Metropolitan Railway Company (1876–77) LR 2 App Cas 666

Facts: B had supplied coal to M for a number of years. There were negotiations for a new contract. M sent B a draft agreement. B filled in the name of an arbitrator and completed some other details, and then returned the document to M. M's representative put the agreement in a desk drawer, and there were no further communications about it. M then ordered coal from B. In the course of a subsequent dispute, B claimed that there was no contract, because M had never communicated acceptance of the agreement which B had sent.

Held: The House of Lords confirmed the view of the courts below that there was a contract. The act of ordering coal indicated M's acceptance of the offer made by B.

Lord Cairns (Lord Chancellor):
'My Lords, there are no cases upon which difference of opinion may more readily be entertained, or which are always more embarrassing to dispose of, than cases where the Court has to decide whether or not, having regard to letters and documents which have not assumed the complete and formal shape of executed and solemn agreements, a contract has really been constituted between the parties. But, on the other hand, there is no principle of law better established than this, that even although

---

parties may intend to have their agreement expressed in the most solemn and complete form that conveyancers and solicitors are able to prepare, still there may be a *consensus* between the parties far short of a complete mode of expressing it, and that *consensus* may be discovered from letters or from other documents of an imperfect and incomplete description; I mean imperfect and incomplete as regards form. . . .

[The] case finds that at that meeting [on 19 December] the representative of the railway company handed over the form of contract or agreement. The date was in blank, the names of the Messrs. Brogden were not filled up, and, in the clause with regard to arbitration, the name of the arbitrator was also left blank; the price was fixed in the way which had been mentioned in the letter at 20s. a ton, and the continuance of the agreement was to be for a twelvemonth, to run on for another twelvemonth if a notice was not given to terminate by the 1st of November, 1872. This draft, or the agreement in this form, was handed over at this meeting; to the Messrs. Brogden or to their agent. On the 21st of December, losing therefore no time, and shewing that the parties at this time were clearly bent upon concluding the business, Mr. Hardman, the agent of Messrs. Brogden, returns the draft agreement with this letter:

> Herewith I beg to return your draft of proposed agreement, *re* new contract for coal, which Mr. Brogden has approved. I am obliged to leave town for *Bristol* to-night, and shall be up again on Monday week. If you have anything farther to communicate letters addressed to Tondu [the Appellants' collieries] will find me.

The last sentence is important. . . .

My Lords, it appears to me that it was with regard to the circumstance that there had been the insertion of this name among other matters, that the letter of the 21st of December contained the words to which I have already called your Lordships' attention, "If you have anything farther to communicate, letters addressed to 'Tondu' will find me." That appears to me to be just what you would have expected . . .

My Lords, that draft having been sent in this form to the railway directors, the statement in the case is that "Mr. Burnett was the proper custodian of contracts for the supply of coke and coal for the Plaintiffs. On receipt of the paper enclosed in Mr. Hardman's letter he put it into his drawer, and it remained there till the 7th of November, 1872, when it was produced to Mr. Alexander Brogden on the occasion hereinafter mentioned."

Now, my Lords, I will call your Lordships' attention to what was done subsequent to this date; but before I do so, there is at the very outset this remarkable circumstance, which your Lordships will bear in mind: these two parties having been in negotiation up to the 22nd of December, both of them clearly bent upon making a contract which was to provide for a supply of coals in the following year, both of them engaged upon it, and so seriously engaged upon it that they had reduced it into writing with very considerable minuteness of detail; according to the view of the Appellants, this agreement, which they were so bent on forming, is said suddenly and without any kind of explanation to have passed entirely out of view, an incomplete and unfinished transaction, as regarded which there never was any *consensus* between them, and no explanation is given in any shape or form of why it was, according to the view of the Appellants, that there never was any reference afterwards to the contract, nor any proceeding taken to have it brought to a definite point. My Lords, it would be, indeed, a very strange matter if, both parties having shewn such earnestness in the business to which they were addressing themselves, they were from the moment of the 22nd of December to be held to have parted without any impression whatever that anything had been done towards accomplishing the object of that act upon which they were bent.

But, my Lords, what took place afterwards was this: On the 22nd of December Mr. Burnett, getting this draft, putting it where the contracts of the company were placed for custody, writes in return to Messrs. Brogden & Sons. He makes no objection to anything which had been done with regard to that document; he is silent upon that subject, but he says, "We shall require 250 tons per week of locomotive coal, commencing not later than the 1st of January next"—the very date which was the date mentioned in the contract for the commencement of the supply—"Reply by wire that you will do this, that we may arrange with other collieries accordingly." My Lords, the contract had provided, with regard to the amount of the supply, that it should be "220 tons of coal, and any farther quantity of coal not exceeding 350 tons per week, at such times and in such quantity as the company shall by writing under their agent's hands from time to time require, such notice to be given to the contractors or agents of the contractors for the time being."

Now reference was made to this letter, and some argument was raised upon it to the effect that it was a letter asking Messrs. Brogden to reply by wire whether they would supply the 250 tons, and that it was therefore inconsistent with a right to order that supply. My Lords, it seems to me to be the most natural letter possible for persons who had a contract to have written. They order a supply within the terms of the contract greater than the minimum, which was 220 tons, but within their power as regards the maximum; and it seems to me that, inasmuch as they had to give notice with regard to the times and the mode of any supply over 220 tons, it was only what men in that position would have done, to ask those who had to make that supply whether they might depend and rely upon their affording it at the times and in the quantity which were thus specified.

My Lords, on the 22nd of December Messrs. Brogden & Sons telegraph to the railway directors, "We have arranged to supply you quantity you name, 250 tons weekly, from 1st January." And without going through the letters as to the change of supply, I may say that the quantity was afterwards changed to a quantity of 350 tons per week, which also was a quantity not beyond the maximum mentioned, but the actual maximum mentioned by the contract.

My Lords, those are the grounds which lead me to think that, there having been clearly a *consensus* between these parties, arrived at and expressed by the document signed by Mr. Brogden, subject only to approbation, on the part of the company, of the additional term which he had introduced with regard to an arbitrator, that approbation was clearly given when the company commenced a course of dealing which is referable in my mind only to the contract, and when that course of dealing was accepted and acted upon by Messrs. Brogden & Co. in the supply of coals. Therefore, my Lords, I am of opinion that the conclusion at which the Court of Common Pleas arrived was correct, as was also the conclusion at which the majority of the Court of Appeal arrived.'

2.2.7.3 Acceptance by silence

What is the position if the offeree makes no response to an offeror, who has said that if nothing more happens the assumption will be that a contract has come into existence? We have seen that verbal communication is not necessary – acceptance can be by conduct – but can silence be sufficient to indicate acceptance. The most frequently cited authority in this area is the old case of *Felthouse v Bindley*

Felthouse v Bindley (1862) 11 CB (NS) 869 (CP)

Facts: An uncle and nephew had been negotiating over the sale of a horse, which the nephew had put up for auction. The uncle offered to buy it at a particular price, and said that he would assume if he heard nothing further that it was his. The nephew instructed the auctioneer to remover the horse from the sale, but did not communicate further with his uncle. The auctioneer by mistake sold the horse at the auction. The uncle sued the auctioneer, claiming that the horse was his under his contract with his nephew.

Held: The uncle was unable to impose a contract on his nephew by indicating that silence would be taken as consent. Communication of an acceptance from the offeree to the offeror was necessary in order for a contract to come into existence.

Willes J:

'. . . The horse in question had belonged to the plaintiff's nephew, John Felthouse. In December, 1860, a conversation took place between the plaintiff and his nephew relative to the purchase of the horse by the former. The uncle seems to have thought that he had on that occasion bought the horse for £30, the nephew that he had sold it for 30 guineas: but there was clearly no complete bargain at that time. On the 1st of January, 1861, the nephew writes, – "I saw my father on Saturday. He told me that you considered you had bought the horse for £30. If so, you are labouring under a mistake, for 30 guineas was the price I put upon him, and you never heard me say less. When you said you would have him, I considered you were aware of the price". To this the uncle replies on the following day – "Your price, I admit, – was 30 guineas. I offered £30; never offered more: and you said the horse was mine. However, as there may be a mistake about him, I will split the difference. If I hear no more about him, I consider the horse mine at £30 15s." It is clear that there was no complete bargain on the 2nd of January; and it is also clear that the uncle had no right to impose upon the nephew a sale of his horse for £30 15s unless he chose to comply with the condition of writing to repudiate the offer. The nephew might, no doubt, have bound his uncle to the bargain by writing to him: the uncle might also have retracted his offer at any time before acceptance. It stood an open offer: and so things remained until the 25th of February, when the nephew was about to sell his farming stock by auction. The horse in question being catalogued with the rest of the stock, the auctioneer (the defendant) was told that it was already sold. It is clear, therefore, that the nephew in his own mind intended his uncle to have the horse at the price which he (the uncle) had named, – £30 15s.: but he had not communicated such his intention to his uncle, or done anything to bind himself. Nothing, therefore, had been done to vest the property in the horse in the plaintiff down to the 25th of February, when the horse was sold by the defendant . . . .'

Keating J:
'I am of the same opinion. Had the question arisen as between the uncle and the nephew, there would probably have been some difficulty. But, as between the uncle and the auctioneer, the only question we have to consider is whether the horse was the property of the plaintiff at the time of the sale on the 25th of February. It seems to me that nothing had been done at that time to pass the property out of the nephew and vest it in the plaintiff. A proposal had been made, but there had before that day been no acceptance binding the nephew.'

The case of *Felthouse v Bindley* has generally been taken to establish that a bilateral contract can never be accepted by silence. Indeed, in *The Leonidas D* [1985] 2 All ER 796; [1985] 1 WLR 925, Robert Goff J noted that 'We have all been brought up to believe it to be axiomatic that acceptance of an offer cannot be inferred from silence, save in the most exceptional circumstances' (p 805; 937). On the other hand, others have suggested that it does depend on the circumstances – in *Felthouse v Bindley* itself, Keating J notes that if the dispute had been between the uncle and nephew 'there would probably have been some difficulty'. The kinds of argument that might be raised in this context are well explored in the following extract from an article by Professor Miller:

Miller CJ, ' *Felthouse v Bindley* Re-visited' (1972), 35 MLR, p 489

An interesting and unresolved point which has given rise to a certain amount of academic discussion is that of the extent to which it is open to an offeror effectively to waive the need for any formal communication of acceptance. Here, it appears, an initial distinction must be drawn between unilateral and bilateral contracts. In the potentially unilateral contract the position is reasonably straightforward. The offeror will normally be impliedly taken to have waived the need for communication and it is clear that it is competent to him to do this. Performance by the offeree of the requested act will generally suffice and notification of an intention to perform is unnecessary. Authority for this general proposition is to be found in the well known case of *Carlill v Carbolic Smoke Ball Co* [1893] 1 QB 256. Here, it may be remembered, the plaintiff successfully claimed that she was entitled to the sum of £100 which had been advertised as being payable to anyone who caught influenza after using the defendant's smoke ball in the prescribed manner and for the prescribed period of time. The Court of Appeal emphatically discounted the need for any communication of acceptance by the offeree and, taking an analogous example of a reward for finding a lost dog, Bowen LJ said,

> The essence of the transaction is that the dog should be found, and it is not necessary under such circumstances, as it seems to me, that in order to make the contract binding there should be any notification of acceptance. It follows from the nature of the thing that the performance of the condition is sufficient acceptance without the notification of it, and a person who makes an offer in an advertisement of that kind makes an offer which must be read in the light of that common-sense reflection. He does, therefore, in his offer impliedly indicate that he does not require notification of the acceptance of the offer.

The position in the potentially bilateral contract is, however, more complicated. Of such cases one can safely say that it is not open to an offer to stipulate as against an unwilling offeree that the latter's silence will be regarded as equivalent to acceptance. He cannot force him to take a positive course of action under penalty of being contractually bound if he does not. Nor, by the same token, can he circumscribe the offeree's freedom of action by providing that a similar significance will be attributed to an ordinary everyday act of an offeree. As Corbin has graphically put it,

> If A offers his land to B for a price, saying that B may signify his acceptance by eating his breakfast or by hanging out his flag on Washington's birthday . . . he does not thereby make such action by B operative as an acceptance against B's will. If B shows that he had no intent to accept, and that he ate his breakfast merely because he was hungry, or hung out his flag because it was his patriotic custom, . . . no contract has been made even though A truly believed that B meant to accept.

Suppose, though, that the offeree is not unwilling and indeed has every intention of agreeing to the terms proposed by the offeror. The question then arises as to whether a contract may be concluded in such circumstances by either conduct which is indicative of this assent or indeed by mere silence. Some authorities certainly suggest that active conduct short of communication will suffice where the offeror has expressly or impliedly waived the need for a communication of acceptance. Thus if A sends unsolicited goods to B it is clear that his offer to supply may be accepted by B's using or consuming the goods without more. This, in effect, occurred in *Weatherby v Banham* (1832) 5 C & P 228 where the plaintiffs recovered the price of periodicals which they had sent unsolicited to the defendant who had received and presumably used them. Similarly if A offers to buy certain goods from B it seems clear that a contract may be concluded by B's dispatching the goods and that they will prima facie be at A's risk from the time of dispatch. An analogous situation was considered in *Taylor v Allon* [1965] 1 All ER 557 where a Divisional Court heard an appeal against a conviction for using a motorcycle on a road without insurance cover against third-party risks. Briefly, the accused's insurance policy had admittedly expired on the relevant day, but he had been issued with a temporary cover note which not having been requested, clearly amounted to no more than an offer to insure. Equally clearly on the facts of the case this offer had not been accepted by the appellant who had intended throughout to insure with another company. Hence no contract was in force and the conviction was upheld. The case is of interest in the present context, however, in that Lord Parker was prepared to envisage that the result might have been different if the appellant *had* taken the car out onto the road in reliance upon the offer. According to his Lordship,

> It may be, although I find it unnecessary to decide in this case, that there can be an acceptance of such an offer by conduct and without communication with the insurance company. It may well be, as it seems to me, that if a man took his motor car out on the road in reliance on this temporary cover note, albeit there had been no communication of that fact to the insurance company, there would be an acceptance.

This, with respect, would appear to be an entirely sensible conclusion which has the added advantage of according with the assumptions of the ordinary driver. It would also lend support to the view that it is open to the offeror to impliedly waive the need for a communication of acceptance in the potentially bilateral contract.

The leading English case of *Felthouse v Bindley* (1862) 11 CB (NS) 869 might, however, be thought to point conclusively in the opposite direction. In this case the plaintiff and his nephew had been negotiating about the sale of a horse and had failed to reach agreement over the price. The plaintiff thereupon wrote to the nephew saying, 'If I hear no more about him, I consider the horse is mine at £30 15s'. The nephew did not reply, but he resolved to accept the offer and informed the defendant auctioneer, who was selling off his farming stock, that the horse in question was not to be disposed of as it had already been sold. The auctioneer mistakenly sold the horse and he was sued by the plaintiff in conversion. The Common Pleas held for the auctioneer on the ground that the plaintiff had no title to sue since at the date of the auction the nephew had not effectively accepted the offer. Given that he had admittedly told the auctioneer that the horse was reserved for his uncle and that the latter had equally assumed that this was so, it is not clear why anything further should have been regarded as essential to the formation of a contract. On balance it is submitted that the approach of the Common Pleas was wrong in principle and that the actual result of the case can only be supported because there had been no delivery, part payment or memorandum in writing to satisfy the then requirements of the Statute of Frauds. This was the alternative reason given by the Common Pleas and it was the reason which appears to have been emphasised by the Exchequer Chamber when affirming the decision on appeal.

If one is prepared to concede that positive conduct falling short of communication is sufficient to conclude a bilateral contract, this still leaves open the question of whether silence coupled with mental assent would be equally sufficient where the offeror has purported to waive the need for notification. The additional difficulty here is, of course, that the lack of any outward expression of assent would effectively enable the offeree to deny or assert the fact of acceptance to suit his own convenience. Lord Denning clearly appreciated the point in *Robophone Facilities v Blank* [1966] 3 All ER 128 when he discussed the effect of a clause providing that, 'This agreement shall become binding on the [plaintiffs] only upon acceptance thereof by signature ... on their behalf'. His Lordship was clear that notwithstanding this terminology,

> Signing without notification is not enough. It would be deplorable if it were. The plaintiffs would be able to keep the form in their office unsigned, and then play fast and loose as they pleased. The defendant would not know whether or not there was a contract binding them to supply or him to take. Just as mental acceptance is not enough, nor is internal acceptance within the plaintiff's office.

This statement accords with the views expressed in the House of Lords in the old case of *Brogden v Metropolitan Railway* (1876) 2 App Cas 666, and it may well be productive of justice where, as in the *Robophone* case itself, the offer is submitted on a standard form agreement drawn up by the offeree. It is not, however, difficult to envisage other situations where insistence on the need for such notification might well work substantial injustice. Thus suppose that A writes to B offering to buy his car for £100 and adding, 'There is no need to reply. If I do not hear from you within the week, I shall assume you accept.' If B wishes to take up the offer and remains silent it would hardly be satisfactory to permit A to deny the existence of a contract on the ground that acceptance had not been notified when he himself had expressly stated that it was unnecessary. Again it would have been equally unsatisfactory if the uncle in *Felthouse v Bindley* could have pointed to the lack of notification if it had been he who was being sued by the nephew for damages for non-acceptance. Presumably if A and the uncle are to be regarded as having entered a contract to purchase then B and the nephew must be regarded as having entered a contract to sell. Notwithstanding the admitted difficulties involved, it is tentatively submitted that in such cases there may be an effective waiver of the need for communication of acceptance, and, moreover, a contract may be concluded without the need for any external manifestation of assent. A similar view is expressed in section 72(1)(b) of the American Restatement on Contracts which reads,

> Where an offeree fails to reply to an offer, his silence and inaction operate as an acceptance ... where the offeror has stated or given the offeree reason to understand that assent may be made by silence and the offeree intends to accept.

2.2.7.4 Acceptance by post

The standard position, as we have seen, is that acceptance must be communicated to be effective. This does not answer all questions, however, once parties start to contract at a distance, through means that may involve delay between one party sending an acceptance and the other being aware of it. This issue first arose in connection with contracts made via the postal service. Application of the standard rule would mean that a posted acceptance had no effect until the person to whom it was addressed read it. But was this the best way of dealing with the situation? Is it right that the acceptor should have to wait for confirmation that his or her letter has been read to know whether or not a contract has been made? The first reported case in which the question was considered dates from before the introduction of the 'penny post'.

Adams v Lindsell (1818) 1 B & Ald 681; 106 ER 250

Facts: The owners of a quantity of wool sent a letter offering it to the plaintiffs. The letter was misdirected and arrived later than would have been expected. The plaintiffs immediately replied by letter accepting the offer. The sellers, however, had sold the wool elsewhere before the letter of acceptance was delivered (though after it had been posted).

Held: The acceptance was effective on posting, and there was a binding contract for the sale of the wool to the plaintiffs at that point.

Action for non-delivery of wool according to agreement. At the trial at the last Lent Assizes for the county of Worcester, before Burrough J it appeared that the defendants, who were dealers in wool, at St. Ives, in the county of Huntingdon, had, on Tuesday the 2nd of September 1817, written the following letter to the plaintiffs, who were woollen manufacturers residing in Bromsgrove, Worcestershire. 'We now offer you eight hundred tods of wether fleeces, of a good fair quality of our country wool, at 35s.6d. per tod, to be delivered at Leicester, and to be paid for by two months' bill in two months, and to be weighed up by your agent within fourteen days, receiving your answer in course of post.'

> This letter was misdirected by the defendants, to Bromsgrove, Leicestershire, in consequence of which it was not received by the plaintiffs in Worcestershire till 7p.m. on Friday, September 5th. On that evening the plaintiffs wrote an answer, agreeing to accept the wool on the terms proposed. The course of the post between St. Ives and Bromsgrove is through London, and consequently this answer was not received by the defendants till Tuesday, September 9th. On the Monday September 8th, the defendants not having, as they expected, received an answer on Sunday September 7th (which in case their letter had not been misdirected, would have been in the usual course of the post), sold the wool in

question to another person. Under these circumstances, the learned judge held, that the delay having been occasioned by the neglect of the defendants, the jury must take it, that the answer did come back in due course of post; and that then the defendants were liable for the loss that had been sustained: and the plaintiffs accordingly recovered a verdict.

Jervis having in Easter term obtained a rule nisi for a new trial, on the ground that there was no binding contract between the parties, Dauncey, Puller, and Richardson, shewed cause. They contended, that at the moment of the acceptance of the offer of the defendants by the plaintiffs, the former became bound. And that was on the Friday evening, when there had been no change of circumstances. They were then stopped by the Court, who called upon Jervis and Campbell in support of the rule. They relied on *Payne v Cave* (1789) 3 Term Rep 148, and more particularly on *Cooke v Oxley* (1790) 3 Term Rep 653. In that case, Oxley who had proposed to sell goods to Cooke, and given him a certain time at his request, to determine whether he would buy them or not, was held not liable to the performance of the contract, even though Cooke, within the specified time, had determined to buy them, and given Oxley notice to that effect. So here the defendants who have proposed by letter to sell this wool, are not to be held liable, even though it be now admitted that the answer did come back in due course of post. Till the plaintiffs' answer was actually received, there could be no binding contract between the parties; and before then, the defendants had retracted their offer, by selling the wool to other persons.

But the court said, that if that were so, no contract could ever be completed by the post. For if the defendants were not bound by their offer when accepted by the plaintiffs till the answer was received, then the plaintiffs ought not to be bound till after they had received the notification that the defendants had received their answer and assented to it. And so it might go on ad infinitum. The defendants must be considered in law as making, during every instant of the time their letter was travelling, the same identical offer to the plaintiffs; and then the contract is completed by the acceptance of it by the latter. Then as to the delay in notifying the acceptance, that arises entirely from the mistake of the defendants, and it therefore must be taken as against them, that the plaintiffs' answer was received in course of post.

Was the court right to suggest that a contract could never be concluded by the post, if an acceptance was not effective until read by the offeror? Surely, once the accepting company had received confirmation of its letter's arrival, then both parties could proceed on the basis that there was a binding contract. The argument has even less force in modern times, when it is easy to check on the arrival of a letter by means of a phone call, text message, or email. Nevertheless, the view taken in *Adams v Lindsell*, that the most business efficient solution was to treat an acceptance as effective on posting was adopted by later cases in the nineteenth century (eg *Dunlop v Higgins* (1848) 1 HLC 384, *Henthorn v Fraser* [1892] 2 Ch 27), and still represents the position of English law on the issue at the start of the twenty-first century.

Gardner has suggested that there may have been reasons other than simple business efficiency, which contributed to the court's enthusiasm for the postal rule.

Gardner, S "Trashing with *Trollope*: a deconstruction of the postal rules" (1992) OJLS 170, pp 178–184

The 1840s Decisions and Postal Reform

1840 was the year in which the uniform penny post was introduced, and the circumstances surrounding this event may have much significance for appreciating the decisions of that decade.

The uniform penny post had been proposed in 1837, in a pamphlet entitled *Post Office Reform: Its Importance and Practicability*, published by Rowland Hill. The idea was that there should be a uniform rate of letter postage of 1d across the whole country. Hill's argument was taken up by Robert Wallace MP, who since 1833 had himself been crusading for the reform of the nation's postal arrangements. In 1835 his efforts had procured the appointment of a Commission of Inquiry, which over the next three years produced ten reports, recommending various improvements, many of which were put into effect during the late 1830s. Wallace now obtained the appointment of a Select Committee of the House of Commons to consider Hill's arguments. In fact, the Committee's report, in 1838, found some of Hill's calculations about revenue rather naïve, and as a result did not altogether support his scheme. Nevertheless, in 1839–40 it was enacted and brought into effect.

It is important to understand that the introduction of the penny post was not a random event. It was—and was contemporarily regarded and supported as—an element in the general programme of liberal reform of the age. Robert Wallace was the new MP for Greenock, a town newly enfranchised under the Reform Act, and Wallace was a free-trader, concerned for the economic development of his constituency. Given its remote location, he felt, an efficient system of postage was essential to providing its traders with what is nowadays called 'a level playing-field'; or perhaps, more positively, to their being able to contribute fully to the prosperity of the nation. Hill too was a liberal, though more of the ideological kind: his designs for the postal service seem to have sprung from his concern for the education and general civilization of the people; he regarded the post as a means of disseminating knowledge, and free trade principles as a means of improving its effectiveness. And it was the huge public support for Hill's scheme, especially from amongst the then Whig government's liberal supporters, which in 1838–9 persuaded the government—somewhat against, as we have seen, the Select Committee's advice—that it should be enacted.

This popular support for Hill's scheme may be an important part of the explanation for the rule which the courts were to adopt by their decisions in the 1840s. The general perception seems to have been that the scheme provided something of a panacea, by which the postal service would become in every way thoroughly wonderful.

Examination shows that Hill's ideas—and especially his handling of Post Office affairs when he was appointed to administer it—left much to be desired, but that is not to detract from the reality of the contemporary enthusiasm for them. And it is quite clear that very substantial improvements in postal efficiency were indeed occurring at this time, partly from the recommendations of the 1835 Commission, but above all from the fact that from 1830 the mail began to be carried on the new railways, which by 1846 had entirely superseded the slower and less reliable coach system on routes to and from London.

This contemporary perception may have played a substantial part in the decisions in which the courts established the acceptance rule in the 1840s. In these terms, the basis of the rule might have been not a preference for posting over delivery as the dispositive act. It might have been an idea that delivery was self-evidently important, but that in the newly prevailing conditions posting and delivery were little different: that once posted, a letter was as good as delivered. But there is a certain weakness about this. Despite the great improvements in efficiency to which reference has been made, equating posting with delivery on purely empirical grounds would have been a little foolish: indeed, the reason why these cases came to court at all was because the equation had failed.

However, some of Hill's other innovations added a further dimension to this constructive identification of posting with delivery. One was a dramatic shift towards prepayment of postage. In March 1839, only 14 per cent of letters sent by the London General Post were prepaid, leaving 86 per cent for which payment had to be collected from the addressee. By February 1840 these figures had been precisely reversed. Prepayment was endorsed by none other than Queen Victoria herself, abandoning the privilege of free use of the mail. A year later still, the unpaid element had fallen further to 8 per cent. A second was the further facilitation of prepayment by the introduction in 1840 of the self-adhesive postage stamp: another measure which entranced the public. Of the February 1841 prepaid total of 92 per cent, 45 per cent comprised letters for which the payment was by this means. A third important innovation was the cutting of letter-boxes in front doors of houses, so that letters no longer needed to be handed to their addressee; this too captured the public imagination.

Taken together, these measures may have great significance. Until 1840, the delivery of a letter typically required that the addressee should manually receive it and pay for it. This was not, of course, a significant practical hurdle, but it sat in symbolic contrast with the new position, whereby the sender had only to affix his stamp and post the letter, and it would go through to its destination *without further subvention from outside the system*. So these three innovations of 1840 may be seen as predicating a radically new perception of the nature of the post: the notional equation of the posting of a letter with its delivery. They may thus have been a very powerful influence towards the courts affirming the acceptance rule in the way that they did in that decade. (The empirical efficiency of the system still matters to some extent, in that the argument would not work unless the system was perceived as at least adequately efficient; but we have seen that in the 1840s this was the case.)

This identification of posting with delivery is to be seen in an episode from Anthony Trollope's novel of 1873, *The Eustace Diamonds*. In a conversation, Frank Greystock has told Lucy Morris of his love for her, but has not proposed marriage to her. After some agonizing, he now decides to do so. He puts his proposal into a letter, which, after further agonizing, he decides to post. 'He walked out of the Temple with it in his hand, and dropped it into a pillar letter-box just outside the gate. As the envelope slipped through his fingers, he felt that he had now bound himself to his fate'. The scene then moves to a conversation between Lucy and Lady Fawn, her employer and mentor. Lucy tells Lady Fawn of her inconclusive conversation with Frank. Lady Fawn takes it to mean that Frank is trifling with Lucy's affections, and advises Lucy to think of him no more. But Lucy shares Frank's feelings, and is discomfited by this advice. The narrator comments: 'If Lucy could only have known of the letter, which was already her own property though lying in the pillar letter-box in Fleet Street, and which had not already been sent down and delivered simply because it was Sunday morning! ... It was so hard on her that she should be so interrogated while that letter was lying in the iron box!'

This material is explicitly along the lines that a letter takes effect on posting, and as such may illuminate the legal rule. To appreciate this, however, we need to explore it in its turn.

Trollope was an employee of the Post Office, and took considerable pride both in his own work there and in the Post Office's service to the public. In *The Eustace Diamonds* (explaining that Lucy's letter was indeed delivered on the Monday morning) he refers to 'that accuracy in the performance of its duties for which it is conspicuous among all offices'. He took pride perhaps above all in having personally secured the introduction of pillar-boxes to this country, in 1852.

Trollope saw pillar-boxes as partnering postage stamps in permitting more convenient use of the postal service: given these two facilities, one no longer needed to go to a post office to mail a letter, either to pay for its postage or, now, to hand it in. (At the same time, he anticipated the fear that letters posted in such boxes might be at risk, and was concerned to rebut it.) These ideas translate very naturally into the notion that, once Frank has put his letter to Lucy into the pillar-box, it is as good as delivered. Even the detail that Frank's letter was held up because it was Sunday is to the same effect. In 1850 the Government had extended Sunday observance to the Post Office, against the latter's wishes. Trollope's presentation of the resulting delay to the letter—and the consequent travail to Lucy's feelings—as the product of an artificial, almost gratuitous inefficiency further emphasizes the underlying identification of posting with delivery. We have already seen how the new postal arrangements captured the public's imagination, so we can surely take it that these ideas would not have been lost on Trollope's readers. If so, the emergent reading of this material in *The Eustace Diamonds* seems to support the view that the 1840s decisions may reflect a common social perception, animated by the contrast with previous arrangements, of a sender having only to post a letter for it automatically to go through to its destination.

Another possible reading of the material in *The Eustace Diamonds* is that it was actually based on the legal rule. Indeed, it comes complete with legal imagery: 'bound', 'property'. Certainly, Trollope was not a legal innocent. In *The Eustace Diamonds* itself he explicitly handles substantive law, having his character Thomas Dove, of the Chancery bar, produce a learned opinion on the subject of heirlooms. This was written for Trollope by a barrister, Charles Merewether, so in itself it by no means indicates that he is likely to have known of the postal rules in contract, but it is not an isolated passage: his novels are full of legal material. Moreover, it was during the 1840s, the period of the seminal decisions on the postal acceptance rule, that (as a postal surveyor in Ireland) his hitherto lackadaisical attitude to his Post Office work changed to one of interest and enthusiasm. It seems plausible that he might well have assimilated the contemporary judicial pronouncements on the subject. The fact that this period also saw the start of his writing may mean that he also began to register their possible symbolic potentialities. So when he was writing *The Eustace Diamonds* in 1870 he may have been drawing on the postal acceptance rule as it had been articulated in the decisions of the 1840s, and conceivably in the obiter dictum in *Hebb's Case* of 1867 (the other cases of this group begin in 1871). However, even if he was drawing on the legal rule here, it seems improbable that Trollope, the great realist, would have used it in this way—not merely as a mode of expression, but as a component of the story itself—unless he judged that it would at least strike a chord with his readers, rather than trying gratuitously to ram a legal curiosity down their throats. Which again returns us to the idea that the judges' rule that a letter takes effect on mailing correlated with a general public consciousness about the post.

The thesis, then, is that the decisions of the 1840s were influenced not so much by internal considerations about offer and acceptance in contract as by a way of regarding the phenomenon of posting as such. It may thus be significant that the first decision of this group—*Stocken v Collin*, which formed the basis of the House of Lords' declaration of the acceptance rule in *Dunlop v Higgins*—was not about the formation of a contract at all, but about notice of the dishonour of a bill of exchange.

2.2.7.5 Limitations on the postal rule

In *Henthorn v Fraser* [1892] 2 Ch 27 it was held that the postal rule would apply wherever it was reasonable to use the post for the acceptance. In that case the offer had been made face to face, but the acceptance was by letter. Lord Herschell stated the position in this way (at p 33):

> Where the circumstances are such that it must have been within the contemplation of the parties that, according to the ordinary usages of mankind, the post might be used as a means of communicating the acceptance of an offer, the acceptance is complete as soon as it is posted.

This envisages a broad scope for the use of the postal rule, and in *Bruner v Moore* [1904] 1 Ch 305 it was extended to apply to telegrams. Moreover, the rule was taken to its logical conclusion in *Household Fire and Carriage Accident Insurance v Grant* (1879) 4 Ex D 216, where it was held that it would apply even if the letter of acceptance was lost in the post and never received by the offeror. Subsequent case law, however, has tended to limit the application of the rule, rather than extend it. In particular, it seems that in relation to the more modern forms of business communication developed in the twentieth century – telex, fax, email, etc. – the postal rule should not apply, and that communication should be required. The starting point is the case of *Entores v Miles Far East Corporation*, where telex was held to be analogous to contracting face to face or over the telephone.

Entores v Miles Far East Corporation [1955] 2 QB 327 (CA)

Facts: A contract was alleged to have been made by exchange of telex between firms operating in England and the Netherlands. The question was whether the contract was made in England or the Netherlands, as this would affect which law governed the transaction.

Held: Where a contract was made by telex, it was formed at the location at which the acceptance was received, not the location from which it was sent.

Denning LJ:

'. . . The plaintiffs are an English company. The defendants are an American corporation with agents all over the world, including a Dutch company in Amsterdam. The plaintiffs say that the contract was made by Telex between the Dutch company in Amsterdam and the English company in London. Communications by Telex are comparatively new. Each company has a teleprinter machine in its office; and each has a Telex number like a telephone number. When one company wishes to send a message to the other, it gets the Post Office to connect up the machines. Then a clerk at one end taps the message on to his machine just as if it were a typewriter, and it is instantaneously passed to the machine at the other end, which automatically types the message onto paper at that end.

The relevant Telex messages in this case were as follows: September 8, 1954: Dutch company: "Offer for account our associates Miles Far East Corporation Tokyo up to 400 tons Japanese cathodes sterling 240 longton c.i.f. shipment Mitsui Line September 28 or October 10 payment by letter of credit. Your reply Telex Amsterdam 12174 or phone 81490 before 4 p.m. invited." English company: "Accept 100 longtons cathodes Japanese shipment latest October 10 sterling £239 10s. longton c.i.f. London/Rotterdam payment letter of credit stop please confirm latest tomorrow." Dutch company: "We received O.K. Thank you." September 9, 1954: English company: "Regarding our telephone conversation a few minutes ago we note that there is a query on the acceptance of our bid for 100 tons payment in sterling and you are ascertaining that your

---

Tokyo office will confirm the price to be longton we therefore await to hear from you further." September 10, 1954: English company: "Is the price for the sterling cathodes understood to be for longton by Japan as you were going to find this out yesterday?" Dutch company: "Yes, price £239 10s. for longton."

At that step there was a completed contract by which the defendants agreed to supply 100 tons of cathodes at a price of £239 10s. a ton. The offer was sent by Telex from England offering to pay £239 10s. a ton for 100 tons, and accepted by Telex from Holland. The question for our determination is where was the contract made?

When a contract is made by post it is clear law throughout the common law countries that the acceptance is complete as soon as the letter is put into the post box, and that is the place where the contract is made. But there is no clear rule about contracts made by telephone or by Telex. Communications by these means are virtually instantaneous and stand on a different footing.

The problem can only be solved by going in stages. Let me first consider a case where two people make a contract by word of mouth in the presence of one another. Suppose, for instance, that I shout an offer to a man across a river or a courtyard but I do not hear his reply because it is drowned by an aircraft flying overhead. There is no contract at that moment. If he wishes to make a contract, he must wait till the aircraft is gone and then shout back his acceptance so that I can hear what he says. Not until I have his answer am I bound. I do not agree with the observations of Hill J in *Newcomb v De Roos* (1859) 2 E & E 271.

Now take a case where two people make a contract by telephone. Suppose, for instance, that I make an offer to a man by telephone and, in the middle of his reply, the line goes "dead" so that I do not hear his words of acceptance. There is no contract at that moment. The other man may not know the precise moment when the line failed. But he will know that the telephone conversation was abruptly broken off: because people usually say something to signify the end of the conversation. If he wishes to make a contract, he must therefore get through again so as to make sure that I heard. Suppose next, that the line does not go dead, but it is nevertheless so indistinct that I do not catch what he says and I ask him to repeat it. He then repeats it and I hear his acceptance. The contract is made, not on the first time when I do not hear, but only the second time when I do hear. If he does not repeat it, there is no contract. The contract is only complete when I have his answer accepting the offer.

Lastly, take the Telex. Suppose a clerk in a London office taps out on the teleprinter an offer which is immediately recorded on a teleprinter in a Manchester office, and a clerk at that end taps out an acceptance. If the line goes dead in the middle of the sentence of acceptance, the teleprinter motor will stop. There is then obviously no contract. The clerk at Manchester must get through again and send his complete sentence. But it may happen that the line does not go dead, yet the message does not get through to London. Thus the clerk at Manchester may tap out his message of acceptance and it will not be recorded in London because the ink at the London end fails, or something of that kind. In that case, the Manchester clerk will not know of the failure but the London clerk will know of it and will immediately send back a message "not receiving". Then, when the fault is rectified, the Manchester clerk will repeat his message. Only then is there a contract. If he does not repeat it, there is no contract. It is not until his message is received that the contract is complete.

In all the instances I have taken so far, the man who sends the message of acceptance knows that it has not been received or he has reason to know it. So he must repeat it. But, suppose that he does not know that his message did not get home. He thinks it has. This may happen if the listener on the telephone does not catch the words of acceptance, but nevertheless does not trouble to ask for them to be repeated: or the ink on the teleprinter fails at the receiving end, but the clerk does not ask for the message to be repeated: so that the man who sends an acceptance reasonably believes that his message has been received. The offeror in such circumstances is clearly bound, because he will be estopped from saying that he did not receive the message of acceptance. It is his own fault that he did not get it. But if there should be a case where the offeror without any fault on his part does not receive the message of acceptance – yet the sender of it reasonably believes it has got home when it has not – then I think there is no contract.

My conclusion is, that the rule about instantaneous communications between the parties is different from the rule about the post. The contract is only complete when the acceptance is received by the offeror; and the contract is made at the place where the acceptance is received . . .'

(Birkett and Parker LJJ concurred)

It is important to note that this case was primarily concerned with *where* the contract was made, not *when*. As regards timing, it is clear that the postal rule cannot apply, because this would imply that the contract was made at the point it was sent, which is contrary to the decision in *Entores*. Indeed, Lord Denning says (above) the contract is only complete when the acceptance is 'received' by the offeror. But when does this occur with a communication sent by telex, fax or email? Is it when the message is delivered to the recipient's telex or fax machine, or email inbox? Or is it when the message is actually read? And what of a message that is sent out of office hours? Some consideration of these issues in relation to telex occurred in *The Brimnes* [1975] QB 929 and *Brinkibon Ltd v Stahag Stahl* [1983] 2 AC 34. In *The Brimnes* the Court of Appeal held that a telex (in this case a withdrawal notice, rather than an acceptance) received on a telex machine during 'normal office hours' should be regarded as having been effective at that point, whether or not it was actually read. In *Brinkibon v Stahag Stahl*, the House of Lords, while approving *Entores v Miles Far East Corporation*, took a more flexible view.

Brinkibon Ltd v Stahag Stahl GMBH [1982] 1 All ER 293 (HL)

Facts: A contract was alleged to have been made by exchange of telexes between London and Vienna, in the form of a counter-offer from Vienna to London (3rd May) and an acceptance from London to Vienna (4th May). The Court of Appeal held that the contract was made in Vienna.

Held: Applying the approach taken in *Entores v Miles Far East Corporation*, the contract was made when and where the acceptance was received, in Vienna, but the House of Lords noted the difficulty of applying a general rule to all situations involving telex communications.

Lord Wilberforce:

'My Lords, the appellants desire to sue in this country the respondents, an Austrian company, for breach of an alleged contract for the supply of steel. In order to do so, they must obtain leave to serve notice of their writ upon the respondents under one or other of the provisions of RSC, Ord. 11, r. 1(1). Those relied upon are paragraphs (f) and (g). To satisfy (f), the appellants must show that the contract was "made within the jurisdiction" . . .

The question whether a contract was made within the jurisdiction will often admit of a simple answer: if both parties are in England at the time of making it, or if it is contained in a single document signed by both parties in England, there is no difficulty. But in the case of contracts involving negotiations, where one party is abroad, the answer may be difficult to find. Sophisticated analysis may be required to decide when the last counter-offer was made into a contract by acceptance, or at what point a clear consensus was reached and by virtue of what words spoken or of what conduct. In the case of successive telephone conversations it may indeed be most artificial to ask where the contract was made: if one asked the parties, they might say they did not know – or care. The place of making a contract is usually irrelevant as regards validity, or interpretation, or enforcement. Unfortunately it remains in Order 11 as a test for purposes of jurisdiction, and courts have to do their best with it.

In the present case it seems that if there was a contract (a question which can only be decided at the trial), it was preceded by and possibly formed by a number of telephone conversations and telexes between London and Vienna, and there are a number of possible combinations upon which reliance can be placed. At this stage we must take the alternatives which provide evidence of a contract in order to see if the test is satisfied. There are two: (i) A telex dated May 3, 1979, from the respondents in Vienna, said to amount to a counter-offer, followed by a telex from the appellants in London to the respondents in Vienna dated May 4, 1979, said to amount to an acceptance. (ii) The above telex dated May 3, 1979, from the respondents followed by action, by way of opening a letter of credit, said to have amounted to an acceptance by conduct.

The first of these alternatives neatly raises the question whether an acceptance by telex sent from London but received in Vienna causes a contract to be made in

London, or in Vienna. If the acceptance had been sent by post, or by telegram, then, on existing authorities, it would have been complete when put into the hands of the post office – in London. If on the other hand it had been telephoned, it would have been complete when heard by the offeror – in Vienna. So in which category is a telex communication to be placed? Existing authority of the Court of Appeal decides in favour of the latter category, i.e. a telex is to be assimilated to other methods of instantaneous communication: see *Entores Ltd v Miles Far East Corporation* [1955] 2 QB 327. The appellants ask that this case, which has stood for 30 years, should now be reviewed.

Now such review as is necessary must be made against the background of the law as to the making of contracts. The general rule, it is hardly necessary to state, is that a contract is formed *when* acceptance of an offer is communicated by the offeree to the offeror. And if it is necessary to determine *where* a contract is formed (as to which I have already commented) it appears logical that this should be at the place where acceptance is communicated to the offeror. In the common case of contracts, whether oral or in writing inter praesentes, there is no difficulty; and again logic demands that even where there is not mutual presence at the same place and at the same time, if communication is instantaneous, for example by telephone or radio communication, the same result should follow.

Then there is the case – very common – of communication at a distance, to meet which the so called "postal rule" has developed. I need not trace its history: it has firmly been in the law at least since *Adams v Lindsell* (1818) 1 B & Ald 681 . . .

In this situation, with a general rule covering instantaneous communication inter praesentes, or at a distance, with an exception applying to non-instantaneous communications at a distance, how should communications by telex be categorised? In *Entores Ltd v Miles Far East Corporation* [1955] 2 QB 327 the Court of Appeal classified them with instantaneous communications. Their ruling, which has passed into the textbooks, including *Williston on Contracts*, 3rd edn, 1957, appears not to have caused either adverse comment, or any difficulty to business men. I would accept it as a general rule. Where the condition of simultaneity is met, and where it appears to be within the mutual intention of the parties that contractual exchanges should take place in this way, I think it a sound rule, but not necessarily a universal rule.

Since 1955 the use of telex communication has been greatly expanded, and there are many variants on it. The senders and recipients may not be the principals to the contemplated contract. They may be servants or agents with limited authority. The message may not reach, or be intended to reach, the designated recipient immediately: messages may be sent out of office hours, or at night, with the intention, or upon the assumption, that they will be read at a later time. There may be some error or default at the recipient's end which prevents receipt at the time contemplated and believed in by the sender. The message may have been sent and/or received through machines operated by third persons. And many other variations may occur. No universal rule can cover all such cases: they must be resolved by reference to the intentions of the parties, by sound business practice and in some cases by a judgment where the risks should lie: see *Household Fire and Carriage Accident Insurance Co. Ltd v Grant* (1879) 4 Ex D 216, 227 *per* Baggallay LJ and *Henthorn v Fraser* [1892] 2 Ch 27 *per* Lord Herschell.

The present case is, as *Entores Ltd v Miles Far East Corporation* [1955] 2 QB 327 itself, the simple case of instantaneous communication between principals, and, in accordance with the general rule, involves that the contract (if any) was made when and where the acceptance was received. This was on May 4, 1979, in Vienna . . .'

[Lord Wilberforce went on to reject the alternative analysis put forward (above, p 118) and affirmed the decision of the Court of Appeal.]

2.2.7.6 Fax, email and websites

It is generally assumed that the approach taken in the telex cases would also be applied to fax and email – but there are as yet no authorities confirming this. As far as contracts made by interaction with a website, however, the position has been affected by a European Directive on Electronic Commerce (2000/31/EC). This has been given effect in the UK by the Electronic Commerce (EC Directive) Regulations 2002. The relevant paragraphs are to be found in Regulations 11, 12 and 15.

Placing the order

11.—(1) Unless parties who are not consumers have agreed otherwise, where the recipient of the service places his order through technological means, a service provider shall–

   (a) acknowledge receipt of the order to the recipient of the service without undue delay and by electronic means; and

   (b) make available to the recipient of the service appropriate, effective and accessible technical means allowing him to identify and correct input errors prior to the placing of the order.

(2) For the purposes of paragraph (1)(a) above—

   (a) the order and the acknowledgement of receipt will be deemed to be received when the parties to whom they are addressed are able to access them; and

   (b) the acknowledgement of receipt may take the form of the provision of the service paid for where that service is an information society service.

(3) The requirements of paragraph (1) above shall not apply to contracts concluded exclusively by exchange of electronic mail or by equivalent individual communications.

Meaning of the term 'order'

12. Except in relation to regulation 9(1)(c) and regulation 11(1)(b) where 'order' shall be the contractual offer, 'order' may be but need not be the contractual offer for the purposes of regulations 9 and 11.

. . .

Right to rescind contract

15. Where a person—

    (a) has entered into a contract to which these Regulations apply, and

    (b) the service provider has not made available means of allowing him to identify and correct input errors in compliance with regulation 11(1)(b), he shall be entitled to rescind the contract unless any court having jurisdiction in relation to the contract in question orders otherwise on the application of the service provider.

The fact that Reg 12 defines 'order' in 11(1)(b) as meaning 'the contractual offer' seems to mean that in this type of transaction it is the customer who makes the offer, and the website operator which accepts it. The power, therefore, lies with the website operator to decide with whom it wishes to contract, and on what terms.

2.2.8 TERMINATION OF OFFERS

How does an offer come to an end, so that it can no longer be accepted? We have seen earlier that a rejection by the offeror, or the making of a counter-offer, will have this effect (above, p 93). If the offeror has put a time limit on acceptance, the expiry of this will end the offer; if no time limit is stated, it will lapse after 'a reasonable time', as in *Ramsgate Victoria Hotel Co v Montefiore* (1866) LR 1 Ex 109 (five months too long for acceptance of an offer to sell shares). The offeror can also, at any time, revoke an offer, provided this revocation is communicated to the offeree.

Byrne & Co v Van Tienhoven & Co (1880) 5 CPD 344 (CP)

Facts: The defendants wrote from Cardiff on 1 October offering goods for sale to the plaintiffs at New York. The plaintiffs received the offer on 11 October. They accepted it by telegram on the same day, and by letter on 15 October. On 8 October the defendants posted to the plaintiffs a letter withdrawing their offer. This letter reached the plaintiffs on 20 October. The plaintiffs sued for breach of contract. The defendants argued that their offer had been withdrawn by the time the plaintiffs purported to accept.

Held: The withdrawal was ineffective. The postal rule did not apply to revocation of acceptance, which had to be communicated.

Lindley J:
'There is no doubt that an offer can be withdrawn before it is accepted, and it is immaterial whether the offer is expressed to be open for acceptance for a given time or not: *Routledge v Grant* (1828) 4 Bing 653. For the decision of the present case, however, it is necessary to consider two other questions, viz.: 1. Whether a withdrawal of an offer has any effect until it is communicated to the person to whom the offer has

---

been sent? 2. Whether posting a letter of withdrawal is a communication to the person to whom the letter is sent?

It is curious that neither of these questions appears to have actually been decided in this country. As regards the first question, I am aware that Pothier and some other writers of celebrity are of opinion that there can be no contract if an offer is withdrawn before it is accepted, although the withdrawal is not communicated to the person to whom the offer has been made. The reason for this opinion is that there is not in fact any such consent by both parties as is essential to constitute a contact between them. Against this view, however, it has been urged that a state of mind not notified cannot be regarded in dealings between man and man; and that an uncommunicated revocation is for all practical purposes and in point of law no revocation at all. This is the view taken in the United States: see *Tayloe v Merchants Fire Insurance Co.* 9 Howard 5 Ct Rep 390 cited in Benjamin on Sales, pp 56–58, and it is adopted by Mr Benjamin. The same view is taken by Mr Pollock in his excellent work on Principles of Contract, ed. ii., p. 10, and by Mr Leake in his Digest of the Law of Contracts, p 43. This view, moreover, appears to me much more in accordance with the general principles of English law than the view maintained by Pothier. I pass, therefore, to the next question, viz., whether posting the letter of revocation was a sufficient communication of it to the plaintiff. The offer was posted on the 1st of October, the withdrawal was posted on the 8th, and did not reach the plaintiff until after he had posted his letter of the 11th, accepting the offer. It may be taken as now settled that where an offer is made and accepted by letters sent through the post, the contract is completed the moment the letter accepting the offer is posted: *Harris' Case* (1872) LR 7 Ch App 587; *Dunlop v Higgins* (1848) 1 HLC 381, even although it never reaches its destination. When, however, these authorities are looked at, it will be seen that they are based upon the principle that the writer of the offer has expressly or impliedly assented to treat an answer to him by a letter duly posted as a sufficient acceptance and notification to himself, or, in other words, he has made the post office his agent to receive the acceptance and notification of it. But this principle appears to me to be inapplicable to the case of the withdrawal of an offer. In this particular case I can find no evidence of any authority in fact given by the plaintiffs to the defendants to notify a withdrawal of their offer by merely posting a letter; and there is no legal principle or decision which compels me to hold, contrary to the fact, that the letter of the 8th of October is to be treated as communicated to the plaintiff on that day or on any day before the 20th, when the letter reached them. But before that letter had reached the plaintiffs they had accepted the offer, both by telegram and by post; and they had themselves resold the tin plates at a profit.

In my opinion the withdrawal by the defendants on the 8th of October of their offer of the 1st was inoperative; and a complete contract binding on both parties was entered into on the 11th of October, when the plaintiffs accepted the offer of the 1st, which they had no reason to suppose had been withdrawn. Before leaving this part of the case it may be as well to point out the extreme injustice and inconvenience which any other conclusion would produce. If the defendants' contention were to prevail no person who had received an offer by post and had accepted it would know his position until he had waited such a time as to be quite sure that a letter withdrawing the offer had not been posted before his acceptance of it. It appears to me that both legal principles, and practical convenience require that a person who has accepted an offer not known to him to have been revoked, shall be in a position safely to act upon the footing that the offer and acceptance constitute a contract binding on both parties.'

It is not essential, however, that the communication of the revocation comes directly from the offeror. As long as the offeree is aware of the fact that the offer has been withdrawn, it seems that that is sufficient. The authority for this is *Dickinson v Dodds*.

Dickinson v Dodds (1876) 2 Ch D 463 (CA)

Facts: On 10 June Dodds offered to sell a property to Dickinson, with the offer to be held open until 12 June. On 11 June, Dickinson learnt from a third party that Dodds was negotiating with Allan. Dickinson made several attempts on the afternoon of 11 June and the morning of 12 June to communicate his acceptance to Dodds, but Dodds had already sold to Allan before he was aware of Dickinson's acceptance.

Held: The offer had been withdrawn before Dickinson had effectively accepted.

Mellish LJ:
'The first question is, whether this document of the 10th of June, 1874, which was signed by Dodds, was an agreement to sell, or only an offer to sell, the property therein mentioned to Dickinson; and I am clearly of opinion that it was only an offer, although it is in the first part of it, independently of the postscript, worded as an agreement . . . Well, then, this being only an offer, the law says – and it is a perfectly clear rule of law – that, although it is said that the offer is to be left open until Friday morning at 9 o'clock, that did not bind Dodds. He was not in point of law bound to hold the offer over until 9 o'clock on Friday morning. He was not so bound either in law or in equity. Well, that being so, when on the next day he made an agreement with Allan to sell the property to him, I am not aware of any ground on which it can be said that that contract with Allan was not as good and binding a contract as ever was made. Assuming Allan to have known (there is some dispute about it, and Allan does not admit that he knew of it, but I will assume that he did) that Dodds had made the offer to Dickinson, and had given him till Friday morning at 9 o'clock to accept it, still in point of law that could not prevent Allan from making a more favourable offer than Dickinson, and entering at once into a binding agreement with Dodds.
   Then Dickinson is informed by Berry that the property has been sold by Dodds to

Allan. Berry does not tell us from whom he heard it, but he says that he did hear it, that he knew it, and that he informed Dickinson of it. Now, stopping there, the question which arises is this – If an offer has been made for the sale of property, and before that offer is accepted, the person who has made the offer enters into a binding agreement to sell the property to somebody else, and the person to whom the offer was first made receives notice in some way that the property has been sold to another person, can he after that make a binding contract by the acceptance of the offer? I am of opinion that he cannot. The law may be right or wrong in saying that a person who has given to another a certain time within which to accept an offer is not bound by his promise to give that time; but, if he is not bound by that promise, and may still sell the property to someone else, and if it be the law that, in order to make a contract, the two minds must be in agreement at some one time, that is, at the time of the acceptance, how is it possible that when the person to whom the offer has been made knows that the person who has made the offer has sold the property to someone else, and that, in fact, he has not remained in the same mind to sell it to him, he can be at liberty to accept the offer and thereby make a binding contract? It seems to me that would be simply absurd. If a man makes an offer to sell a particular horse in his stable, and says, "I will give you until the day after tomorrow to accept the offer", and the next day goes and sells the horse to somebody else, and receives the purchase-money from him, can the person to whom the offer was originally made then come and say, "I accept", so as to make a binding contract, and so as to be entitled to recover damages for the non-delivery of the horse? If the rule of law is that a mere offer to sell property, which can be withdrawn at any time, and which is made dependent on the acceptance of the person to whom it is made, is a mere *nudum pactum*, how is it possible that the person to whom the offer has been made can by acceptance make a binding contract after he knows that the person who has made the offer has sold the property to some one else? It is admitted law that, if a man who makes an offer dies, the offer cannot be accepted after he is dead, and parting with the property has very much the same effect as the death of the owner, for it makes the performance of the offer impossible. I am clearly of opinion that, just as when a man who has made an offer dies before it is accepted it is impossible that it can then be accepted, so when once the person to whom the offer was made knows that the property has been sold to someone else, it is too late for him to accept the offer, and on that ground I am clearly of opinion that there was no binding contract for the sale of this property by Dodds to Dickinson, and even if there had been, it seems to me that the sale of the property to Allan was first in point of time. However, it is not necessary to consider, if there had been two binding contracts, which of them would be entitled to priority in equity, because there is no binding contract between Dodds and Dickinson.'

James LJ and Bagallay JA concurred.

It will be noted that *Dickinson v Dodds* is also authority for the rule that a promise to keep an offer open for a particular time is not generally binding on the offeror (see also: *Routledge v Grant* (1824) 4 Bing 653). This is because there is usually no consideration for such a promise – that is, the offeree has not given or promised anything in exchange. The topic of consideration is dealt with fully in the next chapter.

2.2.8.1 Termination of offers in unilateral contracts

A difficulty arises regarding the termination of offers in unilateral contracts. In such a contract, acceptance is generally taken to be the performance of the requested act – for example, returning the lost dog for which a reward has been offered, using a smoke ball in the directed way. We have just seen that an offeror can withdraw an offer at any time before acceptance. Does this mean that an offeror in a unilateral contract can withdraw an offer even though the other party may have started performance, and may even have nearly completed it? This was held to be the case in the early twentieth century US case of *Petterson v Pattberg* (1928) 248 NY 86. More recent English authority, however, has suggested that, at least where the offeror is aware that the other party has started performance, the offer may not be unreasonably withdrawn. Two cases need to be noted – *Errington v Errington*, and *Daulia v Four Millbank Nominees*.

Errington v Errington & Woods [1952] 1 All ER 149 (CA)

Facts: In 1936 Mr E bought a house for his son and daughter-in-law to live in. He told them that the house would be theirs if they kept up the mortgage payments. They did so for some years. Mr E then died, and under his will the house was left to his wife. She sought possession of the house.

Held: The son and daughter-in-law were entitled to remain in the house while they continued to make the mortgage payments, on the basis of a unilateral contract made with Mr E. This could not be terminated while they continued to perform.

Denning LJ:
'The facts are reasonably clear. In 1936 the father bought the house for his son and daughter-in-law to live in. The father put down £250 in cash and borrowed £500 from a building society on the security of the house, repayable with interest by instalments of 15s. a week. He took the house in his own name and made himself responsible for the instalments. The father told the daughter-in-law that the £250 was a present for them, but he left them to pay the building society instalments of 15s. a week themselves. He handed the building society book to the daughter-in-law and said to her: "Don't part with this book. The house will be your property when the mortgage is paid." He said

---

125

that when he retired he would transfer it into their names. She has, in fact, paid the building society instalments regularly from that day to this with the result that much of the mortgage has been repaid, but there is a good deal yet to be paid . . . It is to be noted that the couple never bound themselves to pay the instalments to the building society, and I see no reason why any such obligation should be implied. It is clear law that the court is not to imply a term unless it is necessary, and I do not see that it is necessary here. Ample content is given to the whole arrangement by holding that the father promised that the house should belong to the couple as soon as they had paid off the mortgage. The parties did not discuss what was to happen if the couple failed to pay the instalments to the building society, but I should have thought it clear that, if they did fail to pay the instalments, the father would not be bound to transfer the house to them. The father's promise was a unilateral contract – a promise of the house in return for their act of paying the instalments. It could not be revoked by him once the couple entered on performance of the act, but it would cease to bind him if they left it incomplete and unperformed, which they have not done. If that was the position during the father's lifetime, so it must be after his death. If the daughter-in-law continues to pay all the building society instalments, the couple will be entitled to have the property transferred to them as soon as the mortgage is paid off, but if she does not do so, then the building society will claim the instalments from the father's estate and the estate will have to pay them. I cannot think that in those circumstances the estate would be bound to transfer the house to them, any more than the father himself would have been.'

Somervell and Hodson LJJ concurred.

Daulia Ltd v Four Millbank Nominees [1978] 2 All ER 557 (CA)

Facts: The parties were negotiating for the sale of some properties. On the afternoon of Tuesday, 21 December the defendants promised that they [the defendants] would enter into a contract for the sale of the properties with the plaintiffs if the plaintiffs procured a Bankers Draft for the deposit, and attended at the defendants' offices before 10.00 am on Wednesday, 22 December and tendered to the defendants the plaintiffs' part of the contract in the terms already agreed and the Bankers Draft. When the plaintiffs arrived with the bankers draft at 10 am on Wednesday, the defendants refused to go through with the transaction.

Held: There was a unilateral contract, and that the defendants could not withdraw their offer until the plaintiffs had a chance to perform, but the contract was in any case unenforceable because it did not comply with the requirements of writing contained in the Law of Property Act 1925 and applying to contracts for the transfer of interests in land.

Goff LJ:
'. . . I therefore turn to the first question. Was there a concluded unilateral contract by the defendants to enter into a contract for sale on the agreed terms?

The concept of a unilateral or "if" contract is somewhat anomalous, because it is clear that, at all events until the offeree starts to perform the condition, there is no contract at all, but merely an offer which the offeror is free to revoke. Doubts have been expressed whether the offeror becomes bound so soon as the offeree starts to perform or satisfy the condition, or only when he has fully done so. In my judgment, however, we are not concerned in this case with any such problem, because in my view the plaintiffs had fully performed or satisfied the condition when they presented themselves at the time and place appointed with a banker's draft for the deposit and their part of the written contract for sale duly engrossed and signed, and then retendered [*sic*] the same, which I understand to mean proffered it for exchange. Actual exchange, which never took place, would not in my view have been part of the satisfaction of the condition but something additional which was inherently necessary to be done by the plaintiffs to enable, not to bind, the defendants to perform the unilateral contract.

Accordingly in my judgment, the answer to the first question must be in the affirmative.

Even if my reasoning so far be wrong the conclusion in my view is still the same for the following reasons. Whilst I think the true view of a unilateral contract must in general be that the offeror is entitled to require full performance of the condition which he has imposed and short of that he is not bound, that must be subject to one important qualification, which stems from the fact that there must be an implied obligation on the part of the offeror not to prevent the condition becoming satisfied, which obligation it seems to me must arise as soon as the offeree starts to perform. Until then the offeror can revoke the whole thing, but once the offeree has embarked on performance it is too late for the offeror to revoke his offer.'

Because the case was decided on other grounds (that is, the agreement's non-compliance with the formal requirements of the Law of Property Act 1925), Goff LJ's statement about the possibility of withdrawing of offers in unilateral contracts is strictly *obiter*, and so not binding on other courts. Taken with the views expressed by Denning LJ in *Errington v Errington*, however, it probably does represent the law in this area.

2.3 ADDITIONAL READING

Evans, DM, 'The Anglo-American mailing rule' (1966) 15 ICLQ 553.

Goodrich, P, 'The posthumous life of the postal rule: requiem and revival of *Adams v Lindsell*', Ch 4 in Mulcahy, L and Wheeler, S, *Feminist Perspectives on Contract Law*, 2005, London: Glasshouse Press.

Hudson, AH, 'Retraction of letters of acceptance' (1966) 82 LQR 169.

McClintock, R, 'Objectivity in contract' (1988–1991) 6 Auckland UL Rev 317.

Mitchell, P and Phillips, J, 'The contractual nexus: is reliance essential?' (2002) 22 OJLS 115.

Rawlings, R, 'The battle of the forms' (1979) 42 MLR 715.

Steyn, J, 'Contract law: fulfilling the reasonable expectations of honest men' (1997) 113 LQR 433.

TESTS OF ENFORCEABILITY

3.1 INTRODUCTION

Not all agreements involving a matching offer and acceptance will be enforceable. English contract law uses two main tests of enforceability: deeds, and 'consideration'. The use of a deed involves the parties putting their agreement into a particular form, and by so doing confirming their intention that it should be enforceable. 'Consideration' is a technical concept that involves finding an element of mutuality, or exchange, in the agreement – each side must bring something to the bargain. If this is present, then an agreement will generally be enforceable. There are also some situations, however, where English law will enforce promises even though there is no deed or consideration. This is through the doctrine of promissory estoppel, which is discussed at the end of this chapter.

There is also an overarching concept of 'intention to create legal relations', which becomes important in certain situations. Discussion of this is left to Chapter 4.

3.2 DEEDS

A 'deed' used to be a formal document, which was signed by the parties, and had a physical 'seal' – made out of wax or paper – attached to it. This explains the origin of the phrase 'signed and sealed'. The modern requirements for the creation of a deed are more relaxed, and are set out in s 1 of the Law of Property (Miscellaneous Provisions) Act 1989.

LAW OF PROPERTY (MISCELLANEOUS PROVISIONS) ACT 1989

s 1 Deeds and their execution

(1) Any rule of law which–

    (a) restricts the substances on which a deed may be written;

    (b) requires a seal for the valid execution of an instrument as a deed by an individual; or

    (c) requires authority by one person to another to deliver an instrument as a deed on his behalf to be given by deed,

is abolished.

(2) An instrument shall not be a deed unless–

    (a) it makes it clear on its face that it is intended to be a deed by the person making it or, as the case may be, by the parties to it (whether by describing itself as a deed or expressing itself to be executed or signed as a deed or otherwise); and

    (b) it is validly executed as a deed by that person or, as the case may be, one or more of those parties.

(2A) For the purposes of subsection (2)(a) above, an instrument shall not be taken to make it clear on its face that it is intended to be a deed merely because it is executed under seal.

(3) An instrument is validly executed as a deed by an individual if, and only if–

    (a) it is signed–

        (i) by him in the presence of a witness who attests the signature; or

        (ii) at his direction and in his presence and the presence of two witnesses who each attest the signature; and

    (b) it is delivered as a deed by him or a person authorised to do so on his behalf.

(4) In subsections (2) and (3) above 'sign', in relation to an instrument, includes making one's mark on the instrument and 'signature' is to be construed accordingly.

(4A) Subsection (3) above applies in the case of an instrument executed by an individual in the name or on behalf of another person whether or not that person is also an individual.

From this it will be seen that the important questions are whether the parties intended to produce a 'deed', whether it has been signed, and whether the signature has been witnessed. There must also be 'delivery', as required by s 1(3)(b).

The position regarding companies incorporated under the Companies Acts is governed by s 36A, and s 36AA of the Companies Act 1985.

COMPANIES ACT 1985

s 36A Execution of documents: England and Wales

(1) Under the law of England and Wales the following provisions have effect with respect to the execution of documents by a company.

(2) A document is executed by a company by the affixing of its common seal.

(3) A company need not have a common seal, however, and the following subsections apply whether it does or not.

(4) A document signed by a director and the secretary of a company, or by two directors of a company, and expressed (in whatever form of words) to be executed by the company has the same effect as if executed under the common seal of the company.

(4A) Where a document is to be signed by a person as a director or the secretary of more than one company, it shall not be taken to be duly signed by that person for the purposes of subsection (4) unless the person signs it separately in each capacity.

(6) In favour of a purchaser a document shall be deemed to have been duly executed by a company if it purports to be signed by a director and the secretary of the company, or by two directors of the company.

A 'purchaser' means a purchaser in good faith for valuable consideration and includes a lessee, mortgagee or other person who for valuable consideration acquires an interest in property.

(7) This section applies in the case of a document which is (or purports to be) executed by a company in the name or on behalf of another person whether or not that person is also a company.

(8) For the purposes of this section, a document is (or purports to be) signed, in the case of a director or the secretary of a company which is not an individual, if it is (or purports to be) signed by an individual authorised by the director or secretary to sign on its behalf.

s 36AA Execution of deeds: England and Wales

(1) A document is validly executed by a company as a deed for the purposes of section 1(2)(b) of the Law of Property (Miscellaneous Provisions) Act 1989, if and only if–

(a) it is duly executed by the company, and

(b) it is delivered as a deed.

(2) A document shall be presumed to be delivered for the purposes of subsection (1)(b) upon its being executed, unless a contrary intention is proved.

For companies, therefore, the document must indicate on its face that it is intended to be a deed, and must be 'executed' in one of the ways set out in s 35A. A seal may be used, but it is also permissible for the document to be signed by directors. It must then be 'delivered as a deed' (s 36AA).

Deeds may be used to create an enforceable obligation that is entirely one-sided – for example, a promise to make a gift at some point in the future. It is also sometimes used in relation to complex contracts in relation to construction and engineering to give the parties the benefit of a longer period for bringing legal action in the event of breach. For an ordinary contract the limitation period is normally six years; for a deed the period is 12 years (Limitation Act 1980, ss 5, 8).

3.3 CONSIDERATION

The main method by which agreements are found to be enforceable under English law is through the finding of 'consideration'. This means that both parties must bring something to the bargain. A promise by A to B for which B gives nothing in return will not generally be enforceable.

3.3.1 DEFINITION OF CONSIDERATION

What is 'consideration'? In *Currie v Misa* (1875) LR 10 it was suggested that:

> A valuable consideration, in the sense of the law, may consist either in some right, interest, profit or benefit accruing to one party or some forbearance, detriment, loss or responsibility, given, suffered or undertaken by the other.

This is sometimes abbreviated to the idea that consideration must involve some benefit to the promisor or some detriment to the promisee. In many cases it will involve both – as where money is exchanged for goods. The seller has the benefit of the money paid (benefit), but loses ownership of the goods (detriment); for the buyer, the position is reversed.

It is more difficult to see 'benefit and detriment' where a contract is made by the exchange of promises, both of which are to be performed in the future. It is clear that such an exchange will create a binding contract – as is confirmed by Lord Dunedin's in the following passage from *Dunlop Pneumatic Tyre Co Ltd v Selfridge & Co Ltd* [1915] AC 847, 855:

> My Lords, I confess that this case is to my mind apt to nip any budding affection which one might have had for the doctrine of consideration. For the effect of that doctrine in the present case is to make it possible for a person to snap his fingers at a bargain deliberately made, a bargain not in itself unfair, and which the person seeking to enforce it has a legitimate interest to enforce. Notwithstanding these considerations I cannot say that I have ever had any doubt that the judgment of the Court of Appeal was right . . .
>
> My Lords, I am content to adopt from a work of Sir Frederick Pollock, to which I have often been under obligation, the following words as to consideration: 'An act or forbearance of one party, or the promise thereof, is the price

for which the promise of the other is bought, and the promise thus given for value is enforceable.' (Pollock on Contracts, 8th edn, p 175.)

Lord Dunedin is clearly of the view, therefore, that, as indicated by Pollock, a 'promise for a promise' results in a binding agreement.

As Atiyah has pointed out, however, the acceptance of a 'promise' as valid consideration does not fit easily with the idea of benefit and detriment.

Atiyah, PS, *Essays on Contract*, 1986, Oxford: Clarendon Press, pp 191–192

Benefit or detriment is not necessary

... I need hardly stress that many promises are given in order to obtain some reciprocal benefit; and that a detriment incurred by a promisee in reliance on the promise is often a very good reason for enforcing a promise. But it seems incorrect to assert that the presence of benefit or detriment is always a necessary prerequisite for the enforcement of a contract. In the first place, an executory bilateral contract is and has for centuries been enforceable by the courts, although neither benefit nor detriment usually arises until the contract has been at least partly performed. It is of course true that once the law has begun to enforce bilateral executory contracts, the mere giving and receipt of the promises may be said to involve a benefit and detriment because they are legally enforceable. But enforceability comes first, and benefit and detriment afterwards; it is purely circular to assert that the presence of benefit and detriment can be a ground for the enforcement of such contracts. It is also true that if an executory bilateral contract is in due course performed the promisor may receive a benefit and the promisee may incur a detriment. But where the promisee sues for damages for breach of an executory bilateral contract the promisor has in fact received no benefit, and the promisee has not necessarily incurred any detriment.

It is common for lawyers to apply the benefit-detriment analysis even to bilateral executory contracts; the inquiry then takes the form of asking if performance of the promise will be, or would have been beneficial to the promisor or detrimental to the promisee. The fact that the answer may be in the negative may well be a factor which leads the court to decide that there is no reason (or consideration) for enforcing the promise. But the fact that the answer is in the affirmative does not and cannot demonstrate that the promise is being enforced because of a factual benefit or detriment, unless that is, it is possible to argue that a promise may be a benefit or a detriment irrespective of its legal enforceability. In the original essay I assumed perhaps too easily that this could not be so, but Professor Treitel argues cogently that promises can be beneficial or detrimental even if they are not legally enforceable; and if we assume a society in which promises are generally performed, and in which their non-performance carries a certain odium, then I am prepared to admit that this may be the case. Nevertheless, there is an element of unreality in treating bilateral executory contracts in this way. Counter-promises are treated by the courts as beneficial (or detrimental) unless it can be demonstrated that there is or was no possibility of any benefit or detriment being derived from the promise. A counter-promise is thus treated more like a formal reason for the enforcement of a promise than a reason of substance, and in most actions for breach of an executory bilateral contract, there is no possibility of the promisor obtaining any benefit, or the promisee suffering any detriment by the time the case comes for trial.

The truth seems to be that bilateral executory contracts are enforced for other reasons (or considerations) than the existence of benefit or detriment. Quite what those other reasons are, whether they are adequate reasons, and whether they extend to all cases of bilateral executory contracts, are all very difficult questions ... In the original version of the present essay I assumed far too readily (again largely under the influence of Corbin) that bilateral executory contracts are enforced because in modern societies business could scarcely be carried on if they were not enforced. Professor Treitel challenges my reasoning here with some justification; though it is a little ironical that he should do so, given that he has no apparent doubts that bilateral executory contracts *should* be enforced, while I have a great many such doubts.

Treitel, on the other hand, has argued that even an unenforceable promise may constitute a benefit or detriment.

Treitel, GH, *Law of Contract,* 2003, 11th edn, Stevens, p 70

Mutual promises

So far we have discussed performance by one party as consideration for the promise of the other: for example, payment by a buyer as the consideration for the seller's promise to deliver, or delivery by a seller as consideration for the buyer's promise to pay. It is, however, also well settled that mutual promises can be consideration for each other. Hence if a seller promises to deliver goods in six months' time and the buyer to pay for them on delivery, there is an immediately binding contract from which neither party can withdraw, though, of course, performance cannot be claimed till the appointed time. Implied, no less than express, promises can constitute consideration for each other.

Some difficulty has been felt in explaining the rule that mutual promises can be consideration for each other. At first sight, it might seem that the mere giving of a promise was not a detriment, nor its receipt a benefit, so as to make the counter-promise binding. It will not do to say that the person making the promise suffers a detriment because he is legally bound to perform it; for if this assumption is made about one of the promises, it must also be made of the other, so that the 'explanation' assumes the very point in issue. Probably the reason for the rule is simpler. A person who makes a commercial promise expects to have to perform it (and is in fact under considerable pressure to do so). Correspondingly, one who receives such a promise expects it to be kept. These expectations, which can exist even where the promise is not legally enforceable, are based on commercial morality, and can properly be called a detriment and a benefit; hence they satisfy the requirement of consideration in the case of mutual promises.

The two options appear to be to downgrade the requirement of 'benefit and detriment', or to accept that a promise to do something which, in performance, will constitute a benefit to the other party or a detriment to the promisor can itself be treated as consideration.

3.3.2 CONSIDERATION NEED NOT BE 'ADEQUATE' BUT MUST BE 'SUFFICIENT'

It is not usually important to the courts whether there is any balance, in financial terms, between what is brought to the contract by each party. They are not interested in whether the consideration is 'adequate' in objective terms, as long as it takes a form that is recognised as being a valid type of consideration – that is, it is 'sufficient'.

The point regarding 'adequacy' as against 'sufficiency' is illustrated by *Thomas v Thomas*.

Thomas v Thomas (1842) 2 QB 851

Facts: Mr Thomas expressed a wish that, following his death, his wife should have his house for the rest of her life. When Mr Thomas died, his executors entered into an agreement to this effect with Mrs Thomas (the plaintiff in the action). The agreement was stated to be 'in consideration' of Mr Thomas's desire, but was subject to the proviso that Mrs Thomas paid the executor's £1 a year towards the ground rent and agreed to keep the house in good repair.

Held: Complying with the desire of Mr Thomas could not constitute consideration, but the payment of £1 a year could – so that the agreement was enforceable as a contract.

Patteson J:
'It would be giving to causa too large a construction if we were to adopt the view urged for the defendant: it would be confounding consideration with motive. Motive is not the same thing with consideration. Consideration means something which is of some value in the eye of the law, moving from the plaintiff: it may be some benefit to the plaintiff or some detriment to the defendant; but at all events it must be moving from the plaintiff. Now that which is suggested as the consideration here, a pious respect for the wishes of the testator, does not in any way move from the

plaintiff; it moves from the testator; therefore, legally speaking, it forms no part of the consideration. Then it is said that, if that be so, there is no consideration at all, it is a mere voluntary gift: but when we look at the agreement we find that this is not a mere proviso that the donee shall take the gift with the burthens; but it is an express agreement to pay what seems to be a fresh apportionment of a ground rent, and which is made payable not to a superior Landlord but to the executors. So that this rent is clearly not something incident to the assignment of the house; for in that case, instead of being payable to the executors, it would have been payable to the land-lord. Then as to the repairs: these houses may very possibly be held under a lease containing covenants to repair; but we know nothing about it: for any thing that appears, the liability to repair is first created by this instrument. The proviso certainly struck me at first as Mr. Williams put it, that the rent and repairs there merely attached to the gift by the donors; and, had the instrument been executed by the donors only, there might have been some ground for that construction; but the fact is not so . . .'

Coleridge J:

'The concessions made in the course of the argument have, in fact, disposed of the case. It is conceded that mere motive need not be stated: and we are not obliged to look for the legal consideration in any particular part of the instrument, merely because the consideration is usually stated in some particular part: ut res magis valeat, we may look to any part. In this instrument, in the part where it is usual to state the consider-ation, nothing certainly is expressed but a wish to fulfil the intentions of the testator: but in another part we find an express agreement to pay an annual sum for a particular purpose; and also a distinct agreement to repair. If these had occurred in the first part of the instrument, it could hardly have been argued that the declaration was not well drawn, and supported by the evidence. As to the suggestion of this being a voluntary conveyance, my impression is that this payment of £1 annually is more than a good consideration: it is a valuable consideration: it is clearly a thing newly created, and not part of the old ground rent.'

In other words, a desire to comply with the wishes of the testator was not 'sufficient' to amount to consideration, but it was irrelevant whether the £1 contribution towards the rent was 'adequate' to pay for the benefit that Mrs Thomas was receiving.

The decision in *Thomas v Thomas* might be taken to suggest that consideration needs to have some economic value, and that is indeed sometimes suggested as a characteristic. This derives mainly from the old case of *White v Bluett* (1853) 23 LJ Ex 36. In this case a father promised not to enforce a promissory note against his son, in return for the son stopping complaining about the distribution of his father's property. It was held that there was no consideration for the father's promise, with Pollock CB commenting (at 37):

The son had no right to complain, for the father might make what distribution of his property he liked: and the son's abstaining from what he had no right to do can be no consideration.

More recent case law, however, indicates that economic value may not be necessary. For example, in *Ward v Byham* [1956] 2 All ER 318, it was suggested that a promise to ensure that a child was happy could amount to good consideration. Furthermore, in *Chappell v Nestlé* it was held by the House of Lords that supplying items which were of no intrinsic value to the promisor could nevertheless amount to consideration.

Chappell & Co v Nestlé & Co [1960] AC 87

Facts: Nestlé offered a promotion with their chocolate, under which a person who sent in three wrappers, plus a small amount of money, would be sent a record – *Rockin' Shoes*. Chappell claimed that this constituted a breach of copyright which they owned in the song. For the purposes of the law of copyright it was important to determine whether the wrappers constituted part of the consideration for the supply of the record.

Held: The wrappers were part of the consideration, even though they would be thrown away by Nestlé. As a result, Nestlé were in breach of copyright.

Lord Reid:
'. . . I can now turn to what appears to me to be the crucial question in this case: was the 1*s*. 6*d*. an "ordinary retail selling price" within the meaning of s. 8? That involves two questions, what was the nature of the contract between the respondents Nestlé and a person who sent 1*s*. 6*d*. plus three wrappers in acceptance of their offer, and what is meant by "ordinary retail selling price" in this context. To determine the nature of the contract, one must find the intention of the parties as shown by what they said and did. The respondents Nestlé's intention can hardly be in any doubt. They were not setting out to trade in gramophone records. They were using these records to increase their sales of chocolate. Their offer was addressed to everyone. It might be accepted by a person who was already a regular buyer of their chocolate; but, much more important to them, it might be accepted by people who might become regular buyers of their chocolate if they could be induced to try it and found they liked it. The inducement was something calculated to look like a bargain, a record at a very cheap price. It is in evidence that the ordinary price for a dance record is 6*l*. 6*d*. It is true that the ordinary record gives much longer playing time than Nestlé's records and it may have other advantages. But the reader of the respondents Nestlé's offer was not in a position to know that. It seems to me clear that the main intention of the offer was to induce people interested in this kind of music to buy (or, perhaps, get others to buy) chocolate which otherwise would not have been bought. It is, of course, true that some wrappers might come from chocolate which had already been bought, or from

137

chocolate which would have been bought without the offer, but that does not seem to me to alter the case. Where there is a large number of transactions – the notice mentions 30,000 records – I do not think we should simply consider an isolated case where it would be impossible to say whether there had been a direct benefit from the acquisition of the wrappers or not. The requirement that wrappers should be sent was of great importance to the respondents Nestlé; there would have been no point in their simply offering records for 1s. 6d. each. It seems to me quite unrealistic to divorce the buying of the chocolate from the supplying of the records. It is a perfectly good contract if a person accepts an offer to supply goods if he (a) does something of value to the supplier and (b) pays money; the consideration is both (a) and (b). There may have been cases where the acquisition of the wrappers conferred no direct benefit on the respondents Nestlé but there must have been many cases where it did. I do not see why the possibility that, in some cases, the acquisition of the wrappers did not directly benefit the respondents Nestlé should require us to exclude from consideration the cases where it did; and even where there was no direct benefit from the acquisition of the wrappers there may have been an indirect benefit by way of advertisement.'

Lord Tucker and Lord Somervell concurred; Viscount Simonds and Lord Keith dissented.

The decision in *Chappell v Nestlé* suggests that only an indirect economic benefit is required if, any at all. The overall promotional scheme was to Nestlé's commercial advantage, in that it would encourage increased sales of chocolate, but the supply of the wrappers themselves could not be said to have provided any economic benefit from that particular transaction – particularly if the chocolate had been bought by someone other than the person who sent them in. The most recent discussion of this aspect of consideration by the Appeal Courts is to be found in the Court of Appeal's decision in *Edmonds v Lawson*. The court here also found an indirect, rather than direct, economic benefit to the promisor.

Edmonds v Lawson [2000] QB 501 (CA)

Facts: The claimant was a pupil barrister, arguing that she was entitled to be paid the minimum wage. As part of that argument, it was necessary for the claimant to establish that she was working under a contract of employment.

Held: There was a contract between the pupil and her chambers (though not with her individual pupil master). The consideration was in effect the general benefit to the chambers of having pupils. The contract was not one of employment, however, so the claimant was not entitled to the minimum wage.

Lord Bingham: . . .

'**19.** The first issue: was there a contract?

20. The claimant contended, and the judge held, that there was a contract between her and all those who were members of Mr. Lawson's chambers on 1 October 1998, made by the chambers' offer of a 12-month pupillage and her acceptance of that offer. Before the judge and on appeal before us the defendants resisted that conclusion. The grounds of resistance were, first, that there was no intent to create legal relations and, secondly, that the pupillage agreement was unsupported by consideration moving from the claimant as promisee and so lacked an essential ingredient of a legally binding contract.

21. Whether the parties intended to enter into legally binding relations is an issue to be determined objectively and not by inquiring into their respective states of mind. The context is all-important. From the defendants' point of view the written offer of pupillage to the claimant came at the end of a long, time-consuming and expensive process. It was also a process of great long-term consequence to them since, although barristers in practice are independent self-employed practitioners, it is of benefit to all, at every level, that chambers as a whole consist of talented and hardworking members, and the defendants, like other chambers, recruit most of their tenants from the pool of those recruited as pupils. So, quite apart from considerations of professional duty and the public interest, it is of direct practical consequence to chambers to attract and select the ablest pupils. That is why, in part at least, many chambers include the defendants' fund pupillages for a proportion of their pupils, sometimes very generously. From the pupil's point of view, obtaining a pupillage in a flourishing set of chambers practising in the pupil's chosen field is a step with potentially immense consequences, both professional and financial, in both the short and the long term. Obtaining a pupillage does not of course guarantee a tenancy, but it guarantees the pupil an opportunity to show his quality and thereby seek a tenancy. When, as the culmination of a long process of application, short-listing and interview an offer is formally made and formally accepted it would in our judgment be surprising to infer that the parties intended to bind themselves in honour only.

22. In arguing that there was no intent to create legal relations Mr. Goudie for the defendants relied on the educational nature of the arrangement, suggesting that it lacked the characteristics of a commercial contract and involved no payment by the pupil. It was a voluntary and gratuitous offer by the chambers to provide education and training. He also relied on the doubt which, he said, existed as to who entered into the arrangement on the chambers' side. There was, he suggested, no need for a contract because the relationship was already regulated by the documents to which reference has been made above, and if chambers should resile from an undertaking to provide pupillage the pupil would have ample redress through the Bar disciplinary machinery, which would in practice preclude such dishonourable behaviour. The absence of written terms and conditions, he argued, pointed strongly against any intention to contract.

23. Neither singularly nor cumulatively do we find these points in any way persuasive on the question of intent. It is true that the content of the arrangement was educational, but as already pointed out the practical implications of the arrangement for both parties were potentially very significant and, subject to the point on consideration discussed below, there is no reason why a binding contract cannot be made for the provision of education and training. Whereas once the arrangement of pupillage was a one-to-one engagement between pupil and pupil master, that has ceased to be so, as evidenced by the responsibility imposed on and accepted by heads of chambers, by the procedure in practice adopted by chambers and by the management of pupillage as a chambers responsibility. The claimant was not interviewed, nor was the offer of pupillage made, by either of those who became her successive pupil masters, and when the offer was made and accepted she did not know who they would be. The regulatory materials governing pupillage (only a small part of which we have quoted) were impliedly incorporated by reference into the arrangement made between the parties, and to that extent the terms of the arrangement were recorded in writing; but the functions and obligations of the parties were so clearly specified in these materials that any detailed negotiation of terms and conditions to be recorded in a written agreement between the parties was rendered unnecessary. It is of course unlikely that any chambers, certainly any reputable chambers, having made an offer of pupillage which has been accepted, would resile from that arrangement without very good reason, but the existence of a disciplinary sanction does not in our view point against the existence of a contract. To our mind this arrangement had all the characteristics of a binding contract. It makes no difference that, if the pupil defaulted, the chambers would be most unlikely to sue; the same is true if an employer engages a junior employee under an employment contract which is undoubtedly binding, and the employee fails to turn up on the appointed day.

24. The defendants' argument on consideration is, we think, much stronger, for while chambers undertake to provide a closely prescribed curriculum of education and training the pupil no longer pays any fee and does not in our view undertake to do anything beyond that which is conducive to his or her education and training. In working on the pupil master's papers (making factual summaries, or drafting chronologies, or writing advices or preparing pleadings) the pupil will be seeking to acquire, under the tutelage of the pupil master, the skills of a professional adviser, pleader and advocate, even though the pupil master will often benefit from the pupil's work and from discussion with him. If the pupil carries out legal research or keeps a note in court, he is again learning and applying professional skills necessary for practice. If the pupil produces any work of real value, whether to the pupil master or any other member of the Bar, the beneficiary is under a professional duty to remunerate the pupil. While any pupil of ordinary common sense would, if asked, carry out mundane tasks (such as photocopying authorities or making a cup of tea) which do not in any way promote his professional development, there is in our view no obligation or duty on the pupil to do anything for the pupil master which is not conducive to his own professional development.

25. This conclusion, if correct, would we think be fatal to any argument that there was a contract between the pupil and the individual pupil master, for the pupil would provide no consideration for the pupil master's educational services. But the claimant does not rely on any contract said to have been made with an individual pupil master and we think a broader view has to be taken of the relationship between chambers and pupil. For reasons on which we have already touched, members of chambers have a strong incentive to attract talented pupils, and their future prospects will to some extent depend on their success in doing so. The funding of awards is not an exercise in pure altruism but reflects an obvious (and wholly unobjectionable) element of self-interest. The agreement of the claimant and other pupils to undertake pupillage at chambers such as the defendants' provides a pool of selected candidates who can be expected to compete with each other for recruitment as tenants. We do not regard this argument as undermined by the fact that some pupils who are accepted as such may be regarded as unlikely candidates for tenancy. The process must be viewed in the round, and not on a pupil by pupil basis, and chambers may well see an advantage in developing close relationships with pupils who plan to practise as employed barristers or to practise overseas. On balance we take the view that pupils such as the claimant provide consideration for the offer made by chambers such as the defendants' by agreeing to enter into the close, important and potentially very productive relationship which pupillage involves.

26. We agree with the judge, although for somewhat different reasons, that the claimant did make a legally binding contract with the defendants.'

Once again, the idea of consideration being required to have some economic value is being applied flexibly. This flexibility has led Treitel to refer to the idea of 'invented consideration'.

Treitel, GH, *Law of Contract* 2003, 11th edn, London: Stevens, p 71

Invented consideration

Normally, a party enters into a contract with a view to obtaining the consideration provided by the other: for example, the buyer wants the goods and the seller the price. In the United States it has been said that this is essential, and that 'Nothing is consideration that is not regarded as such by both parties.' But English courts do not insist on this requirement and often regard an act or forbearance as the consideration for a promise even though it may not have been the object of the promisor to secure it. They may also regard the possibility of some prejudice to the promisee as a detriment without regard to the question whether it has in fact been suffered. These practices may be called 'inventing consideration', and the temptation to adopt one or the other of them is particularly strong when the act or forbearance which was actually bargained for cannot be regarded as consideration for some reason which is thought to be technical and without merit. In such cases the practice of inventing consideration may help to make the operation of the doctrine of consideration more acceptable; but the practice may also be criticised on the ground that it gives the courts a wide discretion to hold promises binding (or not) as they please. Thus the argument that the promisee *might* have suffered prejudice by acting in reliance on a promise is in some cases made a basis of decision, while in others precisely the same argument is rejected. The courts have not been very consistent in the exercise of this discretion and its existence is a source of considerable uncertainty in this branch of the law.

This concept has been roundly rejected by Atiyah, as part of his attack on the orthodox analysis of the doctrine of consideration.

Atiyah, PS, *Essays on Contract*, 1986, Oxford: Clarendon Press, pp 182–183

The notion that consideration means a reason for the enforcement of a promise was largely borrowed in my original essay from Corbin, and although Professor Treitel has objected to this, and insisted that it cannot just be asserted that this is what consideration means, it seems clear to me that it is both a historical and an analytical truth. I will not inquire further into the historical use of the term here, but at least it must be admitted that in modern law the presence of consideration is a necessary condition for the enforceability of a promise, leaving aside promissory estoppel and other 'non-contractual' means of enforcement. To translate that into saying that consideration means a *reason* for the enforcement of a promise only requires us to make the assumption that the law is a rational enterprise. To assert that the law 'will not do A unless B' surely entails, if law is purposive in its nature, that the presence of B is a *reason* for doing A—unless (which can hardly be suggested here) it is merely a condition for the doing of A. Of course this does not carry the implication that the *reason* is always a good one; nor that sometimes the reason ought not to be outweighed by other reasons. But unless the presence of consideration is regarded, in general terms, as a reason for the enforcement of promises, the whole doctrine would have to be treated as mumbo-jumbo. Doubtless the law is sometimes irrational, but to treat a whole doctrine of the law as irrational implies both an extraordinary lack of faith in the intelligence of former judges, and an astonishing perversity in the erection of a system of precedent which requires that their decisions should be followed. I decline to make either of these assumptions.

Professor Treitel's critique of my original essay (and his textbook on the *Law of Contract*) insists that the courts have power to 'invent' consideration, and that this ability is an important phenomenon which I have overlooked and which explains many otherwise puzzling things about the doctrine. I find this a difficult concept to grasp. Is an 'invented' consideration something different from a 'real' consideration or is it the same thing? If it is the same thing, then it is hard to see in what sense it is invented; and if it is not the same thing, then it either violates the rules of law, or it modifies them. Presumably Professor Treitel does not mean to suggest that when judges invent consideration they are defying the law and violating their judicial oaths, but if an invented consideration modifies the rules governing ordinary consideration, then an invented consideration becomes again an ordinary consideration, though the legal significance of the doctrine has now changed. The only other possibility that occurs to me is that the courts might use the concept of 'invented consideration' rather like an equitable or merciful dispensation from the ordinary law, but it is unthinkable that judges should behave in this way. They have no power to invent a consideration in one case and refuse to do so in a relevantly identical case. Thus an invented consideration must in the end be the same thing as an ordinary consideration. I fear that Professor Treitel has himself invented the concept of an invented consideration because he finds it the only way in which he is able to reconcile many decisions with what he takes to be the 'true' or 'real' doctrine. This is, of course, exactly the sort of process against which Corbin warned us, and I give my full allegiance to Corbin on this point.

(Professor Atiyah's views on consideration are discussed further towards the end of this chapter, at p 205.)

3.3.3 PAST CONSIDERATION

It is a general rule of English contract law that 'past consideration is no consideration'. This means that if the action that is alleged to provide consideration for a promise was completed before the promise was made, then the promise will not be enforceable. The reason is that the action needs to have been done in response to the promise – as a means of 'buying' it; the action cannot perform this role if it preceded the promise. An old example of the basic rule is the case of *Roscorla v Thomas*.

Roscorla v Thomas (1842) 3 QB 234

Facts: The plaintiff bought a horse from the defendant. The defendant then promised that the horse was 'sound and free from vice'. This turned out to be untrue, and the plaintiff sued for breach of this promise.

Held: There was no consideration for the promise – the sale had already been completed before it was given.

Lord Denman CJ:
'. . . It may be taken as a general rule, subject to exceptions not applicable to this case, that the promise must be coextensive with the consideration. In the present case, the only promise that would result from the consideration, as stated, and be coextensive

with it, would be to deliver the horse upon request. The precedent sale, without a warranty, though at the request of the defendant, imposes no other duty or obligation upon him. It is clear, therefore, that the consideration stated would not raise an implied promise by the defendant that the horse was sound or free from vice.

But the promise in the present case must be taken to be, as in fact it was, express and the question is, whether that fact will warrant the extension of the promise beyond that which would be implied by law; and whether the consideration, though insufficient to raise an implied promise, will nevertheless support an express one. And we think that it will not.

The cases in which it has been held that, under certain circumstances, a consideration insufficient to raise an implied promise will nevertheless support an express one, will be found collected and reviewed in the note (a) to *Wennall v Adney*, and in the case of *Eastwood v Kenyon*. They are cases of voidable contracts subsequently ratified, of debts barred by operation of law, subsequently revived, and of equitable and moral obligations, which, but for some rule of law, would of themselves have been sufficient to raise an implied promise. All these cases are distinguishable from, and indeed inapplicable to, the present, which appears to us to fall within the general rule, that a consideration past and executed will support no other promise than such as would be implied by law.

The rule for arresting the judgment upon the first count must therefore be made absolute.'

A more recent example of the same principle is to be found in *Re McArdle*.

Re McArdle [1951] Ch 669 (CA)

Facts: William McArdle left a house to his children. One of his sons was living in the house, and he and his wife carried out improvements to it. His wife then got each of the siblings to promise to agree to share the costs of this work.

Held: The promise to pay for the work was unenforceable, because the doing of the work was 'past consideration' in relation to the promise.

Jenkins LJ:

'. . . The document which is said to operate as an equitable assignment is the document of April 30, 1945, signed by the five children of the testator. That document on the face of it purports to be an agreement for valuable consideration under which when Mrs Marjorie McArdle has carried out certain alterations and improvements to the property known as Gravel Hill Poultry Farm, in consideration of her so doing, the five children agree that she is to be paid a sum of £488, representing the cost of the work, out of the testator's estate when distributed. That is what it purports to be; and I think, notwithstanding the argument to the contrary, that it is really perfectly plain, so far as the construction of the document is concerned, that what it contemplates is the doing by Mrs Marjorie McArdle of work yet to be done; and her doing that work is to form the consideration by virtue of which she is to be entitled to receive £488 out of the estate. That is what the document is, and if the document had correctly represented the facts, for my part I have no doubt that it would have operated as a valid equitable assignment of £488, subject to Mrs Marjorie McArdle's performing her part of the bargain by providing the consideration she had contracted to provide in the form of doing the work. There might have been room for difficulty, and for argument, whether the work had been properly done or not, but those matters could have been resolved one way or the other, if necessary by an action; and ultimately, if Mrs McArdle showed that she had done the work contracted for, her title to the £488 would have been complete and, the agreement being for valuable consideration, it would not have mattered that further steps had to be taken in order to perfect her title.

But the true position was that, as the work had in fact all been done and nothing remained to be done by Mrs Marjorie McArdle at all, the consideration was a wholly past consideration, and, therefore, the beneficiaries' agreement for the repayment to her of the £488 out of the estate was *nudum pactum*, a promise with no consideration to support it. That being so, it is impossible for her to rely upon this document as constituting an equitable assignment for valuable consideration.'

Lord Evershed MR, and Hodson LJ concurred.

3.3.3.1 Exceptions

There are some exceptions to the basic rule, both at common law and under statute. The first requirement for such an exception at common law is that the act alleged to constitute consideration was performed at the request of the promisor. This is illustrated by the ancient case of *Lampleigh v Braithwait* (1615) Hob 105; 80 ER 255. The defendant had been convicted of murder, and asked the plaintiff to seek a pardon from the king. After the plaintiff had made attempts to do so, the defendant promised him £100 for his efforts. It was held that this promise was enforceable. The situation must, however, be one in which there was an expectation of payment when the action was requested. This point was emphasised in *Re Casey's Patents*.

Re Casey's Patents [1892] 1 Ch 104 (CA)

Facts: The plaintiff had managed certain patents on behalf of the defendants. They then promised him a one third share in the patents, in return for his efforts.

Held: It was always assumed that the plaintiff would be paid for the work which he was doing. The subsequent promise was simply a formalisation of what that payment should be.

Bowen LJ:

'. . . The document is one by which the signatories agree with Mr Casey to give him "one-third share of the patents above mentioned, the same to take effect from this date". It cannot be denied that that is an equitable assignment if it is anything. It is not an agreement to take effect at some future date. It is an agreement to give him the share as from the date of the document, and it immediately passes in Equity the right to the third share.

But then it was said by Mr Daniel, "But there is no consideration, and this document is not under seal". We will see if there is consideration. The consideration is stated, such as it is. It is, "in consideration of your services as the practical manager in working our patents as above for transit by steamer". Then says Mr Daniel, "Yes, but that is a future consideration, and a future consideration, if nothing were done under it or nothing was proved to be done, would fail". The answer to that is that the consideration is not the rendering of the services, as is plain from the fact that the document is to take effect in Equity from the date. The consideration must be something other than rendering services in the future. It is the promise to render them which those words imply, that constitutes the consideration; and the promise to render future services, if an effectual promise, is certainly good consideration. Then, driven from that, Mr Daniel said, "Oh! but it is past services that it means, and past services are not a consideration for anything". Well, that raises the old question – or might raise it, if there was not an answer to it – of *Lampleigh v Braithwait* (1615) Hob 105, a subject of great interest to every scientific lawyer, as to whether a past service will support a promise. I do not propose to discuss that question, or, perhaps, I should not have finished this week. I should have to examine the whole state of the law as to, and the history of the subject of, consideration, which, I need hardly say, I do not propose to do. But the answer to Mr Daniel's point is clear. Even if it were true, as some scientific students of law believe, that a past service cannot support a future promise, you must look at the document and see if the promise cannot receive a proper effect in some other way. Now, the fact of a past service raises an implication that at the time it was rendered it was to be paid for, and, if it was a service which was to be paid for, when you get in the subsequent document a promise to pay, that promise may be treated either as an admission which evidences or as a positive bargain which fixes the amount of that reasonable remuneration on the faith of which the service was originally rendered. So that here for past services there is ample justification for the promise to give the third share. Therefore, this is an equitable assignment which cannot be impeached.'

Fry LJ, and Lindley LJ concurred.

The current position on the situations in which 'past consideration' will be treated as valid was summed up by Lord Scarman in the following passage from *Pao On v Lau Yiu Long* [1980] AC 614, 629:

An act done before the giving of a promise to make a payment or to confer some other benefit can sometimes be consideration for the promise. The act must have been done at the promisors' request: the parties must have understood that the act was to be remunerated either by a payment or the conferment of some other benefit: and payment, or the conferment of a benefit, must have been legally enforceable had it been promised in advance.

The first of Lord Scarman's requirements appears clearly in *Lampleigh v Braithwait*, and the second in *Re Casey's Patents*. The third seems simply to require that consideration, if supplied before the promise, must be 'sufficient', in the terms discussed above (p 135).

Statutory exceptions include:

BILLS OF EXCHANGE ACT 1882

s 27. Valuable consideration for a bill [of exchange] may be constituted by (a) any consideration sufficient to support a simple contract, (b) an antecedent debt or liability.

Sub-para (b) shows that a debt that precedes the creation of the bill may be good consideration for it.

LIMITATION ACT 1980

s 29 Fresh accrual of action on acknowledgment or part payment
. . . (5) Subject to subsection (6) below, where any right of action has accrued to recover–

(a) any debt or other liquidated pecuniary claim; or
(b) any claim to the personal estate of a deceased person or to any share or interest in any such estate;

and the person liable or accountable for the claim acknowledges the claim or makes any payment in respect of it the right shall be treated as having accrued on and not before the date of the acknowledgment or payment.
(6) A payment of a part of the rent or interest due at any time shall not extend the period for claiming the remainder then due, but any payment of interest shall be treated as a payment in respect of the principal debt.

s 30 Formal provisions as to acknowledgments and part payments

(1) To be effective for the purposes of section 29 of this Act, an acknowledgment must be in writing and signed by the person making it.
(2) For the purposes of section 29, any acknowledgment or payment–
    (a) may be sent by the agent of the person by whom it is required to be made under that section; and
    (b) shall be made to the person, or to an agent of the person, whose title or claim is being acknowledged or, as the case may be, in respect of whose claim the payment is being made.

147

If the acknowledgment under s 29(5) is in the form of a promise, it will have the effect of extending the limitation period for the recovery of a debt, even though no fresh consideration has been given.

3.3.4 PERFORMANCE OF EXISTING DUTIES

This topic – that is, the extent to which the performance of, or promise to perform, an act that the person is already under a duty to perform, can constitute good consideration – needs to be considered under three headings: duties imposed by law; duties owed to a third party; duties owed under a contract with the same promisor.

3.3.4.1 Duties imposed by law

The position here is that, for reasons of public policy, a duty that you owe as a result of some public obligation, cannot constitute valid consideration. The police officer who agreed to make sure that a particular street was free from crime, in return for a promise of payment from a person living there, should not be able to enforce the promise. The potential for corruption is obvious. This applies generally to those who are under public duties. In *Collins v Godefroy,* one of the earliest authorities establishing this principle, was concerned with the payment of witnesses in a legal proceeding.

Collins v Godefroy (1831) 1 B & Ald 950; 120 ER 241

Facts: Collins (an attorney) was subpoenaed to attend a trial as a witness for Godefroy. Collins did so for six days, but was not called. He claimed his 'usual' fee of six guineas as compensation for his lost time.

Held: Collins had not provided any valid consideration for a promise to pay him.

Lord Tenterden CJ:
'Assuming that the offer to pay the six guineas without costs was evidence of an express promise by the defendant to pay that sum to the plaintiff as a compensation to him for his loss of time, still, if the defendant was not bound by law to pay that sum, the offer to do so, not having been accepted, will not avail the plaintiff. If it be a duty imposed by law upon a party regularly subpoenaed, to attend from time to time to give his evidence, then a promise to give him any remuneration for loss of time incurred in such attendance is a promise without consideration. We think that such a duty is imposed by law; and on consideration of the Statute of Elizabeth, and of the cases which have been decided on this subject, we are all of opinion that a party cannot maintain an action for compensation for loss of time in attending a trial as a witness.

We are aware of the practice which has prevailed in certain cases, of allowing, as costs between party and party, so much per day for attendance of professional men; but that practice cannot alter the law. What the effect of our decision may be, is not for our consideration. We think, on principle that an action does not lie for a compensation to a witness for loss of time in attendance under a subpoena.

The Statute of Elizabeth referred to – 5 Eliz c 9, s 12 – allowed for the payment of reasonable costs to witnesses – for example, in relation to travel – but not compensation for lost time.

Lord Denning suggested in two cases – *Ward v Byham* [1956] 2 All ER 318 and *Williams v Williams* [1957] 1 All ER 305 – that it should be good consideration to perform a duty imposed by law, provided that there was no conflict with the public interest. The duties in question were, respectively, that of a mother to look after her illegitimate child, and of a wife who had left her husband to support herself. The other members of the court in each case managed to reach a decision without using this principle. The question whether such duties can be good consideration remains open. What is clear, however, is that doing more than is required by the duty imposed by law can constitute good consideration, as is shown by the next case.

Glasbrook v Glamorgan County Council [1925] AC 270 (HL)

Facts: During a miners' strike, the police were obliged to ensure that workers who had the responsibility of keeping the mines safe and in good repair were not prevented from doing so. The police felt that this could be achieved with a mobile force, but the mine owners insisted that officers should be billeted on the premises. They agreed to pay the additional costs of this, but subsequently refused to do so, relying on the fact that the police were doing no more than their public duty. The council succeeded at trial and in the Court of Appeal. The owners appealed to the House of Lords.

Held: By providing the force billeted on the premises, the police had exceeded their public duty, and were entitled to recover for the additional costs.

Viscount Finlay:

'My Lords, the appellants are the owners of collieries on the Garngoch Common in the county of Glamorgan. In 1921 there was a national coal strike which began on April 1 and lasted till July 4, at which date work was generally resumed. The men at the appellants' collieries were, however, dissatisfied with the terms of settlement and refused to resume work. In these collieries over 1,000 men had been employed, and they remained idle until September 4, 1921. The "safety men", as they are called, who were engaged in working the pumps on which the preservation of the mine from flooding depended, remained at work. If the working of the pumps had been stopped the mine in the course of a few days would have been most seriously damaged by the accumulation of water. The strikers endeavoured to get these "safety men" to join in the strike, the effect of which would have been that in three or four days the mine would have been drowned out. Under these circumstances the agent of the owners, Mr Alfred James, went to the Gowerton Police Station to arrange with the superintendent, Colonel Smith, for police protection. He asked that an adequate force of police should be billeted in the houses in the immediate vicinity of the collieries. Colonel Smith thought that protection would be best afforded by a flying column moving from point to point as required, but Mr Alfred James insisted that a "garrison" near the mines should be provided, and Colonel Smith acquiesced. Mr James in his evidence described what ensued as follows:

Q. Did he then tell you something about a form?

A. Yes.

Q. What did he say exactly about the form?

A. As near as I remember he said: "You will of course have to sign a form of requisition". I said: "Yes – that is the usual procedure in matters of this description" – and he told me it was, so I said: "All right, I will sign the form".

The form was accordingly signed. It is headed: "Form of Requisition for Special Services of Police". It stated that certain men, seventy in all, were required for special duty at the Garngoch and Cape Collieries on the occasion of a strike from 6 p.m. on July 9. The form concluded "I hereby guarantee payment on the conditions specified in Clause 'C' in the Second Schedule to this form".

This was signed by Mr James and addressed to the chief constable. The schedule stated the terms as to payment, accommodation and food.

The seventy men arrived on the evening of the same day. The safety men remained at work, and it was admitted at the trial that police protection in some shape or form was required. No pressure was put upon Mr James to sign the requisition; as his evidence shows, he was prepared to sign it and he knew that it was usual in such cases.

The action in this case was brought to recover the amount due on the terms of the requisition.

The colliery owners repudiated liability on the grounds that there was no consideration for the promise to pay for the police protection and that such an agreement was against public policy. . . .

It appears to me that there is nothing in the first point made for the colliery owners that there was no consideration for the promise. It is clear that there was abundant consideration. The police authorities thought that it would be best to give protection by means of a flying column of police, but the colliery owners wanted the "garrison" and promised to pay for it if it was sent . . .'

Viscount Cave LC:

'. . . I conclude, therefore, that the practice of lending constables for special duty in consideration of payment is not illegal or against public policy; and I pass to the second question – namely, whether in this particular case the lending of the seventy constables to be billeted in the appellants' colliery was a legitimate application of the principle. In this connection I think it important to bear in mind exactly what it was that the learned trial judge had to decide. It was no part of his duty to say – nor did he purport to say – whether in his judgment the billeting of the seventy men at the colliery was necessary for the prevention of violence or the protection of the mines from criminal injury. The duty of determining such questions is cast by law, not upon the courts after the event, but upon the police authorities at the time when the decision has to be taken; and a court which attempted to review such a decision from the point of view of its wisdom or prudence would (I think) be exceeding its proper functions. The question for the court was whether on July 9, 1921, the police authorities, acting reasonably and in good faith, considered a police garrison at the colliery necessary for the protection of life and property from violence, or, in other words, whether the decision of the chief constable in refusing special protection unless paid for was such a decision as a man in his position and with his duties could reasonably take. If in the judgment of the police authorities, formed reasonably and in good faith, the garrison was necessary for the protection of life and property, then they were not entitled to make a charge for it, for that would be to exact payment for the performance of a duty which they clearly owed to the appellants and their servants; but if they thought the garrison a superfluity and only acceded to Mr James' request with a view to meeting his wishes, then in my opinion they were entitled to treat the garrison duty as a special duty and to charge for it. Now, upon this point the Divisional Superintendent Colonel Smith, who was a highly experienced officer, gave specific and detailed evidence; and the learned judge having seen him in the witness box and heard his examination and cross-examination accepted his evidence upon the point, as the following extract from the judgment shows:

> Colonel Smith says that if the matter had been left entirely to him without this requisition, he would have protected this colliery, and he would have protected it amply, but in quite a different way, and I accept his evidence that that is so. He would not have sent his garrison there, and in my judgment, while not desiring for a moment to suggest that it was not the bounden duty of the county council to protect this colliery, and not for one moment suggesting that the performing of a legal duty will support a promise to pay, I have come to the conclusion that when a colliery company or an individual requisitions police protection of a special character for a particular purpose, he must pay for it, and he must pay for it whether he makes a contract to pay or whether he does not – a promise to pay would be implied under those circumstances. In this case, of course, there is an express promise, and in my judgment this promise is not without consideration and must be fulfilled.

Upon this point Sir John Simon in his powerful argument for the appellants contended that the true inference to be drawn from the evidence was that the police authority, having a discretion to elect between protecting the collieries (which admittedly required protection in some form) by means of the "mobile body" to which Colonel Smith referred or by means of a garrison, chose the latter alternative in consideration of payment, and that they could not so (as he put it) "sell their discretion". Upon the evidence, I do not think that they did anything of the kind. Colonel Smith said clearly that the police garrison was no part of his scheme of protection and did not help him in his scheme at all; that he had an ample force by which to protect the collieries from outside and was well able to cope with the situation. It does not appear that the provision of the garrison, who were brought in from distant parts of the county, relieved the force on the spot from any of their duties, or that the local force was reduced in consequence; and I think that the true inference is that the garrison formed an additional and not a substituted or alternative means of protection.'

Lord Shaw concurred; Lord Carson and Lord Blanesburgh dissented.

The position as regards the police is now governed in part by statute:

POLICE ACT 1996

s 25 Provision of special services
(1) The chief officer of police of a police force may provide, at the request of any person, special police services at any premises or in any locality in the police area for which the force is maintained, subject to the payment to the police authority of charges on such scales as may be determined by that authority.

This seems to have the effect that a police force can now receive payment for doing no more than fulfilling its public obligation to 'keep the peace', at least where it is called on to provide a police presence at sporting events or entertainment events. This was confirmed by *Harris v Sheffield Utd FC* [1987] 2 All ER 838 in relation to football matches.

The more general point remains as decided in *Glasbrook v Glamorgan CC*, that is that it is only possible to have an enforceable contract in relation to the performance of public duties, where the performance exceeds the obligation imposed by the law.

3.3.4.2 Existing contractual duty owed to a third party

In contrast to the previous situation, here the courts have had no trouble in finding that the performance, or promise to perform, an obligation under a contract with a third party, can be good consideration. The issue was considered in *Shadwell v Shadwell*.

Shadwell v Shadwell (1860) 9 CB(NS) 159 (Court of Common Bench)

Facts: The plaintiff's uncle had promised, in consideration of the plaintiff marrying one Ellen Nicholl, to pay him £150 a year, until the plaintiff's income exceeded 600 guineas per annum. The plaintiff was at the time seeking a career at the Bar, but later abandoned this. Twelve payments were made, and the uncle then died. The plaintiff sought to enforce the uncle's promise against his uncle's estate. The defence argued that the plaintiff had provided no consideration, because he was already legally obliged to marry Ellen Nicholl (in that she would have been able to sue him for breach of promise of marriage, if he backed out).

Held: The marriage was good consideration for the uncle's promise, which was therefore enforceable.

Erle CJ:

'The question raised by the demurrer to the replication to the fourth plea is, whether there is a consideration which will support the action on the promise to pay the annuity of £150 per annum. . . .

Now, do [the] facts show that the promise was in consideration either of a loss to be sustained by the plaintiff or a benefit to be derived from the plaintiff to the uncle, at his, the uncle's, request? My answer is in the affirmative.

First, do these facts show a loss sustained by the plaintiff at his uncle's request? When I answer this in the affirmative, I am aware that a man's marriage with the woman of his choice is in one sense a boon, and in that sense the reverse of a loss: yet, as between the plaintiff and the party promising to supply an income to support the marriage, it may well be also a loss. The plaintiff may have made a most material change in his position, and induced the object of his affection to do the same, and may have incurred pecuniary liabilities resulting in embarrassments which would be in every sense a loss if the income which had been promised should be withheld; and, if the promise was made in order to induce the parties to marry, the promise so made would be in legal effect a request to marry.

Secondly, do these facts show a benefit derived from the plaintiff to the uncle, at his request? In answering again in the affirmative, I am at liberty to consider the relation in which the parties stood and the interest in the settlement of his nephew which the uncle declares. The marriage primarily affects the parties thereto; but in a secondary degree it may be an object of interest to a near relative, and in that sense a benefit to him. This benefit is also derived from the plaintiff at the uncle's request. If the promise of the annuity was intended as an inducement to the marriage, and the averment that the plaintiff, relying on the promise, married, is an averment that the promise was one inducement to the marriage, this is the consideration averred in the declaration; and it appears to me to be expressed in the letter, construed with the surrounding circumstances.

The second demurrer raises the question whether the plaintiff's continuance at the bar was made a condition precedent to the right of the annuity. I think not. The uncle promises to continue the annuity until the professional income exceeds the sum men-tioned. I find no stipulation that the annuity shall cease if professional diligence ceases – no limitation except a defeasance in case of an amount of income from the other source. If the prospect of success at the bar had failed, a continuance to attend the courts might be an unreasonable expense. My judgment on this demurrer is also for the plaintiff.

The above is the judgment of my Brother Keating and myself.'

Byles J dissented.

It should be noted that the action for breach of promise of marriage was abolished by the Law Reform (Miscellaneous Provisions) Act 1970, so that the issue discussed in *Shadwell v Shadwell* could not now arise in the same way. The principle it set out has, however, been applied in other contexts, including commercial agreements – as shown by *Scotson v Pegg*.

Scotson v Pegg (1861) 6 H&N 295 (Court of Exchequer)

Facts: The plaintiff was contractually bound to a third party to deliver coal to the defendant. The defendant promised to unload it a particular rate – but then failed to do so. The plaintiff sued. The defendant argued that the only alleged consideration for its promise to unload was the plaintiff's delivery of the coal, and this could not be valid because it was an obligation already owed to a third party.

Held: The plaintiff's delivery of the coal was good consideration for the defendant's promise.

Martin B:

'I am of opinion that the plea is bad, both on principle and in law. It is bad in law because the ordinary rule is, that any act done whereby the contracting party receives a benefit is a good consideration for a promise by him. Here the benefit is the delivery of the coals to the defendant. It is consistent with the declaration that there may have been some dispute as to the defendant's right to have the coals, or it may be that the plaintiffs detained them for demurrage; in either case there would be good consider-ation that the plaintiffs, who were in possession of the coals, would allow the defend-ant to take them out of the ship. Then is it any answer that the plaintiffs had entered into a prior contract with other persons to deliver the coals to their order upon the same terms, and that the defendant was a stranger to that contract? In my opinion it is not. We must deal with this case as if no prior contract had been entered into. Suppose the plaintiffs had no chance of getting their money from the other persons who might perhaps have become bankrupt. The defendant gets a benefit by the delivery of the coals to him, and it is immaterial that the plaintiffs had previously contracted with third parties to deliver to their order.'

Wilde B:

'I am also of opinion that the plaintiffs are entitled to judgment. The plaintiffs say, that in consideration that they would deliver to the defendant a cargo of coals from their ship, the defendant promised to discharge the cargo in a certain way. The defendant, in answer, says "You made a previous contract with other persons that they should discharge the cargo in the same way, and therefore there is no consideration for my promise." But why is there no consideration? It is said, because the plaintiffs, in delivering the coals are only performing that which they were already bound to do. But to say that there is no consideration is to say that it is not possible for one man to have an interest in the performance of a contract made by another. But if a person chooses to promise to pay a sum of money in order to induce another to perform that which he has already contracted with a third person to do, I confess I cannot see why such a promise should not be binding. Here the defendant, who was a stranger to the original contract, induced the plaintiffs to part with the cargo, which they might not otherwise have been willing to do, and the delivery of it to the defendant was a benefit to him. I accede to the proposition that if a person contracts with another to do a certain thing, he cannot make the performance of it a consideration for a new promise to the same individual. But there is no authority for the proposition that where there has been a promise to one person to do a certain thing, it is not possible to make a valid promise to another to do the same thing. Therefore, deciding this matter on principle, it is plain to my mind that the delivery of the coals to the defendant was a good consideration for his promise, although the plaintiffs had made a previous contract to deliver them to the order of other persons.'

This principle has been applied more recently in *New Zealand Shipping Co Ltd v Satterthwaite (The Eurymedon)* [1975] AC 154, which is discussed in Chapter 5, p 308. In *Pao On v Lau Yiu Long* [1980] AC 614 the Privy Council suggested that a *promise* to perform an obligation owed to a third party could be good consideration, as well as actual performance. This seems to be in line with the general approach to consideration, which recognises promises as sufficient, in addition to actions.

3.3.4.3 Existing duty to same promisor

The likely scenario for this issue to arise is that A and B have a contract, and B is having difficulty in performing, or in performing on time. What is the situation if A offers B an additional inducement, probably in the form of extra payment, to complete the contract, or to complete it on time? Is the promise of the inducement enforceable? Has B provided any consideration for it? The general answer given by the classical law of contract is 'no, there is no consideration, and the promise is not enforceable'. This is generally said to derive from the early nineteenth century case of *Stilk v Myrick*.

Stilk v Myrick (1809) 2 Camp 317; 170 ER 1168

Facts: The plaintiff had been engaged as part of the crew of a ship, to be paid at £5 a month for a particular voyage. In the course of the voyage two of the crew deserted, and the captain was unable to replace them. At Cronstadt, he entered into an agreement with the rest of the crew, that they should have the wages of the two who had deserted equally divided among them. The ship was worked back to London by the plaintiff and eight more of the original crew, with whom the agreement had been made at Cronstadt. On their return, the ship owners refused to pay the additional wages.

Held: The promise to pay the additional money was not enforceable, because there was no consideration for it.

Lord Ellenborough:

'I think *Harris v Watson* (1791) Peake 102 was rightly decided; but I doubt whether ground of public policy, upon which Lord Kenyon is stated to have proceeded, be the true principle on which the decision is to be supported. Here, I say, the agreement is void for want of consideration. There was no consideration for the ulterior pay promised to the mariners who remained with the ship. Before they sailed from London they had undertaken to do all that they could under all the emergencies of the voyage. They had sold all their services till the voyage should be completed. If they had been at liberty to quit the vessel at Cronstadt, the case would have been quite different; or if the captain had capriciously discharged the two men who were wanting, the others might not have been compellable to take the whole duty on themselves, and their agreeing to do so might have been a sufficient consideration for the promise of an advance of wages. But the desertion of a part of the crew is to be considered an emergency of the voyage as much as their death; and those who remain are bound by the terms of their original contract to exert themselves to the utmost to bring the ship in safety to her destined port. Therefore, without looking to the policy of this agreement, I think it is void for want of consideration, and that the plaintiff can only recover at the rate of £5 a month.'

The principle set out by Lord Ellenborough has been widely accepted as stating the correct approach to be applied, but in fact the case is not uncontroversial. The reference to *Harris v Watson* at the start of his judgment is to a case where a similar situation was dealt with on the basis of 'public policy' – that is, the risk of a crew in this situation 'blackmailing' the captain. This approach is given much more prominence in the other report of this case, by Espinasse (6 Esp 129; 170 ER 851), who was in fact one of the counsel for the plaintiff. This difference has led to much academic comment – just two examples are given here. The first is taken from a lengthy examination of the reasons for, and implications of, the difference between the two reports of the case.

Luther, P, *Campbell, Espinasse and the sailors: text and comment in the common law* **(1999) 19** *Legal Studies* **525, pp 525–528, 550–551**

1 INTRODUCTION

This article scarcely needs any introduction, for it relates to a case which will be familiar to every student of the law of contract: *Stilk v Myrick*. This case raises the question whether a plaintiff who has contracted to perform certain tasks in return for payment can enforce a subsequent promise by the defendant to pay him a higher sum in return for his contractual duties. Stilk was a merchant seaman, who had signed articles to sail to the Baltic and back for £5 a month. Two of his fellow seamen deserted, and the master of the ship (the defendant Myrick or Meyrick), having failed to find replacements at Cronstadt, promised the remaining nine crew-members that he would divide the deserters' wages among them if they would work the ship home. They did so, and on their return Stilk sued to recover his wages under the articles and the bonus he had been promised. Counsel for the defendant referred to the earlier case of *Harris v Watson*, in which Lord Kenyon had refused to enforce a promise of extra pay made by the master of a ship during a storm, on the ground that to do so might lead to sailors coercing their masters by making extravagant demands for extra wages. Lord Kenyon's judgment will be examined in more detail below. Counsel for the plaintiff (the Attorney General Sir Vicary Gibbs, with the law reporter Espinasse as his junior) replied that Myrick, unlike the master in *Harris v Watson*, had made his offer 'in perfect security', not in the face of danger, emergency or coercion. Lord Ellenborough held that Stilk could only recover at the rate of £5 per month. This is where the problems with the case start: the two published reports of the case, in Campbell's and Espinasse's *Reports*, differ; it appears that no other accounts of the case have survived against which these reports might be checked. Despite the familiarity of the material, it is convenient to quote the two versions of the judgment in full, as this article will include a close examination of each. Here is Campbell's version:

[This is reproduced above, at p 156]

This is what Espinasse says:

'Lord Ellenborough ruled, That the plaintiff could not recover this part of his demand. His Lordship said, That he recognised the principle of the case of *Harris v Watson* as founded on just and proper policy. When the defendant [*sic*: it should be "plaintiff"] entered on board the ship, he stipulated to do all the work his situation called upon him to do. Here the voyage was to the Baltick and back, not to Cronstadt only; if the voyage had then terminated, the sailors might have made what terms they pleased. If any part of the crew had died, would not the remainder have been forced to work the ship home? If that accident would have left them liable to do the whole work without any extraordinary remuneration, why should not desertion or casualty equally demand it?'

The orthodox view here is that Espinasse's report is based on considerations of public policy, and that this policy is, in essence, that articulated by Lord Kenyon in *Harris v Watson*: the need to prevent sailors from coercing masters into promising extra pay. Campbell's report, again on the orthodox view, is simply about the doctrine of consideration (and thus capable of general application outside the specific context of sailors' wages). As every law student knows, it is Campbell's version of the judgment – despite frequent criticism of its application – that has, at least until recent times, been generally accepted (even to the extent that his spelling of the master's name, Myrick, has been preferred to Espinasse's Meyrick; the writer has swum with the tide here, though on this point, if no other, one might expect that the opinion of counsel with the papers of the case in front of him would carry more weight than that of an observer). This article looks at some of the questions raised by the case, including the question of how two different reports of a case might come to be written, and the related questions of how one report of a case might come to be preferred, and of how much reliance can be placed upon the words that a reporter has used. Much of the comment on *Stilk v Myrick* has been inclined to be superficial, tending towards statements that 'X is the more reliable reporter', or that 'X's report is right' (and, as noted earlier, for the most part X = Campbell). This article suggests, both in general terms and with specific reference to *Stilk v Myrick*, that the textual problems of reports of the nineteenth century and earlier are more complicated than such comments suggest. It also looks at the policy considerations involving merchant seamen in the eighteenth and nineteenth centuries, and suggests that the avoidance of coercion – while it was undoubtedly a factor when courts considered issues of public policy – was only one strand in an elaborate web of policy considerations surrounding sailors and maritime trade. These issues remain important, despite the fact that *Stilk v Myrick* is almost two centuries old, as can be seen from the reconsideration of the case by the Court of Appeal in *Williams v Roffey Bros & Nicholls*. Although this latter case is itself almost ten years old, the approach taken by the Court to *Stilk* has given rise to difficulties which have yet to be resolved.

. . .

5 CONCLUSION

This article is not intended to be a discussion of the desirability of maintaining the perceived principle of *Stilk v Myrick*. It has merely attempted to show that there are complicating factors, surrounding both the text and context of the case, which modern judges and commentators have tended to ignore. Recent cases – and *Williams v Roffey* is the prime example here – take an over-simplified view of it. As noted earlier, the textual problems (Espinasse v Campbell) are altogether ignored in *Williams v Roffey*, though they are addressed in some earlier cases: see the comment of Mocatta J in *North Ocean Shipping Co Ltd v Hyundai Construction Co Ltd (The 'Atlantic Baron')*, that 'Campbell's reports have the better reputation', or the rather fuller analysis of Lord Scarman in *Pao On v Lau Liu Long*. The Court of Appeal in *Williams v Roffey does* consider the context of the earlier cases, and *is* prepared to admit that the decisions were driven by public policy, but sees this policy as no more than the need to avoid coercion. This is most obvious in the judgment of Purchas LJ:

'The two cases, *Harris v Watson* . . . and *Stilk v Myrick* . . . involved circumstances of a very special nature, namely the extraordinary conditions existing at the turn of the 18th century under which seamen had to serve their contracts of employment on the high seas. There were strong public policy grounds at that time to protect the master and owners of a ship from being held to ransom by disaffected crews.'

Such an analysis has been enthusiastically adopted by commentators. Adams and Brownsword, for example, state that '[t]he better answer . . . must be that *Stilk v Myrick* was a case involving what would nowadays be recognised as economic duress'. Halson similarly sees the sailors' cases as 'a rare articulation of the policy consideration underpinning the law in the area of contractual modifications; the non-enforcement of extorted modifications and the enforcement of freely agreed alterations'.

This approach renders the decision in *Williams v Roffey* open to attack. McKendrick points out that there is 'no evidence that Stilk applied any pressure on the master'. Nor, one might add, is there any evidence that the claimant in *Harris v Watson* applied pressure, and nor did Lord Kenyon say that he had. McKendrick also suggests that if the Court of Appeal in *Williams v Roffey* wished to turn *Stilk v Myrick* into a duress case, they could have done so more easily by relying on Espinasse's report and on *Harris v Watson*. This is true, but it would still have been an over-simple view of the case. Espinasse's report of *Stilk v Myrick* was not solely about duress, though this may well be one strand that runs through it, any more than Campbell's was solely about consideration.

As suggested in the fourth section of this article, *Stilk v Myrick* is a case which must be read in the context of the mass of policy concerns which led the courts, throughout the eighteenth century and into the nineteenth century, to treat merchant seamen as in almost every respect different from other workers. It is also a case, as suggested in the second and third sections, in which we need to be aware of the complexity of the issues which surround the very text. It is not enough to look at the two reports and choose one as 'right', or to look at the two reporters and choose one as 'more reliable'. This is true whether or not the view advanced here, that the difference between the texts may be more apparent than real, is accepted. This article may seem like a perverse attempt to muddy the waters at just the time when we had started to see *Stilk v Myrick* more clearly, but it is only by taking a broader view, both of the text of the case and of its context, that the problems it poses will be resolved.

The next extract considers why it is that *Stilk v Myrick,* and in particular the version of the case to be found in the Campbell report, became a leading authority in the common law of contract.

Grant Gilmore, *The Death of Contract,* 1974, Columbus: Ohio State University Press, pp 24–30

In *Stilk v Myrick* it appeared that two seamen had deserted a ship which was engaged on a Russian voyage. The master was unable to replace the deserters at Cronstadt where the ship had made port. Under these circumstances the master offered to divide the wages of the two deserters among the remaining members of the crew if they had to work the ship back to London shorthanded (as in fact they did). The owners having refused to pay the additional wages, plaintiff (one of the members of the crew) brought suit on the Cronstadt agreement. It was held by Lord Ellenborough that the action did not lie; the plaintiff and his fellows were entitled only to the wages they had originally signed on for.

Now, what is the principle or 'rule' which the case is supposed to illustrate? According to Williston:

Where A and B have entered into a bilateral agreement, it not infrequently happens that one of the parties, becoming dissatisfied with the contract, refuses to perform or to continue performance unless a larger compensation than that provided in the original agreement is promised him. . . . On principle the second agreement [i.e. the Cronstadt agreement on the *Stilk v Myrick facts*] is invalid for the performance by the recalcitrant contractor is no legal detriment to him whether actually given or promised, since, at the time the second agreement was entered into, he was already bound to do the work; nor is the performance under the second agreement a legal benefit to the promisor since he was already entitled to have the work done. In such situations and others identical in principle, the great weight of authority supports this conclusion.

There are of course many cases, old and new, of the type Professor Williston was hypothesizing. Was *Stilk v Myrick* one of them? It seems unlikely that a neutral observer, not yet corrupted by the study of law, would jump to that conclusion. Professor Williston's case is one in which 'one of the parties, becoming dissatisfied with the contract, refuses to perform or to continue performance' unless he is paid more than he had originally agreed to do the work for. We are not told that any of the complaining seamen refused to go forward with the voyage unless they received the wages of the two deserters. It is of course possible that in real life they did refuse to go forward unless the deserters were replaced (or their wages distributed). Counsel, however, did not even attempt to argue that the master had been coerced or threatened. All we can gather from the reports of the case is that the master, having found it impossible to recruit two new hands, voluntarily offered to distribute the wages among the remaining members of the crew.

Williston's hypothetical also assumes that the 'dissatisfied' party insists on the greater pay for doing the same work he had originally agreed to do for less. It is clear enough that the seamen in *Stilk v Myrick* were doing more work on the return voyage than they had agreed to do—their own work plus the work of the two deserters. There is a doctrine of maritime law under which the members of the crew are required to exert extraordinary efforts, indeed to venture their lives, to rescue the ship from an emergency. Lord Ellenborough seems to have assumed that, under this doctrine, the seamen were required to work the ship short-handed for their original wages. To know whether his assumption was correct, we would have to know a great deal more than we are told about the circumstances of the 'desertions', about the state of the labor market in Cronstadt and about the dangers of a return voyage with less than a full crew. We do know that the ship was safe in port at Cronstadt; it was not in imminent peril from the sea. If the ambiguities in the factual situation were resolved in favor of the crew, it is quite possible that, under maritime law, they would have been justified in quitting the service of the ship at Cronstadt rather than work it back to London short-handed. Counsel for the plaintiff made no attempt to investigate these questions. Lord Ellenborough may have been right or counsel, representing impecunious seamen with fairly small claims, may not have been as aggressive and ingenious in behalf of their clients as they should have been.

Stilk v Myrick can hardly be described as a case in which a dissatisfied party insists on more pay for doing the same work. The next point is that Williston supports his statement of the principle quoted above with a long string citation of cases ('the great weight of authority') which begins: '*Harris v Watson, Peake*, 72; *Stilk v Myrick*, 2 Camp. 371. . . .' Williston goes on to cite dozens of cases, English and American, in support of his statement (a few cases, illustrating a 'contrary view' which has prevailed 'in a few jurisdictions' are collected in a separate footnote). However, from the form and style of the citation it is clear that the two English cases are given as the 'root authority'—the 'leading cases.'

Harris v Watson, which had been decided almost twenty years before *Stilk v Myrick*, was another case in which seamen were attempting to collect extra wages which had been promised them by the master. Unlike *Stilk v Myrick*, however, *Harris v Watson* was a classical illustration of the maritime law doctrine which has been referred to. It was proved, according to the statement of the case, that, 'the ship being in danger', the master 'to induce the seamen to exert themselves', promised each of them an extra five guineas over and above their regular wages. Lord Kenyon briefly remarked:

> If this action was to be supported, it would materially affect the navigation of this kingdom.. . . [The] rule [of maritime law] was founded on a principle of policy, for if sailors were in all events to have their wages, and in times of danger were entitled to insist on an extra charge on such a promise as this, they would in many cases suffer a ship to sink, unless the captain would pay any extravagant demand they might think proper to make.

Harris v Watson, it appears, was decided entirely on the rule and 'policy' of the maritime law, with the realistic comment thrown in that the contrary decision would 'materially affect the navigation of this kingdom'.

Harris v Watson was, naturally, the principal authority relied on by counsel for the owners in *Stilk v Myrick*. Counsel for the plaintiff suggested the obvious distinction that the Cronstadt agreement had been made while the ship was in port and 'was not made from the apprehension of danger, nor extorted from the captain; but a voluntary offer on his part for extraordinary service'. Lord Ellenborough, however, was not persuaded and chose to follow *Harris v Watson*.

At this point our understanding of *Stilk v Myrick* becomes entangled in the vagaries of early nineteenth century English case-reporting. According to the report in Espinasse, Lord Ellenborough said that 'he recognized the principle of the case of *Harris v Watson* as founded on just and proper policy', noted that the *Stilk v Myrick* seamen had signed on for the round trip voyage to the Baltic and back, not merely for the voyage to Cronstadt, and concluded that he could see no difference in principle between the two cases. If that was a correct report, there was no more thought given in *Stilk v Myrick* to contract and consideration theory than there had been in *Harris v Watson*; it was a pure 'policy' decision based on the maritime law. However, Lord Ellenborough is quoted quite differently in the Campbell report. There he is made to say:

I think *Harris v Watson* was rightly decided; but I doubt whether the ground of public policy, upon which Lord Kenyon is stated to have proceeded, be the true principle on which the decision is to be supported. Here, I say, the agreement is void for want of consideration.

After noting that the 'mariners' in *Stilk v Myrick* had signed on for the round trip voyage and giving as his opinion that they would not, under the circumstances of the case, have been 'at liberty to quit the vessel at Cronstadt', he concluded:

Therefore, without looking to the policy of this agreement, I think it is void for want of consideration . . . .

What are we to make of the discrepancy in the two reports? I have been told by English colleagues that Espinasse is not held in high regard as a reporter. And it does seem unlikely that Campbell would have made up out of whole cloth the remarks about consideration which he attributes to Lord Ellenborough. If we assume that Campbell was being reasonably accurate, what explanation can there be for Lord Ellenborough's switch from the 'public policy' ground on which *Harris v Watson* had been decided to 'want of consideration'? It is of course true that *Stilk v Myrick* was decided at a time when the reaction against Lord Mansfield's attempt to uproot consideration theory had already set in. 'Want of consideration' as a ground for invalidating a purported contract is a phrase that would have come more readily to the mind of an English judge in 1809 (*Stilk v Myrick*) than in 1791 (*Harris v Watson*). It is also within the bounds of fair comment to suggest that the maritime law rule, which clearly applied to *Harris v Watson* was, at best, of doubtful applicability on the *Stilk v Myrick* facts. As a good common lawyer, Lord Ellenborough may have felt more comfortable with the broader ground for decision, which of course made it unnecessary for him to deal seriously with the distinction argued by counsel.

After this lengthy digression we are in a position to return to the manner in which the case of *Stilk v Myrick* was transmuted into the 'rule of *Stilk v Myrick*'. It was done, of course, by lumping two unlike cases together without stating the facts of either case. Of the two reports of *Stilk v Myrick* Williston cited only the Campbell report. No mention was made of the facts that there is no conceivable way in which *Harris v Watson* can be taken to have been decided on consideration theory (the 'rule') or that there is considerable doubt as to the theory on which *Stilk v Myrick* was decided. Such is the progress of jurisprudence.

I have gone into tedious detail about *Stilk v Myrick* because I think that the devious process by which the 'cases' became the 'rules' of the general theory of contract can be understood only microscopically. We need not concern ourselves with whether the process involved deliberate deception or merely unconscious distortion on the part of the theory-builders. What is clear is that some funny things happened on the way from case report to treatise.

Despite these issues relating to the true basis for the decision in *Stilk v Myrick,* until 1991 there was no English case which seriously questioned the principle for which it was generally accepted to be authority – that is, that a person making a promise to an existing party to the contract, was not bound by that promise, unless the promisee went beyond his or her existing obligations. The fact that exceeding your existing contractual obligations could amount to consideration for a promise of extra payment, for example, was confirmed by *Hartley v Ponsonby* (1857) 7 E & B 872 – a case with very similar facts to *Stilk v Myrick,* but where the level of desertion was to a level which rendered the voyage unsafe. In these circumstances a promise of additional wages for continuing to work the ship was held to be enforceable. As with public duties, therefore, doing more than you are obliged to do will constitute consideration.

In 1991, however, a decision was handed down by the Court of Appeal, which involved a more significant reconsideration of the scope of *Stilk v Myrick*.

Williams v Roffey Bros & Nicholls (Contractors) Ltd [1990] 1 All ER 512 (CA)

Facts: The defendant building contractors engaged the plaintiff to carry out the carpentry work in the refurbishment of 27 flats, at a price of £20,000. When about half the work had been done, it became clear that the plaintiff was in financial difficulties, partly because he had under-quoted for the work. The defendants were concerned that delay would lay them open to a penalty clause in their contract with the developer. They offered the plaintiff extra money at the rate of £575 per completed flat. 8 flats were completed, but the defendant only paid £1,500. The plaintiff then ceased work. The job was completed by other carpenters and the defendant had to pay a time penalty. The plaintiff sought payment of £575 for each flat completed. The defendant resisted on the basis that there was no consideration for the promise of extra payment.

Held: There was a 'practical benefit' for the defendant in the new arrangement for payment, and this was sufficient to constitute consideration for the promise of additional payment.

Glidewell LJ (giving the first judgment at the invitation of Purchas LJ):
'This is an appeal against the decision of Mr Rupert Jackson QC sitting as an assistant recorder given on 31 January 1989 in the Kingston-upon-Thames County Court, entering judgment for the plaintiff for £3,500 damages with £1,400 interest and costs and dismissing the defendants' counterclaim.

The facts
The plaintiff is a carpenter. The defendants are building contractors who in September 1985 had entered into a contract with Shepherd's Bush Housing Association Ltd to refurbish a block of flats called Twynholm Mansions, Lillie Road, London SW6. The defendants were the main contractors for the works. There are 28 flats in Twynholm Mansions, but the work of refurbishment was to be carried out in 27 of the flats.

The defendants engaged the plaintiff to carry out the carpentry work in the refurbishment of the 27 flats, including work to the structure of the roof. Originally, the plaintiff was engaged on three separate sub-contracts, but these were all superseded by a sub-contract in writing made on 21 January 1986 by which the plaintiff undertook to provide the labour for the carpentry work to the roof of the block and for the first and second fix carpentry work required in each of the 27 flats for a total price of £20,000. The judge found that, though there was no express term providing for payment to be made in stages, the contract of 21 January 1986 was subject to an implied term that the defendants would make interim payments to the plaintiff, related to the amount of work done, at reasonable intervals.

The plaintiff and his men began work on 10 October 1985. The judge found that by 9 April 1986 the plaintiff had completed the work to the roof, had carried out the first fix to all 27 flats and had substantially completed the second fix to 9 flats. By this date the defendants had made interim payments totalling £16,200.

It is common ground that by the end of March 1986 the plaintiff was in financial difficulty. The judge found that there were two reasons for this, namely: (i) that the agreed price of £20,000 was too low to enable the plaintiff to operate satisfactorily and at a profit. Mr Cottrell, a surveyor employed by the defendants, said in evidence that a reasonable price for the works would have been £23,783; (ii) that the plaintiff failed to supervise his workmen adequately.

The defendants, as they made clear, were concerned lest the plaintiff did not complete the carpentry work on time. The main contract contained a penalty clause. The judge found that on 9 April 1986 the defendants promised to pay the plaintiff the further sum of £10,300, in addition to the £20,000, to be paid at the rate of £575 for each flat in which the carpentry work was completed.

The plaintiff and his men continued work on the flats until the end of May 1986. By that date the defendants, after their promise on 9 April 1986, had made only one further payment of £1,500. At the end of May the plaintiff ceased work on the flats. I will describe later the work which, according to the judge's findings, then remained to be done. Suffice it to say that the defendants engaged other carpenters to complete the work, but in the result incurred one week's time penalty in their contract with the building owners.

The action
The plaintiff commenced this action by specially endorsed writ on 10 March 1987 . . .

The judge's conclusions
The judge found that the defendants' promise to pay an additional £10,300, at the rate of £575 per completed flat, was part of an oral agreement made between the plaintiff and the defendants on 9 April 1986, by way of variation to the original contract.

The judge also found that before the plaintiff ceased work at the end of May 1986 the carpentry in 17 flats had been substantially (but not totally) completed. This means that between the making of the agreement on 9 April 1986 and the date when the plaintiff ceased work, eight further flats were substantially completed.

The judge calculated that this entitled the plaintiff to receive £4,600 (8 x £575) 'less some small deduction for defective and incomplete items'. He held that the plaintiff was also entitled to a reasonable proportion of the £2,200 which was outstanding from the original contract sum. (I believe this figure should be £2,300, but this makes no practical difference.) Adding these two amounts, he decided that the plaintiff was entitled to further payments totalling £5,000 against which he had only received £1,500, and that the defendants were therefore in breach of contract, entitling the plaintiff to cease work.

The issues
Before us counsel for the defendants advances two arguments. His principal submission is that the defendants' admitted promise to pay an additional £10,300, at the rate of £575 per completed flat, is unenforceable since there was no consideration for it. This issue was not raised in the defence, but we are told that the argument was advanced at the trial without objection, and that there was equally no objection to it being argued before us . . . .

Was there consideration for the defendants' promise made on 9 April 1986 to pay an additional price at the rate of £575 per completed flat?
The judge made the following findings of fact which are relevant on this issue. (i) The sub-contract price agreed was too low to enable the plaintiff to operate satisfactorily and at a profit. Mr Cottrell, the defendants' surveyor, agreed that this was so. (ii) Mr Roffey, the managing director of the defendants, was persuaded by Mr Cottrell that the defendants should pay a bonus to the plaintiff. The figure agreed at the meeting on 9 April 1986 was £10,300.

The judge quoted and accepted the evidence of Mr Cottrell to the effect that a main contractor who agrees too low a price with a sub-contractor is acting contrary to his own interests. He will never get the job finished without paying more money.

The judge therefore concluded:

> In my view where the original sub-contract price is too low, and the parties subsequently agree that the additional moneys shall be paid to the sub-contractor, this agreement is in the interests of both parties. This is what happened in the present case, and in my opinion the agreement of 9 April 1986 does not fail for lack of consideration.

In his address to us counsel for the defendants outlined the benefits to the defendants which arose from their agreement to pay the additional £10,300 as (i) seeking to ensure that the plaintiff continued work and did not stop in breach of the sub-contract, (ii) avoiding the penalty for delay and (iii) avoiding the trouble and expense of engaging other people to complete the carpentry work.

However, counsel submits that, though the defendants may have derived, or hoped to derive, practical benefits from their agreement to pay the "bonus", they derived no benefit in law, since the plaintiff was promising to do no more than he was already bound to do by his sub-contract, ie continue with the carpentry work and complete it on time. Thus there was no consideration for the agreement.

Counsel for the defendants relies on the principle of law which, traditionally, is based on the decision in *Stilk v Myrick* (1809) 2 Camp 317, 170 ER 1168 . . .

In *North Ocean Shipping Co Ltd v Hyundai Construction Co Ltd, The Atlantic Baron* [1978] 3 All ER 1170, [1979] QB 705 Mocatta J regarded the general principle of the decision in *Stilk v Myrick* as still being good law . . .

There is, however, another legal concept of relatively recent development which is relevant, namely that of economic duress. Clearly, if a sub-contractor has agreed to undertake work at a fixed price, and before he has completed the work declines to continue with it unless the contractor agrees to pay an increased price, the sub-contractor may be held guilty of securing the contractor's promise by taking unfair advantage of the difficulties he will cause if he does not complete the work. In such a case an agreement to pay an increased price may well be voidable because it was entered into under duress. Thus this concept may provide another answer in law to the question of policy which has troubled the courts since before *Stilk v Myrick* (1809) 2 Camp 317, 170 ER 1168, and no doubt led at the date of that decision to a rigid adherence to the doctrine of consideration.

This possible application of the concept of economic duress was referred to by Lord Scarman, delivering the judgment of the Judicial Committee of the Privy Council in *Pao On v Lau Yiu* [1979] 3 All ER 65 at 76, [1980] AC 614 at 632. He said:

> Their Lordships do not doubt that a promise to perform, or the performance of, a pre-existing contractual obligation to a third party can be valid consideration. In *New Zealand Shipping Co Ltd v A M Satterthwaite & Co Ltd* [1974] 1 All ER 1015 at 1021, [1975] AC 154 at 168 the rule and the reason for the rule were stated as follows: "An agreement to do an act which the promisor is under an

existing obligation to a third party to do, may quite well amount to valid consideration:. . . the promisee obtains the benefit of a direct obligation. . . This proposition is illustrated and supported by *Scotson v Pegg* (1861) 6 H & N 295, 158 ER 121 which their Lordships consider to be good law." Unless, therefore, the guarantee was void as having been made for an illegal consideration or voidable on the ground of economic duress, the extrinsic evidence establishes that it was supported by valid consideration . . . .

It is true that *Pao On v Lau Yiu* is a case of a tripartite relationship, ie a promise by A to perform a pre-existing contractual obligation owed to B, in return for a promise of payment by C. But Lord Scarman's words seem to me to be of general application, equally applicable to a promise made by one of the original two parties to a contract.

Accordingly . . . the present state of the law on this subject can be expressed in the following proposition: (i) if A has entered into a contract with B to do work for, or to supply goods or services to, B in return of payment by B and (ii) at some stage before A has completely performed his obligations under the contract B has reason to doubt whether A will, or will be able to, complete his side of the bargain and (iii) B thereupon promises A an additional payment in return for A's promise to perform his contractual obligations on time and (iv) as a result of giving his promise B obtains in practice a benefit, or obviates a disbenefit, and (v) B's promise is not given as a result of economic duress or fraud on the part of A, then (vi) the benefit to B is capable of being consideration for B's promise, so that the promise will be legally binding.

As I have said, counsel for the defendants accepts that in the present case by promising to pay the extra £10,300 the defendants secured benefits. There is no finding, and no suggestion, that in this case the promise was given as a result of fraud or duress.

If it be objected that the propositions above contravene the principle in *Stilk v Myrick,* I answer that in my view they do not: they refine and limit the application of that principle, but they leave the principle unscathed, eg where B secures no benefit by his promise. It is not in my view surprising that a principle enunciated in relation to the rigours of seafaring life during the Napoleonic wars should be subjected during the succeeding 180 years to a process of refinement and limitation in its application in the present day.

It is therefore my opinion that on his findings of fact in the present case, the judge was entitled to hold, as he did, that the defendants' promise to pay the extra £10,300 was supported by valuable consideration, and thus constituted an enforceable agreement . . . .'

Russell LJ:

'I agree with and have nothing to add to the judgment of Glidewell L.J. in so far as it relates to the defendants' submission that the plaintiff was not entitled to any part of the £10,300 because none of the eight flats had been completed . . . I have no doubt that the judge was right upon what Mr. Evans, on behalf of the defendants, referred to as his secondary point.

I find his primary argument relating to consideration much more difficult. . . . In the late 20th century I do not believe that the rigid approach to the concept of consideration to be found in *Stilk v Myrick* is either necessary or desirable. Consideration there must still be but, in my judgment, the courts nowadays should be more ready to find its existence so as to reflect the intention of the parties to the contract where the bargaining powers are not unequal and where the finding of consideration reflect the true intention of the parties.

What was the true intention of the parties when they arrived at the agreement pleaded by the defendants in paragraph 5 of the amended defence? The plaintiff had got into financial difficulties. The defendants, through their employee Mr. Cottrell, recognised the price that had been agreed originally with the plaintiff was less than what Mr. Cottrell himself regarded as a reasonable price. There was a desire on Mr. Cottrell's part to retain the services of the plaintiff so that the work could be completed without the need to employ another subcontractor. There was further a need to replace what had hitherto been a haphazard method of payment by a more formalised scheme involving the payment of a specified sum on the completion of each flat. These were all advantages accruing to the defendants which can fairly be said to have been in consideration of their undertaking to pay the additional £10,300. True it was that the plaintiff did not undertake to do any work additional to that which he had originally undertaken to do but the terms upon which he was to carry out the work were varied and, in my judgment, that variation was supported by consideration which a pragmatic approach to the true relationship between the parties readily demonstrates.

For my part I wish to make it plain that I do not base my judgment upon any reservation as to the correctness of the law long ago enunciated in *Stilk v Myrick*. A gratuitous promise, pure and simple, remains unenforceable unless given under seal. But where, as in this case, a party undertakes to make a payment because by so doing it will gain an advantage arising out of the continuing relationship with the promisee the new bargain will not fail for want of consideration. As I read the judgment of the assistant recorder this was his true ratio upon that part of the case wherein the absence of consideration was raised in argument. For the reasons that I have endeavoured to outline, I think that the assistant recorder came to a correct conclusion and I too would dismiss this appeal.'

Purchas LJ agreed.

As will be seen, the Court of Appeal was at pains to stress that it was not intending to overrule *Stilk v Myrick,* but at the very least, *Williams v Roffey* requires a reinterpretation of that case. It is arguable that the captain in *Stilk v Myrick* received a practical benefit from the agreement of the crew to continue working. How is this different from the benefit received by the defendant in *Williams v Roffey*. There has been no review of *Williams v Roffey* by the Court of Appeal or House of Lords, but it has been applied by the lower courts in several reported decisions – for example, *Anangel Atlas Companies Naviera SA v Ishikawajima-Harima Heavy Industries Co Ltd*

(No 2) [1990] 2 Lloyd's Rep 526; *Simon Container Machinery Ltd v Emba Machinery AB* [1998] 2 Lloyd's Rep 429; and *Lee v GEC Plessey Telecommunications* [1993] IRLR 383. To that extent, it seems to have become an established authority. On the other hand, in a recent decision the judge doubted whether it was good law.

South Caribbean Trading Ltd ('SCT') v Trafigura Beheer BV ('Trafigura') [2004] EWHC 2676 (Comm)

Colman J:

'. . . **107.** Had it been necessary to base the question of consideration exclusively on the promise to release the cargo, I should have held that this alone was insufficient to supply consideration. It was SCT's obligation to make delivery under Contract 3053b. In promising to do so they were promising to perform an existing obligation. The authorities on this issue starting with *Stilk v Myrick* (1809) 2 Camp 317 and developing more recently in *Syros Shipping Co SA v Elaghill Trading Co Ltd (The Prodos C)* [1980] 2 Lloyd's Rep 390 and *Atlas Express Ltd v Kafco (Importers and Distributors) Ltd* [1989] 1 QB 833 indicate a firmly established rule of law that a promise to perform an enforceable obligation under a pre-existing contract between the same parties is incapable of amounting to sufficient consideration. The decision of the Court of Appeal in *Williams v Roffey Bros & Nicholls (Contractors) Ltd* [1991] 1 QB1 appears to have introduced some amelioration to the rigidity of this rule in cases where there has been refusal to perform amounting to economic duress by the party who might otherwise be in breach of any existing contract and where the other party will derive a practical benefit from such performance.

108. But for the fact that *Williams v Roffey Bros Ltd*, supra, was a decision of the Court of Appeal, I would not have followed it. That decision is inconsistent with the long-standing rule that consideration, being the price of the promise sued upon, must move from the promisee. The judgment of Glidewell LJ. was substantially based on *Pao On v Lau Yin Long* [1980] AC 614 in which the Judicial Committee of the Privy Council had held a promise by A to B to perform a contractual obligation owed by A to X could be sufficient consideration as against B. At page 15 Glidewell LJ regarded Lord Scarman's reasoning in relation to such tripartite relationship as applicable in principle to a bipartite relationship. But in the former case by the additional promise to B, consideration has moved from A because he has made himself liable to an additional party, whereas in the latter case he has not undertaken anything that he was not already obliged to do for the benefit of the same party. Glidewell LJ substituted for the established rule as to consideration moving from the promisee a completely different principle – that the promisor must by his promise have conferred a benefit on the other party. Purchas LJ at pages 22–23 clearly saw the nonsequitur but was "comforted" by observations from Lord Hailsham LC in *Woodhouse AC Israel Cocoa Ltd v Nigerian Product Marketing Co Ltd* [1972] AC 741 at pages 757–758. Investigation of the correspondence referred to in those observations shows that the latter are not authority for the proposition advanced "with some hesitation" by Purchas LJ.

109. However, seeing that *Williams v Roffey Bros,* supra has not yet been held by the House of Lords to have been wrongly decided, and approaching the validity of consideration on the basis of mutuality of benefit, I would hold that SCT's threat of non-compliance with its delivery obligation under Contract 3053b precluded its reliance on the benefit that its performance by effecting delivery would confer on Trafigura. This threat was analogous to economic duress as contemplated in *Williams v Roffey Bros,* supra because it was not based on any argument that SCT was discharged from its delivery obligation: reliance on clause 7 of Contract 5536 only came later.'

Colman J was bound to apply *Williams v Roffey,* since it is a Court of Appeal decision, but is clearly of the view that it might well be overruled by the House of Lords. Given that the decision has stood without serious challenge in the courts for over 15 years, this is perhaps unlikely. A much stronger possibility is that the House of Lords would distinguish *Williams v Roffey* in a way that narrowed its scope to circumstances very close to those that arose on its facts. There is certainly no move to extend *Williams v Roffey* into other areas – as is shown by its rejection in the case of *Re Selectmove* [1995] 2 All ER 534, which is discussed in the next section.

3.3.5 CONSIDERATION AND THE PART PAYMENT OF DEBTS

A particular aspect of the performance of an existing obligation, and whether this can amount to consideration, arises in relation to the part payment of debts. If one party has a contractual obligation to pay the other a sum of money, can that obligation ever be discharged by the payment of *less* than the amount due? It would follow from the general position on existing obligations – that is, the *Stilk v Myrick* principle – that payment of less than is due would provide no consideration for a promise to take it in satisfaction of the debt. In fact, English law has a separate line of authority dealing specifically with this issue. The starting point is the so-called 'rule in *Pinnel's Case*'.

Pinnel's Case (1602) 5 Co Rep 117a; 77 ER 237 (Common Pleas)

Facts: Pinnel brought an action of debt against Cole, for payment of £8 10s, due on 11 November 1600. The defendant pleaded, that he at the instance of the plaintiff, had paid £5 2s 9d on the 1 October, and that the plaintiff had accepted this in full satisfaction of the debt.

Held: Payment of a less sum on the due date cannot be any satisfaction for the whole. Part payment *before* the day, and acceptance of this, may discharge the whole debt. But in this case the plaintiff succeeded, because the defendant had not pleaded the defence properly.

Judgment:
[I]t was resolved by the whole Court, that payment of a lesser sum on the day in satisfaction of a greater, cannot be any satisfaction for the whole, because it appears to the Judges that by no possibility, a lesser sum can be a satisfaction to the plaintiff for a greater sum: but the gift of a horse, hawk, or robe, etc in satisfaction is good. For it shall be intended that a horse, hawk, or robe, etc might be more beneficial to the plaintiff than the money, in respect of some circumstance, or otherwise the plaintiff would not have accepted of it in satisfaction.

But when the whole sum is due, by no intendment the acceptance of a parcel can be a satisfaction to the Plaintiff: but in the case at Bar it was resolved, that the payment and acceptance of parcel before the day in satisfaction of the whole, would be a good satisfaction in regard of circumstance of time, for peradventure parcel of it before the day would be more beneficial to him than the whole at the day, and the value of the satisfaction is not material: so if I am bound in £20 to pay you £10 at Westminster and you request me to pay you £5 at the day at York, and you will accept it in full satisfaction of the whole, it is a good satisfaction for the whole: for the expenses to pay it at York, is sufficient satisfaction.

Pinnel's Case was not a strong authority, because the plaintiff only succeeded on the basis that the defence had been inadequately pleaded. The principle that part payment cannot in itself discharge a debt was confirmed, however, by the House of Lords in *Foakes v Beer*.

Foakes v Beer (1884) 9 App Cas 605 (HL)

Facts: Mrs Beer had agreed to accept a judgment debt, owed to her by Dr Beer, in instalments. When the instalments had been paid, she sued to recover the interest which she alleged have been accrued by the delay in completing payment. Mrs Beer succeeded in the lower courts. Dr Beer appealed to the House of Lords.

Held: Even if she had promised to take the instalments in full satisfaction, this did not preclude her from recovering the interest. The interest was owed by Dr Beer, and acceptance of part payment could not discharge the whole debt.

Earl of Selborne LC:
'My Lords, upon the construction of the agreement of the 21st of December 1876, I cannot differ from the conclusion in which both the courts below were agreed. If the operative part could properly be controlled by the recitals, I think there would be much

reason to say that the only thing contemplated by the recitals was giving time for payment, without any relinquishment, on the part of the judgment creditor, of any portion of the amount recoverable (whether for principal or for interest) under the judgment. But the agreement of the judgment creditor, which follows the recitals, is that she "will not take any proceedings whatever on the judgment," if a certain condition is fulfilled. What is that condition? Payment of the sum of £150 in every half year, "until the whole of the said sum of £2090 19s" (the aggregate amount of the principal debt and costs, for which judgment had been entered) "shall have been fully paid and satisfied." A particular "sum" is here mentioned, which does not include the interest then due, or future interest. Whatever was meant to be payable at all, under this agreement, was clearly to be payable by half-yearly instalments of £150 each; any other construction must necessarily make the conditional promise nugatory. But to say that the half-yearly payments were to continue till the whole sum of £2090 19s., "and interest thereon," should have been fully paid and satisfied, would be to introduce very important words into the agreement, which are not there, and of which I cannot say that they are necessarily implied. Although, therefore, I may (as indeed I do) very much doubt whether the effect of the agreement, as a conditional waiver of the interest to which she was by law entitled under the judgment, was really present to the mind of the judgment creditor, still I cannot deny that it might have that effect, if capable of being legally enforced. But the question remains, whether the agreement is capable of being legally enforced. Not being under seal, it cannot be legally enforced against the respondent, unless she received consideration for it from the appellant, or unless, though without consideration, it operates by way of accord and satisfaction, so as to extinguish the claim for interest. What is the consideration? On the face of the agreement none is expressed, except a present payment of £500, on account and in part of the larger debt then due and payable by law under the judgment. The appellant did not contract to pay the future instalments of £150 each, at the times therein mentioned; much less did he give any new security, in the shape of negotiable paper, or in any other form. The promise de futuro was only that of the respondent, that if the half-yearly payments of £150 each were regularly paid she would "take no proceedings whatever on the judgment". No doubt if the appellant had been under no antecedent obligation to pay the whole debt, his fulfilment of the condition might have imported some consideration on his part for that promise. But he was under that antecedent obligation; and payment at those deferred dates, by the forbearance and indulgence of the creditor, of the residue of the principal debt and costs, could not (in my opinion) be a consideration for the relinquishment of interest and discharge of the judgment, unless the payment of the £500, at the time of signing the agreement, was such a consideration. As to accord and satisfaction, in point of fact there could be no complete satisfaction, so long as any future instalment remained payable; and I do not see how any mere payments on account could operate in law as a satisfaction ad interim, conditionally upon other payments being afterwards duly made, unless there was a consideration sufficient to support the agreement while still un-executed. Nor was anything, in fact, done by the respondent in this case, on the receipt of the last payment, which could be tantamount to an acquittance, if the agreement did not previously bind her.

The question, therefore, is nakedly raised by this appeal, whether your Lordships are now prepared, not only to overrule, as contrary to the law, the doctrine stated by Sir Edward Coke to have been laid down by all the judges of the Common Pleas in *Pinnel's Case* in 1602, and repeated in his note to Littleton, s. 344(2), but to treat a prospective agreement, not under seal, for satisfaction of a debt, by a series of payments on account to a total amount less than the whole debt, as binding in law, provided those payments are regularly made; the case not being one of a composition with a common debtor, agreed to, inter se, by several creditors. I prefer so to state the question instead of treating it (as it was put at the Bar) as depending on the authority of the case of *Cumber v Wane* (1721) 1 Stra 426, decided in 1718. It may well be that distinctions, which in later cases have been held sufficient to exclude the application of that doctrine, existed and were improperly disregarded in *Cumber v Wane*; and yet that the doctrine itself may be law, rightly recognised in *Cumber v Wane*, and not really contradicted by any later authorities. And this appears to me to be the true state of the case. The doctrine itself, as laid down by Sir Edward Coke, may have been criticised, as questionable in principle, by some persons whose opinions are entitled to respect, but it has never been judicially overruled; on the contrary I think it has always, since the sixteenth century, been accepted as law. If so, I cannot think that your Lordships would do right, if you were now to reverse, as erroneous, a judgment of the Court of Appeal, proceeding upon a doctrine which has been accepted as part of the law of England for 280 years.

The doctrine, as stated in *Pinnel's Case*, is "that payment of a lesser sum on the day" (it would of course be the same after the day), "in satisfaction of a greater, cannot be any satisfaction for the whole, because it appears to the judges, that by no possibility a lesser sum can be a satisfaction to the plaintiff for a greater sum". As stated in Coke Littleton, 212, it is, "where the condition is for payment of £20, the obligor or feoffor cannot at the time appointed pay a lesser sum in satisfaction of the whole, because it is apparent that a lesser sum of money cannot be a satisfaction of a greater;" adding (what is beyond controversy), that an acquittance under seal, in full satisfaction of the whole, would (under like circumstances) be valid and binding.

The distinction between the effect of a deed under seal, and that of an agreement by parol, or by writing not under seal, may seem arbitrary, but it is established in our law; nor is it really unreasonable or practically inconvenient that the law should require particular solemnities to give a gratuitous contract the force of a binding obligation. If the question be (as, in the actual state of the law, I think it is), whether consideration is, or is not, given in a case of this kind, by the debtor who pays down part of the debt presently due from him, for a promise by the creditor to relinquish, after certain further payments on account, the residue of the debt, I cannot say that I think consideration is given, in the sense in which I have always understood that word as used in our law. It might be (and indeed I think it would be) an improvement in our law, if a release or acquittance of the whole debt, on payment of any sum which the creditor might be content to receive by way of accord and satisfaction (though less than the whole), were held to be, generally, binding, though not under seal; nor should I be unwilling to see equal force given to a prospective agreement, like the present, in writing though not under seal; but I think it impossible, without refinements which practically alter the sense of the word, to treat such a release or acquittance as supported by any new consideration proceeding from the debtor. All the authorities subsequent to *Cumber v Wane*, which were relied upon by the appellant at your Lordships' Bar (such as *Sibree v Tripp* (1846) 15 M & W 23, *Curlewis v Clark* (1849) 3 Ex 375, and *Goddard v O'Brien* (1882) 9 QBD 37) have proceeded upon the distinction, that, by giving negotiable paper or otherwise, there had been some new consideration for a new agreement, distinct from mere money payments in or towards discharge of the original liability. I think it unnecessary to go through those cases, or to examine the particular grounds on which each of them was decided. There are no such facts in the case now before your Lordships. What is called "any benefit, or even any legal possibility of benefit," in Mr Smith's notes to *Cumber v Wane*, is not (as I conceive) that sort of benefit which a creditor may derive from getting payment of part of the money due to him from a debtor who might otherwise keep him at arm's length, or possibly become insolvent, but is some independent benefit, actual or contingent, or a kind which might in law be a good and valuable consideration for any other sort of agreement not under seal.

My conclusion is, that the order appealed from should be affirmed, and the appeal dismissed, with costs, and I so move your Lordships.'

The rule set out in *Foakes v Beer* is still good law, and has recently been reaffirmed in *Re Selectmove* [1995] 2 All ER 534 and *Ferguson v Davies* [1997] 1 All ER 315. There are, however, some exceptions to it, both under common law, and under the equitable doctrine of promissory estoppel (which is dealt with at p 183).

Before looking at these exceptions, however, we should note the attempt in *Re Selectmove* to apply the approach taken in *Williams v Roffey* (above, p 163) to the part payment of debts.

Re Selectmove Ltd [1995] 2 All ER 531 (CA)

Facts: In this case the company was trying to enforce an alleged promise by the Inland Revenue ('the Crown') to accept the payment of a tax debt by instalments. It argued that this would be of 'practical benefit' to the Revenue, following the *Williams v Roffey* principle, in that the firm would be able to stay in business, and would be more likely to be able to pay its debts.

Held: Even if the Crown had made the alleged promise, the *Williams v Roffey* approach had no application to the situation of part payment of debts. On the basis of *Foakes v Beer*, the Crown was entitled to recover.

Peter Gibson LJ:

'... There are two elements to the consideration which the company claims was provided by it to the Crown. One is the promise to pay off its existing liability by instalments from 1 February 1992. The other is the promise to pay future PAYE and NIC as they fell due. Mr Nugee suggested that implicit in the latter was the promise to continue trading. But that cannot be spelt out of Mr Fooks' evidence as to what he agreed with Mr Polland. Accordingly, the second element is no more than a promise to pay that which it was bound to pay under the fiscal legislation at the date at which it was bound to make such payment. If the first element is not good consideration, I do not see why the second element should be either.

The judge held that the case fell within the principle of *Foakes v Beer* (1884) 9 App Cas 605, [1881–5] All ER Rep 106. In that case a judgment debtor and creditor agreed that in consideration of the debtor paying part of the judgment debt and costs immediately and the remainder by instalments the creditor would not take any proceedings on the judgment. The House of Lords held that the agreement was nudum pactum, being without consideration, and did not prevent the creditor, after payment of the whole debt and costs, from proceeding to enforce payment of the interest on the judgment. Although their Lordships were unanimous in the result, that case is notable for the powerful speech of Lord Blackburn, who made plain his disagreement with the course the law had taken in and since *Pinnel's Case* (1602) 5 Co Rep 117a, [1558–1774] All ER Rep 612 and which the House of Lords in *Foakes v Beer* decided should not be reversed. Lord Blackburn expressed his conviction that—

> all men of business, whether merchants or tradesmen, do every day recognise and act on the ground that prompt payment of a part of their demand may be more beneficial to them than it would be to insist on their rights and enforce payment of the whole. (See 9 App Cas 605 at 622, [1881–5] All ER Rep 106 at 115.)

Yet it is clear that the House of Lords decided that a practical benefit of that nature is not good consideration in law.

Foakes v Beer has been followed and applied in numerous cases subsequently, of which I shall mention two. In *Vanbergen v St Edmunds Properties Ltd* [1933] 2 KB 223 at 231, [1933] All ER Rep 488 at 491 Lord Hanworth MR said:

> It is a well established principle that a promise to pay a sum which the debtor is already bound by law to pay to the promisee does not afford any consideration to support the contract.

More recently in *D & C Builders Ltd v Rees* [1965] 3 All ER 837 at 841, [1966] 2 QB 617 at 626 this court also applied *Foakes v Beer*, Danckwerts LJ saying that the case—

> settled definitely the rule of law that payment of a lesser sum than the amount of a debt due cannot be a satisfaction of the debt, unless there is some benefit to the creditor added so that there is an accord and satisfaction.

Mr Nugee, however, submitted that an additional benefit to the Crown was conferred by the agreement in that the Crown stood to derive practical benefits therefrom: it was likely to recover more from not enforcing its debt against the company, which was known to be in financial difficulties, than from putting the company into liquidation. He pointed to the fact that the company did in fact pay its further PAYE and NIC liabilities and £7,000 of its arrears. He relied on the decision of this court in *Williams v Roffey Bros & Nicholls (Contractors) Ltd* [1990] 1 All ER 512, [1991] 1 QB 1 for the proposition that a promise to perform an existing obligation can amount to good consideration provided that there are practical benefits to the promisee.

In that case the defendant, which had a building contract, sub-contracted work to the plaintiff at a price which left him in financial difficulty and there was a risk that the work would not be completed by the plaintiff. The defendant agreed to make additional payments to the plaintiff in return for his promise to carry out his existing obligations. The plaintiff sued for payment under the original agreement and the further agreement. The defendant argued that its promise to make additional payments was unenforceable and relied on *Stilk v Myrick* (1809) 2 Camp 317, 170 ER 1168, in which Lord Ellenborough CJ held to be unenforceable for want of consideration a promise by a ship's captain to seamen, hired to crew the ship to and from the Baltic, of extra pay for working the ship back from the Baltic after two men had deserted. This court rejected that argument without overruling *Stilk v Myrick*. Glidewell LJ, with whom Purchas and Russell LJJ agreed, expressed the law to be this:

> . . . (i) if A has entered into a contract with B to do work for, or to supply goods or services to, B in return for payment by B and (ii) at some stage before A has completely performed his obligations under the contract B has reason to doubt whether A will, or will be able to, complete his side of the bargain and (iii) B thereupon promises A an additional payment in return for A's promise to perform his contractual obligations on time and (iv) as a result of giving his promise B obtains in practice a benefit, or obviates a disbenefit, and (v) B's promise is not given as a result of economic duress or fraud on the part of A, then (vi) the benefit to B is capable of being consideration for B's promise, so that the promise will be legally binding. (See [1990] 1 All ER 512 at 521–522, [1991] 1 QB 1 at 15–16.)

Mr Nugee submitted that although Glidewell LJ in terms confined his remarks to a case where B is to do the work for or supply goods or services to A, the same principle must apply where B's obligation is to pay A, and he referred to an article by Adams and Brownsword "Contract, Consideration and the Critical Path" (1990) 53 MLR 536 at 539–540 which suggests that *Foakes v Beer* might need reconsideration. I see the force of the argument, but the difficulty that I feel with it is that if the principle of *Williams'* case is to be extended to an obligation to make payment, it would in effect leave the principle in *Foakes v Beer* without any application. When a creditor and a debtor who are at arm's length reach agreement on the payment of the debt by instalments to accommodate the debtor, the creditor will no doubt always see a practical benefit to himself in so doing. In the absence of authority there would be much to be said for the enforceability of such a contract. But that was a matter expressly considered in *Foakes v Beer* yet held not to constitute good consideration in law. *Foakes v Beer* was not even referred to in *Williams'* case, and it is in my judgment impossible, consistently with the doctrine of precedent, for this court to extend the principle of *Williams'* case to any circumstances governed by the principle of *Foakes v Beer*. If that extension is to be made, it must be by the House of Lords or, perhaps even more appropriately, by Parliament after consideration by the Law Commission.

In my judgment, the judge was right to hold that if there was an agreement between the company and the Crown it was unenforceable for want of consideration.'

Stuart-Smith and Balcombe LJJ concurred.

Having noted this confirmation of the continued strength of the rule in *Foakes v Beer*, we now turn to consider the limited common-law exceptions to it.

3.3.5.1 Common-law exceptions to the rule in *Foakes v Beer*

Pinnel's case itself recognises one set of exceptions to the rule applied in *Foakes v Beer*. That is, that doing something more than simply paying part of the debt – for example paying early, or at a different place, or providing goods as well as or instead of money – will be sufficient to make a promise to discharge the debt enforceable.

There are two other situations that the common law recognises as having the same effect. The first is where a third party makes the part payment.

Hirachand Punamchand v Temple [1911] 2 KB 330

Facts: The plaintiffs were moneylenders, from whom Temple had borrowed money. Temple's father sent them a draft for less than the full amount, in settlement of the debt. The plaintiffs cashed the draft, but then sued for the balance. At trial the plaintiffs succeeded. Temple appealed.

Held: Where part payment was made by a third party, and was accepted by the creditor, the creditor could not then sue the debtor for the balance.

Fletcher Moulton LJ:
'I also think that the plaintiffs' action fails, and that this appeal should be allowed. The facts of this case are such that this result may be arrived at by more than one course of reasoning. I am clearly of opinion that there must be taken to have been an agreement between the plaintiffs and Sir Richard Temple, by which the plaintiffs agreed to accept the money sent by him in satisfaction of the note. No oral testimony was given at the trial, but the facts of the case appear clearly from the correspondence. In the first letter the plaintiffs applied to Sir Richard Temple, the father, in respect of his son's account with them. Then comes a letter from the father's solicitors, in which they offer the

plaintiffs a certain sum in settlement of the plaintiffs' two claims against the son, one of which was on a bond and the other on the promissory note. In answer to this letter, two separate letters were written by the plaintiffs, one with regard to the bond, and the other with regard to the note. I need only refer to the latter, as the purport of the two, mutatis mutandis, is the same. The plaintiffs in that letter say "We shall be glad if you will let us know the amount for which Sir Richard Temple is prepared to settle this debt due from his son." Therefore it is clear that the plaintiffs realized that the father was proposing to settle the whole claim on the note, and that they accordingly asked what amount he was prepared to give. The father's solicitors wrote in answer one letter dealing with both claims. In the paragraph relating to the promissory note, they say: "Our instructions are, therefore, to pay you Rs. 500 in respect of the principal and Rs. 150 in respect of the one year's interest, making together Rs. 650. We enclose draft by the National Bank of India on the Bank of Bombay, Poona, in your favour for this amount, and shall be glad to receive the promissory note in exchange." It is perfectly clear from the previous correspondence that this was an offer made for the full settlement of the claim. The plaintiffs, with knowledge that this was the money of the father, sent to them in full settlement of the claim, took the draft, and cashed it, and kept the money. They must be taken to have known that they could only do this rightly, if they agreed to the terms that it should be in full settlement of the debt. Their action was inconsistent with the duty of an honest man, unless, at the time when they took the money, they accepted the terms on which it was offered. They must have known that they could only possess themselves of this money honestly by accepting those terms, and, knowing that, they possessed themselves of it. That appears to me to be overwhelming evidence of an acceptance by them of the proposal made to them by the father . . .

These being the facts, we have to consider how they affect the debt on the note in point of law. I am of opinion that by that transaction between the plaintiffs and Sir Richard Temple the debt on the promissory note became extinct. I agree with the view expressed by Willes J in *Cook v Lister*. The effect of such an agreement between a creditor and a third party with regard to the debt is to render it impossible for the creditor afterwards to sue the debtor for it. The way in which this is worked out in law may be that it would be an abuse of the process of the Court to allow the creditor under such circumstances to sue, or it may be, and I prefer that view, that there is an extinction of the debt; but, whichever way it is put, it comes to the same thing, namely that, after acceptance by the creditor of a sum offered by a third party in settlement of the claim against the debtor, the creditor cannot maintain an action for the balance.'

Farwell LJ agreed. Vaughan Williams LJ also held for the defendant, but on different grounds.

The reasoning in this case is in part based on the idea that allowing the creditor to recover from the debtor in such circumstances would amount to a fraud on the third party, who has paid the money on the understanding that the debt would be discharged. A similar rationale supports the other common-law exception to *Foakes v Beer*. This arises where a debtor has a number of creditors, and they agree between themselves to take only a proportion of the debt owing – for example, 20p for each pound owing. Such an agreement is known as a 'composition agreement'. Once it has been made, none of the creditors will be allowed to sue the debtor for any more than is due under the composition agreement: *Good v Cheeseman* (1831) 2 B & Ald 328.

3.3.6 CONSIDERATION AND THE VARIATION OF CONTRACTS

The issues considered in the previous two sections are just particular aspects of the approach taken by English contract law to the variation of contractual obligations. It will not infrequently be the case that a contract that lasts for a number of months or years will need to be changed to deal with changed circumstances. The easiest way to achieve this is by what has been described as 'accord and satisfaction'. This effectively means that the parties reach a new agreement, with consideration being provided for any change. So, if one party is seeking to increase the payments, it will have to offer something in exchange for this – for example, more flexibility over delivery. Provided that there is mutuality in the variation, then it will be enforceable. The difficulty arises where the change is one-sided. An approach based on the idea of the 'relational contract' (see Chapter 1, p 22) would have no problem coping with this. The classical law of English contract, however, with its focus on everything being determined by the initial agreement, becomes more complicated. There are, however, two concepts that have been used to make one-sided variations in a contract enforceable. These are 'waiver' and 'promissory estoppel'.

3.3.6.1 Waiver

The concept of waiver involves a party to a contract promising that s/he will suspend his or her strict contractual rights. The rights are to be 'waived'. To this extent it enables the terms of a contract to be varied, though the effect may only be temporary. Thus a buyer who indicates to the seller that late delivery will be accepted will not subsequently be allowed to reject delivery because it is late: *Hartley v Hymans* [1920] 3 KB 475. A relatively recent example of the operation of this concept is to be found in *Charles Rickards Ltd v Oppenheim*.

Charles Rickards Ltd v Oppenheim [1950] 1 All ER 420 (CA)

Facts: The contract was for a car body to be built on a chassis owned by the defendant. The contract was to be completed in a specified time. When this did not occur, the defendant allowed an extension. Eventually, the defendant indicated that the work must be completed by a particular date. The plaintiffs completed the work after that date and sued for payment.

Held: Although the defendant had waived the original date for delivery, he was entitled subsequently to set a firm deadline, which a failure to meet would constitute a repudiatory breach. The defendant was not obliged to pay for the work.

Denning LJ:

'Early in 1947 the defendant, Mr Oppenheim, wanted a new Rolls Royce car, and he placed an order in two parts with the plaintiffs Charles Rickards, Ltd, who are motor car traders. He first ordered the chassis, a Rolls Royce Silver Wraith chassis, for estimated delivery in June, 1947, but he also wanted a body built on the chassis, and he particularly wanted to know the time within which that body could be made. The plaintiffs made inquiries of various firms for an estimated time for building a body on to the chassis. In July, 1947, Rolls Royce themselves estimated twenty-one months, and Park Ward at about the same time estimated fifteen months. Those times were too long for the defendant's satisfaction, so the plaintiffs obtained an estimate from Jones Brothers (Coachbuilders) Ltd, who said that they could do it within "six months or, at the most, seven months". Thereupon, the plaintiffs gave the same time to the defendant and he gave them the order for the body on that footing. The order was placed in July. The plaintiffs sub-contracted it and put out the work with Jones Brothers (Coachbuilders) Ltd. The actual time from which the six or seven months started is not precisely ascertained. The chassis was actually delivered to the sub-contractors on July 30, 1947, and, if that is taken as the date from which the time ran, the seven months would be up at the end of February, 1948, but the specification for the body work was not finally agreed until August 20, 1947. If that date is taken, the latest time for delivery would be March 20, 1948. Whichever date is taken, though, is immaterial, for the time was plainly exceeded. The body was not built on to the chassis by March 20, nor, indeed, until many months later – not until October 18, 1948, was the car completed.

Meanwhile, however, as from 20 March 1948, at least, onwards, the defendant had been pressing for delivery. During the winter of 1947/8 he went to America, and in the autumn of 1947, before he left, he told the plaintiffs that he hoped the car would be ready by the time he came back. He came back in March, and the car was not ready by 20 March 1948. He could have cancelled the contract there and then, but he did not do so. By pressing for delivery he waived the stipulation as to time. He asked for delivery in time for Ascot, but he did not get it. He asked for delivery in time to take the car on his holiday abroad at the beginning of August, 1948. He did not get it. He was given promises from time to time for early delivery – not definite guarantees, but promises which were not fulfilled. These promises were made not so much by the plaintiffs as by the sub-contractors, but the defendant was well justified in dealing direct with the sub-contractors, as, not only were they actually doing the work, but, on 7 August 1947, the plaintiffs had written to them telling them that it was in order for them to accept any instructions with regard to the body that were given by the defendant, and asking them to keep the plaintiffs *au fait* with the situation. It was, therefore, quite natural for the defendant to deal direct with the sub-contractors, to talk to them about the work, and to press them for delivery. He also pressed the plaintiffs for delivery, but they did not go further than to say that the car would be delivered as early as possible.

Eventually, not having got the car for Ascot and wanting it in time to take it abroad at the beginning of August, on 28 June 1948, the defendant saw Mr Musk, the sub-contractors' manager, who told him that it would be ready in two weeks' time. On the next day the defendant wrote to the sub-contractors a letter on which much of this case turns. He sent it "For the attention of the managing director." It says:

> Further to my conversation with Mr. Musk to-day, I regret that I shall be unable, unless my plans change, to accept delivery of the Rolls you are making for me after July 25. For six months I have had a reservation to take a car abroad on Aug. 3 for my holiday and it would appear to me to be impossible for me to alter this date. I shall therefore have to buy another car.

He also asked in the letter whether there was any definite likelihood of receiving the car before July 25. A week later, about 7 July Mr Musk intimated that the car would not even be ready for him to take abroad by 3 August. Thereupon the defendant bought elsewhere another car, a Rolls Bentley, and asked the plaintiffs to return the money which he had paid for the chassis – he was ready to let them keep the chassis and have the advantage of the work that had been done on the body. This request was followed by an interview on 10 July at which, according to the evidence of the plaintiffs, the defendant in effect waived his notice of cancellation and agreed that the plaintiffs should go on with the work and he would take the car later. The judge has negatived any such waiver on the facts, and I do not see any reason to differ from his finding. After that interview the plaintiffs, through the sub-contractors, completed the car. On 18 October 1948, it was finished, but delivery was refused by the defendant. This action is now brought by the plaintiffs for the price of the body, and a counterclaim is made by the defendant claiming the return of the chassis or its value.

It is clear on the findings of the judge that there was an initial stipulation making time of the essence of the contract between the plaintiffs and the defendant, namely, that it was to be completed "in six, or, at the most, seven months". Counsel for the plaintiffs did not seek to disturb that finding – indeed, he could not successfully have done so – but he said that that stipulation was waived. His argument was that, the stipulated time having been waived, the time became at large, and that thereupon the plaintiffs' only obligation was to deliver within a reasonable time. He said that, in accordance with well-known authorities, "a reasonable time" meant a reasonable time in the circumstances as they actually existed, i.e. that the plaintiffs would not exceed a reasonable time if they were prevented from delivering by causes outside their control, such as strikes or the impossibility of getting parts, and so forth, and that, on the evidence in this case, it could not be said that a reasonable time was in that sense exceeded. . . .

I agree that that initial time was waived by reason of the requests for delivery which the defendant made after March, 1948, and that, if delivery had been tendered in compliance with those requests, the defendant could not have refused to accept. Supposing, for instance, delivery had been tendered in April, May, or June 1948, the defendant would have had no answer. It would be true that the plaintiffs could not aver and prove that they were ready and willing to deliver in accordance with the original contract. They would have had, in effect, to rely on the waiver almost as a cause of action . . . If the defendant, as he did, led the plaintiffs to believe that he would not insist on the stipulation as to time, and that, if they carried out the work, he would accept it, and they did it, he could not afterwards set up the stipulation in regard to time against them. Whether it be called waiver or forbearance on his part, or an agreed variation or substituted performance, does not matter. It is a kind of estoppel. . . .

Therefore, if the matter stopped there, the plaintiffs could have said that, notwith-standing that more than seven months had elapsed, the defendant was bound to accept, but the matter does not stop there, because delivery was not given in compli-ance with the requests of the defendant. Time and time again the defendant pressed for delivery, time and time again he was assured that he would have early delivery, but he never got satisfaction, and eventually at the end of June he gave notice saying that, unless the car was delivered by July 25, he would not accept it. The question thus arises whether he was entitled to give such a notice, making time of the essence, and that is the question which counsel for the plaintiffs has argued before us . . .

[I]n my view, it is unnecessary to determine whether it was a contract for the sale of goods or a contract for work and labour, because, whichever it was, the defendant was entitled to give notice bringing the matter to a head. It would be most unreasonable if, having been lenient and having waived the initial expressed time, he should thereby have prevented himself from ever thereafter insisting on reasonably quick delivery. In my judgment, he was entitled to give a reasonable notice making time of the essence of the matter. Adequate protection to the suppliers is given by the requirement that the notice should be reasonable.

. . . In this case, not only did the defendant press continually for delivery, not only was he given promises of speedy delivery, but, on the very day before he gave notice, he was told by the sub-contractors' manager, who was in charge of the work, that it would be ready within two weeks. He then gave a four weeks' notice. The judge found that it was a reasonable notice and, in my judgment, there is no ground on which this court could in any way differ from that finding. The reasonableness of the notice must, of course, be judged at the time at which it is given. It cannot be held to be a bad notice because, after it is given, the suppliers find themselves in unanticipated difficulties in making delivery.

The notice of June 29, 1948, was, therefore, a perfectly good notice so as to make time of the essence of the contract. . . .

The case, therefore, comes down to this. There was a contract by the plaintiffs to supply and fix a body on the chassis within six or seven months. They did not do it. The defendant waived that stipulation. For three months after the time had expired he pressed them for delivery, asking for it first for Ascot and then for his holiday abroad. But still they did not deliver it. Eventually at the end of June, being tired of waiting any longer, he gave a four weeks' notice and said: 'At all events, if you do not supply it at the end of four weeks I must cancel', and he did cancel. I see no injustice to the plaintiffs in saying that that was a reasonable notice. Having originally stipulated for six to seven months, having waited eleven months, and still not getting delivery, the defendant was entitled to cancel the contract.'

Bucknill and Singleton LJJ concurred.

Rickards v Oppenheim illustrates the fact that a 'waiver' of rights may well only be temporary in its effect. The party that has waived its rights may well be able to bring that suspension to an end by giving reasonable notice. In this it has similarities with the next concept used to vary contracts – promissory estoppel. Indeed, Denning LJ clearly saw *Rickards v Oppenheim* as capable of being regarded as an application of that approach, which he himself had put forward a few years earlier in *Central London Property Trust Ltd v High Trees House Ltd* [1947] KB 130. There are some distinctions, however, as will be explained in the next section.

3.3.7 PROMISSORY ESTOPPEL

The doctrine of promissory estoppel can be argued to have taken the place of the concept of 'waiver' in the modern law of contract. It was developed, however, to deal with a situation to which waiver had never been applied – the part payment of debts. As we have seen, the House of Lords in *Foakes v Beer* affirmed the principle that part payment of a debt by the debtor can never in itself provide consideration to support a promise to forgo the balance. The case that provided the starting point for an exception to this was *Central London Property Trust Ltd v High Trees House Ltd*.

Central London Property Trust Ltd v High Trees House Ltd [1947] KB 130 (HC)

Facts: The contract concerned the lease of a block of flats in London. At the start of the Second World War the tenants, the defendants, found it difficult to find people to take the flats. The landlords agreed that because of this the tenants could pay half the rent. After the war, the landlords sought to revert to the original terms of the lease.

Held: The landlords could return to the original terms once the conditions for which the rebate had been granted had ceased to exist. They would not, however, be able to recover in respect of the under-payment during the war years.

Denning J:
'By a lease under seal made on September 24, 1937, the plaintiffs, Central London Property Trust Ltd, granted to the defendants, High Trees House Ltd, a subsidiary of

the plaintiff company, a tenancy of a block of flats for the term of ninety-nine years from September 29, 1937, at a ground rent of £2,500 a year. The block of flats was a new one and had not been fully occupied at the beginning of the war owing to the absence of people from London. With war conditions prevailing, it was apparent to those responsible that the rent reserved under the lease could not be paid out of the profits of the flats and, accordingly, discussions took place between the directors of the two companies concerned, which were closely associated, and an arrangement was made between them which was put into writing. On January 3, 1940, the plaintiffs wrote to the defendants in these terms, "we confirm the arrangement made between us by which the ground rent should be reduced as from the commencement of the lease to £1,250. per annum", and on April 2, 1940, a confirmatory resolution to the same effect was passed by the plaintiff company . . . The defendants paid the reduced rent from 1941 down to the beginning of 1945 by which time all the flats in the block were fully let, and continued to pay it thereafter. In September, 1945, the then receiver of the plaintiff company looked into the matter of the lease and ascertained that the rent actually reserved by it was £2,500. On September 21, 1945, he wrote to the defendants saying that rent must be paid at the full rate and claiming that arrears amounting to £7,916 were due. Subsequently, he instituted the present friendly proceedings to test the legal position in regard to the rate at which rent was payable. In the action the plaintiffs sought to recover £625, being the amount represented by the difference between rent at the rate of £2,500 and £1,250 per annum for the quarters ending September 29, and December 25, 1945. By their defence the defendants pleaded (I.) that the letter of January 3, 1940, constituted an agreement that the rent reserved should be £1,250 only, and that such agreement related to the whole term of the lease, (2.) they pleaded in the alternative that the plaintiff company were estopped from alleging that the rent exceeded £1,250 per annum and (3.) as a further alternative, that by failing to demand rent in excess of £1,250 before their letter of September 21, 1945 (received by the defendants on September 24), they had waived their rights in respect of any rent, in excess of that at the rate of £1,250 which had accrued up to September 24, 1945.

If I were to consider this matter without regard to recent developments in the law, there is no doubt that had the plaintiffs claimed it, they would have been entitled to recover ground rent at the rate of £2,500 a year from the beginning of the term, since the lease under which it was payable was a lease under seal which, according to the old common law, could not be varied by an agreement by parol (whether in writing or not), but only by deed. Equity, however stepped in, and said that if there has been a variation of a deed by a simple contract (which in the case of a lease required to be in writing would have to be evidenced by writing), the courts may give effect to it as is shown in *Berry v Berry* [1929] 2 KB 316. That equitable doctrine, however, could hardly apply in the present case because the variation here might be said to have been made without consideration. With regard to estoppel, the representation made in relation to reducing the rent, was not a representation of an existing fact. It was a representation, in effect, as to the future, namely, that payment of the rent would not be enforced at the full rate but only at the reduced rate. Such a representation would not give rise to an estoppel, because, as was said in *Jorden v Money* (1854) 5 HL 185, a representation as to the future must be embodied as a contract or be nothing.

But what is the position in view of developments in the law in recent years? The law has not been standing still since *Jorden v Money*. There has been a series of decisions over the last fifty years which, although they are said to be cases of estoppel are not really such. They are cases in which a promise was made which was intended to create legal relations and which, to the knowledge of the person making the promise, was going to be acted on by the person to whom it was made, and which was in fact so acted on. In such cases the courts have said that the promise must be honoured. The cases to which I particularly desire to refer are: *Fenner v Blake* [1900] 1 QB 426, *In re Wickham*, [1917] 34 TLR 158, *Re William Porter & Co. Ltd* [1937] 2 All ER 361 and *Buttery v Pickard* [1946] WN 25. As I have said they are not cases of estoppel in the strict sense. They are really promises – promises intended to be binding, intended to be acted on, and in fact acted on. *Jorden v Money* can be distinguished, because there the promisor made it clear that she did not intend to be legally bound, whereas in the cases to which I refer the proper inference was that the promisor did intend to be bound. In each case the court held the promise to be binding on the party making it, even though under the old common law it might be difficult to find any consideration for it. The courts have not gone so far as to give a cause of action in damages for the breach of such a promise, but they have refused to allow the party making it to act inconsistently with it. It is in that sense, and that sense only, that such a promise gives rise to an estoppel. The decisions are a natural result of the fusion of law and equity: for the cases of *Hughes v Metropolitan Ry Co, Birmingham* (1877) 2 App Cas 439 and *District Land Co v London & North Western Ry Co* (1888) 40 Ch D 268 and *Salisbury (Marquess) v Gilmore* [1942] 2 KB 38, afford a sufficient basis for saying that a party would not be allowed in equity to go back on such a promise. In my opinion, the time has now come for the validity of such a promise to be recognised. The logical consequence, no doubt is that a promise to accept a smaller sum in discharge of a larger sum, if acted upon, is binding notwithstanding the absence of consideration: and if the fusion of law and equity leads to this result, so much the better. That aspect was not considered in *Foakes v Beer*. At this time of day however, when law and equity have been joined together for over seventy years, principles must be reconsidered in the light of their combined effect. It is to be noticed that in the Sixth Interim Report of the Law Revision Committee, pars. 35, 40, it is recommended that such a promise as that to which I have referred, should be enforceable in law even though no consideration for it has been given by the promisee. It seems to me that, to the extent I have mentioned, that result has now been achieved by the decisions of the courts.

I am satisfied that a promise such as that to which I have referred is binding and the only question remaining for my consideration is the scope of the promise in the present case. I am satisfied on all the evidence that the promise here was that the ground rent should be reduced to £1,250 a year as a temporary expedient while the block of flats was not fully, or substantially fully let, owing to the conditions prevailing. That means that the reduction in the rent applied throughout the years down to the end of 1944, but early in 1945 it is plain that the flats were fully let, and, indeed the rents received from them (many of them not being affected by the Rent Restrictions Acts), were increased beyond the figure at which it was originally contemplated that they would be let. At all events the rent from them must have been very considerable. I find that the conditions prevailing at the time when the reduction in rent was made, had completely passed away by the early months of 1945. I am satisfied that the promise was understood by all parties only to apply under the conditions prevailing at the time when it was made, namely, when the flats were only partially let, and that it did not extend any further than that. When the flats became fully let, early in 1945, the reduction ceased to apply.

In those circumstances, under the law as I hold it, it seems to me that rent is payable at the full rate for the quarters ending September 29 and December 25, 1945.

If the case had been one of estoppel, it might be said that in any event the estoppel would cease when the conditions to which the representation applied came to an end, or it also might be said that it would only come to an end on notice. In either case it is only a way of ascertaining what is the scope of the representation. I prefer to apply the principle that a promise intended to be binding, intended to be acted on and in fact acted on, is binding so far as its terms properly apply. Here it was binding as covering the period down to the early part of 1945, and as from that time full rent is payable.

I therefore give judgment for the plaintiff company for the amount claimed.'

Denning tries in his judgment to link his decision to earlier authority, but it is clear that he was breaking new ground. None of the earlier authorities cited was concerned with the part payment of debts. Moreover, his dismissal of the problem of *Foakes v Beer* on the basis that it simply did not take account of the principles derived from equity is disingenuous. There is no reason to suppose that the members of the House of Lords in *Foakes v Beer* were unaware of the decision in *Hughes v Metropolitan Railway*, for example, which had been decided only seven years previously. It is clear, then, that *Central London Property Trust v High Trees House* was establishing a new principle in the law of contract. What exactly was this principle? Denning, at the end of his judgment, put it in these terms: 'a promise intended to be binding, intended to be acted on and in fact acted on, is binding so far as its terms properly apply'. In other words, a serious promise, which has been relied on, is legally enforceable. Taken at face value this is a clear contradiction of the doctrine of consideration, which says that such promises are only binding if the promisee has provided something in exchange. Whether Lord Denning intended such a bold attack at the time is open to question. The following extract from his own account of the case clearly indicates that he felt that the doctrine of consideration was in need of significant reform.

**Denning, A, *The Discipline of Law,* 1979, London:
Butterworths, pp 200–205**

We did a lot of commercial work in No. 4 Brick Court, especially with sale of goods and charterparties of ships. Soon after I started I came upon a pathway which led to the *High Trees*. At that time one dominating factor was that every contract of sale of goods of £10 or more in value had to be in writing. The other dominating factor was that no promise was binding unless there was consideration for it. Those two factors caused injustices of all kinds. We used to resort to many subtleties to get round them. When I was still a pupil we came across a very useful case on the subject. It had just been reported, called *Hartley v Hymans*. I noted it in pencil on my copy of Anson and added 'Suggest Estoppel'. It was a decision of Mr. Justice McCardie in which he had examined many authorities. He was the most diligent collector of cases that has ever been on the Bench. In it he made a passing reference to 'the broad rule of justice stated by Lord Cairns LC in *Hughes v Metropolitan Railway Co* [1877] 2 AC 439'. That case had been overlooked for 50 years. None of the textbooks had noticed it. I made a special note of it: and as it has had so much impact on subsequent developments, I will set it out:

> 'It is the first principle upon which all Courts of Equity proceed, that if parties who have entered into definite and distinct terms involving certain legal results – certain penalties or legal forfeiture – afterwards by their own act or with their own consent enter upon a course of negotiation which has the effect of leading one of the parties to suppose that the strict rights arising under the contract will not be enforced, or will be kept in suspense, or held in abeyance, the person who otherwise might have enforced those rights will not be allowed to enforce them where it would be inequitable having regard to the dealings which have thus taken place between the parties'.

I found also that that principle had been explained by Bowen LJ who said that it was not confined to penalties and forfeitures but extended to all cases of contractual rights. That was in a case in 1888 – *Birmingham and District Land Co v London and NW Railway Co*.

The fences in the way

As I went along the pathway towards the *High Trees*, I found many obstacles had been left in the way. I came across them whilst I was waiting for briefs. They came slowly. It took me seven years before I was making £1,000 a year. During this time Sir Willes Chitty, the Senior Master and one of the most learned of men – coming from a long line of lawyers – asked me to join him as one of the editors of *Smith's Leading Cases*. It took up much of my time until it was published in 1929. Each editor took responsibility for the notes to a particular leading case. I learned more law in those years than I have done before or since. In particular I came across two fences barring the path. They had been put up 70 years before. One was that estoped applies only in respect of representations of fact, and not of statements of intention (*Jorden v Money*). The other was that a representation, in order to work an estoppel, must be one of fact and not of law. Somehow or other these fences had to be overcome.

In order to leap these fences, I needed a good horse. It turned up. It was the Report of the Law Revision Committee on the Doctrine of Consideration. It came out in 1937 when I was in very busy practice as a junior. So I had no time to read it then. But on a significant day – All Fools' Day – 1 April 1938, I took silk. I had more time then for a year or two. I read the Report. It was made by the leading lawyers of the day. They included Lord Wright MR, Mr. Justice Goddard, Mr. Justice Asquith and Professor Goodhart. Even to this day it has not been implemented by the Legislature. But it was just the horse to get me over the fences. In particular it exposed the injustice of the rule that estoppel only applies to statements of fact, and of the rule that payment of a lesser sum is no consideration for the discharge of a larger sum. The Committee recommended the abolition of both those rules. They made this recommendation. It got me over the fences which obstructed the way to *High Trees*:

'We therefore recommend that a promise which the promisor knows, or reasonably should know, will be relied upon by the promisee, shall be enforceable if the promisee has altered his position to his detriment in reliance on the promise'.

Being now on the right path, I pointed it out to the Court of Appeal in my argument as King's Counsel in *Salisbury (Marquess) v Gilmore*. Lord Justice Mackinnon was disposed to follow the path. But he did not feel able to do so. The fences were too high for him. In his usual pungent style, he said that the House of Lords – the 'voices of infallibility' – as they spoke in *Jorden v Money* – were binding on the Court of Appeal. So estoppel was still confined to representations of existing fact.

The *High Trees* case itself – promissory estoppel
At last I came in sight of *High Trees*. It was in July 1946. I had only been a Judge in the King's Bench for some six months. During that time I had been mostly out on circuit where it was all fact and no law. But in my first spell in London there came the *Central London Property Trust Ltd v High Trees House Ltd*. It was argued by Mr. Robert Fortune on the one side – 'Frothy Bob' as we used to call him because of his spluttering – and Mr. Ronald Hopkins on the other, a sound and sensible advocate. They argued it well but they had not the reserves at their command as I had. I delivered judgment straight off the reel – with a tidying up afterwards for the Law Reports . . .

There was no appeal. This was probably because the decision could be supported on other grounds. An appeal might have ruined everything.

The principle became known as promissory estoppel.

What is clear is that the doctrine derived from *High Trees* – which has become known as the doctrine of 'promissory estoppel' – has developed in a way that means that it has only a limited impact on the doctrine of consideration. There are three clear limiting factors that have been established by subsequent case law:

1. the need for there to have been an existing legal relationship between the parties;
2. that the doctrine can only be used 'as a shield, not a sword'; and
3. that it must be inequitable for the promisor to go back on the promise.

3.3.7.1 Need for an existing legal relationship

The first two constraints are to some extent linked, and can both be illustrated by the case of *Combe v Combe* – in which Denning himself was one of the judges.

Combe v Combe [1951] 1 All ER 767 (CA)

Facts: H and W divorced. H promised to pay W £100 per annum. He never made any payments. W sued. At trial it was held that W had given no consideration for H's promise, but could recover on the basis of promissory estoppel.

Held: Promissory estoppel cannot be used as the basis for creating a contractual obligation, but only as a means of varying an existing obligation.

Denning LJ:

'In this case a wife who has divorced her husband claims maintenance from him – not in the Divorce Court, but in the King's Bench on an agreement which is said to be embodied in letters. The parties were married in 1915. They separated in 1939. On February 1, 1943, on the wife's petition, a decree *nisi* of divorce was pronounced. Shortly afterwards letters passed between the solicitors with regard to maintenance. On February 9, 1943 (eight days after the decree *nisi*), the solicitor for the wife wrote to the solicitor for the husband:

> With regard to permanent maintenance, we understand that your client is pre-pared to make [the wife] an allowance of £100 per year free of income tax.

In answer, on February 19, 1943, the husband's solicitors wrote:

> The respondent has agreed to allow your client £100 per annum free of tax.

On August 11, 1943, the decree was made absolute. On August 26, 1943, the wife's solicitors wrote to the husband's solicitors, saying:

> Referring to your letter of February 19 last, our client would like the £100 per annum agreed to be paid to her by your client to be remitted to us on her behalf quarterly. We shall be glad if you will kindly let us have a cheque for £25 for the first quarterly instalment and make arrangements for a similar remittance to us on November 11, February 11, May 11 and August 11 in the future.

A reply did not come for nearly two months because the husband was away, and then

---

189

he himself, on October 18, 1943, wrote a letter which was passed on to the wife's solicitors:

> . . . regarding the sum of £25 claimed on behalf of Mrs Combe . . . I would point out that whilst this is paid quarterly as from August 11, 1943, the sum is not due till November 11, 1943, as I can hardly be expected to pay this allowance in advance.

He never paid anything. The wife pressed him for payment, but she did not follow it up by an application to the divorce court. It is to be observed that she herself has an income of her own of between £700 and £800 a year, whereas her husband has only £650 a year. Eventually, after nearly seven years had passed since the decree abso-lute, she brought this action in the King's Bench Division on July 28, 1950, claiming £675 being arrears for six years and three quarters at £100 a year. Byrne J held that the first three quarterly instalments of £25 were barred by the Limitation Act 1939, but he gave judgment for £600 in respect of the instalments which accrued within the six years before the action was brought. He held, on the authority of *Gaisberg v Storr* [1949] 2 All ER 411, that there was no consideration for the husband's promise to pay his wife £100, but, nevertheless, he held that the promise was enforceable on the principle stated in *Central London Property Trust Ltd v High Trees House Ltd* [1947] KB 130 and *Robertson v Minister of Pensions* [1948] 2 All ER 767, because it was an unequivocal acceptance of liability, intended to be binding, intended to be acted on, and, in fact, acted on.

Much as I am inclined to favour the principle of the *High Trees* case, it is important that it should not be stretched too far lest it should be endangered. It does not create new causes of action where none existed before. It only prevents a party from insisting on his strict legal rights when it would be unjust to allow him to do so, having regard to the dealings which have taken place between the parties. That is the way it was put in the case in the House of Lords which first stated the principle – *Hughes v Metropolitan Ry. Co.* (1877) 2 App Cas 439 – and in the case in the Court of Appeal which enlarged it – *Birmingham and District Land Co v London & North Western Ry Co* (1888) 40 ChD 268. It is also implicit in all the modern cases in which the principle has been developed. Sometimes it is a plaintiff who is not allowed to insist on his strict legal rights.

Seeing that the principle never stands alone as giving a cause of action in itself, it can never do away with the necessity of consideration when that is an essential part of the cause of action. The doctrine of consideration is too firmly fixed to be overthrown by a side-wind. Its ill effects have been largely mitigated of late, but it still remains a cardinal necessity of the formation of a contract, although not of its modification or discharge. I fear that it was my failure to make this clear in *Central London Property Trust Ltd v High Trees House Ltd* which misled Byrne J in the present case. He held that the wife could sue on the husband's promise as a separate and independent cause of action by itself, although, as he held, there was no consideration for it. That is not correct. The wife can only enforce the promise if there was consideration for it. That is, therefore, the real question in the case: Was there sufficient consideration to support the promise?

If it were suggested that, in return for the husband's promise, the wife expressly or impliedly promised to forbear from applying to the court for maintenance – that is, a promise in return for a promise – there would clearly be no consideration because the wife's promise would not be binding on her and, therefore, would be worth nothing. Notwithstanding her promise, she could always apply to the divorce court for mainten- ance – perhaps, only with leave – but nevertheless she could apply. No agreement by her could take away that right: *Hyman v Hyman* [1929] AC 601, as interpreted by this court in *Gaisberg v Storr* [1949] 2 All ER 411. There was, however, clearly no promise by the wife, express or implied, to forbear from applying to the court. All that happened was that she did, in fact, forbear – that is, she did an act in return for a promise. Is that sufficient consideration? Unilateral promises of this kind have long been enforced so long as the act or forbearance is done on the faith of the promise and at the request of the promisor, express or implied. The act done is then in itself sufficient consideration for the promise, even though it arises *ex post facto*, as Parker J pointed out in *Wigan v English and Scottish Law Life Assurance Assocn* [1909] 1 Ch 298. If the findings of Byrne J are accepted, they are sufficient to bring this principle into play. His finding that the hus- band's promise was intended to be binding, intended to be acted on, and was, in fact, acted on – although expressed to be a finding on the principle of the *High Trees House* case – is equivalent to a finding that there was consideration within this long-settled rule, because it comes to the same thing expressed in different words: see *Oliver v Davis* [1949] 2 All ER 353. My difficulty, however, is to accept the findings of Byrne J that the promise was "intended to be acted on". I cannot find any evidence of any intention by the husband that the wife should forbear from applying to the court for maintenance, or, in other words, any request by the husband, express or implied, that the wife should so forbear. He left her to apply, if she wished to do so. She did not do so, and I am not surprised, because it is very unlikely that the divorce court would have made any order in her favour, since she had a bigger income than her husband. Her forbearance was not intended by him, nor was it done at his request. It was, therefore, no consideration.

It may be that the wife has suffered some detriment because, after forbearing to apply to the court for seven years, she might not now get leave to apply: *Scott v Scott* [1921] P 107. The court, however, is, nowadays much more ready to give leave than it used to be: *Fisher v Fisher* [1942] 1 All ER 438; *Hasting v Hasting* [1947] 2 All ER 744; and I should have thought that, if the wife fell on hard times, she would still get leave. Assuming, however, that she has suffered some detriment by her forbearance, never- theless, as the forbearance was not at the husband's request, it is no consideration. In *Scott v Scott* where a maintenance agreement was made during divorce proceedings, Scrutton LJ said ([1921] P 127) that he had no doubt about there being consideration for it, but this must now be taken to be erroneous, having regard to *Hyman v Hyman* and *Gaisberg v Storr*.

The doctrine of consideration is sometimes said to work injustice, but I see none in this case, nor was there any in *Oliver v Davis* or *Gaisberg v Storr*. I do not think it would be right for this wife, who is better off than her husband, to take no action for six or seven years and then demand from him the whole £600. The truth is that in these maintenance cases the real remedy of the wife is, not by action in the King's Bench Division, but by application in the Divorce Court. I have always understood that no agreement for maintenance, which is made in the course of divorce proceedings prior to decree absolute, is valid unless it is sanctioned by the court – indeed, I said so in *Emanuel v Emanuel* [1945] 2 All ER 496. I know that such agreements are often made, but their only valid purpose is to serve as a basis for a consent application to the court. The reason why such agreements are invalid, unless approved, is because they are so apt to be collusive. Some wives are tempted to stipulate for extortionate maintenance as the price of giving their husbands their freedom. It is to remove this temptation that the sanction of the court is required. It would be a great pity if this salutory requirement could be evaded by taking action in the King's Bench Division. The Divorce Court can order the husband to pay whatever maintenance is just. Moreover, if justice so requires, it can make the order retrospective to decree absolute. That is the proper remedy of the wife here, and I do not think she has a right to any other. For these reasons I think the appeal should be allowed.'

Birkett LJ:
'I agree. There were two points before the learned judge, both clearly stated and both clearly argued. . . .

   With regard to the second point, we have had the great advantage of hearing Denning LJ deal with *Central London Property Trust Ltd v High Trees House Ltd* and *Robertson v Minister of Pensions* which formed such a prominent part of the judgment of the court below. I am bound to say that reading them for myself I think the description which was given by counsel for the husband in this court, namely, that the doctrine there enunciated was, so to speak, a doctrine which would enable a person to use it as a shield and not as a sword, is a very vivid way of stating what, I think, is the principle underlying both those cases.'

An existing contract is clearly sufficient of a relationship to allow promissory estoppel to operate, though some later cases have suggested that other types of legal relationship may serve the same purpose. In *Durham Fancy Goods Ltd v Michael Jackson (Fancy Goods) Ltd* [1968] 2 QB 839, at 847, Donaldson J suggested that it was enough that 'there is a pre-existing legal relationship which could in certain circumstances give rise to liabilities and penalties', without this relationship needing to be contractual.

3.3.7.2 'Shield not a sword'

This phrase derives from counsel for the husband in *Combe v Combe* (above). It indicates that the most common use of promissory estoppel will be to defend against an action where a promisor is suing, having previously agreed to amend some aspect of the parties' relationship. It need not be used exclusively by defendants, however, as indicated by Halson.

Halson, R, 'The Offensive Limits of Promissory Estoppel' (1999) LMCLQ 256, pp 258–261

PROMISSORY ESTOPPEL: A NEW CAUSE OF ACTION?

One of the most debated issues in promissory estoppel is whether such an estoppel can itself constitute a cause of action. Cases have undoubtedly foundered when it was realized that one party's cause of action was a 'naked' estoppel. Many commentators and judges have said this cannot be done. So why the debate? Two answers come to mind. First, it seems that here, as elsewhere in estoppel, terminological clarity is lacking. The epithet that is most commonly cited to summarize the traditional wisdom on this subject, the shield/sword distinction which has been described judicially as a 'time-honoured phrase', is unhelpfully ambiguous. In truth, the use that can be made of an estoppel can be represented by a spectrum ranging from a defence to the creation of a new cause of action. Courts appear to use the shield/sword dichotomy to refer to some point on this spectrum . . .

A. The estoppel spectrum described

(1) Estoppel can only be used as a defence
This is the least ambitious claim that can be made. New legal doctrines often make their first appearance in a truncated and non-threatening guise. Therefore it should occasion no surprise that in both of the seminal cases, *Hughes v Metropolitan Ry* and *Central London Property Trust Co v High Trees House*, estoppel was relied upon as a defence. Indeed, as recently as 1960 this circumscribed role for estoppel was apparently contemplated in *Beesley v Hallwood Estates Ltd* by Buckley, J., who said:

> As I understand this part of the law, which has been described as promissory estoppel, it is that . . . the doctrine may afford a defence against the enforcement of otherwise enforceable rights. It cannot, in my judgment, be invoked to render enforceable a right which would otherwise be unenforceable.

(2) Estoppel can be used by a party seeking to enforce a claim based upon a recognized cause of action to defeat the defence or counter-claim of the other party
A simple example of this use of promissory estoppel would be provided by a variation of the facts of *High Trees*: the lessor lets directly to an occupying tenant; some time after the representation has been made and reduced rent payments have been accepted, the landlord distrains the tenant's property in order to recover the balance of the rent. Here the tenant could bring an action for conversion; the landlord would reply that he was rightfully distraining, and the tenant could use estoppel to defeat this defence. Academic authority also supports this usage.

A factually more complex example of this use of estoppel occurred in *The Ion*, the relevant facts of which were as follows. The defendant owners chartered their vessel to the plaintiff charterers. The charter incorporated the Hague Rules, which provide in Art III, r 6 that the carrier and the ship shall be discharged from all liability unless an action is brought within one year. There were several cargo claims but proceedings were not instituted within the required period. However, the charterers claimed, *inter alia*, that a letter from the owners' P. & I. club to the charterers' P. & I. club should be construed as amounting to a promissory estoppel to the effect that the owners would not rely on the time bar. The Commercial Court interpreted the letter from the owners' P. & I. club as containing an implied promise not to insist upon the strict time limit, which promise was relied on by the charterers in not making an immediate application under the Arbitration Act 1950, s 27 for an extension of time. In such circumstances the court held that it would be inequitable to allow the owners to enforce their strict legal rights and so the claimed estoppel was established.

Several judicial statements as to the proper limits of the offensive use of promissory estoppel extend further to one of the following two categories.

(3) Estoppel can be used by a party seeking to enforce a claim to prove one element of a recognized cause of action

This appears to be the effect the promissory estoppel was stated to have in *Robertson v Minister of Pensions*, where the plaintiff was relieved of the burden of having to prove that his injury was attributable to war service in order to qualify for a disablement pension because the Ministry were estopped from denying this causal connection. The plaintiff's cause of action was a recognized one; in this case statutory or at least *sui generis*. Yet it could not be said that the estoppel relieved the colonel of the obligation to prove all the elements of his cause of action, e.g., that he had served long enough and in a sufficient capacity to qualify for a pension, that the injury was serious enough to so qualify etc. The estoppel related solely to the question of causation; was the injury attributable to military service? This usage may have been what Denning LJ, was thinking of when, in *Combe v Combe*, commenting upon a number of decisions including the *Robertson* case, he said:

> In none of these cases was the defendant sued on the promise, assurance or assertion as a cause of action in itself: he was sued for some other cause, for example a pension . . . and the promise, assurance or assertion only played a supplementary role—an important role, no doubt, but still a supplementary role.

(4) Estoppel can be used by a party seeking to enforce a claim to prove all the elements of a recognized cause of action

This appears to be the way the promissory estoppel was used in *The Henrik Sif*. The first defendants conducted themselves as if they were a party to a bill of lading, which they were not. This led the plaintiff to allow the limitation period to run out against the second defendant, who was a party to the bill of lading. The judge based his finding for the plaintiff in his action against the first defendants, *inter alia*, upon promissory estoppel. It appears that all the elements (agreement, consideration etc.) of a recognized cause of action (contract) were proved by the estoppel.

The case of *Bruner v Moore*, which, although predating the *High Trees* case, similarly drew upon the *Hughes* principle, may be explained in this way. The plaintiff there was allowed to enforce his option out of time, either because the option had been consensually extended or because an equity arose in his favour as a result of the conduct of the grantor. It would appear that the effect of the equity was to prevent the defendant from denying that the plaintiff had a contractually binding option; the 'equity' provided the plaintiff with all the elements of a recognized cause of action. This decision has been adopted and relied on in Canada. A somewhat more equivocal endorsement has been given by an Australian court. In England the case seems mainly to be cited in connection with the postal rule of acceptance.

3.3.7.3 Inequitable for the promisor to go back on the promise

Promissory estoppel is a doctrine that has its roots in equity; the courts will not, therefore, allow it to be used unless it is to prevent some inequity arising. The most obvious situation that will prevent its use is where the promisee has taken advantage of the promisor in order to extract the promise. This was the situation in *D & C Builders Ltd v Rees*.

D & C Builders Ltd v Rees [1966] 2 QB 617 (CA)

Facts: The plaintiffs were builders who had done work for the defendant. They were owed about £500. The defendant, who knew that the plaintiffs were in financial difficulties, offered them £300, indicating that they would not get any more. The plaintiffs accepted this in settlement of the debt, but later sued for the outstanding balance.

Lord Denning MR:

'. . . In point of law payment of a lesser sum, whether by cash or by cheque, is no discharge of a greater sum.

This doctrine of the common law has come under heavy fire. It was ridiculed by Sir George Jessel in *Couldery v Bartram* (1881) 19 Ch.D. 394, 399. It was said to be mistaken by Lord Blackburn in *Foakes v Beer* 9 App.Cas. 605, 622. It was condemned by the Law Revision Committee (1945 Cmd. 5449), paras. 20 and 21. But a remedy has been found. The harshness of the common law has been relieved. Equity has stretched out a merciful hand to help the debtor. The courts have invoked the broad principle stated by Lord Cairns in *Hughes v Metropolitan Railway Co* (1877) 2 App.Cas. 439, 448:

"It is the first principle upon which all courts of equity proceed, that if parties, who have entered into definite and distinct terms involving certain legal results, afterwards by their own act or with their own consent enter upon a course of negotiation which has the effect of leading one of the parties to suppose that the strict rights arising under the contract will not be enforced, or will be kept in suspense, or held in abeyance, the person who otherwise might have enforced those rights will not be allowed to enforce them when it would be inequitable having regard to the dealings which have taken place between the parties."

It is worth noticing that the principle may be applied, not only so as to suspend strict legal rights, but also so as to preclude the enforcement of them.

This principle has been applied to cases where a creditor agrees to accept a lesser sum in discharge of a greater. So much so that we can now say that, when a creditor and a debtor enter upon a course of negotiation, which leads the debtor to suppose that, on payment of the lesser sum, the creditor will not enforce payment of the balance, and on the faith thereof the debtor pays the lesser sum and the creditor accepts it as satisfaction: then the creditor will not be allowed to enforce payment of the balance when it would be inequitable to do so. This was well illustrated during the last war. Tenants went away to escape the bombs and left their houses unoccupied. The landlords accepted a reduced rent for the time they were empty. It was held that the landlords could not afterwards turn round and sue for the balance, see *Central London Property Trust Ltd v High Trees House Ltd* [1947] 1 K.B. 130; 62 T.L.R. 559; [1956] 1 All E.R. 256. This caused at the time some eyebrows to be raised in high places. But they have been lowered since. The solution was so obviously just that no one could well gainsay it.

In applying this principle, however, we must note the qualification: The creditor is only barred from his legal rights when it would be *inequitable* for him to insist upon them. Where there has been a true *accord*, under which the creditor voluntarily agrees to accept a lesser sum in satisfaction, and the debtor acts upon that accord by paying the lesser sum and the creditor accepts it, then it is inequitable for the creditor afterwards to insist on the balance. But he is not bound unless there has been truly an accord between them.

In the present case, on the facts as found by the judge, it seems to me that there was no true accord. The debtor's wife held the creditor to ransom. The creditor was in need of money to meet his own commitments, and she knew it. When the creditor asked for payment of the £480 due to him, she said to him in effect: "We cannot pay you the £480. But we will pay you £300 if you will accept it in settlement. If you do not accept it on those terms, you will get nothing. £300 is better than nothing." She had no right to say any such thing. She could properly have said: "We cannot pay you more than £300. Please accept it on account." But she had no right to insist on his taking it in settlement. When she said: "We will pay you nothing unless you accept £300 in settlement", she was putting undue pressure on the creditor. She was making a threat to break the contract (by paying nothing) and she was doing it so as to compel the creditor to do what he was unwilling to do (to accept £300 in settlement): and she succeeded. He complied with her demand. That was on recent authority a case of intimidation: see *Rookes v Barnard* and *Stratford (J. T.) & Son Ltd v Lindley*. In these circumstances there was no true accord so as to found a defence of accord and satisfaction: see *Day v McLea*. There is also no equity in the defendant to warrant any

196

departure from the due course of law. No person can insist on a settlement procured by intimidation.'

Danckwerts and Winn LJJ concurred in the result, but without discussing the doctrine of promissory estoppel.

The behaviour of the defendant in *D & C Builders v Rees* was what, in Lord Denning's view, made it not inequitable to allow the plaintiffs to go back on their promise. But wrongdoing by the promisee is not a necessary factor of this aspect of the doctrine of promissory estoppel. In *The Post Chaser*, Robert Goff J held that the speed with which the promise had been withdrawn meant that it was not inequitable to allow the promisor to escape from it, even if the promisee had to some extent relied on it. In the following passage, where Robert Goff refers to 'equitable estoppel', he means the concept that is referred to in this chapter as 'promissory estoppel'.

The Post Chaser [1982] 1 All ER 19 (HC)

Robert Goff J:

'. . . [Having found that there was a representation which was sufficient to constitute an estoppel, he continued]:

However, there next arises the question whether there was any sufficient reliance by the sellers on this representation to give rise to an equitable estoppel. Here there arose a difference between counsel for the sellers and counsel for the buyers as to the degree of reliance which is required. It is plain, however, from the speech of Lord Cairns LC in *Hughes v Metropolitan Rly Co* (1877) 2 App Cas 439 at 448, [1874–80] All ER Rep 187 at 191 that the representor will not be allowed to enforce his rights "where it would be inequitable having regard to the dealings which have taken place between the parties". Accordingly there must be such action, or inaction, by the representee on the faith of the representation as will render it inequitable to permit the representor to enforce his strict legal rights.

On the findings of fact in the award before the court, there is no finding of any reliance by the sellers on the buyers' representation, save the fact that the documents covering the parcel on the Post Chaser were accordingly presented by Kievit (who in this context must be taken to have acted on behalf of the sellers) to Conti. That was done on 20 January; and by 22 January the sellers were informed by the buyers that NOGA had rejected the documents, following which the documents were passed back up the string to the sellers. The question therefore arises whether such action constituted sufficient reliance by the sellers on the buyers' representation to render it inequitable for the buyers thereafter to enforce their right to reject the documents. . . .

I approach the matter as follows. The fundamental principle is that stated by Lord

Cairns LC, viz that the representor will not be allowed to enforce his rights "where it would be inequitable having regard to the dealings which have thus taken place between the parties". To establish such inequity, it is not necessary to show detriment; indeed, the representee may have benefited from the representation, and yet it may be inequitable, at least without reasonable notice, for the representor to enforce his legal rights. Take the facts of *Central London Property Trust Ltd v High Trees House Ltd* (1946) [1956] 1 All ER 256, [1947] KB 130, the case in which Denning J breathed new life into the doctrine of equitable estoppel. The representation was by a lessor to the effect that he would be content to accept a reduced rent. In such a case, although the lessee has benefited from the reduction in rent, it may well be inequitable for the lessor to insist on his legal right to the unpaid rent, because the lessee has conducted his affairs on the basis that he would only have to pay rent at the lower rate; and a court might well think it right to conclude that only after reasonable notice could the lessor return to charging rent at the higher rate specified in the lease. Furthermore it would be open to the court, in any particular case, to infer from the circumstances of the case that the representee must have conducted his affairs in such a way that it would be inequitable for the representor to enforce his rights, or to do so without reasonable notice. But it does not follow that in every case in which the representee has acted, or failed to act, in reliance on the representation, it will be inequitable for the representor to enforce his rights for the nature of the action, or inaction, may be insufficient to give rise to the equity, in which event a necessary requirement stated by Lord Cairns LC for the application of the doctrine would not have been fulfilled.

This, in my judgment, is the principle which I have to apply in the present case. Here, all that happened was that the sellers, through Kievit, presented the documents on the same day as the buyers made their representation; and within two days the documents were rejected. Now on these simple facts, although it is plain that the sellers did actively rely on the buyers' representation, and did conduct their affairs in reliance on it, by presenting the documents, I cannot see anything which would render it inequitable for the buyers thereafter to enforce their legal right to reject the documents. In particular, having regard to the very short time which elapsed between the date of the representation and the date of the presentation of the documents on the one hand and the date of rejection on the other hand, I cannot see that, in the absence of any evidence that the sellers' position had been prejudiced by reason of their action in reliance on the representation, it is possible to infer that they suffered any such prejudice. In these circumstances, a necessary element for the application of the doctrine of equitable estoppel is lacking; and I decide this point in favour of the buyers.'

The way in which Robert Goff J deals with the issue of 'inequitability' in this case, shows that it is related to the issue of whether the promises have 'relied' on the promise. The formulation by Denning in *High Trees*, included the requirement that the promise has been 'acted upon'. Some judges have suggested that this means that the promisee must have acted to his or her detriment in relying on the promise – that is, that 'detrimental reliance' is a requirement for promissory estoppel to be binding. Lord Denning himself addressed this issue in *WJ Alan & Co v El Nasr*. Although in the following passage he discusses the case in terms of 'waiver', it is clear that he regards this concept as being part of the doctrine of promissory estoppel, so that the same approach to the issue of 'detrimental reliance' should apply to that doctrine.

WJ Alan & Co v El Nasr [1972] 2 Q.B. 189

Facts: A contract provided for payment to be made in Kenyan shillings. The buyers made payment under a letter of credit for the contract amount in sterling shillings – a lesser sum. The sellers accepted this, but then sued for the difference between the Kenyan and sterling amounts. The trial judge held that the sellers were not bound by their acceptance of the sterling amount, since the buyers had not acted to their detriment on any promise by the sellers to accept the lesser sum.

Held (per Lord Denning): Detrimental reliance was not necessary, where one party had led the other to believe that its strict rights under a contract would not be enforced, and the other had acted on this. (The other members of the court decided in favour of the sellers without committing themselves on the issue of 'detriment').

Lord Denning:
'. . . There are two cases on this subject. One is *Panoutsos v Raymond Hadley Corporation of New York* [1917] 2 K.B. 473 . . . The other is *Enrico Furst & Co v W E Fischer Ltd* [1960] 2 Lloyd's Rep. 340. In each of those cases the letter of credit did not conform to the contract of sale. In each case the non-conformity was in that it was not a confirmed credit. But the sellers took no objection to the letter of credit on that score. On the contrary, they asked for the letter of credit to be extended: and it was extended. In each case the sellers sought afterwards to cancel the contract on the ground that the letter of credit was not in conformity with the contract. In each case the court held that they could not do so.

What is the true basis of those decisions? is it a variation of the original contract? or a waiver of the strict rights thereunder? or a promissory estoppel precluding the seller from insisting on his strict rights? or what else?

In *Enrico Furst*, Diplock J. said it was a "classic case of waiver." I agree with him. It is an instance of the general principle which was first enunciated by Lord Cairns L.C. in *Hughes v Metropolitan Railway Co* (1877) 2 App.Cas 439, and rescued from oblivion by *Central London Property Trust Ltd v High Trees House Ltd* [1947] K.B. 130. The principle is much wider than waiver itself: but waiver is a good instance of its application.

The principle of waiver is simply this: If one party, by his conduct, leads another to believe that the strict rights arising under the contract will not be insisted upon, intending that the other should act on that belief, and he does act on it, then the first party will not afterwards be allowed to insist on the strict legal rights when it would be inequitable for him to do so: see *Plasticmoda Societa per Azioni v Davidsons (Manchester) Ltd* [1952] 1 Lloyd's Rep. 527, 539. There may be no consideration moving from him who benefits by the waiver. There may be no detriment to him by acting on it. There may be nothing in writing. Nevertheless, the one who waives his strict rights cannot afterwards insist on them. His strict rights are at any rate suspended so long as the waiver lasts . . .

The judge rejected this doctrine because, he said, "there is no evidence of the buyers having acted to their detriment." I know that it has been suggested in some quarters that there must be detriment. But I can find no support for it in the authorities cited by the judge. The nearest approach to it is the statement of Viscount Simonds in the *Tool Metal* case [1955] 1 W.L.R. 761, 764, that the other must have been led "to alter his position," which was adopted by Lord Hodson in *Ajayi v R T Briscoe (Nigeria) Ltd* [1964] 1 W.L.R. 1326, 1330. But that only means that he must have been led to act differently from what he otherwise would have done. And if you study the cases in which the doctrine has been applied, you will see that all that is required is that the one should have "*acted* on the belief induced by the other party." That is how Lord Cohen put it in the *Tool Metal* case [1955] 1 W.L.R. 761, 799, and that is how I would put it myself.'

If Lord Denning's analysis is accepted, then the position seems to be that detriment is not a necessary element in the reliance, in order for promissory estoppel to operate, but that it may be relevant to the question of whether the court will find it inequitable to allow the promisor to go back on the promise. The question is thus not 'has the promisee suffered detriment as a result of the reliance?', but, 'would it now cause significant detriment to the promisee if the promisor were to be allowed to go back on the promise?'

3.3.7.4 Suspensory nature of the doctrine

There is no doubt that in many situations in which it is appropriate for it to be used, the doctrine of promissory estoppel, like waiver, will only be suspensory in its effect. That was the situation in *High Trees* itself – once the conditions that had led to the promise had disappeared, the landlord was entitled to return to the originally agreed rent. In that case, the change in circumstances led to the ending of the promise. What if there is no change in circumstances? Can the promisor simply decide to withdraw the concession, and say that for the future the promisee must perform in accordance with the strict terms of the contract? The issue was considered in *Tool Metal Manufacturing Co v Tungsten Electric Co.*

Tool Metal Manufacturing Co. Ltd v Tungsten Electric Co Ltd
[1955] 2 All ER 657 (HL)

Facts: The defendants were producing metal alloys under a licence from the plaintiffs who owned the patents in the alloys. The defendants were obliged to pay a royalty of 10% of the value of what was produced, plus a further 30% where production exceeded 50 kilograms a month. When production increased significantly because of the outbreak of the war with Germany in 1939, the plaintiffs did not insist on the 30% payment. After the end of the war, the defendants sued the plaintiffs for fraud, and the plaintiffs counterclaimed for payment of the 30%. Both actions were dismissed; the plaintiffs were unsuccessful because they had not given notice of an intention to return to the strict term of the agreement. The plaintiffs then brought a further action to recover the 30%; the trial judge held that the previous counterclaim was sufficient notice; the Court of Appeal disagreed. The plaintiffs appealed to the House of Lords.

Held: The counterclaim was sufficient notice of the intention to revert to the strict terms of the contract, and the plaintiffs were now entitled to succeed.

Viscount Simonds:

'. . . the appellants (hereinafter called "T.M.M.C."), by writ issued on September 11, 1950, claimed from the respondents (hereinafter called "TECO"), as compensation under cl. 5 of the deed as from January 1, 1947, to January 26, 1950, a quantified sum of £84,050, and an account of compensation payable under the same clause from January 26, 1950, to July 27, 1950, when the licence terminated. To this claim TECO put in a number of defences. They pleaded that the provisions of cl. 5 were void on three separate grounds: (a) because they imposed a penalty; (b) because they were an unreasonable restraint of trade; and (c) because they contravened s. 38 of the Patents and Designs Act, 1907. They also pleaded that the delivery of the counterclaim in the first action did not operate as notice to terminate the equitable arrangement which, as was held in that action, existed at any rate until such delivery, and that it was a condition of its termination that the notice determining it (a) should be unequivocal, and (b) should specify the date of termination, and, further, that that date should give them a reasonable time to adjust their business affairs to meet the altered circumstances. To this, in effect, T.M.M.C. replied that the delivery of the counterclaim was a sufficient intimation of their intention to reassert their legal rights and that, that intimation having been given, equity demanded nothing more than that a reasonable time should be allowed before they sought to enforce them. And they further said (nor was this denied by TECO) that, on this footing, a reasonable time was given, since the counterclaim was delivered in March, 1946, and compensation claimed from January, 1947. . . .

My Lords, the decision of the Court of Appeal in the first action was based on nothing else than the principle of equity stated in this House in *Hughes v Metropolitan Ry Co* (1877) 2 App Cas at p 448 and interpreted by Bowen LJ in *Birmingham & District Land Co v London & North Western Ry Co* (1888) 40 ChD at p 286 in these terms:

It seems to me to amount to this, that if persons who have contractual rights against others induce by their conduct those against whom they have such rights to believe that such rights will either not be enforced or will be kept in suspense or abeyance for some particular time, those persons will not be allowed by a court of equity to enforce the rights until such time has elapsed, without at all events placing the parties in the same position as they were before.

These last words are important, for they emphasise that the gist of the equity lies in the fact that one party has by his conduct led the other to alter his position. I lay stress on this, because I would not have it supposed, particularly in commercial transactions, that mere acts of indulgence are apt to create rights, and I do not wish to lend the authority of this House to the statement of the principle which is to be found in *Combe v Combe* ([1951] 1 All ER 767 at p 770) and may well be far too widely stated.

The difficulty in the present case lies in the fact that, in the first action, in which it was held that between these parties the principle applies, neither of them in any pleading or other statement between the delivery of the counterclaim in March, 1946 and judgment in April, 1950, took their stand on its existence. TECO asserted a binding agreement for the complete and final abrogation of any compensation: T.M.M.C., though willing to make some concession in regard to the past, denied any agreement in respect of any period at all. The position of neither of them was compatible with the existence of an equitable arrangement by which the right to receive, and the obligation to pay, compensation were suspended for a period which lasted at least until March, 1946, and for a debatable period thereafter.

My Lords, I think that, at this point, the issue is a very narrow one. On the one hand, it is said that a plea resting on the denial of an agreement cannot be a notice determining that agreement. This is the view taken by Romer LJ, in which the other members of the Court of Appeal concurred. On the other hand, it is urged that, since the suspensory period is due to the gratuitous willingness of the one party to forgo their rights, nothing can be a clearer intimation that they propose no longer to forgo them than a claim which, though it may ask too much, can leave the other party in no doubt that they must not expect further indulgence. The problem may, perhaps, be stated in this way: Did equity require that T.M.M.C. should expressly and unequivocally refer to an equitable arrangement which TECO had not pleaded and they did not recognise? Or was it sufficient for them by a reassertion of their legal rights to proclaim that the period of indulgence was over? In favour of the latter view, it is added that such an attitude on the part of T.M.M.C. could not surprise TECO who had not hesitated to bring against them a serious charge of fraud.

My Lords, it is not clear to me what conclusion the Court of Appeal would have reached but for the authority of *Canadian Pacific Ry Co v Regem* [1931] AC 414, to which I must refer later. For my part, I have, after some hesitation, formed the opinion that, as soon as the counterclaim was delivered, TECO must be taken to know that the suspensory period was at an end and were bound to put their house in order. The position is a very artificial one, but it was their own ignorance of a suspensory period, or at least their failure to plead it, which created the difficulty, and I do not think that they can take advantage of their own ignorance or default and say that they were entitled to a further period of grace until a further notice was given. Equity demands that all the circumstances of the case should be regarded, and I think that the fair and reasonable view is that TECO could not, after they had received the counterclaim, regard themselves as entitled to further indulgence.

It was, however, urged on behalf of TECO that, even if the counterclaim could otherwise be regarded as a sufficient notice that the equitable arrangement was at an end, yet it was defective in that it did not name a certain future date at which it was to take effect. To this the reply was made that equity did not require a future date to be named in the notice, but that what it did require was that a reasonable time should be allowed to elapse before it was sought to enforce it. Here, too, the Court of Appeal favoured the view of TECO, again feeling themselves constrained by the decision in the *Canadian Pacific Railway* case. And here, too, I am forced to the opposite conclusion. Equity is not held in a strait-jacket. There is no universal rule that an equitable arrangement must always be determined in one way. It may, in some cases, be right and fair that a dated notice should be given. But in this case, what was the position in January, 1947, which I take to be the critical date? Then for nine months TECO must, in my opinion, be taken to have been aware that T.M.M.C. proposed to stand on their legal rights. It is not denied that those nine months gave them ample time to readjust their position. I cannot regard it as a requirement of equity that, in such circumstances, they should have been expressly notified in March, 1946, that they would have nine months and no more to take such steps as the altered circumstances required. In coming to this conclusion, I do not think I run counter to any authority that was cited to us, unless it be the *Canadian Pacific Railway* case to which I must now refer.

My Lords, in his judgment in the Court of Appeal, Romer LJ introduced that case with these words ([1954] 2 All ER at p 41):

> In my opinion, although in many cases the equity, to which *Hughes v Metropolitan Ry Co* gave recognition and high authority, is satisfied by merely conforming to the terms in which Lord Cairns (and subsequently Bowen LJ) formulated it, there are other cases where justice requires that the resumption of legal rights which have been suspended for a period must be preceded by a notification to the other party concerned specifying a fixed period of grace during which that party can put his house in order, and that in such cases a notification such as that will be a condition precedent to the valid re-assumption of the owner's legal rights. Such a case was *Canadian Pacific Ry Co v Regem*.

My Lords it is undoubtedly the fact that the *Canadian Pacific Railway* case decided that what I have called a "dated notice" was required in that case to terminate an existing licence, and that the Crown, the licensor, had in that case the duty and the risk of fixing a reasonable period of notice, but I must observe that, not only was the equitable principle, which was recognised in *Hughes'* case not invoked, but Lord Russell of Killowen, in delivering the opinion of the Board, expressly disclaimed any reference to that or any other equitable principle. The relevant problem was that whether a licence to occupy land by placing telegraph poles thereon had been revoked by the institution of proceedings by the Crown, and the question was what term in regard to revocation should be implied in the licence which the Crown was assumed to have granted. I have no doubt that the question is analogous to that which we have to decide in this case, for the implication of a term as to revocation, on which the licence is silent, must depend on what is fair and reasonable between the parties. The court will be guided by the same principles in the one case and the other. The passage which I cited from Bowen LJ's judgment in the *Birmingham* case ended with these words (40 ChD at p 286):

> That is the principle to be applied. I will not say it is not a principle that was recognised by courts of law as well as of equity. It is not necessary to consider how far it was always a principle of common law.

Nor, my Lords, is it necessary today, but in the House of Justice it would be difficult to distinguish between the equitable principle recognised in *Hughes'* case and the rule well established at common law long before the fusion of law and equity that a licensor must give reasonable notice to determine a licence. It was this rule which was applied in the *Canadian Pacific Railway* case and, in applying it, Lord Russell of Killowen said ([1931] AC at p 432):

> Whether any and what restrictions exist on the power of a licensor to determine a revocable licence must, their Lordships think, depend upon the circumstances of each case.

And, as I read the decision, it was the circumstances of that case and nothing else, certainly not any general rule, which led him to say that (ibid., at p 433):

> it will be for the Crown to determine the licence by service of a notice the sufficiency of which, if called in question, will have to be decided, upon proper evidence, in subsequent proceedings. It will be for the Crown, at its risk, to fix the length of notice.

The circumstances of that case were very unusual, and I do not doubt that they fully justified the rule being applied in that way. But so, also, in the present case the circumstances are very unusual: it is hardly possible that they should be repeated, and, even if I apply in the amplest way to the termination of the equitable arrangement between the parties in the case the rule applicable to the revocation of licence, I find nothing in the *Canadian Pacific Railway* case which precludes me from reaching the conclusion which I have already stated, viz., that the appellants gave sufficient notice that the suspensory period was at an end and allowed enough time to elapse before seeking to enforce their rights. For these reasons, I think that this defence fails and that the judgment of the Court of Appeal cannot, on this ground, be upheld. . . .'

Lord Oaksey, Lord Tucker, and Lord Cohen concurred.

The position is, therefore, that a party making a promise that varies a continuing contractual obligation, but to which no time limit has been attached, can bring the variation to an end by giving reasonable notice. In this case, the notice was constituted by the issue of the counterclaim, and the plaintiffs had waited a reasonable time before seeking to enforce it.

This clearly applies where the contract being varied is one involving continuing obligations – such as to pay rent, or royalties. It is difficult to see that it could apply if promissory estoppel is used to reduce a single debt – as in *Alan v El Nasr*. It would not seem to make sense to hold, on the one hand that promissory estoppel prevented the recovery of the full debt, but on the other that the promisor could withdraw the concession by giving reasonable notice. In this type of situation it is submitted that promissory estoppel would operate to extinguish the debt completely, and would not simply be suspensory in its effect.

3.4 ALTERNATIVE TESTS OF ENFORCEABILITY

Some commentators, most notably Atiyah, have argued that English contract law should depart from its insistence on 'consideration' as the hallmark of a contract. Two possible alternative approaches are noted here – the use of 'reliance' as a test of enforceability, and the approach set out in the Principles of European Contract Law.

3.4.1 RELIANCE

A good starting point for discussion of the possibility of using reliance to enforce what otherwise appears to be a gratuitous promise in English law is the argument to this effect by Professor Atiyah.

Atiyah, PS, *Essays on Contract*, 1986, Oxford: Clarendon Press, pp 226–240

The Enforcement of Gratuitous Promises

It is, of course, an integral part of the orthodox doctrine that gratuitous promises are not enforced by the courts except when they are under seal. So long as a 'gratuitous promise' is defined as meaning a promise without any consideration (as that word is in practice understood by the courts), then this conclusion is not merely sound but self-evident. But if the term 'gratuitous promise' means what it means in ordinary speech, namely a promise to make a gift, then the proposition is not sound. No promise is enforced by the courts unless there is some good reason (or consideration) for its enforcement; and the mere desire to make a gift is not a sufficient reason standing alone. Nor, according to the traditional view of the law, is it a sufficient reason that a man may be morally obliged to keep his word. But all this is just as true of commercial promises as it is of gratuitous promises. In both cases some good reason (or consideration) for enforcement must be shown, though it hardly need be stated that such reasons (or considerations) are more commonly found in the former than in the latter case.

I have already discussed one group of gratuitous promises which are regularly enforced by the courts, namely those cases in which the promisee has performed some act in reliance on the promise which makes it just to enforce the promise. I must now go on to consider the area of promissory estoppel.

The frontier between promissory estoppel and unilateral contracts
Orthodox theory draws a firm line between a promise given for consideration, and a promise enforceable on the ground of promissory estoppel. In the case of a promise for an act, the distinction comes down to a very fine point. If the act is stated or specified (or possibly if it is requested) by the promisor, then the promise is enforceable in the ordinary way; the performance of the act is a good consideration. If the act is done by the promisee in reliance on the promise, but it has not been requested or stated or specified by the promisor, then orthodoxy asserts that there is no consideration, though there is a sufficient reason for giving the promise the limited validity recognized by promissory estoppel. It may help to see this distinction in perspective if the following possible fact situations are differentiated:

1. The promisor requests and desires the act, and the act confers a benefit on him, for example A promises commission to an estate agent if the agent introduces a purchaser who buys A's house. This promise is enforceable once the act is done.

2. The promisor requests and desires the act, but it confers no direct benefit on him, though it involves a factual detriment to the promisee, for example A promises to give B the price of a house if B enters into a contract to purchase it from a third party. This promise is enforceable once the act is done.

3. The promisor requests and desires the act though it confers no direct benefit on him and involves no factual detriment to the promisee, for example A promises a reward to the winner of a race. This promise is enforceable by the winner of the race once he has complied with the condition.

4. The promisor states the act to be performed by the promisee, but does not request or desire it; it confers no benefit on him though it might involve a factual detriment to the promisee, for example a father promises to give an allowance to his daughter if she should decide to leave her husband. This promise is, I submit, enforceable if the promisee acts on it.

5. The promisor does not state any act which is to be performed by the promisee but it is reasonably implicit that such an act is requested or desired by him, for example A promises additional payment to his creditor without stating that he asks for more time to pay, but it is reasonably implicit in the circumstances that this is what he wants. This promise is enforceable once some reasonable time has been given. (It would of

course be enforceable at the outset if the creditor expressly or impliedly *promised* to give some reasonable time.)

6. The promisor does not state any act which is to be performed by the promisee but the promisee does act in reliance on the promise in a way which was the natural and foreseeable result of the promise. This promise is said to be not enforceable as a contract, but enforceable to the limited extent recognized by promissory estoppel.

7. The promisor states the act to be performed by the promisee, and the promisee performs some other act which is a necessary step towards the performance of the act stated by the promisor, but he does not perform the act stated. The promisee cannot enforce the principal promise but may in some circumstances be able to enforce an implied subsidiary promise.

8. The promisor does not state any act which is to be performed by the promisee, but the promisee acts in reliance on the promise in a way which the promisor had no reason to anticipate.

9. The promisee does not act on the promise at all.

I do not suggest that the above list is an exhaustive statement of the possibilities; indeed, there are plainly other permutations and combinations, but this list will suffice for my purposes. The crucial cases are 6, 7, and 8. Few, I think, would contend that Case 9 is enforceable in the present state of the law, either as a contract or even as a case of promissory estoppel. Certainly *some* factor must be present in this case beyond the bare fact of the promise, if the promise is to be given any recognition, and none is stated in the facts assumed. Case 8 is not a case which has been much discussed. It is, at any rate, clear that orthodoxy would not allow Case 8 to be enforced as a binding contractual promise. The case I wish to concentrate on is Case 6. This is the case of promissory estoppel, but what I want to examine here is not why this case should be enforceable (to a limited extent) as a case of promissory estoppel, but why it should not be enforced as a case of consideration.

The factual difficulty of defining the frontier

If the law of consideration had been recognized for what I suggest it to be, namely a set of guides for deciding whether there is good reason for the enforcement of a promise, the answer would surely have been clear. There is no natural frontier between Case 5 and Case 6. Indeed, there are frequently great difficulties in drawing the factual distinction between Case 5 and Case 6. *Combe v Combe* is one well-known case in which the act was not stated and the court refused to imply a statement (or request, as it was there put). On the other hand, in the collateral contract cases, the act to be performed by the promisee would rarely be expressly stated, though it would normally be implicit. The man who deals with another by professing to be an agent is clearly impliedly requesting the other to deal with him. The car dealer who gives a collateral promise to a prospective hire-purchaser usually makes it fairly clear what is the act to be done by the promisee. But it is to be observed that the *precise* act need not be stated or specified for a collateral promise to be enforceable. In *Wells v Buckland Sand*, a collateral promise was enforced where the act was the purchase of chrysanthemum sand from a third party who himself acquired the sand from the defendant. It was held that a collateral warranty is enforceable 'notwithstanding that no specific main contract is discussed at the time it is given', although it must be shown that it was contemplated that some such contract would be entered into. No particular contract of sale or hire-purchase thus needs to be identified as the one into which the promisee must enter to make the promise enforceable. But it will be seen that the less precise is the nature of the act stated by the promisor, the closer does Case 5 get to Case 6.

Next, it is to be noted that Case 6 is, or may be, very close to Case 7. In Case 7 the promisee may be given some enforceable contractual right although he has not actually performed the act stated by the promisor—though we have seen that this will only be so in somewhat rare cases. On the other hand in Case 6 the promisee also performs some act other than the act stated, being an act which is the natural result of the promise. The fineness of this distinction in fact is illustrated by the situation in *Hohler v Aston*. In this case the defendant, Mrs A, promised to give a London house to Mr and Mrs R, her niece and husband. She contracted to acquire the property and Mr and Mrs R gave up the lease of their country property and moved into the London house. The defendant then died before the property had been transferred to her or to Mr and Mrs R. Sargant J. was able to decide the case in favour of the plaintiffs without having to consider whether the facts already stated were sufficient to enable Mr and Mrs R to enforce the aunt's promise. But he expressed the view that the promise would probably not have been enforceable, although he acknowledged the hardship which this would have entailed for Mr and Mrs R. If they had given up their country house at Mrs A's request, this would have rendered the promise enforceable, but because this was not actually stated as an act to be performed by them, the promise was (he thought) unenforceable. This distinction is exactly the orthodox doctrine, but the distinction seems so fine as to be virtually unintelligible. It seems most undesirable to decide a case of this kind on such a point because the whole issue would turn on oral evidence as to whether the aunt ever said to Mr and Mrs R that they must give up their country property and come and live in the London house. It is probable that recollection of oral discussions to this degree of accuracy would be impossible, and that the decision would actually turn on findings of fact which are bound to be unreliable. Perhaps if the decision had actually turned on this issue Sargant J. would have been prepared to imply a request. It could not be said that this was a *necessary* implication of the defendant's conduct; doubtless Mr and Mrs R could have retained the lease of their country house while going to live in the London house. But the possibility of implying a request where the court feels it necessary to do justice is another confirmation of the unreality of the factual distinction between Case 5 and Case 6.

Policy arguments for maintaining the frontier

But even if these arguments are not felt to be convincing, it remains to inquire whether there can be any rational ground for distinguishing between Case 5 and Case 6. I have already indicated that this seems to me an impossible line to maintain. So long as it is believed that all contracts are bargains, there is some rational ground for requiring that the act to be performed by the promisee must be stated, if not actually requested, by the promisor; but once it is agreed that many promises are enforced though they are not bargains, it is hard to see what rational purpose is intended to be served by the insistence that the act must be stated. The natural place to draw a line in the above listed cases is not between Case 5 and Case 6 but between Case 7 and Case 8. The difference between an act done by the promisee which is impliedly stated by the promisor, and an act done in natural and foreseeable reliance on the promise seems much less substantial than the distinction between the latter case and an act in reliance which could not have been anticipated by the promisor. That is not to say that even this last case may not, in certain circumstances, be thought to be a promise worthy of enforcement.

The authorities

I turn, now, to inquire whether the orthodox distinction between Case 5 and Case 6 is in fact supported by the actual decisions of the courts. And here we find a somewhat paradoxical situation. By the time of the *High Trees* decision in 1946, orthodox opinion had become so hardened in the view that gratuitous promises were never enforceable and that only bargains could constitute contracts, that orthodox lawyers could not believe that the dicta of Denning J. in that case could be sound law. When the issue came up again in *Combe v Combe*, even Denning LJ (as he had then become) resiled from the view that a *High Trees* type of promise could be fully enforceable as a contractual promise. *Combe v Combe*, it will be recalled, involved the enforceability of a promise by a husband to pay his wife £100 per annum on their separation. The wife did not apply for maintenance to the court, nor did she make any attempt to enforce the husband's promise for a period of some six years. She then sued the husband for £600. At first instance Byrne J. applied the dictum of Denning J. in the *High Trees* case and gave judgment for the wife. The judgment of Byrne J. gives no hint that the learned judge thought that he was doing anything very radical or unprecedented in enforcing the husband's promise. Perhaps he thought that the husband had impliedly requested that the wife should forbear from applying for maintenance. But even if he had thought that there was no such implied request, his decision would have been perfectly explicable in terms of the existing case-law. As we have already seen, a forbearance (or an act) which naturally and foreseeably follows a promise had been previously held to be a good consideration for the enforcement of a promise in a number of situations.

When *Combe v Combe* came before the Court of Appeal, however, that decision was reversed. The court first held that there was no implied request by the husband that the wife should forbear; and even if they were wrong in thinking that a request (as opposed to a statement of the act or forbearance) was necessary, the absence of an implied request must have also led to the view that there was no implied statement in that case. Perhaps the court should have implied a request, as Professor Goodhart cogently argued. Certainly they *could* have done so without doing the least violence to the facts. Why then did they not do so? I submit that they did not do so because they did not feel that the justice of the case required it. Denning LJ himself made no secret of his views as to the merits of the case: 'The doctrine of consideration is sometimes said to work injustice, but I see none in this case . . . I do not think it would be right for this wife, who is better off than her husband, to take no action for six or seven years and then come down on him for the whole £600.' With this statement I find myself in complete sympathy. In recent times it has become clear that the changing moral values of our society mean that a man is not necessarily regarded as under any obligation to maintain a separated wife—especially if she has an income as large as his own. It is true that the addition of an express promise may suffice to create such an obligation but in this situation the length of time which had elapsed since the promise was made had completely altered the nature of the promise which the wife was trying to enforce. What the husband promised was an income of £100 per annum, a matter of £2 per week. What the wife was trying to enforce was payment of a lump sum of £600. While I would freely admit that two views may be possible as to the merits of the case, I find it hard to believe that the Court of Appeal did not regard the merits as with the husband. Had they wished to find in favour of the wife it would have been so easy to imply a requested forbearance that it is hard to believe they did in fact wish to do so.

If we pause here for a moment, what did *Combe v Combe* actually decide? The common (and now orthodox) interpretation of the case is that it decides this: that action by a promisee in reliance on a promise (where the action is not requested or stated) is not directly enforceable by the promisee, but may be set up by him as a defence to proceedings by the promisor. Once again I feel obliged to depart from orthodox doctrine. I would suggest that, on the contrary, the case decided nothing more than this: that an act (or forbearance) which naturally and foreseeably follows from and in reliance on a promise is not a consideration for the enforcement of the promise *where the justice of the case does not require that it should be*. So viewed the decision is perfectly in line with older cases. Among these cases are the ones to which I have already made reference, namely *Dillwyn v Llewellyn*, and the line of authorities following it. There is no doubt that the principle stated in these cases is flatly inconsistent with orthodox doctrine; for these cases stand for the principle that if a man promises to give another some land, and permits the other to build a property on his land, then even though he has not requested or stated that such building is the act on which his promise becomes enforceable, the promise will be enforceable. As I have already pointed out, the judges who decided these cases did not find anything inconsistent between the notion of requiring a consideration for the enforcement of a promise, and yet enforcing the promises in these cases. I have also pointed out that attempts have been made by orthodox lawyers to 'explain' away these decisions, but the need for such 'explanations' only arises because of the conviction that they are inconsistent with some 'doctrine' for which there was (in this respect) no contrary authority.

Today, it must be admitted, the *High Trees* case has itself become the new orthodoxy; or at least it has become the new orthodoxy as orthodoxy interprets *Combe v Combe*. Here is a paradox indeed. The *High Trees* principle, as cut down by the generally accepted interpretation placed on *Combe v Combe*, was not the radical and forward-looking innovation that it was thought by orthodoxy to be. It was, on the contrary, a reactionary step. It did not create new defences to actions which would previously have found the defendant helpless. On the contrary, it refused to recognize as a consideration what earlier courts were willing to recognize as consideration.

I do not rely solely on *Dillwyn v Llewellyn* and the cases following it for my view that an act done in reliance on a promise may be a good consideration even though it is not stated or requested by the promisor as an act to be performed by the promisee. These particular cases may be explained away as anomalous or exceptional. I therefore turn to an examination of the House of Lords' decision in *Jorden v Money*, which lies at the heart of this whole question. The treatment of this case by lawyers during the past fifty years is one of the most extraordinary chapters in the whole law of consideration, and must make one wonder whether lawyers actually read the cases which form the pillars of orthodoxy.

The facts in *Jorden v Money* were as follows. The plaintiff M had executed a bond for £1,200 in favour of one C, and on C's death the bond had passed to the defendant, Miss M, now Mrs J. The defendant had frequently stated to M and others that the debt was gone, and that she would never enforce it; she repeated these statements at a time when M was contemplating marriage. In reliance thereon M did marry; subsequently the defendant married and then demanded payment on the bond. The plaintiff therefore brought a suit in equity asking for an order that the bond be given up and cancelled. It was held that the suit should be dismissed. Now, what did this case decide? The commonly accepted view is that the case decided that a representation of intention cannot be the foundation for an estoppel; estoppel can only arise from a statement of fact. Therefore, although the plaintiff relied on Mrs J's representations of intention by marrying, he could not plead estoppel. Naturally this causes great difficulty to the new orthodoxy which recognizes the defence of promissory estoppel based on a representation of intention. How can this be reconciled with *Jorden v Money*? One suggestion is that that case was a decision at common law, while promissory estoppel is an equitable development. But this will not do; *Jorden v Money* was a decision in equity on appeal from the Chancery Court of Appeal. Another explanation is that *Jorden v Money* does not lay down an absolute rule; exceptions to it may be justified. Another suggestion is that Mrs J did not intend to be legally bound by her promises, and there are remarks by Lord Cranworth which would support this, though the suggestion is difficult to reconcile with some of the evidence, and it would anyhow involve rejection of most of the speeches as erroneous dicta. Another suggestion is that promissory estoppel is not really estoppel at all. Another is that the new promissory estoppel has a more limited effect than a 'real' estoppel, and another is that the decision was wrong.

The truth is that there is a very much simpler explanation of *Jorden v Money* which seems to stare in the face anyone who actually reads the report. Discussions of the case all start with the assumption that the plaintiff could not enforce the defendant's promise in contract because he could show no consideration; and it is for this reason that (it is assumed) the plaintiff relied on estoppel. The truth is precisely the opposite. The plaintiff could have proved a good contract; in fact—it is scarcely too much to say—he *did* show a good contract, and that is precisely why he failed. To understand this paradoxical statement it must be recalled that the Statute of Frauds required at this time that a promise in consideration of marriage must be proved in writing. The only act in reliance on the promise which the plaintiff could show was his marriage; *but he had no written note or memorandum signed by the defendant*. His counsel, therefore, deliberately refrained from arguing his case in contract but relied on estoppel. The whole point of the case (at all events as it developed in the House of Lords) was whether the plaintiff was entitled to do this. Could he evade the Statute of Frauds by calling his cause of action estoppel instead of contract? Had this stratagem succeeded, a blow would have been dealt to the Statute of Frauds greater than anything that had gone before; for it would have meant that any plaintiff who could show that he had altered his position in reliance on the defendant's promise could ignore the statute and rely on estoppel. And since at this time the distinction between estoppel as a cause of action and as a ground of defence was not established, the threatened evasion of the statute would have seemed even wider than it might today. Had *Jorden v Money* gone the other way, the result might well have been to confine the Statute of Frauds to executory contracts. It is, therefore, quite understandable that the House of Lords should not have sanctioned the plaintiff's claim.

That this is the true explanation of the case seems to me borne out by the whole of the report, but as this explanation appears to run counter to everything said about the case since, I must justify my assertion by detailed reference to the report itself. I look first at the arguments and there I find that the plaintiff's counsel, Mr Roundell Palmer (afterwards Lord Chancellor Selborne), argues that the Statute of Frauds does not apply:

MR PALMER: The first question on this point is, whether this is a case in which the Statute of Frauds applies at all. The respondent relies on two grounds of equity; first, that there having been an assurance of the creditor that the bond should not be enforced, a marriage took place on the faith of that assurance. The Statute of Frauds cannot apply to such a case.

THE LORD CHANCELLOR: It does not apply if the party was led into the marriage by a misrepresentation of fact; but the question is, whether, when the creditor says, 'I have abandoned' (supposing her to have said so), she means more than 'I will not enforce'; and then the further question is, whether that is not a contract to which the Statute is applicable.

MR PALMER: It is not: the statute says, 'nor upon any agreement made upon consideration of marriage'. This was not so made: it is a promise with reference to a marriage, a promise of a creditor not to enforce a claim; but it is not a promise the consideration of which, in the legal sense of the words, is a marriage.

The real issue in the case could hardly be more clearly put. Palmer is arguing that a representation of intention followed by marriage in reliance thereon differs from a promise supported by the consideration of the marriage. Lord Cranworth disagrees.

In his judgment Lord Cranworth maintains this opinion:

I think that that doctrine [estoppel] does not apply to a case where the representation is not a representation of a fact, but a statement of something which the party intends or does not intend to do. In the former case it is a contract, in the latter it is not; what is here contended for, is this, that Mrs. Jorden, then Miss Marnell, over and over again represented that she abandoned the debt. Clothe that in any words you please, it means no more than this, that she would never enforce the debt; she does not mean, in saying that she had abandoned it, to say that she had executed a release of the debt so as to preclude her legal right to sue. All that she could mean, was that she positively promised that she never would enforce it. My opinion is, that if all the evidence had come up to the mark, which, for reasons I shall presently state, I do not think it did, that if upon the very eve of the marriage she had said, 'William Money, I never will enforce the bond against you' that would not bring it within these cases. *It might be, if all statutable requisites, so far as there are statutable requisites, had been complied with, that it would have been a very good contract whereby she might have bound herself not to enforce the payment. That, however, is not the way in which it is put here; in short, it could not have been, because it must have been a contract reduced into writing and signed; but that is not the way in which this case is put; it is put entirely upon the ground of representation.* Now my Lords, I think that the not adhering to this statement call it contract or call it representation, is no more fraud than it would be not adhering to her engagement if she had said, 'Mr William Money, you may marry; do not be in fear, you will not be in want; I promise to settle £10,000 Consols upon you.' *If she does not perform that promise, she is guilty of a breach of contract, in respect of which she may be sued, if it is put into a valid form, but not otherwise*; so if she had said, as she did to William Money, 'I mean to give you everything I am worth in the world; I promise to do so', her not doing so, is no fraud in the sense in which these cases speak of fraud; it is no misrepresentation of a fact which the party is afterwards held bound to make good as true; it seems to me that the distinction is founded upon perfectly good sense, and that in truth in the case of what is something future, there is no reason for the application of the rule, because the parties have only to say; 'Enter into a contract,' and then all difficulty is removed.

I do not see how the point could be more clearly put. Estoppel is a necessary part of the law where the misrepresentation is one of fact because that cannot be enforced as a promise. It is unnecessary where the misrepresentation is one of intention because there is no difference between such a misrepresentation followed by reliance and a promise given for consideration. Lord Brougham, the concurring judge, does not expressly deal with the Statute of Frauds but he also makes it plain that in his opinion the defendant *promised* that she would not enforce the bond. I have no doubt that Lord Brougham, like Lord Cranworth, would have regarded that promise as made for consideration and enforceable if it had not been for the Statute of Frauds, subject perhaps to the argument that Mrs Jorden intended to be bound in honour only. The dissenting judge, Lord St Leonards, thought that the principle of estoppel could be applied to a representation of intention. But he too makes it clear that he is not treating promissory estoppel as a doctrine which can only be used when there is no contract, but as a doctrine which may legitimately be used by the courts even where there is a contract which is unenforceable under the Statute of Frauds.

> Your lordships are asked to consider that a representation of an intention is not a binding contract, and that you cannot misrepresent what you intend to do. But if you declare your intention with reference, for example, to a marriage, not to enforce a given right, and the marriage takes place on that declaration, I submit that, in point of law, that is a binding undertaking.

I cannot quote here the whole of Lord St Leonards's judgment but anyone who cares to read it for himself will see that the question to which he adverts throughout is whether the misrepresentation of intention can be sued on despite the Statute of Frauds.

The true view: an unnecessary frontier

It will be seen, therefore, that virtually all modern academic (and much judicial) discussion of promissory estoppel has been entirely beside the point. This discussion invariably takes as its starting point the assumption that the performance of an act in reliance on a promise, not requested or stated by the promisor, cannot be a good consideration. If this assumption is unfounded then there is not, and never was, any need for promissory estoppel. *Jorden v Money*, far from being (as the new orthodoxy would have it) a difficult obstacle in the way of recognition of promissory estoppel, is a clear indication that promissory estoppel was never necessary at all. The facts of *Jorden v Money* are the clearest possible example of my Case 6 that I have been able to find. The plaintiff undoubtedly married in reliance on the defendant's promise but the defendant never requested the marriage nor did she promise to release the debt if and when the plaintiff married. Her promise was, indeed, originally made before any question of marriage was in contemplation; it was repeated time and again and the plaintiff acted upon it by his marriage. I have myself no doubt that, as the law was then understood, this was a good consideration for the enforcement of the promise which would (apart from the Statute of Frauds) have been enforced by the House of Lords in 1854.

I do not, of course, mean to say that nineteenth-century courts would have held that a promise always becomes enforceable whenever the promisee acts in reliance on it (even though the act is not requested or stated by the promisor). But what I suggest is that the courts were at that time prepared to enforce such a promise where they felt that the justice of the case required it. If this was so, then there was good reason (or consideration) for enforcement in the promisee's actions in reliance on the promise. Alas, the new orthodoxy has now itself grown so strong and vigorous that it seems too late for the courts to recognize what they have actually done. In *Crabb v Arun District Council* the Court of Appeal actually 'enforced' (by appropriate equitable decrees) an arrangement (to use a neutral term) in a case where one judge insisted that the whole question was whether there was an agreement between the parties. But this 'agreement' though 'enforced' by court decrees was not regarded as a contract, but merely as a set of representations of intention which were enforceable because they had been relied upon to the plaintiff's prejudice. When I protested that if there was an agreement and it was enforced, this must have been a contract, I was rebuked for failing to understand that contracts are designed to enforce agreements, while estoppel is designed to protect reliance. The reader will (I trust) by now know enough of my views to appreciate that I do not assume that because there was (as I think) a 'contract' in this case, it should have been enforceable without any reliance by the plaintiff. I merely protest at the absurdity of a conceptual analysis which states that the agreement in *Crabb v Arun District Council* was not enforceable because the detrimental reliance was not requested, and therefore failed to comply with the requirements of consideration; and then proceeds to add that the 'agreement' was nevertheless enforceable because the element of reliance did satisfy the doctrine of promissory estoppel. Surely, it would be simpler and more sensible if the law made up its mind what kind of detrimental reliance was sufficient to justify the imposition of some kind of obligation without regard to whether the case should be classified as involving consideration or promissory estoppel.

The present position—what I have called the new orthodoxy—might be more defensible if estoppel, or promissory estoppel, was only called upon to protect reliance, and therefore was confined to cases in which expectations should not be protected. Whether or not these cases should be called 'contracts' therefore would be settled by arbitrary fiat: cases where only reliance interests are to be protected would not be entitled to be called contracts. But the new orthodoxy is far more complex than this. In *Crabb v Arun District Council* (and many similar cases), plaintiffs have had their expectation interests protected by use of promissory (or as it is now called in these cases, proprietary) estoppel, and there are, of course, many genuine contracts in which only reliance interests are protected. Thus the line between promissory estoppel and consideration does not parallel the line between reliance protection and expectation protection.

The present orthodoxy therefore seems to me unnecessarily cumbrous. It would be a great deal simpler if the courts were willing to treat action in reliance which suffices for estoppel as also sufficient to satisfy the requirements of consideration; but it would at the same time be necessary, of course, for the courts to become more sophisticated about when expectation protection is, and when it is not, justified. If American experience is anything to go by, it may well be necessary to retain considerable flexibility as to when to confine contractual redress to the protection of reliance, and when to go further; it is unwise to try to draw this line by fastening on the absurdly narrow and unreal distinction between an action in reliance which is requested, and one which is not requested, but merely foreseeable. Fortunately, in practice it is so easy for a court to 'imply' a request when it wishes to do so, that no court which wishes directly to enforce a promise in this sort of case need find any difficulty in doing so. And I may illustrate that this can and still does happen by referring again to *V/O Rasnoimport v Guthrie & Co Ltd*. The consideration for the enforcement of the promisor's implied warranty of authority in this case was held to be the act of the plaintiffs in taking up the

> bill of lading in due course of business. It seems to strain the meaning of words to say that the defendants requested anyone to take up the bill of lading; it even strains the meaning of words to say that the defendants promised that they had authority to sign the bill of lading and impliedly stated to the world that the promise was to take effect on the taking up of the bill of lading. It is much more in accordance with reality to say that the defendants impliedly warranted their authority and that in the ordinary course of business the plaintiffs relied on this statement by taking up the bill of lading.

The possibility of using reliance on a promise as a test of its enforceability has been recognised much more readily in other common-law jurisdictions. In the USA, for example, the American Restatement of the Law of Contract includes s 90:

> A promise which the promisor should reasonably expect to induce action or forbearance of a definite and substantial character on the part of the promisee and which does induce such action or forbearance is binding if injustice can be avoided only by the enforcement of the promise.

Although the American Restatement also recognises consideration as a basis for enforcing promises, reliance has been part of the United States' law of contract for at least 70 years. There are significant similarities in the above formulation with Denning's statement of the basis of promissory estoppel in *High Trees*. As we have seen, however, promissory estoppel cannot be used as the basis for creating new contractual obligations, but rather only to modify existing ones. Section 90 of the American Restatement clearly has much broader potential for use as the basis for legal action. The same trend can be seen in other parts of the common-law world, notably Australia. The case of *Waltons Stores (Interstate) Ltd v Maher* is particularly significant in this context.

Waltons Stores (Interstate) Ltd v Maher (1988) 164 CLR 406
(High Court of Australia)

Facts: The owners of a piece of land which was expected to form part of a development project were led to believe that the prospective lessees would proceed with the transaction, and that the necessary exchange of contracts would take place. With that expectation they demolished an existing building on the land, in preparation for the construction of a new building to meet the lessees' requirements. In fact the lessees had already decided not to proceed with the agreement. They failed to communicate this to the owners, even though they knew that the work on demolishing the building had started. The owners sought compensation. They succeeded at trial and in the Australian Court of Appeal. The lessees appealed to the High Court of Australia.

Held: The owners could succeed on the basis of promissory estoppel.

Mason CJ and Wilson J:

'. . . The direct enforcement of promises made without consideration by means of promissory estoppel has proceeded apace in the United States.

The *Restatement on Contracts* 2d § 90 states:

(1) A promise which the promisor should reasonably expect to induce action or forbearance on the part of the promisee or a third person and which does induce such action or forbearance is binding if injustice can be avoided only by enforcement of the promise. The remedy granted for breach may be limited as justice requires.

This general proposition developed from the treatment in particular situations of promissory estoppel as the equivalent of consideration. Thus in *Allegheny College v National Chautauqua County Bank* (1927) 246 NY 369 Cardozo CJ said (at 374): "Certain . . . it is that we have adopted the doctrine of promissory estoppel as the equivalent of consideration in connection with our law of charitable subscriptions." See Farnsworth, *Contracts* (1982) § 2.19; Gilmore, *The Death of Contract* (1974), p 129.

However, we need to view the development of the doctrine in the United States with some caution. There promissory estoppel developed partly in response to the limiting effects of the adoption of the bargain theory of consideration which has not been expressly adopted in Australia or England . . . It is perhaps sufficient to say that in the United States, as in Australia, there is an obvious interrelationship between the doctrines of consideration and promissory estoppel, promissory estoppel tending to occupy ground left vacant due to the constraints affecting consideration.

The proposition stated in § 90(1) of the *Restatement* seems on its face to reflect a closer connection with the general law of contract than our doctrine of promissory estoppel, with its origins in the equitable concept of unconscionable conduct, might be thought to allow. This is because in the United States promissory estoppel has become an equivalent or substitute for consideration in contract formation, detriment being an element common to both doctrines. None the less the proposition, by making the enforcement of the promise conditional on (a) a reasonable expectation on the part of the promisor that his promise will induce action or forbearance by the promisee and (b) the impossibility of avoiding injustice by other means, makes it clear that the promise is enforced in circumstances where departure from it is unconscionable. Note that the emphasis is on the promisor's reasonable expectation that his promise will induce action or forbearance, not on the fact that he created or encouraged an expectation in the promisee of performance of the promise . . . .

[Having reviewed various authorities from England, including the Privy Council decision in *Attorney General of Hong Kong v Humphreys Estate Ltd* [1987] 1 AC 114, they continued:]

The foregoing review of the doctrine of promissory estoppel indicates that the doctrine extends to the enforcement of voluntary promises on the footing that a departure from the basic assumptions underlying the transaction between the parties must be unconscionable. As failure to fulfil a promise does not of itself amount to unconscionable conduct, mere reliance on an executory promise to do something, resulting in the promisee changing his position or suffering detriment, does not bring promissory estoppel into play. Something more would be required. *Humphreys Estate* suggests that this may be found, if at all, in the creation or encouragement by the party estopped in the other party of an assumption that a contract will come into existence or a promise will be performed and that the other party relied on that assumption to his detriment to the knowledge of the first party. *Humphreys Estate* referred in terms to an assumption that the plaintiff would not exercise an existing legal right or liberty, the right or liberty to withdraw from the negotiations, but as a matter of substance such an assumption is indistinguishable from an assumption that a binding contract would eventuate. On the other hand the United States experience, distilled in the *Restatement* (2d § 90), suggests that the principle is to be expressed in terms of a reasonable expectation on the part of the promisor that his promise will induce action or forbearance by the promisee, the promise inducing such action or forbearance in circumstances where injustice arising from unconscionable conduct can only be avoided by holding the promisor to his promise.

The application of these principles to the facts of the present case is not without difficulty. The parties were negotiating through their solicitors for an agreement for lease to be concluded by way of customary exchange. *Humphreys Estate* illustrates the difficulty of establishing an estoppel preventing parties from refusing to proceed with a transaction expressed to be "subject to contract". And there is the problem . . . that a voluntary promise will not generally give rise to an estoppel because the promisee may reasonably be expected to appreciate that he cannot safely rely upon it. This problem is magnified in the present case where the parties were represented by their solicitors.

All this may be conceded. But the crucial question remains: was the appellant entitled to stand by in silence when it must have known that the respondents were proceeding on the assumption that they had an agreement and that completion of the exchange was a formality? The mere exercise of its legal right not to exchange contracts could not be said to amount to unconscionable conduct on the part of the appellant. But there were two other factors present in the situation which require to be taken into consideration. The first was the element of urgency that pervaded the negotiation of the terms of the proposed lease. As we have noted, the appellant was bound to give up possession of its existing commercial premises in Nowra in January 1984; the new building was to be available for fitting out by 15 January and completed by 5 February 1984. The respondents' solicitor had said to the appellant's solicitor on 7 November that it would be impossible for Maher to complete the building within the agreed time unless the agreement were concluded "within the next day or two". The outstanding details were agreed within a day or two thereafter, and the work of preparing the site commenced almost immediately.

The second factor of importance is that the respondents executed the counterpart deed and it was forwarded to the appellant's solicitor on 11 November. The assumption on which the respondents acted thereafter was that completion of the necessary exchange was a formality. The next their solicitor heard from the appellant was a letter from its solicitors dated 19 January, informing him that the appellant did not intend to proceed with the matter. It had known, at least since 10 December, that costly work was proceeding on the site.

It seems to us, in the light of these considerations, that the appellant was under an obligation to communicate with the respondents within a reasonable time after receiving the executed counterpart deed and certainly when it learnt on 10 December that demolition was proceeding. It had to choose whether to complete the contract or to warn the respondents that it had not yet decided upon the course it would take. It was not entitled simply to retain the counterpart deed executed by the respondents and do nothing ... The appellant's inaction, in all the circumstances, constituted clear encouragement or inducement to the respondents to continue to act on the basis of the assumption which they had made. It was unconscionable for it, knowing that the respondents were exposing themselves to detriment by acting on the basis of a false assumption, to adopt a course of inaction which encouraged them in the course they had adopted. To express the point in the language of promissory estoppel the appellant is estopped in all the circumstances from retreating from its implied promise to complete the contract ...'

Brennan J:

'... In *Combe v Combe* Denning LJ limited the application of promissory estoppel, as he expounded the doctrine, to ensure that it did not displace the doctrine of consideration. His Lordship's solution of the problem was to hold that the promise should not itself be a cause of action, but merely the foundation of a defensive equity. He said ...: "Seeing that the principle never stands alone as giving a cause of action in itself, it can never do away with the necessity of consideration when that is an essential part of the cause of action. The doctrine of consideration is too firmly fixed to be overthrown by a side wind."

The remedy offered by promissory estoppel has been limited to preventing the enforcement of existing legal rights. In *Crabb v Arun District Council* Lord Denning MR said ... that if a person "by his words or conduct, so behaves as to lead another to believe that he will not insist on his strict legal rights – knowing or intending that the other will act on that belief – and he does so act, that again will raise an equity in favour of the other; and it is for a court of equity to say in what way the equity may be satisfied".

If the object of the principle were to make a promise binding in equity, the need to preserve the doctrine of consideration would require a limitation to be placed on the remedy. But there is a logical difficulty in limiting the principle so that it applies only to promises to suspend or extinguish existing rights. If a promise by A not to enforce an existing right against B is to confer an equitable right on B to compel fulfilment of the promise, why should B be denied the same protection in similar circumstances if the promise is intended to create in B a new legal right against A? There is no logical distinction to be drawn between a change in legal relationships effected by a promise which extinguishes a right and a change in legal relationships effected by a promise which creates one. Why should an equity of the kind to which *Combe v Combe* refers be regarded as a shield but not a sword? The want of logic in the limitation on the remedy is well exposed in Mr David Jackson's essay "Estoppel as a Sword" in (1965) 81 *Law Quarterly Review* 84, 223 at 241–3.

Moreover, unless the cases of proprietary estoppel are attributed to a different equity from that which explains the cases of promissory estoppel, the enforcement of promises to create new proprietary rights cannot be reconciled with a limitation on the enforcement of other promises. If it be unconscionable for an owner of property in certain circumstances to fail to fulfil a non-contractual promise that he will convey an interest in the property to another, is there any reason in principle why it is not unconscionable in similar circumstances for a person to fail to fulfil a non-contractual promise that he will confer a non-proprietary legal right on another? It does not accord with principle to hold that equity, in seeking to avoid detriment occasioned by unconscionable conduct, can give relief in some cases but not in others . . . .

In my opinion, to establish an equitable estoppel, it is necessary for a plaintiff to prove that (1) the plaintiff assumed or expected that a particular legal relationship then existed between the plaintiff and the defendant or expected that a particular legal relationship would exist between them and, in the latter case, that the defendant would not be free to withdraw from the expected legal relationship; (2) the defendant has induced the plaintiff to adopt that assumption or expectation; (3) the plaintiff acts or abstains from acting in reliance on the assumption or expectation; (4) the defendant knew or intended him to do so; (5) the plaintiff's action or inaction will occasion detriment if the assumption or expectation is not fulfilled; and (6) the defendant has failed to act to avoid that detriment whether by fulfilling the assumption or expectation or otherwise. For the purposes of the second element, a defendant who has not actively induced the plaintiff to adopt an assumption or expectation will nevertheless be held to have done so if the assumption or expectation can be fulfilled only by a transfer of the defendant's property, a diminution of his rights or an increase in his obligations and he, knowing that the plaintiff's reliance on the assumption or expectation may cause detriment to the plaintiff if it is not fulfilled, fails to deny to the plaintiff the correctness of the assumption or expectation on which the plaintiff is conducting his affairs.

This is such a case . . .'

[Deane and Gaudron JJ also held for the owners, but on different grounds.]

The case of *Crabb v Arun District Council* [1975] 3 All ER 865, referred to in the above extract, was a case concerning a right of access to land, and is often categorised by English commentators as falling within a distinct category of estoppel – 'proprietary estoppel', which the English courts have been much more willing to allow to be used as the basis for a cause of action.

This distinction between different categories of estoppel was emphasised by the Court of Appeal in *Baird Textile Holdings Ltd v Marks and Spencer plc*, when considering the development of the law approved in *Waltons v Maher*.

Baird Textile Holdings Ltd v Marks and Spencer plc [2001] EWCA Civ 274; [2002] 1 All ER (Comm) 737

Sir Andrew Morritt VC:

'. . . **34.** Counsel for M&S submits that the judge was wrong. He contends, amongst many and varied arguments, that a conclusion to that effect does not involve the reconciliation of numerous cases but the recognition that this court is, as the judge was, bound by three decisions of the Court of Appeal to conclude that the estoppel claim has no real prospect of success either. The three decisions and the propositions they respectively established are: (1) a common law or promissory estoppel cannot create a cause of action (*Combe v Combe* [1951] 1 All ER 767, [1951] 2 KB 215); (2) an estoppel by convention cannot create a cause of action either (*Amalgamated Investment and Property Co Ltd (in liq) v Texas Commerce International Bank Ltd* [1981] 3 All ER 577, [1982] QB 84); and (3) accepting that a proprietary or equitable estoppel may create a cause of action it is limited to cases involving property rights, whether or not confined to land (*Western Fish Products Ltd v Penwith DC* [1981] 2 All ER 204 at 217).

35. Counsel for Baird did not dispute that those cases established the propositions for which M&S contended. Rather, he submitted, it is wrong to categorise particular types of estoppel and then impose limitations in each category not applicable to one or more of the other categories. He suggested that English law permits some cross-fertilisation between one category and another. He contended that English law should follow where the High Court of Australia has led in *Waltons Stores (Interstate) Ltd v Maher* (1988) 164 CLR 387 and *Commonwealth of Australia v Verwayen* (1990) 170 CLR 394 and permit estoppel to create causes of action in non-proprietary cases. In reply counsel for M&S conceded that if the Australian cases, to the effect that promissory estoppel extends to the enforcement of voluntary promises, represent the law of England then the judge was right and the cross-appeal must fail . . .

38. In my view English law, as presently understood does not enable the creation or recognition by estoppel of an enforceable right of the type and in the circumstances relied on in this case. First, it would be necessary for such an obligation to be sufficiently certain to enable the court to give effect to it. That such certainty is required in the field of estoppels such as is claimed in this case as well as in contract was indicated by the House of Lords in *Woodhouse AC Israel Cocoa Ltd SA v Nigerian Produce Marketing Co Ltd* [1972] 2 All ER 271, [1972] AC 741 and by Ralph Gibson LJ in *Troop v Gibson* [1986] 1 EGLR 1 at 6. For the reasons I have already given I do not think that the alleged obligation is sufficiently certain. Second, in my view, the decisions in the three Court of Appeal decisions on which M&S rely do establish that such an enforceable obligation cannot be established by estoppel in the circumstances relied on in this case. This conclusion does not involve the categorisation of estoppels but is a simple application of the principles established by those cases to the obligation relied on in this. I do not consider that any of the dicta in the line of cases relied on by Baird could entitle this court to decline to apply those principles . . . .

39. Counsel for M&S was, at one stage, inclined to concede that if we considered that the House of Lords, after the facts had been found at a trial, might adopt the propositions formulated by Mason CJ, Wilson and Brennan JJ in the *Waltons Stores* case, then it might be said that there was a real prospect of succeeding on the estoppel issue so that judgment under CPR 24.2 should not be given at this stage. In reply he submitted that the possibility that the House of Lords might adopt those propositions was an inadequate reason for allowing a trial. I agree. If I am right in believing that English law, as it now stands, does not permit the enforcement of an estoppel in the form alleged in this case then it is the duty of this court to apply it, notwithstanding that it may be developed by the House of Lords, who are not bound by any of the cases relied on, in the future.'

[Judge and Mance LJJ agreed that the Court of Appeal was bound by decisions which prevented the development of the law so as to allow promissory estoppel to be used as a cause of action.]

3.4.2 PRINCIPLES OF EUROPEAN CONTRACT LAW

The Principles of European Contract Law deal with the conditions for the conclusion of an enforceable contract in Article 2.101. This states:

Article 2:101: Conditions for the Conclusion of a Contract

(1) A contract is concluded if:

    (a) the parties intend to be legally bound; and

    (b) they reach sufficient agreement
        without any further requirement.

(2) A contract need not be concluded or evidenced in writing nor is it subject to any other requirement as to form. The contract may be proved by any means, including witnesses.

Article 2:102: Intention

The intention of a party to be legally bound by contract is to be determined from the party's statements or conduct as they were reasonably understood by the other party.

From this it will be seen that the PECL do not require any test of enforceability other than the intention of the parties. That intention is to be determined from the actions and statements of the parties. There is therefore no room here for strict doctrines of consideration, or any other formal process for determining enforceability. Whether the requirement of intention is capable of dealing with the variety of situations that might be argued to give rise to a contract is questionable. The issue of the intention to create legal relations is discussed in the next chapter.

▋3.5 ADDITIONAL READING

Adams, J and Brownsword, R, 'Contract, consideration and the critical path' (1990) 53 MLR 536.

Atiyah, PS, 'Contracts, promises and the law of obligations' (1978) 94 LQR 340.

Campbell, D, 'The relational constitution of the discrete contract', Ch 3 in Campbell, D and Vincent-Jones, P (eds), *Contract and Economic Organisation*, 1996, Aldershot: Dartmouth.

Fried, C, *Contract as Promise*, 1981, Cambridge, Mass: Harvard University Press.

Halson, R, 'Sailors, sub-contractors and consideration' (1990) 106 LQR 183.

Hird, NJ and Blair, A, 'Minding your own business – *Williams v Roffey* revisited' [1996] JBL 254.

O'Sullivan, J, 'In defence of *Foakes v Beer*' [1996] CLJ 219.

Thompson, MP, 'Representation to expectation: estoppel as a cause of action' (1983) 42 CLJ 257.

Treitel, GH, 'Consideration: a critical analysis of Professor Atiyah's fundamental restatement' (1976) 50 Australian LJ 439.

CHAPTER 4

INTENTION TO CREATE LEGAL RELATIONS

4.1 INTRODUCTION

As well as evidence of an agreement, for a contract to be enforceable, the courts need to be sure that it was intended to be legally binding. In most cases where there is offer, acceptance and consideration, this is not an issue, but in some cases a party to an agreement that has all those characteristics may wish to claim that they did not intend to create legal relations. English law deals with such an assertion by means of presumptions. If the alleged contract is a social or domestic agreement, the courts will presume that it was not intended to be legally binding. If, on the other hand, the alleged contract was a commercial agreement, the courts will presume that it was intended to be legally binding.

In either case the presumption is rebuttable by appropriate evidence, and most of the case law is concerned with what provides sufficient evidence for this.

Statute provides that collective agreements between employers and trade unions should not generally be regarded as intended to be legally binding.

4.2 OBJECTIVE APPROACH TO AGREEMENT

As with most areas within the English law of contract, the courts purport to use an objective approach to the question of determining what the parties 'intended' at the time they entered into an agreement. It is what the parties have said or done, and how a reasonable person would view that, which is important. This was confirmed by Lord Bingham in *Edmonds v Lawson* [2000] 2 WLR 1091, which concerned an alleged contract between a pupil barrister and her chambers (p 1099):

> Whether the parties intended to enter into legally binding relations is an issue to be determined objectively and not by inquiring into their respective states of mind.

Collins has challenged this analysis:

Collins, H, *Law of Contract*, 2003, London: Butterworths, pp 104–105

One of the reasons given in *Balfour v Balfour* for refusing to enforce the agreement was that the parties did not intend to enter a binding contract. In a few instances, the parties may have made it plain that they do not expect to be legally bound. It is a common practice in business, for instance, to issue 'letters of comfort' or 'letters of intent', which contain indications of likely future action and current business strategy, but these are not intended, without more, to create binding obligations, and the courts respect this choice not to enter the market sphere. Similarly, it is normally stated expressly or implied by custom in the UK that the parties to a collective agreement between management and trade unions do not intend to create a legally enforceable agreement. Apart from these clear expressions of intent, however, the libertarian explanation seems to be fatally flawed.

In cases where the issue is litigated, it seems likely that one party intended a legal agreement and the other wanted the agreement to be merely morally binding. This contradiction removes any possibility of justifying the limits on contracts on the basis of the joint intent of the parties. We are forced to the conclusion that the courts must rely upon hidden policy considerations when determining the intent of the parties. The libertarian focus upon the choice of the parties to make contracts in a family context runs the risk of ignoring the obligations imposed by law, which are designed to support the family as a way of life insulated from market considerations. Even if both husband and wife in *Balfour v Balfour* had seriously intended to make a binding contract, the agreement would surely not have been enforceable, because it was likely to subvert the distributive principles of family law, such as depriving the wife of her needs-based right to maintenance.

Although there may well be policy considerations that influence decisions in this area, as in many others in English contract law, the attempt to discern what one party could reasonably have believed to be the intentions of the other from their words and conduct is still a valid exercise. It is adopted, for example, by the Principles of European Contract Law, Art 2.102:

> The intention of a party to be legally bound to a contract is to be determined from the party's statements or conduct as they were reasonably to be understood by the other party.

4.3 DOMESTIC OR SOCIAL AGREEMENTS

The approach to 'domestic' or 'social' agreements is that they are presumed not to involve an intention to create legal relations. This is generally accepted as deriving from the case of *Balfour v Balfour*.

Balfour v Balfour [1919] 2 KB 571 (CA)

Facts: Mr Balfour went to work in Ceylon. Mrs Balfour was not well enough to accompany him. Mr Balfour agreed to pay his wife £30 per month while they were apart. The marriage later broke up, and Mrs Balfour sued to enforce her husband's promise. Mrs Balfour succeeded at first instance, but Mr Balfour appealed.

Held: The agreement, even if Mrs Balfour had provided consideration, was not intended to be legally binding, and could not be enforced.

Duke LJ:
'This is in some respects an important case, and as we differ from the judgment of the Court below I propose to state concisely my views and the grounds which have led me to the conclusion at which I have arrived. Substantially the question is whether the promise of the husband to the wife that while she is living absent from him he will make her a periodical allowance involves in law a consideration on the part of the wife sufficient to convert that promise into a binding agreement. In my opinion it does not . . .

In order to establish a contract there ought to be something more than mere mutual promises having regard to the domestic relations of the parties. It is required that the obligations arising out of that relationship shall be displaced before either of the parties can found a contract upon such promises. The formula which was stated in this case to support the claim of the lady was this: In consideration that you will agree to give me £30 a month I will agree to forego my right to pledge your credit . . . Erle C.J. states this proposition: "But taking the law to be, that the power of the wife to charge her husband is in the capacity of his agent, it is a solecism in reasoning to say that she derives her authority from his will, and at the same time to say that the relation of wife creates the authority against his will, by a *presumptio juris et de jure* from marriage." What is said on the part of the wife in this case is that her arrangement with her husband that she should assent to that which was in his discretion to do or not to do was the consideration moving from her to her husband. The giving up of that which was not a right was not a consideration . . .'

Atkin LJ:

'The defence to this action on the alleged contract is that the defendant, the husband, entered into no contract with his wife, and for the determination of that it is necessary to remember that there are agreements between parties which do not result in contracts within the meaning of that term in our law. The ordinary example is where two parties agree to take a walk together, or where there is an offer and an acceptance of hospitality. Nobody would suggest in ordinary circumstances that those agreements result in what we know as a contract, and one of the most usual forms of agreement which does not constitute a contract appears to me to be the arrangements which are made between husband and wife. It is quite common, and it is the natural and inevitable result of the relationship of husband and wife, that the two spouses should make arrangements between themselves – agreements such as are in dispute in this action – agreements for allowances, by which the husband agrees that he will pay to his wife a certain sum of money, per week, or per month, or per year, to cover either her own expenses or the necessary expenses of the household and of the children of the marriage, and in which the wife promises either expressly or impliedly to apply the allowance for the purpose for which it is given. To my mind those agreements, or many of them, do not result in contracts at all, and they do not result in contracts even though there may be what as between other parties would constitute consideration for the agreement. The consideration, as we know, may consist either in some right, interest, profit or benefit accruing to one party, or some forbearance, detriment, loss or responsibility given, suffered or undertaken by the other. That is a well-known definition, and it constantly happens, I think, that such arrangements made between husband and wife are arrangements in which there are mutual promises, or in which there is consideration in form within the definition that I have mentioned. Nevertheless they are not contracts, and they are not contracts because the parties did not intend that they should be attended by legal consequences. To my mind it would be of the worst possible example to hold that agreements such as this resulted in legal obligations which could be enforced in the courts. It would mean this, that when the husband makes his wife a promise to give her an allowance of 30s. or £2 a week, whatever he can afford to give her, for the maintenance of the household and children, and she promises so to apply it, not only could she sue him for his failure in any week to supply the allowance, but he could sue her for non-performance of the obligation, express or implied, which she had undertaken upon her part. All I can say is that the small courts of this country would have to be multiplied one hundredfold if these arrangements were held to result in legal obligations. They are not sued upon, not because the parties are reluctant to enforce their legal rights when the agreement is broken, but because the parties, in the inception of the arrangement, never intended that they should be sued upon. Agreements such as these are outside the realm of contracts altogether. The common law does not regulate the form of agreements between spouses. Their promises are not sealed with seals and sealing wax. The consideration that really obtains for them is that natural love and affection which counts for so little in these cold courts. The terms may be repudiated, varied or renewed as performance proceeds or as disagreements develop, and the principles of the common law as to exoneration and discharge and accord and satisfaction are such as find no place in the domestic code. The parties themselves are advocates, judges, courts, sheriff's officer and reporter. In respect of these promises each house is a domain into which the King's writ does not seek to run, and to which his officers do not seek to be admitted. The only question in this case is whether or not this promise was of such a class or not. For the reasons given by my brethren it appears to me to be plainly established that the promise here was not intended by either party to be attended by legal consequences. I think the onus was upon the plaintiff, and the plaintiff has not established any contract. The parties were living together, the wife intending to return. The suggestion is that the husband bound himself to pay £30 a month under all circumstances, and she bound herself to be satisfied with that sum under all circumstances, and, although she was in ill-health and alone in the country, that out of that sum she undertook to defray the whole of the medical expenses that might fall upon her, whatever might be the development of her illness, and in whatever expenses it might involve her. To my mind neither party contemplated such a result. I think that the parol evidence upon which the case turns does not establish a contract. I think that the letters do not evidence such a contract, or amplify the oral evidence which was given by the wife, which is not in dispute. For these reasons I think the judgment of the court below was wrong and that this appeal should be allowed.'

Warrington LJ delivered a concurring judgment.

It will be seen from the extract above from the judgment of Duke LJ that his conclusion was based as much on the lack of consideration as the absence of intention to create legal relations. Atkin LJ, however, focuses much more clearly on the 'intention' issue. It is this aspect of the case that has been emphasised subsequently, and *Balfour v Balfour* is thus regarded as the source of the principle that domestic agreements will be regarded as not intended to be binding, unless there is clear evidence to the contrary.

In terms of agreements between husband and wife it is clear that in *Balfour v Balfour* it was regarded by the court as significant that the couple was 'living in amity' at the time of the agreement. One piece of evidence that will be likely to overturn the presumption of lack of intention is if the parties are in the process of splitting up when the agreement is made. This was confirmed by *Merritt v Merritt*.

Merritt v Merritt [1970] 2 All ER 760 (CA)

Facts: H and W were married in 1941. The matrimonial home was subsequently put into joint names. In 1966 H left W. They had a conversation about the future, at the end of which H signed a piece of paper agreeing to transfer the house into W's name, if she paid off the mortgage. When she had done so, H refused to make the transfer, claiming that the agreement was not binding. W succeeded at trial, but H appealed.

Held: The agreement was binding. *Balfour* was distinguishable, because in this case the agreement was made when the parties were in the process of separating.

Lord Denning MR:

'Husband and wife married as long ago as 1941. After the war in 1949 they got a building plot and built a house. It was a freehold house, no. 133, Clayton Road, Hook, Chessington. It was in the husband's name, with a considerable sum on mortgage with a building society. There they lived and brought up their three children, two daughters, aged now 20 and 17, and a boy now 14. The wife went out to work and contributed to the household expenses.

Early in 1966 they came to an agreement whereby the house was to be put in joint names. That was done. It reflected the legal position when a house is acquired by a husband and wife by financial contributions of each.

But, unfortunately, about that time the husband formed an attachment for another woman. He left the house and went to live with her. The wife then pressed the husband for some arrangement to be made for the future. On May 25 they talked it over in the husband's car. The husband said that he would make the wife a monthly payment of £40 and told her that out of it she would have to make the outstanding payments to the building society. There was only £180 outstanding. He handed over the building society's mortgage book to his wife. She was herself going out to work, earning net £7 10s. a week. Before she left the car she insisted that he put down in writing a further agreement. It forms the subject of the present action. He wrote these words on a piece of paper:

> In consideration of the fact that you will pay all charges in connection with the house at 133 Clayton Road, Chessington, Surrey, until such time as the mortgage repayment has been completed, when the mortgage has been completed, I will agree to transfer the property into your sole ownership.
> Signed, John Merritt. May 25, 1966.

The wife took that paper away with her. She did, in fact, over the ensuing months pay off the balance of the mortgage, partly, maybe, out of the money the husband gave her, £40 a month, and partly out of her own earnings. When the mortgage had been paid off, he reduced the £40 a month down to £25 a month.

The wife asked the husband to transfer the house into her sole ownership. He refused to do so. She brought an action in the Chancery Division for a declaration that the house should belong to her and for an order that he should make the conveyance.

The judge made the order; but the husband now appeals to this court.

The first point taken on his behalf by Mr Thompson is that the agreement was not intended to have legal relations. It was, he says, a family arrangement such as was considered by the court in *Balfour v Balfour* [1919] 2 KB 571 and in *Jones v Padavatton* [1969] 1 WLR 328. So the wife could not sue upon it.

I do not think those cases have any application here. The parties there were living together in amity. In such cases their domestic arrangements are ordinarily not intended to create legal relations. It is altogether different when the parties are not living in amity but are separated, or about to separate. They then bargain keenly. They do not rely on honourable understandings. They want everything cut and dried. It may safely be presumed that they intend to create legal relations.

Mr Thompson then relied on the recent case of *Gould v Gould* [1970] 1 QB 275, when the parties had separated, and the husband agreed to pay the wife £12 a week "so long as he could manage it". The majority of the court thought those words introduced such an element of uncertainty that the agreement was not intended to create legal relations. But for that element of uncertainty, I am sure the majority would have held the agreement to be binding. They did not differ from the general proposition which I stated at p 280 that:

> when husband and wife, at arm's length, decide to separate, and the husband promises to pay a sum as maintenance to the wife during the separation, the court does, as a rule, impute to them an intention to create legal relations.

In all these cases the court does not try to discover the intention by looking into the minds of the parties. It looks at the situation in which they were placed and asks itself: Would reasonable people regard the agreement as intended to be binding?

Mr Thompson sought to say that this agreement was uncertain because of the arrangement for £40 a month maintenance. That is obviously untenable. Next he said that there was no consideration for the agreement. That point is no good. The wife paid the outstanding amount to the building society. That was ample consideration. It is true that the husband paid her £40 a month which she may have used to pay the building society. But still her act in paying was good consideration.

Mr Thompson took a small point about rates. There was nothing in it. The rates were adjusted fairly between the parties afterwards.

Finally, Mr Thompson said that, under section 17 of the Act of 1882, this house would be owned by husband and wife jointly: and that, even if this house were transferred to the wife, she should hold it on trust for them both jointly. There is nothing in this point either. This paper which the husband signed dealt with the beneficial ownership of the house. It was intended to belong entirely to the wife.

I find myself in entire agreement with the judgment of Stamp J. This appeal should be dismissed.'

Widgery and Karminski LJJ concurred.

The presumption of non-enforceability does not only apply to agreements between husband and wife. It will also apply as between other family members (as in *Jones v Padavatton*, extracted below), and between friends. It is the type of agreement, as much as the relationship between the parties that is important. An agreement between a group of students sharing a flat as to who is to perform various domestic chores would be unlikely to be regarded as legally binding; if it related to the payment of bills, however, it would be more likely to have this character.

In *Simpkins v Pays* [1955] 3 All ER 10, the agreement between a group who were not all related, concerned the sharing of a prize in a competition that they jointly entered. It was held that there had been an intention from a legally binding agreement that any winnings would be shared. Sellers J commented:

> It may well be there are many family associations where some sort of rough and ready statement is made which would not, in a proper estimate of the circumstances, establish a contract which was contemplated to have legal consequences, but I do not so find here. I think that in the present case there was a mutuality in the arrangement between the parties. It was not very formal, but certainly it was, in effect, agreed that every week the forecast should go in the name of the defendant, and that if there was success, no matter who won, all should share equally. It seems to be the implication from, or the interpretation of, what was said that this was in the nature of a very informal syndicate so that they should all get the benefit of success.

A further example of the presumption being overturned by the evidence is to be found in *Parker v Clark* [1960] 1 All ER 93.

Parker v Clark [1960] 1 All ER 93

Facts: A niece and her husband agreed to live with her aunt and uncle, who were 20 years older, and help to look after them. They were promised that the aunt and uncle's house would be left to them. When the arrangement did not work out, and the younger couple were asked to move, they brought an action for damages for breach of contract. The defendants argued that there was no contract, as the agreement was not intended to create legal relations.

Held: There was sufficient evidence to overturn the presumption that a domestic arrangement between family members was not intended to be legally binding. In particular, the fact that the younger couple had sold their house in order to move in with the defendants was an indication of the seriousness of the commitment being undertaken.

Devlin J:

'. . . The contract relied upon by the plaintiffs is said to be contained in the defendants' letter of September 25 and Commander Parker's acceptance thereof. In this part of the case, since Commander Parker and Mr. Clark were the contractual protagonists, it is convenient to refer to them simply as plaintiff and defendant. The defendants' first submission in answer to the claim is that the letters, construed in the light of the surrounding circumstances, show no intention to enter into a legal relationship or to make a binding contract. No doubt a proposal between relatives to share a house, and a promise to make a bequest of it, may very well amount to no more than a family arrangement of the type considered in *Balfour v Balfour*, which the courts will not enforce. But there is equally no doubt that arrangements of this sort, and in particular a proposal to leave property in a will, can be the subject of a binding contract. . . .

The question must, of course, depend on the intention of the parties, to be inferred from the language they use and from the circumstances in which they use it. On the plaintiff's side, I accept his evidence that he considered that he was making a binding contract. An important factor in this was that he disposed of his own residence. It does not matter for this purpose whether it was or was not a term of the contract that he should sell "The Thimble"; the important thing is that the contract required him to give up his occupation of "The Thimble", and that he was always quite clear, and made it quite clear, that he would not give up occupation unless he also gave up the ownership and parted with the property. He would not have done that, he says – and I believe it – unless he thought that he was securing another permanent home. There is, undoubtedly, in the arrangement a lack of formality, upon which Mr. Park greatly relies. This, I think, is largely explained by the relationship between the parties; it is easier to demand formal documents from a stranger than it is from a relative and friend. It is clear that the plaintiff constantly relied upon the letter as a sort of title to his rights; he kept it and referred to it whenever his rights were called in question. When on October 24, 1957, they were seriously threatened, he went forthwith and consulted a solicitor. He is not, in my judgment, the sort of man who would "think up" a legal action as an afterthought, when he found he was not getting what he wanted.

The plaintiff is not a moneyed man. On the strength of Mr. Clark's promise he, so to speak, put down £672 10s. That is the figure that is agreed as the expense which he incurred in giving up "The Thimble", on the assumption that he could repurchase "The Thimble" or a cottage like it. In addition to that, he tied up £2,000, so that he has never since been in a position to buy another property like "The Thimble", and has never in fact bought one. The defendant knew this, and had plenty of time to reflect upon it between September 25, 1955, when he wrote his letter, and March 1, 1956, when the plaintiffs arrived. If he had thought that all that his letter involved was an amicable arrangement terminable at will, I cannot believe that he would not have enlightened the plaintiff and, as a cautious man himself, have warned him against the folly of what he was doing. I cannot believe either that the defendant really thought that the law would leave him at liberty, if he so chose, to tell the Parkers when they arrived that he had changed his mind, that they could take their furniture away, and that he was indifferent whether they found anywhere else to live or not. Yet this is what the defence means. The defendant gave several answers which show that this was not really his state of mind. He said that the object of the letter was to induce the Parkers to come to "Cramond"; and he agreed also that he made the will in fulfilment of the promise. I am satisfied that an arrangement binding in law was intended by both sides.'

In some cases the dividing line between intention and lack of intention may be hard to discern. In *Jones v Padavatton*, for example, the four judges who considered the case divided equally as to whether there was an intention or not. The majority of the Court of Appeal, however, held that there was no intention, and the plaintiff succeeded in recovering property that was the subject of the agreement. It was probably significant that, since the contract was between mother and daughter, there was a presumption of unenforceability to be overturned. If the burden had been on the plaintiff to prove that the contract was not intended to be binding then it is more likely that the defendant would have succeeded.

Jones v Padavatton [1969] 2 All ER 616, CA

Facts: A mother, living in the West Indies, agreed with her daughter, who was living in the United States, that if the daughter went to London to read for the Bar, the mother would support her. Subsequently, the mother bought a house in London in which the daughter lived rent free, but taking in tenants and using the rent to support herself. After about 5 years, when the daughter had still not passed her Bar exams, the mother sought to recover the house. At trial, the county court judge dismissed the mother's claim, on the basis that her agreement with her daughter was binding. The mother appealed.

Held (by a majority): The agreement was not intended to be legally binding, so the mother was entitled to recover possession of the house.

Danckwerts LJ:
'. . . This is an action between mother, Mrs. Violet Lalgee Jones, and daughter, Mrs. Ruby Padavatton, and one which is really deplorable. The points of difference between the two parties appear to be comparatively small, and it is distressing that they could not settle their differences amicably and avoid the bitterness and expense which is involved in this dispute carried as far as this court . . .

   Of course, there is no difficulty, if they so intend, in members of families entering into legally binding contracts in regard to family affairs. A competent equity draftsman would, if properly instructed, have no difficulty in drafting such a contract. But there is possibly in family affairs a presumption against such an intention (which, of course, can be rebutted). I would refer to Atkin LJ's magnificent exposition of the situation in regard to such arrangements in *Balfour v Balfour* [1919] 2 KB 571, 578–580.

   There is no doubt that this case is a most difficult one, but I have reached a conclusion that the present case is one of those family arrangements which depend on the good faith of the promises which are made and are not intended to be rigid, binding agreements. *Balfour v Balfour* was a case of husband and wife, but there is no doubt that the same principles apply to dealings between other relations, such as father and son and daughter and mother. This, indeed, seems to me a compelling case. Mrs. Jones and her daughter seem to have been on very good terms before 1967. The mother was arranging for a career for her daughter which she hoped would lead to success. This involved a visit to England in conditions which could not be wholly foreseen. What was required was an arrangement which was to be financed by the mother, and was such as would be adaptable to circumstances, as it in fact was. The operation about the house was, in my view, not a completely fresh arrangement, but an adaptation of the mother's financial assistance to her daughter due to the situation which was found to exist in England. It was not a stiff contractual operation any more than the original arrangement.

In the result, of course, on this view, the daughter cannot resist her mother's rights as the owner of the house to the possession of which the mother is entitled.'

Salmon LJ:

'I agree with the conclusion at which my Lord has arrived, but I have reached it by a different route. The first point to be decided is whether or not there was ever a legally binding agreement between the mother and daughter in relation to the daughter's reading for the Bar in England. The daughter alleges that there was such an agreement, and the mother denies it. She says that there was nothing but a loose family arrangement which had no legal effect. The onus is clearly on the daughter. There is no dispute that the parties entered into some sort of arrangement. It really depends upon (a) whether the parties intended it to be legally binding, and (b) if so, whether it was sufficiently certain to be enforceable. . . . Mr. Sparrow has said, quite rightly, that as a rule when arrangements are made between close relations, for example, between husband and wife, parent and child or uncle and nephew in relation to an allowance, there is a presumption against an intention of creating any legal relationship. This is not a presumption of law, but of fact. It derives from experience of life and human nature which shows that in such circumstances men and women usually do not intend to create legal rights and obligations, but intend to rely solely on family ties of mutual trust and affection. This has all been explained by Atkin L.J. in his celebrated judgment in *Balfour v Balfour* [1919] 2 K.B. 571, 578–580. There may, however, be circumstances in which this presumption, like all other presumptions of fact, can be rebutted . . .

On the facts as found by the county court judge this was entirely different from the ordinary case of a mother promising her daughter an allowance whilst the daughter read for the Bar, or a father promising his son an allowance at university if the son passed the necessary examinations to gain admission. The daughter here was thirty-four years of age in 1962. She had left Trinidad and settled in Washington as long ago as 1949. In Washington she had a comfortable flat and was employed as an assistant accountant in the Indian Embassy at a salary of $500 a month (over £2,000 a year). This employment carried a pension. She had a son of seven years of age who was an

American citizen, and had, of course, already begun his education. There were obviously solid reasons for her staying where she was. For some years prior to 1962, however, her mother, who lived in Trinidad, had been trying hard to persuade her to throw up all that she had achieved in Washington and go to London to read for the Bar. The mother would have been very proud to have a barrister for a daughter. She also thought that her plan was in the interest of her grandson, to whom she was much attached. She envisaged that, after her daughter had been called to the Bar, she would practice in Trinidad and thereafter presumably she (the mother) would be able to see much more of her daughter than formerly. The daughter was naturally loth to leave Washington, and did not regard her mother's suggestion as feasible. The mother, however, eventually persuaded the daughter to do as she wished by promising her that, if she threw up her excellent position in Washington and came to study for the Bar in England, she would pay her daughter an allowance of $200 a month until she had completed her studies. The mother's attorney in Trinidad wrote to the daughter to confirm this. I cannot think that either intended that if, after the daughter had been in London, say, for six months, the mother dishonoured her promise and left her daughter destitute, the daughter would have no legal redress.

In the very special circumstances of this case, I consider that the true inference must be that neither the mother nor the daughter could have intended that the daughter should have no legal right to receive, and the mother no legal obligation to pay, the allowance of $200 a month. Then again it is said that the duration of the agreement was not specified. No doubt, but I see no difficulty in implying the usual term that it was to last for a reasonable time. The parties cannot have contemplated that the daughter should go on studying for the Bar and draw the allowance until she was seventy, nor on the other hand that the mother could have discontinued the allowance if the daughter did not pass her examinations within, say, eighteen months. The promise was to pay the allowance until the daughter's studies were completed, and to my mind there was a clear implication that they were to be completed within a reasonable time. Studies are completed either by the student being called to the Bar or giving up the unequal struggle against the examiners.

It may not be easy to decide, especially when there is such a paucity of evidence, what is a reasonable time. The daughter, however, was a well educated intelligent woman capable of earning the equivalent of over £2,000 a year in Washington. It is true that she had a young son to look after, and may well (as the judge thought) have been hampered to some extent by the worry of this litigation. But, making all allowances for these factors and any other distraction, I cannot think that a reasonable time could possibly exceed five years from November 1962, the date when she began her studies . . .'

Fenton-Atkinson LJ:
'. . . The problem is, in my view, a difficult one, because though one would tend to regard a promise by a parent to pay an allowance to a child during a course of study as no more than a family arrangement, on the facts of this case this particular daughter undoubtedly gave up a great deal on the strength of the mother's promise.

In my judgment it is the subsequent history which gives the best guide to the parties' intention at the material time. There are three matters which seem to me important: (1) The daughter thought that her mother was promising her 200 United States dollars, or £70 a month, which she regarded as the minimum necessary for her support. The mother promised 200 dollars, but she had in mind 200 British West Indian dollars, £42 a month, and that was what she in fact paid from November 1962 to December 1964. Those payments were accepted by the daughter without any sort of suggestion at any stage that the mother had legally contracted for the larger sum. (2) When the arrangements for the purchase of No. 181, Highbury Quadrant were being discussed, and the new arrangement was made for maintenance to come out of the rents, many material matters were left open: how much accommodation was the daughter to occupy; how much money was she to have out of the rents; if the rents fell below expectation, was the mother to make up the difference below £42, or £42 less the sum saved by the daughter in rent; for how long was the arrangement to continue, and so on. The whole arrangement was, in my view, far too vague and uncertain to be itself enforceable as a contract; but at no stage did the daughter bring into the discussions her alleged legal right to £42 per month until her studies were completed, and how that right was to be affected by the new arrangement. (3) It is perhaps not without relevance to look at the daughter's evidence in cross-examination. She was asked about the occasion when her mother visited the house, and she, knowing perfectly well that her mother was there, refused for some hours to open the door. She said: "I didn't open the door because a normal mother doesn't sue her daughter in court. Anybody with normal feelings would feel upset by what was happening." Those answers and the daughter's conduct on that occasion provide a strong indication that she had never for a moment contemplated the possibility of her mother or herself going to court to enforce legal obligations, and that she felt it quite intolerable that a purely family arrangement should become the subject of proceedings in a court of law . . .'

Note that Salmon LJ treated the arrangement in relation to the house as separate from the original contract to provide maintenance, and found it too vague to be legally binding. So all members of the Court of Appeal held for the mother against her daughter.

4.4 COMMERCIAL AGREEMENTS

The presumption in relation to commercial agreements is that they are intended to be binding, and this can include arrangements that are primarily concerned with education or training, such as those between a pupil barrister and his or her chambers, as held in *Edmonds v Lawson* [2000] 2 WLR 1091.

The presumption is difficult to overturn, as is indicated by *Edwards v Skyways*.

Edwards v Skyways Ltd [1964] 1 WLR 349, QBD

Facts: The plaintiff was made the offer of an 'ex gratia' payment as part of a redundancy arrangement. The company subsequently refused to make the payment, denying that was legally bound to do so.

Held: The use of the phrase 'ex gratia' was not sufficient to overturn the presumption in commercial dealings that parties intend to be legally bound to their agreements.

Megaw, J:

'. . . In the present case, the subject-matter of the agreement is business relations, not social or domestic matters. There was a meeting of minds – an intention to agree. There was, admittedly, consideration for the company's promise. I accept the propositions of counsel for the plaintiff that in a case of this nature the onus is on the party who asserts that no legal effect was intended, and the onus is a heavy one . . .

[T]he company says, first, as I understand it, that the mere use of the phrase "ex gratia" by itself, as a part of the promise to pay, shows that the parties contemplated that the promise, when accepted, should have no binding force in law. It says, secondly, that even if the first proposition is not correct as a general proposition, nevertheless here there was certain background knowledge, present in the minds of everyone, which gave unambiguous significance to "ex gratia" as excluding legal relationship.

As to the first proposition, the words "ex gratia", in my judgment, do not carry a necessary, or even a probable, implication that the agreement is to be without legal effect. It is, I think, common experience amongst practitioners of the law that litigation or threatened litigation is frequently compromised on the terms that one party shall make to the other a payment described in express terms as "ex gratia" or "without admission of liability". The two phrases are, I think, synonymous. No one would imagine that a settlement, so made, is unenforceable at law. The words "ex gratia" or "without admission of liability" are used simply to indicate – it may be as a matter of amour-propre, or it may be to avoid a precedent in subsequent cases – that the party agreeing to pay does not admit any pre-existing liability on his part; but he is certainly not seeking to preclude the legal enforceability of the settlement itself by describing the contemplated payment as "ex gratia". So here. There are obvious reasons why the phrase might have been used by the company in just such a way. It might have desired to avoid conceding that any such payment was due under the employers' contract of service. It might have wished – perhaps ironically in the event – to show, by using the phrase, its generosity in making a payment beyond what was required by the contract of service. I see nothing in the mere use of the words "ex gratia", unless in the circumstances some very special meaning has to be given to them, to warrant the conclusion that this promise, duly made and accepted, for valid consideration, was not intended by the parties to be enforceable in law.

The company's second proposition seeks to show that in the circumstances here the words "ex gratia" had a special meaning. What is said is this: when a payment such as this is made by an employer to a dismissed employee the question whether it is subject to income tax in the hands of the recipient is important. It was understood by the company and by the association, and by all their respective representatives at the meeting, that if the company's payment were made as the result of a legally binding obligation, it would be taxable in the hands of the recipient; whereas, if it were to be made without legal obligation on the part of the company, it would not be taxable. It was not argued before me whether this assertion is right or wrong in law. It was said by the company that that is quite immaterial; what is material is that the parties so believed. Thus, it is said, the phrase "ex gratia" was used, and was understood by all present to be used, deliberately and advisedly as a formula to achieve that there would be no binding legal obligation on the company to pay, and hence to save the recipient from a tax liability. It is said that the offer was accepted by the association with full knowledge and understanding of these matters. Hence, it is said, the agreement by tacit consent, a consent evidenced by the use of the words "ex gratia" against this background of common understanding, was an agreement from which legal sanction and consequences were excluded.

In my judgment, that submission also fails because the evidence falls far short of showing that this supposed background of avoidance of tax liability was present as an important element in the minds of all, or indeed any, of the persons who attended the meeting of February 8; or, if this be something different, in the minds of the company or of the association; or that they all, or any of them, directed their minds to the significance of the words "ex gratia" which is now suggested on behalf of the company. The question of the liability, and the possible influence thereon of the use of the words "ex gratia", may indeed have been present in some degree, and as one element, in the minds of some of the persons present at the meeting. That, however, is far from sufficient to establish that the parties – both of them – affirmatively intended not to enter into legal relations in respect of the company's promise to pay.'

As Megaw J makes clear at the start of the quoted passage, the burden of proving that there was no intention to create legal relations in an ostensibly commercial contract lies with the party alleging this, and is a heavy one. A similar approach can be seen in the decision of the majority of the House of Lords in *Esso Petroleum Ltd v Commissioners of Customs and Excise* [1976] 1 All ER 117, where a promotion involving the 'gift' of a World Cup coin to motorists buying petrol was held to involve an intention to create legal relations. Indeed, the only way to be certain of avoiding legal effects is to use explicit language, as, for example, is done by companies running football pools competitions. In several cases the use of a phrase such as 'binding in honour only' has been held to indicate that the parties do not intend to enter a binding agreement. In *Jones v Vernons Pools* [1938] 2 All ER 626 the following clause was included on the entry coupon:

It is a basic condition of the sending in and the acceptance of this coupon that it is intended and agreed that the conduct of the pools and everything done in connection therewith and all arrangements relating thereto (whether mentioned in these rules or to be implied) and this coupon and any agreement or transaction entered into or payment made by or under it shall not be attended by or give rise to any legal relationship, rights, duties or consequences whatsoever or be legally enforceable or the subject of litigation, but all such arrangements, agreements and transactions are binding in honour only.

The judge commented on this clause:

That is a clause which seems to me to express in the fullest and clearest way that everything that follows in these rules is subject to that basic or overriding condition that everything that is promised, every statement made with relation to what a person sending the coupon may expect, or may be entitled to, is governed by that clause.

If it means what I think that they intend it to mean, and what certainly everybody who sent a coupon and who took the trouble to read it would understand, it means that they all trusted to the defendants' honour, and to the care they took, and that they fully understood that there should be no claim possible in respect of the transactions.

Even this type of clause may be given a restrictive interpretation in some circumstances. In *Rose and Frank Co v Crompton Bros* [1925] AC 445, it was held that an 'honour' clause applied to an overall agency arrangement between the parties, but not to in relation to particular orders placed under it.

Rose and Frank Co v Crompton Bros [1925] AC 445

Facts: The parties enter into an agreement under which the producers of carbonising tissue paper agreed to sell all their output to one company, which agreed in return only to obtain its paper from these producers. The agreement was stated to last for 3 years, but contained a clause indicating that it was 'binding in honour only'. Orders were placed and honoured, and then a question arose as to the enforceability of the overall agreement. The trial judge held that both the overall agreement and the orders under it were legally binding. The Court of Appeal found that neither was binding.

Held: The honour clause indicated that the overall agreement was not intended to be legally binding, but the orders placed under it were binding contracts.

Lord Phillimore:
'. . . The appellants, Rose and Frank Company, carry on business in the United States as dealers in carbonising tissue paper, which they have been in the habit of buying from England, then treating in some manner and selling in the perfected state.
Their relations with the respondents, James R. Crompton and Brothers, Ld., began as early as 1905; and there were three arrangements, which for the purposes of this

appeal we may assume to have been binding contracts, under which Rose and Frank Company were to be entitled to have the exclusive or nearly exclusive right of selling Crompton and Brothers' carbonising tissues in America, subject to twelve months' notice – a notice which was never given.

In 1913 circumstances led to the relations between the parties being reconsidered; and it was then for the first time brought to the notice of Rose and Frank Company that the respondents, Brittains, Ld., had been interested with Cromptons in supplying the carbonising tissue; and thereupon the three parties entered into the arrangement which has given rise to the present litigation. It is dated July 8, 1913, and in the earlier part of it appears to be a binding agreement, under which the English companies agree to confine the sale of all their carbonising tissue in the U.S. and Canada – subject to certain defined exceptions – and Rose and Frank Company agree to confine their purchases of the same stuff exclusively to the two English companies and to do their best to increase their trade. The arrangement was to last for three years subject to six months' notice. The other supplementary provisions need not be stated; but towards the end of the document appears this remarkable clause:

> "This arrangement is not entered into, nor is this memorandum written, as a formal or legal agreement, and shall not be subject to legal jurisdiction in the Law Courts either of the United States or England, but it is only a definite expression and record of the purpose and intention of the three parties concerned, to which they each honourably pledge themselves with the fullest confidence – based on past business with each other – that it will be carried through by each of the three parties with mutual loyalty and friendly co-operation."

There is no explanation upon the record, and no suggestion was made by counsel at the Bar of any reason for the introduction of this remarkable clause. During the progress of the hearing it occurred to some of your Lordships that it might have been inserted in order to avoid the operation of some American law discouraging monopolies. But this was a mere surmise. For whatever reason it was introduced the clause is there, and it remains for the Courts to give the proper effect to it.

The terms of this arrangement, whatever may be its force or effect, were continued by correspondence for a second three-yearly period and by arrangement in August, 1918, till March 31, 1920.

During the early part of 1919 differences arose between the parties. The respondents thought that the appellants were not conducting the business as they should, and that their (the respondents') interests were suffering. Accordingly on May 5 they demanded by telegram compliance with certain requirements, threatening, if the requirements were not met, to communicate direct with the consumers.

On the same day the appellants telegraphed back that they refused to consent to terminate the agreement and would hold the respondents accountable for any violation of contract, and they demanded immediate shipment of the parcels they had ordered; but on May 9 and 10, by cable and letter, the respondents definitely refused to allow further deliveries to be made.

During the existence of the arrangement the appellants had been giving to the respondents, Cromptons, from time to time, orders for certain numbers of cases of tissues to be delivered at various dates. The documents took this form: an order from the appellants to Cromptons: "Please enter our order for the following goods and ship." Then followed either a specific date – usually the first of the month or, if no specific date, then "as soon as possible," and the port to which they were to be shipped, either New York or sometimes Toronto, and the nature of the articles required. In compliance with these orders the respondents used to ship the goods. A few of the orders sent in this way in the early part of 1919 were complied with, but the others had not actually been complied with by the time of the quarrel and were not fulfilled afterwards.

On November 19, 1919, the appellants brought their action, treating the arrangement as a binding contract and claiming damages for the breach, alternatively averring that the three earlier agreements were still in force and claiming damages for their breach, and as a third alternative relying on the several specific orders for parcels of goods in the early part of 1919 as having been accepted by the respondents, Cromptons, and constituting specific contracts and claiming damages for the non-delivery of these goods. As to this part of their claim, they made no case against the respondents, Brittains, Ld.

The respondents joined in their defence, and contended that the arrangement was not a binding contract, that the earlier agreements were not binding contracts or had expired by loss of time. They also offered an alternative plea that if the respondents, Cromptons, ever made any of the earlier agreements, then "all of such agreements were determined by mutual consent by virtue of or alternatively at the date of the signing of the document referred to in paragraph 8 of the statement of claim and/or alternatively the plaintiffs by signing the said document and acting thereon are estopped from relying on any of the said alleged agreements."

As to the appellants' claim in respect of the specific orders, they denied that these orders gave rise to any contracts, said that the requirements of s 4 of the Sale of Goods Act had not been complied with, and further that these orders and acceptances, if any, were given as part of a specification under the arrangement of 1913, and that if that arrangement did not constitute any legal contract, neither did these orders with provisional acceptances constitute contracts.

They further pleaded misconduct on the part of the appellants justifying them in determining the agreement . . .

These issues were then tried by Bailhache J. He decided that the arrangement of 1913 was a binding contract, and further that if the appellants were ultimately held to fail on this ground, they had a good case as to the orders and acceptances . . .

The present respondents appealed from this order, and the Court of Appeal came unanimously to a different conclusion to that of Bailhache J. with respect to the arrangement of 1913, and by a majority (Bankes and Scrutton L.JJ.; Atkin L.J. dissenting) thought that Bailhache J. was also wrong on the question of orders and acceptances. They declined, however, to determine whether the pre–1913 arrangements were still in existence, and whether if in existence they were enforceable, and said that this matter remained to be tried. They gave the respondents costs of the issues on which they were successful and the costs of the appeal. Appeal and cross appeal have been preferred from this order and are now before your Lordships for decision.

With regard to the first and most important point, that of the legal force or want of force of the arrangement of 1913, your Lordships are, I conceive, of one mind with the Court of Appeal. I do not propose to repeat their reasoning, with which I venture to concur, but I wish to add one observation. I was for a time impressed by the suggestion that as complete legal rights had been created by the earlier part of the document in question, any subsequent clause nullifying those rights ought to be regarded as repugnant and ought to be rejected. This is what happens for instance in cases where an instrument inter vivos purports to pass the whole property in something either real or personal, and there follows a provision purporting to forbid the new owner from exercising the ordinary rights of ownership. In such cases this restriction is dis-regarded. But I think the right answer was made by Scrutton L.J. It is true that when the tribunal has before it for construction an instrument which unquestionably creates a legal interest, and the dispute is only as to the quality and extent of that interest, then later repugnant clauses in the instrument cutting down that interest which the earlier part of it has given are to be rejected, but this doctrine does not apply when the question is whether it is intended to create any legal interest at all. Here, I think, the overriding clause in the document is that which provides that it is to be a contract of honour only and unenforceable at law.

With regard to the next point – namely, the right of the plaintiffs to recover damages for non-delivery of the goods specified in the particular orders for the year 1919 – it should be stated that the defence under the Sale of Goods Act was abandoned at the trial. On this point I agree with your Lordships in preferring the judgments of Bailhache J. and Atkin L.J. to that of the majority of the Court of Appeal.

According to the course of business between the parties which is narrated in the unenforceable agreement, goods were ordered from time to time, shipped, received, and paid for, under an established system; but the agreement being unenforceable, there was no obligation on the American company to order goods or upon the English companies to accept an order. Any actual transaction between the parties, however, gave rise to the ordinary legal rights; for the fact that it was not of obligation to do the transaction did not divest the transaction when done of its ordinary legal significance. This, my Lords, will, I think, be plain if we begin at the latter end of each transaction.

Goods were ordered, shipped, and received. Was there no legal liability to pay for them? One stage further back. Goods were ordered, shipped, and invoiced. Was there no legal liability to take delivery? I apprehend that in each of these cases the American company would be bound. If the goods were short-shipped or inferior in quality, or if the nature of them was such as to be deleterious to other cargo on board or illegal for the American company to bring into their country, the American company would have its usual legal remedies against the English companies or one of them. Business usually begins in some mutual understanding without a previous bargain.

> However, as to this claim for damages for the unfulfilled orders, the respondents have, under the terms of the order of McCardie J. the defence open to them that the conduct of the appellants was such as to justify them in determining the agreements to deliver.
>
> There remains the matter of the cross appeal. This, I think, succeeds.
>
> The unenforceable agreement cannot (it is true) be relied upon as cancelling the previous agreements, because it was to have no legal weight. But the parties who entered into the relations implied by the unenforceable agreement must have previously cancelled, as they could do by mutual consent, all the earlier agreements.
>
> Upon the documents which were before the Court – which were indeed the only materials before the Court – the proper inference to be drawn was that the arrangement of 1913 was, though unenforceable, intended to supersede all previous arrangements or agreements, whether enforceable or unenforceable.
>
> The principle laid down in *Morris v Baron & Co* [1918] A. C. 1, followed in *British and Beningtons v North Western Cachar Tea Co* [1923] A. C. 48, is the one which governs the present case.
>
> It was a pity, I think, that the Court of Appeal determined, apparently against the view of Scrutton L.J., to remit this issue for trial instead of deciding it themselves. I think they should have decided it, and decided it in favour of the respondents and cross appellants.
>
> Upon the whole, I would advise your Lordships to restore the judgment of Bailhache J., except that part of it which declares "that the agreement of July, 1913, mentioned in paragraph 8 of the statement of claim is a legally binding agreement against both defendants". . . . The case should be remitted to the High Court of Justice with a declaration that it be disposed of accordingly.'

▌4.5 COLLECTIVE AGREEMENTS

In the context of employment law, it is not uncommon for an employer, or group of employers, to come to an agreement with a trade union as to the pay or other conditions of service that are to apply to a group of employees. Such an agreement will commonly affect the individual contract of employment of each employee, and to that extent have a binding legal effect. Is it also binding as between the employer and trade union? Since it is an agreement that is clearly 'commercial' rather than 'domestic', the expectation would be that it would be presumed to be binding, on the principles outlined in the previous section. In fact, it was held in *Ford Motor Co Ltd v AEF* [1969] 2 QB 303 that the overall context in which industrial relations were conducted in the United Kingdom meant that such agreements should not be regarded as being intended to be legally enforceable. This approach has subsequently been given statutory effect, and the current provision dealing with this is to be found in the Trade Union and Labour Relations (Consolidation) Act 1992.

TRADE UNION AND LABOUR RELATIONS (CONSOLIDATION) ACT 1992

Section 179

Whether agreement intended to be a legally enforceable contract.

(1) A collective agreement shall be conclusively presumed not to have been intended by the parties to be a legally enforceable contract unless the agreement—

    (a) is in writing, and

    (b) contains a provision which (however expressed) states that the parties intend that the agreement shall be a legally enforceable contract.

(2) A collective agreement which does satisfy those conditions shall be conclusively presumed to have been intended by the parties to be a legally enforceable contract.

(3) If a collective agreement is in writing and contains a provision which (however expressed) states that the parties intend that one or more parts of the agreement specified in that provision, but not the whole of the agreement, shall be a legally enforceable contract, then—

    (a) the specified part or parts shall be conclusively presumed to have been intended by the parties to be a legally enforceable contract, and

    (b) the remainder of the agreement shall be conclusively presumed not to have been intended by the parties to be such a contract.

(4) A part of a collective agreement which by virtue of subsection (3)(b) is not a legally enforceable contract may be referred to for the purpose of interpretating a part of the agreement which is such a contract.

As indicated by this provision, collective agreements are not legally binding unless in writing and specifically stated to be intended to be binding.

▌4.6 IS A REQUIREMENT OF INTENTION NECESSARY?

It has sometimes been argued that the elements of offer, acceptance and consideration should be sufficient to determine the question of whether an agreement is intended to be binding, and that a separate requirement of 'intention' is unnecessary. This approach is exemplified by the arguments put forward by Professor Hepple in the following article.

**Brian Hepple, "*Intention to create legal relations*",
(1970) *CLJ* 122, pp 127–137**

The requirement of an intention to create legal relations, additional to the test of bargain, has been repeatedly criticised by academic commentators. In essence, the objection raised by the critics is that the whole basis of the common law of contract is the notion of bargain, of which offer, acceptance and consideration are indivisible facets. Every offer may be seen as consisting of a promise and a request to the offeree to do some act (which may be the giving of a promise or the rendering of a performance) in exchange for the promise. From the offeree's side the doing of that act is an acceptance of the offer. From the offeror's angle, the response to his request is consideration. For analytical reasons it has become traditional to separate the element of agreement (usually reduced to an offer and acceptance) from the element of consideration. In determining the existence of agreement the courts have sought to find *consensus ad idem* by objective yardsticks, by strict grammatical rules of construction, and by classifications such as 'invitation to treat', 'puff' and 'offer' which provide *a priori* tests of the respective 'intentions' of the parties. The intervention of equity has made this approach workable by preventing 'hardship amounting to injustice' where appearances are too far removed from reality. Consideration has provided the test of enforceability. This separation of agreement from consideration (in part inspired by a desire to contrast consideration with the civil law *causa*) has resulted in a fundamental point being overlooked. This is that the common law recognised at an early stage that parties usually do not define their intention to enter legal relations. Consequently, the fact that they have cast their arrangement into the form of bargain (offer, acceptance, consideration) provides an extremely practical test of that intention. This test of bargain renders superfluous any *additional* proof of intention.

The difficulties which have arisen in reconciling this approach with the remarks of Atkin L.J. (as he then was) in *Balfour v Balfour* have arisen, as the late Professor Unger showed, only because of Atkin L.J.'s definition of consideration. It will be remembered that his Lordship insisted that 'arrangements made between husband and wife are arrangements in which there are mutual promises, or there is consideration in form within the definition that I have mentioned. Nevertheless they are not contracts . . . because the parties do not intend that they should be attended by legal consequences.' He defined consideration as consisting of a benefit received by one party or a loss suffered by the other, but he failed to add that the benefit or loss must be received or suffered as the price for the other. An agreement between spouses may consist of mutual promises and yet not be a contract precisely because the promise of the one party is not given as the price for the other. The same reasoning can be applied to other domestic agreements. In *Shadwell v Shadwell*, for example, the court was agreed that the question they had to answer was, 'Was the plaintiff's marriage at his uncle's request?' Their Lordships differed only on the construction of the particular promise before them.

The courts, aided by all the standard textbooks, have tended to conceal this simple analysis of every offer into a promise and request by the repeated incantation of Atkin L.J.'s dictum without making the essential qualification about the sense in which he defined consideration.

A recent example is *Jones v Padavatton*. At her mother's request and in return for a promise to provide $200 a month maintenance for her, the plaintiff gave up an 'excellent' job and other advantages of living in Washington in order to come to England in 1962 to read for the Bar. In 1964 the mother bought a house in London for the daughter to live in one or two rooms and let the rest to tenants to cover expenses and provide maintenance. After a quarrel with her daughter in 1967, the mother brought legal proceedings for possession of the house. Danckwerts and Fenton Atkinson L.JJ. agreed that there was good consideration for the mother's promise in 1962 but held that the principle in *Balfour v Balfour* applied and that the presumption against an intention to be bound in family matters had not been rebutted. Accordingly, the mother was entitled to possession. Salmon L.J. reached the same result but by a different route. He held that the presumption had been rebutted in the case of the 1962 agreement, but that the agreement in 1964 regarding possession of the house was unenforceable. A close examination of Salmon L.J.'s judgment (like the well-known inquiry of Scrutton L.J. into the alleged bargain in *Wyatt v Kreglinger and Fernau*) reveals that although he stated the problem in the *language* of intention, the test of that intention was in fact that of bargain. The mother's promise of maintenance (confirmed through her attorney) was the decisive factor which led the daughter to respond to the request to live in London. In regard to the second agreement, however, Salmon L.J. said: 'There is no evidence that the mother bargained away her right to dispose of her home, or to evict her daughter (who was a mere licensee) whenever she wished to do so.' Bargain was once again used as the test of contractual intention.

To require, as Danckwerts and Fenton Atkinson L.JJ. did, some further test of intention is to invite confusion and uncertainty. Indeed, their Lordships were not agreed how that intention should be ascertained. Fenton Atkinson L.J. was influenced by the fact that the daughter had said in cross-examination, 'a normal mother doesn't sue her daughter in court', to which Salmon L.J. responded: 'the fact that a contracting party is in some circumstances unlikely to extract his pound of flesh does not mean that he has no right to it'. Fenton Atkinson L.J. also remarked on the failure of the daughter at any stage prior to the institution of proceedings against her to bring into discussion her right to a particular amount of maintenance. This surely goes no further than to confirm Professor Unger's view that 'the family circle differs from the market place in that it is not the setting for bargaining but for gratuitous services'.

It has been argued that 'one cannot tell whether mutual promises are a bargain or an "exchange of gifts" without regard to the intention of the parties'. This attributes unnecessary circularity to the notion of bargain. Once it was conceded that an agreement existed in *Jones v Padavatton*, the only test of intention ought to have been the terms of the promises which were given by mother and daughter. Was there a request to the daughter to come to London in return for the promise of maintenance? Did the daughter respond to that request? This approach would have done much to simplify what Danckwerts L.J. called a 'most difficult' case.

Although Lord Atkin's celebrated judgment has been accepted as authoritative for fifty years, it is interesting to note that when it recently reached the House of Lords, as an incidental issue in *Pettitt v Pettitt*, there was a keen desire to limit its application. It was described as 'an extreme case' and one which 'stretched the doctrine [that in ordinary day-to-day life spouses do not intend to contract] to its limits'. At a time when this cautious approach is evident in the context for which the *Balfour v Balfour* principle was devised, it seems strange that it should be undergoing an extension in another direction to resolve the problems of a very different type of relationship, namely, collective bargaining.

This extension was preceded by the attempt of some textbook writers to rationalise a number of cases involving ordinary business contracts by reference to the *Balfour v Balfour* principle. In my view this attempt was mistaken because all those cases may properly be classed under some other definite rule of the law of contract.

First, there are those cases in which contracts have been distinguished from licences. Although the language of contractual intention has been used, the test in fact employed has been that of bargain. So in *Gore v Van der Lann* the court found that there was a negotiated bargain although the stated intention of the parties was that the free pass issued by Liverpool Corporation 'merely constitutes and grants a licence to the holder to travel on the . . . Corporation's buses'. The crucial fact leading to the inference of a contractual *animus* was that the pass was issued to Mrs. Gore only pursuant to her written application. This distinguished the case from *Wilkie v L.P.T.B.* where Mr. Wilkie, being an employee, received his free pass as a matter of course. The test of contractual intention in both these cases was that of bargain. It might be argued, with some justification, that the Court of Appeal stretched the facts to their limits in finding a contract between Mrs. Gore and the Corporation, but it is clear that no additional proof of intention was required apart from the bilateral nature of the negotiations between the parties.

Secondly, there are those cases in which proof of an *animus contrahendi* has been required to distinguish a mere representation from a contractual warranty (either forming part of a single contract with the main promise or standing as a separate collateral contract). It has been suggested that *Heilbut, Symons & Co v Buckleton* cannot be explained by those who criticise the requirement of additional proof of an intention to create legal relations. The simple answer is that the House of Lords did not ask whether there was offer, acceptance, consideration *and* some additional proof of intention. On the contrary, when Lord Moulton said that a party wishing to establish a collateral contract must clearly prove 'not only the terms of such contracts but the existence of an *animus contrahendi* on the part of all the parties', he was referring to the need to establish an offer (promise and request) and acceptance. This is made particularly clear in the speech of Lord Atkinson who said that the plaintiff's 'own language . . . appears to me to be inconsistent with the idea that he accepted the alleged offer or treated it as part of the bargain'.

In cases where puffs and statements made in jest or anger have been distinguished from binding promises, the legal question has been whether a reasonable person would have understood the words as importing a promise. The judges in that timeless case of *Carlill v Carbolic Smoke Ball Co* had no doubt that in dealing with this question they were inquiring into the existence of a bargain. A. L. Smith L.J. remarked: 'The defendants have contended that [the advertisement] was a promise in honour or an agreement or a contract in honour—whatever that may mean. I understand that if there is no consideration for a promise, it may be a promise in honour, or, as we should call it, a promise without consideration and *nudum pactum*; but if anything else is meant I do not understand it.'

Thirdly, there are those cases in which a driver has given a lift to a friend or workmate in return for the payment of money or contribution to petrol and the courts have denied the existence of a contract on the ground of an absence of intention to create legal relations. Most of the cases have been concerned with the interpretation of section 203 of the Road Traffic Act 1960 which requires insurance 'in the case of a vehicle in which passengers are carried for hire or reward'. *Coward v Motor Insurers' Bureau* is an example of the way in which the common law notion of bargain can be distorted because of the exigencies of statutory interpretation. Can it be seriously argued that had Coward refused to pay the weekly amount promised in return for Cole's lift, the courts would have denied Cole a contractual remedy? Fortunately, the Court of Appeal has now provided a more satisfactory basis on which to rest the decision in *Coward's* case, namely, that section 203 requires insurance only where passengers are *habitually* carried for hire or reward. It is far more satisfactory to ask what purposes were intended by Parliament than to say that a bargain is not a contract. This leaves *Buckpitt v Oates*, which was decided on the basis that if there was a contract between an infant driver and his infant passenger to the effect that the latter should be carried at his own risk this contract would be void (because it would not be to his benefit) and the negligent driver would have to submit to judgment in respect of damage caused by his negligent driving. In order to avoid this consequence it was held that there was no contract, despite the fact of bargain, because of the absence of an intention to create legal relations. It is submitted that this was unnecessary for the decision because even had the agreement been void as a contract, the question could still have been considered whether the terms of that agreement gave the defence of assumption of risk.

Finally, mention must be made of those instances in which the parties have *expressed* an intention not to be bound. These create no problem because the test of bargain is used to establish the contractual character of the promise only if parties are silent as to their intentions. However, expressions of intention can be ambiguous, as in *Edwards v Skyways Ltd*, in which a promise to make an *ex gratia* payment to a redundant pilot fell to be interpreted. In deciding that the words '*ex gratia*' did not imply that the agreement was to be without legal effect, the court went no further, in relation to *Balfour v Balfour*, than to say that 'where the subject-matter . . . is related to business affairs, the parties may, by using *clear words*, show that their intention is to make the transaction binding in honour only and not in law; and the courts will give effect to that expressed intention.'

The conclusions to be drawn from this are as follows:

(1) In ascertaining whether or not the parties have reached agreement the common law inquires how a reasonable person would have understood the words or conduct in issue. The courts may, however, prevent injustice by denying or granting equitable relief.

(2) In ascertaining whether or not the agreement is enforceable the common law applies the test of bargain.

These tests (1) and (2) are sometimes couched in the language of 'intention'. Viewed in this way, they are conclusive evidence of an 'intention to create legal relations'.

(3) Atkin L.J.'s dictum requiring some *additional* proof of an intention to create legal relations must be understood in the light of the special meaning which he attached to 'consideration', and should not be extended to situations in which a bargain in the usual sense of offer, acceptance and consideration is found to exist. Attempts to make such extensions, as in the *Ford* case, inevitably result in the use of unnecessary legal fictions. This cannot be in the interests of the rational development of the law of contract, particularly in such modern contexts as collective labour relations.

(4) The present English rules about the seriousness of promises are inseparable from tests (1) and (2) above.

Bargains and Policy

It would be open to the House of Lords in an appropriate case to review the cases since *Balfour v Balfour* and to reject or modify the requirement of additional proof of an intention to create legal relations. A possible obstacle, however, is that the device of constructive 'intention' is superficially attractive because it enables the courts to cloak policy decisions in the mantle of private contractual autonomy.

In most situations the test of bargain provides a satisfactory answer to the policy question. It also satisfies the theory of contractual autonomy since it is for the parties to cast their transaction in the form of a bargain. For example, Atkin L.J. himself recognised the policy considerations behind the non-enforceability of social and domestic arrangements when he said: 'the small courts of this country would have to be multiplied one hundredfold if these arrangements were held to be legal obligations', and that 'in these cold courts' natural love and affection counted for little. Consequently, 'each house is a domain into which the King's writ does not run'. This policy can be flexibly implemented by applying the test of bargain.

There are, however, other agreements, manifestly cast in the form of bargain, to which the concepts of private contract law seem inappropriate. The main examples are government contracts and collective labour agreements. In dealing with agreements such as these the courts prefer to deny legal enforceability on the grounds of absence of a constructive intention rather than to base their decisions explicitly on policy grounds.

The term 'government contracts' is used here to describe those 'undertakings that are political in character—using the word "political" as referring to promises and undertakings of governments, either to their own citizens, or to other states or governments'. Sometimes the nature of the statutory relationship between the consumer and the government or a public body may lead to the conclusion that there is no consensual bargain at all. So there is no 'sale' of a prescribed drug to an outpatient who is entitled, under National Health Service regulations, to demand it on payment of a nominal charge. The transaction is a creature of statute. Similarly, electricity is supplied in pursuance of a statutory duty; the transaction cannot be treated as the acceptance by the electricity board of an offer by the consumer to take and pay for the supply.

There are other situations, however, in which there appears to be a voluntary assumption of legal responsibility but the courts nevertheless treat the undertaking as non-justiciable. This may be attributed to the status of a government department or public body. For example, the Post Office has been treated as a branch of Revenue created by Act of Parliament and the consequence of this has been said to be that the Post Office does not enter into contractual relations. This was avowedly a policy decision but it has sometimes been thought necessary to explain it on the basis that the parties did not intend, or cannot be regarded as having intended, to subject their agreement to the adjudication of the courts. The 'intention' usually considered in this regard is solely that of the government (which does not want to be held liable) and not that of the private contractor. The justification in terms of absence of intention may be one of the factors which has retarded the development of a separate set of legal rules to deal with the construction and effects of government 'contracts' and may help to account for the meagre role played by the courts in regulating this activity of government.

The rigid classification of the issues on a 'contract/no contract' basis has also precluded the development in England of a separate jurisprudence of the collective labour agreement. This classification was itself a product of the 'intention' theory. The policy implicit in the *Ford* decision was that the parties had arranged their affairs on the basis that the 'peace' obligation in those collective agreements would be enforced by social rather than legal sanctions in the circumstances of the particular dispute. This policy was implemented by saying that no contract had been formed. The assumption was that there either was a contract, in which case it would have to be strictly construed like other contracts, or there was no contract at all.

An alternative approach would have been to assume that the fact of bargain was sufficient to create a legal relationship, but then to find that the distinctive features of collective bargaining give rise to a relationship *sui generis*. These features have often been pointed out. Collective labour agreements partake more of the features of statute or treaty of peace than of commercial bargain. As the Donovan Report pointed out, it is often impossible to fit these agreements into the traditional categories of contract. The continuous nature of the relationship, in which the interpretation of an agreement merges imperceptibly into differences concerning claims, and the 'open-ended' nature of many agreements, means that it is difficult to find 'rights' capable of legal enforcement. The concept of material breach seems meaningless in a situation in which the parties are less interested in deviations from the bargain struck than in the achievement of the just and harmonious operation of an enterprise. Moreover, the power of performance may lie in the hands of employees on the shop floor and not of union officials. The multiplicity of parties (as on the Fords' N.J.N.C.) introduces extremely difficult problems of agency to which the common law provides no clear answers. Many agreements, if treated like ordinary contracts, would run foul of the doctrines of restraint of trade. Nor would traditional contractual remedies be adequate. These and other difficulties reflect the fact that the formative period of the modern law of contract antedated the rise of collective labour relations. Concepts appropriate to private bargains cannot simply be extended to collective agreements.

None of these distinctive features of the collective bargain, however, presents an absolute barrier to legal enforceability. If it did, it would be impossible to account for the enforceability of such agreements in most other countries, or for the fact that even in England the parties may expressly declare themselves to be bound. The real legal difficulty is that the courts, having been led to view the issues through the blinkers of the 'contract/no contract' analysis, may not now be willing or able to develop a separate set of rules for the construction in good faith of collective agreements, nor to create appropriate remedies. This is bound to become an increasingly important problem. The growth of formal, fixed-period plant and company bargains—the central recommendation in the Donovan Report—may lead the courts to find that the climate of opinion adverse to enforceability has changed and that the language of contract has been used. *A fortiori* there will be legal enforcement on the basis of ordinary contract law when the parties declare their intention to be bound.

The question whether or not collective labour agreements should be justiciable is too important and controversial a political matter to be left to the courts. In view of the fact that the courts have rejected the test of bargain, enforceability or non-enforceability, as the case may be, should now be on the basis of an express statutory provision rather than constructive intention. This would leave the way clear for the common law to free itself from the stultifying effects of the requirement of additional proof of an intention to create legal relations.

4.7 ADDITIONAL READING

Allen, D, 'The gentleman's agreement in legal theory and in modern practice' [2000] Anglo-American Law Review 204.

Brown, I, 'The letter of comfort: placebo or promise?' [1990] JBL 281.

Freeman, M, 'Contracting in the haven: *Balfour v Balfour* revisited', in Halson, R (ed), *Exploring the Boundaries of Contract*, 1996, London: Dartmouth.

Hedley, S, 'Keeping contract in its Place: *Balfour v Balfour* and the enforceability of informal agreements' (1985) OJLS 391.

Unger, R, *The Critical Legal Studies Movement*, 1983, Cambridge, Mass: Harvard University Press, pp 60–6.

CHAPTER 5

PRIVITY

5.1 INTRODUCTION

The doctrine of privity states that only the parties to a contract can have rights and obligations under it. It is one of the characteristic doctrines of English contract law, but there are a number of exceptions to it. The most important of these is contained in the Contracts (Rights of Third Parties) Act 1999, which allows contracting parties to confer an enforceable benefit on a third party. There are various other exceptions to the doctrine. These include the ability of a contracting party to recover damages on behalf of non-parties. There has been significant case law on this in recent years. In some situations the courts have found the existence of a trust of a promise. This exception has largely fallen into disuse, because of the difficulty of establishing that the parties intended to create an irrevocable trust. Collateral contracts can be used to create rights or obligations in relation to a person who is not a party to the main contract. There are also some specific statutory exceptions.

A particular approach has been used to give third parties the benefit of an exclusion clause, involving one of the contracting parties being treated as the agent of the third party. This is likely to be less used, now that the same objective can be achieved through the 1999 Act.

There have been far fewer attempts to impose burdens on third parties, but in some circumstances *restrictive covenants* can be used, in relation to land and shipping contracts in particular. The tort of inducing breach of contract can also be of assistance in this area.

5.2 THE BASIC DOCTRINE OF PRIVITY

The common-law doctrine of privity states that only a party to a contract can have rights or obligations under it. The basis of the doctrine of privity may be found in *Tweddle v Atkinson*.

Tweddle v Atkinson (1861) 1 B & S 393; 121 ER 762 (QB)

Facts: The fathers of a couple who were about to get married, made an agreement under which the father of the bride was to pay £200 and the father of the groom £100, to the bridegroom, William Tweddle. William sued his father-in-law for non-payment.

Held: William Tweddle could not sue on the agreement between the fathers, because he was not a party to it, even though he was intended to benefit from it.

Wightman J:

'Some of the old decisions appear to support the proposition that a stranger to the consideration of a contract may maintain an action upon it, if he stands in such a near relationship to the party from whom the consideration proceeds, that he may be considered a party to the consideration. The strongest of those cases is that cited in *Bourne v Mason* (1 Ventr. 6), in which it was held that the daughter of a physician might maintain assumpsit upon a promise to her father to give her a sum of money if he performed a certain cure. But there is no modern case in which the proposition has been supported. On the contrary, it is now established that no stranger to the consideration can take advantage of a contract, although made for his benefit.'

Crompton J:

'It is admitted that the plaintiff cannot succeed unless this case is an exception to the modern and well established doctrine of the action of assumpsit. At the time when the cases which have been cited were decided the action of assumpsit was treated as an action of trespass upon the case, and therefore in the nature of a tort; and the law was not settled, as is now is, that natural love and affection is not a sufficient consideration for a promise upon which an action may be maintained; nor was it settled that the promisee cannot bring an action unless the consideration for the promise moved from him. The modern cases have, in effect, overruled the old decisions; they show that the consideration must move from the party entitled to sue upon the contract. It would be a monstrous proposition to say that a person was a party to the contract for the purpose of suing upon it for his own advantage, and not a party to it for the purpose of being sued. It is said that the father in the present case was agent for the son in making the contract, but that argument ought also to make the son liable upon it. I am prepared to overrule the old decisions, and to hold that, by reason of the principles which now govern the action of assumpsit, the present action is not maintainable.'

Blackburn J concurred.

As these judgments make clear, at the time, the doctrine was founded on the requirement that consideration must move from the promisee. The later affirmation of *Tweddle v Atkinson* by the House of Lords in *Dunlop v Selfridge* focuses more directly on the principle that only a person who is a party to a contract can have rights (or liabilities) under it.

Dunlop Pneumatic Tyre Co Ltd v Selfridge & Co Ltd [1915] AC 847

Facts: Dunlop contracted with D, wholesalers of motor accessories, that D in selling tyres to retailers would require the retailer to observe Dunlop's list price. S entered into such an agreement with D, but then sold tyres at below the list price. Dunlop sought an injunction and damages from S.

Held: Dunlop was not in a contractual relationship with S, and so could not enforce the terms of the agreement between D and S.

Viscount Haldane, LC:
'. . . My Lords, in the law of England certain principles are fundamental. One is that only a person who is a party to a contract can sue on it. Our law knows nothing of a *jus quaesitum tertio* arising by way of contract. Such a right may be conferred by way of property, as, for example, under a trust, but it cannot be conferred on a stranger to a contract as a right to enforce the contract in personam. A second principle is that if a person with whom a contract not under seal has been made is to be able to enforce it consideration must have been given by him to the promisor or to some other person at the promisor's request. These two principles are not recognized in the same fashion by the jurisprudence of certain Continental countries or of Scotland, but here they are well established. A third proposition is that a principal not named in the contract may sue upon it if the promisee really contracted as his agent. But again, in order to entitle him so to sue, he must have given consideration either personally or through the promisee, acting as his agent in giving it.

My Lords, in the case before us, I am of opinion that the consideration, the allowance of what was in reality part of the discount to which Messrs. Dew, the promisees, were entitled as between themselves and the appellants, was to be given by Messrs. Dew on their own account, and was not in substance, any more than in form, an allowance made by the appellants. The case for the appellants is that they permitted and enabled Messrs. Dew, with the knowledge and by the desire of the respondents, to sell to the latter on the terms of the contract of January 2, 1912. But it appears to me that even if this is so the answer is conclusive. Messrs. Dew sold to the respondents goods which they had a title to obtain from the appellants independently of this contract. The consideration by way of discount under the contract of January 2 was to come wholly out of Messrs. Dew's pocket, and neither directly nor indirectly out of that of the appellants. If the appellants enabled them to sell to the respondents on the terms they did, this was not done as any part of the terms of the contract sued on.

No doubt it was provided as part of these terms that the appellants should acquire certain rights, but these rights appear on the face of the contract as *jura quaesita tertio*, which the appellants could not enforce. Moreover, even if this difficulty can be got over by regarding the appellants as the principals of Messrs. Dew in stipulating for the rights in question, the only consideration disclosed by the contract is one given by Messrs. Dew, not as their agents, but as principals acting on their own account.

The conclusion to which I have come on the point as to consideration renders it unnecessary to decide the further question as to whether the appellants can claim that a bargain was made in this contract by Messrs. Dew as their agents; a bargain which, apart from the point as to consideration, they could therefore enforce. If it were necessary to express an opinion on this further question, a difficulty as to the position of Messrs. Dew would have to be considered. Two contracts—one by a man on his own account as principal, and another by the same man as agent—may be validly comprised in the same piece of paper. But they must be two contracts, and not one as here. I do not think that a man can treat one and the same contract as made by him in two capacities. He cannot be regarded as contracting for himself and for another *uno flatu*.

My Lords, the form of the contract which we have to interpret leaves the appellants in this dilemma, that, if they say that Messrs. Dew contracted on their behalf, they gave no consideration, and if they say they gave consideration in the shape of a permission to the respondents to buy, they must set up further stipulations, which are neither to be found in the contract sued upon nor are germane to it, but are really inconsistent with its structure. That contract has been reduced to writing, and it is in the writing that we must look for the whole of the terms made between the parties. These terms cannot, in my opinion consistently with the settled principles of English law, be construed as giving to the appellants any enforceable rights as against the respondents.

I think that the judgment of the Court of Appeal was right, and I move that the appeal be dismissed with costs.'

Lord Dunedin:
'My Lords, I confess that this case is to my mind apt to nip any budding affection which one might have had for the doctrine of consideration. For the effect of that doctrine in the present case is to make it possible for a person to snap his fingers at a bargain deliberately made, a bargain not in itself unfair, and which the person seeking to

enforce it has a legitimate interest to enforce. Notwithstanding these considerations I cannot say that I have ever had any doubt that the judgment of the Court of Appeal was right.'

This was a unanimous decision of a six-person House of Lords, and so firmly established the doctrine. The potential unfairness, however, pointed out by Lord Dunedin, and the fact that preventing an agreement of this kind from operating may well thwart the intentions of all concerned at the time of contract, meant that the doctrine, at least as far as it prevents the conferment of benefits, was the subject of much criticism throughout the twentieth century. The Law Revision Committee, in its Sixth Interim Report (Cmd 5449), recommended legislative reform in 1937. Nevertheless, the House of Lords again confirmed the basic principle in 1968. They were able to do justice in the case despite the doctrine, but also rejected one possible route to reducing its impact, advocated by Lord Denning, and involving a broad interpretation of the effect of s 56 of the Law of Property Act 1925.

Beswick v Beswick [1968] AC 58 (HL)

Facts: Peter Beswick was a coal merchant. When he retired from the business his nephew who took over the business agreed to pay Peter an agreed sum for the rest of Peter's life, and a slightly smaller sum to Peter's widow after Peter's death. When Peter died, the nephew refused to make the agreed payments to his widow.

Held: Although the widow was not a party to the contract, in her capacity of administratrix of her husband's estate, she could obtain specific performance of the contract.

Lord Reid:
'My Lords, before 1962 the respondent's deceased husband carried on business as a coal merchant. By agreement of March 14, 1962, he assigned to his nephew, the appellant, the assets of the business and the appellant undertook first to pay to him £6 10s. per week for the remainder of his life and then to pay to the respondent an annuity of £5 per week in the event of her husband's death. The husband died in November, 1963. Thereupon, the appellant made one payment of £5 to the respondent but he refused to make any further payment to her. The respondent now sues for £175 arrears of the annuity and for an order for specific performance of the continuing obligation to pay the annuity. The Vice-Chancellor of the County Palatine of Lancaster decided against the respondent but the Court of Appeal reversed this decision and, besides ordering payment of the arrears, ordered the appellant to pay to the respondent for the remainder of her life an annuity of £5 per week in accordance with the agreement.
    It so happens that the respondent is administratrix of the estate of her deceased

husband and she sues both in that capacity and in her personal capacity. So it is necessary to consider her rights in each capacity.

For clarity I think it best to begin by considering a simple case where, in consideration of a sale by A to B, B agrees to pay the price of £1,000 to a third party X. Then the first question appears to me to be whether the parties intended that X should receive the money simply as A's nominee so that he would hold the money for behalf of A and be accountable to him for it, or whether the parties intended that X should receive the money for his own behalf and be entitled to keep it. That appears to me to be a question of construction of the agreement read in light of all the circumstances which were known to the parties. There have been several decisions involving this question. I am not sure that any conflicts with the view which I have expressed: but if any does, for example, *In re Engelbach's Estate* [1924] Ch 348, I would not agree with it. I think that *In re Schebsman* [1944] Ch 83 was rightly decided and that the reasoning of Uthwatt J and the Court of Appeal supports what I have just said. In the present case I think it clear that the parties to the agreement intended that the respondent should receive the weekly sums of £5 in her own behalf and should not be accountable to her deceased husband's estate for them. Indeed the contrary was not argued.

Reverting to my simple example the next question appears to me to be: Where the intention was that X should keep the £1,000 as his own, what is the nature of B's obligation and who is entitled to enforce it? It was not argued that the law of England regards B's obligation as a nullity, and I have not observed in any of the authorities any suggestion that it would be a nullity. There may have been a time when the existence of a right depended on whether there was any means of enforcing it, but today the law would be sadly deficient if one found that, although there is a right, the law provides no means for enforcing it. So this obligation of B must be enforceable either by X or by A. I shall leave aside for the moment the question whether section 56(1) of the Law of Property Act, 1925, has any application to such a case, and consider the position at common law.

Lord Denning's view, expressed in this case not for the first time, is that X could enforce this obligation. But the view more commonly held in recent times has been that such a contract confers no right on X and that X could not sue for the £1,000. Leading counsel for the respondent based his case on other grounds, and as I agree that the respondent succeeds on other grounds, this would not be an appropriate case in which to solve this question. It is true that a strong Law Revision Committee recommended so long ago as 1937 (Cmd. 5449):

> That where a contract by its express terms purports to confer a benefit directly on a third party it shall be enforceable by the third party in his own name . . . (p 31).

And, if one had to contemplate a further long period of Parliamentary procrastination, this House might find it necessary to deal with this matter. But if legislation is probable at any early date I would not deal with it in a case where that is not essential. So for the purposes of this case I shall proceed on the footing that the commonly accepted view is right.

What then is A's position? I assume that A has not made himself a trustee for X, because it was not argued in this appeal that any trust had been created. So, if X has no right, A can at any time grant a discharge to B or make some new contract with B. If there were a trust the position would be different. X would have an equitable right and A would be entitled and, indeed, bound to recover the money and account for it to X. And A would have no right to grant a discharge to B. If there is no trust and A wishes to enforce the obligation, how does he set about it? He cannot sue B for the £1,000 because under the contract the money is not payable to him, and, if the contract were performed according to its terms, he would never have any right to get the money. So he must seek to make B pay X.

The argument for the appellant is that A's only remedy is to sue B for damages for B's breach of contract in failing to pay the £1,000 to X. Then the appellant says that A can only recover nominal damages of 40s. because the fact that X has not received the money will generally cause no loss to A: he admits that there may be cases where A would suffer damage if X did not receive the money but says that the present is not such a case.

Applying what I have said to the circumstances of the present case, the respondent in her personal capacity has no right to sue, but she has a right as administratrix of her husband's estate to require the appellant to perform his obligation under the agreement. He has refused to do so and he maintains that the respondent's only right is to sue him for damages for breach of his contract. If that were so, I shall assume that he is right in maintaining that the administratrix could then only recover nominal damages because his breach of contract has caused no loss to the estate of her deceased husband.

If that were the only remedy available the result would be grossly unjust. It would mean that the appellant keeps the business which he bought and for which he has only paid a small part of the price which he agreed to pay. He would avoid paying the rest of the price, the annuity to the respondent, by paying a mere 40s. damages.

The respondent's first answer is that the common law has been radically altered by section 56(1) of the Law of Property Act, 1925, and that that section entitles her to sue in her personal capacity and recover the benefit provided for her in the agreement although she was not a party to it. Extensive alterations of the law were made at that time but it is necessary to examine with some care the way in which this was done. That Act was a consolidation Act and it is the invariable practice of Parliament to require from those who have prepared a consolidation Bill an assurance that it will make no substantial change in the law and to have that checked by a committee. On this assurance the Bill is then passed into law, no amendment being permissible. So, in order to pave the way for the consolidation Act of 1925, earlier Acts were passed in 1922 and 1924 in which were enacted all the substantial amendments which now appear in the Act of 1925 and these amendments were then incorporated in the Bill which became the Act of 1925. Those earlier Acts contain nothing corresponding to section 56 and it is therefore quite certain that those responsible for the preparation of this legislation must have believed and intended that section 56 would make no substantial change in the earlier law, and equally certain that Parliament passed section 56 in reliance on an assurance that it did make no substantial change.

In construing any Act of Parliament we are seeking the intention of Parliament and it is quite true that we must deduce that intention from the words of the Act. If the words of the Act are only capable of one meaning we must give them that meaning no matter how they got there. But if they are capable of having more than one meaning we are, in my view, well entitled to see how they got there. For purely practical reasons we do not permit debates in either House to be cited: it would add greatly to the time and expense involved in preparing cases involving the construction of a statute if counsel were expected to read all the debates in *Hansard*, and it would often be impracticable for counsel to get access to at least the older reports of debates in Select Committees of the House of Commons; moreover, in a very large proportion of cases such a search, even if practicable, would throw no light on the question before the court. But I can see no objection to investigating in the present case the antecedents of section 56.

Section 56 was obviously intended to replace section 5 of the Real Property Act 1845 (8 and 9 Vict. c. 106). That section provided:

> That, under an indenture, executed after October 1, 1845, an immediate estate or interest, in any tenements or hereditaments, and the benefit of a condition or covenant, respecting any tenements or hereditaments, may be taken, although the taker thereof be not named a party to the same indenture. . . .

Section 56(1) now provides:

> A person may take an immediate or other interest in land or other property, or the benefit of any condition, right of entry, covenant or agreement over or respecting land or other property, although he may not be named as a party to the conveyance or other instrument: . . .

If the matter stopped there it would not be difficult to hold that section 56 does not substantially extend or alter the provisions of section 5 of the Act of 1845. But more difficulty is introduced by the definition section of the Act of 1925 (section 205) which provides:

> (1) In this Act unless the context otherwise requires, the following expressions have the meanings hereby assigned to them respectively, that is to say:–. . .
> (xx) "Property" includes any thing in action, and any interest in real or personal property.

Before further considering the meaning of section 56(1) I must set out briefly the views which have been expressed about it in earlier cases. *White v Bijou Mansions Ltd* [1937] 3 All ER 269 dealt with a covenant relating to land. The interpretation of section 56 was not the main issue. Simonds J rejected an argument that section 56 enabled anyone to take advantage of a covenant if he could show that if the covenant were enforced it would redound to his advantage. He said:

> Just as under section 5 of the Act of 1845 only that person could call it in aid who, although not a party, yet was a grantee or convenantee, so under section 56 of this Act only that person can call it in aid who, although not named as a party to the conveyance or other instrument, is yet a person to whom that conveyance or other instrument purports to grant something or with which some agreement or covenant is purported to be made.

He was not concerned to consider whether or in what way the section could be applied to personal property. In the Court of Appeal Sir Wilfred Greene MR said, in rejecting the same argument as Simonds J had rejected:

> Before he can enforce it he must be a person who falls within the scope and benefit of the covenant according to the true construction of the document in question.

Again he was not considering an ordinary contract and I do not think that he can be held to have meant that every person who falls within the "scope and benefit" of any contract is entitled to sue, though not a party to the contract.

In *In re Miller's Agreement* [1947] 2 All ER 78 two partners covenanted with a retiring partner that on his death they would pay certain annuities to his daughters. The Revenue's claim for estate duty was rejected. The decision was clearly right. The daughters, not being parties to the agreement, had no right to sue for their annuities. Whether they received them or not depended on whether the other partners were willing to pay or, if they did not pay, whether the deceased partner's executor was willing to enforce the contract. After citing the earlier cases Wynn-Parry J said:

> I think it emerges from these cases that the section has not the effect of creating rights, but only of assisting the protection of rights shown to exist.

I am bound to say I do not quite understand that. I had thought from what Lord Simonds said in *White's* case that section 5 of the Act of 1845 did enable certain persons to take benefits which they could not have taken without it. If so, it must have given them rights which they did not have without it. And, if that is so, section 56 must now have the same effect. In *Smith and Snipes Hall Farm Ltd v River Douglas Catchment Board* [1949] 2 All ER 179 Denning LJ, after stating his view that a third person can sue on a contract to which he is not a party, referred to section 56 as a clear statutory recognition of this principle, with the consequence that *Miller's* case was wrongly decided. I cannot agree with that. And in *Drive Yourself Hire Co. (London) Ltd v Strutt* [1953] 2 All ER 1475 Denning LJ again expressed similar views about section 56.

I can now return to consider the meaning and scope of section 56. It refers to any "agreement over or respecting land or other property". If "land or other property" means the same thing as "tenements or hereditaments" in the Act of 1845 then this section simply continues the law as it was before the Act of 1925 was passed, for I do not think that the other differences in phraseology can be regarded as making any substantial change. So any obscurities in section 56 are obscurities which originated in 1845. But if its scope is wider, then two points must be considered. The section refers to agreements "over or respecting land or other property". The land is something which existed before and independently of the agreement and the same must apply to the other property. So an agreement between A and B that A will use certain personal property for the benefit of X would be within the scope of the section, but an agreement that if A performs certain services for B, B will pay a sum to X would not be within the scope of the section. Such a capricious distinction would alone throw doubt on this interpretation.

Perhaps more important is the fact that the section does not say that a person may take the benefit of an agreement although he was not a party to it: it says that he may do so although he was not named as a party in the instrument which embodied the agreement. It is true that section 56 says "although he may not be named"; but section 5 of the Act of 1845 says although he "be not named a party". Such a change of phraseology in a consolidation Act cannot involve a change of meaning. I do not profess to have a full understanding of the old English law regarding deeds. But it appears from what Lord Simonds said in *White's* case and from what Vaisey J said in *Chelsea and Waltham Green Building Society v Armstrong* [1951] 2 All ER 250 that being in fact a party to an agreement might not be enough; the person claiming a benefit had to be named a party in the indenture. I have read the explanation of the old law given by my noble and learned friend, Lord Upjohn. I would not venture to criticise it, but I do not think it necessary for me to consider it if it leads to the conclusion that section 56 taken by itself would not assist the present respondent.

But it may be that additional difficulties would arise from the application to section 56 of the definition of property in the definition section. If so, it becomes necessary to consider whether that definition can be applied to section 56. By express provision in the definition section a definition contained in it is not to be applied to the word defined if in the particular case the context otherwise requires. If application of that definition would result in giving to section 56 a meaning going beyond that of the old section, then, in my opinion, the context does require that the definition of "property" shall not be applied to that word in section 56. The context in which this section occurs is a consolidation Act. If the definition is not applied the section is a proper one to appear in such an Act because it can properly be regarded as not substantially altering the pre-existing law. But if the definition is applied the result is to make section 56 go far beyond the pre-existing law. Holding that the section has such an effect would involve holding that the invariable practice of Parliament has been departed from *per incuriam* so that something has got into this consolidation Act which neither the draftsman nor Parliament can have intended to be there. I am reinforced in this view by two facts. The language of section 56 is not at all what one would have expected if the intention had been to bring in all that the application of the definition would bring in. And, secondly, section 56 is one of 25 sections which appear in the Act under the cross-heading "Conveyances and other Instruments". The other twenty-four sections come appropriately under that heading and so does section 56 if it has a limited meaning: but, if its scope is extended by the definition of property, it would be quite inappropriately placed in this part of the Act. For these reasons I am of opinion that section 56 has no application to the present case.

The respondent's second argument is that she is entitled in her capacity of administratrix of her deceased husband's estate to enforce the provision of the agreement for the benefit of herself in her personal capacity, and that a proper way of enforcing that provision is to order specific performance. That would produce a just result, and, unless there is some technical objection, I am of opinion that specific performance ought to be ordered. For the reasons given by your Lordships I would reject the arguments submitted for the appellant that specific performance is not a possible remedy in this case. I am therefore of opinion that the Court of Appeal reached a correct decision and that this appeal should be dismissed.'

Lord Hodson, Lord Guest, Lord Pearce and Lord Upjohn concurred.

5.3 REFORM: CONTRACTS (RIGHTS OF THIRD PARTIES) ACT 1999

There was regular academic criticism of the privity doctrine confirmed in *Beswick v Beswick*. In 1990, Adams and Brownsword proposed that in relation to many complex commercial contracts an approach based on a 'network' of contracts would come closer to what the contracting parties would expect – see Adams, J and Brownsword, R, 'Privity and the concept of a network contract', 1990, 10 *Legal Studies* 12. The Law Commission, however, went further and proposed that there should be a broad exception to the privity doctrine, applying to virtually all contracts where the parties intended to provide a third party with an enforceable benefit.

Law Commission, Report No 242, *Privity of Contract: Contracts for the Benefit of Third Parties*, 1996, Cmnd 3329

1.1 In 1995 in the Court of Appeal in *Darlington Borough Council v Wiltshier Northern Ltd*

Steyn LJ, in criticising the present law, said the following:

'The case for recognising a contract for the benefit of a third party is simple and straightforward. The autonomy of the will of the parties should be respected. The law of contract should give effect to the reasonable expectations of contracting parties. Principle certainly requires that a burden should not be imposed on a third party without his consent. But there is no doctrinal, logical, or policy reason why the law should deny effectiveness to a contract for the benefit of a third party where that is the expressed intention of the parties. Moreover, often the parties, and particularly third parties, organise their affairs on the faith of the contract. They rely on the contract. It is therefore unjust to deny effectiveness to such a contract. I will not struggle with the point further since nobody seriously asserts the contrary.'

1.2 In this Report we make recommendations for the reform of that part of the doctrine of privity of contract which lays down that a contract does not confer rights on some-one who is not a party to the contract (hereinafter referred to as the "third party rule"). Our proposals will mean, for example, that subsequent purchasers or tenants of buildings can be given rights to enforce an architect's or building contractor's contractual obligations without the cost, complexity and inconvenience of a large number of separate contracts; that an employer can take out medical expenses insurance for its employees without there being doubts as to whether the employees can enforce the policy against the insurance company; that a life insurance policy taken out for one's stepchild or cohabitee is enforceable (subject to a term to the contrary) by that named beneficiary; and that a contractual clause limiting or excluding one's liability to a third party (for example, the promisee's subsidiary company or sub-contractor or employee) will be straightforwardly enforceable by that third party.

1.3 The Law Commission first became interested in this subject after the Commission's creation in 1965. Item 1 of the First Programme of Law Reform was the codification of the law of contract. Item 3 included the topic of third party rights. A substantial amount of work was done on this topic in conjunction with work on consideration. At that time it was felt that reform of privity could not usefully be undertaken without reform of the doctrine of consideration. The relationship between the doctrines of privity and of consideration is discussed in Part VI below, where we explain why we believe that reform of the third party rule can be profitably undertaken without reassessing the entire doctrine of consideration.

1.4 In 1973 work was suspended on the production of a contract code which, in its draft form, would have provided for the creation of rights in third parties. The Law Commission's strategy since then has been to tackle problems in the law of contract as separate projects. In arriving at the view that a project on privity was justified, we were influenced by, for example, the continued judicial and academic criticism of the doctrine, by the work of Commonwealth law reform bodies, by insights gained from our work on the rights of buyers of goods carried by sea, and by a more cautious judicial approach in the late 1980s and early 1990s to tort liability for pure economic loss. In short we had little doubt that the continued existence of the third party rule represented a pressing problem for the English law of contract.

1.5 In Consultation Paper No 121, we set out the current law on the third party rule, the case for its reform, and the main issues that would need to be dealt with in any reform.

In an Appendix, we gave an account of the way in which the problem has been dealt with in other jurisdictions. Our provisional conclusion was that the law ought to be reformed and that the reform should be embodied in a detailed legislative scheme. The principal feature of that scheme (that is, the test of enforceability) would be that a third party should be able to enforce a contract where the parties intended that the third party should receive the benefit of the promised performance and also intended to create a legal obligation enforceable by the third party.

1.6 The Consultation Paper attracted 102 replies. A clear majority accepted the validity of our arguments in favour of reform. Our provisional proposals were particularly welcomed by the legal profession and some other professional bodies, academic lawyers, consumer organisations, and the insurance and banking industries. While it was to be expected that the subject of the Consultation Paper would be of great interest to academic lawyers, the wide range of responses from non-academic lawyers and non-lawyers reflects the degree to which the third party rule still causes significant difficulties in practice.

1.7 The minority who opposed the proposals outlined in the Consultation Paper did so in reliance on four main general arguments. First, that reform was unnecessary because the rule caused few problems in practice given that those who were affected by it could use various devices . . . to get round the third party rule. Secondly, that no legislative reform could hope adequately to deal with all the diverse situations where the third party rule is relevant. Thirdly, that the existing legal regime, while complicated, achieved certainty, and that reform would only result in uncertainty and litigation. Fourthly, that the proposals for reform might lead to contracting parties being bound to third parties when this was not their true intention.

1.8 We disagree with the view that the third party rule does not cause significant problems in practice. We cannot ignore those who do not have access to (good) legal advice and, in any event, our proposed reforms will provide a simpler way of affording a third party the right to enforce a contract than the present convoluted techniques. This will not only save the parties costs, it will also save the taxpayer the needless litigation costs caused by the complexity of the present law. Nevertheless the response of the minority who opposed the proposed reform was invaluable in requiring us to reassess whether our proposals were too uncertain and would result in the imposition of unintended liabilities. In certain respects – and especially as regards the test of enforceability – we have modified our provisional recommendations in an attempt to allay those kinds of fears. We should emphasise, at the outset, that our recommendations are not concerned to override the allocation of liability within contracts but rather rest on an underlying policy of effectuating the contracting parties' intentions. At root our recommendations would enable the parties to create enforceable third party rights in contract without the complexities of the devices presently used to circumvent the privity doctrine.

1.9 Our general approach has been to devise moderate reform proposals which can be expected to gain wide support. Some more radical possibilities have been put to one side for fear that the central reform would otherwise be endangered. For example, we do not in this report recommend a special test of enforceability for third parties who are consumers; we do not propose a reform of insurance contracts that goes as far as section 48 of the Australian Insurance Contracts Act 1984; and we do not seek to recast the decision of the House of Lords in *White v Jones* [1995] 2 AC 207 by bringing the claims of disappointed beneficiaries under negligently drafted wills within our proposed Act.

1.10 It has also been important in our thinking that, while we believe that a detailed legislative scheme is the best means of reforming privity, we have no desire to hamper judicial creativity in this area. For example, we have left to the developing common law, what the rights of promisees should be in contracts for the benefit of third parties; and we have left open for the judges to decide what the rights of a joint promisee, who has not provided consideration, should be. In general terms, we see our draft Bill as achieving at a stroke and with certainty and clarity what a progressive House of Lords might well itself have brought about over the course of time. While the draft Bill departs from a long-established common law rule, we hope that it will not be seen as cutting across the underpinning principles of the common law.

The Law Commission's proposals, as outlined in the above report, were given fairly speedy legislative effect, with the consequent Act following very closely the Law Commission's draft Bill.

CONTRACTS (RIGHTS OF THIRD PARTIES) ACT 1999

1.—(1) Subject to the provisions of this Act, a person who is not a party to a contract (a 'third party') may in his own right enforce a term of the contract if—

    (a) the contract expressly provides that he may, or

    (b) subject to subsection (2), the term purports to confer a benefit on him.

(2) Subsection (1)(b) does not apply if on a proper construction of the contract it appears that the parties did not intend the term to be enforceable by the third party.

(3) The third party must be expressly identified in the contract by name, as a member of a class or as answering a particular description but need not be in existence when the contract is entered into.

(4) This section does not confer a right on a third party to enforce a term of a contract otherwise than subject to and in accordance with any other relevant terms of the contract.

(5) For the purpose of exercising his right to enforce a term of the contract, there shall be available to the third party any remedy that would have been available to him in an action for breach of contract if he had been a party to the contract (and the rules

relating to damages, injunctions, specific performance and other relief shall apply accordingly).

(6) Where a term of a contract excludes or limits liability in relation to any matter references in this Act to the third party enforcing the term shall be construed as references to his availing himself of the exclusion or limitation.

(7) In this Act, in relation to a term of a contract which is enforceable by a third party—

'the promisor' means the party to the contract against whom the term is enforceable by the third party, and

'the promisee' means the party to the contract by whom the term is enforceable against the promisor.

2.—(1) Subject to the provisions of this section, where a third party has right under section 1 to enforce a term of the contract, the parties to the contract may not, by agreement, rescind the contract, or vary it in such a way as to extinguish or alter his entitlement under that right, without his consent if—

(a) the third party has communicated his assent to the term to the promisor,

(b) the promisor is aware that the third party has relied on the term, or

(c) the promisor can reasonably be expected to have foreseen that the third party would rely on the term and the third party has in fact relied on it.

(2) The assent referred to in subsection (1)(a)—

(a) may be by words or conduct, and

(b) if sent to the promisor by post or other means, shall not be regarded as communicated to the promisor until received by him.

(3) Subsection (1) is subject to any express term of the contract under which—

(a) the parties to the contract may by agreement rescind or vary the contract without the consent of the third party, or

(b) the consent of the third party is required in circumstances specified in the contract instead of those set out in subsection (1)(a) to (c). . . .

3.—(1) Subsections (2) to (5) apply where, in reliance on section 1, proceedings for the enforcement of a term of a contract are brought by a third party.

(2) The promisor shall have available to him by way of defence or setoff any matter that—

(a) arises from or in connection with the contract and is relevant to the term, and

(b) would have been available to him by way of defence or set-off if the proceedings had been brought by the promisee.

(3) The promisor shall also have available to him by way of defence or set-off any matter if—

(a) an express term of the contract provides for it to be available to him in proceedings brought by the third party, and

(b) it would have been available to him by way of defence or set-off if the proceedings had been brought by the promisee.

(4) The promisor shall also have available to him—

(a) by way of defence or set-off any matter, and

(b) by way of counterclaim

any matter not arising from the contract, that would have been available to him by way of defence or set-off or, as the case may be, by way of counterclaim against the third party if the third party had been a party to the contract.

(5) Subsections (2) and (4) are subject to any express term of the contract as to the matters that are not to be available to the promisor by way of defence, set-off or counterclaim.

(6) Where in any proceedings brought against him a third party seeks in reliance on section 1 to enforce a term of a contract (including, in particular, a term purporting to exclude or limit liability), he may not do so if he could not have done so (whether by reason of any particular circumstances relating to him or otherwise) had he been a party to the contract.

4. Section 1 does not affect any right of the promisee to enforce any term of the contract.

5. Where under section 1 a term of a contract is enforceable by a third party, and the promisee has recovered from the promisor a sum in respect of—

(a) the third party's loss in respect of the term, or
(b) the expense to the promisee of making good to the third party the default of the promisor,

then, in any proceedings brought in reliance on that section by the third party, the court or arbitral tribunal shall reduce any award to the third party to such extent as it thinks appropriate to take account of the sum recovered by the promisee.

6.—(1) Section 1 confers no rights on a third party in the case of a contract on a bill of exchange, promissory note or other negotiable instrument.

(2) Section 1 confers no rights on a third party in the case of any contract binding on a company and its members under section 14 of the 1985 c. 6. Companies Act 1985.

(3) Section 1 confers no right on a third party to enforce—

(a) any term of a contract of employment against an employee,
(b) any term of a worker's contract against a worker (including a home worker), or
(c) any term of a relevant contract against an agency worker . . .

(5) Section 1 confers no rights on a third party in the case of—

(a) a contract for the carriage of goods by sea, or
(b) a contract for the carriage of goods by rail or road, or for the carriage of cargo by air, which is subject to the rules of the appropriate international transport convention,

except that a third party may in reliance on that section avail himself of an exclusion or limitation of liability in such a contract.

(6) In subsection (5) 'contract for the carriage of goods by sea' means a contract of carriage—

(a) contained in or evidenced by a bill of lading, sea waybill or a corresponding electronic transaction, or
(b) under or for the purposes of which there is given an undertaking which is contained in a ship's delivery order or a corresponding electronic transaction . . .

7.—(1) Section 1 does not affect any right or remedy of a third party that exists or is available apart from this Act.

(2) Section 2(2) of the Unfair Contract Terms Act 1977 (restriction on 1977 c. 50. exclusion etc. of liability for negligence) shall not apply where the negligence consists of the breach of an obligation arising from a term of a contract and the person seeking to enforce it is a third party acting in reliance on section 1 . . .

8.—(1) Where—

(a) a right under section 1 to enforce a term ('the substantive term') is subject to a term providing for the submission of disputes to arbitration ('the arbitration agreement'), and

(b) the arbitration agreement is an agreement in writing for the purposes of Part I of the Arbitration Act 1996, the third party shall be treated for the purposes of that Act as a party to the arbitration agreement as regards disputes between himself and the promisor relating to the enforcement of the substantive term by the third party.

(2) Where—

(a) a third party has a right under section 1 to enforce a term providing for one or more descriptions of dispute between the third party and the promisor to be submitted to arbitration ('the arbitration agreement'),

(b) the arbitration agreement is an agreement in writing for the purposes of Part I of the Arbitration Act 1996, and

(c) the third party does not fall to be treated under subsection (1) as a party to the arbitration agreement,

the third party shall, if he exercises the right, be treated for the purposes of that Act as a party to the arbitration agreement in relation to the matter with respect to which the right is exercised, and be treated as having been so immediately before the exercise of the right.

It will be seen that section 1 of this Act provides for a third party to have an enforceable right under a contract where that was the intention of the parties. That intention can be express, or it can be presumed from the fact that the contract purports to confer a benefit, unless the court is satisfied that the benefit was not intended to be legally enforceable. The burden of proving this will, presumably, fall on the party arguing against enforceability. This seems to be the implication of the confirmation in *Nisshin Shipping Co Ltd v Cleaves & Co Ltd* [2003] EWHC 2602; [2004] 1 Lloyd's Rep 38 that the Act creates a rebuttable presumption in favour of third-party enforceability.

Nisshin Shipping Co Ltd v Cleaves & Co Ltd [2003] EWHC 2602; [2004] 1 Lloyd's Rep 38

Facts: Charterparties between N and others, negotiated by C as agents for N, contained a provision for commission to be paid to C, and for disputes to be referred to arbitration. N withheld commission. C argued that the dispute should go to arbitration, on the basis that, applying the 1999 Act, the clauses in the charterparties were for the benefit of C and intended to be enforceable by them.

Held: The clauses were clearly intended to benefit C, and there was a rebuttable presumption, as a result of section 1 of the 1999 Act that this benefit was intended to be legally enforceable. Since the presumption had not been rebutted, the combined effect of sections 1 and 8 of the Act was that C were entitled to insist on arbitration.

Colman J:

'. . . **21.** It is accepted by Miss Philippa Hopkins, on behalf of Cleaves, that the brokers were not parties to the arbitration agreements as a matter of construction of those clauses. Her case is that the effect of s. 8 of the 1999 Act is to impose the arbitration clauses on the owners and the brokers as the means of enforcement of the commission benefit conferred by the commission clause. I shall have to consider this submission more fully when I come to discuss the effect of s. 8. However, for the purposes of the submission in relation to absence of intention to confer a benefit, the wording of the arbitration clauses is, in my judgment, of little or no materiality. First, although the parties to the charter-parties clearly expressed their mutual intention that *their* disputes should be arbitrated, that mutual intention is entirely consistent with a mutual intention that the brokers should be obliged to recover their commission by court action rather than by arbitration. Secondly, if, on the proper construction of the 1999 Act, the third party is obliged to enforce the commission benefit by arbitration, even where the agreement does not on its proper construction provide for any participants in an arbitration other than the parties to the main contract, identification of the intention to be imputed to the parties as to enforceability of the third party commission benefit clearly has to take this into account. That is to say, if, as a matter of law, it makes no difference to the broker's ability to enforce his right to commission benefit that no express provision is made for this in the arbitration agreement, the strength of any inference derived from the absence of such express provision could be little more than negligible.

22. Secondly, it is argued by Mr. Ashcroft on behalf of Nisshin that there is no positive indication in the charter-parties that the parties did intend the brokers to have enforceable rights. There is no suggestion in those contracts that the owners and charterers were mutually in agreement that the brokers should be entitled to claim against the owners as if they were parties to the contract.

23. It is to be noted that s. 1(2) of the 1999 Act does not provide that sub-s. 1(b) is disapplied unless on a proper construction of the contract it appears that the parties intended that the benefit term should be enforceable by the third party. Rather it provides that sub-s. 1(b) is disapplied if, on a proper construction, it appears that the parties did not intend third party enforcement. In other words, if the contract is neutral on this question, sub-s. (2) does not disapply sub-s. 1(b). Whether the contract does express a mutual intention that the third party should not be entitled to enforce the benefit conferred on him or is merely neutral is a matter of construction having regard to all relevant circumstances. The purpose and background of the Law Commission's recommendations in relation to sub-s. (2) are explained in a paper by Professor Andrew Burrows who, as a member of the Law Commission, made a major contribution to the drafting of the bill as enacted. He wrote at [2000] L.M.C.L.Q. 540 at p 544:

> "The second test therefore uses a rebuttable presumption of intention. In doing so, it copies the New Zealand Contracts (Privity) Act, 1982, s. 4, which has used the same approach. It is this rebuttable presumption that provides the essential balance between sufficient certainty for contracting parties and the flexibility required for the reform to deal fairly with a huge range of different situations. The presumption is based on the idea that, if you ask yourself, 'When is it that parties are likely to have intended to confer rights on a third party to enforce a term, albeit that they have not expressly conferred that right', the answer will be: 'Where the term purports to confer a benefit on an expressly identified third party'. That then sets up the presumption. But the presumption can be rebutted if, as a matter of ordinary contractual interpretation, there is something else indicating that the parties did not intend such a right to be given.

24. In the present case, apart from Mr. Ashcroft's third point, the charter-parties are indeed neutral in the sense that they do not express any intention contrary to the entitlement of the brokers to enforce the commission term.

25. Thirdly, Mr. Ashcroft submits that the parties' mutual intention on the proper construction of the contracts was to create a trust of a promise in favour of the brokers – a trust enforceable against the owners at the suit of the charterers as trustees. That being the proper construction of the contracts by reference to the state of the law at the time when the 1999 Act came into force, the very same contract wording did not, subsequently to that, evidence a different mutual intention. Accordingly, the mutual intention evidenced by the contracts was that the enforcement of the promise to pay commission would be at the suit of the charterers who must be joined by the brokers as co-claimants.

26. The starting point for consideration of this point is *Les Affreteurs Reunis S.A. v Leopold Walford (London) Ltd*, [1919] A.C. 801. The House of Lords in that case confirmed the decision in *Robertson v Wait*, (1853) 8 Ex. 299. In relation to that authority Lord Birkenhead, L.C. said this at pp 806–807:

> My Lords, so far as I am aware, that case has not before engaged the attention of this House, and I think it right to say plainly that I agree with that decision and I agree with the reasoning, shortly as it is expressed, upon which the decision was founded. In this connection I would refer to the well-known case of In re Empress Engineering Company. In the judgment of Sir George Jessel M.R. the principle is examined which, in my view, underlies and is the explanation of the decision in *Robertson v Wait*. The Master of the Rolls uses this language: "So, again, it is quite possible that one of the parties to the agreement may be the nominee or trustee of the third person. As Lord Justice James suggested to me in the course

of the argument, a married woman may nominate somebody to contract on her behalf, but then the person makes the contract really as trustee for somebody else, and it is because he contracts in that character that the cestui que trust can take the benefit of the contract."

It appears to me plain that for convenience, and under long established practice, the broker in such cases, in effect, nominates the charterer to contract on his behalf, influenced probably by the circumstances that there is always a contract between charterer and owner in which this stipulation, which is to enure to the benefit of the broker, may very conveniently be inserted. In these cases the broker, on ultimate analysis, appoints the charterer to contract on his behalf. I agree therefore with the conclusion arrived at by all the learned judges in *Robertson v Wait*, that in such cases charterers can sue as trustees on behalf of the broker.

27. Viscount Finlay and Lords Atkinson and Wrenbury adopted identical reasoning.

28. Accordingly, the position in 1853 and 1919 was that when a charter-party was entered into and incorporated a term that the owners would pay commission to the brokers, the only means of enforcement of that promise was an action by the charterers and the brokers as co-plaintiff because, the charterer having contracted for commission on behalf of the broker, once the contract had been signed, the charterer became trustee of the broker's right to recover that commission, the broker being unable to enforce the promise direct and without the charterer's intervention because he was not a party to the contract and therefore had no cause of action available to him against the owner. With regard to this trustee relationship it could then be said that when the charter-party was entered into neither owners nor charterers contemplated that the brokers could sue the owners direct.

29. What is the position arising from the contract itself following the coming into force of the 1999 Act? As a matter of analysis of the underlying relationship between the parties, it must be precisely the same. Thus, the charterer is no less the trustee of the owners' promise to pay the commission, having regard to the fact that the charterer contracts for payment of the commission on behalf of a non-contracting party. Indeed, the only thing that has changed is the coming into force of the 1999 Act and the introduction of the statutory facility of a direct right of action for a non-contracting party on whom a contract purports to confer a benefit.

30. Accordingly, the argument advanced by the owners can only succeed if it is to be inferred from the existence of the underlying trustee relationship that it was the mutual intention of owners and charterers that the broker beneficiary should not be entitled to avail himself of the facility of direct action by the 1999 Act.

31. This proposition is, in my judgment, entirely unsustainable. The fact that prior to the 1999 Act it would be the mutual intention that the only available facility for enforcement would be deployed by the broker does not lead to the conclusion that, once an additional statutory facility for enforcement had been introduced, the broker would not be entitled to use it, but would instead be confined to the use of the pre-existing procedure. Indeed, quite apart from the complete lack of any logical basis for such an inference, the very cumbersome and inconvenient nature of the procedure based on the trustee relationship (described by Lord Wright as a "cumbrous fiction") would point naturally to the preferred use by the broker of the right to sue directly provided by the 1999 Act. Not only would that original procedure be inconvenient, but it might involve risk that the broker would be prevented from recovering his commission, for example, in a case where the charterer had been dissolved in its place of incorporation or where, in the absence of co-operation by the charterer, proceedings had to be served on it outside the jurisdiction and service could not be effected. There are therefore very strong grounds pointing against any mutual intention to confine the brokers to the old procedure and to deny them the right to rely on the 1999 Act.

32. I therefore reject the third ground relied upon by Nisshin. In so doing I reach the same conclusion as the arbitrators.

33. It follows that Cleaves are entitled to enforce the commission clauses in their own right by reason of s. 1 of the 1999 Act.'

5.3.1 CHANGING THE AGREEMENT

The standard position that parties are entitled, by mutual agreement, to change their contract, or bring it to an end whenever they wish is to some extent altered by the Act. The relevant provision is s 2, above. As will be seen, this allows the parties specifically to preserve their right to modify the agreement (s 2(3)). But if they do not do so, the third party will acquire a right that cannot be rescinded by the parties to the contract, provided that the conditions set out in s 2(1), involving either 'assent' or 'reliance' are satisfied.

5.3.2 DEFENCES

The promisor cannot be liable to both the promisee and the third party (s 4). Where the third party is taking action, s 3 deals with the defences available to the promisor. Its effect is that in any action by the third party, the promisor can:

- rely on any defence that would have been available as against the promisee (s 3(2));
- if the contracting parties have so agreed, rely on a right of set-off arising from other dealings between them to be used against the third party (s 3(3);
- rely on any right of defence, set-off, or counterclaim arising from other dealings between the promisor and the third party (s 3(4));

- if sued by the third party for negligent performance, rely on an exclusion clause, without its effect being limited by s 2(2) of the Unfair Contract Terms Act 1977 (for which, see Ch 8, p 487).

Section 3(6) also makes it clear that where a third party, who is being sued, seeks to rely on a clause in a contract between two other parties, the third party will only be able to enforce the term if s/he could have done so had s/he been a party to the contract.

5.3.3 EXCEPTIONS

The types of contract that fall outside the scope of the Act are listed in s 6. Note that although certain types of carriage contract are excluded, this does not apply to third-party reliance on an exclusion clause. The situation which arose in *The Eurymedon* [1975] AC 154 (below, p 308) could now be dealt with under the Act.

5.4 COMMON-LAW EXCEPTIONS TO PRIVITY

The common law has developed a number of ways in which the doctrine of privity can be circumvented. These are not abolished by the 1999 Act, nor are they necessarily redundant. As has been noted, the Act does not apply to all contracts. There may also be situations where the Act will not apply on the facts, but one of the common-law approaches might be used. These must be considered, even if some of them now only justify fairly brief discussion.

5.4.1 DAMAGES ON BEHALF OF ANOTHER

If A and B have agreed that A will provide goods or services that will benefit C, and A breaks the contract, can B recover damages that reflect C's loss? And, if so, is A obliged to hand over any such damages recovered to C? The starting point for answering these questions is *Jackson v Horizon Holidays*.

Jackson v Horizon Holidays [1975] 3 All ER 92 (CA)

Facts: A father booked a holiday for his family, at a cost of about £1,200. The holiday was very unsatisfactory, and the father recovered damages for breach of contract. The trial judge refused to award damages for the distress and discomfort of the rest of the family, but awarded the father a total of £1,100. The holiday company appealed against the level of damages.

Held: Upholding the judge's award, the damages awarded to the father could take account of the distress and discomfort suffered by the rest of the family.

Lord Denning MR:

'Mr Jackson is a young man, in his mid-twenties. He has been very successful in his business. He is married with three small children. In November 1970 there were twin boys of three years of age; and his wife had just had her third child. He had been working very hard. They determined to have a holiday in the sun. He decided upon Ceylon. He inquired of Horizon Holidays Ltd. He made arrangements with their agent, a Mrs Bremner, for a holiday at a hotel, the Pegasus Reef Hotel, Hendala Point, Ceylon. He wrote them a letter which shows that he wanted everything of the highest standard:

> With reference to our telephone conversation would you please confirm that you can arrange for my wife myself and my two twin boys aged three years to stay for 28 days from January 23 at the Hotel Pegasus Reef, Hendala Point, Ceylon. Would you also arrange that the children's room has an adjoining door to our room; this is essential and is a condition of me booking this holiday. Would you please make sure that the balcony is facing the sea and would you also confirm the distance the hotel is from the sea. Would you confirm that the meals are four course with a choice of three or four dishes to each course. Could you confirm that there have been arrangements made that an English speaking doctor would call on the hotel if needed. Would you please make a clear answer to all these questions appreciating that you might have difficulties in answering some of these questions and not to send an evasive answer to any of these questions.

He spoke on the telephone to Mrs Bremner. She led him to believe that the hotel would come up to his expectations. She wrote on the booking form:

> "Remarks Twins" room with connecting door essential. Total charge £1432.

He sent it in and booked the holiday.

In the middle of January it was discovered that the Pegasus Reef Hotel would not be ready in time. So Horizon Holidays recommended a substitute. This was Brown's Beach Hotel. It was described in the advertisement as being:

> superbly situated right on the beach, with all facilities for an enjoyable holiday including mini-golf, excellent restaurant, cocktail lounge, and gift shop. The bed-rooms are well furnished and equipped in modern style. *All rooms have private bath, shower, w.c., sea view and air-conditioning.*

Mr Jackson had some hesitation about this other hotel. But Horizon Holidays assured him that it would be up to his expectation. So Mr Jackson accepted it. But Horizon Holidays reduced the charge. Instead of the price being the total sum of £1,432 it would, because of the change of hotel, be £1,200. That included air travel to Ceylon and back and a holiday for four weeks. So they went there. The courier, Miss Redgrove, met them and took them to the Brown's Beach Hotel. But they were greatly disappointed. Their room had not got a connecting door with the room for the children at all. The room for the children was mildewed – black with mildew, at the bottom. There was fungus growing on the walls. The toilet was stained. The shower was dirty. There was no bath. They could not let the children sleep in the room. So for the first three days they had all the family in one room. The two children were put into one of the single beds and the two adults slept in the other single bed. After the first three days they were moved into what was said to be one of the best suites in the hotel. Even then they had to put the children to sleep in the sitting room and the parents in the bedroom. There was dirty linen on the bed. There was no private bath but only a shower; no mini-golf course; no swimming pool; no beauty salon; no hairdressers' salon. Worst of all was the cooking. There was no choice of dishes. On some occasions, however, curry was served as an alternative to the main dish. They found the food was very distasteful. It appeared to be cooked in coconut oil. There was a pervasive taste because of the manner of cooking. They were so uncomfortable at Brown's Beach Hotel that after a fortnight they moved to the Pegasus Reef Hotel. It appears that by that time it was nearing completion. But a lot of building work was still going on. At any rate, for the second fortnight they were in the Pegasus Reef Hotel, where things were somewhat better than at Brown's Beach Hotel. They stayed out for the four weeks, and came home.

Soon after their return, Mr Jackson wrote a letter setting out all his complaints from the beginning to the end. Then Mr Jackson brought an action for damages in respect of the loss of his holiday for himself, his wife and the two small children. Horizon Holidays admitted liability. The contest was only on the amount of damages.

In *Jarvis v Swans Tours Ltd* [1973] QB 233, it was held by this court that damages for the loss of a holiday may include not only the difference in value between what was promised and what was obtained, but also damages for mental distress, inconvenience, upset, disappointment and frustration caused by the loss of the holiday. The judge directed himself in accordance with the judgments in that case. He eventually awarded a sum of £1,100. Horizon Holidays Ltd appealed. They say it was far too much.

The judge did not divide up the £1,000. Counsel has made suggestions about it. Mr Cheyne for Horizon Holidays suggests that the judge gave £100 for diminution in value and £1,000 for the mental distress. But Mr Davies for Mr Jackson suggested that the judge gave £600 for the diminution in value and £500 for the mental distress. If I were inclined myself to speculate, I think Mr Davies' suggestion may well be right. The judge took the cost of the holiday at £1,200. The family only had about half the value of it. Divide it by two and you get £600. Then add £500 for the mental distress.

On this question a point of law arises. The judge said that he could only consider the mental distress to Mr Jackson himself, and that he could not consider the distress to his wife and children. He said:

> The damages are the plaintiff's. . . . I cannot consider the effect upon his mind of the wife's discomfort, vexation, and the like, although I cannot award a sum which represents her own vexation.

Mr Davies, for Mr Jackson, disputes that proposition. He submits that damages can be given not only for the leader of the party – in this case, Mr Jackson's own distress, discomfort and vexation – but also for that of the rest of the party.

We have had an interesting discussion as to the legal position when one person makes a contract for the benefit of a party. In this case it was a husband making a contract for the benefit of himself, his wife and children. Other cases readily come to mind. A host makes a contract with a restaurant for a dinner for himself and his friends. The vicar makes a contract for a coach trip for the choir. In all these cases there is only one person who makes the contract. It is the husband, the host or the vicar, as the case may be. Sometimes he pays the whole price himself. Occasionally he may get a contribution from the others. But in any case it is he who makes the contract. It would be a fiction to say that the contract was made by all the family, or all the guests, or all the choir, and that he was only an agent for them. Take this very case. It would be absurd to say that the twins of three years old were parties to the contract or that the father was making the contract on their behalf as if they were principals. It would equally be a mistake to say that in any of these instances there was a trust. The transaction bears no resemblance to a trust. There was no trust fund and no trust property. No, the real truth is that in each instance, the father, the host or the vicar, was making a contract himself for the benefit of the whole party. In short, a contract by one for the benefit of third persons.

What is the position when such a contract is broken? At present the law says that the only one who can sue is the one who made the contract. None of the rest of the party can sue, even though the contract was made for their benefit. But when that one does sue, what damages can he recover? Is he limited to his own loss? Or can he recover for the others? Suppose the holiday firm puts the family into a hotel which is only half built and the visitors have to sleep on the floor? Or suppose the restaurant is fully booked and the guests have to go away, hungry and angry, having spent so much on fares to get there? Or suppose the coach leaves the choir stranded halfway and they have to hire cars to get home? None of them individually can sue. Only the father, the host or the vicar can sue. He can, of course, recover his own damages. But can he not recover for the others? I think he can. The case comes within the principle stated by Lush LJ in *Lloyd's v Harper* (1880) 16 ChD 290, 321:

> I consider it to be an established rule of law that where a contract is made with A for the benefit of B, A can sue on the contract for the benefit of B, and recover all that B could have recovered if the contract had been made with B himself.

It has been suggested that Lush LJ was thinking of a contract in which A was trustee for B. But I do not think so. He was a common lawyer speaking of common law. His words were quoted with considerable approval by Lord Pearce in *Beswick v Beswick* [1968] AC 58, 88. I have myself often quoted them. I think they should be accepted as correct, at any rate so long as the law forbids the third person themself from suing for damages. It is the only way in which a just result can be achieved. Take the instance I have put. The guests ought to recover from the restaurant their wasted fares. The choir

277

ought to recover the cost of hiring the taxis home. Then is no one to recover from them except the one who made the contract for their benefit? He should be able to recover the expense to which he has been put, and pay it over to them. Once recovered, it will be money had and received to their use. (They might even, if desired, be joined as plaintiffs.) If he can recover for the expense, he should also be able to recover for the discomfort, vexation and upset which the whole party have suffered by reason of the breach of contract, recompensing them accordingly out of what he recovers.

Applying the principles to this case, I think that the figure of £1,100 was about right. It would, I think, have been excessive if it had been awarded only for the damage suffered by Mr Jackson himself. But when extended to his wife and children, I do not think it is excessive. People look forward to a holiday. They expect the promises to be fulfilled. When it fails, they are greatly disappointed and upset. It is difficult to assess in terms of money; but it is the task of the judges to do the best they can. I see no reason to interfere with the total award of £1,100. I would therefore dismiss the appeal.'

Orr LJ concurred with Lord Denning's judgment; James LJ came to the same conclusion, but on the basis that the father's own loss was increased by the problems suffered by the rest of the family. The view of the majority appeared to open the door to a more general possibility of a claimant being able to claim damages for a third party's loss. In *Woodar v Wimpey* the House of Lords had the opportunity to consider whether this should apply in a commercial contract.

Woodar Investment Development Ltd v Wimpey Construction UK Ltd [1980] 1 All ER 571 (HL)

Facts: In February, the purchasers, W.C. Ltd. entered into a contract to buy certain land from the vendors, W.I.D. Ltd. The purchase price was £850,000 of which £150,000 was to be paid on completion to T.T. Ltd. By a special condition the purchasers reserved the right to rescind if compulsory purchase proceedings were commenced in relation to the land. In March the purchasers sent the vendors a notice purporting to rescind the contract under that condition on the ground that the Secretary of State for the Environment had commenced the procedure for compulsory acquisition of part of the land. At the date of the contract both parties knew that 3 years previously the minister had given the then owner notice of a draft compulsory purchase order. In November a compulsory purchase order was made. The vendors brought an action against the purchasers for a declaration that the condition gave them no right to rescind. By their defence the purchasers contended that on the true construction of the condition the notice of rescission was valid. In a second action the vendors claimed damages for breach of contract by the purchasers in serving the notice and delivering their defence.

The trial judge and the Court of Appeal held that the purchasers were not entitled to invoke the condition and by doing so had wrongfully repudiated the contract and that they were accordingly liable for damages. The purchasers appealed.

Held: (by a 3 to 2 majority): The purchasers' action did not constitute repudiation, and so the issue of damages did not arise. If it had, the vendors would not have been able to recover the sum which was to be paid to the third party, TT.

Lord Wilberforce:

'. . . The second issue in this appeal is one of damages. Both courts below have allowed Woodar to recover substantial damages in respect of condition I under which £150,000 was payable by Wimpey to Transworld Trade Ltd on completion. On the view which I take of the repudiation issue, this question does not require decision, but in view of the unsatisfactory state in which the law would be if the Court of Appeal's decision were to stand I must add three observations.

1. The majority of the Court of Appeal followed, in the case of Goff LJ with expressed reluctance, its previous decision in *Jackson v Horizon Holidays Ltd* [1975] 3 All ER 92. I am not prepared to dissent from the actual decision in that case. It may be supported either as a broad decision on the measure of damages (per James LJ) or possibly as an example of a type of contract, examples of which are persons contracting for family holidays, ordering meals in restaurants for a party, hiring a taxi for a group, calling for special treatment. As I suggested in *New Zealand Shipping Co Ltd v A M Satterthwaite & Co Ltd* [1974] 1 All ER 1015, there are many situations of daily life which do not fit neatly into conceptual analysis, but which require some flexibility in the law of contract. *Jackson's* case may well be one.

I cannot agree with the basis on which Lord Denning MR put his decision in that case. The extract on which he relied from the judgment of Lush LJ in *Lloyd's v Harper* (1880) 16 ChD 290 was part of a passage in which Lush LJ was stating as an "established rule of law" that an agent (sc an insurance broker) may sue on a contract made by him on behalf of the principal (sc the assured) if the contract gives him such a right, and is no authority for the proposition required in *Jackson's* case, still less for the proposition, required here, that if Woodar made a contract for a sum of money to be paid to Transworld, Woodar can, without showing that it has itself suffered loss or that Woodar was agent or trustee for Transworld, sue for damages for non-payment of that sum. That would certainly not be an established rule of law, nor was it quoted as such authority by Lord Pearce in *Beswick v Beswick* [1967] 2 All ER 1197.

2. Assuming that *Jackson's* case was correctly decided (as above), it does not carry the present case, where the factual situation is quite different. I respectfully think therefore that the Court of Appeal need not, and should not have followed it.

3. Whether in a situation such as the present, viz where it is not shown that Woodar was agent or trustee for Transworld, or that Woodar itself sustained any loss, Woodar can recover any damages at all, or any but nominal damages, against Wimpey, and on what principle, is, in my opinion, a question of great doubt and difficulty, no doubt open in this House, but one on which I prefer to reserve my opinion . . . .'

Lord Russell:

'. . . There is no question on this appeal as to quantum of damage save under the heading of damages for breach of special condition I, under which Wimpey agreed on completion of the sale to pay £150,000 to Transworld, a Hong Kong company. Transworld was in some way connected with Mr Cornwell, who died before action. No evidence connects Transworld with Woodar, the party to the contract. No evidence suggests that Woodar could suffer any damage from a failure by Wimpey to pay £150,000 to Transworld. It is clear on the authority of *Beswick v Beswick* that Woodar on completion could have secured an order for specific performance of the agreement to pay £150,000 to Transworld, which the latter could have enforced. That would not have been an order for payment to Woodar, nor (contrary to the form of order below) to Woodar for the use and benefit of Transworld. There was no suggestion of trust or agency of Woodar for Transworld. If it were necessary to decide the point, which in the light of the views of the majority of your Lordships on the first point it is not, I would have concluded that no more than nominal damages had been established by Woodar as a consequence of the refusal by Wimpey to pay Transworld in the light of the law of England as it now stands. I would not have thought that the reasoning of Oliver J in *Radford v De Froberville* [1978] 1 All ER 33 supported Woodar's case for substantial damages. Nor do I think that on this point the Court of Appeal was correct in thinking it was constrained by *Jackson v Horizon Holidays Ltd* to award substantial damages. I do not criticize the outcome of that case: the plaintiff had bought and paid for a high class family holiday; he did not get it, and therefore he was entitled to substantial damages for the failure to supply *him* with one. It is to be observed that the order of the Court of Appeal as drawn up did not suggest that any part of the damages awarded to him were "for the use and benefit of" any member of his family. It was a special case quite different from the instant case on the Transworld point.

I would not, my Lords, wish to leave the *Jackson* case without adverting with respectful disapproval to the reliance there placed by Lord Denning MR, not for the first time, on an extract taken from the judgment of Lush LJ in *Lloyd's v Harper* (1880) 16 ChD 290. That case was plainly a case in which a trustee or agent was enforcing the rights of a beneficiary or principal, there being therefore a fiduciary relationship. Lord Denning MR in *Jackson'* case said this:

> The case comes within the principle stated by Lush LJ in *Lloyd's* v *Harper*. . .. I consider it to be an established rule of law that where a contract is made with A for the benefit of B, A can sue on the contract for the benefit of B, and recover all that B could have recovered if the contract had been made with B himself. [Lord Denning continued:] It has been suggested that Lush LJ was thinking of a contract in which A was trustee for B. But I do not think so. He was a common lawyer speaking of the common law.

I have already indicated that in all the other judgments the matter proceeded on a fiduciary relationship between A and B; and Lush LJ in the same passage made it plain that he did also, for he said:

It is true that the person [B] who employed him [the broker A] has a right, if he pleases, to take action himself and sue upon the contract made by the broker for him, for he [B] *is a principal party to the contract*. (Emphasis mine).

To ignore that passage is to divorce the passage quoted by Lord Denning MR from the fiduciary context in which it was uttered, the context of principal and agent, a field with which it may be assumed Lush LJ was familiar. I venture to suggest that the brief quotation should not be used again as support for a proposition which Lush LJ cannot have intended to advance. . . .'

This decision appeared to have limited the approach taken in *Jackson* to non-commercial situations, where one person, as part of a social or family arrangement, makes a booking on behalf of a group. In 1993, however, the House of Lords opened the door again to the possibility of damages being recovered for a third party, even in a commercial situation.

St. Martins Property Corporation Ltd v Sir Robert McAlpine Ltd [1993] 3 All ER 417 (HL)

[NB this case involved appeals in two separate actions, and is found in the law reports under the name of the other action – *Linden Gardens Ltd v Lenesta Sludge Disposals Ltd.*]

Facts: There was a building contract between a developer, P, and a construction company, C. Before the work was complete, P assigned its interest to T. This did not, however, create any contractual relationship between T and C, since it was done without T's consent. Defective work, done after the assignment, cost about £800,000 to repair. P sued, but it was argued that it had suffered no loss, because its interests had been assigned to T.

Held: Since it was known from the start that the building would in the end be occupied by a third party, rather than P, C could foresee that defective work would cause loss to a third party. In the circumstances, P could recover damages on behalf of T.

Lord Browne-Wilkinson:

'. . . *The facts in the St. Martins case*
In 1968 the first plaintiffs, St. Martins Property Corporation Ltd. ("Corporation") began to develop a site at King Street, Hammersmith, London. The development was to include shops, offices, and flats. On 17 May 1968, Corporation entered into a written agreement with the local authority whereby, upon completion of the development, Corporation would be entitled to the grant of a 150-year lease of the site.
On 29 October 1974 Corporation entered into a building contract with Sir Robert

McAlpine and Sons Ltd. ("McAlpine") which incorporated the Joint Contracts Tribunal, Standard Form of Building Contract, Private Edition with Quantities, 1963 edn. (July 1972 rev.). Clause 17 of such contract was, for all practical purposes, in terms identical to those in clause 17 in the Linden Gardens case.

Corporation is a wholly owned subsidiary of St. Martins Holdings Ltd. which is itself wholly owned by the State of Kuwait. In the mid–1970s a scheme was implemented for tax reasons whereunder all the property interests of the State of Kuwait were to be vested in another wholly owned subsidiary of St. Martins Holdings Ltd., the second plaintiff, St. Martins Property Investments Ltd. ("Investments"). Pursuant to that scheme a deed of assignment dated 25 March 1976 was executed under which Corporation for full value assigned to Investments all Corporation's interests in the property under the agreement with the local authority of 17 May 1968. It further purported to assign to Investments:

"the full benefit of all the contracts and engagements whatsoever entered into by the assignor and existing at the date hereof for the construction of and completion of the development."

As in the Linden Gardens case, the consent of McAlpine's to the assignment of the benefit of the building contract was neither sought nor given. No notice of the assignment was given to McAlpine until 10 years later on 3 March 1986.

At the time of the assignment there were no subsisting relevant breaches of the building contract. In November 1976 Investments appointed Corporation to be its agent to manage the property and the development. Practical completion of the works took place in 1980.

In 1981 part of the development, the podium deck, was found to be leaking. It is alleged that this is due to breaches of contract by McAlpine occurring after the date of assignment to Investment. Remedial works have been carried out at a cost of some £800,000 plus VAT which, although originally paid by Corporation, has been recovered by Corporation from Investments.

In the action Corporation and Investments sue McAlpine for breach of contract. The following points should be noted. First, as in the Linden Gardens case, no consent to the assignment was obtained. Second, unlike the Linden Gardens case the breaches of contract all took place after the date of the assignment, that is to say at a time when Corporation had no interest in the property. Third, unlike the Linden Gardens case, the original contracting party, Corporation, is a party to the action and is claiming substantial damages notwithstanding that Corporation is not out of pocket as a result of the McAlpine breaches.

Therefore the main issues which arise in this case are first, whether notwithstanding clause 17 of the building contract the assignment to Investments was effective. Second, whether Corporation is entitled to substantial damages for breach of contract. Judge Bowsher Q.C. held that the assignment to Investments was ineffective and that Corporation was only entitled to nominal damages. The appeal to the Court of Appeal was heard at the same time as the appeal in the Linden Gardens case. The Court of Appeal held by a majority (Staughton L.J. dissenting) that the assignment was invalid, the case differing from the Linden Gardens case in that, at the date of the assignment, there were no accrued causes of action which could be assigned. However the Court of Appeal held unanimously that Corporation was entitled to substantial damages. McAlpine appeal and Investments cross-appeal to this House . . . .

(6) What is the measure of damages in the claim by Corporation?

McAlpine accept that, since the attempted assignment by Corporation of its rights under the contract to Investments was ineffective, Corporation has retained those rights and is entitled to judgment against McAlpine for any breach of contract. But, McAlpine submits, Corporation is only entitled to nominal damages. Corporation has suffered no loss: it had parted with its interest in the property (and therefore with the works when completed) before any breach of the building contract; moreover Corporation received full value for that interest on its disposal to Investments. Therefore, it is said, neither of the plaintiffs has any right to substantial damages: Investments has incurred damage (being the cost of rectifying the faulty work) but has no cause of action; Corporation has a cause of action but has suffered no loss. If this is right, in the words of my noble and learned friend, Lord Keith of Kinkel in *GUS Property Management Ltd v Littlewoods Mail Order Stores Ltd*, 1982 S.L.T. 533, 538, "the claim to damages would disappear. . .into some legal black hole, so that the wrongdoer escaped scot-free."

The Court of Appeal was able to avoid this result by reason of the continuing liability on Corporation to indemnify Investments against the cost of remedying the defects. McAlpine accepted, and still accept, that Corporation is liable to Investments in damages for Corporation's breach of contract in failing to obtain the consent of McAlpine to the assignment of the benefit of the building contract. The measure of the damages payable by Corporation to Investments for such breach would be the cost of remedying the defects since, if the assignment had been valid, Investments could have recovered such cost from McAlpine. Therefore, the Court of Appeal held, Corporation have suffered substantial loss by reason of McAlpine's breach, such loss being the liability to indemnify Investments.

Attractive as this argument is, Mr. Fernyhough for McAlpine has satisfied me that it is erroneous because the damage being claimed is too remote. The loss so identified as having been suffered by Corporation flows from the attempt by Corporation to assign the benefit of the building contract in breach of clause 17 of the contract. However the rule in *Hadley v Baxendale* (1854) 9 Exch. 341 is formulated, in my judgment it is impossible to say that such damage arose naturally according to the usual course of things, or was in the contemplation of, or foreseeable by, McAlpine, or that McAlpine ought to have realised that such damage was "not unlikely". The contract for the breach of which damages are sought expressly prohibited Corporation from making such assignment. One party to a contract cannot be liable for damages flowing from the doing of an act by the other party which the contract itself expressly forbids.

It is therefore necessary to consider Mr. Fernyhough's principle argument in some detail. He starts from the well known proposition that the measure of damages is generally "that sum of money which will put the party who has been injured, or who has suffered, in the same position he would have been in if he had not sustained the wrong for which he is now getting his compensation or reparation:" *per* Lord Blackburn in *Livingstone v Rawyards Coal Co* (1880) 5 App.Cas. 25, 39.

Since, before the date of any breach of contract by McAlpine, Corporation had disposed of all its interest in the property on which the building works were carried out, Corporation has suffered no loss. Corporation received the full value of the property from Investments. The measure of damages for defective performance of a building contract is the diminution in value of the plaintiff's property, which diminution is usually properly reflected by the cost of carrying out the repairs necessary to effect reinstatement: *East Ham Corporation v Bernard Sunley & Sons Ltd* [1966] A.C. 406. Since at the date of breach Corporation did not own the property, Corporation suffered no loss by any diminution in its value nor could Corporation carry out any works of reinstatement. Therefore, it is said, Corporation has suffered no loss.

Mr. Fernyhough accepted that central to his argument is the fact that at the date of breach Corporation no longer owned the property. He distinguished the decision in *Newton Abbot Development Co Ltd v Stockman Bros* (1931) 47 T.L.R. 616 on that ground. In that case the plaintiffs, as developers, had contracted with the defendants as contractors for the construction of a number of houses. After completion of the works, the plaintiffs had sold the houses to individual purchasers at a profit. Thereafter defects due to faulty construction by the defendants appeared in the houses. The plaintiffs, although under no legal liability to do so, had remedied these defects. They were held entitled to recover from the defendants not the cost of effecting the remedial work but the difference between the value of the houses as they ought to have been completed and their actual value as in fact completed. Mr. Fernyhough explains this case on the basis that, although in fact the plaintiff suffered no commercial loss, they were the owners of the houses at the date of breach and therefore entitled to the diminution in value of that property, the sale on by the plaintiffs being irrelevant as res inter alios acta. In support of the proposition that only nominal damages are recoverable by a plaintiff who has parted with ownership of the property at the date of breach, Mr. Fernyhough further relied on two cases concerned with breach of contract for the carriage of goods, *The Albazero* [1977] A.C. 774 and *Obestain Inc v National Mineral Development Corporation Ltd* [1987] 1 Lloyd's Rep. 465.

This is a formidable, if unmeritorious, argument since it is apparently soundly based on principle and is supported by authority. In *The Albazero* the plaintiffs chartered the defendant's vessel for the carriage of oil. The carriage was covered by a bill of lading which named the plaintiffs as consignees. In the course of the voyage the vessel and cargo became a total loss. However on the day before that loss, the plaintiffs endorsed the bill of lading to a third party: the property in the goods and the right to sue the defendants were thereby vested in the third party. The plaintiffs, although having no property in the goods at the date of breach of the contract of carriage, sued the defendants for the full value of the goods. This House held that the plaintiffs were not entitled to substantial damages. Lord Diplock treated the general rule as being clear: a party who has no property in the goods at the date of breach has suffered no loss.

However he recognised that there were exceptions to this general rule and I will consider those exceptions later.

Notwithstanding the apparent logic of Mr. Fernyhough's submission, I have considerable doubts whether it is correct. A contract for the supply of goods or of work, labour and materials (a supply contract) is not the same as a contract for the carriage of goods. A breach of a supply contract involves a failure to provide the very goods or services which the defendant had contracted to supply and for which the plaintiff has paid or agreed to pay. If the breach is discovered before payment of the contract price, the price is abated by the cost of making good the defects: see as to sale of goods *Mondel v Steel* (1841) 8 M. & W. 858 and Sale of Goods Act 1979, section 53(1); as to building contracts *Modern Engineering (Bristol) Ltd v Gilbert-Ash (Northern) Ltd* [1974] A.C. 689. Mr. Fernyhough accepted that this right to abatement of the price does not depend on ownership by the plaintiff of the goods and it would be odd if the plaintiff's rights arising from breach varied according to whether the breach was discovered before or after the payment of the price. No such similar principle of abatement applies to freight charges: the freight charges have to be paid in full leaving the consignor to bring a separate action for damages for breach of the contract of carriage: *Colonial Bank v European Grain and Shipping Ltd* [1989] A.C. 1056, 1067–1068.

In contracts for the sale of goods, the purchaser is entitled to damages for delivery of defective goods assessed by reference to the difference between the contract price and the market price of the defective goods, irrespective of whether he has managed to sell on the goods to a third party without loss: *Slater v Hoyle & Smith Ltd* [1920] 2 K.B. 11; see also as to non-delivery *William Bros v ED T Agius Ltd* [1914] A.C. 510. In those cases the judgments contained no consideration of the person in whom the property in the goods was vested although it appears that some of the subcontracts had been made prior to the breach of contract.

If the law were to be established that damages for breach of a supply contract were not quantifiable by reference to the beneficial ownership of goods or enjoyment of the services contracted for but by reference to the difference in value between that which was contracted for and that which is in fact supplied, it might also provide a satisfactory answer to the problems raised where a man contracts and pays for a supply to others, e.g., a man contracts with a restaurant for a meal for himself and his guests or with a travel company for a holiday for his family. It is apparently established that, if a defective meal or holiday is supplied, the contracting party can recover damages not only for his own bad meal or unhappy holiday but also for that of his guests or family: see *Jackson v Horizon Holidays Ltd* [1975] 1 W.L.R. 1468 as explained in *Woodar Investment Development Ltd v Wimpey Construction UK Ltd* [1980] 1 W.L.R. 277, 283–284, 293–294, 297, 300–301.

There is therefore much to be said for drawing a distinction between cases where the ownership of goods or property is relevant to prove that the plaintiff has suffered loss through the breach of a contract other than a contract to supply those goods or property and the measure of damages in a supply contract where the contractual obligation itself requires the provision of those goods or services. I am reluctant to express a concluded view on this point since it may have profound effects on commercial contracts which effects were not fully explored in argument. In my view the point merits exposure to academic consideration before it is decided by this House. Nor do I find it necessary to decide the point since, on any view, the facts of this case bring it within the class of exceptions to the general rule to which Lord Diplock referred in *The Albazero*.

In *The Albazero* Lord Diplock said [1977] A.C. 774, 846:

"Nevertheless, although it is exceptional at common law that a plaintiff in an action for breach of contract, although he himself has not suffered any loss, should be entitled to recover damages on behalf of some third person who is not a party to the action for a loss which that third person has sustained, the notion that there may be circumstances in which he is entitled to do so was not entirely unfamiliar to the common law and particularly to that part of it which, under the influence of Lord Mansfield and his successors, Lord Ellenborough and Lord Tenterden, had been appropriated from the law merchant. "I have already mentioned the right of the bailee, which has been recognised from the earliest period of our law, to sue in detinue or trespass for loss or damage to his bailor's goods although he cannot be compelled by his bailor to do so and he is not himself liable to the bailor for the loss or damage: *The Winkfield* [1902] P. 42. Nevertheless, he becomes accountable to his bailor for the proceeds of the judgment in an action by his bailor for money had and received. So too the doctrine of subrogation in the case of insurers, which was adopted from the law merchant by the common law in the eighteenth century, involved the concept of the nominal party to an action at common law suing for a loss which he had not himself sustained and being accountable to his insurer for the proceeds to the extent that he had been indemnified against the loss by the insurer. In this instance of a plaintiff being able to recover as damages for breach of contract for the benefit of a third person a loss which that person had sustained and he had not, the insurer is entitled to compel an assured to whom he has paid a total or partial indemnity to bring the action. A third example, once again in the field of mercantile law, is the right of an assured to recover in an action on a policy of insurance upon goods the full amount of loss or damage to them, on behalf of anyone who may be entitled to an interest in the goods at the time when the loss or damage occurs, provided that it appears from the terms of the policy that he intended to cover their interests."

In addition, the decision in *The Albazero* itself established a further exception. This House was concerned with the status of a long-established principle based on the decision in *Dunlop v Lambert* (1839) 6 Cl. & F. 600 that a consignor of goods who had parted with the property in the goods before the date of breach could even so recover substantial damages for the failure to deliver the goods. Lord Diplock, identified, at p 847, the rationale of that rule as being:

"The only way in which I find it possible to rationalise the rule in *Dunlop v Lambert* so that it may fit into the pattern of the English law is to treat it as an application of the principle, accepted also in relation to policies of insurance upon goods, that in a commercial contract concerning goods where it is in the contemplation of the parties that the proprietary interests in the goods may be transferred from one owner to another after the contract has been entered into and before the breach which causes loss or damage to the goods, an original party to the contract, if such be the intention of them both, is to be treated in law as having entered into the contract for the benefit of all persons who have or may acquire an interest in the goods before they are lost or damaged, and is entitled to recover by way of damages for breach of contract the actual loss sustained by those for whose benefit the contract is entered into."

In *The Albazero* it was held that the principle in *Dunlop v Lambert* no longer applied to goods consigned under a bill of lading because both the property in the goods and the cause of action for breach of the contract of carriage passes to the consignee or endorsee by reason of the consignment or endorsement; therefore, since the consignee or endorsee will in any event be entitled to enforce the contract direct there is no ground on which one can impute to the parties an intention that the consignor is entering into the contract for the benefit of others who will acquire the property in the goods but no right of action for breach of contract.

However, this House was careful to limit its decision to cases of carriage by sea under a bill of lading, leaving in force the principle in *Dunlop v Lambert* in relation to other contracts for the carriage of goods where such automatic assignment of the rights of action for breach does not take place. Lord Diplock, after the passage referring to the exceptions which I have already quoted, said, at pp 846–847:

"My Lords, in the light of these other exceptions, particularly in the field of mercantile law, to the general rule of English law that apart from nominal damages the plaintiff can only recover in an action for breach of contract the actual loss he has himself sustained, I do not think that the fact that the rule which it is generally accepted was laid down by this House in *Dunlop v Lambert*, 6 Cl. & F. 600 would add one more exception would justify your Lordships in declaring the rule to be no longer law. Nor do I think that the almost complete absence of reliance on the rule by litigants in actions between 1839 and 1962 provides a sufficient reason for abolishing it entirely. The development of the law of negligence since 1839 does not provide a complete substituted remedy for some types of loss caused by breach of a contract of carriage. Late delivery is the most obvious example of these. The Bills of Lading Act 1855 and the subsequent development of the doctrine laid down in *Brandt v Liverpool, Brazil and River Plate Steam Navigation Co Ltd* [1924] 1 K.B. 575, have reduced the scope and utility of the rule in *Dunlop v Lambert* . . . where goods are carried under a bill of lading. But the rule extends to all forms of carriage including carriage by sea itself where no bill of lading has been issued, and there may still be occasional cases in which the rule would provide a remedy where no other would be available to a person sustaining loss which under a rational legal system ought to be compensated by the person who has caused it. For my part, I am not persuaded that your Lordships ought to go out of your way to jettison the rule."

In my judgment the present case falls within the rationale of the exceptions to the general rule that a plaintiff can only recover damages for his own loss. The contract was for a large development of property which, to the knowledge of both Corporation and McAlpine, was going to be occupied, and possibly purchased, by third parties and not by Corporation itself. Therefore it could be foreseen that damage caused by a breach would cause loss to a later owner and not merely to the original contracting party, Corporation. As in contracts for the carriage of goods by land, there would be no automatic vesting in the occupier or owners of the property for the time being who sustained the loss of any right of suit against McAlpine. On the contrary, McAlpine had specifically contracted that the rights of action under the building contract *could* not without McAlpine's consent be transferred to third parties who became owners or occupiers and might suffer loss. In such a case, it seems to me proper, as in the case of the carriage of goods by land, to treat the parties as having entered into the contract on the footing that Corporation would be entitled to enforce contractual rights for the benefit of those who suffered from defective performance but who, under the terms of the contract, could not acquire any right to hold McAlpine liable for breach. It is truly a case in which the rule provides "a remedy where no other would be available to a person sustaining loss which under a rational legal system ought to be compensated by the person who has caused it."

Mr. Fernyhough submitted that it would be wrong to distort the law in order to meet what he described as being an exceptional case. He said that this was a one-off or exceptional case since the development was sold before any breach of contract had occurred and there was an express contractual prohibition on assignment. He submitted that to give Corporation a right to substantial damages in this case would produce chaos when applied to other cases where the contractors have entered into direct warranties with the ultimate purchasers of the individual parts of a development. I am not impressed by these submissions. I am far from satisfied that this is a one off or exceptional case. We are concerned with standard forms of building contracts which prohibit the assignment of the benefit of building contracts to the ultimate purchasers. In the prolonged period of recession in the property market which this country has experienced many developments have had to be sold off before completion, thereby producing the risk that the ownership of the property may have become divided from the right to sue on the building contract at a date before any breach occurs. As to the warranties given by contractors to subsequent purchasers, they will not, in my judgment, give rise to difficulty. If, pursuant to the terms of the original building contract, the contractors have undertaken liability to the ultimate purchasers to remedy defects appearing after they acquired the property, it is manifest the case will not fall within the rationale of *Dunlop v Lambert*, 6 Cl. & F. 600. If the ultimate purchaser is given a direct cause of action against the contractor (as is the consignee or endorsee under a bill of lading) the case falls outside the rationale of the rule. The original building owner will not be entitled to recover damages for loss suffered by others who can themselves sue for such loss. I would therefore hold that Corporation is entitled to substantial damages for any breach by McAlpine of the building contract.'

The majority of the House of Lords adopted Lord Browne-Wilkinson's analysis. A broader approach was put forward by Lord Griffiths, more directly challenging the assumption that the normal position should be in this type of situation that the promisee can only recover nominal damages. He supported this with the following example (at pp 119–120):

I cannot accept that in a contract of this nature, namely for work, labour and the supply of materials, the recovery of more than nominal damages for breach of contract is dependent upon the plaintiff having a proprietary interest in the subject matter of the contract at the date of breach. In everyday life contracts for work and labour are constantly being placed by those who have no proprietary interest in the subject matter of the contract. To take a common example, the matrimonial home is owned by the wife and the couple's remaining assets are owned by the husband and he is the sole earner. The house requires a new roof and the husband places a contract with a builder to carry out the work. The husband is not acting as agent for his wife; he makes the contract as principal because only he can pay for it. The builder fails to replace the roof properly and the husband has to call in and pay another builder to complete the work. Is it to be said that the husband has suffered no damage because he does not own the property? Such a result would in my view be absurd and the answer is that the husband has suffered loss because he did not receive the bargain for which he had contracted with the first builder and the measure of damages is the cost of securing the performance of that bargain by completing the roof repairs properly by the second builder. To put this simple example closer to the facts of this appeal – at the time the husband employs the builder he owns the house but just after the builder starts work the couple are advised to divide their assets so the husband transfers the house to his wife. This is no concern of the builder whose bargain is with the husband. If the roof turns out to be defective the husband can recover from the builder the cost of putting it right and thus obtain the benefit of the bargain that the builder had promised to deliver. It was suggested in argument that the answer to the example I have given is that the husband could assign the benefit of the contract to the wife. But what if, as in this case, the builder has a clause in the contract forbidding assignment without his consent and refuses to give consent as McAlpine has done. It is then said that neither husband nor wife can recover damages; this seems to me to be so unjust a result that the law cannot tolerate it.

To adopt Lord Griffiths approach would involve a much more significant departure from the traditional doctrine of privity than that taken by the majority. It would also run counter to the prevailing doctrine in relation to contract damages – that is, that they are awarded for losses actually suffered as the consequence of a breach, not simply for the breach itself. When the matter fell to be considered again by the House of Lords in *Panatown Ltd v Alfred McAlpine Construction Ltd* a minority of the panel would have been prepared to adopt Lord Griffiths' approach, but the majority thought that the narrower ground for allowing damages to be recovered for a third-party's loss was the right approach.

Alfred McAlpine Construction Ltd v Panatown Ltd [2001] AC 518 (HL)

Facts: M, a building contractor, entered into a contract with P to construct an office building and car park on land owned by U, a company within the same group of companies as P. The reason for this arrangement was to avoid (legitimately) the payment of VAT. There was also a 'duty of care deed' (DCD) executed between U and M which gave U a right to sue M for negligence in performance of the building contract. The DCD was assignable to those to whom the U might later transfer the property. When problems arose, P initiated arbitration proceedings under its contract with M. M sought to argue as a preliminary point that as P had no proprietary interest in the site, it had suffered no loss. The arbitrator held for P; the trial judge for M; and the Court of Appeal for P. M appealed.

Held: (Lords Goff and Millett dissenting) On the facts, P could not succeed on the contract, because the existence of the DCD meant that the case was not one where the claim would otherwise fall into the 'black hole', with no party being able to claim. The majority confirmed the 'narrow ground' identified in the *St Martin's* case as a possible basis for recovery on behalf of a third party, but was sceptical as to Lord Griffiths' 'broader ground'.

Lord Clyde:
'. . . The justification for the exception to the general rule that one can only sue for damages for a loss which he has himself suffered was explained by Lord Diplock in *The Albazero* [1977] AC 774, 847. His Lordship noted that the scope and utility of what he referred to as the rule in *Dunlop v Lambert*, 6 Cl & F 600 in its application to carriage by sea under a bill of lading had been much reduced by the passing of the Bills of Lading Act 1855 and the subsequent development of the law, but that the rule extended to all forms of carriage, including carriage by sea where there was no bill of lading:

and there may still be occasional cases in which the rule would provide a remedy where no other would be available to a person sustaining loss which under a rational legal system ought to be compensated by the person who has caused it.

The justification for *The Albazero* exception is thus the necessity of avoiding the disappearance of a substantial claim into what was described by Lord Stewart in *GUS Property Management Ltd v Littlewoods Mail Order Stores Ltd*, 1982 SC(HL) 157, 166 as a legal black hole, an expression subsequently taken up by Lord Keith of Kinkel in this House, at p 177.

In *The Albazero* [1977] AC 774, 847 Lord Diplock sought to "rationalise the rule in *Dunlop v Lambert*" so that it might fit into the pattern of English law. He did so by treating it:

> as an application of the principle, accepted also in relation to policies of insurance upon goods, that in a commercial contract concerning goods where it is in the contemplation of the parties that the proprietary interests in the goods may be transferred from one owner to another after the contract has been entered into and before the breach which causes loss or damage to the goods, an original party to the contract, if such be the intention of them both, is to be treated in law as having entered into the contract for the benefit of all persons who have or may acquire an interest in the goods before they are lost or damaged, and is entitled to recover by way of damages for breach of contract the actual loss sustained by those for whose benefit the contract is entered into.

It is particularly this passage in Lord Diplock's speech which has given rise to a question discussed in the present appeal whether *The Albazero* exception is a rule of law or is based upon the intention of the parties. The issue was identified by my noble and learned friend, Lord Goff of Chieveley, in his speech in *White v Jones* [1995] 2 AC 207, 267. The problem arises from two phrases in the speech of Lord Diplock the mutual relationship between which may not be immediately obvious. The two phrases, in the reverse order than that in which they appear, are "is to be treated in law as having entered into the contract" and "if such be the intention of the parties". In my view it is preferable to regard it as a solution imposed by the law and not as arising from the supposed intention of the parties, who may in reality not have applied their minds to the point. On the other hand if they deliberately provided for a remedy for a third party it can readily be concluded that they have intended to exclude the operation of the solution which would otherwise have been imposed by law. The terms and provisions of the contract will then require to be studied to see if the parties have excluded the operation of the exception.

That appears to have been the conclusion adopted in *Linden Gardens Trust Ltd v Lenesta Sludge Disposals Ltd*; *St Martins Property Corpn Ltd v Sir Robert McAlpine Ltd* [1994] 1 AC 85 (the *St Martins* case), where my noble and learned friend, Lord Browne-Wilkinson, observed, at p 115:

> In such a case, it seems to me proper, as in the case of the carriage of goods by land, to treat the parties as having entered into the contract on the footing that

Corporation would be entitled to enforce contractual rights for the benefit of those who suffered from defective performance but who, under the terms of the contract, could not acquire any right to hold McAlpine liable for breach.

In that case the point was made that the contractor and the employer were both aware that the property was going to be occupied and possibly purchased by third parties so that it could be foreseen that a breach of the contract might cause loss to others than the employer. But such foresight may be an unnecessary factor in the applicability of the exception. So also an intention of the parties to benefit a third person may be unnecessary. Foreseeablility may be relevant to the question of damages under the rule in *Hadley v Baxendale* (1854) 9 Exch 341, but in the context of liability it is a concept which is more at home in the law of tort than in the law of contract. If the exception is founded primarily upon a principle of law, and not upon the particular knowledge of the parties to the contract, then it is not easy to see why the necessity for the contemplation of the parties that there will be potential losses by third parties is essential. It appears that in the *St Martins* case [1994] 1 AC 85 the damages claimed were in respect of the cost of remedial work which had been carried out. I see no reason why consequential losses should not also be recoverable under this exception where such loss occurs and the third party should have a right to recover for himself all the damages won by the original party on his behalf.

The Albazero exception will plainly not apply where the parties contemplate that the carrier will enter into separate contracts of carriage with the later owners of the goods, identical to the contract with the consignor. Even more clearly, as Lord Diplock explained [1977] AC 774, 848, will the exception be excluded if other contracts of carriage are made in terms different from those in the original contract. In *The Albazero* the separate contracts which were mentioned were contracts of carriage. That is understandable in the context of carriage by sea involving a charterparty and bills of lading. But the counterpart in a building contract to a right of suit under a bill of lading should be the provision of a direct entitlement in a third party to sue the contractor in the event of a failure in the contractor's performance. In the context of a building contract one does not require to look for a second building contract to exclude the exception. It would be sufficient to find the provision of a right to sue. Thus as my noble and learned friend, Lord Browne-Wilkinson, observed in the *St Martins* case [1994] 1 AC 85 115:

> If, pursuant to the terms of the original building contract, the contractors have undertaken liability to the ultimate purchasers to remedy defects appearing after they acquired the property, it is manifest the case will not fall within the rationale of *Dunlop v Lambert* 6 Cl & F 600. If the ultimate purchaser is given a direct cause of action against the contractor (as is the consignee or endorsee under a bill of lading) the case falls outside the rationale of the rule.

In the *St Martins* case the employer started off as the owner of the property and subsequently conveyed it to another company. In the present case the employer never was the owner. But that has not featured as a critical consideration in the present appeal and I do not see that that factor affects the application of the exception. In the *St Martins* case there was a contractual bar on the assignment of rights of action without the consent of the contractor. In the present case the extra qualification was added that the consent should not be unreasonably withheld. But again I do not see that difference as of significance. It does not follow that the presence of a provision enabling assignment without the consent of the contractor excludes the exception. As was held in *Darlington Borough Council v Wiltshier Northern Ltd* [1995] 1 WLR 68 where there is a right to have an assignment of any cause of action accruing to the employer against the contractor, the exception may still apply so as to enable the assignee to recover substantial damages. It may be that the exception could be excluded through some contractual arrangement between the employer and the third party who sustained the actual loss, but the law would probably be slow to find such an intention established where it would leave the black hole. At least an express provision for assignment of the employer's rights will not suffice.

I have no difficulty in holding in the present case that the exception cannot apply. As part of the contractual arrangements entered into between Panatown and McAlpine there was a clear contemplation that separate contracts would be entered into by McAlpine, the contracts of the deed of duty of care and the collateral warranties. The duty of care deed and the collateral warranties were of course not in themselves building contracts. But they did form an integral part of the package of arrangements which the employer and the contractor agreed upon and in that respect should be viewed as reflecting the intentions of all the parties engaged in the arrangements that the third party should have a direct cause of action to the exclusion of any substantial claim by the employer, and accordingly that the exception should not apply. There was some dispute upon the difference in substance between the remedies available under the contract and those available under the duty of care deed. Even if it is accepted that in the circumstances of the present case where the eventual issue may relate particularly to matters of reasonable skill and care, the remedies do not absolutely coincide, the express provision of the direct remedy for the third party is fatal to the application of *The Albazero* exception. On a more general approach the difference between a strict contractual basis of claim and a basis of reasonable care makes the express remedy more clearly a substitution for the operation of the exception. Panatown cannot then in the light of these deeds be treated as having contracted with McAlpine for the benefit of the owner or later owners of the land and the exception is plainly excluded.

I turn accordingly to what was referred to in the argument as the broader ground. But the label requires more careful definition. The approach under *The Albazero* exception has been one of recognising an entitlement to sue by the innocent party to a contract which has been breached, where the innocent party is treated as suing on behalf of or for the benefit of some other person or persons, not parties to the contract, who have sustained loss as a result of the breach. In such a case the innocent party to the contract is bound to account to the person suffering the loss for the damages which the former has recovered for the benefit of the latter. But the so-called broader ground involves a significantly different approach. What it proposes is that the innocent party

293

to the contract should recover damages for himself as a compensation for what is seen to be his own loss. In this context no question of accounting to anyone else arises. This approach however seems to me to have been developed into two formulations.

The first formulation, and the seeds of the second, are found in the speech of Lord Griffiths in the *St Martins* case [1994] 1 AC 85, 96. At the outset his Lordship expressed the opinion that Corporation, faced with a breach by McAlpine of their contractual duty to perform the contract with sound materials and with all reasonable skill and care, would be entitled to recover from McAlpine the cost of remedying the defect in the work as the normal measure of damages. He then dealt with two possible objections. First, it should not matter that the work was not being done on property owned by Corporation. Where a husband instructs repairs to the roof of the matrimonial home it cannot be said that he has not suffered damage because he did not own the property. He suffers the damage measured by the cost of a proper completion of the repair:

> "In cases such as the present the person who places the contract has suffered financial loss because he has to spend money to give him the benefit of the bargain which the defendant had promised but failed to deliver." (See p 97.)

The second objection, that Corporation had in fact been reimbursed for the cost of the repairs was answered by the consideration that the person who actually pays for the repairs is of no concern to the party who broke the contract. But Lord Griffiths added, at p 97:

> The court will of course wish to be satisfied that the repairs have been or are likely to be carried out but if they are carried out the cost of doing them must fall upon the defendant who broke his contract.

In the first formulation this approach can be seen as identifying a loss upon the innocent party who requires to instruct the remedial work. That loss is, or may be measured by, the cost of the repair. The essential for this formulation appears to be that the repair work is to be, or at least is likely to be, carried out. This consideration does not appear to be simply relevant to the reasonableness of allowing the damages to be measured by the cost of repair. It is an essential condition for the application of the approach, so as to establish a loss on the part of the plaintiff. Thus far the approach appears to be consistent with principle, and in particular with the principle of privity. It can cover the case where A contracts with B to pay a sum of money to C and B fails to do so. The loss to A is in the necessity to find other funds to pay to C and provided that he is going to pay C, or indeed has done so, he should be able to recover the sum by way of damages for breach of contract from B. If it was evident that A had no intention to pay C, having perhaps changed his mind, then he would not be able to recover the amount from B because he would have sustained no loss, and his damages would at best be nominal.

But there can also be found in Lord Griffiths's speech the idea that the loss is not just constituted by the failure in performance but indeed consists in that failure. This is the "second formulation". In relation to the suggestion that the husband who instructs repair work to the roof of his wife's house and has to pay for another builder to make good the faulty repair work has sustained no damage Lord Griffiths observed, at p 97:

> Such a result would in my view be absurd and the answer is that the husband has suffered loss because he did not receive the bargain for which he had contracted with the first builder and the measure of damages is the cost of securing the performance of that bargain by completing the roof repairs properly by the second builder.

That is to say that the fact that the innocent party did not receive the bargain for which he contracted is itself a loss. As Steyn LJ put it in *Darlington Borough Council v Wiltshier Northern Ltd* [1995] 1 WLR 68, 80: "He suffers a loss of bargain or of expectation interest." In this more radical formulation it does not matter whether the repairs are or are not carried out, and indeed in the Darlington case that qualification is seen as unnecessary. In that respect the disposal of the damages is treated as res inter alios acta. Nevertheless on this approach the intention to repair may cast light on the reasonableness of the measure of damages adopted. In order to follow through this aspect of the second formulation in Lord Griffiths's speech it would be necessary to understand his references to the carrying out of the repairs to be relevant only to that consideration.

I find some difficulty in adopting the second formulation as a sound way forward. First, if the loss is the disappointment at there not being provided what was contracted for, it seems to me difficult to measure that loss by consideration of the cost of repair. A more apt assessment of the compensation for the loss of what was expected should rather be the difference in value between what was contracted for and what was supplied. Secondly, the loss constituted by the supposed disappointment may well not include all the loss which the breach of contract has caused. It may not be able to embrace consequential losses, or losses falling within the second head of *Hadley v Baxendale* 9 Exch 341. The inability of the wife to let one of the rooms in the house caused by the inadequacy of the repair, does not seem readily to be something for which the husband could claim as his loss. Thirdly, there is no obligation on the successful plaintiff to account to anyone who may have sustained actual loss as a result of the faulty performance. Some further mechanism would then be required for the court to achieve the proper disposal of the monies awarded to avoid a double jeopardy. Alternatively, in order to achieve an effective solution, it would seem to be necessary to add an obligation to account on the part of the person recovering the damages. But once that step is taken the approach begins to approximate to *The Albazero* exception. Fourthly, the "loss" constituted by a breach of contract has usually been recognised as calling for an award of nominal damages, not substantial damages.

The loss of an expectation which is here referred to seems to me to be coming very close to a way of describing a breach of contract. A breach of contract may cause a loss, but is not in itself a loss in any meaningful sense. When one refers to a loss in the context of a breach of contract, one is in my view referring to the incidence of some personal or patrimonial damage. A loss of expectation might be a loss in the proper sense if damages were awarded for the distress or inconvenience caused by the disappointment. Professor Coote ("Contract Damages, *Ruxley* and the Performance Interest" [1997] CLJ 537) draws a distinction between benefits in law, that is bargained-for contractual rights, and benefits in fact, that is the enjoyment of the fruits of performance. Certainly the former may constitute an asset with a commercial value. But while frustration may destroy the rights altogether so that the contract is no longer enforceable, a failure in the obligation to perform does not destroy the asset. On the contrary it remains as the necessary legal basis for a remedy. A failure in performance of a contractual obligation does not entail a loss of the bargained-for contractual rights. Those rights remain so as to enable performance of the contract to be enforced, as by an order for specific performance. If one party to a contract repudiates it and that repudiation is accepted, then, to quote Lord Porter in *Heyman v Darwins Ltd* [1942] AC 356, 399, "By that acceptance he is discharged from further performance and may bring an action for damages, but the contract itself is not rescinded." The primary obligations under the contract may come to an end, but secondary obligations then arise, among them being the obligation to compensate the innocent party. The original rights may not then be enforced. But a consequential right arises in the innocent party to obtain a remedy from the party who repudiated the contract for his failure in performance.

Both of these two formulations seek to remedy the problem of the legal black hole. At the heart of the problem is the doctrine of privity of contract which excludes the ready development of a solution along the lines of a jus quaesitum tertio. It might well be thought that such a solution would be more direct and simple. In the context of the domestic and familial situations, such as the husband instructing the repairs to the roof of his wife's house, or the holiday which results in disappointment to all the members of the family, the jus quaesitum tertio may provide a satisfactory means of redress, enabling compensation to be paid to the people who have suffered the loss. Such an approach is available in Germany: see W Lorenz, "Contract Beneficiaries in German Law" in The Gradual Convergence: Foreign Ideas, Foreign Influences, and English Law on the Eve of the 21st Century, edited by Markesinis (1994), pp 65, 78, 79. It may also be available in Scotland (*Carmichael v Carmichael's Executrix*, 1920 SC(HL) 195). But we were not asked to adopt it in the present case and so radical a step cannot easily be achieved without legislative action. Since Parliament has recently made some inroad into the principle of privity but has stopped short of admitting a solution to a situation such as the present, it would plainly be inappropriate to enlarge the statutory provision by judicial innovation. The alternative has to be the adoption of what Lord Diplock in *Swain v The Law Society* [1983] 1 AC 598, 611 described as a juristic subterfuge "to mitigate the effect of the lacuna resulting from the non-recognition of a jus quaesitum tertio". The solution, achieved by the operation of law, may carry with it some element of artificiality and may not be supportable on any clear or single principle. If the entitlement to sue is not to be permitted to the party who has suffered the loss, the law has to treat the person who is entitled to sue as doing so on behalf of the third party. As Lord Wilberforce observed in *Woodar Investment Development Ltd v Wimpey Construction*

UK Ltd [1980] 1 WLR 277, 283, "there are many situations of daily life which do not fit neatly into conceptual analysis, but which require some flexibility in the law of contract".

It seems to me that a more realistic and practical solution is to permit the contracting party to recover damages for the loss which he and a third party has suffered, being duly accountable to them in respect of their actual loss, than to construct a theoretical loss in law on the part of the contracting party, for which he may be under no duty to account to anyone since it is to be seen as his own loss. The solution is required where the law will not tolerate a loss caused by a breach of contract to go uncompensated through an absence of privity between the party suffering the loss and the party causing it. In such a case, to avoid the legal black hole, the law will deem the innocent party to be claiming on behalf of himself and any others who have suffered loss. It does not matter that he is not the owner of the property affected, nor that he has not himself suffered any economic loss. He sues for all the loss which has been sustained and is accountable to the others to the extent of their particular losses. While it may be that there is no necessary right in the third party to compel the innocent employer to sue the contractor, in the many cases of the domestic or familial situation that consideration should not be a realistic problem. In the commercial field, in relation to the interests of such persons as remoter future proprietors who are not related to the original employer, it may be that a solution by way of collateral warranty would still be required. If there is an anxiety lest the exception would permit an employer to receive excessive damages, that should be set at rest by the recognition of the basic requirement for reasonableness which underlies the quantification of an award of damages.

The problem which has arisen in the present case is one which is most likely to arise in the context of the domestic affairs of a family group or the commercial affairs of a group of companies. How the members of such a group choose to arrange their own affairs among themselves should not be a matter of necessary concern to a third party who has undertaken to one of their number to perform services in which they all have some interest. It should not be a ground of escaping liability that the party who instructed the work should not be the one who sustained the loss or all of the loss which in whole or part has fallen on another member or members of the group. But the resolution of the problem in any particular case has to be reached in light of its own circumstances. In the present case the decision that Panatown should be the employer under the building contract although another company in the group owned the land was made in order to minimise charges of VAT. No doubt thought was given as to the mechanics to be adopted for the building project in order to achieve the course most advantageous to the group. Where for its own purposes a group of companies decides which of its members is to be the contracting party in a project which is of concern and interest to the whole group I should be reluctant to refuse an entitlement to sue on the contract on the ground simply that the member who entered the contract was not the party who suffered the loss on a breach of the contract. But whether such an entitlement is to be admitted must depend upon the arrangements which the group and its members have decided to make both among themselves and with the other party to the contract. In the present case there was a plain and deliberate course adopted whereby the company with the potential risk of loss was given a distinct entitlement directly to sue the contractor and the professional advisers. In the light of such a clear and deliberate course I do not consider that an exception can be admitted to the general rule that substantial damages can only be claimed by a party who has suffered substantial loss.

I agree that the appeal should be allowed.'

The fact that the majority in *Panatown* decided the case on the basis of the existence of the DCD means that the decision will not necessarily be held to be decisive on the more general issues. It seems, however, that it is the narrower ground for recovery, rather than Lord Griffiths' broader ground, which is more favoured. The possibility that parties can now, if they so wish, give a third party a direct right of action under the Contracts (Rights of Third Parties) Act 1999 may well mean that the courts will be reluctant to extend this common-law exception any further. Whether the Act would have assisted the parties in the cases discussed above is, however, doubted by Harris, Campbell and Halson:

Harris, D, Campbell, D, and Halson, R, *Remedies in Contract and Tort*, pp 80–81

The problem addressed by the courts in the above cases was described as being caused by the fact that the party who has a cause of action for breach of contract is not the same as the person who has most immediately suffered the loss caused by that breach. The courts have shown great ingenuity in their attempt to permit recovery by the party who has the benefit of a direct cause of action. A different approach has been taken by the legislature, which has introduced a general right of action for third parties. In other words the party who has undoubtedly suffered the loss is given a new cause of action. The Contracts (Rights of Third Parties) Act 1999, s 1 provides that a third party to a contract may 'in his own right' enforce a term of a contract if 'the contract expressly provides that he may' or 'purports to confer [such] a benefit on him'. This section creates two distinct categories of third party claimant who can enforce a contract. An illustration of the first would be where X contracts to sell his boat to D in exchange for D's promise to pay C £20k 'who shall enjoy the direct right to enforce D's promise'. Such express provision is likely to be rare particularly in regard to contracts where it is not usual for X to seek legal advice. Therefore the second category of third party claimant is of greater practical importance. The effect of the provision is to create a rebuttable presumption in favour of there being a third party right whenever a contract seeks to confer a benefit on an expressly specified third party. A simple example might be where X contracts to sell his boat as above absent the express conferral on

C of a right to sue. The intentions of the original contracting parties, D and X must be ascertained by other means. However, the burden of proof will effectively be borne by D who will have to show that the parties' intention was not to confer an enforceable right on C.

It is unclear whether, if the Act were in force at the time, it would have been of assistance to the third parties in the cases considered above. In *Linden Gardens*, the third party (the new building owner) was not identified in the original contract and so would fall outside s 1. In the *McAlpine* case, it could be convincingly argued that the direct right of action enjoyed by X under the deed would indicate a clear intention that that document should exhaustively define X's rights. However what would be the position where the rights conferred on the third party were more limited? Where third parties do acquire a right under the Act they are entitled to whatever remedy they would be able to exercise if they were a party to the contract. This implies that the limitations (remoteness, mitigation etc) appropriate to an action for damages by a party to the contract will also be applicable to any action by the third party.

5.4.2 THE TRUST OF A PROMISE

At one time it appeared that the courts were prepared to use the concept of the 'trust' – that is, where a party who is the legal owner of property has an obligation to use it for the benefit of another – as a means of providing an exception to privity. This possibility was approved by the House of Lords in *Les Affréteurs Réunis SA v Leopold Walford (London) Ltd*.

Les Affréteurs Réunis SA v Leopold Walford (London) Ltd [1919] AC 801

Facts: A contract for the hire of a ship included a clause promising a commission to the broker, W, who had arranged the contract. W was not a party to the contract, and the parties argued that he could not enforce the promise of commission.

Held: The charterers, to whom the promise had been made, were trustees of this promise, so that it could be enforced by them on behalf of the broker.

Lord Birkenhead LC:

'... My Lords, the issues under debate seem to me to be so plain that they may conveniently be disposed of at once. This is an appeal from a decision of the Court of Appeal delivered on July 9, 1918, reversing a decision of Bailhache J. delivered on April 10, whereby he directed judgment to be entered for the defendants with costs. It follows from what I have said that the defendants are the appellants before your Lordships' House.

The facts are very simple. The charterers' brokers claim commission from the ship-owners under a charterparty dated September 28, 1916, which was a continuation of an earlier charterparty dated December 9, 1915, by which the SS *Flore* was demised. The owners were Les Affréteurs Réunis Société Anonyme and the charterers were the Lubricating and Fuel Oils, Ld. The relevant clause in the charterparty is No. 29, and is as follows: "A commission of three per cent. on the estimated gross amount of hire is due to Leopold Walford (London), Ld., on signing this charter (ship lost or not lost)."

Your Lordships are not troubled here with any question of amount.

My Lords, the first charterparty, that of December 9, 1915, would have ended on March 5, 1917, but its duration proved longer than the twelve months originally contemplated owing to an interruption with the details of which your Lordships are not concerned. The second charterparty would, if matters had remained normal, have commenced on March 5, but in the month of January the French Government requisitioned the ship. The first charterparty came to an end and the second never became effective. The second charterparty was entered into after an agreement between the owners and the charterers dated September 28, 1916, which contained the following clause: "The brokers will continue their good services to either party, but their total brokerage fixed for the charterparty at 5 per cent. will be reduced for the extension period to 3 per cent. For all other conditions of detail the brokers of the respective parties will have to fix together the final clauses, it being understood that the question of principle expressed above will be faithfully observed according to the good faith of the parties, and in accordance with the business customs in shipping matters and the spirit of the present agreement." Clause 34 of the second charterparty incorporated clause 26 of this agreement, and indeed the whole of this agreement, and should, I think, for clearness, be read: "This charterparty is in extension of that of December 9, 1915, and will take effect at the day and hour at which the earlier charterparty will terminate. Both charterparties are for their due fulfilment subject to the conditions and stipulations contained in the special agreement signed in Paris on September 28, 1916, by the two parties exactly as if these conditions and stipulations were embodied in the present charterparty itself."

My Lords, under those circumstances, the document must be read, in my judgment, as one whole, containing the clause of the French agreement to which I have directed attention. I do not, therefore, read the agreement in this matter as if your Lordships had to deal with a clause in the charterparty on the one hand, and an independent agreement known as the French agreement on the other. Having regard to the undeniable circumstance that the French agreement is incorporated in the charterparty it is impossible to consider that an independent agreement, in relation to the second charterparty, existed at all. A charterparty is, of course, a contract between owners and charterers, and it is elementary that, so far as the brokers are concerned, it is res inter alios acta; but the parties in the present case, by an interlocutory and very sensible arrangement, have agreed that the matter shall be dealt with as if the charterers were co-plaintiffs. The question therefore is, can the charterers succeed in such circumstances as the present in such an action against owners?

My Lords, it was decided nearly seventy years ago in the case of *Robertson v Wait* 8 Ex. 299 that charterers can sue under an agreement of this character as trustees for the broker. I am unable to distinguish between the decision in *Robertson v Wait* 8 Ex. 299 and the conclusion which, in my view, should be reached in the present case. It was conceded by Mr. Wright that unless there was a special and independent agreement in this case he was unable to distinguish the facts in this case from those which were considered in *Robertson v Wait*. In my opinion Mr. Wright has failed to establish the existence of an independent agreement.

My Lords, so far as I am aware, that case has not before engaged the attention of this House, and I think it right to say plainly that I agree with that decision and I agree with the reasoning, shortly as it is expressed, upon which the decision was founded. In this connection I would refer to the well-known case of *In re Empress Engineering Company* 16 Ch. D. 125, 129. In the judgment of Sir George Jessel M.R., the principle is examined which, in my view, underlies and is the explanation of the decision in *Robertson v Wait*. The Master of the Rolls uses this language: "So, again, it is quite possible that one of the parties to the agreement may be the nominee or trustee of the third person. As Lord Justice James suggested to me in the course of the argument, a married woman may nominate somebody to contract on her behalf, but then the person makes the contract really as trustee for somebody else, and it is because he contracts in that character that the cestui que trust can take the benefit of the contract."

It appears to me plain that for convenience, and under long-established practice, the broker in such cases, in effect, nominates the charterer to contract on his behalf, influenced probably by the circumstance that there is always a contract between charterer and owner in which this stipulation, which is to enure to the benefit of the broker, may very conveniently be inserted. In these cases the broker, on ultimate analysis, appoints the charterer to contract on his behalf. I agree therefore with the conclusion arrived at by all the learned judges in *Robertson v Wait*, that in such cases charterers can sue as trustees on behalf of the broker.'

Although there are other examples in the reported cases of the courts using the trust device as a means of circumventing the privity doctrine, it came to be held that it could only be used where there was a clear intention to create a trust, and one that was moreover irrevocable. Both of these factors influenced the court in *Re Schebsman*.

Re Schebsman [1944] Ch 83 (CA)

Facts: S's employer agreed on his retirement to pay him £5,500 in instalments over six years. If he died within that period, certain sums were to be payable to his widow. S did die within the six years, shortly after being declared bankrupt. His trustee in bankruptcy argued that the payments to Mrs S were made on the basis of a trust, and should form part of S's estate, going to pay off his creditors. The trial judge rejected this argument, the trustee appealed.

Lord Greene, MR:

'. . . The first question which arises is whether or not the debtor was a trustee for his wife and daughter of the benefit of the undertaking given by the English company in their favour. An examination of the decided cases does, it is true, show that the courts have on occasions adopted what may be called a liberal view on questions of this character, but in the present case I cannot find in the contract anything to justify the conclusion that a trust was intended. It is not legitimate to import into the contract the idea of a trust when the parties have given no indication that such was their intention. To interpret this contract as creating a trust would, in my judgment, be to disregard the dividing line between the case of a trust and the simple case of a contract made between two persons for the benefit of a third. That dividing line exists, although it may not always be easy to determine where it is to be drawn. In the present case I find no difficulty. . . .'

Du Parcq LJ:

'. . . I may now summarize the position at common law as follows: 1. It is the right, as well as the duty, of the company to make the prescribed payments to Mrs. Schebsman and to no other person. 2. Mrs. Schebsman may dispose of the sums so received as she pleases and is not accountable for them to the personal representatives of the debtor or to anyone claiming to stand in the shoes of the debtor. 3. If anyone standing in the shoes of the debtor were to intercept the sums payable to Mrs. Schebsman and refuse to account to her for them, he would be guilty of a breach of the debtor's contract with the company. 4. The obligation undertaken by the company cannot be varied at the will of the other party to the contract, but may be varied consensually at any time although the debtor is no longer living, as it could have been in his life-time.

It now remains to consider the question whether, and if so to what extent, the principles of equity affect the position of the parties. It was argued by Mr. Denning that one effect of the agreement of September 20, 1940, was that a trust was thereby created, and that the debtor constituted himself trustee for Mrs. Schebsman of the benefit of the covenant under which payments were to be made to her. Uthwatt J. rejected this contention, and the argument has not satisfied me that he was wrong. It is true that, by the use possibly of unguarded language, a person may create a trust, as Monsieur Jourdain talked prose, without knowing it, but unless an intention to create a trust is clearly to be collected from the language used and the circumstances of the case, I think that the court ought not to be astute to discover indications of such an intention. I have little doubt that in the present case both parties (and certainly the debtor) intended to keep alive their common law right to vary consensually the terms of the obligation undertaken by the company, and if circumstances had changed in the debtor's life-time injustice might have been done by holding that a trust had been created and that those terms were accordingly unalterable. On this point, therefore, I agree with Uthwatt J.'

There are no recent reported cases of a trust being successfully used as a means of circumventing privity and it is probably safe to treat this particular exception as effectively obsolete. It seems clear that the majority of judges did not regard it with enthusiasm.

The rise and fall of the trust as a means of circumventing privity is summarised in the following extract.

Smith, S, *Atiyah's Introduction to the Law of Contract*, 2006, 6th edn, Oxford: Clarendon Press, pp 348–50

6. Trusts

It has already been mentioned that the law of trusts, being closely associated with the law of property, is not subject to all the restrictions of the privity doctrine. So A and B can create a trust for the benefit of C without the participation of C at all. Indeed, it might happen that C is not even in existence when the trust is created, as frequently used to happen with the classic marriage settlement, where the beneficiaries would include the unborn children of the marriage. Nevertheless, such trusts were enforceable, and the doctrine of privity of contract was, and remains, irrelevant. The trust creates proprietary rights, so that the creation of the trust operates to transfer property rights to C, rather than to create merely personal rights in favour of C. Even if the trust is not completely constituted, so that it has to take effect as a contract, and not as an actual transfer of property (e.g. where the settlor merely covenants to transfer future property to the trustees, rather than making an actual transfer then and there), C will be able to enforce the trust if he is a child of the marriage in question. Despite his being a stranger to the contract and supplying no valuable consideration, he is said to be 'within the marriage consideration'. Any other person, however, who attempted to enforce an imperfectly constituted trust would be met by the plea that he was no party to the contract and had supplied no consideration.

Towards the end of the nineteenth century attempts were made to use the device of the trust as a general method to escape the doctrine of privity. Thus it came to be suggested that, whenever a contract purported to confer rights on third parties, the third parties could claim that a trust over such rights (a so-called 'trust of the promise') had been created in their favour; and could enforce their rights by way of trust. This was more or less the process by which assignments first came to be enforceable, for here also the common law at first refused to permit an assignee to sue on the contract because he was no party to it. In equity, the assignor came to be treated as a trustee for the assignee, and, once this result was reached, it became possible for the assignee to enforce the assignment himself. At first this had to be done in the name of the assignor, but after the Judicature Act 1873 even this was usually unnecessary.

For a time it looked as if a third party beneficiary might be treated in a similar way to an assignee. Specifically, there seemed to be a possibility that the third party would be able to enforce a contract by characterizing the promisee as a trustee. But in the twentieth century, the judicial attitude to this method of circumventing privity gradually

---

hardened until it was almost rejected altogether. While it is, of course, still open to a person to enforce a genuine trust of a contractual right without having been a party to its creation, it is no longer possible (unless the circumstances are wholly exceptional) to allege a fictitious trust merely as a device for the enforcement of contractual rights by a third party. Moreover, although it may be possible to find that a genuine trust has been created without the word 'trust' having been used, the cases show that this is an unlikely eventuality.

It is no doubt correct that in most contracts made for the benefit of a third party the contracting parties did not intend to create a trust or (what amounts to the same thing) to create an arrangement with the same legal consequences of a trust. But the validity of the trust in English law shows that English courts are willing to recognize the possibility of individuals obtaining legally enforceable rights by virtue of consensual arrangements to which they were not a party. Indeed, in legal systems that do not recognize trusts, an English trust is generally regarded as a contract for the benefit of a third party.

It should also be noted that there are a number of situations in which the courts are still willing to impose a 'constructive' (or 'fictional') trust on parties who did not intend to make a trust; this is done in order to give the intended beneficiary of the arrangement the same protection she would have had under a genuine trust. For example, where husband and wife make 'mutual wills' under which they agree to leave all their property in an agreed way, it is possible (subject to various limitations) to enforce the arrangements after the death of one of the parties by means of a constructive trust. One reason that courts have refused to take a similar approach in privity cases is that a trust, once constituted, is prima facie irrevocable except with the consent of the beneficiaries; and if some of the beneficiaries are under-age, or still unborn, it may be irrevocable altogether. If a contract between A and B which professes to confer rights on X is treated as creating a trust, it would follow (the courts have reasoned) that the contract was irrevocable as soon as it was made. So, for instance, if a man makes a contract with his employer that the employer will pay the employee's widow a pension if the employee dies in his employment after (say) twenty years' service, the courts have refused to treat the widow's claim to the pension as enforceable by way of trust. The reason given for this is that the employer and the employee might have wanted to vary or rescind the pension arrangements.

Despite the courts' (sensible) concern that implying a trust in these situations would serve to render contractual terms irrevocable, there are at least two ways such a result could have been avoided. First, they could have held that a contract for the benefit of a third party does create a trust, but a revocable trust. The concept of a revocable trust is by no means unknown to the law; and if it is legitimate to 'imply' a trust in order to do justice, there is no greater difficulty in 'implying' a power to revoke the trust for the same purpose. Alternatively, the courts could have held that the promisee holds the right of action to enforce the contract on trust for the third party. It is unnecessary to regard the contract itself as creating a trust in its inception; the need to invoke the concept of a trust only arises when enforcement is sought. At that date the third party could be treated as the beneficiary of a trust.

Thus, it can be seen that here, as so often in the law, results which appear to be dictated by the logic of legal principle are not so dictated at all. Legal rules can often be made to yield up a wide variety of results without any violation of fundamental principles; whether they do so or not depends to a large extent on the willingness of the courts to mould the law to new conditions. Sometimes—as in this area—the courts have taken the easy (one is tempted to say 'lazy') way out and refused to modify the law at all. On other occasions, in different areas of the law, the courts have been much more willing to adapt rules to new situations.

5.4.3 COLLATERAL CONTRACTS

One way of avoiding the effect of privity is to find that there is in fact a collateral contract between one of the main contracting parties and the third party. Since these two parties are now found to be in a contractual relationship, privity becomes irrelevant. The type of situation in which this can be used is illustrated by *Shanklin Pier v Detel Products*, in which the manufacturer of paint was held responsible for defects in it to someone who had specified that it should be used on a particular project.

Shanklin Pier Ltd v Detel Products Ltd [1951] 2 KB 854 (KBD)

Facts: S, the owners of a pier, were promised by D that D's paint, if used to repaint the pier would last for seven years. S specified to its painters that D's paint was to be used. The paint deteriorated after 3 months. There appeared to be no contract between S and D, so that S was without a remedy against D. The only contract relating to the paint, was that between D and S's painters.

Held: There was a collateral contract between S and D. In consideration for D's guarantee that the payment would last, S promised to specify the paint for use on the pier.

McNair J:

'. . . This case raises an interesting and comparatively novel question whether or not an enforceable warranty can arise as between parties other than parties to the main contract for the sale of the article in respect of which the warranty is alleged to have been given . . . .

The defence, stated broadly, is that no warranty such as is alleged in the statement of claim was ever given and that, if given, it would give rise to no cause of action between these parties. Accordingly, the first question which I have to determine is whether any such warranty was ever given . . . .

In the result, I am satisfied that, if a direct contract of purchase and sale of the DMU had then been made between the plaintiffs and the defendants, the correct conclusion on the facts would have been that the defendants gave to the plaintiffs the warranties substantially in the form alleged in the statement of claim. In reaching this conclusion, I adopt the principles stated by Holt, C.J., in *Crosse v Gardner* (1688) Comb. 142 and *Medina v Stoughton* (1700) 1 Salkeld 210 that an affirmation at the time of sale is a warranty, provided it appears on evidence to have been so intended.

Counsel for the defendants submitted that in law a warranty could give rise to no enforceable cause of action except between the same parties as the parties to the main contract in relation to which the warranty was given. In principle this submission seems to me to be unsound. If, as is elementary, the consideration for the warranty in the usual case is the entering into of the main contract in relation to which the warranty is given, I see no reason why there may not be an enforceable warranty between A and B supported by the consideration that B should cause C to enter into a contract with A or that B should do some other act for the benefit of A.

Counsel for the defendants, however, relied upon the decision of the Court of Appeal in *Drury v Victor Buckland LD* [1941] 1 All E. R. 269 and particularly upon the judgment of Scott, L.J. In that case the plaintiff, who had been approached by an agent of the defendants, dealers in refrigerating machines, agreed to purchase such a machine, but, being unable or unwilling to pay forthwith the whole of the purchase price, the deal was put through by the defendants' selling the machine to a finance company, who in turn entered into a hire-purchase agreement with the plaintiff, under which she eventually, when the whole of the hire-purchase instalments had been paid, acquired title to the machine. The machine proving unsatisfactory, the plaintiff sued the defendants, claiming damages for breach of the implied warranty or condition under s. 14, sub-s. 1, of the Sale of Goods Act, 1893.

The claim failed, Scott, L.J., saying: "It was a sale by the Buckland Company [the defendants] to the hire-purchase company. The property passed to them on the terms that they [the defendants] would get paid by the hire-purchase company. Therefore, the claim against them [the defendants] for damages for breach of warranty is a cause of action unsupported by any contract of sale which would carry it". This judgment can readily be understood in relation to its subject matter, namely, an implied statutory condition or warranty arising out of a contract of sale, and one can well understand it being said that, as there was no contract of sale between the plaintiff and defendants, no such implied warranty or condition could arise between them; but I do not read it as affording any support for the wider proposition for which counsel for the defendants contended.

The same view of the effect of this judgment as I have indicated was, I think, taken by Jones, J., in *Brown v Sheen and Richmond Car Sales LD* [1950] W. N. 316; [1950] 1 All E. R. 1102, a case in which the judge entered judgment against a motor car dealer on an express oral warranty given in relation to the purchase of a car, the transaction, as in Drury's case [1941] 1 All E. R. 269, being carried through with the assistance of a finance company. It was here sought to distinguish Brown's case on the ground that in the statement of facts in the report in All England Law Reports it was stated that "the plaintiff agreed to buy" the motor car from the defendants, but the pleadings in Brown's case, which I have examined, lend no support for suggesting that in that case there was in any legal sense any agreement to sell between the plaintiff and the defendants. The judgment of Hilbery, J., in *Parker v Oloxo LD* [1937] 3 All E. R. 524, 529 also, I think, negatives the defendants' submission in the present case.

Accordingly, in my judgment the plaintiffs are entitled to recover against the defendants damages for breach of the express warranties alleged.

In the similar case of *Wells Ltd v Buckland Sand and Silica Co Ltd* [1965] 2 QB 170 the same approach was applied, even though there was no specific contract in prospect when the supplier of sand made a promise as to its iron oxide content. It was held that the plaintiff, who later bought a quantity of the defendants' sand from a third party, could sue the defendant on the basis of a collateral contract. It was sufficient that there was a clear understanding that a purchase of the sand was planned for the near future (*animo contrahendi*).

5.4.4 AGENCY

English law has long recognised the usefulness of the concept of agency, whereby one person (the agent) may be given the authority to make contracts on behalf of another (the principal). This has the effect of bringing the third party with whom the agent deals into a direct contractual relationship with the principal. Everyday examples of agents include:

- most shop assistants – the contract is made between the customer and the shop-owner, not the shop assistant personally;
- company directors – they act on behalf of the company, which being inanimate, cannot physically sign documents, make agreements, etc.;
- estate agents – though it should be noted that they do not generally have the power to commit their principal to a contract.

In some situations there is no obligation for the agent to disclose to the third party that the contract is in fact being made with the principal. As far as the third party is concerned the contract is made with the person that s/he has been dealing with. To the extent that the undisclosed principal is given rights and obligations in relation to the contract, this appears to be an exception to the doctrine of privity.

The concept has also been combined with the idea of the collateral contract to enable a third party to take advantage of an exclusion clause in a contract between two other parties.

New Zealand Shipping Co. Ltd v Satterthwaite & Co. Ltd, The Eurymedon
[1975] AC 154 (PC)

Facts: A contract (comprised in a bill of lading) between the consignee of goods and the carrier purported to give stevedores, who had contracted with the carrier to unload the goods, the benefit of a limitation of liability provision. It was argued that the stevedores were not party to the contract between the consignee and the carrier, and so could not benefit from the clause.

Held: The carrier contracted as agent for the stevedores, so as to form a unilateral contract between the consignee and the stevedores, by which the consignee agreed to give the stevedore the benefit of the exclusion clause, in exchange for the stevedores unloading the goods.

Lord Wilberforce:
'The facts of this case are not in dispute. An expensive drilling machine was received on board the ship *Eurymedon* at Liverpool for transhipment to Wellington pursuant to the terms of a bill of lading no. 1262 dated June 5, 1964. The shipper was the maker of the drill, Ajax Machine Tool Co. Ltd ("the consignor"). The bill of lading was issued by agents for the Federal Steam Navigation Co. Ltd ("the carrier"). The consignee was A. M. Satterthwaite & Co. Ltd of Christchurch, New Zealand ("the consignee"). For several years before 1964 the New Zealand Shipping Co. Ltd ("the stevedore") had carried out all stevedoring work in Wellington in respect of the ships owned by the carrier, which was a wholly owned subsidiary of the stevedore. In addition to this stevedoring work the stevedore generally acted as agent for the carrier in New Zealand; and in such capacity as general agent (not in the course of their stevedoring functions) the stevedore received the bill of lading at Wellington on July 31, 1964. Clause 1 of the bill of lading, on the construction of which this case turns, was in the same terms as bills of lading usually issued by the stevedore and its associated companies in respect of ordinary cargo carried by their ships from the United Kingdom to New Zealand. The consignee became the holder of the bill of lading and owner of the drill prior to August 14, 1964. On that day the drill was damaged as a result of the stevedore's negligence during unloading.

At the foot of the first page of the bill of lading the following words were printed in small capitals:

> In accepting this bill of lading the shipper, consignee and the owners of the goods, and the holders of this bill of lading agree to be bound by all of its conditions, exceptions and provisions whether written, printed or stamped on the front or back hereof.

... The incorporation in the bill of lading of the rules scheduled to the Carriage of Goods by Sea Act 1924 meant that the carrier and the ship were discharged from all liability in respect of the damage to the drill unless suit was brought against them within one year after delivery. No action was commenced until April 1967, when the consignee sued the stevedore in negligence, claiming £880 the cost of repairing the damaged drill.

The question in the appeal is whether the stevedore can take the benefit of the time limitation provision. The starting point, in discussion of this question, is provided by the House of Lords decision in *Midland Silicones Ltd v Scruttons Ltd* [1962] AC. 446. There is no need to question or even to qualify that case in so far as it affirms the general proposition that a contract between two parties cannot be sued on by a third person even though the contract is expressed to be for his benefit. Nor is it necessary to disagree with anything which was said to the same effect in the Australian case of *Wilson v Darling Island Stevedoring and Lighterage Co Ltd* (1956) 95 C.L.R. 43. Each of these cases was dealing with a simple case of a contract the benefit of which was sought to be taken by a third person not a party to it, and the emphatic pronouncements in the speeches and judgments were directed to this situation. But *Midland Silicones* left open the case where one of the parties contracts as agent for the third person: in particular Lord Reid's speech spelt out, in four propositions, the prerequisites for the validity of such an agency contract. There is of course nothing unique to this case in the conception of agency contracts: well known and common instances exist in the field of hire purchase, of bankers' commercial credits and other transactions. Lord Reid said, at p 474:

> "I can see a possibility of success of the agency argument if (first) the bill of lading makes it clear that the stevedore is intended to be protected by the provisions in it which limit liability, (secondly) the bill of lading makes it clear that the carrier, in addition to contracting for these provisions on his own behalf, is also contracting as agent for the stevedore that these provisions should apply to the stevedore, (thirdly) the carrier has authority from the stevedore to do that, or perhaps later ratification by the stevedore would suffice, and (fourthly) that any difficulties about consideration moving from the stevedore were overcome and then to affect the consignee it would be necessary to show that the provisions of the Bills of Lading Act 1855 apply."

The question in this appeal is whether the contract satisfies these propositions. Clause 1 of the bill of lading, whatever the defects in its drafting, is clear in its relevant terms. The carrier, on his own account, stipulates for certain exemptions and immunities: among these is that conferred by article III, rule 6, of the Hague Rules which discharges the carrier from all liability for loss or damage unless suit is brought within one year after delivery. In addition to these stipulations on his own account, the carrier as agent for, inter alios, independent contractors stipulates for the same exemptions.

Much was made of the fact that the carrier also contracts as agent for numerous other persons; the relevance of this argument is not apparent. It cannot be disputed that among such independent contractors, for whom, as agent, the carrier contracted, is the appellant company which habitually acts as stevedore in New Zealand by arrangement with the carrier and which is, moreover, the parent company of the carrier. The carrier was, indisputably, authorised by the appellant to contract as its agent for the purposes of clause 1. All of this is quite straightforward and was accepted by all the judges in New Zealand. The only question was, and is, the fourth question presented by Lord Reid, namely that of consideration.

It was on this point that the Court of Appeal differed from Beattie J holding that it had not been shown that any consideration for the shipper's promise as to exemption moved from the promisee, i.e., the appellant company.

If the choice, and the antithesis, is between a gratuitous promise, and a promise for consideration, as it must be in the absence of a tertium quid, there can be little doubt which, in commercial reality, this is. The whole contract is of a commercial character, involving service on one side, rates of payment on the other, and qualifying stipulations as to both. The relations of all parties to each other are commercial relations entered into for business reasons of ultimate profit. To describe one set of promises, in this context, as gratuitous, or nudum pactum, seems paradoxical and is prima facie implausible. It is only the precise analysis of this complex of relations into the classical offer and acceptance, with identifiable consideration, that seems to present difficulty, but this same difficulty exists in many situations of daily life, e.g., sales at auction; supermarket purchases; boarding an omnibus; purchasing a train ticket; tenders for the supply of goods; offers of rewards; acceptance by post; warranties of authority by agents; manufacturers' guarantees; gratuitous bailments; bankers' commercial credits. These are all examples which show that English law, having committed itself to a rather technical and schematic doctrine of contract in application takes a practical approach, often at the cost of forcing the facts to fit uneasily into the marked slots of offer, acceptance and consideration.

In their Lordships' opinion the present contract presents much less difficulty than many of those above referred to. It is one of carriage from Liverpool to Wellington. The carrier assumes an obligation to transport the goods and to discharge at the port of arrival. The goods are to be carried and discharged, so the transaction is inherently contractual. It is contemplated that a part of this contract, viz. discharge, may be performed by independent contractors – viz. the appellant. By clause 1 of the bill of lading the shipper agrees to exempt from liability the carrier, his servants and independent contractors in respect of the performance of this contract of carriage. Thus, if the carriage, including the discharge, is wholly carried out by the carrier, he is exempt. If part is carried out by him and part by his servants, he and they are exempt. If part is carried out by him and part by an independent contractor, he and the independent contractor are exempt. The exemption is designed to cover the whole carriage from loading to discharge, by whomsoever it is performed: the performance attracts the exemption or immunity in favour of whoever the performer turns out to be. There is possibly more than one way of analysing this business transaction into the necessary components; that which their Lordships would accept is to say that the bill of lading brought into existence a bargain initially unilateral but capable of becoming mutual, between the shipper and the appellant, made through the carrier as agent. This became a full contract when the appellant performed services by discharging the goods. The performance of these services for the benefit of the shipper was the consideration for the agreement by the shipper that the appellant should have the benefit of the exemptions and limitations contained in the bill of lading. The conception of a "unilateral" contract of this kind was recognized in *Great Northern Railway Co v Witham* (1873) LR 9 CP 16 and is well established. This way of regarding the matter is very close to if not identical to that accepted by Beattie J in the Supreme Court: he analysed the transaction as one of an offer open to acceptance by action such as was found in *Carlill v Carbolic Smoke Ball Co* [1893] 1 QB 256. But whether one describes the shippers' promise to exempt as an offer to be accepted by performance or as a promise in exchange for an act seems in the present context to be a matter of semantics. The words of Bowen LJ in *Carlill v Carbolic Smoke Ball Co* [1893] 1 QB 256, 268: "why should not an offer be made to all the world which is to ripen into a contract with anybody who comes forward and performs the condition?" seem to bridge both conceptions: he certainly seems to draw no distinction between an offer which matures into a contract when accepted and a promise which matures into a contract after performance, and, though in some special contexts (such as in connection with the right to withdraw) some further refinement may be needed, either analysis may be equally valid. On the main point in the appeal, their Lordships are in substantial agreement with Beattie J.

The following points require mention. 1. In their Lordships' opinion, consideration may quite well be provided by the appellant, as suggested, even though (or if) it was already under an obligation to discharge to the carrier. (There is no direct evidence of the existence or nature of this obligation, but their Lordships are prepared to assume it.) An agreement to do an act which the promisor is under an existing obligation to a third party to do, may quite well amount to valid consideration and does so in the present case: the promisee obtains the benefit of a direct obligation which he can enforce. This proposition is illustrated and supported by *Scotson v Pegg* (1861) 6 H & N 295 which their Lordships consider to be good law . . . .'

Viscount Dilhorne and Lord Simon of Glaisdale dissented from the above majority judgment.

The approach taken in the above case was also adopted in *The New York Star* [1981] 1 WLR 138. In *The Mahkutai* [1996] AC 650, while accepting the general principle established in the earlier cases, the Privy Council suggested that it might be time for a more general exception to privity to be adopted, rather than relying on the technical arguments based on agency and consideration set out in *New Zealand Shipping Company v Satterthwaite.*

The Mahkutai [1996] AC 650

Lord Goff of Chievely:

'. . . *Critique of the Eurymedon principle*
In *The New York Star* [1981] 1 W.L.R. 138, 144, Lord Wilberforce discouraged "a search

for fine distinctions which would diminish the general applicability, in the light of established commercial practice, of the principle." He was there, of course, speaking of the application of the principle in the case of stevedores. It has however to be recognised that, so long as the principle continues to be understood to rest upon an enforceable contract as between the cargo owners and the stevedores entered into through the agency of the shipowner, it is inevitable that technical points of contract and agency law will continue to be invoked by cargo owners seeking to enforce tortious remedies against stevedores and others uninhibited by the exceptions and limitations in the relevant bill of lading contract. Indeed, in the present case their Lordships have seen such an exercise being legitimately undertaken by Mr. Aikens on behalf of the cargo owners. In this connection their Lordships wish to refer to the very helpful consideration of the principle in *Palmer on Bailment*, 2nd edn. (1991), at pp 1610–1625, which reveals many of the problems which may arise, and refers to a number of cases, both in England and in Commonwealth countries, in which the courts have grappled with those problems. In some cases, notably but by no means exclusively in England, courts have felt impelled by the established principles of the law of contract or of agency to reject the application of the principle in the particular case before them. In others, courts have felt free to follow the lead of Lord Wilberforce in *The Eurymedon* [1975] A.C. 154, and of Lord Wilberforce and Barwick C.J. in *The New York Star* [1981] 1 W.L.R. 138; [1979] 1 Lloyd's Rep. 298, and so to discover the existence of a contract (nowadays a bilateral contract of the kind identified by Barwick C.J.) in circumstances in which lawyers of a previous generation would have been unwilling to do so.

Nevertheless there can be no doubt of the commercial need of some such principle as this, and not only in cases concerned with stevedores; and the bold step taken by the Privy Council in *The Eurymedon* [1975] A.C. 154, and later developed in *The New York Star* [1981] 1 W.L.R. 138, has been widely welcomed. But it is legitimate to wonder whether that development is yet complete. Here their Lordships have in mind not only Lord Wilberforce's discouragement of fine distinctions, but also the fact that the law is now approaching the position where, provided that the bill of lading contract clearly provides that (for example) independent contractors such as stevedores are to have the benefit of exceptions and limitations contained in that contract, they will be able to enjoy the protection of those terms as against the cargo owners. This is because (1) the problem of consideration in these cases is regarded as having been solved on the basis that a bilateral agreement between the stevedores and the cargo owners, entered into through the agency of the shipowners, may, though itself unsupported by consideration, be rendered enforceable by consideration subsequently furnished by the stevedores in the form of performance of their duties as stevedores for the shipowners; (2) the problem of authority from the stevedores to the shipowners to contract on their behalf can, in the majority of cases, be solved by recourse to the principle of ratification; and (3) consignees of the cargo may be held to be bound on the principle in *Brandt v Liverpool, Brazil and River Plate Steam Navigation Co Ltd* [1924] 1 K.B. 575. Though these solutions are now perceived to be generally effective for their purpose, their technical nature is all too apparent; and the time may well come when, in an appropriate case, it will fall to be considered whether the courts should take what may legitimately be perceived to be the final, and perhaps inevitable, step in this development, and recognise in these cases a fully-fledged exception to the doctrine of privity of contract, thus escaping from all the technicalities with which courts are now faced in English law. It is not far from their Lordships' minds that, if the English courts were minded to take that step, they would be following in the footsteps of the Supreme Court of Canada: see *London Drugs Ltd v Kuehne & Nagel International Ltd* (1992) 97 D.L.R. (4th) 261 and, in a different context, the High Court of Australia: see *Trident General Insurance Co Ltd v McNiece Bros Pty Ltd* (1988) 165 C.L.R. 107. Their Lordships have given consideration to the question whether they should face up to this question in the present appeal. However, they have come to the conclusion that it would not be appropriate for them to do so, first, because they have not heard argument specifically directed towards this fundamental question, and second because, as will become clear in due course, they are satisfied that the appeal must in any event be dismissed.'

It may well be that the enactment of the statutory exception in the Contracts (Rights of Third Parties) Act 1999, which enables parties to achieve the end result of giving third parties the benefit of an exclusion clause by more direct means, will mean that the courts will be reluctant to take the step suggested by Lord Goff in the above extract, in creating a more general common-law exception to privity.

5.5 IMPOSITION OF OBLIGATIONS

The main exception to the aspect of privity, which prevents a contract imposing obligations on a third party, falls within land law. The seller of a piece of land is able to control the uses to which subsequent purchasers put the land, by means of a 'restrictive covenant', attached to the initial transfer of ownership. This principle derives from the case of *Tulk v Moxhay* (1848) 2 Ph 774; 41 ER 1143, but its application in the context of land transactions is not discussed further here. In *Taddy v Sterious* an attempt to apply this approach more generally to the law of contract was firmly rejected.

Taddy v Sterious [1904] 1 Ch 354

Facts: The manufacturers of tobacco attached a notice to packets indicating that they were not to be sold below the stipulated price. Acceptance of the goods was deemed to be the acceptance of these conditions, and where the goods were bought from a wholesaler, the wholesaler was deemed to be the agent of the manufacturer.

Held: The purchaser of the tobacco from a wholesaler was not bound by the price stipulation clause.

Swinfen Eady J:

'In this case the plaintiffs are manufacturers of tobacco. There are two defendants – Sterious & Co., who are retail tobacconists at Southend, and James Netten, a wholesale dealer. The plaintiffs submit to have their action dismissed with costs as against Netten; there only remains, therefore, their action against Sterious & Co. The object of the action is to obtain a declaration that these defendants are not entitled to sell any packet tobaccos manufactured by the plaintiffs except at such prices and generally upon terms and conditions of supply as were specified and contained in their invoices, price-lists, and catalogues, and also in labels and notices attached to the boxes in which the tobacco was sold, and an injunction . . . .

The defendants have dealt in the plaintiffs' tobaccos for some time. It is not suggested that they were ignorant of the terms and conditions issued by the plaintiffs. Complaints were made on several occasions of the defendants selling under the minimum price, and since the writ was issued the defendant Netten has agreed not to sell them any more of this tobacco, and the supply from that source has ceased. But the claim made by Taddy & Co. is not confined to tobacco obtained by Sterious & Co. from Netten, but is quite general. The plaintiffs put their case in two ways. First, they contended that the conditions constituted a contract made by Sterious & Co. with Netten as the plaintiffs' agents, and that they are entitled to restrain Sterious & Co. from acting in breach of that contract. Secondly, they contended that the goods were sold subject to certain conditions, and that even if Netten or any one else had purported to sell them free from the conditions, Sterious & Co., having notice of the conditions, could not sell the goods except according to the conditions, and the plaintiffs were entitled to restrain them from doing so.

With regard to this last contention, there is a short answer. Conditions of this kind do not run with goods, and cannot be imposed upon them. Subsequent purchasers, therefore, do not take subject to any conditions which the Court can enforce. If there was a breach of contract, the plaintiffs could no doubt sue. The question remains, therefore, whether there was any contract. There was no direct contract between Sterious & Co. and Taddy & Co., and the question does not arise as to the effect of a sale by Taddy & Co. direct to a retail trader subject to these terms as to minimum retail price. The part of the conditions now in question is: "In the case of a purchase by a retail dealer through a wholesale dealer, the latter shall be deemed to be the agent of Taddy & Co." Now it is quite clear that Taddy & Co. sell to wholesale dealers out and out. The wholesale dealers are not Taddy & Co.'s agents to sell the goods; they buy them out and out, and sell them for their own profit. It was argued that the words in the special condition, "purchase by a retail dealer through a wholesale dealer", can only refer to cases where the wholesale dealers really are the agents of Taddy & Co., and do not apply to cases where the wholesale dealers first bought and then resold. That seems to be the right construction. If, however, the condition ought to be construed as applying to a purchase from as well as through a wholesale dealer – even then, a wholesale dealer selling for his own profit would not be an agent of Taddy & Co. in the ordinary sense of that term. Nor can it be said that the wholesale dealer was selling the goods for his own profit, and at the same time entered into a collateral contract with the purchaser, as to the subsequent dealing with the goods, as the agent of Taddy & Co. No such collateral contract was in fact entered into. In my opinion, when the wholesale dealer sold the goods for his own profit, he was not in any sense whatever the agent of Taddy & Co., and the mere insertion in the condition of the words that he was to be deemed to be an agent could not make him one. Whatever may be the case as between Taddy & Co. and Netten, there is no contract between Taddy & Co. and Sterious & Co.'

Despite this rejection of any general application of a 'restrictive covenant' approach outside the area of land law, in some cases a similar principle was successfully applied in some shipping contracts. In *Port Line v Ben Line Ltd*, however, Diplock J took the view that these cases were explicable as examples of the tort of wrongful interference with contractual rights, rather than an equitable principle analogous to restrictive covenants.

Port Line Ltd v Ben Line Steamers Ltd [1957 P. No. 85.]; [1958] 2 W.L.R. 551

Diplock J:
'The plaintiffs' charterparty with Silver Line was a gross time charter, not one by demise. It gave the plaintiffs no right of property in or to possession of the vessel. It was one by which Silver Line agreed with the plaintiffs that for 30 months from March 9, 1955, they would render services by their servants and crew to carry the goods which were put on the vessel by the plaintiffs: see *per* MacKinnon L.J. in *Sea and Land Securities Ltd v William Dickinson & Co Ltd* [1942] 2 K.B. 65, 69; 58 T.L.R. 210; [1942] 1 All E.R. 503. By parting with their property in the vessel on February 8, 1956, and retaining a right to possession and use which terminated on its requisition, Silver Line put it out of their power to continue to perform their contractual services after the vessel was requisitioned. It is true that during the period of requisition (which is the only period with which I am concerned) Silver Line could not have performed their contractual services to the plaintiffs anyway, but the plaintiffs would have been entitled under section 4 (3) of the Compensation (Defence) Act, 1939, to the bareboat element of any compensation received by Silver Line from the Crown, and would have had to pay to Silver Line a rather larger sum by way of hire under the charterparty. It would seem, therefore, that so far as the period of requisition itself is concerned, the plaintiffs would have gained rather than lost by any breach of the contract by Silver Line which relieved the plaintiffs from paying to Silver Line the chartered hire. This, however, is a

matter between Silver Line and the plaintiffs with which I am not called upon to deal except in so far (if at all) as it may be relevant to the determination of the plaintiffs' rights against the defendants. There was no privity of contract between the plaintiffs and the defendants. On what ground, therefore, can they assert against the defendants all or any of the contractual rights they had against Silver Line, or any statutory rights which they would have had against Silver Line by virtue of the existence of such contractual rights?

It is contended that the plaintiffs' rights against the defendants stem from the principle laid down by Knight Bruce L.J. in *De Mattos v Gibson* (1858) 4 De G. & J. 276 in 1858 as approved by the Privy Council in the Lord Strathcona case. [1926] A.C. 108. The principle laid down by Knight Bruce L.J. in *De Mattos v Gibson* in granting on appeal an interlocutory injunction to restrain a mortgagee of a ship who had acquired his mortgage with knowledge of the plaintiffs' subsisting charterparty from interfering with the performance of a subsisting voyage charter was in the following oft-quoted terms: "Reason and justice seem to prescribe that, at least as a general rule, where a man, by gift or purchase, acquires property from another, with knowledge of a previous contract, lawfully and for valuable consideration made by him with a third person, to use and employ the property for a particular purpose in a specified manner, the acquirer shall not, to the material damage of the third person, in opposition to the contract and inconsistently with it, use and employ the property in a manner not allowable to the giver or seller." In 1858 this was new law in *Tulk v Moxhay* (1848) 2 Ph. 774 decided 10 years before, on which Knight Bruce L.J.'s statement has been assumed to be based, Lord Cottenham L.C.'s ratio decidendi was based on the retention by the covenantee of land the value of which would be diminished by breach of the covenant. Turner L.J., who sat with Knight Bruce L.J. in the interlocutory appeal in *De Mattos v Gibson*, gave a separate judgment which was subsequently treated as correctly propounding the questions to be determined at the trial, and expressed no concurrence with Knight Bruce L.J.'s reasons. When the action came for trial before the Lord Chancellor, Lord Chelmsford L.C. did not grant an injunction. It would appear on analysis of his judgment that he treated the right to an injunction as depending on the same principle as the right to damages in *Lumley v Gye*, (1853) 2 E. & B. 216 decided five years before, namely, that it is a tort knowingly to procure a breach of contract by another person.

De Mattos v Gibson was followed five years later with expressed reluctance by Wood V.-C. in *Messageries Imperiales Co v Baines*, (1863) 7 L.T. 763 but I am inclined to think on the principle laid down by Lord Chelmsford L.C. rather than that laid down by Knight Bruce L.J. The broad principle as laid down by Knight Bruce L.J. applies to all species of property – real property, chattels and choses in action alike. It was applied (or at any rate treated as correct) in a number of cases relating to each of those species up to the turn of the century, but as a doctrine dependent upon notice alone was finally discredited in *London County Council v Allen* [1914] 3 K.B. 642. Scrutton L.J. there shed a tear over its demise as respects real property, but five years later in *Barker v Stickney* [1919] 1 K.B. 121 he regarded the period of mourning as over, and his judgment conveniently lists (and so saves me from citing) the cases which he considered had buried it as respects each class of property. In 1926, however, it rose from the grave in the Strathcona case which, being a decision of the Privy Council, is not binding upon me, but being, one of a Board which included Lords Haldane, Wrenbury and Blanesburgh, in addition to Lord Shaw, is (so far as it deals with questions of equity) entitled to respect which in a common law lawyer borders upon awe.

It may be relevant to note that in the Strathcona case the buyers of the vessel subject to the time charter in favour of the plaintiffs had express notice of the terms of the charter, and had covenanted with the sellers to perform and accept all responsibilities under it. It was, as the Board said, not a mere case of notice of the existence of a covenant affecting the use of the property sold, but a case of acceptance of the property expressly sub conditione. The initial emphasis on this, and the reference at a later stage to the possibility that a shipowner might declare himself a trustee of his obligations under a charterparty so as to bind his assignee might suggest as a possible ratio decidendi that the Strathcona case was one where either the purchaser used expressions which amounted to a declaration of trust in favour of the charterers, or the vendor himself accepted the benefit of the covenant as trustee for the charterers. But an examination of the Board's opinion as a whole seems to indicate that they accepted the full doctrine of Knight Bruce L.J. as respects chattels, namely, that mere notice does give rise to the equity, the only qualification that the Board imposed being that "an interest must remain" (sc. in the person seeking the remedy) "in the subject matter of the covenant before a right can be conceded to an injunction against the violation by another of the covenant in question." The only remedy which the Board in terms recognized is a remedy by injunction against the use of the ship by the purchaser inconsistent with the charterparty, but they said, in a passage on which Mr. Roskill for the plaintiffs strongly relies, that the purchaser "appears to be plainly in the position of a constructive trustee with obligations which a court of equity will not permit him to violate."

These passages pose several problems: (1) If, as the Board state, the ship is the "subject-matter" of the covenant of which the violation by another is to be restrained, it is difficult to see in what sense a charterer under a gross time charter has an interest in that subject-matter except in the broad sense that it is to his commercial advantage that his covenantor should continue to use the ship to perform the services which he has covenanted to perform. But the time charter is a contract for services. The time charterer has no proprietary or possessory rights in the ship, and if the covenantee's commercial advantage in the observance of the covenant is sufficient to constitute an "interest" in the chattel to which the covenant relates, it is difficult to see why the principle does not apply to price fixing cases such as *Dunlop Pneumatic Tyre Co Ltd v Selfridge & Co Ltd*. The Board explain cases like Dunlop's case, which had been cited to them, as cases where the plaintiff had no interest in the subject-matter of the contract. They say that the charterer has and will have during the continuance of the charterparty "a plain interest" (in the ship) "so long as she is fit to go to sea". Plain though it may be, if the expression "interest" is used colloquially, the Board nowhere explain what the legal nature of that interest is.

(2) Whether the reference to the subsequent purchaser with notice as being, also "plainly", in the position of a constructive trustee imports that equity provides other remedies against him by his cestui que trust, such as the right to an account, the making of a vesting order or the appointment of a new trustee is nowhere discussed in the Strathcona case; but the whole trend of the opinion, the actual order made and the observation of the Board: "It is incredible that the owners will lay up the vessel rather than permit its use under the contract" all strongly suggest that the only remedy in the view of the Board that the charterer acquired against the subsequent purchaser was the purely negative remedy, namely, to restrain a user of the vessel inconsistent with the terms of his charter with the former owner, and the obligations of the purchaser which a court of equity will not allow him to violate are the negative obligation not to make such inconsistent user of the vessel. As a "constructive trustee" the subsequent purchaser seems to be one sui generis, and I should hesitate as a common law lawyer to seek to devise other remedies against him which did not apparently occur to the Board

(3) The Board in the Strathcona case, beyond saying that that case was not one of "mere notice", did not discuss what kind of notice to the purchaser of the charterer's rights gives rise to the equity, namely, whether at the time of his acquisition of his interest in the vessel he must have actual knowledge of the charterer's rights against the seller, the violation of which it is sought to restrain, or whether "constructive notice" will suffice. "Reason and justice" – the sole though weighty grounds on which Knight Bruce L.J. based the equity – do not seem to me to prescribe the introduction into commercial matters such as the sale of a ship of the doctrine of constructive notice. I respectfully agree with Lindley L.J.'s observations in *Manchester Trust v Furness* [1895] 2 Q.B. 539, 545. Furthermore, as between vendor and purchaser of real property, where the doctrine has been developed, constructive notice – like estoppel in less esoteric matters – is a shield not a weapon of offence. It protects an already existing equitable interest from being defeated by a purchaser for value without notice. It is not itself the source of an equitable interest.

The Strathcona case, although decided over 30 years ago, has never been followed in the English courts, and has never come up for direct consideration. In *Clore v Theatrical Properties Ltd* [1936] 3 All E.R. 483, 490 Lord Wright M.R. suggested in passing that it might be peculiar to ships, but no such suggestion is to be found in the Strathcona case itself. In *Greenhalgh v Mallard* [1943] 2 All E.R. 234 Lord Greene M.R., in a judgment concurred in by Luxmoore L.J. and Goddard L.J., was clearly of opinion that it was wrongly decided, although it is only fair to add that as recently as 1952, Denning L.J. gave it a not unfriendly passing glance in *Bendall v McWhirter* [1952] 2 Q.B. 466; [1952] 1 T.L.R. 1332; [1952] 1 All E.R. 1307.

It seems, therefore, that it is in this case for the first time after more than 30 years that an English court has to grapple with the problem of what principle was really laid down in the Strathcona case, and whether that case was rightly decided. The difficulty I have found in ascertaining its ratio decidendi, the impossibility which I find of reconciling the actual decision with well-established principles of law, the unsolved and, to me, insoluble problems which that decision raises combine to satisfy me that it was wrongly decided. I do not propose to follow it. I naturally express this opinion with great diffidence, but having reached a clear conclusion it is my duty to express it.

If I am wrong in my view that the case was wrongly decided, I am certainly averse from extending it one iota beyond that which, as I understand it, it purported to decide. In particular, I do not think that it purported to decide (1) that anything short of actual knowledge by the subsequent purchaser at the time of the purchase of the charterer's rights, the violation of which it is sought to restrain, is sufficient to give rise to the equity; (2) that the charterer has any remedy against the subsequent purchaser with notice except a right to restrain the use of the vessel by such purchaser in a manner inconsistent with the terms of the charter; (3) that the charterer has any positive right against the subsequent purchaser to have the vessel used in accordance with the terms of his charter. The third proposition follows from the second; ubi jus ibi remedium. For failure by the subsequent purchaser to use the vessel in accordance with the terms of the charter entered into by his seller there is no remedy by specific performance as was held in the Strathcona case itself. There is equally no remedy in damages, a consideration which distinguishes the Strathcona case from such cases as *Lumley v Wagner* and *Lumley v Gye*. The charterer's only right is coterminous with his remedy, namely, not to have the ship used by the purchaser in violation of his charter.'

The trial judge in *Swiss Bank Corporation v Lloyds Bank Ltd* [1979] Ch 548 held that where there was a specifically enforceable obligation to deal with property in a particular way, this could give the party to whom the obligation was owed an equitable right over the property concerned, and that this would bind a third party. The Court of Appeal and House of Lords decided the case on other grounds, and no subsequent case has picked up on it, so it seems that the approach taken in *Port Line v Ben Line* is still likely to represent the current law in this area.

5.6 PRIVITY UNDER THE PRINCIPLES OF EUROPEAN CONTRACT LAW

The provisions of the Principles of European Contract Law dealing with privity are very similar to those to be found in the Contracts (Rights of Third Parties) Act 1999, though much less detailed. They are set out in Article 6.110.

Article 6.110 – Stipulation in Favour of a Third Party

(1) A third party may require performance of a contractual obligation when its right to do so has been expressly agreed upon between the promisor and the promisee, or when such agreement is to be inferred from the purpose of the contract or the circumstances of the case. The third party need not be identified at the time the agreement is concluded.

(2) If the third party renounces the right to performance the right is treated as never having accrued to it.

(3) The promisee may by notice to the promisor deprive the third party of the right to performance unless:

    (a) the third party has received notice from the promisee that the right has been made irrevocable, or

    (b) the promisor or the promisee has received notice from the third party that the latter accepts the right.

5.7 ADDITIONAL READING

Adams, J and Brownsword, R, 'Privity and the concept of a network contract' (1990) 10 Legal Studies 12.

Adams, J, Beyleveld, D and Brownsword, R, 'Privity of contract – the benefits and burdens of law reform' (1997) 60 MLR 238.

Burrows, A, 'The Contracts (Rights of Third Parties) Act and its implications for commercial contracts' [2000] LMCLQ 540.

Flannigan, R, 'Privity – the end of an era (error)' (1987) 103 LQR 564.

Law Commission, Consultation Paper No 121, *Privity of Contract: Contracts for the benefit of third parties'*, 1991.

Law Revision Committee, 6th Interim Report, 1937, Cmnd 5449.

Smith, S, 'Contracts for the benefit of third parties: in defence of the Third-Party Rule' (1997) OJLS 643.

Waddams, S, 'Johanna Wagner and the rival opera houses' (2001) 117 LQR 431.

CAPACITY

▌6.1 INTRODUCTION

In certain situations the courts will refuse to enforce a contract that appears to be valid because of the lack of capacity of one of the parties. This chapter considers three situations where this issue can arise: where one party is a 'minor' (under the age of 18); where one party is intoxicated; and where one party suffers from some mental disability. In all three cases the subject matter of the contract may be important. In particular, it will generally be the case that contracts that have involved the supply of 'necessary' goods to a party lacking capacity will be enforceable by the other party. In relation to minors' contracts, certain other contracts, such as beneficial contracts of service, are also enforceable.

Lack of capacity, which may arise through the doctrine of 'ultra vires' in relation to companies, is not dealt with in this text. The area is largely governed by statute and is more properly the concern of company law.

The order of treatment is to look first at minors' contracts, which is the most significant area, then at mental disability, and finally at intoxication.

6.2 MINORS' CONTRACTS

For the purposes of English law a 'minor' is a person under the age of 18. This was reduced from 21 by the Family Law Reform Act 1969. Some of the older case law refers to 'infants' ' contracts, but the more modern terminology has been in use for at least 20 years. The rationale of the law is to ensure that young people are not exploited by older contracting parties, and do not enter into contractual commitments that are inappropriate to their circumstances. It provides an exception to the general policy of 'freedom of contract', which underpins much of English contract law. The law in these circumstances is not simply acting as a 'referee', supervising the implementation of freely made agreements, but intervenes to provide protection from one of the contracting parties.

The starting point is that a contract made with a minor is unenforceable by the adult party (though may well be enforceable by the minor). Two main exceptions exist, relating to:

1. The supply of necessary goods or services;
2. Beneficial contracts of service (employment).

6.2.1 NECESSARIES

It is reasonable that a minor should be able to make valid contracts to obtain the essentials of life – food, clothing, accommodation – particularly when it is considered that a person under the age of 18 may well be married, and have responsibilities as a parent. It would be unacceptable for such individuals to have to rely on their parents or other adults to make contracts on their behalf. From the point of view of the law, such essentials of life fall into the category of 'necessary' goods and services. The definition of what constitutes 'necessaries' is to be found in a mixture of case law and statute.

Chapple v Cooper (1844) 3 M & W 252

Facts: A widow, who was a minor, contracted with the plaintiff, an undertaker, in relation to her husband's funeral. When the undertaker sought payment, she resisted on the basis that she lacked capacity to make the contract.

Held: The contract was for necessary services, and so was enforceable against the minor.

Alderson, B:
'We took time to consider this case, which, in the course of the last term, was argued before my Brothers Gurney and Rolfe and myself. The declaration was in the ordinary

form for work and labour and materials found. To this the defendant pleaded infancy; and the replication stated that the goods were necessaries. At the trial, it appeared that the plaintiff, being an undertaker, had, by the defendant's order, conducted the funeral of her husband. The jury, under my Brother Gurney's direction, found a verdict for the plaintiff, damages £10, being the reasonable amount of such expenses.

On the motion to enter a verdict for the defendant, the various authorities have been brought before us. My Brother Byles, in his argument, ingeniously suggested a variety of cases in which such expenses as these might become necessaries from the peculiar situation of the infant, as if she were sick and had only one apartment in which the body lay, and so the removal of the offence therefrom arising might be as much a necessary to her as medicine for her sickness. But it is manifest that such cases would be determined on their special circumstances, and it is a sufficient answer to this argument to say that no such special circumstances exist here. This question, therefore, must depend on the general principles by which the validity of an infant's contracts are to governed. Now it seems clear that an infant can contract so as to bind himself in those cases where it is necessary for him to have the things for which he contracts; or where the contract is, at the time he makes it, plainly and unequivocally for his benefit. It is with the former class that we are concerned. Things necessary are those without which an individual cannot reasonably exist. In the first place, food, raiment, lodging, and the like. About these there is no doubt. Again, as the proper cultivation of the mind is as expedient as the support of the body, instruction in art or trade, or intellectual, moral, and religious information may be a necessary also. Again, as man lives in society, the assistance and attendance of others may be a necessary to his well-being. Hence attendance may be the subject of an infant's contract. Then the classes being established, the subject-matter and extent of the contract may vary according to the state and condition of the infant himself. His clothes may be fine or coarse according to his rank; his education may vary according to the station he is to fill; and the medicines will depend on the illness with which he is afflicted, and the extent of his probable means when of age. So, again, the nature and extent of the attendance will depend on his position in society; and a servant in livery may be allowed to a rich infant, because such attendance is commonly appropriated to persons in his rank of life. But in all these cases, it must first be made out that the class itself is one in which the things furnished are essential to the existence and reasonable advantage and comfort of the infant contractor. Thus, articles of mere luxury are always excluded, though luxurious articles of utility are in some cases allowed. So, contracts for charitable assistance to others, though highly to be praised, cannot be allowed to be binding, because they do not relate to his own personal advantage. In all cases there must be personal advantage from the contract derived to the infant himself.

It is manifest, we think, that this principle alone would not be sufficient to decide the present case. For it would be difficult to say that there is any personal advantage necessarily derived to an infant from the mere burial of a deceased person. But there is another consideration which arises out of the circumstances of this case, which may, we think, materially affect the defendant's liability. This is the case of an infant widow, and the burial that of her husband, who has left no property to be administered. Now the law permits an infant to make a valid contract of marriage, and all necessaries furnished to those with whom he becomes one person by or through the contract of marriage are, in point of law, necessaries to the infant himself. Thus, a contract for necessaries to an infant's wife and lawful children, is used by Lord Bacon as one of the illustrations of the maxim, persona conjuncta æquiparatur interesse proprio (Bac. Law Maxims, p 86). 'If a man', says Lord Bacon, 'under the years of twenty-one, contract for the nursing of his lawful child, this contract is good, and shall not be avoided by infancy, no more than if he had contracted for his own ailments or education.' Now there are many authorities which lay it down that decent Christian burial is a part of a man's own rights; and we think it is no great extension of the rule to say, that it may be classed as a personal advantage, and reasonably necessary to him. His property, if he leaves any, is liable to be appropriated by his administrator to the performance of this proper ceremonial. If then this be so, the decent Christian burial of his wife and lawful children, who are the personæ conjunctæ with him, is also a personal advantage and reasonably necessary to him; and then the rule of law applies, that he may make a binding contract for it. This seems to us to be a proper and legitimate consequence from the proposition that the law allows an infant to make a valid contract of marriage. If this be correct, then an infant husband or parent may contract for the burial of his wife or lawful children; and then the question arises, whether an infant widow is in a similar situation. It may be said that she is not, because during the coverture she is incapable of contracting, and after the death of the husband the relation of marriage has ceased. But we think this is not so. In the case of the husband, the contract will be made after the death of the wife or child, and so after the relation which gives validity to the contract is at an end to some purposes. But if the husband can contract for this, it is because a contract for the burial of those who are personæ conjunctæ with him by reason of the marriage, is as a contract for his own personal benefit, and if that be so, we do not see why the contract for the burial of the husband should not be the same as a contract by the widow for her own personal benefit. Her coverture is at an end, and so she may contract, and her infancy is, for the above reasons, no defence, if the contract be for her personal benefit.

It may be observed, that as the ground of our decision arises out of the infant's previous contract of marriage, it will not follow from it that an infant child, or more distant relation, would be responsible upon a contract for the burial of his parent or relative.

SALE OF GOODS ACT 1979

S 3

... 'necessaries' means goods suitable to the condition in life of the minor and to his actual requirements at the time of sale and delivery.

The statutory definition makes it clear that it is not simply a question of deciding whether the goods are appropriate for the minor, but also whether the minor is already adequately supplied with goods of this type. The application of this is to be seen in *Nash v Inman*, where the section under consideration was the predecessor to s 3 of the Sale of Goods Act 1979, that is, s 2 of the Sale of Goods Act 1893.

Nash v Inman [1908] 2 KB 1

Facts: An undergraduate at Cambridge University ordered 11 fancy waistcoats from a tailor. The tailor sued for payment, and the undergraduate pleaded lack of capacity.

Held: Although the waistcoats, constituting clothing, could have fallen within the category of necessaries, it was up to the tailor to prove that the minor was not already adequately supplied. Since the tailor was unable to do so, the contract was unenforceable.

Cozens-Hardy Mr:
'This case is undoubtedly one of difficulty and also, I think, one of importance. It is an action by a tailor against Mr. Inman, who was at the date of the transactions in question an infant. There were no pleadings in the action. There was merely a writ and an application under Order XIV., and the action was adjourned into Court, and came on for trial before Ridley J. and a special jury. In substance the position is this: The plaintiff sues the defendant for goods sold and delivered. The defendant pleads infancy at the date of the sale, and his plea is proved. What is the consequence of that? The consequence of that is that the Infants' Relief Act, 1874, becomes applicable. Under that Act all contracts for goods supplied are absolutely void, the only exception being contracts for necessaries. Then s. 2 of the Sale of Goods Act, 1893, provides as follows: "Capacity to buy and sell is regulated by the general law concerning capacity to contract, and to transfer and acquire property." That, of course, includes the Act of 1874. Then follows this proviso: "Provided that where necessaries are sold and delivered to an infant, or minor, or to a person who by reason of mental incapacity or drunkenness is incompetent to contract, he must pay a reasonable price therefor." The section then defines necessaries as follows: "Necessaries in this section mean goods suitable to the condition in life of such infant or minor or other person, and to his actual requirements at the time of the sale and delivery." What is the effect of that? The plaintiff sues for goods sold and delivered. The defendant pleads infancy. The plaintiff must then reply, "The goods sold were necessaries within the meaning of the definition in s. 2 of the Sale of Goods Act, 1893." It is not sufficient, in my view, for him to say, "I have discharged the onus which rests upon me if I simply shew that the goods supplied were suitable to the condition in life of the infant at the time." There is another branch of the definition which cannot be disregarded. Having shewn that the goods were suitable to the condition in life of the infant, he must then go on to shew that they were suitable to his actual requirements at the time of the sale and delivery. Unless he establishes that fact, either by evidence adduced by himself or by cross-examination

of the defendant's witnesses, as the case may be, in my opinion he has not discharged the burden which the law imposes upon him. Our attention has been called by Mr. McCardie, in his very able and learned argument, to a number of authorities going back for a very long period, which he said established that the burden on a plaintiff who supplied goods to an infant was simply to shew that the goods were of a class which might be necessaries, having regard to the position in life of the defendant and his family, and that, unless the judge withdrew the case from the jury on the ground that the articles in question could not be necessaries, it was for the jury to find as a matter of fact, Aye or No, were these articles necessaries? It had never, he said, been the law that the plaintiff was required to go into the question, which might present great difficulties, of whether or not the goods were actually required by the defendant at the date of the sale, or, in other words, to say what was the state of the defendant's wardrobe at the time when the goods were ordered. I think there is very great force up to a certain point in that argument. But it must be remembered that the law on this subject has been developed and altered in the course of the last century. It was until quite recently doubted whether it was even admissible to prove that the infant was supplied with goods of the class – being goods which might properly be necessaries – at the date when the contract was made, so that he really did not want any more. It was not until the decision of the Divisional Court in *Barnes v Toye* 13 Q. B. D. 410 in 1884, overruling the direction given by A. L. Smith J., that it could be said to be at all established that that was even admissible evidence unless you went further and proved that the plaintiff knew he was sufficiently supplied. The point arose again in *Johnstone v Marks* 19 Q. B. D. 509 before what was no doubt a Divisional Court, but it was composed of three members of the Court of Appeal, Lord Esher M.R., Lindley L.J., and Lopes L.J. In that case the county court judge had rejected evidence to prove that the defendant was sufficiently supplied with clothes at the time of the sale. Lord Esher said: "I am of opinion that the evidence was improperly rejected. It lies upon the plaintiff to prove, not that the goods supplied belong to the class of necessaries as distinguished from that of luxuries, but that the goods supplied when supplied were necessaries to the infant. The circumstance that the infant was sufficiently supplied at the time of the additional supply is obviously material to this issue, as well as fatal to the contention of the plaintiff with respect to it." Lindley L.J. said: "If an infant can be made liable for articles which may be necessaries without proof that they are necessaries, there is an end to the protection which the law gives him. If he has enough of such articles, more cannot possibly be necessary to him." Although it may be true that the language which I have just read from the judgments of Lord Esher and Lindley L.J. goes further than was absolutely necessary for the decision of the case, that language is perfectly clear and unambiguous, and seems to me to be logically involved in the definition of necessaries. After those two decisions there was passed in the year 1893 an Act of Parliament which defines, in a manner that admits of no doubt, what are those necessaries for which, and for which alone, an infant can be made liable on assumpsit, and that definition in terms includes the second element which Lord Esher and Lindley L.J. said was involved in the term "necessaries", and the burden of proving which, they said, rested on the plaintiff. That being so, how does the matter stand? The plaintiff called evidence to prove the delivery of the goods. It is not of course contended, and it could not be contended, that the infant would be liable for the credit price or for the cash price of the goods, because by the terms of the statute he is only liable for a reasonable price, but that is a subsidiary point. There being no pleadings, the infancy of the defendant was not admitted, and the father was called to prove the date of his son's birth. There was no cross-examination as to that, and the infancy is not disputed. Then he went on to give evidence, which was quite clear and explicit and was not shaken in cross-examination, that the infant, who was an undergraduate at Cambridge, and had just gone up to the university when these goods were supplied, was in fact supplied with clothes suitable and necessary and proper for his condition in life, and for his position as an undergraduate of Trinity College, Cambridge. The learned judge ruled as a matter of law that there was no evidence fit to be submitted to the jury that these articles, or any of them, were necessaries within the meaning of the statutory definition, and, thinking as I do that there was no evidence in support of that which was a necessary issue, I cannot say that the learned judge was wrong in the view which he took. We have scarcely heard any suggestion that there was even a scintilla of evidence to support that which is an affirmative issue, that the goods were suitable to the requirements of the infant. Nay more, I think, if the matter had been left to the jury, and the jury had found that they were suitable to the requirements of the infant at that time, and application had been made for a new trial, it would have been the duty of this Court to grant a new trial on the ground that there was no evidence to support the verdict, and that it was perverse. Under these circumstances it seems to me that this appeal fails, and that there is no ground for interfering with the judgment which was entered for the defendant.

6.2.2 BENEFICIAL CONTRACTS OF SERVICE

Since a person can leave school at 16, it is only reasonable that they should be able to seek employment before reaching the age of 18, and to make binding contracts in this respect. The contract of employment must be one that is, overall, beneficial to the minor.

De Francesco v Barnum (1889) 45 Ch D 430

Facts: A girl of 14 entered into a seven-year contract of apprenticeship with the plaintiff. The terms of the apprenticeship were onerous, including restrictions on the minor's ability to marry and not containing any guarantee that work would be provided by the plaintiff.

Held: The contract was not overall beneficial to the minor, and was unenforceable.

Fry LJ:

'... The most important question in this case is the first of those propositions which has been urged at the Bar on Mr. Barnum's behalf. Is there or is there not in this case a valid contract between the infants and Signor De Francesco? Now, from a very early date it has been held that one exception as to the incapacity of an infant to bind himself relates to a contract for his good teaching or instruction whereby he may profit himself afterwards, to use Lord Coke's language. There is another exception, which is based on the desirableness of infants employing themselves in labour; therefore, where you get a contract for labour and you have a remuneration of wages, that contract, I think, must be taken to be, prima facie, binding upon an infant. At any rate, it is plain that the contract by which an infant binds himself to learn an art or trade to his own future profit is, prima facie, valid and binding. But no doubt the law has grafted on that general principle certain well-known and defined exceptions. It has been held from the time of Lord Coke, that an infant cannot bind himself to be liable to a penalty; that the contract to impose a penalty on an infant is void. Again, it has been held that a contract by which an infant renders his vested interest subject to forfeiture is void against the infant; and again, I think it may be taken that, wherever you find extraordinary or unusual stipulations contained in a contract, either of apprenticeship or of service, there the Court at least must be on the watch lest the infant should be held to be bound by a contract which is not reasonable and which is not good in law and which is not maintainable.

Now I approach this subject with the observation that it appears to me that the question is this, Is the contract for the benefit of the infant? Not, Is any one particular stipulation for the benefit of the infant? Because it is obvious that the contract of apprenticeship or the contract of labour must, like any other contract, contain some stipulations for the benefit of the one contracting party, and some for the benefit of the other. It is not because you can lay your hand on a particular stipulation which you may say is against the infant's benefit, that therefore the whole contract is not for the benefit of the infant. The Court must look at the whole contract, having regard to the circumstances of the case, and determine, subject to any principles of law which may be ascertained by the cases, whether the contract is or is not beneficial. That appears to me to be in substance a question of fact.

Now in the present case I must bear in mind that the two girls who were apprenticed in the year 1886 were at that time not ignorant of the art of dancing. It appears they had learnt something of it from their mother, who herself had been connected with the theatre, and also from friends who were familiar with the art of dancing. By this indenture, which I have already mentioned, dated December, 1886, the Defendant, Helen Maude Parnell, with the consent of her parent, put herself apprentice to Signor De Francesco, to learn from the 6th day of December, 1886, until the full end of the term of seven years from thence next following, during which term the apprentice should her master faithfully serve, and so forth, with the usual stipulations with regard to faithful service. There is the further stipulation that she shall not contract matrimony within the said term, and further that she shall not accept professional engagements unless with the full written permission of her master. Now, so far, the contract, with the exception of the stipulation about matrimony, seems to be of a usual description. But then we come to the clauses by which Signor De Francesco undertakes his duties towards the child. In the first place, he agrees that he will, with qualified assistants, instruct the apprentice in what are described as "the higher branches of the choreographic art", which I understand to be dancing, "for the term of seven years". Then he agrees to pay the apprentice "the following remuneration for all or any choreographic engagements of the said apprentice during the said term, namely, in London and suburbs, for the first three years, 9d. per night, and 6d. for each *matinée*; and for the remainder of the said term, 1s. per night, and 6d. for each *matinée*". Then, further, he shall have the right to engage the apprentice to performances in America or any foreign or colonial state, and shall pay to the apprentice, during the maintenance of such engagement abroad, the sum of 5s. a week, and provide the apprentice with board and lodging during such last-mentioned engagement.

It is obvious that that is a very unusual stipulation. There is no provision for remuneration of any sort or kind, except during the engagement. There are no wages to be paid to the girls except during the engagement. The matter, therefore, rests with Signor De Francesco as to how far those children shall take any wages at all. Nor can it be entirely put out of consideration that he has a right to send these apprentices for performances to any foreign state or foreign country, a power which, if exercised, would remove the infants, or probably would remove the infants from maternal care. Now perhaps it is right at this point that I should say that, so far as the evidence goes, I am satisfied that the establishment of Signor De Francesco is carried on in a thoroughly careful and respectable manner. It appears that whenever the girls go anywhere out of London they are placed under the care of matrons, whose duty it is to look after them, and that a similar care has been extended to them when there has been a performance at the Crystal Palace, and they had to take the journey between London and Sydenham. The mother, who was in the witness-box, says explicitly, so long as regards the care whilst the children had been under Signor De Francesco's management, she has no complaint to make whatever. I say that by way of parenthesis. At the same time it is obvious that the clause I have read places a very large power indeed in the hands of Signor De Francesco.

The next provision is, that if there is not sufficient dancing the apprentice may be required to do utility business and receive certain remuneration. That would not seem unreasonable. Then it is provided: "The services of the apprentice shall be entirely at the disposal of Signor De Francesco, and the said apprentice shall not during the said term of seven years enter into any professional engagements without the permission in writing of the said Signor De Francesco." Be it observed there is no corresponding obligation on the part of Signor De Francesco. He requires the infant to enter into no engagements without his permission, but does not in any corresponding way bind himself to any extent to provide engagements or employment for the infant.

Then comes the provision with regard to the apprentices receiving lessons, and a provision as to the rules and regulations of the theatre. They all seem reasonable; and then there is a provision which is praiseworthy, requiring the infant to conform to the *Education Act*, and then comes the 8th clause: "In case the said Giuseppe de Francesco shall at any time during the said term be of opinion (after a fair trial) that the said apprentice is unfit from any cause whatever (either physical or otherwise) to pursue the avocation of stage dancing, the said Signor De Francesco may put an end to these presents and every matter and thing, herein contained by giving to the parents and the said apprentice notice in writing to that effect." Now, be it observed that that clause is provided to operate throughout the whole seven years. It might be put in force at any time, subject only to this, that it must be after a fair trial. But what is a fair trial? How long, after the fair trial this notice may be given is not stipulated for in any manner whatsoever. We have therefore, to put it shortly, the contract under which the infant is placed, I might almost say absolutely, at the disposal of the teacher. The child may be required to undertake any engagements at any theatre in England, or any theatre in the United Kingdom, or anywhere else in the world. The child is to receive no remuneration, no maintenance except when employed; there is no correlative obligation on Signor De Francesco to find employment for the child; there is power in him to put an end to a child's chances of success at any time after trial.

Those are stipulations of an extraordinary and an unusual character, which throw, or appear to throw, an inordinate power into the hands of the master without any correlative obligation on the part of the master. I cannot, therefore, say that on the face of this instrument it appears to be one which the Court ought to hold to be for the benefit of the infant.

Now, I will suppose myself sitting in Chambers administering the jurisdiction in this division of the Court over infants; and I ask myself whether I should approve of such a contract as that as being for the benefit of an infant ward of Court – assuming of course, in so doing, that the infant ward of Court was one whom it was desirable to apprentice to the art of a ballet-dancer. I cannot say that I should hold anything of the kind. It may be that evidence could be tendered which would shew me that no other form of contract is available, that the same contract prevails in every school, and that no person can hope to enter the profession of a ballet-dancer except by apprenticeship in these terms. That may be so. But no evidence of the sort has been tendered before me. I have undoubtedly this in favour of upholding it, that the school of the Plaintiff is said by Mrs. Parnell to be a very excellent school, and, for anything I know, it may be the best in London, and, I have already said, Signor De Francesco is a person who is well able to, and does, protect the interest of the girls who are under his care. At the same time, this contract seems to me to place in his hands an inordinate power, which, except under the pressure of some evidence which has not been given, I cannot help being of opinion is not for the infants' benefit.

I hold, therefore, this instrument is one by which the infants are not bound; and consequently Mr. Barnum, having only enticed them away from an employment or contract of a nature which is not binding upon them, no action can be maintained against Mr. Barnum.'

Fry LJ's insistence that the overall effect of the contract, rather than particular provisions, must be considered is important. By way of contrast, consider:

Clements v London and NW Rly [1894] 2 QB 482

Facts: The minor was employed as a porter. He agreed to forgo certain statutory rights to compensation for injury at work, but was part of an insurance scheme run by the employer, which provided lower levels of compensation.

Held: Although the compensation levels were lower, the insurance scheme covered a wider range of situations. Overall the contract was not disadvantageous to the minor, and was enforceable.

Kay LJ:

'Some questions have been argued in this case of general interest relating to contracts made by infants. The law which relates to such contracts has been a great deal discussed, perhaps more than was necessary for the decision of the case before us; but it was long ago settled that all such contracts are not void. In Coke upon Littleton, 172a, the note as to the power of an infant to bind himself by a writing states that there are some exceptions to his general inability, as "an infant may bind himself to pay for his necessary meat, drink, apparel, necessary physicke, and such other necessaries, and likewise for his good teaching or instruction, whereby he may profit himself afterwards". It has been since held, in *Peters v Fleming* [FN11], that under the term "necessaries" are included such articles as are useful and suitable to the state and condition of life of the party, and not merely such as are requisite for bare subsistence. It has been clearly held that contracts of apprenticeship and with regard to labour are not contracts to an action on which the plea of infancy is a complete defence, and the question has always been, both at law and in equity, whether the contract, when carefully examined in all its terms, is for the benefit of the infant. If it is so, the Court before which the question comes will not allow the infant to repudiate it . . . .

In this case the contract entered into was this. The men in the employ of the London and North Western Railway Company formed an insurance society, the object of which was to compensate any of the members who might sustain an injury, either temporary or permanent, and to pay a fixed sum in the case of the death of any member from accident. The society gives to its members an advantage greater than the law gives, because it enables them to obtain compensation even where the injury was not caused by the negligence of the company or of a superior workman under whose control the injured man was working. The compensation fixed may not be so large as the amount that could be obtained from a jury; but there was this advantage, that it would be payable in cases where there would be no remedy against the company nor, possibly, against any one else.

The plaintiff seems to have been in the employment of the company for a week, and then to have signed the form which made him a member of the insurance society. We are told that this is made a condition of service by the company. I think, therefore, that the case has been rightly treated on the footing that this was part of the terms of a labour contract entered into between the plaintiff and the company, and I agree with the Divisional Court that, on examination of the whole contract, it is for the benefit of the infant, although it contains terms that, standing alone, would not be for his advantage. There is, therefore, no right on the part of the infant to repudiate the contract. One of the terms is, that while he was bound by it he would not bring such an action as this. Obviously the railway company, who give nearly one-half the funds which the insurance society has to dispose of, were bound to make that condition in their own interest. This condition is part of the contract which the plaintiff entered into with the railway company, and, as such a clause does not prevent the contract as a whole being for the benefit of the infant he is bound by the condition, and it is an answer to this action.'

6.2.3 OTHER CONTRACTS RELATED TO WORK

The general approach taken to employment contracts will be applied to other contracts related to the way in which the minor earns a living. Provided these are in general terms beneficial, they will be enforceable. This is illustrated by the next two cases.

Doyle v White City Stadium [1935] 1 KB 110

Facts: The contract under which a boxer obtained a licence from the British Boxing Board of Control operated to his disadvantage in that the boxer was unable to claim his purse if disqualified in a bout.

Held: The licensing arrangement was overall beneficial to the boxer, and was enforceable.

Lord Hanworth MR:
'This case has been fully argued and raises some interesting points. The action was brought by Joseph Doyle (professionally known as Jack Doyle) who is an infant by his next friend. The statement of claim says:

  "The plaintiff is an infant and he obtains his livelihood by professional boxing."

The pleading then goes on to say that certain terms were arranged for a boxing match which was to take place, and in fact did take place, on 12th July, 1933. Para. 4 says:

  "The said contest took place between the plaintiff and the said Petersen as agreed, on 12th July, 1933, and the said Petersen was declared the winner."

The statement of claim further sets out that by terms which are contained in a letter written by Mr. Gentle to the plaintiff:

"You are to receive £3000 after the fight. This is of course clear to you and is exclusive of percentage and training expenses",

and that is accepted by Mr. Doyle. More than that, there is a letter from Mr. Doyle which states the terms. The letter I refer to is in the statement of claim and says: "I am to receive £3000 win, lose or draw, after the Petersen fight." That fight took place under the auspices of and under the rules and conditions laid down by the British Boxing Board of Control, of which the stewards are persons of some eminence who are established as a board to control boxing. The objects for which it is stated to be formed are:

"To control and regulate professional boxing in the United Kingdom and to act as a Board of Appeal" and "To promote and safeguard the interests of British professional boxers throughout the world."

The Board requires that if persons are to take part in fights to which they give countenance, there shall be licences granted to the fighters and also that the promoters are to be members of this association. In effect the rules which are before us clearly indicate that the Board have taken steps to secure that all persons, whether promoters or managers or boxers, shall all of them be members of this society or association and under the control of the board. This fight was a fight recognized by the Board. The secretary wrote on June 23, 1933, to Messrs. Jeff Dickson: "The Board" – that is the administrative stewards – "at a meeting yesterday decided to recognize the above mentioned contest" – that is the contest which ultimately took place on July 12 – "as being for the heavyweight championship of Great Britain. Officials for the contest will be appointed later", and the Board give a personal notice of this to Mr. Jack Doyle, c/o Mr. Sullivan, his manager, and a similar letter was written to Mr. Petersen.

The result of those letters and the facts which are not in dispute is that this fight was one in which the heavyweight championship of Great Britain was in issue and one which was subject to the regulations of the Board of Control. It will be found that at the end of the rules there are a number of boxing rules relating to the contests. They contain minutiae in respect of the contests, such as, for instance:

"All contests to be decided in a roped ring not less than 14 ft. or more than 20 ft. square."

Powers are given to the referee, including power to disqualify a contestant for any of the acts there set out. Then it is provided:

"The breaking of any of these rules by a contestant or his seconds shall render such contestant liable to disqualification. A contestant disqualified for any cause whatever shall not be entitled to any prize, except in accordance with regulation 20, paragraph 16",

and reg. 20, para. 16, provides:

"Boxers in case of disqualification are only entitled to receive bare travelling expenses, pending the decision of the board or branch on the circumstances of the case, when the board or branch may deal with the money as it thinks fit. Every disqualification must be reported to the board or branch by the referee within twenty-four hours of the contest taking place."

It will be seen, therefore, that these rules are framed for the purpose of securing what I will call clean fighting by disqualifying persons who use certain strokes such as hitting below the belt, using the pivot blow, and using a number of other technical strokes which are barred by the regulations. It is plain therefore that the Board does endeavour to promote and safeguard the interests of professional boxers throughout the world by laying down these rules.

In fact a sum of £3000 was put up for the plaintiff whatever happened in the course of the fight, win, lose or draw. But the rules I have read contain the definite statement that a boxer who is disqualified shall only be entitled to receive bare travelling expenses, and that the board may deal with the money as it thinks fit. There is no question at all that on July 12, 1933, the plaintiff was disqualified in the contest at the second round, and he was called upon to go before the Board or their representatives for them to investigate the circumstances; and it is in evidence that he apologized for his conduct. The learned judge's note of the plaintiff's evidence on that point is:

"I appeared before the Board. I apologized for my conduct. I did not appeal under the rules."

A great number of points have been raised in the course of the case, but I should like first of all to consider what is the meaning and purpose of these rules and of the adhesion of the plaintiff to them. That adhesion was secured by the plaintiff's becoming a licensee of the Board. In order to do that he made application for a licence. That application was made in March, 1932, and approved on March 15, 1932, and the year for which the licence ran began on March 5, 1932. He is said to have been an infant at the time aged eighteen years – though perhaps the term "boy" which was used by Serjeant Sullivan was a little inapt, because his exact fighting weight at the time of the application for the licence was fifteen stone. The licence was granted on the terms of his application, which was as follows:

"I hereby apply for a licence as a boxer and, if this licence is granted me I declare to adhere strictly to the rules of The British Boxing Board of Control (1929) as printed, and abide by any further rules or alteration to existing rules as may be passed. I agree to pay the fee in accordance with the above."

The licence granted ran until March 4, 1933, and it was then extended and ran until March 3, 1934. So that when the fight took place on July 12, 1933, the plaintiff entered the ring as a licensee of the Board and as one who had agreed to adhere strictly to the rules of the Board of Control and to abide by any further rules, or alteration to existing rules . . .

In fact the plaintiff, having been disqualified, the Board after inquiry and after the plaintiff had appeared before them and apologized, decided to withhold the £3000 as they had power to do under this rule in their discretion. This action was brought to recover the money, it being alleged that the particular defendants, that is the individual members of the Board against whom the action succeeded, were not entitled to intervene and stop the money from being handed over to the plaintiff. The action was brought, alternatively, against the White City Stadium Ld.; but the learned judge held that there was no cause of action against them and judgment was entered for them. There is no appeal as to that. The appeal is brought by those individual members of the Board, the administrative stewards of the Board, against whom judgment was given for the sum of £3000.

The learned judge first had to consider whether or not the rules in their original form were rules which bound the plaintiff, who is an infant, and he came to the conclusion that the contract was "so nearly concerned with his entering upon a form or employment or occupation that I think I ought to hold that it is within the type of contract which, if found to be for his benefit, the Court ought to hold is not voidable by the infant". . . .

I turn back now to consider whether or not the contract as found by the learned judge – the contract that is contained or partly contained in the terms on which the licence was asked for – is good and binding upon the infant. It was argued with force by Serjeant Sullivan and Mr. O'Connor that no contract with an infant can be supported other than a contract as to necessaries including employment and services to be rendered by the infant's labour, when the law will presume an obligation on the part of the infant to pay. Serjeant Sullivan bases his contention that only this limited range of contracts is binding upon the infant upon passages to be found in Sir Edward Coke's Institutes, and confirmed in a number of the Digests. Of these a number of illustrations are to be found in cases to which our attention has been called. To my mind that statement of the law is too narrow. It is unnecessary at the present moment to decide it, but I confess that as at present advised I find difficulty in acceding to the view that there is nothing that can properly be called a valid contract on the part of an infant – that all that can be inferred is an obligation on his part, which is improperly termed a contract, to repay money spent in supplying necessaries . . .

I turn to three cases which to my mind are binding upon this Court. The first is De Francesco v Barnum, where Fry L.J. says:

"I approach this subject with the observation that it appears to me that the question is this, Is the contract for the benefit of the infant? Not, Is any one particular stipulation for the benefit of the infant? Because it is obvious that the contract of apprenticeship or the contract of labour must, like any other contract, contain some stipulations for the benefit of the one contracting party, and some for the benefit of the other. It is not because you can lay your hand on a particular stipulation which you may say is against the infant's benefit, that therefore the whole contract is not for the benefit of the infant. The Court must look at the whole contract, having regard to the circumstances of the case, and determine, subject to any principles of law which may be ascertained by the cases, whether the contract is or is not beneficial. That appears to me to be in substance a question of fact."

In *Corn v Matthews* [1893] 1 Q. B. 310 the matter came again before the Court of Appeal, and Lord Esher M.R. definitely said:

"It seems to me that the judgment of Fry L.J. is one with which one would agree, and, although it makes the major premise larger than it had been previously enunciated in such cases, it does not alter the law applicable to them",

and he repeats what Fry L.J. had said, and particularly that the mere fact that some of the conditions in the deed are against an apprentice, does not enable the Court on that ground to say that the agreement is void. He says that the question is whether or not the terms are such as would on the whole be beneficial to the infant, and it seemed to him in the particular case that there was a term which was so unfair to the infant and solely in favour of the master that it made the whole contract unfair. The term was one that if there was either a strike, or what we now call a lock-out, the master could cease to pay the apprentice's wages though the master himself had caused the lock-out, and it was on the ground of this term that the Court held the contract to be unreasonable and against the interest of the infant; but Corn v Matthews definitely confirms the principles laid down by Fry L.J.

Then in *Clements v London & North Western Ry Co* we have once more the statement made that the whole contract is to be looked at. That was a case in which the infant whilst employed by the railway company joined an insurance society formed among the employees of the railway company towards the funds of which the railway company contributed, and in return for being a member and getting that contribution, the infant agreed not to bring any proceedings under the Employers' Liability Act; he set aside, in other words, a very considerable advantage given to him by statute, but it was held by Lord Esher that the contract was one which was for the benefit of the infant, and he says:

"I am of opinion, without going again through the cases that have been cited, that the answer to this proposition depends on whether, on the true construction of the contract as a whole, it was for his advantage. If it was not so, he can repudiate it; but if it was for his advantage, it was not a voidable contract, but one binding on him, which he had no right to repudiate." . . .

It was therefore held effective and binding. Those cases are binding upon us. The learned judge on the question of fact has held that the terms of the agreement in this case are favourable and to the advantage of the infant, and it seems therefore that the application of the rules cannot be held to be prevented by reason of the plaintiff's infancy.

I should just like to add a few more words by way of emphasis to show that I have both appreciated and at the same time reject the view which has been advanced by Serjeant Sullivan. He spoke of the position of the plaintiff as if he was one who had agreed to render services, indeed I think he said that the plaintiff provided an exhibition for the defendants on the terms that win, lose or draw he should receive £3000, that he was therefore entitled in any event to receive that sum for services rendered, that the withholding of the money was in the nature of a penalty and that a penalty could not be to the infant's advantage so as to be binding on him. To my mind all those observations involve a complete misreading of these rules and of the terms and conditions under which the fight took place. It is as much in the interests of the plaintiff himself as of any other contestant that there should be rules for clean fighting, and that he should be protected against his adversary's misconduct in hitting below the belt or doing anything of the sort. There is no question of his rendering services to employers. The position is that he himself has been given the opportunity of making his livelihood by professional boxing on terms and conditions which safeguard him as a contestant from any improper conduct on the part of those with whom he may engage in fight. Moreover the rules contain specific provisions under which the interests of the boxer are safeguarded in respect of any conduct of the promoter or manager with whom or through whom he may have to make arrangements and terms.

On all these grounds, therefore, I come to the same conclusion as that of the learned judge – namely, that this plea of infancy does not avail to prevent the plaintiff from being bound by the rules and conditions provided for in his application for a licence.'

Although the rules of the Board operated to Doyle's disadvantage in this case, the view was that overall they were beneficial to boxers, in providing the framework under which fights took place, and discouraging 'improper conduct'. A similar approach was taken in the rather different circumstances of *Chaplin v Leslie Frewin*, where a publication contract was held to be for the benefit of the minor author, even though the contents of the book did not cast him in a good light.

Chaplin v Leslie Frewin [1966] Ch 71

Facts: The minor was the son of the film star, Charlie Chaplin. He entered into a contract for the publication of his autobiography, which he later wished to withdraw from.

Held: (Lord Denning MR dissenting): Despite the fact that the book dealt with unedifying conduct by the minor, the contract was overall for his advantage, and was enforceable.

Danckwerts LJ:
'This is an action brought by Michael John Chaplin (a young man $19\frac{1}{2}$ years of age) somewhat comically by his wife, Patrice Frances Chaplin (who is 25) as his next friend. The object of the action is to prevent the defendants reproducing or selling a literary work called by the unattractive title: "I Couldn't Smoke the Grass on My Father's Lawn."

The origin of the matter was the discovery by the press that the plaintiff, the son of a famous film actor and director, and his wife and a child, were living in England on

National Assistance. The idea was then conceived by someone and was taken up by Leslie Frewin (Publishers) Ltd. that the plaintiff should produce a kind of auto-biography, with the assistance of two "ghost writers" (as they are called), and that this work should be published by the defendant publishers. The other defendants are the printers. No one among the participants (leaving out the printers) emerges from the affair with any credit. The book itself seems to me to be worthless from a literary point of view, and, in addition to its many other shortcomings, contains on page 9 (the first page) and on page 91 passages of cheap and silly blasphemy. It is a sneering kind of book. The style in which the book is written is atrocious, and for this no doubt the ghost writers are responsible. The writers are, I suppose, experts in illiterate literature. But the evidence is that they were attempting to reproduce what they had been told by the plaintiff in the language which it was supposed that a young man of the plaintiff's type would write. The publishers were plainly endeavouring to exploit for profit the notoriety attaching to the plaintiff, and the plaintiff, who appears to be a conceited and unreliable young man, was only too glad to take advantage of the chance of obtaining money out of the situation. As I have said, the contents and style of the book are objectionable; but we are neither censors nor arbiters of taste, and presumably the publishers are satisfied that there is a market for this kind of vulgar trash . . .

The plaintiff's case is that, subject to certain classes of exceptions, a contract made by an infant is voidable by him during infancy or within a reasonable time after attaining full age. It is said that the present case does not fall within any of the excepted classes, and that, even if the contract could fall within any of those classes, the contract is so detrimental to the plaintiff's reputation and so liable to expose him to actions for defamation that it cannot be for his benefit.

On behalf of the defendants four main points have been taken: (1) The contract falls within the cases analogous to contracts of service in that the contract enabled the plaintiff to earn his living and so is binding on the infant. (2) If the contract is voidable, nonetheless the infant cannot recover interests or rights which have been transferred by him for value during the contract's existence. (3) On a proper construction of the contract the contract contained an assignment of the copyright to the publishers. (4) If not an assignment, it is at least an exclusive licence which, by virtue of section 19 of the Copyright Act, 1956, is an interest of a substantial nature analogous to a transfer and is irrevocable.

I propose to deal with the first proposition last. The other three propositions are related to each other.

If the contract is capable of being a transfer, it could not effect a transfer at law but only in equity until the work came into existence. But once the work came into existence, the transfer would be complete at law. There can, of course, be no question of possession because copyright is a chose in action, that is to say, a collection of rights recognised by the law. There is, therefore, very little difference between assignment of the copyright and the grant of an exclusive licence. Further, it is to be observed that a transfer of copyright does not require a deed. The statutory method of assignment of copyright is by writing signed by the copyright owner, and so that form of transfer is fully effective at law. In the result, in my view, during the period while the contract admittedly was in force, the plaintiff had fully performed what was required of him. The question of future works had not arisen, and except for that improbable detail, so far as the plaintiff was concerned the contract was wholly executed, and when the attempted revocation came, it was no longer executory on his side. All that was left were the obligations of the publishers to publish and sell the book and make the payments to the plaintiff and his wife.

On the question of construction we were referred to certain cases in which it was held on construction that copyright had been assigned: *Messager v British Broadcasting Corporation* [1929] A.C. 151; 45 T.L.R. 50, H.L.(E.); *British Actors Film Co v Glover* [1918] 1 K.B. 299; 34 T.L.R. 162; *Jonathan Cape Ltd v Consolidated Press Ltd* [1954] 1 W.L.R. 1313; [1954] 3 All E.R. 253; and *Loew's Incorporated v Littler* [1958] Ch. 650; [1958] 2 W.L.R. 787; [1958] 2 All E.R. 200, C.A. Mr. Roche sought to distinguish these cases as containing the express word "grant", which he contended was the essential or proper word to use in an assignment. The most obvious word is "assign". But even if the words "grant" or "assign" are not used, the intention to assign the copyright may appear from the context. I think that the words in clause 1 of the contract, "The publishers shall during the legal term of the copyright have the exclusive right of producing, publishing and selling the said work" (which are the rights conferred by statute on the owner of the copyright), are ample and effective to constitute an assignment of the copyright to the publishers. The use of the word "assigns" in other clauses and the absence of an express provision for reverter in clause 8 does not seem to me to affect the matter. It would, I think, be reasonable to imply a reverter where necessary.

Mr. Hirst had the further point on section 19 (1) of the Copyright Act, 1956. The effect of that subsection is that the grantee of an exclusive licence has all the rights of a copyright owner and the copyright owner is left only with the right to sue other persons for infringement. Clearly this gives to the grantee a most important interest in the copyright. The provisions in section 36 describing assignments and licences as personal or movable property hardly seem to be necessary. Mr. Hirst has, in my view, a further effective point under the section.

The point of all this is, of course, that Mr. Hirst contends that if an infant revokes a contract, the property and interests which have previously been transferred by him cannot be recovered by the infant. I think that Mr. Hirst's contention is correct on this point and that the transfers of property made by the plaintiff remain effective against him, even if the contract is otherwise revocable. This, I think, is the true effect of the authorities cited to us. If that is correct, it is an end of the matter. The copyright is no longer at the plaintiff's disposal.

I now turn to the first question – whether the contract is revocable or is binding on the infant. On this question we were referred to *Doyle v White City Stadium* [1935] 1 K.B. 110 in which Doyle (an infant) had agreed to be bound by the rules regulating professional boxing because otherwise he could not pursue the career of a professional boxer. The contract and the rules were held binding upon him. It is plain that it was a case treated as within or analogous to the exceptions to the general rule in respect of infants' contracts and the contract was held binding on the infant because it enabled him to earn his living and so was for his benefit.

I think the principle of that case applies to the present case. The advantage of the contract to the plaintiff in the present case was that it would enable the plaintiff to make a start as an author and thus earn money to keep himself and his wife. The time to judge the question of whether the contract is beneficial must, I think, be the date when the contract is made: see *Halsbury's Laws of England*, 3rd edn. (1957), Vol. 21, p 145. It cannot be right to enable a contract made in good faith to be avoided because it turns out at a later date that the benefits are not as great as the parties anticipated.

It was contended by Mr. Roche that this contract could not be beneficial to the plaintiff because (1) the book exposed him to the risk of actions for defamation, and (2) the book presented the plaintiff himself as being a bad character. As regards the first, the defendants allege that they can justify, and on this ground the judge declined, according to practice, to grant an injunction. As regards the second ground, the contract did confer substantial benefits. I find it difficult to sympathise with a person who, for the purpose of gain, has approved of a book which is calculated to denigrate his character and afterwards wishes to change his mind. How far the book will affect readers I do not know, but it may be that the publicity which the book has now received will increase the sales of the book and thus increase the benefits to the plaintiff which were the object of the contract. The mud may cling but the profits will be secured. Taste is a matter of opinion.'

This area has importance for young musicians and sports people, who may be tempted by contracts offered by record companies, managers or agents, not all of which will wholly beneficial. It is clear that the fact that some terms are ungenerous will not in itself render the contract unenforceable, provided that overall it is seen to be for the minor's benefit. This is likely to be the approach taken where the agent or manager is involved in finding work for the minor, as will generally be the case with musicians and actors. If, however, the agent's role is not crucial to the minor's employment, as may be the case with some agents for sportspeople, then the contract may be regarded as not being for 'necessary services', and so unenforceable. This was the position regarding a contract entered into by the footballer Wayne Rooney, as discussed in *Proform Sports Management Ltd v Proactive Sports Management Ltd.*

Proform Sports Management Ltd v Proactive Sports Management Ltd.
[2006] EWHC 2812 (Ch); [2007] 1 All ER 542

Facts: In 2000, when he was 15, Rooney entered into a representation agreement with the claimant. In 2002, Rooney terminated that agreement, and entered into an agreement with the defendant. The claimant sued the defendant for the tort of interference with contractual relations, and inducing or procuring a breach of contract.

Held: The 2000 agreement was not contract for necessary services. Rooney was already with a football club at the time, which subsequently employed him. The 2000 agreement was therefore voidable, and there was no liability in tort for inducing or facilitating the breach of a voidable contract.

Hodge J:

[Having held that it was not a tort to induce a breach of a voidable contract, the judge continued] – '[**34.**] It then becomes necessary to consider the next stage in Mr Joffe's argument. He submits that the law as to minors' contracts is correctly stated in Chitty vol 1, p 581 (paras 8–004, 8–005). Paragraph 8–004 identifies the only contracts which are binding on the minor as contracts for necessaries. However, a diversity of meanings has been given to the word "necessaries". In one sense the term is confined to necessary goods and services supplied to the minor, but in another it extends to contracts for the minor's benefit and in particular to contracts of apprenticeship, education and service. Paragraph 8–005 provides that apart from contracts for necessaries and contracts of apprenticeship education and service, the general rule at common law is that a minor's contract is voidable at his option; ie not binding on the minor, but binding on the other party.

[**35.**] As to other beneficial contracts, Mr Joffe relies on para 8–028 (p 591). I quote:

> "The principle that contracts beneficial to a minor are binding on him is not confined to contracts for necessaries and contracts of employment, apprenticeship or education in a strict sense. It extends also to other contracts which in a broad sense may be treated as analogous to contracts of service, apprenticeship or education. So, for instance, a contract by a minor (who was a professional boxer) with the British Boxing Board of Control whereby he agreed to adhere to the rules of the Board was held binding on him because he could not have earned his living as a boxer without entering into the agreement."

The authority cited is *Doyle v White City Stadium Ltd* [1935] 1 KB 110, [1934] All ER Rep 252.

> "Similarly, it has been held that an agreement between a minor and a publisher for the publication of the minor's biography which was to be written by a 'ghost writer', was binding on the minor."

The authority cited is *Chaplin v Leslie Frewin (Publishers) Ltd* [1965] 3 All ER 764, [1966] Ch 71.

> "So also, a contract between a group of under-age musicians (known as 'The Kinks') whereby they appointed a company as their manager and agent was held binding as analogous to a contract of employment."

The authority cited is the first instance decision in *Denmark Productions Ltd v Boscobel Productions Ltd* reported only at (1967) 111 Sol Jo 715 and reversed on other grounds by the Court of Appeal ([1968] 3 All ER 513, [1969] 1 QB 699). The footnote goes on to contrast from that case the case of *Shears v Mendeloff* (1914) 30 TLR 342, where the contract contained oppressive terms and was void. The text goes on:

> "On the other hand there is no general principle to the effect that any contract beneficial to a minor is binding on him. So a minor's trading contracts are not binding on him, even if beneficial."

[**36.**] Thus, two questions arise. First, whether the contract between Wayne Rooney and Proform falls within the class of contracts analogous to contracts for necessaries and contracts of employment, apprenticeship or education. If so, secondly, and only if the first question is answered in a positive sense, whether this particular contract was one which was beneficial to Wayne Rooney. Mr Joffe submits that a contract analogous to one of apprenticeship, education or employment is only enforceable against a minor if it is of benefit to him at the time when he enters into it. Where the contract contains terms, some of which are beneficial to him and others not, the question is whether, taken as a whole, the contract is to his advantage. The burden of showing benefit is always on the party seeking to uphold the contract. At para 31 of his written skeleton argument, Mr Joffe poses the question whether the Proform agreement fell within the class of minors' contracts which were analogous to those of apprenticeship, education and service. At sub-para 6 he proposes a negative answer to that question. He says that Proform cannot show that the contract is so analogous. At the time when it was signed, Mr Rooney was already with a club, Everton, that was providing him with training. He had no need for any training from Proform. He submits that the Proform agreement makes no provision for training, education or instruction in any way.

[**37.**] The absence of such provision was, he submits, the basis of the decision in *Shears v Mendeloff* that the contract could not be construed as one for necessaries. *Shears v Mendeloff* was of course the case before Avory J, where a minor who was a professional boxer had appointed the plaintiff his sole manager on commission and agreed not to take any engagements under any other management without the plaintiff's consent for three years. Such a contract was held unenforceable against the infant, on the grounds that it was a trading contract, and also as one which could not be construed as being beneficial to him. Mr Joffe contrasts such a case with the decision in *Roberts v Gray* [1913] 1 KB 520, [1911–13] All ER Rep 870, where the infant had entered into a contract to go on a tour as a professional billiard player. That contract was held to be one for necessaries and for his benefit. The Court of Appeal held the contract to be binding on him as a whole. Mr Joffe submits that the basis of the decision in that case was clearly that the contract could be construed as one for necessaries, because it was for teaching, instruction and employment. By contrast, he submits that the Proform agreement contains nothing which can be said to be analogous to instruction, education or training. Nor did the Proform agreement permit Mr Rooney to make a start as a footballer or enable him to earn a living. It is on that basis that he distinguishes the cases of *Chaplin v Leslie Frewin (Publishers) Ltd* [1965] 3 All ER 764, [1966] Ch 71 and *Doyle v White City Stadium Ltd* [1935] 1 KB 110, [1934] All ER Rep 252, which are authorities relied upon by Mr King. Mr Joffe submits that in those two cases the minor was enabled to earn a living by reason of a contract he entered into. That is not the position here. There was no payment being made to him. He was already contracted to Everton. That was all that he needed. He had no need of a contract to represent him as a professional footballer. He would on turning 17 be in a position to earn his living via a contract with Everton Football Club or any other club, and he had no need of an agreement with an agent to enable him to do so. Certainly he did not need to be bound to such an agent for two years. After all, he could not under the Football Association Rules sign a professional contract at the earliest until he was 17, assuming he was not then in full-time education; and he had no need of representation in his work as a professional footballer, as cl 1 of the Proform agreement stated.

[**38.**] Mr King submits that the terms of the Proform contract speak for themselves. He relies upon the terms of Mr McIntosh's witness statement, which record that Proform was providing all the functions in respect of personal representation and management, advice and negotiation for the benefit of Wayne Rooney. That was intended to encompass all aspects of the services undertaken by the claimant for a player aged 17 years or under. He submits that the case falls squarely within the principle stated at para 8–028 of Chitty, that contracts beneficial to a minor, and which can thus be upheld, are not confined to contracts for necessaries and contracts of employment, apprenticeship or education in a strict sense. They extend also to other contracts which in a broad sense may be treated as analogous to contracts of service, apprenticeship or education. In any event, he submits that the defendants cannot establish – and the burden is upon them – that the claimant has no real prospect at trial of bringing the agreement within these principles. Whether the agreement is within the same must, he submits, be a mixed question of construction and fact.

[**39.**] I am conscious that on this issue I have, as Mr King submits, to be satisfied that the claimant has no real prospect of succeeding in establishing that the Proform agreement falls within the class of contracts analogous to those described as contracts for necessaries, contracts of employment, apprenticeship or education. Clearly Wayne Rooney's agreement with Everton Football Club would fall squarely within the class of contracts identified at para 8–028 of Chitty. However, it does seem to me that the same cannot be said of the Proform agreement. On the evidence, Mr Rooney was already engaged with Everton. Under the terms of the Football Association rules, he could not enter into any contract of employment until he was 17, if then not in full-time education. Even if he entered into a contract with Everton when he was 17, that contract, if not for his benefit, would of course be voidable at his election. It does not seem to me that a contract in the terms of the Proform agreement, whereby Proform was to act as his executive agent and to carry out all the functions in respect of personal representation on behalf of his work as a professional football player, falls to be considered as analogous to the class of contracts considered at para 8–028 of Chitty. As I say, Mr Rooney was already with Everton on Mr McIntosh's own evidence (see para 18 of his witness statement). At this time, and indeed in 2002, Wayne Rooney only wanted to play for Everton; he did not wish to play for any other club. He was already doing so.

[**40.**] It does seem to me that the Proform agreement is much more analogous to the contract considered by Avory J in *Shears v Mendeloff* (1914) 30 TLR 342 than it is to the class of contract considered in cases such as *Doyle v White City Stadium Ltd* [1935] 1 KB 110, [1934] All ER Rep 252 and *Chaplin v Leslie Frewin (Publishers) Ltd* [1965] 3 All ER 764, [1966] Ch 71 and *Denmark Productions Ltd v Boscobel Productions Ltd* [1968] 3 All ER 513, [1969] 1 QB 699. As Mr Joffe submitted, music group managers are very different from players' representatives. Music group managers organise matters that are essential to the very business of the musical artiste. Players' representatives do not undertake matters that are essential to the player's training or his livelihood. They do not enable the minor to earn a living or to advance his skills as a professional footballer. In my judgment, cases such as *Chaplin v Leslie Frewin (Publishers) Ltd* and *Doyle v White City Stadium Ltd* make it clear that the basis of the class of analogous contracts is that the minor is entitled to earn his living or to start to do so. It does not seem to me that the Proform agreement is analogous to such a contract. I say that particularly bearing in mind the fact that, under the Football Association rules, no contract can be entered into by a player as young as Wayne Rooney then was. No contract could properly be entered into by him until a time less than two months before this representation agreement was due to expire; and even if entered into by Wayne Rooney at that time, it would have been voidable at his instance if not genuinely for his benefit. That would have continued to be so throughout the remaining short duration of the management and agency agreement. It seems to me that the Proform agreement is at one remove from the class of contract that has been treated in the authorities as being subject to the exception to the general voidability of minors' contracts, applicable where such a contract is for the minor's benefit. As para 8–028 of Chitty makes clear, "A minor's trading contracts are not binding on him, even if beneficial". It seems to me that this case falls within the general principle that merely because a contract is beneficial to a minor, if such is the case, it is not binding on him unless it falls within a particular category.

[**41.**] So for those reasons, it seems to me that Mr Joffe is correct in saying that the Proform agreement does not fall within the class of minors' contracts which are analogous to contracts of apprenticeship, education and service.'

A further type of employment-related contract, which the courts refuse to enforce, is a 'trading' contract. In other words, self-employed minors who set up a business may have difficulty making binding contracts in relation to it.

Mercantile Union Guarantee v Ball [1937] 2 KB 498

Facts: The minor ran a haulage business, and entered into a hire purchase contract in connection with this.

Held: The contract was not enforceable against the minor.

Finlay J:

'This is an appeal from a judgment of Judge Ruegg given in the Hanley county court. The action was brought by the plaintiffs claiming a sum of £96. 7s. 6d., arrears due under a hire purchase agreement in respect of a motor lorry. The total price of the lorry was £666. It is unnecessary to refer in detail to the terms, which were those common in such contracts.

The defendant was, at the time of the making of the contract, an infant, being aged twenty. He had been carrying on business as a haulage contractor for about two years. He got into financial difficulties and fell into arrears with his instalments. Being sued he raised two defences, but to one only of these – that of infancy – is it necessary here to refer. The learned judge has held that this defence succeeded and we think that he was right in so holding.

The law on this matter has been discussed in many cases. The position is thus stated in Coke upon Littleton, p 172a:

> "An infant may bind himselfe to pay for his necessary meat, drinke, apparell, necessary physicke, and such other necessaries, and likewise for his good teaching or instruction, whereby he may profit himselfe afterwards."

To this enumeration some addition has in the course of years been made, particularly, as pointed out by Slesser L.J. in *Doyle v White City Stadium Ltd* with reference to contracts of service. Our attention was drawn to several modern cases: *Walter v Everard* [1891] 2 Q. B. 369; *Clements v London & North Western Ry Co*; *Cowern v Nield* [1912] 2 K. B. 419. In this last case the law is thus laid down by Bray J.: "It is true that there are certain contracts which, if they are for the infant's benefit, can be enforced against him; and it is said this trading contract was for the benefit of the infant because it was for the benefit of the infant that he should learn how to carry on a trade. But in my opinion there is no authority for saying that a trading contract, even if for the benefit of the infant, is an exception to the rule that an infant is not, except in certain cases, liable on contracts made by him." The most recent case appears to be *Doyle v White City Stadium Ltd* [1935] 1 K. B. 110, 131.

Applying the law laid down in these cases it seems to us in the first place that this contract is not one of the class by which an infant can be bound. It is not a contract for necessaries within the enumeration of Lord Coke. Nor is it a contract of service or apprenticeship or analogous to any of these. But there is a further and in our view an insuperable difficulty in the plaintiffs' way. The contract must be not only within the class of contracts by which an infant may be bound, but it must be one beneficial to the infant, and whether it is so is a question to be decided on the facts of each particular case. The judge here has found that the contract was not for the benefit of the infant. Even if it be assumed, contrary to our view, that the contract is one of the class by which an infant could be bound, we find it quite impossible to differ from his view that a contract for a large and expensive lorry on onerous hire purchase terms was not a contract for the benefit of the infant.

For these reasons we are of opinion that the judgment of Judge Ruegg was perfectly correct, that it should be affirmed and this appeal dismissed with costs.'

The policy underlying this restriction on minors' contracts is understandable – that is, that minors should not be exposed to the significant financial risks that may attach to business contracts. It is questionable, however, whether a society, which (currently) allows those over the age of 16 to leave school, should put barriers in the way of those of that age with the entrepreneurial flair to establish their own businesses. Other businesses are likely to be wary of contracting with such a person, because of the risk that their contracts will not be enforceable against the minor.

6.2.4 VOIDABLE CONTRACTS

Certain types of contract that involve continuing interests in property are valid, unless the minor repudiates them while still a minor, or within a reasonable period of attaining majority. Contracts falling within this rule include partnership agreements, marriage settlements and leases. The question of what is a 'reasonable time' is one of fact, and was considered in *Edwards v Carter*, a case on marriage settlements.

Edwards v Carter [1893] AC 360

Facts: A man who had entered into a marriage settlement while still a minor, sought to repudiate it, when its provisions operated to his disadvantage.

Held: Repudiation must occur within a reasonable time, and on these facts, a period of four years and eight months was too long to be reasonable.

Lord Herschell LC:

'My Lords, the point for determination in this appeal may be very shortly stated. On the 16th of October 1883 a settlement was executed in contemplation of a marriage between Martin Albert Silber and Lady Lucy Vaughan. At the time of its execution Martin Albert Silber the intending bridegroom was an infant; he did not come of age until the 19th of November 1883, just over a month afterwards. By the deed his father Albert Marcius Silber covenanted to pay the trustees of the settlement £1500 a year "during the life of Lady Lucy Vaughan and during such further period (if any) as there should be living any child or grandchild of the intended marriage". The trustees were to pay the yearly sum of £1500 to Martin Albert Silber during his life or until he should become bankrupt, and after the determination of his interest upon the trusts declared for the benefit of Lady Lucy Vaughan and the issue of the marriage. I need not trouble your Lordships with those trusts; they were for the most part, such as are commonly found in settlements of this description. Nor need I dwell upon the provisions relating to a policy of insurance. But by the settlement it was further agreed and declared that if Martin Albert Silber then was, or if he or the trustees for the time being, should become entitled to any property under any settlement executed, or to be executed, by Albert Marcius Silber, or under any appointment made or to be made, in exercise of any power in any such settlement contained or to be contained, or under or by virtue of the will of Albert Marcius Silber, or the will of Amelia Silber his wife, or any codicil thereto, or by virtue of the intestacy of either of them, then, unless such settlement or appointment, or will or codicil, should otherwise direct, such property, if not thereby given to the trustees, should be vested in them upon such trusts for sale or conversion as might be necessary or expedient, and subject thereto upon the trusts, and with and subject to the powers contained with respect to the moneys assured by or to become payable under the policy of insurance, except that the ultimate trust should be in favour of Martin Albert Silber instead of Albert Marcius Silber (his father), "and the amount or value of all property so acquired by the trustees should be deemed to fall within the operation of the clause or provision lastly thereinbefore contained, and be applicable accordingly by way of satisfaction, pro tanto at the rate aforesaid, of the yearly sum so covenanted to be paid by Albert Marcius Silber"; the effect of this provision being that, if any money was left to Martin Albert Silber under the will of Albert Marcius Silber, the father, that money was to pass to the trustees of the settlement and be held by them upon the trusts of the settlement, to the extent to which it was sufficient to do so, in lieu of the obligation and covenant to pay the £1500 a year.

My Lords, the settlement having been executed, and the infant having come of age on the 19th of November 1883, the father made a will leaving his two sons residuary legatees. The father died on the 14th of May 1887, and his will and codicil were proved in July 1887. There was nothing which can be regarded as a repudiation by Martin Albert Silber until July 1888. Now, my Lords, it is not disputed that this contract executed and entered into by Martin Albert Silber was not absolutely void, but was voidable only, that is to say, that after he came of age it was as binding as if he had been of age at the time when he executed it, subject only to this, that the law enabled him to avoid his obligations provided he did so within a reasonable time.

My Lords, I did not understand the learned counsel for the appellants really to dispute the proposition that the repudiation in order that the obligations may be got rid of must be within a reasonable time after the minor ceases to be a minor. The controversy has been as to what elements may be taken into account in determining whether more than a reasonable time has elapsed. In the present case, as I have shewn your Lordships, there was no repudiation at all during the lifetime of the father. Down to the death of the father nothing had been done by the son; and it is impossible not to see that if the son had repudiated in the lifetime of the father it is in the highest degree probable that the disposition made by the father would have been different from what it was, as it is certain that the position of those taking, or at all events of one of those taking, under the will of the father was altered for the worse by reason of this repudiation if the repudiation was effective.

Now, my Lords, the first question is whether the infant was entitled to wait until an actual sum of money came to him to which this covenant could apply before he made the repudiation. I think that is a proposition which it is absolutely impossible to regard with seriousness – that this covenant being binding unless he repudiates it within a reasonable time, he is entitled to wait to see how in respect of any particular sum of money the covenant will operate, and when he has made up his mind whether with regard to that sum of money it will be beneficial to him or not, he can then, and not till then, be said to have his proper opportunity of making the determination!

Then it is said that in considering whether a reasonable time has elapsed you must take into account the fact that he did not know what were the terms of the settlement, and that it contained this particular covenant. He knew that he had executed a deed – he must be taken to have known that that deed though binding upon him could be repudiated when he came of age. And, my Lords, it seems to me that in measuring a reasonable time, whether in point of fact he had or had not acquainted himself with the nature of the obligations which he had undertaken is wholly immaterial. The time must be measured in precisely the same way whether he had so made himself acquainted or not. I do not say that he was under any obligation to make himself acquainted with the nature of the deed which, having executed as an infant, he might or might not at his pleasure repudiate when he came of age. All I say is this, that he cannot maintain that the reasonable time when measured must be a longer time because he has chosen not to make himself acquainted with the nature of the deed which he has executed.

My Lords, having put aside those two contentions, the only question comes to be, Has a reasonable time been exceeded? The learned judges in the court below expressed their opinion that the period which elapsed, a period of between four and five years, was more than a reasonable time. It is not at all necessary for your Lordships to lay down what would have been a reasonable time in this case. It is enough to say that in my opinion it is impossible to hold that the learned judges in the court below have in any way erred in saying that more than a reasonable time had elapsed.'

6.3 EFFECTS OF ENTERING INTO A CONTRACT WITH A MINOR

6.3.1 VOID CONTRACTS

A void contract – for example, for the purchase of non-necessary goods or services – can be ratified by the minor on attaining majority. This will make the contract fully enforceable by both parties.

The position regarding the effect of actions performed in reliance on a void contract, is partly governed by the provisions of the Minors' Contracts Act 1987.

MINORS' CONTRACTS ACT 1987

s 3(1) Where—

(a) a person ('the plaintiff') has after the commencement of this Act entered into a contract with another ('the defendant'), and

(b) the contract is unenforceable against the defendant (or he repudiates it) because he was a minor when the contract was made,

the court may, if it is just and equitable to do so, require the defendant to transfer to the plaintiff any property acquired by the defendant under the contract, or any property representing it.

(2) Nothing in this section shall be taken to prejudice any other remedy available to the plaintiff.

The result is that:

- A fully executed contract cannot be undone. It will be effective to transfer ownership of money or goods exchanged under it;
- If only the minor has performed, then damages for breach can be claimed from the adult, but not specific performance;
- If the adult party has transferred property, then s 3 allows the court to require the minor to return the property, or any property representing it, if it is just and equitable to do so.

Where non-necessary services have been provided, the adult is without a remedy, since s 3 only applies to property.

Where a contract is void, the courts will not generally allow indirect enforcement through a tortious remedy. Thus the minor who misrepresents his or her age cannot be sued for deceit.

Stocks v Wilson [1913] 2 KB 235

Facts: The defendant, an infant, by fraudulently representing that he was of full age, induced the plaintiff to sell and deliver to him certain furniture and effects of which she was the owner. The goods were not necessaries. They were assigned to the defendant by an instrument which was a bill of sale within the Bills of Sale Act, 1878. It contained a promise by the defendant to pay the purchase-money at a future date and a licence to the plaintiff to resume possession of the goods if the price was not then paid. After the purchase the defendant sold some of the goods for £30 and, with the knowledge and assent of the plaintiff or her agent, granted a bill of sale of the residue as security for an advance of £100.

Held: The defendant was not liable on the contract, on in tort for deceit, but was liable to account for the £130 obtained for the goods.

Lush J:

'. . . The next question, which is the one that has caused me some difficulty, is whether under the peculiar circumstances of this case the plaintiff has a claim for equitable relief, and if so to what amount. That an infant who appears to be of full age, and who has made an express representation that he is of full age fraudulently and to deceive some other person, incurs an equitable liability under some circumstances is clear enough. He cannot be sued for damages although he is generally speaking liable for a tort; the reason being that a temptation would be offered both to the infant himself and to other persons to enter into contracts if the other party were able by obtaining a representation of majority by the infant to make the contract practically effective. For the more complete protection of the infant, the law prevents the other contracting party not only from suing on the contract, but also from suing for damages, if the fraud is connected with and forms the inducement to the contract. Nor is the infant estopped from proving the true facts, which again, if such an estoppel were permitted, would deprive the infant of the protection necessary for his security. What the Court of Equity has done in cases of this kind is to prevent the infant from retaining the benefit of what he has obtained by reason of his fraud. It has done no more than this, and this is a very different thing from making him liable to pay damages or compensation for the loss of the other party's bargain. If the infant has obtained property by fraud he can be compelled to restore it; if he has obtained money he can be compelled to refund it. If he has not obtained either, but has only purported to bind himself by an obligation to transfer property or to pay money, neither in a Court of law nor a Court of Equity can he be compelled to make good his promise or to make satisfaction for its breach.

6.3.2 VOIDABLE CONTRACTS

Repudiation of a voidable contract will remove any future obligation, but will leave intact those that have already been performed. Regarding obligations that should have been performed prior to repudiation, but have not, the position is unclear, but was considered in *obiter dicta* in *North Western Rail Co v McMichael* (1850) 5 Ex 114, a case concerned with calls on shares, and in particular, the provisions of the Railways Acts, which made shareholders absolutely liable to pay calls. Parke B commented (p 125):

We consider . . . that this statute did not mean, by general words, to deprive infants of the protection which the law gave them, against improvident bargains. Under this statute, therefore, our opinion is, that an infant is not absolutely bound, but is in same situation as an infant acquiring real estate, or any other permanent interest: he is not deprived of the right which the law gives every infant, of waiving and disagreeing to a purchase which he has made: and if he waives it, the estate acquired by the purchase is at an end, and with it his liability to pay calls, *though the avoidance may not have taken place until the call was due*. [emphasis added]

This seems to indicate that the repudiation of a voidable contract can be, to this extent, retrospective.

6.3.2.1 Enforceable contracts

Where a minor has been supplied with necessary goods, there is an obligation to pay a reasonable price for them – s 3, Sale of Goods Act 1979 (above, p 324). There is no obligation in relation to goods that have not been received.

As regards the services, however, the position appears to be different, on the basis of the decision in *Roberts v Gray*. It seems to be possible in this case for the adult to recover damages, even if no services have been provided.

Roberts v Gray [1913] 1 KB 520 (CA)

Facts: The defendant was an aspiring billiards player, who made a contract to go on world tour with the plaintiff, an experienced player. The defendant backed out before the tour began, and the plaintiff sued for breach of contract. The defendant argued, by analogy with the position in relation to the supply of goods, that the adult should not be able to recover other than a reasonable price for services actually provided.

Held: In this type of case the adult was entitled to damages based on the full losses involved in organising the world tour.

Cozens-Hardy Mr:
'. . . .Now, what is the effect of a contract which is entered into by an infant with reference to necessaries, including instruction and education? We have heard an argument forcibly put before us that such a contract may be good so far as the consideration has been executed, but that it cannot be enforced so far as it is executory. For that proposition I think there is no authority, and I certainly think that it is not open to this Court to say that there is any such rule . . .

If, therefore, this is a contract falling within a class to which the doctrine of necessaries applies, and if, taken as a whole, it is for the infant's benefit, I see no foundation whatever for the argument that the infant is not liable for damages in the event of his repudiating or declining to perform the contract entered into. The Court has acted upon that in *Gadd v Thompson* [1894] 2 Q. B. 482 to the extent of granting an injunction to restrain an infant from being guilty of a breach of a clause in a contract of service after he has left the employment. Here only damages are claimed and have been given.

It only remains, therefore, to consider that which I think is not really a very difficult

---

problem. What is the nature of this contract? What was the station of the parties and what is the meaning of the agreement?'

[His Lordship went through the contract, and was clearly of opinion that playing billiards in company with a noted player like John Roberts must be instruction of the most valuable kind for an infant who desired to make playing billiards the occupation of his life; and agreed with the Lord Chief Justice that the agreement was in effect for teaching, instruction and employment, and was reasonable and for the benefit of the infant.]

'That being so, the Lord Chief Justice gave judgment for the plaintiff against the infant, and in my opinion the judgment which he gave was perfectly right and cannot be interfered with.'

The same applies to beneficial contracts of service; it is only in relation to the supply of necessary goods that the adult can recover only where he or she has performed his or her part of the contract (and then only a reasonable price, rather than the contract price).

6.4 MENTAL DISABILITY

MENTAL CAPACITY ACT 2005

s 7 *Payment for necessary goods and services*

(1) If necessary goods or services are supplied to a person who lacks capacity to contract for the supply, he must pay a reasonable price for them.
(2) 'Nece ssary' means suitable to a person's condition in life and to his actual requirements at the time when the goods or services are supplied.

This applies the same rule as operates in relation to contracts for necessary goods under s 3, Sale of Goods Act 1979. Note, however, that here the rule applies to services, as well as goods.

This approach will apply to those who are either under the control of the court because of their mental disability, or who are unable to appreciate the nature of the transaction they are entering into because of such disability.

In cases falling outside the scope of s 7, the fully competent party will be able to enforce the contract, unless it is proved that s/he was aware of the incapacity of the disabled party. The Privy Council in *Hart v O'Connor* confirmed this.

Hart v O'Connor [1985] 2 All ER 880 (PC)

Facts: H entered into an agreement to purchase land. The seller, J's, signature on the agreement was obtained by J's solicitor. At the time, unknown to H, J was of unsound mind. At trial the judge held that the contract was unenforceable because of J's incapacity, although H was unaware of this. H appealed to the New Zealand Court of Appeal, and then to the Privy Council.

Held: Where a contracting party was unaware of the mental incapacity of the other party, the contract was enforceable.

Lord Brightman:

'. . . The judge in *Archer v Cutler* [1980] 1 N.Z.L.R. 386 relied on the statement of Lopes L.J. that the mental incapacity of a lunatic must be known to the other contracting party "in order to avoid a *fair* contract on the ground of insanity", as implying that such knowledge is unnecessary in order to avoid a contract which is unfair in the sense of contractual imbalance. But in their Lordships' view "fair" was quite appropriately used by Lopes L.J. so as to except the case of the apparently sane person who is imposed upon in a manner which equity regards as unconscionable, and was not intended to permit an inquiry into the balance of the terms of the contract. The quotation from Lopes L.J. which the judge in *Archer v Cutler* relied upon, at p 398, omits the succeeding sentence where Lopes L.J. repeats the rule without any reference to "fairness" and says in unqualified terms [1892] 1 Q.B. 599, 603:

"A defendant who seeks to avoid a contract on the ground of his insanity, must plead and prove, not merely his incapacity, but also the plaintiff's knowledge of that fact, and unless he proves these two things he cannot succeed."

In the face of that statement of the rule, it seems to their Lordships impossible to suppose that Lopes L.J. regarded proof of contractual imbalance as a permissible alternative to knowledge of insanity where a person of unsound mind seeks to set aside an agreement which was made in good faith.

. . . In *Imperial Loan Co Ltd v Stone* [1892] 1 Q.B. 599 a person of unsound mind was sued on a promissory note which he had signed as surety. The jury found that he was insane when he signed the note but there was no finding as to the creditor's knowledge of such insanity. Nevertheless the judge entered a verdict against the creditor. On appeal it was submitted that there was no authority that a man could be sued and made liable on an executory contract which he had made when of unsound mind, except in the case of a contract for necessaries. This submission was rejected, and a new trial was directed. Lord Esher M.R. said, at p. 601:

"When a person enters into a contract, and afterwards alleges that he was so insane at the time that he did not know what he was doing, and proves the allegation, the contract is as binding on him in every respect, whether it is executory or executed, as if he had been sane when he made it, unless he can prove further that the person with whom he contracted knew him to be so insane as not to be capable of understanding what he was about."

Fry L.J. said, at p 602:

"It thus appears that there has been grafted on the old rule the exception that the contracts of a person who is non compos mentis may be avoided when his condition can be shewn to have been known to the plaintiff. So far as I know, that is the only exception." . . .

Imperial Loan Co Ltd v Stone [1892] 1 Q.B. 599 was considered and accepted as correct by the High Court of Australia in *McLaughlin v Daily Telegraph Newspaper Co Ltd (No. 2)* (1904) 1 C.L.R. 243, where Griffith C.J. delivering the judgment of the court said of the Imperial Loan case and its predecessor *Molton v Camroux*, at p 272:

"The principle of the decision seems, however, to be the same in both cases, which, in our judgment, establish that a contract made by a person actually of unsound, but apparently of sound, mind with another who deals with him directly, and who has no knowledge of the unsoundness of mind, is as valid as if the unsoundness of mind had not existed. If the man dealing with the person of unsound mind is aware of his insanity, the contract is voidable at the option of the latter, but the party who takes advantage of the other cannot himself set up the incapacity. In this respect the matter is treated on the same footing as cases of fraud inducing a contract. There is, indeed, authority for saying that the equitable doctrines governing the validity or invalidity of a contract made with an insane person are only a particular instance of the general doctrines relating to fraudulent contracts. In the cases last mentioned no unfairness of dealing could be imputed to the persons who sought to take advantage of the contract, which was, in fact, made, in each case, with an apparently sane person. The principle appears to be that the validity of a contract made with an apparently sane person is to be determined by the application of the same rules as are applied in ordinary cases." . . .

Their Lordships must also refer to *Tremills v Benton* (1892) 18 V.L.R. 607 which the judge in *Archer v Cutler*, at p 401, mentioned as an Australian case where "lack of fairness has been held to be a material element" in a contract entered into with a lunatic who was ostensibly sane. The action was by the personal representative of Tremills to set aside deeds whereby Tremills had granted land and buildings to Mr. and Mrs. Benton, reserving to himself a life interest, in return for his keep. He was 86 years of age, in bad health and died 12 days later. The administrator sought to set aside the deeds on the ground that their execution was obtained by undue influence, and secondly on the ground that Tremills was, to the knowledge of the Bentons, of unsound mind. The judge found that although Tremills was in full possession of his faculties, he suffered from delusions; he was not however acting in subjection to any undue influence. The Full Court upheld these findings. Higinbotham C.J. said, at p 620:

"Was the contract itself, which was entered into by the parties, a fair and bona fide contract? If it was, this case is clearly within the legal and the equitable rule by which such a contract, if executed and completed, is to be upheld, although it has been made by a person of unsound mind with another person who has no knowledge that he is contracting with a lunatic. In determining whether a contract is or is not unfair, the adequacy of the consideration is, as the learned primary judge observed, one of the elements to be regarded; but it should be added that it is only one element, and that in order to justify the avoidance of a contract on this ground, the inadequacy of the consideration must be so great as to be unconscionable, and to amount in itself to conclusive and decisive evidence of over-reaching or fraud."

Higinbotham C.J. accepted the judge's finding that the consideration given by the defendants was "altogether inadequate", and that neither the deceased nor the defendants regarded the matter as a bargain in which the former expected to receive or the latter supposed they were giving full value. He concluded, at p 621:

"Holding, as we are bound to do, that proof of undue influence on the part of the defendants has failed, and that the deceased had full possession of his faculties, and perfectly comprehended what he was doing, I cannot find any evidence whatever that the transaction between these parties was in itself wanting in fairness and bona fides. The deceased, who was advised by his solicitor, had a single, definite object in view. Under the influence of an insane delusion, he wished to deprive his son of his property after his own death, while at the same time he sanely and prudently desired to retain full possession of it during the remainder of his life, and also to secure for himself the benefits and comforts of a home. He bargained for this as a condition of his gift, and the defendants complied with his wish, and covenanted to carry it into effect. The burden of the covenant was in the event small in proportion to the money value of the gift, but the disparity was not caused by the act or demand or undue influence of the defendants. They gave the consideration they were asked to give, and that was all that the deceased in his insane delusion, and in his prudent regard for himself, thought of requiring. The bargain was made a legal and binding bargain by the act of the deceased, and apart from the suspicion, which we must hold to be unfounded, of undue influence having been employed to bring it about, presents no trace of fraud or over-reaching on the part of the defendants, although they undoubtedly reaped the larger share of the benefit of the bargain. I think that we should be departing from the principles on which courts of equity have acted in similar cases if these deeds should now be set aside at the instance of the administrator."

Holroyd J. said, at pp 621–622:

"After much hesitation, and examining carefully all the authorities that were cited, I have come to the conclusion that a contract entered into with a lunatic by a person who does not know him to be, or suspect him to be, a lunatic, cannot be avoided by the lunatic or by his representatives after his death on the ground merely of the insufficiency of the consideration; but that some fraud or imposition must have been practised by the party who desires to uphold the contract, or something done by him which would render it unconscientious on his part to take advantage of the bargain, to afford a ground for setting it aside. For that reason only I differ from the learned primary judge."

Finally Hodges J. said, at pp 622–623:

"The learned judge has found, and in my opinion has so found on sufficient evidence, that there was not undue influence, that there was bona fides on the part of the defendants, and that the defendants did not know that H. Tremills was insane; but he has declared the deeds void on the ground that H. Tremills was insane at the time that he executed them, and that they were not 'fair' within the meaning of that word as used in the judgment in *Hassard v Smith* (1872) 6 I.R.Eq. 429, 433, and it is against this decision that the defendants have appealed. The learned judge appears to have acted on the following passage, which he quoted from the case of *Hassard v Smith*: 'The rule which now prevails, both at law and in equity, in reference to contracts entered into by a person of apparently sound mind, and not known by the other contracting party to be insane, is, that such contracts, if executed and completed, and if fair and bona fide, will not be held void or set aside.' This, I think, correctly states the law if the word 'fair' be understood in the sense in which the Vice-Chancellor [Chatterton] must be taken from the context to have intended that it should be understood and by 'fair' I understand him to mean not unfair, not unconscientious, not over-reaching. I think it refers to a contract not obtained by imposition, but I do not think that it would correctly give the Vice-Chancellor's meaning to substitute for the word 'fair' the words 'for full consideration'."

The words "if executed and completed" should of course now be disregarded. Then, picking up the word "fairly" in *Beavan v M'Donnell*, 9 Exch. 309, he said, at p 623:

"There the word 'fairly' could not, I think, be referring to a perfect equality of the consideration given by each party to the contract. Again, a little further on, the Vice-Chancellor quotes with approval the following passage from *Story*: 'The ground upon which courts of equity now interfere to set aside the contracts and other acts, however solemn, of persons who are idiots, lunatics, and otherwise non compotes mentis, is fraud.' The Vice-Chancellor could not quote, with approval, Story's opinion that the ground on which courts of equity set aside these contracts is *fraud*, if he was deciding that inequality of consideration was a sufficient ground for setting aside such contracts. Again, the Vice-Chancellor a little further on again quotes with approval Story's view that 'If a purchase is made without any knowledge of the incapacity, and no advantage has been taken, courts of equity will not interfere to set aside the contract, etc.' Here again the Vice-Chancellor shows that what invalidates these contracts is not mere inequality of consideration, but the taking of an advantage. If an advantage is taken, the contract is not 'fair'."

This case appears to their Lordships to be directly contrary to the proposition adopted in *Archer v Cutler* [1980] 1 N.Z.L.R. 386, because it plainly recognises that a contract with an unsuspected lunatic will not be set aside short of equitable fraud.

In the opinion of their Lordships, to accept the proposition enunciated in *Archer v Cutler* that a contract with a person ostensibly sane but actually of unsound mind can be set aside because it is "unfair" to the person of unsound mind in the sense of contractual imbalance, is unsupported by authority, is illogical and would distinguish the law of New Zealand from the law of Australia, as exemplified in McLaughlin's case (1904) 1 C.L.R. 243 and Tremills' case, 18 V.L.R. 607, for no good reason, as well as from the law of England from which the law of Australia and New Zealand and other "common law" countries has stemmed. In so saying their Lordships differ with profound respect from the contrary view so strongly expressed by the New Zealand courts.

To sum the matter up, in the opinion of their Lordships, the validity of a contract entered into by a lunatic who is ostensibly sane is to be judged by the same standards as a contract by a person of sound mind, and is not voidable by the lunatic or his representatives by reason of "unfairness" unless such unfairness amounts to equitable fraud which would have enabled the complaining party to avoid the contract even if he had been sane.

Their Lordships turn finally to . . . whether the plaintiffs are entitled to have the contract set aside as an "unconscionable bargain". This issue must also be answered in the negative, because the defendant was guilty of no unconscionable conduct. Indeed, as is conceded, he acted with complete innocence throughout. He was unaware of the vendor's unsoundness of mind. The vendor was ostensibly advised by his own solicitor. The defendant had no means of knowing or cause to suspect that the vendor was not in receipt of and acting in accordance with the most full and careful advice. The terms of the bargain were the terms proposed by the vendor's solicitor, not terms imposed by the defendant or his solicitor. There was no equitable fraud, no victimisation, no taking advantage, no overreaching or other description of unconscionable doings which might have justified the intervention of equity to restrain an action by the defendant at law. The plaintiffs have in the opinion of their Lordships failed to make out any case for denying to the defendant the benefit of a bargain which was struck with complete propriety on his side.'

6.5 INTOXICATION

The position in relation to the supply of necessary goods to those incompetent to contract through intoxication is governed by s 3 Sale of Goods Act 1979 – as set out above (p 324). Otherwise, it would seem that the same approach should apply as is used in relation to mental disability – including the fact that the sober party needs to be aware of the other party's lack of capacity before the contract is rendered unenforceable.

It is assumed, in the absence of authority, that the same rules will apply whether the intoxication is the result of alcohol or drugs.

6.6 ADDITIONAL READING

Collins, H, *Regulating Contracts*, 1999, Oxford: OUP, pp 116–17.
Hudson, AH, 'Mental Incapacity Revisited' [1986] *Conveyancer and Property Lawyer* 178.

CHAPTER 7

CONTENTS OF THE CONTRACT

7.1 INTRODUCTION

Once the formation of a contract has been established the next issue to deal with is the contents of the contract. What are the parties' respective rights and obligations under the contract? In practice, this is an extremely important issue for the parties.

Problems may arise in a number of ways. First, the contract may have been preceded by a lengthy period of negotiation. If so, it will be important for the parties to ascertain which precontractual statements have been incorporated into the contract and which have not. The contract may have been oral, written or a combination of both. Even if the contract is written, one of the parties might allege that the written document does not represent their true intentions. In such cases, the job of the court is to interpret the contract so as to ascertain the true meaning of the language used. In fulfilling this role, the court can take into account evidence of the surrounding factual context – known as the 'factual matrix'. In addition, the court's approach will be influenced by other factors including the relative bargaining power of the parties and, in some situations, statutory regulation. If the contract is entirely verbal the court will have to determine what has been said. The problems that arise here are likely to be evidential and are beyond the scope of this book. Nevertheless, issues of construction may arise here in a similar way to written contracts. Problems may also occur in respect of implied terms. In addition to terms expressly incorporated into the contract, terms may be implied into the contract either by the courts or by statute. In certain situations, terms will be implied by statute, irrespective of the wishes or intentions of the parties. This is part of a legislative policy to protect the reasonable expectations of vulnerable parties.

The chapter is divided into three parts. First, the distinction between precontractual representations and terms will be considered. Second, the approach to express terms and their interpretation will be analysed. Finally, the rules relating to the implication of terms, both at common law and by statute, will be discussed.

7.2 DISTINCTION BETWEEN REPRESENTATIONS AND TERMS

It is extremely important to ascertain whether a statement made by one party to the other prior to the formation of the contract has been incorporated into the contract as a term. If it has, then a person who fails to comply with the statement will be liable to the full range of contractual remedies as discussed in Chapter 17. If the statement has not been incorporated as a term, then liability cannot be for breach of contract and the claimant will have to pursue a claim for misrepresentation.

This distinction was once highly significant because of the different remedial consequences that attach to a breach of contract and a misrepresentation. Following a breach of contract, the claimant will normally be entitled to damages, which will compensate him for any profits that may have been lost as a result of the broken promise. Following a misrepresentation, the remedies available to a claimant will be much more restricted. Indeed, prior to the decision of the House of Lords in *Hedley Byrne & Co Ltd v Heller & Partners* [1964] AC 465 and the enactment of the Misrepresentation Act 1967, damages were only recoverable in English law for fraudulent misrepresentations. This meant that a claimant who wished to claim damages prior to these developments had either to prove fraud (which was notoriously difficult) or prove that the statement had been incorporated into the contract (thus giving rise to a claim for breach of contract). Because of these difficulties, the courts often adopted a generous approach to finding that a statement was a term of the contract in order to award damages to a deserving claimant (see, for example, *De Laselle v Guildford* [1901] 2 KB 215). Now that damages are available for negligent misrepresentation, the need to adopt such an approach has diminished.

7.2.1 INCORPORATION AS A TERM OF THE AGREEMENT

The basic test as to whether or not a statement has been incorporated into a contract is one of intention. Did the parties intend for the statement to be a term? In ascertaining intention the courts take into account a number of factors in determining whether a statement was intended to be a term. Some of these factors have been afforded a greater importance than others, but none of them are decisive of the issue. They are merely aids to establishing the parties' intention.

7.2.1.1 Importance of the statement

The first factor that might be relevant is the importance of the statement. This was seen in the case of *Bannerman v White*.

Bannerman v White (1861) 10 CB(NS) 844; 142 ER 685

Facts: White asked Bannerman if the hops he was selling had been treated with sulphur stating that if they had been so treated, he would not be willing to purchase them. Bannerman said that they had not been treated with sulphur which he believed to be the case. Later, White discovered that 5 out of 300 acres had been treated with sulphur.

Held: There had been no fraudulent misrepresentation. However, the statement had become a term of the contract, and Bannerman was in breach of the term.

Erle CJ:
'[The statement] was a preliminary stipulation; and if it had not been given, the defendants would not have gone on with the treaty which resulted in the sale. In this sense it was the condition upon which the defendants contracted; and it would be contrary to the intention expressed by this stipulation that the contract should remain valid if sulphur had been used. The intention of the parties governs in the making and in the construction of all contracts. If the parties so intend, the sale may be absolute, with a warranty superadded; or the sale may be conditional, to be null if the warranty is broke. And, upon this statement of facts, we think that the intention appears that the contract should be null if sulphur had been used . . .'

It was crucial that the statement was a 'preliminary stipulation'. In the absence of the statement, White would not have been prepared to purchase the hops. Due to the importance of the statement it was construed to be a term of the contract.

7.2.1.2 Requirement of independent verification

It should be noted that, even where the matter is of importance to the representee, it will not be construed as a term of the contract if the maker of the statement made clear that the truth should be verified independently.

Ecay v Godfrey (1947) 80 Lloyd's Law Reports 286

Facts: Señor José Paniego Ecay, Spanish Vice-consul at Newcastle upon Tyne, agreed to purchase a boat from Mr Godfrey, who stated that the *Tio Pepe* was 'sea-going and capable of going overseas, in excellent condition and with a sound hull'. Prior to the sale, Godfrey recommended that Ecay have the boat surveyed. The boat was not sea-going or capable of going overseas, and in view of her condition the plaintiff had to sell the boat at a significantly lower price than that at which he had bought her. The plaintiff brought a claim for breach of contract.

Held: The High Court held that, in light of Godfrey's recommendation that Ecay should have the boat surveyed, Godfrey could not have intended his statement as to the ship's condition to have formed part of the contract.

Lord Goddard CJ:
'What you have got to think of is: If the parties sat down here and wrote out their contract, would you find in that contract an undertaking by the defendant that so and so existed or so and so was the fact? If we apply that test to the case here, having heard all the evidence, I think it is impossible to come to the conclusion that if these two parties had sat down and written out their contract, intending thereby to put down on paper exactly what they bargained about and all the terms of their bargain, Mr. Godfrey would have said, "And I promise you . . . that the vessel is in good condition." It would be quite inconsistent, I think, with his statement to the plaintiff at the time, "Aren't you going to have a survey?" . . . because if he was intending to warrant at the time that this boat was in good condition, there would be no point in having a survey.'

The same principle will apply where such verification would normally be expected, even if it had not been actively encouraged. For example, this will normally be the position in relation to the sale of real property, where a purchaser will generally be expected to commission a homebuyer's survey, rather than relying upon the vendor's statements.

7.2.1.3 Contract terms stated in writing

The third factor that might be relevant is the fact that the parties have committed their contract to writing. If the parties have done this, the courts will be very reluctant to incorporate a term into the contract that was not included in the written terms. This was seen in the case of *Routledge v McKay*.

Routledge v McKay [1954] 1 WLR 615

Facts: McKay sold a Douglas motor-cycle to Routledge. Prior to the sale, McKay told Routledge that the motor-cycle was a 1942 model. Routledge prepared a 'written memorandum' at the time of the sale, but this was silent as to the age of the motor-cycle. After the sale, Routledge discovered that the motor-cycle was a 1930 model and he brought a claim for breach of warranty. The county court judge held that there had been a breach of warranty and gave judgment for Routledge.

Held: The Court of Appeal allowed the appeal on the ground that the evidence did not establish a collateral contract by which a warranty was given that the motor-cycle was a 1942 model. It was particularly important to the Court of Appeal that the date of the motor-cycle had not been included in the written memorandum.

Lord Evershed MR:
'[The written memorandum] represents prima facie the record of what the parties intended to agree when the actual transaction took place. Counsel for the defendant has contended that the terms of it necessarily exclude any warranty – that is to say, any collateral bargain, either contemporary or earlier in date. I am not sure that I would go as far . . . in that respect. But I think that, as a matter of construction, it would be extremely difficult to say that such an agreement was consistent with a warranty being given at the same time and so as to be intended to form a part of the bargain then made.'

The rule is not an absolute one, however, and if the party can show that the term that was not included was of the utmost importance, then the courts may be prepared to incorporate it. This is particularly likely where the written contract is in the standard terms of one of the parties.

Evans J & Son (Portsmouth) Ltd v Andrea Merzario Ltd [1976] 1 WLR 1078

Facts: The plaintiffs were English importers of machines from Italy. Since 1959 they had arranged for the carriage of the machines to England under contracts with the defendants. The contracts were in a standard printed form and included conditions allowing for freight to be carried on deck. In 1967 the plaintiffs explained to the defendants that it was of great importance that the machinery should not be carried on deck. The defendants gave an oral assurance that the plaintiff's machinery would be carried below deck. In October 1968 the defendants loaded one of the plaintiffs' machines, valued at nearly £3,000, packed in a container, onto the deck of the ship. Owing to a swell at sea, the container fell overboard and was a total loss. The plaintiffs brought an action claiming damages of £2,720. The forwarding agents denied liability, relying on the exemptions in the printed conditions of carriage. At first instance the judge found for the defendants holding that the oral assurance was not a legally binding warranty such as would override the standard conditions.

Held: The Court of Appeal held that the verbal promise that the machines would be carried below deck took precedence over the written conditions. The defendants were in breach of that promise and were liable to the plaintiffs in damages.

Roskill LJ:

'[I]t seems to me that the contract was this: "If we continue to give you our business, you will ensure that those goods in containers are shipped under deck"; and the defendants agreed that this would be so. Thus there was a breach of that contract by the defendants when this container was shipped on deck; and it seems to me to be plain that the damage which the plaintiffs suffered resulted from that breach . . . It is suggested that even so these exemption clauses [in the printed written terms] apply. I ventured to ask [counsel for the defendants] what the position would have been if when the defendants' first quotation had come along there had been stamped on the face of that quotation: "No containers to be shipped on deck": and this container had then been shipped on deck. He bravely said that the exemption clauses would still have applied. With great respect, I think that is an impossible argument. In the words which Devlin J used in *Firestone Tyre and Rubber Co Ltd v Vokins & Co Ltd* [1951] 1 Lloyd's Rep 32, 39, and approved by Lord Denning MR in *Mendelssohn v Normand Ltd* [1970] 1 QB 177, 184, the defendants' promise that the container would be shipped under deck would be wholly illusory . . . Interpreting the contract as I find it to have been, I feel driven to the conclusion that none of these exemption clauses can be applied, because one has to treat the promise that no container would be shipped on deck as overriding any question of exempting conditions. Otherwise, as I have already said, the promise would be illusory.'

7.2.1.4 Expert knowledge of one of the parties

The relative knowledge of the parties may also be a relevant factor in considering whether a statement is a term or merely a representation. The court will be more inclined to find that a statement is a term if it was made by the person in the best position to have ascertained the truth. The following two cases will illustrate this point.

Oscar Chess v Williams [1957] 1 WLR 370

Facts: Williams, a private individual, sold a Morris car to Oscar Chess, a car dealership. In the pre-contractual negotiations, Williams innocently described the car as a

1948 Morris and produced the registration book for the car. The salesman checked the registration book and it showed that 1948 was the date of the first registration. On this basis he offered Williams a trade-in allowance of £290 against the purchase of a new car. It later turned out that the car was a 1939 model which was only worth £175. The plaintiffs sought to recover from the defendant damages of £115, calculated as the difference in value between £290 and £175. The county court judge held that the assumption that the car was a 1948 model was a fundamental condition of the contract, breach of which entitled the car dealers to damages.

Held: A majority of the Court of Appeal (Morris LJ dissenting) allowed the appeal on the ground that that there was no evidence to support the conclusion that the statement made by the defendant was intended to be a term of the contract; it was a mere innocent misrepresentation.

Denning LJ:

'It must have been obvious to both that the seller had himself no personal knowledge of the year when the car was made. He only became owner after a great number of changes. He must have been relying on the registration book. It is unlikely that such a person would warrant the year of manufacture. The most he would do would be to state his belief, and then produce the registration book in verification of it. In these circumstances the intelligent bystander would, I suggest, say that the seller did not intend to bind himself so as to warrant that it was a 1948 model. If the seller was asked to pledge himself to it, he would at once have said "I cannot do that. I have only the log-book to go by, the same as you . . ."

It seems to me clear that the motor-dealers who bought the car relied on the year stated in the log-book. If they had wished to make sure of it, they could have checked it then and there, by taking the engine number and chassis number and writing to the makers. They did not do so at the time, but only eight months later. They are experts, and, not having made that check at the time, I do not think they should now be allowed to recover against the innocent seller who produced to them all the evidence he had, namely, the registration book. I agree that it is hard on the dealers to have paid more than the car is worth: but it would be equally hard on the seller to make him pay the difference.'

Denning LJ applied an objective test, referring to the 'intelligent bystander', to determine whether the statement was a term or a representation. The court therefore looked at what the parties said and did rather than what they thought. Of crucial importance was the fact that it was unlikely, in light of his state of knowledge, that the defendant would have guaranteed the age of the car. Furthermore, Denning LJ placed emphasis on the fact that the plaintiffs, as car dealers, could have taken further steps to verify the age of the car. The significance of the knowledge and expertise of the parties is apparent when one compares the facts of *Oscar Chess* with those of *Dick Bentley Productions v Harold Smith (Motors)*.

Dick Bentley Productions Ltd v Harold Smith (Motors) Ltd
[1965] 1 WLR 623, CA

Facts: Harold Smith (Motors) sold Dick Bentley Productions a Park Ward drop-head coupé Bentley motor car for the sum of £1,850. The car had recently been fitted with a new engine and gearbox and in the pre-contractual negotiations, Harold Smith innocently stated that the car had only done 20,000 miles with the new engine and gearbox. In fact, the car had done very near to 100,000 miles. The county court judge held that the statement as to mileage was a warranty. That warranty had been broken and the judge awarded Bentley £400 in damages.

Held: The Court of Appeal dismissed the appeal on the ground that the statement as to mileage was intended and understood as a legally binding promise.

Lord Denning MR:

'I endeavoured to explain in *Oscar Chess Ltd* [1957] 1 WLR 370, 375, that the question whether a warranty was intended depends on the conduct of the parties, on their words and behaviour, rather than on their thoughts. If an intelligent bystander would reasonably infer that a warranty was intended, that will suffice . . . [I]t seems to me that if a representation is made in the course of dealings for a contract for the very purpose of inducing the other party to act upon it, and actually inducing him to act upon it, by entering into the contract, that is prima facie ground for inferring that it was intended as a warranty. It is not necessary to speak of it as being collateral. Suffice it that it was intended to be acted upon and was in fact acted on. But the maker of the representation can rebut this inference if he can show that it really was an innocent misrepresentation, in that he was in fact innocent of fault in making it, and that it would not be reasonable in the circumstances for him to be bound by it. In the *Oscar Chess* case the inference was rebutted. There a man had bought a second-hand car and received with it a log-book which stated the year of the car, 1948. He afterwards resold the car. When he resold it he simply repeated what was in the log-book and passed it on to the buyer. He honestly believed on reasonable grounds that it was true. He was completely innocent of any fault. There was no warranty by him, but only an innocent misrepresentation. Whereas in the present case it is very different. The inference is not rebutted. Here we have a dealer, Smith, who was in a position to know, or at least to find out, the history of the car. He could get it by writing to the makers. He did not do so. Indeed, it was done later. When the history of this car was examined, his statement turned out to be quite wrong. He ought to have known better. There was no reasonable foundation for it.'

It seems that the distinction between *Oscar Chess* and *Dick Bentley* was that, in the former case, the defendant had no knowledge of the age of the car and had made his statement in all innocence. In the latter case, however, the defendant was a car dealer who was in a better position than the purchaser to check the history of the car. Because of this the defendant was prevented from asserting that his statement was a mere representation. The Court of Appeal held that, on the basis of Harold Smith's position as a car dealer, it could be inferred that the parties intended the statement as to mileage to be incorporated into the contract as a term.

It should be noted that if the facts of *Dick Bentley* occurred today, it is highly likely that the case would be dealt with as a negligent misrepresentation under s 2(1) of the Misrepresentation Act 1967 (see Chapter 9). That section imposes liability in damages for a misrepresentation where the misrepresentation induces the other party into the contract unless the misrepresentor can prove that he had reasonable grounds to believe – and did believe up to the time the contract was made – that the facts as represented were true. The defendants in *Dick Bentley* would have struggled to prove that they had reasonable grounds for their belief but, at the time, of course, damages for negligent misrepresentation were not available. Therefore, the plaintiff's only recourse was a claim for breach of contract. Even today, a claim for breach of contract may be preferable because it enables the claimant to recover his expectation loss. Damages for misrepresentation merely compensate the claimant for his reliance loss (*Doyle v Olby* [1969] 2 QB 158, 167).

7.2.2 INCORPORATION IN A COLLATERAL CONTRACT

It is extremely rare for the courts to find that an oral statement has been incorporated as a term in the main contract. Prior to the enactment of the Misrepresentation Act 1967, this could lead to considerable hardship for claimants. For this reason, the courts developed a number of ingenious measures to enable claimants to obtain adequate remedies. One such measure was finding that the oral statement had been incorporated into a collateral contract between the parties. The House of Lords considered the use of such collateral contracts in *Heilbut Symons & Co v Buckleton*.

Heilbut Symons & Co v Buckleton [1913] AC 30

Facts: Heilbut were rubber merchants who underwrote shares in a new rubber company. The manager saw a prospectus claiming that the company had a certain number of rubber trees. On this basis, the manager of Heilbut indicated to Buckleton that the new company was a sound proposition and Buckleton bought 6000 shares in it. Later on it was discovered that there was a large deficiency in the rubber trees which were said in the prospectus to exist, and the shares fell in value. Buckleton brought a claim against Heilbut for fraudulent misrepresentation, and alternatively for damages for breach of contract. At first instance, it was held that there had been no fraudulent misrepresentation but that the representation had been incorporated into the contract as a term which had been breached.

Held: The House of Lords allowed the appeal on the ground that there had been no fraudulent misrepresentation and that the statement had not been incorporated as a term of the main contract. Their Lordships considered the possibility that the statement had been incorporated into a collateral agreement between the manager and Buckleton but concluded that it had not.

Lord Moulton:

'It is evident, both on principle and on authority, that there may be a contract the consideration for which is the making of some other contract . . . It is collateral to the main contract, but each has an independent existence, and they do not differ in respect of their possessing to the full the character and status of a contract. But such collateral contracts must from their very nature be rare . . . Such collateral contracts, the sole effect of which is to vary or add to the terms of the principal contract, are viewed with suspicion by the law. They must be proved strictly. Not only the terms of such contracts but the existence of an animus contrahendi on the part of all the parties to them must be clearly shewn. Any laxity . . . would enable parties to escape from the full performance of the obligations of contracts unquestionably entered into by them and more especially would have the effect of lessening the authority of written contracts by making it possible to vary them by suggesting the existence of verbal collateral agreements relating to the same subject-matter. There is in the present case an entire absence of any evidence to support the existence of such a collateral contract.'

On the facts of *Heilbut*, the House of Lords were unwilling to find a collateral contract, but in more recent times the courts have adopted a more flexible approach.

City of Westminster Properties v Mudd [1959] Ch 129

Facts: Mudd became the tenant of an antique shop for a term of three years during which he was allowed by the landlords, City of Westminster Properties, to sleep in an office behind the shop. When the lease came up for renewal, the landlord tried to insert a clause stating that the premises could not be used as a place for lodging, dwelling or sleeping. Mudd objected, but was assured orally that if he signed the lease, he would be allowed to continue to live there. Due to an oversight the new clause was omitted, but a provision requiring the premises only to be used for business activities remained. The landlord subsequently sought to forfeit the lease on the basis that Mudd was still living in the shop in breach of the clause.

Held: The High Court held that the oral statement that Mudd could live in the premises constituted a collateral agreement that overrode the clause in the lease itself.

Harman J:

'If the defendant's evidence is to be accepted, as I hold it is, it is a case of a promise made to him before the execution of the lease that, if he would execute it in the form put before him, the landlord would not seek to enforce against him personally the covenant about using the property as a shop only. The defendant says that it was in reliance on this promise that he executed the lease and entered on the onerous obligations contained in it. He says, moreover, that but for the promise made he would not have executed the lease, but would have moved to other premises available to him at the time. If these be the facts, there was a clear contract acted upon by the defendant to his detriment and from which the plaintiffs cannot be allowed to resile . . . The plea that this was a mere licence retractable at the plaintiffs' will does not bear examination. The promise was that so long as the defendant personally was tenant, so long would the landlords forbear to exercise the rights which they would have if he signed the lease. He did sign the lease on this promise and is therefore entitled to rely on it so long as he is personally in occupation of the shop.'

In the following case, Lord Denning MR went even further than Harman J in *Mudd* and recommended the wide-scale use of collateral contracts where experts make statements of fact.

Esso Petroleum v Mardon [1976] QB 801

Facts: Mr Mardon was a prospective tenant of a petrol filling station. One of Esso's employees, Mr Leith, who had forty years' experience in the petrol trade, stated that the estimated throughput of the station was 200,000 gallons per year. This estimate failed to take into account the fact that the local authority had refused to allow the pumps at the station to front on to the main street, thus requiring the station to be built back to front. Mr Mardon was dubious as to the accuracy of the estimate, but accepted it on the basis of the greater experience and expertise of Mr Leith. He entered the lease but the throughput never exceeded 78,000 gallons per year. Mr Mardon brought an action in contract for breach of warranty as to the potential throughput, and alternatively in tort for negligent misrepresentation. At first instance, Lawson J held that the statement as to potential throughput was not a contractual warranty such as to give the defendant a cause of action for breach of contract but that Esso was liable for negligent misrepresentation.

Held: The Court of Appeal allowed the appeal on the ground that Mr Leith's statement was a warranty that Esso had breached. The cross-appeal against Esso's liability for negligent misrepresentation was dismissed.

Per Lord Denning MR:

'Collateral warranty
Ever since *Heilbut, Symons & Co v Buckleton* [1913] AC 30, we have had to contend with the law as laid down by the House of Lords that an innocent misrepresentation

gives no right to damages. In order to escape from that rule, the pleader used to allege – I often did it myself – that the misrepresentation was fraudulent, or alternatively a collateral warranty. At the trial we nearly always succeeded on collateral warranty. We had to reckon, of course, with the dictum of Lord Moulton, at p. 47, that "such collateral contracts must from their very nature be rare". But more often than not the court elevated the innocent misrepresentation into a collateral warranty: and thereby did justice – in advance of the Misrepresentation Act 1967. I remember scores of cases of that kind, especially on the sale of a business. A representation as to the profits that had been made in the past was invariably held to be a warranty. Besides that experience, there have been many cases since I have sat in this court where we have readily held a representation – which induces a person to enter into a contract – to be a warranty sounding in damages. I summarised them in *Dick Bentley Productions v Harold Smith (Motors) Ltd* [1965] 1 WLR 623, 627, when I said:

> "Looking at the cases once more, as we have done so often, it seems to me that if a representation is made in the course of dealings for a contract for the very purpose of inducing the other party to act upon it, and actually inducing him to act upon it, by entering into the contract, that is prima facie ground for inferring that it was intended as a warranty. It is not necessary to speak of it as being collateral. Suffice it that it was intended to be acted upon and was in fact acted on."

[Counsel for Esso], retaliated, however, by citing *Bisset v Wilkinson* [1927] AC 177, where the Privy Council said that a statement by a New Zealand farmer that an area of land "would carry 2,000 sheep" was only an expression of opinion. He submitted that the forecast here of 200,000 gallons was an expression of opinion and not a statement of fact: and that it could not be interpreted as a warranty or promise.

Now I would quite agree with [counsel for the appellant] that it was not a warranty – in this sense – that it did not *guarantee* that the throughput *would* be 200,000 gallons. But, nevertheless, it was a forecast made by a party – Esso – who had special knowledge and skill. It was the yardstick (the estimated annual consumption) by which they measured the worth of a filling station. They knew the facts. They knew the traffic in the town. They knew the throughput of comparable stations. They had much experience and expertise at their disposal. They were in a much better position than Mr Mardon to make a forecast. It seems to me that if such a person makes a forecast, intending that the other should act upon it – and he does act upon it, it can well be interpreted as a warranty that the forecast is sound and reliable in the sense that they made it with reasonable care and skill. It is just as if Esso said to Mr Mardon: "Our forecast of throughput is 200,000 gallons. You can rely upon it as being a sound forecast of what the service station should do. The rent is calculated on that footing." If the forecast turned out to be an unsound forecast such as no person of skill or experience should have made, there is a breach of warranty. Just as there is a breach of warranty when a forecast is made – "expected to load" by a certain date – if the maker has no reasonable grounds for it: see *Samuel Sanday and Co v Keighley, Maxted and Co* (1922) 27

ComCas 296; or bunkers "expected 600/700 tons": see *Efploia Shipping Corporation Ltd v Canadian Transport Co Ltd (The Pantanassa* [1958] 2 Lloyd's Rep 449, 455–457 by Diplock J. It is very different from the New Zealand case where the land had never been used as a sheep farm and both parties were equally able to form an opinion as to its carrying capacity: see particularly *Bisset v Wilkinson* [1927] AC 177, 183–184.

In the present case it seems to me that there was a warranty that the forecast was sound, that is, Esso made it with reasonable care and skill. That warranty was broken. Most negligently Esso made a "fatal error" in the forecast they stated to Mr. Mardon, and on which he took the tenancy. For this they are liable in damages. The judge, however, declined to find a warranty. So I must go further.

Negligent misrepresentation

Assuming that there was no warranty, the question arises whether Esso are liable for negligent misstatement under the doctrine of *Hedley Byrne & Co Ltd v Heller & Partners Ltd* [1964] AC 465 . . . It seems to me that *Hedley Byrne & Co Ltd v Heller & Partners Ltd* [1964] AC 465, properly understood, covers this particular proposition: if a man, who has or professes to have special knowledge or skill, makes a representation by virtue thereof to another – be it advice, information or opinion – with the intention of inducing him to enter into a contract with him, he is under a duty to use reasonable care to see that the representation is correct, and that the advice, information or opinion is reliable. If he negligently gives unsound advice or misleading information or expresses an erroneous opinion, and thereby induces the other side to enter into a contract with him, he is liable in damages. This proposition is in line with what I said in *Candler v Crane, Christmas & Co* [1951] 2 KB 164, 179–180, which was approved by the majority of the Privy Council in *Mutual Life and Citizens' Assurance Co Ltd v Evatt* [1971] AC 793 . . .

Applying this principle, it is plain that Esso professed to have – and did in fact have – special knowledge or skill in estimating the throughput of a filling station. They made the representation – they forecast a throughput of 200,000 gallons – intending to induce Mr Mardon to enter into a tenancy on the faith of it. They made it negligently. It was a 'fatal error' and thereby induced Mr. Mardon to enter into a contract of tenancy that was disastrous to him. For this misrepresentation they are liable in damages.

The measure of damages

Mr Mardon is not to be compensated here for "loss of a bargain". He was given no bargain that the throughput *would* amount to 200,000 gallons a year. He is only to be compensated for having been induced to enter into a contract which turned out to be disastrous for him. Whether it be called breach of warranty or negligent misrepresentation, its effect was *not* to warrant the throughput, but only to induce him to enter the contract. So the damages in either case are to be measured by the loss he suffered. Just as in *Doyle v Olby (Ironmongers) Ltd* [1969] 2 QB 158, 167 he can say: ". . . I would not have entered into this contract at all but for your representation. Owing to it, I have lost all the capital I put into it. I also incurred a large overdraft. I have spent four years of my life in wasted endeavour without reward: and it will take me some time to re-establish myself."

For all such loss he is entitled to recover damages. It is to be measured in a similar way as the loss due to a personal injury. You should look into the future so as to forecast what would have been likely to happen if he had never entered into this contract: and contrast it with his position as it is now as a result of entering into it. The future is necessarily problematical and can only be a rough-and-ready estimate. But it must be done in assessing the loss.'

The judgment of the Court of Appeal in *Esso v Mardon* demonstrates the willingness of the courts to manipulate legal concepts in order to achieve their desired result. Esso were found liable to Mr Mardon on two grounds: breach of contractual warranty and negligent misrepresentation. The similarities between the alternative claims are of particular interest to us. Following the decision of the House of Lords in *Hedley Byrne*, Mr Mardon was able to seek damages for non-fraudulent misrepresentation as an alternative to his claim for breach of warranty. Both claims gave rise to a right to recover damages.

What is more surprising is that the court held that the same measure of damages was available for both claims. Traditionally, damages for breach of contract protect the innocent party's expectation interest, by placing him in the position he would have occupied had the contract been performed. By contrast, damages for misrepresentation protect the innocent party's reliance interest, by placing him in the position he would have occupied had there been no misrepresentation. However, in *Esso v Mardon*, the Court of Appeal awarded reliance damages for Esso's breach of contractual warranty. This was because, on the facts, the warranty was not a guarantee that the throughput of the station would reach 200,000 gallons per year. Instead, it was a promise that the forecast had been made with reasonable care and skill. Therefore, the measure of damages for breach of the term was not the profit that Mr Mardon expected to make on the projected throughput, but the losses he suffered by relying on Esso's negligent forecast.

It can be argued that the court's assessment of damages demonstrates that the claim for breach of warranty should have failed. There is no doubt that Mr Mardon's expectations had been disappointed – on the basis of Mr Leith's forecast Mr Mardon had expected that the filling station would have generated significant profit. However, the Court of Appeal refused to protect these expectations by an award of damages. Instead, their Lordships ordered Esso to compensate Mr Mardon for the loss caused by his reliance on Mr Leith's statement. Such an award is consistent with construing Mr Leith's statement as a precontractual representation, not a contractual promise.

Given that Mr Mardon already had a damages claim for negligent misrepresentation, it is somewhat surprising that the Court of Appeal went to such lengths to find a collateral contract. Indeed, it could be argued that, following the recognition of damages for negligent misrepresentation, the courts should refrain from artificially construing the facts to find a collateral contract. While the distinction between the claim for breach of contract and the claim for negligent misrepresentation made no difference on the facts of *Esso v Mardon*, the distinction may be more significant in other cases. For example, a claim for misrepresentation provides the claimant with the possibility of rescinding the main contract; a claim for breach of a collateral contract does not. Moreover, the remoteness test applied in actions for breach of contract is more restrictive than the test applied in actions for deceit, or under s 2(1) of the Misrepresentation Act 1967 (see Chapter 9).

7.2.3 SUMMARY

As we have seen, there are a number of actions that may be available in relation to precontractual statements. The statement may be incorporated into the main contract, giving rise to a claim for breach of contract. In ascertaining whether this was the intention of the parties the courts will take into account a number of factors including: the importance of the statement, any requirement of independent verification, the written terms of the contract and the relative knowledge of the parties. Alternatively, the statement might be construed to form a collateral contract, giving rise to an action for damages. Nowadays, following the recognition of damages for negligent misrepresentation, it will rarely be necessary for the court to construe the statement as a contractual term. However, if the statement is not susceptible to construction as a statement of fact, an action for breach of a contractual term may still be the only course open to a claimant.

7.3 EXPRESS TERMS

Having noted the importance of distinguishing between terms of a contract and precontractual representations, we turn to examine express terms – clauses that have been put forward by one or other of the parties as a term of the contract. Contracts are normally made up of various express terms, differing in character and importance. The courts are often called upon to decide which terms have been incorporated into a contract, what those terms mean and what the consequences are of breach. In each of these situations the court seeks to determine the parties' intention from an objective perspective. We will look at each of these issues in turn.

7.3.1 INCORPORATION

The question of whether a term has been incorporated into the contract is an important issue for the parties, particularly when the term in question is an exclusion clause. There are three main ways in which a term can be incorporated into a contract: by signed consent, by notice of printed terms and by common course of dealings.

7.3.1.1 Signed consent

A signature by a living person normally operates as a definitive statement of the terms of the written contract, whether or not the party signing the contract has read or understood the terms. This can lead to harsh results as seen in *L'Estrange v Graucob*.

L'Estrange v Graucob [1934] 2 KB 394

Facts: L'Estrange, a café owner in Llandudno, bought a cigarette vending machine from Graucob. She signed a sales agreement, without reading it, which contained in small print certain special terms one of which was 'any express or implied condition, statement, or warranty, statutory or otherwise not stated herein is hereby excluded'. The machine was delivered to L'Estrange but it did not work satisfactorily, so she brought an action against Graucob in the county court claiming damages for breach of an implied warranty that the machine was fit for the purpose for which it was sold. Graucob argued that the contract expressly excluded all implied warranties.

Held: The Divisional Court reversed the judgment of the county court judge, and held that the exclusion clause was enforceable even though it was written in small print and L'Estrange had not read it.

Scrutton LJ:
'The main question raised in the present case is whether [the exclusion clause] formed part of the contract. If it did, it clearly excluded any condition or warranty . . . When a document containing contractual terms is signed, then, in the absence of fraud, or, I will add, misrepresentation, the party signing it is bound, and it is wholly immaterial whether he has read the document or not.

The plaintiff contended at the trial that she was induced by misrepresentation to sign the contract without knowing its terms, and that on that ground they are not binding upon her. The learned judge in his judgment makes no mention of that contention of the plaintiff, and he pronounces no finding as to the alleged misrepresentation. There is a further difficulty. Fraud is not mentioned in the pleadings, and I strongly object to deal with allegations of fraud where fraud is not expressly pleaded. I have read the evidence with care, and it contains no material upon which fraud could be found. The plaintiff no doubt alleged that the defendants' agent represented to her that the document which was given her to be signed was an order form, but according to the defendants'

---

evidence no such statement was made to her by the agent. Moreover, whether the plaintiff was or was not told that the document was an order form, it was in fact an order form, and an order form is a contractual document. It may be either an acceptance or a proposal which may be accepted, but it always contains some contractual terms. There is no evidence that the plaintiff was induced to sign the contract by misrepresentation.

In this case the plaintiff has signed a document headed "Sales Agreement", which she admits had to do with an intended purchase, and which contained a clause excluding all conditions and warranties. That being so, the plaintiff, having put her signature to the document and not having been induced to do so by any fraud or misrepresentation, cannot be heard to say that she is not bound by the terms of the document because she has not read them.'

Maugham LJ:
'I regret the decision to which I have come, but I am bound by legal rules and cannot decide the case on other considerations . . .

I deal with this case on the footing that when the order confirmation was signed by the defendants confirming the order form which had been signed by the plaintiff, there was then a signed contract in writing between the parties. If that is so, then, subject to certain contingencies, there is no doubt that it was wholly immaterial whether the plaintiff read the small print or not . . .

There are, however, two possibilities to be kept in view. The first is that it might be proved that the document, though signed by the plaintiff, was signed in circumstances which made it not her act. That is known as the case of *Non est factum*. I do not think it is necessary to add anything to what Scrutton LJ has already said about that, the written document admittedly related to the purchase of the machine by the plaintiff. Even if she was told that it was an order form, she could not be heard to say that it did not affect her because she did not know its contents.

Another possibility is that the plaintiff might have been induced to sign the document by misrepresentation. She contended that she was so induced to sign the document inasmuch as (i.) she was assured that it was an order form, (ii.) that at the time when she signed it she knew nothing of the conditions which it contained. The second of these contentions is unavailing by reason of the fact that the document was in writing signed by the plaintiff. As to the first contention it is true that the document was an order form. But further, if the statement that it was an order form could be treated as a representation that it contained no clause expressly excluding all conditions and warranties, the answer would be that there is no evidence to prove that that statement was made by or on behalf of the defendants.

In this case it is, in my view, an irrelevant circumstance that the plaintiff did not read, or hear of, the parts of the sales document which are in small print, and that document should have effect according to its terms. I may add, however, that I could wish that the contract had been in a simpler and more usual form. It is unfortunate that the important clause excluding conditions and warranties is in such small print. I also think that the order confirmation form should have contained an express statement to the effect that it was exclusive of all conditions and warranties.'

The rule in *L'Estrange v Graucob* may be considered to operate harshly, but it should be noted that there are exceptions to the rule, as recognised by the Court of Appeal. First, if the signature is obtained by fraud or a misrepresentation, the terms are not enforceable and the oral statement supersedes the writing. This was seen in *Curtis v Chemical Cleaning & Dyeing Co.*

Curtis v Chemical Cleaning & Dyeing Co [1951] 1 KB 805

Facts: Mrs Curtis took a white satin wedding dress trimmed in beads and sequins to the defendant dry cleaners for cleaning. She was asked to sign a 'receipt' by the assistant. When she asked what the significance of the document was, the assistant replied that it excluded liability for the beads and sequins. Mrs Curtis signed the document. The receipt actually contained a general exclusion clause stating that the dress was 'accepted on condition that the company is not liable for any damage howsoever arising'. When the dress was returned to Mrs Curtis it was badly stained. She brought a claim against the dry cleaners and they sought to rely on the general exclusion clause.

Held: The Court of Appeal held that the defendants could not rely on the exclusion clause in light of the innocent misrepresentation made by the shop assistant prior to the plaintiff signing the document.

Denning LJ:
'This case is of importance because of the many cases nowadays when people sign printed forms without reading them, only to find afterwards that they contain stringent clauses exempting the other side from their common-law liabilities . . . If the party . . . signs a written document, knowing it to be a contract which governs the relations between them, his signature is irrefragable evidence of his assent to the whole contract, including the exempting clauses, unless the signature is shown to be obtained by fraud or misrepresentation: *L'Estrange v Graucob* [1934] 2 KB 394. But what is a sufficient misrepresentation for this purpose?

In my opinion any behaviour, by words or conduct, is sufficient to be a misrepresentation if it is such as to mislead the other party about the existence or extent of the exemption. If it conveys a false impression, that is enough. If the false impression is created knowingly, it is a fraudulent misrepresentation; if it is created unwittingly, it is an innocent misrepresentation; but either is sufficient to disentitle the creator of it to the benefit of the exemption. In *Rex v Kylsant (Lord)* [1932] 1 KB 443 it was held that a representation might be literally true but practically false, not because of what it said, but because of what it left unsaid; in short, because of what it implied. This is as true of an innocent misrepresentation as it is of a fraudulent misrepresentation. When one party puts forward a printed form for signature, failure by him to draw attention to the existence or extent of the exemption clause may in some circumstances convey the impression that there is no exemption at all, or at any rate not so wide an exemption as that which is in fact contained in the document. The present case is a good illustration. The customer said in evidence: "When I was asked to sign the document I asked why? The assistant said I was to accept any responsibility for damage to beads and sequins. I did not read it all before I signed it." In those circumstances, by failing to draw attention to the width of the exemption clause, the assistant created the false impression that the exemption only related to the beads and sequins, and that it did not extend to the material of which the dress was made. It was done perfectly innocently, but nevertheless a false impression was created . . . It was a sufficient misrepresentation to disentitle the cleaners from relying on the exemption, except in regard to beads and sequins.'

Second, subsequent cases have also shown that the rule in *L'Estrange v Graucob* only operates when the signed document is contractual in effect.

Grogan v Robin Meredith Plant Hire [1996] 15 Tr LR 371

Facts: The plaintiff was injured by a machine used to lay pipes in North Wales. The machine and driver had been hired from Meredith Plant Hire by Triact, a firm of civil engineers. Mr Patten, the site agent for Triact, had arranged the hire and each week he signed the driver's 'time sheet', a form which kept a record of the hours that the driver had worked. The time sheet contained the words 'all hire undertaken under CPA (Contractors Plant Association) conditions. Copies available on request'. Those conditions included an indemnity from Triact to Meredith against liability to third parties incurred in the course of hire. At the time of entering into the contract of hire no terms had been mentioned and there had been no suggestion that the contract was under CPA conditions. At first instance, Pill J held that the clause contained in the time sheet was binding and ordered Triact to indemnify Meredith.

Held: The Court of Appeal allowed the appeal. The verbal contract had not been varied by the site agent's signature of the time sheets and therefore Triact was not obliged to indemnify Meredith.

Auld LJ:
'The central question . . . is whether the time sheet in this case comes within the class of document which the party receiving it knew contained, or which a reasonable man would expect to contain, relevant contractual conditions. Another way of putting it, as Kerr J did in *Bahamas Oil Refining Co v Kristiansands Tankrederie A/S (The Polyduke)*

> [1978] 1 Lloyd's Rep 211 at 215–216, is whether "the document purport[ed] to have contractual effect" . . .
>
> Documents such as a time sheet, an invoice or a statement of account . . . do not normally have a contractual effect in the sense of making or varying a contract. The purpose of time sheets is not normally to contain or evidence the terms of a contract, but to record a party's performance of an existing obligation under a contract.'

The rule in *L'Estrange v Graucob* is therefore subject to a number of exceptions that seriously limit its scope. Maugham LJ clearly regretted the outcome but felt that he was 'bound by legal rules' to come to the decision. This conclusion has been doubted by several commentators, including J R Spencer, who has argued that the rule was based on a misapplication of the parol evidence rule (see below) and the defence of *non est factum*. He suggests that the claimant should not be bound by the clause where 'he did not mean to consent to the disputed term, and although he appeared to consent to it, the other party either caused or connived at his mistake' (J R Spencer, 'Signature, Consent and the Rule in *L'Estrange v Graucob*' [1973] CLJ 104, 121). The Ontario Court of Appeal has adopted Spencer's criticisms and refused to follow *L'Estrange v Graucob*.

Tilden Rent-A-Car Co v Clendenning (1978) 83 DLR (3d) 400

Facts: Mr Clendenning rented a car from the office of Tilden-Rent-A-Car at Vancouver Airport. He was an experienced traveller and had used Tilden on many prior occasions. The clerk asked him whether he desired additional insurance coverage, and, as was his practice, he replied that he did. He was given a form to sign which he signed without reading, as would have been apparent to the clerk. The form contained an exemption clause which had the effect of imposing liability on Mr Clendenning for any damage caused to the car. The question for the court was whether Mr Clendenning was bound by this clause.

Held: The Ontario Court of Appeal held that Mr Clendenning was not bound by the clause because there was no *consensus ad idem*.

Dublin JA:
'It was urged that the rights of the parties were governed by what has come to be known as "the rule in *L'Estrange v F Graucob, Ltd*" . . .

Consensus ad idem is as much a part of the law of written contracts as it is of oral contracts. The signature to a contract is only one way of manifesting assent to contractual terms. However, in the case of *L'Estrange v F Graucob*, there was in fact no *consensus ad idem*. Miss L'Estrange was a proprietor of a café. Two salesmen of the defendant company persuaded her to order a cigarette machine to be sold to her by their employer. They produced an order form which Miss L'Estrange signed without reading all of its terms. Amongst the many clauses in the document signed by her, there was included a paragraph, with respect to which she was completely unaware, which stated "any express or implied condition, statement, or warranty, statutory or otherwise not stated herein is hereby excluded". In her action against the company she alleged that the article sold to her was unfit for the purposes for which it was sold and contrary to the Sale of Goods Act. The company successfully defended on the basis of that exemption clause.

Although the subject of critical analysis by learned authors (see, for example, J R Spencer, "Signature, Consent, and the Rule in *L'Estrange v Graucob*", [1973] CLJ 104), the case has survived, and it is now said that it applies to all contracts irrespective of the circumstances under which they are entered into, if they are signed by the party who seeks to escape their provisions . . .

As is pointed out in Waddams, *The Law of Contracts*, at p 191:

> "From the 19th century until recent times an extraordinary status has been accorded to the signed document that will be seen in retrospect, it is suggested, to have been excessive."

The justification for the rule in *L'Estrange v F Graucob Ltd*, appears to have been founded upon the objective theory of contracts, by which means parties are bound to a contract in writing by measuring their conduct by outward appearance rather than what the parties inwardly meant to decide . . .

Even accepting the objective theory to determine whether Mr. Clendenning had entered into a contract which included all the terms of the written instrument, it is to be observed that an essential part of that test is whether the other party entered into the contract in the belief that Mr. Clendenning was assenting to all such terms. In the instant case, it was apparent to the employee of Tilden-Rent-A-Car that Mr Clendenning had not in fact read the document in its entirety before he signed it. It follows under such circumstances that Tilden-Rent-A-Car cannot rely on provisions of the contract which it had no reason to believe were being assented to by the other contracting party.

As stated in Waddams, *The Law Contracts*, p 191:

> "One who signs a written document cannot complain if the other party reasonably relies on the signature as a manifestation of assent to the contents, or ascribes to words he uses their reasonable meaning. But the other side of the same coin is that only a reasonable expectation will be protected. If the party seeking to enforce the document knew or had reason to know of the other's mistake the document should not be enforced."

In ordinary commercial practice where there is frequently a sense of formality in the transaction, and where there is a full opportunity for the parties to consider the terms of the proposed contract submitted for signature, it might well be safe to assume that the party who attaches his signature to the contract intends by so doing to acknowledge his acquiescence to its terms, and that the other party entered into the contract upon that belief. This can hardly be said, however, where the contract is entered into in circumstances such as were present in this case.

A transaction, such as this one, is invariably carried out in a hurried, informal manner. The speed with which the transaction is completed is said to be one of the attractive features of the services provided.

The clauses relied on in this case . . . are inconsistent with the over-all purpose for which the contract is entered into by the hirer. Under such circumstances, something more should be done by the party submitting the contract for signature than merely handing it over to be signed.

An analysis of the Canadian cases . . . indicates that the approach in this country has not been so rigid [as that in England and Wales]. In the case of *Colonial Investment Co of Winnipeg, Man v Borland* [1911] 1 WWR 171 at p 189, 19 WLR 588, 5 Alta LR at p 72 [affirmed 6 DLR 21, 2 WWR 960, 22 WLR 145, 5 Alta LR 71] Beck, J, set forth the following propositions:

> "*Consensus ad idem* is essential to the creation of a contract, whether oral, in writing or under seal, subject to this, that as between the immediate parties (and merely voluntary assigns) apparent – as distinguished from real – consent will on the ground of estoppel effect a binding obligation unless the party denying the obligation proves:
>
> (1) That the other party knew at the time of the making of the alleged contract that the mind of the denying party did not accompany the expression of his consent; or
>
> (2) Such facts and circumstances as show that it was not reasonable and natural for the other party to suppose that the denying party was giving his real consent and he did not in fact give it;"

In commenting on the *Colonial Investment Co of Winnipeg v Borland* case, Spencer, in the article above cited, observes at p 121:

> "It is instructive to compare a Canadian approach to the problem of confusing documents which are signed but not fully understood."

And at p 122 the author concludes his article with the following analysis:

> "Policy considerations, but of different kinds, no doubt lay behind both the Canadian and the English approaches to this problem. The Canadian court was impressed by the abuses which would result – and, in England, have resulted – from enabling companies to hold ignorant signatories to the letter of sweeping exemption clauses contained in contracts in standard form. The English courts, however, were much more impressed with the danger of furnishing an easy line of defence by which liars could evade contractual liabilities freely assumed. It would be very dangerous to allow a man over the age of legal infancy to escape from the legal effect of a document he has, after reading it, signed, in the absence of any express misrepresentation by the other party of that legal effect.

> Forty years later, most lawyers would admit that the English courts made a bad choice between two evils . . ."
>
> In modern commercial practice, many standard form printed documents are signed without being read or understood. In many cases the parties seeking to rely on the terms of the contract know or ought to know that the signature of a party to the contract does not represent the true intention of the signer, and that the party signing is unaware of the stringent and onerous provisions which the standard form contains. Under such circumstances, I am of the opinion that the party seeking to rely on such terms should not be able to do so in the absence of first having taken reasonable measures to draw such terms to the attention of the other party, and, in the absence of such reasonable measures, it is not necessary for the party denying knowledge of such terms to prove either fraud, misrepresentation or *non est factum*.
>
> In the case at bar, Tilden Rent-A-Car took no steps to alert Mr Clendenning to the onerous provisions in the standard form of contract presented by it. The clerk could not help but have known that Mr Clendenning had not in fact read the contract before signing it. Indeed the form of the contract itself with the important provisions on the reverse side and in very small type would discourage even the most cautious customer from endeavouring to read and understand it. Mr Clendenning was in fact unaware of the exempting provisions. Under such circumstances, it was not open to Tilden Rent-A-Car to rely on those clauses, and it was not incumbent on Mr Clendenning to establish fraud, misrepresentation or non est factum. Having paid the premium, he was not liable for any damage to the vehicle while being driven by him.
>
> As Lord Denning stated in *Neuchatel Asphalte Co Ltd v Barnett* [1957] 1 WLR 356 at p 360: "We do not allow printed forms to be made a trap for the unwary." '

As J R Spencer noted the choice to be made was a choice between two evils: either allowing companies to hold ignorant signatories to the letter of sweeping exemption clauses, or allowing liars to evade contractual liabilities freely assumed. The former evil would undermine justice, the latter would undermine the certainty created by a signed contractual document. The English courts have decided to accept the former evil in preference to the latter (the High Court of Australia has recently affirmed the approach adopted by the English courts: *Toll (FGCT) Pty Ltd v Alphapharm Pty Ltd* (2004) 219 CLR 165). This may be wise since the Unfair Contract Terms Act 1977 and the Unfair Terms in Consumer Contract Regulations 1999 already provide mechanisms for dealing with unfair exemption clauses. However, the 'hands-off' approach adopted by the courts in respect of signed contracts is hard to reconcile with the stricter approach adopted in cases concerned with the incorporation of terms by notice.

7.3.1.2 Notice of printed terms

Terms can also be incorporated into a contract by notice. A party wishing to incorporate printed terms must take reasonable steps to bring the terms to the other party's attention or knowledge. The burden of showing that the terms have been incorporated is on the party seeking to rely on them. Once again, the courts adopt an objective approach. If it can be shown that the party seeking to rely on the printed terms has taken reasonable steps to bring them to the attention of the other party, the terms will be incorporated into the contract regardless of whether the other party has read or understood the terms.

Parker v South Eastern Railway (1877) 2 CPD 416

Facts: Mr Parker deposited his bag in a station cloakroom. He paid 2 pence and was given a ticket which said, on the front, 'see back'. On the back of the ticket was an exclusion clause which stated that 'The Company will not be responsible for any package exceeding the value of £10'. His bag was stolen. The trial judge left two questions to the jury: '1. Did the plaintiff read or was he aware of the special condition upon which the article was deposited? 2. Was the plaintiff, under the circumstances, under any obligation, in the exercise of reasonable and proper caution, to read or to make himself aware of the condition?' The jury answered both the questions in the negative, and judgment was directed for the plaintiff. The defendant appealed.

Held: The Court of Appeal ordered a new trial, on the ground that there had been a misdirection by the judge. There was no obligation on the plaintiff to read the condition and the second question left to the jury ought to have been, whether the company did that which was reasonably sufficient to bring the clause to the attention of the plaintiff.

Mellish LJ:

'I am of opinion . . . that the proper direction to leave to the jury in these cases is, that if the person receiving the ticket did not see or know that there was any writing on the ticket, he is not bound by the conditions; that if he knew there was writing, and knew or believed that the writing contained conditions, then he is bound by the conditions; that if he knew there was writing on the ticket, but did not know or believe that the writing contained conditions, nevertheless he would be bound, if the delivering of the ticket to him in such a manner that he could see there was writing upon it, was, in the opinion of the jury, reasonable notice that the writing contained conditions.

I have lastly to consider whether the direction of the learned judge was correct, namely, "Was the plaintiff, under the circumstances, under any obligation, in the exercise of reasonable and proper caution, to read or to make himself aware of the condition?" I think that this direction was not strictly accurate, and was calculated to mislead the jury. The plaintiff was certainly under no obligation to read the ticket, but was entitled to leave it unread if he pleased, and the question does not appear to me to direct the attention of the jury to the real question, namely, whether the railway company did what was reasonably sufficient to give the plaintiff notice of the condition.'

The test to be applied by the court is whether the party seeking to rely upon the term has made a reasonable effort to give the claimant notice of the term. This is an objective test, and in determining whether or not reasonable steps have been taken, the courts have regard to a number of factors including: the location of the notice, the form it takes and the point in time at which it is displayed. The courts have made clear that, in order to be incorporated, terms must have been contained or referred to in a document that was intended to have contractual effect.

Chapelton v Barry UDC [1940] 1 KB 532

Facts: Mr Chapelton wished to hire a deck chair on a beach. The defendant council had placed a notice next to the deck chairs advising members of the public of the cost of the chairs and requesting that they obtain tickets for their chairs from the chair attendants. The notice contained no exclusion clause. Mr Chapelton obtained two chairs from the attendant and received two tickets. He glanced at the tickets and put them in his pocket. On the back of the tickets were the words: 'The council will not be liable for any accident or damage arising from the hire of the chair.' When Mr Chapelton sat on his chair it gave way. He brought an action against the defendants for negligence. The county court found that the accident was due to the defendant's negligence but that they were exempted from liability as the plaintiff had sufficient notice of the exclusion clause printed on the ticket.

Held: The Court of Appeal allowed the appeal on the ground that the ticket was a mere voucher or receipt for the money paid for the hire of the chair. The conditions for hire were to be found on the notice put up next to the pile of chairs and that notice contained no clause excluding the defendant's liability.

Goddard LJ:
'In this case the appellant paid 2d in order to have the right to sit on a chair on the beach, and he was asked to take a ticket in the form of a receipt for that purpose . . . I cannot imagine that anybody paying 2d under those circumstances for the privilege of sitting in a chair on the beach would think for one moment that some conditions were being imposed upon him which would limit his ordinary rights, or that the document he received when paying his 2d was a contractual document in any shape or form. I think the ticket he received was nothing but a receipt for his 2d – a receipt which showed him how long he might use the chair.'

It is also necessary for the terms to be brought to the other party's attention prior to the formation of the contract. If communication of the terms comes after the moment in time at which the contract is agreed, the terms will not be effectively incorporated, as seen in *Olley v Marlborough Court Ltd* and *Thornton v Shoe Lane Parking*.

Olley v Marlborough Court Ltd [1949] 1 KB 532

Facts: A man and his wife checked into a hotel, and paid a week's board and residence in advance. They went upstairs to their bedroom where a notice was displayed as follows: 'The proprietors will not hold themselves responsible for articles lost or stolen, unless handed to the manageress for safe custody. Valuables should be deposited for safe custody in a sealed package and a receipt obtained.' The wife's furs were stolen from her room due to the negligence of the hotel's employees who left her key unguarded on the key-board at the reception. The defendant claimed that the notice displayed in the room had effectively excluded their liability for negligence.

Held: The Court of Appeal held that the terms of the notice in the bedroom formed no part of the contract because the contract had been made before the guests could see the notice.

Denning LJ:

'The first question is whether that notice formed part of the contract. Now people who rely on a contract to exempt themselves from their common law liability must prove that contract strictly. Not only must the terms of the contract be clearly proved, but also the intention to create legal relations – the intention to be legally bound – must also be clearly proved. The best way of proving it is by a written document signed by the party to be bound. Another way is by handing him before or at the time of the contract a written notice specifying its terms and making it clear to him that the contract is on those terms. A prominent public notice which is plain for him to see when he makes the contract or an express oral stipulation would, no doubt, have the same effect. But nothing short of one of these three ways will suffice. It has been held that mere notices put on receipts for money do not make a contract (see *Chapelton v Barry UDC* [1940] 1 KB 532). So, also, in my opinion, notices put up in bedrooms do not of themselves make a contract. As a rule, the guest does not see them until after he has been accepted as a guest. The hotel company no doubt hope that the guest will be held bound by them, but the hope is vain unless they clearly show that he agreed to be bound by them, which is rarely the case.'

Thornton v Shoe Lane Parking [1971] 2 QB 163

Facts: Mr Thornton drove his car into a new multi-storey car park which he had not been in before. A notice on the outside gave the charges and stated that all cars were 'parked at owner's risk'. As he drove in a light changed from red to green and a ticket was issued by a machine. He put it in his pocket without fully reading it. The ticket said that it was issued subject to conditions displayed on notices inside the car park. The notices contained a clause excluding all liability for personal injury inside the car park. When Mr Thornton returned to collect his car he was injured in the car park as a result of Shoe Lane's negligence. Thornton claimed damages for the injury but the defendants contended that the ticket incorporated a condition exempting them from liability.

Held: The Court of Appeal held that since Thornton did not know of the exemption clause and Shoe Lane Parking had not done what was reasonably sufficient to bring it to his notice it did not exempt them from liability.

Lord Denning MR:
'The customer pays his money and gets a ticket. He cannot refuse it. He cannot get his money back. He may protest to the machine, even swear at it. But it will remain unmoved. He is committed beyond recall. He was committed at the very moment when he put his money into the machine. The contract was concluded at that time. It can be translated into offer and acceptance in this way: the offer is made when the proprietor of the machine holds it out as being ready to receive the money. The acceptance takes place when the customer puts his money into the slot. The terms of the offer are contained in the notice placed on or near the machine stating what is offered for the money. The customer is bound by those terms as long as they are sufficiently brought to his notice beforehand, but not otherwise. He is not bound by the terms printed on the ticket if they differ from the notice, because the ticket comes too late. The contract has already been made: see *Olley v Marlborough Court Ltd* [1949] 1 KB 532.'

In *Thornton v Shoe Lane Parking*, the exemption clause was not incorporated into the contract because Shoe Lane Parking failed to bring the clause to Mr Thornton's attention prior to the formation of the contract. It is possible for terms to be incorporated into a contract by reference to another document, but this will only occur if that other document is available for inspection at the time of contracting.

Hollingworth v Southern Ferries Ltd (The 'Eagle') [1977] 2 Lloyd's Rep 70

Facts: The plaintiff wished to go on holiday to Spain. She asked her friend, who was travelling with her, to make the necessary travel arrangements. He went to a travel agent who gave him a copy of the defendants' brochure which stated that the conditions of carriage were printed on the inside of the ticket covers. Some time later, the plaintiff's friend purchased a ticket. The ticket contained a general exclusion clause. Midway through the voyage the ship encountered a storm. At the time

Mrs Hollingworth was sitting down in the ship's restaurant eating a meal. Her seat toppled over and she fell hitting her head on a hot cupboard. She brought a negligence action against the defendants for the injuries she sustained. The defendants denied liability and relied on the exclusion clause printed on the ticket.

Held: The exclusion clause was not incorporated into the contract.

Deputy Judge Mr Michael Ogden QC:
'[I]t seems clear . . . that if the defendants are entitled to rely upon that exclusion clause it is a valid exclusion clause which would result in the plaintiff failing in this action, notwithstanding my finding that the defendants had been negligent . . . In the present case [Mrs Hollingworth's friend] was not shown the brochure by the defendants at the time when the contract was made, nor just before it was made, so as to make the terms referred to in the brochure part of the contract. Of course, he knew that the defendants had said in the brochure which he collected some time before that they contracted on the basis of conditions of carriage, but in my view that is not enough to make such conditions terms of the contract . . . I do not consider that merely seeing a statement of this kind in a brochure makes that statement in effect of the same import as would be the case if one were shown that document at the time when one was making the contract; the statement in the brochure merely gives an intending passenger advance notice of the terms which he may expect to find when he enters into the contract.'

A notice displaying printed terms is sufficient to incorporate those terms into a contract if the notice is in the form of a contractual document and presented to the other party at or before the time of contracting. A notice can also have the direct effect of forming a unilateral contract if the notice can be construed as making an offer which the customer accepts. This was seen in *Bowerman v Association of British Travel Agents*.

Bowerman v Association of British Travel Agents [1996] CLC 451

Facts: The plaintiff was planning to go on a school ski trip, but before the trip began the tour operator became insolvent. The tour operator was a member of the Association of British Travel Agents (ABTA) which displayed the following notice in the offices of ABTA members: 'Where holidays or other travel arrangements have not yet commenced at the time of failure [of the tour operator], ABTA arranges for you to be reimbursed the money you would have paid in respect of your holiday arrangements.' The question was whether this notice created a contract between the plaintiff and ABTA.

Held: A majority of the Court of Appeal held that, construed objectively, the notice evinced sufficient intention to create legal relations and constituted an offer that was accepted by the plaintiff.

Hobhouse LJ:

'[The notice] satisfies the criteria for a unilateral contract and contains promises which are sufficiently clear to be capable of legal enforcement. The principles established in *Carlill* apply.'

7.3.1.3 Common course of dealings

It is not always necessary for the terms of the contract to be explicitly stated by the parties. If the parties have dealt with each other on the same terms on a number of previous occasions, it is reasonable to assume that the parties are aware of the terms of the contract. Thus the terms can be incorporated by a 'common course of dealings'. The leading case on this is *McCutcheon v David MacBrayne Ltd*.

McCutcheon v David MacBrayne Ltd [1964] 1 WLR 430

Facts: Mr McCutcheon asked his brother-in-law, Mr McSporran, to arrange for his car to be shipped to the mainland. Mr McSporran called at the office of David MacBrayne Ltd and booked a place for the car on a ferry. The usual practice of MacBrayne was to ask Mr McSporran to sign a risk note containing various exclusion clauses. On this occasion, MacBrayne forgot and merely gave Mr McSporran a receipt stating that the goods were carried subject to the conditions set out in the notices in MacBrayne's offices. Neither Mr McCutcheon nor Mr McSporran had ever read the words on the receipt or the notices. During the voyage, the ship hit a rock and sank through the negligence of MacBrayne's employees. Mr McSporran brought an action in negligence against MacBrayne, who sought to rely on an exclusion clause contained in their conditions of carriage on the basis that that Mr McSporran had signed risk notes on previous occasions.

Held: The House of Lords held that MacBrayne's terms had not been incorporated into the contract. There was no consistent course of dealings, as on the day in question when the accident occurred, McSporran was offered an oral contract without reference to the conditions usually contained in the risk note.

Lord Reid:

'Mr McSporran had consigned goods of various kinds on a number of previous occasions. He said that sometimes he had signed a note, sometimes he had not. On one occasion he had sent his own car. A risk note for that consignment was produced signed by him. He had never read the risk notes signed by him. He said: "I sort of just signed it at the time as a matter of form." He admitted that he knew he was signing in connection with some conditions but he did not know what they were. In particular, he did not know that he was agreeing to send the goods at owner's risk. [Mr McCutcheon] had consigned goods on four previous occasions. On three of them he was acting on behalf of his employer. On the other occasion he had sent his own car. Each time he had signed a risk note. He also admitted that he knew there were conditions but said that he did not know what they were.

The respondents contend that, by reason of the knowledge thus gained by the appellant and his agent in these previous transactions, the appellant is bound by their conditions. But this case differs essentially from the ticket cases. There, the carrier in making the contract hands over a document containing or referring to conditions which he intends to be part of the contract. So if the consignor or passenger, when accepting the document, knows or ought as a reasonable man to know that that is the carrier's intention, he can hardly deny that the conditions are part of the contract, or claim, in the absence of special circumstances, to be in a better position than he would be if he had read the document. But here, in making the contract neither party referred to, or indeed had in mind, any additional terms, and the contract was complete and fully effective without any additional terms. If it could be said that when making the contract Mr McSporran knew that the respondents always required a risk note to be signed and knew that the purser was simply forgetting to put it before him for signature, then it might be said that neither he nor his principal could take advantage of the error of the other party of which he was aware. But counsel frankly admitted that he could not put his case as high as that.

The only other ground on which it would seem possible to import these conditions is that based on a course of dealing. If two parties have made a series of similar contracts each containing certain conditions, and then they make another without expressly referring to those conditions it may be that those conditions ought to be implied. If the officious bystander had asked them whether they had intended to leave out the conditions this time, both must, as honest men, have said "of course not". But again the facts here will not support that ground. According to Mr. McSporran, there had been no constant course of dealing; sometimes he was asked to sign and sometimes not. And, moreover, he did not know what the conditions were. This time he was offered an oral contract without any reference to conditions, and he accepted the offer in good faith.

The respondents also rely on [Mr McCutcheon's] previous knowledge. I doubt whether it is possible to spell out a course of dealing in his case. In all but one of the previous cases he had been acting on behalf of his employer in sending a different kind of goods and he did not know that the respondents always sought to insist on excluding liability for their own negligence. So it cannot be said that when he asked his agent to make a contract for him he knew that this or, indeed, any other special term would be included in it. He left his agent a free hand to contract, and I see nothing to prevent him from taking advantage of the contract which his agent in fact made.

"The judicial task is not to discover the actual intentions of each party; it is to decide what each was reasonably entitled to conclude from the attitude of the other" (*Gloag on Contract*, 2nd ed, p 7).

In this case I do not think that either party was reasonably bound or entitled to conclude from the attitude of the other, as known to him, that these conditions were intended by the other party to be part of this contract. I would therefore allow the appeal and restore the interlocutor of the Lord Ordinary.'

Lord Guest:
'All that the previous dealings in the present case can show is that the appellant and his agent knew that the previous practice of the respondents was to impose special conditions. But knowledge on their part did not and could not by itself import acceptance by them of these conditions, the exact terms of which they were unaware, into a contract which was different in character from those in the previous course of dealing. The practice of the respondents was to insist on a written contract incorporated in the risk note. On the occasion in question a verbal contract was made without reference to the conditions.'

The key to establishing a common course of dealings is demonstrating that there has been both a frequency and consistency of dealing between the parties. This is what MacBrayne failed to prove. Although Mr McCutcheon had always been asked to sign a risk note by MacBrayne, Mr McSporran stated in evidence that sometimes he was asked to sign a risk note and sometimes he was not. This appeared to be conclusive for Lord Reid in finding that there was insufficient consistency in dealings between the parties to justify incorporating MacBrayne's conditions into the oral contract. The facts of McCutcheon can be contrasted with those of *British Crane Hire Co Ltd v Ipswich Plant Hire Ltd*.

British Crane Hire Co Ltd v Ipswich Plant Hire Ltd [1975] QB 303

Facts: British Crane Hire (BCH) hired out heavy earth-moving equipment. Ipswich Plant Hire were doing drainage work and hired a dragline crane from BCH over the telephone. Nothing was said on the telephone about the terms and conditions of hire. BCH did send the defendants their standard hire terms and conditions but before they signed them the crane sank into marshy ground. BCH sought to recover from the defendants the cost of recovering the crane on the ground that their written terms and conditions required the defendant to indemnify them against such losses. BCH claimed that the terms and conditions were known to the defendants because they were customarily used in the trade.

Held: The Court of Appeal held that BCH's terms and conditions were incorporated into the contract of hire.

Lord Denning MR:
'In support of the course of dealing, the plaintiffs relied on two previous transactions in which the defendants had hired cranes from the plaintiffs. One was February 20, 1969;

and the other October 6, 1969. Each was on a printed form which set out the hiring of a crane, the price, the site, and so forth; and also setting out the conditions the same as those here. There were thus only two transactions many months before and they were not known to the defendants' manager who ordered this crane. In the circumstances I doubt whether those two would be sufficient to show a course of dealing . . .

But here the parties were both in the trade and were of equal bargaining power. Each was a firm of plant hirers who hired out plant. The defendants themselves knew that firms in the plant-hiring trade always imposed conditions in regard to the hiring of plant: and that their conditions were on much the same lines . . .

[I]t is clear that both parties knew quite well that conditions were habitually imposed by the supplier of these machines: and both parties knew the substance of those conditions. In particular that if the crane sank in soft ground it was the hirer's job to recover it: and that there was an indemnity clause. In these circumstances, I think the conditions on the form should be regarded as incorporated into the contract. I would not put it so much on the course of dealing, but rather on the common understanding which is to be derived from the conduct of the parties, namely, that the hiring was to be on the terms of the plaintiffs' usual conditions.

As Lord Reid said in *McCutcheon v David MacBrayne Ltd* [1964] 1 WLR 125, 128 quoting from the Scottish textbook, *Gloag on Contract*, 2nd ed. (1929), p 7:

"The judicial task is not to discover the actual intentions of each party; it is to decide what each was reasonably entitled to conclude from the attitude of the other."

It seems to me that, in view of the relationship of the parties, when the defendants requested this crane urgently and it was supplied at once – before the usual form was received – the plaintiffs were entitled to conclude that the defendants were accepting it on the terms of the plaintiffs' own printed conditions – which would follow in a day or two. It is just as if the plaintiffs had said: "We will supply it on our usual conditions", and the defendants said "Of course, that is quite understood." '

Two factors influenced the Court of Appeal in coming to its decision. First, it was relevant that Ipswich had previously contracted with BCH on the same terms. This was important but not, in itself, conclusive. Second, there was evidence that it was the normal practice in the trade for liability to be placed on the hirer, rather than the owner. For Lord Denning, it was the combination of these two factors that provided a satisfactory basis for incorporating MacBrayne's terms into the contract.

The issue in such cases is primarily one of fact: Is there evidence of a common course of dealing, either on the basis of past experience or general trade practice, that would lead the parties to reasonably believe that the standard terms had been incorporated into their contract? The answer to this question will depend on the context of the case. It is relatively easy to demonstrate a common course of dealing in the context of a commercial contract but far more difficult when the contract is between a consumer and a business.

Hollier v Rambler Motors (AMC) Ltd [1972] 2 QB 71

Facts: Rambler Motors had repaired Mr Hollier's car on three or four occasions over a period of five years. On at least two of the occasions, Mr Hollier had signed a form containing Rambler's standard terms which included a clause excluding liability for damage caused by fire to customer's cars on the premises. In this instance the parties contracted over the telephone, without any mention of the standard terms. Whilst the car was in the garage it was damaged by fire due to Rambler's negligence. Mr Hollier claimed damages for breach of an implied term that Rambler would take reasonable care of his car. The defendants argued that the term excluding liability for damage caused by fire was incorporated into the oral contract because of the previous course of dealing between the parties. At first instance it was held that the term was incorporated into the contract and excluded the defendants' liability for negligence.

Held: The Court of Appeal allowed the appeal on the ground that the course of dealing on three or four occasions over five years was not sufficient to incorporate the term into the contract.

Salmon LJ:
'I am bound to say that, for my part, I do not know of any other case in which it has been decided or even argued that a term could be implied into an oral contract on the strength of a course of dealing (if it can be so called) which consisted at the most of three or four transactions over a period of five years . . .

It seems to me that if it was impossible to rely on a course of dealing in *McCutcheon v David MacBrayne Ltd*, still less would it be possible to do so in this case, when the so-called course of dealing consisted only of three or four transactions in the course of five years.'

7.3.1.4 Onerous or unusual conditions

In determining whether reasonable steps have been taken to bring the term to the attention of the other party the courts will take into account the nature of the term. If the term is particularly onerous or unusual, greater steps will be required to incorporate the term into the contract or to give effect to its provisions. This rule of 'special notice' was suggested by Lord Denning MR in *Thornton v Shoe Lane Parking* [1971] 2 QB 163:

'I do not pause to inquire whether the exempting condition is void for unreasonableness. All I say is that it is so wide and so destructive of rights that the court should not hold any man bound by it unless it is drawn to his attention in the most explicit way. It is an instance of what I had in mind in *J Spurling Ltd v Bradshaw* [1956] 1 WLR 461, 466. In order to give sufficient notice, it would need to be printed in red ink with a red hand pointing to it – or something equally startling.'

The requirement of special notice was further considered by the Court of Appeal in *Interfoto v Stiletto Visual Programmes*.

Interfoto v Stiletto Visual Programmes [1989] 1 QB 433

Facts: Stiletto were an advertising agency which needed some photographs of the 1950s for a presentation. They telephoned Interfoto, who had a library of photographs. They had never dealt with Interfoto before. Interfoto sent out some photographs in a bag containing a delivery note upon which were printed a number of conditions in small but visible print. Condition 2 stated that 'a holding fee of £5 plus VAT per day will be charged for each transparency which is retained ... longer than ... 14 days'. The daily rate per transparency was far greater than usual in the market but nothing was done by Interfoto to draw Stiletto's attention particularly to the condition. Stiletto forgot to return the photos on time and were presented with a bill for £3,783.50.

Held: The Court of Appeal held that the clause was not incorporated into the contract because Interfoto had not done what was reasonably necessary to draw the clause to the attention of Stiletto. Interfoto could only recover a holding fee assessed on the basis of a *quantum meruit* which was held to be £3.50 per week per transparency beyond the 14-day period.

Bingham LJ:
'In many civil law systems, and perhaps in most legal systems outside the common law world, the law of obligations recognises and enforces an overriding principle that in making and carrying out contracts parties should act in good faith. This does not simply mean that they should not deceive each other, a principle which any legal system must recognise; its effect is perhaps most aptly conveyed by such metaphorical colloquialisms as "playing fair", "coming clean" or "putting one's cards face upwards on the table". It is in essence a principle of fair and open dealing. In such a forum it might, I think, be held on the facts of this case that the plaintiffs were under a duty in all fairness to draw the defendants' attention specifically to the high price payable if the transparencies were not returned in time and, when the 14 days had expired, to point out to the defendants the high cost of continued failure to return them.

English law has, characteristically, committed itself to no such overriding principle but has developed piecemeal solutions in response to demonstrated problems of unfairness. Many examples could be given. Thus equity has intervened to strike down unconscionable bargains. Parliament has stepped in to regulate the imposition of exemption clauses and the form of certain hire-purchase agreements. The common law also has made its contribution, by holding that certain classes of contract require the utmost good faith, by treating as irrecoverable what purport to be agreed estimates of damage but are in truth a disguised penalty for breach, and in many other ways.

The well-known cases on sufficiency of notice are in my view properly to be read in this context. At one level they are concerned with a question of pure contractual analysis, whether one party has done enough to give the other notice of the incorporation of a term in the contract. At another level they are concerned with a somewhat different question, whether it would in all the circumstances be fair (or reasonable) to hold a party bound by any conditions or by a particular condition of an unusual and stringent nature.

[he reviewed the authorities on incorporation of terms]

These authoritative passages appear to base the law very firmly on consideration of what is fair in all the circumstances.

J Spurling Ltd v Bradshaw [1956] 1 WLR 461 concerned an exemption clause in a warehousing contract. The case is now remembered for the observations of Denning LJ, at p 466:

> "This brings me to the question whether this clause was part of the contract. Mr Sofer urged us to hold that the warehousemen did not do what was reasonably sufficient to give notice of the conditions within *Parker v South Eastern Railway Co*, 2 CPD 416. I quite agree that the more unreasonable a clause is, the greater the notice which must be given of it. Some clauses which I have seen would need to be printed in red ink on the face of the document with a red hand pointing to it before the notice could be held to be sufficient."

Here, therefore, is made explicit . . . that what would be good notice of one condition would not be notice of another. The reason is that the more outlandish the clause the greater the notice which the other party, if he is to be bound must in all fairness be given . . .

The tendency of the English authorities has, I think, been to look at the nature of the transaction in question and the character of the parties to it; to consider what notice the party alleged to be bound was given of the particular condition said to bind him; and to resolve whether in all the circumstances it is fair to hold him bound by the condition in question. This may yield a result not very different from the civil law principle of good faith, at any rate so far as the formation of the contract is concerned.

Turning to the present case, I am satisfied . . . that no contract was made on the telephone when the defendants made their initial request. I am equally satisfied that no contract was made on delivery of the transparencies to the defendants before the opening of the jiffy bag in which they were contained. Once the jiffy bag was opened and the transparencies taken out with the delivery note, it is in my judgment an inescapable inference that the defendants would have recognised the delivery note as a document of a kind likely to contain contractual terms and would have seen that there were conditions printed in small but visible lettering on the face of the document. To the extent that the conditions so displayed were common form or usual terms regularly encountered in this business, I do not think the defendants could successfully contend that they were not incorporated into the contract.

The crucial question in the case is whether the plaintiffs can be said fairly and reasonably to have brought condition 2 to the notice of the defendants ... In my opinion the plaintiffs did not do so ... The defendants are not to be relieved of that liability because they did not read the condition, although doubtless they did not; but in my judgment they are to be relieved because the plaintiffs did not do what was necessary to draw this unreasonable and extortionate clause fairly to their attention. I would accordingly allow the defendants' appeal and substitute for the judge's award the sum which he assessed upon the alternative basis of quantum meruit.'

In his judgment, Bingham LJ clearly indicates that the courts adopt a flexible approach in determining whether a term has been incorporated into a contract. The court seeks to do what is fair. This means that the test will vary, depending on the nature of the term: 'what would be good notice of one condition would not be notice of another'. Bingham LJ emphasised that this approach was rooted in well-established authorities. That may be true, but it is surely questionable whether this approach is justified as a matter of principle. The real issue, as Bingham LJ identified, is the principle of fair dealing. It is doubtful whether the doctrine of incorporation of terms is the most appropriate mechanism to deal with unfair bargains. Surely, the courts should tackle the problem at its root by striking out unfair terms on substantive grounds. Indeed, following the enactment of the Unfair Contract Terms Act 1977 and the Unfair Terms in Consumer Contract Regulations 1999 (see Chapter 8), there seems to be little need for the special notice rule for incorporation of onerous or unusual terms. This was noted by Hobhouse LJ (dissenting) in *AEG (UK) Ltd v Logic Resource Ltd.*

AEG (UK) Ltd v Logic Resource Ltd [1996] CLC 265

Hobhouse LJ:
'It is desirable as a matter of principle to keep what was said in the *Interfoto* case within its proper bounds. A wide range of clauses are commonly incorporated into

contracts by general words. If it is to be the policy of English law that in every case those clauses are to be gone through with, in effect, a toothcomb to see whether they were entirely usual and entirely desirable in the particular contract, then one is completely distorting the contractual relationship between the parties and the ordinary mechanisms of making contracts. It will introduce uncertainty into the law of contract.

In the past there may have been a tendency to introduce more strict criteria but this is no longer necessary in view of the Unfair Contract Terms Act. The reasonableness of clauses is the subject matter of the Unfair Contract Terms Act and it is under the provisions of that Act that problems of unreasonable clauses should be addressed and the solution found.'

Furthermore, the Court of Appeal has recently doubted the application of the 'red-hand rule' to commercial contracts.

Ocean Chemical Transport Inc v Exnor Craggs Ltd [2000] 1 Lloyd's Rep 446

Facts: The claimants owned ships. By an exchange of faxes on 7 February 1995, they entered into a contract with the defendants for the supply of bunkers for one of their ships. One of the faxes from the defendants stated that the sale was subject to its general terms and conditions. One of the terms, clause 10, stated: 'All liability whatsoever on our part shall cease unless suit is brought within six months after delivery of the good or the date when the goods should have been delivered'. In July 1996, the claimants discovered that there was a defect in the title to the bunkers and brought an action against the defendants for breach of an implied to the effect that the seller had a right to sell the goods. The defendants denied liability and alleged that the claim was time barred by clause 10 of their general terms and conditions. The claimants argued that the clause had not been incorporated because the defendants had not taken adequate steps to bring the clause to the claimants' attention.

Held: The Court of Appeal held that the claimant's cause of action was time barred because clause 10 had been incorporated into the contract. The defendants had discharged their duty to bring the existence of the term to the attention of the claimants.

Evans LJ:
'[Counsel for the claimant] submits that the *Interfoto* test, as he called it, has to be applied, even in a case where the other party has signed an acknowledgement of the terms and conditions and their incorporation. It seems to me that [he] could be right in what might be regarded as an extreme case, where a signature was obtained under pressure of time or other circumstances, and where it was possible to satisfy the

Interfoto test; that is to say, that the clause was one which was particularly onerous or unusual for incorporation in the contract in question. I would prefer to put the matter more broadly and to say that the question is whether the defendants have discharged the duty which lies upon them of bringing the existence of the clause upon which they rely . . . to the notice of the other party in the circumstances of the particular case.

As I have indicated, in some extreme circumstances, even a signature might not be enough. On the other hand, in the present case there was an express acknowledgement. It seems to me that, given the nature of this term and condition and its effect, as relied upon by the respondents, it cannot be said that the respondents failed in their duty to bring the existence of that term to the notice of the buyers . . . [Counsel for the claimant] does not hesitate to submit that the clause in question should have had, as he puts it, the red-hand approach. I would doubt very much whether that is practical in the context of a commercial contract such as this. In my view, the respondents did, in this particular case, where there was an express acknowledgement of the existence of the terms, certainly discharge their duty of bringing it sufficiently to the notice of the buyers for the clause to form part of the contract.'

In light of this decision, it is doubtful whether the red-hand rule will ever again be applied to a commercial contract. Furthermore, it is clear that the courts will be reluctant to find that a term is onerous or unusual, even in a consumer contract.

O'Brien v MGN Ltd [2002] CLC 33

Facts: The claim concerned a 'scratchcard' game operated by the defendants, Mirror Group Newspapers. The claimant had obtained one of the scratchcards from a newspaper. It was a winning card and he telephoned the 'Mystery Bonus Hotline' number as directed. A recorded message told him that the mystery bonus cash amount for that day was £50,000. Unfortunately for him, a mistake had been made by the defendant. Instead of there being only one winner of the £50,000 prize on that day there were 1,472. Once the mistake was realised, the defendants refused to pay out to all the 'winners' and they relied on Rule 5 of the competition rules which stated that, 'should more prizes be claimed than are available in any prize category for any reason, a separate draw will take place for the prize'. At first instance, the judge held that the defendants had made a contractual offer in the newspaper and that the claimant had accepted the offer by telephoning the defendants to claim the prize. The judge held that the claimant must have seen the rules and that Rule 5 was not sufficiently onerous and unusual as to require special notice.

Held: The Court of Appeal dismissed the appeal. Rule 5 was neither 'onerous' nor 'unusual' and the defendant had taken reasonable steps to bring the term to the attention of the claimant.

Hale LJ:

'The offer and therefore the contract clearly incorporated the term "Normal Mirror Group rules apply". The words were there to be read and it makes no difference whether or not the claimant actually read or paid attention to them.

The question, therefore, is whether those words, in the circumstances, were enough to incorporate the Rules, including Rule 5, into the contract. In the words of Bingham LJ in *Interfoto Library Ltd v Stiletto Ltd* [1989] 1 QB 433, at p 445E, can the defendant "be said fairly and reasonably to have brought [those rules] to the notice of" the claimant? This is a question of fact . . . [W]hat is fair and reasonable notice will depend upon the nature of the transaction and upon the nature of the term . . .

In my view, although Rule 5 does turn an apparent winner into a loser, it cannot by any normal use of language be called "onerous" or "outlandish". It does not impose any extra burden upon the claimant, unlike the clause in *Interfoto*. It does not seek to absolve the defendant from liability for personal injuries negligently caused, unlike the clause in *Thornton v Shoe Lane Parking*. It merely deprives the claimant of a windfall for which he has done very little in return. He bought two newspapers, although in fact he could have acquired a card and discovered the hotline number without doing either. He made a call to a premium rate number, which will have cost him some money and gained the newspaper some, but only a matter of pennies, not pounds.

The more difficult question is whether the rule is "unusual" in this context. The judge found that the claimant knew that there was a limit on the number of prizes and that there were relevant rules. [Evidence was given] that these games and competitions always have rules. Indeed I would accept that this is common knowledge. This is not a situation in which players of the game would assume that the newspaper bore the risk of any mistake of any kind which might lead to more people making a claim than had been intended. Some people might assume that the "get out" rule would provide for the prize to be shared amongst the claimants. Some might assume that it would provide for the drawing of lots. In the case of a single prize some might think drawing lots more appropriate; but it seems to me impossible to say that either solution would be "unusual". There is simply no evidence to that effect. Such evidence as there is was to the effect that such rules are not unusual.

In any event, the words "onerous or unusual" are not terms of art. They are simply one way of putting the general proposition that reasonable steps must be taken to draw the particular term in question to the notice of those who are to be bound by it and that more is required in relation to certain terms than to others depending on their effect. In the particular context of this particular game, I consider that the defendants did just enough to bring the Rules to the claimant's attention. There was a clear reference to rules on the face of the card he used. There was a clear reference to rules in the paper containing the offer of a telephone prize. There was evidence that those rules could be discovered either from the newspaper offices or from back issues of the paper. The claimant had been able to discover them when the problem arose.'

The Court of Appeal had a great deal of sympathy for Mr O'Brien, noting that he was, 'a thoroughly decent young man who must have suffered a cruel disappointment when his hopes were raised only to be dashed'. Nevertheless, the court held that Rule 5 did not require special notice because its effect was merely to disappoint Mr O'Brien's expectations. The term did not impose any extra burden upon Mr O'Brien, nor did it constitute an unreasonable exclusion of liability. It merely deprived Mr O'Brien of a prize for which he had done very little in return. As such, the special notice doctrine had no application. It is clear that, following *O'Brien v MGN*, the scope of the special notice doctrine has been seriously limited.

7.3.2 INTERPRETATION

Having established which terms have been incorporated into the contract the next task for the court is to ascertain the meaning of those terms. The focus is on what the parties intended the terms to mean and, again, the courts adopt an objective approach. This means that, if the contract is put in written form, the written document will be regarded as very strong evidence of what the parties intended.

7.3.2.1 Parol evidence rule

The parties to a contract will not be permitted to give evidence claiming that their real intention was contrary to the ordinary meaning of the written provisions. This rule is known as the 'parol evidence rule'.

Lovell and Christmas Ltd v Wall (1911) 104 LT 85

Facts: Mr Wall was a director of Lovell and Christmas which made and sold margarine in Liverpool. When he became a director he agreed to a restraint of trade clause which stated that, for five years he would not, at any time, solely or jointly, directly or indirectly, carry on or be engaged or concerned or interested in the business of a 'provision merchant'. Before the five years had elapsed, he ceased to be a director and threatened to carry on trade as a margarine manufacturer. Lovell and Christmas sought an injunction to restrain him. At first instance Eve J refused to grant an injunction because a margarine manufacturer did not fall within the meaning of the words 'provision merchant'.

Held: The Court of Appeal dismissed the appeal.

Cozens-Hardy MR:

'If there is one principle more clearly established than another in English law it is surely this: It is for the court to construe a written document. It is irrelevant and improper to ask what the parties, prior to the execution of the instrument, intended or understood. What is the meaning of the language they have used therein? That is the problem, and the only problem. In saying that, I do not mean to assert than no evidence can be admitted. Indeed, the contrary is clear. If a deed relates to Black Acre, you may have evidence to show what are the parcels. If a document is in a foreign language, you may have an interpreter. If it contains technical terms, an expert may explain them. If, according to the custom of a trade or the usage of the market, a word has acquired a secondary meaning, evidence may be given to prove it. A well-known instance is where in a particular trade 1,000 rabbits meant 1,200. But unless the case can be brought within some or one of these exceptions, it is the duty of the court, which is presumed to understand the English language, to construe the document according to the ordinary grammatical meaning of the words used therein, and without reference to anything which has previously passed between the parties to it.

. . . [I]n considering clause 13, I am entitled to receive evidence that in the term "provision merchant" there is a secondary meaning attached to the word "provision" so as to exclude many articles which in its primary sense would be included, such as bread, fruit, and vegetables, but to include margarine. Such evidence was rightly admitted by Eve J. Enlightened by that evidence I ask myself whether a margarine manufacturer – as distinguished from a dealer in margarine – falls within the meaning of the word "provision merchant", and I hold that he does not.'

7.3.2.2 Exceptions

Although the purpose of the rule is to promote certainty and to save time and money in the conduct of litigation the rule can operate very harshly. Because of this, the rule has been made subject to a number of exceptions:

7.3.2.2.1 *Identifying the subject matter of the contract*
In *Lovell*, Cozens-Hardy MR noted that extrinsic evidence would be admissible in order to identify the subject matter of the contract. This was seen in *Freeguard v Rogers*.

Freeguard v Rogers [1999] 1 WLR 375

Facts: The case concerned an agreement by which the vendors of a house and garden in Chichester granted purchasers an option to buy 'the property known as 9, Graffham Close, Chichester, West Sussex'. The question was whether the Court was entitled to take into account extrinsic evidence as to what exactly the property was and whether it included an adjoining garage.

Held: The Court of Appeal held that extrinsic evidence could be admitted to identify the subject matter of the contract.

Peter Gibson LJ:
'In my judgment, when a property, the subject matter of a conveyancing document, is described as "the property known as . . .", it is permissible, indeed inevitable, that recourse will be had to extrinsic evidence to identify the property so known. In *Spall v Owen* (1981) 44 P & CR 36 at page 43, in which there was a description of a property as "the property known as plot number 1", I said that such a description cried aloud for evidence of the surrounding circumstances. That dictum was quoted by this court in the *Targett* case with approval.

In my judgment, it was permissible for the Deputy Master to have regard to the appearance of the property in determining what property was known as 9, Graffham Close. . . . In these circumstances, in my judgment, it was open to the Deputy Master, on the material available before him, to reach the conclusion that the property known as 9, Graffham Close did include the garage as well as the house itself.'

7.3.2.2.2 *Custom*

Cozens-Hardy MR also recognised that extrinsic evidence could be admitted in order to interpret a particular word or phrase when its meaning in a particular trade or market does not accord with its ordinary linguistic meaning. His Lordship cited the case of *Smith v Wilson* (1832) 3 B & Ad 611, where evidence was allowed to establish a local custom to the effect that the phrase '1,000 rabbits' meant '2,000 rabbits'. Custom may also be used to fill out an aspect of the contract on which the written document is silent. This was seen in *Hutton v Warren*.

Hutton v Warren (1836) 1 M & W 466; 150 ER 517

Facts: The plaintiff was tenant of land belonging to the defendant's father. In October 1832, the defendant's father resigned from his job and the land passed to the defendant as landlord. In October 1833, the defendant served a notice to quit on the plaintiff. The plaintiff quit the land and sought compensation for the sowing of the arable land. The lease contained no provision as to such compensation but the plaintiff demonstrated that there was custom of the country entitling the tenant of a farm to receive from the landlord a reasonable allowance for seeds and labour bestowed on the arable land in the last year of the tenancy.

Held: The custom was incorporated into the lease.

Parke B:

'The custom of the country as to cultivation and the term of quitting with respect to allowances for seed and labour, is clearly applicable to a tenancy from year to year and, therefore, if this custom was, by implication, imported into the lease, the plaintiff and defendant were bound by it after the lease expired. We are of opinion that this custom was, by implication, imported into the lease. It has long been settled that, in commercial transactions, extrinsic evidence of custom and usage is admissible to annex incidents to written contracts in matters with respect to which they are silent. The same rule has also been applied to contracts in other transactions of life, in which known usages have been established and prevailed. This has been done on the principle of presumption that, in such transactions, the parties did not mean to express in writing the whole of the contract by which they intended to be bound, but a contract with reference to those known usages.'

This use of custom in the interpretation of contracts overlaps with the use of custom to imply terms into the contract, considered in greater detail below.

7.3.2.2.3 *Existence of a condition precedent*

Extrinsic evidence may be admitted to prove that the contract has not yet entered into force because of a condition precedent to the agreement.

Pym v Campbell (1856) 6 E & B 370

Facts: Pym invented a 'Crushing, Washing and Amalgamating Machine'. Campbell proposed to purchase Pym's invention and arranged a meeting at which two engineers would inspect and approve the invention. Pym arrived late for the meeting and the engineers had already left. It was agreed that, since the parties were together, if the engineers could be found, the sale would go ahead. Ferguson was found and approved of the invention, but Abernethie could not be found. To conclude the deal, Campbell drew up a written document which both he and Pym signed and it was agreed that if later Abernethie approved the invention the paper should be an agreement and if he did not it should not be one. Abernethie did not approve.

Held: Oral evidence could be admitted to prove the existence of a condition precedent.

Erle J:

'The point made is that this is a written agreement, absolute on the face of it, and that evidence was admitted to shew it was conditional: and if that had been so it would have been wrong. But I am of opinion that the evidence shewed that in fact there was never any agreement at all. The production of a paper purporting to be an agreement by a party, with his signature attached, affords a strong presumption that it is his written agreement; and, if in fact he did sign the paper *animo contrahendi*, the terms contained in it are conclusive, and cannot be varied by parol evidence: but in the present case the defence begins one step earlier: the parties met and expressly stated to each other that, though for convenience they would then sign the memorandum of the terms, yet they were not to sign it as an agreement until Abernethie was consulted . . . The distinction in point of law is that evidence to vary the terms of an agreement in writing is not admissible, but evidence to shew that there is not an agreement at all is admissible.'

7.3.2.2.4 *Written agreement incomplete*

A major exception to the parol evidence rule is the fact that a party can lead oral evidence to show that the written agreement was incomplete and that it was the parties' intention to supplement the written agreement with oral terms. A good example of this is the Scottish case of *Irons v Partick Thistle Football Club Ltd.*

Irons v Partick Thistle Football Club Ltd (1997) SLT 983

Facts: David Irons was a professional footballer who signed for Partick Thistle FC and later alleged that certain terms were agreed between himself and the manager, John Lambie, relating to a signing-on fee and a bonus on £20,000 if Partick Thistle were promoted. These statements were not included in the standard form written contract which he signed. In fact, different figures were later inserted into blank spaces in the contract. Partick Thistle alleged that only lower bonuses had been agreed and that these figures were stated in the document.

Held: The Outer House of the Court of Session held that while normally oral evidence was not admissible to contradict the terms of a written contract, as a result of the football club's admission that a bonus of some sort was payable, oral evidence was admissible because both parties had agreed that the written document was incomplete and did not constitute the entire agreement between them.

In this case the court objectively found that the written agreement was incomplete and that it was the parties' intention to supplement the agreement with additional terms. The parties can avoid such a finding by inserting an 'entire agreement' clause into the written agreement: see *The Inntrepreneur Pub Co (GL) v East Crown Ltd* [2000] 2 Lloyd's Rep 611.

7.3.2.2.5 *Collateral contract*

Finally, extrinsic evidence will be admitted to prove the existence of a collateral contract. We have already seen an example of this in the case of *City of Westminster Properties v Mudd* [1959] Ch 129. It is arguable that this is not a true exception to the parol evidence rule since the case did not directly concern the interpretation of a contract; the main issue was which of two inconsistent contracts was to be given priority.

It is clear that the parol evidence rule is subject to a number of wide exceptions. This led the Law Commission to doubt whether it really was a legal rule at all.

> **Law Commission, 'The law of contract: the parol evidence rule',
> Report no 154, Cmnd 9700, 1986 at para 2.7**
>
> 'We have concluded that although a proposition of law can be stated which can be described as the "parol evidence rule" it is not a rule of law which, correctly applied, could lead to evidence being unjustly excluded. Rather, it is a proposition of law which is no more than a circular statement: *when it is proved or admitted that the parties to a contract intended that all the express terms of their agreement should be as recorded in a particular document or documents, evidence will be inadmissible (because irrelevant) if it is tendered only for the purpose of adding to, varying, subtracting from or contradicting the express terms of the contract.* We have considerable doubts whether such a proposition should be characterised as a "rule" at all, but several leading textbook writers and judges have referred to it as a "rule" and we are content to adopt their terminology for the purposes of this report.

This observation about the circularity of the parol evidence rule (which is doubted by Professor Treitel: see *Law of Contract* (2003) pp 193–194) explains why the Law Commission changed its view on the need for reform. Ten years earlier, in its Working Paper (Law Com WP No 76 (1976)), the Law Commission recommended legislation to abolish the rule stating that it was, 'a technical rule of uncertain ambit which, at least, adds to the complications of litigation without affecting the outcome and, at worst, prevents the courts getting at the truth'. By the time the Law Commission published its report its position had changed. It was of the view that there was no need for legislation since, 'there is no *rule of law* that evidence is rendered inadmissible or is to be ignored solely because a document exists which looks like a complete contract. Whether it is a complete contract depends upon the intention of the parties, objectively judged and not on any rule of law' (at para 2.17).

In summary, the parol evidence rule is merely a presumption that a written document contains all the terms of the contract. That presumption is, of course, capable of rebuttal by evidence of a contrary intention.

7.3.2.3 The move from literal to contextual methods of interpretation

The parol evidence rule was part of a more general literalist approach to contractual interpretation. As Cozens-Hardy MR noted in *Lovell*: '[T]he duty of the court . . . [is] to construe the document according to the ordinary grammatical meaning of the words used therein.' The assumption was that contracting parties had an obligation to use correct and appropriate language to convey their objectives. If they used words or phrases that bore alternative meanings, the court would not look behind the words to discover the real intention of the parties.

On the face of it, this was an entirely sensible approach to contractual interpretation, since it enabled the parties to obtain a quick and relatively inexpensive decision on the meaning of a disputed term. However, the approach is ultimately unsatisfactory because it assumes that communication takes place in a vacuum. In reality, the meaning of a communication can only be understood once its context is considered. For example, the utterance 'two fat ladies', has a very different meaning when spoken in a bingo hall than when spoken on the street. In the former situation you are likely to hear a cheer; in the latter you are likely to receive a slap!

The courts have recognised the limitations of the literalist approach and rejected it in favour of a more contextual approach. The landmark judgment was that of Lord Wilberforce in *Prenn v Simmonds*.

Prenn v Simmonds [1971] 1 WLR 1381

Facts: Dr Simmonds brought an action against Mr Prenn in which he claimed that, under the terms of an agreement, he was entitled to acquire from Mr Prenn for a price of £6,600 a 4% stake in Radio & Television Trust Ltd ('RTT'). Mr Prenn disputed the claim on the ground that a necessary condition of the agreement had not been satisfied because less than £300,000 profits available for dividend on the ordinary stock of the company had been earned. The central question in the case was whether 'profits' meant: (1) the profits of RTT alone in which case the amount fell short of the £300,000 by less than £10,000; or (b) the consolidated profits of the group consisting of RTT and subsidiaries in which case the amount was largely exceeded.

Held: The House of Lords held that, in construing a written agreement, the court should consider evidence of the factual background known to both parties but not evidence relating to prior negotiations between the parties. Applying this principle of construction, their Lordships found that the word 'profits' meant 'consolidated profits'.

Lord Wilberforce:
'The time has long passed when agreements, even those under seal, were isolated from the matrix of facts in which they were set and interpreted purely on internal linguistic considerations. There is no need to appeal here to any modern, anti-literal, tendencies, for Lord Blackburn's well-known judgment in *River Wear Commissioners v Adamson* (1877) 2 App Cas 743,763, provides ample warrant for a liberal approach. We must, as he said, inquire beyond the language and see what the circumstances were with reference to which the words were used, and the object, appearing from those circumstances, which the person using them had in view. Moreover, at any rate since 1859 (*Macdonald v Longbottom*, 1 E & E 977) it has been clear enough that evidence of mutually known facts may be admitted to identify the meaning of a descriptive term.'

This approach was confirmed by Lord Wilberforce in *Reardon Smith Line Ltd v Hansen-Tangen*.

Reardon Smith Line Ltd v Hansen-Tangen [1976] 1 WLR 989

Lord Wilberforce:
'No contracts are made in a vacuum: there is always a setting in which they have to be placed. The nature of what is legitimate to have regard to is usually described as "the surrounding circumstances" but this phrase is imprecise: it can be illustrated but hardly defined. In a commercial contract it is certainly right that the Court should know the commercial purpose of the contract and this in turn presupposes knowledge of the genesis of the transaction, the background, the context, the market in which the parties are operating . . .

It is often said that, in order to be admissible in aid of construction, these extrinsic facts must be within the knowledge of both parties to the contract, but this requirement should not be stated in too narrow a sense. When one speaks of the intention of the parties to the contract, one is speaking objectively – the parties cannot themselves give direct evidence of what their intention was – and what must be ascertained is what is to be taken as the intention which reasonable people would have had if placed in the situation of the parties. Similarly when one is speaking of aim, or object, or commercial purpose, one is speaking objectively of what reasonable persons would have in mind in the situation of the parties . . .

[W]hat the Court must do must be to place itself in thought in the same factual matrix as that in which the parties were. [I]n the search for the relevant background, there may be facts, which form part of the circumstances in which the parties contract in which one, or both, may take no particular interest, their minds being addressed to or concentrated on other facts, so that if asked they would assert that they did not have these facts in the forefront of their mind, but that will not prevent those facts from forming part of an objective setting in which the contract is to be construed.'

It is clear that a literal approach to contractual interpretation has been rejected in favour of a purposive approach that takes into account that 'factual matrix' in which the contract was formed. The modern approach has now been set out fully by Lord Hoffman in *Investors Compensation Scheme Ltd v West Bromwich Building Society*.

Investors Compensation Scheme Ltd v West Bromwich Building Society [1998] 1 WLR 896

Lord Hoffman:

'I think I should preface my explanation of my reasons with some general remarks about the principles by which contractual documents are nowadays construed. I do not think that the fundamental change which has overtaken this branch of the law, particularly as a result of the speeches of Lord Wilberforce in *Prenn v Simmonds* [1971] 1 WLR 1381, 1384–1386 and *Reardon Smith Line v Hansen-Tangen* [1976] 1 WLR 989, is always sufficiently appreciated. The result has been, subject to one important exception, to assimilate the way in which such documents are interpreted by judges to the common sense principles by which any serious utterance would be interpreted in ordinary life. Almost all the old intellectual baggage of "legal" interpretation has been discarded. The principles may be summarised as follows.

(1) Interpretation is the ascertainment of the meaning which the document would convey to a reasonable person having all the background knowledge which would reasonably have been available to the parties in the situation in which they were at the time of the contract.

(2) The background was famously referred to by Lord Wilberforce as the "matrix of fact", but this phrase is, if anything, an understated description of what the background may include. Subject to the requirement that it should have been reasonably available to the parties and to the exception to be mentioned next, it includes absolutely anything which would have affected the way in which the language of the document would have been understood by a reasonable man.

(3) The law excludes from the admissible background the previous negotiations of the parties and their declarations of subjective intent. They are admissible only in an action for rectification. The law makes this distinction for reasons of practical policy and, in this respect only, legal interpretation differs from the way we would interpret utterances in ordinary life. The boundaries of this exception are in some respects unclear. But this is not the occasion on which to explore them.

(4) The meaning which a document (or any other utterance) would convey to a reasonable man is not the same thing as the meaning of its words. The meaning of
words is a matter of dictionaries and grammars; the meaning of the document is
what the parties using those words against the relevant background would
reasonably have been understood to mean. The background may not merely
enable the reasonable man to choose between the possible meanings of words
which are ambiguous but even (as occasionally happens in ordinary life) to conclude that the parties must, for whatever reason, have used the wrong words or
syntax: see *Mannai Investments Co Ltd v Eagle Star Life Assurance Co Ltd* [1997]
AC 749.

(5) The "rule" that words should be given their "natural and ordinary meaning" reflects
the common sense proposition that we do not easily accept that people have
made linguistic mistakes, particularly in formal documents. On the other hand, if
one would nevertheless conclude from the background that something must have
gone wrong with the language, the law does not require judges to attribute to the
parties an intention which they plainly could not have had. Lord Diplock made this
point more vigorously when he said in *Antaios Compania Naviera SA v Salen
Rederierna AB* [1985] AC 191, 201:

> "if detailed semantic and syntactical analysis of words in a commercial con-
> tract is going to lead to a conclusion that flouts business commonsense, it
> must be made to yield to business commonsense." '

The factual background that can be taken into account in construing a contract
includes 'absolutely everything reasonably available to the parties which would have
affected the way in which the language of the document would have been understood by a reasonable man'. The only exceptions are evidence relating to previous
negotiations of the parties and declarations of their subjective intent. Lord Hoffman
did not give reasons for these restrictions, but Lord Wilberforce in *Prenn v Simmonds*
[1971] 1 WLR 1381, said the following:

'The reason for not admitting evidence of these exchanges . . . is simply that
such evidence is unhelpful. By the nature of things, where negotiations are
difficult, the parties' positions, with each passing letter, are changing and
until the final agreement, though converging, still divergent. It is only the
final document which records a consensus . . . Far more, and indeed totally,
dangerous is it to admit evidence of one party's objective – even if this is
known to the other party. However strongly pursued this may be, the other
party may only be willing to give it partial recognition, and in a world of give
and take, men often have to be satisfied with less than they want. So, again, it
would be a matter of speculation how far the common intention was that the
particular objective should be realised.'

In *Sirius International Insurance Co (Publ) v FAI General Insurance Ltd* [2004] 1 WLR 3251, Lord Steyn explained the process to be applied in the following terms:

> 'The aim of the inquiry is not to probe the real intentions of the parties but to ascertain the contextual meaning of the relevant contractual language. The inquiry is objective: the question is what a reasonable person, circumstanced as the actual parties were, would have understood the parties to have meant by the use of specific language. The answer to that question is to be gathered from the text under consideration and its relevant contextual scene.'

The approach embodied by Lord Hoffman's five principles is to be welcomed since it advocates a 'common-sense' approach to understanding words within their factual context. Undoubtedly, this is preferable to an over-literal approach, which fails to take into account pragmatic inferences drawn from the factual context. Kramer has argued in favour of Lord Hoffman's five principles, claiming that they are a helpful restatement of the principles that the courts have been applying for years.

Kramer, A, 'Common sense principles of contract interpretation (and how we've been using them all along)' (2003) 23 OJLS 173, 177–179, 184–186, 188–190

Beyond the Text: the 'Matrix of Fact'

... [O]ur shared method of interpretation that makes communication possible is a sophisticated process of pragmatic inference. This process allows a more extensive meaning than the linguistic meaning to be gleaned from an utterance, and, given that the communicator designs the utterance accordingly, allows a meaning more extensive than the linguistic meaning to be communicated. But how can this work? Since an utterance is only a set of words, what more can be extracted from the utterance than the linguistic meaning?

The answer is provided by Lord Justice Steyn (as he then was): '[d]ictionaries never solve concrete problems of construction. The meaning of words cannot be ascertained divorced from their context.' If the interpreter only processes the text, she can get little more than the linguistic meaning of the text out of the interpretative process. However, by harnessing, and then processing, more information than merely the text, more meaning can be extracted at the other end of the interpretative process. The other information is the 'context' (meaning 'with the text') ...

In contract law, it is now well-established that the context is important in interpreting documents, such context being most often referred to by the label 'matrix of facts'. The context has also been referred to as the 'surrounding circumstances', 'relevant circumstances', 'factual background', and by the elegant statement that the court must 'place itself in thought in the same position as the parties to the contract were placed, in fact, when they made it'. Lord Hoffmann in the *ICS* case described the relevant contextual information as:

> 'all the background knowledge which would reasonably have been available to the parties in the situation in which they were at the time of the contract' . . .

This definition of the factual matrix (absolutely anything . . .) is rightly without any fixed boundary; the context, alongside the text itself, is part of the relevant source-material that is the utterance, and so anything in the context that was used by the communicator in his design of the utterance should be used by the interpreter in her interpretation of it.

Consequently, it is clear that the contextual information, to be relevant, must be shared. An interpreter will only process contextual information that the communicator knew since only that information will have been used in designing the utterance (and conversely, a communicator will not factor into his design any contextual information that the interpreter does not have since she will not be able to interpret it) . . . Henceforth, such mutually held information (knowledge, beliefs, assumptions) will be referred to as 'mutual context' . . .

The Use of Pragmatic Inference to Supplement the Linguistic Meaning
The interpreter will need to supplement the linguistic meaning in four types of situation, the first two of which are:

Deixis. This arises whenever an indexical term—a label that refers to and identifies something that exists in the world (such as 'John Smith' or 'the blue Robin Reliant with registration A305 RCA') is used.
Linguistic ambiguity. This arises whenever a word (or, sometimes, a grammatical construction) has more than one ordinary (*i.e.* conventional) meaning.

An example of how the process of pragmatic inference works in such cases can be found by looking at the case of *The Karen Oltmann*, heard before Kerr J in 1976. In that case a two year charterparty permitted an option to redeliver the vessel to be exercised by the charterers 'after 12 months' trading'. Linguistically, this phrase is ambiguous, as it could denote either that early redelivery is permissible at any time after 12 months' trading (the defendant charterers' contention), or that early redelivery is permissible only at the specific point of time marked by the passage of 12 months' trading (the plaintiff shipowner's contention). Significantly, no normal contractor would be ambivalent as which way this important issue is resolved, and so clearly the intended meaning goes beyond the ambiguous linguistic meaning. In such cases there is an implied licence to supplement the linguistic meaning through pragmatic inference to the extent that it appears that the utterance's meaning was intended to go; here an implied licence to disambiguate.

The next step is to determine what it would be normal to intend by the words 'after 12 months' trading' in the circumstances. One relevant factor, particularly in the interpretation of carefully designed utterances such as commercial documents, is the so-called Choice Principle. This principle, following from the assumption of optimal design, allows the interpreter to draw conclusions from the communicator's selection of particular words and grammatical constructions instead of others. Even though the charterparty could have been drafted to indicate either meaning more clearly, Kerr J was rightly persuaded that the omission of the words 'at any time' before the words 'after 12 months trading' made it apparent that the parties intended to refer to a specific instance and not a period of time beginning after 12 months. This is persuasive for two reasons. The first is that, as Kerr J observed, it is common in charterparties to include the words 'at any time' when that is what is meant. Since the parties would have mutually known this (allowing for the specialist knowledge that the parties' lawyers bring to them), the failure to include these words is an important indication that the parties did not intend their meaning. The second reason for the persuasiveness of the omission is that it would have been simpler to include such words to point to the charterers' contended meaning than it would be to use extra words to point to the shipowners' contended meaning. The omission to do either points more strongly towards the shipowners' contended meaning being intended . . .

The other two types of situation in which the linguistic meaning requires supplementation provide more room for interpreter error:

Linguistic vagueness. This arises whenever the conventional meaning of a word is indeterminate and hence uncertain, in that there exist borderline cases which cannot be said to fall within the meaning of the utterance nor can they be said to fall without that meaning.

Things that go without saying. This situation arises whenever pragmatic inference can point to something that would usually be meant even though it is not part of the linguistic meaning (and so has not been 'said').

Unlike in cases of deixis or ambiguity, it is not always clear in these categories of case whether, and to what extent, the intended meaning extends further than the linguistic meaning. In other words, it is not always clear to what extent a licence to supplement can be implied.

A famous example of a vagueness arose in *Arcos v Ronaasen*, heard by the House of Lords in 1933. In this case two contracts for the sale of a quantity of Russian timber, c.i.f. the River Thames, were concluded. Since a wrongful rejection of the documents by the buyer, the staves had lain on an open wharf exposed to rain. Six months after delivery, in a falling market, the buyers sought to reject the goods on the grounds that they did not conform to the contract description, which specified that the staves should be ½ inch thick (as well as specifying a length for the staves, and a range within which the breadth of the staves must fall). The goods were not measured at the time of delivery, but when the umpire inspected the goods after some nine or ten months' exposure to the elements on the wharf, it was found that the staves were mostly over the required ½ inch thickness (although over 75% were less than $\frac{1}{16}$ inch over). The umpire found (or at least the House of Lords interpreted his statements as finding) that although when delivered the staves had been thinner than at the time of inspection, still they had been mostly over ½ inch thick.

The problems in this case arise from the vagueness of the linguistic meaning of the word 'inch' . . . Lord Atkin was of the opinion that 'if the seller wants a margin he *must and in my experience does* stipulate for it' [italics added] and therefore the contract was for staves of ½ inch thick, permitting only 'microscopic deviations' (in Lord Warrington's words, deviations 'so slight as to be negligible'). The important part of this statement is the italicised part. If, as Lord Atkin seems to believe, there is a trade practice or reasonable expectation amongst commercial traders or the drafters of commercial contracts that, unless a margin is stipulated, specifications are strict with only microscopic deviations permissible (since, after all, the parties are commercial adversaries at arm's length), this would form part of the communal mutual context and would inform the reasonable interpretation of the contract. It would then be necessary to decide what size of deviation is 'negligible' — which itself depends upon the specific case and upon norms that were not presented in evidence (since in some industries a literally 'microscopic' deviation may be significant), and is not an easy matter once the aid to construction that is communicator's purpose has been abandoned . . .

The other type of supplementation occurs when, without the indication that deixis, ambiguity or vagueness provide, nevertheless there is something that would normally go without saying . . . A brief example of such supplementation can be found in the case of *BCCI v Ali*. The appeal involved a release by Mr. Naeem of his former employer BCCI's liability for 'any or all claims whether under statute, Common Law or in Equity of whatsoever nature that exist or may exist', and whether that release extended to the dismissed employee's claim for stigma damages (available after *Mahmud v BCCI*) — a claim that neither party were or could have been aware at the time of contracting . . . Lord Hoffmann . . . believed the words to be as clear as they could have been in intending to preclude the implication of qualifications, and believed that the lack of a dispute between the parties meant that there was no further limit that would be normally intended and so could be inferred. He was impressed by the mutually obvious lack of a commercial purpose that the agreement would have if it did not apply to claims of which the parties were unaware, since there were no claims of which they were aware . . .

The Use of Pragmatic Inference to Replace the Linguistic Meaning

Sometimes the communicator will (apparently) intend part of the linguistic meaning to be actually replaced by meaning from another source, rather than merely supplemented. Most usually, this will occur in cases of dialect — whereby a variation of a language has been used by the parties themselves (what the law calls a 'course of dealing') or is in use by a community of which the parties are members (what the law calls 'custom', 'trade usage' or 'scientific terms'). Whenever words in an utterance could take a dialectual as well as the basic linguistic meaning, the interpreter must decide, given the mutual context, which meaning it would be more normal to intend. Unless the parties have expressly defined a personal meaning for the term, the

> balancing will depend upon which meaning is more likely to have been intended given the communicator's apparent purpose, as well as whether the dialect is apropos to the topic or situation of the utterance. In *The Karen Oltmann*, discussed above, the meaning of 'after 12 months' trading' that the parties had used in pre-contractual negotiations provided a personal meaning that, in a contract to which the negotiations were pursuant, it would be normal to continue to intend in the absence of disavowal. Standard trade clauses and legal terms of art make up particular dialects used by the legal community. These dialects are apposite to the need for precision and certainty in commercial documents, and their mutual knowledge is easily inferable among the legally-trained, thus there should be a strong presumption that the specialist meaning of such clauses or terms is intended to displace the linguistic meaning.

As Kramer notes, Lord Hoffman's principles should be taken seriously because they reflect the reality of what people do when they interpret communications. This does not mean, however, that the principles are easy to apply to actual cases.

Kramer refers to the case of *Bank of Credit Commerce International SA v Ali* [2002] 1 AC 352 in which the House of Lords was asked to interpret a release clause in a redundancy arrangement that stated that the employees would not pursue any further claims against their employers. The question for the House of Lords was whether this clause precluded the employees from pursuing a claim for 'stigma' damages – a claim that neither party were or could have been aware of at the time the contract was formed. All five members of the House of Lords purported to apply Lord Hoffman's principles, but Lord Hoffman, himself, was in a minority of one in holding that the agreement on its proper construction precluded any action for the former employees. He asserted (at [38]):

> The language of the document is very wide. The impression it conveys is that the draftsman meant business. He has gone to some trouble to avoid leaving anything out. He uses traditional style: pairs of words like 'full and final settlement', 'all or any claims', 'that exist or may exist' and phrases like 'whether under statute, common law or in equity' and 'of whatsoever nature'. Admittedly, he could have gone further . . . and I have seen American documents in which the release covers an entire page. But most people in this country would regard this as overkill.

The majority of the House of Lords disagreed, holding that the agreement should not be taken to have excluded causes of action that had not even been recognised at the time of entry into the release. Lord Bingham delivered the leading speech and said (at [13] and [21]):

> . . . [A] long and in my view salutary line of authority shows that, in the

absence of clear language, the court will be very slow to infer that a party intended to surrender rights and claims of which he was unaware and could not have been aware . . . On a fair construction of this document I cannot conclude that the parties intended to provide for the release of rights and the surrender of claims which they could never have had in contemplation at all. If the parties had sought to achieve so extravagant a result they should in my opinion have used language which left no room for doubt and which might at least have alerted Mr Naeem to the true effect of what (on that hypothesis) he was agreeing.

The case shows how, even when operating under the same principles, judges can come to very different conclusions on the interpretation of contracts. Undoubtedly, Lord Hoffman's five principles have brought clarity to the law by providing a helpful exposition of the approach to be adopted when interpreting contracts. Uncertainty will remain, however, in regard to how these principles will be applied in practice. To this extent, there is still scope for the exercise of judicial discretion in the interpretation of contracts.

7.3.2.4 Contractual interpretation under the Principles of European Contract Law

The approach to contract interpretation in the Principles of European Contract Law is found in Chapter 5 of the draft. It states the following:

Article 5:101: General Rules of Interpretation
(1) A contract is to be interpreted according to the common intention of the parties even if this differs from the literal meaning of the words.
(2) If it is established that one party intended the contract to have a particular meaning, and at the time of the conclusion of the contract the other party could not have been unaware of the first party's intention, the contract is to be interpreted in the way intended by the first party.
(3) If an intention cannot be established according to (1) or (2), the contract is to be interpreted according to the meaning that reasonable persons of the same kind as the parties would give to it in the same circumstances.

Article 5:102: Relevant Circumstances
In interpreting the contract, regard shall be had, in particular, to:

(a) the circumstances in which it was concluded, including the preliminary negotiations;
(b) the conduct of the parties, even subsequent to the conclusion of the contract;
(c) the nature and purpose of the contract;
(d) the interpretation which has already been given to similar clauses by the parties and the practices they have established between themselves;
(e) the meaning commonly given to terms and expressions in the branch of activity concerned and the interpretation similar clauses may already have received;

(f)   usages; and

(g)   good faith and fair dealing

Article 5.103: Contra Proferentem Rule

Where there is doubt about the meaning of a contract term not individually negotiated, an interpretation of the term against the party who supplied it is to be preferred.

Article 5:104: Preference to Negotiated Terms

Terms which have been individually negotiated take preference over those which are not.

Article 5:105: Reference to Contract as a Whole

Terms are interpreted in the light of the whole contract in which they appear.

Article 5:106: Terms to Be Given (Full) Effect

An interpretation which renders the terms of the contract lawful, or effective, is to be preferred to one which would not.

Article 5:107: Linguistic Discrepancies

Where a contract is drawn up in two or more language versions none of which is stated to be authoritative, there is, in case of discrepancy between the versions, a preference for the interpretation according to the version in which the contract was originally drawn up.

The approach suggested by the Principles is, on the whole, very similar to that adopted in the English courts. One principal difference is that the relevant circumstances to be taken into consideration under paragraphs (a) and (b) of Article 5–102 go beyond what English law currently permits (see *Prenn v Simmonds* [1971] 1 WLR 1381, 1384–5). Of course, it could be argued that the position adopted by the Principles is preferable since precontractual negotiations are part of the surrounding circumstances that are used to design, and hence interpret, the meaning of a document (see Kramer (2003) 23 OJLS 173, 180; McMeel (2003) 119 LQR 272; Nicholls (2005) 121 LQR 577). The Principles may indeed indicate the direction in which English law is progressing. In the recent case of *ProForce Recruit Ltd v The Rugby Group Ltd* [2006] EWCA Civ 69, the Court of Appeal held that evidence of precontractual negotiations was admissible to determine the meaning of the expression 'preferred supplier status'. Arden LJ said:

'55. In this case, the parties have used a very unusual combination of words ('preferred supplier status'). These words are undefined and they are not introduced or accompanied by any words of explanation. In those circumstances it is in my judgment reasonably arguable that on their true interpretation those words bear the meaning that the parties in common gave them in their communications leading up to the signing of the agreement. In admitting evidence as to those communications, the court would be hearing that evidence not with a view to taking the parties' subjective intent into account for the purposes of interpretation (a purpose precluded by the principles laid down by Lord Hoffmann in the *ICS* case) but for the purpose of identifying the meaning that the parties in effect incorporated into their agreement in circumstances where the court was satisfied that on their true interpretation the terms of the agreement were to have this effect . . .

57. Evidence as to negotiations between the parties to a contract leading up to the making of that contract may be admissible for the purposes of interpretation in wider circumstances than I have indicated above, but it is unnecessary for me to go further than those circumstances for the purpose of this appeal. Lord Hoffmann recognises in the *ICS* case that the boundaries of the rule excluding evidence of pre-contractual negotiations on questions of interpretation is unclear. Moreover, Lord Nicholls has argued ['My Kingdom for a Horse: the Meaning of Words' (2005) 121 LQR 577, 583] that the rule should be relaxed. The exclusion of pre-contractual negotiations is not on the face of it consistent with the general principle that a contract should be interpreted in the light of its context. Nor, on the face of it, is the application of a meaning which is not that which the parties themselves gave to a term consistent with the general approach of contract law, which is to respect party autonomy. The results may be anomalous. If the judge's ruling in this case expresses the general position in law, the result would be that the parties' meaning would be adopted if they defined the term in their written contract but not if they only did so only in the course of pre-contractual negotiations. Moreover, in that latter event, the meaning given to the term by the court would prevail, and (if the court's meaning is one which is different from that on which both parties in fact proceeded) a party would be able to avoid its contractual obligations deriving from the parties' meaning. That may be the law but, if it is, it is not, on the face of it, an attractive result. There are considerations that may go the other way. Lord Hoffmann's holding is that the exclusionary rule is based on reasons of practical policy . . . That policy would have to be carefully considered if evidence of pre-contractual negotiations is to be admitted in evidence in interpretation questions in the future on any wider basis than the law presently permits. In that sense there may be parallels to be drawn with the use of legislative history in the interpretation of statutes. In addition, careful consideration may have to be given to the aims to be achieved by contractual interpretation and the precise extent to which the law requires an objective interpretation.'

It has also recently been held that evidence of the conduct of the parties subsequent to the conclusion of the contract may be admitted in order to establish the content of an oral contract. In *Maggs (t/a BM Builders) v Marsh* [2006] EWCA Civ 1058, Smith LJ said:

'Determining the terms of an oral contract is a question of fact. Establishing the facts will usually . . . depend upon the recollections of the parties and other witnesses. The accuracy of those recollections may be tested and elucidated by things said and done by the parties or witnesses after the agreement has been concluded. Receiving evidence of such words or actions does not mean that the judge is losing sight of his task of deciding what the parties agreed at the time of the contract. It is simply helping him to decide whose recollection is right. It is not surprising to me that the editor of *Lewison on the Interpretation of Contracts*, 3rd edition, should observe that there is nothing in the authorities to prevent the court from looking at post contract actions of the parties. As a matter of principle, I can see every reason why such evidence should be received.'

A further difference between the Principles and the current approach in English law is that paragraph (g) of the Principles recognises a substantive doctrine of 'good faith and fair dealing'. Whether such a doctrine is desirable will be considered in Chapter 12.

7.3.3 CATEGORIES OF TERMS

There are three types of express term: conditions, warranties and innominate terms. The word condition can have a number of meanings, but, in this context, it means a 'promissory condition'. When contrasted with warranties or innominate terms, the label of 'promissory condition' is being used to indicate the legal consequence of a breach, in the sense of whether the injured party has a right to terminate the contract because of the breach. When a party breaches a term that is a condition, the injured party has a right to terminate the contract as well as to claim damages. In contrast, when a party breaches a warranty this only gives rise to the right to claim damages. The consequences of breach of an innominate term will depend upon the seriousness of the breach. If the breach is merely trivial, the injured party will only be entitled to damages. If it is more serious, termination of the contract may be available. The distinction between conditions, warranties and innominate terms was explained by Diplock LJ in *Hong Kong Fir Shipping v Kawasaki Kisen Kaisha*.

Hong Kong Fir Shipping v Kawasaki Kisen Kaisha [1962] 2 QB 26

Diplock LJ:

'[T]here are many simple contractual undertakings, sometimes express but more often because of their very simplicity ("It goes without saying") to be implied, of which it can be predicated that every breach of such an undertaking must give rise to an event which will deprive the party not in default of substantially the whole benefit which it was intended that he should obtain from the contract; and such a stipulation, unless the parties have agreed that breach of it shall not entitle the non-defaulting party to treat the contract as repudiated, is a "condition". So too there may be other simple contractual undertakings of which it can be predicated that no breach can give rise to an event which will deprive the party not in default of substantially the whole benefit which it was intended that he should obtain from the contract; and such a stipulation, unless the parties have agreed that breach of it shall entitle the non-defaulting party to treat the contract as repudiated, is a "warranty".

There are, however, many contractual undertakings of a more complex character which cannot be categorised as being "conditions" or "warranties", . . . Of such undertakings all that can be predicated is that some breaches will and others will not give rise to an event which will deprive the party not in default of substantially the whole benefit which it was intended that he should obtain from the contract; and the legal consequences of a breach of such an undertaking, unless provided for expressly in the contract, depend upon the nature of the event to which the breach gives rise and do not follow automatically from a prior classification of the undertaking as a "condition" or a "warranty".'

Whether a term is classified as a condition or a warranty usually depends on the importance of the term. If the parties refer to a term as a 'condition', this may well indicate that the parties intend that breach of the term should entitle the non-defaulting party to treat the contract as discharged. However, use of such labels is not conclusive and the presumption can be rebutted by contrary evidence (see *Schuler AG v Wickman Machine Tools* [1974] AC 235). The distinction between conditions, warranties and innominate terms will be discussed in Chapter 16, which deals with issues of performance and breach. At this point, it is important to note that the parties should have these issues in mind when drafting the contract. They can, if they wish, include an express term stating the consequences that will follow from breach of particular obligations. Such a term will provide greater certainty than leaving it to the court to determine the consequences of breach.

7.4 IMPLIED TERMS

It would be unrealistic to expect every term in a contract to be written down or expressed in words. Indeed, if they were, contracts would be absurdly lengthy documents. Therefore, in certain situations a term or terms may be implied into a contract. Parliament has intervened to imply terms into certain types of contract, for example: contracts for the sale and supply of goods, employment contracts and contracts between a landlord and tenant. In the absence of intervention by Parliament, it is left to the courts to imply terms. The relationship between express and implied terms was considered by Lord Diplock in *Photo Production v Securicor Transport* [1980] AC 827:

> 'A basic principle of the common law of contract . . . is that parties to a contract are free to determine for themselves what primary obligations they will accept. They may state these in express words in the contract itself, and, where they do, the statement is determinative; but in practice a commercial contract never states all the primary obligations of the parties in full; many are left to be incorporated by implication of law from the legal nature of the contract into which the parties are entering. But if the parties wish to reject or modify primary obligations which would otherwise be so incorporated, they are fully at liberty to do so by express words.'

As we will see there are some terms implied by statute that cannot be excluded because they are necessary for the protection of vulnerable parties, but as Lord Diplock notes, all other implied terms can be excluded by the express words of the parties. There are two sources of implied terms: the courts and Parliament. We will consider terms implied by the courts first.

7.4.1 TERMS IMPLIED BY THE COURTS

The courts imply terms into contracts on the ground that they are purporting to realise the presumed intention of the parties. The test is strict. As Lord Bingham said in *Phillips Electronique Grand Public SA v British Sky Broadcasting Ltd* [1995] EMLR 472, 481, 'it is because the implication of terms is so potentially intrusive that the law imposes strict constraints on the exercise of this extraordinary power'. The courts are understandably reluctant to give any encouragement to parties to try to escape from contractual obligations on the basis of some term which was not stated, but which is now alleged to be of great significance. There are certain situations, however, where the courts will be willing to imply terms.

7.4.1.1 Terms implied by custom

The first basis on which the courts will imply terms is where the implication of the term derives from a local trade or custom. Such implications have an important role to play in the commercial law. The requirements for implying a term derived from trade or custom were expounded by Ungoed-Thomas J in *Cunliffe-Owen v Teather & Greenwood* [1967] 1 WLR 1421:

' "Usage" [or custom] may be admitted to explain the language used in a written contract or to add an implied incident to it, provided that if expressed in the written contract it would not make its terms or its tenor insensible or inconsistent ... "Usage" as a practice which the court will recognise is a mixed question of fact and law. For the practice to amount to such a recognised usage, it must be certain, in the sense that the practice is clearly established; it must be notorious, in the sense that it is so well known, in the market in which it is alleged to exist, that those who conduct business in that market contract with the usage as an implied term; and it must be reasonable.

The burden lies on those alleging "usage" to establish it ... The practice that has to be established consists of a continuity of acts, and those acts have to be established by persons familiar with them ... Arrangements or compromises to the same effect as the alleged usage do not establish usage; they contradict it. They may be the precursors of usage; but usage presupposes that arrangements and compromises are no longer required ... What is necessary is that for a practice to be a recognised usage it should be established as a practice having binding effect.'

To imply a term derived from custom it must be shown that the term is: (1) certain, (2) notorious, (3) reasonable and (4) recognised as binding. An early example of such a term is seen in the case of *Hutton v Warren*.

Hutton v Warren (1836) 1 M & W 466; All ER Rep 151

Facts: See above.

Parke B:
'The custom of the country as to cultivation and the term of quitting with respect to allowances for seed and labour, is clearly applicable to a tenancy from year to year and, therefore, if this custom was, by implication, imported into the lease, the plaintiff and defendant were bound by it after the lease expired. We are of opinion that this custom was, by implication, imported into the lease. It has long been settled that, in commercial transactions, extrinsic evidence of custom and usage is admissible to annex incidents to written contracts in matters with respect to which they are silent. The same rule has also been applied to contracts in other transactions of life, in which known usages have been established and prevailed. This has been done on the principle of presumption that, in such transactions, the parties did not mean to express in writing the whole of the contract by which they intended to be bound, but a contract with reference to those known usages.'

Implication of a term by custom will not be possible if the contract contains an express term that is inconsistent with the custom. In that case the express term prevails over the implied term.

Les Affréteurs Réunis SA v Leopold Walford (London) Ltd [1919] AC 801

Facts: A clause in a time charterparty provided that 'a commission of three per cent on the estimated gross amount of hire is due to Leopold Walford (London), Limited, on signing this charter (ship lost or not lost)'. The charterers brought an action for payment of the commission. At first instance, Bailhache J found for the ship owners on the ground that no hire had in fact been earned under the charterparty and there was a custom in operation that a broker's commission was payable only in relation to hire which had been earned under the charter.

Held: The House of Lords held that the charterers could enforce the express clause because the ship owners could not lawfully set up a custom which was inconsistent with the express terms of the charterparty.

Lord Birkenhead:
'The learned judge, in my judgment (and here I think the comments of the learned Lords Justices in the Court of Appeal are perfectly well-founded and in no way exaggerated), has in effect declared that a custom may be given effect to in commercial matters which is entirely inconsistent with the plain words of an agreement into which commercial men, certainly acquainted with so well known a custom, have nevertheless thought proper to enter. Much evidence would be necessary to convince me of the existence of such a custom, and, if it were forthcoming, I should nevertheless hold the custom to be bad on grounds which seem to me to be both notorious and elementary.'

7.4.1.2 Terms implied in fact

Terms may be implied into an apparently complete contract from the factual context of the agreement. Terms implied in fact are implied into the contract to give effect to the unexpressed intentions of the parties. In other words, the term is implied not as a matter of law, but as a matter of fact to give effect to what the parties had agreed, although the agreement was implicit rather than explicit. Because of this, terms implied in fact will usually be specific to the particular transaction between the parties.

Traditionally the courts have been reluctant to imply a term into a contract as a matter of fact. This is because of concerns about protecting freedom of contract. It is undesirable for the courts to rewrite the contract for the parties. Terms will only be implied in fact where it is 'necessary' to do so. Two tests have emerged:

(i)   the business efficacy test
(ii) the officious bystander test

They are basically different shades of the same test as to what is 'necessary' to make the contract work.

7.4.1.2.1 *The business efficacy test*

The Moorcock (1889) LR 14 PD 64

Facts: The defendant agreed to allow the plaintiff's ship to unload cargo at the defendant's Thames wharf. It was well known that ships normally ran aground at low tide on the Thames, but unfortunately the plaintiff's ship was damaged because of the unevenness of the river bed at the defendant's wharf. The contract between the parties contained no express term as to the suitability of the river bed for mooring a ship. The plaintiff brought an action for damages against the defendants. At first instance, Butt J held that the defendants were liable for breach of an implied term to take 'reasonable care to ascertain that the bottom of the river at the jetty was in such a condition as not to endanger the vessel using their premises in the ordinary way.'

Held: The Court of Appeal dismissed the defendant's appeal.

Bowen LJ:
'The question which arises here is whether when a contract is made to let the use of this jetty to a ship which can only use it, as is known by both parties, by taking the ground, there is any implied warranty on the part of the owners of the jetty, and if so, what is the extent of the warranty. Now, an implied warranty, or, as it is called, a covenant in law, as distinguished from an express contract or express warranty, really is in all cases founded on the presumed intention of the parties, and upon reason. The implication which the law draws from what must obviously have been the intention of the parties, the law draws with the object of giving efficacy to the transaction and preventing such a failure of consideration as cannot have been within the contemplation of either side; and I believe if one were to take all the cases, and they are many, of implied warranties or covenants in law, it will be found that in all of them the law is raising an implication from the presumed intention of the parties with the object of giving to the transaction such efficacy as both parties must have intended that at all events it should have. In business transactions such as this, what the law desires to effect by the implication is to give such business efficacy to the transaction as must have been intended at all events by both parties who are business men; not to impose on one side all the perils of the transaction, or to emancipate one side from all the chances of failure, but to make each party promise in law as much, at all events, as it must have been in the contemplation of both parties that he should be responsible for in respect of those perils or chances.
    Now what did each party in a case like this know? For if we are examining into their

presumed intention we must examine into their minds as to what the transaction was. Both parties knew that this jetty was let out for hire, and knew that it could only be used under the contract by the ship taking the ground. They must have known that it was by grounding that she used the jetty; in fact, except so far as the transport to the jetty of the cargo in the ship was concerned, they must have known, both of them, that unless the ground was safe the ship would be simply buying an opportunity of danger, and that all consideration would fail unless some care had been taken to see that the ground was safe. In fact the business of the jetty could not be carried on except upon such a basis. The parties also knew that with regard to the safety of the ground outside the jetty the ship-owner could know nothing at all, and the jetty owner might with reasonable care know everything. The owners of the jetty, or their servants, were there at high and low tide, and with little trouble they could satisfy themselves, in case of doubt, as to whether the berth was reasonably safe. The ship's owner, on the other hand, had not the means of verifying the state of the jetty, because the berth itself opposite the jetty might be occupied by another ship at any moment.

Now the question is how much of the peril of the safety of this berth is it necessary to assume that the ship-owner and the jetty owner intended respectively to bear – in order that such a minimum of efficacy should be secured for the transaction, as both parties must have intended it to bear? Assume that the berth outside had been absolutely under the control of the owners of the jetty, that they could have repaired it and made it fit for the purpose of the unloading and the loading. If this had been the case, then the case of *The Mersey Docks Trustees v Gibbs* Law Rep 1 H L 93 shews that those who owned the jetty, who took money for the use of the jetty, and who had under their control the *locus in quo*, would have been bound to take all reasonable care to prevent danger to those who were using the jetty – either to make the berth outside good, or else not to invite ships to go there – either to make the berth safe, or to advise persons not to go there. But there is a distinction in the present instance. The berth outside the jetty was not under the actual control of the jetty owners. It is in the bed of the river, and it may be said that those who owned the jetty had no duty cast upon them by statute or common law to repair the bed of the river, and that they had no power to interfere with the bed of the river unless under the licence of the Conservators. Now it does make a difference, it seems to me, where the entire control of the *locus in quo* – be it canal, or be it dock, or be it river berth – is not under the control of the persons who are taking toll for accommodation which involves its user, and, to a certain extent, the view must be modified of the necessary implication which the law would make about the duties of the parties receiving the remuneration. This must be done exactly for the reason laid down by Lord Holt in his judgment in *Coggs v Bernard* Ld Raym 909 (918), where he says "it would be unreasonable to charge persons with a trust further than the nature of the thing puts it in their power to perform." Applying that modification, which is one of reason, to this case, it may well be said that the law will not imply that the persons who have not the control of the place have taken reasonable care to make it good, but it does not follow that they are relieved from all responsibility. They are on the spot. They must know that the jetty cannot be used unless reasonable care is taken, if not to make it safe, at all events to see whether it is safe. No one can tell whether reasonable safety has been secured except themselves, and I think if they let out their jetty for use they at all events imply that they have taken reasonable care to see whether the berth, which is the essential part of the use of the jetty, is safe, and if it is not safe, and if they have not taken such reasonable care, it is their duty to warn persons with whom they have dealings that they have not done so. This is a business transaction as to which at any moment the parties may make any bargain they please, and either side may by the contract throw upon the other the burden of the unseen and existing danger. The question is what inference is to be drawn where the parties are dealing with each other on the assumption that the negotiations are to have some fruit, and where they say nothing about the burden of this kind of unseen peril, leaving the law to raise such inferences as are reasonable from the very nature of the transaction. So far as I am concerned I do not wish it to be understood that I at all consider this is a case of any duty on the part of the owners of the jetty to see to the access to the jetty being kept clear. The difference between access to the jetty and the actual use of the jetty seems to me, as [counsel for the defendants] says it is, only a question of degree, but when you are dealing with implications which the law directs, you cannot afford to neglect questions of degree, and it is just that difference of degree which brings one case on the line and prevents the other from approaching it. I confess that on the broad view of the case I think that business could not be carried on unless there was an implication to the extent I have laid down, at all events in the case where a jetty like the present is so to be used, and, although the case is a novel one, and the cases which have been cited do not assist us, I feel no difficulty in drawing the inference that this case comes within the line.'

According to Bowen LJ, the purpose of implying terms in fact, 'is to give such business efficacy to the transaction as must have been intended at all events by both parties who are business men'. In other words, a term will be implied in fact if, without it, the contract would be rendered unworkable. This is a stringent test. It is based on the presumed intentions of the parties but, on the facts of *The Moorcock*, this was assessed by reference to what was 'necessary' to make the contract work; not by reference to what would be 'reasonably expected'. *The Moorcock* thus establishes a test of 'necessity' in relation to terms implied in fact. The test is not without its difficulties, however, because it rests on the assumption that the parties are agreed as to the objectives of the contract, which is often not true.

H Collins, *The Law of Contract*, 4th edn, 2003, Cambridge: CUP, p 240

Implied terms are often presented as default rules, ie rules which the parties would agree were the costs of negotiation low or absent. Yet in all probability the parties have not failed to reach agreement on this point because of shortage of time and resources, but have simply not wished to enter into such detailed specification for fear of failure to reach agreement. The attempt to resolve this problem by means of a reification of the purpose of the contract in the business efficacy test only serves to obscure the problem. If the commercial motives of the parties for entering the contract diverge, as they usually will outside the realm of symbiotic contracts such as partnership and joint ventures, the performance of the contract without the implied term might easily satisfy the commercial objective of one party whilst simultaneously frustrating the objective of the other. Although these tests have been hallowed by constant judicial use for over a century, we must doubt whether they always provide a convincing justification for the insertion of additional obligations.

7.4.1.2.2 The 'officious bystander' test

The officious bystander test was put forward by Mackinnon LJ in *Shirlaw v Southern Foundries*.

Shirlaw v Southern Foundries [1939] 2 KB 206

Facts: In 1933 Mr Shirlaw was appointed managing director of Southern Foundries for a term of ten years. Three years later the beneficial owners of the company removed him from his directorship. The question for the court was whether there existed an implied term that he would not be removed from his directorship.

Held: The Court of Appeal held that such a term would be implied into the contract.

MacKinnon LJ:
'The question is whether this termination was a breach by the Southern Company of the agreement of December 21, 1933, caused or procured by the Federated Company.

I think that Humphreys J was right in holding that it was, for, as by the contract and the then existing articles, the company had no right to remove Mr Shirlaw from being a director during the ten years, I think it was an implied term that they would not by any alteration of the articles create such a right and exercise it during that period.

I recognise that the right or duty of a Court to find the existence of an implied term or implied terms in a written contract is a matter to be exercised with care; and a Court is too often invited to do so upon vague and uncertain grounds. Too often also such an invitation is backed by the citation of a sentence or two from the judgment of Bowen LJ in *The Moorcock* (1889) 14 PD 64. They are sentences from an extempore judgment as sound and sensible as all the utterances of that great judge; but I fancy that he would have been rather surprised if he could have foreseen that these general remarks of his would come to be a favourite citation of a supposed principle of law, and I even think that he might sympathise with the occasional impatience of his successors when *The Moorcock* (1889) 14 PD 64 is so often flushed for them in that guise.

For my part, I think that there is a test that may be at least as useful as such generalities. If I may quote from an essay which I wrote some years ago, I then said: "Prima facie that which in any contract is left to be implied and need not be expressed is something so obvious that it goes without saying; so that, if, while the parties were making their bargain, an officious bystander were to suggest some express provision for it in their agreement, they would testily suppress him with a common "Oh, of course!" '

At least it is true, I think, that, if a term were never implied by a judge unless it could pass that test, he could not be held to be wrong.

Applying that in this case, I ask myself what would have happened if, when this contract had been drafted and was awaiting signature, a third party reading the draft had said: "Would it not be well to put in a provision that the company shall not exercise or create any right to remove Mr Shirlaw from his directorship, and he have no right to resign his directorship?" I am satisfied that they would both have assented to this as implied already, and agreed to its expression for greater certainty. Mr Shirlaw would certainly have said: "Of course that is implied. If I am to be bound by this agreement, including the barring of my activities under clauses 11 and 12 when I cease to be managing director, obviously the company must not have, or create, the power to remove me at any moment from the Board and so disqualify me from that post"; and the company, which must be presumed to have been then desirous of binding him to serve them as managing director for ten years, would, I think, with equal alacrity have said: "Of course that is implied. If you were tempted by some offer elsewhere, it would be monstrous for you to be able to resign your directorship and, by so disqualifying yourself from being managing director, put an end to this agreement." '

The officious bystander test is again a strict one, emphasising that the standard is one of necessity, not reasonableness. This was noted in *Hughes v Greenwich LBC*.

Hughes v Greenwich LBC [1994] 1 AC 170

Lord Lowry:

'In order that a term may be implied, there has to be a compelling reason for deeming that term to form part of the contract . . . . I may perhaps illustrate my view by referring to what I said in the Court of Appeal in *JM Reilly Ltd v Belfast Corporation* [1970] NI 68, 83–84, in a passage which has no claim to originality of thought:

"It is not enough for the court to conclude, (and I guard myself against doing so), that such a term would have made the contract more reasonable; terms will be implied not in order to make for the parties a contract which the court considers fair, but only to make effective the contract which the parties have made for themselves. The principle is clearly and authoritatively stated in *Luxor*

> *(Eastbourne) Ltd v Cooper* [1941] AC 108, and even in *Devonald v Rosser* [1906]
> 2 KB 728, which may at first sight appear to give a more liberal expression to the
> doctrine, one finds on analysis a loyal adherence to the rule of *necessary implica-*
> *tion* in the passage (at p 743) where Farwell LJ asks, 'What, then, are we to infer
> would be a reasonable bargain such as the parties, being businessmen, *must*
> *have intended* to make?' " '

7.4.1.2.3 *The relationship between the two tests*

There is considerable overlap between the two tests. In theory, a term could satisfy
the 'officious bystander' test but not the 'business efficacy' test if, without the term
the contract would still have been workable, but both parties, as reasonable persons,
would have agreed to the term's inclusion had it been suggested to them. In
practice, however, differing commercial objectives will often preclude implication
under both tests.

Ashmore v Corporation of Lloyd's (No 2) [1992] 2 Lloyd's Rep 620

Facts: Ashmore, a Lloyd's name, claimed breach of contract against Lloyd's following
losses sustained on a number of insurance contracts. Ashmore contended that his
contract with Lloyd's contained an implied term that Lloyd's would take reasonable
steps to alert names about matters likely to affect their interests.

Held: Gatehouse J dismissed the action. The implied term could not pass the 'business efficacy' test because the Lloyd's names had always operated under the same
contractual arrangements as at present and it was impossible to say that the contract
would be unworkable without those implied terms. Nor did it pass the 'officious
bystander' test because it was impossible to contemplate an officious bystander
thinking of such a term.

Gatehouse J:
'The . . . two tests will often overlap and, indeed, have in the past been regarded as a
single test embodying both aspects . . .

[Regarding] the *Moorcock* "business efficacy" . . . I am driven to the conclusion that
neither of the terms contended for by the plaintiffs comes within measurable distance
of passing it. Very many thousands of people over the years have been or are
now Names at Lloyd's under the same contractual arrangements and it is obviously
impossible to say that without these implied terms the contract will not work.

Turning to the officious bystander test, in my judgment the same result follows. With
regard to the alleged "Duty to alert", I have already remarked on the complexity of the
question posed, in its final and alternative form, and the successive versions put forward in the process of reaching it. I sympathise with the plaintiffs' legal advisers,

---

striving to formulate a term which is at the same time sufficiently circumscribed to qualify as both reasonable and necessary, but also sufficiently wide to cover the actual events alleged in the remainder of the points of claim and on which the remedy of damages and indemnity is founded . . .

The plain fact is that the more the plaintiffs' advisers strove to bring the implied term within the bounds of reasonableness and necessity, the more divorced from reality the question became. To start with, I find it impossible to contemplate an officious bystander at the Rota Committee being capable of thinking up so complex a question; one which has taken a team of skilled lawyers so long and so many attempts to formulate. Even if he could, the answer of both parties would certainly not be, "Oh, of course! That is something that is so obvious that it goes without saying". If Lloyd's had not dismissed the suggestion out of hand, the Rota Committee would at least have required the question to be written down for detailed consideration, no doubt with their lawyers' advice. The eventual answer would, I believe, have been an uncompromising, "No". At least, I am wholly unpersuaded that it would have been, "Yes, of course": and certainly such acceptance would not have been given unhesitatingly at the time the question was asked.'

7.4.1.2.4 Necessity or reasonableness

It is repeatedly emphasised in the cases that 'the touchstone [for implication] is always *necessity* and not merely *reasonableness*' (*Liverpool City Council v Irwin* [1977] AC 239, 266 per Lord Edmund-Davies). However, this distinction may be difficult to maintain in practice because contracts are very rarely unworkable without revision. More often than not, the real problem is that the contract is manifestly unreasonable without the implication of a term.

Equitable Life Assurance Society v Hyman [2000] 3 WLR 529

Facts: Hyman was a representative of approximately 90,000 policyholders who held life assurance policies containing a guaranteed annuity rate (GAR) with Equitable Life Assurance Society. The issue was whether Equitable Life could decide to reduce the level of bonus which certain of its policyholders would receive. This was contrary to past practice and the expectations of the policyholders. The articles of association of the society, however, appeared to permit the directors of the society to take such an action. At first instance the judge held that the directors' policy was in accord with the society's articles of association. The Court of Appeal reversed that decision.

Held: The House of Lords held that, although the society's articles gave the directors a very broad discretion in relation to bonuses, a term should be implied into the articles to the effect that the society would not exercise its discretion under the articles so as to defeat the reasonable expectations of the parties, which included the expectation that the discretion would not be exercised in a way that prejudiced the rights of a particular group of policyholders.

Lord Steyn:

'[T]he question is whether the implication is strictly necessary. My Lords, as counsel for the GAR policyholders observed, final bonuses are not bounty. They are a significant part of the consideration for the premiums paid. And the directors' discretions as to the amount and distribution of bonuses are conferred for the benefit of policyholders. In this context the self-evident commercial object of the inclusion of guaranteed rates in the policy is to protect the policyholder against a fall in market annuity rates by ensuring that if the fall occurs he will be better off than he would have been with market rates. The choice is given to the GAR policyholder and not to the Society. It cannot be seriously doubted that the provision for guaranteed annuity rates was a good selling point in the marketing by the Society of the GAR policies. It is also obvious that it would have been a significant attraction for purchasers of GAR policies. The Society points out that no special charge was made for the inclusion in the policy of GAR provisions. So be it. This factor does not alter the reasonable expectations of the parties. The supposition of the parties must be presumed to have been that the directors would not exercise their discretion in conflict with contractual rights. These are the circumstances in which the directors of the Society resolved upon a differential policy which was designed to deprive the relevant guarantees of any substantial value. In my judgment an implication precluding the use of the directors' discretion in this way is strictly necessary. The implication is essential to give effect to the reasonable expectations of the parties. The stringent test applicable to the implication of terms is satisfied.'

Lord Steyn insisted that the term was implied on the basis of its 'necessity'. But the term was not really necessary to make the contract workable (the business efficacy test) and it was not so necessary that it went without saying (the officious bystander test). Rather, in the words of Lord Steyn, it was 'essential to give effect to the reasonable expectations of the parties'. The touchstone of the implication of the term was the 'reasonable expectations of the parties', not necessity.

Paragon Finance plc v Nash [2002] 1 WLR 685.

Facts: Paragon Finance loaned money to Nash under two mortgage agreements which contained variable interest clauses. Nash defaulted on the mortgages and Paragon Finance claimed possession. Nash raised a number of defences including the claim that the agreements contained an implied term that Paragon Finance was bound to exercise its discretion in varying interest rates fairly, honestly, in good faith, and not arbitrarily, capriciously or unreasonably, having regard to all relevant matters and ignoring the irrelevant.

Held: The Court of Appeal held that the discretion to vary interest rates on the mortgages was not completely unfettered and was subject to the implied term contended for by Nash. However, the fact that Paragon Finance had set interest rates without reference to those of other market lenders did not place Paragon Finance in breach of the implied term and therefore the appeal was dismissed.

Dyson LJ:

'I would hold that there were terms to be implied in both agreements that the rates of interest would not be set dishonestly, for an improper purpose, capriciously or arbitrarily. I have no doubt that such an implied term is necessary in order to give effect to the reasonable expectations of the parties. I am equally in no doubt that such an implied term is one of which it could be said that "it goes without saying". If asked at the time of the making of the agreements whether it accepted that the discretion to fix rates of interest could be exercised dishonestly, for an improper purpose, capriciously or arbitrarily, I have no doubt that the claimant would have said "of course not".'

In *Paragon Finance*, Dyson LJ stated that the implied term was 'necessary in order to give effect to the reasonable expectations of the parties'. Once again it seems like this is reasonableness paraded in the clothes of necessity. In an interesting article, Bryan and Ellinghaus have argued that the true test is one of 'objective necessity'. They contend that the law is rightly moving from the test of the 'officious bystander' to the test of the 'reasonable bystander'.

Bryan, M & Ellinghaus, F, 'Fault lines in the law of obligations: *Roxborough v Rothmans of Pall Mall Australia Ltd*' (2000) 22 Syd LR 636, 645 and 647

It is important to bear in mind that in asking, via the bystander, what the parties would have decided had they addressed the issue the court is asking a hypothetical question. It is not inquiring into the actual intention of the parties. If it can be shown that the parties actually intended to include a term in their contract there will be no need to imply that term; it is included by virtue of their agreement. If there is a written document from which the term has been omitted, that document will be rectified so as to include it. 'Implication' begins where the ascertainment of intention leaves off. It assumes that the parties did not actually have any agreed intention on the point in issue. So the matter has to be resolved by hypothesis.

Once this is clearly understood, an alternative conception of the bystander suggests itself. It is that of the 'reasonable bystander', or in other words the reasonable person, on whom the law traditionally relies when hypotheses about human conduct are called for. Substituting the 'reasonable bystander' for the 'officious bystander' involves a reversal of the roles of the bystander and the parties. The bystander's role is no longer that of an interrogator who elicits from the parties whether they would have instant-aneously agreed on the term sought to be implied by one of them. Rather the bystander replaces the parties as the source of any implied term. The bystander does not ask for a response from the parties, but rather decides what, if anything, reasonable parties would have agreed on in the circumstances . . .

It is also striking to note that the objective conception of the bystander is applied when the inclusion of an express term of the contract is in issue. For example, whether a statement of the parties is promissory is decided according to the objective judg-ment of the reasonable (or 'intelligent') bystander. There is no obvious reason why implied terms should be treated differently.

In our view, the time has come to give the 'officious' bystander, conceived of as the interrogator of the contracting parties, 'a decent burial', and to replace him (if he is to be retained at all) with an unequivocally 'reasonable' bystander, conceived of as the objective arbiter of what reasonable parties would have accepted (or would now accept) as appropriate in the circumstances.

Whether the officious bystander will be buried and replaced by the reasonable bystander remains to be seen. What is clear is that the courts are increasingly concerned to satisfy the reasonable expectations of the parties. This has led some to argue that implication in fact is really part of contractual interpretation by pragmatic inference.

Kramer, A, 'Implication in fact as an instance of contractual interpretation' [2004] 63 CLJ 384, 395–402

The following are examples of some contract cases in which the apparently intended meaning goes further than the linguistically encoded meaning, and so pragmatic inference has been used to supplement the linguistically encoded meaning:

(i)   In *The Karen Oltmann* a charterparty states, ambiguously, that the charterers have an option to redeliver the vessel "after 12 months' trading". The court found, after looking at the pre-contractual negotiations and the norms of com-munication, that the option was intended to be exercisable at the specific point of time defined by the passage of 12 months' trading, rather than at any time after 12 months' trading had been completed.

(ii) In *BCCI v Ali* an employee's release of "any or all claims" against his employer was intended to be qualified such that it did not apply to those claims that were unforeseeable at the time of contracting (claims for stigma damages).

(iii) In *Equitable Life Assurance Society v Hyman* a pension company's general dis-cretion was held to be intended to include an implied restriction preventing its exercise so as to deprive the guarantees of annual rate of any value. In *Paragon*

Finance v Nash, a mortgage lender's variable interest clause was held to include an implied restriction preventing its exercise dishonestly, for an improper purpose, capriciously, arbitrarily or in a Wednesbury unreasonable manner.

(iv)   In *The Moorcock* an agreement to unload a vessel at a wharf was intended to include an implied warranty that the wharfingers had taken reasonable care to see that the river bottom was not in a dangerous condition.

(v)   In *Malik v BCCI* an employment contract was held to be intended to include a promise by the employer not to engage in conduct likely to undermine the trust and confidence required if the employment relationship is to continue in the manner the employment contract implicitly envisages. Consequently, an employer is held to intend to promise to take reasonable care when writing an employee's reference (*Spring v Guardian Assurance*).

(vi)   In *Hutton v Warren* a lease was held to include a landlord's duty to compensate the tenant for seed and labour since the tenant had sown the land before quitting (upon notice to quit served by the landlord), such a duty being customary.

(vii) In *Liverpool CC v Irwin* a lease was held to include an implied obligation on the landlord to take reasonable care to keep in reasonable repair and usability the staircase, lifts and rubbish chutes, as well as implied rights in the tenants to use such facilities.

All of the above are cases of supplementation of the linguistic meaning by a process of pragmatic inference. In such cases there is an apparently intended licence to supplement because it would be normal to intend more than the linguistic meaning. However the interesting thing about law's treatment of these cases, all cases of the same linguistic process, is that they are divided by our principles of contract law into two categories. The cases outlined in headings (i) and (ii) are characterised by courts as cases of interpretation, and hence governed by the rules set down by Lord Hoffmann in the *Investors Compensation Scheme v West Bromwich Building Society* case. The cases under headings (iii) to (vii) are characterised by the courts as cases of implication of terms, and hence governed by the officious bystander test of *Shirlaw v Southern Foundries (1926) Ltd* and/or the business efficacy test of *The Moorcock*, and/or the test for implying from custom, and/or the principles of implication in law.

It is, at least at first sight, puzzling that we should have two sets of rules to govern what is as a single task, that of supplementation by inference. Lord Steyn has said, extra-judicially, "The implication of terms is also part of the process of interpretation of written contracts". Lord Hoffmann has said that "As in the case of any implied term, the process is one of construction of the agreement as a while in its commercial setting", and extra-judicially, "the implication of terms into a contract is in essence a question of construction like any other". Kim Lewison has observed that the implication of terms is "part of the province of the interpretation of contracts", but rightly observes that "if the implication of terms is part of a continuous spectrum beginning with the construction of express terms, it would seem to follow that at some point in the spectrum there is a radical change in approach. The location of that point is uncertain". Certainly, it is difficult to explain why the situation in (ii) is on a different side of the point of radical change to the situations in (iii), why this point of radical change exists and how it can be identified. An attempt will be made . . . to answer these questions by using the analysis of supplementation by pragmatic inference . . . Ultimately it will be shown to what degree the rules of implied terms are merely a special instance of interpretation of express terms, and whether a "bright line" separating the two tests and two categories can be justified . . .

As is well known, there are two common tests (or two formulations of one test) for the implication of terms in fact. The first is the "business efficacy test" of Bowen LJ in *The Moorcock* . . . The second is the officious bystander test of MacKinnon LJ in *Shirlaw v Southern Foundries (1926) Ltd* . . .

[I]t seems fairly clear that the test is at least based upon presumed intention of some sort. If this is so, then we must ask (after Glanville Williams) whether this is this an intention that was presumed to be actually held, or a hypothetical intention that the parties would have held if they had foreseen and considered the matter? Even if the implication of terms is not founded upon principles of interpretation, it is sufficiently similar a project that it must be governed by the objective principle to avoid confusion and incoherence in the law. If this is so, then Williams' distinction should be reformulated as that between, on the one hand, implying terms that reasonably appear to have been in fact intended, and, on the other hand, implying terms that reasonably appear to be what the parties would have intended if they had put their mind to the matter. This nice distinction fades away when we realise that one can intend something without it crossing one's mind—applying intended principles to interpolate or extrapolate from what is expressed is to find out what was intended even if it was not consciously considered.

If this is correct, then at their hearts the tests of implication in fact require that the term to be implied be one that reasonably appears to have been intended—the same test as that for interpretation of express terms by supplementation. This is consistent with the raft of rules surrounding the implication of terms, for example that a term cannot be implied where it is inconsistent with the express terms (in other words, where it is inconsistent with linguistically encoded material and that which is implied in interpreting such material). This stands to reason—it cannot reasonably appear to have been intended if the linguistically encoded material, which clearly was intended, is inconsistent with it. The business efficacy test, as a neither necessary nor sufficient guide to what terms can be implied, fits with the basic common sense principles of interpretation: all students of contractual interpretation know that the court should be slow to construe a commercial agreement in a way that produces an uncommercial or absurd result because it is very unlikely to have been intended. To say that any term that is necessary for business efficacy is likely to have been intended is merely an application of this principle.

Yet the officious bystander test appears to be stricter than the basic objective principle of interpretation ("does it reasonably appear that the term was intended by both parties") rather than merely a colourful recounting of it, and it is usually understood in that way. Should implied terms have a stricter test than the implication of supplementary material through interpretation, and if so why? This is perhaps the real mystery of implied terms, and the main obstacle to seeing implication in fact as part of the rules interpretation.

Explaining why the test for implication of terms is stricter than the basic objective test

... Crucially for an understanding of why the implication of terms tests are stricter than the basic interpretation tests, there is a principled difference between the implication of terms and the interpretation of express terms, although the distinction cannot be drawn with a bright line ... [P]rimary information is that which is more independent, which forms the skeleton of the preferences or goals of the communicator, and which identifies new issues rather than relating to other issues in an utterance. Such information is important and the inference of such information is more unreliable than the inference of secondary information. For these reasons, the benefits of expressing such information are by far outweighed by the costs of doing so, and so primary information is less likely to be intended to go without saying than secondary information.

With this in mind, the stricter (implication of terms in fact) test of supplementation can be justified by reconceptualising it as an instance of the application of the basic interpretation principles (the objective test etc.) to the special situation of primary information. The test is strict because the information inferred is primary and so less likely to be intended to go without saying: information characterised as a new term to be implied is more primary than information characterised as detail to be inferred in interpretation of an existing linguistically encoded term. As new terms are more primary than details supplementing existing terms, the licence to supplement by inference is much harder to infer in the case of the implication of terms than in the case of the interpretation of terms.

The narrow formulation of the implication in fact test seeks to point to the narrow range of situations in which it is credible to believe that such primary information went without saying—to wit, those situations in which a term is easy to identify (i.e. "so obvious that it goes without saying") and those situations in which it appears that the communicators may have forgotten to express the term (hence their testy suppression of the officious bystander's reminder).

It is thus submitted that this difference between primary and secondary information explains the existence of a separate and strict test for the implication of terms in fact. The test for the implication of terms is thus a special instance of contractual interpretation; a special application of the common sense principles (particularly the objective principle). Terms that are implied in fact are really terms that are tacitly intended, the process of implication being the same as the process by which information is imported through interpretation, but the type of information implied being different.

The relevance of the 'reasonable expectations of the parties' will be returned to at the end of the chapter when we consider the underlying rationale for implying terms into a contract.

7.4.1.3 Terms implied in law

There is a fundamental distinction between terms implied in fact and terms implied in law. Terms implied in fact are designed to supplement the unexpressed but supposed actual intentions of the parties. Terms implied in law, on the other hand, arise where precedent has incorporated such terms into particular types of contract in the absence of intention. The distinction was explained by Lord Wright in *Luxor (Eastbourne) Ltd v Cooper* [1941] AC 108:

> 'The expression "implied term" is used in different senses. Sometimes it denotes some term which does not depend on the actual intention of the parties but on a rule of law, such as the terms, warranties or conditions which, if not expressly excluded, the law imports, as for instance under the Sale of Goods Act and the Marine Insurance Act . . . But a case like the present is different because what it is sought to imply is based on an intention imputed to the parties from their actual circumstances.'

The distinction between terms implied in fact and terms implied in law was also considered by the Court of Appeal on the facts of *Shell (UK) Ltd v Lostock Garage Ltd*.

Shell (UK) Ltd v Lostock Garage Ltd [1976] 1 WLR 1187

Facts: Lostock Garage entered into a 'solus agreement' to buy petrol exclusively from Shell. During the petrol price war of 1975 Shell had a temporary support scheme to enable their petrol to be sold at 70p per gallon, and the neighbouring garages were enabled to sell their petrol at that price. Shell, however, insisted on the terms of Lostock Garage's solus agreement, so that Lostock Garage could only reduce their price to 75p. This was having a disastrous effect on their business so Lostock Garage argued that a term should be implied into the solus agreement to the effect that Shell would not discriminate against the garage in the terms on which it supplied the petrol.

Held: The Court of Appeal held that there was no implied term in the contract such as to enable the defendants to terminate the contract.

Lord Denning MR:
'It was submitted by [counsel for the appellant] that there was to be implied in the solus agreement a term that Shell, as the supplier, should not abnormally discriminate

against the buyer and/or should supply petrol to the buyer on terms which did not abnormally discriminate against him. He said that Shell had broken that implied term by giving support to the two Shell garages and refusing it to Lostock: that, on that ground, Shell were in breach of the solus agreement: and that Lostock were entitled to terminate it.

This submission makes it necessary once again to consider the law as to implied terms . . . [T]here are two broad categories of implied terms.

(i) The first category

The first category comprehends all those relationships which are of common occurrence. Such as the relationship of seller and buyer, owner and hirer, master and servant, landlord and tenant, carrier by land or by sea, contractor for building works, and so forth. In all those relationships the courts have imposed obligations on one party or the other, saying they are "implied terms". These obligations are not founded on the intention of the parties, actual or presumed, but on more general considerations: see *Luxor (Eastbourne) Ltd v Cooper* [1941] AC 108, 137 by Lord Wright; *Lister v Romford Ice and Cold Storage Co Ltd* [1957] AC 555, 576 by Viscount Simonds, and at p 594 by Lord Tucker (both of whom give interesting illustrations); and *Liverpool City Council v Irwin* [1976] 2 WLR 562, 571 by Lord Cross of Chelsea, and at p 579 by Lord Edmund-Davies. In such relationships the problem is not to be solved by asking what did the parties intend? Or would they have unhesitatingly agreed to it, if asked? It is to be solved by asking: has the law already defined the obligation or the extent of it? If so, let it be followed. If not, look to see what would be reasonable in the general run of such cases . . . In these relationships the parties can exclude or modify the obligation by express words; but unless they do so, the obligation is a legal incident of the relationship which is attached by the law itself and not by reason of any implied term . . .

(ii) The second category

The second category comprehends those cases which are not within the first category. These are cases – not of common occurrence – in which from the particular circumstances a term is to be implied. In these cases the implication is based on an intention imputed to the parties from their actual circumstances: *Luxor (Eastbourne) Ltd v Cooper* [1941] AC 108, 137 by Lord Wright. Such an imputation is only to be made when it is necessary to imply a term to give efficacy to the contract and make it a workable agreement in such manner as the parties would clearly have done if they had applied their mind to the contingency which has arisen. These are the "officious bystander" types of case: see *Lister v Romford Ice and Cold Storage Co Ltd* [1957] AC 555, 594, by Lord Tucker. In such cases a term is not to be implied on the ground that it would be reasonable: but only when it is necessary and can be formulated with a sufficient degree of precision. This was the test applied by the majority of this court in *Liverpool City Council v Irwin* [1976] QB 319 and they were emphatically upheld by the House on this point: see [1976] 2 WLR 562, 571D–H by Lord Cross of Chelsea; p 578G–579A by Lord Edmund-Davies . . .

Into which of the two categories does the present case come? I am tempted to say that a solus agreement between supplier and buyer is of such common occurrence nowadays that it could be put into the first category: so that the law could imply a term based on general considerations. But I do not think this would be found acceptable. Nor do I think the case can be brought within the second category. If the Shell company had been asked at the beginning: "Will you agree not to discriminate abnormally against the buyer?" I think they would have declined. It might be a reasonable term, but it is not a necessary term. Nor can it be formulated with sufficient precision.'

Lord Denning emphasised that terms implied in law do not depend on determining the intention of the parties. The term will be imposed on the parties regardless of whether they would have agreed to it or not. Two conditions must be fulfilled, however:

1.   The contract has to be of a sufficiently common type, for example, seller/buyer, owner/hirer, master/servant, landlord/tenant;
2.   The matter to which the implied term relates must not have been addressed in the contract.

In *Shell v Lostock*, it seems that the garage owner failed on the first test because solus agreements were not sufficiently common that typical terms could be identified. The claimant in *Ashmore v Corporation of Lloyd's (No 2)* (see above) failed for the same reason. He argued, as an alternative claim to implication in fact, that there were so many contracts in identical terms between 'names' and Lloyd's that this constituted a category of contracts and, as such, it was an appropriate situation in which to imply a term in law. Gatehouse J disagreed. Although there were many contracts between names and Lloyd's, running into the thousands, they were all the same and did not form part of a larger category, or genus, of contracts. On the contrary, they were *sui generis*, and for this reason Gatehouse J was not prepared to imply a term in law. It is therefore clear that to fulfil the first condition the claimant must prove that the type of contract is not merely numerous but also part of a broad category or type of relationship.

The second condition mentioned by Lord Denning requires qualification. As a general rule, it is true that a term will not be implied in law if it relates to a matter that is governed by the contract. The majority of terms implied in law are default rules, which the parties can 'contract out' of. Some implied terms, however, are mandatory and cannot be excluded by the parties' express agreement. In *Johnstone v Bloomsbury Health Authority* [1992] QB 333, a junior hospital doctor's employment contract allowed the defendant health authority to require him to work up to

88 hours per week. The Court of Appeal held that the defendant's power was subject to an implied term that the defendant would exercise reasonable care not to endanger the employee's health and safety. Stuart Smith LJ said that the implied term would prevail over the express term, if necessary, since the express term would amount to an exclusion of liability for personal injury or death, which is void under s 2(1) of the Unfair Contract Terms Act 1977. Other provisions of the Act restrict the parties' ability to 'contract out' of terms implied in law (see Chapter 8).

7.4.1.3.1 *The necessity test*

Once the two conditions for implication of a term in law have been fulfilled, the court must consider whether a term should be implied and, if so, what the content of that term ought to be.

Lister v Romford Ice and Cold Storage Co Ltd [1957] AC 555

Facts: In 1949 the defendant, a lorry driver employed by the plaintiffs, drove their lorry to a slaughterhouse in order to collect some waste. He took his father with him, and injured him by backing the lorry into him in the slaughterhouse yard. The father recovered damages from the plaintiffs who then obtained indemnity from the defendant on the basis that he had broken an implied term in his contract of employment to drive with reasonable skill and care. The defendant appealed arguing that the contract also contained an implied term that the employers would indemnify the driver if they were insured.

Held: The House of Lords dismissed the appeal and held that no such term could be implied into the contract of employment.

Viscount Simmonds:
'It was contended ... that a term should not be implied by law of which the social consequences would be harmful. The common law demands that the servant should exercise his proper skill and care in the performance of his duty: the graver the consequences of any dereliction, the more important it is that the sanction which the law imposes should be maintained. That sanction is that he should be liable in damages to his master: other sanctions there may be, dismissal perhaps and loss of character and difficulty of getting fresh employment, but an action for damages, whether for tort or for breach of contract, has, even if rarely used, for centuries been available to the master, and now to grant the servant immunity from such an action would tend to create a feeling of irresponsibility in a class of persons from whom, perhaps more than any other, constant vigilance is owed to the community.'

The reasons given for refusing to imply the term proposed by the defendant were partly based on the fact that the implication was not necessary to give business efficacy to the contract, that is, the test for implication in fact. Also weighing heavily on the House of Lords, as the extract above shows, were questions of policy. Viscount Simmonds considered it to be undesirable to allow a driver to recover an indemnity from his employer as he might then drive less carefully. It is now clear that the policy test for whether a term should be implied in law is one of 'necessity'.

Liverpool City Council v Irwin [1977] AC 239

Facts: The case concerned a tenancy agreement for a flat in a council tower block. The agreement contained no express provisions about the common parts of the block and the facilities. The lifts were often broken, the lighting on the stairs did not work, and the rubbish chutes were often blocked. This led to a rent strike. The tenants claimed that a term should be implied into the agreement that the City Council was responsible to keep the common parts of the building in repair.

Held: The House of Lords held that a term would be implied into the tenancy agreement with the effect that the council was responsible to keep the common parts of the building in reasonable repair. However, on the facts, the council was not in breach of that duty.

Lord Wilberforce:
'The court here is simply concerned to establish what the contract is, the parties not having themselves fully stated the terms. In this sense the court is searching for what must be implied.

What then should this contract be held to be? There must first be implied a letting, that is, a grant of the right of exclusive possession to the tenants. With this there must, I would suppose, be implied a covenant for quiet enjoyment, as a necessary incident of the letting. The difficulty begins when we consider the common parts . . .

[I]t is necessary to define what test is to be applied, and I do not find this difficult. In my opinion such obligation should be read into the contract as the nature of the contract itself implicitly requires, no more, no less: a test, in other words, of necessity. The relationship accepted by the corporation is that of landlord and tenant: the tenant accepts obligations accordingly, in relation inter alia to the stairs, the lifts and the chutes. All these are not just facilities, or conveniences provided at discretion: they are essentials of the tenancy without which life in the dwellings, as a tenant, is not possible. To leave the landlord free of contractual obligation as regards these matters, and subject only to administrative or political pressure, is, in my opinion, inconsistent totally with the nature of this relationship. The subject matter of the lease (high rise blocks) and the relationship created by the tenancy demand, of their nature, some contractual obligation on the landlord. . . .

It remains to define the standard. My Lords, if, as I think, the test of the existence of the term is necessity the standard must surely not exceed what is necessary having regard to the circumstances. To imply an absolute obligation to repair would go beyond what is a necessary legal incident and would indeed be unreasonable. An obligation to take reasonable care to keep in reasonable repair and usability is what fits the requirements of the case. Such a definition involves – and I think rightly – recognition that the tenants themselves have their responsibilities. What it is reasonable to expect of a landlord has a clear relation to what a reasonable set of tenants should do for themselves.'

Lord Cross:

'When it implies a term in a contract the court is sometimes laying down a general rule that in all contracts of a certain type – sale of goods, master and servant, landlord and tenant and so on – some provision is to be implied unless the parties have expressly excluded it. In deciding whether or not to lay down such a prima facie rule the court will naturally ask itself whether in the general run of such cases the term in question would be one which it would be reasonable to insert. Sometimes, however, there is no question of laying down any prima facie rule applicable to all cases of a defined type but what the court is being in effect asked to do is to rectify a particular – often a very detailed – contract by inserting in it a term which the parties have not expressed. Here it is not enough for the court to say that the suggested term is a reasonable one the presence of which would make the contract a better or fairer one; it must be able to say that the insertion of the term is necessary to give – as it is put – 'business efficacy' to the contract and that if its absence had been pointed out at the time both parties – assuming them to have been reasonable men – would have agreed without hesitation to its insertion. The distinction between the two types of case was pointed out by Viscount Simonds and Lord Tucker in their speeches *Lister v Romford Ice and Cold Storage Ltd* [1957] AC 555, 579, 594, but I think that Lord Denning MR in proceeding – albeit with some trepidation – to 'kill off' MacKinnon LJ's "officious bystander" . . . must have overlooked it. Counsel for the appellant did not in fact rely on this passage in the speech of Lord Denning. His main argument was that when a landlord lets a number of flats or offices to a number of different tenants giving all of them rights to use the staircases, corridors and lifts there is to be implied, in the absence of any provision to the contrary, an obligation on the landlord to keep the "common parts" in repair and the lifts in working order. But, for good measure, he also submitted that he could succeed on the 'officious bystander' test.

I have no hesitation in rejecting this alternative submission. We are not here dealing with an ordinary commercial contract by which a property company is letting one of its flats for profit. The respondent council is a public body charged by law with the duty of providing housing for members of the public selected because of their need for it at rents which are subsidised by the general body of ratepayers. Moreover the officials in the council's housing department would know very well that some of the tenants in any given block might subject the chutes and lifts to rough treatment and that there was an ever present danger of deliberate damage by young "vandals" – some of whom might in fact be children of the tenants in that or neighbouring blocks. In these circumstances, if at the time when the respondents were granted their tenancy one of them had said to the council's representative: "I suppose that the council will be under a legal liability to us to keep the chutes and the lifts in working order and the staircases properly lighted", the answer might well have been – indeed I think, as Roskill LJ thought [1976] Q.B. 319, 338, in all probability would have been – "Certainly not" . . .

I turn . . . to consider the main argument advanced by the appellants. One starts with the general principle that the law does not impose on a servient owner any liability to keep the servient property in repair for the benefit of the owner of an easement. . . . But must it follow that the same principle must be applied to the case where a landlord lets off parts of his property to a number of different tenants retaining in his ownership "common parts" – halls, staircases, corridors and so on – which are used by all the tenants? I think that it would be contrary to common sense to press the general principle so far. In such a case I think that the implication should be the other way and that, instead of the landlord being under no obligation to keep the common parts in repair and such facilities as lifts and chutes in working order unless he has expressly contracted to do so, he should – at all events in the case of ordinary commercial lettings – be under some obligation to keep the common parts in repair and the facilities in working order unless he has expressly excluded any such obligation . . . I agree, however, with your Lordships that the obligation to be implied in such cases is not an absolute one but only a duty to use reasonable care to keep the common parts and facilities in a state of reasonable repair and efficiency.'

Lord Salmon:

'I find it difficult to think of any term which it could be more necessary to imply than one without which the whole transaction would become futile, inefficacious and absurd as it would do if in a 15 storey block of flats or maisonettes, such as the present, the landlords were under no legal duty to take reasonable care to keep the lifts in working order and the staircases lit.'

Although there was some disagreement on the issue in the Court of Appeal, the House of Lords was in full agreement that the term sought to be implied by the tenants could not be implied in fact because neither the 'officious bystander' test nor the 'business efficacy' test were satisfied (see, the speech of Lord Cross, above). The term was implied into the contract in law because the nature of the relationship made it desirable to place some obligation on the landlord to maintain the common parts of the premises. There was some divergence among their Lordships as to what was the appropriate test. Lord Wilberforce was of the view that the test was one of necessity: the term 'should be read into the contract as the nature of the contract itself implicitly requires, no more, no less: a test in other words of necessity'. Lords Salmon, Edmund-Davies and Fraser agreed. Lord Cross, on the other hand, applied a test of reasonableness: 'the court will naturally ask itself whether in the general run of such cases the term in question would be one which it would be reasonable to insert'. In subsequent cases this conflict seems to have been resolved in favour of the test of necessity. It is clear, however, that the test for necessity in the context of terms implied in law involves wider issues and differs from the test applied in relation to terms implied in fact.

Scally v Southern Health and Social Services Board [1992] 1 AC 294

Lord Bridge:
'A clear distinction is drawn . . . between the search for an implied term necessary to give business efficacy to a particular contract and the search, based on wider considerations, for a term which the law will imply as a necessary incident of a definable category of contractual relationship.'

It seems that the 'necessity' test in this context encompasses issues of justice and public policy. This was seen in *Malik v BCCI*.

Malik v BCCI [1998] AC 20

Facts: Malik had worked for the Bank of Credit and Commerce International which collapsed in 1991. He claimed damages for injury to his reputation and consequent difficulties in finding new employment, which he alleged were caused by BCCI conducting its business in a dishonest and corrupt way.

Held: The House of Lords allowed the appeal, holding that BCCI was under an implied obligation not to conduct a corrupt and dishonest business, being one aspect of a general implied contractual obligation not to engage in conduct likely to undermine the relationship of confidence and trust between employer and employee.

Lord Steyn:
'[The employees] rely on a standardised term implied by law, that is, on a term which is said to be an incident of all contracts of employment: *Scally v Southern Health and Social Services Board* [1992] 1 AC 294, 307B. Such implied terms operate as default rules. The parties are free to exclude or modify them. But it is common ground that in the present case the particular terms of the contracts of employment of the two applicants could not affect an implied obligation of mutual trust and confidence . . .

For convenience I will set out the term again. It is expressed to impose an obligation that the employer shall not:

"without reasonable and proper cause, conduct itself in a manner calculated and

---

likely to destroy or seriously damage the relationship of confidence and trust between employer and employee" . . .

A useful anthology of the cases applying this term, or something like it, is given in *Sweet & Maxwell's Encyclopedia of Employment Law* (looseleaf ed), vol 1, para 1.5107, pp 1467–1470. The evolution of the term is a comparatively recent development. The obligation probably has its origin in the general duty of co-operation between contracting parties: Hepple & O'Higgins, *Employment Law*, 4th ed (1981), pp 134–135, paras 291–292. The reason for this development is part of the history of the development of employment law in this century. The notion of a "master and servant" relationship became obsolete. Lord Slynn of Hadley recently noted "the changes which have taken place in the employer-employee relationship, with far greater duties imposed on the employer than in the past, whether by statute or by judicial decision, to care for the physical, financial and even psychological welfare of the employee": *Spring v Guardian Assurance Plc* [1995] 2 AC 296, 335B. A striking illustration of this change is *Scally's Case* [1992] 1 AC 294, to which I have already referred, where the House of Lords implied a term that all employees in a certain category had to be notified by an employer of their entitlement to certain benefits. It was the change in legal culture which made possible the evolution of the implied term of trust and confidence.

There was some debate at the hearing about the possible interaction of the implied obligation of confidence and trust with other more specific terms implied by law. It is true that the implied term adds little to the employee's implied obligations to serve his employer loyally and not to act contrary to his employer's interests. The major importance of the implied duty of trust and confidence lies in its impact on the obligations of the employer: Douglas Brodie, "Recent cases, Commentary, The Heart of the Matter: Mutual Trust and Confidence" (1996) 25 ILJ 121. And the implied obligation as formulated is apt to cover the great diversity of situations in which a balance has to be struck between an employer's interest in managing his business as he sees fit and the employee's interest in not being unfairly and improperly exploited.

The evolution of the implied term of trust and confidence is a fact. It has not yet been endorsed by your Lordships' House. It has proved a workable principle in practice. It has not been the subject of adverse criticism in any decided cases and it has been welcomed in academic writings. I regard the emergence of the implied obligation of mutual trust and confidence as a sound development.'

In light of Lord Steyn's observations in *Malik* it appears that the courts adopt an extremely flexible approach to implying terms in law. Although the courts claim to use a test of necessity their decisions are based more on considerations of justice and policy. Indeed, it could be contended that this actually amounts to a test of reasonableness since the fair and reasonable man should act in a just manner. The importance of issues of public policy was confirmed by Dyson LJ in the recent case of *Crossley v Faithful & Gould Holdings Ltd* [2004] 4 All ER 447:

It seems to me that, rather than focus on the elusive concept of necessity, it is better to recognise that, to some extent at least, the existence and scope of standardised implied terms raise questions of reasonableness, fairness and the balancing of competing policy considerations: see Elisabeth Peden, 'Policy Concerns behind Implication of Terms in Law' (2001) 117 LQR 459, 467–475.

7.4.2 TERMS IMPLIED BY STATUTE

Terms may be implied into contracts by statute. There are two main reasons why it may be appropriate for Parliament to enact such legislation:

1. **Efficiency**. This reason is based on the presumed intention of the parties. If it is standard practice for certain terms to be used in particular contractual relationships, it is inefficient for the parties to be required to expressly agree to them on every occasion. By means of statute, Parliament can provide a form of words on which the parties can rely as representing their obligations. If this is the reason for the statutory enactment, the parties should be allowed to depart from the statutory wording, if they so wish.

2. **Protection**. This reason is based on the protection of one of the parties. It may be thought that a particular type of contractual relationship is likely to involve inequality of bargaining power. Parliament implies terms into such contracts to provide protection for the weaker party. If this is the reason for the implication, then it may well be that the obligation to include the term should be absolute, with no possibility of exclusion by the parties.

Terms have been implied by Parliament into a broad range of contracts, for example, contracts for the sale of goods, contracts for the supply of services and hire-purchase agreements. In this section, we will focus on contracts for the sale of goods.

SALE OF GOODS ACT (SGA) 1979

S 12 Implied terms about title, etc.

(1) In a contract of sale, other than one to which subsection (3) below applies, there is an implied term on the part of the seller that in the case of a sale he has a right to sell the goods, and in the case of an agreement to sell he will have such a right at the time when the property is to pass.

(2) In a contract of sale, other than one to which subsection (3) below applies, there is also an implied term that –

    (a) the goods are free, and will remain free until the time when the property is to pass, from any charge or encumbrance not disclosed or known to the buyer before the contract is made, and

    (b) the buyer will enjoy quiet possession of the goods except so far as it may be disturbed by the owner or other person entitled to the benefit of any charge or encumbrance so disclosed or known.

(3) This subsection applies to a contract of sale in the case of which there appears from the contract or is to be inferred from its circumstances an intention that the seller should transfer only such title as he or a third person may have.

(4) In a contract to which subsection (3) above applies there is an implied term that all charges or encumbrances known to the seller and not known to the buyer have been disclosed to the buyer before the contract is made.

(5) In a contract to which subsection (3) above applies there is also an implied term that none of the following will disturb the buyer's quiet possession of the goods, namely –

(a) the seller;

(b) in a case where the parties to the contract intend that the seller should transfer only such title as a third person may have, that person;

(c) anyone claiming through or under the seller or that third person otherwise than under a charge or encumbrance disclosed or known to the buyer before the contract is made.

(5A) As regards England and Wales and Northern Ireland, the term implied by subsection (1) above is a condition and the terms implied by subsections (2), (4) and (5) above are warranties.

S 13 Sale by description

(1) Where there is a contract for the sale of goods by description, there is an implied term that the goods will correspond with the description.

(1A) As regards England and Wales and Northern Ireland, the term implied by subsection (1) above is a condition.

(2) If the sale is by sample as well as by description it is not sufficient that the bulk of the goods corresponds with the sample if the goods do not also correspond with the description.

(3) A sale of goods is not prevented from being a sale by description by reason only that, being exposed for sale or hire, they are selected by the buyer.

S 14 Implied terms about quality or fitness

(1) Except as provided by this section and section 15 below and subject to any other enactment, there is no implied term about the quality or fitness for any particular purpose of goods supplied under a contract of sale.

(2) Where the seller sells goods in the course of a business, there is an implied term that the goods supplied under the contract are of satisfactory quality.

(2A) For the purposes of this Act, goods are of satisfactory quality if they meet the standard that a reasonable person would regard as satisfactory, taking account of any description of the goods, the price (if relevant) and all the other relevant circumstances.

(2B) For the purposes of this Act, the quality of goods includes their state and condition and the following (among others) are in appropriate cases aspects of the quality of goods –

(a) fitness for all the purposes for which goods of the kind in question are commonly supplied.

(b) appearance and finish,

(c) freedom from minor defects,

(d) safety, and

(e) durability.

(2C) The term implied by subsection (2) above does not extend to any matter making the quality of goods unsatisfactory –

(a) which is specifically drawn to the buyer's attention before the contract is made,

(b) where the buyer examines the goods before the contract is made, which that examination ought to reveal, or

(c) in the case of a contract for sale by sample, which would have been apparent on a reasonable examination of the sample.

(2D) If the buyer deals as consumer or, in Scotland, if a contract of sale is a consumer contract, the relevant circumstances mentioned in subsection (2A) above include any public statements on the specific characteristics of the goods made about them by the seller, the producer or his representative, particularly in advertising or on labelling.

(2E) A public statement is not by virtue of subsection (2D) above a relevant circumstance for the purposes of subsection (2A) above in the case of a contract of sale, if the seller shows that –

(a) at the time the contract was made, he was not, and could not reasonably have been, aware of the statement,

(b) before the contract was made, the statement had been withdrawn in public or, to the extent that it contained anything which was incorrect or misleading, it had been corrected in public, or

(c) the decision to buy the goods could not have been influenced by the statement.

(2F) Subsections (2D) and (2E) above do not prevent any public statement from being a relevant circumstance for the purposes of subsection (2A) above (whether or not the buyer deals as consumer or, in Scotland, whether or not the contract of sale is a consumer contract) if the statement would have been such a circumstance apart from those subsections.

(3) Where the seller sells goods in the course of a business and the buyer, expressly or by implication, makes known –

(a) to the seller, or

(b) where the purchase price or part of it is payable by instalments and the goods were previously sold by a credit-broker to the seller, to that credit-broker, any particular purpose for which the goods are being bought, there is an implied term that the goods supplied under the contract are reasonably fit for that purpose, whether or not that is a purpose for which such goods are commonly supplied, except where the circumstances show that the buyer does not rely, or that it is unreasonable for him to rely, on the skill or judgment of the seller or credit-broker.

(4) An implied term about quality or fitness for a particular purpose may be annexed to a contract of sale by usage.

(5) The preceding provisions of this section apply to a sale by a person who in the course of a business is acting as agent for another as they apply to a sale by a principal in the course of a business, except where that other is not selling in the course of a business and either the buyer knows that fact or reasonable steps are taken to bring it to the notice of the buyer before the contract is made.

(6) As regards England and Wales and Northern Ireland, the terms implied by subsection (2) and (3) above are conditions.

S 15 Sale by sample

(1) A contract of sale is a contract for sale by sample where there is an express or implied term to that effect in the contract.

(2) In the case of a contract for sale by sample there is an implied term –

(a) that the bulk will correspond with the sample in quality;

. . .

(c) that the goods will be free from any defect, making their quality unsatisfactory, which would not be apparent on reasonable examination of the sample.

(3) As regards England and Wales and Northern Ireland, the term implied by subsection (2) above is a condition.

The SGA 1979 is an important piece of legislation because it confers upon buyers of goods a number of significant rights. These rights are contained within implied terms, which have the effect of reversing the presumption of *caveat emptor* (let the buyer beware). Prior to the enactment of the original SGA 1893, it was necessary for the buyer to obtain a specific undertaking from the seller as to the quality of the goods. Such undertakings are no longer necessary because the implied terms contained in sections 12–15 of the SGA 1979 provide buyers with a significant bundle of rights. We will briefly examine the contents of each of these sections.

Section 12(1) of the SGA 1979 is concerned with 'title'. It gives the buyer a remedy against a seller who does not have the right to sell the goods that he has contracted to sell. The implied term is a condition, which means that the buyer has a right to repudiate the contract for breach. This is so even when the buyer has made use of the goods prior to discovery that the seller did not have good title.

Rowland v Divall [1923] 2 KB 500

Facts: The plaintiff car dealer had bought a motor car from the defendant and used it for several months. Unknown to both parties, the car had been stolen. The plaintiff resold the car to a third party, from whom it was reclaimed, some months later, by the true owner's insurance company. The plaintiff had to repay the purchase price to the third party and then sought to recover the purchase price he had paid to the defendant.

Held: The Court of Appeal held that notwithstanding that the plaintiff had had the use of the car for several months the consideration had totally failed, and he was entitled to get the purchase money back. The plaintiff had contracted for the property in and lawful possession of the car, neither of which he had received.

Scrutton LJ:

'[T]he Sale of Goods Act . . . re-enacted that rule . . . as a condition, not as a warranty. Sect. 12 says in express terms that there shall be "An implied condition on the part of the seller that . . . . he has a right to sell the goods." It being now a condition, wherever that condition is broken the contract can be rescinded, and with the rescission the buyer can demand a return of the purchase money . . .'

Section 12 also contains warranties of freedom from encumbrances and quiet possession.

Section 13 concerns the sale of goods by description and implies a condition that the goods will match the description. Section 13(3) makes it clear that the condition will apply even though the buyer has seen the goods and may have even selected the goods himself. The section will only operate, however, if the buyer has entered into the contract in reliance upon the description provided by the seller. In *Harlingdon and Leinster Enterprises v Christopher Hull Fine Art Ltd* [1991] 1 QB 564, the buyer had purchased a painting that turned out not to be by the artist to whom it was attributed in the catalogue. It was found as a matter of fact that the buyer had not relied upon the attribution in the catalogue and, as a result, this was not a sale by description. Not all descriptive words are a description within the meaning of section 13. The words used must identify the subject matter of the contract (*Reardon Smith Line Ltd v Yngvar Hansen-Tangen* [1976] 1 WLR 989).

Section 15 is similar to section 13 and concerns sale by sample. Two conditions are implied. First that the bulk will correspond with the sample in quality and second that the goods will be free from any defect, making their quality unsatisfactory, which would not be apparent on a reasonable examination of the sample. An example of this second condition can be found in the case of *Godley v Perry*.

Godley v Perry [1960] 1 WLR 9

Facts: A six-year-old boy purchased a toy catapult from a shop. It was made of brittle plastic and fractured when the boy fired it, blinding him in one eye. The boy claimed damages against the retailer for breach of s 15 of the SGA.

Held: It was held that the retailer was liable for damages because the defect was not apparent on reasonable examination of the sample.

Edmund Davies J:

'Counsel . . . . demonstrated that by squeezing together the two prongs of the catapult in the hand they could be fractured, and further suggested that by holding the toy down with one's foot and then pulling on the elastic its safety could be tested and, as I understand it, its inherent fragility would thereby inevitably be discovered. True, the potential customer might have done any of these things. He might also, I suppose, have tried biting the catapult, or hitting it with a hammer, or applying a lighted match to ensure its non-inflammability, experiments which, with all respect, are but slightly more bizarre than those suggested by counsel. But, looking at the matter realistically, as one must, in my judgment none of those tests are called for by a process of "reasonable examination", as that phrase would be understood by the common-sense standards of everyday life.'

Section 14 implies two different conditions into contracts for the sale of goods. Section 14(2) implies a condition of satisfactory quality. The test of satisfactory quality was substituted for the previous test of 'merchantable quality' by the Sale and Supply of Goods Act 1994 and was further amended by the Sale and Supply of Goods to Consumers Regulations 2002 (SI 2002 No 3045). Because of this, the previous case law on s 14(2) is only of limited assistance in the interpretation of the section. Section 14(2B) provides a list of factors that will be relevant in applying the new test.

The second condition is found in section 14(3) and states that the goods must be reasonably fit for their purpose. The seller does not provide a guarantee that the goods will be fit for any purpose. If the buyer intends to use the goods for some unusual purpose then he must make the seller aware of that purpose prior to entering into the contract if he wishes to rely on section 14(3). The condition contained in section 14(3) is merely that the goods will be 'reasonably' fit for their purpose. Therefore, if the goods prove to be unfit for their purpose due to some unexpected occurrence, unknown to the seller, section 14(3) will not operate.

Slater v Finning Ltd [1997] AC 473

Facts: The defendants supplied and fitted a camshaft to the engine of the plaintiff's fishing boat. It failed, so the defendants fitted a second camshaft, and again it broke. A third camshaft was fitted but the problems persisted. In the end, the plaintiffs gave up and sold the engine. The new purchasers fitted it to another fishing boat in which it was apparently used without a problem. At first instance, the judge found that the problem of the failure of the camshaft had been caused by some unexplained idiosyncrasy of the plaintiffs' fishing boat. He concluded therefore that the damage observed in the camshafts was not due to their unfitness to fulfil the purpose.

Held: The finding of the judge was upheld by the House of Lords. It was held that there was no breach of s 14(3) where the failure of the goods to meet the intended purpose arose from an abnormal feature or idiosyncrasy, not made known to the seller. It was irrelevant whether the idiosyncrasy was known to the buyer.

The two conditions contained in section 14 are only implied where a sale of goods contract is made in the course of business. The scope of the phrase 'in the course of business', was considered by the Court of Appeal in *Stevenson v Rogers*.

Stevenson v Rogers [1999] QB 1028

Facts: Mr Rogers, a fisherman, had owned a boat called the 'Jelle' for some time before selling it to Mr Stevenson. Mr Rogers had intended to replace the 'Jelle' with a custom-built boat. However, he changed his mind and bought another boat instead. Mr Stevenson contended that, since Mr Rogers had sold and replaced the very thing without which he could have no fishing business, the sale should have been regarded as being in the course of business for the purposes of s 14(2).

Held: The Court of Appeal allowed the appeal. Their Lordships noted that the original SGA 1893 had limited liability to situations in which the seller dealt 'in goods of that description'. This limitation, however, had been removed by the SGA 1979. The court held that there was no justification for the re-introduction of such a qualification on the apparently wide scope and purpose of s 14. Therefore, on the facts, s 14(2) applied even though the fisherman was not regularly in the business of selling fishing boats. *R and B Customs Brokers v UDT* [1988] 1 WLR 321 and the test applied under UCTA 1977 were distinguished.

The two implied conditions of s 14 overlap because they both refer to fitness for the purpose for which the goods were supplied. There are important differences, however, and in the following case the Court of Appeal emphasised the need to distinguish between s 14(2) (satisfactory quality) and s 14(3) (fitness for a particular purpose).

Jewson Ltd v Boyhan [2004] 1 Lloyd's Rep 505

Facts: The claimants had supplied and fitted electric boilers as part of a project to convert a former convent school into 13 self-contained flats. The boilers all worked satisfactorily. However, the defendant refused to pay the claimants for the boilers. He contended that the claimants were in breach of the terms implied by s 14(2) and (3) of the SGA 1979 because the boilers reduced the energy efficiency of the flats and made them difficult to sell. The trial judge found the claimants in breach of both s 14(2) and s 14(3).

Held: The Court of Appeal allowed the appeal. There was no breach of s 14(2) because the boilers were of satisfactory quality as boilers for flats, ignoring the particular circumstances which gave rise to problems in the specific case. There was no breach of section 14(3) since, although it was reasonable for the defendant to rely on the claimant's skill and judgment in regard to the intrinsic quality of the boilers, it was not reasonable for him to rely on them as regards the suitability of the boilers for the particular flats. The claimants had insufficient information for it to be reasonable for the defendant to rely on them for this purpose.

Clarke LJ:
'[Counsel for the claimants] submissions may be summarized as follows:

(i) There is a considerable overlap between subsections 14(2) and 14(3) but they perform different functions. The function of s 14(2) is to establish a general standard which goods are required to reach, whereas the function of s 14(3) is to impose a particular (higher) standard which is appropriate where the buyer (to the knowledge of the seller) buys the goods for a particular purpose and relies on the seller's skill and judgment for that purpose.

(ii) Goods are satisfactory if they meet the standard which a reasonable person would regard as satisfactory: s 14(2A).

(iii) In determining the standard that a reasonable person would regard as satisfactory, the circumstances which must be taken into account are any description of the goods, the price and all the other relevant circumstances: s 14(2A).

(iv) In appropriate circumstances, certain defined features may be regarded as aspects of the quality of the goods, including fitness for all purposes for which goods of the kind in question are commonly supplied: s 14(2B).

I would accept those submissions. It seems to me that under the statutory scheme set out in s 14 it is the function of s 14(3), not s 14(2), to impose a particular obligation tailored to the particular circumstances of the case.'

At the start of this section we noted that there were two main reasons why Parliament enacts legislation to imply terms into contracts: efficiency and protection. What is the basis underlying the terms implied by the SGA 1979? The argument that the terms are implied for the sake of efficiency, to express the parties' presumed intentions, is unconvincing. If that really was the reason then equivalent terms would be implied into contracts for the sale of real property. In actual fact, English law does not imply terms of satisfactory quality or even habitability into contracts for the sale or lease of a house. Furthermore, the efficiency basis is difficult to reconcile with the presumption of *caveat emptor* that operated throughout the nineteenth century. If the implied terms found in the SGA 1979 really do represent the presumed intentions of the parties, it is inexplicable why the contrary presumption played such a dominant role in the nineteenth-century market.

It seems that the protective function lies behind the terms implied by the SGA 1979. The terms seek to protect the 'reasonable expectations' of buyers of goods and to counter unequal bargaining power. This is confirmed by the fact that Parliament has intervened by enacting Unfair Contract Terms Act 1977 to make it impossible for the parties to exclude these terms in consumer contracts and prohibiting their exclusion from commercial contracts, unless it is shown to be reasonable to do so (see Chapter 8). The Unfair Terms in Consumer Contracts Regulations 1999 have provided further protection to consumers by voiding unfair contract terms. The fact that it is impossible to exclude such terms demonstrates that the terms are implied to protect the reasonable expectations of the parties rather than to express their presumed intentions.

7.4.3 The justification for implied terms

As we have seen there are four main categories of implied terms: (1) terms implied by custom, (2) terms implied in fact, (3) terms implied in law, and (4) terms implied by statute. Terms are implied under each of these heads on different bases: necessity, notoriety, reasonableness and protection. It is arguable, however, that the same justification underlies all implied terms: protection of the reasonable expectations of the contracting parties.

Lord Steyn, 'Contract Law: Fulfilling the Reasonable Expectations of Honest Men' (1997) 113 LQR 433, 441–442

In systems of law where there is a general duty of good faith in the performance of contracts the need to supplement the written contract by implied terms is less than in the English system. In our system, however, the implication of terms fulfils an important function in promoting the reasonable expectations of parties. Three categories of implied terms can be identified. First, there are terms implied by virtue of the usages of trade and commerce. The assumption is that usages are taken for granted and therefore not spelled out in writing. The recognition of trade usages protects the reasonable expectations of the parties. Secondly, there are terms implied in fact, i.e. from the contextual scene of the particular contract. Such implied terms fulfil the role of ad hoc gap fillers. Often the expectations of the parties would be defeated if a term were not implied, e.g. sometimes a contract simply will not work unless a particular duty to co-operate is implied. The law has evolved practical tests for the permissibility of such an implication, such as the test of whether the term is necessary to give business efficacy to the contract or the less stringent test whether the conventional bystander, when faced with the problem, would immediately say 'yes, it is obvious that there is such an implied term'. The legal test for the implication of a term is the standard of strict necessity. And it is right that it should be so since courts ought not to supplement a contract by an implication unless it is perfectly obvious that it is necessary to give effect to the reasonable expectations of parties. It is, however, a myth to regard such an implied term as based on an inference of the actual intention of the parties. The reasonable expectations of the parties in an objective sense are controlling: they sometimes demand that such terms be imputed to the parties. The third category is terms implied by law. This occurs when incidents are impliedly annexed to particular forms of contracts, e.g. contracts for building work, contracts of sale, hire, etc. Such implied terms operate as default rules. By and large such implied terms have crystal-lised in statute or case law. But there is scope for further development. In such new cases a broader approach than applied in the case of terms implied in fact must necessarily prevail. The proposed implication must fit the generality of cases. Indeed, despite some confusion in the authorities, it is tolerably clear that the court may take into account considerations of reasonableness in laying down the scope of terms to be implied in contracts of common occurrence. This function of the court is essential in providing a reasonable and fair framework for contracting. After all, there are many incidents of contracts of common occurrence which the parties cannot always be expected to reproduce in writing. This type of supplementation of contracts also fulfils an essential function in promoting the reasonable expectations of the parties.

7.5 ADDITIONAL READING

Goode, R, 'Usage and its reception in transnational commercial law' (1997) 46 ICLQ 1.

Macdonald, E, 'Incorporation of contract terms by a "consistent course of dealing" ' (1988) 8 LS 48.

McKendrick, E, 'The interpretation of contracts: Lord Hoffman's re-statement' (2003) in S Worthington (ed), *Commercial Law and Commercial Practice*, Oxford: Hart, p 139.

Mitchell, C, 'Leading a life of its own? The roles of reasonable expectation in contract law' (2003) 23 OJLS 639.

Nicholls, D, 'My kingdom for a horse: the meaning of words' (2005) 121 LQR 577.

Peden, E, 'Policy concerns behind implication of terms in law' (2001) 117 LQR 459.

Peden, E and Carter, JW, 'Incorporation of terms by signature: *L'Estrange* Rules!' (2005) 21 JCL 96.

Phang, A, 'Implied terms, business efficacy and the officious bystander – a modern history' [1998] JBL 1.

Riley, C, 'Designing default rules in contract law' (2000) 20 OJLS 367.

Staughton, C, 'How do the courts interpret commercial contracts?' [1999] CLJ 303.

CHAPTER 8

CLAUSES EXCLUDING OR LIMITING LIABILITY

CONTENTS	

8.1 INTRODUCTION

In the previous chapter we considered the contents of a contract and the rules that are applied by the courts in ascertaining what obligations have been assumed by the parties. In this chapter we deal with a particular type of contract term – those that purport to exclude or limit the liability of the contracting parties in contract or tort. In theory, there is nothing inherently objectionable about clauses of this kind. Indeed, they provide an invaluable mechanism for allocating risks within transactions. For example, in contracts for the carriage of goods it may have been agreed that the owner should be responsible for insuring the goods against loss or damage in transit. In such circumstances, it may be entirely reasonable for the carrier to exclude or limit his liability for loss or damage to the goods being carried. Exclusion clauses also perform an important role in high-risk contracts, where the consequential losses might far exceed the contract price. For example, in a contract for the supply of an air-conditioning unit the supplier of a faulty unit to a factory may incur liability for personal injury to the factory employees, damage to goods stored in the factory and loss of profits caused by closure of the factory. A small business would not be able to bear such extensive loss, so may need to rely on an exclusion or limitation clause in order to contain their potential liability.

Provided that an exclusion clause has been included in the contract as a result of a clear voluntary agreement between the parties, it should be upheld. Problems arise when there is no such equality of bargaining power and the clause has been forced upon the weaker party by the strong. In the previous chapter, we saw an example of this in *Parker v South Eastern Railway* (1877) 2 CPD 416, where a railway company incorporated a broad-sweeping exclusion clause into contracts with its passengers. Today, exclusion clauses frequently appear in standard form contracts where the other party has little choice as to whether to accept or reject it. There is usually no discussion of the contents of the contract and the other party simply has to agree to the terms offered in a 'take it or leave it' fashion. Here, there is a compelling case for control.

Law Commission, Report No 69, *Second Report on Exemption Clauses in Contracts*, 1975, para 11

It is clear that exemption clauses are much used both in dealings with private individuals and in purely commercial transactions. We are in no doubt that in many cases they operate against the public interest and that the prevailing judicial attitude of suspicion, or indeed hostility, to such clauses is well founded. All too often they are introduced in ways which result in the party affected by them remaining ignorant of their presence or import until it is too late. That party, even if he knows of the exemption clause will often be unable to appreciate what he may lose by accepting it. In any case, he may not have sufficient bargaining strength to refuse to accept it. The result is that the risk; of carelessness or of failure to achieve satisfactory standards of performance is thrown onto the party who is not responsible for it or who is unable to guard against it. Moreover, by excluding liability for such carelessness or failure the economic pressures to maintain high standards of performance are reduced. There is no doubt that the misuse of these clauses is objectionable. Some are unjustified. Others, however, may operate fairly or unfairly, efficiently or inefficiently depending on the circumstances: for example, the cost and practicability of insurance may be factors in determining how liability should be apportioned between the two contracting parties. The problem of devising methods of controlling the use of these clauses, and indeed of identifying some of them, has proved both difficult and complicated.

The Law Commission recognised that exclusion clauses frequently operate against the public interest, especially in circumstances where they are imposed on parties who do not have sufficient bargaining strength to refuse to accept them. Regulation is necessary but often difficult. This is sometimes due to the difficulty that exists in distinguishing between clauses that limit liability and those that simply determine the obligations under the contract. To illustrate the point, consider a contract for the regular servicing of a motorcar. Michael, the owner of the car, wishes for any spare parts used in the servicing to be manufactured and supplied by Ferrari. The garage, Dodge G Motors, knows that there is no guarantee that such parts will be available when needed. The situation can be dealt with in one of two ways. A clause might be incorporated stating that: 'Dodge G will use parts manufactured and supplied by Ferrari when available, but may substitute equivalent parts if necessary to complete the service within a reasonable time'. Such a clause would define Dodge G's obligations under the contract. Alternatively the clause might be drafted in the following way: 'Dodge G will use parts manufactured and supplied by Ferrari, but in the event that such parts are unavailable, Dodge G will not be liable for any loss arising from the use of equivalent parts'. Such a clause is drafted in the form of a limitation on Dodge G's liability, but in practice it achieves the same purpose as the previous clause. It is generally possible to rewrite any clause that purports to limit liability for a breach of contract as a clause that defines the parties' obligations under the contract.

Indeed, some commentators go further than that and argue that the true function of all exclusion clauses is to define liability, not to provide a defence to liability.

Coote, B, *Exception Clauses*, 1964, London: Sweet & Maxwell, pp 10–11, 17–18

If we suppose, for example, a promise in general terms, and a series of particular exceptions from that promise, we have a case where an exception clause is directly limiting the substantive contractual content of a promise, or more technically, perhaps, is negativing any primary right to performance of those matters excluded from the promise. Thus, where a horse is sold warranted sound 'except for hunting', a purchaser will have no primary right to call a horse sound for hunting. An exception may have the same effect indirectly, through the operation of the proposition that it is impossible to create valid contractual rights while at the same time agreeing that they shall be at all times unenforceable. A total exclusion, either of sanctioning rights or of procedural rights of enforcement, would have the effect of making the apparent primary right unenforceable. In so far as the 'unenforceable right' would be illusory (that is, would have no existence as a contractual right), exceptions of this type would, accordingly, have the effect on primary rights of preventing their accrual. Thus, if the vendor of a horse should represent that the animal is sound but stipulate that he shall not be required to make compensation if it should prove to be unsound, then unless he is merely contradicting himself, he is indicating thereby that his representation is a 'mere' representation and that he refuses to contract as to the horse's soundness. In other words, by excluding sanctioning rights he is indirectly preventing the purchaser from acquiring any contractual primary right as to soundness . . .

[I]t follows that the true juristic function and effect of exception clauses are quite different from those currently ascribed to them, by the courts. Instead of being mere shields to claims based on breach of accrued rights, exception clauses substantively delimit the rights themselves. A large class of them prevent those rights from ever arising in the first place. As it has been put in an American publication: 'the ordinary function of an exception is to take out of the contract that which otherwise would have been in it . . .'

People who adopt Professor Coote's position contend that exclusion clauses should be treated in exactly the same way as other clauses of the contract. The courts have not adopted this approach, however, and have (as the Law Commission report notes) insisted that exclusion clauses should be treated differently. In the absence of direct means to regulate exclusion clauses the courts have resorted to indirect means, most notably the rules relating to incorporation and interpretation.

More recently, Parliament has intervened to add a statutory layer of controls on top of the common-law rules (the Unfair Contract Terms Act (UCTA) 1977 and the Unfair Terms in Consumer Contracts Regulations (UTCCR) 1999). Unlike the common-law rules, these controls do not draw such a sharp distinction between terms that purport to exclude liability and terms that seek to define contractual obligations (although the distinction is not abolished altogether). The controls also distinguish between consumer and business contracts in recognition of the fact that the 'fairness' of a term is often dependent upon its context.

This chapter is divided into three sections. In the first, we will consider the common-law rules that have been applied to regulate exclusion clauses. In the second, we will consider the UCTA 1977 and in the third we will examine the UTCCR 1999.

8.2 COMMON LAW

Due to the traditional emphasis on freedom of contract, the courts have been unable to directly assess exclusion clauses on their merits. Instead, they have regulated exclusion clauses indirectly by manipulating the rules relating to the determination of the contents of the contract and the scope of the clauses contained in it. The main rules that are used for this purpose are those of 'incorporation', 'interpretation' and the doctrine of 'fundamental breach.'

8.2.1 INCORPORATION

Incorporation was discussed in detail in Chapter 7. Many of the cases discussed in that chapter concerned the incorporation of exclusion clauses. As we saw, the courts have generally been reluctant to conclude that an exclusion clause has been incorporated into a contract. One of the devices used for this purpose was the 'red-hand rule', which required 'unusual' or 'onerous' terms to be given special notice (see *Thornton v Shoe Lane Parking* [1971] 2 QB 163; *Interfoto v Stiletto Visual Programmes* [1989] QB 433). Following the enactment of the UCTA 1977 and the UTCCR 1999, the importance of the special notice rule has diminished (see *AEG (UK) Ltd v Logic Resource Ltd* [1996] CLC 265).

8.2.2 INTERPRETATION

Once the court has concluded that the clause has been incorporated into the contract, it is necessary to determine whether it covers the breach that has occurred. This is a matter of interpretation: does the wording of the clause cover the situation that has arisen? The rules of interpretation, like the rules of incorporation, are of general application and can be used in relation to all clauses within a contract, not just exclusion clauses. In Chapter 7 we considered the more general issues relating to interpretation. In the context of exclusion clauses, the courts have generally adopted a stricter approach to interpretation than elsewhere. Here, we will examine the main rules of interpretation that have been applied by the courts and we will consider what impact *Investors Corporation v West Bromwich Building Society* [1998] 1 WLR 896, has had on those rules.

8.2.2.1 Strict interpretation

The first rule of interpretation that is applied to exclusion clauses is that plain words will be given no wider meaning than their ambit requires. In *Wallis, Son and Wells v Pratt & Haynes* [1910] 2 KB 1003, the Court of Appeal held that a clause stating that the suppliers of seed gave no 'warranty' in relation to its 'growth, description or any other matters' did not protect them from being liable for a breach of condition. The clause was to be given no wider meaning that its ambit required and for that reason it only covered warranties, not conditions. This rule was applied by the House of Lords in *Beck v Szymanowski*.

Beck v Szymanowski [1924] AC 43

Facts: The defendants agreed to supply the plaintiffs with 2000 '200 yards reels' of sewing cotton. The contract contained the following exclusion clause: 'The goods delivered shall be deemed to be in all respects in accordance with the contract and the buyers shall be bound to accept and pay for the same accordingly unless the sellers shall within fourteen days after the arrival of the goods at their destination receive from the buyers notice of any matter or thing by reason whereof they may allege that the goods are not in accordance with the contract'. Eighteen months after delivery, the plaintiffs discovered that the length of cotton per reel was only 188 yards and they brought an action against the defendants for breach of contract. The defendants argued that they were protected by the exclusion clause.

Held: The House of Lords held (Lord Buckmaster dissenting) that the exclusion clause applied to quality only and not quantity. The clause referred to 'goods delivered'. The problem was that the goods had been short delivered and therefore the 14-day notification period did not apply here.

Lord Shaw of Dunfermline:
'The clause applies to "the goods delivered", saying that they shall be deemed to be in all respects according to contract.

But one may stop there; for the damages are claimed not in respect of the goods delivered but in respect of goods which were not delivered. And when fourteen days are given for notice of any "matter or thing of reason whereof they may allege that the goods are not in accordance with the contract" the expression "the goods" can only mean "the goods delivered", to which alone the clause applies.

Anything else would mean that the sale was in substance a sale of reels and was not in substance a sale of cotton thread. I think this is to confound make up with substance. And the results would be extraordinary; if a seller innocently sent forward the number of reels with only half the thread that should be upon them, the clause would cover that portion, and the seller would, barring objection within fourteen days, keep the price for the whole thread, although he had only supplied half . . .

[I]n my opinion the clause can never be used so as to convert goods undelivered into goods delivered or to warrant an implication to the effect that non-delivery in length or small measure was included in the objections which should, within the time fixed, be made to goods delivered. I am totally unable to make such an implication out of anything in the bargain between these parties – an implication which would seriously affect the security of business dealings.'

More recently this rule has been applied by the Court of Appeal in holding that a clause to exclude liability for 'indirect or consequential loss' does not cover lost profits arising directly from the breach.

Hotel Services Ltd v Hilton International Hotels (UK) Ltd [2000] BLR 235

Facts: The defendants agreed to supply the claimants with 'Robobars' for their hotels. A 'Robobar' was a device developed and marketed by the defendants, which electronically registered on the guests account any use of its contents. The 'Robobars' proved to be defective in that their chillers leaked ammonia which both corroded the equipment and created a small risk of injury or even fatality to guests. The claimants dismantled and removed the 'Robobars' from their hotels and brought a claim against the defendants for the cost of the removal and storage of the chiller units and cabinets and the loss of profit on the minibars. The defendants sought to rely on an exclusion clause which stated: 'The Company [HSL] will not in any circumstances be liable for any indirect or consequential loss, damage or liability arising from any defect in or failure of the System or any part thereof or the performance of this Agreement or any breach hereof by the Company or its employees'.

Held: The Court of Appeal held that this clause was ineffective to exclude liability for the losses claimed by the claimants.

Sedley LJ:

'[Counsel for the claimants] contends that a solid body of authority treats indirect or consequential damage as loss arising out of mutually known special circumstances, leaving all naturally occurring loss in the category of direct or immediate damage. [Counsel for the defendants] submits that this simplistic allocation of contractual intent between the two limbs of *Hadley v Baxendale* is erroneous . . .

The rule in *Hadley v Baxendale* (1854) 9 Ex 341, known to every law student, is this: Where two parties have made a contract which one of them has broken, the damages which the other party ought to receive in respect of such a breach of contract should be such as may fairly and reasonably be considered either arising naturally, i.e. according to the usual course of things, from such breach of contract itself, or such as may reasonably be supposed to have been in the contemplation of both parties, at the time they made the contract, as the probable result of the breach of it. (per Alderson B at 354).

This is not a dichotomous but a continuous classification, bringing into the region of recoverability all loss which the parties must in the nature of things or for known reasons have anticipated. It is the framing of exclusion clauses which has made it necessary to divide up its elements in order to keep the contractual effects within acceptable bounds . . . Direct damage is that which flows naturally from the breach without other intervening cause and independently of special circumstances, while indirect damage does not so flow . . .

[I]n *Victoria Laundry (Windsor) Ltd v Newman Industries Ltd* [1949] 2 KB 528 where, adopting the *Hadley v Baxendale* description of recoverable damage, this court reversed the trial judges decision that loss of profit was a special circumstance not drawn to the defendants' attention as a potential consequence of breach. It held that, knowing what they did of the plaintiffs' business, the defendants must be regarded as having known that some loss of profit was liable to result from their breach, though not profit on other contracts of which they knew nothing . . .

We prefer . . . to decide this case, much as *Victoria Laundry* was decided, on the direct ground that if equipment rented out for selling drinks without defalcations turns out to be unusable and possibly dangerous, it requires no special mutually known fact to establish the immediacy both of the consequent cost of putting it where it can do no harm and – if when in use it was showing a direct profit of the consequent loss of profit. Such losses are not embraced by the exclusion clause, read in its documentary and commercial context.'

The Court of Appeal adopted an extremely narrow interpretation of 'indirect or consequential loss'. For Sedley LJ, the clause only covered losses falling within the second limb of *Hadley v Baxendale* (1854) 9 Exch 341 (see Chapter 17), that is, losses that did not directly arise from the breach of contract but were within the contemplation of the parties at the time of entering into the contract. This provided very limited protection to the defendant since the category of losses that fall within the second limb of *Hadley v Baxendale* is extremely limited. On the facts of the case, all the losses sustained by the claimant fell within the first limb.

The Court's interpretation of the clause was extremely narrow and arguably inconsistent with the ordinary meaning of 'consequential loss'. All loss of profit is ultimately loss consequential on breach and thus the loss sustained in *Hotel Services Ltd* should have been excluded by the clause. The decision has been doubted by Lord Hoffman in *Caledonia North Sea Ltd v British Telecommunications Plc* [2002] 1 Lloyd's Rep 553, where his Lordship indicated that he wished 'to reserve the question of whether, in the context of the contracts in the *Hotel Services* and similar cases, the construction adopted by the Court of Appeal was correct'. It is submitted that the interpretation adopted in *Hotel Services* distorted the plain meaning of the clause in order to exclude loss that clearly fell within its ambit. Instead of relying on the indirect means of interpretation to regulate the clause, the Court of Appeal should have resorted to the direct controls contained within UCTA.

8.2.2.2 *Contra proferentem* rule

The second rule of interpretation is that exclusion clauses will be interpreted *contra proferentem*. This means that, if there is ambiguity in the language used, the clause will be construed against the party seeking to rely on it.

Lee (John) & Son (Grantham) Ltd v Railway Executive [1949] 2 All ER 581

Facts: The plaintiffs were the tenants of a warehouse in which they stored certain goods. The goods were damaged by a fire owing to the alleged negligence of the defendant landlords who allowed a spark to be ejected by one of their railway engines. By clause 10 of the tenancy agreement the landlords were released from all liability for damage to property 'however caused . . . which but for the tenancy hereby created or anything done pursuant to the provisions hereof would not have arisen'. The defendants claimed that the clause exempted them from liability.

Held: The Court of Appeal applied the *contra proferentem* rule and held that the words 'which but for the tenancy hereby created . . . would not have arisen' limited the exclusion to liabilities arising only by reason of the relationship of landlord and tenant created by the lease. The clause was capable of bearing a broader meaning but it had to be construed against the defendant.

Sir Raymond Evershed MR:
'We are presented with two alternative readings of this document and the reading which one should adopt is to be determined, among other things, by a consideration of the fact that the defendants put forward the document. They have put forward a clause which is by no means free from obscurity and have contended that, on the view for which they argued, it has a remarkably, if not an extravagantly, wide scope, and I think that the rule *contra proferentem* should be applied and that the result is that the present claim is not one which obliges the first plaintiffs to give to the defendants a release and an indemnity.'

8.2.2.2.1 *Exclusion of negligence liability*

The *contra proferentem* rule has often been used in the context of liability for negligence. The presumption is that a party has not excluded liability for his or her own negligence unless express words have been used. The principles to be applied here were set out by the Privy Council in *Canada Steamship Lines Ltd v The King* [1952] AC 192. The court was dealing with Canadian law but it has been confirmed that the principles are equally applicable to English law (see *Shell Chemical v P & O Tankers* [1995] 1 Lloyd's Rep 297). Lord Morton of Henryton said:

'Their Lordships think that the duty of a court in approaching the consideration of such clauses may be summarised as follows:

(1) If the clause contains language which expressly exempts the person in whose favour it is made (hereafter called "the *proferens*") from the consequence of the negligence of his own servants, effect must be given to that provision . . .

(2) If there is no express reference to negligence, the court must consider whether the words used are wide enough, in their ordinary meaning, to cover negligence on the part of the servants of the proferens . . .

(3) If the words used are wide enough for the above purpose, the court must then consider whether "the head of damage may be based on some ground other than that of negligence" . . . The "other ground" must not be so fanciful or remote that the proferens cannot be supposed to have

desired protection against it; but subject to this qualification . . . the existence of a possible head of damage other than that of negligence is fatal to the proferens even if the words used are prima facie wide enough to cover negligence on the part of his servants.

The first of these principles is relatively straightforward. If a clause expressly exempts a party from the consequences of his/her negligence then the clause is effective to exclude liability for negligence. The use of the word 'negligence' is obviously sufficient, but synonyms (such as carelessness) may also be enough. In *Monarch Airlines Ltd v London Luton Airport* [1998] 1 Lloyd's Rep 403, Clarke J held that the phrase 'act, omission, neglect or default' was clearly intended to include negligent acts.

Problems arise with the second and third principles because they rest on the assumption that a party does not intend to exclude negligence unless s/he explicitly says so. This is obviously a dubious assumption since the majority of contract drafters omit to explicitly refer to negligence for fear of putting the other party off of the transaction. Instead they use general words such as 'any loss howsoever caused'. While the natural meaning of such a phrase may be taken to include loss caused by both negligent and non-negligent acts, Lord Morton's third principle dictates that the phrase will be construed to cover only non-negligent sources of liability unless negligently inflicted loss is the only loss likely to be suffered by the claimant. The application of this principle can be seen in *Hollier v Rambler Motors*.

Hollier v Rambler Motors [1972] 2 QB 71

Facts: Hollier regularly took his car to Rambler Motors, who were garage proprietors, to have it repaired. Normally he would sign an 'invoice' which contained a clause stating: 'The company is not responsible for damage caused by fire to customers' cars on the premises'. On this occasion he did not sign the form. His car was damaged by a fire which was caused by Rambler's negligence. Hollier claimed damages for breach of the implied term that Rambler Motors would take reasonable care of his car. Rambler relied on the exclusion clause claiming that it had been incorporated into the contract because of the previous course of dealing between the parties. At first instance, the judge held that the clause had been incorporated into the contract and excluded Rambler's liability for negligence.

Held: The Court of Appeal held that the exclusion clause was not incorporated into the contract because there was no sufficient course of dealing. In any event, the language of the clause was not sufficient to exclude liability for their negligence.

Salmon LJ:
'[I]n case I am wrong on the view that I have formed, without any hesitation, I may say, that the course of dealing did not import the so-called exclusion clause, I think I should

deal with the point as to whether or not the words on the bottom of the form, had they been incorporated in the contract, would have excluded the defendants' liability to compensate the plaintiff for damage caused to the plaintiff's car by a fire which in turn had been caused by the defendants' own negligence. It is well settled that a clause excluding liability for negligence should make its meaning plain on its face to any ordinarily literate and sensible person. The easiest way of doing that, of course, is to state expressly that the garage, tradesman or merchant, as the case may be, will not be responsible for any damage caused by his own negligence. No doubt merchants, tradesmen, garage proprietors and the like are a little shy of writing in an exclusion clause quite so bluntly as that. Clearly it would not tend to attract customers, and might even put many off. I am not saying that an exclusion clause cannot be effective to exclude negligence unless it does so expressly, but in order for the clause to be effective the language should be so plain that it clearly bears that meaning. I do not think that defendants should be allowed to shelter behind language which might lull the customer into a false sense of security by letting him think – unless perhaps he happens to be a lawyer – that he would have redress against the man with whom he was dealing for any damage which he, the customer, might suffer by the negligence of that person.

The principles are stated by Scrutton LJ with his usual clarity in *Rutter v Palmer* [1922] 2 KB 87, 92:

> "For the present purposes a rougher test will serve. In construing an exemption clause certain general rules may be applied: First the defendant is not exempted from liability for the negligence of his servants unless adequate words are used; secondly, the liability of the defendant apart from the exempting words must be ascertained; then the particular clause in question must be considered; and if the only liability of the party pleading the exemption is a liability for negligence, the clause will more readily operate to exempt him."

Scrutton LJ was far too great a lawyer, and had far too much robust common sense, if I may be permitted to say so, to put it higher than that "if the only liability of the party pleading the exemption is a liability for negligence, the clause will more readily operate to exempt him". He does not say that "if the only liability of the party pleading the exemption is a liability for negligence, the clause will necessarily exempt him". After all, there are many cases in the books dealing with exemption clauses, and in every case it comes down to a question of construing the alleged exemption clause which is then before the court. It seems to me that in *Rutter v Palmer* although the word "negligence" was never used in the exemption clause, the exemption clause would have conveyed to any ordinary, literate and sensible person that the garage in that case was inserting a clause in the contract which excluded their liability for the negligence of their drivers. The clause being considered in that case – and it was without any doubt incorporated in the contract – was: "Customers' cars are driven by your staff at customers' sole risk". Any ordinary man knows that when a car is damaged it is not infrequently damaged because the driver has driven it negligently. He also knows, I suppose, that if he sends it to a garage and a driver in the employ of the garage takes the car on the road for some purpose in connection with the work which the customer has entrusted the garage to do, the garage could not conceivably be liable for the car being damaged in an accident unless the driver was at fault. It follows that no sensible man could have thought that the words in that case had any meaning except that the garage would not be liable for the negligence of their own drivers. That is a typical case where, on the construction of the clause in question, the meaning for which the defendant was there contending was the obvious meaning of the clause.

The next case to which I wish to refer is the well-known case of *Alderslade v Hendon Laundry Ltd* [1945] 1 KB 189. In that case articles were sent by the plaintiff to the defendants' laundry to be washed, and they were lost. In an action by the plaintiff against the defendants for damages, the defendants relied on the following condition to limit their liability: "The maximum amount allowed for lost or damaged articles is 20 times the charge made for laundering". Again, this was a case where negligence was not expressly excluded. The question was: what do the words mean? I have no doubt that they would mean to the ordinary housewife who was sending her washing to the laundry that, if the goods were lost or damaged in the course of being washed through the negligence of the laundry, the laundry would not be liable for more than 20 times the charge made for the laundering. I say that for this reason. It is, I think, obvious that when a laundry loses or damages goods it is almost invariably because there has been some neglect or default on the part of the laundry; it is said that thieves break in and steal, and the goods (in that case handkerchiefs) might have been stolen by thieves. That of course is possible, but I should hardly think that a laundry would be a great allurement to burglars. It is a little far-fetched to think of burglars breaking into a laundry to steal the washing when there are banks, jewellers, post offices, factories, offices and homes likely to contain money and articles far more attractive to burglars. I think that the ordinary sensible housewife, or indeed anyone else who sends washing to the laundry, who saw that clause must have appreciated that almost always goods are lost or damaged because of the laundry's negligence, and therefore this clause could apply only to limit the liability of the laundry, when they were in fault or negligent.

But [counsel for the defendant] has drawn our attention to the way in which the matter was put by Lord Greene MR in delivering the leading judgment in this court, and he contends that Lord Greene MR was in fact making a considerable extension to the law as laid down by Scrutton LJ in the case to which I have referred. For this proposition he relies on the following passage in Lord Greene MR's judgment, at p 192:

> "The effect of those authorities can I think be stated as follows: Where the head of damage in respect of which limitation of liability is sought to be imposed by such a clause is one which rests on negligence and nothing else, the clause must be construed as extending to that head of damage, because it would otherwise lack subject matter."

If one takes that word "must" *au pied de la lettre* that passage does support [counsel for the defendant's] contention. However, we are not here construing a statute, but a passage in an unreserved judgment of Lord Greene MR, who was clearly intending no more than to re-state the effect of the authorities as they then stood. It is to be observed that MacKinnon LJ, who gave the other judgment in this court, set out the rule or principle which he said was very admirably stated by Scrutton LJ in *Rutter v Palmer* [1922] 2 KB 87. He said, at p 195:

> "Applying that principle to the facts of the case, I think that the clause in question does avail to protect the proprietors of the laundry in respect of liability for negligence which must be assumed to be the cause of these handkerchiefs having disappeared."

And clearly it did, for the reasons that I have already given. I do not think that Lord Greene MR was intending to extend the law in the sense for which [counsel for the defendant] contends. If it were so extended, it would make the law entirely artificial by ignoring that rules of construction are merely our guides and not our masters; in the end you are driven back to construing the clause in question to see what it means. Applying the principles laid down by Scrutton LJ, they lead to the result at which the court arrived in *Alderslade v Hendon Laundry Ltd* [1945] 1 KB 189.

In my judgment these principles lead to a very different result in the present case. The words are: "The company is not responsible for damage caused by fire to customers' cars on the premises". What would that mean to any ordinarily literate and sensible car owner? I do not suppose that any such, unless he is a trained lawyer, has an intimate or indeed any knowledge of the liability of bailees in law. If you asked the ordinary man or woman: "Supposing you send your car to the garage to be repaired, and there is a fire, would you suppose that the garage would be liable?" I should be surprised if many of them did not answer, quite wrongly: "Of course they are liable if there is a fire". Others might be more cautious and say: "Well, I had better ask my solicitor", or, "I do not know. I suppose they may well be liable". That is the crucial difference, to my mind, between the present case and *Alderslade v Hendon Laundry Ltd* and *Rutter v Palmer*. In those two cases, any ordinary man or woman reading the conditions would have known that all that was being excluded was the negligence of the laundry, in the one case, and the garage, in the other. But here I think the ordinary man or woman would be equally surprised and horrified to learn that if the garage was so negligent that a fire was caused which damaged their car, they would be without remedy because of the words in the condition. I can quite understand that the ordinary man or woman would consider that, because of these words, the mere fact that there was a fire would not make the garage liable. Fires can occur from a large variety of causes, only one of which is negligence on the part of the occupier of the premises, and that is by no means the most frequent cause. The ordinary man would I think say to himself: "Well, what they are telling me is that if there is a fire due to any cause other than their own negligence they are not responsible for it". To my mind, if the defendants were seeking to exclude their responsibility for a fire caused by their own negligence, they ought to have done so in far plainer language than the language here used.'

> Stamp LJ:
>
> 'On the question of construction, I reach the same conclusion as Salmon LJ, but by, I think, a slightly different route. As I understand the law, it is settled that where in a contract such as this you find a provision excluding liability capable of two constructions, one of which will make it applicable where there is no negligence by the defendant, and the other will make it applicable where there is negligence by the defendant, it requires special words or special circumstances to make the clause exclude liability in case of negligence: see, for example, *Price & Co v Union Lighterage Co* [1904] 1 KB 412. Similarly, I would hold that, where the words relied upon by the defendant are susceptible either to a construction under which they become a statement of fact in the nature of a warning or to a construction which will exempt the defendant from liability for negligence, the former construction is to be preferred. The words here, "the company is not responsible for damage caused by fire to customer's cars on the premises", are, in my judgment, certainly susceptible to a construction which would regard them as a mere statement in the nature of a warning, and reinforced by the principle that I have stated, I would hold that that is how they ought to be construed in this case. If this be correct, I do not find it necessary to consider the cases which have been decided upon the footing that the clause under consideration was a term of the contract excluding some liability: for on the view that I have formed, the clause on its true construction is not a clause of that nature.'

Salmon LJ's statement of general principle sounds entirely sensible. He is right to insist that 'a clause excluding liability for negligence should make its meaning plain on its face to any ordinarily literate and sensible person'. That said, it is difficult to comprehend why the clause used by Rambler Motors did not achieve this purpose. According to the Court of Appeal, the reasonable customer would assume that the clause related only to fires that arose without negligence on the part of the defendant (even though as a matter of law no liability would arise in such a case). Thus the clause was not really an exclusion of liability at all. It was merely a 'warning' that the defendant was not, as a matter of law, liable for non-negligent fire damage. But surely the clause purported to do much more than that. Furthermore, the distinction drawn between the present case and *Alderslade v Hendon Laundry Ltd* is far from convincing. Contract drafters are left in a profound state of uncertainty and it is probably sensible for them to make explicit reference to 'negligence' if they wish to exclude such liability.

8.2.2.2.2 *Exclusion of fraudulent liability*
It is clear that the *contra proferentem* rule will operate to ensure that a general exclusion clause is not construed to apply to fraud.

Motis Exports Ltd v Dampskibsselskabet AF 1912 Aktieselskab
[2000] 1 Lloyd's Rep 211

Facts: The plaintiff was the shipper of various consignments of goods under a number of bills of lading at ports in China and Hong Kong. A clause in the bill of lading stated: '. . . the Carrier shall have no liability whatsoever for any loss or damage to the goods while in its actual or constructive possession before loading or after discharge over ship's rail, or if applicable, on the ship's ramp, however caused.' The goods were carried to West Africa in ships owned and operated by the defendants. The issue for decision was whether the defendants were liable for the loss of the goods after discharge from their vessels, where the cause of that loss was the use of forged bills of lading to obtain delivery orders in respect of, and thus delivery of, the goods at the discharge port.

Held: The Court of Appeal held that the natural subject matter of the exclusion clause consisted in loss or damage caused to the goods while in the carrier's custody but not deliberate delivery up of the goods against a forged bill of lading.

Stuart-Smith LJ:
'In my judgment [the clause] is not apt on its natural meaning to cover delivery by the carrier or his agent, albeit the delivery was obtained by fraud. I also agree with the Judge that even if the language was apt to cover such a case, it is not a construction which should be adopted, involving as it does excuse from performing an obligation of such fundamental importance. As a matter of construction the Courts lean against such a result if adequate content can be given to the clause. In my view it can . . . it is wide enough also to cover loss caused by negligence, provided the loss is of the appropriate kind.'

8.2.2.2.3 Strict interpretation should not be strained
Although the *contra proferentem* rule states that exclusion clauses will be read strictly against the person seeking to rely upon them, the construction applied will not be strained and the words will be given their natural meaning.

Ailsa Craig Fishing Co Ltd v Malvern Fishing Co Ltd [1983] 1 WLR 964

Facts: Securicor agreed to provide a security service to Ailsa Craig's fishing boats moored in Aberdeen harbour. Due to Securicor's negligent failure to provide the service contracted for, a fishing boat belonging to Ailsa Craig sank, dragging down another boat owned by Malvern Fishing. The contract contained a clause limiting liability to £1,000. Ailsa Craig argued that since Securicor had failed to provide a security service they should not be able to hide behind the clause.

Held: The House of Lords held that the limitation clause was effective because its terms were clear and unambiguous and wide enough to cover the liability of Securicor for their negligence.

Lord Wilberforce:
'Whether a clause limiting liability is effective or not is a question of construction of that clause in the context of the contract as a whole. If it is to exclude liability for negligence, it must be most clearly and unambiguously expressed, and in such a contract as this, must be construed *contra proferentem*. I do not think that there is any doubt so far. But I venture to add one further qualification, or at least clarification: one must not strive to create ambiguities by strained construction, as I think that the appellants have striven to do. The relevant words must be given, if possible, their natural, plain meaning.'

As Lord Wilberforce confirmed, the *contra proferentem* rule does not countenance finding ambiguity where none exists. This was confirmed by Lord Bridge in *Mitchell (George) (Chesterhall) Ltd v Finney Lock Seeds Ltd* [1983] 2 AC 803, where his Lordship confirmed the need for straightforward interpretation:

'The relevant condition, read as a whole, unambiguously limits the appellants' liability to replacement of the seeds or refund of the price. It is only possible to read an ambiguity into it by the process of strained construction which was deprecated by Lord Diplock in the *Photo Production* case and by Lord Wilberforce in *Ailsa Craig*.'

8.2.2.3 Exclusion and limitation clauses

It has been held that a less rigorous approach should be applied to construing clauses that merely limit liability rather than excluding liability altogether. In *Ailsa Craig Fishing* Lord Wilberforce said:

'Clauses of limitation are not regarded by the courts with the same hostility as clauses of exclusion: this is because they must be related to other contractual terms, in particular to the risks to which the defending party may be exposed, the remuneration which he receives and possibly also the opportunity of the other party to insure.'

Lord Fraser of Tulybelton agreed:

'There are . . . authorities which lay down very strict principles to be applied when considering the effect of clauses of exclusion or of indemnity . . . In my opinion these principles are not applicable in their full rigour when considering the effect of clauses merely limiting liability. Such clauses will of course be read *contra proferentem* and must be clearly expressed, but there is no reason why they should be judged by the specially exacting standards which are applied to exclusion and indemnity clauses. The reason for imposing such standards on these clauses is the inherent improbability that the other party to a contract including such a clause intended to release the proferens from a liability that would otherwise fall upon him. But there is no such high degree of improbability that he would agree to a limitation of the liability of the proferens, especially when . . . the potential losses that might be caused by the negligence of the proferens or its servants are so great in proportion to the sums that can reasonably be charged for the services contracted for. It is enough in the present case that the clause must be clear and unambiguous.'

The reasons given for distinguishing between exclusion clauses and limitation clauses are unconvincing. In particular, it is unclear why only limitation clauses are 'related to other contractual terms' and to 'the opportunity of the other party to insure'. It is also unclear why a party is any more likely to agree to a limitation clause than to an exclusion clause. In practice, the difference between the two may be nonexistent. For example, a clause limiting compensation to one penny is virtually indistinguishable from a total exclusion of liability. In *Atlantic Shipping & Trading Company v Louis Dreyfus & Company* [1922] 2 AC 250, Lord Sumner said: 'There is no difference in principle between words which save [contractors] from having to pay at all and words which save them from paying as much as they would otherwise have had to pay'.

It is submitted that the courts should look to the substance of the clause rather than to the form of words used. A sensible approach was advocated by Evans LJ in *BHP Petroleum Ltd v British Steel plc* [2000] 2 Lloyd's Rep 277: '[T]he more extreme the consequences are, in terms of excluding or modifying the liability which would otherwise arise, then the more stringent the Court's approach should be in requiring that the exclusion or limit should be clearly and unambiguously expressed'.

8.2.2.4 Relaxation of the rules of interpretation

Following the enactment of statutory controls to regulate the use of exclusion clauses, the courts have increasingly taken the view that there is no longer a need to manipulate the rules of interpretation to provide indirect regulation. Consumer and standard form contracts are now dealt with by the UCTA 1977 and the UTCCR 1999. Businesses are expected to be able to look after themselves and it is presumed that if they enter into contracts containing exclusion clauses, they will know what they are doing. In *Photo Production Ltd v Securicor Transport Ltd* [1980] AC 827, Lord Wilberforce commented that:

'. . . after [UCTA 1977], in commercial matters generally, when the parties are not of unequal bargaining power, and when risks are normally borne by insurance, not only is the case for judicial intervention undemonstrated, but there is everything to be said, and this seems to have been Parliament's intention, for leaving the parties free to apportion the risks as they think fit and for respecting their decisions.'

Lord Diplock agreed with Lord Wilberforce, commenting that the need for judicial distortion of the English language has been banished by Parliament's enactment of UCTA 1977:

'In commercial contracts negotiated between business-men capable of looking after their own interests and of deciding how risks inherent in the performance of various kinds of contract can be most economically borne (generally by insurance), it is, in my view, wrong to place a strained construction upon words in an exclusion clause which are clear and fairly susceptible of one meaning only even after due allowance has been made for the presumption in favour of the implied primary and secondary obligations.'

The interpretation of exclusion clauses in commercial contracts should now also take into account the principles set out by Lord Hoffman in *Investors Compensation Scheme Ltd v West Bromwich Building Society* [1998] 1 WLR 896. There he said that 'almost all the old intellectual baggage of "legal" interpretation has been discarded'. What this meant in the context of the interpretation of exclusion clauses was explained by Lord Hoffman in his dissenting speech in *BCCI v Ali* [2002] 1 AC 251:

'My Lords, the lesson which I would draw from the development of the rules for construing exemption clauses is that the judicial creativity, bordering on judicial legislation, which the application of that doctrine involved is a desperate remedy, to be invoked only if it is necessary to remedy a widespread injustice. Otherwise there is much to be said for giving effect to what on ordinary principles of construction the parties agreed . . .

The disappearance of artificial rules for the construction of exemption clauses seems to me in accordance with the general trend in matters of construction, which has been to try to assimilate judicial techniques of construction to those which would be used by a reasonable speaker of the language in the interpretation of any serious utterance in ordinary life. In *Investors Compensation Scheme Ltd v West Bromwich Building Society* [1998] 1 WLR 896, 912, I said with the concurrence of three other members of the House: "Almost all the old intellectual baggage of 'legal' interpretation has been discarded". But if [counsel for the claimant's] submissions on the rules of construction are accepted, a substantial piece of baggage will have been retrieved. Lord Keeper Henley's ghost (*Salkeld v Vernon* 1 Eden 64) will have struck back. I think it would be an unfortunate retreat into formalism if the outcome of this case were to require employers using the services of Acas to add verbiage to the form of release in order to attain the comprehensiveness which it is obviously intended to achieve.'

The authority of this statement is somewhat difficult to predict. It was clearly obiter because the case concerned the interpretation of a release clause, not the interpretation of an exclusion clause. In addition, the statement was made in the context of a dissenting speech. Nevertheless, the comments were of significance because they were made in respect of Lord Hoffman's majority speech in *Investors Compensation Scheme*. More recently, in *Keele University v Price Waterhouse* [2004] PNLR 43, the Court of Appeal confirmed that exclusion clauses must be interpreted in accordance with the principles of interpretation set out by Lord Hoffmann in *Investors Compensation Scheme*. The court's primary purpose is to give effect to the intention of the parties. If the old rules of interpretation are found to be contrary to that purpose they will not be applied (also see *HIH Casualty and General Insurance v Chase Manhattan Bank* [2003] 1 All ER (Comm) 349).

8.2.3 FUNDAMENTAL BREACH

A further rule that the common law sought to introduce to restrict the impact of exclusion clauses was the doctrine of fundamental breach. The rule stated that some breaches of contract are so serious that no exclusion clause can cover them. The idea is rooted in the English tradition that there is a core obligation, the consideration for the contract, which is more fundamental than any condition or warranty and therefore cannot be excluded. Lord Denning, in the Court of Appeal, championed the fundamental breach doctrine and its operation can be seen in *Karsales (Harrow) Ltd v Wallis*.

Karsales (Harrow) Ltd v Wallis [1956] 1 WLR 936

Facts: The defendant, Frank Wallis, purchased a second-hand Buick car. When he inspected the car prior to purchase he found it to be in an excellent condition. However, when the car was delivered (late at night) he found that it was in a deplorable state: it had to be towed to his premises because it was incapable of self-propulsion, the cylinder head had been removed, the valves were burnt out, and two of the pistons had been broken. Wallis refused to accept the car. The plaintiff sued Wallis for payment and relied upon a clause in the agreement which stated the following: 'No condition or warranty that the vehicle is roadworthy or as to its age, condition or fitness for any purpose is given by the owner or implied herein'. The county court held for the plaintiff.

Held: The Court of Appeal allowed the appeal, holding that the thing that had been delivered was not a 'car', which by definition had to be capable of movement.

Denning LJ:

'Notwithstanding earlier cases which might suggest the contrary, it is now settled that exempting clauses of this kind, no matter how widely they are expressed, only avail the party when he is carrying out his contract in its essential respects. He is not allowed to use them as a cover for misconduct or indifference or to enable him to turn a blind eye to his obligations. They do not avail him when he is guilty of a breach which goes to the root of the contract. The thing to do is to look at the contract apart from the exempting clauses and see what are the terms, express or implied, which impose an obligation on the party. If he has been guilty of a breach of those obligations in a respect which goes to the very root of the contract, he cannot rely on the exempting clauses ... The principle is sometimes said to be that the party cannot rely on an exempting clause when he delivers something "different in kind" from that contracted for, or has broken a "fundamental term" or a "fundamental contractual obligation", but these are, I think, all comprehended by the general principle that a breach which goes to the root of the contract disentitles the party from relying on the exempting clause. In the present case the lender was in breach of the implied obligation that I have mentioned. When the defendant inspected the car before signing the application form, the car was in excellent condition and would go: whereas the car which was subsequently delivered to him was no doubt the same car, but it was in a deplorable state and would not go. That breach went, I think, to the root of the contract and disentitles the lender from relying on the exempting clause.'

Birkett LJ:

'Clearly it was the duty of the [plaintiff] ... to supply to the defendant a "car", in the ordinary sense of that term, and not something that needed towing, because in the true meaning of words a car that would not go was not a car at all; and on the evidence before the county court judge that was the kind of article which was supplied.

... I think that it was quite clearly here shown that there was a fundamental breach – indeed, those are the very words that were the words of the submission that was made. It may be put in alternative forms – that the thing delivered was not the thing contracted for, or words of that kind; but it seems to me that the [plaintiff], being in breach, and fundamentally in breach, cannot rely, as they have sought to rely, on the provisions of [the exclusion clause] in the written agreement. In those circumstances, therefore, I think that the defendant is entitled to succeed and should have succeeded in the court below. I would allow the appeal.

Parker LJ:

'Applying that to the facts of this case it seems to me that the vehicle delivered in effect is not properly described (as the agreement describes it) as a motor vehicle, "Buick", giving the chassis and engine number. By that I am not saying that every defect in a car which renders it for the moment unusable on the road amounts to a breach of a fundamental term; but where, as here, a vehicle is delivered incapable of

> self-propulsion except after a complete overhaul and in the condition referred to by my Lord, it seems to me that it is abundantly clear that there was a breach of a fundamental term and that, accordingly, the exceptions in [the exclusion clause] do not apply.'

Denning LJ reached the same conclusion as the majority but on slightly different reasoning. The majority decided the case on the basis that the thing delivered was not a 'car'. Denning LJ did not agree with this conclusion but held that the plaintiffs were nevertheless disentitled from relying on the exclusion clause because the breach went to the 'root' of the contract. This doctrine of fundamental breach was reapplied by Lord Denning 14 years later in *Harbutt's Plasticine Ltd v Wayne Tank and Pump Co Ltd*.

Harbutt's Plasticine Ltd v Wayne Tank and Pump Co Ltd [1970] 1 QB 447

Facts: The defendants agreed to design and install pipe work in the plaintiffs' factory for storing and dispensing a heavy wax. The contract contained printed conditions including a condition 15 which stated that liability would be limited to the contract price of the work. The defendants installed pipe work which was wholly unsuitable for the purpose. This resulted in a fire which destroyed the plaintiffs' factory. The trial judge held that there had been a fundamental breach of contract which disentitled the defendants from relying on the limitation clause.

Held: The Court of Appeal dismissed the appeal.

Lord Denning MR:

'Fundamental Breach
Assuming that condition 15 does, in terms, purport to limit the liability of the defendants, the next question is whether the defendants were guilty of a fundamental breach of contract which disentitled them from relying on it. I eschew in this context the word "repudiation" because it is applied so differently in so many different contexts, as Lord Wright explained in *Heyman v Darwins Ltd* [1942] AC 356, 378. There was no repudiation in this case by the defendants – not, at any rate, in its proper sense of denying they are bound by the contract. The defendants have always acknowledged the contract. All that has happened is that they have broken it. If they have broken it in a way that goes to the very root of it, then it is a fundamental breach. If they have broken it in a lesser way, then the breach is not fundamental.

In considering the consequences of a fundamental breach, it is necessary to draw a distinction between a fundamental breach which still leaves the contract open to be performed, and a fundamental breach which itself brings the contract to an end.

(i) The first group
In cases where the contract is still open to be performed, the effect of a fundamental breach is this: it gives the innocent party, when he gets to know of it, an option either to

affirm the contract or to disaffirm it. If he elects to *affirm* it, then it remains in being *for the future* on both sides. Each has a right to sue for damages for *past or future* breaches. If he elects to disaffirm it (namely, accepts the fundamental breach as determining the contract), then it is at an end from that moment. It does not continue into the future. All that is left is the right to sue for past breaches or for the fundamental breach, but there is no right to sue for *future* breaches.

(ii) The second group

In cases where the fundamental breach itself brings the contract to an end, there is no room for any option in the innocent party. The present case is typical of this group. The fire was so disastrous that it destroyed the mill itself. If the fire had been accidental, it would certainly have meant that the contract was frustrated and brought to an end by a supervening event; just as in the leading case in 1863 when the Surrey Music Hall was burnt down: see *Taylor v Caldwell* (1863) 3 B & S 826 . . .

All that I have said thus far is so obvious that it needs no authority. But now I come to the great question. When a contract is brought to an end by a fundamental breach by one of the parties, can the guilty party rely on an exclusion or limitation clause so as to avoid or limit his liability for the breach?

I propose to take first the group of cases when the fundamental breach does not automatically bring the contract to an end, but it has to be accepted by the innocent party as doing so. Such a case was *Karsales (Harrow) Ltd v Wallis* [1956] 1 WLR 936, where the hirer, on discovering the fundamental breach, at once rejected the car. In this group it is settled that once he accepts it, the innocent party can sue for the breach and the guilty party cannot rely on the exclusion or limitation clause. That clearly appears from the speeches in the House of Lords in *Suisse Atlantique Société d'Armement Maritime SA v NV Rotterdamsche Kolen Centrale* [1967] 1 AC 361. Lord Reid said, at p 398:

> "If fundamental breach is established the next question is what effect, if any, that has on the applicability of other terms of the contract. This question has often arisen with regard to clauses excluding liability, in whole or in part, of the party in breach. I do not think there is generally much difficulty where the innocent party has elected to treat the breach as a repudiation, bring the contract to an end and sue for damages. Then the whole contract has ceased to exist including the exclusion clause, and I do not see how that clause can then be used to exclude an action for loss which will be suffered by the innocent party after it has ceased to exist, such as loss of the profit which would have accrued if the contract had run its full term." . . .

When their Lordships said the contract "is at an end", they meant, of course, for the future. Such an ending disentitles the guilty party from relying on an exclusion clause in respect of the breach. Such, then, is established as law when there is "a fundamental breach accepted by the innocent party", that is, when the innocent party has an election to treat the contract as at an end and does so. The position must, I think, be the same when the defendant has been guilty of such a fundamental breach that the contract is *automatically* at an end without the innocent party having an election. The innocent party is entitled to sue for damages for the breach, and the guilty party cannot rely on the exclusion or limitation clause: for the simple reason that he, by his own breach, has brought the contract to an end; with the result that he cannot rely on the clause to exempt or limit his liability for that breach.

The one question in this case is, therefore: Were the defendants guilty of a fundamental breach which brought the contract to an end? For, if so, they cannot rely on the limitation clause. It was suggested that, in order to determine whether a breach is fundamental or not, you must look at the quality of it, and not at the results. I do not accept this suggestion. It is not the breach itself which counts so much, but the event resulting from it . . .

So I come to the question: were the breaches by the defendants and the consequences of them so fundamental as to bring the contract to an end, and thus disentitle the defendants from relying on the limitation clause? The judge thought that they were. I agree with him . . .

Before leaving this part of the case, I would just like to say what, in my opinion, is the result of the *Suisse Atlantique* case. It affirms the long line of cases in this court that when one party has been guilty of a fundamental breach of the contract, that is, a breach which goes to the very root of it, and the other side accepts it, so that the contract comes to an end – or if it comes to an end anyway by reason of the breach – then the guilty party cannot rely on an exception or limitation clause to escape from his liability for the breach.

If the innocent party, on getting to know of the breach, does not accept it, but keeps the contract in being (as in *Charterhouse Credit Co Ltd v Tolly* [1963] 2 QB 683), then it is a matter of construction whether the guilty party can rely on the exception or limitation clause, always remembering that it is not to be supposed that the parties intended to give a guilty party a blanket to cover up his own misconduct or indifference, or to enable him to turn a blind eye to his obligations. . .'.

Lord Denning's reliance on *Suisse Atlantique* was misplaced and his summary of the decision faulty. In *Suisse Atlantique*, the House of Lords actually expressly disapproved of the argument that the doctrine of fundamental breach was a substantive rule of law precluding reliance on an exclusion clause. Viscount Dilhourne said:

'In my view, it is not right to say that the law prohibits and nullifies a clause exempting or limiting liability for a fundamental breach or breach of a fundamental term. Such a rule of law would involve a restriction on freedom of contract and in the older cases I can find no trace of it.'

According to the House of Lords, the doctrine of fundamental breach was a rule of construction, not a rule of law. It was relevant to the question of whether the clause covered the breach in question – the more serious the breach the more specific the wording of the clause would need to be. It did not, however, act as a rule of law prohibiting reliance on exemption clauses in cases of fundamental breach.

In *Harbutt's Plasticine*, the Court of Appeal sought to distinguish *Suisse Atlantique* on the ground that the claimant in that case had affirmed the contract following the alleged breach. Lord Denning suggested that the parties following the breach should only follow the approach adopted in *Suisse Atlantique* in cases where there was an affirmation of the contract, and not where the breach itself brought the contract to the end. In cases that fell into this latter category, including *Harbutt's Plasticine*, his Lordship suggested that reliance on an exclusion clause should be prohibited. The problem with Lord Denning's argument is that it ignores the well-established legal principle that a breach of contract never in itself brings a contract to an end. It merely gives rise to an option at the behest of the innocent party, either to accept the breach and terminate the contract or to affirm the contract and claim for damages (see Chapter 16). Contrary to this well-established principle, the Court of Appeal in *Harbutt's Plasticine*, claimed that this did not apply to certain fundamental breaches, which themselves brought the contract to an end without the need for repudiation by the innocent party. This view, and the fundamental breach doctrine that it supported, was later categorically rejected by the House of Lords in *Photo Production Ltd v Securicor Transport Ltd*.

Photo Production Ltd v Securicor Transport Ltd [1980] AC 827

Facts: Photo Production had a contract with Securicor whereby a security guard visited their factory on a night patrol. Unfortunately, one of the guards employed by Securicor to carry out these duties started a fire at the premises which got out of control and destroyed Photo Production's factory. The loss caused was £615,000. There was an exclusion clause in the contract stating: 'Under no circumstances shall (Securicor) be responsible for any injurious act or default by any employee of the Company unless such act or default could have been foreseen and avoided by the exercise of due diligence on the part of the Company as his employer . . .'. It was clear on the facts that Securicor had not been negligent in employing the guard who started the fire. The question arose as to whether the clause was nullified by a fundamental breach. The Court of Appeal held that it was.

Held: The House of Lords allowed the appeal and held that the exclusion clause applied despite the fact that a fundamental breach had occurred.

Lord Wilberforce:
'I have no second thoughts as to the main proposition that the question whether, and to what extent, an exclusion clause is to be applied to a fundamental breach, or a breach of a fundamental term, or indeed to any breach of contract, is a matter of construction of the contract. Many difficult questions arise and will continue to arise in

the infinitely varied situations in which contracts come to be breached – by repudiatory breaches, accepted or not, by anticipatory breaches, by breaches of conditions or of various terms and whether by negligent, or deliberate action or otherwise. But there are ample resources in the normal rules of contract law for dealing with these without the superimposition of a judicially invented rule of law. I am content to leave the matter there with some supplementary observations:

1. The doctrine of "fundamental breach" in spite of its imperfections and doubtful parentage has served a useful purpose. There was a large number of problems, productive of injustice, in which it was worse than unsatisfactory to leave exception clauses to operate . . . But since then Parliament has taken a hand: it has passed the Unfair Contract Terms Act 1977. This Act applies to consumer contracts and those based on standard terms and enables exception clauses to be applied with regard to what is just and reasonable . . .

    At the stage of negotiation as to the consequences of a breach, there is everything to be said for allowing the parties to estimate their respective claims according to the contractual provisions they have themselves made, rather than for facing them with a legal complex so uncertain as the doctrine of fundamental breach must be. What, for example, would have been the position of the respondents' factory if instead of being destroyed it had been damaged, slightly or moderately or severely? At what point does the doctrine (with what logical justification I have not understood) decide, *ex post facto*, that the breach was (factually) fundamental before going on to ask whether legally it is to be regarded as fundamental? . . .

2. The case of *Harbutt* [1970] 1 QB 447 must clearly be overruled. It would be enough to put that upon its radical inconsistency with the *Suisse Atlantique* case [1967] 1 AC 361. But even if the matter were *res integra* I would find the decision to be based upon unsatisfactory reasoning as to the "termination" of the contract and the effect of "termination" on the plaintiffs' claim for damage. I have, indeed, been unable to understand how the doctrine can be reconciled with the well accepted principle of law, stated by the highest modern authority, that when in the context of a breach of contract one speaks of "termination", what is meant is no more than that the innocent party or, in some cases, both parties, are excused from further performance. Damages, in such cases, are then claimed under the contract, so what reason in principle can there be for disregarding what the contract itself says about damages – whether it "liquidates" them, or limits them, or excludes them?'

The decision of the House of Lords in *Photo Production* appeared to 'put to bed' the doctrine of fundamental breach (see the comments of Lord Bridge in *Mitchell (George) (Chesterhall) Ltd v Finney Lock Seeds Ltd* [1983] 2 AC 803, 813 and, more recently, Judge Peter Coulson QC in *Decoma UK Limited v Haden Drysys* [2005] EWHC 2948). Their Lordships concluded that the doctrine was no longer necessary following the enactment of the UCTA 1977 and *Harbutt's Plasticine* was explicitly overruled.

Nevertheless, the seriousness of the breach continues to be of relevance to the issue of interpretation and, at times, the courts have come perilously close to reintroducing the fundamental breach doctrine through the back door. It is arguable that this is precisely what Stuart Smith LJ did in *Motis Exports v Dampskibsselsk* [2000] 1 Lloyd's Rep 211. We have already considered the facts of the case. In coming to the conclusion that the exclusion clause did not cover a fraudulent breach of contract, Stuart Smith LJ said:

> 'I also agree with the Judge [at first instance] that even if the language was apt to cover such a case, it is not a construction which should be adopted, involving as it does excuse from performing an obligation of such fundamental importance. As a matter of construction the Courts lean against such a result if adequate content can be given to the clause.'

In practice, there may not be much difference between the substantive doctrine of fundamental breach and the interpretation approach approved by the House of Lords in *Photo Production*.

8.3 THE UNFAIR CONTRACT TERMS ACT

In the previous section we considered the common-law techniques used by the courts to regulate exclusion clauses. To a large extent these have proven to be either flawed or ineffective and in 1977 Parliament intervened to enact the Unfair Contract Terms Act 1977. The effect of this Act was to render certain exclusion clauses ineffective and to subject others to a test of reasonableness. In the last couple of years the Law Commission has recommended substantial revision of the 1977 Act. This is largely due to the impact of the Unfair Terms in Consumer Contract Regulations 1994, later repealed and replaced by the Unfair Terms in Consumer Contract Regulations 1999. These regulations and the reforms that have been recommended by the Law Commission will be considered in greater detail below.

In most cases concerning an exclusion clause in a consumer contract, or an exclusion clause in the defendant's written standard terms, it is likely that the statutory provisions will prove to be determinative of the outcome of the case. Indeed, in many cases the statutory provisions will be considered first of all because they are the most significant issue. This is not always the case, however, because if the term has not been incorporated into the contract or does not cover the breach that has occurred then the clause will have no effect at all and the statutory provisions will be irrelevant.

University of Keele v Price Waterhouse [2004] PNLR 43

Facts: Price Waterhouse contracted with the University of Keele to implement a profit related pay scheme. After the scheme had been operated for some three years, it came to light that it did not meet the Inland Revenue's requirements, and it was cancelled. University of Keele brought a claim against Price Waterhouse for the tax it had to pay after cancellation, the savings it would have made had the scheme been valid and the professional fees expended. Price Waterhouse sought to rely on a clause in the contract which stated the following: 'Subject to the preceding paragraph we accept liability to pay damages in respect of loss or damage suffered by you as a direct result of our providing the Services. All other liability is expressly excluded, in particular consequential loss, failure to realise anticipated savings or benefits and a failure to obtain registration of the scheme.' University of Keele contended that the clause did not cover the claimed losses, and that if it did, the clause was ineffective under UCTA 1977.

Held: The Court of Appeal held that on the plain meaning of the clause the relevant loss was not excluded. Therefore the question of whether the clause was ineffective under UCTA 1977 was a moot point and did not need to be discussed.

8.3.1 SCOPE

Although the UCTA 1977 has had a very significant effect on the law relating to exclusion clauses it must be remembered that the Act does not apply to all contracts. Indeed, the name of the Act is rather misleading in this respect, as George Appleby has explained (*Contract Law*, 2001, p 283, London: Sweet & Maxwell):

'It only deals with exemption clauses and does not impose a fairness test. It is not restricted to contract law but deals with liability for negligence and other forms of liability, such as that of occupiers of business premises. Although it was created largely as a measure of consumer protection, the 1977 Act, in several important areas, also deals with some exemptions where both parties are in business. A more accurately descriptive title would therefore be the Void and Unreasonable Exemptions Act.'

Before discussing the main protective provisions of the Act, it is important to note which contracts and which clauses are excluded from the remit of the Act.

8.3.1.1 Business liability

Scope of Part I
Section 1

(3) In the case of both contract and tort, sections 2 to 7 apply (except where the contrary is stated in section 6(4)) only to business liability, that is liability for breach of obligations or duties arising –

(a) from things done or to be done by a person in the course of a business (whether his own business or another's); or

(b) from the occupation of premises used for business purposes of the occupier;

and references to liability are to be read accordingly but liability of an occupier of premises for breach of an obligation or duty towards a person obtaining access to the premises for recreational or educational purposes, being liability for loss or damage suffered by reason of the dangerous state of the premises, is not a business liability of the occupier unless granting that person such access for the purposes concerned falls within the business purposes of the occupier.

This section makes it clear that the protective provisions of the Act only apply to attempts to exclude or restrict business liability. A nonbusiness contractor is free to include exclusion clauses, without fear of their being declared ineffective under the Act. There is no comprehensive definition of business in the Act, although s 14 does provide the following:

Interpretation of Part I
Section 14
In this Part of this Act –

'business' includes a profession and the activities of any government department or local or public authority

It is unclear whether organisations such as charities or universities, fall within this definition of business. It is clear that such organisations often carry out business activities, but they may not be regarded as contracting 'in the course of business'.

There is one notable exception to the 'business' requirement of section 1(3). Under section 6(4) any contract for the sale of goods or hire purchase, even one not involving a business, must satisfy the requirement of the Act. This includes a private individual not acting in the course of business. We will consider this in greater detail below.

8.3.1.2 Exclusions

There are certain contracts, listed in Schedule 1, which are not within the scope of the main protective provisions of the UCTA 1977.

Schedule 1

1. Sections 2 to 4 of this Act do not extend to –

   (a) any contract of insurance (including a contract to pay an annuity on human life);

   (b) any contract so far as it relates to the creation or transfer of an interest in land, or to the termination of such an interest, whether by extinction, merger, surrender, forfeiture or otherwise;

   (c) any contract so far as it relates to the creation or transfer of a right or interest in any patent, trade mark, copyright [or design right], registered design, technical or commercial information or other intellectual property, or relates to the termination of any such right or interest;

   (d) any contract so far as it relates –

       (i) to the formation or dissolution of a company (which means any body corporate or unincorporated association and includes a partnership), or

       (ii) to its constitution or the rights or obligations of its corporators or members;

   (e) any contract so far as it relates to the creation or transfer of securities or of any right or interest in securities.

2. Section 1(1) extends to –

   (a) any contract of marine salvage or towage;

   (b) any charterparty of a ship or hovercraft; and

   (c) any contract for the carriage of goods by ship or hovercraft;

   but subject to this sections 2 to 4 and 7 do not extend to any such contract except in favour of a person dealing as consumer.

   . . .

4. Section 2(1) and (2) do not extend to a contract of employment, except in favour of the employee.

The most significant exclusions contained in Schedule 1 include:

- Contracts of insurance;
- Contracts relating to the creation, transfer or termination of an interest in land. This includes continuing covenants under a lease: *Electricity Supply Nominees v IAF Group* [1993] 1 WLR 1059;
- Contracts concerning the creation, transfer or termination of intellectual property rights.

It should also be noted that under paragraph 2, the UCTA only has limited application in relation to various types of shipping contract. Under paragraph 4, s 2(1) and (2) (which deal with the exclusion of liability for negligence) do not apply other than in favour of the employee (see *Bridgen v American Express* [2000] IRLR 94). Finally s 26 states that the Act does not apply to liability arising under an international supply contract.

8.3.1.3 Clauses covered

At the start of this chapter it was noted that it is often difficult to distinguish between clauses that limit liability and those that simply determine the obligations under the contract. Thus a party can exclude liability by simply defining the obligations arising under the contract restrictively. Section 13 of the UCTA seeks to bring such terms within the scope of the Act.

Varieties of exemption clause
Section 13

(1) To the extent that this Part of this Act prevents the exclusion or restriction of any liability it also prevents –

    (a) making the liability or its enforcement subject to restrictive or onerous conditions;

    (b) excluding or restricting any right or remedy in respect of the liability, or subjecting a person to any prejudice in consequence of his pursuing any such right or remedy;

    (c) excluding or restricting rules of evidence or procedure;

    and (to that extent) sections 2 and 5 to 7 also prevent excluding or restricting liability by reference to terms and notices which exclude or restrict the relevant obligation or duty.

(2) But an agreement in writing to submit present or future differences to arbitration is not to be treated under this Part of this Act as excluding or restricting any liability.

The function of s 13 is to extend the scope of ss 2 and 5–7 of the Act. It does not apply to ss 3 and 4. This is probably because s 3, which is concerned primarily with non-negligent contractual liability, is already wide enough to cover clauses that define contractual obligations (see s 3(2) (b)). Section 4 merely concerns one particular type of exclusion clause, the indemnity clause, so it is probably not necessary for s 13 to apply. The operation of s 13 can be seen in *Smith v Eric S Bush.*

Smith v Eric S Bush [1990] 1 AC 831

Facts: The plaintiff applied to a building society for a mortgage to assist her in purchasing a home. The building society instructed the defendants, a firm of surveyors, to prepare a report on the property as to its value and condition. The defendants' valuer, who carried out the inspection, noticed that two chimney breasts had been removed but he negligently failed to check whether the chimneys above had been left adequately supported. The chimneys were not adequately supported and one of them subsequently collapsed causing widespread damage to the rest of the house. The plaintiff claimed damages from the defendants for the loss sustained as a result of the negligent report. The defendants contended that they had excluded liability for negligence by a notice in the contract stating that neither the society nor the surveyor would accept responsibility for the surveyor's report.

Held: The House of Lords held that whilst the surveyor could seek to disclaim liability for negligence by an exclusion notice, such a notice was subject to s 2(2) UCTA. The court said that there could be no difference between a clause that sought to restrict the negligence obligation, and one which sought to exclude negligence liability

Lord Templeman:

'In these circumstances it is necessary to consider . . . whether the disclaimers of liability are notices which fall within the Unfair Contract Terms Act 1977. In *Harris v Wyre Forest Council* [1988] QB 835, the Court of Appeal (Kerr and Nourse LJJ and Caulfield J) accepted an argument that the Act of 1977 did not apply because the council by their express disclaimer refused to obtain a valuation save on terms that the valuer would not be under any obligation to Mr and Mrs Harris to take reasonable care or exercise reasonable skill. The council did not exclude liability for negligence but excluded negligence so that the valuer and the council never came under a duty of care to Mr and Mrs Harris and could not be guilty of negligence. This construction would not give effect to the manifest intention of the Act but would emasculate the Act. The construction would provide no control over standard form exclusion clauses which individual members of the public are obliged to accept. A party to a contract or a tortfeasor could opt out of the Act of 1977 by declining in the words of Nourse LJ, at p 845, to recognise 'their own answerability to the plaintiff . . .

Section 13(1) of the Act prevents the exclusion of any right or remedy and (to that extent) section 2 also prevents the exclusion of liability:

"by reference to . . . notices which exclude . . . the relevant obligation or duty."

. . . In my opinion both these provisions support the view that the Act of 1977 requires that all exclusion notices which would in common law provide a defence to an action for negligence must satisfy the requirement of reasonableness.

The answer to the second question involved in these appeals is that the disclaimer of liability made by the council on its own behalf in the *Harris* case and by the Abbey National on behalf of the appellants in the *Smith* case, constitute notices which fall within the Unfair Contract Terms Act 1977 and must satisfy the requirement of reasonableness.'

It is clear that, under s 13, the test for an exclusion clause is based upon the nature and substance of the clause, not merely upon its form. But this in itself creates problems. Once it is admitted that some obligation-defining clauses fall within the scope of the Act, it is difficult to know where to draw the line. All contract terms are obligation-defining to a certain extent. What test can be applied to make an appropriate 'form and substance' distinction for the purposes of s 13(1)? Professor MacDonald has suggested the following test as outlined below.

MacDonald, E, *Exemption Clauses and Unfair Terms*, 2nd ed, 2006, pp 105–108, Horsham: Tottel Publishing

Is there some distinction 'in nature' between exclusion clauses and those defining obligations which could provide a form and substance distinction for the purposes of the Act? It can be contended that what must be looked at is the creation, or origin, of the obligations and the relationship of the term (or notice) in question to that creation. In other words, the distinction which must be made is between the exclusion of an obligation purely because of the status of the words in question and its circumstantial displacement. If there is circumstantial displacement, the term or notice in question is 'in nature' part of the definition of the obligation. If the displacement is purely because of the status of the words, then the term or notice – the words in question – is, in nature, an exclusion of liability. In order to consider whether the displacement is 'circumstantial' or merely due to the status of the words as a term, the situation must be viewed absent the artificialities which the law has placed upon it. Artificialities can occur in the very drafting of terms (although less so since *Investors*) and in almost every form of incorporation, and can lead to a situation in which 'the relatively unsophisticated or unwary party will not realise what or how little has been promised' and such artificialities can be recognised even when the situation is viewed objectively, as will normally be required . . .

Section 10 of the UCTA 1977 prevents evasion of the provisions of the Act by means of a secondary contract.

Evasion by means of secondary contract
Section 10
A person is not bound by any contract term prejudicing or taking away rights of his which arise under, or in connection with the performance of, another contract, so far as those rights extend to the enforcement of another's liability which this Part of this Act prevents that other from excluding or restricting.

In *Tudor Grange Holdings Ltd v Citibank NA* [1992] Ch 53, it was held that s 10 did not apply to a compromise or waiver of an existing contractual dispute. Sir Nicholas Browne-Wilkinson VC said:

'The textbooks, to my mind correctly, identify at least one case which section 10 is designed to cover. Under contract 1, the supplier (S) contracts to supply a customer (C) with a product. Contract 1 contains no exemption clause. However, C enters into a servicing contract, contract 2, with another party (X). Under contract 2, C is precluded from exercising certain of his rights against S under contract 1. In such a case section 10 operates to preclude X from enforcing contract 2 against C so as to prevent C enforcing his rights against S under contract 1 . . . Although as a matter of language the words of the section are capable of referring to anyone other than C, in my judgment, read in context and having regard to the purpose both of the Act and of the section itself, the reference to "another" plainly means someone other than X, that is to say someone other than the party to the secondary contract. In my judgment section 10 does not apply where the parties to both contacts are the same.'

With respect, the suggestion that s 10 will not apply when the parties to both contracts are the same is rather doubtful. Such a rule would create a significant loophole in the Act and would surely be contrary to the clear intention of the original drafters. While *Tudor Grange* is good authority that s 10 will not be applied to a contract of settlement, it is doubtful whether the general rule expounded by Browne-Wilkinson VC will be followed in the future.

8.3.2 PROTECTIVE PROVISIONS

Having looked at the scope of the Act, we now need to consider the various forms of liability that it covers. The Act covers most contractual obligations, namely those arising from express or implied terms, in addition to negligence liability and liability for the sale and supply of goods. It is necessary for the claimant to identify the defendant's liability under one of the protective provisions of the Act.

8.3.2.1 Liability for negligence

Section 2 of the UCTA 1977 is concerned with clauses that purport to exclude business liability for 'negligence', which is defined in s 1(1) as follows:

Scope of Part I

Section 1

(1) For the purposes of this Part of this Act, 'negligence' means the breach –

    (a) of any obligation, arising from the express or implied terms of a contract, to take reasonable care or exercise reasonable skill in the performance of the contract;

    (b) of any common law duty to take reasonable care or exercise reasonable skill (but not any stricter duty);

    (c) of the common duty of care imposed by the Occupiers' Liability Act 1957 or the Occupiers' Liability Act (Northern Ireland) 1957.

(4) In relation to any breach of duty or obligation, it is immaterial for any purpose of this Part of this Act whether the breach was inadvertent or intentional, or whether liability for it arises directly or vicariously.

This section confirms that the Act encompasses both contractual negligence, that is, liability arising from breach of a contractual duty of care, and tortious negligence, that is, liability arising in the tort of negligence independent of any contract. Section 1(1)(c) recognises liability arising under the statutory duty of care imposed on occupiers towards lawful visitors.

Subsection (4) expands the definition of negligence by confirming that it is immaterial whether the breach was inadvertent or intentional, or whether liability for it arose directly or vicariously. The definition does not include strict liability, however. Therefore, the section cannot be used to regulate clauses that purport to exclude or restrict strict liability.

Negligence liability
Section 2

(1)   A person cannot by reference to any contract term or to a notice given to persons generally or to particular persons exclude or restrict his liability for death or personal injury resulting from negligence.

(2)   In the case of other loss or damage, a person cannot so exclude or restrict his liability for negligence except in so far as the term or notice satisfies the requirement of reasonableness.

(3)   Where a contract term or notice purports to exclude or restrict liability for negligence a person's agreement to or awareness of it is not of itself to be taken as indicating his voluntary acceptance of any risk.

The level of control imposed by s 2 depends on the consequences of the negligent act. Any attempt to exclude liability for death or personal injury resulting from negligence will be totally ineffective (s 2(1)). In respect of other types of loss, a term that purports to exclude liability for negligence will be effective to the extent that it satisfies the 'requirement of reasonableness' (s 2(2)). The test of reasonableness that is to be applied in this context is contained in s 11 and Schedule 2 of the Act. These provisions will be considered in greater detail below. The purpose of s 2(3) is to prevent the defendant from relying on an exclusion clause to establish the defence of *volenti non fit injuria*. A defendant is not permitted to point to a term or notice that the claimant is aware of in order to establish that the claimant has consented to the risk of suffering injury. In practice, this makes it extremely difficult to establish the defence of *volenti non fit injuria*. Finally, subsection (1) makes it clear that the section only applies to clauses that 'exclude or restrict' liability. This means that the section does not cover clauses that purport to transfer liability from one party to another.

Thompson v T Lohan (Plant Hire) [1987] 1 WLR 649

Facts: The defendants, Lohan, hired an excavator with a driver to a third party called Hurdiss for use in its quarry. Clause 8 of the Contractors Plant Association conditions placed liability for the acts of the driver onto the hirer. The driver drove negligently and killed Mr Thompson. Mrs Thompson, as her husband's personal representative brought a claim against Lohan and won damages and costs. Lohan then sought an indemnity from Hurdiss pursuant to clause 8. Hurdiss denied liability on the basis that clause 8 was ineffective under s 2(1) of the UCTA 1977.

Held: The Court of Appeal held that s 2(1) had no application to clause 8 because the clause did not purport to restrict or limit liability.

Fox LJ:

'The plaintiff is not prejudiced in any way by the operation sought to be established of clause 8. All that has happened is that Lohan and the third party have agreed between themselves who is to bear the consequences of Mr Hill's negligent acts. I can see nothing in section 2(1) of the Act of 1977 to prevent that. In my opinion, section 2(1) is concerned with protecting the victim of negligence and, of course, those who claim under him. It is not concerned with arrangements made by the wrongdoer with other persons as to the sharing or bearing of the burden of compensating the victim. In such a case it seems to me there is no exclusion or restriction of the liability at all. The liability has been established by Hodgson J. It is not in dispute and is now unalterable. The circumstance that the defendants have between themselves chosen to bear the liability in a particular way does not affect that liability; it does not exclude it, and it does not restrict it. The liability to the plaintiff is the only relevant liability in the case, as it seems to me, and that liability is still in existence and will continue until discharge by payment to the plaintiff. Nothing is excluded in relation to the liability, and the liability is not restricted in any way whatever. The liability of Lohan to the plaintiff remains intact. The liability of Hamstead to Phillips was sought to be excluded.

In those circumstances it seems to me that, looking at the language of section 2(1), this case does not fall within its prohibition.'

For the Court of Appeal it was crucial that clause 8 did not prevent the injured party from making a claim (contrast *Phillips Products Ltd v Hyland* [1987] 1 WLR 659); it merely transferred liability to a third party. This approach is consistent with the claimant-focused emphasis of the Act. The UCTA 1977 was designed to provide 'protection' to claimants, not to inflict 'punishment' on defendants. Therefore, a clause is not caught by the Act so long as the injured party is not prevented from making a claim.

8.3.2.2 Liability in contract

Section 3 covers liability arising in contract.

Liability arising in contract
Section 3

(1) This section applies as between contracting parties where one of them deals as consumer or on the other's written standard terms of business.

(2) As against that party, the other cannot by reference to any contract term –

   (a) when himself in breach of contract, exclude or restrict any liability of his in respect of the breach; or

   (b) claim to be entitled –

   (i) to render a contractual performance substantially different from that which was reasonably expected of him, or

   (ii) in respect of the whole or any part of his contractual obligation, to render no performance at all,

   except in so far as (in any of the cases mentioned above in this subsection) the contract term satisfies the requirement of reasonableness.

The section is directed at situations where there is an inequality of bargaining power. In such situations it is probable that the claimant had no real choice as to whether or not to accept the exclusion clause. Two types of contract are identified in which it is assumed that there is an inequality of bargaining power: (1) contracts where the claimant 'deals as a consumer'; and (2) contracts concluded on the other party's 'written standard terms of business'.

8.3.2.2.1 Deals as a consumer

The definition of 'deals as a consumer' is to be found in s 12.

'Dealing as consumer'
s 12

(1) A party to a contract 'deals as consumer' in relation to another party if –

   (a) he neither makes the contract in the course of a business nor holds himself out as doing so; and

   (b) the other party does make the contract in the course of a business; and

   (c) in the case of a contract governed by the law of sale of goods or hire-purchase, or by section 7 of this Act, the goods passing under or in pursuance of the contract are of a type ordinarily supplied for private use or consumption.

(1A) But if the first party mentioned in subsection (1) is an individual paragraph (c) of that subsection must be ignored.

   . . .

(3) Subject to this, it is for those claiming that a party does not deal as consumer to show that he does not.

To establish that he deals as a consumer the claimant must satisfy two requirements. First, he must show that he neither made the contract in the course of business nor held himself out as doing so. Second, he must show that the other party to the contract did make the contract in the course of a business. Guidance on the meaning of the phrase 'in the course of a business' has been given by the Court of Appeal in *R & B Customs Brokers v United Dominions Trust Ltd*.

R & B Customs Brokers v United Dominions Trust Ltd [1988] 1 WLR 321

Facts: The plaintiff company purchased a Colt Shogun car from the defendant financial company. It was bought for the personal and business use of one of the plaintiff's directors. The contract excluded liability for breach of any implied terms as to the condition or quality of the car or as to its fitness for any particular purpose. The plaintiff discovered that the roof of the car leaked and after the dealer failed to rectify the problem the plaintiff rejected the car and claimed damages for breach of contract.

Held: The Court of Appeal held that the exclusion clause was prohibited by s 6(2) of the UCTA 1977. The car was not bought 'in the course of a business,' because the plaintiff's business was not that of buying and selling cars.

Dillon LJ:

'[T]here are some transactions which are clearly integral parts of the businesses concerned, and these should be held to have been carried out in the course of those businesses; this would cover, apart from much else, the instance of a one-off adventure in the nature of trade, where the transaction itself would constitute a trade or business. There are other transactions, however, such as the purchase of the car in the present case, which are at highest only incidental to the carrying on of the relevant business; here a degree of regularity is required before it can be said that they are an integral part of the business carried on, and so entered into in the course of that business.

Applying the test thus indicated to the facts of the present case, I have no doubt that the requisite degree of regularity is not made out on the facts. Mr Bell's evidence that the car was the second or third vehicle acquired on credit terms was in my judgment and in the context of this case not enough. Accordingly, I agree with the judge that, in entering into the conditional sale agreement with the defendants, the company was "dealing as consumer." '

The Court of Appeal held that a sale would be deemed to be made 'in the course of business' if it was either: (a) an integral part of the business; or (b) incidental to the business but of a type regularly carried out by the buyer. On the facts the purchase was only incidental to the business of the company and there was insufficient regularity (it was only the second or third vehicle acquired by the plaintiffs) for it to be deemed a purchase in the course of the plaintiff's business. Thus the plaintiff was deemed to 'deal as a consumer' and the exclusion clause was prohibited by s 6(2) of the UCTA 1977 (which deals with liability for the sale of goods – see below).

Some doubt was cast over the decision in *R & B Customs* by the Court of Appeal in *Stevenson v Rogers* [1999] QB 1028. The case concerned the question of whether a sale was 'in the course of business' for the purpose of s 14(2) of the Sale of Goods Act 1979. The court held that the ratio of the earlier case was limited to its context, namely the interpretation of s 12 of the UCTA 1977, and not necessarily applicable elsewhere. Potter LJ insisted that a broader interpretation should be given to the phrase under s 14(2):

> 'As to the proper construction of section 14(2), given the clear view which I have formed, I do not consider it right to displace that construction simply to achieve harmony with a decision upon the meaning of section 12 of the Act of 1977. Section 14(2) as amended by the Act of 1973 was itself a piece of consumer protection intended to afford wider protection to a buyer than that provided in the Act of 1893. Indeed, there is a sense in which the decision in the *R &B Customs* case can be said to be in harmony with that intention. It dealt with the position of consumer *buyers* and the effect of adopting the construction . . . in relation to section 12(1)(a) of the Act of 1977 was to further such buyers' protection. In the context of its statutory history, section 14(2), as amended by the Act of 1973 and re-enacted in the Act of 1979, is the primary provision in the overall scheme of increased protection for buyers which the Act of 1973 initiated. To apply the reasoning in the *R &B Customs* case [1988] 1 WLR 321 in the interests only of consistency, thereby under-mining the wide protection for buyers which section 14(2) was intended to introduce, would in my view be an unacceptable example of the tail wagging the dog.'

Despite the Court of Appeal's refusal to follow *R & B Customs* in the context of s 14(2) of the Sale of Goods Act 1979, the Court of Appeal has held itself to be bound by the decision in respect of the meaning of the 1977 Act (*Feldaroll Foundry Plc v Hermes Leasing (London) Ltd* [2004] EWCA Civ 747). It remains the case, therefore, that pending a decision to the contrary by the House of Lords, the interpretation of 'in the course of business' given by the Court of Appeal in *R & B Customs* remains the correct approach under the UCTA 1977.

Section 12(1)(c) of the Act states that where the contract is concerned with the supply of goods, a business will only be treated as dealing as a consumer where the goods are 'of a type ordinarily supplied for private use or consumption'. This represents a significant limitation on the definition of 'dealing as a consumer' and will mean that a large number of business purchases will not be considered as 'consumer contracts', even though the business does not generally deal in the goods concerned. The restriction contained in subsection 12(1)(c) only applies to business buyers; it does not apply where the buyer is an individual (s 12 (1A)). Finally, s 12(3) states that the burden of proof is on the party claiming that a person is not dealing as a consumer.

8.3.2.2.2 Written standard terms of business

Section 3(1) also states that the section applies where one of the parties deals on the other party's 'written standard terms of business'. This category is unlikely to be used by the private individual because in most situations s/he will deal 'as a consumer', and will therefore be within the first category covered by s 3. Instead the category is likely to be used by commercial parties who wish to bring their contract within the regulatory scope of the Act.

The meaning of 'written standard terms of business' is not given in the Act. It is clear, however, that the individual negotiation of some of the terms will not prevent them from being 'standard'. In *St Albans City and District Council v International Computers Ltd* [1996] 4 All ER 481, the Court of Appeal held that a contract to purchase computer software was concluded on the defendant's standard terms of business even though the terms had been negotiated prior to agreement. Nourse LJ said:

'[The judge at first instance] dealt with this question as one of fact, finding that the defendant's general conditions remained effectively untouched in the negotiations and that the plaintiffs accordingly dealt on the defendant's written standard terms for the purposes of s 3(1); see p 706. I respectfully agree with him. The consequence of that finding is that the defendant cannot rely on clause 9(c) except in so far as it satisfies the requirement of reasonableness.'

For the terms to be 'standard' it is not necessary that they are *always* used by the party wishing to rely on them, so long as they are *habitually* used. In *Chester Grosvenor Hotel Company Ltd v Alfred McAlpine Management Ltd* (1991) 56 Build LR 115, Judge Stannard said:

'I accept that where a party invariably contracts in the same written terms without material variation, those terms will become its "standard form contract" or "written standard terms of business". However, it does not follow that because terms are not employed invariably, or without material variation, they cannot be standard terms. If this were not so the statute would be emasculated, since it could be excluded by showing that, although the same terms had been employed without modification on a multitude of occasions, and were employed on the occasion in question, previously on one or more isolated occasions they had been modified or not employed at all. In my judgment the question is one of fact and degree. What are alleged to be standard terms may be used so infrequently in comparison with other terms that they cannot realistically be regarded as standard, or on any particular occasion may be so added to or mutilated that they must be regarded as having lost their essential identity. What is required for terms to be standard is that they should be regarded by the party which advances them as its standard terms and that it should habitually contract in those terms. If it contracts also in other terms, it must be determined in any given case, and as a matter of fact, whether this has occurred so frequently that the terms in question cannot be regarded as standard, and if on any occasion a party has substantially modified its prepared terms, it is a question of fact whether those terms have been so altered that they must be regarded as not having been employed on that occasion.'

If the terms used are those of a trade association, which are simply adopted by the mutual consent of the parties, then they can still be treated as standard terms if the claimant can show that the defendant habitually used such terms in its contracts (see *British Fermentation Products v Compair Reavell Ltd* [1999] BLR 352).

8.3.2.2.3 The effect of section 3
The effect of s 3 is found is sub-s 2:

Liability arising in contract
Section 3

(2) As against that party, the other cannot by reference to any contract term –

    (a) when himself in breach of contract, exclude or restrict any liability of his in respect of the breach; or

    (b) claim to be entitled –

        (i) to render a contractual performance substantially different from that which was reasonably expected of him, or

        (ii) in respect of the whole or any part of his contractual obligation, to render no performance at all,

except in so far as (in any of the cases mentioned above in this subsection) the contract term satisfies the requirement of reasonableness.

Section 3(2)(a) confirms that any attempt to exclude or restrict liability by a non-consumer, or a party putting forward their own standard terms, will be subject to the requirement of reasonableness. Section 3(2)(b) extends this to any term that seeks to exclude liability indirectly by narrowly defining a party's obligations under the contract. It would apply, for example, if a travel agent agrees to provide a holiday for a consumer on a certain cruise ship, but nevertheless reserves the right, in certain circumstances, to substitute the cruise ship for another, or to cancel the holiday in whole or in part. Such clauses would be permissible, but only to the extent that they satisfy the requirement of reasonableness.

Section 3(2)(b) enables the courts to distinguish between clauses that are a legitimate attempt to define the parties' obligations and those that are, in reality, attempts to evade liability. The scope of s 3(2)(b) was considered by the Court of Appeal in *Timeload Ltd v British Telecommunications plc.*

Timeload Ltd v British Telecommunications plc [1995] EMLR 459

Facts: The plaintiff set up a free telephone inquiry service for people needing particular professional or commercial services. BT sought to disconnect the plaintiff's freephone line and sought to rely on clause 18 of the contract which provided that at any time the contract could be terminated by BT on one month's notice. The plaintiff applied for an interlocutory injunction to restrain BT from terminating the contract. The reason why the plaintiff sought an injunction was that they wished to keep their telephone number (which was included on their publicity) and termination of the contract would have led to the number being withdrawn. The plaintiff argued that by virtue of s 3(2) of the UCTA 1977, BT was not entitled to rely on clause 18 to deliver a performance substantially different from that reasonably expected of it.

Held: The Court of Appeal granted an interlocutory injunction. Although at this stage it was not necessary to finally resolve the issue.

Sir Thomas Bingham MR:
'Mr Hobbs [counsel for BT] says that section 3(2)(a) is directed to an exemption clause of the classic type exonerating a contractual party in default from the ordinary consequences of the default. I agree, and it seems clear that that subsection has no application here.

The argument accordingly turns on section 3(2)(b) and that I find more difficult. Mr Hobbs submits that the subsection cannot apply where, as here, the clause under consideration defines the service to be provided and does not purport to permit substandard or partial performance. He says that the customer cannot reasonably expect that which the contract does not purport to offer, namely enjoyment of telephone service under a given number for an indefinite period. That may indeed be so, but I find the construction and ambit of this subsection by no means clear. If a customer reasonably expects a service to continue until BT has substantial reason to terminate it, it seems to me at least arguable that a clause purporting to authorise BT to terminate without reason purports to permit partial or different performance from that which the customer expected.'

Sir Thomas Bingham MR took a very broad approach to what constitutes 'performance' of the contract. A more cautious approach was taken by the Court of Appeal in *Paragon Finance v Staunton & Another.*

Paragon Finance plc v Staunton & Another [2002] 1 WLR 685

Facts: The claimant made loans to the defendants under a number of mortgage agreements. The agreements contained variable interest clauses which gave the claimant freedom to vary the interest payable at will. The defendant sought to argue that these clauses fell within s 3(2)(b) of the UCTA 1977.

Held: The Court of Appeal held that the fixing of interest rates under the variable interest clauses was not 'contractual performance' within the meaning of s 3(2)(b) since there was no relevant obligation on the claimant to perform a service and therefore nothing that could qualify as 'contractual performance'.

Dyson LJ:

'It is submitted on behalf of the defendants that they were reasonably entitled to expect that, in performing their side of the bargain, the claimant would not apply rates which were substantially out of line with rates applied by comparable lenders to borrowers in comparable situations to the defendants. It is contended that the setting of interest rates is "contractual performance" within the meaning of section 3(2)(b)(i) of the 1977 Act, and that the claimant set interest rates that defeated that expectation.

The first question is whether the fixing of rates of interest under a discretion given by the contract was "contractual performance" within the meaning of section 3(2)(b)(i). [Counsel for the defendants] submits that it is. He relies on two authorities. The first is *Timeload Ltd v British Telecommunications plc* [1995] EMLR 459 . . . It was held by the Court of Appeal that it was at least arguable that a clause purporting to authorise BT to terminate without reason purported to permit partial or different performance from that which the plaintiff was entitled to expect, and that section 3(2) of the 1977 Act applied. But the licence agreement imposed clear performance obligations on BT. Thus, clause 1.1 obliged BT to provide the various services there set out. In these circumstances, it is not difficult to see why the court thought that it was at least arguable that a clause authorising termination of the obligation to provide those services for no good reason purported to permit a contractual performance different from that which the customer might reasonably expect.

The second authority is *Zockoll Group Ltd v Mercury Communications Ltd (No 2)* [1999] EMLR 385. This was another telecommunications case. The plaintiff planned to set up a network of franchisees to provide goods and services to the public in response to telephone inquiries. It entered into a contract with Mercury under which it obtained a number of telephone numbers. Mercury wished to withdraw one number from the plaintiff and asserted that it was entitled to do so at its sole discretion. The plaintiff brought proceedings and relied on section 3(2)(b)(i) of the 1977 Act. The court held that the withdrawal of the disputed number did not render the contractual performance substantially different from what was expected. [Counsel for the defendants] points out that it is implicit in the decision of the court that it was accepted that the withdrawal of the disputed number was *capable of being* contractual performance substantially different from that which it was reasonable to expect.

In my judgment, neither of these authorities assists [counsel for the defendants'] submission. In both cases, the defendant telecommunications provider was contractually bound to provide a service. The question was whether the withdrawal of the service in the particular circumstances of the case was such as to render the contract performance (ie the provision of that service) substantially different from that which it was reasonable for the other contracting party to expect. The present cases are quite different. Here, there is no relevant obligation on the claimant, and therefore nothing that can qualify as "contractual performance" for the purposes of section 3(2)(b)(i). Even if that is wrong, by fixing the rate of interest at a particular level the claimant is not altering the performance of any obligation assumed by it under the contract. Rather, it is altering the performance required of the defendants.

There appears to be no authority in which the application of section 3(2)(b)(i) to a situation similar to that which exists in this case has been considered. The editors of *Chitty on Contracts*, 28th edn (1999) offer this view, at para 14–071:

"Nevertheless it seems unlikely that a contract term entitling one party to terminate the contract in the event of a material breach by the other (eg failure to pay by the due date) would fall within paragraph (b), or, if it did so, would be adjudged not to satisfy the requirement of reasonableness. Nor, it is submitted, would that provision extend to a contract term which entitled one party, not to alter the performance expected of himself, but to alter the performance required of the other party (eg a term by which a seller of goods is entitled to increase the price payable by the buyer to the price ruling at the date of delivery, or a term by which a person advancing a loan is entitled to vary the interest payable by the borrower on the loan)."

In my judgment, this passage accurately states the law. The contract term must be one which has an effect (indeed a substantial effect) on the contractual performance reasonably expected of the party who relies on the term. The key word is "performance".'

The Court of Appeal distinguished *Timeload* on the basis that it involved a positive obligation to provide something, whereas the clause in *Paragon Finance* enabled the claimant to alter the performance required by the defendant. This distinction has not been maintained, however, and in a recent decision of an Employment Appeal Tribunal it was held that a clause imposing a positive obligation fell outside the scope of s 3(2)(b). *Peninsula Business Services Ltd v Sweeney* [2004] IRLR 49 concerned a term in an employment contract, which stated that 'an employee has no claim whatsoever on any commission payments that would otherwise have been generated and paid, if they are not in employment on the date when they would normally have been paid'. Sweeney resigned his post with the defendants and forfeited substantial commission payments that he otherwise would have been entitled to receive. He argued that the term amounted to an attempt by the defendants to render a performance substantially different from that which was reasonably expected of them. The Employment Appeal Tribunal rejected this argument. Rimer J said:

> 'All that the paying party has done is to operate the contract in accordance with the terms to which the receiving party agreed at the outset. In this case, [the term] simply defined the limits of Mr Sweeney's rights, and there is no basis on which he could ever have reasonably expected any rights greater than those that section B gave him. This is not a case in which Peninsula has endeavoured to cut down or restrict his rights in any way.'

This reasoning is wholly unsatisfactory because the majority of terms that fall under s 3(2)(b) are likely to define the limits of the party's rights. Indeed, this is precisely what the clause in *Timeload* did. The real point of distinction between this case and *Timeload* is that the tribunal did not believe that Sweeney could have reasonably expected to receive greater rights than those conferred under the contract. But how are we to identify the situations in which the party has reasonable expectations other than those created by the contract? On the one hand, it is arguable that the parties' expectations are only ever *reasonable* to the extent that they correspond to the enforceable rights contained in the contract. On the other, it is clear that reasonable expectation must extend beyond those contained in the contract, otherwise s 3(2)(b) would be rendered meaningless. Until the source of these extra-contractual expectations is identified there will continue to be confusion and uncertainty as to the scope of s 3(2)(b).

8.3.2.3 Liability for indemnities

Unreasonable indemnity clauses
Section 4

(1) A person dealing as consumer cannot by reference to any contract term be made to indemnify another person (whether a party to the contract or not) in respect of liability that may be incurred by the other for negligence or breach of contract, except in so far as the contract term satisfies the requirement of reasonableness.

(2) This section applies whether the liability in question –

   (a) is directly that of the person to be indemnified or is incurred by him vicariously;

   (b) is to the person dealing as consumer or to someone else.

This section deals with attempts to impose liability on a consumer by means of an indemnity clause. An indemnity clause is a clause by which one party agrees to pay a sum of money to another party in respect of any liability that the other party might incur to third parties. For example, if B agrees to build an extension to A's house, B might ask A for an indemnity against any liability he may incur towards C,

A's neighbour, in respect of the work done. Assuming that A is a consumer, s 4 will operate and subject the clause to the requirement of reasonableness. If A were a business, however, s 4 would not operate and A would have to argue that the clause fell within the scope of s 2 of the Act (see *Phillips Products Ltd v Hyland* [1987] 1 WLR 659). As we have seen, this can be extremely difficult because of the distinction drawn under s 2 between clauses that exclude liability and those that transfer liability (see *Thompson v T Lohan (Hire) Ltd* [1987] 1 WLR 649).

8.3.2.4 Liability arising from guarantees of consumer goods

'Guarantee' of consumer goods
Section 5

(1) In the case of goods of a type ordinarily supplied for private use or consumption, where loss or damage –

   (a) arises from the goods proving defective while in consumer use; and

   (b) results from the negligence of a person concerned in the manufacture or distribution of the goods,

liability for the loss or damage cannot be excluded or restricted by reference to any contract term or notice contained in or operating by reference to a guarantee of the goods.

(2) For these purposes –

   (a) goods are to be regarded as 'in consumer use' when a person is using them, or has them in his possession for use, otherwise than exclusively for the purposes of a business; and

   (b) anything in writing is a guarantee if it contains or purports to contain some promise or assurance (however worded or presented) that defects will be made good by complete or partial replacement, or by repair, monetary compensation or otherwise.

(3) This section does not apply as between the parties to a contract under or in pursuance of which possession or ownership of the goods passed.

Section 5 deals with guarantees given by the manufacturers of consumer goods. Such guarantees are common and are sometimes used to limit the consumer's rights by giving, for example, a right to a refund or a replacement, but denying any other liability. Section 5(1) provides that such limitations are ineffective where the goods have proved defective while in 'consumer use', and this results from the negligence of the manufacturer or distributor. The section does not cover guarantees given by a seller or hirer of goods. Such terms are covered by ss 6 and 7, which are discussed below.

8.3.2.5 Liability arising from contracts for the supply of goods

Sale and hire-purchase

Section 6

(1) Liability for breach of the obligations arising from –

   (a) section 12 of the Sale of Goods Act 1979 (seller's implied undertakings as to title, etc.);

   (b) section 8 of the Supply of Goods (Implied Terms) Act 1973 (the corresponding thing in relation to hire-purchase),

cannot be excluded or restricted by reference to any contract term.

(2) As against a person dealing as consumer, liability for breach of the obligations arising from –

   (a) section 13, 14 or 15 of the 1979 Act (seller's implied undertakings as to conformity of goods with description or sample, or as to their quality or fitness for a particular purpose);

   (b) section 9, 10 or 11 of the 1973 Act (the corresponding things in relation to hire-purchase),

cannot be excluded or restricted by reference to any contract term.

(3) As against a person dealing otherwise than as consumer, the liability specified in sub-section (2) above can be excluded or restricted by reference to a contract term, but only in so far as the term satisfies the requirement of reasonableness.

(4) The liabilities referred to in this section are not only the business liabilities defined by section 1(3), but include those arising under any contract of sale of goods or hire-purchase agreement.

Section 6 deals with exclusion clauses that purport to exclude or limit liability for breach of implied terms arising in contracts for the sale of goods and contracts of hire purchase. The effect of the section will depend upon whether the contract is a 'consumer sale' (on the meaning of 'consumer sale' see discussion of s 12 above), in which case attempts to exclude terms implied by ss 13–15 of the Sale of Goods Act 1979 or ss 9–11 of the Supply of Goods (Implied Terms) Act 1973, will be ineffective; or a 'non-consumer sale', in which case the clause will be subject to the requirement of reasonableness. Section 6(1) states that liability arising under s 12 of the Sale of Goods Act 1979 and s 8 of the Supply of Goods (Implied Terms) Act 1973, which both concern the seller's implied undertaking as to title, cannot be excluded in any contract, whether a consumer or non-consumer sale. Section 6(4) extends the scope of the section to include attempts to exclude or limit nonbusiness liability.

Miscellaneous contracts under which goods pass

Section 7

(1) Where the possession or ownership of goods passes under or in pursuance of a contract not governed by the law of sale of goods or hire-purchase, subsections (2) to (4) below apply as regards the effect (if any) to be given to contract terms excluding or restricting liability for breach of obligation arising by implication of law from the nature of the contract.

(2) As against a person dealing as consumer, liability in respect of the goods' correspondence with description or sample, or their quality or fitness for any particular purpose, cannot be excluded or restricted by reference to any such term.

(3) As against a person dealing otherwise than as consumer, that liability can be excluded or restricted by reference to such a term, but only in so far as the term satisfies the requirement of reasonableness.

(3A) Liability for breach of the obligations arising under section 2 of the Supply of Goods and Services Act 1982 (implied terms about title etc. in certain contracts for the transfer of the property in goods) cannot be excluded or restricted by reference to any such term.

(4) Liability in respect of –

(a) the right to transfer ownership of the goods, or give possession; or

(b) the assurance of quiet possession to a person taking goods in pursuance of the contract,

cannot (in a case to which subsection (3A) above does not apply) be excluded or restricted by reference to any such term except in so far as the term satisfies the requirement of reasonableness.

Section 7 performs the same function as s 6, but covers contracts for the hire of goods and contracts for the supply of work and materials (such as a building contract). Again, a distinction is drawn between consumer contracts where any attempt to exclude liability for breach of an implied term as to description, quality, fitness for purpose, or compliance with sample is ineffective, and nonconsumer contracts where such exclusion clauses are subject to the requirement of reasonableness. Section 7(3A) operates in the same way as s 6(1) to prevent exclusions of liability for breach of an implied term as to title arising under s 2(1) of the Supply of Goods and Services Act 1982.

8.3.2.6 Liability arising from misrepresentation

Section 8 of the Unfair Contract Terms Act 1977 amended s 3 of the Misrepresentation Act 1967. This amendment requires clauses purporting to exclude or limit liability for a misrepresentation to satisfy the requirement of reasonableness. The effect of this change is dealt with in Chapter 9.

8.3.3 THE REQUIREMENT OF REASONABLENESS

The test for reasonableness is contained in s 11 of the UCTA 1977.

The 'reasonableness' test
Section 11

(1) In relation to a contract term, the requirement of reasonableness for the purposes of this Part of this Act, section 3 of the Misrepresentation Act 1967 and section 3 of the Misrepresentation Act (Northern Ireland) 1967 is that the term shall have been a fair and reasonable one to be included having regard to the circumstances which were, or ought reasonably to have been, known to or in the contemplation of the parties when the contract was made.

(2) In determining for the purposes of section 6 or 7 above whether a contract term satisfies the requirement of reasonableness, regard shall be had in particular to the matters specified in Schedule 2 to this Act; but this subsection does not prevent the court or arbitrator from holding, in accordance with any rule of law, that a term which purports to exclude or restrict any relevant liability is not a term of the contract.

(3) In relation to a notice (not being a notice having contractual effect), the requirement of reasonableness under this Act is that it should be fair and reasonable to allow reliance on it, having regard to all the circumstances obtaining when the liability arose or (but for the notice) would have arisen.

(4) Where by reference to a contract term or notice a person seeks to restrict liability to a specified sum of money, and the question arises (under this or any other Act) whether the term or notice satisfies the requirement of reasonableness, regard shall be had in particular (but without prejudice to subsection (2) above in the case of contract terms) to –

   (a) the resources which he could expect to be available to him for the purpose of meeting the liability should it arise; and

   (b) how far it was open to him to cover himself by insurance.

(5) It is for those claiming that a contract term or notice satisfies the requirement of reasonableness to show that it does.

Section 11(1) makes it clear that the point at which the reasonableness of the term is to be assessed is the date on which the contract was made, and the court will assess the term itself, not any particular application of it. This means that, when considering the reasonableness of the term, the court should take no account of subsequent events. In particular, the court should not consider the actual breach that has occurred and for which the term is claimed to provide exclusion or limitation of liability. This can have the peculiar result of a court finding that the defendant was reasonable to exclude liability for the particular breach, but that the term used was ineffective, due to it having been drafted in unreasonably broad terms. Such an outcome is entirely consistent with the judicial policy of discouraging unnecessarily wide clauses. It is also consistent with the courts refusal to sever or rewrite unreasonably broad exclusion clauses.

Stewart Gill Ltd v Horatio Myer & Co Ltd [1992] QB 600

Facts: The plaintiffs agreed to supply, install and test an overhead conveyor system at the defendants' premises. Clause 12.4 of the contract stated: 'The customer shall not be entitled to withhold payment of any amount due to the company under the contract by reason of any payment credit set off counterclaim allegation of incorrect or defective goods or for any other reason whatsoever which the customer may allege excuses him from performing his obligations hereunder'. The defendants refused to pay alleging that the plaintiffs had breached the contract. The plaintiffs brought a claim for the outstanding payments.

Held: The Court of Appeal held that clause 12.4 was unreasonable because it could be used to prevent the defendant from setting off a payment already made and would extend to a defence based on fraud.

Stuart-Smith LJ:

'In my judgment it is the term as a whole that has to be reasonable and not merely some part of it. Throughout the Act the expression used is "by reference to any contract term", the contract "term satisfies the requirement of reasonableness": see sections 3 and 7 and in section 11(1) the reasonableness test is laid down as:

> "In relation to a contract term, the requirement of reasonableness . . . is that the term shall have been a fair and reasonable one to be included having regard to the circumstances which were, or ought reasonably to have been, known to or in the contemplation of the parties when the contract was made."

Although the question of reasonableness is primarily one for the court when the contract term is challenged, it seems to me that the parties must also be in a position to judge this at the time the contract is made. If this is so, I find it difficult to see how such an appreciation can be made if the customer has to guess whether some, and if so which, part of the term will alone be relied upon. Section 11(2) of the Act requires the court which is determining the question of reasonableness for the purpose of sections 6 and 7 to have regard in particular to the matters specified in Schedule 2. Although Schedule 2 does not apply in the present case, the considerations there set out are usually regarded as being of general application to the question of reasonableness. Two paragraphs of these guidelines would in my judgment be unworkable unless the whole term is being considered.

Paragraph (b) provides:

> "whether the customer received an inducement to agree to the term, or in accepting it had an opportunity of entering into a similar contract with other persons, but without having to accept a similar term; . . ."

If there was an inducement, it would I think be quite impossible in most cases to say that it related only to the words which the party seeking to establish reasonableness relies upon as opposed to those he wishes to delete. It is equally unreal to suppose that the customer could divine which part the vendor will ultimately seek to rely upon so as to decide whether other persons are willing to contract without the term.

Paragraph (c) provides:

"whether the customer knew or ought reasonably to have known of the existence and extent of the term (having regard, among other things, to any custom of the trade and any previous course of dealing between the parties); . . ."

In my judgment the customer would be most unlikely ever to know the extent of the term if the vendor is entitled, when it is questioned as to reasonableness, to rely on only part of it.

These examples in my judgment support the construction of the word term as being the whole term or clause as drafted, and not merely that part of it which may eventually be taken to be relevant to the case in point.

Nor does it appear to me to be consistent with the policy and purpose of the Act to permit a contract or to impose a contractual term, which taken as a whole is completely unreasonable to put a blue pencil through the most offensive parts and say that what is left is reasonable and sufficient to exclude or restrict his liability in a manner relied upon.'

The Court of Appeal was unwilling to separate out the 'unreasonable' parts of the exclusion clause from the 'reasonable' parts. It is of course open to the drafters of the contract to do this themselves. Instead of drafting the exclusion of liability as a single clause they might draft it as a number of separate subclauses. If they take this approach, the court will apply the requirement of reasonableness to each subclause individually and will not allow the unreasonableness of one clause to effect the enforceability of the others (*Watford Electronics v Sanderson CFL Ltd* [2001] 1 All ER Comm 696).

Section 11(3) states that the test of reasonableness for notices differs from that applicable to contract terms. The test is whether it is 'fair and reasonable' to rely on the notice and the court can have regard to all the circumstances obtaining when the liability arose or (but for the notice) would have arisen.

Section 11(4) directs the court to take into account two matters when considering the reasonableness of clauses that purport to limit liability to a specific sum of money, rather than excluding it altogether. This recognises that it may be entirely reasonable for a contracting party to limit their liability, particularly when they are underresourced or engaging in a high-risk activity.

Finally s 11(5) places the burden of proof in relation to reasonableness on the party seeking to rely on the clause.

8.3.3.1 Guidelines in Schedule 2

As Stuart Smith LJ noted in *Stewart Gill*, s 11(2) of the Act permits the courts to take into account the matters listed in Schedule 2 when considering the requirement of reasonableness under ss 6 and 7.

'Guidelines' for application of reasonableness test
Schedule 2
The matters to which regard is to be had in particular for the purposes of sections 6(3), 7(3) and (4), 20 and 21 are any of the following which appear to be relevant –

(a) the strength of the bargaining positions of the parties relative to each other, taking into account (among other things) alternative means by which the customer's requirements could have been met;

(b) whether the customer received an inducement to agree to the term, or in accepting it had an opportunity of entering into a similar contract with other persons, but without having to accept a similar term;

(c) whether the customer knew or ought reasonably to have known of the existence and extent of the term (having regard, among other things, to any custom of the trade and any previous course of dealing between the parties);

(d) where the term excludes or restricts any relevant liability if some condition is not complied with, whether it was reasonable at the time of the contract to expect that compliance with that condition would by practicable;

(e) whether the goods were manufactured, processed or adapted to the special order of the customer.

In practice, the courts have been willing to have regard to the 'guidelines' contained in Schedule 2 in cases that do not fall within the scope of ss 6 and 7 (see *Overseas Medical Supplies Ltd v Orient Transport Services Ltd* [1999] 2 Lloyd's Rep 273, discussed in detail below). The matters contained in Schedule 2 are only 'guidelines' and therefore there is no obligation on the court to look to them at all. Indeed, it is highly unlikely that the Court of Appeal would overturn a judge's decision on the reasonableness issue simply because one of the above guidelines had not been considered, even if the case concerned a clause covered by ss 6 or 7. Furthermore, the list of considerations is not exhaustive. The court will take into account a number of other factors that have been held to be relevant in the task of assessing reasonableness.

8.3.3.2 'Reasonableness' in the House of Lords

In this section and the next we will consider a number of cases in which the courts have sought to apply the test of reasonableness. We will see that the courts have regard to a broad range of factors. The duty of the judge is to balance these factors in a sagacious manner. In practice, the trial judge is afforded a considerable degree of latitude in undertaking this task and it will be very rare for his decision to be overturned by an appeal court.

In this section, we will consider two decisions of the House of Lords – one applying a test of reasonableness that predated the UCTA 1977, the other dealing with the UCTA 1977 itself.

George Mitchell (Chesterhall) Ltd v Finney Lock Seeds Ltd
[1983] 2 AC 803

Facts: The plaintiffs were farmers in East Lothian who ordered a quantity of Finney's Late Dutch Special cabbage seed from the defendants. The seed supplied was not Finney's Late Dutch Special or any other variety of Dutch winter white cabbage, but a variety of autumn cabbage. The seed germinated and the cabbage grew but it proved to be commercially useless and had to be ploughed in. A limitation clause in the contract provided a maximum liability of no more than the price of seeds which was just over £200. The farmer claimed the loss of his profits calculated at £61,000.

Held: The House of Lords held that the limitation clause was ineffective because it failed the reasonableness test contained in s 55(4) of the Sale of Goods Act 1979 as set out in Sched 1 of the 1979 Act, para 11 (now superseded by the UCTA 1977).

Lord Bridge of Harwich:
'The relevant subsections of the modified section 55 provide as follows:

"(1) Where a right, duty or liability would arise under a contract of sale of goods by implication of law, it may be negatived or varied by express agreement . . . but the preceding provision has effect subject to the following provisions of this section. . . . (4) In the case of a contract of sale of goods, any term of that or any other contract exempting from all or any of the provisions of section 13, 14 or 15 above is void in the case of a consumer sale and is, in any other case, not enforceable to the extent that it is shown that it would not be fair or reasonable to allow reliance on the term. (5) In determining for the purposes of subsection (4) above whether or not reliance on any such term would be fair or reasonable regard shall be had to all the circumstances of the case and in particular to the following matters – (a) the strength of the bargaining positions of the seller and buyer relative to each other, taking into account, among other things, the availability of suitable alternative products and sources of supply; (b) whether the buyer received an inducement to agree to the term or in accepting it had an opportunity of buying the goods or suitable alternatives without it from any source of supply; (c) whether the buyer knew or ought reasonably to have known of the existence and extent of the term (having regard, among other things, to any custom of the trade and any previous course of dealing between the parties); (d) where the term exempts from all or any of the provisions of section 13, 14, or 15 above if some condition is not complied with, whether it was reasonable at the time of the contract to expect that compliance with that condition would be practicable; (e) whether the goods were manufactured, processed, or adapted to the special order of the buyer. . . ."

The statutory issue . . . turns on the words in subsection (4) "to the extent that it is shown that it would not be fair or reasonable to allow reliance on" this restriction of the appellants' liabilities, having regard to the matters referred to in subsection (5).

This is the first time your Lordships' House has had to consider a modern statutory provision giving the court power to override contractual terms excluding or restricting liability, which depends on the court's view of what is "fair and reasonable". The particular provision of the modified section 55 of the Act of 1979 which applies in the instant case is of limited and diminishing importance. But the several provisions of the Unfair Contract Terms Act 1977 which depend on "the requirement of reasonable-ness", defined in section 11 by reference to what is "fair and reasonable", albeit in a different context, are likely to come before the courts with increasing frequency. It may, therefore, be appropriate to consider how an original decision as to what is "fair and reasonable" made in the application of any of these provisions should be approached by an appellate court. It would not be accurate to describe such a decision as an exercise of discretion. But a decision under any of the provisions referred to will have this in common with the exercise of a discretion, that, in having regard to the various matters to which the modified section 55(5) of the Act of 1979, or section 11 of the Act of 1977 direct attention, the court must entertain a whole range of considerations, put them in the scales on one side or the other, and decide at the end of the day on which side the balance comes down. There will sometimes be room for a legitimate differ-ence of judicial opinion as to what the answer should be, where it will be impossible to say that one view is demonstrably wrong and the other demonstrably right. It must follow, in my view, that, when asked to review such a decision on appeal, the appellate court should treat the original decision with the utmost respect and refrain from inter-ference with it unless satisfied that it proceeded upon some erroneous principle or was plainly and obviously wrong.

Turning back to the modified section 55 of the Act of 1979, it is common ground that the onus was on the respondents to show that it would not be fair or reasonable to allow the appellants to rely on the relevant condition as limiting their liability . . .

My Lords . . . I turn to the application of the statutory language to the circumstances of the case. Of the particular matters to which attention is directed by paragraphs (a) to (e) of section 55(5), only those in (a) to (c) are relevant. As to paragraph (c), the respondents admittedly knew of the relevant condition (they had dealt with the appel-lants for many years) and, if they had read it, particularly clause 2, they would, I think, as laymen rather than lawyers, have had no difficulty in understanding what it said. This and the magnitude of the damages claimed in proportion to the price of the seeds sold are factors which weigh in the scales in the appellants' favour. The question of relative bargaining strength under paragraph (a) and of the opportunity to buy seeds without a limitation of the seedsman's liability under paragraph (b) were inter-related. The evidence was that a similar limitation of liability was universally embodied in the terms of trade between seedsmen and farmers and had been so for very many years. The limitation had never been negotiated between representative bodies but, on the other hand, had not been the subject of any protest by the National Farmers' Union. These factors, if considered in isolation, might have been equivocal. The decisive factor, however, appears from the evidence of four witnesses called for the appellants, two independent seedsmen, the chairman of the appellant company, and a director of a sister company (both being wholly-owned subsidiaries of the same parent). They said that it had always been their practice, unsuccessfully attempted in the instant case, to negotiate settlements of farmers' claims for damages in excess of the price of the seeds, if they thought that the claims were "genuine" and "justified". This evidence indicated a clear recognition by seedsmen in general, and the appellants in particular, that reliance on the limitation of liability imposed by the relevant condition would not be fair or reasonable.

Two further factors, if more were needed, weight the scales in favour of the respondents. The supply of autumn, instead of winter, cabbage seeds was due to the negligence of the appellants' sister company. Irrespective of its quality, the autumn variety supplied could not, according to the appellants' own evidence, be grown commercially in East Lothian. Finally, as the trial judge found, seedsmen could insure against the risk of crop failure caused by supplying the wrong variety of seeds without materially increasing the price of seeds.

My Lords, even if I felt doubts about the statutory issue, I should not, for the reasons explained earlier, think it right to interfere with the unanimous original decision of that issue by the Court of Appeal. As it is, I feel no such doubts. If I were making the original decision, I should conclude without hesitation that it would not be fair or reasonable to allow the appellants to rely on the contractual limitation of their liability.'

Lord Bridge confirmed that the test of reasonableness was a balancing exercise in which the court must entertain a whole range of considerations and balance them against each other. Three factors weighed in favour of the seed sellers:

1. The clause was clear and understandable.
2. The clause was common in the trade, and had never been objected to by the National Farmers' Union.
3. The magnitude of the damages claimed in proportion to the price of the seeds sold weighed heavily in favour of the sellers.

Four considerations weighed in favour of the farmers, however:

1. The clause had been inserted by the seller; there had been no real negotiation.
2. The loss of the crop had been caused by negligence (albeit the negligence of the sellers' sister company, rather than the sellers themselves).
3. The trial judge had found that seedsmen could insure against the risk of crop

failure caused by supplying the wrong variety of seeds without significantly increasing the price of seeds.

4.   There was evidence from a number of witnesses (including the chairman of the defendant company) that it was the general practice of the trade not to rely on the clause, but to use it as the basis for negotiating more substantial compensation.

For Lord Bridge, the final consideration was the most important. He considered that it was conclusive evidence that seedsman in general and the defendants in particular did not believe that reliance on the clause would be fair and reasonable.

The House of Lords upheld the verdicts delivered at first instance and in the Court of Appeal. Lord Bridge emphasised that there was room for legitimate disagreement as to whether a clause was reasonable. For this reason, he said that the appellate courts should refrain from interference with a first instance decision 'unless satisfied that it proceeded upon some erroneous principle or was plainly and obviously wrong'.

Smith v Eric S Bush [1990] 1 AC 831

Facts: See p 483.

Held: The House of Lords held that a clause purporting to exclude liability for the negligent performance of a survey was subject to s 2(2) of the UCTA 1977. On the facts of the case the clause did not meet the requirement of reasonableness.

Lord Griffiths:

'[T]he question is whether the exclusion of liability contained in the disclaimer satisfies the requirement of reasonableness provided by section 2(2) of the Act of 1977. The meaning of reasonableness and the burden of proof are both dealt with in section 11(3) which provides:

"In relation to a notice (not being a notice having contractual effect), the requirement of reasonableness under this Act is that it should be fair and reasonable to allow reliance on it, having regard to all the circumstances obtaining when the liability arose or (but for the notice) would have arisen."

It is clear, then, that the burden is upon the surveyor to establish that in all the circumstances it is fair and reasonable that he should be allowed to rely upon his disclaimer of liability.

I believe that it is impossible to draw up an exhaustive list of the factors that must be taken into account when a judge is faced with this very difficult decision. Nevertheless, the following matters should, in my view, always be considered.

1.   Were the parties of equal bargaining power? If the court is dealing with a one-off situation between parties of equal bargaining power the requirement of

reasonableness would be more easily discharged than in a case such as the present where the disclaimer is imposed upon the purchaser who has no effective power to object.

2. In the case of advice would it have been reasonably practicable to obtain the advice from an alternative source taking into account considerations of costs and time. In the present case it is urged on behalf of the surveyor that it would have been easy for the purchaser to have obtained his own report on the condition of the house, to which the purchaser replies, that he would then be required to pay twice for the same advice and that people buying at the bottom end of the market, many of whom will be young first-time buyers, are likely to be under considerable financial pressure without the money to go paying twice for the same service.

3. How difficult is the task being undertaken for which liability is being excluded. When a very difficult or dangerous undertaking is involved there may be a high risk of failure which would certainly be a pointer towards the reasonableness of excluding liability as a condition of doing the work. A valuation, on the other hand, should present no difficulty if the work is undertaken with reasonable skill and care. It is only defects which are observable by a careful visual examination that have to be taken into account and I cannot see that it places any unreasonable burden on the valuer to require him to accept responsibility for the fairly elementary degree of skill and care involved in observing, following-up and reporting on such defects. Surely it is work at the lower end of the surveyor's field of professional expertise.

4. What are the practical consequences of the decision on the question of reasonableness. This must involve the sums of money potentially at stake and the ability of the parties to bear the loss involved, which, in its turn, raises the question of insurance. There was once a time when it was considered improper even to mention the possible existence of insurance cover in a lawsuit. But those days are long past. Everyone knows that all prudent, professional men carry insurance, and the availability and cost of insurance must be a relevant factor when considering which of two parties should be required to bear the risk of a loss. We are dealing in this case with a loss which will be limited to the value of a modest house and against which it can be expected that the surveyor will be insured. Bearing the loss will be unlikely to cause significant hardship if it has to be borne by the surveyor but it is, on the other hand, quite possible that it will be a financial catastrophe for the purchaser who may be left with a valueless house and no money to buy another. If the law in these circumstances denies the surveyor the right to exclude his liability, it may result in a few more claims but I do not think so poorly of the surveyor's profession as to believe that the floodgates will be opened. There may be some increase in surveyors' insurance premiums which will be passed on to the public, but I cannot think that it will be anything approaching the figures involved in the difference between the Abbey National's offer of a valuation without liability and a valuation with liability discussed in the speech of my noble and learned friend, Lord Templeman. The result of denying a surveyor, in the circumstances of this case, the right to exclude liability, will result in distributing the risk

of his negligence among all house purchasers through an increase in his fees to cover insurance, rather than allowing the whole of the risk to fall upon the one unfortunate purchaser.

I would not, however, wish it to be thought that I would consider it unreasonable for professional men in all circumstances to seek to exclude or limit their liability for negligence. Sometimes breathtaking sums of money may turn on professional advice against which it would be impossible for the adviser to obtain adequate insurance cover and which would ruin him if he were to be held personally liable. In these circumstances it may indeed be reasonable to give the advice upon a basis of no liability or possibly of liability limited to the extent of the adviser's insurance cover.

In addition to the foregoing four factors, which will always have to be considered, there is in this case the additional feature that the surveyor is only employed in the first place because the purchaser wishes to buy the house and the purchaser in fact provides or contributes to the surveyor's fees. No one has argued that if the purchaser had employed and paid the surveyor himself, it would have been reasonable for the surveyor to exclude liability for negligence, and the present situation is not far removed from that of a direct contract between the surveyor and the purchaser. The evaluation of the foregoing matters leads me to the clear conclusion that it would not be fair and reasonable for the surveyor to be permitted to exclude liability in the circumstances of this case. I would therefore dismiss this appeal.'

Once again, the availability of insurance was a significant factor for the House of Lords. The surveyor could have quite easily obtained insurance to cover his liability. This was an individual private house purchase, not a deal in relation to commercial property and while it would have been a financial catastrophe for the purchaser to be left with a valueless house, the loss could have quite easily been absorbed by the surveyor and his insurer. Better to spread the risk through an increase in insurance premiums than to allow the whole of the risk to fall on the one unfortunate purchaser.

8.3.3.3 'Reasonableness' in the Court of Appeal

Repeatedly the Court of Appeal has emphasised its reluctance to interfere with the decision of the trial judge on the issue of reasonableness. In both *Phillips Products Ltd v Hyland* [1987] 1 WLR 659 and *St Albans City and District Council v International Computers Ltd* [1996] 4 All ER 481, the Court of Appeal refused to overturn the decision at first instance because it had not been shown to be 'plainly or obviously wrong'.

Subsequent cases have sought to give some guidance as to factors that are relevant in applying the test.

Schenkers Ltd v Overland Shoes Ltd [1998] 1 Lloyd's Rep 498

Facts: The plaintiffs were the freight carriers for the defendants who imported shoes from the Far East into the European Community. The contract stated that the plaintiffs were to reclaim the VAT payable to the Portuguese authorities and repay it to the defendants. They failed to do this and the defendants purported to set-off the sum of VAT against the money they owed to the plaintiffs. The contract between the parties contained a number of standard trading conditions of the British International Freight Association. Clause 23(A) stated: 'The Customer shall pay to the Company in cash or as otherwise agreed all sums immediately when due, without reduction or defer-ment on account of any claim, counterclaim or set-off'. The issue for consideration was whether clause 23(A), which prohibited set-off, satisfied the requirement of reasonableness in the UCTA 1977.

Held: The Court of Appeal held that the plaintiffs had satisfied the burden on them of establishing that clause 23(A) in the circumstances satisfied the requirement of reasonableness.

Pill LJ:

'In my judgment, the plaintiffs have satisfied the burden upon them of establishing that cl 23(A) in the circumstances satisfies the requirement of reasonableness. The clause was in common use and well known in the trade following comprehensive discussions between reputable and representative bodies mindful of the considerations involved. It reflects a general view as to what is reasonable in the trade concerned. It was suf-ficiently well known that any failure by the defendant's officers, in the course of long and substantial dealings, to put their minds to the clause cannot be relied on to establish that it was unfair or unreasonable to include it in the contracts. I regard the level of disbursements as a factor which assists the plaintiffs to establish that it was fair and reasonable to include the term but not in itself a conclusive one. In a situation in which there was no significant inequality of bargaining position, the customs of the trade were an important factor. The parties were well aware of the circumstances in which busi-ness was conducted, the heads of expenditure to be incurred and the risks involved.

In present circumstances, I see little merit in the defendants' argument that the clause had not in practice been relied upon. The give and take practised by the parties in the course of substantial dealings upon the running account was admirable and conducive to a good business relationship but did not in my judgment prevent the plaintiffs, when the dispute arose, relying upon the term agreed. In *George Mitchell*, there was evidence that neither party expected the limitation of liability clause to be applied literally and a recognition that reliance on the clause was unreasonable. While there was evidence in the present case that there was no ready or frequent resort to the clause, there was no such recognition. I cannot find conduct which permits the defendants to claim that reliance on the clause would be unfair or unreasonable. For those reasons I would dismiss these appeals.'

Of particular relevance to the Court of Appeal was the fact that there was equality of bargaining power and that the clause was in common use and well known in the trade. It did not matter that there was 'no ready or frequent resort to the clause', because this was due to the 'admirable give and take practised by the parties in the course of substantial dealings'. Unlike the *George Mitchell* case, it was not due to a recognition in the trade that the clause was unreasonable.

A clause contained in the British International Freight Association's standard terms also came up for consideration in *Overseas Medical Supplies Ltd v Orient Transport Services Ltd*.

Overseas Medical Supplies Ltd v Orient Transport Services Ltd
[1999] 2 Lloyd's Rep 273

Facts: The clause in this case stated the following: '[T]he Company's liability how-soever arising and notwithstanding that the cause of loss or damage be unexplained shall not exceed

(i) in the case of claims for loss or damage to goods (a) the value of any goods lost or damaged or (b) a sum at the rate of two Special Drawing Rights as defined by the International Monetary Fund (hereinafter referred to as SDRs), per kilo of gross weight of any goods lost or damaged whichever shall be the least;

(ii) in the case of all other claims (a) the value of the goods the subject of the relevant transaction between the Company and its Customer or (b) a sum at the rate of two SDRs per kilo of the gross weight of the goods the subject of the said transaction, or (c) 75,000 SDRs in respect of any one transaction whichever shall be the least the value of SDRs shall be calculated as at the date when the claim is received by the Company in writing.'

The trial judge held that the clause was unreasonable.

Held: The Court of Appeal dismissed the appeal and held that the clause was unreasonable.

Potter LJ:
'First, so far as this Court is concerned, while the hearing of this appeal is in the form of a re-hearing and the Court is entitled to reach its own view on the evidence, its approach is constrained by a natural reluctance to disturb a first instance decision as to what is reasonable in all the circumstances of a particular case, bearing in mind that views on reasonableness may properly differ and that, in any matter where the decision depends not merely on argument but also on the effect of oral evidence, the first instance Judge has the advantage of hearing such evidence at first hand . . .

The treatment of various factors going to the question of reasonableness has been considered in a number of authorities from which the following observations of relevance emerge.

(1) The way in which the relevant conditions came into being and are used generally is relevant: *Singer Co (UK) Ltd v Tees and Hartlepool Port Authority* [1988] 2 Lloyd's Rep 164, at 169, applied by the Court of Appeal in *Schenkers Ltd v Overland Shoes Ltd* [1998] 1 Lloyd's Rep 498 (a case concerning an entirely different aspect of the BIFA terms).

(2) Although not specifically applicable to cases falling within s 3 of the 1977 Act, the five guidelines as to reasonableness set out in Schedule 2 are nonetheless relevant to the question of reasonableness, while bearing in mind that the Court is dealing with a commercial and not a consumer transaction. They ought therefore to be taken into account: *Stewart Gill Ltd v Horatio Myer and Co Ltd* [1992] QB 600 at p 608. Those which are relevant in this case are (a) the strength of the bargaining positions of the parties relative to each other, taking into account (among other things) alternative means by which the customer's requirements could have been met; (b) whether the customer received an inducement to agree to the term or, in accepting it, had an opportunity of entering into a similar contract with other persons, but without having to accept similar terms; (c) whether the customer knew or ought to have known of the existence and extent of the term (having regard, among other things, to any custom of the trade and any previous course of dealing between the parties).

(3) In relation to the question of equality of bargaining position, the Court will have regard not only to the question of whether the customer was obliged to use the services of the supplier but also to the question of how far it would have been practicable and convenient to go elsewhere: *Singer v Tees* at p 169 and *St Alban's City and District Council v International Computers Ltd*, (1995) XXI FSR 686 at p 708.

(4) The question of reasonableness must be assessed having regard to the relevant clause viewed as a whole: it is not right to take any particular part of the clause in isolation, although it must also be viewed against a breach of contract which is the subject matter of the present case: *AEG (UK) Ltd v Logic Resource Ltd* (Unreported save by New Law on Line, Court of Appeal, Oct 20, 1995) per Lord Justice Hobhouse.

(5) The reality of the consent of the customer to the supplier's clause will be a significant consideration (ibid: see also the *St Alban's City* case at pp 709–711).

(6) In cases of limitation rather than exclusion of liability, the size of the limit compared with other limits in widely used standard terms may also be relevant: *Sonicare International Ltd v East Anglia Freight Terminal Ltd* [1997] 2 Lloyd's Rep 48 at 55, per Judge Hallgarten, QC.

(7) While the availability of insurance to the supplier is relevant, it is by no means a decisive factor: see *Singer v Tees* at p 170 and *The Flamar Pride* [1990] 1 Lloyd's Rep 434, 439.

(8) The presence of a term allowing for an option to contract without the limitation clause but with a price increase in lieu is important: see *Singer v Tees* at p 170. However, as suggested in *Yates: Contracts for the Carriage of Goods* par. 7.2.25.13, if the condition works in such a way as to leave little time to put such option into effect, this may effectively eliminate the option as a factor indicating reasonableness, cf *Phillips Products Ltd v Hyland* [1987] 1 WLR 659.'

The eight factors set out by Potter LJ are entirely sensible. Once again, his Lordship chose to emphasise the relevance of the bargaining position of the parties, the availability of insurance and the common use of such clauses. With respect, however, his reference to the relevance of breach in the second half of observation (4) is impossible to reconcile with the clear wording of s 11(1). As we have seen, the assessment of reasonableness is to be based on the state of knowledge of the parties at the time the contract was formed. Since the breach takes place after that point it should not be taken into account. Potter LJ's statement to the contrary, which is clearly obiter, should be treated with extreme caution until the House of Lords revisit the issue.

In all the cases we have looked at so far, the appeal court has refused to overturn the decision of the trial judge at first instance. This is because, as Lord Bridge indicated in *George Mitchell*, the appellate court will 'treat the original decision with the utmost respect'. The appeal court will intervene, however, if it is convinced that the judge has misdirected himself as to the proper basis for applying the reasonableness test.

Watford Electronics Ltd v Sanderson CFL Ltd [2001] 1 All ER (Comm) 696

Facts: The defendants agreed to sell the claimants a number of computer products which turned out to be faulty. The contract contained an exclusion clause stating: 'Neither the Company nor the Customer shall be liable to the other for any claims for indirect or consequential losses whether arising from negligence or otherwise. In no event shall the Company's liability under the Contract exceed the price paid by the Customer to the Company for the Equipment connected with any claim'. The trial judge held that the clause did not satisfy the requirement of reasonableness under s 3 of the UCTA 1977.

Held: The Court of Appeal allowed the appeal.

Chadwick LJ:

'Where experienced businessmen representing substantial companies of equal bargaining power negotiate an agreement, they may be taken to have had regard to the matters known to them. They should, in my view be taken to be the best judge of the commercial fairness of the agreement which they have made; including the fairness of each of the terms in that agreement. They should be taken to be the best judge on the question whether the terms of the agreement are reasonable. The court should not assume that either is likely to commit his company to an agreement which he thinks is unfair, or which he thinks includes unreasonable terms. Unless satisfied that one party has, in effect, taken unfair advantage of the other – or that a term is so unreasonable that it cannot properly have been understood or considered – the court should not interfere.

In the present case the parties did negotiate as to the price. Mr Jessa, on behalf of Watford, secured substantial concessions on price from Mr Broderick. The parties negotiated, also, as to which of them should bear the risk (or the cost of insurance against the risk) of making good the loss of profits, and other indirect or consequential loss, which Watford might suffer if the product failed to perform as intended. Mr Jessa was less successful in obtaining from Mr Broderick the concession which he wanted. The most that he could get was an undertaking that Sanderson would use its best endeavours to allocate appropriate resources to ensuring that the product performed according to specification. But, for the reasons which I have sought to explain, that was worth something to Watford; and Mr Jessa decided that he would be content with what he could get. In my view it is impossible to hold, in the circumstances of the present case, that Sanderson took unfair advantage of Watford; or that Watford, through Mr Jessa, did not properly understand and consider the effect of the term excluding indirect loss.

It follows that I would hold that the term excluding indirect loss, applicable in the circumstances which I have described, was a fair and reasonable one to include in the contract.'

The decision represents a 'hands-off' approach to the supervision of exclusion clauses in commercial contracts. The Court of Appeal was willing to overturn the trial judge's finding that the clause was unreasonable because the judge had failed to give due weight to the following factors:

1. There had been considerable negotiation between the parties as to which of them should bear the risk of making good the loss of profits.
2. The purchaser had successfully obtained an undertaking that the seller would use its best endeavours to allocate appropriate resources to ensuring that the product performed according to specification.
3. There was no significant difference in bargaining power between the parties.

For the Court of Appeal, the clause was reasonable because it was openly negotiated between two parties who were well capable of looking after their own interests. In high-risk contracts the parties should be left to allocate the risk between themselves (*Frans Maas (UK) Ltd v Samsung Electronics (UK) Ltd* [2004] 2 Lloyd's Rep 251).

This 'hands-off' approach to regulating commercial contracts was rejected by Tomlinson J on the facts of *Britvic Soft Drinks Ltd v Messer UK Ltd* [2002] 1 Lloyd's Rep 20. The case concerned the exclusion of liability for CO_2 not being of satisfactory quality. Tomlinson J considered the comments of Chadwick LJ in *Watford Electronics*, but concluded that on the facts of the case before him it would be 'wholly unreasonable for the supplier of a bulk commodity such as CO_2 for a food application to seek to exclude liability for the commodity not being of satisfactory quality or being unfit for its purpose where that has come about as a result of a breakdown

515

in the manufacturing process allowing the inadvertent introduction of a redundant carcinogen.'

While it is true that the court will consider each case on its merits it seems that the courts are increasingly reluctant to intervene in commercial agreements on the basis of the UCTA 1977. This was recently confirmed by Tuckey LJ in *Granville Chemicals Ltd v Davis Turner & Co Ltd* [2003] 2 Lloyd's Rep 356, who concluded his judgment with these words:

'The 1977 Act obviously plays a very important role in protecting vulnerable consumers from the effects of draconian contract terms. But I am less enthusiastic about its intrusion into contracts between commercial parties of equal bargaining strength, who should generally be considered capable of being able to make contracts of their choosing and expect to be bound by their terms.'

8.4 UNFAIR TERMS IN CONSUMER CONTRACTS REGULATIONS

As a result of the European Union (EU) Directive on Unfair Terms in Consumer Contracts (Directive 93/13/EC), the United Kingdom implemented the Unfair Terms in Consumer Contracts Regulations in 1994. These were later amended and replaced by the Unfair Terms in Consumer Contracts Regulations 1999 (UTCCR 1999), which were intended to reflect more closely the aims of the Directive.

8.4.1 SCOPE

The scope of the Regulations is outlined in the following provisions:

Terms to which these Regulations apply
Reg 4
(1) These Regulations apply in relation to unfair terms in contracts concluded between a seller or a supplier and a consumer.
(2) These Regulations do not apply to contractual terms which reflect –

    (a) mandatory statutory or regulatory provisions (including such provisions under the law of any Member State or in Community legislation having effect in the United Kingdom without further enactment);
    (b) the provisions or principles of international conventions to which the Member States or the Community are party.

The scope of the Regulations is in some respects narrower than the scope of the UCTA 1977. The most important restriction is that it only applies to contracts between a seller or supplier and a 'consumer'. The definition of a consumer for the purpose of the Regulations is found in reg 3(1), which states that a consumer is 'any natural person who, in contracts covered by these Regulations, is acting for purposes which are outside his trade, business or profession'. Unlike the UCTA 1977, the Regulations do not apply to business-to-business (B2B) contracts, and only a natural person can be a consumer for the purpose of the Regulations.

Regulation 4(2) confirms that contract terms inserted into the contract in compliance with a statutory or regulatory requirement or an international convention do not fall under the jurisdiction of the Regulations. This is potentially a very broad exception and its precise scope depends on how the subsection will be interpreted. In particular, the word 'reflect' is extremely vague and susceptible to expansive interpretation.

Unfair Terms
Reg 5

(1) A contractual term which has not been individually negotiated shall be regarded as unfair if, contrary to the requirement of good faith, it causes a significant imbalance in the parties' rights and obligations arising under the contract, to the detriment of the consumer.

(2) A term shall always be regarded as not having been individually negotiated where it has been drafted in advance and the consumer has therefore not been able to influence the substance of the term.

(3) Notwithstanding that a specific term or certain aspects of it in a contract has been individually negotiated, these Regulations shall apply to the rest of a contract if an overall assessment of it indicates that it is a pre-formulated standard contract.

(4) It shall be for any seller or supplier who claims that a term was individually negotiated to show that it was.

. . .

Assessment of unfair terms
Reg 6

. . .

(2) In so far as it is in plain intelligible language, the assessment of fairness of a term shall not relate –

(a) to the definition of the main subject matter of the contract, or

(b) to the adequacy of the price or remuneration, as against the goods or services supplied in exchange.

The UTCCR 1999 have a wider scope than the UCTA 1977 to the extent that they apply to all types of contract term, not just exclusion clauses. The Regulations do not apply, however, to clauses which: (1) define the main subject matter of the contract; or (2) concern the adequacy of the price or remuneration (reg 6(2)).

A further limitation on the scope of the Regulations is that they do not apply to any clause which has been 'individually negotiated' (reg 5(1)). In other words, they target standard form consumer contracts. Regulation 5(2)–(4) explains precisely what is meant by a term 'which has not been individually negotiated'. The burden of proof falls on the seller or supplier (reg 5(4)). Regulation 5(3) prevents the seller from relying on the fact that one term has been individually negotiated to remove the contract from the jurisdiction of the Regulations.

8.4.2 CONTROL

8.4.2.1 Unfair terms

Unfair Terms

Reg 5

(1) A contractual term which has not been individually negotiated shall be regarded as unfair if, contrary to the requirement of good faith, it causes a significant imbalance in the parties' rights and obligations arising under the contract, to the detriment of the consumer.

Effect of unfair term

Reg 8

(1) An unfair term in a contract concluded with a consumer by a seller or supplier shall not be binding on the consumer.

(2) The contract shall continue to bind the parties if it is capable of continuing in existence without the unfair term.

Regulation 8 states that an unfair term will not be binding on the consumer, although the contract will continue to bind the parties if it is capable of continuing in existence without the unfair term.

The test of 'unfairness' is contained in reg 5(1). It makes reference to two concepts: 'good faith' and 'significant imbalance'. While the latter concept is familiar to English lawyers and used in the UCTA 1977 jurisprudence, the former concept has a much more European flavour and is less familiar to English lawyers. The 1994 Regulations contained some guidance about factors to be taken into account in assessing the issue of good faith:

Schedule 2

In making an assessment of good faith, regard shall be had in particular to – (a) the strength of the bargaining positions of the parties; (b) whether the consumer had an inducement to agree to the term; (c) whether the goods or services were sold or supplied to the special order of the consumer, and (d) the extent to which the seller or supplier has dealt fairly and equitably with the consumer.

This list has not been reproduced in the 1999 Regulations, but since it consists of common-sense principles it is inevitable that these will still be taken into account by the courts when assessing the issue of good faith.

The 1994 Regulations also contained an indicative list of terms that may be regarded as unfair (contained in Schedule 3). This was reproduced in the 1999 Regulations.

INDICATIVE AND NON-EXHAUSTIVE LIST OF TERMS WHICH MAY BE REGARDED AS UNFAIR

Schedule 2

1   Terms which have the object or effect of –

(a)   excluding or limiting the legal liability of a seller or supplier in the event of the death of a consumer or personal injury to the latter resulting from an act or omission of that seller or supplier;

(b)   inappropriately excluding or limiting the legal rights of the consumer vis-a-vis the seller or supplier or another party in the event of total or partial non-performance or inadequate performance by the seller or supplier of any of the contractual obligations, including the option of offsetting a debt owed to the seller or supplier against any claim which the consumer may have against him;

(c)   making an agreement binding on the consumer whereas provision of services by the seller or supplier is subject to a condition whose realisation depends on his own will alone;

(d)   permitting the seller or supplier to retain sums paid by the consumer where the latter decides not to conclude or perform the contract, without providing for the consumer to receive compensation of an equivalent amount from the seller or supplier where the latter is the party cancelling the contract;

(e)   requiring any consumer who fails to fulfil his obligation to pay a disproportionately high sum in compensation;

(f)   authorising the seller or supplier to dissolve the contract on a discretionary basis where the same facility is not granted to the consumer, or permitting the seller or supplier to retain the sums paid for services not yet supplied by him where it is the seller or supplier himself who dissolves the contract;

(g)   enabling the seller or supplier to terminate a contract of indeterminate duration without reasonable notice except where there are serious grounds for doing so;

(h)   automatically extending a contract of fixed duration where the consumer does not indicate otherwise, when the deadline fixed for the consumer to express his desire not to extend the contract is unreasonably early;

(i)   irrevocably binding the consumer to terms with which he had no real opportunity of becoming acquainted before the conclusion of the contract;

(j)   enabling the seller or supplier to alter the terms of the contract unilaterally without a valid reason which is specified in the contract;

(k)   enabling the seller or supplier to alter unilaterally without a valid reason any characteristics of the product or service to be provided;

(l) providing for the price of goods to be determined at the time of delivery or allowing a seller of goods or supplier of services to increase their price without in both cases giving the consumer the corresponding right to cancel the contract if the final price is too high in relation to the price agreed when the contract was concluded;

(m) giving the seller or supplier the right to determine whether the goods or services supplied are in conformity with the contract, or giving him the exclusive right to interpret any term of the contract;

(n) limiting the seller's or supplier's obligation to respect commitments undertaken by his agents or making his commitments subject to compliance with a particular formality;

(o) obliging the consumer to fulfil all his obligations where the seller or supplier does not perform his,

(p) giving the seller or supplier the possibility of transferring his rights and obligations under the contract, where this may serve to reduce the guarantees for the consumer, without the latter's agreement;

(q) excluding or hindering the consumer's right to take legal action or exercise any other legal remedy, particularly by requiring the consumer to take disputes exclusively to arbitration not covered by legal provisions, unduly restricting the evidence available to him or imposing on him a burden of proof which, according to the applicable law, should lie with another party to the contract.

The significance of the list remains unclear. In particular, it is uncertain whether inclusion on the list creates a rebuttable presumption that the term is unfair. If it does, then the burden of proof will shift from the claimant onto the seller. If not, the list constitutes no more than a useful guide. The Office of Fair Trading (Office of Fair Trading Bulletin 4) has described the list in the following way:

> 'It is not a "black list" but the exact shade of grey is debatable. Our view is that if a term appears in the list it is under substantial suspicion, but that correspondence with an item in the list cannot of itself determine the issue of unfairness.'

The list is stated to be nonexhaustive, which means that a clause of a type that is not featured on the list may nevertheless be found to be unfair. Many of the clauses featured are familiar to us from the discussion of the UCTA 1977, for example, para 1 (a), (b), (f), (g), (k), (l), (m), (o) and (q). Paragraph 1(e) overlaps with the common-law rules on penalties (see Chapter 17). The terms referred to in the list are stated by reference to their 'object or effect', indicating that the courts should look to the substance of the clause, not its form. This means that a term may be under suspicion, even if it does not look like a term on the list, so long as it has the same affect on consumers.

The first reported case to consider the 1994 Regulations concerned a term in a loan agreement issued by a bank and is detailed below.

Director General of Fair Trading v First National Bank plc [2002] 1 AC 481

Facts: The defendant bank included in its loan agreement a term which stated that, should the borrower default on his repayments, interest would continue to be charged at the contractual rate until any judgment obtained by the bank was discharged. This meant that a court might order the consumer to pay off the debt by specified instalments, but the contractually agreed interest would continue to accrue while the instalments were being paid. The Director General of Fair Trading considered that the term was unfair for the purposes of regulation 4 of the Unfair Terms in Consumer Contracts Regulations 1994. The trial judge held that the term was not unfair. The Court of Appeal allowed the appeal, holding that the term was unfair to the extent that it created unfair surprise and caused a significant imbalance in the rights and obligations between the parties.

Held: The House of Lords allowed the bank's appeal and held that the term was not unfair.

Lord Bingham:
'**10.** In reliance on regulation 3(2)(b) Lord Goodhart, on behalf of the bank, submitted that no assessment might be made of the fairness of the term because it concerns the adequacy of the bank's remuneration as against the services supplied, namely the loan of money. A bank's remuneration under a credit agreement is the receipt of interest. The term, by entitling the bank to post-judgment interest, concerns the quantum and thus the adequacy of that remuneration . . .

11. To this submission Mr Crow, representing the Director, gave two short answers. First, condition 8, of which the term forms part, is a default provision. Its purpose, and its only purpose, is to prescribe the consequences of a default by the borrower. It does not lay down the rate of interest which the bank is entitled to receive and the borrower bound to pay. It is an ancillary term, well outside the bounds of regulation 3(2)(b) . . .

12. In agreement with the judge and the Court of Appeal, I do not accept the bank's submission on this issue. The Regulations, as Professor Sir Guenter Treitel QC has aptly observed (Treitel, *The Law of Contract*, 10th edn (1999), p 248), "are not intended to operate as a mechanism of quality or price control" and regulation 3(2) is of "crucial importance in recognising the parties' freedom of contract with respect to the essential features of their bargain": p 249. But there is an important "distinction between the term or terms which express the substance of the bargain and 'incidental' (if important) terms which surround them": *Chitty on Contracts*, 28th edn (1999), vol 1, ch 15 "Unfair Terms in Consumer Contracts", p 747, para 15–025. The object of the Regulations and the Directive is to protect consumers against the inclusion of unfair and prejudicial terms in standard-form contracts into which they enter, and that object would plainly be frustrated if regulation 3(2)(b) were so broadly interpreted as to cover any terms other than those falling squarely within it. In my opinion the term, as part of a provision prescribing the consequences of default, plainly does not fall within it. It does not concern the adequacy of the interest earned by the bank as its remuneration but is designed to ensure that the bank's entitlement to interest does not come to an end on the entry of judgment. I do not think the bank's argument on merger advances its case. It appears that some judges in the past have been readier than I would be to infer that a borrower's covenant to pay interest was not intended to extend beyond the entry of judgment. But even if a borrower's obligation were ordinarily understood to extend beyond judgment even in the absence of an independent covenant, it would not alter my view of the term as an ancillary provision and not one concerned with the adequacy of the bank's remuneration as against the services supplied. It is therefore necessary to address the second question.

17. The test laid down by regulation 4(1), deriving as it does from article 3(1) of the Directive, has understandably attracted much discussion in academic and professional circles and helpful submissions were made to the House on it. It is plain from the recitals to the Directive that one of its objectives was partially to harmonise the law in this important field among all member states of the European Union. The member states have no common concept of fairness or good faith, and the Directive does not purport to state the law of any single member state. It lays down a test to be applied, whatever their pre-existing law, by all member states. If the meaning of the test were doubtful, or vulnerable to the possibility of differing interpretations in differing member states, it might be desirable or necessary to seek a ruling from the European Court of Justice on its interpretation. But the language used in expressing the test, so far as applicable in this case, is in my opinion clear and not reasonably capable of differing interpretations. A term falling within the scope of the Regulations is unfair if it causes a significant imbalance in the parties' rights and obligations under the contract to the detriment of the consumer in a manner or to an extent which is contrary to the requirement of good faith. The requirement of significant imbalance is met if a term is so weighted in favour of the supplier as to tilt the parties' rights and obligations under the contract significantly in his favour. This may be by the granting to the supplier of a beneficial option or discretion or power, or by the imposing on the consumer of a disadvantageous burden or risk or duty. The illustrative terms set out in Schedule 3 to the Regulations provide very good examples of terms which may be regarded as unfair; whether a given term is or is not to be so regarded depends on whether it causes a significant imbalance in the parties' rights and obligations under the contract. This involves looking at the contract as a whole. But the imbalance must be to the detriment of the consumer; a significant imbalance to the detriment of the supplier, assumed to be the stronger party, is not a mischief which the Regulations seek to address. The requirement of good faith in this context is one of fair and open dealing. Openness requires that the terms should be expressed fully, clearly and legibly, containing no concealed pitfalls or traps. Appropriate prominence should be given to terms which might operate disadvantageously to the customer. Fair dealing requires that a supplier should not, whether deliberately or unconsciously, take advantage of the consumer's necessity, indigence, lack of experience, unfamiliarity with the subject matter of the contract, weak bargaining position or any other factor listed in or analogous to those listed in Schedule 2 to the Regulations. Good faith in this context is not an artificial or technical concept; nor, since Lord Mansfield was its champion, is it a concept wholly unfamiliar to British lawyers. It looks to good standards of commercial morality and practice. Regulation 4(1) lays down a composite test, covering both the making and the substance of the contract, and must be applied bearing clearly in mind the objective which the Regulations are designed to promote.

. . . **20.** In judging the fairness of the term it is necessary to consider the position of typical parties when the contract is made. The borrower wants to borrow a sum of money, often quite a modest sum, often for purposes of improving his home. He discloses an income sufficient to finance repayment by instalments over the contract term. If he cannot do that, the bank will be unwilling to lend. The essential bargain is that the bank will make funds available to the borrower which the borrower will repay, over a period, with interest. Neither party could suppose that the bank would willingly forgo any part of its principal or interest. If the bank thought that outcome at all likely, it would not lend. If there were any room for doubt about the borrower's obligation to repay the principal in full with interest, that obligation is very clearly and unambiguously expressed in the conditions of contract. There is nothing unbalanced or detrimental to the consumer in that obligation; the absence of such a term would unbalance the contract to the detriment of the lender.

. . . **22.** Should it then be said that the provisions of the 1991 Order render the term unfair, providing as it does for a continuing obligation to pay interest after judgment notwithstanding the payment of instalments by the borrower in accordance with a court order? It is, I think, pertinent that the [Consumer Credit Act 1974], which laid down a number of stipulations with which regulated agreements must comply, did not prohibit terms providing for post-judgment interest even though it required claims to enforce regulated agreements to be brought in the county court which could not at the time award statutory interest in any circumstances. The 1974 Act was passed to pro-tect consumers and such a prohibition would no doubt have been enacted had it been recognised as a necessary or desirable form of protection. The Crowther Committee, on whose report (Cmnd 4596, March 1971) the Act was based, did not recommend such a prohibition; indeed, it contemplated the recovery of contractual interest: see paragraphs 5.4.3, 6.6.33, 6.6.44(iv) and 6.7.16. It is also pertinent that judgments based on regulated agreements appear to have been excluded from the scope of the county court's power to award statutory interest in response to observations of Lord Donaldson of Lymington MR in *Forward Trust Ltd v Whymark* [1990] 2 QB 670, 681: but that was a case based on a flat rate agreement, in which the judgment in default would include a sum for future interest not yet accrued, in contrast with a simple rate agree-ment of the present kind (see [2001] 1 WLR 98, 110–111; [2000] QB 672, 679); the logic underpinning exclusion of statutory interest in the one case would not apply, at any rate with the same force, in the other. It is understandable that when a court is exercising a statutory power to order payment by instalments it should not also be empowered to order payment of statutory interest if the instalments are duly paid, but the term is directed to the recovery of contractual and not statutory interest. I do not think that the term can be stigmatised as unfair on the ground that it violates or undermines a statutory regime enacted for the protection of consumers.

23. It is of course foreseeable that a borrower, no matter how honourable and realistic his intentions when entering into a credit agreement, may fall on hard times and find himself unable to honour his obligations. The bank's standard conditions recognise that possibility by providing for the contingency of default. The 1974 Act even more fully recognises that possibility, by providing for time orders to be made and providing that when a time order is made the terms of the underlying agreement may also be amended. These provisions are clearly framed for the relief not of the borrower who, having the means to meet his contractual obligations, chooses not to do so, but for the relief of those who cannot pay or cannot pay without more time. Properly applied, these provisions enable the undeserving borrower to be distinguished from the deserving and for the contractual obligations of the deserving to be re-drawn in terms which reasonably reflect such ability, if any, as he may then have to repay within a reasonable period. Where problems arise in practice, it as to be because borrowers do not know of the effect of sections 129 and 136; neither the procedure for giving notice of default to the borrower nor the prescribed county court forms draw attention to them; and judgments will routinely be entered in the county court without the court considering whether to exercise its power under the sections.

24. I have no hesitation in accepting the proposition, inherent in the Director's submissions, that this situation is unacceptable. I have much greater difficulty in deciding whether the difficulties derive, as the Court of Appeal concluded, from the unfairness of the term or from the absence of procedural safeguards for the consumer at the stage of default. When the contract is made, default is a foreseeable contingency, not an expected outcome. It is not customary, even in consumer contracts, for notice to be given to the consumer of statutory reliefs open to him if he defaults. The 1974 Act does not require that notice of the effect of sections 129 and 136 be given. The evidence contains examples of clauses used by over 30 other lenders providing for the payment of interest after judgment, and none alerts the borrower to these potential grounds of relief. Regulation 4 is directed to the unfairness of a contract term, not the use which a supplier may make of a term which is in itself fair. It is readily understandable that a borrower may be disagreeably surprised if he finds that his contractual interest obligation continues to mount despite his duly paying the instalments ordered by the court, but it appears that the bank seeks to prevent that surprise by sending what is described in the evidence as a standard form of letter:

> "You need only pay the amount ordered by the court under the terms of the judgment but you should be aware that under the terms of the agreement interest continues to accrue on your account. It is therefore in your interest to increase the instalment paid as soon as possible otherwise a much greater balance than the judgment debt may quickly build up."

On balance, I do not consider that the term can properly be said to cause a significant imbalance in the parties' rights and obligations under the contract to the detriment of the consumer in a manner or to an extent which is contrary to the requirement of good faith.

25. I do not think that the issues raised in this appeal raise any question on which the House requires a ruling from the European Court of Justice to enable it to give judgment and I would not accordingly order a reference to be made.

26. For the reasons I have given, and those given by each of my noble and learned friends, I would allow the bank's appeal with costs in the House and the Court of Appeal and restore the order of the judge.'

Lord Steyn:

'**30.** My Lords, this is the first occasion on which the House has had the opportunity to examine an important branch of consumer law. It is therefore appropriate to consider the framework in which the questions before the House must be considered.

31. As between the Directive and the domestic implementing Regulations, the former is the dominant text. Fortunately, the 1994 Regulations, and even more so the Unfair Terms in Consumer Contracts Regulations 1999, appear to have implemented the Directive in domestic law in a manner which ought not to cause serious difficulty . . .

33. The Directive made provision for a dual system of *ex casu* challenges and pre-emptive or collective challenges by appropriate bodies: see article 7. This system was domestically enacted in the 1994 Regulations, with the Director General of Fair Trading as the administering official to investigate and take action on complaints: see regulation 8. The 1999 Regulations extended the system of enforcement by including other bodies as qualified to undertake pre-emptive challenges. The system of pre-emptive challenges is a more effective way of preventing the continuing use of unfair terms and changing contracting practice than *ex casu* actions: see Susan Bright, 'Winning the battle against unfair contract terms' (2000) 20 LS 331, 333–338. It is, however, to be noted that in a pre-emptive challenge there is not a direct *lis* between the consumer and the other contracting party. The Directive and the Regulations do not always distinguish between the two situations. This point is illustrated by the emphasis in article 4.1 of the Directive and regulation 4(2) on the relevance of particular circumstances affecting a contractual relationship. The Directive and the Regulations must be made to work sensibly and effectively and this can only be done by taking into account the effects of contemplated or typical relationships between the contracting parties. Inevitably, the primary focus of such a pre-emptive challenge is on issues of substantive unfairness.

34. Under the Regulations, a term in a standard form contract that is unfair is not binding on the consumer. But certain provisions, sometimes called core terms, have been excepted from the regulatory regime. Regulation 3(2) so provides:

"In so far as it is in plain, intelligible language, no assessment shall be made of the fairness of any term which – (a) defines the main subject matter of the contract, or (b) concerns the adequacy of the price or remuneration, as against the goods or services sold or supplied."

Clause 8 of the contract, the only provision in dispute, is a default provision. It prescribes remedies which only become available to the lender upon the default of the consumer. For this reason the escape route of regulation 3(2) is not available to the bank. So far as the description of terms covered by regulation 3(2) as core terms is helpful at all, I would say that clause 8 of the contract is a subsidiary term. In any event, regulation 3(2) must be given a restrictive interpretation. Unless that is done regulation 3(2)(a) will enable the main purpose of the scheme to be frustrated by endless formalistic arguments as to whether a provision is a definitional or an exclusionary provision. Similarly, regulation 3(2)(b) dealing with "the adequacy of the price or remuneration" must be given a restrictive interpretation. After all, in a broad sense all terms of the contract are in some way related to the price or remuneration. That is not what is intended. Even price escalation clauses have been treated by the Director as subject to the fairness provision: see Susan Bright 20 LS 331, 345 and 349. It would be a gaping hole in the system if such clauses were not subject to the fairness requirement. For these further reasons I would reject the argument of the bank that regulation 3(2), and in particular 3(2)(b), take clause 8 outside the scope of the Regulations.

35. Given these conclusions the attack on the merger principle mounted by the bank was misplaced. In any event, I am not willing to uphold criticism by the bank of the well tried and tested principle of merger. I would therefore reject the bank's submissions under this heading.

36. It is now necessary to refer to the provisions which prescribe how it should be determined whether a term is unfair. Implementing article 3(1) of the Directive regulation 4(1) provides:

> " 'unfair term' means any term which contrary to the requirement of good faith causes a significant imbalance in the parties' rights and obligations under the contract to the detriment of the consumer."

There are three independent requirements. But the element of detriment to the consumer may not add much. But it serves to make clear that the Directive is aimed at significant imbalance against the consumer, rather than the seller or supplier. The twin requirements of good faith and significant imbalance will in practice be determinative. Schedule 2 to the Regulations, which explains the concept of good faith, provides that regard must be had, amongst other things, to the extent to which the seller or supplier has dealt fairly and equitably with the consumer. It is an objective criterion. Good faith imports, as Lord Bingham of Cornhill has observed in his opinion, the notion of open and fair dealing: see also *Interfoto Picture Library Ltd v Stiletto Visual Programmes Ltd* [1989] QB 433. And helpfully the commentary to Lando & Beale, *Principles of European Contract Law, Parts I and II* (combined and revised 2000), p 113 prepared by the Commission of European Contract Law, explains that the purpose of the provision of good faith and fair dealing is "to enforce community standards of decency, fairness and reasonableness in commercial transactions"; *a fortiori* that is true of consumer transactions. Schedule 3 to the Regulations (which corresponds to the annexe to the Directive) is best regarded as a check list of terms which must be regarded as potentially vulnerable. The examples given in Schedule 3 convincingly demonstrate that the argument of the bank that good faith is predominantly concerned with procedural defects in negotiating procedures cannot be sustained. Any purely procedural or even predominantly procedural interpretation of the requirement of good faith must be rejected.

37. That brings me to the element of significant imbalance. It has been pointed out by Hugh Collins that the test "of a significant imbalance of the obligations obviously directs attention to the substantive unfairness of the contract": 'Good Faith in European Contract Law' (1994) 14 Oxford Journal of Legal Studies 229, 249. It is however, also right to say that there is a large area of overlap between the concepts of good faith and significant imbalance.

38. It is now necessary to turn to the application of these requirements to the facts of the present case. The point is a relatively narrow one. I agree that the starting point is that a lender ought to be able to recover interest at the contractual rate until the date of payment, and this applies both before and after judgment. On the other hand, counsel for the Director advanced a contrary argument. Adopting the test of asking what the position of a consumer is in the contract under consideration with or without clause 8, he said that the consumer is in a significantly worse position than he would have been if there had been no such provision. Certainly, the consumer is worse off. The difficulty facing counsel, however, is that this disadvantage to the consumer appears to be the consequence not of clause 8 but of the County Courts (Interest on Judgment Debts) Order 1991. Under this Order no statutory interest is payable on a county court judgment given in proceedings to recover money due under a regulated agreement: see article 2. Counsel said that for policy reasons it was decided that in such a case no interest may be recovered after judgment. He said that it is not open to the House to criticise directly or indirectly this legal context. In these circumstances he submitted that it is not legitimate for a court to conclude that fairness requires that a lender must be able to insist on a stipulation designed to avoid the statutory regime under the 1991 Order. Initially I was inclined to uphold this policy argument. On reflection, however, I have been persuaded that this argument cannot prevail in circumstances where the legislature has neither expressly nor by necessary implication barred a stipulation that interest may continue to accrue after judgment until payment in full.

39. For these reasons as well as the reasons given by Lord Bingham I agree that clause 8 is not unfair and I would also make the order which Lord Bingham proposes.

Lord Hope of Craighead:

'**40.** My Lords, I have had the advantage of reading in draft the speech of my noble and learned friend, Lord Bingham of Cornhill. I agree with it, and for reasons which he has given I too would allow the appeal . . .

44. The primary reason which the Director has given for maintaining that the term is unfair is the uncertainty, confusion and hardship which has been shown to result from the bank's practice of claiming contractual interest from its borrowers after judgment has been given for the principal. Particular unfairness is said to arise where an order is made to pay the debt by instalments, whether under section 71 of the County Courts

Act 1984 or a time order under section 129 of the 1974 Act, and where no consideration has been given to making an order under section 136 of the 1974 Act to amend the agreement so as to prevent the accrual of contractual interest on instalments which are paid when they fall due. The fact that it is commonplace for no consideration to be given to the use of section 136 when payment by instalments is being ordered is not in dispute. So it is not surprising that borrowers, on finding that they are liable for further amounts in addition to the instalments provided for in judgments obtained against them by the bank, have complained to the Director.

45. I am not persuaded that, despite these consequences, the term is unfair. The meaning to be given to the word "unfair" in this context is laid down in regulation 4(1) of the 1994 Regulations. Guidance as to how the words used in that paragraph are to be understood is to be found in the sixteenth recital to the Directive. The recital explains what "constitutes the requirement of good faith". It states that an assessment of the unfair character of unfair terms must be supplemented by an overall evaluation of the different interests involved. Regulation 4(2) indicates the wide range of circumstances to be taken into account in the assessment. It provides that the assessment is to be done as at the time of the conclusion of the contract. But an appreciation of how the term will affect each party when the contract is put into effect must clearly form part of the exercise. It has been pointed out that there are considerable differences between the legal systems of the member states as to how extensive and how powerful the penetration has been of the principle of good faith and fair dealing: Lando & Beale, *Principles of European Contract Law, Parts I and II* (combined and revised, 2000), p 116. But in the present context there is no need to explore this topic in any depth. The Directive provides all the guidance that it needed as to its application.

46. Following this approach it does not seem to me that there is a significant imbalance to the detriment of the borrower in the stipulation that the interest which is payable in terms of the first part of the last sentence is to be charged after as well as before any judgment and that this obligation is not to merge in the judgment. The primary obligation in condition 4 is to pay interest on the outstanding balance due to the bank. The plain fact is that, in the event of a default by the borrower, the bank will not have recovered all of its money until the entire balance on the borrower's account has been paid. The main purpose of the last sentence is to ensure that the borrower does not enjoy the benefit of the outstanding balance after judgment without fulfilling the corresponding obligation which he has undertaken to pay interest on it as provided for in the contract. While the working out of that purpose may give rise to uncertainty in practice, the term itself does not seem to me to be unfair.'

Lord Millett:

'53. My Lords, I have had the advantage of reading in draft the speech of my noble and learned friend, Lord Bingham of Cornhill. I agree with it, and for the reasons he gives I too would allow the appeal. Because of the importance of the case, and because the real source of the problem remains to be tackled, I propose to add a few brief observations of my own.

54. A contractual term in a consumer contract is unfair if "contrary to the require-ment of good faith [it] causes a significant imbalance in the parties' rights and obliga-tions under the contract to the detriment of the consumer". There can be no one single test of this. It is obviously useful to assess the impact of an impugned term on the parties' rights and obligations by comparing the effect of the contract with the term and the effect it would have without it. But the inquiry cannot stop there. It may also be necessary to consider the effect of the inclusion of the term on the substance or core of the transaction; whether if it were drawn to his attention the consumer would be likely to be surprised by it; whether the term is a standard term, not merely in similar non-negotiable consumer contracts, but in commercial contracts freely negotiated between parties acting on level terms and at arms' length; and whether, in such cases, the party adversely affected by the inclusion of the term or his lawyer might reasonably be expected to object to its inclusion and press for its deletion. The list is not necessarily exhaustive; other approaches may sometimes be more appropriate.

55. The substance of the transaction in the present case is self-evident. It is a loan repayable by instalments with interest on the balance from time to time outstanding until the whole of the principal is repaid. The borrower would have no difficulty in understanding this. Nor would he think it unfair. If his attention were drawn to the impugned term, ie that interest should continue to be paid on the outstanding balance after as well as before judgment, he might well be surprised at the need to spell this out, but he would surely not be at all surprised by the fact. It is what he would expect. The term does not affect the substance of the transaction, which is that the borrower should continue to pay interest on the principal from time to time outstanding, nor does it impose any further or unexpected liability upon him not inherent in the basic transac-tion. It is included only to protect the lender from the (to modern eyes artificial) meaning placed on a covenant to pay interest by the Court of Appeal in *In re Sneyd; Ex p Fewings* (1883) 25 ChD 338, where a covenant to pay interest on the balance of the principal sum from time to time remaining unpaid was construed as meaning remaining due under the covenant, so that it fell when the covenant was subsumed in the judgment.

56. The term is not only a standard term in non-negotiable loans to consumers, but in commercial loans freely negotiated between parties on equal terms and acting with pro-fessional advice. I venture to think that no lawyer advising a commercial borrower would dream of objecting to the inclusion of such a term, which merely reinforces and carries into effect what the parties themselves would regard as the essence of the transaction.

57. I am satisfied, therefore, that the term is not unfair. It does not cause an im-balance in the parties' rights and obligations; and the lender did not act in bad faith by taking advantage of the borrower's weakness of bargaining power or lack of professional advice to insist upon a term which would otherwise have been omitted.'

Lord Rodger of Earlsferry:
'**62.** My Lords, I have had the opportunity of reading the speech of my noble and learned friend, Lord Bingham in draft and, for the reasons which he gives, I too would allow the appeal . . .'

The first issue for the House of Lords to consider was whether the term fell within the scope of the Regulations. As we have seen, reg 6(2) (reg 3(2) under the 1994 Regulations) states that the test of fairness will not apply to clauses that define the main subject matter of the contract, or concern the adequacy of the price, provided that they meet the criterion of 'plain intelligible language'. In other words, the Regulations govern the fairness of the terms, not the fairness of the bargain. The question for the House of Lords was whether the provision as to the payment of interest following a court judgment fell under the reg 6(2) exclusions. Lord Steyn emphasised that reg 6(2) 'must be given a restrictive interpretation', otherwise the main purpose of the Regulations would be frustrated by 'endless formalistic arguments as to whether a provision is a definitional or an exclusionary provision'. Lord Bingham agreed, stating that:

> 'The object of the Regulations and the Directive is to protect consumers against the inclusion of unfair and prejudicial terms in standard-form contracts into which they enter, and that object would plainly be frustrated if regulation 3(2)(b) were so broadly interpreted as to cover any terms other than those falling squarely within it.'

Lord Bingham noted with approval the distinction identified by *Chitty* 'between the term or terms which express the substance of the bargain and "incidental" (if important) terms which surround them'. Applying this distinction to the facts before him, Lord Bingham concluded that the term specifying the rate of interest payable after judgment was 'an ancillary provision and not one concerned with the adequacy of the bank's remuneration as against the services supplied'. For both Lord Bingham [12] and Lord Steyn [34] it was significant that the term dealt with the consequences following breach. This weighed in favour of the conclusion that the term was merely incidental or ancillary to the 'core obligation' of the contract.

The restrictive interpretation given to reg 6(2) is to be welcomed since it maintains the integrity and effectiveness of the Regulations. As Gross J explained in the recent case of *Bairstow Eves v Smith* [2004] EWHC 263: '[R]egulation 6(2) must be given a restrictive interpretation; otherwise a coach and horses could be driven through the regulations.' Nevertheless, the House of Lords' conclusion that the term did not fall under reg 6(2) is rather more questionable. The term concerned the payment of interest. In a loan agreement, the main consideration provided by the debtor is the payment of interest. Thus, provisions as to such payment should be regarded as dealing with the 'adequacy of the remuneration' received by the creditor and therefore fall under reg 6(2)(b). This is not the conclusion reached by the House of Lords, however.

Having determined that the term was subject to review under the Regulations, their Lordships turned to consider the issue of fairness. Lord Bingham, with whom the other Law Lords agreed, noted that reg 5(1) (formerly reg 4(1) under the

1994 Regulations) identified two separate requirements: 'significant imbalance' and 'good faith'. For Lord Bingham the former requirement is predominantly concerned with the substance of the agreement. It 'involves looking at the contract as a whole' and the significant imbalance must operate 'to the detriment of the consumer'. The test of 'good faith' on the other hand, is more concerned with procedural fairness. The court must ask whether the supplier has taken advantage of the consumer's 'necessity, indigence, lack of experience, unfamiliarity with the subject matter of the contract, weak bargaining position'. All these matters relate to procedural fairness in the making of the agreement. For Lord Bingham, reg 4(1) 'lays down a composite test, covering both the making and the substance of the contract'.

Lord Steyn took a rather different view, holding that the issue of good faith was concerned with substance as well as procedure. For his Lordship, the examples given in Schedule 2 (Schedule 3 under the 1994 Regulations) were conclusive evidence against the argument that good faith merely concerned procedure (at [36]). Lord Steyn's position appears to be preferable since the wording of reg 5(1) clearly envisages 'significant imbalance' as just one element in an overall test of 'good faith'. The other members of the House of Lords concurred with Lord Bingham, however, and expressed no specific view on the issue, which probably means that his analysis reflects the view of the majority. In practice, this will probably make little difference since the substantive issues will still be considered under the test of 'significant imbalance'. The Court of Appeal has recently confirmed that reg 5(1) sets out a composite test requiring both procedural and substantive unfairness. In *Bryen & Langley Ltd v Boston* [2005] EWCA Civ 973, Rimer LJ said (at [45]):

> '[I]n assessing whether a term that has not been individually negotiated is "unfair" for the purposes of Regulation 5(1) it is necessary to consider not merely the commercial effects of the term on the relative rights of the parties but, in particular, whether the term has been imposed on the consumer in circumstances which justify a conclusion that the supplier has fallen short of the requirements of fair dealing.'

Given the uncertainty that surrounds the concept of 'unfairness', it is perhaps surprising that their Lordships declined to make an Article 234 reference to the European Court of Justice (ECJ) for a preliminary ruling on its meaning. Lord Bingham thought that such a reference was unnecessary because the language used was 'clear and not reasonably capable of differing interpretations'. This conclusion is rather doubtful, however, given the lack of consensus that exists within Member States as to the meaning of 'good faith'. Meryll Dean ('Defining Unfair Terms in Consumer Contracts – Crystal Ball Gazing? *Director General of Fair Trading v First National Bank plc* (2002) 65 MLR 773, 776–7) has written the following:

'[Lord Bingham's] confidence in the obvious meaning of the test and the unlikely divergence of interpretation is to be respected but, in the light of comparative research, may be somewhat misplaced. In the leading comparative analysis of the subject, Zimmerman and Whittaker studied the concept of good faith in 15 legal systems and applied it to 30 hypothetical cases. They came to the conclusion that the concept meant different things within a particular legal system as well as between legal systems. Similarly, Lando and Beale, whilst accepting that "the principle of good faith and fair dealing is recognised or at least appears to be acted on as a guideline for contractual behaviour in all EC countries", nevertheless acknowledge the "considerable difference between the legal systems as to how extensive and how powerful the penetration of the principle has been". . . . There is no doubt that, whilst the concept may be identified as present in a variety of forms in EC legal systems, good faith means different things to different courts . . . *First National Bank* was one of those situations where the House of Lords should have recognised the importance of the reference in a broader European context. As Markesinis has observed, "the task the modern courts face is formidable; the responsibility awesome; their opportunity to harmonise legal systems indisputable". In other words, national myopia needs to give way to a broader vision based on the Europeanisation of contract law.'

It is to be hoped that when the issue is revisited by the House of Lords their Lordships will make a reference to the ECJ in order to obtain clarification of the meaning of 'good faith and fair dealing'.

The House of Lords was unanimous in holding that the term did not contravene the Regulations. Such clauses were common in loan agreements. The obligation created by it was clear and unambiguous and involved nothing 'unbalanced or detrimental to the consumer'. Indeed, in Lord Bingham's view, 'the absence of such a term would unbalance the contract to the detriment of the lender' (at [20]). For Lord Bingham and Lord Steyn the problem lay, not in the contract term itself, but in consumers' understanding of the regulatory framework established by the Consumer Credit Act 1974. In particular, there was a need to draw attention to the courts' powers under ss 129 and 136 of the 1974 Act to redraw the terms of the contract in appropriate circumstances. These provisions would allow the court to incorporate the recovery of interest into the calculation of the instalment payments for the judgment. Catherine MacMillan ('Evolution or Revolution? Unfair Terms in Consumer Contracts' [2002] CLJ 22, 24) has provided the following helpful summary of the case:

'The decision is a welcome one. A strange aspect to this case is that while consumers could face an unpleasant state of affairs, this occurred within an existing regulatory framework. The 1974 Act arguably provides a greater degree of protection to consumers than the Directive'.

In recent years, a number of other cases have considered the operation of reg 5(1). In *Westminster Building Co Ltd v Beckingham* [2004] EWHC 138, the High Court upheld an adjudication clause in a contract for the renovation of a London house. Judge Thornton QC explained his decision as follows (at [31]):

'I was referred to a number of authorities of which the most helpful were *Director General of Fair Trading v First National Bank plc* [2002] 1 AC 481, HL, particularly the speech of Lord Bingham at page 494, and *Lovell Projects Ltd v Legg and Carver* [2003] BLR 452, Judge Moseley QC, particularly at paragraphs 24–31. From these authorities, I derive the following guidance as applicable to the facts of this case:

1. The terms in this case were not individually negotiated but were couched in plain and intelligible language.

2. The terms of the contract were decided upon by Mr Beckingham's agent, who are chartered surveyors, and Mr Beckingham had, or had available to him, competent and objective advice as to the existence and effect of the adjudication clause before he proffered and entered into the contract. Westminster did no more than accept the contract terms offered and had no reasonable need to draw to Mr Beckingham's attention the potential pitfalls to be found in the adjudication clause and in its operation during the course of the work. The clause did not, therefore contravene the requirement of good faith (see especially the speech of Lord Bingham in the *Director General of Fair Trading* case at page 494).

3. The clause did not, if considered at the time of making the contract, constitute a significant imbalance as to Mr Beckingham's rights . . .

4. The clause does not significantly exclude or hinder the consumer's right to take legal action or other legal remedy or restrict the evidence available to him . . .

For all these reasons, I conclude that the adjudication clause, on the facts of this case, is not unfair and is binding on Mr Beckingham.'

While the Regulations have been successfully used to challenge the validity of an adjudication clause (*Picardi v Cuniberti* [2003] BLR 487), this will be extremely difficult where the consumer has received professional advice (*Westminster Building Co Ltd v Beckingham* [2004] EWHC 138; *Allen Wilson Shopfitters v Buckingham* [2005] EWHC 1165), or where s/he has put forward the terms of the contract (*Bryen & Langley Ltd v Boston* [2005] EWCA Civ 973).

A standard form contract issued by the Royal Institute of British Architects was successfully challenged by a consumer in *Munkenbeck & Marshall v Harold*.

Munkenbeck & Marshall v Harold [2005] EWHC 356

Facts: The defendant consumer engaged the claimant firm of architects to undertake architectural services. The claimant's letter of appointment stated that they were appointed on the standard terms of the Royal Institute of British Architects. The terms included the following:

'5.13 Any sums due and remaining unpaid at the expiry of 30 days after the date of issue of an account from the Architect shall bear interest. Interest shall be payable at 8% over Bank of England base rate current at the date of issue of the account.

9.6 The Client shall indemnify the Architect in respect of his legal and other costs in any action or proceedings, together with a reasonable sum in respect of his time spent in connection with such action or proceedings or any part thereof, if:

(1) the Architect obtains a judgment of the court or an Arbitrator's award in his favour for the recovery of fees and/or expenses under the Agreement; or

(2) the Client fails to obtain a judgment of the court or an Arbitrator's award in the Client's favour for any claim or any part of any claim against the Architect.'

In reliance on these terms, the claimant brought an action to recover unpaid fees and the costs involved in bringing the claim. The defendant challenged the terms under reg 5(1).

Held: The Court held that the terms were unfair and were not enforceable.

Judge Richard Havery QC:

'My conclusion on these points is this. The terms in question, 5.13 and 9.6, are unusual and onerous. They are unusual, in my judgment, notwithstanding that they form part of profession-wide standard terms. They were not drawn to the attention of Mr. Harold, who was unaware of them. There is force in the argument that clause 9.6 is there to protect the architect against unfair treatment by the client. The same may be said for the high interest rate. Those points are relevant to the question whether the requirement of good faith mentioned in regulation 5(1) has been satisfied. There is the further point that Mr. Harold was by no means without bargaining power. He negotiated a reduction in the claimant's fees from 10 per cent to 9.5 per cent of final cost. But there is an imbalance, as submitted by Mr. Roberts, and it runs to the detriment of the consumer. That imbalance is not required by the requirement to protect the position of the architect. I conclude that the terms in question are unfair in this case, and fall within regulation 5(1). By reason of regulation 8(1), they are not contractually enforceable.'

It is significant to note that there was evidence of both procedural and substantive unfairness on the facts of the case.

8.4.2.2 The requirement of 'plain, intelligible language'

Written contracts

Reg 7

(1) A seller or supplier shall ensure that any written term of a contract is expressed in plain, intelligible language.

(2) If there is doubt about the meaning of a written term, the interpretation which is most favourable to the consumer shall prevail but this rule shall not apply in proceedings brought under regulation 12.

Regulation 7 applies to all written terms (including terms excluded by reg 6(2)) and requires the seller or supplier to ensure that the terms are expressed in 'plain, intelligible language'. The problem with the provision is that it does not prescribe any sanction for breach and therefore its status as a requirement remains unclear. Elizabeth MacDonald (*Exemption Clauses and Unfair Terms*, 2nd edn, 2006, p 227, Horsham: Tottel Publishing) has noted the following:

'[I]t is difficult to see it as a requirement in any formal sense when the Directive and the Regulations do not state any penalty for failure to draft in plain intelligible language beyond that of interpretation favourable to the consumer (and that is only applicable in the context of the particular contract and not at the level of preventive actions). The point might be made that a penalty could now be seen as provided as the Consumer Injunctions Directive requires injunctive relief to be available in certain circumstances where there is 'any act contrary' to a listed Directive, including the Unfair Terms in Consumer Contracts Directive. However, clearly the ECJ in *EC Commission v Spain* [2004] ECR I–7999, did not take the view that there was any distinct requirement, as such, for terms to be in 'plain intelligible language' which would allow them to be dealt with simply because of their lack of "plain intelligible language" '

It therefore seems that failure to meet the requirement of reg 7 does not of itself render the term unfair although it is inevitable that such matters will be taken into account by the courts when considering the fairness of the term.

Regulation 7(2) simply gives statutory effect to the common-law *contra proferentem* rule. If a term is ambiguous in its meaning, it will be construed in favour of the consumer.

8.4.3 ENFORCEMENT

The primary role in supervising compliance with the Regulations lies with the Office of Fair Trading (OFT).

Complaints – consideration by Director
Reg 10

(1) It shall be the duty of the Director to consider any complaint made to him that any contract term drawn up for general use is unfair, unless –

    (a) the complaint appears to the Director to be frivolous or vexatious; or

    (b) a qualifying body has notified the Director that it agrees to consider the complaint.

(2) The Director shall give reasons for his decision to apply or not to apply, as the case may be, for an injunction under regulation 12 in relation to any complaint which these Regulations require him to consider.

(3) In deciding whether or not to apply for an injunction in respect of a term which the Director considers to be unfair, he may, if he considers it appropriate to do so, have regard to any undertakings given to him by or on behalf of any person as to the continued use of such a term in contracts concluded with consumers.

Complaints – consideration by qualifying bodies
Reg 11

(1) If a qualifying body specified in Part One of Schedule 1 notifies the Director that it agrees to consider a complaint that any contract term drawn up for general use is unfair, it shall be under a duty to consider that complaint.

(2) Regulation 10(2) and (3) shall apply to a qualifying body which is under a duty to consider a complaint as they apply to the Director.

Injunctions to prevent continued use of unfair terms
Reg 12

(1) The Director or, subject to paragraph (2), any qualifying body may apply for an injunction (including an interim injunction) against any person appearing to the Director or that body to be using, or recommending use of, an unfair term drawn up for general use in contracts concluded with consumers.

(2) A qualifying body may apply for an injunction only where –

    (a) it has notified the Director of its intention to apply at least fourteen days before the date on which the application is made, beginning with the date on which the notification was given; or

    (b) the Director consents to the application being made within a shorter period.

(3) The court on an application under this regulation may grant an injunction on such terms as it thinks fit.

(4) An injunction may relate not only to use of a particular contract term drawn up for general use but to any similar term, or a term having like effect, used or recommended for use by any person.

Powers of the Director and qualifying bodies to obtain documents and information
Reg 13

(1) The Director may exercise the power conferred by this regulation for the purpose of –

    (a) facilitating his consideration of a complaint that a contract term drawn up for general use is unfair; or

    (b)   ascertaining whether a person has complied with an undertaking or court order as to the continued use, or recommendation for use, of a term in contracts concluded with consumers.

(2)   A qualifying body specified in Part One of Schedule 1 may exercise the power conferred by this regulation for the purpose of –

    (a)   facilitating its consideration of a complaint that a contract term drawn up for general use is unfair; or

    (b)   ascertaining whether a person has complied with –

        (i)   an undertaking given to it or to the court following an application by that body, or

        (ii)   a court order made on an application by that body,

    as to the continued use, or recommendation for use, of a term in contracts concluded with consumers.

(3)   The Director may require any person to supply to him, and a qualifying body specified in Part One of Schedule 1 may require any person to supply to it –

    (a)   a copy of any document which that person has used or recommended for use, at the time the notice referred to in paragraph (4) below is given, as a pre-formulated standard contract in dealings with consumers;

    (b)   information about the use, or recommendation for use, by that person of that document or any other such document in dealings with consumers.

(4)   The power conferred by this regulation is to be exercised by a notice in writing which may –

    (a)   specify the way in which and the time within which it is to be complied with; and

    (b)   be varied or revoked by a subsequent notice.

(5)   Nothing in this regulation compels a person to supply any document or information which he would be entitled to refuse to produce or give in civil proceedings before the court.

(6)   If a person makes default in complying with a notice under this regulation, the court may, on the application of the Director or of the qualifying body, make such order as the court thinks fit for requiring the default to be made good, and any such order may provide that all the costs or expenses of and incidental to the application shall be borne by the person in default or by any officers of a company or other association who are responsible for its default.

Publication, information and advice
Reg 15

(1)   The Director shall arrange for the publication in such form and manner as he considers appropriate, of –

    (a)   details of any undertaking or order notified to him under regulation 14;

    (b)   details of any undertaking given to him by or on behalf of any person as to the continued use of a term which the Director considers to be unfair in contracts concluded with consumers;

    (c)   details of any application made by him under regulation 12, and of the terms of any undertaking given to, or order made by, the court;

    (d)   details of any application made by the Director to enforce a previous order of the
          court.

(2)   The Director shall inform any person on request whether a particular term to which these
     Regulations apply has been –

    (a)   the subject of an undertaking given to the Director or notified to him by a qualifying
          body; or

    (b)   the subject of an order of the court made upon application by him or notified to him
          by a qualifying body;

    and shall give that person details of the undertaking or a copy of the order, as the case
    may be, together with a copy of any amendments which the person giving the undertak-
    ing has agreed to make to the term in question.

(3)   The Director may arrange for the dissemination in such form and manner as he con-
    siders appropriate of such information and advice concerning the operation of these
    Regulations as may appear to him to be expedient to give to the public and to all
    persons likely to be affected by these Regulations.

The power of supervision previously lay with the Director General of Fair Trading but, by virtue of the Enterprise Act 2002, all powers have now been transferred to the OFT. The supervisory role created by the Regulations includes the duty to consider complaints (reg 10) and the power to publish information and advice about the operation of the Regulations. Under reg 12, the Director has the power to apply to the court for an injunction to restrain the use of unfair terms, and reg 13 provides for a new power to obtain documents and information from traders in relation to the use of unfair terms.

Although *Director General of Fair Trading v First National Bank* concerned an application by the Director General for an injunction under reg 12, the vast major-ity of cases do not reach the courts. Instead they are resolved at a much earlier stage through negotiation between the Unfair Contract Terms Unit of the OFT and the businesses concerned.

Bright, S, 'Winning the Battle Against Unfair Terms' (2000) 20 LS 331–333–338

ENFORCEMENT OF THE UNFAIR TERMS IN CONSUMER
CONTRACTS REGULATIONS
Although the UK Regulations can be relied on in private law disputes involving consumers, it is the Unfair Contract Terms Unit that has been at the forefront of action
against unfair contract terms. Private law enforcement does not provide an effective
way of regulating the standard inclusion of unfair terms in adhesion contracts: it is
true that success in an individual action will mean that the term is not binding upon
that consumer, but its impact beyond that consumer will be limited, and there is no

significant pressure on the business to discontinue future use of that term. Further, there will only ever be a trickle of private law actions, as most consumers prefer to deal with matters informally or not at all, rather than pursue complaints by formal legal mechanisms in which the costs of litigation (financial and otherwise) exceed the benefits that stand to be achieved. So far there has only been a handful of cases in which the consumer has, with mixed success, relied upon the 1994 Regulations.

The administrative model of enforcement created by the 1994 Regulations (and extended by the 1999 Regulations) is a much more effective way of preventing the continuing use of unfair terms and changing contracting practice. Investigation into allegedly unfair terms usually follows a complaint made to the Director General of Fair Trading, who is under a duty to investigate unless it is 'frivolous or vexatious'. There is a strong flow of complaints made to the Unfair Contract Terms Unit, about half of which come from local authority trading standards departments and consumer advice organisations. The Unit has adopted a proactive response to complaints; not only will the particular term complained about be looked into, but the contract as a whole will be investigated. Indeed, investigations often spread beyond the particular contract to involve trade associations, and the Unit has initiated a number of sectoral investigations so that contracts used by traders in a similar line of business can be looked at together. So, for example, there has been notable success in securing the amendment of terms in mobile phone contracts, the sector about which there has been most complaint. By way of illustration, numerous amendments were agreed in relation to Vodafone contracts, including adjustment of the notice requirement (which had required three months' notice in addition to the minimum 12-month term), deletion of a clause providing for a substantial disconnection charge, and a reduction in the level of compensation payable by a consumer who terminates early. Other sectors which have been focused upon include the home improvement industry, vehicle rental, package holidays and, most recently, the Director General of Fair Trading has announced that he is investigating conditions of airline use. Discussions with trade associations are not always a response to complaints and may be on the initiative of the Office of Fair Trading.

In practice, the vast majority of cases are dealt with by negotiation and if the contract term is found to be unfair the Unfair Contract Terms Unit will require the business to provide an undertaking to discontinue the use of the unfair term. Court action has been seen as a last resort. Although the Director General of Fair Trading has power to apply for an injunction to restrain the use of unfair terms, this has, so far, occurred only once. This is a little surprising, given that the issues at stake are not insignificant. In relation to mortgages, for example, the Office of Fair Trading persuaded the City Mortgage Corporation (CMC) to reduce its dual interest rates and the manner of calculating the premium due on early redemption of the mortgage. The financial costs to CMC must be great. It is interesting to speculate just why this course of action has been so successful and why traders have, with varying degrees of willingness, complied with the requests to abandon or amend terms without forcing the issue to court. Presumably, the fear of bad publicity plays a part. There is also the fact that many of the terms are fair in part: by rewriting them the trader can still secure the protection needed whilst also being fair to the consumer; if left unamended, the terms may be wholly unenforceable against the consumer. Dealing with trade associations is also an efficient way of reaching businesses: as the representative figure within that sectoral activity, associations will often be anxious to present a positive public image and to maintain good working relationships with the Office of Fair Trading. Agreements reached at this level will be passed through to the trading bodies who use the association's standard contract. By way of example, the Office of Fair Trading agreed a revised model contract for use by members of the British Vehicle Rental and Leasing Association. About 85% of companies in the industry belong to that association. It is also less costly to proceed by way of undertaking than by paying the costs of going to court. However, what has been the practice over the last five years will not necessarily be the pattern of the future; if it emerges over time that the courts adopt a less consumer-orientated interpretation of the Regulations, there is the possibility that fewer cases will be settled by negotiation alone.

This administrative model of enforcement was not prescribed by the Directive. Although the Directive specifies that mechanisms must be in place to prevent the continued use of unfair terms in consumer contracts, the method deployed to achieve this end is left to member states. States could therefore select not only to hand this role to a public official (as in the United Kingdom and in Nordic countries), but to permit consumer organisations to bring actions to prevent the continued use of unfair terms (as in Germany and France), or (possibly) to use criminal sanctions. The route chosen in the United Kingdom has proven effective, as already seen, but there were complaints that the 1994 Regulations failed to give a voice to consumer organisations. Article 7 of the Unfair Terms Directive requires member states to ensure that 'adequate and effective means exist to prevent the continued use of unfair terms' and that the means shall 'include provisions whereby persons or organisations, having a legitimate interest under national law in protecting consumers' may take action to have terms declared unfair. In 1995 the Consumers' Association sought to have the exclusion of bodies such as theirs declared to be an unlawful implementation of the Directive. The judge, Hidden J, referred the question raised by the Consumers' Association's action to the European Court of Justice for a ruling on the Community law, but the point was never pursued, as the UK government announced its intention to address their concerns through an amendment to the 1994 Regulations.

There are various models that could have been used to extend the enforcement powers beyond the Director General of Fair Trading. The approach adopted in the 1999 Regulations is to list additional specific bodies (statutory regulators, trading standards departments and the Consumers' Association) as having powers to apply for an injunction to prevent the continued use of unfair terms. With the exception of the Consumers' Association, these bodies can also notify the Director General of Fair Trading that they will investigate a complaint, and will then be under an obligation to do so . . .

The extension of powers beyond the Director General of Fair Trading meant that measures had to be put in place to ensure that there would be consistent approaches taken to unfair terms, effective co-ordination between the enforcement bodies, and to protect traders from multiple challenges. To this end, if a qualifying body intends to apply for an injunction, it must give the Director General of Fair Trading notice and then, unless a shorter period is authorised, cannot commence the action within 14 days. In addition, the qualifying body must inform the Director General of Fair Trading of all undertakings it receives and of the result of any applications for an injunction. The fact that there is only a small number of bodies authorised to act does minimise the risk of a trader being in negotiation with several 'enforcers'. The Director General of Fair Trading will remain the primary investigator and, as all investigations have to be reported to him, he will have an overview of all complaints. He retains a duty to disseminate information about the operation of the Regulations, not only about his own actions but also reporting on undertakings given to, and actions brought by, other qualifying bodies. In practice, dissemination has taken place through the issue of regular bulletins containing details of case reports, coupled with press releases reporting significant 'triumphs'.

It is anticipated that the widening of the enforcement provisions, and the ability to apply for injunctive relief in the County Court, will increase the number of cases taken to court. This may well impact upon the application of the Regulations. To date, the Office of Fair Trading has largely operated with a free hand, exercising a wide discretion to apply the Regulations in the interests of consumers. Judicial intervention may impose more checks and balances into their application . . .

Susan Bright's article highlights the important role played by the OFT in the regulation of unfair terms. Most cases are resolved not in the courts but in the OFT itself.

An important change brought about by the 1999 Regulations was the inclusion of a number of other bodies in the enforcement framework. The list of 'qualifying bodies' is contained in Schedule 1. It includes various statutory regulators, local authority trading standards departments and the Consumers' Association. These 'qualifying bodies' are given the power to apply for an injunction under reg 12(2) and to obtain documents and information under reg 13(2). As Bright notes, the success of this extension of powers will largely depend on how well the qualifying bodies co-ordinate with one other. Section 14 ensures that the OFT is kept informed of any enforcement action being taken.

8.5 UNFAIR TERMS UNDER THE PRINCIPLES OF EUROPEAN CONTRACT LAW

The Principles of European Contract Law contain a number of provisions that deal with unfair terms and good faith in the law of contract.

Article 1.201: Good Faith and Fair Dealing
(1) Each party must act in accordance with good faith and fair dealing.
(2) The parties may not exclude or limit this duty.

Article 1.201 provides that the parties to a contract must act in accordance with 'good faith and fair dealing'. This is a general duty that cannot be excluded or limited by the parties.

The Principles also contain some more specific provisions relating to unfair terms:

Article 4:110: Unfair Terms not Individually Negotiated
(1) A party may avoid a term which has not been individually negotiated if, contrary to the requirements of good faith and fair dealing, it causes a significant imbalance in the parties' rights and obligations arising under the contract to the detriment of that party, taking into account the nature of the performance to be rendered under the contract, all the other terms of the contract and the circumstances at the time the contract was concluded.
(2) This Article does not apply to:

   (a) a term which defines the main subject matter of the contract, provided the term is in plain and intelligible language; or to
   (b) the adequacy in value of one party's obligations compared to the value of the obligations of the other party.

Article 4.110 deals with unfair terms that have not been individually negotiated. The Article is very similar to reg 6 of the UTTCR 1999 and uses the same language: good faith, fair dealing and significant imbalance. As with reg 6, the Article does not apply to terms that define the subject matter of the contract, or the adequacy in value of one party's obligations compared to the other party's obligations. The main difference between Art 4.110 and reg 6 is that Art 4.110 applies to all types of contract, not just to consumer contracts.

Article 4:118: Exclusion or Restriction of Remedies
(1) Remedies for fraud, threats and excessive benefit or unfair advantage-taking, and the right to avoid an unfair term which has not been individually negotiated, cannot be excluded or restricted.
(2) Remedies for mistake and incorrect information may be excluded or restricted unless the exclusion or restriction is contrary to good faith and fair dealing.

Article 4.118 limits the power to exclude or limit remedies. Importantly, this includes attempts to limit the right to avoid an unfair term under Art 4.110. Remedies for mistake and incorrect information can be excluded or restricted so long as such an exclusion or restriction would not be contrary to good faith and fair dealing.

Article 8:109: Clause Excluding or Restricting Remedies
Remedies for non-performance may be excluded or restricted unless it would be contrary to good faith and fair dealing to invoke the exclusion or restriction.

Art 8.109 permits the exclusion or restriction of remedies for nonperformance so long as such an exclusion or restriction would not be contrary to good faith and fair dealing.

The Principles of European Contract Law provide for broad control of unfair terms, not just in consumer contracts, but in commercial contracts as well. In keeping with the UTCCR 1999, the Principles operate by reference to the concepts of 'good faith and fair dealing'. As we have seen in *Director General of Fair Trading v First National Bank*, the English courts are just beginning to come to terms with these concepts and we may require an ECJ reference in order to provide further clarification.

8.6 REFORM

There is a significant degree of overlap between the UCTA 1977 and the UTCCR 1999, but due to the use of different language and concepts the two pieces of legislation sometimes lead to different outcomes. The key differences are set out in the table on p 544.

The Law Commission (*Unfair Terms in Contracts*, 2005, Law Com No 292, Scot Law Com, No 199, Cm 6464, para 1.14) has described the UCTA 1977 in the following terms:

'UCTA is a complex statute. As we know from our own experience, it is difficult to understand fully without very careful reading. Given the complexity of its subject matter, UCTA is structured in a way that is very economical, but that structure is not easy to grasp. Frequently, a single provision will apply to a number of different types of contract and to a variety of different situations: this makes it difficult to see the effect of the statute, particularly for a reader without legal training.'

The Law Commission's opinion of the UTCCR 1999 was slightly more positive, but it still criticised the Regulations for using terminology 'that is alien to English and Scots readers, lawyers and non-lawyers alike' (para 1.15). In addition, the Commission expressed concern that the unfair terms legislation provided inadequate protection to small businesses.

In 2001, the Department of Trade and Industry (DTI) asked the Law Commission and the Scottish Law Commission to review the law of unfair contract terms. The review has now been completed and a report and draft Bill was published in

Table 1

	Unfair Contract Terms Act 1977	Unfair Terms in Consumer Contracts Regulations 1999
Scope:	Wide scope covering consumer and commercial contracts, and some forms of liability in tort and under statute (ss 1–8).	Narrow scope covering only consumer contracts (reg 4(1)).
Application:	Narrow application just to clauses excluding or limiting liability, or performance modification clauses (ss 3, 13).	Wide application to all clauses except: (i) those defining the main subject matter of the contract and (ii) those concerning the adequacy of the price or remuneration (reg 6(2)).
Trigger:	Triggered by clauses excluding or restricting liability for negligence, breach of contract, breach of terms implied by statute and misrepresentation (ss 2–8).	Triggered only by terms that have not been individually negotiated (reg 5 and Sched 2).
Control:	Two-tier control rendering some clauses automatically ineffective and others subject to the requirement of reasonableness (ss 2–8, 11).	One-tier control subjecting clauses to 'good faith' requirement (reg 5(1)).
Burden of proof:	The burden of proof is placed on the party seeking to rely on the clause.	The burden of proof is on the consumer to show that the clause is unfair.
Effect:	Renders some clauses ineffective and subjects others to the requirement of 'reasonableness'.	Renders unfair terms unenforceable against the consumer although the contract can continue without the unfair term (reg 8).
Consumer:	Narrow definition of 'consumer', but includes legal and natural persons (s 12).	Wide definition of 'consumer', but restricted to natural persons (reg 3(1)).
Language of contract:	None required, but must satisfy reasonableness test (if applicable).	Written in plain and intelligible language (reg 7(1)).
Interpretation provisions:	Contains no strict interpretation provisions.	Contains contra proferentem rule (reg 7(2)).
Policing provisions:	Contains no policing provisions.	Contains detailed policing provisions to be exercised by the OFT and other 'qualifying bodies' (regs 10–15 plus Sched 1).
Jurisdictions:	Has separate provisions for Scotland (Part II).	Applies to the UK as a whole.

February 2005. It is, as yet, unclear whether the government will implement the proposals recommended by the Law Commission. The Report was accompanied by the following summary.

Unfair Terms in Contracts, 2005, Law Com No 292, Scot Law Com, No 199, Cm 6464

SUMMARY

1. In 2001, the Department of Trade and Industry asked the Law Commission and Scottish Law Commission to rewrite the law of unfair contract terms as a single regime, in a clearer and more accessible style. At the same time we were asked to consider whether to extend the legislation to protect businesses, particularly small businesses.

2. On 24 February we published a final report setting out our detailed recommendations, together with a draft Bill.

THE PROBLEM

3. As the law currently stands, there are two major pieces of legislation dealing with unfair contract terms. The Unfair Contract Terms Act 1977 sets out the traditional UK approach, while the Unfair Terms in Consumer Contracts Regulations 1999 implement the 1993 EU Directive. The two laws contain inconsistent and overlapping provisions, using different language and concepts to produce similar but not identical effects. A law that affects ordinary people in their everyday lives had been made unnecessarily complicated and difficult.

4. The 1977 Act is written in a particularly dense style, which even specialist lawyers find difficult to follow. This is made even more complicated by the fact that the Act contains two Parts: one for England, Wales and Northern Ireland, and one for Scotland. The two Parts produce almost the same effect but use different language to do so. Meanwhile the 1999 Regulations use European concepts that are unfamiliar to UK lawyers. The combination of legislation has led to widespread confusion among consumers, businesses and their advisers.

5. The draft Bill rewrites both laws for the whole of the UK in a way that is much clearer and easier to follow. We have also plugged some gaps in protection.

THE CURRENT LAW: DIFFERENCES BETWEEN THE ACT AND REGULATIONS

6. The 1977 Act extends to a wide range of contracts, including consumer, business, private and employment contracts. However, it only covers a narrow range of terms. It is designed to control exclusion clauses, where one party attempts to exclude or limit their normal liability for negligence or breach of contract, or tries to 'render a contractual performance substantially different from that which was reasonably expected'. The 1999 Regulations cover a much wider range of terms, extending to any term other than the main subject matter or the price. However, they only apply to consumer contracts.

7. Under the 1977 Act some terms are automatically ineffective. Under the Regulations, no term is automatically unfair. Instead, they are all subject to a fairness test. However the Regulations permit the Office of Fair Trading (OFT) and other bodies to go to court to prevent unfair terms from being used. These preventive powers have proved to be an important way of regulating the market.

8. The Act and Regulations also differ in their treatment of negotiated clauses; in the way they phrase the fairness test; and in their burden of proof.

CONSUMER CONTRACTS

9. Our aim is to produce a single, unified regime to cover the whole of the UK that preserves the existing level of consumer protection. Where the Act and Regulations differ, we have rounded up rather than rounded down. Thus for consumer contracts, the draft Bill

(1) extends to all the terms currently covered by the Regulations (not just exclusion clauses);

(2) continues to hold that terms which limit liability for death or personal injury, or which exclude basic undertakings about the quality and fitness of goods are ineffective;

(3) includes negotiated clauses as well as standard clauses (as does the 1977 Act). This closes a current loophole by which some businesses can, for example, demand unreasonable deposits by saying that they are prepared to negotiate the amount from 100% to 75%;

(4) states that in claims brought by consumers, the burden of proof lies on the business to show that the term is fair. Again this follows the 1977 Act. The business will generally have far greater resources than the consumer so, where the fairness of a term is in issue, it should be required to justify its position. This is not the case in preventive powers, where it will still be up to the OFT or other body to show that the term is unfair;

10. The OFT and other bodies will gain some additional powers to take action against notices. For example, the OFT would be able to demand that a sign in a store car-park saying 'no liability is accepted for injury' is taken down. Such signs have long been ineffective in legal terms but organisations continue to use them, presumably in an attempt to discourage people from claiming their rights.

PROTECTING SMALL BUSINESSES

11. The report also recommends improved protection for small businesses. At present, where a business contracts on the other party's standard written terms of business, it may challenge unfair exclusion clauses. This means that the court may review the fairness of a term that excludes or limits liability for negligence or breach of contract, or purports to allow the other party to render a contractual performance substantially different from that which was reasonably expected.

12. We were told that small businesses frequently find themselves signing contracts that contain other unfair terms, which the law does not allow to be challenged. This is

especially true where a small farmer, manufacturer or builder supplies a much larger business. The small business may be required to indemnify the larger business for losses that are not their fault, or forfeit deposits, or accept variations of price after the contract has been agreed. They may find that the larger business has reserved the right to terminate a contract at will, or for only a minor default, while the small business is bound more rigorously by the contract.

13. We do not wish to interfere with business contracts that are genuinely negotiated between the parties. However, there is a problem when one party imposes its standard terms on a vulnerable small business. The small business may not understand the term or its consequences; and even if it does understand the term it will often lack the bargaining strength to change it.

14. The draft Bill includes special protection for the smallest and most vulnerable businesses, commonly referred to as 'micro businesses'. We define these as businesses with nine or fewer staff.

15. Under our proposals, these very small businesses will be able to challenge any standard term of the contract that has not been altered through negotiation, and is not the main subject matter of the contract or the price.

16. However, we do not wish to interfere where contracts are already sufficiently regulated, or where the business is sufficiently sophisticated to look after its interests. We therefore set out a number of exceptions to the new small business protections. We exclude contracts for financial services, contracts over £500,000 and situations where the apparently small business is associated with other businesses, so that overall the group has more than nine employees. We also recommend that the exemptions currently in the 1977 Act should apply to the new controls on small business contracts. These exclude, for example, contracts for land, intellectual property, or security interests or contracts to form or dissolve contracts. Here people will usually seek legal advice.

17. In an ideal world, a well-resourced organisation would use preventive powers to protect small businesses generally, by challenging those that imposed unfair standard terms on them. However, we have not been able to find an organisation with the resources to take on this task. The draft Bill does not presently include preventive powers to be used on behalf of small businesses. However, if resources could be found, this would provide useful protection. Many small businesses told us about unfair terms that could be challenged under the present law, but which are still used because the small business lacks the ability to bring court action.

OTHER CONTRACTS

18. At present, the 1977 Act includes several other types of contract, such as contracts between larger businesses, employment contracts and private sales. Here our aim is to preserve the effect of the current law, while setting it out in a way that is clearer and easier to understand.

19. We do, however, recommend some small reductions in the way that the 1977 Act regulates negotiated contracts between businesses. At present, the Act allows courts to review any term that limits the effect of the implied undertakings in the Sale of

Goods Act 1979, which state that goods should match their description or sample, be of satisfactory quality and fit for their purpose. These controls apply to negotiated terms as well as to standard terms. We think it would be very unlikely for a court to find that a clause is unfair when it had been genuinely negotiated between businesses, and we are not aware that any cases have been brought to challenge negotiated terms under these provisions. Under our proposals, businesses will generally be allowed to negotiate to limit contractual liability: the controls will only apply to standard terms.

INTERNATIONAL CONTRACTS AND CHOICE OF LAW

20. Much criticism has been levelled at how the 1977 Act deals with business contracts involving the cross-border sale of goods. Although the avowed aim of section 26 was to exempt export contracts while protecting UK importers, it was drafted in a way that exempted many import contracts and applied the legislation to some exporters. The Draft Bill rewrites this section to exempt only those contracts under which goods are exported or supplied abroad.

21. For consumer contracts, the Draft Bill prevents businesses from using non-UK law if the consumer was living in the UK when the contract was made and took all the steps necessary to conclude the contract there.

The Law Commission Report contains more detailed provisions but the Summary helpfully highlights the main changes that will be brought about by the proposals. The unified regime will provide greater certainty and clarity, and will avoid the confusion of having two pieces of legislation governing the one area. The proposals extend the scope of protection so that it covers all terms currently covered by the UTCCR (not just exclusion clauses). The definition of 'consumer' is narrowed, however. Non-natural persons (for example, companies) will no longer be regarded as consumers and it will be necessary for the consumer to demonstrate that s/he was not acting for purposes related to any business which s/he may run. The new Act will include an Indicative List of 'unfair and unreasonable' clauses, similar to that included in the UTCCR 1999. This should help to provide clarification of what amounts to an 'unfair and unreasonable' clause. The burden of proving 'fairness and reasonableness' in a consumer contract will rest on the party seeking to rely on the clause.

It will be interesting to see how the courts respond to the extension of their jurisdiction to regulate terms given to small businesses. Some may fear that this will lead to commercial uncertainty, but this is unlikely, given the courts' historic reluctance to intervene in business-to-business contracts: see *Watford Electronics Ltd v Sanderson CFL Ltd* [2001] 1 All ER (Comm) 696 and *Granville Chemicals Ltd v Davis Turner & Co Ltd* [2003] 2 Lloyd's Rep 356. Only time will tell whether the new provisions will encourage a more interventionist approach.

8.7 ADDITIONAL READING

Adams, J, and Brownsword, R, 'The Unfair Contract Terms Act: a decade of discretion' (1988) 104 LQR 94.

Bradgate, R, 'Unreasonable standard terms' (1997) 60 MLR 582.

Beale, H, 'Unfair contracts in Britain and Europe' [1989] CLP 197.

Beale, H, 'Legislative control of fairness: The Directive on Unfair Terms in Consumer Contracts', in Beatson J, and Friedmann, D (eds), *Good Faith and Fault in Contract Law*, 1995, Oxford: Clarendon.

Collins, H, 'Good faith in European contract law' (1994) 14 OJLS 229.

MacDonald, E, 'Unifying unfair terms legislation' (2004) 67 MLR 69.

Palmer, N, and Yates, D, 'The future of the Unfair Contract Terms Act 1977' (1981) 40 CLJ 108.

Von Mehren, A, 'General limits on the use of contract', Vol vii, *International Encyclopaedia of Comparative Law*, 1982, The Hague: Mohr/Nijhoff.

Yates, D, *Exclusion Clauses in Contracts*, 2nd edn, 1982, London: Sweet & Maxwell.

MISREPRESENTATION

In this chapter and the following three we deal with the period prior to the formation of the contract and the problems that may arise due to the parties' conduct. Following formation of an apparently valid contract, one of the parties might decide that it should not be enforced, due to the conduct of the other party or some fact unknown to both parties. In the following four chapters we will consider four categories of legal rule that govern these situations: misrepresentation (the subject of this chapter), mistake (Chapter 10), duress (Chapter 11) and undue influence (Chapter 12). The first two categories can be grouped together because misrepresentation is effectively the law of induced mistake and the latter two categories can be grouped together because undue influence is the sister doctrine of duress.

9.1 INTRODUCTION

English law recognises no general duty of good faith in the negotiation of a contract. This is in stark contrast to the Principles of European Contract Law, which state the following:

Article 2:301 – Negotiations Contrary to Good Faith

(1) A party is free to negotiate and is not liable for failure to reach an agreement.
(2) However, a party who has negotiated or broken off negotiations contrary to good faith and fair dealing is liable for the losses caused to the other party.
(3) It is contrary to good faith and fair dealing, in particular, for a party to enter into or continue negotiations with no real intention of reaching an agreement with the other party.

Although the Article recognises that negotiation does not always lead to the formation of a contract, it does make a party liable, who in negotiating it has no real intention of reaching an agreement. Furthermore, paragraph 2 imposes a positive duty of 'good faith and fair dealing' on the parties. No such positive duty exists in English law. Parties are free to enter and leave negotiations without fear of being penalised. Likewise, there is no positive duty to negotiate in good faith (this concept was rejected by the House of Lords in *Walford v Miles* [1992] 2 AC 128). Instead, English law imposes a negative duty upon contracting parties, not to make false statements of fact to each other, which thereby induce the other party to enter the contract.

The law of misrepresentation is somewhat complicated by the fact that it straddles the boundary between contract, tort and unjust enrichment. The claimant will have an action for damages in the law of tort if the misrepresentation was either fraudulent or negligent. In addition, s/he will have an action in unjust enrichment (see Chapter 18) to recover the benefits transferred under the contract if s/he elects to rescind. The law is further complicated by the fact that it involves a complex interplay between the rules of common law, equity and statute. All this will be considered in greater detail when we look at the remedial consequences of a misrepresentation.

Before moving on to consider the law of misrepresentation it should be noted that there are a number of other remedies available for precontractual statements. For example, in the context of consumer contracts, s 44 of the Consumer Credit Act 1974 imposes criminal sanctions on creditors that breach the stated regulations (Consumer Credit Advertisement Regulations 1989/ SI 1989/1125) as to the form and content of credit advertisements. The purpose of these Regulations is to ensure that advertisements convey a fair and reasonably comprehensive indication of the nature of the credit facilities offered by the advertiser and of their true cost to persons using them. Criminal liability is also imposed on retailers who give misleading information as to the price of their goods, services or facilities (s 20 Consumer Protection Act 1987).

In addition to these remedies under statute and in the law of misrepresentation, a remedy may also be available if the statement is incorporated into the contract as a term. In such circumstances the claimant will have an action for breach of contract in the event of breach of the term and the usual contract remedies will be available. Alternatively, the statement may be found to form a collateral contract, of the form – 'If you enter into a contract with me, I promise to do this for you'. These issues have been discussed in Chapters 5 and 7 and will not be pursued further here.

This chapter is divided up into five sections. First, we will consider what constitutes an actionable representation; we will then consider the requirement that the misrepresentation induced the other party to enter into the contract; next we will look at the four categories of misrepresentation; and then we will consider the remedies available for each; and finally, we will examine the law on exclusion of liability for misrepresentation.

▌9.2 ACTIONABLE REPRESENTATIONS

For a statement to be actionable it must be made by, or on behalf, of the other contracting party. If the statement is made by a third party, this will generally have no effect on the contract. In the rest of this section we will consider what statements can be actionable as misrepresentations.

9.2.1 STATEMENTS OF FACT

It is clear that unambiguous statements of fact are actionable as misrepresentations.

Curtis v Chemical Cleaning & Dyeing [1951] 1 KB 805

Facts: Mrs Curtis took a white satin wedding dress trimmed in beads and sequins to a dry cleaner for cleaning. The shop assistant asked her to sign a 'receipt'. When she asked what the significance of the document was, the assistant replied that it excluded liability for damage by or to the beads and sequins. Mrs Curtis signed the document and left the dress with the assistant. The document actually contained a general exclusion clause, excluding all liability for damages howsoever caused. When Mrs Curtis returned for the dress she discovered that it was badly stained. She was awarded damages by the county court judge, who held that the defendants had been guilty of negligence and were not protected by their exclusion clause because of the misrepresentation as to its character.

Held: The Court of Appeal dismissed the defendants' appeal holding that they could not rely on the general exclusion clause because it had been superseded by the shop assistant's misrepresentation.

Denning LJ:
'In my opinion, any behaviour by words or conduct is sufficient to be a misrepresentation if it is such as to mislead the other party about the existence or extent of the exemption. If the false impression is created knowingly, it is a fraudulent misrepresentation; if it is created unwittingly, it is an innocent misrepresentation; but either is sufficient to disentitle the creator of it to the benefit of the exemption.'

9.2.2 STATEMENTS OF INTENTION

Statements of intention cannot, of themselves, constitute an actionable misrepresentation. However, a statement of intention carries with it an implied statement of fact as to the state of mind of the representor and this can constitute an actionable representation.

Edgington v Fitzmaurice (1885) 24 Ch D 459

Facts: The directors of a company issued a prospectus inviting subscriptions for debentures. The prospectus stated that it was intended to use the money obtained to make improvements in the company by altering buildings, purchasing horses and vans, and developing the trade of the company. The real intention was to use the money obtained to pay off existing debts of the company.

Held: The Court of Appeal held the statement of intention was a misrepresentation of fact as to the state of mind of the directors because there had never been an intention to use the money in the manner stated.

Bowen LJ:
'There must be a misstatement of an existing fact: but the state of a man's mind is as much a fact as the state of his digestion. It is true that it is very difficult to prove what the state of a man's mind at a particular time is, but if it can be ascertained it is as much a fact as anything else. A misrepresentation as to the state of a man's mind is, therefore, a misstatement of fact.'

9.2.3 REPRESENTATIONS OF OPINION

A mere statement of opinion is not an actionable misrepresentation. This was seen in *Bisset v Wilkinson.*

Bisset v Wilkinson [1927] AC 177

Facts: Mr Wilkinson agreed to purchase certain land from Mr Bisset, on the Southern Island of New Zealand, for the purpose of sheep farming. Bisset told Wilkinson that the land would support 2,000 sheep. However, neither Bisset nor anyone else had used the land for sheep farming. Wilkinson bought the land and it failed to support 2,000 sheep. He refused to pay the outstanding balance of the purchase price and sought rescission on the ground of misrepresentation.

Held: The Judicial Committee of the Privy Council held that the statement was merely a statement of opinion which Bisset honestly held and accordingly refused to order rescission.

Lord Merrivale:
'In the present case ... the material facts of the transaction, the knowledge of the parties respectively, and their relative positions, the words of representation used, and the actual condition of the subject-matter spoken of, are relevant to the two inquiries necessary to be made: What was the meaning of the representation? Was it true?

In ascertaining what meaning was conveyed to the minds of the now respondents by the appellant's statement as to the two thousand sheep, the most material fact to be remembered is that, as both parties were aware, the appellant had not and, so far as appears, no other person had at any time carried on sheep-farming upon the unit of land in question. That land as a distinct holding had never constituted a sheep-farm ...'

The fact that neither Bisset nor anyone else had ever used the land for sheep farming was highly significant to the Privy Council. This is because a statement of opinion may be actionable if it is contradicted by other facts known to the person giving it.

Smith v Land & House Property Corp (1884) 28 Ch D 7

Facts: The plaintiff put up a hotel for sale. The particulars stated that it was 'let to Mr F Fleck (a most desirable tenant)', at a rental of £400 per annum, for an unexpired term of twenty-seven and a half years. Mr Fleck was a very undesirable tenant; he had not been paying his rent on time and was in arrears.

Held: The Court of Appeal held that the description of Mr Fleck as a most desirable tenant was not a mere expression of opinion, but contained an implied statement of fact that the vendors knew of no facts leading to the conclusion that he was not. The late payment of rent demonstrated that he was not a desirable tenant.

Bowen LJ:
'In considering whether there was a misrepresentation, I will first deal with the

argument that the particulars only contain a statement of opinion about the tenant. It is material to observe that it is often fallaciously assumed that a statement of opinion cannot involve the statement of a fact. In a case where the facts are equally well known to both parties, what one of them says to the other is frequently nothing but an expression of opinion. The statement of such opinion is in a sense a statement of a fact, about the condition of the man's own mind, but only of an irrelevant fact, for it is of no consequence what the opinion is. But if the facts are not equally known to both sides, then a statement of opinion by the one who knows the facts best involves very often a statement of a material fact, for he impliedly states that he knows facts which justify his opinion. Now a landlord knows the relations between himself and his tenant, other persons either do not know them at all or do not know them equally well, and if the landlord says that he considers that the relations between himself and his tenant are satisfactory, he really avers that the facts peculiarly within his knowledge are such as to render that opinion reasonable. Now are the statements here statements which involve such a representation of material facts? They are statements on a subject as to which *prima facie* the vendors know everything and the purchasers nothing. The vendors state that the property is let to a most desirable tenant. What does that mean? I agree that it is not a guarantee that the tenant will go on paying his rent, but it is to my mind a guarantee of a different sort, and amounts at least to an assertion that nothing has occurred in the relations between the landlords and the tenant which can be considered to make the tenant an unsatisfactory one. That is an assertion of a specific fact. Was it a true assertion? Having regard to what took place between Lady Day and Midsummer [Fleck's failure to pay rent], I think that it was not.'

There were two grounds for the decision in this case. The statement of opinion contained an implied statement of fact that the vendors knew of no information that would contradict the statement. On the facts of the case, the vendors knew that Mr Fleck had failed to pay his rent and this contradicted their statement of opinion. The second ground is found in Bowen LJ's judgment: 'if the facts are not equally known to both sides, then a statement of opinion by the one who knows the facts best involves very often a statement of a material fact'. Because the vendors, as landlord of the hotel, were in the best position to know the suitability of the tenant, their statement of opinion was treated as a statement of fact. Statements of opinion by experts are often treated as statements of fact because experts are in the best position to ascertain the truth of the matter.

Esso Petroleum v Mardon [1976] 2 All ER 5

Facts: A representative of Esso told Mardon, a prospective tenant of a petrol filling station, that the throughput of petrol at the station was likely to reach 200,000 gallons.

In giving this estimate, the representative had negligently overlooked the fact that the local planning authority had refused permission for the petrol pumps to front on to the main street. As a result of this the throughput of the station was only 78,000 gallons per year. Mardon sued Esso for negligent misrepresentation. Esso argued that their statement as to the throughput of petrol was merely a statement of opinion and therefore not actionable.

Held: The Court of Appeal held that Esso's statement as to the throughput of petrol involved a representation that reasonable care had been taken to ensure that the estimate was correct, and that this was a misrepresentation of fact.

Lord Denning MR:

'It seems to me that *Hedley Byrne & Co Ltd v Heller & Partners Ltd* [1964] AC 465, properly understood, covers this particular proposition: if a man, who has or professes to have special knowledge or skill, makes a representation by virtue thereof to another – be it advice, information or opinion – with the intention of inducing him to enter into a contract with him, he is under a duty to use reasonable care to see that the representation is correct, and that the advice, information or opinion is reliable. If he negligently gives unsound advice or misleading information or expresses an erroneous opinion, and thereby induces the other side to enter into a contract with him, he is liable in damages . . . Applying this principle, it is plain that Esso professed to have – and did in fact have – special knowledge or skill in estimating the throughput of a filling station. They made the representation – they forecast a throughput of 200,000 gallons – intending to induce Mr Mardon to enter into a tenancy on the faith of it. They made it negligently. It was a "fatal error" and thereby induced Mr Mardon to enter into a contract of tenancy that was disastrous to him. For this misrepresentation they are liable in damages.'

A statement of opinion will not be actionable if the representee did not have reasonable grounds to rely on the representor's opinion.

Kyle Bay Limited (T/A Astons Nightclub) v Underwriters Subscribing Under Policy No. 019057/08/01 [2006] EWHC 607 (Comm)

Facts: Kyle Bay settled an insurance claim in reliance on a letter from the Underwriters which stated that the policy was not declaration linked. Kyle Bay had access to the policy documents and could have verified this for themselves. A schedule to the policy in fact stated that the sum insured was declaration linked.

Held: The Court held that the Underwriters' letter was merely putting forward an argument as to its understanding of the policy. If the letter was a representation, it was merely a representation of opinion and Kyle Bay had no reasonable grounds for relying on it.

Jonathan Hirst QC:

'52. . . .I do not construe the letter as being a representation as to the contents of the policy . . . but rather as a statement of Underwriters' understanding of the overall effect of policy, namely that it was not declaration linked and average applied. I interpret the letter as being more of an argument or a contention than a representation, but if a representation, at most one as to the Underwriters' opinion . . . If the letter is to be treated as merely an argument or contention, then there was no representation.

53. Even if, contrary to my primary view, the letter is to be read as a representation of the Underwriters' opinion, it accurately reported Mr Ing's opinion, which was based on his original quotation on a gross profits basis. It was not suggested that the Underwriters or CGS were acting other than in perfect good faith and, having heard Mr Ing and Mr Stafford give evidence, I am quite satisfied that they were acting in good faith. So there was no misrepresentation.

54. A representation as to belief or opinion can sometimes be treated as including a representation that it is based on reasonable grounds – see *Brown v Raphael* [1958] Ch 636 and Chitty §§6–004–6–007 – but that was not pleaded or argued before me, rightly in my view. I do not think that any such implication would be justified . . . This was a commercial negotiation being conducted by experienced professionals on both sides. Both had equal access to the papers and were well able to form their own opinion . . .

56. So, in my judgment the misrepresentation case fails. There was no misrepresentation. Questions as to whether there was any inducement (as would in my judgment be necessary although presumptions could apply) are academic, but I am satisfied there was no inducement. Mr Dymant treated the Underwriters contentions as exactly that and decided for reasons that I have not managed to fathom that the claim should be settled on the basis proposed by the Underwriters, rather than investigating the point further, as he had ample opportunity to do. He appears to have decided to defer further investigation until after the compromise had been reached, but by doing that, he left it too late.'

9.2.4 REPRESENTATIONS OF LAW

It had previously been thought that a false statement of law was not actionable as a misrepresentation. This led to a number of contradictory decisions as the courts struggled to distinguish between representations of law and representations of fact. A couple of cases from the mid-twentieth century illustrate the point well.

In *Territorial & Auxiliary Forces Association v Nichols* [1949] 1 KB 35, a statement that the Rent Acts applied to a house that was known to be in the occupation of the Crown was held to be a misrepresentation of law because it involved a false proposition of law that the Rent Acts bound the Crown. However, in *Solle v Butcher* [1950] 1 KB 671, a statement that the Rent Acts did not apply to a flat because its identity had been changed by work done to it was held by the Court of Appeal to be a misrepresentation of fact.

The traditional rule that false statements of law are not actionable as misrepresentations has been called into question by the decision of the House of Lords in *Kleinwort Benson v Lincoln City Council* [1999] 2 AC 349 (see Chapter 18). This case overturned the well-established rule that a claimant could recover restitution of money paid under a mistake of fact, but not for money paid under a mistake of law. Their Lordships did not comment on the law of misrepresentation but having abolished the distinction between 'fact' and 'law' in the context of mistake it is difficult to maintain the distinction in the law of misrepresentation. In *Pankhania v Hackney LBC* [2002] EWHC 2441, the High Court expressed the view that, following *Kleinwort Benson*, misrepresentations of law were actionable. Rex Tedd QC said:

'I have concluded that the "misrepresentation of law" rule has not survived the decision in *Kleinwort Benson Ltd v Lincoln City Council*. Its historical origin is as an off-shoot of the "mistake of law" rule, created by analogy with it, and the two are logically inter-dependent . . . The distinction between fact and law in the context of relief from misrepresentation has no more underlying principle to it than it does in the context of relief from mistake . . . The survival of the "misrepresentation of law" rule following the demise of the "mistake of law" rule would be no more than a quixotic anachronism.'

9.2.5 SILENCE

9.2.5.1 The rule

The general rule is that there is no misrepresentation by silence.

Turner v Green [1895] 2 Ch 205

Facts: Turner and Green were engaged in a legal dispute. Turner's solicitor, Fowler, reached a settlement with Green on behalf of his client. Shortly before concluding that agreement, Fowler received a telegram informing him of certain proceedings in the action that made the settlement disadvantageous to Green. He failed to disclose this to Green. When Turner claimed specific enforcement of the agreement, Green attempted to rely upon the non-disclosure to resist the claim.

Held: The High Court held that mere non-disclosure of a material fact did not constitute a misrepresentation. Therefore rescission of the agreement was not available.

Chitty J:

'The distinction between suppression of a fact and mere silence is a very old one, and is to be found in a passage from Cicero (De Off lib iii c 13), which is cited by Sir Edward

Fry in his book (3rd edn p 329): "Aliud est celare, aliud tacere; neque enim id est celare quicquid reticeas." The obligation to speak is at the root of this proposition.

In *Walters v Morgan*, where specific performance of an agreement for a lease was being sought, Campbell LC said: "There being no fiduciary relation between vendor and purchaser in the negotiation, the purchaser is not bound to disclose any fact exclusively within his knowledge which might reasonably be expected to influence the price of the subject to be sold. Simple reticence does not amount to legal fraud, however it may be viewed by moralists. But a single word, or (I may add) a nod or a wink, or a shake of the head, or a smile from the purchaser intended to induce the vendor to believe the existence of a non-existing fact, which might influence the price of the subject to be sold, would be sufficient ground for a Court of Equity to refuse a decree for a specific performance of the agreement." That is a correct statement of the law, and one which, it appears to me, is not to be confined to the sale of lands or goods, but is of general application, except perhaps in the case of contracts requiring *uberrima fides*, which involve a duty to make full disclosure.'

It is clear that English law does not recognise a duty to disclose material facts known to one party but not to the other. This is because English law does not impose any general duty of good faith. There are, however, a number of exceptions to this general rule.

9.2.5.2 Exceptions

First, a misrepresentation may be inferred from silence where there has been an active attempt to conceal a defect. In *Horsfall v Thomas* (1862) 1 H & C 90, Thomas purchased a gun from Horsfall. The gun had a defect in it, which made it worthless. Horsfall attempted to conceal the defect by inserting a metal plug over the soft spot in the metal. The Court of Appeal held that the concealment was actionable, but for other reasons that will be considered in due course, the court held that there was no misrepresentation.

Second, a partial non-disclosure may amount to an actionable misrepresentation. This arises when a party makes a statement that is literally true, but is nevertheless misleading, because the representor fails to disclose all the relevant information. In short, it is a half-truth.

Nottingham Patent Brick and Tile Co v Butler (1886) 16 QBD 778

Facts: Butler wished to sell a piece of land that was subject to a number of restrictive covenants, one of which precluded its use as a brickyard. The plaintiff company, which manufactured bricks, wished to purchase the land to use in its business. The company inquired of Butler's solicitor whether the land was subject to any restrictive covenants. The solicitor stated that he was not aware of any but omitted to mention that he had not inspected the relevant documents. The company entered into a contract for the purchase of the land and paid the deposit. On discovery of the restrictive covenants they attempted to rescind the contract and recover the deposit.

Held: The Court of Appeal held there had been a misrepresentation which entitled the purchaser to rescind the contract.

Lord Esher MR:

'The evidence has been read to us, and I am sorry to say that I have come to the conclusion that the defendant's solicitor allowed himself to be carried away by his zeal for his client, and that he did not act with that candour to the other side with which a solicitor is bound to act under such circumstances. He allowed himself, in his zeal for his client, to make statements which were calculated to lead the other side to believe that he was stating facts within his own knowledge, and his statements in fact misled them, so that what he said amounts to a mis-statement of facts.'

Clinicare Ltd v Orchard Homes & Developments Ltd [2004] EWHC 1694

Facts: The claimant agreed to lease premises from the defendant. The lease imposed on the tenant a full repairing obligation. The claimant contended that it entered into the lease in reliance upon the defendant's fraudulent misrepresentation that it was unaware of the presence of dry rot and an implied negligent misrepresentation that reasonable steps had been taken to see whether dry rot existed. The defendant argued that its subsequent verbal statement about the historic existence of dry rot had corrected its initial misrepresentation.

Held: The court held that the negligent misrepresentation had not been corrected by the subsequent statement about the historic existence of dry rot.

Moses J:

'**20.** The representation that the defendant was not aware of "woodworm, rising damp, wet or dry rot or other infestation" was plainly false . . . Moreover, the representation was fraudulent in that the person who made it did so knowingly and cannot have believed in its truth. It was, at the very least, made recklessly in the sense that the person making the representation must have been careless whether it be true or false . . .

22. Of equal importance is the implied representation, which the representation, that the vendor was not aware of any dry rot, carries. It is alleged that the representation amounts to a representation that Orchard had made such investigations as could reasonably be expected of them . . .

25. The representation that Orchard had made such investigations as to the existence of dry rot as could reasonably be expected of it was made negligently . . .

27. Orchard's first substantial defence to Clinicare's allegations relies upon Mr Eagle's oral statement to Mr Dukes that dry rot had been discovered in the staircase but that the staircase had been stripped out and replaced . . .

28. [I]n my view the oral information given by Mr Eagle . . . did not correct the implied representation that Orchard had made such investigations as could be reasonably be expected of them. Indeed, it tended to confirm that such investigations had been made. The oral statement of Mr Eagle carried with it the implication that the dry rot no longer existed, so far as Orchard was aware. That statement itself carried the further implication that in undertaking the replacement of the staircase Orchard had taken reasonable steps to see that replacement cured the problem of dry rot. This was wholly contradicted by the advice Orchard had been given by Armour. Orchard had chosen to ignore the advice it had been given. The implied representation contained in the oral correction that the dry rot had been cured was false, particularly when Orchard had deliberately declined to do that which it had been advised to do . . .'

Third, silence will be actionable as a misrepresentation if a person has made a statement that was true at the time it was made but has subsequently, to his knowledge, become false.

With v O'Flanagan [1936] Ch 575

Facts: O'Flanagan wished to sell his medical practice. In January 1934 he told With that the takings of the practice were £2,000 a year. The contract for the sale was signed in May 1934, but by that time the circumstances had changed. O'Flanagan had been unwell and, as a result of his absence, the practice had become virtually worthless. In the three weeks preceding the sale the takings of the practice averaged only £5 a week. When With took possession of the practice he discovered what had happened and brought an action for rescission of the contract.

Held: The Court of Appeal held that the change of facts should have been disclosed and that failure to do so meant that the contract could be rescinded.

Lord Wright MR:
'As to the law, which has been challenged, I want to say this. I take the law to be as it was stated by Fry J in D*avies v London and Provincial Marine Insurance Co* 8 Ch D 469, where it is perhaps most fully expressed. In that case certain friends of an agent had agreed to deposit a sum of money for what was alleged to have been defaults on his part. The company who had employed him were under the belief and were advised that the default of the agent constituted felony, but they were later advised that these acts did not amount to felony and they withdrew the order for his arrest, and then still later in the day the friends of the agent agreed to deposit a sum of money on the footing of what they had been told earlier in the day before the arrest had been withdrawn – these

statements had not been corrected – and on that footing it was held by Fry J "that the change of circumstances ought to have been stated to the intending sureties, and that the agreement must be rescinded and the money returned to the sureties." . . .

Very much the same was said by the same learned judge, when a Lord Justice, in *re Scottish Petroleum Co* 23 Ch D 413 . . . In these cases – I need not refer to others on this point – the position is based upon the duty to communicate the change of circumstances. The matter, however, may be put in another way though with the same effect, and that is on the ground that a representation made as a matter of inducement to enter into a contract is to be treated as a continuing representation. That view of the position was put in *Smith v Kay* 7 HLC 750, 769, by Lord Cranworth. He says of a representation made in negotiation some time before the date of a contract: "It is a continuing representation. The representation does not end for ever when the representation is once made; it continues on. The pleader who drew the bill, or the young man himself, in stating his case, would say, 'Before I executed the bond I had been led to believe, and I therefore continued to believe, that it was executed pursuant to the arrangement.' "

The underlying principle is also stated again in a slightly different application by Lord Blackburn in *Brownlie v Campbell* 5 App Cas 925, 950. I need only quote a very short passage. Lord Blackburn says:

> "when a statement or representation has been made in the *bona fide* belief that it is true, and the party who has made it afterwards comes to find out that it is untrue, and discovers what he should have said, he can no longer honestly keep up that silence on the subject after that has come to his knowledge, thereby allowing the other party to go on, and still more, inducing him to go on, upon a statement which was honestly made at the time when it was made, but which he has not now retracted when he has become aware that it can be no longer honestly persevered in." . . .

On these grounds, with great respect to the learned judge, I think he ought to have come to the conclusion that the plaintiffs have established their case and there ought to be a declaration rescinding the contract with the consequences which follow upon such a declaration.'

There were two alternative grounds for the decision: either (1) there was a duty on O'Flanagan to notify With of the change of circumstances; or (2) the statement was a continuing representation that became untrue. On either ground, O'Flanagan was liable for misrepresentation and the contract could be rescinded.

In the above extract from his judgment in *Turner v Green*, Chitty J referred to the fourth exception to the general rule – contracts *uberrimae fidei* (of the utmost good faith). These types of contract, which include contracts of insurance, require full disclosure of all material facts. Such disclosure is necessary even if the other party has not requested it.

Lambert v Co-operative Insurance [1975] 2 Lloyd's Rep 485

Facts: Mrs Lambert signed a proposal form for an insurance policy with Co-operative Insurance to cover her own and her husband's jewellery. The form contained no questions about the applicant's previous convictions and Lambert gave no information even though, to her knowledge, her husband had been convicted of a crime of dishonesty some years earlier. The policy was issued and the documents stated that it would be void if there was any omission to state any fact material for estimating the risk. The policy was renewed each year. Eight years after the policy commenced Lambert's husband was imprisoned for an offence of dishonesty. She did not disclose this to Co-Operative Insurance when the policy was renewed. One year later Lambert made a claim for £311 for jewellery lost or stolen. The insurer refused to pay the claim on the grounds that Lambert had failed to disclose her husband's convictions.

Held: The Court of Appeal held that Lambert was not entitled to claim under the policy due to her non-disclosure of a material fact.

MacKenna J:

'Everyone agrees that the assured is under a duty of disclosure and that the duty is the same when he is applying for a renewal as it is when he is applying for the original policy. The extent of that duty is the matter in controversy. There are, at least in theory, four possible rules or tests which I shall state. (1) The duty is to disclose such facts only as the particular assured believes to be material. (2) It is to disclose such facts as a reasonable man would believe to be material. (3) It is to disclose such facts as the particular insurer would regard as material. (4) It is to disclose such facts as a reasonable or prudent insurer might have treated as material. Section 18 of the Marine Insurance Act 1906, chooses the fourth. Sub-section (1) of that section provides that: The assured must disclose to the insurer, before the contract is concluded, every material circumstance which is known to the assured, and the assured is deemed to know every circumstance which, in the ordinary course of business, ought to be known by him. If the assured fails to make such disclosure, the insurer may avoid the contract.

Sub-section (2) is in these words:

"Every circumstance is material which would influence the judgment of a prudent insurer in fixing the premium or determining whether he will take the risk . . ."

I would only add to this long judgment the expression of my personal regret . . . The present case shows the unsatisfactory state of the law. Mrs Lambert is unlikely to have thought that it was necessary to disclose the distressing fact of her husband's recent conviction when she was renewing the policy on her little store of jewellery. She is not an underwriter and has presumably no experience in these matters. The defendant company would act decently if, having established the point of principle, they were to pay her. It might be thought a heartless thing if they did not, but that is their business, not mine.

The Court of Appeal confirmed that the obligation imposed on the insured is to disclose all such facts as a reasonable insurer might have treated as material. This test is taken from the law of marine insurance. Their Lordships thought that the test should be generally applicable to all types of insurance contract. It seems that the test will be applied strictly.

Woolcott v Sun Alliance & London Insurance Ltd [1978] 1 WLR 493

Facts: Mr Woolcott was granted a mortgage advance by a building society whose application form, completed by Mr Woolcott, stated that the society would insure the property. No information was requested from Mr Woolcott for the purposes of the insurance, which was arranged under a block policy held by the society with Sun Alliance. The property was duly insured for £30,000, including the society's interest which was £12,000. The property was destroyed by fire and although the insurers indemnified the society they refused the claim of Mr Woolcott on the grounds that he had failed to disclose a material fact, namely that he had been convicted of robbery some 10 years previously.

Held: The High Court held that Sun Alliance was entitled to avoid the policy on the grounds of non-disclosure of a material fact.

Caulfield J:

'I accept that the criminal record of an assured can affect the moral hazard which insurers have to assess; indeed this is almost self-evident. I therefore hold that on the particular facts of this case the non-disclosure of a serious criminal offence like robbery by the plaintiff was a material non-disclosure. For these reasons the defendants, in my judgment, are entitled to avoid the policy in so far as that policy affects the plaintiff's separate interest.'

Although Caulfield J insisted that it was self-evident that the criminal record could affect the moral hazard that the insurers were asked to assess, it is not immediately obvious why this is so. It is clear that the materiality test does not require proof that the particular circumstance would have had a *decisive* effect on the decision of the prudent insurer. Lord Slynn confirmed this in *Pan Atlantic Insurance v Pine Top Insurance* [1995] 1 AC 501:

'[A] circumstance may be material for the purposes of an insurance contract (whether marine or non-marine) even though had it been fully and accurately disclosed it would not have had a decisive effect on the prudent underwriter's decision whether to accept the risk and if so at what premium, but that an underwriter who is not induced by the misrepresentation or non-disclosure of a material fact to make the contract cannot rely on the misrepresentation or non-disclosure to avoid the contract.'

The category of contracts *uberrimae fidei* has been regarded as strictly limited and now closed. As we have seen, it includes contracts of insurance as well as family settlements (*Gordon v Gordon* (1816–2) 3 Swans 400; 36 ER 910) and contracts of guarantee (*Credit Lyonnais Bank Nederland NV v Export Credit Guarantee Department* [1996] 1 Lloyd's Rep 200). It does not, however, include contracts for the division of property upon the breakdown of a marriage (*Wales v Wadham* [1977] 1 WLR 199).

Finally, contracts entered into between persons in a fiduciary relationship entail a duty of disclosure. Included in this category are contracts between agent and principal (*Armstrong v Jackson* [1917] 2 KB 822), solicitor and client (*Boardman v Phipps* [1967] 2 AC 46), and a company and its directors (*Regal Hastings v Gulliver* [1967] 2 AC 134).

9.2.6 CONDUCT

A misrepresentation might also stem from conduct where nothing has been said.

Spice Girls Ltd v Aprilia World Services BV [2002] EMLR 27

Facts: The claimants, Spice Girls Ltd, entered into a contract with the defendants, Aprilia, for the promotion of Aprilia's new scooters – to be known as 'Spice Sonic Scooters'. The original five Spice Girls, including Geri Halliwell, participated in a commercial advertising shoot, and two days later contracted with Aprilia in relation to the use of that material. The band had known prior to the making of this agreement that Geri Halliwell intended to leave the band after the US tour in September 1998. The advertising material was due to be released after that date. Aprilia claimed that they had been induced to enter into the contract on the basis of a misrepresentation by conduct, that the Spice Girls did not know and had no reasonable grounds to believe, at or before the time of the agreement, that any of the Spice Girls had an existing declared intention to leave the group.

At first instance, Arden J found a misrepresentation by conduct. She concluded:

'Given that the benefits of the commercial shoot could not be enjoyed by Aprilia if one of the Spice Girls left the group before March 1999, participation in the shoot . . . carried with it a representation by conduct that the Spice Girls Ltd did not know, and had no reasonable grounds to believe, that any of the Spice Girls had an existing declared intention to leave the group before that date.'

Held: The Court of Appeal dismissed the appeal and upheld the decision of Arden J but on the basis of a broader survey of the facts.

Morritt VC:

'The representation for which AWS [Aprilia World Services] has contended ever since it amended its defence and counterclaim in December 1999 is that "SGL [Spice Girls Ltd] did not know and had no reasonable grounds to believe at or before the time of entry into the agreement that any of the Spice Girls had an existing declared intention to leave the group during the minimum term of the Agreement", *i.e.* before March 1999. This was accepted by the judge (J1, paragraph 112) but only in respect of the commercial shoot on May 4, 1998 and "other promotional material depicting the five Spice Girls which was intended to be used at any time during the period of the agreement".

In our view the judge took too limited a view of the effect of the course of the negotiations as a whole and the specific documents and conduct relied on . . . [A]t this stage it is sufficient to highlight the most salient facts and events.

First, shortly after the conclusion of the heads of agreement on March 4, 1998 SGL supplied the logos, images and designs depicting each of the Spice Girls which were to be used by Aprilia in the promotion of the scooters. It must have been quite obvious from all such material and the judge's finding . . . that the same five girls were required for all of them. AWS was entitled to use them throughout the period of 12 months . . . As we understand it such material was consistently used thereafter so as to generate a connection in the public eye between the Spice Girls and the scooters. In our view the representation contended for is necessarily implicit in that conduct from early March 1998 onwards. In, seemingly, connecting such material only to the commercial shoot on May 4, 1998, in our view, the judge seriously understated its significance.

Second, the events of March 9, 1998 were such as to bring to the attention of four of the other five directors of SGL the fact that Ms Halliwell had declared her intention to leave in September 1998. It follows that the representation implicit in the approval and use of the promotional material was false when made, or to the extent it was made before March 9, became false on March 9, 1998 . . .

Third, the subsequent events merely served to affirm, not correct, the initial representation and its falsity. Thus, the photocalls in Madrid, Munich and Paris held on or between March 16 and 26 May have been unsatisfactory to Ms Fuzzi but they took place and their effect was no different to the other promotional material. There were five Spice Girls each with her 'distinct and individual image, style and personality'.

Fourth, the fax of March 30, 1998 was sent by Mr Pettett in the light of the information given to him by Ms Halliwell and the tour manager . . . In our view it was an express assurance that each Spice Girl was fully committed to all the matters contained in the heads of agreement and in the draft agreement then circulating for the full term of 12 months. There is implicit in such assurance the representation for which AWS contends. That representation was false when made because of the declaration of intention made by Ms Halliwell on March 9, 1998 and never qualified or withdrawn . . .

Fifth, the events of the meeting held at Wembley on April 25, 1998 demonstrated quite conclusively the falsity of all the representations previously made. Whichever formulation of the principle enunciated in *With v O'Flanagan* is adopted and whatever view is taken of the declaration made by Ms Halliwell on March 9, 1998 it is quite clear

> that SGL could no longer deal with AWS on the previous basis without disclosing Ms Halliwell's expressed intention . . .
>
> Sixth, it is clear that far from correcting the previous misrepresentations SGL continued and affirmed them . . .
>
> Seventh, as the judge held, participation in the commercial shoot necessarily carried the same implication and was likewise false. It did nothing to correct the previous misrepresentations, indeed it gave them additional force . . .
>
> Whilst it is necessary to give each episode separate consideration it is also necessary to have regard to their cumulative effect. This is not a case of an isolated representation made at an early stage of ongoing negotiations. It is the case of a series of continuing representations made throughout the two months' negotiations leading to the Agreement. Later representations gave added force to the earlier ones; earlier representations gave focus to the later ones . . .'

The Court of Appeal took a broader view of the facts than Arden J at first instance and listed seven factors that contributed to the conclusion that the Spice Girls had made a misrepresentation by conduct. As the last paragraph of the judgment makes clear, none of these factors standing alone would have been decisive, but the cumulative effect of all the factors was that there was an actionable misrepresentation. Of course such a convoluted analysis would not have been necessary if English law had recognised a general duty of good faith.

9.3 MISREPRESENTATION MUST INDUCE THE CONTRACT

9.3.1 THE GENERAL RULE

Having established that the defendant made an actionable misrepresentation, the claimant is then required to show that the misrepresentation induced the formation of the contract.

JEB Fasteners Ltd v Marks, Bloom & Co [1983] 1 All ER 583

Facts: The defendants negligently prepared the accounts of a company which was taken over by the claimants. The accounts had been made available to the claimants, who had reservations about them, but they nevertheless decided to proceed with the take-over because they wished to acquire the services of two of the directors of the company. The take-over was a commercial failure. In an attempt to recover their losses, the claimants brought an action against the defendants alleging that the negligently prepared accounts had induced them into the take-over.

Held: The Court of Appeal dismissed the action on the ground that the defendants' representation did not play a 'real and substantial' part in inducing the claimants to act. They had taken over the company, not in reliance upon the accounts but because they wished to acquire the services of the two directors.

9.3.2 MATERIALITY

The burden of proving that the misrepresentation induced the contract rests upon the claimant. It is sometimes suggested that the claimant must also prove that the misrepresentation was 'material', that is, that it would have influenced the reasonable person in deciding whether to enter into the contract or not. In *Smith v Chadwick* (1884) 9 App Cas 187, 196, Lord Blackburn said:

'I think that if it is proved that the defendants with a view to induce the plaintiff to enter into a contract made a statement to the plaintiff of such a nature as would be likely to induce a person to enter into a contract, and if it is proved that the plaintiff did enter into the contract, it is a fair inference of fact that he was induced to do so by the statement.'

It seems that if the representation is one on which a reasonable person would have relied, this creates a rebuttable presumption that the claimant did in fact rely on the representation (*Barton v County NatWest Ltd* [1999] Lloyd's Rep Bank 408). The reverse is not true, however. Evidence that reliance on the representation was unreasonable does not bar a claim.

Museprime Properties Ltd v Adhill Properties Ltd (1991) 61 P & CR 111

Facts: The defendants sold property that they owned in Finchley by auction to the plaintiffs. The auction particulars stated that the rent reviews of three leases to which the properties were subject had not been finalised. This was inaccurate but the statement was later reaffirmed by the auctioneer. The plaintiffs sought to rescind the contract for misrepresentation. The defendants argued that rescission should not be allowed because the misrepresentation was not material since no reasonable bidder would have allowed it to influence his bid.

Held: The High Court held that as long as the plaintiffs were in fact induced by the misrepresentation, which they were on the facts, that was sufficient to entitle them to rescission of the contract.

Scott J:

'A representation is material, in my opinion, if it is something that induces the person to whom it is made, whether solely or in conjunction with other inducements, to contract on the terms on which he does contract. I would gratefully adopt the view expressed in Goff and Jones on the *Law of Restitution*, (1986) 3rd edn, p 168 which reads:

> "In our view any misrepresentation which induces a person to enter into a contract should be a ground for rescission of that contract. If the misrepresentation would have induced a reasonable person to enter into the contract then the court will, as we have seen, presume that the representee was so induced and the onus will be on the representor to show that the representee did not rely on the misrepresentation either wholly or in part. If, however, the misrepresentation would not have induced a reasonable person to contract, the onus will be on the representee to show that the misrepresentation induced him to act as he did. But these considerations relate to the onus of proof. To disguise them under the cloak of materiality is misleading and unnecessary."

And, as the learned editors say a little way above that passage, the cases have tended to treat materiality as synonymous with inducement.

I respectfully agree with that view of the law and propose to apply it in this case. I do not decide as between Mr. Welch and Mr. Maunder-Taylor whether Mr. Maunder-Taylor's reliance on his ability to negotiate or succeed in obtaining on arbitration rent levels higher than those specified in the January 4, 1988, notices was reasonable or unreasonable. I will assume for present purposes that it was unreasonable, in which case the onus is on Mr. Maunder-Taylor to satisfy me that that factor did induce him, and through him Mr. Henley, and through the two of them the plaintiff company, to bid the £490,000 at the auction. Mr. Maunder-Taylor's evidence has satisfied me of that and indeed I think Mr. Primost accepted that that was the only possible conclusion from his evidence, very firmly given as it was . . .'

It is clear that materiality (the reasonableness of the claimant's reliance on the misrepresentation) is only of relevance to the burden of proof. If the misrepresentation would have induced a reasonable person to enter into the contract, the burden of proof shifts to the representor to prove that the representee did not in fact rely upon the misrepresentation. If, however, a reasonable person would not have been induced to enter into the contract on the basis of the misrepresentation, the burden of proof remains with the representee to prove that s/he was in fact induced to enter into the contract. Materiality is not a further requirement; it is merely supporting evidence for the existence of inducement.

9.3.3 THREE REQUIREMENTS OF INDUCEMENT

To demonstrate that the representation induced the representee to enter into the contract the claimant must show that the representation was:

(1) known to the representee;
(2) intended to be acted on;
(3) actually acted on.

We will examine each of these three requirements:

9.3.3.1 Known to representee

In *Horsfall v Thomas* (1862) 1 H & C 90, the facts of which were considered above, Thomas was unsuccessful in his claim for misrepresentation. This was because he had never inspected the gun and thus the attempted concealment did not operate upon his mind. Bramwell B said:

> 'If the plug, which it was said was put in to conceal the defect, had never been there, his position would have been the same; for, as he did not examine the gun or form any opinion as to whether it was sound, its condition did not affect him.'

A misrepresentation may be assumed to be known to a person, even if it was not specifically addressed to him/her, if it would be reasonable to assume that the representation would have been relied on by a third party.

Smith v Eric S Bush [1990] 1 AC 831

Facts: The plaintiff applied to a building society for a mortgage to assist her in purchasing a home. The building society instructed the defendants, a firm of surveyors, to prepare a report on the property as to its value and condition. The defendants' valuer, who carried out the inspection, noticed that two chimney breasts had been removed but he negligently failed to check whether the chimneys above had been left adequately supported. His report stated that no essential repairs were necessary. The plaintiff paid for the surveyor's report and in accordance with the terms of the mortgage agreement, received a copy of the report. In reliance on this report she proceeded with the purchase of the house without obtaining a further survey. The chimneys were not adequately supported and one of them subsequently collapsed causing widespread damage to the rest of the house. The plaintiff claimed damages from the defendants for the loss sustained as a result of the negligent report.

Held: The House of Lords upheld the plaintiff's claim, holding that a valuer owed a duty of care to a prospective mortgagor if he was aware that the mortgagor would probably purchase the house in reliance on the valuation without an independent survey.

Lord Templemann:
'In general I am of the opinion that in the absence of a disclaimer of liability the valuer who values a house for the purpose of a mortgage, knowing that the mortgagee will rely and the mortgagor will probably rely on the valuation, knowing that the purchaser mortgagor has in effect paid for the valuation, is under a duty to exercise reasonable skill and care and that duty is owed to both parties to the mortgage for which the valuation is made.'

9.3.3.2 Intended to be acted on

In addition to demonstrating that the representee knew the representation it must also be shown that the representation was intended to be acted upon.

Peek v Gurney (1873) LR 6 HL 377

Facts: The defendants prepared a prospectus for an intended company with the aim of attracting initial investors. The prospectus contained a number of misrepresentations of fact which were known to be untrue by the defendants. Mr Peek was a subsequent purchaser of shares who relied on the prospectus in forming his decision to purchase shares from one of the original allottees. He brought an action against the defendant claiming damages for the losses which he had suffered in consequence of the purchase.

Held: The House of Lords held that Mr Peek could not recover damages because the prospectus was not intended to be acted upon by subsequent purchasers of shares.

Lord Cairns:
'The allotment having been completed, the prospectus, as it seems to me, had done its work; it was exhausted. The share list was full; the directors had obtained from the company the money which they desired to obtain ... How can the directors of a company be liable, after the full original allotment of shares, for all the subsequent dealings which may take place with regard to those shares upon the Stock Exchange? If the argument of the Appellant is right, they must be liable *ad infinitum*, for I know no means of pointing out any time at which the liability would, in point of fact, cease. Not only so, but if the argument be right, they must be liable, no matter what the premium may be at which the shares may be sold. That premium may rise from time to time from circumstances altogether unconnected with the prospectus, and yet, if the argument be right, the Appellant would be entitled to call upon the directors to indemnify him up to the highest point at which the shares may be sold, for all that he may expend in buying the shares. My Lords, I ask, is there any authority for this proposition? I am aware of none.'

A similar result was reached in the case of *Caparo Industries Plc v Dickman* [1990] 1 AC 831, where the House of Lords held that the audited accounts of a company were not intended to be acted upon for the purpose of a takeover bid. Lord Oliver of Aylmerton said:

'[I]t is almost always foreseeable that someone, somewhere and in some circumstances, may choose to alter his position upon the faith of the accuracy of a statement or report which comes to his attention and it is always foreseeable that a report – even a confidential report – may come to be communicated to persons other than the original or intended recipient. To apply as a test of liability only the foreseeability of possible damage without some further control would be to create a liability wholly indefinite in area, duration and amount and would open up a limitless vista of uninsurable risk for the professional man.'

In the recent case of *Peekay Intermark Ltd v Australia & New Zealand Banking Group Ltd* [2006] EWCA Civ, the Court of Appeal held that an investor could not claim that it was induced into an investment by a misrepresentation as to its nature when the investor had signed a document containing the final terms and conditions. Chadwick LJ held that, in such circumstances, the investor was not entitled to rely on the earlier misrepresentation:

'65. The Deputy Judge held, at paragraph 92 of his judgment, that Peekay was induced to invest "by Mrs B's misrepresentation as to the nature of the product" . . .

66. It is important to keep in mind that Mrs Balasubramaniam made no representation as to the actual contents of the FTCs. She had not seen those documents at the time of her telephone conversations with Mr Pawani on 1 and 2 February 1998. The effect of those conversations, as the judge found, was that Mr Pawani was given a "rough and ready" description of the product that he would be offered. But it could not be said that Mr Pawani – an experienced investor in emerging markets – was under any misapprehension, following the telephone conversations, as to the need for a definitive and detailed description of the financial instrument to be employed (the "product"); nor that he would have made an investment decision on behalf of Peekay if he had not received documents which he understood to contain the definitive and detailed description which he needed. And the judge made no finding to the contrary.

67. The judge found that Mr Pawani did no more than glance at the FTCs and the Risk Disclosure Statement. On the basis of that finding, the judge must be taken to have accepted that Peekay entered into the investment contract in the knowledge that the terms of that contract were to be found in

those documents, but without knowing what those terms were. In holding that Peekay was induced to invest by Mrs Balasubramaniam's misrepresentation as to the nature of the product the judge inferred that Mr Pawani was entitled to, and did, assume that the terms which (as Mr Pawani knew) were to be found in the documents would not differ materially from the "rough and ready" description which Mrs Balasubramaniam had given him a few days earlier. As he put it at paragraph 88 of his judgment: "Mr Pawani . . . evidently had no prior cause to think that the FTCs would contain any nasty surprises".

68. I am satisfied that that inference was not open to the judge. There are three reasons which lead me to that conclusion. First, given the importance which Mr Pawani professed to place on the potential for exerting influence, as an investor, on the means by which the underlying investment was liquidated or realised in the event of sovereign default in payment of the Note or of default by the counter-party to the currency hedge, it was necessary for him to give careful consideration to the FTCs. It was in those documents – and not in the "rough and ready" description which he had been given by Mrs Balasubramaniam – that he would find the provisions that would apply in the event of default. He could not say that he was entitled to or did assume that the documents were a formality.

69. Second, it is clear that Mr Pawani, himself, regarded the documents which he had signed and returned as important. It was he who had added the words "as per the attached document" to Mrs Balasubramaniam's draft letter of instructions . . .

70. Third, Peekay could not be heard to say (through Mr Pawani) that it had thought it unnecessary to read and understand the FTCs. The Risk Disclosure Statement was a contractual document – as Mr Pawani recognised when he returned it, signed, with the letter of 7 February 1998. ANZ accepted the investment instructions in that letter on the basis of the investor's confirmation that it had read and understood the terms of the Statement. That confirmation, as it seems to me, operates as a contractual estoppel to prevent Peekay from asserting in litigation that it had not, in fact read and understood the Risk Disclosure Statement.'

9.3.3.3 Actually acted on

Finally, it must be shown that the representee actually acted on the representation. If this cannot be established then his/her claim will fail.

> ### *Attwood v Small* (1838) 6 Cl & Fin 232
>
> **Facts:** Attwood wished to sell a mine. He made exaggerated and untrue statements as to the mine's earning capacity. Before agreeing to purchase the mine, Small sent his own experts to assess the mine's capacity, who in error agreed with Attwood's assessment. When the true situation was discovered six months later Small claimed to rescind the contract on the grounds of misrepresentation.
>
> **Held:** The House of Lords held that the action for misrepresentation failed because the purchaser had relied on his own experts rather than Attwood's misrepresentation.

While the above case shows that the representee must have actually acted upon the representation, it is clear that the representation need not have been the sole factor inducing the contract in order for it to be operative. In *Edgington v Fitzmaurice* (1885) 24 ChD 459, the facts of which we have already considered, the plaintiff was induced to take debentures in a company partly on the basis of a misrepresentation in the company prospectus and partly because of his own mistaken belief that the debenture holders would have a charge on the company's leasehold property. The Court of Appeal held that the plaintiff was entitled to damages for fraudulent misrepresentation even though the misrepresentation was not the sole cause of his entering into the contract. Cotton LJ said:

'It is not necessary to show that the misstatement was the sole cause of his acting as he did. If he acted on that misstatement, though he was also influenced by an erroneous supposition, the Defendants will be still liable.'

Bowen LJ agreed, stating the test to be applied thus:

'The real question is, what was the state of the Plaintiff's mind, and if his mind was disturbed by the misstatement of the Defendants, and such disturbance was in part the cause of what he did, the mere fact of his also making a mistake himself could make no difference. It resolves itself into a mere question of fact.'

Similarly, in *Clinicare Ltd v Orchard Homes & Developments Ltd* [2004] EWHC 1694 (see above), the fact that the claimant had commissioned its own survey, which advised further investigation, did not bar its claim for misrepresentation. This was because the claimant's decision to enter the lease without further investigation demonstrated that the claimant had actually acted upon the defendant's negligent misrepresentation.

A misrepresentation cannot be held to have induced a contract where the representee knew that it was untrue prior to the formation of the contract. The misrepresentation will still be effective, however, if there was merely an opportunity to discover the truth and that opportunity was not taken.

Redgrave v Hurd (1881) 20 ChD 1

Facts: Mr Redgrave, a solicitor in Birmingham, placed an advertisement in the *Law Times* for the sale of his practice. Mr Hurd wished to establish himself in practice as a solicitor and had a meeting with Redgrave where he asked for details about the takings of the practice. Redgrave told him that the practice brought in £300–£400 a year. Hurd asked for information about the amount of business done for the last three years. At a subsequent meeting, Redgrave provided documents showing business of just under £200 a year. Hurd asked how the difference was made up, and Redgrave showed him a number of papers which he said related to other business not included in the summaries. These papers, which Hurd did not examine, showed only a small amount of business, and the gross returns of the business were in fact only about £200 a year. Hurd took possession of the practice but on finding that the business was worthless, refused to complete. Redgrave brought an action for specific performance. At first instance, Fry J held that Redgrave was entitled to specific performance because Hurd, having had the opportunity to discover the truth of Redgrave's representation, had not done so and therefore must be taken not to have relied on the representations.

Held: The Court of Appeal allowed the appeal and held that Hurd was entitled to rescind the contract. The mere opportunity to discover the truth does not preclude rescission provided that the plaintiff had relied upon the misrepresentation

Lord Jessel MR:
'If a man is induced to enter into a contract by a false representation it is not a sufficient answer to him to say, "If you had used due diligence you would have found out that the statement was untrue. You had the means afforded you of discovering its falsity, and did not choose to avail yourself of them" . . . Nothing can be plainer, I take it, on the authorities in equity than that the effect of false representation is not got rid of on the ground that the person to whom it was made has been guilty of negligence. One of the most familiar instances in modern times is where men issue a prospectus in which they make false statements of the contracts made before the formation of a company, and then say that the contracts themselves may be inspected at the offices of the solicitors. It has always been held that those who accepted those false statements as true were not deprived of their remedy merely because they neglected to go and look at the contracts. Another instance with which we are familiar is where a vendor makes a false statement as to the contents of a lease, as, for instance, that it contains no covenant preventing the carrying on of the trade which the purchaser is known by the vendor to be desirous of carrying on upon the property. Although the lease itself might be produced at the sale, or might have been open to the inspection of the purchaser long previously to the sale, it has been repeatedly held that the vendor cannot be allowed to say, "You were not entitled to give credit to my statement."

Although a representee is not precluded from making a claim for misrepresentation on the grounds of his failure to take the opportunity to discover the truth, his carelessness may be taken into account when assessing damages. The role played by contributory negligence in the law of misrepresentation will be discussed in greater detail later in the chapter.

9.4 CATEGORIES OF MISREPRESENTATION

Once it has been established that there is an actionable misrepresentation that has induced the formation of the contract it is necessary to consider the state of mind of the person who made the misrepresentation. Misrepresentations fall into three categories:

(1) fraudulent misrepresentations;
(2) negligent misrepresentations;
(3) innocent misrepresentations.

It is important to ascertain which category the misrepresentation falls into in order to determine which remedies are available. Rescission is available for all three types of misrepresentation. Damages are only available for negligent and fraudulent mis-representations and the measure of damages differs between the categories. In this section we will consider the requirements for each of the categories.

9.4.1 FRAUDULENT MISREPRESENTATION

Fraud was defined by Lord Herschell in *Derry v Peek*.

Derry v Peek (1889) 14 App Cas 337

Facts: A company obtained a statutory right to operate trams moved by animal power, or, with the consent of the Board of Trade, steam power. The directors assumed that the Board would give this consent as a matter of course because they had already submitted plans to the Board without any objection being made. The directors issued a prospectus containing a statement that they had the right to use steam power instead of horses. The plaintiff purchased shares in the company in reliance on this statement. The Board of Trade eventually refused their consent to the use of steam power and the company was wound up. The plaintiff brought an action against the directors for fraudulent misrepresentation.

Held: The House of Lords held that the defendants were not liable because the statement as to steam power had been made by them in the honest belief that it was true.

Lord Herschell:

'I think the authorities establish the following propositions: First, in order to sustain an action of deceit, there must be proof of fraud, and nothing short of that will suffice. Secondly, fraud is proved when it is shewn that a false representation has been made (1) knowingly, or (2) without belief in its truth, or (3) recklessly, careless whether it be true or false. Although I have treated the second and third as distinct cases, I think the third is but an instance of the second, for one who makes a statement under such circumstances can have no real belief in the truth of what he states. To prevent a false statement being fraudulent, there must, I think, always be an honest belief in its truth. And this probably covers the whole ground, for one who knowingly alleges that which is false, has obviously no such honest belief. Thirdly, if fraud be proved, the motive of the person guilty of it is immaterial. It matters not that there was no intention to cheat or injure the person to whom the statement was made . . . In my opinion making a false statement through want of care falls far short of, and is a very different thing from, fraud, and the same may be said of a false representation honestly believed though on insufficient grounds.

Lord Herschell made a clear distinction between negligence and fraud. A false statement honestly believed does not constitute fraud. The reasonableness of the representor's belief is relevant, however, in so far as it assists the court in ascertaining whether the representor really did have an honest belief in the truth of the statement. The less reasonable the belief, the less likely it is to be honest. On the facts of *Derry v Peek*, the House of Lords concluded that there were reasons why the directors honestly believed that their statement was a true and fair representation of the facts.

The test for fraud is subjective. It must be shown that the representor himself knew that his statement was false. Consequently, the statement must be analysed from the point of view of the representor.

Akerhielm v De Mare [1959] AC 789

Facts: Mr De Mare bought shares in Dantile Ltd after Baron Akerhielm had informed him that 'about one third of the capital has already been subscribed in Denmark'. In fact some of this one third had been issued fully paid to persons resident in Kenya for services rendered in Denmark in connection with the formation of the company. The company went into insolvency and Mr De Mare brought an action for fraudulent misrepresentation, claiming that the statement indicated that the one-third of the capital had been subscribed in cash.

Held: The House of Lords held that the statement must be construed in the sense that Baron Akerhielm understood it and, on this construction, 'subscribed' did not mean subscribed in cash.

Lord Jenkins:

'The question is not whether the defendant in any given case honestly believed the representation to be true in the sense assigned to it by the court on an objective consideration of its truth or falsity, but whether he honestly believed the representation to be true in the sense in which he understood it albeit erroneously when it was made. This general proposition is no doubt subject to limitations. For instance, the meaning placed by the defendant on the representation made may be so far removed from the sense in which it would be understood by any reasonable person as to make it impossible to hold that the defendant honestly understood the representation to bear the meaning claimed by him and honestly believed it in that sense to be true. But that is not this case.'

Again, the reasonableness of the representor's understanding of his statement is only relevant in so far as it indicates whether the representor honestly understood the representation to bear the meaning claimed by him.

Finally, it has been held that the motive of the person making the representation is irrelevant to the issue of fraud. In *Polhill v Walter* (1832) 3 B & Ad 114, the representor, an agent, made a statement which he knew to be false with the sole intention of benefiting his principal. His intention was neither to benefit himself nor to injure anyone else. Notwithstanding his good motives, the representor was held liable in the tort of deceit (also, see *Standard Chartered Bank v Pakistan National Shipping Corp (No 2)* [2000] 1 Lloyd's Rep 218).

Fraud is an extremely difficult matter to prove and because of this it is rarely invoked in the courts.

9.4.2 NEGLIGENT MISREPRESENTATION

Negligent misrepresentation can be subdivided into two categories: (1) negligent misrepresentation at common law; and (2) negligent misrepresentation under statute. We will consider the reason for this subdivision when we examine negligent misrepresentation under statute.

9.4.2.1 At common law

Professor Treitel (G Treitel, *The Law of Contract* (2003, 11th edn, Sweet & Maxwell) describes a negligent misrepresentation in the following terms:

'A misrepresentation is negligent if it is made carelessly and in breach of a duty owed by the representor to the representee to take reasonable care that the representation is accurate.'

The law governing negligent misrepresentation at common law is derived from the decision of the House of Lords in *Hedley Byrne v Heller & Partners*.

Hedley Byrne v Heller & Partners [1964] AC 465

Facts: The claimants were advertising agents who booked substantial advertising space on behalf of their clients, Easipower Ltd, on terms stating that they were personally liable if Easipower defaulted. Hedley Byrne became concerned about the financial standing of Easipower and asked the defendants, who were Easipower's bankers, to give a reference on the financial standing of Easipower. The defendant replied that Easipower were 'considered good for its ordinary business transactions'. In reliance upon this reference, the claimants placed orders which, because of the subsequent default of Easipower, resulted in a loss to them of £17,000. The claimant alleged that Heller were negligent in their preparation of the reference and were therefore liable for damages.

Held: The House of Lords held that the defendant was not liable in negligence because it had included an exclusion clause stating that the reference was made 'without responsibility'. It was held, however, that in the absence of this exclusion the defendant would have been liable.

Lord Devlin:
'I think, therefore, that there is ample authority to justify your Lordships in saying now that the categories of special relationships which may give rise to a duty to take care in word as well as in deed are not limited to contractual relationships or to relationships of fiduciary duty, but include also relationships which in the words of Lord Shaw in *Nocton v Lord Ashburton* [1914] AC 932, 972, are "equivalent to contract", that is, where there is an assumption of responsibility in circumstances in which, but for the absence of consideration, there would be a contract. . .

I have had the advantage of reading all the opinions prepared by your Lordships and of studying the terms which your Lordships have framed by way of definition of the sort of relationship which gives rise to a responsibility towards those who act upon information or advice and so creates a duty of care towards them. I do not understand any of your Lordships to hold that it is a responsibility imposed by law upon certain types of persons or in certain sorts of situations. It is a responsibility that is voluntarily accepted or undertaken, either generally where a general relationship, such as that of solicitor and client or banker and customer, is created, or specifically in relation to a particular transaction. In the present case the appellants were not, as in *Woods v Martins Bank Ltd*, [1959] 1 QB 55, the customers or potential customers of the bank. Responsibility can attach only to the single act, that is, the giving of the reference, and only if the doing of that act implied a voluntary undertaking to assume responsibility. This is a point of great importance because it is, as I understand it, the foundation for the ground on which in the end the House dismisses the appeal. I do not think it possible to formulate with exactitude all the conditions under which the law will in a specific case imply a voluntary undertaking any more than it is possible to formulate those in which the law will imply a contract . . .'

The case established the possibility of bringing an action in negligence for statements made without reasonable care and attention. For this to be possible, a 'duty of care' must be established between the maker of the statement and the person who has acted on it. It is clear that the principle is not restricted to statements that induce a contract. Indeed, *Hedley Byrne* was not such a case and their Lordships did not directly consider the impact of the decision on the law relating to misrepresentation.

Much of the subsequent case law in this area has been concerned with the question of when a 'duty of care' arises. The language used in *Hedley Byrne* was that of a 'special relationship' between the representor and the representee. Initially, it was assumed that such a relationship would arise whenever the representor could reasonably foresee that the representee would rely on the statement, and would suffer loss if it turned out to be untrue (*Anns v Merton London Borough Council* [1978] AC 728). This expansive view of liability threatened to lead to indeterminate liability, however, and the House of Lords provided a much more restrictive test in *Caparo Industries v Dickman* [1990] 2 AC 605. Lord Bridge said the following:

'In addition to the foreseeability of damage, necessary ingredients in any situation giving rise to a duty of care are that there should exist between the party owing the duty and the party to whom it is owed a relationship characterized by the law as one of "proximity" or "neighbourhood" and that the situation should be one in which the court considers it fair, just and reasonable that the law should impose a duty of a given scope on the one party for the benefit of the other'.

The *Caparo* test essentially has three stages:

(1) the damage should be foreseeable;
(2) the representor and representee should be proximate;
(3) the imposition of a special relationship should be 'fair, just and reasonable'.

Stage 2 provides a significant limitation on liability, although it will normally be satisfied where the statement is made in a context where the parties anticipate that a contract will be made between them.

9.4.2.2 Under the 1967 statute

In addition to the common law action for negligent misstatement there is also a statutory action under s 2(1) of the Misrepresentation Act 1967. To understand why we have two separate actions we need to consider the history of the statute. Back in 1962, the Law Reform Committee issued its 10th report (Cmnd 1782), in which it recommended that damages should be available for negligent misrepresentation. Parliament was slow to enact implementing legislation, however, and by the time the Misrepresentation Act 1967 appeared on the statute book, the House of Lords had already decided *Hedley Byrne & Co v Heller* [1964] AC 465, and recognised the common-law action for negligent misstatement.

MISREPRESENTATION ACT 1967

Section 2

(1) Where a person has entered into a contract after a misrepresentation has been made to him by another party thereto and as a result thereof he has suffered loss, then, if the person making the misrepresentation would be liable to damages in respect thereof had the misrepresentation been made fraudulently, that person shall be so liable notwithstanding that the misrepresentation was not made fraudulently, unless he proves that he had reasonable grounds to believe and did believe up to the time the contract was made that the facts represented were true.

The action for negligent misrepresentation under s 2(1) differs from the action at common law in two significant ways. First, it reverses the burden of proof. Under *Hedley Byrne v Heller* the burden is placed on the representee to establish that the representor made the representation without having reasonable grounds to believe in its truth. Under s 2(1) the burden is reversed and the claim is much easier to prove. All the representee has to show is that he entered into the contract in reliance upon a misrepresentation made by the other party. The burden will then shift to the representor to demonstrate that, until the time the contract was made, he had reasonable grounds to believe in the truth of the representation.

Second, unlike the common law action for negligent misstatement, section 2(1) does not require a duty of care to have existed between the representor and the representee. It merely requires proof that the misrepresentation led to the formation of a contract between the representor and the representee.

The operation of s 2(1) is illustrated by the case of *Howard Marine & Dredging Co Ltd v Ogden*.

Howard Marine & Dredging Co Ltd v Ogden [1978] QB 574

Facts: Ogden wished to hire barges from Howard Marine. During the negotiations an employee of Howard Marine, O'Loughlin, told Ogden that the carrying capacity of the barges was 1,600 tonnes. O'Loughlin based that figure on an entry in the Lloyd's Register. There was a mistake in the register, however, and the correct figure was 1,055 tonnes. The correct figure was stated in the ship's documents which were in Howard's possession. Ogden and Howard Marine concluded a contract of hire. Ogden used the barges, and the work for which they were required fell behind schedule. Ogden discovered the true carrying capacity of the barges and refused to continue paying the hire charge. Howard sued Ogden for the hire charge and Ogden counterclaimed under s 2(1) and in the tort of negligent misstatement. At first instance, the trial judge held that Howard was not liable and that Ogden were liable to pay for the hire of the barges.

Held: The Court of Appeal (Lord Denning MR dissenting) allowed the appeal and held that Ogden succeeded under 2(1).

Lord Denning MR:
'Negligent misrepresentations
Ogdens contended next that the representations by Howards, as to the carrying capacity of the barges, were made negligently: and that Howards are liable in damages for negligent misrepresentation on the principles laid down in *Hedley Byrne v Heller & Partners* [1964] AC 465.

This raises the vexed question of the scope of the doctrine of *Hedley Byrne*. It was much discussed in the Privy Council in *Mutual Life and Citizens' Assurance Co Ltd v Evatt* [1971] AC 793 and in this court in *Esso Petroleum Co Ltd v Mardon* [1976] QB 801. To my mind one of the most helpful passages is to be found in the speech of Lord Pearce in *Hedley Byrne v Heller & Partners* [1964] AC 465, 539:

> "... To import such a duty [of care] the representation must normally, I think, concern a business or professional transaction whose nature makes clear the gravity of the inquiry and the importance and influence attached to the answer ... A most important circumstance is the form of the inquiry and of the answer."

To this I would add the principle stated by Lord Reid and Lord Morris of Borth-y-Gest in the Privy Council case, *Mutual Life and Citizens' Assurance Co Ltd v Evatt* [1971] AC 793, 812, which I would adopt in preference to that stated by the majority:

> "... when an inquirer consults a business man in the course of his business and makes it plain to him that he is seeking considered advice and intends to act on it in a particular way ... his action in giving such advice ... (gives rise to) ... a legal obligation to take such care as is reasonable in the whole circumstances."

Those principles speak of the "gravity of the inquiry" and the seeking of "considered advice". Those words are used so as to exclude representations made during a casual conversation in the street; or in a railway carriage; or an impromptu opinion given offhand; or "off the cuff" on the telephone. To put it more generally, the duty is one of honesty and no more whenever the opinion, information or advice is given in circumstances in which it appears that it is unconsidered and it would not be reasonable for the recipient to act on it without taking further steps to check it . . .

Applying this test, it seems to me that at these various conversations Mr O'Loughlin was under a duty to be honest, but no more. Take the first two conversations. They were on the telephone. The callers from the north wanted to know what was the capacity of the barges. Mr O'Loughlin answered it offhand as best he could, without looking up the file. If they had wanted considered advice, they should have written a letter and got it in writing. Take the last conversation. It was on an occasion when Mr O'Loughlin went up to the north to discuss all sorts of things. In the course of it, he was asked again the capacity of the barges. He had not got the file with him, so he answered as best he could from memory. To my mind in those circumstances it was not reasonable for Ogdens to act on his answers without checking them. They ought either to have got him to put it in writing – that would have stressed the gravity and importance of it – or they ought to have got expert advice on their own behalf – especially in a matter of such importance to them. So I agree with the judge that there was not such a situation here as to give rise to a duty of care: or to make Howards liable for negligent misrepresentation at common law.

The Misrepresentation Act 1967

Alternatively Ogdens claim damages for innocent misrepresentation under the Misrepresentation Act 1967 . . .

This enactment imposes a new and serious liability on anyone who makes a representation of fact in the course of negotiations for a contract. If that representation turns out to be mistaken – then however innocent he may be – he is just as liable as if he made it fraudulently. But how different from times past! For years he was not liable in damages at all for innocent misrepresentation: see *Heilbut, Symons & Co v Buckleton* [1913] AC 30. Quite recently he was made liable if he was proved to have made it negligently: see *Esso Petroleum Co Ltd v Mardon* [1976] QB 801. But now with this Act he is made liable – unless he proves – and the burden is on him to prove – that he had reasonable ground to believe and did in fact believe that it was true.

Section 2(1) certainly applies to the representation made by Mr. O'Loughlin on July 11, 1974, when he told Ogdens that each barge could carry 1,600 tonnes. The judge found that it was a misrepresentation: that he said it with the object of getting the hire contract for Howards. They got it: and, as a result, Ogdens suffered loss. But the judge found that Mr. O'Loughlin was not negligent: and so Howards were not liable for it.

The judge's finding was criticised before us: because he asked himself the question: was Mr. O'Loughlin negligent? Whereas he should have asked himself: did Mr. O'Loughlin have reasonable ground to believe that the representation was true? I think that criticism is not fair to the judge. By the word "negligent" he was only using shorthand for the longer phrase contained in section 2(1) which he had before him. And the judge, I am sure, had the burden of proof in mind: for he had come to the conclusion that Mr. O'Loughlin was not negligent. The judge said in effect: "I am satisfied that Mr. O'Loughlin was not negligent": and being so satisfied, the burden need not be further considered: see *Robins v National Trust Co Ltd* [1927] AC 515, 520.

It seems to me that when one examines the details, the judge's view was entirely justified. He found that Mr O'Loughlin's state of mind was this: Mr O'Loughlin had examined Lloyd's Register and had seen there that the deadweight capacity of each barge was 1,800 tonnes. That figure stuck in his mind. The judge found that "the 1,600 tonnes was arrived at by knocking off what he considered a reasonable margin for fuel, and so on, from the 1,800 tonnes summer deadweight figure in Lloyd's Register, which was in the back of his mind." The judge said that Mr O'Loughlin had seen at some time the German shipping documents and had seen the deadweight figure of 1,055.135 tonnes: but it did not register. All that was in his mind was the 1,800 tonnes in Lloyd's Register which was regarded in shipping circles as the Bible. That afforded reasonable ground for him to believe that the barges could each carry 1,600 tonnes payload: and that is what Mr. O'Loughlin believed.

So on this point, too, I do not think we should fault the judge. It is not right to pick his judgment to pieces – by subjecting it – or the shorthand note – to literal analysis. Viewing it fairly, the judge (who had section 2(1) in front of him) must have been of opinion that the burden of proof was discharged.'

Bridge LJ:

'I will consider first the position under the statute . . . It is unfortunate that the judge never directed his mind to the question whether Mr O'Loughlin had any reasonable ground for his belief. The question he asked himself, in considering liability under the Misrepresentation Act 1967, was whether the innocent misrepresentation was negligent. He concluded that if Mr O'Loughlin had given the inaccurate information in the course of the April telephone conversations he would have been negligent to do so but that in the circumstances obtaining at the Otley interview in July there was no negligence. I take it that he meant by this that on the earlier occasions the circumstances were such that he would have been under a duty to check the accuracy of his information, but on the later occasions he was exempt from any such duty. I appreciate the basis of this distinction, but it seems to me, with respect, quite irrelevant to any question of liability under the statute. If the representee proves a misrepresentation which, if fraudulent, would have sounded in damages, the onus passes immediately to the representor to prove that he had reasonable ground to believe the facts represented. In other words the liability of the representor does not depend upon his being under a duty of care the extent of which may vary according to the circumstances in which the representation is made. In the course of negotiations leading to a contract the statute imposes an absolute obligation not to state facts which the representor cannot prove he had reasonable ground to believe.

[Bridge LJ considered the grounds for the reasonableness of O'Loughlin's belief by reference to the transcript of the judgment at first instance]

I am fully alive to the dangers of trial by transcript and it is to be assumed that Mr O'Loughlin was perfectly honest throughout. But the question remains whether his evidence, however benevolently viewed, is sufficient to show that he had an objectively reasonable ground to disregard the figure in the ship's documents and to prefer the Lloyd's Register figure. I think it is not. The fact that he was more interested in cubic capacity could not justify reliance on one figure of deadweight capacity in preference to another. The fact that the deadweight figure in the ship's documents was a freshwater figure was of no significance since, as he knew, the difference between freshwater and sea water deadweight capacity was minimal. Accordingly I conclude that Howards failed to prove that Mr O'Loughlin had reasonable ground to believe the truth of his misrepresentation to Mr Redpath.

Having reached a conclusion favourable to Ogdens on the issue of liability under the Misrepresentation Act 1967, I do not find it necessary to express a concluded view on the issue of negligence at common law. As at present advised I doubt if the circumstances surrounding the misrepresentation at the Otley interview were such as to impose on Howards a common law duty of care for the accuracy of the statement. If there was such a duty, I doubt if the evidence established a breach of it.'

Shaw LJ:
'I turn next to the question of liability for negligence. I would respectfully adopt what Lord Denning MR has already said in preferring the minority opinion in *Mutual Life and Citizens' Assurance Co Ltd v Evatt* [1971] AC 793 and I would approach the problem as he has done from the standpoint of the passage he has cited from the speech of Lord Pearce in *Hedley Byrne v Heller & Partners* [1964] AC 465, 539.

Now it does seem to me that the chartering of barges for the purpose of carrying clay out to sea and there dumping it is a business transaction whose nature makes clear the importance and influence of an answer to the question: "What is their carrying capacity in the context of the purpose of the prospective charterparties?" That the question was only asked over the telephone in April and later repeated at an interview in July does not of itself, as I see it, render the subject matter of the question less material or the impact of the answer less important. The information sought would govern the performance by Ogdens of their contract with the authority and this must have been apparent to any man of business, let alone Mr O'Loughlin. The judge so held. The information which had been asked for more than once cannot be regarded as other than important whatever the circumstances in which it was sought and given. Moreover, it was not expert advice that was sought which might honestly and reasonably have assumed different forms according to the source of it. What was asked for was a specific fact. Ogdens had not themselves any direct means of ascertaining what the fact was. Certainly they had no such ready and facile means as were available to Mr O'Loughlin. These factors in association with the relationship of the parties as owners and prospective charterers of barges to be employed for a specific purpose known to the owners did in my judgment give rise to a duty upon the owners to exercise reasonable care to be accurate in giving information of a material character which was peculiarly within their knowledge. All Mr O'Loughlin had to do was to look at documents in Howard's possession and to read them accurately. Had he done so there would have been no room for error of fact or for misconceived opinion or wrong advice. That he chose to answer an important question from mere recollection "off the cuff" does not in my view diminish, if I may adopt the language of Lord Pearce, the "gravity of the inquiry or the importance and influence attached to the answer".

It is with considerable diffidence that I express this view since it is not shared by either of the other members of this court and was not held by Bristow J. None the less I would venture to hold that Ogdens have a cause of action in negligence at common law. This is not, in my judgment, affected by the exception clause which does not purport to grant absolution from the consequences of negligence on the part of the owners.

There remains the issue raised by the claim under section 2(1) of the Misrepresentation Act 1967. I do not regard the telephone conversation of April and the interview of July 11, 1974, as being so casual as to give rise to no legal consequences. Certainly I find myself unable to dismiss what was said at the interview in July as inconsequential. I share the opinion expressed in this regard in the judgment of Bridge LJ which is based on the finding of the judge. I entirely agree, furthermore, with Bridge LJ's analysis of the evidence, together with the judge's findings in this regard, and I agree also with the views expressed by Bridge LJ as to the operation and effect of the relevant provisions of the Misrepresentation Act. I cannot do better than respectfully to adopt his reasoning without seeking to repeat it, and I agree with his conclusions.'

The case illustrates the advantages of a claim under s 2(1). Ogden succeeded on the basis that the majority of the Court of Appeal (Shaw and Bridge LJJ) held that Howard had failed to demonstrate that it had reasonable grounds for belief in the truth of its statement. Crucial to this finding was the fact that Howard had the correct information in its possession at the relevant time. Lord Denning MR dissented, holding that it was reasonable for Howard to rely on the entry in the Lloyd's register, the mariner's 'Bible' as he put it.

Importantly, had the case been decided prior to the enactment of the Misrepresentation Act 1967, Ogden would have lost. Lord Denning MR and Bridge LJ agreed that no duty of care existed between Howard Marine and Ogden. Furthermore, even if there had been a duty of care, Bridge LJ thought that there was insufficient evidence to establish that Howard Marine had been negligent and breached that duty of care.

It is clear that in most situations a claim under s 2(1) will be more advantageous than a claim for negligent misstatement. Nevertheless, there are two reasons why a person may wish to pursue a claim in negligence. First, the claimant will not have to prove the existence of a contract. This will be beneficial if the claim is against a third party, such as the claim in *Hedley Byrne* itself. It will also be beneficial when the contract has been found to be void and therefore no longer in existence. Second, a claim in negligence is not dependent upon there being a misrepresentation as defined in section 2, above. Therefore a claim can be brought for a statement of intention or opinion.

A further problem with a claim under s 2(1) is that the section specifies that the misrepresentation must be 'made' to the other party. It has been argued that this language is inapt to cover the situation where the misrepresentation is in the form of silence. In *Banque Financière de la Cité v Westgate Insurance* [1990] 1 QB 665, Slade LJ said:

> 'The expression "misrepresentation . . . made" (which is repeated in several later sections of the Act of 1967) would, in our judgment, on the ordinary meaning of words be inapt to refer to a misrepresentation which had not been made in fact but was (at most) merely deemed by the common law to have been made. If it had been the intention of the legislature that a mere failure to discharge the duty of disclosure in the case of a contract *uberrimae fidei* would fail to be treated as the "making" of a representation within the meaning of the Act of 1967, we are of the opinion that the legislature would have said so.'

9.4.3 INNOCENT MISREPRESENTATION

Historically, all non-fraudulent misrepresentations were known as innocent misrepresentations. Following the recognition of liability for negligent misrepresentation an innocent misrepresentation is now any misrepresentation, which is neither fraudulent nor negligent. As we will see the remedies available for an innocent misrepresentation are strictly limited. The claimant may be entitled to rescind the contract or to claim damages in lieu of rescission, but s/he will not be entitled to claim damages in addition to rescission.

9.5 REMEDIES

The remedies available for misrepresentation differ between the three categories.

9.5.1 RESCISSION

Under the common law, rescission was available only for fraudulent misrepresentation. Equity extended this right to all categories of operative misrepresentation. Thus any type of misrepresentation, whether fraudulent, negligent, or innocent, renders a contract voidable. The party misled is given the option either to have the contract set aside or, alternatively, to affirm it. If s/he elects to rescind the contract it will be set aside both retrospectively and prospectively. The parties will be restored, so far as it is possible, to their precontractual positions. This view of the effect of misrepresentation makes sense if the false statement is viewed as having undermined the agreement between the parties. If the agreement has been reached on a false basis, the parties should not be bound to their obligations under it.

Prior to the Misrepresentation Act 1967, rescission was unavailable where either the misrepresentation had become a term of the contract or where the contract had been performed. This was changed by s 1 of the Misrepresentation Act 1967.

S 1 Removal of certain bars to rescission for innocent misrepresentation

Where a person has entered into a contract after a misrepresentation has been made to him, and:

(a) the misrepresentation has become a term of the contract; or
(b) the contract has been performed;

or both, then, if otherwise he would be entitled to rescind the contract without alleging fraud, he shall be so entitled, subject to the provisions of this Act, notwithstanding the matters mentioned in paragraphs (a) and (b) of this section.

9.5.1.1 Operation of rescission

The representee will not always require the assistance of the court in order to effect rescission. If the contract remains executory, that is, nothing has been done under the contract, the representee will be able to effect rescission simply by informing the other party that s/he intends to rescind. If performance has already commenced, however, the representee will often require an order of the court to ensure the co-operation of the other party.

To rescind the contract, the innocent party will normally be expected to give notice to the other party. In some situations, however, particularly where the misrepresentation was fraudulent, the innocent party may no longer be able to find the maker of the false statement. In such situations, there is authority that other reasonable steps, which clearly indicate an intention to rescind, will be sufficient.

Car and Universal Finance Co Ltd v Caldwell [1965] 1 QB 525

Facts: The defendant, Mr Caldwell, sold his Jaguar car to a rogue named Mr Norrris. Norris paid by cheque, and when this proved to be worthless, Caldwell sought to rescind the contract. He could not find either Norris or the car so he informed the police and the Automobile Association about the fraud and asked them to trace the car. Norris subsequently sold the car to a motor dealer who had notice of the fraud, but the car then changed hands on a number of occasions until it was eventually purchased in good faith by the plaintiff. The car was eventually seized by the police and the plaintiff sought to recover it on the ground that the contract had not been validly rescinded prior to the date that it purchased the car.

Held: The Court of Appeal held that rescission had occurred on the day that Mr Caldwell informed the police and the AA. Thus, the plaintiff had not obtained good title to the car.

Sellers LJ:

'This appeal raises a primary point in the law of contract. The question has arisen whether a contract which is voidable by one party can in any circumstances be terminated by that party without his rescission being communicated to the other party . . .

An affirmation of a voidable contract may be established by any conduct which unequivocally manifests an intention to affirm it by the party who has the right to affirm or disaffirm. Communication of an acceptance of a contract after knowledge of a fundamental breach of it by the other party or of fraud affecting it is, of course, evidence establishing affirmation but it is not essential evidence. A party cannot reject goods sold and delivered if he uses them after knowledge of a right to reject, and the judgment cites a case where an instruction to a broker to re-sell was sufficient affirmation of the contract in question even though that conduct was not communicated. It may be said that a contract may be more readily approved and accepted than it can be terminated where a unilateral right to affirm or disaffirm arises. The disaffirmation or election to avoid a contract changes the relationship of the parties and brings their respective obligations to an end, whereas an affirmation leaves the contract effective though subject to a claim for damages for its breach. Where a contracting party could be communicated with, and modern facilities make communication practically world-wide and almost immediate, it would be unlikely that a party could be held to have disaffirmed a contract unless he went so far as to communicate his decision so to do. It would be what the other contracting party would normally require and unless communication were made the party's intention to rescind would not have been unequivocally or clearly demonstrated or made manifest. But in circumstances such as the present case, the other contracting party, a fraudulent rogue who would know that the vendor would want his car back as soon as he knew of the fraud, would not expect to be communicated with as a matter of right or requirement, and would deliberately, as here, do all he could to evade any such communication being made to him. In such exceptional contractual circumstances, it does not seem to me appropriate to hold that a party so acting can claim any right to have a decision to rescind communicated to him before the contract is terminated. To hold that he could would involve that the defrauding party, if skilful enough to keep out of the way, could deprive the other party to the contract of his right to rescind, a right to which he was entitled and which he would wish to exercise, as the defrauding party would well know or at least confidently suspect. The position has to be viewed, as I see it, between the two contracting parties involved in the particular contract in question. That another innocent party or parties may suffer does not in my view of the matter justify imposing on a defrauded seller an impossible task. He has to establish, clearly and unequivocally, that he terminates the contract and is no longer to be bound by it. If he cannot communicate his decision he may still satisfy a judge or jury that he had made a final and irrevocable decision and ended the contract. I am in agreement with Lord Denning MR who asked "How is a man in the position of Caldwell ever to be able to rescind the contract when a fraudulent person absconds as Norris did here?" and answered that he can do so "... if he at once, on discovering the fraud, takes all possible steps to regain the goods even though he cannot find the rogue nor communicate with him." '

Davies LJ:

'On the facts of this case Norris must be taken to have known that the defendant might, on ascertaining the fraud, wish to rescind the contract. Norris disappeared; and so did the car. The defendant could, therefore, neither communicate with Norris nor retake the car. It must, therefore, I think, be taken to be implied in the transaction between Norris and the defendant that in the event of the defendant's wishing to rescind he should be entitled to do so by the best other means possible. *Lex non cogit ad impossibilia.* It is true that it was conceivably possible that the defendant might decide not to rescind but to sue on the cheque instead; but it is most doubtful whether on the facts of this case such a possibility could have occurred to Norris as a real one. The fact that Norris knew that he was a rogue and that, therefore, the defendant was likely to be after him distinguishes this case from that of an innocent misrepresentor. It would not occur to the latter that the other party to the contract would have any right or desire to rescind, so that there would be no such implication as that which I have suggested arose in the present case.

The decision in *Caldwell* was controversial because it was effectively a decision as to which of two innocent parties should bear the loss caused by the actions of a fraudulent third party. The Court of Appeal concluded that the plaintiff should bear the loss because the defendant had taken reasonable steps to inform the fraudster of his intention to rescind. The outcome is somewhat harsh on the plaintiff who bought the car in good faith and paid in cash. Surely, in the circumstances, it would have been fairer for the loss to fall on the defendant, who had naively accepted a cheque in exchange for the car. The rule in *Caldwell* is extremely harsh on innocent third parties and probably should not be extended beyond fraudulent misrepresentations. Indeed, the Law Reform Committee recommended in 1966 that the rule should be reversed (12th Report (Cmnd, 2958), para 16). This is already the position in Scots law, where in *Macleod v Ker*, 1965 SC 253, the Court of Session decided a very similar case in favour of the third party.

9.5.1.2 Bars to rescission

The law has placed a number of limitations on the right to rescind. We will consider the four main bars to rescission. If any of these bars are present the claimant will be precluded from rescinding the contract and will be left to rely on his/her remedy in damages.

9.5.1.2.1 Intervention of third-party rights

Caldwell provides an excellent example of the operation of this bar. On the facts of the case it was held that Caldwell had rescinded the contract prior to the purchase of the car by the plaintiff. Had he not, rescission would have been barred because of the intervention of third-party rights. This is because rescission is a restitutionary claim for which the defence of 'bona fide purchaser for value without notice' is available (see *Phillips v Brooks Ltd* [1919] 2 KB 243). The only avenue open to a claimant in such a situation is to argue that the contract is void for mistake rather than voidable for misrepresentation. In practice, this is rarely successful because of the difficulty of proving that the representee was mistaken as to the identity of the representor (see Chapter 10). *Ingram v Little* [1961] 1 QB 31, provides a rare example of a claim being successfully made on this basis.

9.5.1.2.2 Counter-restitution is impossible

A party will not be permitted to rescind a contract if s/he is unable or unwilling to give back what s/he has received under the contract. The purpose of this limitation is to prevent the unjust enrichment of the party seeking to rescind. For example, suppose I purchase a car from you on the basis of a misrepresentation. Prima facie, I am entitled to rescind the contract and recover the money I have paid. But this would result in my unjust enrichment if I am unwilling to return the car because my wife still likes it, or unable to return the car because it has been stolen from my driveway.

The common law took an extremely strict approach to the operation of this bar.

Clarke v Dickson (1858) EB & E 148 (HC)

Facts: The plaintiff was induced to purchase shares in a company following a mis-representation by the defendants. Subsequently the company was registered as a company with limited liability. On discovering the misrepresentation the plaintiff sought to rescind the contract.

Held: The court held that rescission was not available because the plaintiff could not restore the defendant to his pre-contractual position. The shares in the limited liability company were different in nature and status to the shares that existed prior to the formation of the contract.

Crompton J:
'When once it is settled that a contract induced by fraud is not void, but voidable at the option of the party defrauded, it seems to me to follow that, when that party exercises his option to rescind the contract, he must be in a state to rescind; that is, he must be in such a situation to be able to put the parties into their original state before the contract. Now here I will assume, what is not clear to me, that the plaintiff bought his shares from

591

the defendants and not from the Company, and that he might at one time have been able to restore the shares to the defendants if he could, and demand the price from them. But then what did he buy? Shares in a partnership with others. He cannot return those; he has become bound to those others. Still stronger, he has changed their nature: what he now has and offers to restore are shares in a quasi corporation now in process of being wound up. That is quite enough to decide this case. The plaintiff must rescind *in toto* or not at all: he cannot both keep the shares and recover the whole price.'

The facts of the case demonstrate that the bar can often operate very harshly. A more flexible approach has been taken in equity.

Erlanger v New Sombrero Phosphate Co (1878) 3 App Cas 1218

Facts: The defendants, who were in a fiduciary relationship with the plaintiff, sold a phosphate mine to the plaintiff for £110,000. After working the mine for a period of time, the plaintiff sought to rescind the contract on the grounds that the defendants had breached their fiduciary duty by failing to disclose the fact that they had purchased the mine for £55,000 a few days prior to the sale. The defendants argued that rescission was unavailable because the plaintiff could not return the mine in its original condition.

Held: The House of Lords allowed the plaintiff to rescind the contract and recover the purchase price on the condition that they returned the mine and accounted for the profits they had made from working the mine.

Lord Blackburn said:

'[A Court of Equity] can take account of profits, and make allowance for deterioration. And I think the practice has always been for a Court of Equity to give this relief whenever, by the exercise of its powers, it can do what is *practically just*, though it cannot restore the parties precisely to the state they were in before the contract.'

The key theme in Lord Blackburn's speech seems to be 'practical justice' – the court will do whatever is 'practically just'. Instead of rigidly insisting that the parties be restored to their precontractual positions, the court will aim to ensure that the claimant is not unjustly enriched as a result of rescission. In many cases this will be possible simply by ordering the claimant to provide a money allowance for the benefits s/he has received, but cannot give back. While the courts have generally adopted a more flexible approach to the counter-restitution bar, it is important to remember that the claimant does not have a right to provide a money allowance instead of making counter-restitution. The court retains the discretion to make whatever judgment it sees fit to meet the 'practical justice' of the case. In *Spence v Crawford* [1939] 3 All ER 271, Lord Wright explained the approach in the following terms:

> 'The court will be less ready to pull a transaction to pieces where the defendant is innocent, whereas in the case of fraud the court will exercise its jurisdiction to the full in order, if possible, to prevent the defendant from enjoying the benefits of his fraud at the expense of the innocent plaintiff.'

9.5.1.2.3 *Affirmation*

Rescission will be barred if the person to whom the statement was made has affirmed the contract either expressly through spoken word or impliedly by conduct.

Long v Lloyd [1958] 1 WLR 753

Facts: The plaintiff purchased a lorry from the defendant, Lloyd, in reliance on the defendant's assurance that it was in 'first-class condition'. On the first journey after the sale, the dynamo broke and the plaintiff noticed a number of other serious defects including a broken oil seal and a crack in one of the wheels. The defendant offered to contribute towards the costs of the repairs. The plaintiff accepted this offer, and later sent the lorry on a journey to Middlesbrough during which it broke down. The plaintiff sought to rescind the contract on the ground of innocent misrepresentation.

Held: The Court of Appeal held that rescission was barred because the plaintiff's dispatch of the lorry to Middlesbrough amounted to an affirmation of the contract.

Pearce LJ:
'[T]he plaintiff, knowing all that he did about the condition and performance of the lorry, dispatched it, driven by his brother, on a business trip to Middlesbrough. That step, at all events, appears to us to have amounted, in all circumstances of the case, to a final acceptance of the lorry by the plaintiff for better or for worse, and to have conclusively extinguished any right of rescission remaining to the plaintiff after completion of the sale.'

9.5.1.2.4 *Lapse of time*

Lapse of time may operate as evidence of affirmation, but this will rarely be so because knowledge is usually required for affirmation.

Armstrong v Jackson [1917] 2 KB 822

Facts: The defendant, a stockbroker, purported to purchase specified shares for the plaintiff but instead sold the plaintiff his own shares. After a six-year delay the plaintiff discovered the fraud and sought to rescind the contract, notwithstanding that the value of the shares had considerably decreased between the date of the sale and the date of the action for rescission. The defendant claimed that rescission should be barred for delay.

Held: The High Court held that, on the facts, delay was not a bar to rescission.

McCardie J:
'In cases like the present the right of the party defrauded is not affected by the mere lapse of time so long as he remains in ignorance of the fraud.'

It is clear that in cases of fraudulent misrepresentation, lapse of time without knowledge of the fraud will not constitute a bar to rescission. Exceptionally, however, in cases of innocent misrepresentation, mere lapse of time may act as a bar to rescission.

Leaf v International Galleries [1950] 2 KB 86

Facts: In 1944, Mr Leaf paid £85 to International Galleries for a picture of Salisbury Cathedral. Prior to the sale, International Galleries had innocently represented to Mr Leaf that the painting was by John Constable. Five years later, in 1949, Leaf sought to re-sell the painting and discovered that it was not a Constable. He attempted to return the picture to International Galleries but they refused to accept it, so Mr Leaf brought a claim for rescission of the contract of sale.

Held: The Court of Appeal held that rescission was barred for lapse of time.

Jenkins LJ:
'[C]ontracts such as this cannot be kept open and subject to the possibility of rescission indefinitely . . . it behoves the purchaser either to verify or, as the case may be, to disprove the representation within a reasonable time, or else stand or fall by it. If he is allowed to wait five, ten or twenty years and then reopen the bargain, there can be no finality at all. I, for my part, do not think that equity will intervene in such a case, more especially as in the present case it cannot be said that, apart from rescission, the plaintiff would have been without remedy. The county court judge was of opinion, and it seems to me that he was clearly right, that the representation that the picture was a Constable amounted to a warranty. If it amounted to a warranty, and that was broken, as on the findings of the county court judge it was, then the plaintiff had a right at law in the shape of damages for breach of warranty. That remedy he did not choose to

exercise, and, although he was invited at the hearing to amend his claim so as to include a claim for breach of warranty, he declined that opportunity. That being so, it seems to me that he has no justification at all for now coming to equity five years after the event and claiming rescission. Accordingly, it seems to me that this is not a case in which the equitable remedy of rescission, assuming it to be available in the absence of fraud in respect of a completed sale of chattels, should be allowed to the plaintiff. For these reasons, I agree that the appeal fails and should be dismissed.

It seems that the justification for the lapse of time bar is the desirability of certainty and finality in contractual relationships. For Jenkins LJ, it was significant that the representation had been incorporated into the contract, giving rise to an action for damages. Given that the plaintiff was unwilling to pursue this claim, the Court of Appeal was not prepared to order rescission five years after the completion of the contract. It seems clear that the lapse of time bar will only operate in respect of innocent misrepresentations.

9.5.2 DAMAGES

In addition or as an alternative to rescission the representee may also claim damages for misrepresentation. Historically, damages were only available in relation to fraudulent misrepresentations, under the tort of deceit. However, following *Hedley Byrne v Heller* and the enactment of the Misrepresentation Act 1967, damages have become available for negligent misrepresentation as well. In the following section we will see the different methods of assessment of damages that the courts apply to each category of misrepresentation.

9.5.2.1 Fraudulent misrepresentation

Damages for fraudulent misrepresentation may be recovered in the tort of deceit. The Court of Appeal tackled the question of how such damages are to be calculated in *Doyle v Olby (Ironmongers) Ltd.*

Doyle v Olby (Ironmongers) Ltd [1969] 2 All ER 119

Facts: The plaintiff bought an ironmongers' business from the defendants. The defendants had made several fraudulent misrepresentations to the plaintiff concerning annual profits, sales and future competition. Specifically, the defendants told the plaintiff that most of the trade was over the counter in the ironmongers' shop. The plaintiff purchased the business subject to a covenant which stated that the defendants would not engage in a similar business within a 10-mile radius for five years. Following the purchase the plaintiff invested £7,000 into the business. He soon discovered that the turnover had been misrepresented and, in particular, that half the trade had been obtained by the defendant's brother acting as a part-time travelling salesman. It also became apparent that a company associated to the defendants had begun canvassing the defendants' former customers in the area.

The plaintiff brought an action for fraudulent misrepresentation. At first instance, Swanwick J found all the defendants liable for fraud and awarded the plaintiff damages of £1,500 calculated as equivalent to the cost of making good the representation or the reduction in the value of the goodwill. The plaintiff appealed against the amount of damages.

Held: The Court of Appeal allowed the appeal, holding that damages should be measured on a tort basis, not a contractual basis. The proper measure of damages was £5,500, measured by reference to all the losses directly flowing from the fraud.

Lord Denning:

'The judge awarded Mr. Doyle £1,500 damages. Mr. Doyle appeals against that award. He says it is far too small . . . It appears . . . that . . . the judge accepted that the proper measure of damages was the "cost of making good the representation", or what came to the same thing, "the reduction in value of the goodwill" due to the misrepresentation. In so doing, he treated the representation as if it were a contractual promise, that is, as if there were a contractual term to the effect "The trade is all over the counter. There is no need to employ a traveller." I think it was the wrong measure. Damages for fraud and conspiracy are assessed differently from damages for breach of contract . . .

The second question is what is the proper measure of damages for fraud, as distinct from damages for breach of contract. It was discussed during the argument in *Hadley v Baxendale* (1854) 9 Ex 341, and finds a place in the notes to *Smith's Leading Cases*, 13th edn (1929) at p 563, where it is suggested there is no difference. But in *McConnel v Wright* [1903] 1 Ch 546, 554, Lord Collins MR pointed out the difference. It was an action for fraudulent statements in a prospectus whereby a man was induced to take up shares. Lord Collins said of the action for fraud:

"It is not an action for breach of contract, and, therefore, no damages in respect of prospective gains which the person contracting was entitled by his contract to expect to come in, but it is an action of tort – it is an action for a wrong done whereby the plaintiff was tricked out of certain money in his pocket, and, therefore, prima facie, the highest limit of his damages is the whole extent of his loss, and that loss is measured by the money which was in his pocket and is now in the pocket of the company."

But that statement was the subject of comment by Lord Atkin in *Clark v Urquhart* [1930] AC 28, 67–68. He said:

"I find it difficult to suppose that there is any difference in the measure of damages in an action of deceit depending upon the nature of the transaction into which the plaintiff is fraudulently induced to enter. Whether he buys shares or buys sugar, whether he subscribes for shares, or agrees to enter into a partner-ship, or in any other way alters his position to his detriment, in principle, the measure of damages should be the same, and whether estimated by a jury or a judge. I should have thought it would be based on the actual damage directly flowing from the fraudulent inducement. The formula in *McConnel v Wright* [1903] 1 Ch 546, may be correct or it may be expressed in too rigid terms."

I think that Lord Collins did express himself in too rigid terms. He seems to have overlooked consequential damages. On principle the distinction seems to be this: in contract, the defendant has made a promise and broken it. The object of damages is to put the plaintiff in as good a position, as far as money can do it, as if the promise had been performed. In fraud, the defendant has been guilty of a deliberate wrong by inducing the plaintiff to act to his detriment. The object of damages is to compensate the plaintiff for all the loss he has suffered, so far, again, as money can do it. In contract, the damages are limited to what may reasonably be supposed to have been in the contemplation of the parties. In fraud, they are not so limited. The defendant is bound to make reparation for all the actual damages directly flowing from the fraudulent inducement. The person who has been defrauded is entitled to say:

"I would not have entered into this bargain at all but for your representation. Owing to your fraud, I have not only lost all the money I paid you, but, what is more, I have been put to a large amount of extra expense as well and suffered this or that extra damages."

All such damages can be recovered: and it does not lie in the mouth of the fraudulent person to say that they could not reasonably have been foreseen. For instance, in this very case Mr. Doyle has not only lost the money which he paid for the business, which he would never have done if there had been no fraud: he put all that money in and lost it; but also he has been put to expense and loss in trying to run a business which has turned out to be a disaster for him. He is entitled to damages for all his loss, subject, of course to giving credit for any benefit that he has received. There is nothing to be taken off in mitigation: for there is nothing more that he could have done to reduce his loss. He did all that he could reasonably be expected to do.'

Winn LJ:
'If a man in this country is made the victim of a fraudulent misrepresentation that a business in Bangkok, Hongkong, Manila or the Fiji Islands has certain equipment, certain assets, certain goodwill, certain trade contracts and profits, and is thereby induced to pay for that business, it being, of course, understood by both parties to the transaction of sale, for the procurement of which a fraudulent misrepresentation is made, that he will set out to that remote place with his family and, it may be, his household goods, at very considerable expense, and on arrival will acquire living accommodation and, perhaps, have to buy additional furniture and engage staff or servants; and if he acts upon the representations and incurs all such expenses,

and the business is found to be very different from that which it was fraudulently represented to be, so that he cannot survive out in the remote place to which he has gone, and is bound to come back again, then I, speaking for myself, would not hesitate to give him all the outgoings from his pocket of the kinds which I have indicated, up to such time as he should sensibly have come home again, and had the money to come back again, less, of course, by way of set-off, any benefit which he has derived from the exploitation of such assets as he found there upon his arrival.'

The Court of Appeal confirmed that damages for fraudulent misrepresentation will be measured according to the tortious measure, not the contractual measure. Damages in contract, if applied in the context of misrepresentation, would aim to put the innocent party in the position s/he would have been in had the statement been true (see Chapter 17). Damages in tort aim to put the innocent party in the position s/he would have been in had the statement not been made at all.

The key issue for the court was whether the plaintiff could recover damages for all his consequential losses flowing from the fraud, or whether his damages were limited by a rule of remoteness. In the law of negligence, a claimant can only recover damages for losses that were reasonably foreseeable (*Overseas Tankship (UK) v Morts Dock & Engineering Co (The Wagon Mound)* [1961] AC 388). The court refused to apply this test to the tort of deceit, insisting that the defendants were liable for all the plaintiff's losses, regardless of whether they were foreseeable. This stricter measure of damages, focusing on causation rather than remoteness, seems to be justified on the public policy ground that the courts should actively deter deliberate wrongdoing.

The effect of the rule was demonstrated in the House of Lords' decision in *Smith New Court Securities v Scrimgeour Vickers*.

Smith New Court Securities v Scrimgeour Vickers [1997] AC 254

Facts: The plaintiffs were persuaded to purchase 28 million shares in a company called Ferranti by the fraudulent misrepresentation of the defendants that there were other possible purchasers in the market. The price paid by the plaintiffs was 82.25p per share at a time when the shares were trading at 78p per share. It later transpired that Ferranti had been the victim of a major fraud (unrelated to the fraudulent misrepresentation) which caused the company's share price to plummet. The plaintiffs eventually sold the shares for between 40p and 30p per share – making a combined loss of over £11 million. The plaintiffs claimed this sum in damages from the defendants. The defendants argued that damages should be limited to the difference between the price that the plaintiffs paid (82.25p) and the price that they would have paid in the absence of the misrepresentation (78p). The Court of Appeal applied the measure contended for by the defendants.

Held: The House of Lords allowed the appeal and held that the plaintiffs were entitled to recover all the loss directly caused by the fraudulent misrepresentation, whether or not it was foreseeable.

Lord Steyn:

'Damages
Given the fact that the subsequent dramatic fall in the value of Ferranti shares was caused by the disclosure of an earlier fraud practised on Ferranti by a third party the question is whether Smith is entitled to recover against Citibank the entire loss arising from the fraudulently induced transaction. Smith submits that the Court of Appeal adopted the wrong measure. Smith seeks to recover damages calculated on the basis of the price paid less the aggregate of subsequent realisations. Citibank contends that the loss attributable to the subsequent disclosure of the fraud by a third party is a misfortune risk and is irrecoverable. Citibank argues that the Court of Appeal adopted the correct measure . . . .

The justification for distinguishing between deceit and negligence
That brings me to the question of policy whether there is a justification for differentiating between the extent of liability for civil wrongs depending on where in the sliding scale from strict liability to intentional wrongdoing the particular civil wrong fits in. It may be said that logical symmetry and a policy of not punishing intentional wrongdoers by civil remedies favour a uniform rule. On the other hand, it is a rational and defensible strategy to impose wider liability on an intentional wrongdoer. As *Hart and Honoré, Causation in the Law*, 2nd edn (1985), p 304 observed, an innocent plaintiff may, not without reason, call on a morally reprehensible defendant to pay the whole of the loss he caused. The exclusion of heads of loss in the law of negligence, which reflects considerations of legal policy, does not necessarily avail the intentional wrongdoer. Such a policy of imposing more stringent remedies on an intentional wrongdoer serves two purposes. First it serves a deterrent purpose in discouraging fraud. Counsel for Citibank argued that the sole purpose of the law of tort generally, and the tort of deceit in particular, should be to compensate the victims of civil wrongs. That is far too narrow a view. Professor Glanville Williams identified four possible purposes of an action for damages in tort: appeasement, justice, deterrence and compensation: see 'The Aims of the Law of Tort' (1951) 4 CLP 137. He concluded, at p 172: "Where possible the law seems to like to ride two or three horses at once; but occasionally a situation occurs where one must be selected. The tendency is then to choose the deterrent purpose for tort of intention, the compensatory purpose for other torts", and in the battle against fraud civil remedies can play a useful and beneficial role. Secondly, as between the fraudster and the innocent party, moral considerations militate in favour of requiring the fraudster to bear the risk of misfortunes directly caused by his fraud. I make no

apology for referring to moral considerations. The law and morality are inextricably interwoven. To a large extent the law is simply formulated and declared morality. And, as Oliver Wendell Holmes, *The Common Law* (ed M De W Howe), p 106, observed, the very notion of deceit with its overtones of wickedness is drawn from the moral world . . .'

Doyle v Olby (Ironmongers) Ltd

'. . . The logic of the decision in *Doyle v Olby (Ironmongers) Ltd*, justifies the following propositions.

(1) The plaintiff in an action for deceit is not entitled to be compensated in accordance with the contractual measure of damage, i.e. the benefit of the bargain measure. He is not entitled to be protected in respect of his positive interest in the bargain.

(2) The plaintiff in an action for deceit is, however, entitled to be compensated in respect of his negative interest. The aim is to put the plaintiff into the position he would have been in if no false representation had been made.

(3) The practical difference between the two measures was lucidly explained in a contemporary case note on *Doyle v Olby (Ironmongers) Ltd*: G.H. Treitel, 'Damages for Deceit' (1969) 32 MLR 556, 558–559. The author said:

> "If the plaintiff's bargain would have been a bad one, even on the assumption that the representation was true, he will do best under the tortious measure. If, on the assumption that the representation was true, his bargain would have been a good one, he will do best under the first contractual measure (under which he may recover something even if the actual value of what he has recovered is greater than the price)."

(4) Concentrating on the tort measure, the remoteness test whether the loss was reasonably foreseeable had been authoritatively laid down in *The Wagon Mound* in respect of the tort of negligence a few years before *Doyle v Olby (Ironmongers) Ltd* was decided . . . *Doyle v Olby (Ironmongers) Ltd* settled that a wider test applies in an action for deceit.

(5) The dicta in all three judgments, as well as the actual calculation of damages in *Doyle v Olby (Ironmongers) Ltd* make clear that the victim of the fraud is entitled to compensation for all the actual loss directly flowing from the transaction induced by the wrongdoer. That includes heads of consequential loss.

(6) Significantly in the present context the rule in the previous paragraph is not tied to any process of valuation at the date of the transaction. It is squarely based on the overriding compensatory principle, widened in view of the fraud to cover all direct consequences. The legal measure is to compare the position of the plaintiff as it was before the fraudulent statement was made to him with his position as it became as a result of his reliance on the fraudulent statement . . .'

Damages for fraudulent misrepresentation can also include an element of compensation for lost profits if the loss flows directly from the misrepresentation. In *East v Maurer* [1991] 2 All ER 733, the plaintiffs purchased a hair salon in reliance on a fraudulent misrepresentation that the seller had no intention of regularly working at another salon in the same town. The defendant did in fact open up a new salon in the town and the plaintiffs sued the defendant for their loss of profits. At first instance, the judge awarded the plaintiffs damages calculated by reference to the profit they would have made had the defendant not set up the new business. The Court of Appeal allowed the appeal, holding that the judge had wrongly applied the contract measure of damages. However, the court did take into account lost profits in its own assessment of damages. Beldam LJ said:

'It seems to me that [the judge] should have begun by considering the kind of profit which the second defendant might have made if the representation which induced her to buy the business at Exeter Road had not been made, and that involved considering the kind of profits which *she* might have expected to make in another hairdressing business bought for a similar sum.'

The measure of damages so framed looks very much like damages for breach of contract. This is not a problem, however, as Sedley LJ explained in *Clef Aquitaine v Sovereign Chemical Industries* [2000] 3 All ER 493: '[I]t does not follow that the proper mode of ascertaining damage in certain cases of tort may not mimic reasoning more familiar in contract'.

Finally, following the abolition of the 'cause of action' limitation in *Kuddus v Chief Constable of Leicestershire Constabulary* [2002] 2 AC 122 (considered in Chapter 17), punitive damages are now potentially available for fraudulent misrepresentation.

9.5.2.2 Negligent misstatement

Damages for negligent misrepresentation are subject to the normal tort principles of remoteness.

South Australia Asset Management Corp v York Montague Ltd [1997] AC 191

Facts: The plaintiff asked the defendants to value properties on the security of which they were considering advancing money by way of mortgage. The defendants negligently overvalued the properties and in reliance on these valuations the plaintiffs loaned money which they would not otherwise have done. The borrowers defaulted on their repayments and the plaintiffs suffered significant losses as a result. The losses were magnified due to the collapse of the property market. The plaintiffs sued the defendants for negligent misstatement and sought to recover the whole of their loss on the basis that they would not have entered into the transactions at all but for the negligent valuation. The Court of Appeal allowed the plaintiffs' claim.

Held: The House of Lords allowed the appeal, holding that the plaintiffs could only recover the loss which foreseeably flowed from the negligent valuation.

Lord Hoffman:
'Rules which make the wrongdoer liable for all the consequences of his wrongful conduct are exceptional and need to be justified by some special policy. Normally the law limits liability to those consequences which are attributable to that which made the act wrongful. In the case of liability in negligence for providing inaccurate information, this would mean liability for the consequences of the information being inaccurate.'

9.5.2.3 Misrepresentation Act 1967 s 2(1)

Section 2(1) of the 1967 Act states that: 'the person making the misrepresentation [will] be liable to damages in respect thereof had the misrepresentation been made fraudulently'. In other words, a person liable under s 2(1) will be treated as if they had made the misrepresentation fraudulently. This equation with fraud raises difficult questions concerning the measure of damages. Initially, there was some suggestion that the measure should be contractual (*Watts v Spence* [1976] Ch 165), but this approach was rejected by the Court of Appeal in *Sharneyford v Edge* [1987] Ch 305, in favour of the tortious approach. The express wording of the Act seems to suggest that the fraud measure should apply and this approach received support from the Court of Appeal in the leading case on the issue.

Royscott Trust v Rogerson [1991] 2 QB 297

Facts: The defendant car dealer told the plaintiff finance company that a prospective hire-purchaser had paid a 20% deposit. The finance company would not have loaned as much money as it did had it known the true value of the deposit. The hire-purchaser defaulted on repayments and dishonestly sold the car. The plaintiff brought an action against the defendant for misrepresentation under s 2(1).

Held: The Court of Appeal held that the fraud measure applied and the plaintiff could recover the unpaid instalments whether or not they were foreseeable.

Balcombe LJ:
'The first main issue before us was: accepting that the tortious measure is the right measure, is it the measure where the tort is that of fraudulent misrepresentation, or is it

the measure where the tort is negligence at common law? The difference is that in cases of fraud a plaintiff is entitled to any loss which flowed from the defendant's fraud, even if the loss could not have been foreseen: see *Doyle v Olby (Ironmongers) Ltd* [1969] 2 QB 158. In my judgment the wording of the subsection is clear: the person making the innocent misrepresentation shall be "so liable," i.e., liable to damages as if the representation had been made fraudulently. This was the conclusion to which Walton J came in *F & B Entertainments Ltd v Leisure Enterprises Ltd* (1976) 240 EG 455, 461. See also the decision of Sir Douglas Frank QC, sitting as a High Court judge, in *McNally v Welltrade International Ltd* [1978] IRLR 497. In each of these cases the judge held that the basis for the assessment of damages under section 2(1) of the Act of 1967 is that established in *Doyle v Olby (Ironmongers) Ltd* . . . By 'so liable' I take it to mean liable as he would be if the misrepresentation had been made fraudulently.

This was also the original view of the academic writers. In an article, "The Misrepresentation Act 1967" (1967) 30 MLR 369 by P S Atiyah and G H Treitel, the authors say, at pp 373–374:

"The measure of damages in the statutory action will apparently be that in an action of deceit . . . But more probably the damages recoverable in the new action are the same as those recoverable in an action of deceit . . ."

Professor Treitel has since changed his view. In Treitel, *The Law of Contract*, 7th edn (1987), p 278, he says:

"Where the action is brought under section 2(1) of the Misrepresentation Act, one possible view is that the deceit rule will be applied by virtue of the fiction of fraud. But the preferable view is that the severity of the deceit rule can only be justified in cases of actual fraud and that remoteness under section 2(1) should depend, as in actions based on negligence, on the test of foreseeability."

Professor Furmston in *Cheshire, Fifoot and Furmston's Law of Contract*, 11th edn (1986), p 286, says:

"It has been suggested" – and the reference is to the passage in Atiyah and Treitel's article cited above – "that damages under section 2(1) should be calculated on the same principles as govern the tort of deceit. This suggestion is based on a theory that section 2(1) is based on a 'fiction of fraud'. We have already suggested that this theory is misconceived. On the other hand the action created by section 2(1) does look much more like an action in tort than one in contract and it is suggested that the rules for negligence are the natural ones to apply." . . .

The suggestion that the "fiction of fraud" theory is misconceived occurs at p 271, in a passage which includes:

"Though it would be quixotic to defend the drafting of the section, it is suggested that there is no such 'fiction of fraud' since the section does not say that a negligent misrepresentor shall be treated for all purposes as if he were fraudulent. No doubt the wording seeks to incorporate by reference some of the rules relating to fraud but, for instance, nothing in the wording of the subsection requires the measure of damages for deceit to be applied to the statutory action."

With all respect to the various learned authors whose works I have cited above, it seems to me that to suggest that a different measure of damage applies to an action for innocent misrepresentation under the section than that which applies to an action for fraudulent misrepresentation (deceit) at common law is to ignore the plain words of the subsection and is inconsistent with the cases to which I have referred. In my judgment, therefore, the finance company is entitled to recover from the dealer all the losses which it suffered as a result of its entering into the agreements with the dealer and the customer, even if those losses were unforeseeable, provided that they were not otherwise too remote.'

The 'fiction of fraud' interpretation of s 2(1) can lead to some startling results, particularly in light of the fact that the defendant may not even have acted negligently – remember that the burden of proof is on the defendant to prove that he had reasonable grounds for belief in the truth of his statement. Nevertheless, the Court of Appeal felt that this interpretation was the only one consistent with the plain meaning of the words used in the subsection. Richard Hooley challenged this aspect of the judgment in the following article.

R Hooley, 'Damages and the Misrepresentation Act 1967' (1991) 107 LQR 547, 549–551

Section 2(1) extends liability to the negligent misrepresentor without requiring his victim to establish either fraud or a duty of care. The effect of the Court of Appeal's decision is to treat the foolish but honest man as if he were dishonest. Repugnant as this may appear, if the wording of the Act is clear there is nothing for the court to do but to apply the statute: *Shepheard v Broome* [1904] AC 342, *per* Lord Lindley (at p 346). It was at all times assumed by Balcombe and Ralph Gibson LJJ that section 2(1) is so clearly worded. But is it? It is certainly arguable that the words 'that person shall be so liable', mean merely, 'that person shall be liable in damages notwithstanding that at common law damages were only available for misrepresentations proved to be fraudulent' (see Taylor (1982) 45 MLR 139 at p 141). On this interpretation the subsection establishes liability in damages but not their quantum.

There are a number of arguments to be made against this alternative interpretation of section 2(1). The first is that it leaves the door open to the argument that the appropriate measure of damages under section 2(1) is contractual. But it is submitted that so long as the courts recognise the essential nature of a mere representation as opposed to a term of the contract the tortious measure will prevail. Secondly, it ignores the fact that before the Act of 1967 common law damages were recoverable for negligent misrepresentation under *Hedley Byrne & Co Ltd v Heller & Partners Ltd* [1964] AC 465. However, when the Misrepresentation Act was passed it was generally believed that *Hedley Byrne* could not be used to impose liability for pre-contractual statements. Although this understanding was later shown to be false (*Esso Petroleum Co Ltd v Mardon* [1976] QB 801, per Lord Denning MR at p 820), section 2(1) was designed to establish liability in damages for negligent misrepresentation in those circumstances. Thirdly, the alternative interpretation flies in the face of the wealth of authority cited by Balcombe LJ in favour of his interpretation of section 2(1). Yet in all reported cases applying the *Doyle v Olby* measure of damages to section 2(1) there is no report of this alternative interpretation of section 2(1) being considered by the court.

Even if the arguments against this alternative interpretation prevail it is submitted that there is a strong case for Parliament to intervene and remove the reference to fraudulent misrepresentation from section 2(1). Fraudulent misrepresentation is an intentional tort where the public policy of deterring deliberate wrongdoing dictates the shift in emphasis from foreseeability to causation. No such considerations dictate that the same emphasis apply under section 2(1). On the contrary, section 2(1) has much closer links to liability under *Hedley Byrne*; and the effect of applying *Doyle v Olby* to it means that the primary basis for recovery of damages for common law negligent misstatement is foreseeability, whereas for negligent misrepresentation under the statute it is causation. It is submitted that there is no justification for this distinction.

Making liability to damages under section 2(1) the same as for fraudulent misrepresentation could have bizarre consequences. If exemplary damages are recoverable for deceit, and Peter Pain J in *Archer v Brown* [1985] QB 401 at p 423 leaves this possibility open, then are they also recoverable under section 2(1)? It is hoped not. It is also hoped that damages awarded in lieu of rescission under section 2(2) of the Misrepresentation Act 1967 continue to exclude consequential loss in the same way it is excluded from the award of an equitable indemnity on rescission. One of the main arguments for the exclusion of consequential loss from an award under section 2(2) was that by the wording of section 2(3) damages under section 2(2) are meant to be less than damages under section 2(1). If the test of remoteness under both subsections 2(1) and (2) is that of foreseeability then it has been submitted that to make damages less under subsection (2) consequential loss is not recoverable under that subsection. If damages under section 2(1) are governed by *Doyle v Olby* and those under section 2(2) by foreseeability then this particular argument goes out of the window (see Treitel, *Law of Contract* (7th edn) at p 279).

605

Hooley's criticism of the judgments in *Royscott* is compelling. In addition, it should be noted that the court's interpretation of s 2(1) was not strictly necessary to the decision in the case. This is because the act of selling on the car by the hire-purchaser was held to be a reasonably foreseeable consequence and thus damages would have been recoverable under the negligence test. The decision has also been questioned by Lord Steyn in *Smith New Court Securities v Scrimgeour Vickers* [1997] AC 254:

> 'The question is whether the rather loose wording of the statute compels the court to treat a person who was morally innocent as if he was guilty of fraud when it comes to the measure of damages. There has been trenchant academic criticism of the Royscott case: see Richard Hooley, "Damages and the Misrepresentation Act 1967" (1991) 107 LQR 547.'

His Lordship indicated that the decision in *Royscott* might be revisited, but stopped short of making any specific recommendations due to the fact that the issue was not directly before him.

Despite the doubts that have been cast on the decision in *Royscott* it appears that it remains good law and it was recently applied by the High Court in *Pankhania v Hackney LBC (Damages)* [2004] EWHC 323; [2004] 1 EGLR 135. Geoffrey Vos QC said:

> 'Though this decision has been the subject of some academic criticism (see, for example, Lord Steyn in *Smith New Court*), and [counsel for the defendants] wished to reserve his position as to its correctness, it was accepted that it was a decision binding on me, and that I should follow it.'

9.5.2.4 Contributory negligence

Further doubt is cast on the correctness of the decision in *Royscott* by the law on contributory negligence. It is clear that, in respect of negligent misstatement, damages may be reduced on the grounds of contributory negligence, where the representee has also been at fault.

LAW REFORM (CONTRIBUTORY NEGLIGENCE) ACT 1945

Section 1

(1) Where any person suffers damage as the result partly of the fault of any other person or persons, a claim in respect of that damage shall not be defeated by reason of the fault of the person suffering the damage, but the damages recoverable in respect thereof shall be reduced to such an extent as the court thinks just and equitable having regard to the claimant's share in the responsibility of the damage.

The availability of a reduction in damages for contributory negligence was extended to misrepresentation under s 2(1) of the 1967 Act in *Gran Gelato Ltd v Richcliff (Group) Ltd* [1992] Ch 560. Sir Donald Nicholls VC said:

> '. . . in short, liability under the 1967 Act is essentially founded on negligence, in the sense that the defendant, the representor, did not have reasonable grounds to believe that the facts represented were true. (Of course, if he did not so believe the facts represented were true he will be liable for fraud.) This being so, it would be very odd if the defence of contributory negligence were not available to a claim under that Act. It would be very odd if contributory negligence were available as a defence to a claim for damages based on breach of duty to take care in and about the making of a particular representation, but not available to a claim for damages under the 1967 Act in respect of the same representation.'

This 'equation with negligence' approach is impossible to reconcile with the 'fiction of fraud' analysis applied to the law of damages under s 2(1) in *Royscott*. It has been held that a reduction for contributory negligence is not available for an action based on deceit (*Standard Chartered Bank v Pakistan National Shipping* [2003] 1 AC 959). Therefore, assuming the 'fiction of fraud' analysis is correct, a reduction should not be available under s 2(1). It is clear that the decisions in *Royscott* and *Gran Gelato* are irreconcilable, but it may be the former that was wrongly decided rather than the latter.

9.5.3 DAMAGES UNDER S 2(2) MISREPRESENTATION ACT 1967

MISREPRESENTATION ACT 1967

Section 2

(2) Where a person has entered into a contract after a misrepresentation has been made to him otherwise than fraudulently, and he would be entitled, by reason of the misrepresentation, to rescind the contract, then, if it is claimed, in any proceedings arising out of the contract, that the contract ought to be or has been rescinded, the court or arbitrator may declare the contract subsisting and award damages in lieu of rescission, if of opinion that it would be equitable to do so, having regard to the nature of the misrepresentation and the loss that would be caused by it if the contract were upheld, as well as to the loss that rescission would cause to the other party.

This section gives the court a discretion to award damages as an alternative to rescission. The exercise of the court's discretion under s 2(2) was considered by the Court of Appeal in *William Sindall Plc v Cambridgeshire County Council*.

William Sindall Plc v Cambridgeshire County Council [1994] 1 WLR 1016

Facts: The claimants purchased a piece of land from the defendant council. The defendant innocently failed to disclose the existence of a private foul sewer running across the land, and on discovery of the sewer, the claimants sought to withdraw from the contract. This was very much in their interests because, following the sale, there had been a major property slump and the price of the land had more than halved. At first instance, a misrepresentation was found and rescission was allowed.

Held: The Court of Appeal allowed the appeal and held that there had been no misrepresentation. It was not strictly necessary to consider the operation of s 2(2) but the court did consider obiter how s 2(2) Misrepresentation Act 1967 would have been applied had an operative misrepresentation been found.

Evans LJ:

'Section 2(3) makes it clear that the statutory power to award damages under section 2(2) is distinct from the plaintiff's right to recover damages under section 2(1). Quoting from section 2(2) itself, such damages are awarded "in lieu of rescission" and the court has to have regard to three factors in particular, namely, the nature of the misrepresentation, the loss that would be caused by it (sc. the misrepresentation) if the contract was upheld, and the loss that rescission would cause to the other party (sc. the non-fraudulent author of the misrepresentation). It has not been suggested that these three are the only factors which the court may take into account. The discretion is expressed in broad terms – "if of opinion that it would be equitable to do so". The three factors, however, in all but an exceptional case, are likely to be the ones to which most weight would be given, even if the subsection were silent in this respect . . .

. . . [I]t would be substantially unjust, in my judgment, to deprive Cambridgeshire of the bargain which it made in 1988, albeit that the bargain was induced by a misrepresentation innocently made, but which was of little importance in relation to the contract as a whole. That misrepresentation apart, Sindall made what has proved to be so far an unfortunate bargain for them (although they remain owners of an important potential development site in what is a notoriously cyclical market). To permit them to transfer the financial consequences to Cambridgeshire, in the circumstances of this case, could properly be described as a windfall for them.

For the above reasons, and taking into account the nature of the alleged representation and the history of the matter generally, including Sindall's deliberate failure to make any serious attempt to find a solution to the difficulty which arose when the sewer was discovered, the equitable balance, in my judgment, lies in favour of upholding the contract and awarding damages in lieu of rescission in this case. If there were a live issue under section 2(2), I would award damages in lieu of rescission and order the amount of such damages to be assessed.

There remains the question of whether these damages should include the decline in the market value of the land since the contract was made. . . . [I]n my judgment they should not. This conclusion may be inconsistent with the view expressed in *McGregor on Damages*, 15th edn (1988), para 1752, and in deference to the distinguished author I should explain my reasons briefly. He suggests that the measure to be adopted is

> "the same as the normal measure of damages in tort where the plaintiff has been induced to contract by fraudulent or negligent misrepresentation . . . The overall result, therefore, is that the damages will be held to be the difference between the value transferred and the value received . . . no recovery being possible for consequential losses."

If the "value transferred" (meaning the price paid by the plaintiff, to whom the representation was made) was the market value of the property, then there is no difference between this formula and what *McGregor* calls the contract measure, that is to say, the difference between the actual value received and the value which the property would have had, if the representation had been true: see paragraph 1718. By adopting the tort measure, therefore, as he does in paragraph 1752 in the paragraph already quoted, the author impliedly rejects the contract measure, whereas in my judgment that becomes the correct measure in circumstances where the plaintiff is entitled to an order for rescission, but rescission is refused under section 2(2) of the Act. This is because the difference in value between what the plaintiff was misled into believing that he was acquiring, and the value of what he in fact received, seems to me to be the measure of the loss caused to him by the misrepresentation in a case where he cannot rescind the contract and therefore retains the property which he received.

As *McGregor on Damages* points out, the tortious measure benefits a plaintiff who made a bad bargain, that is to say, who agreed to pay more than the market value of the property in the state in which he believed it to be, more so than the contract measure would do. Conversely, it dis-benefits one who paid less than the market value, because it disentitles him from recovering the whole of the difference which the contract measure would otherwise produce. Likewise, the right to rescind benefits a plaintiff who has paid, or agreed to pay more than, with hindsight, he should have done. The period of hindsight may be short or long; where it is long, and the value has fallen in line with the market and therefore for reasons unconnected with the misrepresentation, there is no justification, in my view, for holding that the author of the misrepresentation is liable to compensate the plaintiff for that loss, in a case where rescission is refused.'

Hoffman LJ:
'Under section 2(1), the measure of damages is the same as for fraudulent misrepresentation, i.e. all loss caused by the plaintiff having been induced to enter into the contract: *Cemo Properties (UK) Ltd v Dentsply Research & Development Corporation* [1991] EGLR 197. This means that the misrepresentor is invariably deprived of the benefit of the bargain (e.g. any difference between the price paid and the value of the

thing sold) and may have to pay additional damages for consequential loss suffered by the representee on account of having entered into the contract. In my judgment, however, it is clear that this will not necessarily be the measure of damages under section 2(2).

First, section 2(1) provides for damages to be awarded to a person who "has entered into a contract after a misrepresentation has been made to him by another party and as a result thereof" – sic of having entered into the contract – "he has suffered loss". In contrast, section 2(2) speaks of "the loss which would be caused by it" – sic the misrepresentation – "if the contract were upheld". In my view, section 2(1) is concerned with the damage flowing from having entered into the contract, while section 2(2) is concerned with damage caused by the property not being what it was represented to be.

Secondly, section 2(3) contemplates that damages under section 2(2) may be less than damages under section 2(1) and should be taken into account when assessing damages under the latter subsection. This only makes sense if the measure of damages may be different.

Thirdly, the Law Reform Committee report makes it clear that section 2(2) was enacted because it was thought that it might be a hardship to the representor to be deprived of the whole benefit of the bargain on account of a minor misrepresentation. It could not possibly have intended the damages in lieu to be assessed on a principle which would invariably have the same effect.

The Law Reform Committee drew attention to the anomaly which already existed by which a minor misrepresentation gave rise to a right of rescission whereas a warranty in the same terms would have grounded no more than a claim for modest damages. It said that this anomaly would be exaggerated if its recommendation for abolition of the bar on rescission after completion were to be implemented. I think that section 2(2) was intended to give the court a power to eliminate this anomaly by upholding the contract and compensating the plaintiff for the loss he has suffered on account of the property not having been what it was represented to be. In other words, damages under section 2(2) should never exceed the sum which would have been awarded if the representation had been a warranty. It is not necessary for present purposes to discuss the circumstances in which they may be less.'

Evans LJ suggested that there were three basic factors to which the court had regard when considering whether to exercise its discretion under s 2(2):

(1) the nature of the misrepresentation;
(2) the loss that would be caused by the misrepresentation if the contract was upheld;
(3) the loss that would be caused to the representor by rescission.

On the facts, the Court of Appeal unanimously concluded that it would have exercised its discretion to grant damages in lieu of rescission, because the misrepresentation was relatively insignificant and the loss caused to the claimants was trifling in comparison to the loss that would have been sustained by the defendant had the contract been rescinded.

On the issue of the measure of damages, Hoffman and Evans LJJ agreed that the measure under s 2(2) should be less than the measure under s 2(1), because the representee is less culpable. It seems that the purpose of an award of damages under s 2(2) is to compensate the representee for the loss caused by the refusal of rescission, not the loss caused by entering into the contract in reliance on the misrepresentation. The comments of Evans LJ to the effect that the contract measure ought to be applied under s 2(2) are somewhat doubtful, given that this could easily exceed the measure of damages available under s 2(1). What seems to be clear is that account will not be taken of consequential losses or losses due to a general fall in market values after the contract is made. These losses are only relevant to damages assessed under s 2(1). This was confirmed by Jacob J in *Thomas Witter Ltd v TBP Industries Ltd* [1996] 2 All ER 575:

> 'It is fair to say as *Chitty* para 6–059, p 373 observes, that 'the Act gives little clue as to how damages are to be assessed under this section if they are not to be assessed in the same way as under subsection (1)'. However both *Chitty* and Treitel *Law of Contract* (8th edn, 1991) p 326 (see also Atiyah and Treitel [1967] MLR 369 at 376) suggest that damages under s 2(2) may be limited to the loss in value of what is bought under the contract whereas s 2(1) damages may also include consequential loss.'

It should also be noted that the award of damages in lieu of rescission is entirely at the discretion of the court. The representee does not have a right to recover damages under s 2(2) (see *UCB Corporate Services Ltd v Thomason* [2005] EWCA Civ 225 where no substantial damages were awarded in lieu of rescission). Moreover, the court can only exercise its discretion to award damages under s 2(2) while it continues to have jurisdiction to order rescission. If the claimant has lost the right to rescission due to lapse of time or the intervention of third-party rights, damages under 2(2) will not be available either (*Floods of Queensferry Ltd v Shand Construction Ltd* [2000] BLR 8; *Government of Zanzibar v British Aerospace (Lancaster House) Ltd* [2000] 1 WLR 2333. But, contrast *Thomas Witter Ltd v TBP Industries Ltd* [1996] 2 All ER 575).

9.5.4 INDEMNITY AT COMMON LAW

In addition to rescission, the common law also provided a remedy known as an indemnity. An indemnity is a money remedy, which can be used alongside rescission to help to put the representee back in the position s/he was in before the contract was made. Thus it is restitutionary in effect. Unlike damages, an indemnity is available for all types of misrepresentation, including innocent misrepresentations. It is a far more restricted remedy than damages and only entitles the representee to recover the cost to him/her of the obligations created by the contract with the representor. This is illustrated by the facts of *Newbigging v Adam* (1887) 34 Ch D 582, where the plaintiff was induced to enter a partnership agreement by false representations. The Court of Appeal ordered rescission; the partnership was dissolved and the plaintiff recovered the capital he had invested in the partnership. He was also granted an indemnity against the liabilities he had incurred while a partner.

The distinction between damages and an indemnity is illustrated by the facts of *Whittington v Seal-Hayne*.

Whittington v Seal-Hayne (1900) 82 LT 49

Facts: The plaintiffs, who were breeders of prize poultry, leased premises from the defendant, relying on his statement that the premises were in a sanitary condition. Under the lease the plaintiffs covenanted to execute all such works as might be required by the local authority. The water supply was contaminated due to the unsanitary condition of the premises. The plaintiffs' manager and his family became ill, the poultry died or became valueless for breeding, and the local authority required the drains to be put in good order and the house to be made fit for human habitation. The plaintiffs claimed, in addition to a refund of the rent, compensation in relation to rates paid, repairs carried out, stock lost, medical and removal expenses.

Held: Farewell J held that the plaintiffs were entitled to have the lease rescinded and to recover what they had spent on the rent, rates and repairs since these were obligations created by the contract. They could not recover compensation for the other items of loss because these losses were not necessarily incurred as a result of entering into the contract – the lease contained no obligation to use the land for poultry farming. Therefore these items of loss fell in the category of damages and were not recoverable.

Now that damages are available for negligent misrepresentation at common law and under statute, the only situation in which a claimant may wish to claim an indemnity is where the contract is being rescinded for a wholly innocent, non-negligent, misrepresentation.

9.6 EXCLUSION OF LIABILITY FOR MISREPRESENTATION

Section 3 of the Misrepresentation Act 1967, as amended by s 8 of the Unfair Contract Terms Act 1977, restricts the freedom to exclude liability for misrepresentation.

MISREPRESENTATION ACT 1967

Section 3

If a contract contains a term which would exclude or restrict:

(a) any liability to which a party to a contract may be subject by reason of any misrepresentation made by him before the contract was made; or

(b) any remedy available to another party to the contract by reason of such a misrepresentation,

that term shall be of no effect except in so far as it satisfies the requirement of reasonableness as stated in section 11(1) of the Unfair Contract Terms Act 1977; and it is for those claiming that the term satisfies that requirement to show that it does.

The section states that any clause which purports to exclude or restrict either liability for misrepresentation or any remedy in respect thereof, will only be effective in so far as it satisfies the requirement of reasonableness under s 11 of the UCTA 1977 (see Chapter 8). In *HIH Casualty and General Insurance Ltd v Chase Manhattan Bank* [2003] UKHL 6; [2003] 2 Lloyd's Rep 61, the House of Lords confirmed that a clause purporting to exclude liability for fraudulent misrepresentation will be held to be unreasonable (although their Lordships did leave open the possibility of excluding such liability for a statement made by an agent, provided that sufficiently clear language was used). The position in relation to non-fraudulent misrepresentations was stated by the High Court in *Walker v Boyle*.

Walker v Boyle [1982] 1 WLR 495

Facts: The plaintiff agreed to purchase a house from the defendant for £105,000 and paid a deposit. The agreement was subject to the National Conditions of Sale (19th edn), condition 17 (1) of which provided that 'no error, mis-statement or omission in any preliminary answer concerning the property . . . shall annul the sale . . .'. In response to a question raised prior to the agreement the defendant had told the plaintiff that she was not aware of any boundary dispute. There was in fact a boundary dispute but the defendant had mistakenly believed that it had been settled. The plaintiff sought to recover the deposit he had paid. The defendant claimed that the contract excluded liability for misrepresentation.

Held: The court held that condition 17 of the National Conditions of Sale did not satisfy the reasonableness test even though it was in common use.

Dillon J;

'If condition 17 has any validity or relevance in the circumstances of this case, it is a term which would exclude liabilities to which Mrs Boyle would be subject by reason of misrepresentation, and so section 3 is applicable. The requirement of reasonableness in section 11 of the Unfair Contract Terms Act 1977 is that the term shall have been a fair and reasonable one to be included, having regard to the circumstances which were or ought reasonably to have been known to or in the contemplation of the parties when the contract was made. I do not regard condition 17 as satisfying that requirement in the circumstances of this case. Another way of putting it is that Mrs. Boyle has not shown that it does satisfy that requirement . . .

It has . . . been submitted by [counsel for the defendant] that the court should be very slow to hold that a common form clause like condition 17 is not fair and reasonable. Of course it is true that there are common form clauses which have been evolved by negotiation between trade associations, associations of merchants or associations of growers or trade unions or other such bodies concerned to pro-tect the rights of their members, which can be regarded as representing what con-sensus in the trade regards as fair and reasonable. Again, the National Conditions of Sale are not the product of negotiation between such bodies and it is plain from the conditions I have cited in the *Nottingham Patent Brick and Tile Co.* case, 16 Q.B.D. 778 and Clauson J's case of *Charles Hunt v Palmer* [1931] 2 Ch 287 that what now appears in condition 17 has come down through the ages despite very drastic limita-tions imposed on it by the courts. I do not think it can be said that its precarious survival until 1977 entitles it to the automatic accolade of fairness and reasonableness.'

In a recent commercial case, a clause excluding liability for misrepresentation was upheld by the High Court.

Six Continents Hotels Inc v Event Hotels GmbH [2006] EWHC 2317

Facts: The claimant, the owner of the Holiday Inn trademark, brought an action against the defendant for unpaid licence fees in relation to its use of the Holiday Inn trademark in Germany. The defendant counter-claimed for damages for fraudulent/negligent misrepresentation. The alleged misrepresentations were as follows: (1) that all other franchisees operating under the Holiday Inn Trademark Name in Germany did not pay lower franchise fees than the defendant; and (2) that the claimant had decided that in respect of new franchise agreements, it would impose higher fees than those agreed for the defendant. The claimant denied making the misrepresentations and sought to rely on an exclusion clause in the contract which stated that: 'Each of the parties agrees that it shall not commence any lawsuit or assert any claim . . . based on actions, discussions or agreements . . . which occurred prior to the signing of this Agreement.'

Held: The Court held that there had been no misrepresentations, and even if there had, the claimant was entitled to rely on the exclusion clause.

Gloster J:

'54. I would . . . in this context have held that, insofar as [the exclusion clause] falls to be tested against section 3 of the 1967 Act, it passes the test of reasonableness. The Agreements were sophisticated agreements that were entered into by substantial entities in respect of a major transaction. There was no inequality of bargaining power. As Chadwick LJ said in *Grimstead & Son Ltd v McGarrigan* [1999] CA Transcript 1733 (27 October 1999):

> "There are, as it seems to me, at least two good reasons why the courts should not refuse to give effect to an acknowledgement of non-reliance in a commercial contract between experienced parties of equal bargaining power—a fortiori, where those parties have the benefit of professional advice. First, it is reasonable to assume that the parties desire commercial certainty. They want to order their affairs on the basis that the bargain between them can be found within the document which they have signed. They want to avoid the uncertainty of litigation based on allegations as to the content of oral discussions at pre-contractual meetings. Second, it is reasonable to assume that the price to be paid reflects the commercial risk which each party—or, more usually, the purchaser—is willing to accept. The risk is determined, in part at least, by the warranties which the vendor is prepared to give. The tighter the warranties, the less the risk and (in principle at least) the greater the price the vendor will require and which the purchaser will be prepared to pay. It is legitimate and commercially desirable, that both parties should be able to measure the risk, and agree the price, on the basis of the warranties which have been given and accepted."

I respectfully agree.

55. Accordingly, had it been relevant, I would have held against Event on this issue also.'

A difficult issue that has arisen is the status of clauses that seek to deny the existence of any precontractual representations, or state that no reliance is to be placed on any such representations.

Overbrooke Estates Ltd v Glencombe Properties Ltd [1974] 1 WLR 1335

Facts: The plaintiffs offered certain freehold property for sale by auction. The conditions for sale stated: 'The vendors do not make or give and neither the auctioneers nor any person in the employment of the auctioneers has any authority to make or give any representation or warranty in relation to these properties.' The auctioneers, as agents for the plaintiffs, told the defendants that neither the local authority nor the Greater London Council had any plans for the property and were not interested in it for compulsory purchase. It transpired that the property was within an area likely to be included in a slum clearance scheme and the defendants attempted to withdraw from the contract. The plaintiffs sought to rely on the exclusion clause in the conditions of sale and the defendants claimed that this was an unreasonable exclusion clause and thus without effect under s 3 of the Misrepresentation Act 1967.

Held: The court held that the clause was not an exclusion of liability but merely a limitation on the authority of the plaintiff's agent. Therefore s 3 of the 1967 Act did not apply.

Brightman J:
'In my judgment section 3 of the Act ... only applies to a provision which would exclude or restrict liability for a misrepresentation made by a party or his duly authorised agent, including of course an agent with ostensible authority. The section does not, in my judgment, in any way qualify the right of a principal publicly to limit the otherwise ostensible authority of his agent.'

It appears that the approach adopted in *Overbrooke* will not be applied when the representation is made directly by the vendor, rather than by the vendor's agent.

Cremdean Properties Ltd v Nash (1977) 244 EG 547

Facts: The plaintiffs sought rescission of a contract for the sale of two properties, alleging that the defendants had made an innocent misrepresentation as to the area of lettable office space. The contract contained a clause stating: 'These particulars are prepared for the convenience of the intending purchaser or tenant and although they are believed to be correct their accuracy is not guaranteed and any error, omission or misdescription shall not annul the sale or the grounds on which compensation may be claimed and neither do they constitute any part of any offer of a contract. Any intending purchaser or tenant must satisfy himself by inspection or otherwise as to the correctness of the statements contained in these particulars.' The defendants argued that the aim of this clause was not to exclude liability, but rather to bring about a situation as if no representation at all had been made.

Held: The Court of Appeal rejected the defendant's argument and held that the clause was subject to the reasonableness test.

Bridge LJ:

'It is one thing to say that s 3 [of the Misrepresentation Act 1967] does not inhibit a principal from publicly giving notice limiting the ostensible authority of his agents; it is quite another thing to say that a principal can circumvent the plainly intended effect of s 3 by a clause excluding his own liability for a representation which he has undoubtedly made.'

The approach taken in *Cremdean* was subsequently followed by the courts in *South Western General Property Co Ltd v Marton* (1982) 263 EG 1090, *Thomas Witter Ltd v TBP Industries Ltd* [1996] 2 All ER 573, and *Inntreprenenur Pub Co (GL) v East Crown Ltd* [2000] 2 Lloyd's LR 611. Following this line of cases, it was assumed that 'entire agreement' clauses still fell within the scope of s 3 to the extent that they sought to exclude liability for misrepresentation. More recently, however, the Court of Appeal has suggested that an 'entire agreement' clause might have the effect of creating an evidential estoppel, thus side-stepping s 3.

Watford Electronics v Sanderson CFL Ltd [2001] 1 All ER (Comm) 696

Facts: The defendants agreed to sell the claimants a number of computer products. The contract for sale included an entire agreement clause which stated: 'The parties agree that these terms and conditions (together with any other terms and conditions expressly incorporated in the Contract) represent the entire agreement between the parties relating to the sale and purchase of the Equipment and that no statement or representations made by either party have been relied upon by the other in agreeing to enter into the Contract.'

Held: The Court of Appeal held that the effect of the clause was to prevent the person to whom a misrepresentation was made from asserting that he relied on it. Such a clause is not an exclusion to which section 3 of the Misrepresentation Act is applicable.

Chadwick LJ:

'The entire agreement clause – clause 14 in the Terms and Conditions of Sale, clause 15 in the Terms and Conditions of Software Licence – is . . . in two parts. The second part of the clause contains an acknowledgment by the parties that "no statements or representations made by either party have been relied upon by the other in agreeing to enter into the contract".

[A]n acknowledgment of non-reliance does not purport to prevent a party from proving that a representation was made, nor that it was false. What the acknowledgment seeks to do is to prevent the person to whom the representation was made from asserting that he relied upon it. If it is to have that effect, it will be necessary – as I sought to point out in *Grimstead v McGarrigan* – for the party who seeks to set up the acknowledgment as an evidential estoppel to plead and prove that the three requirements identified by this Court in *Lowe v Lombank Ltd* [1960] 1 WLR 196 are satisfied. That may present insuperable difficulties; not least because it may be impossible for a party who has made representations which he intended should be relied upon to satisfy the court that he entered into the contract in the belief that a statement by the other party that he had not relied upon those representations was true. But the fact that, on particular facts, the acknowledgment of non-reliance may not achieve its purpose does not lead to the conclusion that the acknowledgment is "in substance an exclusion clause to which section 3 of the Misrepresentation Act is applicable" . . .'

The effect of the decision is somewhat difficult to predict. As Chadwick LJ notes, it will be extremely difficult for a representor to establish that s/he truly believed the entire agreement clause, that is, that s/he believed that the representee was not relying on his/her statement. Thus it may be that the decision will have very little practical impact on the current law. Nevertheless, it is to be regretted that Chadwick LJ chose to focus on the form of the clause rather than on its substance as Edwin Peel explains below.

Peel, E, 'Reasonable exemption clauses' (2001) 117 LQR 545, 549

It is submitted that, bar any amendment to section 3 of the 1967 Act, the 'substance' approach taken by the [first instance] judge in *Watford Electronics* is to be preferred. This is not to deny the importance to be attached to non-reliance clauses in commercial contracts. They allow the parties 'to order their affairs on the basis that the bargain between them can be found within the document they have signed' and avoid 'the uncertainty of litigation based on allegations as to the content of oral discussions at pre-contractual meetings' (per Chadwick L.J., in *Grimstead*, p 35A–C). These are matters which should be reflected in the application of the reasonableness test and which should normally lead to the conclusion that, as between parties of relatively equal bargaining power, such clauses are reasonable. If they persuade the court not to apply the reasonableness test at all, by rejecting the 'substance' test, they will leave the court with no opportunity to police such clauses when they are used against consumers, or parties of unequal bargaining power. An incompleteness in the drafting of the legislation would have been allowed to undermine its clearly intended effect. This can, and should, be avoided by the courts.

We must wait to see whether the courts in later cases will follow the approach adopted by the Court of Appeal in *Watford Electronics*. It is to be hoped that the courts will decide to bring non-reliance clauses back under their supervisory jurisdiction by looking at the substance of the clause, rather than at its form.

9.7 ADDITIONAL READING

Allen, D, *Misrepresentation*, 1988, London: Sweet & Maxwell.

Atiyah, P and Treitel, G, 'Misrepresentation Act 1967' (1967) 30 MLR 369.

Beale, H, 'Damages in lieu of rescission for misrepresentation' (1995) 111 LQR 60.

Beale, H, 'Points on misrepresentation' (1995) 111 LQR 385.

Cartwright, J, *Misrepresentation*, 2000, London: Sweet & Maxwell.

Chandler, A and Higgins, S, 'Contributory negligence and the Misrepresentation Act 1967, s.2 (1)' [1994] LMCLQ 326.

Taylor, R, 'Expectation, reliance and misrepresentation' (1982) 45 MLR 139.

MISTAKE

CONTENTS

10.1 INTRODUCTION

In this chapter we will examine the situations in which a mistake by either or both parties may render a contract void or voidable. The law of mistake is notoriously complex and brings together a number of situations that are both varied and lacking in conceptual unity. Professor JC Smith ('Contracts: mistake, frustration and implied terms' (1994) 110 LQR 400) famously wrote:

'One of the greatest difficulties for students of the law of contract has always, in my teaching experience, been the law relating to mistake. The brilliant analysis of the subject by Cheshire and Fifoot did an enormous amount to clarify thinking about it. But the presentation of mistake as a separate subject in a large and complex chapter through 12 editions of their admirable textbook has, I believe, unnecessarily exacerbated the inherent difficulties. The problems are generally soluble by the application of the law relating to the formation of contracts or that relating to implied terms. This is the way the late Professor Tony Thomas and I approached the problem during the gestation of Smith and Thomas and I remain convinced of its soundness.'

While it is true that there is a considerable overlap between the law of mistake and other areas of the law of contract – such as offer and acceptance, misrepresentation, implied terms and frustration – there is sufficient commonality between the different types of mistake to justify their inclusion in a single chapter on 'mistake'.

The English courts have traditionally been very reluctant to allow a contract to be set aside on the ground of 'mistake'. This is unsurprising, given the judicial desire to promote certainty in commercial transactions. It would clearly be unsatisfactory if a party to a contract was permitted to have the transaction set aside merely by saying, 'I'm sorry, I made a mistake'. Having said that, the courts are also concerned to give effect to the true intentions of the parties. Many of the judgments emphasise the need for a *consensus ad idem* – a meeting of the minds. If either, or both, of the parties are mistaken as to the nature of the agreement, enforcing the contract would compel the parties to do something that they did not intend to do. For this reason, the English courts recognise the possibility of a mistake affecting the validity of a contractual obligation, but use this power to intervene with considerable caution.

10.2 CATEGORIES OF MISTAKE

Contractual mistakes take many different forms. They may relate to the subject matter, the identity of the other party or the specific terms of the contract. The different categories of mistake were recently summarised by Lord Phillips of Matravers MR in *Great Peace Shipping Ltd v Tsavliris Salvage (International) Ltd*.

Great Peace Shipping Ltd v Tsavliris Salvage (International) Ltd [2003] QB 679

Lord Phillips MR:
'28. A mistake can be simply defined as an erroneous belief. Mistakes have relevance in the law of contract in a number of different circumstances. They may prevent the mutuality of agreement that is necessary for the formation of a contract. In order for two parties to conclude a contract binding in law each must agree with the other the terms of the contract. Whether two parties have entered into a contract in this way must be judged objectively, having regard to all the material facts. It may be that each party mistakenly believes that he has entered into such a contract in circumstances

where an objective appraisal of the facts reveals that no agreement has been reached as to the terms of the contract. Such a case was *Raffles v Wichelhaus* (1864) 2 H & C 906 . . .

29. *Raffles v Wichelhaus* was a case of latent ambiguity. More commonly an objective appraisal of the negotiations between the parties may disclose that they were at cross-purposes, so that no agreement was ever reached. In such a case there will be a mutual mistake in that each party will erroneously believe that the other had agreed to his terms. This case is not concerned with the kind of mistake that prevents the formation of agreement.

30. Another type of mistake is that where the parties erroneously spell out their contract in terms which do not give effect to an antecedent agreement that they have reached. Such a mistake can result in rectification of the contract. Again, this case is not concerned with that type of mistake.

31. In the present case the parties were agreed as to the express terms of the contract. The defendants agreed that the *Great Peace* would deviate towards the *Cape Providence* and, on reaching her, escort her so as to be on hand to save the lives of her crew, should she founder. The contractual services would terminate when the salvage tug came up with the casualty. The mistake relied upon by the defendants is as to an assumption that they claim underlay the terms expressly agreed. This was that the *Great Peace* was within a few hours sailing of the *Cape Providence*. They contend that this mistake was fundamental in that it would take the *Great Peace* about 39 hours to reach a position where she could render the services which were the object of the contractual adventure.

32. Thus what we are here concerned with is an allegation of a common mistaken assumption of fact which renders the service that will be provided if the contract is performed in accordance with its terms something different from the performance that the parties contemplated. This is the type of mistake which fell to be considered in *Bell v Lever Bros Ltd* [1932] AC 161. We shall describe it as "common mistake", although it is often alternatively described as "mutual mistake".

33. Mr Reeder for the defendants puts his case in two alternative ways. First he submits that performance of the contract in the circumstances as they turned out to be would have been fundamentally different from the performance contemplated by the parties, so much so that the effect of the mistake was to deprive the agreement of the consideration underlying it. Under common law, so he submits, the effect of such a mistake is to render the contract void. Mr Reeder draws a close analogy with the test to be applied when deciding whether a contract has been frustrated or whether there has been a fundamental breach. The foundation for this submission is *Bell v Lever Bros Ltd*.

34. If the facts of this case do not meet that test, Mr Reeder submits that they none the less give rise to a right of rescission in equity. He submits that such a right arises whenever the parties contract under a common mistake as to a matter that can properly be described as "fundamental" or "material" to the agreement in question. Here he draws an analogy with the test for rescission where one party, by innocent misrepresentation, induces the other to enter into a contract – indeed that is one situation where the parties contract under a common mistake. The foundation for this submission is *Solle v Butcher* [1950] 1 KB 671.'

Great Peace Shipping is an extremely important case to which we will return in due course. For now it will suffice to note the various categories of mistake identified by Lord Phillips MR in his judgment.

10.2.1 COMMON-LAW MISTAKE

Lord Phillips MR distinguished between two categories of common law mistake.

10.2.1.1 Mistakes that negative consent

In [28] and [29], his Lordship referred to mistakes that prevent a contract from ever existing. These are mistakes in the formation of the contract that Lord Atkin referred to in *Bell v Lever Bros* [1932] AC 161, as mistakes that 'negative consent'. Within this general category, there are two situations that need to be distinguished.

First, there is the situation in which the parties are at cross-purposes – neither party being aware that the other party is contracting on the basis of a different assumption about the terms of the contract. This category is often referred to as a 'mutual mistake' (see Lord Phillips at [29] and *Cheshire, Fifoot and Furmston's Law of Contract*, 15th edn, 2006, Oxford: OUP, p 304), although the phrase is sometimes also and confusingly used to refer to the second category of common-law mistake (see Lord Phillips at [32] and *Anson's Law of Contract*, 28th edn, 2002, Oxford: OUP, p 311), which in this chapter will be labelled 'common mistake'.

The second type of situation where the mistake 'negatives consent' arises is where the mistake of one party is known to the other party, who may indeed have encouraged it. We will refer to this type of mistake as a 'unilateral mistake'. Here there is a clear overlap with the law of misrepresentation. In practice, an action based on mistake will only be brought where the remedies for misrepresentation would be inadequate. The classic example of such a situation is where third-party rights have intervened to bar rescission: see *Ingram v Little* [1961] 1 QB 31.

10.2.1.2 Mistakes that nullify consent

In [31] and [32], Lord Phillips MR refers to the second category of common law mistake, which he describes as 'common mistake' in preference to 'mutual mistake'. Here the parties enter into a contract on the basis of a common assumption as to the surrounding facts, which later turns out to be false. The mistake in such situations does not preclude the formation of the contract, but instead provides the basis for having the contract set aside post-formation. In the words of Lord Atkin in *Bell v Lever Bros*, the mistake 'nullifies consent'.

Professor Collins has argued (Collins, H, *The Law of Contract*, 4th edn, 2003, Cambridge: CUP, p 125) that this type of mistake is better analysed as involving an implied condition precedent that has failed:

'It is . . . possible to view these authorities as merely deciding that where a contract contains an express or implied term that it will only be enforceable if a particular circumstance or state of affairs exists, the failure of the condition precedent will prevent a binding contract arising. Strictly speaking, however, on this analysis a contract has been entered into but one of its terms, which is enforceable, declares that certain events shall render the contract unenforceable and without any legal effect. There is ascription of contractual responsibility to a conditional contract, and, on failure of the condition, the contract provides that it should have no legal effect. This analysis has the potential to explain all the English cases which seem to give credence to the doctrine of mistake.'

Although this theory is attractive, it was rejected by the Court of Appeal in *Great Peace Shipping* at [73].

Common mistake is closely linked to the doctrine of frustration (discussed in Chapter 15). Both concern the occurrence of an extraneous event that renders the performance of the contract impossible. The difference lies in the timing of the event. In cases of common mistake the event occurs pre-formation while in cases of frustration the event occurs post-formation (see *Amalgamated Investment and Property Co Ltd v John Walker & Sons* [1977] 1 WLR 164).

10.2.2 EQUITABLE MISTAKE

In [34], Lord Phillips MR noted that a wider doctrine of mistake had developed in equity following the decision of the Court of Appeal in *Solle v Butcher* [1950] 1 KB 671. This enabled the court to rescind a contract in equity (equitable mistake rendered the contract voidable while common law mistake rendered the contract void), even though the facts did not meet the requirements set out by the House of Lords in *Bell v Lever Bros*. This development was radically halted by the Court of Appeal in *Great Peace Shipping*, where it was held that the doctrine of equitable mistake was inconsistent with the law set out by the House of Lords in *Bell v Lever Bros*.

Despite this important decision, it is clear that equity still has a role to play in a number of other situations. For example, as Lord Phillips MR noted at [30], the equitable remedy of rectification is sometimes available. If an agreement has been reduced to writing and the written document contains an inaccuracy, in the form of an error or an omission, the parties may ask the court to rectify the document in order for it to conform to their oral agreement. The court also has an equitable discretion to refuse specific performance of a contract entered into under a mistake (*Malins v Freeman* (1837) 2 Keen 25).

10.2.3 *NON EST FACTUM*

The final category of mistake concerns cases where a person has signed a contract without reading or understanding it. Generally, English law holds parties to agreements that they have signed (*L'Etsrange v Graucob* [1934] 2 KB 394), but there are some exceptional circumstances where the courts will accept a plea of *non est factum* – 'it is not my deed'.

In this chapter we will consider each of these categories in turn. We will see that the common link between cases of mistake is that they all concern an 'agreement failure', that is to say that the mistake renders performance of the contract either physically impossible or 'radically different' to that which was intended. The chapter will also consider the remedial consequences of mistake and analyse whether the Principles of European Contract Law might provide a more flexible and desirable alternative to the current law.

▌10.3 MISTAKES THAT NEGATIVE CONSENT

As noted above, there are two main types of mistake that negative consent: mutual mistake and unilateral mistake. We will consider each of these in turn.

10.3.1 MUTUAL MISTAKE

The classic example of a situation that might give rise to a mutual mistake is to be found in the case of *Raffles v Wichelhaus*.

Raffles v Wichelhaus (1864) 2 H & C 906; 159 ER 375

Declaration: For that it was agreed between the plaintiff and the defendants, to wit, at Liverpool, that the plaintiff should sell to the defendants, and the defendants buy of the plaintiff, certain goods, to wit, 125 bales of Surat cotton, guaranteed middling fair merchant's Dhollorah, to arrive ex 'Peerless' from Bombay; and that the cotton should

---

be taken from the quay, and that the defendants would pay the plaintiff for the same at a certain rate, to wit, at the rate of 171/4d per pound, within a certain time then agreed upon after the arrival of the said goods in England. Averments that the said goods did arrive by the said ship from Bombay in England to wit, at Liverpool, and the plaintiff was then and there ready, and willing and offered to deliver the said goods to the defendants, & c. Breach: that the defendants refused to accept the said goods or pay the plaintiff for them.

Plea: That the said ship mentioned in the said agreement was meant and intended by the defendants to be the ship called the 'Peerless', which sailed from Bombay, to wit, in October; and that the plaintiff was not ready and willing and did not offer to deliver to the defendants any bales of cotton which arrived by the last mentioned ship, but instead thereof was only ready and willing and offered to deliver to the defendants 125 bales of Surat cotton which arrived by another and different ship, which was also called the 'Peerless', and which sailed from Bombay, to wit, in December.

Demurrer, and joinder therein

Milward, in support of the demurrer. The contract was for the sale of a number of bales of cotton of a particular description, which the plaintiff was ready to deliver. It is immaterial by what ship the cotton was to arrive, so that it was a ship called the 'Peerless'. The words 'to arrive ex "Peerless" ', only mean that if the vessel is lost on the voyage, the contract is to be at an end. [Pollock CB. It would be a question for the jury whether both parties meant the same ship called the 'Peerless'] That would be so if the contract was for the sale of a ship called the 'Peerless', but it is for the sale of cotton on board a ship of that name. [Pollock CB. The defendant only bought that cotton which was to arrive by a particular ship. It may *as* well be said, that if there is a contract for the purchase of certain goods in warehouse A, that is satisfied by the delivery of goods of the same description in warehouse B.] In that case there would be goods in both warehouses, here it does not appear that the plaintiff had any goods on board the other 'Peerless'. [Martin B. It is imposing on the defendant a contract different from that which he entered into. Pollock CB. It is like a contract for the purchase of wine coming from a particular estate in France or Spain, where there are two estates of that name.] The defendant has no right to contradict by parol evidence a written contract good upon the face of it. He does not impute misrepresentation or fraud, but only says that he fancied the ship was a different one. Intention is of no avail, unless stated at the time of the contract. [Pollock CB. One vessel sailed in October and the other in December]. The time of sailing is no part of the contract.

   Mellish (Cohen with him), in support of the plea. There is nothing on the face of the contract to shew that any particular ship called the 'Peerless' was meant, but the moment it appears that two ships called the 'Peerless' were about to sail from Bombay there is a latent ambiguity, and parol evidence may be given for the purpose of shewing that the defendant meant one 'Peerless', and the plaintiff another. That being so, there was no consensus ad idem, and therefore no binding contract. He was then stopped by the Court.

> Per Curiam. There must be judgment for the defendants
>
> *Judgment for the defendants.*

Since the court stopped counsel's argument and provided no
impossible to be certain of the exact basis of the decision. It may be limited to the
finding that the defendants could introduce parol evidence of their intentions
because of the latent ambiguity in the agreement. Later cases, however, have gone
further and suggested that the court in *Raffles* accepted the argument that the latent
ambiguity negatived consent. In *Smith v Hughes* (1871) LR 6 QB 597, Hannen J
said:

'It is essential to the creation of a contract that both parties should agree to the
same thing in the same sense. Thus, if two persons enter into an apparent
contract concerning a particular person or ship, and it turns out that each of
them, misled by a similarity of name, had a different person or ship in his
mind, no contract would exist between them: *Raffles v Wichelhaus* 2 H & C
906; 33 LJ (Ex) 160.'

More recently, in *Great Peace Shipping*, Lord Phillips MR treated *Raffles v Wichelhaus*
as a case of mutual mistake where the parties were at cross-purposes.

The case is probably most famous for the debate it triggered concerning the
question of whether English law adopts a subjective approach to contract formation
or an objective approach. Writers, such as Pollock, argued that the court's emphasis
on *consensus ad idem* showed that the law adopts a subjective approach. Other writers,
such as Holmes, claimed that the case supported an objective approach. For
Holmes, the case merely decided that parol evidence could be introduced. It was
then left to the jury to decide, from an objective standpoint, whether the parties'
intentions could be determined. Unfortunately, the case itself provides no guidance
as to which of these two approaches is correct. As Professor Simpson has argued
('The Beauty of Obscurity: *Raffles v Wichelhaus and Busch* (1864)' in *Leading Cases in
the Common Law*, 1995, Oxford: OUP, p 139), looking for an answer to this question
in the report of *Raffles* is like looking to see 'whether Macbeth suffered from
athlete's foot' in the text of *Macbeth*.

Although *Raffles* is rather obscure on the point, later cases have confirmed that an
objective approach will be adopted. This means that a contract will be found to
exist if, from an objective standpoint, a third party would reasonably believe that
the contract had been formed on particular terms.

Frederick E Rose (London) Ltd v William H Pim Jnr & Co Ltd [1953] 2 QB 450

Facts: The plaintiffs were asked by an English firm in Egypt whether they could supply 'feveroles'. The plaintiffs did not know what these were and they asked the defendants who replied that they were just horsebeans. The plaintiffs entered into a contract with the defendants to purchase five hundred tons of Tunisian horsebeans. These were then supplied to the customer in Egypt who complained that the beans were 'feves' (a larger and less valuable horsebean) instead of 'feveroles'. The customer claimed damages for breach of contract. To cover themselves against this claim, the plaintiffs started proceedings in the High Court to have the contract between themselves and the defendants rectified so as to read 'feveroles' after the word 'horsebeans'.

Held: The Court of Appeal held that rectification was not available because the oral agreement between the parties and the written contracts were in the same terms.

Denning LJ:

'The parties no doubt intended that the goods should satisfy the inquiry of the Egyptian buyers, namely, "horsebeans described in Egypt as feveroles". They assumed that they would do so, but they made no contract to that effect. Their agreement, as outwardly expressed, both orally and in writing, was for "horsebeans". That is all that the defendants ever committed themselves to supply, and all they should be bound to. There was, no doubt, an erroneous assumption underlying the contract – an assumption for which it might have been set aside on the ground of misrepresentation or mistake – but that is very different from an erroneous expression of the contract, such as to give rise to rectification.'

Morris LJ:

'It seems to me clear beyond doubt that both parties proceeded on the basis that "feveroles" and "horsebeans" were the same. The plaintiffs' representative expressed the matter succinctly when he said: "I had agreed to buy because feveroles were horsebeans and horsebeans were feveroles". In that belief the parties came to agreement, and the formal written contracts were prepared and signed. The parties had throughout a clear common intention and purpose of buying and selling horsebeans, and their written agreements faithfully embodied and exactly recorded what they had agreed. In these circumstances it seems to me that no claim for rectification can succeed.

Both parties thought that the result of what they clearly understood and clearly expressed would be that the plaintiffs as buyers would be able to satisfy the inquiry which, as the defendants knew, had been received. In that they were mistaken as a result of the advice honestly given by the defendants' market clerk. But the fact that they were under a mistaken impression as to what their agreement would achieve does not disturb the clarity and the fixity of the agreement which they in fact made. The defendants intended to offer horsebeans and the plaintiffs intended to accept horsebeans: the written agreements correctly reflected and incorporated what they had agreed.

The judge said that "both the plaintiffs and the defendants made an oral agreement in which they intended to deal in horsebeans of the feverole type". With respect, that was not quite the position. There was no question of contracting in reference to a "type" of horsebeans. There was a joint understanding that they should contract in reference to "horsebeans" simpliciter which they thought were the same as "feveroles". If, as now appears to be the case, they were wrong, it appears probable that they would not have acted as they did had they been enlightened. But this does not enable one party to convert the contract into something different from what it was.

On the assumption that "feveroles" are different from "horsebeans", it cannot be said that the parties agreed on the sale of a commodity of the separate existence of which they had no knowledge. The defendants were selling "horsebeans", and in order to sell they would have to acquire "horsebeans". If "feveroles" are different, then the defendants, and equally the plaintiffs, never even gave their minds at all to the question of a sale of some products which are different from "horsebeans".'

John Spencer has criticised the use of the 'detached objectivity' approach in *Rose v Pim*. He labels it the 'fly on the wall' approach and contends that it can lead to absurd results.

Spencer, J R, 'Signature, Consent, and the Rule in *L'Estrange v Graucob'* (1973) 32 CLJ 104, 108–110, 112–114

. . . In recent years an even more objective theory of agreement has emerged, according to which A's words must be judged, not as they appeared to B, but as they would have appeared to C, a reasonable man eavesdropping on the negotiations. The test is not what the other party would have thought, but how things would have appeared to the reasonable fly on the wall . . .

The dissemination of the 'fly on the wall' theory of agreement appears to be largely the work of Lord Denning MR. In *Solle v Butcher* he said:

> 'once a contract has been made, that is to say, once the parties, whatever their inmost states of mind, have to all outward appearances agreed with sufficient certainty in the same terms on the same subject-matter, then the contract is good unless and until it is set aside for failure of some condition on which the existence of the contract depends, or for fraud, or on some equitable ground. Neither party can rely on his own mistake to say it was a nullity from the beginning, no matter that it was a mistake which to his mind was fundamental, *and no matter that the other party knew that he was under a mistake.*'

To support this theory, Denning LJ invoked the authority of the House of Lords in *Bell v*

Lever Bros. It is hard to criticise him for taking this view of *Bell v Lever Bros*; it would, however, be equally hard to criticise him for taking any other view of *Bell v Lever Bros*. 'The case is, of course, a final authority for whatever it decides, but there has been considerable discussion as to what this is'. The real origin of the 'fly on the wall' theory appears to be not the House of Lords, but Williston on Contracts, ss. 1536, 1537. He loudly proclaimed an extreme 'objective' theory of consent, which has had wide influence on legal thinking in the United States, and which is reflected to some extent in the American Law Institute's *Restatement of the Law of Contract*. Indeed, so far from being based on English case law, the 'fly on the wall' theory goes against the English cases almost without exception . . .

Not only is the 'fly on the wall' theory of agreement apparently contrary to authority, it is often difficult and uncertain to apply. It will work well enough where the parties are negotiating face to face. Then the reasonable eavesdropper is notionally at the keyhole, enthusiastically drawing inferences from what he hears within. But what if one of the parties is at Land's End and the other at Llandudno? At whose keyhole is the reasonable eavesdropper notionally listening then? – at the offeror's, or at the offeree's – or has he ears on infinitely extensible leads, enabling him to apply one to each keyhole simultaneously? The difficulty is that the inference he will draw will depend on how much he knows, and what he will know will often depend on where he is. Furthermore, unless *Solle v Butcher* has reversed a long line of cases, the reasonable eavesdropper will need a good deal of specialised and esoteric knowledge. He must have overheard all the previous negotiations, he will need to know all the ships sailing from Bombay to Liverpool, he will need to be an expert in cracking codes, and if we bring other Canadian cases into consideration, he will have to understand fluent German, Ukrainian and Finnish. In the law of tort the reasonable man has to be imbued with qualities which are said to include the agility of an acrobat and the foresight of a Hebrew prophet. To fit him for his new role as the eavesdropper in the law of contract, 'this excellent but odious creature' will also need the omnipresence of Puck and the learning of the *Encyclopaedia Britannica*. These difficulties arise from importing the fiction that a third party is listening to the negotiations when he is not, and they disappear if we abandon that fiction. We run into all sorts of difficulties if we ask ourselves 'how would C, overhearing A and B's negotiations, have interpreted them?' which never arise if we ask the more sensible question, 'How should B, the other party, have interpreted what A said?'

The 'fly on the wall' theory is also open to the objection that it leads to absurd results. What happens if the parties are inwardly agreed, but outwardly at variance, or agreed on something else? Suppose, for example, that Ali and Benedetto, two immigrants with little knowledge of English, agree on the purchase and sale of a 'bull', both of them intending to deal with a cow, and in the belief that the word 'bull' means the female of the species. According to the 'fly on the wall' theory of agreement, they have made a contract to buy and sell a bull, although A does not want one and B has not got one to sell. This is ridiculous. Yet this is the result reached in the Court of Appeal by Denning LJ in *Rose v Pim*. The facts as interpreted by Denning LJ were that A and B made a written agreement for the purchase and sale of 'horsebeans', by which both A and B meant 'feveroles', which, again according to Denning LJ, are something 'essentially different'. Denning LJ held that although both parties meant to deal with feveroles, they were contractually bound to buy and sell horsebeans, because their agreement as outwardly expressed, both orally and in writing, was for 'horsebeans'. It is a platitude to say that the law of contract exists to enforce agreements, and that agreements are what people have agreed to do, not what officious people with no interest in the matter would think they had agreed to do. It may be acceptable for the law occasionally to force upon one of the parties an agreement he did not want; but surely there is something wrong with a theory which forces upon both of the parties an agreement which neither of them wants: If the 'fly on the wall' theory does this, that is an excellent reason for rejecting it.

There are two points to note here. First, Spencer's statement of the facts of *Rose v Pim* is slightly misleading. As Beale, Bishop and Furmston note (*Contract Cases and Materials*, 4th edn, 2001, London: Lexis-Nexis, p 312) it was not that the parties intended to deal in feveroles; rather they intended to deal in horsebeans, which they wrongly believed to be the same thing as feveroles. Had the parties intended to deal in feveroles (which is akin to Spencer's cow and bull example) the outcome may well have been different. This is because, second, the objective approach to formation should not be applied in a way that ignores the context and the surrounding circumstances. To take *Raffles v Wichelhaus* as an example, if the parol evidence could have been used to show that the parties were in agreement as to which ship was intended, the contract would have been upheld. It would not have mattered that in the absence of such additional evidence, the objective approach would not have been able to determine which ship was intended. Applying this approach to the bull and the cow example, a court could surely take into account the fact that the parties used the word 'bull' to refer to a 'cow'.

If, however, it is impossible to ascertain what the parties intended, even with the use of additional information, the contract will be held to be void for mutual mistake. In *Scriven Bros v Hindley* [1913] 3 KB 564, the plaintiffs instructed an auctioneer to sell a number of bales of hemp and tow. The auction catalogue did not distinguish between the bales of hemp and the bales of tow and the defendant successfully bid for the lots of tow at a price that was extravagantly high for tow. The jury held that there had been a mutual mistake: the auctioneer intended to sell tow and the defendant intended to bid for hemp. On this ground the contract was void for mistake.

In *Smith v Hughes*, another case that involved an alleged mutual mistake as to the subject matter of the contract, a different view was taken.

Smith v Hughes (1871) LR 6 QB 597

Facts: The plaintiff farmer offered to sell to the defendant horse trainer a quantity of oats. He showed the defendant a sample of the oats and on the following day the defendant agreed to purchase the whole quantity. When the oats were delivered, the defendant discovered that they were new oats and refused to accept them on the ground that he thought he was buying old oats. There was a conflict of evidence as to whether the plaintiff had referred to the oats as 'old'. In summing up, the trial judge left two questions to the jury: first, whether the word 'old' had been used with reference to the oats in the conversation between the plaintiff and the defendant's manager; second, whether the plaintiff had believed that the defendant believed, or was under the impression, that he was contracting for old oats; in either of which cases he directed the jury to find for the defendant. The jury found for the defendant and the plaintiff appealed the correctness of the judge's direction to the jury.

Held: The Court of Queen's Bench held that there had been a misdirection on the second question and ordered that there should be a new trial.

Cockburn CJ:

'It is to be regretted that the jury were not required to give specific answers to the questions so left to them. For, it is quite possible that their verdict may have been given for the defendant on the first ground; in which case there could, I think, be no doubt as to the propriety of the judge's direction; whereas now, as it is possible that the verdict of the jury – or at all events of some of them – may have proceeded on the second ground, we are called upon to consider and decide whether the ruling of the learned judge with reference to the second question was right.

For this purpose we must assume that nothing was said on the subject of the defendant's manager desiring to buy *old* oats, nor of the oats having been said to be old; while, on the other hand, we must assume that the defendant's manager believed the oats to be old oats, and that the plaintiff was conscious of the existence of such belief, but did nothing, directly or indirectly, to bring it about, simply offering his oats and exhibiting his sample, remaining perfectly passive as to what was passing in the mind of the other party. The question is whether, under such circumstances, the passive acquiescence of the seller in the self-deception of the buyer will entitle the latter to avoid the contract. I am of opinion that it will not . . .

In the case before us it must be taken that, as the defendant, on a portion of the oats being delivered, was able by inspection to ascertain that they were new oats, his manager might, by due inspection of the sample, have arrived at the same result. The case is, therefore, one of the sale and purchase of a specific article after inspection by the buyer. Under these circumstances the rule caveat emptor clearly applies; more especially as this cannot be put as a case of latent defect, but simply as one in which the seller did not make known to the buyer a circumstance affecting the quality of the thing sold. The oats in question were in no sense defective, on the contrary they were good oats, and all that can be said is that they had not acquired the quality which greater age would have given them. There is not, so far as I am aware, any authority for the position that a vendor who submits the subject-matter of sale to the inspection of the vendee, is bound to state circumstances which may tend to detract from the estimate which the buyer may injudiciously have formed of its value . . .

It only remains to deal with an argument which was pressed upon us, that the defendant in the present case intended to buy old oats, and the plaintiff to sell new, so the two minds were not *ad idem*; and that consequently there was no contract. This argument proceeds on the fallacy of confounding what was merely a motive operating on the buyer to induce him to buy with one of the essential conditions of the contract. Both parties were agreed as to the sale and purchase of this particular parcel of oats. The defendant believed the oats to be old, and was thus induced to agree to buy them, but he omitted to make their age a condition of the contract. All that can be said is, that the two minds were not *ad idem* as to the age of the oats; they certainly were *ad idem* as to the sale and purchase of them. Suppose a person to buy a horse without a warranty, believing him to be sound, and the horse turns out unsound, could it be contended that it would be open to him to say that, as he had intended to buy a sound horse, and the seller to sell an unsound one, the contract was void, because the seller must have known from the price the buyer was willing to give, or from his general habits as a buyer of horses, that he thought the horse was sound? The cases are exactly parallel.

The result is that, in my opinion, the learned judge of the county court was wrong in leaving the second question to the jury, and that, consequently, the case must go down to a new trial.

Blackburn J:
'I apprehend that if one of the parties intends to make a contract on one set of terms, and the other intends to make a contract on another set of terms, or, as it is sometimes expressed, if the parties are not *ad idem*, there is no contract, unless the circumstances are such as to preclude one of the parties from denying that he has agreed to the terms of the other. The rule of law is that stated in *Freeman v Cooke* 2 Ex at p. 663; 18 LJ (Ex) at p 119. If, whatever a man's real intention may be, he so conducts himself that a reasonable man would believe that he was assenting to the terms proposed by the other party, and that other party upon that belief enters into the contract with him, the man thus conducting himself would be equally bound as if he had intended to agree to the other party's terms.

The jury were directed that, if they believed the word "old" was used, they should find for the defendant – and this was right; for if that was the case, it is obvious that neither did the defendant intend to enter into a contract on the plaintiff's terms, that is, to buy this parcel of oats without any stipulation as to their quality; nor could the plaintiff have been led to believe he was intending to do so.

But the second direction raises the difficulty. I think that, if from that direction the jury would understand that they were first to consider whether they were satisfied that the defendant intended to buy this parcel of oats on the terms that it was part of his contract with the plaintiff that they were old oats, so as to have the warranty of the plaintiff to that effect, they were properly told that, if that was so, the defendant could not be bound to a contract without any such warranty unless the plaintiff was misled. But I doubt whether the direction would bring to the minds of the jury the distinction between agreeing to take the oats under the belief that they were old, and agreeing to take the oats under the belief that the plaintiff contracted that they were old. The difference is the same as that between buying a horse believed to be sound, and buying one believed to be warranted sound; but I doubt if it was made obvious to the jury, and I doubt this the more because I do not see much evidence to justify a finding for the defendant on this latter ground if the word "old" was not used. There may have been more evidence than is stated in the case; and the demeanour of the witnesses may have strengthened the impression produced by the evidence there was; but it does not seem a very satisfactory verdict if it proceeded on this latter ground. I agree, therefore, in the result that there should be a new trial.'

Hannen J:

'It is essential to the creation of a contract that both parties should agree to the same thing in the same sense. Thus, if two persons enter into an apparent contract concerning a particular person or ship, and it turns out that each of them, misled by a similarity of name, had a different person or ship in his mind, no contract would exist between them: *Raffles v Wichelhaus* 2 H & C 906; 33 LJ (Ex) 160.

But one of the parties to an apparent contract may, by his own fault, be precluded from setting up that he had entered into it in a different sense to that in which it was understood by the other party. Thus in the case of a sale by sample where the vendor, by mistake, exhibited a wrong sample, it was held that the contract was not avoided by this error of the vendor: *Scott v Littledale* 8 E & B 815; 27 LJ (QB) 201.

But if in the last-mentioned case the purchaser, in the course of the negotiations preliminary to the contract, had discovered that the vendor was under a misapprehension as to the sample he was offering, the vendor would have been entitled to shew that he had not intended to enter into the contract by which the purchaser sought to bind him. The rule of law applicable to such a case is a corollary from the rule of morality which Mr Pollock cited from Paley, that a promise is to be performed "in that sense in which the promiser apprehended at the time the promisee received it", and may be thus expressed: "The promiser is not bound to fulfil a promise in a sense in which the promisee knew at the time the promiser did not intend it". And in considering the question, in what sense a promisee is entitled to enforce a promise, it matters not in what way the knowledge of the meaning in which the promiser made it is brought to the mind of the promisee, whether by express words, or by conduct, or previous dealings, or other circumstances. If by any means he knows that there was no real agreement between him and the promiser, he is not entitled to insist that the promise shall be fulfilled in a sense to which the mind of the promiser did not assent.

If, therefore, in the present case, the plaintiff knew that the defendant, in dealing with him for oats, did so on the assumption that the plaintiff was contracting to sell him old oats, he was aware that the defendant apprehended the contract in a different sense to that in which he meant it, and he is thereby deprived of the right to insist that the defendant shall be bound by that which was only the apparent, and not the real bargain.

This was the question which the learned judge intended to leave to the jury; and, as I have already said, I do not think it was incorrect in its terms, but I think that it was likely to be misunderstood by the jury. The jury were asked, "whether they were of opinion, on the whole of the evidence, that the plaintiff believed the defendant to believe, or to be under the impression that he was contracting for the purchase of old oats? If so, there would be a verdict for the defendant". The jury may have understood this to mean that, if the plaintiff believed the defendant to believe that he was buying old oats, the defendant would be entitled to the verdict; but a belief on the part of the plaintiff that the defendant was making a contract to buy the oats, of which he offered him a sample, under a mistaken belief that they were old, would not relieve the defendant from liability unless his mistaken belief were induced by some misrepresentation of the plaintiff, or concealment by him of a fact which it became his duty to communicate. In order to relieve the defendant it was necessary that the jury should find not merely that the plaintiff believed the defendant to believe that he was buying old oats, but that he believed the defendant to believe that he, the plaintiff, was contracting to sell old oats.

I am the more disposed to think that the jury did not understand the question in this last sense because I can find very little, if any, evidence to support a finding upon it in favour of the defendant . . . I therefore think there should be a new trial.'

The judgments in *Smith v Hughes* are rather confusing because their lordships moved between an analysis of 'mutual' mistake, and an analysis of 'unilateral' mistake, with no apparent distinction. In this section we will consider the decision in respect of mutual mistake and in the next we will analyse their lordships' views on unilateral mistake.

The court held that there was no mutual mistake because, looked at objectively, the contract was for the sale of a specific parcel of oats, about which there was no ambiguity. Cockburn CJ said: 'Both parties were agreed as to the sale and purchase of this particular parcel of oats. . . . All that can be said is, that the two minds were not *ad idem* as to the age of the oats; they certainly were *ad idem* as to the sale and purchase of them.' The case turned on the fact that the age of the oats did not appear to be a term of the contract. The buyer may have expected to receive old oats and the seller may have expected to deliver new oats, but neither party intended the age of the oats to be a term of the contract. This is the point that Blackburn J makes in the third paragraph of the extract from his judgment. He concluded that the judge's direction was unsound because it did not 'bring to the minds of the jury the distinction between agreeing to take the oats under the belief that they were old, and agreeing to take the oats under the belief that the plaintiff contracted that they were old'. For there to be a mutual mistake, it is not sufficient for the parties to be at cross-purposes as to their expectations; they must be at cross-purposes as to the specific terms of the contract. On the facts of *Smith v Hughes*, they were not.

10.3.2 UNILATERAL MISTAKE

In *Smith v Hughes*, the Court of Queen's Bench also considered whether there had been a unilateral mistake. This type of mistake arises where one party is aware that the other is mistaken about an important aspect of the contract. Cockburn CJ noted that the law of contract does not generally intervene merely because one party is more knowledgeable than the other. It is an important aspect of commercial enterprise that individuals should be free to take advantage of superior knowledge or information. To prohibit such practices would be to stultify wealth creation. However, the law does not allow a party to 'snap up' a bargain which he knew was not intended for him. Citing *Paley*, Hannen J put the principle as follows: 'The promiser is not bound to fulfil a promise in a sense in which the promisee knew at the time the promiser did not intend it'. On the facts of *Smith v Hughes*, the trial judge had erred in failing to ask the jury whether the plaintiff was aware that the defendant apprehended the contract in a different sense to that in which he meant it. A contract was found to be void for a unilateral mistake in *Hartog v Colin & Shields*.

Hartog v Colin & Shields [1939] 3 All ER 566

Facts: The defendants agreed to sell to the plaintiff 30,000 Argentine hare skins. The price quoted by the seller was stated to be 'per pound'. This was a mistake, since the price should have been 'per piece'. The mistake meant that the skins were being offered at a price two thirds lower than would have been expected. Expert evidence was given that Argentine hare skins were generally sold at prices per piece. The plaintiff accepted the defendants' offer in the terms stated, but the defendants refused to supply on this basis, on the ground that the plaintiff was taking advantage of the defendants' mistake.

Held: The court held that the plaintiff must have realised that a mistake had been made in the offer and therefore there was no binding contract.

Singleton J:

'In this case, the plaintiff, a Belgian subject, claims damages against the defendants because he says they broke a contract into which they entered with him for the sale of Argentine hare skins. The defendants' answer to that claim is: "There really was no contract, because you knew that the document which went forward to you, in the form of an offer, contained a material mistake. You realised that, and you sought to take advantage of it".

Counsel for the defendants took upon himself the onus of satisfying me that the plaintiff knew that there was a mistake and sought to take advantage of that mistake. In other words, realising that there was a mistake, the plaintiff did that which James LJ, in *Tamplin v James*, at p 221, described as "snapping up the offer". It is important, I think, to realise that in the verbal negotiations which took place in this country, and in all the discussions there had ever been, the prices of Argentine hare skins had been discussed per piece, and later, when correspondence took place, the matter was always discussed at the price per piece, and never at a price per pound. Those witnesses who were called on behalf of the plaintiff have had comparatively little experience of dealing in Argentine hare skins. Even the expert witness who was called had had very little . . . Even allowing that the market was bound to fall a little, I find it difficult to believe that anyone could receive an offer for a large quantity of Argentine hares at a price so low as 3d per piece without having the gravest doubts of it.

I cannot help thinking that, when this quotation in pence per pound reached Mr Hartog, the plaintiff, he must have realised . . . that there was a mistake. Otherwise I cannot understand the quotation. There was an absolute difference from anything which had gone before – a difference in the manner of quotation, in that the skins are offered per pound instead of per piece . . . The offer was wrongly expressed, and the defendants by their evidence, and by the correspondence, have satisfied me that the plaintiff could not reasonably have supposed that that offer contained the offerers' real intention. Indeed, I am satisfied to the contrary. That means that there must be judgment for the defendants.'

The case fulfils the two requirements set out in *Smith v Hughes*:

1. The mistake was as to a term of the contract – the price of the hare skins;
2. The plaintiff was aware that the defendants had made a mistake in regard to this term.

On the question of what level of knowledge is required, a recent decision of the Singapore Court of Appeal is instructive. *Chwee Kin Keong v Digilandmall.com Pte Ltd* [2005] 1 SLR 502, concerned the sale of six Hewlett Packard laser printers. The defendants had advertised the printers on their website at a price of $66. They were really worth $3,854. On the question of whether the plaintiffs were aware of the mistake, Chao Hick Tin JA said:

'It is clear that the state of a person's mind is a question of fact. It has to be proved like any other fact . . . As is so often alluded to in the cases, in the absence of an express admission or incontrovertible evidence, the fact of knowledge would invariably have to be inferred from all the surrounding circumstances, including the experiences and idiosyncrasies of the person and what a reasonable person would have known in a similar situation. If a court, upon weighing all the circumstances, thinks that the non-mistaken party is probably aware of the error made by the mistaken party, it is entitled to find, as a fact, that the former party has actual knowledge of the error. Following from that holding, the court should declare the contract so formed as void on the ground of unilateral mistake.

In order to enable the court to come to the conclusion that the non-mistaken party had actual knowledge of the mistake, the court would go through a process of reasoning where it may consider what a reasonable person, placed in the similar situation, would have known. In this connection, we would refer to what is called "Nelsonian knowledge", namely, wilful blindness or shutting one's eyes to the obvious. Clearly, if the court finds that the non-mistaken party is guilty of wilful blindness, it will be in line with logic and reason to hold that that party had actual knowledge.

This then gives rise to the question as to the circumstances under which a party should make inquiry. When should such a party make inquiries failing which he would be considered to be shutting his eyes to the obvious? We do not think this question is amenable to a clear definitive answer. Situations in which such a question could arise are infinite. But we could accept what Mance J said in *OT Africa Line Ltd v Vickers Plc* [1996] 1 Lloyd's Rep 700 ("*OT Africa*") at 703 that there must be a "real reason to suppose the existence of a mistake". What would constitute "real reason" must again depend on the circumstances of each case. Academicians may well query whether this should be based on an "objective" or "subjective" test. At the end of the day, the court must approach it sensibly. The court must be satisfied that the non-mistaken party is, in fact, privy to a "real reason" that warrants the making of an inquiry.

Here, we would reiterate that expressions such as "taking advantage", "good faith", "snapping up", used by the courts to describe the situations under consideration were often just the bases upon which the court, in each case, had come to its conclusions as to whether the non-mistaken party had actual knowledge of the error made by the mistaken party. While we recognise that the distinction between actual knowledge and constructive knowledge can be a fine one and can often be difficult to discern, it is nonetheless not something unfamiliar to the courts. The courts are accustomed to making such a distinction.'

In summary, actual knowledge is required although actual knowledge can be inferred from the surrounding circumstances. The non-mistaken party is not permitted to wilfully close his eyes to the other party's mistake.

10.3.2.1 Unilateral mistake as to identity

Although unilateral mistake may arise in relation to any aspect of the contract the majority of reported cases concern mistakes as to the identity of the other contracting party. This is usually because a fraudulent party (a rogue) misrepresents his or her identity in order to obtain goods on credit or in exchange for a cheque. In the majority of cases, these goods will then be sold on to an innocent third party. As a result of the misrepresentations, the contract will be voidable, but the mistaken party will not know to rescind until after the third party has purchased the goods, by which time it will be too late. The mistaken party will therefore need to argue that the contract was void for mistake, thus meaning that no property rights passed to the rogue. Since one cannot give what one does not have (*nemo dat quod non habet*), any purported sale by the rogue to a third party will be ineffective and the mistaken party will be able to assert his or her property rights against the third party and reclaim possession of the property in the tort of conversion.

It is generally accepted that the law in this area is in an unsatisfactory state. For a mistake to be operative and to render the contract void it must relate to the *identity* of the other party, not merely to his or her *attributes*. In practice, this distinction is very difficult to apply, as Lord Denning explained in *Lewis v Averay* [1972] 1 QB 198:

> A mistake as to identity, it is said, avoids a contract: whereas a mistake as to attributes does not. But this is a distinction without a difference. A man's very name is one of his attributes. It is also a key to his identity. If then, he gives a false name, is it a mistake as to his identity or a mistake as to his attributes? These fine distinctions do no good to the law.'

The distinction between identity and attributes has led to a further distinction being drawn between contracts concluded by face-to-face negotiations and contracts concluded by written correspondence. In the former situation, it is presumed that there is an intention to contract with the person present and therefore the mistake will not be operative. In the latter situation, it is presumed that the true identity of the person is of fundamental importance to the contract, and therefore the mistake will be operative.

It is generally accepted that this distinction is rather false. Nevertheless, it was recently reaffirmed by the House of Lords in *Shogun Finance Ltd v Hudson* [2004] 1 AC 919. We will consider that landmark decision in due course, but first we must survey the case law that preceded it.

10.3.2.1.1 *Contracts concluded by written correspondence*
An early example of a written contract void for mistake as to identity is to be found in the case of *Boulton v Jones*.

Boulton v Jones (1857) 2 H & N 564

Facts: The defendant sent an order for three 50 ft leather hoses to Brocklehurst, against whom he had arranged a set-off. Unknown to the defendant, Brocklehurst had just sold his business to the plaintiff who fulfilled the order. The plaintiff sent an invoice to the defendant who resisted the claim for payment on the basis that he did not intend to contract with the plaintiff.

Held: The court held that the contract was void for mistake.

Pollock CB:

'It is a rule of law, that if a person intends to contract with A, B cannot give himself any right under it. Here the order in writing was given to Brocklehurst.'

Bramwell B:

'The admitted facts are, that the defendants sent to a shop an order for goods, supposing they were dealing with Brocklehurst. The plaintiff who supplied the goods, did not undeceive them. If the plaintiff were now at liberty to sue the defendants, they would be deprived of their right of set-off as against Brocklehurst. When a contract is made, in which the personality of the contracting party is or may be of importance, as a contract with a man to write a book, or the like, or where there might be a set-off, no other person can interpose and adopt the contract.

As to the difficulty that the defendants need not pay anybody, I do not see why they should, unless they have made a contract either express or implied. I decide the case on the ground that the defendants did not know that the plaintiff was the person who supplied the goods, and that allowing the plaintiff to treat the contract as made with him would be a prejudice to the defendants.

It seems that the existence of the set-off meant that the identity of the other party was of crucial importance to the defendants. The result may appear a little harsh towards the plaintiff who was not attempting to take advantage of the defendant. It is likely that were the facts to arise again today, the plaintiff would be entitled to recover restitution for the defendants' unjust enrichment (see Chapter 18).

A more common example of a contract void for mistake is to be found in *Cundy v Lindsay*.

Cundy v Lindsay (1878) 3 App Cas 459

Facts: A rogue named Blenkarn placed large orders for handkerchiefs with the plaintiffs. Blenkarn, who gave his address as 37 Wood Street, signed the order in a manner which made it look like he was 'Blenkiron & Co', a highly respectable firm which also had its business in Wood Street. The plaintiffs sent the goods on credit to 'Messrs

Blenkiron & Co, 37 Wood Street'. Blenkarn never paid for the goods and he sold them on the defendant, an innocent third party. The plaintiffs brought an action against the defendants for conversion, which required them to prove that the contract with Blenkarn was void for mistake.

Held: The House of Lords held that the contract was void for mistake as to identity.

Lord Cairns LC:

'My Lords, the question ... in the present case ... really becomes the very short and simple one which I am about to state. Was there any contract which, with regard to the goods in question in this case, had passed the property in the goods from the Messrs Lindsay to Alfred Blenkarn? If there was any contract passing that property, even although, as I have said, that contract might afterwards be open to a process of reduction, upon the ground of fraud, still, in the meantime, *Blenkarn* might have conveyed a good title for valuable consideration to the present Appellants.

[The jury] found that by the form of the signatures to the letters which were written by *Blenkarn*, by the mode in which his letters and his applications to the Respondents were made out, and by the way in which he left uncorrected the mode and form in which, in turn, he was addressed by the Respondents; that by all those means he led, and intended to lead, the Respondents to believe, and they did believe, that the person with whom they were communicating was not *Blenkarn*, the dishonest and irresponsible man, but was a well known and solvent house of *Blenkiron & Co*, doing business in the same street. My Lords, those things are found as matters of fact, and they are placed beyond the range of dispute and controversy in the case.

If that is so, what is the consequence? ... I ask the question, how is it possible to imagine that in that state of things any contract could have arisen between the Respondents and *Blenkarn*, the dishonest man? Of him they knew nothing, and of him they never thought. With him they never intended to deal. Their minds never, even for an instant of time rested upon him, and as between him and them there was no consensus of mind which could lead to any agreement or any contract whatever. As between him and them there was merely the one side to a contract, where, in order to produce a contract, two sides would be required. With the firm of Blenkiron & Co of course there was no contract, for as to them the matter was entirely unknown, and therefore the pretence of a contract was a failure.

The result, therefore, my Lords, is this, that your Lordships have not here to deal with one of those cases in which there is de facto a contract made which may afterwards be impeached and set aside, on the ground of fraud; but you have to deal with a case which ranges itself under a completely different chapter of law, the case namely in which the contract never comes into existence. My Lords, that being so, it is idle to talk of the property passing. The property remained, as it originally had been, the property of the Respondents, and the title which was attempted to be given to the Appellants was a title which could not be given to them.

> My Lords, I therefore move your Lordships that this appeal be dismissed with costs, and the judgment of the Court of Appeal affirmed.'

Lord Cairns' judgment adopted a rather subjective approach to agreement, although even from an objective point of view (in light of the fact that all of the correspondence was addressed to Blenkiron & Co), it is clear that the plaintiffs were mistaken as to the identity of whom they were dealing with.

It was significant in *Cundy v Lindsay* that the plaintiffs were able to identify the party whom they intended to contract with. If the mistaken party is unable to do this, the contract will not be set aside for mistake. In *King's Norton Metal Co v Edridge, Merrett & Co* (1897) 14 TLR 98, a rogue named Wallis fraudulently induced the plaintiffs to supply him with brass rivet wire on credit by pretending to be a firm called Hallam & Co. Wallis then sold the goods on to the defendants, who were innocent third parties. When the plaintiffs discovered Wallis' fraud they brought an action against the defendants in conversion. The Court of Appeal held that the action failed because the contract between Wallis and the plaintiffs was not void. The firm 'Hallam & Co' was a pure invention, created by Wallis. For this reason it was impossible to say that the plaintiffs intended to deal with a separate entity called Hallam & Co; no such firm existed. The mistake was one as to attributes, not as to identity. The plaintiffs thought that they were dealing with a firm, when in fact they were dealing with a rogue individual.

10.3.2.1.2 Contracts concluded face to face

There are three main cases on mistake in contracts concluded between parties who negotiated with one another face to face. Horridge J decided the first in the early twentieth century.

Phillips v Brooks [1919] 2 KB 243

Facts: A man called North went to a jeweller's shop and asked to see some pearls and some rings. He selected some pearls at the price of £2,550 and a ring at the price of £450. As he was writing a cheque in payment he said: 'You see who I am, I am Sir George Bullough', and he gave an address in St James's Square. After checking in a directory to confirm that Sir George lived at the address mentioned, the plaintiff allowed North to leave with the ring. The cheque was dishonoured, and North was subsequently convicted of obtaining the ring by false pretences. In the meantime, North had pledged the ring to the defendant pawnbrokers who had acted without notice. The plaintiff brought a claim for the value of the ring against the defendant.

What seems plain to me is that the presumption cannot in the present case be rebutted by piling up the evidence to show that Miss Ingram would never have contracted with H unless she had thought him to be PGM Hutchinson. That fact is conceded and, whether it is proved simpliciter or proved to the hilt, it does not go any further than to show that she was the victim of fraud. With great respect to the judge, the question that he propounded as the test is not calculated to show any more than that. He said: "Is it to be seriously suggested that they were willing to accept the cheque of the rogue other than in the belief, created by the rogue himself, that he, the rogue, was in fact the honest PGM Hutchinson of the address in Caterham with the telephone number which they had verified?" In my judgment, there is everything to show that Miss Ingram would never have accepted H's offer if she had known the truth, but nothing to rebut the ordinary presumption that she was addressing her acceptance, in law as well as in fact, to the person to whom she was speaking. I think, therefore, that there was offer and acceptance in form.

There can be no doubt . . . that the dividing line between voidness and voidability, between fundamental mistake and incidental deceit, is a very fine one. That a fine and difficult distinction has to be drawn is not necessarily any reproach to the law. But need the rights of the parties in a case like this depend on such a distinction? The great virtue of the common law is that it sets out to solve legal problems by the application to them of principles which the ordinary man is expected to recognise as sensible and just; their application in any particular case may produce what seems to him a hard result, but as principles they should be within his understanding and merit his approval. But here, contrary to its habit, the common law, instead of looking for a principle that is simple and just, rests on theoretical distinctions. Why should the question whether the defendant should or should not pay the plaintiff damages for conversion depend upon voidness or voidability, and upon inferences to be drawn from a conversation in which the defendant took no part? The true spirit of the common law is to override theoretical distinctions when they stand in the way of doing practical justice. For the doing of justice, the relevant question in this sort of case is not whether the contract was void or voidable, but which of two innocent parties shall suffer for the fraud of a third. The plain answer is that the loss should be divided between them in such proportion as is just in all the circumstances. If it be pure misfortune, the loss should be borne equally; if the fault or imprudence of either party has caused or contributed to the loss, it should be borne by that party in the whole or in the greater part. In saying this, I am suggesting nothing novel, for this sort of observation has often been made. But it is only in comparatively recent times that the idea of giving to a court power to apportion loss has found a place in our law. I have in mind particularly the Law Reform Acts of 1935, 1943 and 1945, that dealt respectively with joint tortfeasors, frustrated contracts and contributory negligence. These statutes, which I believe to have worked satisfactorily, show a modern inclination towards a decision based on a just apportionment rather than one given in black or in white according to the logic of the law. I believe it would be useful if Parliament were now to consider whether or not it is practicable by means of a similar act of law reform to provide for the victims of a fraud a better way of adjusting their mutual loss than that which has grown out of the common law.'

There are two points to note here. First, it is extremely difficult to distinguish between the facts of *Ingram v Little* and those of *Phillips v Brooks*. Various attempts have been made, but none have proven convincing. Second, the real problem in cases such as these is that the court is faced with the unfortunate task of deciding which of two innocent parties should shoulder the burden of the rogue's fraud. Devlin LJ suggested an alternative approach to this conundrum in his dissenting judgment. We will return to this and to the difficulty of reconciling the authorities after we have considered our third case, *Lewis v Averay*.

Lewis v Averay [1972] 1 KB 198

Facts: The plaintiff put an advertisement in the newspaper offering his Austin Cooper 'S' motor car for sale. A rogue came to see the car who claimed to be Robert Greene, a well-known actor who played Robin Hood in the 'Robin Hood' series. They agreed a price of £450 and the rogue wrote out a cheque for the full amount. He wanted to take the car immediately but the plaintiff refused. The rogue then produced a 'pass' from Pinewood Film Studios, which carried his photograph and an official stamp. On seeing the pass, the plaintiff was satisfied and let the rogue have the car in exchange for the cheque. The cheque had come from a stolen cheque book and was not honoured. By the time the plaintiff discovered the fraud, the defendant had sold the car to the defendant who bought it in good faith. The plaintiff sued the defendant in conversion for the return of the vehicle, or its value in damages.

Held: The Court of Appeal held that the contract was voidable for fraud but not void for mistake. The presumption that the plaintiff intended to deal with the person physically present had not been rebutted.

Lord Denning MR:
'The real question in the case is whether on May 8, 1969, there was a contract of sale under which the property in the car passed from Mr Lewis to the rogue. If there was such a contract, then, even though it was voidable for fraud, nevertheless Mr Averay would get a good title to the car. But if there was no contract of sale by Mr Lewis to the rogue – either because there was, on the face of it, no agreement between the parties, or because any apparent agreement was a nullity and void ab initio for mistake, then no property would pass from Mr Lewis to the rogue. Mr Averay would not get a good title because the rogue had no property to pass to him.

There is no doubt that Mr Lewis was mistaken as to the identity of the person who handed him the cheque . . . What is the effect of this mistake? . . . Who is entitled to the goods? The original seller? Or the ultimate buyer? The courts have given different answers. In *Phillips v Brooks*, the ultimate buyer was held to be entitled to the ring. In *Ingram v Little* the original seller was held to be entitled to the car. In the present case the deputy county court judge has held the original seller entitled.

It seems to me that the material facts in each case are quite indistinguishable the one from the other. In each case there was, to all outward appearance, a contract: but there was a mistake by the seller as to the identity of the buyer. This mistake was fundamental. In each case it led to the handing over of the goods. Without it the seller would not have parted with them. This case therefore raises the question: What is the effect of a mistake by one party as to the identity of the other? It has sometimes been said that if a party makes a mistake as to the identity of the person with whom he is contracting there is no contract, or, if there is a contract, it is a nullity and void, so that no property can pass under it. This has been supported by a reference to the French jurist Pothier; but I have said before, and I repeat now, his statement is no part of English law . . . it is time it was dead and buried together.

For instance, in *Ingram v Little* the majority of the court suggested that the difference between *Phillips v Brooks* and *Ingram v Little* was that in *Phillips v Brooks* the contract of sale was concluded (so as to pass the property to the rogue) before the rogue made the fraudulent misrepresentation: see [1961] 1 QB 31, 51, 60: whereas in *Ingram v Little* the rogue made the fraudulent misrepresentation before the contract was concluded. My own view is that in each case the property in the goods did not pass until the seller let the rogue have the goods. Again it has been suggested that a mistake as to the identity of a person is one thing: and a mistake as to his attributes is another. A mistake as to identity, it is said, avoids a contract: whereas a mistake as to attributes does not. But this is a distinction without a difference. A man's very name is one of his attributes . . .

As I listened to the argument in this case, I felt it wrong that an innocent purchaser (who knew nothing of what passed between the seller and the rogue) should have his title depend on such refinements. After all, he has acted with complete circumspection and in entire good faith: whereas it was the seller who let the rogue have the goods and thus enabled him to commit the fraud. I do not, therefore, accept the theory that a mistake as to identity renders a contract void. I think the true principle is that which underlies the decision of this court in *King's Norton Metal Co Ltd v Edridge Merrett & Co Ltd* (1897) 14 TLR 98 and of Horridge J in *Phillips v Brooks* [1919] 2 KB 243, which has stood for these last 50 years. It is this: When two parties have come to a contract – or rather what appears, on the face of it, to be a contract – the fact that one party is mistaken as to the identity of the other does not mean that there is no contract, or that the contract is a nullity and void from the beginning. It only means that the contract is voidable, that is, liable to be set aside at the instance of the mistaken person, so long as he does so before third parties have in good faith acquired rights under it.

Applied to the cases such as the present, this principle is in full accord with the presumption stated by Pearce LJ and also Devlin LJ in *Ingram v Little* [1961] 1 QB 31, 61, 66. When a dealing is had between a seller like Mr. Lewis and a person who is actually there present before him, then the presumption in law is that there is a contract, even though there is a fraudulent impersonation by the buyer representing himself as a different man than he is. There is a contract made with the very person there, who is present in person. It is liable no doubt to be avoided for fraud, but it is still a good contract under which title will pass unless and until it is avoided . . .

Megaw LJ:

'For myself, with very great respect, I find it difficult to understand the basis, either in logic or in practical considerations, of the test laid down by the majority of the court in *Ingram v Little* [1961] 1 QB 31. That test is, I think, accurately recorded in the headnote, as follows:

> "– where a person physically present and negotiating to buy a chattel fraudulently assumed the identity of an existing third person, the test to determine to whom the offer was addressed was how ought the promisee to have interpreted the promise."

The promisee, be it noted, is the rogue. The question of the existence of a contract and therefore the passing of property, and therefore the right of third parties, if this test is correct, is made to depend upon the view which some rogue should have formed, presumably knowing that he is a rogue, as to the state of mind of the opposite party to the negotiation, who does not know that he is dealing with a rogue.

However that may be, and assuming that the test so stated is indeed valid, in my view this appeal can be decided on a short and simple point . . . The well-known textbook *Cheshire and Fifoot* on the *Law of Contract* 7th edn (1969), 213 and 214, deals with the question of invalidity of a contract by virtue of unilateral mistake, and in particular unilateral mistake relating to mistaken identity. The editors describe what in their submission are certain facts that must be established in order to enable one to avoid a contract on the basis of unilateral mistake by him as to the identity of the opposite party. The first of those facts is that at the time when he made the offer he regarded the identity of the offeree as a matter of vital importance. To translate that into the facts of the present case, it must be established that at the time of offering to sell his car to the rogue, Mr Lewis regarded the identity of the rogue as a matter of vital importance. In my view, Mr Titheridge is abundantly justified, on the notes of the evidence and on the findings of the judge, in his submission that the mistake of Mr Lewis went no further than a mistake as to the attributes of the rogue. It was simply a mistake as to the creditworthiness of the man who was there present and who described himself as Mr Green . . .'

Lord Denning said that the material facts of *Phillips v Brooks* and *Ingram v Little* were indistinguishable from each other. Elsewhere in his judgment he suggested that the cases were irreconcilable. Is this true? In *Ingram v Little*, Pearce LJ attempted to distinguish the facts of *Phillips v Brooks* on the ground that the contract in that case was concluded before there was any mention of 'Sir George Bullough', whereas the contract in the case before him was only concluded after the plaintiffs had verified that PGM Hutchinson did indeed live at the address they had been given. This view of *Phillips v Brooks* was first intimated by Viscount Haldane in *Lake v Simmons* [1927] AC 487. The theory is, however, difficult to reconcile with the facts of the case (see Treitel, G, *The Law of Contract*, 11th edn, 2003, p 300, London: Sweet & Maxwell).

In reality, all three cases were identical. They involved a contract concluded by face-to-face negotiations in which the plaintiff was tricked into parting with his property by the fraudulent misrepresentation of a rogue. In all three cases there was a prima facie presumption that the plaintiff intended to contract with the person physically present and in each case the plaintiff attempted to verify the identify of the rogue. Yet, for some reason, the presumption in *Ingram v Little* was held to be rebutted while the presumption in the other two cases was not. Why? It is hard to avoid the conclusion that the decisions were motivated more by policy consider-ations than by principle. The court had to decide which of two innocent parties should bear the loss brought about by the fraud. In *Phillips v Brooks* and *Lewis v Averary*, as in most cases, the original owner was marginally less innocent than the third party, because he had the opportunity to uncover the fraud and stop it before it was carried out. *Ingram v Little* was a little different, however. The third-party purchaser in that case was a large car dealer who was easily able to absorb the loss caused by the fraud, while the original owners were vulnerable old ladies who had far more limited means.

If this is correct and the decision is best explained on policy grounds, it is to be regretted that the Court of Appeal did not unanimously adopt the approach pro-posed by Devlin LJ (in his dissent), which would have reached the same end (albeit through legislation) by a much more principled and consistent means. Devlin LJ expressed the view that decisions as to who should bear the loss caused by a fraud should not rest on theoretical distinctions between void and voidable contract, but instead on an assessment of the circumstances of each case: 'If it be pure misfortune, the loss should be borne equally; if the fault or imprudence of either party has caused or contributed to the loss, it should be borne by that party in the whole or in the greater part.' Devlin LJ's loss apportionment proposal was considered and rejected by the Law Reform Committee in its Twelfth Report (*Transfer of Title to Chattels*, Cmnd 2958, 1966, London: HMSO). The Committee noted that opinion was divided on the proposal, but rejected it on the ground that it was impractical and unworkable. The Committee did, however, recommend that anomalies in the law should be removed by rendering contracts entered into under a mistake as to identity voidable rather than void. Such a reform would have ensured greater protection for innocent third-party purchasers. This proposal was never imple-mented by Parliament, although it clearly won the approval of Lord Denning in

Lewis v Averay and was adopted by the drafters of the Principles of European Contract Law (see below).

10.3.2.1.3 *The decision of the House of Lords in* Shogun Finance

As the cases above show, the law governing mistake as to identity is in a mess. In *Shogun Finance Ltd v Hudson* [2002] QB 834, 842, Sedley LJ said the following:

'We have been shown the Committee's Twelfth Report on the *Transfer of Title to Chattels* (1966) (Cmnd 2958). The conclusion of its distinguished members did not chime with that of Lord Devlin (as he by then was). It was that apportionment of consequential loss was not practicable; that the loser of stolen goods should retain title unless they were bought in good faith by retail or at auction; but that a contract made under a mistake as to the buyer's identity should be voidable as against honest third parties and not void. If the last of these proposals had been adopted, it would have produced the outcome at which Lord Denning MR arrived in *Lewis v Averay* [1972] 1 QB 198. Instead, the illogical and sometimes barely perceptible distinctions made in earlier decisions, some of them representing an unarticulated judicial policy on the incidence of loss as between innocent parties, continue to represent the law.'

The problems that exist in the law are twofold. First, the cases draw an unjustifiable distinction between contracts concluded face-to-face and those concluded by written correspondence. Second, the cases dealing with face-to-face negotiations appear to contradict each other, with a mistake as to identity rendering a contract void in *Ingram v Little*, but not in *Phillips v Brooks* or *Lewis v Averay*. The House of Lords sought to resolve these problems and to clarify the law in *Shogun Finance*. The extent to which they were successful in this endeavour is open to question.

Shogun Finance Ltd v Hudson [2004] 1 AC 919

Facts: A motor dealer agreed to sell a Mitsubishi Shogun car on hire-purchase to a rogue who produced a stolen driving licence as proof of his identity (the driving licence belonged to a Mr Durlabh Patel). The dealer faxed a draft hire-purchase agreement to the claimant hire-purchase company including a copy of the stolen driving licence. The hire-purchase agreement had been signed by the rogue, forging the signature on the driving licence. The claimant checked Mr Patel's credit rating and approved the sale. The rogue then paid a deposit and was allowed to take away the car. The following day, the rogue sold the car to the defendant who purchased it in good faith. When the claimants discovered the fraud they brought a claim against the defendant in the tort of conversion. The defendant counterclaimed that he had acquired good title to the vehicle within the meaning of section 27 of the Hire Purchase Act 1964. Ordinarily in a hire-purchase contract, the hire-purchaser will not acquire title to the goods until after he has made all the payments. Nevertheless, s 27 provides an exception to the *nemo dat* rule that allows the rogue to give good title to an innocent third party provided that the rogue is a 'debtor' under the hire purchase agreement. Thus the case turned on the question of whether there was a valid contract between the claimant and the rogue.

The judge at first instance gave judgment for the claimant. The Court of Appeal dismissed the defendant's appeal on the ground that, since he was not the hirer named in the written hire-purchase agreement, the rogue was not the 'debtor' within the meaning of section 27 of the 1964 Act. The Court of Appeal (Sedley LJ dissenting) also rejected the claimant's alternative argument that the dealer was acting as an agent for the claimant, thereby raising the presumption that the claimants intended to deal with the rogue, as the person physically present.

Held: The House of Lords dismissed the appeal (Lords Nicholls and Millett dissenting). The title to the car had at all material times been in the claimant and accordingly the defendant could not have acquired title to it from the rogue. The rogue was not named in the agreement, nor could oral evidence be admitted to contradict the express terms of the written agreement. There was no *consensus ad idem* between the claimant and the rogue and, accordingly, the rogue had not become a 'debtor' within the meaning of s 27 of the 1964 Act.

Lord Nicholls of Birkenhead:
'The choice
33. In my view [Cundy v Lindsay (1878) 3 App Cas 459] is not reconcilable with *Phillips v Brooks* [1919] 2 KB 243 or with *Lewis v Averay* [1972] 1 QB 198 or with the starting point "presumption" formulated by Devlin LJ in *Ingram v Little* [1961] 1 QB 31. The legal principle applicable in these cases cannot sensibly differ according to whether the transaction is negotiated face-to-face, or by letter, or by fax, or by e-mail, or over the telephone or by video link or video telephone. Typically today a purchaser pays for goods with a credit or debit card. He produces the card in person in a shop or provides details of the card over the telephone or by e-mail or by fax. When a credit or debit card is fraudulently misused in this way the essence of the transaction is the same in each case. It does not differ from one means of communication to the next. The essence of the transaction in each case is that the owner of the goods agrees to part with his goods on the basis of a fraudulent misrepresentation made by the other regarding his identity. Since the essence of the transaction is the same in each case, the law in its response should apply the same principle in each case, irrespective of the precise mode of communication of offer and acceptance.

34. Accordingly, if the law of contract is to be coherent and rescued from its present unsatisfactory and unprincipled state, the House has to make a choice: either to uphold the approach adopted in *Cundy v Lindsay* and overrule the decisions in *Phillips v Brooks* and *Lewis v Averay*, or to prefer these later decisions to *Cundy v Lindsay*.

35. I consider the latter course is the right one, for a combination of reasons. It is in line with the direction in which, under the more recent decisions, the law has now been moving for some time. It accords better with basic principle regarding the effect of fraud on the formation of a contract. It seems preferable as a matter of legal policy. As between two innocent persons the loss is more appropriately borne by the person who takes the risks inherent in parting with his goods without receiving payment. This approach fits comfortably with the intention of Parliament in enacting the limited statutory exceptions to the proprietary principle of *nemo dat quod non habet*. Thus, by section 23 of the 1979 Act Parliament protected an innocent buyer from a seller with a voidable title. The classic instance of a person with a voidable title is a person who acquired the goods by fraud: see per Bramwell LJ in *Babcock v Lawson* (1880) 5 QBD 284, 286. Further, this course is supported by writers of the distinction of Sir Jack Beatson: see *Anson's Law of Contract*, 28th edn (2002), p 332. It is consistent with the approach adopted elsewhere in the common law world, notably in the United States of America in the Uniform Commercial Code, 14th edn (1995), section 2–403. And this course makes practical sense. In a case such as the present the owner of goods has no interest in the identity of the buyer. He is interested only in creditworthiness. It is little short of absurd that a subsequent purchaser's rights depend on the precise manner in which the crook seeks to persuade the owner of his creditworthiness and permit him to take the goods away with him. This ought not to be so. The purchaser's rights should not depend upon the precise form the crook's misrepresentation takes.

36. *Cundy v Lindsay* has stood for a long time. But I see no reason to fear that adopting this conclusion will unsettle the law of contract. In practice the problems surrounding *Cundy v Lindsay* arise only when third parties' rights are in issue. To bring the law here into line with the law already existing in "face-to-face" cases will rid the law of an anomaly. Devlin LJ's starting point presumption is a workable foundation which should apply in all cases. A person is presumed to intend to contract with the person with whom he is actually dealing, whatever be the mode of communication.

37. Although expressed by Devlin LJ as a presumption, it is not easy to think of practical circumstances where, once in point, the presumption will be displaced. The factual postulate necessary to bring the presumption into operation is that a person (O) believes that the person with whom he is dealing is the person the latter has represented himself to be. Evidence that the other's identity was of importance to O, and evidence of the steps taken to check the other's identity, will lead nowhere if the transaction proceeds on the basis of the underlying factual postulate.

The present case

38. It follows that I would allow this appeal . . .

41. One further point may be noted. Some time was taken up in this case with arguments on whether the dealer was an agent for the finance company and for what purposes. This was in an endeavour to bring the case within the "face-to-face" principle. The need for such singularly sterile arguments underlines the practical absurdity of a principle bounded in this way. The practical reality is that in the instant case the presence or absence of a representative of the finance company in the dealer's showroom made no difference to the course of events. Had an authorised representative of the finance company been present no doubt he would have inspected the driving licence himself and himself obtained the information needed by his company. As it was, a copy of the licence, together with the necessary information, were faxed to the finance company. I can see no sensible basis on which these different modes of communication should affect the outcome of this case. I would set aside the orders of the assistant recorder and the Court of Appeal, and dismiss this action. Mr Hudson acquired a good title to the car under section 27 of the 1964 Act.

Lord Hobhouse of Woodborough:

'44. The relevant question is . . .: "Was R a debtor under the hire-purchase agreement relating to the car?" Mr Hudson contends that R was; the finance company contends that he was not. The judge and the majority of the Court of Appeal found that he was not; Sedley LJ would have held that he was.

45. What was the "hire-purchase" agreement relied on? It was a written agreement on a standard hire-purchase printed form purporting to be signed as the "customer" by one Durlabh Patel, the person who lived at 45 Mayflower Road, Leicester, to whom driving licence no 'PATEL506018DJ9FM' had been issued and with a date of birth 01/06/58. This was an accurate identification of the real Mr Durlabh Patel, but in no respect of R who was not the person who lived at that address, not the person to whom the driving licence had been issued and (one suspects) not a twin in age of the real Mr Patel. R forged Mr Patel's signature so as to make the signature on the hire-purchase "agreement" appear to be the same as that on the driving licence. The parties to the written "agreement" are Mr Patel (the "customer"), and Shogun Finance Ltd (the creditor). There is also an offer and acceptance clause (clause 1):

> "You [the customer named overleaf] are offering to make a legal agreement by signing this document. We [the creditor] can reject your offer, or accept it by signing it ourselves . . . If we sign this document it will become legally binding at once (even before we send you a signed copy) . . ."

46. The effect of this is that: (i) it re-emphasises that the customer/hirer is, and is only, the person *named* on the front of the document; (ii) it makes it clear that the agreement is the written agreement contained in the written document; (iii) the offer being accepted by the creditor is the offer contained in the document and that alone, that is to say, the offer of Mr Durlabh Patel of the address in Leicester and to whom the driving licence was issued; (iv) for a valid offer to be made, the form must have been signed by Mr Durlabh Patel; and, (v) most importantly of all, the question in issue becomes a question of the construction of this written document, not a question of factual investigation and evaluation . . .

50. The [defendant's] argument also fails on another ground. There was no *consensus ad idem* between the finance company and the rogue. Leaving on one side the fact that the rogue never had any intention himself to contract with the finance company, the hire-purchase "agreement" to which Mr Hudson pins his argument

was one purportedly made by the acceptance by the finance company, by signing the creditor's box in the form, of a written offer by Mr Durlabh Patel to enter into the hire-purchase agreement. This faces Mr Hudson with a dilemma: either the contract created by that acceptance was a contract with Mr Durlabh Patel or there was no *consensus ad idem*, the rogue having no honest belief or contractual intent whatsoever and the finance company believing that it was accepting an offer by Mr Durlabh Patel. On neither alternative was there a hire-purchase agreement with the rogue.

54. It follows that the appeal must be dismissed and the majority judgment of the Court of Appeal affirmed.

Lord Millett (dissenting):

'**68.** [T]he real objection to the present state of the law, in my view, is that the distinction between the face-to-face contract and other contracts is unrealistic. I leave aside the criticism of the face-to-face rule made by *Corbin on Contracts*, at p 620, that it is "somewhat fanciful to hold that B intends to sell the goods to the physical body of A in front of him, although that body is indeed part of what we call 'identity'". My difficulty is that I cannot see that there is any difference in principle between the two situations . . .

69. In *Ingram v Little* [1961] 1 QB 31 Devlin LJ said, at p 66, that "the presumption that a person is intending to contract with the person to whom he is actually addressing the words of contract seems to me to be a simple and sensible one . . ." I respectfully agree. But why should it be adopted only in the case of a contract entered into between persons who deal in the physical presence of each other? If the offeree's words of acceptance are taken to be addressed to the physical person standing in his presence who made the offer, what is the position where they deal with each other by telephone? Is the disembodied voice to be equated with physical presence? Is it sufficient that the parties are in the hearing of each other? Does it make a difference if the dealing is by televisual link, so that the parties are in the hearing and sight but not the presence of each other? New means of communication make the distinction untenable.

70. But in truth the distinction was always unsound. If the offeree's words of acceptance are taken to be addressed to the physical person standing in his presence who made the offer, why is the contract entered into by correspondence different? . . .

71. In my opinion there are only two principled solutions to the problem. The law must give preference, either to the person for whom the offer or acceptance is intended, or to the person to whom it is directed, and must do so in all cases as a matter of law. The difficulty is in deciding which solution should be adopted, for there is much to commend each of them.

72. The first solution, which gives preference to the person for whom the offer or acceptance is intended, possibly accords more closely to the existing authorities, which treat the face-to-face transaction as an exception to the general rule, and with the decision in *Cundy v Lindsay* 3 App Cas 459, the only case on the subject which has come before the House. It also accords more closely with the parties' subjective intentions, for B intends to deal with C, especially if he has checked his creditworthiness, and not with A, of whom he has never heard; while A has no intention of being bound by contract at all. From his point of view the supposed contract is merely a pretence to enable him to get hold of goods without paying for them. He does not need a contract, for he is content with possession without title. In the days when the law distinguished between trickery and deception, he would have obtained possession by a trick rather than title by false pretences.

73. The strongest argument in favour of this solution, I suppose, is that it could be said to be based on the parties' own assessment of what they mean by the counterparty's "identity" . . . [A]s Treitel observes (*The Law of Contract*, 10th edn, p 277) a person may be identified by reference to any one of his attributes. He may be identified as "the person in the room", "the person who spoke on the telephone", "the person who appended the illegible signature", "the writer of the letter under reply", or "the person who made the offer"; but he may also be identified, and sometimes more relevantly, as "the person whose creditworthiness has been checked and found to be satisfactory". Any of these may be the means of identifying a unique person . . .

75. Given the equivocal nature of a person's "identity", there is something to be said for selecting those aspects of the offeror's identity which are material in causing the other party to accept the offer. In the present case, for example, Mr Patel's name address and date of birth had no intrinsic relevance in themselves. The claimant would have entered into the transaction with anyone, whatever his name and address or date of birth, so long as it was satisfied that he was worthy of credit. Mr Patel's personal details were merely the information which enabled it to conduct inquiries into the credit of the person it assumed to be its customer. It makes commercial sense to treat a contract made in these circumstances as purporting to be made between the finance company and the subject of its inquiries rather than with the person who merely produced the information necessary to enable it to make them.

76. Nevertheless I have come to the conclusion that it is the second solution which ought to be adopted. All the considerations which I have mentioned, and which seem to favour the first solution, when properly analysed go to the mechanics of the deception and its materiality rather than to the identity of the offeror. They ought to come into play when consideration is given to the second question, whether the contract is voidable, rather than to the first, whether there is sufficient correlation between offer and acceptance ("*consensus ad idem*") to bring a contract into existence. Until the fraud is exposed and it is discovered that A is *not* C, the existence of a contract is not in doubt. The fraud is relevant to the question whether the contract is enforceable against B rather than its existence.

81. . . . In my opinion, once one accepts that there are two questions involved: (i) did a contract come into existence at all? and (ii) if so was the contract vitiated by fraud or mistake? there is only one principled conclusion. Whatever the medium of communication, a contract comes into existence if, on an objective appraisal of the facts, there is sufficient correlation between offer and acceptance to make it possible to say that the impostor's offer has been accepted by the person to whom it was addressed. While a person cannot intercept and accept an offer made to someone else, he should normally be treated as intending to contract with the person with whom he is dealing. Provided that the offer is made to him, then whether his acceptance of the offer is obtained by deception or mistake, and whether his mistake is as to the identity of the offeror or some material attribute of his, the transaction should result in a contract, albeit one which is voidable.

82. This rule is easy to apply and accords with principle by distinguishing between the formation of a contract as a question of fact to be determined objectively and the consequences of mistake or fraud which depend on its effect on the mind of the person affected. It avoids undesirable refinements and gives a measure of protection to innocent third parties. Of course, someone has to bear the loss where there is fraud, but it is surely fairer that the party who was actually swindled and who had an opportunity to uncover the fraud should bear the loss rather than a party who entered the picture only after the swindle had been carried out and who had none. In the present case, the claimant could easily have exposed the fraud by writing to Mr Patel, whose address it had been given, and asking him to confirm his intention to proceed with the proposed transaction. If it had been one for which statute required a cooling-off period, it no doubt it would have done.

84. We cannot leave the law as it is. It is neither fair nor principled, and not all the authorities from which it is derived can be reconciled; some, at least, must be overruled if it is to be extricated from the present quagmire. If the law is to be rationalised and placed on a proper footing, the formulation which I have proposed has the merit of according with the recommendations made in the Twelfth Report of the Law Reform Committee on the *Transfer of Title to Chattels* (Cmnd 2958) and in *Anson's Law of Contract*, 28th edn, p 332. It would also bring English law into line with the law both in the United States and in Germany . . .

87. Where does this leave the authorities? Most of those which are concerned with face-to-face transactions can stand with the exception of the decision of the majority of the Court of Appeal in *Ingram v Little* [1961] 1 QB 31, which is inconsistent with *Lewis v Averay* [1972] 1 QB 198 and should be overruled. I would confirm the decision in *Phillips v Brook Ltd* [1919] 2 KB 243 . . .

90. The principal obstacle which has prevented the courts from rationalising this branch of the law has been *Cundy v Lindsay* . . . As an authority on the formation of contract the decision is, with respect, unconvincing. That the plaintiffs did not wish or intend to have any dealings with Blenkarn is beyond dispute; but it is far from obvious that they did not actually have such a dealing even though it was only as a result of the deception practised on them . . .

93. In my view the proper conclusion on these facts is that the plaintiffs contracted with Blenkarn in the mistaken belief, induced by his fraud, that they were dealing with Blenkiron & Co, and that the resulting contract was voidable for fraud. If the plaintiffs' subjective state of mind, induced by the fraud, is put on one side, there is no justification for the question-begging assumption that the plaintiffs' letter of acceptance was directed to Blenkiron & Co and that it was the name which was right and the address which was wrong. Nor is there any justification for the suggestion that the signature was a forgery. Blenkarn, who signed the letter, did not claim that it was someone else's signature; he acknowledged and asserted that it was his own. Even those who consider that the case was rightly decided concede that the rogue could have been sued for the price of the goods: see Treitel, *The Law of Contract*, p 284. But that presupposes that there was sufficient correlation between offer and acceptance to bring a contract into existence, albeit one which was void (or voidable) at the instance of the party deceived. Yet this was the very proposition which the House rejected . . .

103. [O]nce it is established that the person whose name and other personal details are stated in the contract and the person who stated them and signed the contract are not the same, the question immediately arises: which of them should be treated as the counterparty? Do the name and other details included in the contract refer to the person to whom they belong or to the impostor who included them in order to identify himself? This is not simply a question of construction. It is partly a question of fact and partly a question of law. To say, as my noble and learned friend, Lord Hobhouse of Woodborough, does, that it is a question of construction which admits of only one answer, with respect simply begs the question.

104. How should the question be answered in the present case? . . . If there was a contract with the rogue, it was voidable for fraud.

105. But was there such a contact at all? The contact came into being when the claimant executed its part of the agreement. The two parts corresponded in every material particular . . .

106. The object of the deception was to misdirect the claimant's credit inquiries. In this it succeeded. Having satisfied itself that Mr Durlabh Patel, whom it believed to be its customer, was worthy of credit, it accepted the offer which the impostor had made, signed its part of the agreement, and authorised the dealer to deliver possession of the car to his customer as hirer under the agreement.

107. But who was his customer? It was not Mr Durlabh Patel. In my opinion it was plainly the impostor. Any other conclusion would mean that the dealer parted with the vehicle to the impostor without authority and would, presumably, be liable in conversion if the vehicle proved to be irrecoverable. This is far removed from reality. The claimant and the dealer both believed that the customer who was hiring the car and Mr Durlabh Patel were one and the same; but the claimant did not make that a condition of the dealer's authority to part with the car. From first to last it believed that the impostor who attended the dealer's showroom, gave his name as Mr Durlabh Patel, and signed the agreement in that name, was indeed Mr Durlabh Patel; in that belief it entered into a hiring agreement and authorised the dealer to deliver possession of the car to the customer who had so identified himself. In my opinion, the claimant not only took a credit risk, but also took the risk that the customer who was hiring the car was not Mr Durlabh Patel and that its credit inquiries had been fraudulently misdirected. I would hold that there was a hiring, and the impostor was the hirer.

108. This conclusion involves a departure from *Cundy v Lindsay* 3 App Cas 459, a decision of this House which has stood for more than 120 years. But its reasoning is unsound. It is vitiated by its subjective approach to the formation of contract and the necessary correlation between offer and acceptance; which may be why textbook writers treat it as an example of unilateral mistake even though this was not the basis on which it was decided. For the same reason it cannot be regarded as authoritative on the question whether a contract otherwise properly entered into is void for mistake rather than voidable. It has had an unfortunate influence on the development of the law, leading to an unprincipled distinction between face-to-face transactions and others and the indefensible conclusion that an innocent purchaser's position depends on the nature of the mistake of a third party or the precise mechanics of the fraud which had been perpetrated on him. In my view it should now be discarded and the law put on a simpler and more principled and defensible basis.

109. In my opinion only the decision in *Cundy v Lindsay* stands in the way of a rational and coherent restatement of the law. My noble and learned friend, Lord Phillips of Worth Matravers, has expressed the view that the conclusion to which Lord Nicholls and I have come conflicts not only with that case but with the approach in almost all the numerous cases which he has cited. If they had preceded *Cundy v Lindsay*, that would be a strong reason for not adopting it. But they were merely following a decision of this House by which they were bound.'

Lord Phillips of Worth Matravers

'119. The critical issue in this case is whether a hire-purchase agreement was ever concluded between Shogun and the rogue. If an agreement was concluded, then the rogue was the "debtor" under section 27 of the 1964 Act and passed good title in the vehicle to Mr Hudson. If no agreement was concluded, then the rogue stole the vehicle by deception and passed no title to Mr Hudson . . .

Formation of contract

123. A contract is normally concluded when an offer made by one party ("the offeror") is accepted by the party to whom the offer has been made ("the offeree"). Normally the contract is only concluded when the acceptance is communicated by the offeree to the offeror. A contract will not be concluded unless the parties are agreed as to its material terms. There must be "*consensus ad idem*". Whether the parties have reached agreement on the terms is not determined by evidence of the subjective intention of each party. It is, in large measure, determined by making an objective appraisal of the exchanges between the parties. If an offeree understands an offer in accordance with its natural meaning and accepts it, the offeror cannot be heard to say that he intended the words of his offer to have a different meaning. The contract stands according to the natural meaning of the words used. There is one important exception to this principle. If the offeree knows that the offeror does not intend the terms of the offer to be those that the natural meaning of the words would suggest, he cannot, by purporting to accept the offer, bind the offeror to a contract: *Hartog v Colin & Shields* [1939] 3 All ER 566; *Smith v Hughes* (1871) LR 6 QB 597. Thus the task of ascertaining whether the parties have reached agreement as to the terms of a contract can involve quite a complex amalgam of the objective and the subjective and involve the application of a principle that bears close comparison with the doctrine of estoppel. Normally,

however, the task involves no more than an objective analysis of the words used by the parties. The object of the exercise is to determine what each party *intended,* or must be deemed to have *intended.*

124. The task of ascertaining whether the parties have reached agreement as to the terms of a contract largely overlaps with the task of ascertaining what it is that the parties have agreed. The approach is the same. It requires the construction of the words used by the parties in order to deduce the *intention* of the parties – see *Chitty on Contracts,* 28th edn (1999), vol 1, p 604, paras 12–042, 12–043 and the cases there cited. This is true, whether the contract is oral or in writing. The words used fall to be construed having regard to the relevant background facts and extrinsic evidence may be admitted to explain or interpret the words used. Equally, extrinsic evidence may be necessary to identify the subject matter of the contract to which the words refer.

125. Just as the parties must be shown to have agreed on the terms of the contract, so they must also be shown to have agreed the one with the other. If A makes an offer to B, but C purports to accept it, there will be no contract. Equally, if A makes an offer to B and B addresses his acceptance to C there will be no contract. Where there is an issue as to whether two persons have reached an agreement, the one with the other, the courts have tended to adopt the same approach to resolving that issue as they adopt when considering whether there has been agreement as to the terms of the contract. The court asks the question whether each *intended,* or must be deemed to have *intended,* to contract with the other. That approach gives rise to a problem where one person is mistaken as to the identity of the person with whom he is dealing, as the cases demonstrate . . .

The decided cases

[His Lordship considered *Boulton v Jones* (1857) 27 LJ Ex 117; *Hardman v Booth* (1863) 1 H & C 803; *Cundy v Lindsay* (1878) 3 App Cas 459; *King's Norton Metal Co Ltd v Edridge, Merrett & Co Ltd* (1897) 14 TLR 98; *Phillips v Brooks Ltd* [1919] 2 KB 243; *Lake v Simmons* [1927] AC 487; *Ingram v Little* [1961] 1 QB 31 and *Lewis v Averay* [1972] 1 QB 198. He expressed preference for *Phillips v Brooks* over *Ingram v Little* and continued:]

152. Lord Denning MR did not apply the approach of attempting to identify the intention of the plaintiff. He proceeded on the simple basis that, to all outward appearances, the plaintiff entered into an agreement with the rogue, with whom he was dealing. Both he and Phillimore LJ considered that the case was on all fours with *Phillips v Brooks* which had been rightly decided.

153. The difficulty in applying a test of *intention* to the identification of the parties to a contract arises, so it seems to me, only where the parties conduct their dealings in some form of inter-personal contact, and where one purports to have the identity of a third party. There the innocent party will have in mind, when considering with whom he is contracting, both the person with whom he is in contact and the third party whom he imagines that person to be.

154. The same problem will not normally arise where the dealings are carried out exclusively in writing. The process of construction of the written instruments, making appropriate use of extrinsic evidence, will normally enable the court to reach a firm conclusion as to the person with whom a party intends to contract. This was the position in *Boulton v Jones* 27 LJ Ex 117, *Cundy v Lindsay* 3 App Cas 459 and *King's Norton Metal Co Ltd v Edridge, Merrett & Co Ltd* 14 TLR 98. There is a substantial body of authority that demonstrates that the identity of a party to a contract in writing falls to be determined by a process of construction of the putative contract itself. I shall refer to some examples.

[His Lordship referred to a number of cases on the construction of written contracts and continued:]

161. The effect of these authorities is that a person carrying on negotiations in writing can, by describing as one of the parties to the putative agreement an individual who is unequivocally identifiable from that description, preclude any finding that the party to the putative agreement is other than the person so described. The process of construction will lead inexorably to the conclusion that the person with whom the other party intended to contract was the person thus described . . .

The result in the present case

167. I have had the advantage of reading in draft the opinions of my noble and learned friends who have sat with me on this appeal. Lord Hobhouse of Woodborough and Lord Walker of Gestingthorpe have concluded that, as the contract was a written document, the identity of the hirer falls to be ascertained by construing that document. Adopting that approach, the hirer was, or more accurately purported to be, Mr Patel. As he had not authorised the conclusion of the contract, it was void.

168. Lord Nicholls of Birkenhead and Lord Millett have adopted a different approach. They point out the illogicality of applying a special approach to face-to-face dealings. What of dealings on the telephone, or by videolink? There also it could be said that each of the parties to the dealings is seeking to make a contract with the other party to the dealings. And this can even be said when the dealings are conducted by correspondence. If A writes to B making an offer and B writes back responding to that offer, B is intending to contract with the person who made that offer. If a contract is concluded in face-to-face dealings, notwithstanding that one party is masquerading as a third party, why should the result be different when the dealings are by letter?

169. Lord Nicholls of Birkenhead and Lord Millett propose an elegant solution to this illogicality. Where two individuals *deal with each other*, by whatever medium, and agree terms of a contract, then a contract will be concluded between them, notwithstanding that one has deceived the other into thinking that he has the identity of a third party. In such a situation the contract will be voidable but not void. While they accept that this approach cannot be reconciled with *Cundy v Lindsay* 3 App Cas 459, they conclude that *Cundy v Lindsay* was wrongly decided and should no longer be followed.

170. While I was strongly attracted to this solution, I have found myself unable to adopt it. *Cundy v Lindsay* exemplifies the application by English law of the same approach to identifying the parties as is applied to identifying the terms of the contract. In essence this focuses on deducing the intention of the parties from their words and conduct. Where there is some form of personal contact between individuals who are conducting negotiations, this approach gives rise to problems. In such a situation I would favour the application of a strong presumption that each intends to contract with the other, with whom he is dealing. Where, however, the dealings are exclusively conducted in writing, there is no scope or need for such a presumption. This can be illustrated by a slight adaption of the facts of the present case. Assume that the rogue had himself filled in the application form and sent it and a photocopy of Mr Patel's driving licence to Shogun. Assume further that he had been authorised to do so by Mr Patel. There can be no doubt that a contract would have been concluded between Shogun and Mr Patel. Mr Patel would have intended to contract with Shogun; Shogun would have intended to contract with Mr Patel; and this would have been demonstrated by the application form.

171. Assume now that the rogue had wrongly understood that he had been requested by Mr Patel to fill in and submit the application form on his behalf, but in fact had no authority to do so. In this situation, according to established principles of the law of agency, an apparent contract would have been concluded between Shogun and Mr Patel but, being concluded without the latter's authority, it would be a nullity. Shogun might have a claim against the rogue for breach of warranty of authority, but could not have demonstrated that a contract had been concluded with the rogue.

172. Turning to the true position – that the rogue knew he had no authority to conclude a contract in the name of Mr Patel, but fraudulently wished to induce Shogun to believe that they were entering into such a contract – I do not see by what legal principle this change in the mental attitude of the rogue could result in a binding contract being concluded with him.

173. The position is not, of course, as simple as that. Negotiations between the rogue and Shogun were not conducted exclusively by written correspondence. They were conducted with the aid of the dealer and the use of fax and telephone communications. Acceptance of the offer was conveyed by telephone via the dealer – and this might have been capable of concluding a contract, notwithstanding that clause 1 of the standard terms provided for acceptance by signature: see the discussion in *Chitty on Contracts*, 28th edn, vol 1, p 117, para 2–062. Sedley LJ considered that the dealings were analogous to face-to-face dealings and that the dealer was, in effect, the face of Shogun Finance Ltd. He considered that the face-to-face presumption should be applied.

174. The majority of the Court of Appeal considered that *Hector v Lyons* 58 P & CR required them to determine the identity of the parties to the putative contract as a simple question of construction. On that basis they concluded that the putative hirer was Mr Patel and that, as the apparent contract was concluded without his authority, it was a nullity.

175. Dyson LJ considered what the result would have been had the negotiations been treated as face-to-face. He concluded [2002] QB 834, 853–854, paras 45–46 that the presumption would have been displaced by the importance that Shogun attached to the identity of the person with whom they were contracting.

176. My Lords . . . Shogun's representatives were aware of the presence of the prospective hirer in the dealer's showrooms in Leicester. To an extent the dealings were interpersonal through the medium of the dealer. Should one treat them as comparable to face-to-face dealings and conclude that there was a presumption that Shogun intended to contract with the man with whom they were dealing? Should one treat the written agreement as no more than peripheral to the dealings and conclude that it does not override that presumption? I have concluded that the answer to these questions is "no".

177. . . . . Shogun put in place a system for concluding contracts that required both regulated and unregulated agreements to be entered into in writing in a form which provided essential information, including the identity of the parties to the agreement.

178. These considerations lead me to conclude that the correct approach in the present case is to treat the agreement as one concluded in writing and to approach the identification of the parties to that agreement as turning upon its construction. The particulars given in the agreement are only capable of applying to Mr Patel. It was the intention of the rogue that they should identify Mr Patel as the hirer. The hirer was so identified by Shogun. Before deciding to enter into the agreement they checked that Mr Patel existed and that he was worthy of credit. On that basis they decided to contract with him and with no one else. Mr Patel was the hirer under the agreement. As the agreement was concluded without his authority, it was a nullity. The rogue took no title under it and was in no position to convey any title to Mr Hudson.

179. For these reasons I would dismiss this appeal.

Lord Walker of Gestingthorpe:

'**180.** My Lords, I have had the advantage of reading in draft the opinion of my noble and learned friend, Lord Hobhouse of Woodborough. I agree with him that this appeal should be dismissed for the reasons given in his opinion. But because of the interest of this appeal, and the differing views among your Lordships, I wish to add some observations of my own. I begin with two general points.

181. A recurring theme in the authorities, starting with the very first sentence of the speech of Lord Cairns LC in *Cundy v Lindsay* 3 App Cas 459, 463, is the court's difficulty in deciding which of two innocent parties should bear the loss caused by the fraud of a third person (who may be beyond the reach of the law). Typically one innocent party is a seller who has parted with goods to a rogue, without obtaining payment in cash, and the other innocent party has bought the same goods from the rogue for cash. But although the court recognises both as innocent there is sometimes an inclination to regard the eventual buyer from the rogue as the more deserving of sympathy . . . But your Lordships have to lay down a general rule to cover the generality of cases, and it would not be right to make any general assumption as to one innocent party being more deserving than the other. That is especially true in this case which is concerned, not with a sale but with a hire-purchase transaction, and in which the issue to be decided is (as Lord Hobhouse has pointed out) ultimately a question of statutory construction.

183. The other general point is that (in agreement, I think, with all your Lordships) I regard the issue in this appeal as essentially a problem about offer and acceptance; and in determining whether or not a contract has been formed by offer and acceptance, the court adopts an objective approach, and does not inquire into what either party actually intended, but into the effect, objectively assessed, of what they said or wrote . . .

185. The principle to be applied in the case of face-to-face negotiations has sometimes been treated as an exception, but to my mind it is the best starting-point, as it exemplifies the simplest form of oral contract. The principle was first spelled out in England in *Phillips v Brooks Ltd* [1919] 2 KB 243, 247, following the Chief Justice of Massachusetts (Morton CJ) in *Edmunds v Merchants' Despatch Transportation* Co 135 Mass 283, 283–284:

> "The fact that the seller was induced to sell by fraud of the buyer made the sale voidable, but not void. He could not have supposed that he was selling to any other person; his intention was to sell to the person present, and identified by sight and hearing; it does not defeat the sale because the buyer assumed a false name or practised any other deceit to induce the vendor to sell."

The only case out of line with the principle is *Ingram v Little*. The reasoning in Devlin LJ's powerful dissenting judgment is in my view unanswerable. I consider that *Ingram v Little* was wrongly decided.

[His Lordship considered whether the principle should be viewed as a presumption or a rule of law and continued]

187. If the principle is no more than a presumption, it is a strong presumption, and exceptions to it would be rare (in *Ingram v Little* Devlin LJ himself, at p 67, was content to leave this point open). I would hesitate to state it as an inflexible rule (apart from cases of agency) because the notion of one individual impersonating another covers a wide range of factual situations (broadly corresponding to the wide range of meaning conveyed by saying that one person knows, or knows of, another). At one end of the spectrum is the confidence trickster who falsely but convincingly asserts that he is a baronet (or a barrister, or a brain surgeon) in order to inspire confidence and obtain credit. Then there are cases like *Phillips v Brooks Ltd* and *Ingram v Little*, where the rogue falsely gives the name and address of a real person whose existence the other party can and does check (but whom the other party does not actually know by sight, or the deception would fail). The most audacious form of impersonation would be where a rogue (such as the Tichborne claimant was held to be) attempts, face-to-face, to deceive a member of the family of which he claims to be part, or someone else personally acquainted with the individual whom the rogue is impersonating. Impersonation of that sort must be very rare indeed, and probably limited to deception of those whose senses are impaired (as Isaac was when, according to chapter 27 of Genesis, Jacob successfully impersonated his elder twin brother Esau). I would not exclude the possibility that impersonation of that sort might be outside the presumption . . .

188. I return to the question, which is of central importance to this appeal, whether (as Lord Nicholls and Lord Millett propose) the face-to-face principle should be applied much more generally. It may be that it should apply to an oral contract alleged to have been made on the telephone, where the parties are identified by hearing, although not by sight. An alleged oral contract made by telephone might be a case where the presumption applied, but was rebuttable. But to extend the principle to cases where the only contract was by written communication sent by post or by e-mail would be going far beyond identification by sight and hearing. Where there is an alleged contract reached by correspondence, offer and acceptance must be found, if they are to be found at all, in the terms of the documents . . .

191. [Turning to the facts of the present appeal] Shogun Finance had no doubt never heard of the real Mr Patel before the day on which the written contract was signed by the rogue, forging Mr Patel's signature. But by the time it accepted the written offer it had, by efficient information technology, confirmed that Mr Patel existed and had learned a good deal of relevant information about him, including his creditworthiness. The form of contract made quite clear that Shogun Finance's intention was to accept an offer made by the real Mr Patel, and no one else. The appellant's attempt to analyse the matter as a face-to-face contract (effected through the agency of the car salesman) was accepted by Sedley LJ but in my view it must fail, for the reasons stated by Lord Hobhouse . . .'

We will begin by considering a point on which their Lordships seemed to be in agreement. Both the majority and the dissenters agreed that the doctrine of unilateral mistake really concerns the question of whether, from an objective standpoint, there is correspondence of the offer and the acceptance. Lord Millett summarised the approach as follows:

'Whatever the medium of communication, a contract comes into existence if, on an objective appraisal of the facts, there is sufficient correlation between offer and acceptance to make it possible to say that the impostor's offer has been accepted by the person to whom it was addressed.'

The rules on unilateral mistake are designed to ascertain who it reasonably appears that the offer is being made to. The language of reasonableness is used because the approach to be applied is objective; looking at what the parties did rather than what they subjectively intended. It must be shown that the reasonable man would have realised: (1) that the offeror was mistaken; and (2) that the mistake meant that the offer was not intended to be open to him. Their Lordships were agreed that these were the questions that needed to be asked, but disagreed as to how they were to be answered.

Within the majority speeches there were two distinct approaches. Lord Phillips and Lord Walker upheld the traditional distinction between contracts concluded by face-to-face negotiations where the reasonable man would presume that the offer was intended to be open to him, and contracts concluded by written correspondence where the reasonable man would presume that the offer was only intended to be open to the named offeree. Lord Hobhouse was of the view that he did not even need to engage with this discussion. For him, the case was concerned only with the construction of a written document, which should be given certainty. Since the written contract named Mr Patel and purported to be an offer by Mr Patel, the claimant's acceptance could only relate to that offer. Parol evidence was inadmissible to contradict the terms of the written agreement. This emphasis on the written terms of the contract has since been noted by the Court of Appeal in *Dumford Trading AG v OAO Atlantrybflot* [2005] 1 Lloyd's Rep 289. Rix LJ said that *Shogun Finance* 'appears to emphasise the importance of construction of the written document even in matters of the identity of parties, and also to underline the danger of using extrinsic material in what is fundamentally the role of construction'.

With respect, it is submitted that Lord Hobhouse was wrong to believe that the case could be disposed of merely by reliance on the parole evidence rule. As Christopher Hare has noted ('Identity Mistakes: A Missed Opportunity' (2004) 67 MLR 993, 1006):

'Whilst commercial certainty generally demands that a written agreement should be taken at face value, the parole evidence rule is neither absolute in application nor without its critics. In particular, as Lord Nicholls suggested, the majority's application of the rule, completely ignored the fact that there had been a misrepresentation as to the identity of one of the contracting parties. It is uncontroversial that it must be possible to adduce evidence that an agreement was induced by a misrepresentation, even when that agreement has been reduced to writing.'

Lord Hobhouse's analysis does not help us to answer the crucial question: Would the reasonable man take the written name to refer to the rogue who assumed the name, or the person to whom the name truly refers?

Lord Nicholls and Lord Millett, dissenting, held that the distinction between written correspondence and face-to-face dealings was arbitrary and impossible to sustain. Lord Millett commented:

'If the offeree's words of acceptance are taken to be addressed to the physical person standing in his presence who made the offer, what is the position where they deal with each other by telephone? Is the disembodied voice to be equated with physical presence? Is it sufficient that the parties are in the hearing of each other? Does it make a difference if the dealing is by tele-visual link, so that the parties are in the hearing and sight but not the presence of each other? New means of communication make the distinction untenable.'

Their Lordships favoured a two-step approach involving two questions: (1) Did a contract come into existence at all? and (2) If so, was the contract vitiated by fraud or mistake? Lord Millett held that whatever the medium of communication, a contract is formed if, on an objective appraisal of the facts, there is sufficient correlation between offer and acceptance to make it possible to say that the rogue's offer has been accepted by the other party. Thus, while the majority held that the fraud prevented the contract from being formed, the minority held that the fraud merely rendered the contract voidable.

It is submitted that the minority's approach is to be preferred for a number of reasons. First, the distinction between written correspondence and face-to-face dealings is arbitrary and unworkable. Second, the minority's approach would remove the illogical distinction between misrepresentations as to identity, which are capable of preventing a contract from being formed (if the misrepresentation is in writing), and misrepresentations as to subject-matter, which will only render a contract voidable. Finally, the minority's approach would ensure a greater level of protection for third-party purchasers. This would surely be desirable because, as Lord Nicholls observed, 'the loss is more appropriately borne by the person who takes the risks inherent in parting with his goods without receiving payment.'

It seems that the majority did not share Lord Nicholls' concern that the purchaser should not be burdened with the loss (see also Phang, Lee and Koh, 'Mistaken Identity in the House of Lords' (2004) 63 CLJ 24, 26). Lord Walker cautioned that, 'your Lordships have to lay down a general rule to cover the generality of cases, and it would not be right to make any general assumption as to one innocent party being more deserving than the other'. Their Lordships considered that the trad-itional distinction between written contracts and oral contracts was sensible and ought to be retained. Given that this decision is unlikely to be revisited in the near future we are left with two further issues to consider. They both relate to the application of the majority's approach.

First, what forms of communication will constitute written correspondence? This is by no means an easy question to answer. The minority wrestled with the question and even Lord Phillips devoted six paragraphs ([173]–[178]) to considering whether the contract between Shogun and the rogue was concluded in writing. It seems that a contract concluded by fax falls within the definition of a written contract, but according to Lord Walker a contract made by telephone does not (at

[188]). What about a contract concluded by email, or text message, or over the internet (*Chwee Kin Keong v Digilandmall.com Pte Ltd* [2005] 1 SLR 502), or on interactive television? These are hard questions to answer, but guidance is needed if the majority's approach is to be applied to modern forms of communication.

The second point to consider is the position, post-*Shogun*, of contracts concluded by face-to-face negotiations. The majority held that there is a strong presumption that a contracting party intends to deal with the person who is physically present in front of him. This presumption is not easily rebutted. *Phillips v Brooks* and *Lewis v Averay* were cited with approval and *Ingram v Little* appears to have been dealt a fatal blow. Lord Millett declared that the case should be overruled (at [47]) and Lord Walker opined that it had been 'wrongly decided' (at [185]). Lord Nicholls and Lord Phillips were less forthright but both seemed to prefer the dissenting judgment of Devlin LJ (at [22] and [145], respectively). It therefore seems that the presumption will not be rebutted merely by evidence that the mistaken party did not intend to deal with the person physically present. Something more is needed. An example given by Lord Walker is the infamous case of Arthur Orton who impersonated Roger Tichborne in order to claim money from Roger's mother, Lady Tichborne. Such cases are, however, extremely rare.

10.4 MISTAKES THAT NULLIFY CONSENT

A common mistake is a mistake that is shared by both parties to the contract. It operates post-formation and provides a ground for having the contract set aside. The general rule is that a contract will be void for common mistake if the mistake is 'fundamental'. The clearest example of such a mistake is where the parties make a contract about an item that has ceased to exist at the time the contract is made. For example, if A agrees to sell to B his boat, which unknown to the parties has been wrecked in a crash the day before the contract was made, the agreement will be void for common mistake. There is valid consent, but the consent is nullified by the destruction of the subject matter of the contract.

The following case is frequently cited as a classic example of a contract void for common mistake although, as we will see, there are some doubts about the underlying basis for the decision.

Couturier v Hastie (1856) 5 HL Cas 673

Facts: The defendants agreed to sell a cargo of corn to the plaintiffs. At the time the contract was made both parties assumed that the cargo existed. In fact, one month earlier it had begun to deteriorate and the captain of the ship had unloaded and sold the corn to a third party. The plaintiff repudiated the contract and the defendant brought a claim against him for the price of the goods.

Held: The House of Lords affirmed the decision of the Court of Exchequer, holding that the plaintiffs were not obliged to pay for goods because they were not in existence at the time the contract was made.

The Lord Chancellor:

'I have no hesitation in advising your Lordships, and at once moving that the judgment of the Court below should be affirmed. It is hardly necessary, and it has not ordinarily been usual for your Lordships to go much into the merits of a judgment which is thus unanimously affirmed by the Judges who are called in to consider it, and to assist the House in forming its judgment. But I may state shortly that the whole question turns upon the construction of the contract which was entered into between the parties . . . [L]ooking to the contract itself alone, it appears to me clearly that what the parties contemplated, those who bought and those who sold, was that there was an existing something to be sold and bought, and if sold and bought, then the benefit of insurance should go with it . . . The contract plainly imports that there was something which was to be sold at the time of the contract, and something to be purchased. No such thing existing, I think the Court of Exchequer Chamber has come to the only reasonable conclusion upon it, and consequently that there must be judgment given by your Lordships for the Defendants in Error.'

The case has often been cited as authority that a contract entered into under a common mistake as to the existence of the subject matter is void. Indeed this was the interpretation placed on the case by the drafters of the Sale of Goods Act (SGA) 1893. Section 6 of the 1979 Act provides the following:

> Where there is a contract for the sale of specific goods, and the goods without the knowledge of the seller have perished at the time when the contract is made, the contract is void.

However, the Lord Chancellor did not declare the contract to be void in *Couturier v Hastie*. He merely said that the plaintiffs were not liable to pay the price of the cargo. Nor did he use the word 'mistake' in his speech. It is quite possible that the case was decided on a different basis altogether – after all his Lordship did expressly declare that 'the whole question turns upon the construction of the contract which was entered into between the parties'. Whatever the true basis for the decision in *Couturier v Hastie*, it is now clear, by virtue of the SGA 1979, that a contract will be void for common mistake if its subject matter has ceased to exist at the time when the contract is made.

10.4.1 SUBJECT MATTER NEVER EXISTED

Section 6 of the SGA 1979 appears to assume that the goods did at one time exist. It therefore seems that the section will not apply in a situation where the goods *never* in fact existed.

McRae v Commonwealth Disposals Commission (1951) 84 CLR 377

Facts: The Commission had invited tenders for a salvage operation in relation to an oil tanker, said to be 'lying on the Journmand Reef, which is approximately 100 miles north of Samarai'. The plaintiffs were successful in their tender, but on arrival discovered that neither the tanker nor the reef existed. The plaintiffs sought damages for breach of contract. The Commission claimed that the contract was void for mistake.

Held: The High Court of Australia held that the Commission was in breach of its contractual warranty that there was an oil tanker at the location.

Dixon and Fullagar JJ:

'. . . The first question to be determined is whether a contract was made between the plaintiffs and the Commission. The argument that the contract was void, or, in other words, that there was no contract, was based, as has been observed, on *Couturier v Hastie*. It is true that *Couturier v Hastie* has been commonly treated in the text-books as a case of a contract avoided by mutual mistake, and it is found cited in the company of such cases as *Gompertz v Bartlett* and *Strickland v Turner*. Section 7 of the English Sale of Goods Act 1893 is generally regarded as expressing the effect of the case. The case has not, however, been universally regarded as resting on mistake . . .

In considering *Couturier v Hastie* it is necessary to remember that it was, in substance, a case in which a vendor was suing for the price of goods which he was unable to deliver . . . [T]he vendor founded his claim on the provision for "payment upon handing over shipping documents". He was not called upon to prove a tender of the documents, because the defendant had "repudiated" the contract, but he was able and willing to hand them over, and his argument was, in effect, that by handing them over he would be doing all that the contract required of him. The question thus raised would seem to depend entirely on the construction of the contract, and it appears really to have been so treated throughout . . .

In the House of Lords . . . the Lord Chancellor, in giving judgment, said: "The whole question turns upon the meaning and construction of the contract". A little later he said: "What the parties contemplated. . . was that there was an existing something to be sold and bought, and, if sold and bought, then the benefit of insurance should go with it." In other words, there was not an absolute obligation to pay the price on delivery of the shipping documents (as the plaintiff contended), but an obligation to pay on delivery of those documents only if they represented at the time of the making of the contract goods in existence and capable of delivery . . .

671

The truth is that the question whether the contract was void, or the vendor excused from performance by reason of the non-existence of the supposed subject matter, did not arise in *Couturier v Hastie*. It would have arisen if the purchaser had suffered loss through non-delivery of the corn and had sued the vendor for damages. If it had so arisen, we think that the real question would have been whether the contract was subject to an implied condition precedent that the goods were in existence. Prima facie, one would think, there would be no such implied condition precedent, the position being simply that the vendor promised that the goods were in existence . . .

The position so far, then, may be summed up as follows. It was not decided in *Couturier v Hastie* that the contract in that case was void. The question whether it was void or not did not arise. If it had arisen, as in an action by the purchaser for damages, it would have turned on the ulterior question whether the contract was subject to an implied condition precedent. Whatever might then have been held on the facts of *Couturier v Hastie*, it is impossible in this case to imply any such term. The terms of the contract and the surrounding circumstances clearly exclude any such implication. The buyers relied upon, and acted upon, the assertion of the seller that there was a tanker in existence. It is not a case in which the parties can be seen to have proceeded on the basis of a common assumption of fact so as to justify the conclusion that the correct-ness of the assumption was intended by both parties to be a condition precedent to the creation of contractual obligations. The officers of the Commission made an assumption, but the plaintiffs did not make an assumption in the same sense. They knew nothing except what the Commission had told them. If they had been asked, they would certainly not have said: "Of course, if there is no tanker, there is no contract". They would have said: "We shall have to go and take possession of the tanker. We simply accept the Commission's assurance that there is a tanker and the Commis-sion's promise to give us that tanker." The only proper construction of the contract is that it included a promise by the Commission that there was a tanker in the position specified. The Commission contracted that there was a tanker there . . . If, on the other hand, the case of *Couturier v Hastie* and this case ought to be treated as cases raising a question of "mistake", then the Commission cannot in this case rely on any mistake as avoiding the contract, because any mistake was induced by the serious fault of their own servants, who asserted the existence of a tanker recklessly and without any reasonable ground. There was a contract, and the Commission con-tracted that a tanker existed in the position specified. Since there was no such tanker, there has been a breach of contract, and the plaintiffs are entitled to damages for that breach.

Before proceeding to consider the measure of damages, one other matter should be briefly mentioned. The contract was made in Melbourne, and it would seem that its proper law is Victorian law. Section 11 of the Victorian Goods Act 1928 corresponds to s 6 of the English Sale of Goods Act 1893, and provides that "where there is a contract for the sale of specific goods, and the goods without the knowledge of the seller have perished at the time when the contract is made the contract is void". This has been generally supposed to represent the legislature's view of the effect of *Couturier v Hastie*. Whether it correctly represents the effect of the decision in that case or not, it seems clear that the section has no application to the facts of the present case. Here the goods never existed, and the seller ought to have known that they did not exist.'

There are three points to note from the decision in *McRae*. First, the High Court of Australia did not accept that the decision in *Couturier v Hastie* was based on 'mistake'. The House of Lords merely concluded that the plaintiff was under no obligation to pay for the goods, which were not in existence at the time of the making of the contract. Second, the court held that the doctrine of mistake has no role to play where one party specifically promises that the subject matter of the contract exists. In such cases the other party may bring a claim for breach of that promise. Third, the court held that the Victorian equivalent of s 6 of the SGA did not apply to the facts of the case before them because the goods had in fact never existed. Section 6 only has application where the goods did once exist, but have since ceased to exist prior to the formation of the contract.

The second principle is important. On the facts of *McRae*, the plaintiff had undertaken an expensive salvage operation in reliance on the defendant's promise that there was an oil tanker on the Jourmand Reef. The defendant was in the best position to ascertain whether the tanker in fact existed and it seems appropriate in the circumstances to hold the defendant liable for the plaintiff's reliance losses. If the contract had been held to be void for mistake, the plaintiff would not have been able to recover.

A rather vexed question exists as to whether the *McRae* principle applies when the case falls under s 6 of the SGA, that is, in situations where the goods did at one time exist, but have since ceased to exist. Section 6 states that the contract is void and the section contains no provision for the parties to agree to the contrary. Professor Atiyah ('*Couturier v Hastie* and the sale of non-existent goods' (1957) 73 LQR 340, 348–349) has suggested that s 6 is merely a rule of construction which can be overturned by a contrary intention of the parties. This approach has the merit of bringing s 6 into line with the *McRae* principle and removing the illogical distinction between cases where the goods have perished and cases where they have never existed at all. Unfortunately, the approach appears to contradict the express wording of the section. While other provisions of the Act expressly state that they are subject to the contrary intention of the parties there is no such statement in s 6. Perhaps the only action open to a promisee in such a situation is a claim for negligent misrepresentation. Although damages for misrepresentation are assessed on a different basis to those for breach of contract, they would cover reliance losses like those suffered in *McRae*.

10.4.2 IMPOSSIBILITY OF PERFORMANCE

A contract may be void for common mistake if the parties believe that the contract is capable of performance when in fact it is not. Performance may be physically impossible, as in *Sheikh Bros Ltd v Ochsner* [1957] AC 136, where land was not capable of producing the quantity of sisal fibre contracted for. Alternatively, it may be legally impossible. In *Bell v Lever Bros* [1932] AC 161, 218 Lord Atkin gave the example of a contract for the sale of property which the purchaser already owns. Finally, the contract may be commercially impossible if the commercial object has been defeated (*Griffith v Brymer* (1903) 19 TLR 434). In such cases, it could be said that the mistake is as to the quality of the subject matter (see Treitel, G, *The Law of Contract*, 11th edn, 2003, p 288, London: Sweet & Maxwell), which brings us on to the next category of common mistake.

10.4.3 COMMON MISTAKE AS TO QUALITY

Will a contract be void for mistake if both parties are mistaken as to the quality of the subject matter? The leading House of Lords authority on the issue states that the contract will not be void unless the mistake renders the subject matter essentially different from the thing, as it was believed to be.

Bell v Lever Brothers Ltd [1932] AC 161

Facts: Lever Brothers employed Bell and Snelling to serve for five years as the chairman and vice-chairman of their subsidiary company, Niger. While acting in this capacity, Bell and Snelling entered into secret speculations in cocoa, a commodity in which the Niger Company dealt. This was a breach of their employment contracts and would have justified Lever Brothers terminating their contracts without compensation. Some time later, the Niger Company became amalgamated with another company, and the services of Bell and Snelling were no longer required. Unaware of the previous breaches of duty, Lever Brothers agreed to pay Bell and Snelling compensation of £30,000 and £20,000 respectively.

On discovering the breaches of duty Lever Brothers sought to recover the compensation they had paid. They claimed damages and rescission of the contract on the ground of fraudulent misrepresentation and, in the alternative, brought a claim for unilateral mistake induced by fraud. At trial, the jury found that Bell and Snelling had not been fraudulent. The trial judge, however, held that the compensation agreements were void, having been made under a mutual mistake (meaning 'common mistake') as to the legal relation between the parties, each party believing, contrary to the truth, that the one was entitled to claim and the other was bound to pay compensation.

Held: The House of Lords held (Viscount Haldane and Lord Warrington of Clyffe dissenting) that the compensation agreements were not void because the mistake was as to the quality of the service contracts.

Lord Warrington of Clyffe:

'It is in my opinion clear that each party believed that the remunerative offices, compensation for the loss of which was the subject of the negotiations, were offices which could not be determined except by the consent of the holder thereof, and further believed that the other party was under the same belief and was treating on that footing.

The real question, therefore, is whether the erroneous assumption on the part of both parties to the agreements that the service contracts were undeterminable except by agreement was of such a fundamental character as to constitute an underlying assumption without which the parties would not have made the contract they in fact made, or whether it was only a common error as to a material element, but one not going to the root of the matter and not affecting the substance of the consideration.

With the knowledge that I am differing from the majority of your Lordships, I am unable to arrive at any conclusion except that in this case the erroneous assumption was essential to the contract which without it would not have been made.

It is true that the error was not one as to the terms of the service agreements, but it was one which, having regard to the matter on which the parties were negotiating – namely, the terms on which the service agreements were to be prematurely determined and the compensation to be paid therefor, was in my opinion as fundamental to the bargain as any error one can imagine.

The compensation agreed to be paid was in each case the amount of the full salary for the two years and a half unexpired with the addition in Mr Bell's case of £10,000 and in Mr Snelling's of £5,000. It is difficult to believe that the jury were otherwise than correct in their answer to the second branch of the group of questions numbered 5 – namely, that had Levers known of the actings of the appellants in regard to the dealings in question they would not have made the agreements now impeached or either of them . . .'

Lord Atkin:

'Mistake as to quality of the thing contracted for raises . . . difficult questions. In such a case a mistake will not affect assent unless it is the mistake of both parties, and is as to the existence of some quality which makes the thing without the quality essentially different from the thing as it was believed to be. Of course it may appear that the parties contracted that the article should possess the quality which one or other or both mistakenly believed it to possess. But in such a case there is a contract and the inquiry is a different one, being whether the contract as to quality amounts to a condition or a warranty, a different branch of the law. The principles to be applied are to be found in two cases which, as far as my knowledge goes, have always been treated as authoritative expositions of the law. The first is *Kennedy v Panama Royal Mail Co* LR 2 QB 580, 586.

In that case the plaintiff had applied for shares in the defendant company on the faith of a prospectus which stated falsely but innocently that the company had a binding contract with the Government of New Zealand for the carriage of mails. On discovering the true facts the plaintiff brought an action for the recovery of the sums he had paid on calls. The defendants brought a cross action for further calls . . . The Court came to the conclusion in that case that, though there was a misapprehension as to that which was a material part of the motive inducing the applicant to ask for the shares, it did not prevent the shares from being in substance those he applied for.

The next case is *Smith v Hughes* LR 6 QB 597, 604, 606, the well known case as to new and old oats . . . The Court ordered a new trial. It is not quite clear whether they considered that if the defendant's contention was correct, the parties were not *ad idem* or there was a contractual condition that the oats sold were old oats. In either case the defendant would succeed in defeating the claim.

In these cases I am inclined to think that the true analysis is that there is a contract, but that the one party is not able to supply the very thing whether goods or services that the other party contracted to take; and therefore the contract is unenforceable by the one if executory, while if executed the other can recover back money paid on the ground of failure of the consideration.

We are now in a position to apply to the facts of this case the law as to mistake so far as it has been stated . . . Is an agreement to terminate a broken contract different in kind from an agreement to terminate an unbroken contract, assuming that the breach has given the one party the right to declare the contract at an end? I feel the weight of the plaintiffs' contention that a contract immediately determinable is a different thing from a contract for an unexpired term, and that the difference in kind can be illustrated by the immense price of release from the longer contract as compared with the shorter . . . But, on the whole, I have come to the conclusion that it would be wrong to decide that an agreement to terminate a definite specified contract is void if it turns out that the agreement had already been broken and could have been terminated otherwise. The contract released is the identical contract in both cases, and the party paying for release gets exactly what he bargains for. It seems immaterial that he could have got the same result in another way, or that if he had known the true facts he would not have entered into the bargain. A buys B's horse; he thinks the horse is sound and he pays the price of a sound horse; he would certainly not have bought the horse if he had known as the fact is that the horse is unsound. If B has made no representation as to soundness and has not contracted that the horse is sound, A is bound and cannot recover back the price. A buys a picture from B; both A and B believe it to be the work of an old master, and a high price is paid. It turns out to be a modern copy. A has no remedy in the absence of representation or warranty. A agrees to take on lease or to buy from B an unfurnished dwelling-house. The house is in fact uninhabitable. A would never have entered into the bargain if he had known the fact. A has no remedy, and the position is the same whether B knew the facts or not, so long as he made no representation or gave no warranty. A buys a roadside garage business from B abutting on a public thoroughfare: unknown to A, but known to B, it has already been decided to construct a bypass road which will divert substantially the whole of the traffic from passing A's garage. Again A has no remedy. All these cases involve hardship on A and benefit B., as most people would say, unjustly. They can be supported on the ground that it is of paramount importance that contracts should be observed, and that if parties honestly comply with the essentials of the formation of contracts – ie, agree in the same terms on the same subject-matter – they are bound, and must rely on the stipulations of the contract for protection from the effect of facts unknown to them.

This brings the discussion to the alternative mode of expressing the result of a mutual mistake. It is said that in such a case as the present there is to be implied a stipulation in the contract that a condition of its efficacy is that the facts should be as understood by both parties – namely, that the contract could not be terminated till the end of the current term . . . [I]f the contract expressly or impliedly contains a term that a particular assumption is a condition of the contract, the contract is avoided if the assumption is not true. But we have not advanced far on the inquiry how to ascertain whether the contract does contain such a condition. Various words are to be found to define the state of things which make a condition. "In the contemplation of both parties fundamental to the continued validity of the contract", "a foundation essential to its existence", "a fundamental reason for making it", are phrases found in the important judgment of Scrutton LJ in the present case. The first two phrases appear to me to be unexceptionable. They cover the case of a contract to serve in a particular place, the existence of which is fundamental to the service, or to procure the services of a professional vocalist, whose continued health is essential to performance. But "a fundamental reason for making a contract" may, with respect, be misleading. The reason of one party only is presumedly not intended, but in the cases I have suggested above, of the sale of a horse or of a picture, it might be said that the fundamental reason for making the contract was the belief of both parties that the horse was sound or the picture an old master, yet in neither case would the condition as I think exist. Nothing is more dangerous than to allow oneself liberty to construct for the parties contracts which they have not in terms made by importing implications which would appear to make the contract more businesslike or more just. The implications to be made are to be no more than are "necessary" for giving business efficacy to the transaction, and it appears to me that, both as to existing facts and future facts, a condition would not be implied unless the new state of facts makes the contract something different in kind from the contract in the original state of facts . . . We therefore get a common standard for mutual mistake, and implied conditions whether as to existing or as to future facts. Does the state of the new facts destroy the identity of the subject-matter as it was in the original state of facts? To apply the principle to the infinite combinations of facts that arise in actual experience will continue to be difficult, but if this case results in establishing order into what has been a somewhat confused and difficult branch of the law it will have served a useful purpose.'

Lord Atkin said that a contract will be void if the mistake is 'as to the existence of some quality which makes the thing without the quality essentially different from the thing as it was believed to be'. In most cases this test will not be satisfied. The examples given by Lord Atkin bear this out. We do well to note the example given of a picture mistakenly believed to be the work of an old master. Such a case came before the Court of Appeal for consideration in *Leaf v International Galleries* [1950] 2 KB 86. Their lordships held that the buyer's only remedy was for innocent misrepresentation (see Chapter 9).

On the facts of *Bell v Lever Brothers* it was held that the mistake was insufficient to render the contract void for mistake. Lever Brothers still received exactly what they had bargained for, the termination of the contracts with Bell and Snelling. It did not matter that the same result could have been achieved without having to pay compensation to the defendants. With respect, this reasoning is unconvincing. As Lord Atkin noted in his speech, Lever Brothers would not have entered into the agreement had they known of the true state of affairs. The mistake did not merely make the agreement less desirable; it made the agreement of such a nature that Lever Brothers would never have entered into it (see MacMillan, C, (2003) 119 LQR 625, 658). As Lord Warrington noted in his speech, the mistake was 'as fundamental to the bargain as any error one can imagine'.

Catherine MacMillan ('How Temptation Led to Mistake: an Explanation of *Bell v Lever Bros Ltd*' (2003) 119 LQR 625) has argued that *Bell v Lever Bros* was wrongly decided, largely as a result of the subsidiary nature of the mistake claim. She concludes as follows:

'An examination of the historical surrounding to the facts behind the case of *Bell v Lever Bros* reveals that the case is not the stable bedrock necessary to support a functioning doctrine of mistake. Some of the fractures appear in the speeches of the Law Lords. One fracture is the conduct of the case by Lever Brothers in amending their pleadings to allege conduct of a near criminal nature. That they were unable to prove these new allegations did not assist their case. This pleadings point reveals yet another fracture. *Bell v Lever Brothers* was a failed case of fraudulent misrepresentation and concealment. Mistake was pleaded in the alternative and left largely unaddressed during the conduct of the trial. The result was that the evidence in the case was not what it could have been. Indeed, the case did not become a mistake case until virtually the close of the proceedings at first instance. Another fracture is that counsel themselves found the mistake cases difficult to reconcile and apply. The consideration of mistake was, thus, not entirely desirable. Yet this is a hairline fracture running along an even greater fracture – that this was a case about conduct. The lawsuit was brought because of Bell and Snelling's conduct in carrying out personal cocoa trades. Cooper, as head of Lever Brothers, believed that it was impossible for a company that permitted such conduct to function. The problem presented by the conduct was what consequences should attend upon a misdeed committed by two senior managers who had also rendered invaluable services to their employers. Upon this point, different courts reached different conclusions. The ultimate conclusion should, however, be examined in light of the difficult facts of the case.

Bell and Snelling made a terrible mistake when they succumbed to temptation. There is no reason for the common law to perpetuate the legacy of this mistake by maintaining an overly rigid doctrine of contractual mistake. The application of the principles in *Bell v Lever Brothers* must be understood in light of, and limited by, the unfortunate circumstances of the case.'

Despite the problems with the decision in *Bell v Lever Brothers*, it was assumed for a long time that the House of Lords had closed the door on operative mistakes as to quality. Many years later, however, Steyn J confirmed that this was not the case.

Associated Japanese Bank (International) Ltd v Credit Du Nord SA [1989] 1 WLR 255

Facts: Bennett entered into a sale and lease back agreement with the plaintiff under which the plaintiff would purchase four specified packaging machines for £1 million. The defendant bank entered into a separate agreement with the plaintiff to guarantee Bennett's obligations under the leaseback agreement. Both banks believed that the machines were in existence at the time the contract was made. Bennett defaulted on the payments under the lease and the plaintiff sought to enforce the guarantee against the defendant. By this time it had been discovered that the machines did not in fact exist.

Held: The court held that on a true construction of the guarantee agreement there was an express condition precedent that the lease related to existing machines. Since the machines did not exist the guarantee could not be enforced against the defendant.

Steyn J:
'The landmark decision is undoubtedly *Bell v Lever Brothers Ltd*. Normally a judge of first instance would simply content himself with applying the law stated by the House of Lords. There has, however, been substantial controversy about the rule established in that case . . . Lord Atkin held, at p. 218:

"a mistake will not affect assent unless it is the mistake of both parties, and is as to the existence of some quality which makes the thing without the quality essentially different from the thing as it was believed to be."

In my view none of the other passages in Lord Atkin's speech detracts from that statement of the law . . . [I]n *Solle v Butcher* [1950] 1 KB 671, 693, Denning LJ interpreted *Bell v Lever Brothers Ltd* differently. He said that a common mistake, even on a most fundamental matter, does not make the contract void at law. That was an individual opinion. Neither Bucknill LJ (who agreed in the result) nor Jenkins LJ (who dissented) even mentioned *Bell v Lever Brothers Ltd* . . . With the profoundest respect to the former Master of the Rolls I am constrained to say that in my view his interpretation of *Bell v Lever Brothers Ltd* does not do justice to the speeches of the majority . . . In substance the argument was that the actual decision in *Bell v Lever Brothers Ltd* contradicts the language of the speeches. If the test was not satisfied there, so the argument runs, it is difficult to see how it could ever be satisfied . . . This is a point worth examining because at first glance it may seem persuasive . . . Lord Atkin clearly regarded it as a hard case on the facts, but concluded "on the whole", that the plea of common mistake must fail: see p 223. It is noteworthy that Lord Atkin commented upon the scarcity of evidence as to the subsidiaries from the boards of which the two employees resigned: see p 212. Lord Blanesburgh's speech was directed to his conclusion that the amendment ought not to be allowed. He did, however, make clear that "The mistake must go to the whole consideration", and pointed to the advantages (other than the release from the service agreements) which Lever Brothers received: see pp 197 and 181. Lord Blanesburgh emphasised that Lever Brothers secured the future co-operation of the two employees for the carrying through of the amalgamation: see p 181. And the burden, of course, rested squarely on Lever Brothers. With due deference to the distinguished authors, who have argued that the actual decision in *Bell v Lever Brothers Ltd* contradicts the principle enunciated in the speeches, it seems to me that their analysis is altogether too simplistic, and that the actual decision was rooted in the particular facts of the case. In my judgment there is no reason to doubt the substantive reasons emerging from the speeches of the majority . . .

It is clear, of course, that in this case both parties – the creditors and the guarantors – acted on the assumption that the lease related to existing machines. If they had been informed that the machines might not exist, neither the plaintiffs nor the defendants would for one moment have contemplated entering into the transaction. That by itself, I accept, is not enough to sustain the plea of common law mistake . . . The real question is whether the subject matter of the guarantee (as opposed to the sale and lease) was essentially different from what it was reasonably believed to be. The real security of the guarantors was the machines. The existence of the machines, being profit-earning chattels, made it more likely that the debtor would be able to service the debt. More importantly, if the debtor defaulted, and the creditors repossessed the machines the creditors had to give credit for 97½ per cent of the value of the machines. If the creditors sued the guarantors first, and the guarantors paid, the guarantors were entitled to be subrogated to the creditors' rights in respect of recovery against the debtor: see Goff and Jones, The Law of Restitution, 3rd edn (1986), p 533 et seq. No doubt the guarantors relied to some extent on the creditworthiness of Mr. Bennett. But I find that the prime security to which the guarantors looked was the existence of the four machines as described to both parties. For both parties the guarantee of obligations under a lease with non-existent machines was essentially different from a guarantee of a lease with four machines which both parties at the time of the contract believed to exist. The guarantee is an accessory contract. The non-existence of the subject matter of the principal contract is therefore of fundamental importance. Indeed the analogy of the classic *res extincta* cases, so much discussed in the authorities, is fairly close. In my judgment the stringent test of common law mistake is satisfied: the guarantee is void ab initio.'

This was not a contract where the subject matter had ceased to exist (*res extincta*) since the machines were not the subject matter of the guarantee. Rather the subject matter was a contract concerning the sale and leaseback of the machines, which was guaranteed, by the contract between the plaintiff and the defendant. Despite this, there was a strong analogy with the *res extincta* cases and Steyn J was satisfied that the nonexistence of the machines rendered the guarantee essentially different to that which the parties thought that they had agreed to.

It is thus clear that a mistake as to the quality of the subject matter of the contract can, in exceptional cases, give rise to an operative mistake. The scarcity of cases in which such a mistake has been found, however, indicates that mistake as to quality has a very limited role to play in English law. This has been confirmed by the most recent decision of the Court of Appeal on common mistake in *Great Peace Shipping Ltd v Tsavliris Salvage (International) Ltd*.

Great Peace Shipping Ltd v Tsavliris Salvage (International) Ltd ('The Great Peace') [2003] QB 679

Facts: The defendants agreed to provide salvage services for a vessel, the *Cape Providence*, which had suffered serious structural damage in the South Indian Ocean. They were given the names of four vessels reported to be in the area. The nearest was said to be the *Great Peace*, a vessel owned by the claimants, and believed to be about 35 miles away from the stricken vessel. The defendants contacted the claimants and agreed to hire the *Great Peace* for a minimum of five days to escort and stand by the *Cape Providence* for the purpose of saving life. It was discovered that the vessels were in fact 410 miles apart, not 35 miles as previously understood. Once a nearer vessel was found the claimants sought to avoid the contract for the *Great Peace* on the ground that it was void for common mistake – both parties believing at the time of entering into the contract that the vessels were in close proximity. At first instance, Toulson J gave judgment for the claimants.

Held: The Court of Appeal dismissed the appeal holding that the issue of whether there had been a common mistake turned on whether the mistake as to the distance between the two vessels had the effect that the service that the *Great Peace* was in a position to provide was essentially different from which the parties had agreed to. The fact that the defendants did not cancel the hire of the *Great Peace* until after another vessel had been obtained and the fact that the *Great Peace* would have arrived in time to provide several days of escort service demonstrated that performance of the contract had not been impossible. Accordingly, the contract was not void for common mistake and the defendants were liable to pay the cancellation fee.

Lord Phillips of Worth Matravers MR:

'**50.** It is generally accepted that the principles of the law of common mistake expounded by Lord Atkin in *Bell v Lever Bros Ltd* [1932] AC 161 were based on the common law . . . The first step is to identify the nature of the common law doctrine of mistake that was identified, or established, by *Bell v Lever Bros Ltd*.

51. Lord Atkin and Lord Thankerton were breaking no new ground in holding void a contract where, unknown to the parties, the subject matter of the contract no longer existed at the time that the contract was concluded. The Sale of Goods Act 1893 (56 & 57 Vict c 71) was a statute which set out to codify the common law. Section 6, to which Lord Atkin referred, provided: "When there is a contract for the sale of specific goods, and the goods without the knowledge of the seller have perished at the time when the contract is made, the contract is void".

52. Judge Chalmers, the draftsman of the Act, commented in the first edition of his book on the Act, The Sale of Goods Act 1893 (1894), p 17: "The rule may be based either on the ground of mutual mistake, or on the ground of impossibility of performance".

55. Where that which is expressly identified as the subject of a contract does not exist, the contract will necessarily be one which cannot be performed. Such a situation can readily be identified. The position is very different where there is "a mistake as to the existence of some quality of the subject matter which makes the thing without the quality essentially different from the thing as it was believed to be". In such a situation it may be possible to perform the letter of the contract. In support of the proposition that a contract is void in such circumstances, Lord Atkin cited two authorities, in which he said that the principles to be applied were to be found. The first was Lord Kennedy v Panama, New Zealand and Australian Royal Mail Co Ltd LR 2 QB 580 . . .

60. The other case to which Lord Atkin referred was *Smith v Hughes* (1871) LR 6 QB 597. On no view did that difficult case deal with common mistake and we are not able to see how it supported the test formulated by Lord Atkin, as set out at paragraph 47 above. Indeed, Lord Atkin himself commented [1932] AC 161, 222: "In these cases I am inclined to think that the true analysis is that there is a contract, but that the one party is not able to supply the very thing whether goods or services that the other party contracted to take; and therefore the contract is unenforceable by the one if executory, while if executed the other can recover back money paid on the ground of failure of the consideration."

61. We conclude that the two authorities to which Lord Atkin referred provided an insubstantial basis for his formulation of the test of common mistake in relation to the quality of the subject matter of a contract. Lord Atkin advanced an alternative basis for his test: the implication of a term of the same nature as that which was applied under the doctrine of frustration, as it was then understood. In so doing he adopted the analysis of Scrutton LJ in the Court of Appeal. It seems to us that this was a more solid jurisprudential basis for the test of common mistake that Lord Atkin was proposing. At the time of *Bell v Lever Bros Ltd* [1932] AC 161 the law of frustration and common mistake had advanced hand in hand on the foundation of a common principle. Thereafter frustration proved a more fertile ground for the development of this principle than common mistake, and consideration of the development of the law of frustration assists with the analysis of the law of common mistake . . .

[His Lordship then discussed various cases on frustration]

73. What do these developments in the law of frustration have to tell us about the law of common mistake? First that the theory of the implied term is as unrealistic when considering common mistake as when considering frustration. Where a fundamental assumption upon which an agreement is founded proves to be mistaken, it is not realistic to ask whether the parties impliedly agreed that in those circumstances the contract would not be binding. The avoidance of a contract on the ground of common mistake results from a rule of law under which, if it transpires that one or both of the parties have agreed to do something which it is impossible to perform, no obligation arises out of that agreement.

74. In considering whether performance of the contract is impossible, it is necessary to identify what it is that the parties agreed would be performed. This involves looking not only at the express terms, but at any implications that may arise out of the surrounding circumstances. In some cases it will be possible to identify details of the "contractual adventure" which go beyond the terms that are expressly spelt out, in others it will not.

75. Just as the doctrine of frustration only applies if the contract contains no provision that covers the situation, the same should be true of common mistake. If, on true construction of the contract, a party warrants that the subject matter of the contract exists, or that it will be possible to perform the contract, there will be no scope to hold the contract void on the ground of common mistake.

76. [T]he following elements must be present if common mistake is to avoid a contract: (i) there must be a common assumption as to the existence of a state of affairs; (ii) there must be no warranty by either party that that state of affairs exists; (iii) the non-existence of the state of affairs must not be attributable to the fault of either party; (iv) the non-existence of the state of affairs must render performance of the contract impossible; (v) the state of affairs may be the existence, or a vital attribute, of the consideration to be provided or circumstances which must subsist if performance of the contractual adventure is to be possible.

77. The second and third of these elements are well exemplified by the decision of the High Court of Australia in *McRae v Commonwealth Disposals Commission* (1951) 84 CLR 377 . . .

82. [W]hile we do not consider that the doctrine of common mistake can be satisfactorily explained by an implied term, an allegation that a contract is void for common mistake will often raise important issues of construction. Where it is possible to perform the letter of the contract, but it is alleged that there was a common mistake in relation to a fundamental assumption which renders performance of the essence of the obligation impossible, it will be necessary, by construing the contract in the light of all the material circumstances, to decide whether this is indeed the case . . .

84. Once the court determines that unforeseen circumstances have, indeed, resulted in the contract being impossible of performance, it is next necessary to determine whether, on true construction of the contract, one or other party has undertaken responsibility for the subsistence of the assumed state of affairs. This is another way of asking whether one or other party has undertaken the risk that it may not prove possible to perform the contract, and the answer to this question may well be the same as the answer to the question of whether the impossibility of performance is attributable to the fault of one or other of the parties.

85. Circumstances where a contract is void as a result of common mistake are likely to be less common than instances of frustration. Supervening events which defeat the contractual adventure will frequently not be the responsibility of either party. Where, however, the parties agree that something shall be done which is impossible at the time of making the agreement, it is much more likely that, on true construction of the agreement, one or other will have undertaken responsibility for the mistaken state of affairs. This may well explain why cases where contracts have been found to be void in consequence of common mistake are few and far between . . .

90. [In *Associated Japanese Bank (International) Ltd v Credit Du Nord SA* [1989] 1 WLR 255] Steyn J . . . after reviewing the authorities on common mistake . . . reached the following formulation of the law, at p 268:

> "The first imperative must be that the law ought to uphold rather than destroy apparent contracts. Secondly, the common law rules as to a mistake regarding the quality of the subject matter, like the common law rules regarding commercial frustration, are designed to cope with the impact of unexpected and wholly exceptional circumstances on apparent contracts. Thirdly, such a mistake in order to attract legal consequences must substantially be shared by both parties, and must relate to facts as they existed at the time the contract was made. Fourthly, and this is the point established by *Bell v Lever Bros Ltd* [1932] AC 161, the mistake must render the subject matter of the contract essentially and radically different from the subject matter which the parties believed to exist. While the civilian distinction between the substance and attributes of the subject matter of a contract has played a role in the development of our law (and was cited in speeches in *Bell v Lever Bros Ltd*), the principle enunciated in *Bell v Lever Bros Ltd* is markedly narrower in scope than the civilian doctrine. It is therefore no longer useful to invoke the civilian distinction. The principles enunciated by Lord Atkin and Lord Thankerton represent the ratio decidendi of *Bell v Lever Bros Ltd*. Fifthly, there is a requirement which was not specifically discussed in *Bell v Lever Bros Ltd*. What happens if the party, who is seeking to rely on the mistake, had no reasonable grounds for his belief? An extreme example is

that of the man who makes a contract with minimal knowledge of the facts to which the mistake relates but is content that it is a good speculative risk. In my judgment a party cannot be allowed to rely on a common mistake where the mistake consists of a belief which is entertained by him without any reasonable grounds for such belief: cf *McRae v Commonwealth Disposals Commissions* 84 CLR 377, 408. That is not because principles such as estoppel or negligence require it, but simply because policy and good sense dictate that the positive rules regarding common mistake should be so qualified."

91. The detailed analysis that we have carried out leads us to concur in this summary, subject to the proviso that the result in *McRae's* case can, we believe, be explained on the basis of construction, as demonstrated above. In agreeing with the analysis of Steyn J, we recognise that it is at odds with comments that Lord Denning MR made on more than one occasion about *Bell v Lever Bros Ltd* [1932] AC 161 to the effect that "a common mistake, even on a most fundamental matter, does not make a contract void at law" . . .

94. Our conclusions have marched in parallel with those of Toulson J. We admire the clarity with which he has set out his conclusions, which emphasise the importance of a careful analysis of the contract and of the rights and obligations created by it as an essential precursor to consideration of the effect of an alleged mistake. We agree with him that, on the facts of the present case, the issue in relation to common mistake turns on the question of whether the mistake as to the distance apart of the two vessels had the effect that the services that the *Great Peace* was in a position to provide were something essentially different from that to which the parties had agreed. We shall defer answering that question until we have considered whether principles of equity provide a second string to the defendants' bow . . .

162. We revert to the question that we left unanswered at paragraph 94. It was unquestionably a common assumption of both parties when the contract was concluded that the two vessels were in sufficiently close proximity to enable the *Great Peace* to carry out the service that she was engaged to perform. Was the distance between the two vessels so great as to confound that assumption and to render the contractual adventure impossible of performance? If so, the defendants would have an arguable case that the contract was void under the principle in *Bell v Lever Bros Ltd* [1932] AC 161.

163. Toulson J addressed this issue, at para 56:

"Was the *Great Peace* so far away from the *Cape Providence* at the time of the contract as to defeat the contractual purpose – or in other words to turn it into something essentially different from that for which the parties bargained? This is a question of fact and degree, but in my view the answer is No. If it had been thought really necessary, the *Cape Providence* could have altered course so that both vessels were heading toward each other. At a closing speed of 19 knots, it would have taken them about 22 hours to meet. A telling point is the reaction of the defendants on learning the true positions of the vessels. They did not want to cancel the agreement until they knew if they could find a nearer vessel to assist. Evidently the defendants did not regard the contract as devoid of purpose, or they would have cancelled at once." . . .

165. . . . This reaction was a telling indication that the fact that the vessels were considerably further apart than the defendants had believed did not mean that the services that the *Great Peace* was in a position to provide were essentially different from those which the parties had envisaged when the contract was concluded. The *Great Peace* would arrive in time to provide several days of escort service. The defendants would have wished the contract to be performed but for the adventitious arrival on the scene of a vessel prepared to perform the same services. The fact that the vessels were further apart than both parties had appreciated did not mean that it was impossible to perform the contractual adventure.

166. The parties entered into a binding contract for the hire of the *Great Peace*. That contract gave the defendants an express right to cancel the contract subject to the obligation to pay the "cancellation fee" of five days' hire. When they engaged the *Nordfarer* they cancelled the *Great Peace*. They became liable in consequence to pay the cancellation fee. There is no injustice in this result.

167. For the reasons that we have given, we would dismiss this appeal.'

The Court of Appeal took the opportunity to review the whole basis for the doctrine of common mistake. In *Bell v Lever Bros*, Lord Atkin had spoken of implied terms as 'the alternative mode of expressing the result of a mutual [common] mistake' (see final paragraph of extract above). Some commentators (see Slade, 'The Myth of Mistake' (1954) 70 LQR 386; Collins, *The Law of Contract*, 4th edn, 2003, London: Lexis-Nexis, at p 125) have relied on these dicta to argue that an independent doctrine of common mistake is a 'myth'. All the cases, they argue, can be reanalysed as involving an implied condition precedent that the contract will not be enforceable unless a particular circumstance or state of affairs exists. The Court of Appeal in *Great Peace* rejected this view. Lord Phillips MR emphasised that cases of common mistake were analogous to cases of frustration (where the implied term theory has been rejected – see *Davis Contractors Ltd v Fareham UDC* [1956] 2 All ER 145). They both relate to the occurrence of unforeseen circumstances that render the contract impossible to perform. The difference lies in the timing of the event. His lordship reasoned 'that the theory of the implied term is as unrealistic when considering common mistake as when considering frustration' (at [73]). Both doctrines, Lord Phillips insisted, rely on an independent rule of law that a contract will not be enforceable if its performance is impossible.

In [76], Lord Phillips set out the requirements for common mistake. Requirement (i) is straightforward and merely states that there must be a common assumption as to the existence of a state of affairs. This will be easy to establish.

Requirements (ii) and (iii) are derived from *McRae v Commonwealth Commission* (see above). The court must decide, as a question of construction, whether one of the parties has expressly or impliedly taken the risk of the assumption being mistaken. If they have, the contract will not be void for mistake. Lord Phillips noted that the circumstances where a contract will be void for common mistake are likely to be less common than instances of frustration (at [85]). This is because cases of common mistake involve events existing at the time of contracting. It is much easier to allocate the risk of one of these events occurring than it is to allocate the risk of a subsequent event, which is far harder to predict. Lord Phillips gave no opinion as to whether requirement (ii) applies to cases falling under s 6 of the SGA 1979 (requirement (iii) is explicit in the wording of the section). In his silence on the issue, we must assume that the current understanding of the section (see above) remains unchanged.

The reference to 'impossibility' in requirement (iv) may be rather misleading. Although there is some support for the view that the contract will only be void if performance is literally impossible (see *Brennan v Bolt Burdon* [2005] 1 QB 303, 314 per Kay LJ; *EIC Services Ltd v Phipps* [2005] 1 WLR 1377), the statement in *Great Peace* must be read in light of the analogies that the court was drawing with the doctrine of frustration. In the law of frustration, it is only necessary to show that performance in the circumstances would be something essentially different from that to which the parties had agreed. As Chandler, Devenney and Poole have noted ('Common Mistake: Theoretical Justification and Remedial Inflexibility' [2004] JBL 34, 47), the frustration cases demonstrate that, in determining the 'impossibility' issue, the courts will be influenced by the 'justice' of the case. Such considerations seem to have influenced the mind of Lord Phillips as well since he concluded his judgment with the words: 'There is no injustice in this result' (at [166]). Furthermore, the Court of Appeal's treatment of mistakes as to quality suggests that something less than literal impossibility is sufficient. Requirement (v) refers to a 'vital attribute', which may not have existence. This clearly extends the doctrine of common mistake beyond the *res extincta* cases. The Court of Appeal also approved of the decision in *Associated Japanese Bank*, where Steyn J recognised that there could be a common mistake as to quality if the mistake was such as to render the subject matter 'essentially and radically different' from that which the parties believed to exist (see the recent affirmation of this test in *Kyle Bay Limited v Underwriters Subscribing Under Policy No. 019057/08/01* [2006] EWHC 607 (Comm) at [43]). It is therefore clear that the 'impossibility' requirement does not preclude the recognition of common mistakes as to quality in exceptional cases.

10.5 MISTAKE IN EQUITY

From the above commentary it is apparent that the common law rules for identifying an operative common mistake are both inflexible and restrictive. In *Solle v Butcher* [1950] 1 KB 671, Denning LJ sought to avoid the inflexibility of the traditional rules by claiming that *Bell v Lever Brothers* was only authority on the scope of the common law doctrine of mistake. He claimed that there was a much more flexible doctrine of mistake in equity, which could be applied to the facts of the case before him.

Solle v Butcher [1950] 1 KB 671

Facts: The plaintiff let a flat from the defendant at a rent of £250 per year. Both the parties believed that the flat was not subject to control under the Rent Restriction Acts, and that accordingly £250 was a legal rent. Later it was discovered that the flat was in fact controlled by the Rent Restriction Acts and that the maximum legal rent was £140 per year. The plaintiff brought proceedings in the country court for a declaration that the standard rent of the flat was £140 per year. The defendant claimed that the lease should be rescinded on the ground of common mistake of fact. The trial judge held that there had been no mistake of fact, though possibly there had been one of law since both parties imagined that the Rent Restriction Acts did not apply.

Held: The Court of Appeal held (Jenkins LJ dissenting) that judgment should be given for the defendant on terms that the plaintiff must elect between rescission and paying the full rent.

Denning LJ

'It is quite plain that the parties were under a mistake. They thought that the flat was not tied down to a controlled rent, whereas in fact it was. In order to see whether the lease can be avoided for this mistake it is necessary to remember that mistake is of two kinds: first, mistake which renders the contract void, that is, a nullity from the beginning, which is the kind of mistake which was dealt with by the courts of common law; and, secondly, mistake which renders the contract not void, but voidable, that is, liable to be set aside on such terms as the court thinks fit, which is the kind of mistake which was dealt with by the courts of equity. Much of the difficulty which has attended this subject has arisen because, before the fusion of law and equity, the courts of common law, in order to do justice in the case in hand, extended this doctrine of mistake beyond its proper limits and held contracts to be void which were really only voidable, a process which was capable of being attended with much injustice to third persons who had bought goods or otherwise committed themselves on the faith that there was a contract. In the well-known case of *Cundy v Lindsay*, Cundy suffered such an injustice. He bought the handkerchiefs from the rogue, Blenkarn, before the Judicature Acts came into operation. Since the fusion of law and equity, there is no reason to continue this process, and it will be found that only those contracts are now held void in which the mistake was such as to prevent the formation of any contract at all.

Let me first consider mistakes which render a contract a nullity. All previous decisions on this subject must now be read in the light of *Bell v Lever Bros Ltd*. The correct interpretation of that case, to my mind, is that, once a contract has been made, that is to say, once the parties, whatever their inmost states of mind, have to all outward appearances agreed with sufficient certainty in the same terms on the same subject matter, then the contract is good unless and until it is set aside for failure of some condition on which the existence of the contract depends, or for fraud, or on some equitable ground. Neither party can rely on his own mistake to say it was a nullity from the beginning, no matter that it was a mistake which to his mind was fundamental, and no matter that the other party knew that he was under a mistake. *A fortiori*, if the other party did not know of the mistake, but shared it. The cases where goods have perished at the time of sale, or belong to the buyer, are really contracts which are not void for mistake but are void by reason of an implied condition precedent, because the contract proceeded on the basic assumption that it was possible of performance . . .

Applying these principles, it is clear that here there was a contract. The parties agreed in the same terms on the same subject-matter. It is true that the landlord was under a mistake which was to him fundamental: he would not for one moment have considered letting the flat for seven years if it meant that he could only charge 140 a year for it. He made the fundamental mistake of believing that the rent he could charge was not tied down to a controlled rent; but, whether it was his own mistake or a mistake common to both him and the tenant, it is not a ground for saying that the lease was from the beginning a nullity. Any other view would lead to remarkable results, for it would mean that, in the many cases where the parties mistakenly think a house is outside the Rent Restriction Acts when it is really within them, the tenancy would be a nullity, and the tenant would have to go; with the result that the tenants would not dare to seek to have their rents reduced to the permitted amounts lest they should be turned out.

Let me next consider mistakes which render a contract voidable, that is, liable to be set aside on some equitable ground. Whilst presupposing that a contract was good at law, or at any rate not void, the court of equity would often relieve a party from the consequences of his own mistake, so long as it could do so without injustice to third parties. The court, it was said, had power to set aside the contract whenever it was of opinion that it was unconscientious for the other party to avail himself of the legal advantage which he had obtained: *Torrance v Bolton* (1872) LR 8 Ch 118, 124, *per* James LJ.

The court had, of course, to define what it considered to be unconscientious, but in this respect equity has shown a progressive development. It is now clear that a contract will be set aside if the mistake of the one party has been induced by a material misrepresentation of the other, even though it was not fraudulent or fundamental; or if one party, knowing that the other is mistaken about the terms of an offer, or the identity of the person by whom it is made, lets him remain under his delusion and concludes a contract on the mistaken terms instead of pointing out the mistake. That is, I venture to think, the ground on which the defendant in *Smith v Hughes* would be exempted nowadays, and on which, according to the view by Blackburn J of the facts, the contract in *Lindsay v Cundy*, was voidable and not void; and on which the lease in *Sowler v Potter* [1940] 1 KB 271, was, in my opinion, voidable and not void.

A contract is also liable in equity to be set aside if the parties were under a common misapprehension either as to facts or as to their relative and respective rights, provided that the misapprehension was fundamental and that the party seeking to set it aside was not himself at fault . . .

The principle so established by *Cooper v Phibbs* (1867) LR 2 HL 149 has been repeatedly acted on . . .

Applying that principle to this case, the facts are that the plaintiff, the tenant, was a surveyor who was employed by the defendant, the landlord, not only to arrange finance for the purchase of the building and to negotiate with the rating authorities as to the new rateable values, but also to let the flats. He was the agent for letting, and he clearly formed the view that the building was not controlled. He told the valuation officer so. He advised the defendant what were the rents which could be charged. He read to the defendant an opinion of counsel relating to the matter, and told him that in his opinion he could charge £250 and that there was no previous control. He said that the flats came outside the Act and that the defendant was "clear". The defendant relied on what the plaintiff told him, and authorized the plaintiff to let at the rentals which he had suggested. The plaintiff not only let the four other flats to other people for a long period of years at the new rentals, but also took one himself for seven years at £250 a year. Now he turns round and says, quite unashamedly, that he wants to take advantage of the mistake to get the flat at £140 a year for seven years instead of the £250 a year, which is not only the rent he agreed to pay but also the fair and economic rent; and it is also the rent permitted by the Acts on compliance with the necessary formalities. If the rules of equity have become so rigid that they cannot remedy such an injustice, it is time we had a new equity, to make good the omissions of the old. But, in my view, the established rules are amply sufficient for this case . . .

Cooper v Phibbs affords ample authority for saying that, by reason of the common misapprehension, this lease can be set aside on such terms as the court thinks fit . . . In the ordinary way, of course, rescission is only granted when the parties can be restored to substantially the same position as that in which they were before the contract was made; but, as Lord Blackburn said in *Erlanger v New Sombrero Phosphate Co* (1878) 3 App. Cas. 1218, 1278–9: "The practice has always been for a court of equity to give this relief whenever, by the exercise of its powers, it can do what is practically just, though it cannot restore the parties precisely to the state they were in before the contract". That indeed was what was done in *Cooper v Phibbs*. Terms were imposed so as to do what was practically just. What terms then, should be imposed here?

If the lease were set aside without any terms being imposed, it would mean that the plaintiff, the tenant, would have to go out and would have to pay a reasonable sum for

> his use and occupation ... I think that this court should follow these examples and should impose terms which will enable the tenant to choose either to stay on at the proper rent or to go out.'

The Court of Appeal held that there was a wider and more flexible doctrine of mistake in equity. It was wider in its scope in that it applied to mistakes that would not be operative at common law and it was more flexible in its effect. Not only did it render the contract voidable rather than void, but it also permitted the court to order rescission on terms, as the Court of Appeal in fact did on the facts of *Solle v Butcher*.

The doctrine of equitable mistake was accepted by the High Court and the Court of Appeal in numerous subsequent cases (*Rose v Pim* [1953] 2 QB 450; *Grist v Bailey* [1967] Ch 532l; *Magee v Pennine Insurance* [1969] 2 QB 507; *William Sindall Plc v Cambridgeshire CC* [1994] 1 WLR 1016; *Nutt v Read* [2000] 32 HLR 761; *Clarion Ltd v National Provident Institution* [2000] 1 WLR 1888; *West Sussex Properties Ltd v Chichester DC* [2000] NPC 74). It was never really clear, however, why the rules that apply to mistake in equity should be different to those that apply to mistake at law. Furthermore, it was difficult to reconcile *Solle v Butcher* with the decision of the House of Lords in *Bell v Lever Brothers*. If equity allows a broader range of mistakes to lead to the setting aside of a contract, why was this not even discussed in *Bell v Lever Bros*? Indeed, given that none of the usual bars to rescission applied in that case, why didn't the House of Lords set aside the contract between Bell and Lever Brothers on the ground of equitable mistake? A further problem exists as to the scope of mistake in equity. Denning LJ said that the mistake has to be 'fundamental', but this is the same terminology as the House of Lords used to describe common law mistake in *Bell v Lever Brothers*. When is a mistake fundamental enough to be operative in equity but not sufficiently fundamental to be operative at common law? There is no easy answer to this question and, as a result, the scope of equitable mistake has proved impossible to determine (see *Associated Japanese Bank (International) Ltd v Credit Du Nord SA* [1989] 1 WLR 255, 268 per Steyn J; *William Sindall Plc v Cambridgeshire CC* [1994] 1 WLR 1016, 1042 per Evans LJ; *Clarion Ltd v National Provident Institution* [2000] 1 WLR 1888, 1904 per Rimer J).

In *Great Peace Shipping*, the Court of Appeal took the opportunity to review the law on equitable mistake. Lord Phillips considered the cases prior to *Bell v Lever Brothers*, focusing particularly on the decision of the House of Lords in *Cooper v Phibbs* (1867) LR 2 HL. He then considered the effect of *Bell v Lever Brothers* on mistake in equity.

Great Peace Shipping Ltd v Tsavliris Salvage (International) Ltd ('The Great Peace') [2003] QB 679

Lord Phillips of Worth Matravers MR

'113. In the House of Lords [1932] AC 161 the report shows that the appellants relied on both common law authorities and *Cooper v Phibbs* LR 2 HL 149 in support of the submission that a common mistake had to be as to the existence of the subject matter of the contract if it was to render it void. The respondents do not appear to have suggested that equity might provide relief where common law would not . . .

114. Lord Blanesburgh, when considering the pleadings, remarked [1932] AC 161, 190: "the claim made by the heads of claim is for rescission of the agreements of settlement, relief properly consequent upon a case of voidability either for fraud or unilateral mistake induced by fraud. But if the allegation, even alternative, was that the agreements were entered into under mutual mistake of fact, then these agreements were not voidable but void ab initio, and no order on that footing is even hinted at in the relief sought" . . .

116. Lord Atkin, at p 218, cited *Cooper v Phibbs* LR 2 HL 149 as an example of mistake as to the subject matter of the contract: "This is the case of *Cooper v Phibbs*, where A agreed to take a lease of a fishery from B, though contrary to the belief of both parties at the time A was tenant for life of the fishery and B appears to have had no title at all. To such a case Lord Westbury applied the principle that if parties contract under a mutual mistake and misapprehension as to their relative and respective rights the result is that the agreement is liable to be set aside as having proceeded upon a common mistake. Applied to the context the statement is only subject to the criticism that the agreement would appear to be void rather than voidable" . . .

118. These passages demonstrate that the House of Lords in *Bell v Lever Brothers* [1932] AC 161 considered that the intervention of equity, as demonstrated in *Cooper v Phibbs* LR 2 HL 149, took place in circumstances where the common law would have ruled the contract void for mistake. We do not find it conceivable that the House of Lords overlooked an equitable right in Lever Bros to rescind the agreement, notwithstanding that the agreement was not void for mistake at common law. The jurisprudence established no such right. Lord Atkin's test for common mistake that avoided a contract, while narrow, broadly reflected the circumstances where equity had intervened to excuse performance of a contract assumed to be binding in law.'

[Having concluded that the House of Lords in *Bell v Lever Brothers* considered that the intervention of equity only took place in circumstances where the common law would have ruled the contract void for mistake, Lord Phillips moved on to consider *Solle v Butcher* and the line of cases flowing from it.]

'153. A number of cases, albeit a small number, in the course of the last 50 years have purported to follow *Solle v Butcher* [1950] 1 KB 671, yet none of them defines the test of mistake that gives rise to the equitable jurisdiction to rescind in a manner that distinguishes this from the test of a mistake that renders a contract void in law, as identified in *Bell v Lever Bros Ltd* [1932] AC 161. This is, perhaps, not surprising, for Denning LJ, the author of the test in *Solle v Butcher*, set *Bell v Lever Bros Ltd* at nought. It is possible to reconcile *Solle v Butcher* and *Magee v Pennine Insurance Co Ltd* [1969] 2 QB 507 with *Bell v Lever Bros Ltd* only by postulating that there are two categories of mistake, one that renders a contract void at law and one that renders it voidable in equity. Although later cases have proceeded on this basis, it is not possible to identify that proposition in the judgment of any of the three Lords Justices, Denning, Bucknill and Fenton Atkinson, who participated in the majority decisions in the former two cases. Nor, over 50 years, has it proved possible to define satisfactorily two different qualities of mistake, one operating in law and one in equity.

154. In *Solle v Butcher* Denning LJ identified the requirement of a common misapprehension that was "fundamental", and that adjective has been used to describe the mistake in those cases which have followed *Solle v Butcher*. We do not find it possible to distinguish, by a process of definition, a mistake which is "fundamental" from Lord Atkin's mistake as to quality which "makes the thing [contracted for] essentially different from the thing [that] it was believed to be": [1932] AC 161, 218.

155. A common factor in *Solle v Butcher* and the cases which have followed it can be identified. The effect of the mistake has been to make the contract a particularly bad bargain for one of the parties. Is there a principle of equity which justifies the court in rescinding a contract where a common mistake has produced this result? . . .

156. [T]he premise of equity's intrusion into the effects of the common law is that the common law rule in question is seen in the particular case to work injustice, and for some reason the common law cannot cure itself. But it is difficult to see how that can apply here. Cases of fraud and misrepresentation, and undue influence, are all catered for under other existing and uncontentious equitable rules. We are *only* concerned with the question whether relief might be given for common mistake in circumstances wider than those stipulated in *Bell v Lever Bros Ltd* [1932] AC 161. But that, surely, is a question as to where the common law should draw the line; not whether, given the common law rule, it needs to be mitigated by application of some other doctrine. The common law has drawn the line in *Bell v Lever Bros Ltd*. The effect of *Solle v Butcher* [1950] 1 KB 671 is not to supplement or mitigate the common law: it is to say that *Bell v Lever Bros Ltd* was wrongly decided.

157. Our conclusion is that it is impossible to reconcile *Solle v Butcher* with *Bell v Lever Bros Ltd*. The jurisdiction asserted in the former case has not developed. It has been a fertile source of academic debate, but in practice it has given rise to a handful of cases that have merely emphasised the confusion of this area of our jurisprudence . . .

160. . . . We are very conscious that we are not only scrutinising the reasoning of Lord Denning MR in *Solle v Butcher* and in *Magee v Pennine Insurance Co Ltd* [1969] 2 QB 507 but are also faced with a number of later decisions in which Lord Denning MR's approach has been approved and followed. Further, a division of this court has made it clear in *West Sussex Properties Ltd v Chichester District Council* 28 June 2000 that they felt bound by *Solle v Butcher*. However, it is to be noticed that while junior counsel in the court below in the *West Sussex Properties* case had sought to challenge the correctness of *Solle v Butcher*, in the Court of Appeal leading counsel accepted that it was good law unless and until overturned by their Lordships' House. In this case we have heard full argument, which has provided what we believe has been the first opportunity in this court for a full and mature consideration of the relation between *Bell v Lever Bros Ltd* [1932] AC 161 and *Solle v Butcher*. In the light of that consideration we can see no way that *Solle v Butcher* can stand with *Bell v Lever Bros Ltd*. In these circumstances we can see no option but so to hold.

161. We can understand why the decision in *Bell v Lever Bros Ltd* did not find favour with Lord Denning MR. An equitable jurisdiction to grant rescission on terms where a common fundamental mistake has induced a contract gives greater flexibility than a doctrine of common law which holds the contract void in such circumstances. Just as the Law Reform (Frustrated Contracts) Act 1943 was needed to temper the effect of the common law doctrine of frustration, so there is scope for legislation to give greater flexibility to our law of mistake than the common law allows.'

Interestingly, on the facts of *Great Peace*, there almost certainly was not an operative mistake, either in law or in equity. The *Great Peace* was only two days away from the *Cape Providence* and it is doubtful whether such a mistake would have satisfied the test laid down by Denning LJ in *Solle v Butcher*.

On the issue of whether the Court of Appeal was correct to disapprove of *Solle*, the response has been more mixed. On the one hand, it is quite clear that *Solle* is difficult to reconcile with *Bell v Lever Brothers*. It generated uncertainty in the law and was based on a questionable use of authority. On the other hand, the Court of Appeal in numerous subsequent cases has followed *Solle*. It was not strictly necessary for the Court of Appeal to decide the point in *Great Peace* and it is arguable that the issue should only have been determined by the House of Lords. Professor McCamus provided a scathing criticism of the decision in the following article (McCamus, JD, 'Mistaken Assumptions in Equity: Sound Doctrine or Chimera?' (2004) 40 Can Bus LJ 46, 75–76):

'[T]he decision in *The Great Peace* appears to be an unfortunate one for a variety of reasons. First, the test for operative mistake defined by the Court of Appeal in *The Great Peace* appears unduly restrictive and is likely, therefore, to lead to the manipulations characteristic of the earlier narrow versions of the test. Moreover, by failing to address the very problem identified by Denning LJ in *Solle v Butcher* – the impact of the common law void for mistake doctrine on the interests of third parties – the Court of Appeal has breathed renewed life into a doctrine that is quite unattractive from a policy perspective. Further, the attempted suppression of the equitable doctrine carries with it, at least for the purposes of English law, the suppression of the remedial flexibility afforded by that doctrine. The result is to leave mistaken assumptions doctrine in a very unsatisfactory state as, indeed, the Court of Appeal appears to concede in this case. Finally, the handling of matters of precedent and the impression the reader is given of the Court of Appeal's sense of the appropriate role of an appellate court in dealing with matters of this kind may appear troubling to some observers.'

The argument concerning equity's role in protecting the rights of innocent third parties is rather difficult to understand. While such an argument makes sense in the context of unilateral mistake (see *Cundy v Lindsay* and *Ingram v Little*), it is less compelling in cases of common mistake. This is because third-party rights are rarely affected in such cases. Who were the innocent third parties in *Great Peace* or *Solle v Butcher*? In both cases the only rights affected were those belonging to the parties to the contract.

McCamus' criticisms concerning the handling of precedent and the suppression of remedial flexibility are more forceful. We have already considered the issue of precedent above. Interestingly, the Court of Appeal itself appeared to concede the force of Denning LJ's reservations about the remedial inflexibility of the common-law doctrine (at [161]). The solution proposed by Lord Phillips was statutory reform along the lines of the Law Reform (Frustrated Contracts) Act 1943. However, as Professor Reynolds has observed (Reynolds, FMB, 'Reconsider the Contract Textbook (2003) 199 LQR 177, 179): 'It is not clear why a statute (hardly an item of priority for law reformers) would do any better than a careful judicial interpretation of Lord Denning's doctrine, which is after all but a slight extension of lines of existing equity cases on misrepresentation and unconscionability in general'. Professor McCamus agrees ((2004) 40 Can Bus LJ 46, 81–82) stating that, 'it may be questioned whether the legislature is the ideal instrument for refashioning as subtle and complex an area of private law doctrine as the law of mistaken assumptions. It is at least a possible view of the division of responsibility between the legislature and the judiciary that the latter is, as a general matter, the appropriate instrument for the gradual refinement and modification of common law doctrine that is a hallmark of the common law system'. We will return to the issue of remedial flexibility at the end of this chapter when we consider Art 4:103 of the Principles of European Contract Law.

▌10.6 FORMS OF EQUITABLE RELIEF

Although the remedy of rescission on terms appears to be no longer available following the decision of the Court of Appeal in *Great Peace*, equity will still intervene to take account of the mistake in two ways. First, the mistake may constitute a ground for refusing an order specific performance and, second, a mistake in a written document may give rise to the equitable remedy of rectification.

10.6.1 REFUSAL OF SPECIFIC PERFORMANCE

Specific performance is a discretionary remedy (see Chapter 17) and in deciding whether to order specific performance, the court will take into account any mistake that was made by the parties prior to formation of the contract. The court will balance the hardship caused by enforcing the contract against the uncertainty caused by refusing to do so. In *Malins v Freeman* (1837) 2 Keen 25, the defendant purchased a piece of land at auction under the mistaken impression that he was bidding for another lot. The court refused to order specific performance of the contract and left the plaintiff to his remedy in damages. In contract, in *Tamplin v James* (1879) 15 Ch D 215, the Court of Appeal held that the mistake was insufficient to justify refusing specific performance. In this case, the defendant had bid for an inn and a saddler's shop in the mistaken belief that the land included two gardens. James LJ said:

'If a man will not take reasonable care to ascertain what he is buying, he must take the consequences. The defence on the ground of mistake cannot be sustained . . . Perhaps some of the cases on this subject go too far, but for the most part the cases where a Defendant has escaped on the ground of a mistake not contributed to by the Plaintiff, have been cases where a hardship amounting to injustice would have been inflicted upon him by holding him to his bargain, and it was unreasonable to hold him to it.'

It seems that the courts will only refuse specific performance if such an order would be 'a hardship amounting to injustice'. Presumably specific performance would constitute such a hardship if the mistake is as to the identity of the subject matter (*Malins v Freeman*), but not if it is merely as to its extent (*Tamplin v James*).

10.6.2 RECTIFICATION

The court has the equitable power to rectify a written agreement if it does not accurately reflect what the parties agreed to. In *Lovell and Christmas Ltd v Wall* (1911) 104 LT 85, Cozens-Hardy MR said: 'The essence of rectification is to bring the document which was expressed and intended to be in pursuance of a prior agreement into harmony with that prior agreement'. Denning LJ explained the approach to be applied in *Rose (Frederick E) (London) Ltd v William H Pim Jnr & Co Ltd* [1953] 2 QB 450:

'Rectification is concerned with contracts and documents, not with intentions. In order to get rectification it is necessary to show that the parties were in complete agreement on the terms of their contract, but by an error wrote them down wrongly; and in this regard, in order to ascertain the terms of their contract, you do not look into the inner minds of the parties – into their intentions – any more than you do in the formation of any other contract. You look at their outward acts, that is, at what they said or wrote to one another in coming to their agreement, and then compare it with the document which they have signed. If you can predicate with certainty what their contract was, and that it is, by a common mistake, wrongly expressed in the document, then you rectify the document; but nothing less will suffice.'

We have already considered the facts of *Rose v Pim*. The Court of Appeal concluded that, on the facts, rectification was not available because the oral agreement was on the same terms as the written agreement.

For some time it was unclear whether it was necessary to find a binding oral contract between the parties antecedent to the written agreement that they sought to rectify. This issue was later resolved by the Court of Appeal in *Joscelyne v Nissen*.

Joscelyne v Nissen [1970] 2 QB 86

Facts: The plaintiff father lived with his daughter, the defendant. They agreed that the plaintiff would transfer his car-hire business to the defendant, and in return the defendant would pay him a weekly pension and also cover various household expenses such as the gas, electricity and coal bills and the cost of the necessary home help. The written agreement transferring the business to the defendant stated that she 'shall discharge all expenses in connection with the whole premises . . . and shall indemnify [the plaintiff] from and against any claim arising in respect of the same.' The defendant initially paid the household bills but then stopped, claiming that the agreement, on its true construction did not require such payments. At first instance, the county court judge found that although there had been no prior oral contract between the parties, the written agreement should be rectified so as to specifically include the obligation to pay household expenses.

Held: The Court of Appeal dismissed the appeal, holding that it was not necessary to find a concluded contract antecedent to the written agreement. It was sufficient if there was a common continuing agreement and the written document diverged from that agreement.

Russell LJ:
'[His Lordship relied on the following extract form the judgment of Simonds J in *Crane v Hegeman-Harris Co Inc* [1939] 1 All ER 662, 664]

"I am clear that I must follow the decision of Clauson J, as he then was, in *Shipley Urban District Council v Bradford Corpn* [1936] 1 Ch 375, the point of which is that, in order that this court may exercise its jurisdiction to rectify a written instrument, it is not necessary to find a concluded and binding contract between the parties antecedent to the agreement which it is sought to rectify. The judge held, and I respectfully concur with his reasoning and his conclusion, that it is sufficient to find a common continuing intention in regard to a particular provision or aspect of the agreement. If one finds that, in regard to a particular point, the parties were in agreement up to the moment when they executed their formal instrument, and the formal instrument does not conform with that common agreement, then this court has jurisdiction to rectify, although it may be that there was, until the formal instrument was executed, no concluded and binding contract between the parties. That is what the judge decided, and, as I say, with his reasoning I wholly concur, and I can add nothing to his authority in the matter, except that I would say that, if it were not so, it would be a strange thing, for the result would be that two parties binding themselves by a mistake to which each had equally contributed, by an instrument which did not express their real intention, would yet be bound by it. That is a state of affairs which I hold is not the law, and, until a higher court tells me it is the law, I shall continue to exercise the jurisdiction which Clauson J, as I think rightly, held might be entertained by this court.

Secondly, I want to say this upon the principle of the jurisdiction. It is a jurisdiction which is to be exercised only upon convincing proof that the concluded instrument does not represent the common intention of the parties. That is particularly the case where one finds prolonged negotiations between the parties eventually assuming the shape of a formal instrument in which they have been advised by their respective skilled legal advisers. The assumption is very strong in such a case that the instrument does represent their real intention, and it must be only upon proof which Lord Eldon, I think, in a somewhat picturesque phrase described as "irrefragable" that the court can act. I would rather, I think, say that the court can only act if it is satisfied beyond all reasonable doubt that the instrument does not represent their common intention, and is further satisfied as to what their common intention was. For let it be clear that it is not sufficient to show that the written instrument does not represent their common intention unless positively also one can show what their common intention was . . ."

In our judgment the law is as expounded by Simonds J in *Crane's* case with the qualification that some outward expression of accord is required. We do not wish to attempt to state in any different phrases that with which we entirely agree, except to say that it is in our view better to use only the phrase "convincing proof" without echoing an old-fashioned word such as "irrefragable" and without importing from the criminal law the phrase "beyond all reasonable doubt". Remembering always the strong burden of proof that lies on the shoulders of those seeking rectification, and that the requisite accord and continuance of accord of intention may be the more difficult to establish if a complete antecedent concluded contract be not shown, it would be a sorry state of affairs if when that burden is discharged a party to a written contract could, on discovery that the written language chosen for the document did not on its true construction reflect the accord of the parties on a particular point, take advantage of the fact.

The contention in law for the daughter would, we apprehend, involve this proposition, that if all the important terms of an agreement were set out in correspondence with clarity, but expressly "subject to contract", and the contract by a slip of the copyist unnoticed by either party departed from what had been "agreed", there could not be rectification . . .'

The Court of Appeal set down a number of requirements that must be fulfilled if the court is to rectify a written document:

1. Although it is not necessary to show that there was a complete oral contract antecedent to the written document, there must have been a 'common intention' in regard to a particular provision of the agreement.
2. The common intention must have been continuing. A claim for rectification will fail if there is evidence that the parties varied their original intention and the written document accurately records what they finally agreed (see *Marquess of Breadalbane v Marquess of Chandos* (1837) 2 My & Cr 711).
3. There must be evidence of an 'outward expression of accord'. This focus on the objective intentions of the parties has been criticised by Mr Bromley QC (Bromley, L, 'Rectification in Equity' (1971) 87 LQR 532) and there is evidence of a more subjective approach to rectification in Australia (see *Bishopsgate Insurance Australia Ltd v Commonwealth Engineering (NSW) Pty Ltd* [1981] 1 NSWLR 429). Recently, Marcus Smith has provided a convincing defence of the objective approach arguing that it is more workable than the subjective approach, more certain and more likely to lead to the contract being rectified (Smith, M, 'Rectification of Contracts for Common Mistake, *Joscelyne v Nissen*, and the Subjective States of Mind' (2007) 123 LQR 116).
4. The 'common intention' must be proved by 'convincing proof'. If the evidence of oral negotiations leading up to the written agreement is vague or inconclusive the written document will be taken to be the accurate record of what was agreed by the parties.

Because the remedy is equitable, it may be lost if the claimant has excessively delayed in seeking it or if rectification will affect the rights of an innocent third party (*Smith v Jones* [1954] 1 WLR 1089).

Rectification is available if both parties to the contract have missed the error (common mistake). It will not be available if one party can satisfy the court that the written document is an accurate record of what he understood the agreement to be (mutual mistake): see *Riverplate Properties Ltd v Paul* [1975] Ch 133. If, however, it can be shown that the party knew of the other party's mistake (unilateral mistake) rectification will be available. In *Roberts v Leicestershire County Council* [1961] Ch 555, a construction contract, which contained a completion date a year later than the contractor had believed it to be, was rectified on the ground that the other party was well aware of the contractor's mistake. In *Commission for New Towns v Cooper (GB) Ltd* [1995] Ch 259, Stuart Smith LJ said:

> '[T]he court will intervene if there are "additional circumstances that render unconscionable reliance on the document by the party who has intended that it should have effect according to its terms": Spry, *Equitable Remedies*, 4th edn (1990), p 599. The debate in this case turns on what amounts to unconscionable conduct. The judge held that nothing less than actual knowledge of [the] mistake was sufficient . . . It was common ground in this court that fraud, in the form of a dishonest misrepresentation, will also amount to unconscionable behaviour . . . I would hold that where A intends B to be mistaken as to the construction of the agreement, so conducts himself that he diverts B's attention from discovering the mistake by making false and misleading statements, and B in fact makes the very mistake that A intends, then notwithstanding that A does not actually know, but merely suspects, that B is mistaken, and it cannot be shown that the mistake was induced by any misrepresentation, rectification may be granted. A's conduct is unconscionable and he cannot insist on performance in accordance to the strict letter of the contract; that is sufficient for rescission. But it may also not be unjust or inequitable to insist that the contract be performed according to B's understanding, where that was the meaning that A intended that B should put upon it.'

Rectification was refused in the recent case of *George Wimpey UK Ltd v VI Construction Ltd* [2005] Build LR 135, on the ground that the claimant had failed to conclusively prove that the defendant had knowledge of the claimant's mistake. The claimant had entered into a contract with the defendant to purchase a piece of land. The price for the land was calculated by an intricate formula that took into account the profit that the claimant would make from developing the land. The defendant faxed a revised formula to the claimant, but failed to draw their attention to the changes that had been made. The claimant signed the agreement without noticing the changes. On discovery of the mistake, the claimant sought rectification. The Court of Appeal refused this. Peter Gibson LJ said that the claimant had 'failed to provide convincing evidence that [the defendant] shut its eyes to the obvious or wilfully and recklessly failed to do what an honest and reasonable person would have done in the circumstances'. Particularly relevant was the fact that the claimant was a large property developer, which could have been expected to look after its own interests. This strongly supported the conclusion that the claimant had not acted unconscionably. Sedley LJ concluded as follows: 'If ever a party was entitled to assume that its opponent knew what it was doing, it was [the defendant] in its negotiations with one of the country's largest construction and development enterprises. In my judgment the mistake made by [the claimant] was a result of their own corporate neglect for which [the defendant] bore no legal or – so far as it matters – moral responsibility.'

10.7 *NON EST FACTUM*

In exceptional circumstances a person who has signed a written document may be allowed a plea of *non est factum* ('it is not my deed'). A successful plea renders the contract void and unenforceable. This obviously has a significant impact on the rights of third parties and for that reason the courts have narrowly construed the plea. It must be shown that the person relying on the plea is permanently or temporarily unable, through no fault of his or her own, to have, without explanation, any real understanding of the document they are signing. It must also be shown that the document being signed is 'radically different' to the document which the person believed he was signing. The principles to be applied were set out by the House of Lords in *Saunders v Anglia Building Society*.

> ### *Saunders v Anglia Building Society (sub nom Gallie v Lee)* [1971] AC 1004
>
> **Facts:** Mrs Gallie, a widow aged 78, wished to enable her nephew to raise money on the security of her house. She knew that her nephew's business associate, Mr Lee, was to collaborate with the nephew in raising the money. Mrs Gallie was asked to sign a document assigning her interest in the house to Mr Lee. She had broken her reading glasses and so she asked Mr Lee what it was. He replied that it was a deed of gift to her nephew. She signed it, in that belief, and the nephew witnessed the signature, it being his plan for Mr Lee to raise money on the house and then repay it to him in instalments. Mr Lee subsequently mortgaged the house for £2,000 and used the money to pay off his debts. He defaulted on the mortgage instalments and the building society sought to obtain possession of the house. Mrs Gallie pleaded *non est factum* and sought a declaration that the assignment was void and that the title deeds should be delivered to her. At first instance, the judge found that the plea of *non est factum* had been established and granted the declaration requested. The Court of Appeal reversed the decision.

Held: The House of Lords dismissed the appeal. The transaction Mrs Gallie had entered into was not radically different in substance from that which she had intended.

Lord Reid:

'The plea of *non est factum* obviously applies when the person sought to be held liable did not in fact sign the document. But at least since the sixteenth century it has also been held to apply in certain cases so as to enable a person who in fact signed a document to say that it is not his deed. Obviously any such extension must be kept within narrow limits if it is not to shake the confidence of those who habitually and rightly rely on signatures when there is no obvious reason to doubt their validity. Originally this extension appears to have been made in favour of those who were unable to read owing to blindness or illiteracy and who therefore had to trust someone to tell them what they were signing. I think it must also apply in favour of those who are permanently or temporarily unable through no fault of their own to have without explanation any real understanding of the purport of a particular document, whether that be from defective education, illness or innate incapacity.

But that does not excuse them from taking such precautions as they reasonably can. The matter generally arises where an innocent third party has relied on a signed document in ignorance of the circumstances in which it was signed, and where he will suffer loss if the maker of the document is allowed to have it declared a nullity. So there must be a heavy burden of proof on the person who seeks to invoke this remedy. He must prove all the circumstances necessary to justify its being granted to him, and that necessarily involves his proving that he took all reasonable precautions in the circumstances. I do not say that the remedy can never be available to a man of full capacity. But that could only be in very exceptional circumstances: certainly not where his reason for not scrutinising the document before signing it was that he was too busy or too lazy. In general I do not think he can be heard to say that he signed in reliance on someone he trusted. But, particularly when he was led to believe that the document which he signed was not one which affected his legal rights, there may be cases where this plea can properly be applied in favour of a man of full capacity.

The plea cannot be available to anyone who was content to sign without taking the trouble to try to find out at least the general effect of the document. Many people do frequently sign documents put before them for signature by their solicitor or other trusted advisers without making any inquiry as to their purpose or effect. But the essence of the plea *non est factum* is that the person signing believed that the document he signed had one character or one effect whereas in fact its character or effect was quite different. He could not have such a belief unless he had taken steps or been given information which gave him some grounds for his belief. The amount of information he must have and the sufficiency of the particularity of his belief must depend on the circumstances of each case.

Further, the plea cannot be available to a person whose mistake was really a mistake as to the legal effect of the document, whether that was his own mistake or that of his adviser. That has always been the law and in this branch of the law at least I see no reason for any change . . .

Finally, there is the question as to what extent or in what way must there be a difference between that which in fact he signed and that which he believed he was signing. In an endeavour to keep the plea within bounds there have been many attempts to lay down a dividing line. But any dividing line suggested has been difficult to apply in practice and has sometimes led to unreasonable results. In particular I do not think that the modern division between the character and the contents of a document is at all satisfactory. Some of the older authorities suggest a more flexible test so that one can take all factors into consideration. There was a period when here, as elsewhere in the law, hard-and-fast dividing lines were sought, but I think that experience has shown that often they do not produce certainty but do produce unreasonable results.

I think that in the older authorities difference in practical result was more important than difference in legal character. If a man thinks he is signing a document which will cost him £10 and the actual document would cost him £1,000 it could not be right to deny him this remedy simply because the legal character of the two was the same. It is true that we must then deal with questions of degree, but that is a familiar task for the courts and I would not expect it to give rise to a flood of litigation.

There must, I think, be a radical difference between what he signed and what he thought he was signing – or one could use the words "fundamental" or "serious" or "very substantial". But what amounts to a radical difference will depend on all the circumstances. If he thinks he is giving property to A whereas the document gives it to B, the difference may often be of vital importance, but in the circumstances of the present case I do not think that it is. I think that it must be left to the courts to determine in each case in light of all the facts whether there was or was not a sufficiently great difference. The plea *non est factum* is in a sense illogical when applied to a case where the man in fact signed the deed. But it is none the worse for that if applied in a reasonable way.

I would dismiss this appeal.

Policy issues were very much at the fore in *Saunders*. The House of Lords had to balance the interests of Mrs Gallie against the interests of the building society that had advanced money to Mr Lee in reliance on Mrs Gallie's signature. Lord Reid opined that, in order to protect the interests of third parties, the law imposes a 'heavy burden of proof' on those seeking to rely on *non est factum*.

It is now clear that the defence is not limited to the blind and illiterate. It can be invoked by anyone, although the defence will be lost if it can be shown that the claimant has been careless in signing the document (*United Dominions Trust Ltd v Western* [1976] QB 513). The House of Lords also rejected the traditional division between cases where the mistake was as to the 'character' of the document and cases where the mistake was as to its 'contents' (*Howatson v Webb* [1907] 1 Ch 537). Lord

Reid suggested that the division had produced unreasonable results in the past. Their Lordships preferred a more flexible approach, asking whether there was a 'radical' ('fundamental', 'serious' or 'very substantial') difference between what was signed and what the claimant thought he was signing.

A rare and relatively recent example of a successful plea of *non est factum* is to be found in *Lloyds Bank plc v Waterhouse*.

Lloyds Bank plc v Waterhouse [1990] Fam Law 23

Facts: The defendant, who was illiterate, signed a guarantee for a loan with the plaintiff. He believed this to relate solely to his son's purchase of a farm, but in fact it also covered an overdraft facility in favour of the son. The negotiations for the loan were fairly lengthy and during meetings with the bank the father had asked questions about the guarantee and its effect if the son should default. The son did default on the loan and the plaintiff brought a claim against the defendant on the guarantee. At first instance, judgment was given for the plaintiff. It was held that the difference between the document as it was and as it was believed to be was not fundamental. The trial judge also held that the defendant had been careless in not having the document read to him.

Held: The Court of Appeal allowed the appeal. The mistake as to the extent of the guarantee was sufficient to support the plea of *non est factum*. The defendant had not been careless in signing the document since he had asked questions of the bank in order to ascertain his liability under the guarantee.

Purchas LJ:
'[I]t appears that in order for this defence to succeed the father must establish three things: (a) that he was under a disability, in this case illiteracy. There is no challenge to this as an existing fact. For this purpose it is irrelevant that the bank were not aware of this disability; (b) that the document which the father in fact signed was "fundamentally different" or "radically different" or "totally different" from the document which he thought he was signing; and (c) that he was not careless (see per Lord Pearson) or that he did not fail to take precautions which he ought to have taken in the circumstances to ascertain the contents or significance of the document he was signing. Before the defence can succeed the defendant must establish strictly each component, particularly the third one.

   (a) above needs no further elaboration and is not in dispute so I turn immediately to consider (b). . . In considering this requirement of the defence, in my judgment one must look at the respective liabilities which each type of document would have imposed on the person seeking to take advantage of the defence, rather than what in fact happened subsequently. The liabilities or potential liabilities are to be assessed at the moment of signing or execution of the document. The effect of the guarantee which the father signed would have exposed him up to a limit of £110,000 to indemnify the bank for Paul's indebtedness even if this was occasioned by profligate activities totally disassociated from farming. In other words, even if Paul's farming activities had proved to be an immense financial success but he had nevertheless dissipated his profits on riotous living rather than in reducing his indebtedness to the bank, the father would remain liable under the guarantee. In my judgment, this liability can properly be described (in the terms approved by Lord Pearson [in *Saunders v Anglia Building Society (sub nom Gallie v Lee)* [1971] AC 1004]) as fundamentally different, radically different or totally different from indebtedness accruing from the loan account established in order to purchase the farm and the interest thereon, which the father was entitled to believe was the liability which he was to guarantee as a result of his conversation with Mr Farmer . . .

Thus, in my judgment, the father has established his incapacity in the form of illiteracy and on the findings of the Judge that the document which he signed was different within the concept of *non est factum* from the document which he thought he was signing. There remains, however, the third hurdle which the father must surmount before he can establish his defence of *non est factum*. As described in the speech of Lord Reid [in *Saunders v Anglia Building Society (sub nom Gallie v Lee)* [1971] AC 1004], he must take such precautions as he reasonably can to avoid the impact of his incapacity when signing a document in ignorance of its contents . . . From the passages in the evidence . . . to which I have already made reference, it is clear that from the outset the father was anxiously enquiring as to what the true position would be in relation to the guarantee which he was being invited to give . . . [I]n the defence of *non est factum* the consideration of carelessness is subjective to the person proposing the defence and has no element in which the knowledge or state of mind of the other party becomes relevant. The defence is a simple one in concept, namely did the defendant's mind go with the act of signature to the document? The intention, state of knowledge or position of the other party in such a consideration cannot be relevant. Indeed it is the position of an innocent third party which is frequently under consideration. After a very careful review of the position and, I trust, not going against any specific finding by the Judge, . . . I have formed the conclusion that there was ample evidence before the Judge which would discharge the onus of proof, strict as it is in these particular circumstances, imposed upon the father in order to establish his defence of *non est factum*.'

10.8 MISTAKE UNDER THE PRINCIPLES OF EUROPEAN CONTRACT LAW

The Principles of European Contract Law deal with mistake in Art 4.103, which provides the following:

Article 4.103 (ex art. 6.103) – Mistake as to facts or law

(1) A party may avoid a contract for mistake of fact or law existing when the contract was concluded if:

  (a) (i)   the mistake was caused by information given by the other party; or

  (ii) the other party knew or ought to have known of the mistake and it was contrary to good faith and fair dealing to leave the mistaken party in error; or

  (iii) the other party made the same mistake, and

  (b) the other party knew or ought to have known that the mistaken party, had it known the truth, would not have entered the contract or would have done so only on fundamentally different terms.

(2) However a party may not avoid the contract if:

  (a) in the circumstances its mistake was inexcusable, or

  (b) the risk of the mistake was assumed, or in the circumstances should be borne, by it.

There are three points to note. First, the Article only deals with common mistake (para 1(a)(iii)) and unilateral mistake (para 1(a)(i) and (ii)). The Article makes no reference to mutual mistake, where the parties are at cross-purposes. Why is this? Presumably it is because such mistakes are left to be dealt with by the provisions on formation. If this is the reason then it is interesting to note that unilateral mistake is dealt with by Art 4.103. It is just as arguable that in those situations there is no agreement. Perhaps the reason why Art 4.103 deals with unilateral mistake is because it is felt that the mistaken party should have the option of continuing with the contract if it is in their interests to do so.

Second, para 2 provides two limitations on the general power to avoid a contract for mistake. The first limitation prevents an imprudent mistake from being used to avoid a contract. The second limitation ensures that the rules on mistake do not undermine the contractual allocation of risk (see *McRae v Commonwealth Disposals Commission* (1951) 84 CLR 377).

Third, the article states that contracts falling within its scope are voidable, rather than void. As we have seen, if there is an operative mistake, the common law treats the contract as void *ab initio* (from the beginning), with the result that third-party purchasers may fall foul of the *nemo dat* rule. By treating mistakes as rendering a contract voidable rather than void, the Principles introduce much needed remedial flexibility into the law. Lando and Beale's commentary suggests that a shared mistake under Art 4.103 'usually results in the resulting losses being divided between the parties, if only in a rough and ready way' (Lando, O, and Beale, H, *Principles of European Contract Law Parts I and II*, 2000, p 233, The Hague: Kluwer Law International). Damages are available if the mistake is based on a misrepresentation by one of the parties (Art 4.106), or if one of the parties knew or ought to have known of the mistake (Art 4.117). Art 4.115 provides for restitution following avoidance of the contract. Additional remedial flexibility is provided by Art

4.105(3), which states that 'where both parties have made the same mistake, the court may at the request of either party bring the contract into accordance with what might reasonably have been agreed had the mistake not occurred'. Such adaptation is not available where either, it is clear that, but for the mistake, the parties would not have entered the contract or where there has been a subsequent change in one party's position (Lando and Beale at p 247).

10.9 ADDITIONAL READING

Atiyah, PS and Bennion, F, 'Mistake in the construction of contracts' (1961) 24 MLR 421.

Chandler, A and Devenney, J, 'Mistake as to identity and the threads of objectivity' (2004) 1 JOR 7.

De Gregorio, M, 'Impossible performance or excused performance? Common mistake and frustration after *Great Peace Shipping*' (2005) 16 KCLJ 69.

Goodhart, A, 'Mistake as to identify in the law of contract (1941) LQR 228.

Phang, A, 'Common mistake in English law: the proposed merger of common law and equity' (1989) 9 LS 291.

Simpson, AWB, 'Contracts for cotton to arrive: the case of the two ships *Peerless*' (1989) 11 Cardozo L Rev 287.

Stone, J, 'The limits of *non est factum* after *Gallie v Lee*' (1972) 88 LQR 190.

Treitel, GH, 'Mistake in contract' (1988) 104 LQR 501.

DURESS

<table>
<tr><td colspan="3" align="center">CONTENTS</td></tr>
</table>

▌11.1 INTRODUCTION

This chapter is concerned with the law of duress, which governs situations where one party has been induced to enter into a contract as a result of illegitimate pressure of some kind. Historically, the law of duress was restricted to pressure in the form of threats of violence or threats to goods. More recently, the courts have recognised that illegitimate pressure may include 'economic' threats (such as a threat to break a contract). This has created new problems, however, due to the difficulty of ascertaining what constitutes *illegitimate* economic pressure. In commercial dealings, threats are often made in precontractual negotiations as a means of encouraging the other party to enter into the contract. For example, a party might say, 'If you do not enter into this contract we will not deal with you again in the future', or 'If you do not buy these goods from us we will not renew your credit facility next year'. These threats clearly impose pressure on the other party but it is not clear whether the pressure is illegitimate. It is also unclear whether the same requirements for duress apply across all the different categories. For example, it is sometimes suggested that a more restrictive test of causation ought to apply in cases of economic duress. These issues will be considered in further detail below.

If it is shown that a contract has been entered into as a result of duress the contract is rendered voidable. It is generally accepted that there are two elements to a duress claim. These were identified by Lord Scarman in *Universe Tankships v International Transport Workers Federation* [1983] AC 366: '(1) pressure amounting to compulsion of the will of the victim; and (2) the illegitimacy of the pressure exerted'. The first element focuses on the complainant (who will be referred to as the claimant, even though s/he may on the facts of the case be the defendant): was the claimant's consent truly given? The second element focuses on the defendant: did the defendant use illegitimate pressure to procure the contract? One commentator has suggested that either of these two elements is sufficient to establish duress:

S Smith, 'Contracting under pressure: a theory of duress' [1997] CLJ 343, 371–373

By way of a summary description of the main features of the account of duress developed in this article, the questions that a court should ask in the most complex variant of a pressure case, a contractual modification case, will be described briefly. The first question is whether the plaintiff is barred from enforcing the modification because it was obtained as a result of his wrongdoing. In assessing wrongdoing in a modification context, the wrong, if there has been a wrong, is almost always a threat to breach the original contract. If the court establishes that the plaintiff made a threat to breach (and not merely a warning, request, or offer), the next question is whether that threat was operative in the sense that it was a necessary element of a set of actual conditions sufficient for the occurrence of the result. An affirmative answer means that the plaintiff is precluded from enforcing the contract by virtue of the wrongdoing principle. If the answer is negative, or if the plaintiff did not make a threat, then the wrongdoing principle does not apply. This will often be the conclusion reached in modification cases, since modifications are frequently the consequence of the plaintiff's impending bankruptcy or the defendant's wish to maintain a good reputation.

If operative wrongdoing is not established, the court must then consider whether the contract should be invalidated because the defendant's consent was impaired. The defendant is unlikely to be able to establish that his consent was impaired by a wrongful threat because, if the case has gone this far, either no wrongful threat was made or that threat was not operative in the weak sense required under the wrongdoing principle. Only if the defendant can show that there was a risk of non-performance (say because of the plaintiff's impending bankruptcy) and that this risk placed him in a necessitous situation, in the sense that he would suffer an unavoidable loss if the contract was not performed, is a plea of impaired consent possible. Such facts can often be established in modification cases, the parties being in a bilateral monopoly from which neither can exit without incurring losses. If a lack of options is made out, then the defendant must further prove that the lack of options was operative in his decision to renegotiate. The existence of the required but-for causation will typically turn upon the fairness of the contract terms: if the terms are unfair, causation normally is established. Finally, if the contract is invalid, the plaintiff may have a claim for restitution of benefits conferred or for reliance-based losses.

The contractual modification example illustrates the main themes of this article: that pressure cases typically raise two concerns, one for wrongdoing and the other for autonomy and that, while these concerns often overlap and require courts to ask similar questions (Was there a threat to harm? Was the threat operative?), the overlap is not perfect and the questions not identical. In particular, the scope of the concerns diverge where the reason a contracting party was under pressure was not because the other party acted wrongly, in other words, in necessity cases.

That English courts have thus far not distinguished clearly between wrongdoing and lack of consent in pressure cases is understandable. In many pressure cases it is clear that the contract should be invalidated, but less clear whether the reason for invalidity is wrongdoing or lack of consent or both wrongdoing and lack of consent. The distinctions between, for example, wrongful and non-wrongful threats, non-wrongful threats and wrongly exerting pressure other than by threats, and but-for and NESS causation, can be difficult to apply. Second, some of the questions relevant to establishing no consent (e.g., Did the defendant have a non-bad alternative to contracting? Was the contract price fair?) are questions that courts traditionally and for good reasons have been cautious to address. Third, failing to identify the precise reason a contract is invalid has little consequence as far as contract law is concerned so long as it clear, as it often will be, that the contract is invalid.

The main consequence of the failure to distinguish wrongdoing from lack of consent is the underdevelopment of the latter defence. This underdevelopment may be significant when considering possible restitutionary claims following a finding of contractual invalidity since the amount of relief awarded may depend in part on whether or not the enriched party acted wrongly. More importantly, at least from the perspective of contract law, the failure to develop a coherent defence of no consent has resulted in the failure to develop a defence of duress by necessity. A sophisticated approach to pressure cases must therefore distinguish clearly between wrongdoing and lack of consent and, a related matter, take seriously the meaning and value of consent.

As we will see, the courts have rejected Professor Smith's position and insisted that both elements must be established in order to render a contract voidable for duress. The difficulty lies in establishing what constitutes a 'vitiation of consent' and what amounts to 'illegitimate pressure'. We will consider these issues in greater detail in our discussion of economic duress. First, we will consider the more straightforward categories of duress: duress of the person and duress of goods.

11.2 DURESS OF THE PERSON

Actual or threatened violence to the person is the most obvious form of duress. It is illustrated by the case of *Barton v Armstrong*.

Barton v Armstrong [1976] AC 104

Facts: Barton, the managing director of Landmark Corporation Ltd, executed a deed on behalf of the company agreeing to pay $320,000 to Armstrong, in order to remove him from the board of directors. Barton entered into this agreement partly for commercial reasons and partly because Armstrong had threatened to have him murdered if he did not. At first instance, the judge found that Armstrong had threatened Barton, but that the primary and predominant reason why Barton executed the deed was because of the commercial necessity of so acting. The Court of Appeal of New South Wales dismissed the appeal on the ground that Barton had failed to discharge the burden of proving that he would not have entered into the agreement but for the threats.

Held: The Privy Council, by a majority (Lord Wilberforce and Lord Simon of Glaisdale dissenting), allowed the appeal on the ground that Armstrong's threats were a reason why Barton had entered the agreement and it did not matter that Barton might have entered the agreement even if Armstrong had not made any threats. The deeds were executed under duress and were therefore void.

Lord Cross:

'Their Lordships turn now to consider the question of law which provoked a difference of opinion in the Court of Appeal Division. It is hardly surprising that there is no direct authority on the point, for if A threatens B with death if he does not execute some document and B, who takes A's threats seriously, executes the document it can be only in the most unusual circumstances that there can be any doubt whether the threats operated to induce him to execute the document. But this is a most unusual case and the findings of fact made below do undoubtedly raise the question whether it was necessary for Barton in order to obtain relief to establish that he would not have executed the deed in question but for the threats. In answering this question in favour of Barton, Jacobs JA relied both on a number of old common law authorities on the subject of "duress" and also – by way of analogy – on later decisions in equity with regard to the avoidance of deeds on the ground of fraud. Their Lordships do not think that the common law authorities are of any real assistance for it seems most unlikely that the authors of the statements relied on had the sort of problem which has arisen here in mind at all. On the other hand they think that the conclusion to which Jacobs JA came was right and that it is supported by the equity decisions. The scope of common law duress was very limited and at a comparatively early date equity began to grant relief in cases where the disposition in question had been procured by the exercise of pressure which the Chancellor considered to be illegitimate – although it did not amount to common law duress. There was a parallel development in the field of dispositions induced by fraud. At common law the only remedy available to the man defrauded was an action for deceit but equity in the same period in which it was building up the doctrine of "undue influence" came to entertain proceedings to set aside dispositions which had been obtained by fraud: see Holdsworth, *A History of English Law*, vol V (1924), pp 328–329. There is an obvious analogy between setting aside a disposition for duress or undue influence and setting it aside for fraud. In each case – to quote the words of Holmes J in *Fairbanks v Snow* (1887) 13 NE 596, 598 – "the party has been subjected to an improper motive for action". Again the similarity of the effect in law of metus and dolus in connection with dispositions of property is noted by Stair in his *Institutions of the Law of Scotland*, New edn. (1832), Book IV, title 40.25. Had Armstrong made a fraudulent misrepresentation to Barton for the purpose of inducing him to execute the deed of January 17, 1967, the answer to the problem which has arisen would have been clear. If it were established that Barton did not allow the representation to affect his judgment then he could not make it a ground for relief even though the representation was designed and known by Barton to be designed to affect his judgment. If on the other hand Barton relied on the misrepresentation Armstrong could not have defeated his claim to relief by showing that there were other more weighty causes which contributed to his decision to execute the deed, for in this field the court does not allow an examination into the relative importance of contributory causes. "Once make out that there has been anything like deception, and no contract resting in any degree on that foundation can stand": *per* Lord Cranworth LJ in *Reynell v Sprye* (1852) 1 De GM & G 660, 708 – see also the other cases referred to in Cheshire and Fifoot's *Law of Contract*, 8th edn (1972), pp 250–251. Their Lordships think that the same rule should apply in cases of duress and that if Armstrong's threats were "a" reason for Barton's executing the deed he is entitled to relief even though he might well have entered into the contract if Armstrong had uttered no threats to induce him to do so.

It remains to apply the law to the facts. What was the state of Barton's mind when he executed the deed is, of course, a question of fact and a question the answer to which depended largely on Barton's own evidence . . . If Barton had to establish that he would not have made the agreement but for Armstrong's threats, then their Lordships would not dissent from the view that he had not made out his case. But no such onus lay on him. On the contrary it was for Armstrong to establish, if he could, that the threats which he was making and the unlawful pressure which he was exerting for the purpose of inducing Barton to sign the agreement and which Barton knew were being made and exerted for this purpose in fact contributed nothing to Barton's decision to sign. The judge has found that during the 10 days or so before the documents were executed Barton was in genuine fear that Armstrong was planning to have him killed if the agreement was not signed. His state of mind was described by the judge as one of "very real mental torment" and he believed that his fears would be at end when once the documents were executed . . . It is true that on the facts as their Lordships assume them to have been Armstrong's threats may have been unnecessary, but it would be unrealistic to hold that they played no part in making Barton decide to execute the documents. The proper inference to be drawn from the facts found is, their Lordships think, that though it may be that Barton would have executed the documents even if Armstrong had made no threats and exerted no unlawful pressure to induce him to do so the threats and unlawful pressure in fact contributed to his decision to sign the documents and to recommend their execution by Landmark and the other parties to them. It may be, of course, that Barton's fear of Armstrong had evaporated before he issued his writ in this action but Armstrong – understandably enough – expressly disclaimed reliance on the defence of delay on Barton's part in repudiating the deed.

In the result therefore the appeal should be allowed and a declaration made that the deeds in question were executed by Barton under duress and are void so far as concerns him. Their Lordships express no view as to what, if any, effect this may have on the rights or obligations inter se of the other parties to the deeds – and the order should include liberty to any of them to apply to the court of first instance for the determination of any questions which may arise between them in that regard . . .'

Lord Wilberforce and Lord Simon of Glaisdale (dissenting):
'The reason why we do not agree with the majority decision is, briefly, that we regard the issues in this case as essentially issues of fact, issues moreover of a character particularly within the sphere of the trial judge bearing, as they do, upon motivation and credibility. On all important issues, clear findings have been made by Street J. and concurred in by the Court of Appeal either unanimously or by majority. Accepted rules of practice and, such rules apart, sound principle should, in our opinion, prevent a second court of appeal from reviewing them in the absence of some miscarriage of justice, or some manifest and important error of law or misdirection. In our view no such circumstance exists in this case . . .

The action is one to set aside an apparently complete and valid agreement on the ground of duress. The basis of the plaintiff's claim is, thus, that though there was apparent consent there was no true consent to the agreement: that the agreement was not voluntary.

This involves consideration of what the law regards as voluntary, or its opposite; for in life, including the life of commerce and finance, many acts are done under pressure, sometimes overwhelming pressure, so that one can say that the actor had no choice but to act. Absence of choice in this sense does not negate consent in law: for this the pressure must be one of a kind which the law does not regard as legitimate. Thus, out of the various means by which consent may be obtained – advice, persuasion, influence, inducement, representation, commercial pressure – the law has come to select some which it will not accept as a reason for voluntary action: fraud, abuse of relation of confidence, undue influence, duress or coercion. In this the law, under the influence of equity, has developed from the old common law conception of duress – threat to life and limb – and it has arrived at the modern generalisation expressed by Holmes J – "subjected to an improper motive for action": *Fairbanks v Snow*, 13 NE Reporter 596, 598.

In an action such as the present, then, the first step required of the plaintiff is to show that some illegitimate means of persuasion was used. That there were threats to Barton's life was found by the judge, though he did not accept Barton's evidence in important respects. We shall return to this point in detail later.

The next necessary step would be to establish the relationship between the illegitimate means used and the action taken. For the purposes of the present case (reserving our opinion as to cases which may arise in other contexts) we are prepared to accept, as the formula most favourable to the appellant, the test proposed by the majority, namely, that the illegitimate means used was a reason (not *the* reason, nor the *predominant* reason nor the *clinching* reason) why the complainant acted as he did. We are also prepared to accept that a decisive answer is not obtainable by asking the question whether the contract would have been made even if there had been no threats because, even if the answer to this question is affirmative, that does not prove that the contract was not made because of the threats.

Assuming therefore that what has to be decided is whether the illegitimate means used was a reason why the complainant acted as he did, it follows that his reason for acting must (unless the case is one of automatism which this is not) be a conscious reason so that the complainant can give evidence of it: "I acted because I was forced". If his evidence is honest and accepted, that will normally conclude the issue. If, moreover, he gives evidence, it is necessary for the court to evaluate his evidence by testing it against his credibility and his actions.

In this case Barton gave evidence – his was, for practical purposes, the only evidence supporting his case. The judge rejected it in important respects and accepted it in others. The issues as to Barton's motivations were issues purely of fact (that motivation is a question of fact hardly needs authority, but see *Cox v Smail* [1912] VLR 274 *per* Cussen J.): the findings as to motivation were largely, if not entirely, findings as to credibility. It would be difficult to find matters more peculiarly than these within the field of the trial judge who saw both contestants in the box, and who dealt carefully and at length with the credibility, or lack of credibility, of each of them . . .

The judge's findings were also accepted, after careful examination by Taylor A-JA – ". . . the conclusion", he finds, "that Barton entered into this agreement because he wanted to and from commercial motives only is, I think undoubtedly correct." The appeal cannot succeed unless these most explicit findings are overturned. We consider that no basis exists for doing so.

In our opinion the case is far from being one in which a second appellate court should reverse findings made below and endorsed by a Court of Appeal. Respect for such findings – particularly where the issues depend so much upon credibility and an estimate of rival personalities – appears to us to be a central pillar of the appellate process. It is perhaps otiose, but also fair to the judges below, to say that we have no ground for thinking that the factual conclusions which they reached after so prolonged a search did not represent the truth of the situation – or at least the nearest approximation to truth that was attainable.

We would dismiss the appeal.

The Privy Council set out an extremely broad test for establishing causation in cases of duress. In the words of Lord Cross, all Barton needed to show was that 'Armstrong's threats were "a" reason for Barton's executing the deed'. In their dissenting speech, Lord Wilberforce and Lord Simon of Glaisdale agreed with this test, noting that it was sufficient to show that the illegitimate means used 'was a reason (not *the* reason, nor the *predominant* reason nor the *clinching* reason) why the complainant acted as he did'. In other words it is not necessary to establish 'but for causation'. This means that a party, who procures a contract by means of illegitimate pressure, is not entitled to excuse his conduct by introducing evidence that the claimant had other reasons for entering into the contract. Several commentators have criticised this test for setting the threshold too low. While the analogy between duress and fraudulent misrepresentation might be sustainable in relation to threats to the person it falls away once the threat relates to economic circumstances. There is a clear difference between economic pressure and deceit. For this reason, it has been suggested that a more stringent test of causation, requiring the illegitimate pressure to be a 'significant cause' (see Mance J in *Huyton SA v Peter Cremer GmbH & Co* [1999] 1 Lloyd's Rep 620), applies in cases of economic duress. This will be considered in further detail below.

A further point to note is that Lord Cross referred to the deeds as void, not voidable, as a consequence of the duress. With respect, it is rather difficult to know whether this is really what Lord Cross meant. Elsewhere in his speech he referred to the contract being 'set aside' as for fraud. Moreover, he recognised the potential availability of delay as a defence to repudiation of the deed, which is consistent with the view that duress renders a contract voidable. In addition, the minority appeared to take the view that the effect of duress was to render the contract voidable. Lord Wilberforce and Lord Simon of Glaisdale described the action as one to 'set aside an apparently complete and valid agreement on the ground of duress'. Nevertheless, it has been argued that Lord Cross was correct to state that the effect of duress is to render a contract void.

Lanham, D, 'Duress and void contracts' (1966) 29 MLR 615, 617–620

The first reason why common law duress should be regarded as rendering all contracts void is that a marriage induced by such duress is void for lack of consent. Consent (or the appearance of consent) is just as vital to contracts other than marriage as it is to the marriage contract, and the courts have said that the same rule governs both kinds of contract . . .

Secondly, where the effect of a contract (or a gift, to which the same rules of consent apply) would be to pass property, common law duress must render the transaction void in order to avoid a direct clash with the law relating to larceny by intimidation and robbery. It is well settled that if a person takes property from another having secured his consent by intimidation he will be guilty of larceny or robbery. For a conviction on either head it is necessary to show that property had not passed to the accused. This is the position in criminal law where intimidation is present and it would be the same in civil law if the transaction (be it contract or gift) is held void for duress. If the criminal cases are right and the position in civil law is still that a transaction is voidable for duress, we have the absurd situation that a man can be guilty of larceny by intimidation on the ground that the property in question did not pass to him and yet be in a position to give a good title on the ground that it did. Such absurdity cannot be imputed to the common law. It might be possible to argue that there is one rule for contracts under which property is to pass and a different rule for other kinds of contracts. But in all contracts it is essential that there should be consent, or at least the appearance of consent. Not even the officious bystander would care to testify that a person with a gun to his head appeared to consent to the transaction in hand, whatever kind of contract was involved. American law draws a line between cases where there is no consent (e.g., where A grasps B's hand, forcing it to make a mark or signature signifying B's consent) and cases where there is apparent consent. Into the latter category the gun-to-the-head situation is placed. It does not appear to whom consent in the second situation is apparent – certainly not to anyone present. If the test is persons not present, then consent may be apparent in both types of case. The American position does not seem tenable except on the view that in the latter type of case the law has been content to evaporate out of contract all notion of consent. This still leaves the difficulty of reconciling the position in civil law with that in the law of larceny.

Thirdly, there is the question of rescission. It is well established that a voidable contract (other than a marriage contract) may be rescinded without the intervention of a court of law. It is also settled that it is a sufficient act of rescission for the innocent party to notify the guilty party of his desire to terminate the contract. Though the right to rescission may be lost in certain circumstances, especially if a third party would be injured by its exercise, there is no time too early for the right to be exercised and no special form necessary for the rescission to be effective. All that is required is that the desire to terminate is clear to the guilty party. These rules operate satisfactorily for the usual forms of voidable contract. In cases of broken conditions, fraudulent or innocent misrepresentation and even infancy there is a period of time – often substantial – during which the innocent party consents to the transaction. Only later, when the innocent party is apprised of the true facts, or in the case of infancy, when the infant realises he has made a bad bargain, does the question of rescission arise. It is then that he must examine the situation again and decide whether to confirm the consent he once gave or to revoke it. If he decides to rescind the contract he must make this clear to the other party. Even in cases of fraud the fact that consent is withdrawn will not be clear to the guilty party until he is told. In cases of duress, on the other hand, there is no moment of time in which the guilty party is in any doubt as to the desire of the other party to rescind the contract. Even as the 'contract' is being made it is clear that the innocent party wishes to rescind it. This sounds absurd but it must be the position if duress makes a contract voidable and if a voidable contract can be rescinded at any time before the right to rescission is lost. The problem does not arise if it is recognised that a contract is void for duress. There is then no question of revoking the consent because there never was a consent. Without consent there can be no contract. Common law recognised this. The only remaining question is how far equity has modified the common law rule.

Lanham's argument rests on the assumption that there is no real consent in cases of duress. The claimant's will is 'overborne' and thus the claimant is unable to consent to entering into the contract. This view of the absence of consent in cases of duress has since been rejected (see *Universe Tankships Inc of Monrovia v International Transport Workers Federation, The Universe Sentinel* [1983] 1 AC 366; *Attorney General v R* [2003] EMLR 24), and because of this the preferred view is that duress renders a contract voidable, not void.

11.3 DURESS OF GOODS

Historically it was believed that threats in relation to property were insufficient to constitute duress.

Skeate v Beale (1840) 11 Ad & El 983

Facts: A landlord took goods belonging to his tenant because of unpaid rent and threatened to sell them. The tenant agreed that if his landlord would withdraw a distress of £19 10 shillings in respect of rent, he would pay £3 7 shillings 6 pence at once and the remainder within one month. The tenant did not pay the remainder, claiming that he only owed £3 7 shillings 6 pence, and had entered into the agreement for the remainder in order to prevent the landlord from selling his goods. He sought to have the agreement set aside for duress.

Held: The court held that the agreement could not be set aside for duress and the tenant was required to pay the outstanding sum.

Denman CJ:
'We consider the law to be clear, and founded on good reason, that an agreement is not void because made under duress of goods. There is no distinction in this respect between a deed and an agreement not under seal; and, with regard to the former, the law is laid down in 2 Inst 483, and Sheppard's Touchstone, p 61, and the distinction

pointed out between duress of, or menace to, the person, and duress of goods. The former is a constraining force, which not only takes away the free agency, but may leave no appeal to the law for a remedy: a man, therefore, is not bound by the agreement which he enters into under such circumstances: but the fear that goods can be taken or injured does not deprive any one of his free agency who possessed that ordinary degree of firmness that the law requires all to exert.'

This perspective on duress appears rather outdated now. In particular, it seems unreasonable to expect those subject to duress of goods to appeal to the law for a remedy. In practice, it may be just as difficult to appeal to the law in cases of duress of goods as it is in cases of duress of the person. The requirement of bravery, expressed as the 'ordinary degree of firmness' by Denman CJ, is surely unreasonable in modern commercial practice. Furthermore, the decision in *Skeate v Beale* is difficult to reconcile with a line of cases, which permit the recovery of money, paid under duress of goods.

Maskell v Horner [1915] 3 KB 106

Facts: Maskell set up in business as a dealer in produce near Spitalfields Market. Horner, the owner of the market, demanded tolls from Maskell and threatened to seize his goods if he refused to pay. Maskell refused to pay and his goods were seized. He then consulted a solicitor and upon learning that other dealers outside the market paid tolls, he paid the tolls under protest for a period of twelve years. In another case, *Attorney-General v Horner (No 2)* [1913] 2 Ch 140, it was held that the tolls charged by Horner were unlawful, and Maskell sought to recover the money he had paid.

Held: The Court of Appeal held that the money could be recovered because it was paid to avoid the seizure of goods.

Lord Reading CJ:

'[T]he plaintiff asserts that he paid the money not voluntarily but under the pressure of actual or threatened seizure of his goods, and that he is therefore entitled to recover it as money had and received. If the facts proved support this assertion the plaintiff would, in my opinion, be entitled to succeed in this action.

If a person with knowledge of the facts pays money, which he is not in law bound to pay, and in circumstances implying that he is paying it voluntarily to close the transaction, he cannot recover it. Such a payment is in law like a gift, and the transaction cannot be reopened. If a person pays money, which he is not bound to pay, under the compulsion of urgent and pressing necessity or of seizure, actual or threatened, of his goods he can recover it as money had and received. The money is paid not under duress in the strict sense of the term, as that implies duress of person, but under the pressure of seizure or detention of goods which is analogous to that of duress. Payment under such pressure establishes that the payment is not made voluntarily to close the transaction (per Lord Abinger CB and per Parke B in *Atlee v Backhouse*). The payment is made for the purpose of averting a threatened evil and is made not with the intention of giving up a right but under immediate necessity and with the intention of preserving the right to dispute the legality of the demand (*per* Tindal CJ in *Valpy v Manley*). There are numerous instances in the books of successful claims in this form of action to recover money paid to relieve goods from seizure. Other familiar instances are cases such as *Parker v Great Western Ry Co*, where the money was paid to the railway company under protest in order to induce them to carry goods which they were refusing to carry except at rates in excess of those they were legally entitled to demand. These payments were made throughout a period of twelve months, always accompanied by the assertion that they were made under protest, and it was held that the plaintiffs were entitled to recover the excess payments as money had and received, on the ground that the payments were made under the compulsion of urgent and pressing necessity . . .

I come to the conclusion that the plaintiff never intended to depart, and never did depart, from the course taken by him at the commencement of the dispute. In order to preserve his right to recover, it is not, in my opinion, necessary that on every occasion there should be a refusal to pay by the plaintiff followed by seizure. It was not necessary to go through this form. The circumstances of these payments and the conduct of the plaintiff throughout the period of years satisfy me that he never made the payments voluntarily, that he never intended to give up his right to recover the sums paid, and that he only paid because he knew that a refusal to pay would be immediately followed by seizure of his goods, as in fact did happen whenever he disputed the defendant's right and refused to pay. The pressure of seizure was always present to his mind, and never ceased to operate upon it whenever demand for tolls was made. I am also satisfied that the circumstances of the payments and the conduct of the plaintiff were a sufficient indication to the defendant that the plaintiff did not intend to give up his right to recover. If any assertion or declaration of his intentions was necessary it was made to the defendant at the time and in the circumstances of the payments.'

The decisions in *Skeate* and *Maskell* set up an unhappy distinction between cases in which a party *agrees* to pay a sum of money under duress of goods and cases in which a party *actually pays* a sum of money under duress of goods. In the former situation the contract remains enforceable; in the latter the complainant is entitled to recover the money paid. This distinction is unjustifiable and it has been criticised by Professor Beatson.

Beatson, J, 'Duress as a vitiating factor in contract' [1974] CLJ 97, 106–108

It seems clear that payments made by reason of duress may be recovered, and 'for this purpose there is no difference whether the duress be of goods and chattels, or of real property, or of the person.' A payment under duress of goods '. . . is no more voluntary than a donation to a beggar who presents a pistol'.

It is submitted that there is no conceptual distinction between such a situation and the situation in which the coerced party agrees to pay money. An agreement to pay must always exist in the *scintilla temporis* that exists between the demand and the compliance. On the facts of *Astley v Reynolds*, for instance, A did not respond to the demand immediately, but only after his tender of a lesser sum had been twice refused, and at 'some months distance' from the original demand. At some point in that time A must have agreed to comply with the demand. One can apply this reasoning to all payments following a demand, however small the time lag is.

This conclusion is supported by the fact that the usual justification for the view that agreements induced by duress of goods cannot be set aside is either that there is greater coercive force in a threat of physical violence, or that there is no time for the victim to appeal to the courts for a remedy when he is facing a physical danger. Neither of these can rationally be confined to agreements, as opposed to payments.

If the view that an agreement made as the result of duress of goods by a party (who knew, and made it clear, that the 'club' used by the other party was wrongful) is valid and fully binding is accepted, one is forced to recognise that a promise to end a wrongful state of affairs amounts to good consideration. This is surely contrary to principle. If the worthlessness of the claim is clear to the parties, or if its worthlessness has been asserted by the 'victim' in such a way as to make it clear that he is not conceding to or compromising the claim, there is not sufficient consideration to support a contract. Normally the promise to perform an existing duty owed to the promisee does not amount to consideration so as to constitute a contract. *Tamvaco v Simpson* supports this contention. A cargo of coal was shipped aboard S's vessel. T had paid half the freight to a third party, who in turn provided S with a negotiable instrument. The master of the vessel heard that the third party was virtually bankrupt and demanded the full freight or a guarantee for its payment from T, refusing to release the cargo until this was done. T tendered the difference between the sum demanded and the sum paid to the third party, but this was refused. Eventually T gave the required guarantee, and the cargo was released. Later the freight was paid. The Court of Exchequer Chamber affirmed the judgment of the Court of Common Pleas allowing T to recover what had not been due. In this case there was no confusion with either the compromise doctrine or the process of law doctrine. The owner had received a negotiable instrument for half the freight and his lien only extended to the other half. As this had been tendered, continued possession of the cargo was clearly wrongful, and the protests of T's agents made it clear that they did not recognise the validity of the claim. *Skeate v Beale* was not referred to, probably because it was not thought to be relevant. As T recovered a payment made after he had obtained possession of the cargo, surely S could not have maintained an action based on the agreement if T had failed to pay when he did. The fact that S had been given a negotiable instrument was emphasised by Blackburn J, and it is possible that the case would have gone the other way had this been dishonoured at the time the master refused to part with the cargo. However, this merely shows that it will be difficult to displace the wide area covered by the compromise and process of law doctrines.

It is submitted that there is no reason for making a distinction between actual payments and agreements to pay. If that is so there is nothing to prevent a court from finding that duress of goods is a ground upon which the validity of a contract can be impeached. Furthermore, *Tamvaco v Simpson* provides positive authority in favour of the proposition.

[This article is reproduced in Beatson, J, *The Use and Abuse of Unjust Enrichment*, 1991, Oxford: Clarendon, Chapter 5]

The idea that duress of goods does not render a contract voidable is untenable and has been rejected in modern times.

Vantage Navigation Corporation v Suhail and Saud Bahwan Building Materials LLC, The 'Alev' [1989] 1 Lloyd's Rep 138

Facts: The plaintiffs' ship was chartered to carry a cargo of steel. The charterers were not financially sound and defaulted on their payments. Meanwhile, the property in the steel had passed from the charterers to the defendants. In negotiations, the plaintiffs told the defendants that unless they agreed to pay all outstanding sums owed by the charterers, they would not receive their cargo. The defendants agreed to this demand but later sought to have the agreement set aside for duress.

Held: The High Court held that the agreement could be avoided because it had been entered into under the illegitimate threat of economic duress and duress of goods.

Hobhouse J:

'The principle that agreements can be avoided if entered into under duress of goods or economic duress is now well established. See the sequence of modern authorities from *The Siboen v The Sibotre* [1976] 1 Lloyd's Rep 293 to *B & S Contracts v VG Publications* [1984] ICR 419 . . .

In the present case it is clear that the agreement falls within the principles of economic duress and for that matter duress of goods. The plaintiffs did make a threat which was illegitimate, and, if it be relevant, they knew it to be illegitimate. They were under an obligation to carry the cargo to Mina Qaboos and deliver it there to the defendants. They had no right to refuse to do so or to assert any inconsistent right over the goods. They did refuse to carry the goods to Mina Qaboos and deliver them to the

> defendants unless the defendants met their demands. They did assert a dominion over the defendants' goods; they refused to recognize the defendants' right to have the goods. The consent of the defendants was overborne. There was a coercion of their will. They neither in law nor in fact entered into the agreement voluntarily.
>
> . . . On the facts this is a clear example of the situation where the legal remedies are inadequate to meet the victim's legitimate commercial needs or to negate the compulsion operating upon him. There was no reasonable alternative open to the defendants.
>
> The defendants have established their right to rely upon the defence of duress. The plaintiffs' claim must fail.'

The judge concluded that the plaintiffs' action constituted both economic duress and duress of goods. Following the recognition of economic duress (see below), it was inevitable that duress of goods would also be recognised by the courts. The decision in *The Alev* merely confirmed this.

11.4 ECONOMIC DURESS

Economic duress refers to illegitimate commercial pressure – the threat of 'catastrophic' financial consequences. English law was slow to develop a doctrine of economic duress, largely due to the difficulty of distinguishing between legitimate and illegitimate commercial pressure. The first seeds of the doctrine were sown in the case of *D & C Builders v Rees* [1966] 2 QB 617. The plaintiff builders had undertaken work for the defendants and were owed nearly £500. The defendant knew that the plaintiffs were in financial difficulties and offered to pay them £300, telling them that they were unlikely to receive any more. The plaintiffs accepted the part-payment, but later sought to recover the balance of the debt. The Court of Appeal held that the plaintiffs could recover the balance of the debt because their consent to acceptance of part-payment was no true accord. Lord Denning MR said: 'The debtor's wife held the creditor to ransom. The creditor was in need of money to meet his own commitments and she knew it.'

The first recognition of economic duress as a basis for allowing a party to set aside a contract is probably to be found in the obiter comments of Kerr J in *Occidental Worldwide Investment Corp v Skibs A/S Avanti, The Siboen and The Sibotre* [1976] 1 Lloyd's Rep 293:

> '[A]ssuming, as I think, that our law is open to further development in relation to contracts concluded under some form of compulsion not amounting to duress to the person, the Court must in every case at least be satisfied that the consent of the other party was overborne by compulsion so as to deprive him of any *animus contrahendi*.'

The High Court also recognised that a contract could be set aside for economic duress on the facts of *North Ocean Shipping Co Ltd v Hyundai Construction Co Ltd*.

North Ocean Shipping Co Ltd v Hyundai Construction Co Ltd, The Atlantic Baron [1979] QB 705

Facts: The defendant shipbuilder agreed to build a tanker for the plaintiff ship owners. The contract stated a fixed price in US dollars with payment to be made in five instalments. After the plaintiffs had paid the first instalment, the dollar was devalued by 10% and the defendants threatened not to deliver the ship unless the remaining instalments were increased by 10%. The plaintiffs were advised that there was no legal ground on which the claim could be made and suggested that the matter should be referred to arbitration. The defendants declined this offer and insisted that the plaintiffs pay the increased amount. The plaintiffs were anxious that they might lose a very lucrative charter for the ship which they had arranged with Shell and so replied that although they were under no obligation to make increased payments, they would do so 'without prejudice' to their rights. The plaintiffs made the increased payments and the tanker was delivered in November 1974. In July 1975 the plaintiffs sought to recover the extra 10% they had paid. They claimed that they had delayed in their claim because they were concerned that the delivery of another ship that was being built for them might be affected.

Held: The High Court held that the defendant's threat to terminate the contract unless the plaintiffs increased their payments by 10% amounted to economic duress. The plaintiffs were not entitled to rescind the agreement, however, because they had affirmed it by making the final payments without protest and delaying their claim.

Mocatta J:

'I must next consider whether even if that agreement, varying the terms of the original shipbuilding contract of April 10, 1972, was made under a threat to break that original contract and the various increased instalments were made consequently under the varied agreement, the increased sums can be recovered as money had and received. [Counsel for the plaintiffs] submitted that they could be, provided they were involuntary payments and not made, albeit perhaps with some grumbling, to close the transaction.

Certainly this is the well-established position if payments are made, for example, to avoid the wrongful seizure of goods where there is no prior agreement to make such payments. The best known English case to this effect is probably *Maskell v Horner* [1915] 3 KB 106 . . .

There are a number of well-known examples in the books of English cases where the payments made have been involuntary by reason of some wrongful threatened action or inaction in relation to goods and have subsequently been recovered, but where the issue has not been complicated by the payments having been made under a contract. Some of these cases have concerned threats to seize, seizure or wrongful detention of goods, *Maskell v Horner* being the best known modern example of the former two categories and *Astley v Reynolds* (1731) 2 Str 915 a good example of the latter category, where a pawnbroker refused to release plate when the plaintiff tendered the money lent and, on demand, more than the legal rate of interest, since without this the pawnbroker would not release the plaintiff's plate. The plaintiff recovered the excess, as having paid it under compulsion and it was held no answer that an alternative remedy might lie in trover.

[Counsel for the plaintiffs] referred me to other cases decided in this country bordering upon what he called economic duress as distinct from duress to goods. Thus in *Parker v Great Western Railway Co* (1844) 7 Man & G 253, approved in *Great Western Railway Co v Sutton* (1869) LR 4 HL 226, it was held that the railway was not entitled to differentiate adversely between charges on goods made against one carrier or packer using the railway and others. Excess charges payable by such persons were recovered. In advising the House of Lords in the latter case, Willes J said, at p 249:

"... I have always understood that when a man pays more than he is bound to do by law for the performance of a duty which the law says is owed to him for nothing, or for less than he has paid, there is a compulsion or concussion in respect of which he is entitled to recover the excess by *condictio indebiti*, or action for money had and received. This is every day's practice as to excess freight."

There has been considerable discussion in the books whether, if an agreement is made under duress of goods to pay a sum of money and there is some consideration for the agreement, the excess sum can be recovered. The authority for this suggested distinction is *Skeate v Beale* (1841) 11 Ad & El 983. It was there said by Lord Denman CJ that an agreement was not void because made under duress of goods, the distinction between that case and the cases of money paid to recover goods wrongfully seized being said to be obvious in that the agreement was not compulsorily but voluntarily entered into ... Kerr J in *Occidental Worldwide Investment Corp v Skibs A/S Avanti, The Siboen and The Sibotre* [1976] 1 Lloyd's Rep 293, 335, gave strong expression to the view that the suggested distinction based on *Skeate v Beale* would not be observed today ... I was referred to a number of cases decided overseas ... Perhaps their greatest importance, however, is the quotation in the first mentioned from the judgment of Isaacs J in *Smith v William Charlick Ltd* (1924) 34 CLR 38, 56 where he said:

"It is conceded that the only ground on which the promise to repay could be implied is 'compulsion'. The payment is said by the respondent not to have been 'voluntary' but 'forced' from it within the contemplation of the law ... 'Compulsion' in relation to a payment of which refund is sought, and whether it is also variously called 'coercion', 'extortion', 'exaction' or 'force', includes every species of duress or conduct analogous to duress, actual or threatened, exerted by or on behalf of the payee and applied to the person or the property or any right of the person who pays. ... Such compulsion is a legal wrong, and the law provides a remedy by raising a fictional promise to repay."

These cases do not, however, expressly deal with the position arising when the threat or compulsion result in a new or varied contract. This was, or something very like it, however, the position in *Sundell's case*, 56 SR (NSW) 323 . . . It would seem . . . that the Australian courts would be prepared to allow the recovery of excess money paid, even under a new contract, as the result of a threat to break an earlier contract, since the threat or compulsion would be applied to the original contractual right of the party subject to the compulsion or economic duress. This also seems to be the view in the United States, where this was one of the grounds of decision in *King Construction Co v WM Smith Electric Co* (1961) 350 SW 2d 940. This view also accords with what was said in *D & C Builders v Rees* [1966] 2 QB 617, 625, *per* Lord Denning MR: "No person can insist on a settlement procured by intimidation." . . .

Before proceeding further it may be useful to summarise the conclusions I have so far reached. First, I do not take the view that the recovery of money paid under duress other than to the person is necessarily limited to duress to goods falling within one of the categories hitherto established by the English cases. I would respectfully follow and adopt the broad statement of principle laid down by Isaacs J cited earlier and frequently quoted and applied in the Australian cases. Secondly, from this it follows that the compulsion may take the form of "economic duress" if the necessary facts are proved. A threat to break a contract may amount to such "economic duress". Thirdly, if there has been such a form of duress leading to a contract for consideration, I think that contract is a voidable one which can be avoided and the excess money paid under it recovered.

I think the facts found in this case do establish that the agreement to increase the price by 10 per cent reached at the end of June 1973 was caused by what may be called "economic duress". The Yard were adamant in insisting on the increased price without having any legal justification for so doing and the owners realised that the Yard would not accept anything other than an unqualified agreement to the increase. The owners might have claimed damages in arbitration against the Yard with all the inherent unavoidable uncertainties of litigation, but in view of the position of the Yard vis-à-vis their relations with Shell it would be unreasonable to hold that this is the course they should have taken: see *Astley v Reynolds* (1731) 2 Str 915. The owners made a very reasonable offer of arbitration coupled with security for any award in the Yard's favour that might be made, but this was refused. They then made their agreement, which can truly I think be said to have been made under compulsion, by the telex of June 28 without prejudice to their rights. I do not consider the Yard's ignorance of the Shell charter material. It may well be that had they known of it they would have been even more exigent.

If I am right in the conclusion reached with some doubt earlier that there was consideration for the 10 per cent increase agreement reached at the end of June 1973, and it be right to regard this as having been reached under a kind of duress in the form of economic pressure, then what is said in *Chitty on Contracts*, 24th edn (1977), vol 1, para 442, p 207, to which both counsel referred me, is relevant, namely, that a contract entered into under duress is voidable and not void:

"... consequently a person who has entered into a contract under duress, may either affirm or avoid such contract after the duress has ceased; and if he has so voluntarily acted under it with a full knowledge of all the circumstances he may be held bound on the ground of ratification, or if, after escaping from the duress, he takes no steps to set aside the transaction, he may be found to have affirmed it." ...

I have already stated that no protest of any kind was made by the owners after their telex of June 28, 1973, before their claim in this arbitration on July 30, 1975, shortly after in July of that year the *Atlantic Baroness*, a sister ship of the *Atlantic Baron*, had been tendered, though, as I understand it, she was not accepted and arbitration proceedings in regard to her are in consequence taking place. There was therefore a delay between November 27, 1974, when the *Atlantic Baron* was delivered and July 30, 1975, before the owners put forward their claim.

The owners were, therefore, free from the duress on November 27, 1974, and took no action by way of protest or otherwise between their important telex of June 28, 1973, and their formal claim for the return of the excess 10 per cent paid of July 30, 1975, when they nominated their arbitrator. One cannot dismiss this delay as of no significance, though I would not consider it conclusive by itself. I do not attach any special importance to the lack of protest made at the time of the assignment, since the documents made no reference to the increased 10 per cent. However, by the time the *Atlantic Baron* was due for delivery in November 1974, market conditions had changed radically, as is found in paragraph 39 of the special case and the owners must have been aware of this. The special case finds in paragraph 40, as stated earlier, that the owners did not believe that if they made any protest in the protocol of delivery and acceptance that the Yard would have refused to deliver the vessel or the *Atlantic Baroness* and had no reason so to believe. [Counsel for the plaintiffs] naturally stressed that in the rather carefully expressed findings in paragraphs 39 to 44 of the special case, there is no finding that if at the time of the final payments the owners had withheld payment of the additional 10 per cent the Yard would not have delivered the vessel. However, after careful consideration, I have come to the conclusion that the important points here are that since there was no danger at this time in registering a protest, the final payments were made without any qualification and were followed by a delay until July 31, 1975, before the owners put forward their claim, the correct inference to draw, taking an objective view of the facts, is that the action and inaction of the owners can only be regarded as an affirmation of the variation in June 1973 of the terms of the original contract by the agreement to pay the additional 10 per cent. In reaching this conclusion I have not, of course, overlooked the findings in paragraph 45 of the special case, but I do not think that an intention on the part of the owners not to affirm the agreement for the extra payments not indicated to the Yard can avail them in the view of their overt acts ...'

The case is authority for the proposition that a threatened breach of contract can constitute economic duress. On the facts, the defendants' threat amounted to duress because it had no legal justification and it left the plaintiffs with no realistic alternative other than to pay the extra 10%. Mocatta J held that duress rendered the contract voidable, not void (cf *Barton v Armstrong*). As such, the plaintiffs' right to have the contract set aside was subject to the usual bars to rescission, including delay and affirmation. On the facts, the plaintiff's delay of eight months was held to infer that the plaintiffs had affirmed the variation to the contract. This provides a stark reminder of the importance of bringing a claim as soon as practicably possible.

11.4.1 REQUIREMENTS TO ESTABLISH A CLAIM FOR ECONOMIC DURESS

In the leading case on economic duress it was held that there are two elements that are required to establish duress.

Universe Tankships Inc of Monrovia v International Transport Workers' Federation, The Universe Sentinel [1983] 1 AC 366

Facts: The plaintiffs' ship, the Universe Sentinel, was boycotted by the defendant union, the ITF. The plaintiffs paid $6,500 to ITF's welfare fund in order to get the ship released. They later sought to recover the money. ITF admitted economic duress but claimed that the threat had been made in furtherance of a trade dispute and so was protected by s 13 of the Trade Union Labour Relations Act 1974.

Held: The House of Lords (Lord Scarman and Lord Brandon dissenting) held that the action was not protected by the Trade Union Relations Act 1974 and therefore the money could be recovered.

Lord Diplock:
'My Lords, I turn to the second ground on which repayment of the $6,480 is claimed, which I will call the duress point. It is not disputed that the circumstances in which ITF demanded that the shipowners should enter into the special agreement and the typescript agreement and should pay the moneys of which the latter documents acknowledge receipt, amounted to economic duress upon the shipowners; that is to say, it is conceded that the financial consequences to the shipowners of the Universe Sentinel continuing to be rendered off-hire under her time charter to Texaco, while the blacking continued, were so catastrophic as to amount to a coercion of the ship-owners' will which vitiated their consent to those agreements and to the payments made by them to ITF. This concession makes it unnecessary for your Lordships to use the instant appeal as the occasion for a general consideration of the developing law of economic duress as a ground for treating contracts as voidable and obtaining restitution of money paid under economic duress as money had and received to the plaintiffs' use. That economic duress may constitute a ground for such redress was recognised,

albeit obiter, by the Privy Council in *Pao On v Lau Yiu Long* [1980] AC 614. The Board in that case referred with approval to two judgments at first instance in the commercial court which recognised that commercial pressure may constitute duress: one by Kerr J. in *Occidental Worldwide Investment Corp v Skibs A/S Avanti, The Siboen and The Sibotre*, the other by Mocatta J in *North Ocean Shipping Co Ltd v Hyundai Construction Co Ltd, The Atlantic Baron* [1979] QB 705, which traces the development of this branch of the law from its origin in the eighteenth and early nineteenth-century cases.

It is, however, in my view crucial to the decision of the instant appeal to identify the rationale of this development of the common law. It is not that the party seeking to avoid the contract which he has entered into with another party, or to recover money that he has paid to another party in response to a demand, did not know the nature or the precise terms of the contract at the time when he entered into it or did not understand the purpose for which the payment was demanded. The rationale is that his apparent consent was induced by pressure exercised upon him by that other party which the law does not regard as legitimate, with the consequence that the consent is treated in law as revocable unless approbated either expressly or by implication after the illegitimate pressure has ceased to operate on his mind. It is a rationale similar to that which underlies the avoidability of contracts entered into and the recovery of money exacted under colour of office, or under undue influence or in consequence of threats of physical duress.

Commercial pressure, in some degree, exists wherever one party to a commercial transaction is in a stronger bargaining position than the other party. It is not, however, in my view, necessary, nor would it be appropriate in the instant appeal, to enter into the general question of the kinds of circumstances, if any, in which commercial pressure, even though it amounts to a coercion of the will of a party in the weaker bargaining position, may be treated as legitimate and, accordingly, as not giving rise to any legal right of redress. In the instant appeal the economic duress complained of was exercised in the field of industrial relations to which very special considerations apply . . .'

Lord Scarman (dissenting):
'It is, I think, already established law that economic pressure can in law amount to duress; and that duress, if proved, not only renders voidable a transaction into which a person has entered under its compulsion but is actionable as a tort, if it causes damage or loss: *Barton v Armstrong* [1976] AC 104 and *Pao On v Lau Yiu Long* [1980] AC 614. The authorities upon which these two cases were based reveal two elements in the wrong of duress: (1) pressure amounting to compulsion of the will of the victim; and (2) the illegitimacy of the pressure exerted. There must be pressure, the practical effect of which is compulsion or the absence of choice. Compulsion is variously described in the authorities as coercion or the vitiation of consent. The classic case of duress is, however, not the lack of will to submit but the victim's intentional submission arising from the realisation that there is no other practical

choice open to him. This is the thread of principle which links the early law of duress (threat to life or limb) with later developments when the law came also to recognise as duress first the threat to property and now the threat to a man's business or trade. The development is well traced in *Goff and Jones, The Law of Restitution*, 2nd edn (1978), chapter 9.

The absence of choice can be proved in various ways, e.g. by protest, by the absence of independent advice, or by a declaration of intention to go to law to recover the money paid or the property transferred: see *Maskell v Horner* [1915] 3 KB 106. But none of these evidential matters goes to the essence of duress. The victim's silence will not assist the bully, if the lack of any practicable choice but to submit is proved. The present case is an excellent illustration. There was no protest at the time, but only a determination to do whatever was needed as rapidly as possible to release the ship. Yet nobody challenges the judge's finding that the owner acted under compulsion. He put it thus [1981] I.C.R. 129, 143:

> "It was a matter of the most urgent commercial necessity that the plaintiffs should regain the use of their vessel. They were advised that their prospects of obtaining an injunction were minimal, the vessel would not have been released unless the payment was made, and they sought recovery of the money with sufficient speed once the duress had terminated."

The real issue in the appeal is, therefore, as to the second element in the wrong duress: was the pressure applied by the ITF in the circumstances of this case one which the law recognises as legitimate? For, as Lord Wilberforce and Lord Simon of Glaisdale said in *Barton v Armstrong* [1976] AC 104, 121D: "the pressure must be one of a kind which the law does not regard as legitimate".

As the two noble and learned Lords remarked at p 121D, in life, including the life of commerce and finance, many acts are done "under pressure, sometimes overwhelming pressure": but they are not necessarily done under duress. That depends on whether the circumstances are such that the law regards the pressure as legitimate.

In determining what is legitimate two matters may have to be considered. The first is as to the nature of the pressure. In many cases this will be decisive, though not in every case. And so the second question may have to be considered, namely, the nature of the demand which the pressure is applied to support.

The origin of the doctrine of duress in threats to life or limb, or to property, suggests strongly that the law regards the threat of unlawful action as illegitimate, whatever the demand. Duress can, of course, exist even if the threat is one of lawful action: whether it does so depends upon the nature of the demand. Blackmail is often a demand supported by a threat to do what is lawful, e.g. to report criminal conduct to the police. In many cases, therefore, "What [one] has to justify is not the threat, but the demand . . .": see *per* Lord Atkin in *Thorne v Motor Trade Association* [1937] AC 797, 806.

The present is a case in which the nature of the demand determines whether the pressure threatened or applied, ie the blacking, was lawful or unlawful. If it was unlawful, it is conceded that the owner acted under duress and can recover. If it was lawful, it is conceded that there was no duress and the sum sought by the owner is irrecoverable. The lawfulness or otherwise of the demand depends upon whether it was an act done in contemplation or furtherance of a trade dispute. If it was, it would not be actionable in tort: section 13 (1) of the Act. Although no question of tortious liability arises in this case and section 13 (1) is not, therefore, directly in point, it is not possible, in my view, to say of acts which are protected by statute from suit in tort that they nevertheless can amount to duress. Parliament having enacted that such acts are not actionable in tort, it would be inconsistent with legislative policy to say that, when the remedy sought is not damages for tort but recovery of money paid, they become unlawful.

In order to determine whether the making of the demand was an act done in contemplation or furtherance of a trade dispute, it is necessary to refer to section 29 which sets out the statutory meaning of "trade dispute".

The issue therefore is reduced to the one question. Was the demand for contributions to the welfare fund connected with one or more of the matters specified in section 29 of the Act? It is common ground that unless the demand was connected with "terms and conditions of employment" it was not within the section . . .

[His Lordship considered whether the demand related to the terms and conditions of employment]

I conclude that the demand for contributions related to the terms and conditions of employment on the ship, and, if it had been resisted by the owner, would have led to a trade dispute. Blacking the ship in support of the demand was, therefore, not actionable in tort. It was, accordingly, a legitimate exercise of pressure and did not constitute duress. The owner cannot recover the contributions. I would dismiss the appeal.'

The minority in the House of Lords dissented on the issue of whether the ITF's conduct amounted to illegitimate pressure, but agreed that there are two requirements that must be satisfied if relief is to be available on the ground of duress:

(1) Compulsion of the will;
(2) Illegitimate pressure.

We will consider each of these requirements in turn.

11.4.1.1 Compulsion of the will

For duress to be established it must be shown that the claimant was put under pressure that amounted to a coercion of his will. In defining this requirement the courts have spoken of the pressure being such as to overbear the claimant's will so as to vitiate (cancel) his/her consent.

Pao On v Lau Yiu Long [1980] AC 614

Facts: The plaintiffs agreed to sell a building under construction to the defendants. Payment for the building was to be made by an exchange of shares. To avoid depressing the market in the defendants' shares, the plaintiffs agreed to retain 60% of the shares for one year. To guarantee the plaintiffs against a fall in the share value the defendants entered a subsidiary agreement to buy back the shares at $2.5 per share after one year. The plaintiffs then realised that if the shares increased in value over $2.5 per share they would lose profit. Therefore, the plaintiffs threatened to terminate the main contract unless the subsidiary agreement was cancelled and replaced by an agreement to indemnify the plaintiffs against any reduction in the value of the shares below $2.5 per share. The defendants feared losing the building and so agreed to the plaintiffs' terms. The shares fell in value, and the plaintiffs brought a claim under the indemnity agreement to recover their loss.

Held: The Privy Council rejected the defendants' argument that the indemnity agreement should be set aside for duress because the defendant could not demonstrate that the commercial pressure had coerced their will so as to vitiate their consent.

Lord Scarman:
'Duress, whatever form it takes, is a coercion of the will so as to vitiate consent. Their Lordships agree with the observation of Kerr J in *Occidental Worldwide Investment Corp v Skibs A/S Avanti, The Siboen and The Sibotre* [1976] 1 Lloyd's Rep 293, 336 that in a contractual situation commercial pressure is not enough. There must be present some factor "which could in law be regarded as a coercion of his will so as to vitiate his consent" . . . In determining whether there was a coercion of will such that there was no true consent, it is material to inquire whether the person alleged to have been coerced did or did not protest; whether, at the time he was allegedly coerced into making the contract, he did or did not have an alternative course open to him such as an adequate legal remedy; whether he was independently advised; and whether after entering the contract he took steps to avoid it. All these matters are, as was recognised in *Maskell v Horner* [1915] 3 KB 106, relevant in determining whether he acted voluntarily or not.

In the present case there is unanimity amongst the judges below that there was no coercion of the first defendant's will. In the Court of Appeal the trial judge's finding (already quoted) that the first defendant considered the matter thoroughly, chose to avoid litigation, and formed the opinion that the risk in giving the guarantee was more apparent than real was upheld. In short, there was commercial pressure, but no coercion. Even if this Board was disposed, which it is not, to take a different view, it would not substitute its opinion for that of the judges below on this question of fact.

. . . Recently two English judges have recognised that commercial pressure may constitute duress the pressure of which can render a contract voidable: Kerr J in *Occidental Worldwide Investment Corp v Skibs A/S Avanti, The Siboen and The Sibotre* [1976] 1 Lloyd's Rep 293 and Mocatta J in *North Ocean Shipping Co Ltd v Hyundai Construction Co Ltd, The Atlantic Baron* [1979] QB 705. Both stressed that the pressure must be such that the victim's consent to the contract was not a voluntary act on his part. In their Lordships' view, there is nothing contrary to principle in recognising economic duress as a factor which may render a contract voidable, provided always that the basis of such recognition is that it must amount to a coercion of will, which vitiates consent. It must be shown that the payment made or the contract entered into was not a voluntary act.'

The test prescribed by Lord Scarman requires the pressure to 'amount to a coercion of the will, which vitiates consent'. This test has caused a certain degree of controversy because it suggests that there has to be a total lack of consent (see Atiyah, 'Economic duress and the "overborne will"' (1982) 98 LQR 197; Beatson, *The Use and Abuse of Unjust Enrichment*, 1991, pp 113–17, Oxford: Clarendon). But, as Professor Enonchong has shown (Enonchong, *Duress, Undue Influence and Unconscionable Dealing*, 2006, p 37, London: Sweet & Maxwell) this is to misunderstand the meaning of 'vitiation' of consent. Vitiation does not mean that the consent is negatived or destroyed; the claimant does not lose his will to act and become an automaton. Rather, his consent is tainted or 'deflected' (*Huyton SA v Peter Cremer GmbH & Co* [1999] 1 Lloyd's Rep 620, 638 *per* Mance J). The claimant is perfectly aware of what he is doing but because of the pressure exerted on him he feels that he has no 'real' choice. His will is 'redirected'. Lord Scarman helpfully explained the meaning of this in *Universe Tankships v ITF* (see above):

'Compulsion is variously described in the authorities as coercion or the vitiation of consent. The classic case of duress is, however, not the lack of will to submit but the victim's intentional submission arising from the realisation that there is no other practical choice open to him.'

There should be 'no other practical choice open' to the claimant. Pressure will only amount to duress if it caused the victim to enter into the contract. The court must ask the question: 'Did the victim have any "practical" or "reasonable" alternative?'

B & S Contracts and Design Ltd v Victor Green Publications Ltd [1984] ICR 419

Facts: The plaintiffs agreed to erect stands for the defendants at Olympia. They planned to use employees who were to be made redundant after completion of the work. The employees refused to erect the stands unless their demand for £9,000 severance pay (to which they were not entitled) was met. The plaintiffs agreed to pay the employees £4,500 and told the defendants that they would have to terminate the contract unless the defendants agreed to pay the remaining £4,500, in addition to the contract price. If the stands were not erected the defendants faced disastrous financial consequences so they agreed to pay the employees and the contract was performed. The defendants later sought to deduct the £4,500 from the contract price and the plaintiffs sued them for breach of contract. At first instance, the trial judge dismissed the plaintiff's claim on the ground that the money had been paid under duress.

Held: The Court of Appeal dismissed the appeal.

Griffiths LJ:
'The facts of this case appear to me to be as follows. The plaintiffs intended to break their contract . . . by allowing their workforce to walk off the job in circumstances in which they could not possibly replace it with another workforce. The defendants offered to advance the sum of £4,500 on the contract price, which would have enabled the plaintiffs to pay the men a sufficient extra sum of money to induce them to remain on the job. The plaintiffs refused this sum of money. There is no question that they refused to pay as a matter of principle. They refused to pay because they did not want to reduce the sum they would receive for the contract. They said to the defendants, "If you will give us £4,500 we will complete the contract". The defendants, faced with this demand, were in an impossible position. If they refused to hand over the sum of £4,500 they would not be able to erect the stands in this part of the exhibition, which would have clearly caused grave damage to their reputation and I would have thought might have exposed them to very heavy claims from the exhibitors who had leased space from them and hoped to use those stands in the ensuing exhibition. They seem to me to have been placed in the position envisaged by Lord Scarman in the Privy Council decision in *Pao On v Lau Yiu Long* [1980] AC 614, in which they were faced with no alternative course of action but to pay the sum demanded of them. It was submitted to us that there was no overt demand, but it was implicit in negotiations between the parties that the plaintiffs were putting the defendants into a corner and it was quite apparent to the defendants, by reason of the plaintiffs' conduct, that unless they handed over £4,500 the plaintiffs would walk off the job. This is, in my view, a situation in which the judge was fully entitled to find in the circumstances of this case that there was duress. As the defendants' director said, he was over a barrel, he had no alternative but to pay; he had no chance of going to any other source of labour to erect the stands . . . fails.'

Kerr LJ
'I . . . bear in mind that a threat to break a contract unless money is paid by the other party can, but by no means always will, constitute duress. It appears from the authorities that it will only constitute duress if the consequences of a refusal would be serious and immediate so that there is no reasonable alternative open, such as by legal redress, obtaining an injunction, etc . . . [T]here was no other practical choice open to the defendants in the present case, and accordingly I agree that this is a case where money has been paid under duress, which was accordingly recoverable by the defendants provided they acted promptly as they did, and which they have recovered

> by deducting it from the contract price. In these circumstances the plaintiffs' claim for this additional sum must fail.'

On the facts of the case it was not strictly true that the defendants had no alternative other than to pay the £4,500. They could have refused to pay and brought a claim for breach of contract. But this would not have been a 'reasonable' or 'practical' alternative because failure to erect the stands would have caused grave damage to the plaintiffs' reputation and would have exposed them to heavy claims from the exhibitors who had already agreed to lease the stands from the plaintiffs at the trade exhibition.

11.4.1.1.1 *The test of causation*

It was noted earlier in the chapter that the test of causation may differ depending on the type of duress under consideration. *Barton v Armstrong* confirmed that the test applicable in cases of duress of the person was that the pressure should be '*a* reason (not *the* reason, nor the *predominant* reason nor the *clinching* reason) why the complainant acted as he did'. This test set a very low threshold for causation and subsequent cases have suggested that the bar may be raised in cases of economic duress. Lord Goff made the following comments in *Dimskal Shipping Co SA v International Transport Workers Federation, The Evia Luck* [1992] 2 AC 152:

> 'We are here concerned with a case of economic duress. It was at one time thought that, at common law, the only form of duress which would entitle a party to avoid a contract on that ground was duress of the person. The origin for this view lay in the decision of the Court of Exchequer in *Skeate v Beale* (1841) 11 Ad & El 983. However, since the decisions of Kerr J in *Occidental Worldwide Investment Corp v Skibs A/S Avanti, The Siboen and The Sibotre* [1976] 1 Lloyd's Rep 293, of Mocatta J in *North Ocean Shipping Co Ltd v Hyundai Construction Co Ltd, The Atlantic Baron* [1979] QB 705, and of the Judicial Committee of the Privy Council in *Pao On v Lau Yiu Long* [1980] AC 614, that limitation has been discarded; and it is now accepted that economic pressure may be sufficient to amount to duress for this purpose, provided at least that the economic pressure may be characterised as illegitimate and has constituted a significant cause inducing the plaintiff to enter into the relevant contract (see *Barton v Armstrong* [1976] AC 104, 121, *per* Lord Wilberforce and Lord Simon of Glaisdale (referred to with approval in *Pao On v Lau Yiu Long* [1980] AC 614, 635, *per* Lord Scarman) and *Crescendo Management Pty Ltd v Westpac Banking Corporation* (1988) 19 NSWLR 40, 46, *per* McHugh JA).'

Lord Goff inserted the word 'significant' before 'cause'. This led Mance J to conclude in *Huyton SA v Peter Cremer GmbH & Co* [1999] 1 Lloyd's Rep 620, that there is a difference between the test advocated for duress to the person in *Barton v Armstrong*, and that advocated for economic duress in *Dimskal Shipping*:

'I start with the requirement that the illegitimate pressure must, in cases of economic duress, constitute "a significant cause" (cf *per* Lord Goff in *The Evia Luck*, at p 120; p 165, cited above). This is contrasted in Goff and Jones on *The Law of Restitution* (4th edn) p 251, footnote 59 with the lesser requirement that it should be "a" reason which applies in the context of duress to the person. The relevant authority in the latter context is *Barton v Armstrong* [1976] AC 104 (a case of threats to kill) . . .

The use of the phrase "a significant cause" by Lord Goff in *The Evia Luck*, supported by the weighty observation in the footnote in Goff & Jones, suggests that this relaxed view of causation in the special context of duress to the person cannot prevail in the less serious context of economic duress. The minimum basic test of subjective causation in economic duress ought, it appears to me, to be a "but for" test. The illegitimate pressure must have been such as actually caused the making of the agreement, in the sense that it would not otherwise have been made either at all or, at least, in the terms in which it was made. In that sense, the pressure must have been decisive or clinching.'

The 'significant' cause test has also been adopted in two subsequent decisions (*DSND Subsea v Petroleum Geo-Services* [2000] BLR 530; *Carillion Construction Ltd v Felix (UK) Ltd* [2001] BLR 1). It has been subjected to academic criticism, however, in terms of its basis in both authority and principle:

Enonchong, N, *Duress, Undue Influence and Unconscionable Dealing*, 2006, pp 40–41, London: Sweet & Maxwell

Authority. Although Mance J's test relies of Lord Goff's statement in *Dimskal Shipping*, it is not clear that Lord Goff intended any difference between his test and that laid down in *Barton v Armstrong*. On the contrary, there is reason for suspecting that, although his language is different, Lord Goff intended no such difference. This is because the three cases cited by Lord Goff in support of his view that the pressure must be 'a significant cause' are all in line with the test in *Barton v Armstrong*. The first is *Barton v Armstrong* itself and Lord Goff refers specifically to the judgment of Lord Wilberforce and Lord Simon of Glaisdale and in particular to the page where they set out the test that the pressure must be 'a reason (not *the* reason, nor the *predominant* reason nor the *clinching* reason)'. Surely if Lord Goff had intended to state a different test (for economic duress) he would have said so clearly rather than rely for support on the same judgment with which he seeks to differ. The second case cited by Lord Goff is *Pao On v Lau Yiu Long* and he refers to the page where the Board expressly approved of the page where the *Barton* test is stated in the judgment of Lord

Wilberforce and Lord Simon of Glaisdale in *Barton v Armstrong*. Finally, Lord Goff's reliance on the judgment of McHugh JA in *Crescendo Management Pty Ltd v Westpac Banking Corporation* shows very clearly that he did not intend to depart from the test in *Barton v Armstrong*. For McHugh JA, in a case concerned with economic duress, clearly states, in the page referred to by Lord Goff, that it is not necessary to establish that the pressure was 'the sole reason' for entering into the contract: 'It is sufficient that the illegitimate pressure was *one of the reasons* for the person entering into the agreement.' If Lord Goff intended to state a different test he may still have referred to these judgments but only to contrast them with the different test that he was enunciating. Yet he made no contrasting statement at all. It is difficult to believe that, if he intended to depart from all these cases, Lord Goff would not have done so expressly with an explanation of the reasons for selecting a different test.

Moreover in *Dorimex SRL v Visage Imports Ltd*, a case of economic duress, the *Barton* test was applied at first instance where the judge held that the agreement was vitiated by economic duress because the pressure 'was one of several causes' of the agreement. On appeal the Court of Appeal did not criticise the judge.

Principle. Quite apart from authority, it is doubtful whether as a matter of principle there should be different tests of causation for different types of duress. The only reason advanced by Mance J for the view that a different test should apply in the context of economic duress is that economic pressure is less serious than death threats or other threats to the person. He stated that the *Barton* 'relaxed view of causation in the special context of duress to the person cannot prevail in the less serious context of economic duress'. It is true that threats of violence to the person are more serious than threats of economic harm. But it is not clear how it follows from this that the test for whether the threat caused a person to act in the way he did should be different. There seems no sound basis for saying that the test for causation should differ according to the type of duress, with duress to the person requiring a more relaxed test than economic duress.

Such a view smacks of the once received notion that only a threat to the person was sufficient to amount to duress. That notion has now been discredited and abandoned. It should not be allowed to re-appear in a modified form though the idea that a different test of causation should apply in the case of economic duress so as to make it more difficult to establish economic duress than duress to the person. If it is believed that the test laid down in *Barton v Armstrong* is too relaxed and there is a need to raise the hurdle, then the question should be whether a new test is desirable. But it should be one that applies to all types of duress. Once the law has drawn the line between legitimate and illegitimate pressure, it should not discriminate further by making distinctions between different categories of illegitimate pressure when considering the question of causation. The question of causation should not be confused with the evidential question of what the coercive effect of a particular type of pressure is likely to be. It is recognised that a court is more likely to accept that a particular type of pressure caused the victim to act the way he did because the type of pressure is generally known to have such a coercive effect. For example, a court will recognise that a threat to kill the victim is likely to have a more coercive effect than a threat to refuse to repay a loan of a small amount. However, that is an evidential matter rather than a satisfactory basis for saying that the test of causation should be different according to whether the threat is to kill or to refuse to pay a small debt.

Professor Enonchong's argument from principle is surely correct. The nature of the pressure is relevant to the evidential question (whether the pressure affected the claimant's will) in much the same way as the claimant's subjective circumstances are relevant, such as her age, financial position, business experience and access to legal advice (see *Daniel v Drew* [2005] EWCA Civ 507). The causation question does not concern such matters, however, and the test to be applied should be identical, regardless of the form of duress.

With respect, Professor Enonchong's criticisms on the point of authority are less convincing. Mance J's interpretation of Lord Goff in *Dimskal Shipping* is supported by a footnote in Goff & Jones, *The Law of Restitution*, 4th edn, London: Sweet & Maxwell. Lord Goff was the co-author of that work and it is to be expected that it provides the most reliable commentary on the meaning of his Lordship's speech in *Dimskal Shipping*.

11.4.1.2 Illegitimate pressure

The second element of a claim for duress is the illegitimacy of the pressure used. For some people, the word 'illegitimate' has associations with wrongdoing, but in the context of duress illegitimacy is not synonymous with wrongdoing. Illegitimate pressure may include a threatened breach of contract (*North Ocean Shipping Co Ltd v Hyundai Construction Co Ltd, The Atlantic Baron* [1979] QB 705) and even a threatened lawful act (*CTN Cash and Carry v Gallaher* [1994] 4 All ER 714). The question to ask in every situation is: Does the behaviour go beyond what a reasonable person would regard as acceptable in all the circumstances?

In *Universe Tankships Inc of Monrovia v International Transport Workers' Federation, The Universe Sentinel* [1983] 1 AC 366, the House of Lords focused its attention on whether the industrial action was unlawful under English law. Their Lordships concluded that it was and on this basis held that the contract could be set aside for duress. This approach was followed in *Dimskal Fishing v International Transport Workers' Federation, The Evia Luck* [1980] AC 614. Again, the case involved industrial action by the ITF. This time the action was lawful in Sweden where it took place, but unlawful in England. The House of Lords held (Lord Templemann dissenting) that the law to be applied in deciding the issue of legitimacy was English law and on this basis the contracts could be set aside for duress. Lord Goff made the following observations:

'If a person enters into . . . a contract, he has for most purposes to accept the regime of the proper law of the contract; and if under that regime a particular form of conduct constitutes duress, or for that matter undue influence, rendering the contact voidable wherever the relevant conduct occurs, he has in my opinion to accept the consequences of his conduct under that system of law. He should not assume that, simply because his conduct is lawful in the place overseas where it is performed, it cannot for that reason render English contract voidable for duress.'

It is clear that a threatened breach of contract can also constitute illegitimate pressure, although it may be harder for the victim to show that the pressure amounted to a coercion of his will.

Atlas Express Ltd v Kafco (Importers and Distributors) Ltd [1989] 1 QB 833

Facts: The plaintiffs, a national road carrier, agreed with the defendants, a basketware importing company, to deliver their baskets to branches of Woolworths. The original contract price for delivery was £110 per trailer of baskets. After the first load had been delivered, the plaintiffs told the defendants that they would not carry any further loads unless the defendants agreed to increase the price to a minimum of £440 per trailer. The defendants relied heavily on the contract with Woolworths, and reasonably believed that it would be impossible to make alternative arrangements for carriage, so felt compelled to sign the new agreement. Later, the defendants refused to pay the increased rate and the plaintiffs brought a claim for breach of contract.

Held: The court held that the pressure exerted on the defendants amounted to economic duress. Furthermore, since the plaintiffs were already contractually bound to deliver the defendant's goods, there was no consideration for the new agreement. The defendants were not liable to pay the minimum charge of £440 per trailer.

Tucker J:
'The issue which I have to determine is whether the defendants are bound by the agreement signed on their behalf on 18 November 1986. The defendants contend that they are not bound, for two reasons: first because the agreement was signed under duress; second because there was no consideration for it.

The first question raises a particularly interesting point of law – whether economic duress is a concept known to English law. Economic duress must be distinguished from commercial pressure, which on any view is not sufficient to vitiate consent. The borderline between the two may in some cases be indistinct. But the authors of *Chitty* on Contracts and of Goff and Jones, The Law of Restitution appear to recognise that in appropriate cases economic duress may afford a defence, and in my judgment it does. It is clear to me that in a number of English cases judges have acknowledged the existence of this concept.

[The judge considered the leading cases on economic duress]

Reverting to the case before me, I find that the defendants' apparent consent to the agreement was induced by pressure which was illegitimate and I find that it was not approbated. In my judgment that pressure can properly be described as economic duress, which is a concept recognised by English law, and which in the circumstances of the present case vitiates the defendants' apparent consent to the agreement.

In any event, I find that there was no consideration for the new agreement. The plaintiffs were already obliged to deliver the defendants' goods at the rates agreed under the terms of the original agreement. There was no consideration for the increased minimum charge of £440 per trailer.'

The judge concluded that a threatened breach of contract can amount to illegitimate pressure. This finding is supported by the dicta of Lord Scarman in *Pao On v Lau You Long*, where it was held that threatened breach of contract could, in principle, amount to economic duress. On the facts of *Pao On*, however, it was held that there was no economic duress because the threat did not amount to a coercion of the victim's will. This highlights the complex relationship between the two elements of a duress claim. In principle, the two elements are independent, but in practice the more illegitimate the pressure, the easier it is to demonstrate coercion of the will. In *Atlas Express*, the court accepted the defendants' argument that the threatened breach of contract had coerced the defendants' will, because it left them with 'no practical alternative'. The contract with Woolworths was extremely valuable to the defendants and it could have been lost had the plaintiffs carried through their threat to cease delivering the defendants' baskets.

It is interesting to note the alternative ground relied upon by the defendants to refuse the plaintiffs' claim. The defendants argued that there was no consideration for their promise to pay £440 per trailer (see *Stilk v Myrick* (1809) 2 Camp 317; 170 ER 1168). Tucker J agreed, holding that the plaintiffs were already contractually obliged to deliver the defendants' goods and had provided no consideration for the increased charge (a similar argument was unsuccessfully made in *North Ocean Shipping Co Ltd v Hyundai Construction Co Ltd, The Atlantic Baron* [1979] QB 705). The scope for making this argument in the future is likely to be seriously diminished following the decision of the Court of Appeal in *Williams v Roffey Bros & Nicholls (Contractors) Ltd* [1991] QB 833 (see Chapter 3). The recognition that the 'practical benefit' of obtaining the timely performance of an existing obligation is sufficient to form consideration for a new promise means that consideration is likely to be found in most duress situations. The claimant will probably have made the additional payment in order to avoid undesirable consequences. In most cases, it is likely that the avoidance of those consequences will be regarded as a 'practical benefit' and therefore good consideration. As a result, the doctrine of duress will become increasingly important in dealing with this type of situation (see for example *South Caribbean Trading Ltd v Trafigura Beheer BV* [2004] EWHC 2676 (Comm); [2005] 1 Lloyd's Rep 128).

So far, all the examples of duress that we have considered have involved conduct that is, in some respects, a breach of the law. The conduct might be a crime, a tort, or a breach of conduct. But can lawful actions constitute illegitimate pressure? Lord Scarman suggested that they could in *Universe Tankships Inc of Monrovia v International Transport Workers' Federation ('The Universe Sentinel')* [1983] 1 AC 366:

'The origin of the doctrine of duress in threats to life or limb, or to property, suggests strongly that the law regards the threat of unlawful action as illegitimate, whatever the demand. Duress can, of course, exist even if the threat is one of lawful action: whether it does so depends upon the nature of the demand. Blackmail is often a demand supported by a threat to do what is lawful, e.g. to report criminal conduct to the police. In many cases, therefore, "What [one] has to justify is not the threat, but the demand . . .": see *per* Lord Atkin in *Thorne v Motor Trade Association* [1937] AC 797, 806.'

This was followed by the Court of Appeal in *CTN Cash and Carry v Gallaher*.

CTN Cash and Carry v Gallaher [1994] 4 All ER 714

Facts: The plaintiff company, which ran a cash and carry warehouse, agreed to purchase a consignment of cigarettes from the defendants. The defendants mistakenly delivered the cigarettes to the wrong warehouse. Before they could be redelivered the cigarettes were stolen. The defendants invoiced the plaintiffs for the stolen cigarettes maintaining that the cigarettes were at the plaintiffs' risk at the time they were taken. In later negotiations the defendants threatened to withdraw the plaintiffs' credit facility if it did not pay. The defendants were perfectly entitled to do this and it did not amount to an unlawful act. Eventually the plaintiffs agreed to pay for the cigarettes, but when they discovered the goods had not been at their risk they claimed repayment on the grounds that the money had been paid because of economic duress. At first instance the plaintiffs' claim was dismissed.

Held: The Court of Appeal dismissed the plaintiffs' appeal, holding that there had been no economic duress.

Steyn LJ:

'A . . . characteristic of the case is that the defendants were in law entitled to refuse to enter into any future contracts with the plaintiffs for any reason whatever or for no reason at all. Such a decision not to deal with the plaintiffs would have been financially damaging to the defendants, but it would have been lawful. A fortiori, it was lawful for the defendants, for any reason or for no reason, to insist that they would no longer grant credit to the plaintiffs. The defendants' demand for payment of the invoice, coupled with the threat to withdraw credit, was neither a breach of contract nor a tort.

A . . . critically important characteristic of the case is the fact that the defendants bona fide thought that the goods were at the risk of the plaintiffs and that the plaintiffs owed the defendants the sum in question. The defendants exerted commercial pressure on the plaintiffs in order to obtain payment of a sum which they bona fide considered due to them. The defendants' motive in threatening withdrawal of credit facilities was commercial self-interest in obtaining a sum that they considered due to them . . .

I . . . readily accept that the fact that the defendants have used lawful means does not by itself remove the case from the scope of the doctrine of economic duress. Professor Birks, in *An Introduction to the Law of Restitution* (1989) p 177, lucidly explains:

> "Can lawful pressures also count? This is a difficult question, because, if the answer is that they can, the only viable basis for discriminating between acceptable and unacceptable pressures is not positive law but social morality. In other words, the judges must say what pressures (though lawful outside the restitutionary context) are improper as contrary to prevailing standards. That makes the judges, not the law or the legislature, the arbiters of social evaluation. On the other hand, if the answer is that lawful pressures are always exempt, those who devise outrageous but technically lawful means of compulsion must always escape restitution until the legislature declares the abuse unlawful. It is tolerably clear that, at least where they can be confident of a general consensus in favour of their evaluation, the courts are willing to apply a standard of impropriety rather than technical unlawfulness."

And there are a number of cases where English courts have accepted that a threat may be illegitimate when coupled with a demand for payment even if the threat is one of lawful action (see *Thorne v Motor Trade Association* [1937] 3 All ER 157 at 160–161, [1937] AC 797 at 806–807, *Mutual Finance Ltd v John Wetton & Sons Ltd* [1937] 2 All ER 657, [1937] 2 KB 389 and *Universe Tankships Inc of Monrovia v International Transport Workers' Federation* [1982] 2 All ER 67 at 76, 89, [1983] 1 AC 366 at 384, 401). On the other hand, Goff and Jones, *Law of Restitution* (3rd edn, 1986) p 240 observed that English courts have wisely not accepted any general principle that a threat not to contract with another, except on certain terms, may amount to duress.

We are being asked to extend the categories of duress of which the law will take cognisance. That is not necessarily objectionable, but it seems to me that an extension capable of covering the present case, involving "lawful act duress" in a commercial context in pursuit of a bona fide claim, would be a radical one with far-reaching implications. It would introduce a substantial and undesirable element of uncertainty in the commercial bargaining process. Moreover, it will often enable bona fide settled accounts to be reopened when parties to commercial dealings fall out. The aim of our commercial law ought to be to encourage fair dealing between parties. But it is a mistake for the law to set its sights too highly when the critical inquiry is not whether the conduct is lawful but whether it is morally or socially unacceptable. That is the inquiry in which we are engaged. In my view there are policy considerations which militate against ruling that the defendants obtained payment of the disputed invoice by duress.

Outside the field of protected relationships, and in a purely commercial context, it might be a relatively rare case in which "lawful act duress" can be established. And it might be particularly difficult to establish duress if the defendant bona fide considered that his demand was valid. In this complex and changing branch of the law I deliberately refrain from saying "never". But as the law stands, I am satisfied that the defendants' conduct in this case did not amount to duress.

It is an unattractive result, inasmuch as the defendants are allowed to retain a sum which at the trial they became aware was not in truth due to them. But in my view the law compels the result.

For these reasons, I would dismiss the appeal.'

The Court of Appeal held that a refusal to contract does not constitute illegitimate pressure. Once more we are reminded that there is no duty of good faith in the negotiation of a contract. Steyn LJ did accept, however, that a threat to commit a lawful act can, in appropriate circumstances, amount to economic duress. His Lordship thought that such a concession was essential, in order to prevent 'those who devise outrageous but technically lawful means of compulsion' from escaping the doctrine of duress.

In assessing the legitimacy of the threat, the court must consider both the nature of the pressure and the nature of the demand, which the pressure is applied to support. The pressure itself might be lawful, but it will be illegitimate if it is applied for certain purposes. A bribe is a classic example of such a case. On the facts of *CTN*, the pressure was applied in order to obtain payment of a sum that the defendants bona fide considered due to them. Thus both the pressure and the demand were legitimate. Had the defendants not honestly believed that the goods were held at the plaintiff's risk, the outcome of the case might have been very different. The Court of Appeal's comments on this issue are of course obiter but they are supported by the views of the Privy Council (again obiter) in *Attorney-General for England and Wales v R*.

Attorney-General for England and Wales v R [2003] UKPC 22; [2003] EMLR 499

Facts: The defendant was a New Zealander and a former member of the SAS. Following the publication of a number of books concerning the activities of the Bravo Two Zero patrol in the Gulf War of 1991, the defendant and other members of his squadron were told to sign a 'confidentiality agreement', restricting their right to publish information about their experiences in the SAS. They were told that if they did not sign the agreement they would be returned to unit ('RTU'). Involuntary RTU was normally only imposed as a penalty for some disciplinary offence and involved exclusion from the social life of the regiment and the loss of its higher rates of pay. The defendant signed the agreement but six months later left the Army and returned to New Zealand. In 1998 he entered into a contract with a New Zealand publisher to publish his own account of Bravo Two Zero. The New Zealand publishers offered the UK rights to a UK publisher who sent a copy of the manuscript to the Ministry of Defence. The Attorney-General then brought proceedings against the defendant in the New Zealand High Court for breach of contract. The judge held that the agreement had been obtained by duress and undue influence and was therefore unenforceable. The Court of Appeal allowed the Attorney-General's appeal but refused to grant an injunction. The defendant appealed to the Privy Council.

Held: The Privy Council (Lord Scott dissenting on the issue of undue influence) dismissed the appeal.

Lord Hoffman (delivering the judgment for the majority of the Privy Council):
'**15.** In *Universe Tankships Inc of Monrovia v International Transport Workers Federation* [1983] 1 AC 366, 400 Lord Scarman said that there were two elements in the wrong of duress. One was pressure amounting to compulsion of the will of the victim and the second was the illegitimacy of the pressure. R says that to offer him the alternative of being returned to unit, which was regarded in the SAS as a public humiliation, was compulsion of his will. It left him no practical alternative. Their Lordships are content to assume that this was the case. But, as Lord Wilberforce and Lord Simon of Glaisdale said in *Barton v Armstrong* [1976] AC 104, 121:

"in life . . . many acts are done under pressure, sometimes overwhelming pressure, so that one can say that the actor had no choice but to act. Absence of choice in this sense does not negate consent in law: for this the pressure must be one of a kind which the law does not regard as legitimate."

16. The legitimacy of the pressure must be examined from two aspects: first, the nature of the pressure and secondly, the nature of the demand which the pressure is applied to support: see Lord Scarman in the *Universe Tankships* case, at 401. Generally speaking, the threat of any form of unlawful action will be regarded as illegitimate. On the other hand, the fact that the threat is lawful does not necessarily make the pressure legitimate. As Lord Atkin said in *Thorne v Motor Trade Association* [1937] AC 797, 806:

> "The ordinary blackmailer normally threatens to do what he has a perfect right to do – namely, communicate some compromising conduct to a person whose knowledge is likely to affect the person threatened . . . What he has to justify is not the threat, but the demand of money."

17. In this case, the threat was lawful. Although return to unit was not ordinarily used except on grounds of delinquency or unsuitability and was perceived by members of the SAS as a severe penalty, there is no doubt that the Crown was entitled at its discretion to transfer any member of the SAS to another unit. Furthermore, the judge found, in para [123]:

> "The MOD could not be criticised for its motivation in introducing the contracts. They were introduced because of the concerns about the increasing number of unauthorised disclosures by former UKSF personnel and the concern that those disclosures were threatening the security of operations and personnel and were undermining the effectiveness and employability of the UKSF. Those are legitimate concerns for the MOD to have."

18. It would follow that the MOD was reasonably entitled to regard anyone unwilling to accept the obligation of confidentiality as unsuitable for the SAS. Thus the threat was lawful and the demand supported by the threat could be justified. But the judge held that the demand was unlawful because it exceeded the powers of the Crown over a serviceman under military law. It was an attempt to restrict his freedom of expression after he had left the service and was no longer subject to military discipline.

19. The judge's reasoning was that R had signed the contract because he had been ordered to do so. The MOD could not give a serviceman an order which, as a matter of military law, he was obliged to obey after he had left the service and therefore it was an abuse of power for the MOD to try to extend the temporal reach of its orders by ordering the serviceman to sign a contract which could be enforced after he had left.

20. If R had signed the contract because as a matter of military law he had been obliged to do so, their Lordships would see much force in this reasoning. But they agree with the Court of Appeal that this was not the case. There was no order in the sense of a command which created an obligation to obey under military law. Instead, R was faced with a choice which may have constituted "overwhelming pressure" but was not an exercise by the MOD of its legal powers over him. The legitimacy of the pressure therefore falls to be examined by normal criteria and as neither of the courts in New Zealand considered either the threat to be unlawful or the demand unreasonable, it follows that the contract was not obtained by duress.

The starting point for the Privy Council was the two elements of duress identified by Lord Scarman in *Universe Tankships v ITF*: compulsion of the will and illegitimate pressure. Their Lordships were willing to accept that there was compulsion of the soldier's will. The only alternative offered to him was that of being returned to unit, which, given the humiliation involved, was no alternative at all. Regarding the second element, Lord Hoffman said that the legitimacy of the pressure must be examined from two perspectives:

(1) the nature of the pressure; and
(2) the nature of the demand which the pressure is applied to support.

Applying this test to the facts before them, the Privy Council took the view that the threat was in itself lawful. Although return to unit was not ordinarily used for non-disciplinary matters, there was no doubt that the Crown could at its absolute discretion transfer any member of the SAS to another unit. Furthermore, the nature of the demand in support of which the pressure was applied was also legitimate. It was entirely reasonable for the Ministry of Defence (MOD) to seek to restrict the disclosure of confidential information relating to its military operations.

A final point to note is the overlap between the law of duress and its sister doctrine, undue influence, both of which were pleaded in *Attorney-General v R*. As we will see in the next chapter, the law of undue influence deals with situations where the threats are implied, whereas the law of duress deals with situations where the threats are explicit.

The case law remains rather unclear as to when a lawful action may constitute illegitimate pressure. Professor Enonchong (Enonchong, *Duress, Undue Influence and Unconscionable Dealing*, 2006, pp 25–26, London: Sweet & Maxwell) has suggested that four factors emerge from the cases as being relevant:

'The first is where the threat involves an abuse of the legal process. The second is where the demand is not made bona fide. The third is where the demand is unreasonable. The fourth is where the threat is considered unconscionable in the light of all the circumstances.'

These factors are helpful for identifying the circumstances in which a threat of lawful action might be deemed to be morally or socially unacceptable and therefore illegitimate. It should be remembered, however, that the courts will exercise a great deal of caution in this area so as not to upset the expectations of commercial parties. As Steyn LJ said in *CTN Cash and Carry v Gallaher*, 'it is a mistake for the law to set its sights too highly when the critical inquiry is not whether the conduct is lawful but whether it is morally or socially unacceptable'.

11.5 REMEDIES

Although there has been some disagreement in the cases (see *Barton v Armstrong*), it appears that duress renders a contract voidable, not void – in other words the victim is entitled to rescind the contract. As we have seen in the chapters on mistake (Chapter 10) and misrepresentation (Chapter 9), the right to rescission may be lost due to the existence of a bar to rescission, for example, affirmation, delay, the impossibility of counter-restitution or the intervention of third-party rights. It seems that all four of these bars apply to rescission for duress. In *North Ocean Shipping v Hyundai* excessive delay on the part of the plaintiffs was said to bar rescission for duress. In *Halpern v Halpern* [2007] EWCA Civ 291, the Court of Appeal held that an inability to make counter-restitution would be a bar to rescission for duress. The Court did, however, note (at [74]–[75]) that counter-restitution would often be possible through the payment of a monetary equivalent to restitution (citing *Erlanger v New Sombrero Phosphate Company* (1878) 3 AC 1218).

11.6 DURESS UNDER THE PRINCIPLES OF EUROPEAN CONTRACT LAW

The approach to duress in the Principles of European Contract Law is found in Chapter 4 of the draft. It states the following:

Article 4:108: Threats
A party may avoid a contract when it has been led to conclude it by the other party's imminent and serious threat of an act:

(a) which is wrongful in itself, or
(b) which it is wrongful to use as a means to obtain the conclusion of the contract, unless in the circumstances the first party had a reasonable alternative.

Article 4:113 (ex art. 4.113): Time limits
(1) Notice of avoidance must be given within a reasonable time, with due regard to the circumstances, after the avoiding party knew or ought to have known of the relevant facts or became capable of acting freely.

Article 4:114 (ex art. 6.114): Confirmation
If the party who is entitled to avoid a contract confirms it, expressly or impliedly, after it knows of the ground for avoidance, or becomes capable of acting freely, avoidance of the contract is excluded.

Article 4:115 (ex art. 6.116): Effect of avoidance
On avoidance either party may claim restitution of whatever he has supplied under the

contract or the part of it avoided, provided he makes concurrent restitution of whatever he has received under the contract or the part of it avoided. If restitution cannot be made in kind for any reason, a reasonable sum must be paid for what has been received.

Article 4:117 (ex art. 6.117): Damages

(1) A party who avoids a contract under this Chapter may recover from the other party damages so as to put the avoiding party as nearly as possible into the same position as if it had not concluded the contract, provided that the other party knew or ought to have known of the mistake, fraud, threat or taking of excessive benefit or unfair advantage.

(2) If a party has the right to avoid a contract under this Chapter, but does not exercise its right or has lost its right under the provisions of Articles 4:113 or 4:114, it may recover, subject to paragraph (1), damages limited to the loss caused to it by the mistake, fraud, threat or taking of excessive benefit or unfair advantage. The same measure of damages shall apply when the party was misled by incorrect information in the sense of Article 4:106.

(3) In other respects, the damages shall be in accordance with the relevant provisions of Chapter 9, Section 5, with appropriate adaptations.

Article 4:108 largely corresponds with the approach to duress under English law. The Principles contain no definition of 'wrongful', but the annotations indicate that wrongful threats include threats of financial loss. Thus the Principles are in line with the current English position, which normally requires the commission of a crime, tort or breach of contract. Lawful act duress is covered by subparagraph (b) and again the position under the Principles corresponds to that under English law.

Article 4:108 states that a party may avoid a contract when it is entered into under duress. The right to rescission will be lost if there is excessive delay (4:113) or affirmation/confirmation of the contract (4:114). Article 4:115 requires the claimant to make counter-restitution. If counter-restitution is impossible, the claimant will be permitted to make a reasonable payment for the benefits received (this corresponds with the flexible approach to counter-restitution in equity: *Erlanger v New Sombrero Phosphate* (1878) 3 AC 1218).

Article 4:117 provides that damages can be recovered either in addition to, or in lieu of, rescission. These damages aim to put the avoiding party as nearly as possible into the position he would have been in had he not entered into the contract. Damages are not currently available for duress in English law and this would mark a significant departure from current practice.

11.7 ADDITIONAL READING

Bigwood, R, *Exploitative Contracts*, 2003, Oxford: OUP.

Birks, P, 'The travails of duress' [1990] LMCLQ 342.

Friedman, D, 'The objective principle and mistake and involuntariness in contract and Restitution' (2003) 119 LQR 68.

Halson, R, 'Opportunism, economic duress and contractual modifications' (1991) 107 LQR 649.

Nolan, D, 'Economic duress and the availability of a reasonable alternative' [2000] RLR 105.

Tiplady, D, 'Concepts of duress' (1983) 99 LQR 188.

CHAPTER 12

UNDUE INFLUENCE

CONTENTS

▌12.1 INTRODUCTION

Undue influence is the equitable sister doctrine of duress. It operates to release parties from contracts that they have entered into as a result of being 'influenced' by the other party. In the leading case of *Royal Bank of Scotland plc v Etridge (No 2)* [2002] 2 AC 773 Lord Nicholls made the following observations about undue influence:

'Undue influence is one of the grounds of relief developed by the courts of equity as a court of conscience. The objective is to ensure that the influence of one person over another is not abused. In everyday life people constantly seek to influence the decisions of others. They seek to persuade those with whom they are dealing to enter into transactions, whether great or small. The law has set limits to the means properly employable for this purpose. To this end the common law developed a principle of duress. Originally this was narrow in its scope, restricted to the more blatant forms of physical coercion, such as personal violence.

Here, as elsewhere in the law, equity supplemented the common law. Equity extended the reach of the law to other unacceptable forms of persuasion. The law will investigate the manner in which the intention to enter into the transaction was secured: "how the intention was produced", in the oft repeated words of Lord Eldon LC, from as long ago as 1807 (*Huguenin v Baseley* 14 Ves 273, 300). If the intention was produced by an unacceptable means, the law will not permit the transaction to stand. The means used is regarded as an exercise of improper or "undue" influence, and hence unacceptable, whenever the consent thus procured ought not fairly to be treated as the expression of a person's free will. It is impossible to be more precise or definitive. The circumstances in which one person acquires influence over another, and the manner in which influence may be exercised, vary too widely to permit of any more specific criterion.'

As Lord Nicholls notes, one of the main difficulties with the doctrine of undue influence is ascertaining the limits of legitimate persuasion. The legitimacy of persuasion differs between contexts so that although it may be legitimate for a sales representative to persuade me to purchase a washing machine, it may not be legitimate for my father to persuade me to sell my house to him at a discount price. The difficulty lies in ascertaining when influence becomes 'undue' so as to justify the intervention of the law.

12.1.1 THE RELATIONSHIP WITH DURESS

As Lord Nicholls notes there is a close relationship between the common-law doctrine of duress and the equitable doctrine of undue influence. This is examined by Professor Enonchong in the following extract:

Enonchong, N, *Duress, Undue Influence and Unconscionable Dealing*, 2006, pp 82–83, London: Sweet & Maxwell

The objective of undue influence is similar to that of the common law doctrine of duress, namely, to draw a line between acceptable and unacceptable pressure. However, since the scope of relief on the ground of duress was originally very narrow, limited as it was to more blatant forms of physical coercion, equity supplements the common law by means of the doctrine of undue influence. Relief was granted on the ground of undue influence in cases where equity considered the pressure to be improper or unacceptable although it did not amount to duress at common law. Like the law of duress, the law of undue influence examines the manner in which the intention to enter into a transaction was produced. If the intention was produced by an unacceptable means, the law of undue influence will not permit the transaction to stand. However, since a range of conduct that was not regarded as unacceptable at law was so regarded by equity, there was a protection gap between the two doctrines, with equity providing wider protection through undue influence than the common law could through duress. In the past this protection gap was very wide, but the greater expansion in the scope of duress in recent times has resulted in considerable overlap between the two doctrines, since both deal with overt acts of improper pressure such as unlawful threats. However, undue influence applies even in cases where there is no overt act of pressure as where there is a presumption of undue influence. This is the case where the relationship between two persons is such that one has acquired a degree of influence or ascendancy over the other so that the one is disposed to agree to a proposal of the ascendant party without any specific acts of persuasion . . . Many of the cases of undue influence are of this nature and to this extent undue influence differs from common law duress.

A number of early undue influence cases concerned overt threats and pressure. In *Williams v Bayley* (1866) LR 1 HL 200, for example, a father agreed to give an equitable mortgage over his colliery in exchange for a promise by the plaintiff bankers not to prosecute his son for forging his father's signature on promissory notes. In response to this threat, the father replied, 'What be I to do? How can I help myself? You see these men will have their money'. The House of Lords held that the agreement should be set aside as being obtained by undue influence. Similarly, in *Mutual Finance Ltd v John Wetton & Sons Ltd* [1937] 2 KB 389, a guarantee was obtained from a family company under an implied, though not explicit, threat to prosecute a member of the family who was alleged to have forged the signature of the company on a previous guarantee. The guarantee was set aside as having been obtained by undue influence. Both of these cases involved pressure being placed on one party by the other in much the same way as occurs with duress. Following the expansion in the types of threats that are now treated as potentially giving rise to duress, it is possible to argue that facts such as these should now be dealt with under the doctrine of duress. The problem with this analysis, however, is that duress is still limited to overt threats, not implied threats (see observation of Porter J *Mutual Finance Ltd v John Wetton & Sons Ltd* [1937] 2 KB 389, 395). For this reason, some commentators have argued that the scope of duress should be expanded to include both express and implied threats, leaving undue influence to deal with relationships where one party has acquired a degree of ascendancy over the other party without explicit threats.

Birks, P and Chin, NY, 'On the nature of undue influence' in Beatson, J and Friedmann, D (eds), *Good Faith and Fault in Contract Law*, 1995, pp 63–64, Oxford: Clarendon

Some years ago Professor Malcolm Cope suggested that all cases of duress should be treated as undue influence. We believe the decanting should go the other way: all cases of pressure should be treated as duress. It is unfortunate if this must still be expressed as transferring them from equity to common law. It is time that in this field we overcome the old jurisdictional duality. It would be better to say simply that pressure should be litigated as pressure, or as 'duress' if that synonym is preferred. The reasons are, first, that pressure or duress is a relatively easily understood and distinct notion; secondly, that pressure had been allowed to dominate the picture and has concealed the nature of relational undue influence; and, thirdly, whatever the precise future of the requirement of manifest disadvantage in the context of undue influence, nobody has ever suggested that it has any role whatever in duress.

A consolidation of the law relating to pressure would not have been possible in earlier times because of the narrowness of the concept of operative duress. Duress to goods and other economic duress was thought not to give relief from a contract. Thanks in large measure to an influential article by Professor Beatson, that picture has been transformed. Nowadays it is clear that duress includes all illegitimate pressure and that all forms of duress can ground relief from a contract . . .

It is now difficult to conceive of any pressure which will not be relieved satisfactorily, if it should be relieved at all, within the category of duress. To suggest otherwise would be to claim relief for a species of pressure which could not be characterized as illegitimate.

Although the approach of Professor Birks and Professor Chin would bring clarity and consistency to the law, it has yet to be adopted by the courts. As a result, there continues to be considerable overlap between duress and undue influence in cases concerning explicit threats.

12.1.2 THE MEANING OF 'UNDUE'

The law will only intervene when 'influence' becomes 'undue'. But what does the word 'undue' mean? In the context of influence it has two potential meanings:

1. The influence is 'undue' because it is 'illegitimate' or 'unconscionable'. This focuses on the conduct of the influencer. It is defendant-focused.
2. The influence is 'undue' because it is 'overbearing' or 'too high' and causes the influenced party to lose autonomy in deciding whether to enter into the contract. This focuses on the effect that the influence has on the influenced person's state of mind. It is claimant-focused.

The second meaning of 'undue' was adopted by the High Court of Australia in the case of *Commercial Bank of Australia Ltd v Amadio* (1983) 151 CLR 447. This definition of undue influence was used to distinguish the doctrine from unconscionability (discussed at the end of this chapter). Deane J put it in the following terms:

'The equitable principles relating to relief against unconscionable dealing and the principles relating to undue influence are closely related. The two doctrines are, however, distinct. Undue influence, like common law duress, looks to the quality of the consent or assent of the weaker party . . . Unconscionable dealing looks to the conduct of the stronger party in attempting to enforce, or retain the benefit of, a dealing with a person under a special disability in circumstances where it is not consistent with equity or good conscience that he should do so.'

Professor Birks and Professor Chin have argued strongly that the approach taken in *Amadio* should be followed in this country.

> **Birks, P and Chin, NY, 'On the nature of undue influence', in Beatson, J and Friedmann, D (eds), *Good Faith and Fault in Contract Law*, 1995, p 95, Oxford: Clarendon**
>
> Some jurists will still be attracted by the simplicity of the defendant-sided analysis, and they will point out, correctly, that the number of cases in which there is no unconscionable behaviour will be very small. However, the rationality of the law cannot tolerate abbreviations or approximations. If there are two doctrines, there are two doctrines; and the fact that one might do perhaps ninety-five per cent of the work is no reason for pretending that the other does not exist. The correct approach will be to treat both undue influence and duress as plaintiff-sided factors which ground relief on a degree of impairment of the plaintiff's capacity to make decisions. In every case we should accept not a dogma of priority or subsidiarity, but a voluntary intellectual discipline of exhausting the plaintiff-sided analysis before proceeding to the question whether relief might be rested on unconscientious behaviour on the part of the defendant. That discipline will serve to protect all plaintiff-sided grounds for relief – spontaneous and innocently induced mistake no less than undue influence and duress, not to mention others – and will avert the unnecessary injustice which happens when plaintiffs lose cases because lawyers fail to see their winning argument.

There is some judicial support for a claimant-focused approach to undue influence (most notably in the decisions of the Court of Appeal in *Allcard v Skinner* (1887) 36 Ch D 145 and *Pesticcio v Niersmans* [2004] EWCA Civ 372). Nevertheless, the majority of recent cases have emphasised the relevance of wrongdoing, thus suggesting a defendant-focused approach. In *Royal Bank of Scotland v Etridge (No 2)*, their Lordships spoke of undue influence as being an 'abuse' of a position of influence. Likewise, in *R v Attorney-General for England and Wales* [2003] UKPC 22, Lord Hoffman described undue influence as involving 'consent . . . obtained by unacceptable means' and 'the unfair exploitation by one party of a relationship which gives him ascendancy or influence over the other'. In *National Commercial Bank (Jamaica) Ltd v Hew* [2003] UKPC 51, Lord Millet described undue influence as involving 'abuse', 'victimisation' and 'exploitation', and in *UCB Corporate Services Ltd v Williams* [2002] EWCA Civ 555; [2003] 1 P & CR 12, Jonathan Parker LJ described the concept as involving 'improper means of persuasion'. All of these judgments suggest that the courts look to the conduct of the defendant in order to determine whether the influence exerted was 'undue'.

It is important to note that undue influence is concerned with procedural fairness, not substantive fairness. When considering whether undue influence has been exercised the courts will examine the process by which the agreement came into existence, not the agreement itself. This was explained by Lindley LJ in *Allcard v Skinner* (1887) 36 Ch D 145:

> 'What then is the principle? Is it that it is right and expedient to save persons from the consequence of their own folly? Or is it that it is right and expedient to save them from being victimised by other people? In my opinion the doctrine of undue influence is founded upon the second of these two principles . . . to protect people from being forced, tricked or misled in any way by others into parting with their property is one of the most legitimate objects of all laws . . .'

The law of undue influence seeks to prevent 'victimisation'; it is concerned with procedural unfairness. Was the agreement entered into as a result of the exercise of improper influence? To answer this question the court will examine both the nature of the relationship between the parties and the form of influence applied.

12.1.3 THE STRUCTURE OF THIS CHAPTER

In the last 15 years, the House of Lords has twice provided a thorough examination of the law of undue influence, that is, in 1993, in *Barclays Bank plc v O'Brien* [1994] 1 AC 180, and in 2001, in *Royal Bank of Scotland plc v Etridge (No 2)* [2002] 2 AC 773. These two cases contain the most detailed and authoritative statements of the law in this area and for that reason the main focus of this chapter will be on the speeches of their Lordships in those cases, particularly in *Etridge*.

First, we will examine the two categories of undue influence. Next, we will consider how the courts resolve cases in which the undue influence has been exerted by a third party and not by the defendant. Third, we will undertake a detailed analysis of the views expressed by the House of Lords in *Etridge*. We will then consider the remedies available for undue influence. Fifth, we will consider the doctrine of unconscionability and its relationship to the law of undue influence. Finally, we will examine the position taken by the Principles of European Contract Law.

▌12.2 TWO CATEGORIES OF UNDUE INFLUENCE

In *Barclays Bank plc v O'Brien* [1994] 1 AC 180, Lord Browne-Wilkinson divided undue influence into two categories:

'A person who has been induced to enter into a transaction by the undue influence of another ("the wrongdoer") is entitled to set that transaction aside as against the wrongdoer. Such undue influence is either actual or presumed. In *Bank of Credit and Commerce International SA v Aboody* [1990] 1 QB 923, 953, the Court of Appeal helpfully adopted the following classification.

Class 1: Actual undue influence
In these cases it is necessary for the claimant to prove affirmatively that the wrongdoer exerted undue influence on the complainant to enter into the particular transaction which is impugned.

Class 2: Presumed undue influence
In these cases the complainant only has to show, in the first instance, that there was a relationship of trust and confidence between the complainant and the wrongdoer of such a nature that it is fair to presume that the wrongdoer abused that relationship in procuring the complainant to enter into the impugned transaction. In Class 2 cases therefore there is no need to produce evidence that actual undue influence was exerted in relation to the particular transaction impugned: once a confidential relationship has been proved, the burden then shifts to the wrongdoer to prove that the complainant entered into the impugned transaction freely, for example by showing that the complainant had independent advice. Such a confidential relationship can be established in two ways, viz.,

Class 2(A)
Certain relationships (for example solicitor and client, medical advisor and patient) as a matter of law raise the presumption that undue influence has been exercised.

Class 2(B)
Even if there is no relationship falling within Class 2(A), if the complainant proves the *de facto* existence of a relationship under which the complainant

generally reposed trust and confidence in the wrongdoer, the existence of such relationship raises the presumption of undue influence. In a Class 2(B) case therefore, in the absence of evidence disproving undue influence, the complainant will succeed in setting aside the impugned transaction merely by proof that the complainant reposed trust and confidence in the wrongdoer without having to prove that the wrongdoer exerted actual undue influence or otherwise abused such trust and confidence in relation to the particular transaction impugned.'

While the division between actual and presumed under influence remains good law, the House of Lords has since doubted the usefulness of the division between Class 2(A) and Class 2(B) undue influence. We will consider the reasons for this in our discussion of *Etridge*.

12.2.1 ACTUAL UNDUE INFLUENCE

To make out a case for actual undue influence it must be affirmatively proved that one party exercised influence over the other and thus procured a contract that would otherwise not have been made. The influence exercised may be much more subtle than duress and it includes psychological means. There is no need to show that there was a previous history of such influence and there is no requirement of a special relationship, although such a relationship may exist on the facts. An example of this type of undue influence is to be found on the facts of *Bank of Credit & Commerce International SA v Aboody*.

> ### *Bank of Credit & Commerce International SA v Aboody* [1990] 1 QB 923
>
> **Facts:** The defendants were husband and wife. Mrs Aboody was 20 years younger than her husband and had married him when she was 17. She was nominally a director of her husband's business and over a number of years she had signed various documents relating to the business without reading them or questioning her husband about them. The documents that gave rise to the litigation were three guarantees and charges over the wife's home that were made in favour of the bank in order to support loans made to the husband's business. Mrs Aboody claimed that she had signed these agreements under the undue influence of her husband. She had taken no independent advice and her husband had deliberately concealed matters from her. The judge at first instance held that there had been actual undue influence but refused to set aside the guarantees because it had not been proved that they were manifestly disadvantageous to the wife.
>
> **Held:** The Court of Appeal dismissed the appeal. Although Mr Aboody had not acted with any improper motive, he had unduly influenced his wife. Nevertheless, the Court

of Appeal refused to set aside the guarantees because it had not been shown that the transactions were to the manifest disadvantage of Mrs Aboody.

Slade LJ:

'Since Mrs Aboody's claim in the present case is based exclusively on undue influence, it thus becomes necessary to consider whether, contrary to the judge's view, she has shown that all or any of the six transactions were manifestly disadvantageous to her . . . [O]n a fair reading of the judgment, we think it clear that the judge, while not embarking on a full scale repetition of the principal relevant factors in conducting the balancing exercise in respect of each of the six transactions, had them well in mind on each occasion. While there were substantial potential liabilities, and the risk of the loss of the family home, to be put in the balance on the debit side, there was also much to put in on the credit side. Eratex Ltd was the family business and the sole or principal means of support of Mr and Mrs Aboody. Eratex Ltd might still have collapsed with or without the facilities covered by the six transactions. But at least these facilities gave it some hope of survival. The judge found that, as at the date of the 1976 guarantee, it had "more than an equal chance of surviving", and that, even as at December 1979, it had "at least a reasonably good chance of surviving". If it had survived, the potential benefits to Mrs. Aboody would have been substantial.

In the end, we can see no sufficient grounds for disagreeing with his conclusion that on balance a manifest disadvantage has not been shown by Mrs Aboody in respect of any of the six transactions.

Our conclusions on [the issue of manifest disadvantage] must lead to the dismissal of this appeal. Nevertheless, though this is not necessary for our decision, we propose to say something about the allegation of actual undue influence . . .

Lindley LJ in *Allcard v Skinner*, 36 ChD 145, 183, said that no court has ever attempted to define undue influence. Lord Scarman gave a warning against any attempt at comprehensive definition in *National Westminster Bank plc v Morgan* [1985] AC 686, 709. We heed this warning. Nevertheless, for the purpose of dealing with [this] issue, it is necessary briefly to consider what has to be shown if an allegation of actual undue influence is to be made out.

Leaving aside proof of manifest disadvantage, we think that a person relying on a plea of actual undue influence must show that (a) the other party to the transaction (or someone who induced the transaction for his own benefit) had the capacity to influence the complainant; (b) the influence was exercised; (c) its exercise was undue; (d) its exercise brought about the transaction . . . On the evidence there appears to be no doubt that conditions (a) and (b) are satisfied. The findings of the judge show that Mrs Aboody at the invitation of her husband was habitually prepared to sign documents relating to the affairs of Eratex Ltd without considering their contents because she trusted him. They also show that he invited her to enter into the first five transactions. The present issue, therefore, resolves itself to the question whether the exercise of Mr Aboody's influence was on the facts undue . . . If, contrary to our view, the five transactions were manifestly disadvantageous to Mrs Aboody, we do not see how it could be disputed that unfair advantage had been taken of her by her husband. In this context we cite a brief passage from the judge's judgment:

> "There was more than a situation of trust; there was actual influence founded on that trust and [Mr Aboody] used it intentionally. He intended and knew that without any discussion or consideration of risk [Mrs Aboody] would sign security documents for a series of increasingly large overdrafts of the company. He never offered her any choice of her own. She was deprived altogether of the free use of any independent and informed judgment in the transaction. He never mentioned risk at all even if he thought it was a slight one. The only judgment that she could be said to have exercised was her mistaken judgment of Mr Aboody and his business capacity and probity."

When one couples with these findings the fact that it was Mr Aboody who suggested to his wife that she should enter into the first five transactions, the unfair advantage taken of her by him became apparent. If he had positively misrepresented to her the extent of the risks involved, a plea based on misrepresentation might well have been available to her. The mere fact that in order to get his own way he chose deliberately to say nothing as to the risks, rather than to misrepresent them, would not, in our judgment, save his conduct from being unconscionable or absolve him from a charge of actual undue influence, bearing in mind that it was he who invited her to enter into them.'

Slade LJ's judgment in *Aboody* provides a helpful summary of the requirements for a claim of actual undue influence. The requirement of 'manifest disadvantage' has since been rejected by the House of Lords in *CIBC Mortgages plc v Pitt* [1994] AC 200. In that case, Lord Browne-Wilkinson declared:

> 'Actual undue influence is a species of fraud. Like any other victim of fraud, a person who has been induced by undue influence to carry out a transaction which he did not freely and knowingly enter into is entitled to have that transaction set aside as of right.'

In light of this decision, if similar facts were to recur today, Mrs Aboody would be likely to succeed in having the transactions set aside.

12.2.2 PRESUMED UNDUE INFLUENCE

To establish presumed undue influence, the influenced party must demonstrate two things:

1. A relationship of trust and confidence. This raises a presumption of 'influence';
2. A transaction that 'calls for an explanation'. This raises a presumption of 'undue' influence.

Having established a presumption of undue influence the court must then consider whether the presumption has been rebutted. We will consider each of these requirements in turn.

12.2.2.1 A relationship of trust and confidence

Traditionally, presumed undue influence was divided into two classes. The first class (class 2(A)) consisted of relationships in which the law presumed that one party had exercised influence over the other. The class included the relationship between parent and child (*Bainbrigge v Brown* (1881) Ch D 188); guardian and ward (*Hylton v Hylton* (1754) 2 Ves Sen 547); doctor and patient (*Mitchell v Homfray* (1881) 8 QBD 587); solicitor and client (*Wright v Carter* [1903] 1 Ch 27); trustee and beneficiary (*Beningfield v Baxter* (1886) 12 App Cas 167); and spiritual adviser and follower (*Allcard v Skinner* (1887) 36 Ch D 145). Notably, it did not include the relationship between a husband and wife.

If a relationship did not fall within class 2(A) it was possible to argue that it fell within class 2(B). This class consisted of cases where one party could show, on the facts of the case, that it was a relationship in which they had reposed trust and confidence in the other. The relationship between a husband and wife could fall into this category. In *Barclays Bank v O'Brien*, Lord Browne-Wilkinson said:

> 'Although there is no Class 2(A) presumption of undue influence as between husband and wife, it should be emphasised that in any particular case a wife may well be able to demonstrate that de facto she did leave decisions on financial affairs to her husband thereby bringing herself within Class 2(B) i.e. that the relationship between husband and wife in the particular case was such that the wife reposed confidence and trust in her husband in relation to their financial affairs and therefore undue influence is to be presumed.'

Following the decision of the House of Lords in *Etridge*, the terminology of class 2(A) and class 2(B) should no longer be used. Although relationships within class 2(A) still raise a presumption of influence, it is doubtful whether class 2(B) serves any useful purpose. We will consider these issues in greater detail when we examine the speeches in *Etridge*.

12.2.2.2 A transaction which is not readily explicable by the relationship between the parties

As we have seen, it is no longer necessary for a claimant to show that a transaction was to his 'manifest disadvantage' in order to have it set aside for actual undue influence. Prior to the decision of the House of Lords in *Etridge*, it was assumed that the requirement still existed in relation to cases of presumed undue influence, whether they were class 2(A) or class 2(B). In *Etridge*, however, their Lordships discarded the phrase 'manifest disadvantage' and indicated that the nature of the transaction is only of relevance to the evidential issue of whether it can be presumed that *undue* influence has been exerted. In other words, if the transaction is one which calls for an explanation (for example, because it benefits one party with no corresponding benefit to the other), then this will impose a burden on the dominant party to demonstrate that the transaction was not in fact obtained by the exercise of undue influence, that is, by an abuse of the relationship of trust and confidence.

It is clear that the disadvantage of the transaction is still of relevance in determining whether the transaction is one that calls for an explanation. This can be seen by contrasting two recent cases concerning the 'Right to Buy' scheme.

Popowski v Popowski [2004] EWHC 668 (Ch) (Unreported)

Facts: Mr and Mrs Popowski bought their council house at a 60 per cent discount against the market value under the 'Right to Buy' scheme. The purchase price was funded by a mortgage. The couple entered into an agreement with their son, Janek Popowski, whereby he would pay the sums due under the mortgage. The agreement provided that Mr and Mrs Popowski would be allowed to live in the house rent free for the duration of their lives and in return Janek would have the entire beneficial interest in the property. After the death of Mr Popowski, Mrs Popowski claimed that the agreement was unfair and that she should have been entitled to a 60 per cent share in the house by virtue of the Right to Buy discount. She argued that, in light of the relationship between the parties and the disadvantage of the transaction, it must be presumed that Janek exerted undue influence in obtaining the agreement.

Held: The Deputy Judge held that there was sufficient evidence of a relationship of trust and confidence. As to the requirement of a transaction that calls for an explanation, the judge said that Mrs Popowski 'has to satisfy me that the transaction constituted a disadvantage sufficiently serious to require evidence to rebut the presumption that in the circumstances of the parties' relationship it was procured by the exercise of undue influence'. In deciding the issue the judge balanced the advantage to Janek of obtaining the whole beneficial interest in the property with the facts that he paid the mortgage repayments and gave his parents a rent-free home for life. It was relevant that the purchase of the house would not have gone ahead but for Janek's agreement to fund the purchase price. Whilst the judge acknowledged that the loss of the benefit of the 60 per cent discount could be deemed to be a significant disadvantage this had to be balanced against the right to live in the property rent free for life, which was clearly a right of considerable value in terms of both security and financial advantage. The Deputy Judge concluded: 'In my judgment, this is a right which balances out the value of any disadvantage to Mrs Popowski arising from any loss of her right to the benefit of the 60% discount'. On this basis, it was held that the presumption of undue influence did not apply.

Humphreys v Humphreys [2004] EWHC 2201 (Ch) (Unreported)

Facts: The facts were very similar to those in *Popowski v Popowski*. It involved an agreement between a mother and son in relation to the purchase of the mother's council house under the 'Right to Buy' scheme. The son agreed to pay the sums due under the mortgage in exchange for a reversionary interest in the house. A big difference between this case and *Popowski* was that the agreement contained no forfeiture provision to protect the mother in the event of the son forfeiting on the mortgage repayments.

Held: The High Court held that the transaction was 'a very one-sided one' and for that reason it called for an explanation. The presumption of undue influence was raised and it had not been rebutted on the facts.

Rimer J:

'**89.** There is no dispute that Mrs Humphreys reposed the requisite degree of trust and confidence in Dennis, and I understand Dennis's concession on this to mean that such reposing was in relation to the whole matter of the purchase of the house. The main area of difference between the parties is as to the second hurdle that Mrs Humphreys has to surmount. On that I was referred to *Popowski v Popowski* [2004] EWHC 668 (Ch), unreported, a decision of Mr Richard Sheldon QC sitting as a deputy High Court Judge in the Chancery Division . . .

90. The judge directed himself by reference to Lord Nicholls's speech in *Etridge*. He held that Mrs Popowski had proved that she placed relevant trust and confidence in Janek. He then (at paragraph 29) turned to consider "whether the transaction constituted a disadvantage sufficiently serious to require evidence to rebut the presumption [of undue influence]", drawing on paragraph 25 of Lord Nicholls's speech . . .

93. I found the arguments each way on this issue to be fairly finely balanced and they have caused me some anxiety. I have, however, come to the conclusion that, in all the circumstances, the transaction effected by the trust deed does call for an explanation from Dennis. I find that it does give rise to a presumption of undue influence and that the burden is therefore on Dennis to rebut it.

94. Viewing the transaction from Dennis's viewpoint, it was very beneficial. At a cost to him of 40% of the value of the house he acquired a reversionary interest in 100% of the house . . . Dennis's investment was obviously a very good one, as I have no doubt he regarded it. Apart from the mortgage his further obligations in relation to the house were virtually nil. In particular, whilst I accept that he has in practice done material works to it, both internally and externally, I also find that he assumed no enforceable obligation to carry them out.

95. Viewing the transaction from Mrs Humphreys' viewpoint, the benefits are less obvious. The purchase extinguished her prior obligation to pay rent, but as almost the whole of her rent was being paid by her housing benefit that represented only a marginal advantage . . . Whereas previously she enjoyed the security of tenure which her tenancy gave her, her security in the house became dependent on Dennis duly honouring the mortgage obligations . . . A continuing default by Dennis carried the risk of dispossession by the Nationwide, and the net proceeds of a subsequent sale would, under the trust deed, belong wholly to Dennis: Mrs Humphreys would not be entitled to a penny. And although part of Mrs Humphreys' longer term expectations were to sell the house and to buy another in its place for her continued occupation, the trust deed made that operation dependent on Dennis's consent . . .

96. In my judgment, therefore, the transaction reflected in the trust deed is a very one-sided one. I consider that it raises real questions as to whether, from Mrs Humphreys' viewpoint, it was a fair or sensible transaction; and it seems to me obvious that, if the purchase of the house with Dennis was to be pursued, there were several respects in which Mrs Humphreys' position could, and on one view should, have been improved. In particular, consideration could and should have been given to the vulnerability flowing from her reliance on Dennis punctually meeting the mortgage payments . . .

98. Taking account of all these matters, I have concluded that the transaction effected by the trust deed does call for an explanation by Dennis. The effect of my findings is that the burden shifts to Dennis to satisfy the court that Mrs Humphreys entered into the trust deed with a full understanding of its merits and demerits and of her own free and uninfluenced will. I have probably said enough to indicate that I find that Dennis has not discharged that burden. In the particular circumstances of this case I consider that he could probably only have done so if he was able to show that Mrs Humphreys had first been given comprehensive and independent legal advice about all aspects of the proposed transaction. He was not able to show that. I find, therefore, that the trust deed was induced by Dennis's undue influence.'

12.2.2.3 Rebutting the presumption of undue influence

In *Humphreys v Humphreys*, Rimer J noted that once the presumption of undue influence has been raised the court must then consider whether the presumption has been rebutted. On the facts of *Humphreys*, there was insufficient evidence to do this.

The most obvious way to rebut the presumption of undue influence is to show that the vulnerable party received independent advice as to the nature and effect of the transaction. Independent advice will not always be sufficient to rebut the presumption. In *Pesticcio v Niersmans* [2004] EWCA Civ 372, Mummery LJ said:

'It is the case, as held in *Inche Noriah v Omar* [1929] AC 127 at 135, that the presumption of undue influence may be rebutted by showing that the transaction was entered into "after the nature and effect of the transaction had been fully explained to the donor by some independent qualified person". The participation of a solicitor is not, however, a precaution which is guaranteed to work in every case. It is necessary for the court to be satisfied that the advice and explanation by, for example, a solicitor, was relevant and effective to free the donor from the impairment of the influence on his free will and to give him the necessary independence of judgment and freedom to make choices with a full appreciation of what he was doing.'

Independent advice will usually be legal but does not have to be so. In exceptional cases where the presumption of undue influence is particularly heavy it may be necessary to show, in addition to the fact that the vulnerable party received independent legal advice, that he was free to act on it. In *Allcard v Skinner* (1887) 36 Ch D 145, Lindley LJ said:

'[T]he gifts made . . . cannot be supported in the absence of proof that the Plaintiff could have obtained independent advice if she wished for it, and that she knew that she would have been allowed to obtain such advice if she had desired to do so. I doubt whether the gifts could have been supported if such proof had been given, unless there was also proof that she was free to act on the advice which might be given to her.'

Although the usual means of rebutting the presumption of undue influence will be evidence that the vulnerable party received independent competent advice, it is possible to rebut the presumption without such evidence. In *Johnson v EBS Pensioner Trustees Ltd* (2001) 82 P & CR DG2, Patten J held that the presumption had been rebutted even though independent advice had not been provided. The complainant was an experienced businessman and Patten J held that 'he was at all relevant times fully aware of what he was entering into and more to the point did so independently of any pressure stemming from his relationship with [the other party]'. In most cases, however, it will be very difficult to rebut the presumption of undue influence without evidence of independent advice (see *Hammond v Osborn* [2002] EWCA Civ 885).

▌12.3 UNDUE INFLUENCE AND THIRD PARTIES

The majority of recent cases on undue influence have been concerned with the effect on a transaction of undue influence by a third party. The classic example of this is where a husband and wife agree to remortgage the matrimonial home in order to raise capital for the husband's business. If the husband has exercised undue influence over his wife, can the mortgage be set aside as against the bank? The answer would usually be 'no', because the husband is not a party to the transaction and the doctrine of privity would operate. Nevertheless, in certain situations, the courts have been prepared to intervene to find that the mortgage can be set aside due to the bank having had notice of the husband's undue influence.

Barclays Bank plc v O'Brien [1994] 1 AC 180

Facts: Mr and Mrs O'Brien agreed to execute a second mortgage of their matrimonial home as security for an overdraft facility extended by Barclays Bank to Mr O'Brien's company. The employee of the bank who presented the documents for the wife's signature failed to follow his manager's instructions to ensure that both defendants were fully aware of the nature of the documents and to suggest that they take legal advice if either of them were unsure about the transaction. Mrs O'Brien signed the papers without reading them in reliance on her husband's statement that the security was limited to £60,000, whereas in fact it was for £130,000. When the company's overdraft exceeded £154,000 the bank sought to realise the security and obtained a registrar's order for possession. The judge dismissed the wife's appeal on the grounds that Mr O'Brien was not acting on behalf of the bank and therefore they could not be held responsible for his misrepresentation. The Court of Appeal allowed Mrs O'Brien's appeal. Their Lordships found that Mrs O'Brien was an intelligent and independent minded woman, who had not been unduly influenced by Mr O'Brien. They did hold, however, that the guarantee had been entered into in reliance on an actionable misrepresentation by Mr O'Brien, and that Mrs O'Brien was entitled to special protection in equity. For this reason, the legal charge was not enforceable by the bank against Mrs O'Brien save to the extent of the £60,000 which she had thought she was agreeing to secure.

Held: The House of Lords dismissed the bank's appeal. Although their Lordships held that there was no basis for providing special protection in equity to Mrs O'Brien, the appeal was dismissed on the grounds that the bank had constructive notice of Mr O'Brien's misrepresentation.

Lord Browne-Wilkinson:
'Conclusions
(a) Wives. My starting point is to clarify the basis of the law. Should wives (and perhaps others) be accorded special rights in relation to surety transactions by the recognition of a special equity applicable only to such persons engaged in such transactions? Or should they enjoy only the same protection as they would enjoy in relation to their other dealings? In my judgment, the special equity theory should be rejected. First, I can find no basis in principle for affording special protection to a limited class in relation to one type of transaction only. Second, to require the creditor

to prove knowledge and understanding by the wife in all cases is to reintroduce by the back door either a presumption of undue influence of Class 2(A) (which has been decisively rejected) or the Romilly heresy (which has long been treated as bad law). Third, although Scott LJ found that there were two lines of cases one of which supported the special equity theory, on analysis although many decisions are not inconsistent with that theory the only two cases which support it are *Yerkey v Jones*, 63 CLR 649, and the decision of the Court of Appeal in the present case. Finally, it is not necessary to have recourse to a special equity theory for the proper protection of the legitimate interests of wives as I will seek to show.

In my judgment, if the doctrine of notice is properly applied, there is no need for the introduction of a special equity in these types of cases. A wife who has been induced to stand as a surety for her husband's debts by his undue influence, misrepresentation or some other legal wrong has an equity as against him to set aside that transaction. Under the ordinary principles of equity, her right to set aside that transaction will be enforceable against third parties (e.g. against a creditor) if either the husband was acting as the third party's agent or the third party had actual or constructive notice of the facts giving rise to her equity. Although there may be cases where, without artificiality, it can properly be held that the husband was acting as the agent of the creditor in procuring the wife to stand as surety, such cases will be of very rare occurrence. The key to the problem is to identify the circumstances in which the creditor will be taken to have had notice of the wife's equity to set aside the transaction.

The doctrine of notice lies at the heart of equity. Given that there are two innocent parties, each enjoying rights, the earlier right prevails against the later right if the acquirer of the later right knows of the earlier right (actual notice) or would have discovered it had he taken proper steps (constructive notice). In particular, if the party asserting that he takes free of the earlier rights of another knows of certain facts which put him on inquiry as to the possible existence of the rights of that other and he fails to make such inquiry or take such other steps as are reasonable to verify whether such earlier right does or does not exist, he will have constructive notice of the earlier right and take subject to it. Therefore where a wife has agreed to stand surety for her husband's debts as a result of undue influence or misrepresentation, the creditor will take subject to the wife's equity to set aside the transaction if the circumstances are such as to put the creditor on inquiry as to the circumstances in which she agreed to stand surety.

It is at this stage that, in my view, the "invalidating tendency" or the law's "tender treatment" of married women, becomes relevant ... [T]his tenderness of the law towards married women is due to the fact that, even today, many wives repose confidence and trust in their husbands in relation to their financial affairs. This tenderness of the law is reflected by the fact that voluntary dispositions by the wife in favour of her husband are more likely to be set aside than other dispositions by her: a wife is more likely to establish presumed undue influence of Class 2(B) by her husband than by others because, in practice, many wives do repose in their husbands trust and confidence in relation to their financial affairs. Moreover the informality of business dealings between spouses raises a substantial risk that the husband has not accurately stated to the wife the nature of the liability she is undertaking, i.e., he has misrepresented the position, albeit negligently.

Therefore in my judgment a creditor is put on inquiry when a wife offers to stand surety for her husband's debts by the combination of two factors: (a) the transaction is on its face not to the financial advantage of the wife; and (b) there is a substantial risk in transactions of that kind that, in procuring the wife to act as surety, the husband has committed a legal or equitable wrong that entitles the wife to set aside the transaction.

It follows that unless the creditor who is put on inquiry takes reasonable steps to satisfy himself that the wife's agreement to stand surety has been properly obtained, the creditor will have constructive notice of the wife's rights.

What, then are the reasonable steps which the creditor should take to ensure that it does not have constructive notice of the wife's rights, if any? Normally the reasonable steps necessary to avoid being fixed with constructive notice consist of making inquiry of the person who may have the earlier right (ie the wife) to see whether such right is asserted. It is plainly impossible to require of banks and other financial institutions that they should inquire of one spouse whether he or she has been unduly influenced or misled by the other. But in my judgment the creditor, in order to avoid being fixed with constructive notice, can reasonably be expected to take steps to bring home to the wife the risk she is running by standing as surety and to advise her to take independent advice. As to past transactions, it will depend on the facts of each case whether the steps taken by the creditor satisfy this test. However for the future in my judgment a creditor will have satisfied these requirements if it insists that the wife attend a private meeting (in the absence of the husband) with a representative of the creditor at which she is told of the extent of her liability as surety, warned of the risk she is running and urged to take independent legal advice. If these steps are taken in my judgment the creditor will have taken such reasonable steps as are necessary to preclude a subsequent claim that it had constructive notice of the wife's rights. I should make it clear that I have been considering the ordinary case where the creditor knows only that the wife is to stand surety for her husband's debts. I would not exclude exceptional cases where a creditor has knowledge of further facts which render the presence of undue influence not only possible but probable. In such cases, the creditor to be safe will have to insist that the wife is separately advised . . .

If the law is established as I have suggested, it will hold the balance fairly between on the one hand the vulnerability of the wife who relies implicitly on her husband and, on the other hand, the practical problems of financial institutions asked to accept a secured or unsecured surety obligation from the wife for her husband's debts. In the context of suretyship, the wife will not have any right to disown her obligations just because subsequently she proves that she did not fully understand the transaction: she will, as in all other areas of her affairs, be bound by her obligations unless her husband has, by misrepresentation, undue influence or other wrong, committed an actionable wrong against her. In the normal case, a financial institution will be able to lend with confidence in reliance on the wife's surety obligation provided that it warns her (in the absence of the husband) of the amount of her potential liability and of the risk of standing surety and advises her to take independent advice . . .

(b) Other persons. I have hitherto dealt only with the position where a wife stands surety for her husband's debts. But in my judgment the same principles are applicable to all other cases where there is an emotional relationship between cohabitees. The "tenderness" shown by the law to married women is not based on the marriage ceremony but reflects the underlying risk of one cohabitee exploiting the emotional involvement and trust of the other. Now that unmarried cohabitation, whether heterosexual or homosexual, is widespread in our society, the law should recognise this. Legal wives are not the only group which are now exposed to the emotional pressure of cohabitation. Therefore if, but only if, the creditor is aware that the surety is cohabiting with the principal debtor, in my judgment the same principles should apply to them as apply to husband and wife.

In addition to the cases of cohabitees, the decision of the Court of Appeal in *Avon Finance Co Ltd v Bridger* [1985] 2 All ER 281 shows (rightly in my view) that other relationships can give rise to a similar result. In that case a son, by means of misrepresentation, persuaded his elderly parents to stand surety for his debts. The surety obligation was held to be unenforceable by the creditor *inter alia* because to the bank's knowledge the parents trusted the son in their financial dealings. In my judgment that case was rightly decided: in a case where the creditor is aware that the surety reposes trust and confidence in the principal debtor in relation to his financial affairs, the creditor is put on inquiry in just the same way as it is in relation to husband and wife.

Summary
I can therefore summarise my views as follows. Where one cohabitee has entered into an obligation to stand as surety for the debts of the other cohabitee and the creditor is aware that they are cohabitees: (1) the surety obligation will be valid and enforceable by the creditor unless the suretyship was procured by the undue influence, misrepresentation or other legal wrong of the principal debtor; (2) if there has been undue influence, misrepresentation or other legal wrong by the principal debtor, unless the creditor has taken reasonable steps to satisfy himself that the surety entered into the obligation freely and in knowledge of the true facts, the creditor will be unable to enforce the surety obligation because he will be fixed with constructive notice of the surety's right to set aside the transaction; (3) unless there are special exceptional circumstances, a creditor will have taken such reasonable steps to avoid being fixed with constructive notice if the creditor warns the surety (at a meeting not attended by the principal debtor) of the amount of her potential liability and of the risks involved and advises the surety to take independent legal advice.

I should make it clear that in referring to the husband's debts I include the debts of a company in which the husband (but not the wife) has a direct financial interest.

The decision of this case
Applying those principles to this case, to the knowledge of the bank Mr and Mrs O'Brien were man and wife. The bank took a surety obligation from Mrs O'Brien,

secured on the matrimonial home, to secure the debts of a company in which Mr O'Brien was interested but in which Mrs O'Brien had no direct pecuniary interest. The bank should therefore have been put on inquiry as to the circumstances in which Mrs O'Brien had agreed to stand as surety for the debt of her husband. If the Burnham branch had properly carried out the instructions from Mr Tucker of the Woolwich branch, Mrs O'Brien would have been informed that she and the matrimonial home were potentially liable for the debts of a company which had an existing liability of £107,000 and which was to be afforded an overdraft facility of £135,000. If she had been told this, it would have counteracted Mr O'Brien's misrepresentation that the liability was limited to £60,000 and would last for only three weeks. In addition according to the side letter she would have been recommended to take independent legal advice.

Unfortunately Mr Tucker's instructions were not followed and to the knowledge of the bank (through the clerk at the Burnham branch) Mrs O'Brien signed the documents without any warning of the risks or any recommendation to take legal advice. In the circumstances the bank (having failed to take reasonable steps) is fixed with constructive notice of the wrongful misrepresentation made by Mr O'Brien to Mrs O'Brien. Mrs O'Brien is therefore entitled as against the bank to set aside the legal charge on the matrimonial home securing her husband's liability to the bank.

For these reasons I would dismiss the appeal with costs.'

In the context of cohabitees, where one cohabitee has agreed to stand surety for the other, and the creditor is aware that the parties are cohabitees, Lord Browne-Wilkinson outlined three stages to a claim to have the transaction set aside as against the creditor:

1. The surety must show that the transaction was procured by a wrong committed by the principal debtor. On the facts of *O'Brien*, the wrong was a misrepresentation – Mr O'Brien had told Mrs O'Brien that the security was limited to £60,000, whereas in fact it was for £130,000. It is clear that the principles expounded by Lord Browne-Wilkinson are equally applicable where the wrong committed is undue influence.

2. The surety must show that the creditor has been put on notice of the possibility of wrongdoing by the principal debtor. The creditor will be put on constructive notice if:

   (a) the transaction is, on its face, not to the financial advantage of the surety; and

   (b) there is a substantial risk in transactions of that kind that the principal debtor has committed a legal or equitable wrong that entitles the surety to set aside the transaction.

3. Once put on notice, the creditor must take reasonable steps to ensure that the surety's agreement to the transaction was freely given. These steps include:

    (a) warning the surety (not in the presence of the debtor) of the amount of her potential liability; and

    (b) advising the surety to take independent legal advice.

It is important to note that the basis for setting aside the transaction as against the bank in *O'Brien* was not the wrong committed by Mr O'Brien but the fact that the bank was fixed with notice of the wrong and did not take reasonable steps to ensure that Mrs O'Brien's agreement to the transaction was freely given.

Lord Browne-Wilkinson saw no reason to confine his principles to wives. He was of the view that they apply to any situation where the creditor is aware that the surety places trust and confidence in the debtor. The only difference is that, whereas with cohabitees the risk of undue influence or misrepresentation can be inferred from the combination of the relationship and the nature of the transaction, in other situations it would need to be shown that the creditor had actual knowledge that the surety placed trust and confidence in the principal debtor.

The House of Lords, in *Etridge*, has now restated the law on undue influence in third-party situations. This seminal case also did much to clarify the law of undue influence as a whole.

12.4 THE *ETRIDGE* CASE

Royal Bank of Scotland plc v Etridge (No 2) [2002] 2 AC 773

Facts: The case concerned eight conjoined appeals. Each appeal arose out of a transaction in which a wife charged her interest in her home in favour of a bank as security for her husband's indebtedness or the indebtedness of a company through which he carried on business. Seven of the appeals concerned claims by a wife that a charge which she had signed should be set aside on the ground of undue influence and the eighth concerned a claim by a wife for damages from a solicitor for negligent advice prior to signing a charge. The importance of the decision lies not so much in the specific facts of each case but in the statements of general principle to be applied by the courts in subsequent cases.

Held: The House of Lords held that the appeals would be allowed in the second, third, fifth, seventh and eighth cases and dismissed in the first, fourth and sixth cases.

Lord Bingham of Cornhill:
'**1.** My Lords, I have had the great advantage of reading in draft the opinions prepared by each of my noble and learned friends.

3. . . . While the opinions of Lord Nicholls and Lord Scott show some difference of expression and approach, I do not myself discern any significant difference of legal principle applicable to these cases, and I agree with both opinions. But if I am wrong and such differences exist, it is plain that the opinion of Lord Nicholls commands the unqualified support of all members of the House.'

Lord Nicholls of Birkenhead:
'*Undue influence*
6. The issues raised by these appeals make it necessary to go back to first principles. Undue influence is one of the grounds of relief developed by the courts of equity as a court of conscience. The objective is to ensure that the influence of one person over another is not abused. In everyday life people constantly seek to influence the decisions of others. They seek to persuade those with whom they are dealing to enter into transactions, whether great or small. The law has set limits to the means properly employable for this purpose. To this end the common law developed a principle of duress. Originally this was narrow in its scope, restricted to the more blatant forms of physical coercion, such as personal violence.

7. Here, as elsewhere in the law, equity supplemented the common law. Equity extended the reach of the law to other unacceptable forms of persuasion. The law will investigate the manner in which the intention to enter into the transaction was secured: "how the intention was produced", in the oft repeated words of Lord Eldon LC, from as long ago as 1807 (*Huguenin v Baseley* 14 Ves 273, 300). If the intention was produced by an unacceptable means, the law will not permit the transaction to stand. The means used is regarded as an exercise of improper or "undue" influence, and hence unacceptable, whenever the consent thus procured ought not fairly to be treated as the expression of a person's free will. It is impossible to be more precise or definitive. The circumstances in which one person acquires influence over another, and the manner in which influence may be exercised, vary too widely to permit of any more specific criterion.

8. Equity identified broadly two forms of unacceptable conduct. The first comprises overt acts of improper pressure or coercion such as unlawful threats. Today there is much overlap with the principle of duress as this principle has subsequently developed. The second form arises out of a relationship between two persons where one has acquired over another a measure of influence, or ascendancy, of which the ascendant person then takes unfair advantage. An example from the 19th century, when much of this law developed, is a case where an impoverished father prevailed upon his inexperienced children to charge their reversionary interests under their parents' marriage settlement with payment of his mortgage debts: see *Bainbrigge v Browne* (1881) 18 Ch D 188.

9. In cases of this latter nature the influence one person has over another provides scope for misuse without any specific overt acts of persuasion. The relationship between two individuals may be such that, without more, one of them is disposed to agree a course of action proposed by the other. Typically this occurs when one person places trust in another to look after his affairs and interests, and the latter betrays this trust by preferring his own interests. He abuses the influence he has acquired . . .

10. The law has long recognised the need to prevent abuse of influence in these "relationship" cases despite the absence of evidence of overt acts of persuasive conduct. The types of relationship, such as parent and child, in which this principle falls to be applied cannot be listed exhaustively. Relationships are infinitely various. Sir Guenter Treitel QC has rightly noted that the question is whether one party has reposed sufficient trust and confidence in the other, rather than whether the relationship between the parties belongs to a particular type: see Treitel, *The Law of Contract*, 10th edn (1999), pp 380–381. For example, the relation of banker and customer will not normally meet this criterion, but exceptionally it may: see *National Westminster Bank plc v Morgan* [1985] AC 686, 707–709.

11. Even this test is not comprehensive. The principle is not confined to cases of abuse of trust and confidence. It also includes, for instance, cases where a vulnerable person has been exploited. Indeed, there is no single touchstone for determining whether the principle is applicable. Several expressions have been used in an endeavour to encapsulate the essence: trust and confidence, reliance, dependence or vulnerability on the one hand and ascendancy, domination or control on the other. None of these descriptions is perfect. None is all embracing. Each has its proper place.

12. In *CIBC Mortgages plc v Pitt* [1994] 1 AC 200 your Lordships' House decided that in cases of undue influence disadvantage is not a necessary ingredient of the cause of action. It is not essential that the transaction should be disadvantageous to the pressurised or influenced person, either in financial terms or in any other way. However, in the nature of things, questions of undue influence will not usually arise, and the exercise of undue influence is unlikely to occur, where the transaction is innocuous. The issue is likely to arise only when, in some respect, the transaction was disadvantageous either from the outset or as matters turned out.

Burden of proof and presumptions

13. Whether a transaction was brought about by the exercise of undue influence is a question of fact. Here, as elsewhere, the general principle is that he who asserts a wrong has been committed must prove it. The burden of proving an allegation of undue influence rests upon the person who claims to have been wronged. This is the general rule. The evidence required to discharge the burden of proof depends on the nature of the alleged undue influence, the personality of the parties, their relationship, the extent to which the transaction cannot readily be accounted for by the ordinary motives of ordinary persons in that relationship, and all the circumstances of the case.

14. Proof that the complainant placed trust and confidence in the other party in relation to the management of the complainant's financial affairs, coupled with a transaction which calls for explanation, will normally be sufficient, failing satisfactory evidence to the contrary, to discharge the burden of proof. On proof of these two matters the stage is set for the court to infer that, in the absence of a satisfactory explanation, the transaction can only have been procured by undue influence. In other words, proof of these two facts is prima facie evidence that the defendant abused the influence he acquired in the parties' relationship. He preferred his own interests. He did not behave fairly to the other. So the evidential burden then shifts to him. It is for him to produce evidence to counter the inference which otherwise should be drawn.

15. *Bainbrigge v Browne* 18 Ch D 188, already mentioned, provides a good illustration of this commonplace type of forensic exercise . . .

16. Generations of equity lawyers have conventionally described this situation as one in which a presumption of undue influence arises. This use of the term "presumption" is descriptive of a shift in the evidential onus on a question of fact. When a plaintiff succeeds by this route he does so because he has succeeded in establishing a case of undue influence. The court has drawn appropriate inferences of fact upon a balanced consideration of the whole of the evidence at the end of a trial in which the burden of proof rested upon the plaintiff. The use, in the course of the trial, of the forensic tool of a shift in the evidential burden of proof should not be permitted to obscure the overall position. These cases are the equitable counterpart of common law cases where the principle of *res ipsa loquitur* is invoked. There is a rebuttable evidential presumption of undue influence.

17. The availability of this forensic tool in cases founded on abuse of influence arising from the parties' relationship has led to this type of case sometimes being labelled "presumed undue influence". This is by way of contrast with cases involving actual pressure or the like, which are labelled "actual undue influence": see *Bank of Credit and Commerce International SA v Aboody* [1990] 1 QB 923, 953, and *Royal Bank of Scotland plc v Etridge (No 2)* [1998] 4 All ER 705, 711–712, paras 5–7. This usage can be a little confusing. In many cases where a plaintiff has claimed that the defendant abused the influence he acquired in a relationship of trust and confidence the plaintiff has succeeded by recourse to the rebuttable evidential presumption. But this need not be so. Such a plaintiff may succeed even where this presumption is not available to him; for instance, where the impugned transaction was not one which called for an explanation.

18. The evidential presumption discussed above is to be distinguished sharply from a different form of presumption which arises in some cases. The law has adopted a sternly protective attitude towards certain types of relationship in which one party acquires influence over another who is vulnerable and dependent and where, moreover, substantial gifts by the influenced or vulnerable person are not normally to be expected. Examples of relationships within this special class are parent and child, guardian and ward, trustee and beneficiary, solicitor and client, and medical adviser and patient. In these cases the law presumes, irrebuttably, that one party had influence over the other. The complainant need not prove he actually reposed trust and confidence in the other party. It is sufficient for him to prove the existence of the type of relationship.

19. It is now well established that husband and wife is not one of the relationships to which this latter principle applies . . . Although there is no presumption, the court will nevertheless note, as a matter of fact, the opportunities for abuse which flow from a wife's confidence in her husband. The court will take this into account with all the other evidence in the case . . .

Independent advice

20. Proof that the complainant received advice from a third party before entering into the impugned transaction is one of the matters a court takes into account when weighing all the evidence. The weight, or importance, to be attached to such advice depends on all the circumstances. In the normal course, advice from a solicitor or other outside adviser can be expected to bring home to a complainant a proper understanding of what he or she is about to do. But a person may understand fully the implications of a proposed transaction, for instance, a substantial gift, and yet still be acting under the undue influence of another. Proof of outside advice does not, of itself, necessarily show that the subsequent completion of the transaction was free from the exercise of undue influence. Whether it will be proper to infer that outside advice had an emancipating effect, so that the transaction was not brought about by the exercise of undue influence, is a question of fact to be decided having regard to all the evidence in the case.

Manifest disadvantage

21. As already noted, there are two prerequisites to the evidential shift in the burden of proof from the complainant to the other party. First, that the complainant reposed trust and confidence in the other party, or the other party acquired ascendancy over the complainant. Second, that the transaction is not readily explicable by the relationship of the parties.

22. Lindley LJ summarised this second prerequisite in the leading authority of *Allcard v Skinner* 36 Ch D 145, where the donor parted with almost all her property. Lindley LJ pointed out that where a gift of a small amount is made to a person standing in a confidential relationship to the donor, some proof of the exercise of the influence of the donee must be given. The mere existence of the influence is not enough. He continued, at p 185 "But if the gift is so large as not to be reasonably accounted for on the ground of friendship, relationship, charity, or other ordinary motives on which ordinary men act, the burden is upon the donee to support the gift." . . .

24. . . . The second prerequisite, as expressed by Lindley LJ, is good sense. It is a necessary limitation upon the width of the first prerequisite. It would be absurd for the law to presume that every gift by a child to a parent, or every transaction between a client and his solicitor or between a patient and his doctor, was brought about by undue influence unless the contrary is affirmatively proved. Such a presumption would be too far-reaching. The law would be out of touch with everyday life if the presumption were to apply to every Christmas or birthday gift by a child to a parent, or to an agreement whereby a client or patient agrees to be responsible for the reasonable fees of his legal or medical adviser. The law would be rightly open to ridicule, for transactions such as these are unexceptionable. They do not suggest that something may be amiss. So something more is needed before the law reverses the burden of proof, something which calls for an explanation. When that something more is present, the greater the disadvantage to the vulnerable person, the more cogent must be the explanation before the presumption will be regarded as rebutted.

25. This was the approach adopted by Lord Scarman in *National Westminster Bank plc v Morgan* [1985] AC 686, 703–707. He cited Lindley LJ's observations in *Allcard v Skinner* 36 Ch D 145, 185, which I have set out above . . . Lord Scarman concluded, at p 704: "the Court of Appeal erred in law in holding that the presumption of undue influence can arise from the evidence of the relationship of the parties without also evidence that the transaction itself was wrongful in that it constituted *an advantage taken of the person subjected to the influence which, failing proof to the contrary, was explicable only on the basis that undue influence had been exercised to procure it*." (Emphasis added.)

26. Lord Scarman attached the label "manifest disadvantage" to this second ingredient necessary to raise the presumption. This label has been causing difficulty. It may be apt enough when applied to straightforward transactions such as a substantial gift or a sale at an undervalue. But experience has now shown that this expression can give rise to misunderstanding. The label is being understood and applied in a way which does not accord with the meaning intended by Lord Scarman, its originator.

27. The problem has arisen in the context of wives guaranteeing payment of their husband's business debts. In recent years judge after judge has grappled with the baffling question whether a wife's guarantee of her husband's bank overdraft, together with a charge on her share of the matrimonial home, was a transaction manifestly to her disadvantage.

28. In a narrow sense, such a transaction plainly ("manifestly") is disadvantageous to the wife. She undertakes a serious financial obligation, and in return she personally receives nothing. But that would be to take an unrealistically blinkered view of such a transaction. Unlike the relationship of solicitor and client or medical adviser and patient, in the case of husband and wife there are inherent reasons why such a transaction may well be for her benefit. Ordinarily, the fortunes of husband and wife are bound up together . . .

29. Which, then, is the correct approach to adopt in deciding whether a transaction is disadvantageous to the wife: the narrow approach, or the wider approach? The answer is neither. The answer lies in discarding a label which gives rise to this sort of ambiguity. The better approach is to adhere more directly to the test outlined by Lindley LJ in *Allcard v Skinner* 36 Ch D 145, and adopted by Lord Scarman in *National Westminster Bank plc v Morgan* [1985] AC 686, in the passages I have cited.

30. I return to husband and wife cases. I do not think that, in the ordinary course, a guarantee of the character I have mentioned is to be regarded as a transaction which, failing proof to the contrary, is explicable only on the basis that it has been procured by the exercise of undue influence by the husband . . .

31. I have emphasised the phrase "in the ordinary course". There will be cases where a wife's signature of a guarantee or a charge of her share in the matrimonial home does call for explanation. Nothing I have said above is directed at such a case.

A cautionary note

32. I add a cautionary note, prompted by some of the first instance judgments in the cases currently being considered by the House. It concerns the general approach to be adopted by a court when considering whether a wife's guarantee of her husband's bank overdraft was procured by her husband's undue influence. Undue influence has a connotation of impropriety. In the eye of the law, undue influence means that influence has been misused. Statements or conduct by a husband which do not pass beyond the bounds of what may be expected of a reasonable husband in the circumstances should not, without more, be castigated as undue influence. Similarly, when a husband is forecasting the future of his business, and expressing his hopes or fears, a degree of hyperbole may be only natural. Courts should not too readily treat such exaggerations as misstatements.

33. Inaccurate explanations of a proposed transaction are a different matter. So are cases where a husband, in whom a wife has reposed trust and confidence for the management of their financial affairs, prefers his interests to hers and makes a choice for both of them on that footing. Such a husband abuses the influence he has. He fails to discharge the obligation of candour and fairness he owes a wife who is looking to him to make the major financial decisions.

The complainant and third parties: suretyship transactions

35. If the freedom of home-owners to make economic use of their homes is not to be frustrated, a bank must be able to have confidence that a wife's signature of the necessary guarantee and charge will be as binding upon her as is the signature of anyone else on documents which he or she may sign. Otherwise banks will not be willing to lend money on the security of a jointly owned house or flat.

36. At the same time, the high degree of trust and confidence and emotional interdependence which normally characterises a marriage relationship provides scope for abuse . . .

37. In *O'Brien*'s case this House decided where the balance should be held between these competing interests. On the one side, there is the need to protect a wife against a husband's undue influence. On the other side, there is the need for the bank to be able to have reasonable confidence in the strength of its security. Otherwise it would not provide the required money. The problem lies in finding the course best designed to protect wives in a minority of cases without unreasonably hampering the giving and taking of security. The House produced a practical solution . . . Like every compromise, the outcome falls short of achieving in full the objectives of either of the two competing interests. In particular, the steps required of banks will not guarantee that, in future, wives will not be subjected to undue influence or misled when standing as sureties. Short of prohibiting this type of suretyship transaction altogether, there is no way of achieving that result, desirable although it is . . .

38. The jurisprudential route by which the House reached its conclusion in *O'Brien*'s case has attracted criticism from some commentators . . . In *O'Brien*, Lord Browne-Wilkinson prayed in aid the doctrine of constructive notice. In circumstances he identified, a creditor is put on inquiry. When that is so, the creditor "will have constructive notice of the wife's rights" unless the creditor takes reasonable steps to satisfy himself that the wife's agreement to stand surety has been properly obtained: see [1994] 1 AC 180, 196.

39. Lord Browne-Wilkinson would be the first to recognise this is not a conventional use of the equitable concept of constructive notice . . .

40. The traditional view of equity in this tripartite situation seems to be that a person in the position of the wife will only be relieved of her bargain if the other party to the transaction (the bank, in the present instance) was privy to the conduct which led to the wife's entry into the transaction. Knowledge is required . . . The law imposes no obligation on one party to a transaction to check whether the other party's concurrence was obtained by undue influence. But *O'Brien* has introduced into the law the concept that, in certain circumstances, a party to a contract may lose the benefit of his contract, entered into in good faith, if he ought to have known that the other's concurrence had been procured by the misconduct of a third party.

41. There is a further respect in which *O'Brien* departed from conventional concepts. Traditionally, a person is deemed to have notice (that is, he has "constructive" notice) of a prior right when he does not actually know of it but would have learned of it had he made the requisite inquiries. A purchaser will be treated as having constructive notice of all that a reasonably prudent purchaser would have discovered. In the present type of case, the steps a bank is required to take, lest it have constructive notice that the wife's concurrence was procured improperly by her husband, do not consist of making inquiries. Rather, *O'Brien* envisages that the steps taken by the bank will reduce, or even eliminate, the risk of the wife entering into the transaction under any misapprehension or as a result of undue influence by her husband. The steps are not concerned to discover whether the wife has been wronged by her husband in this way. The steps are concerned to minimise the risk that such a wrong may be committed . . .

43. The route selected in *O'Brien* ought not to have an unsettling effect on established principles of contract. *O'Brien* concerned suretyship transactions. These are tripartite transactions. They involve the debtor as well as the creditor and the guarantor. The guarantor enters into the transaction at the request of the debtor. The guarantor assumes obligations. On the face of the transaction the guarantor usually receives no benefit in return, unless the guarantee is being given on a commercial basis. Leaving aside cases where the relationship between the surety and the debtor is commercial, a guarantee transaction is one-sided so far as the guarantor is concerned. The creditor knows this. Thus the decision in *O'Brien* is directed at a class of contracts which has special features of its own . . .

The threshold: when the bank is put on inquiry

44. . . . The House set a low level for the threshold which must be crossed before a bank is put on inquiry. For practical reasons the level is set much lower than is required to satisfy a court that, failing contrary evidence, the court may infer that the transaction was procured by undue influence. Lord Browne-Wilkinson said [1994] 1 AC 180, 196:

"Therefore in my judgment a creditor is put on inquiry when a wife offers to stand surety for her husband's debts by the combination of two factors: (a) the transaction is on its face not to the financial advantage of the wife; and (b) there is a substantial risk in transactions of that kind that, in procuring the wife to act as surety, the husband has committed a legal or equitable wrong that entitles the wife to set aside the transaction."

In my view, this passage, read in context, is to be taken to mean, quite simply, that a bank is put on inquiry whenever a wife offers to stand surety for her husband's debts . . .

47. The position is likewise if the husband stands surety for his wife's debts. Similarly, in the case of unmarried couples, whether heterosexual or homosexual, where the bank is aware of the relationship . . . Cohabitation is not essential.

48. As to the type of transactions where a bank is put on inquiry, the case where a wife becomes surety for her husband's debts is, in this context, a straightforward case. The bank is put on inquiry. On the other side of the line is the case where money is being advanced, or has been advanced, to husband and wife jointly. In such a case the bank is not put on inquiry, unless the bank is aware the loan is being made for the husband's purposes, as distinct from their joint purposes . . .

49. Less clear cut is the case where the wife becomes surety for the debts of a company whose shares are held by her and her husband. Her shareholding may be nominal, or she may have a minority shareholding or an equal shareholding with her husband. In my view the bank is put on inquiry in such cases, even when the wife is a director or secretary of the company. Such cases cannot be equated with joint loans . . .

The steps a bank should take

50. The principal area of controversy on these appeals concerns the steps a bank should take when it has been put on inquiry. In *O'Brien* [1994] 1 AC 180, 196–197 Lord Browne-Wilkinson said that a bank can reasonably be expected to take steps to bring home to the wife the risk she is running by standing as surety and to advise her to take independent advice. That test is applicable to past transactions. All the cases now before your Lordships' House fall into this category. For the future a bank satisfies these requirements if it insists that the wife attend a private meeting with a representative of the bank at which she is told of the extent of her liability as surety, warned of the risk she is running and urged to take independent legal advice. In exceptional cases the bank, to be safe, has to insist that the wife is separately advised . . .

53. My Lords, it is plainly neither desirable nor practicable that banks should be required to attempt to discover for themselves whether a wife's consent is being procured by the exercise of undue influence of her husband. This is not a step the banks should be expected to take. Nor, further, is it desirable or practicable that banks should be expected to insist on confirmation from a solicitor that the solicitor has satisfied himself that the wife's consent has not been procured by undue influence. As already noted, the circumstances in which banks are put on inquiry are extremely wide. They embrace every case where a wife is entering into a suretyship transaction in respect of her husband's debts. Many, if not most, wives would be understandably outraged by having to respond to the sort of questioning which would be appropriate before a responsible solicitor could give such a confirmation. In any event, solicitors are not equipped to carry out such an exercise in any really worthwhile way, and they will usually lack the necessary materials . . .

54. The furthest a bank can be expected to go is to take reasonable steps to satisfy itself that the wife has had brought home to her, in a meaningful way, the practical implications of the proposed transaction. This does not wholly eliminate the risk of undue influence or misrepresentation. But it does mean that a wife enters into a transaction with her eyes open so far as the basic elements of the transaction are concerned.

55. . . . A bank may itself provide the necessary information directly to the wife. Indeed, it is best equipped to do so. But banks are not following that course . . . It seems to me that, provided a suitable alternative is available, banks ought not to be compelled to take this course . . . It is not unreasonable for the banks to prefer that this task should be undertaken by an independent legal adviser.

56. . . . Ordinarily it will be reasonable that a bank should be able to rely upon confirmation from a solicitor, acting for the wife, that he has advised the wife appropriately.

57. The position will be otherwise if the bank knows that the solicitor has not duly advised the wife or, I would add, if the bank knows facts from which it ought to have realised that the wife has not received the appropriate advice. In such circumstances the bank will proceed at its own risk.

The content of the legal advice

61. . . . [I]n the present type of case it is not for the solicitor to veto the transaction by declining to confirm to the bank that he has explained the documents to the wife and the risks she is taking upon herself. If the solicitor considers the transaction is not in the wife's best interests, he will give reasoned advice to the wife to that effect. But at the end of the day the decision on whether to proceed is the decision of the client, not the solicitor. A wife is not to be precluded from entering into a financially unwise transaction if, for her own reasons, she wishes to do so.

62. That is the general rule. There may, of course, be exceptional circumstances where it is glaringly obvious that the wife is being grievously wronged. In such a case the solicitor should decline to act further . . .

64. I turn to consider the scope of the responsibilities of a solicitor who is advising the wife . . . As a first step the solicitor will need to explain to the wife the purpose for which he has become involved at all. He should explain that, should it ever become necessary, the bank will rely upon his involvement to counter any suggestion that the wife was overborne by her husband or that she did not properly understand the implications of the transaction . . .

65. . . . Typically, the advice a solicitor can be expected to give should cover the

following matters as the core minimum. (1) He will need to explain the nature of the documents and the practical consequences these will have for the wife if she signs them. She could lose her home if her husband's business does not prosper. Her home may be her only substantial asset, as well as the family's home. She could be made bankrupt. (2) He will need to point out the seriousness of the risks involved. The wife should be told the purpose of the proposed new facility, the amount and principal terms of the new facility, and that the bank might increase the amount of the facility, or change its terms, or grant a new facility, without reference to her. She should be told the amount of her liability under her guarantee. The solicitor should discuss the wife's financial means, including her understanding of the value of the property being charged. The solicitor should discuss whether the wife or her husband has any other assets out of which repayment could be made if the husband's business should fail. These matters are relevant to the seriousness of the risks involved. (3) The solicitor will need to state clearly that the wife has a choice. The decision is hers and hers alone. Explanation of the choice facing the wife will call for some discussion of the present financial position, including the amount of the husband's present indebtedness, and the amount of his current overdraft facility. (4) The solicitor should check whether the wife wishes to proceed. She should be asked whether she is content that the solicitor should write to the bank confirming he has explained to her the nature of the documents and the practical implications they may have for her, or whether, for instance, she would prefer him to negotiate with the bank on the terms of the transaction. Matters for negotiation could include the sequence in which the various securities will be called upon or a specific or lower limit to her liabilities. The solicitor should not give any confirmation to the bank without the wife's authority.

66. The solicitor's discussion with the wife should take place at a face-to-face meeting, in the absence of the husband. It goes without saying that the solicitor's explanations should be couched in suitably non-technical language. It also goes without saying that the solicitor's task is an important one. It is not a formality.

67. The solicitor should obtain from the bank any information he needs. If the bank fails for any reason to provide information requested by the solicitor, the solicitor should decline to provide the confirmation sought by the bank.

68. As already noted, the advice which a solicitor can be expected to give must depend on the particular facts of the case. But I have set out this "core minimum" in some detail, because the quality of the legal advice is the most disturbing feature of some of the present appeals . . .

Independent advice

69. I turn next to the much-vexed question whether the solicitor advising the wife must act for the wife alone . . .

74. . . . The advantages attendant upon the employment of a solicitor acting solely for the wife do not justify the additional expense this would involve for the husband. When accepting instructions to advise the wife the solicitor assumes responsibilities directly to her, both at law and professionally. These duties, and this is central to the reasoning on this point, are owed to the wife alone. In advising the wife the solicitor is acting for the wife alone. He is concerned only with her interests. I emphasise, therefore, that in every case the solicitor must consider carefully whether there is any conflict of duty or interest and, more widely, whether it would be in the best interests of the wife for him to accept instructions from her. If he decides to accept instructions, his assumption of legal and professional responsibilities to her ought, in the ordinary course of things, to provide sufficient assurance that he will give the requisite advice fully, carefully and conscientiously. Especially so, now that the nature of the advice called for has been clarified. If at any stage the solicitor becomes concerned that there is a real risk that other interests or duties may inhibit his advice to the wife he must cease to act for her.

Agency

75. No system ever works perfectly. There will always be cases where things go wrong, sometimes seriously wrong. The next question concerns the position when a solicitor has accepted instructions to advise a wife but he fails to do so properly. . . .

76. Mr Sher contended that, depending on the facts, the solicitor should be regarded as the agent of the bank . . .

77. I cannot accept this analysis. Confirmation from the solicitor that he has advised the wife is one of the bank's preconditions for completion of the transaction. But it is central to this arrangement that in advising the wife the solicitor is acting for the wife and no one else.

78. In the ordinary case, therefore, deficiencies in the advice given are a matter between the wife and her solicitor. The bank is entitled to proceed on the assumption that a solicitor advising the wife has done his job properly . . .

Obtaining the solicitor's confirmation

79. I now return to the steps a bank should take when it has been put on inquiry and for its protection is looking to the fact that the wife has been advised independently by a solicitor.

(1) . . . Since the bank is looking for its protection to legal advice given to the wife by a solicitor who, in this respect, is acting solely for her, I consider the bank should take steps to check directly with the wife the name of the solicitor she wishes to act for her. To this end, in future the bank should communicate directly with the wife, informing her that for its own protection it will require written confirmation from a solicitor, acting for her, to the effect that the solicitor has fully explained to her the nature of the documents and the practical implications they will have for her. She should be told that the purpose of this requirement is that thereafter she should not be able to dispute she is legally bound by the documents once she has signed them. She should be asked to nominate a solicitor whom she is willing to instruct to advise her, separately from her husband, and act for her in giving the necessary confirmation to the bank. She should be told that, if she wishes, the solicitor may be the same solicitor as is acting for her husband in the transaction. If a solicitor is already acting for the husband and the wife, she should be asked whether she would prefer that a different solicitor should act for

her regarding the bank's requirement for confirmation from a solicitor. The bank should not proceed with the transaction until it has received an appropriate response directly from the wife.

(2) . . . [I]t should become routine practice for banks, if relying on confirmation from a solicitor for their protection, to send to the solicitor the necessary financial information. What is required must depend on the facts of the case. Ordinarily this will include information on the purpose for which the proposed new facility has been requested, the current amount of the husband's indebtedness, the amount of his current overdraft facility, and the amount and terms of any new facility. If the bank's request for security arose from a written application by the husband for a facility, a copy of the application should be sent to the solicitor. The bank will, of course, need first to obtain the consent of its customer to this circulation of confidential information. If this consent is not forthcoming the transaction will not be able to proceed.

(3) Exceptionally there may be a case where the bank believes or suspects that the wife has been misled by her husband or is not entering into the transaction of her own free will. If such a case occurs the bank must inform the wife's solicitors of the facts giving rise to its belief or suspicion.

(4) The bank should in every case obtain from the wife's solicitor a written confirmation to the effect mentioned above.

80. These steps will be applicable to future transactions. In respect of past transactions, the bank will ordinarily be regarded as having discharged its obligations if a solicitor who was acting for the wife in the transaction gave the bank confirmation to the effect that he had brought home to the wife the risks she was running by standing as surety . . .

A wider principle

82. . . . The *O'Brien* decision cannot sensibly be regarded as confined to sexual relationships, although these are likely to be its main field of application at present. What is appropriate for sexual relationships ought, in principle, to be appropriate also for other relationships where trust and confidence are likely to exist.

83. The courts have already recognised this. Further application, or development, of the *O'Brien* principle has already taken place. In *Credit Lyonnais Bank Nederland NV v Burch* [1997] 1 All ER 144 the same principle was applied where the relationship was employer and employee. . . .

84. The crucially important question raised by this wider application of the *O'Brien* principle concerns the circumstances which will put a bank on inquiry. A bank is put on inquiry whenever a wife stands as surety for her husband's debts. It is sufficient that the bank knows of the husband–wife relationship. That bare fact is enough . . . What, then, of other relationships where there is an increased risk of undue influence, such as parent and child? Is it enough that the bank knows of the relationship? . . . A bank should not be called upon to evaluate highly personal matters such as the degree of trust and confidence existing between the father and his daughter, with the bank put on inquiry in one case and not in another. As with wives, so with daughters, whether a bank is put on inquiry should not depend on the degree of trust and confidence the particular daughter places in her father in relation to financial matters . . . [K]nowledge by the bank of the relationship of father and daughter should suffice to put the bank on inquiry. When the bank knows of the relationship, it must then take reasonable steps to ensure the daughter knows what she is letting herself into.

87. [T]here is no rational cut-off point, with certain types of relationship being susceptible to the *O'Brien* principle and others not. Further, if a bank is not to be required to evaluate the extent to which its customer has influence over a proposed guarantor, the only practical way forward is to regard banks as "put on inquiry" in every case where the relationship between the surety and the debtor is non-commercial . . .

88. Different considerations apply where the relationship between the debtor and guarantor is commercial, as where a guarantor is being paid a fee, or a company is guaranteeing the debts of another company in the same group. Those engaged in business can be regarded as capable of looking after themselves and understanding the risks involved in the giving of guarantees.'

Lord Clyde:

'**91.** My Lords, I have had the opportunity of reading in draft the speech of my noble and learned friend, Lord Nicholls of Birkenhead, and agree with it. I add a few observations of my own because of the importance of the appeals which we have heard.

92. I question the wisdom of the practice which has grown up, particularly since *Bank of Credit and Commerce International SA v Aboody* [1990] 1 QB 923 of attempting to make classifications of cases of undue influence. That concept is in any event not easy to define . . . [T]he attempt to build up classes or categories may lead to confusion. The confusion is aggravated if the names used to identify the classes do not bear their actual meaning. Thus on the face of it a division into cases of "actual" and "presumed" undue influence appears illogical. It appears to confuse definition and proof. There is also room for uncertainty whether the presumption is of the existence of an influence or of its quality as being undue. I would also dispute the utility of the further sophistication of subdividing "presumed undue influence" into further categories. All these classifications to my mind add mystery rather than illumination.'

Lord Hobhouse of Woodborough:

'*Introduction*

100. . . . To the end that lenders, those advising parties and, indeed, judges should have clear statements of the law on which to base themselves, I will state at the outset that in this speech I shall agree with my noble and learned friend Lord Nicholls and, specifically, the guidance which he gives concerning the role of the burden of proof, the duties of solicitors towards their clients (paragraphs 64–68, and paragraph 74), and the steps which a lender which has been put on inquiry should take (paragraph 79). I would stress that this guidance should not be treated as optional, to be watered down when it proves inconvenient (as may be thought to have been the fate of Lord Browne-Wilkinson's equally carefully crafted scheme). Nor should it be regarded as something which will only apply to future transactions; it has represented, and continues to represent, the reasonable response to being put on inquiry . . . I will, in the course of this speech and without qualifying the scope of my agreement with Lord Nicholls, mention certain points in the hope that it will add to the clarity and accuracy of the analysis. I must also express my gratitude to my noble and learned friend Lord Scott of Foscote, whose speech I have read in draft, for his summary of the facts of the eight individual cases before the House.

(1) Presumed undue influence

103. The division between presumed and actual undue influence derives from the judgments in *Allcard v Skinner*. Actual undue influence presents no relevant problem. It is an equitable wrong committed by the dominant party against the other which makes it unconscionable for the dominant party to enforce his legal rights against the other. It is typically some express conduct overbearing the other party's will . . . Actual undue influence does not depend upon some preexisting relationship between the two parties though it is most commonly associated with and derives from such a relationship. He who alleges actual undue influence must prove it.

104. Presumed undue influence is different in that it necessarily involves some legally recognised relationship between the two parties. As a result of that relationship one party is treated as owing a special duty to deal fairly with the other. It is not necessary for present purposes to define the limits of the relationships which give rise to this duty. Typically they are fiduciary or closely analogous relationships. A solicitor owes a legal duty to deal fairly with his client and he must, if challenged, be prepared to show that he has done so . . . Such legal relationships can be described as relationships where one party is legally presumed to repose trust and confidence in the other – the other side of the coin to the duty not to abuse that confidence. But there is no presumption properly so called that the confidence has been abused. It is a matter of evidence. If all that has happened is that, say, a client has left a small bequest to his family solicitor or that a solicitor has made a reasonable charge for professional services rendered to the client, no inference of abuse or unfair dealing will arise . . . Thus, at the trial the judge will decide on the evidence whether he is in fact satisfied that there was no abuse of confidence. It will be appreciated that the relevance of the concept of "manifest disadvantage" is evidential. It is relevant to the question whether there is any issue of abuse which can properly be raised . . . It is a fallacy to argue from the terminology normally used, "presumed undue influence", to the position, not of presuming that one party reposed trust and confidence in the other, but of presuming that an abuse of that relationship has occurred; factual inference, yes, once the issue has been properly raised, but not a presumption.

105. The Court of Appeal in *Aboody* [1990] 1 QB 923 and Lord Browne-Wilkinson classified cases where there was a legal relationship between the parties which the law presumed to be one of trust and confidence as "presumed undue influence: class 2(A)". They then made the logical extrapolation that there should be a class 2(B) to cover those cases where it was proved by evidence that one party had in fact reposed trust and confidence in the other. It was then said that the same consequences flowed from this factual relationship as from the legal class 2(A) relationship . . .

107. In agreement with what I understand to be the view of your Lordships, I consider that the so-called class 2(B) presumption should not be adopted. It is not a useful forensic tool. The wife or other person alleging that the relevant agreement or charge is not enforceable must prove her case. She can do this by proving that she was the victim of an equitable wrong. This wrong may be an overt wrong, such as oppression; or it may be the failure to perform an equitable duty, such as a failure by one in whom trust and confidence is reposed not to abuse that trust by failing to deal fairly with her and have proper regard to her interests. Although the general burden of proof is, and remains, upon her, she can discharge that burden of proof by establishing a sufficient prima facie case to justify a decision in her favour on the balance of probabilities, the court drawing appropriate inferences from the primary facts proved. Evidentially the opposite party will then be faced with the necessity to adduce evidence sufficient to displace that conclusion. Provided it is remembered that the burden is an evidential one, the comparison with the operation of the doctrine *res ipsa loquitur* is useful.

(2) Put on inquiry

111. Before turning to discuss what are the reasonable steps to be taken by a lender who had been put on inquiry, I will pause to look at some of the practical aspects . . . The need to guard against lack of comprehension is important . . . But it is not the same as guarding against undue influence. It may be a first step but it is a fallacy to confuse the two. Comprehension is essential for any legal documents of this complexity and obscurity. But for the purpose of negativing undue influence it is necessary to be satisfied that the agreement was, also, given freely in knowledge of the true facts. It must be remembered that the equitable doctrine of undue influence has been created for the protection of those who are *sui juris* and competent to undertake legal obligations but are nevertheless vulnerable and liable to have their will unduly influenced. It is their weakness which is being protected not their inability to comprehend. I regret that I must specifically disagree with my noble and learned friend Lord Scott when (in his summary) he treats a belief on the part of a lender that the wife has understood the nature and effect of the transaction as sufficient to exonerate the lender from inquiry or as treating this as the effect of the scheme laid out by Lord Nicholls in the paragraphs to which I have referred earlier.'

Lord Scott of Foscote:

'*Undue influence*

161. . . . For my part, I doubt the utility of the Class 2B classification. Class 2A is useful in identifying particular relationships where the presumption arises. The presumption in Class 2B cases, however, is doing no more than recognising that evidence of the relationship between the dominant and subservient parties, coupled with whatever other evidence is for the time being available, may be sufficient to justify a finding of undue influence on the balance of probabilities. The onus shifts to the defendant.

Unless the defendant introduces evidence to counteract the inference of undue influence that the complainant's evidence justifies, the complainant will succeed. In my opinion, the presumption of undue influence in Class 2B cases has the same function in undue influence cases as *res ipsa loquitur* has in negligence cases. It recognises an evidential state of affairs in which the onus has shifted.

162. In the surety wife cases it should, in my opinion, be recognised that undue influence, though a possible explanation for the wife's agreement to become surety, is a relatively unlikely one. *O'Brien* itself was a misrepresentation case. Undue influence had been alleged but the undoubted pressure which the husband had brought to bear to persuade his reluctant wife to sign was not regarded by the judge or the Court of Appeal as constituting undue influence. The wife's will had not been overborne by her husband. Nor was *O'Brien* a case in which, in my opinion, there would have been at any stage in the case a presumption of undue influence.

Summary

191. My Lords I think, given the regrettable length of this opinion, I should try and summarise my views about the principles that apply and the practice that should be followed in surety wife cases.

(1) The issue as between the surety wife and the lender bank is whether the bank may rely on the apparent consent of the wife to the suretyship transaction.

(2) If the bank knows that the surety wife's consent to the transaction has been procured by undue influence or misrepresentation, or if it has shut its eyes to the likelihood that that was so, it may not rely on her apparent consent.

(3) If the wife's consent has in fact been procured by undue influence or misrepresentation, the bank may not rely on her apparent consent unless it has good reason to believe that she understands the nature and effect of the transaction.

(4) Unless the case has some special feature, the bank's knowledge that a solicitor is acting for the wife and has advised her about the nature and effect of the transaction will provide a good reason for the purposes of (3) above. That will also be so if the bank has a reasonable belief that a solicitor is acting for her and has so advised her. Written confirmation by a solicitor acting for the wife that he has so advised her will entitle the bank to hold that reasonable belief.

(5) So, too, a sufficient explanation of the nature and effect of the transaction given by a senior bank official would constitute good reason for the purposes of (3) above.

(6) If there are any facts known to the bank which increase the inherent risk that the wife's consent to the transaction may have been procured by the husband's undue influence or misrepresentation, it may be necessary for the bank to be satisfied that the wife has received advice about the transaction from a solicitor independent of the husband before the bank can reasonably rely on the wife's apparent consent.

(7) If the bank has not taken reasonable steps to satisfy itself that the wife understands the nature and effect of the transaction, the wife will, subject to such matters as delay, acquiescence, change of position etc, be able to set aside the transaction if her consent was in fact procured by undue influence or misrepresentation.

(8) Subject to special instructions or special circumstances, the duty of a solicitor instructed to act for a wife proposing to stand as surety, or to give security, for her husband's debts is to try and make sure that she understands the nature and effect of the transaction.

(9) In all surety wife cases the bank should disclose to the surety wife, or to the solicitor acting for her, the amount of the existing indebtedness of the principal debtor to the bank and the amount of the proposed new loan or drawing facility.

(10) Subject to (9) above, a creditor has no greater duty of disclosure to a surety wife than to any other intending surety.

192. I am in full agreement with the analysis of the applicable principles of law and with the conclusions expressed in the opinion of my noble and learned friend, Lord Nicholls of Birkenhead. I believe the analysis I have sought to give in this opinion and my conclusions are consistent with them.'

The speeches delivered in *Etridge* are of enormous significance to the law of undue influence. Not only do they provide much needed guidance to banks and solicitors as to the procedures to be adopted in surety cases, but they also provide searching analysis of the law of undue influence in relation to two-party cases.

We will consider four separate issues. First, we will identify which of the five speeches most accurately reflects the opinion of the court. Second, we will take note of their Lordships' observations concerning the categories of undue influence. Third, we will examine the doctrine of notice and finally we will consider the steps that must be taken by the bank once it has been put on inquiry.

12.4.1 THE SPEECHES

In *Etridge*, five separate speeches were delivered by the House of Lords. As is usual in such situations, the speeches differed in expression and approach. Lord Bingham (at [3]) sought to deal with these differences by insisting that the speeches of Lord Nicholls and Lord Scott evidenced no significant difference of legal opinion. With respect, this is somewhat doubtful. Whilst Lord Hobhouse expressed his unqualified agreement with Lord Nicholls he explicitly disagreed with Lord Scott in relation to the steps a creditor must take to avoid being fixed with notice (at [111]). This is irreconcilable with Lord Bingham's position. It is therefore significant that Lord Bingham concluded at [3] with these words: '[I]f I am wrong and such differences exist, it is plain that the opinion of Lord Nicholls commands the unqualified support of all members of the House.' In light of this, it is clear that to the extent that any differences do exists, it is Lord Nicholls' speech that is to be followed.

12.4.2 THE CATEGORIES OF UNDUE INFLUENCE

The House of Lords considered the *Aboody* classification of undue influence (Class 1, 2(A), 2(B)) and unanimously rejected it. Lord Clyde said that the division into cases of 'actual' and 'presumed' undue influence appears 'illogical' and the subdivision of presumed undue influence 'added mystery rather than illumination' (at [92.]). Lord Scott agreed, expressing the view that the classification set out in *Aboody* had set the law on the wrong track (at [158]). In particular, their Lordships expressed concern about the class 2(B) presumption. Lord Nicholls emphasised the evidential nature of presumed undue influence. In a statement with which Lord Hobhouse and Lord Scott agreed, Lord Nicholls said that the term 'presumption' is merely descriptive of a shift in the evidential burden from the complainant to the alleged wrongdoer (at [16]). It is thus misleading to describe the situation as one of presumed undue influence because undue influence is only established if the presumption is incapable of being rebutted. Likewise, if the relationship falls outside of class 2(A) or class 2(B), a claim for undue influence can still succeed if the complainant is able to prove actual undue influence.

In a rather confusing section of his speech (at [18]), Lord Nicholls distinguished between cases that traditionally fell within class 2(A) and those that fell within class 2(B). He said that 'the law has adopted a sternly protective attitude towards certain types of relationship' and 'in these cases the law presumes, irrebuttably, that one party had influence over the other'. On the face if it, this passage appears to state that all relationships that previously fell within Class 2(A), including the relationship between fiancé and fiancée (*Leeder v Stevens* [2005] EWCA Civ 50), but not the relationship between husband and wife (*Etridge* at [19], [106], and [159]–[160]), give rise to a presumption of undue influence. But this is clearly not what Lord Nicholls intended. Two pages later, at [24] Lord Nicholls said the following: 'It would be absurd for the law to presume that every gift by a child to a parent, or every transaction between a patient and his doctor, was brought about by undue influence unless the contrary is affirmatively proved. Such a presumption is too far-reaching. The law would be out of touch with everyday life . . .'. It is therefore clear that the irrebuttable presumption of [18] is a presumption of 'influence', not of '*undue* influence'. Certain relationships (traditionally falling within class 2(A)) automatically raise an irrebuttable presumption of influence. Other relationships (traditionally falling within class 2(B)) require additional evidence in order to raise the presumption of influence. The complainant must lead evidence that they reposed trust and confidence in the other party.

Having raised a presumption of influence, the complainant must then raise a presumption of *undue* influence. Traditionally, the concept of 'manifest disadvantage' was used for this purpose (*National Westminster Bank v Morgan* [1985] AC 686). In more recent years, however, this label has caused difficulty as, in the words of Lord

Nicholls, 'judge after judge has grappled with the baffling question whether a wife's guarantee of her husband's bank overdraft, together with a charge on her share of the matrimonial home, was a transaction manifestly to her disadvantage' (at [27]). On one level, such transactions are clearly disadvantageous because the wife undertakes a serious financial obligation and receives nothing in return. On another, the transaction is often beneficial to the wife because her financial interests are inextricably bound up with her husband's. Due to this ambiguity, Lord Nicholls recommended discarding the label 'manifest disadvantage' in favour of the approach adopted in *Allcard v Skinner* [1887] 36 Ch D 145. There it was stated that the courts should ask whether, 'the transaction itself was wrongful in that it constituted an advantage taken of the person subjected to the influence which, failing proof to the contrary, was explicable only on the basis that undue influence had been exercised to procure it'. Stated more succinctly, the test is whether the transaction is one that 'calls for an explanation' (Lord Nicholls at [24] and Lord Scott at [155]). The Court of Appeal in *Macklin v Dowsett* [2004] EWCA Civ 904, [2004] 2 EGLR 75, has recently confirmed that it is no longer necessary to establish manifest disadvantage in order to raise the presumption of undue influence.

To summarise, in order to raise the presumption of undue influence it is necessary to prove two things:

(1) A relationship of trust and confidence – either through the automatic presumption of a class 2(A) relationship or through evidence relating to the specific relationship;

(2) A transaction that calls for an explanation.

Once these two elements are established the burden of proof shifts to the alleged wrongdoer. Lord Nicholls (at [16]), Lord Hobhouse (at [107]), and Lord Scott [161] all compared this evidential presumption to the common law negligence doctrine of *res ipsa loquitur* – 'the thing speaks for itself'.

In cases like *Etridge*, where a wife stands surety for her husband's debts, it may be extremely difficult to raise the evidential presumption of undue influence. This is for two reasons. First, the relationship between a husband and wife does not fall within class 2(A). Thus it is necessary for the wife to lead specific evidence to prove that she reposed trust and confidence in her husband. Second, in the ordinary course, a guarantee by a wife of her husband's debts is not a transaction that calls for an explanation (Lord Nicholls at [30]). It can be explained on the ground of their relationship and therefore does not give rise to a presumption of undue influence.

12.4.3 THE DOCTRINE OF NOTICE

Seven of the appeals in *Etridge* concerned claims by the surety against the creditor. As we noted above, the surety must prove both that the principle debtor exerted undue influence and that the creditor had notice of such influence. Lord Nicholls set a low threshold for such notice. He said that a creditor is put on inquiry whenever 'a wife offers to stand surety for her husband's debts' (at [44]). This includes situations that she stands surety for the debts of her husband's business, even when she is a shareholder or director of the company (Lord Nicholls was of the view that such factors were an unreliable guide as to who runs the business).

In addition, Lord Nicholls refused to limit the principle to married couples. Cohabitation is not necessary and nor is a sexual relationship. Given that banks should not be called upon to evaluate highly personal matters between the parties, Lord Nicholls suggested that the only practical way forward was to regard a bank as being put on inquiry in all cases where the bank knows that 'the relationship between the surety and the debtor is non-commercial' (at [87]). This is a very expansive approach to notice that places a significant burden on banks and lending institutions. Nevertheless, it is to be welcomed since it removes the uncertainty that previously existed in the law and enables both the lender and the surety to know where they stand.

12.4.4 THE PRECAUTIONS TO BE TAKEN BY THE BANK

Once put on inquiry the bank must take a number of steps in order to protect itself. These were outlined by Lord Nicholls at [79] of his speech. Lord Hobhouse stressed that these guidelines were not to be 'watered down' or regarded as 'optional' (at [100]). In particular, the bank should communicate directly with the wife, informing her that for its own protection it will require written confirmation from a solicitor, acting for her, to the effect that the solicitor has fully explained to her the nature of the documents and the practical implications they will have for her. The bank is under an obligation to provide the solicitor with the financial information needed to advise the wife. If the bank knows of any information that leads it to suspect that the wife is being misled by her husband or is not entering into the transaction of her own free will, it must inform the wife's solicitors of those facts. The bank should in every case obtain a written confirmation from the wife's solicitor. If it does so, it will be protected. Since the solicitor is not an agent of the bank, any deficiencies in the advice given by the solicitor will not affect the validity of the charge as against the bank. The wife's only form of recourse will be to pursue an action in negligence against the solicitor.

Turning to the advice to be offered by solicitors, Lord Nicholls commented at [52] that 'the quality of the legal advice is the most disturbing feature' of some of the appeals before the House. On the much-vexed question of whether the solicitor acting for the wife must act for the wife alone, Lord Nicholls concluded that this was unnecessary because the benefits of such a rule were outweighed by the additional expense it would entail for the husband (at [74]). Lord Nicholls said that the solicitor should meet with the wife face-to-face and in the absence of the husband. He should explain the transaction and its implications in 'suitably non-technical language'. His advice should include the 'core minimum' set out by Lord Nicholls at [65] of his speech. The solicitor must not give any confirmation to the bank without the wife's specific authority. The purpose of these guidelines is to ensure that the wife is fully informed of the nature of the transaction she is entering into.

In his speech (at [2]), Lord Bingham succinctly summarised the main issues influencing their Lordships:

> 'It is important that a wife (or anyone in a like position) should not charge her interest in the matrimonial home to secure the borrowing of her husband (or anyone in a like position) without fully understanding the nature and effect of the proposed transaction and that the decision is hers, to agree or not to agree. It is important that lenders should feel able to advance money, in run-of-the-mill cases with no abnormal features, on the security of the wife's interest in the matrimonial home in reasonable confidence that, if appropriate procedures have been followed in obtaining the security, it will be enforceable if the need for enforcement arises. The law must afford both parties a measure of protection. It cannot prescribe a code which will be proof against error, misunderstanding or mishap. But it can indicate minimum requirements which, if met, will reduce the risk of error, misunderstanding or mishap to an acceptable level. The paramount need in this important field is that these minimum requirements should be clear, simple and practically operable.'

It is submitted that these aims have been met by the guidelines set down in *Etridge*. The threshold for when banks will be put on notice has been lowered, thus increasing the protection afforded to sureties. At the same time, the House of Lords has provided a set of steps for avoiding liability that is clear, simple and sufficiently formulaic to keep compliance costs low. Although these steps cannot guarantee that sureties will never enter transactions under undue influence, they will certainly do much to reduce the risk of this. Furthermore, it is to be hoped that the clarity of the guidance given in *Etridge* will stem the flow of litigants seeking to set aside transactions on the ground of third-party undue influence.

12.5 REMEDIES FOR UNDUE INFLUENCE

In most of the cases discussed so far the influenced party has been in the position of the defendant, seeking to use the alleged undue influence to escape from his contractual obligations. The primary remedy in such cases is the refusal of the courts to enforce the agreement against the person influenced.

12.5.1 RESCISSION

If the contract is non-executory, that is, it has already been performed, the influenced party will need to seek rescission. The usual bars apply including: affirmation (*Mitchell v Homfray* (1881) 8 QBD 587; *Goldsworthy v Brickell* [1987] 1 Ch 378; *First National Bank v Walker* [2001] 1 FLR 505), delay *(Turner v Collins (1871) LR 7 Ch App 329; Allcard v Skinner* (1887) 36 Ch D 145), counter restitution impossible (in recent years the courts have adopted a more flexible approach to this bar, see: *O'Sullivan v Management Agency and Music Ltd* [1985] 1 QB 328), and the intervention of third-party rights *(Cobbett v Brock* (1855) 20 Beav 524; 52 ER 706; *Bridgeman v Green* (1755) Wilm 58; 97 ER 22).

The transaction will normally be rescinded in its entirety:

TSB Bank plc v Camfield [1995] 1 All ER 951

Facts: The defendant entered into an agreement with the plaintiff bank to execute a charge over her matrimonial home in relation to her husband's debts. Her husband had innocently misrepresented that the maximum liability under this charge would be £15,000. In fact, the liability was unlimited. The bank failed to provide independent advice to the defendant in the absence of her husband and for this reason it was held to have had constructive notice of the husband's misrepresentation. The defendant argued that the charge should be set aside in its entirety. The plaintiff countered that the wife should remain liable for £15,000 since she had been willing to agree to a charge for this amount. At first instance, the judge entered judgment against the wife for £15,000 and made an order for possession subject to payment in full within six months.

Held: The Court of Appeal allowed the appeal holding that the charge should be set aside in its entirety as against the defendant.

Roch LJ:
'The judge found that had the true nature of the legal charge been made known to Mrs Camfield she would not have entered into the charge and her enjoyment of her home would never have been at risk. But for the bank's failure to take reasonable steps, Mrs Camfield would have known the true nature of the proposed legal charge and the potential risk to her interest in the family home, and she would have refused to enter into that transaction. Mrs Camfield is entitled to be placed in the position she would have been in had the misrepresentation not been made and had she been made aware of the true nature of the legal charge.'

The decision in *Camfield* is rather controversial. It appears to be incompatible with another line of authority stemming from *Bristol & West Building Society v Henning*, [1985] 1 WLR 778.

**Ferguson, P, 'Partial rescission for misrepresentation rejected' (1995)
111 LQR 555, 556–558**

In these cases, the claimant of a beneficial interest in a property purchased with the aid of a mortgage was held impliedly to have consented to the subordination of any beneficial interest to the rights of the mortgagee. The mortgagee's claim was in all cases upheld to the extent of the claimant's understanding of the amount of the proposed mortgage; and in one case in which the mortgage advance was far beyond what the claimant believed would be raised, the mortgagee was nonetheless permitted to recover in full (see *Abbey National Building Society v Cann* [1991] 1 AC 56, 94). The contrast with *Camfield*, in which the chargee received nothing at all, is striking. Further, the evidence from which consent could be implied was, if anything, stronger in *Camfield* than in the *Henning* authorities: Mrs Camfield was given legal advice, even if she did not in fact fully understand it, and signed a document giving the chargee exactly that priority over her beneficial interest which was at issue in Henning . . .

[I]n Camfield there was actual consent to a charge up to £15,000, and the bank had perfectly reasonable grounds for assuming this to be the case, given Mrs Camfield's execution of the charge document after legal advice had been given to her . . . Granted, Mrs Camfield would not have executed the charge had she known that it was not limited to £15,000; nonetheless, it is also true that she would have done so if it had been limited to that amount. There is actual consent to the priority of the bank's rights up to that limit, and a strong argument that she is estopped from claiming rescission except insofar as the liability exceeded the £15,000 she was – to the bank's knowledge – willing to risk.

The approach taken in *Camfield* was rejected by the High Court of Australia in favour of granting partial rescission in appropriate cases (*Vadasz v Pioneer Concrete (SA) Pty Ltd* (1995) 184 CLR 102). Similar proposals have been made in this country based around the doctrine of estoppel by convention (see Poole, J and Keyser, A, 'Justifying partial rescission in English law' (2005) 121 LQR 273). Nevertheless, the Court of Appeal continues to be bound by its own decision in *Camfield* (see *Bank Melli Iran v Samadi-Rad* [1995] 2 FLR 367).

It is important to note that the claimant in *Camfield* received no benefit from the loan transaction. If she had received a benefit, the right to rescission would have been conditional upon her making counter-restitution.

Dunbar Bank plc v Nadeem [1998] 3 All ER 876

Facts: The defendant and her husband signed a joint loan facility with the claimant for the purchase of a new leasehold of the matrimonial property. At the time, the defendant's husband had been the sole lessee of the property. The loan was secured by a charge against the home. When the defendant's husband fell into arrears on the payments, the claimant brought an action for possession of the property. At first instance, the judge ordered rescission of the agreement for presumed undue influence on condition that the defendant repay the claimant half the sum advanced to purchase the property. The defendant appealed this decision and the claimant cross-appealed against the order to set aside the charge for presumed undue influence.

Held: The defendant's appeal was dismissed and the claimant's cross-appeal was allowed granting an order for possession. The Court of Appeal held that the transaction should not be set aside at all, because it was not manifestly disadvantageous to the defendant, and her husband had not taken any unfair advantage of her. If there had been undue influence, the Court of Appeal suggested (*obiter*) that the defendant could have made counter-restitution by giving up her interest in the property (which would have reverted to her husband).

Millett LJ:

'In the present case it is inescapable that there must have been two agreements . . . By the first agreement Mrs Nadeem obtained a half interest in the equity of redemption subject to the bank's legal charge, and by the second she obtained jointly with her husband an advance of £260,000 on the terms that £210,000 would be used to buy the property which she and her husband should jointly charge in favour of the bank to secure repayment of the advance. By the second agreement she did not obtain a free-standing loan, whether of £210,000 or £105,000, which she was free to use as she thought fit. There was no possibility of her applying the advance except for the purpose of acquiring the property so that she could join in giving security to the bank for the money advanced with which to acquire it.

Accordingly, in my judgment, the extent of Mrs Nadeem's enrichment, should the legal charge be set aside, is not the money which was advanced to her and her husband jointly, but the interest in the equity of redemption which she obtained by the use of the bank's money. That is the extent of her enrichment. And it is that, in my opinion, of which she must make counter restitution.

In my judgment, however, there was no need to impose conditions on the setting aside of the legal charge in order to achieve counter restitution. On the unusual facts of the present case it would have been automatic. Mrs Nadeem cannot retain her beneficial interest in the property in priority to the bank's charge and at the same time reject the liability to repay the advance by which the property was obtained. Once the legal charge is set aside, the source of her beneficial interest in the property must be her husband. He had nothing to give her except an interest in the equity of redemption. She had no need to make counter restitution because, having set aside the legal charge, she cannot assert a beneficial interest in the property in priority to the bank's legal charge to secure repayment of the money with which the property was acquired.

In my judgment, therefore, the only effect of setting aside the legal charge would be to eliminate any personal liability on the part of Mrs Nadeem.'

Rescission on terms may also be ordered where the value of the property transferred under the transaction has changed.

Cheese v Thomas [1994] 1 WLR 129

Facts: The plaintiff entered into an agreement with the defendant, his great-nephew, to purchase a house for £83,000, the plaintiff contributing £43,000, and the defendant providing £40,000 by means of a building society loan. The agreement was for the plaintiff to occupy the house for the rest of his life and, thereafter, for the house to pass unencumbered to the defendant. After he had moved into the house the plaintiff became worried that the defendant was failing to pay the mortgage instalments. He brought an action seeking to set aside the transaction for undue influence and claimed repayment of the £43,000 with interest. At first instance, the judge set aside the transaction and ordered the sale of the house. Because the housing market had slumped, the property eventually sold for £55,400. The judge ordered that the plaintiff and defendant should bear the loss on the sale of the house in the same proportions as they had contributed to the purchase price. The plaintiff appealed against this decision.

Held: The Court of Appeal dismissed the appeal holding that the court was concerned to achieve practical justice between the parties. Since the personal conduct of the defendant was not open to criticism, it was appropriate for the loss on the value of the house to be shared.

Sir Donald Nicholls VC:
'I approach the matter in this way. Restitution has to be made, not damages paid. Damages look at the plaintiff's loss, whereas restitution is concerned with the recovery back from the defendant of what he received under the transaction. If the transaction is set aside, the plaintiff also must return what he received. Each party must hand back what he obtained under the contract. There has to be a giving back and a taking back on both sides . . . It is well established that a court of equity grants this type of relief even when it cannot restore the parties precisely to the state they were in before the contract. The court will grant relief whenever, by directing accounts and making allowances, it can do what is practically just: see *Erlanger v New Sombrero Phosphate Co* (1878) 3 App Cas 1218, 1278–1279, *per* Lord Blackburn. Here justice requires that each party should be returned as near to his original position as is now possible. Each should get back a proportionate share of the net proceeds of the house, before deducting the amount paid to the building society. Thus the £55,400 should be divided between Mr Cheese and Mr Thomas in the proportions of 43:40. Mr. Cheese should receive about £28,700 and Mr. Thomas £26,700.'

A number of factors meant that it was appropriate to order rescission on terms. First, the transaction was in the nature of a joint venture. Both parties had contributed to the purchase price and both parties acquired rights under the transaction. Second, the Court of Appeal emphasised that there was no hint of wrongdoing in the case. The defendant was an 'innocent fiduciary', who had been anxious to provide his great uncle with a home. In the circumstances it would have been unduly harsh to require the defendant to bear the full loss flowing from the slump in the property market. It should be emphasised that *Cheese v Thomas* is not an example of loss apportionment. The case involved a restitutionary claim for benefits transferred under a rescinded contract. The apportionment concerned the valuation of those benefits, not the assessment of loss.

12.5.2 ACCOUNT OF PROFITS

The remedy of account of profits is also available for undue influence, although it may be subject to a reasonable allowance for the work and skill of the person exercising the influence.

O'Sullivan v Management Agency & Music Ltd [1985] QB 428

Facts: The plaintiff, a young singer, entered into a management agreement with the defendant, a highly experienced, internationally recognised manager and producer of popular music. It was subsequently held that the agreements had been obtained by undue influence. However, by the time the case came to court all the agreements had been performed and counter-restitution was impossible.

Held: The Court of Appeal rejected the argument that the agreements could not be set aside because counter-restitution was impossible. Instead the court held that the agreements should be rescinded and ordered the defendants to account for their profits.

Fox LJ:
'It is said on behalf of the plaintiffs that, if the principle of equity is that the fiduciary must account for profits obtained through the abuse of the fiduciary relationship there is no scope for the operation of anything resembling *restitutio in integrum*. The profits must simply be given up. I think that goes too far and that the law has for long had regard to the justice of the matter. If, for example, a person is by undue influence persuaded to make a gift of a house to another and that other spent money on improving the house, I apprehend that credit could be given for the improvements . . .

Accordingly, it seems to me that the principle that the court will do what is practically just as between the parties is applicable to a case of undue influence even though the parties cannot be restored to their original position. That is, in my view, applicable to the present case. The question is not whether the parties can be restored to their original position; it is what does the justice of the case require? . . .

> The next question is, it seems to me, the recompensing of the defendants . . . Once it is accepted that the court can make an appropriate allowance to a fiduciary for his skill and labour I do not see why, in principle, it should not be able to give him some part of the profit of the venture if it was thought that justice as between the parties demanded that . . . I am not satisfied that it would be proper to exclude Mr Mills and the MAM companies from all reward for their efforts. I find it impossible to believe that they did not make a significant contribution to Mr O'Sullivan's success. It would be unjust to deny them a recompense for that. I would, therefore, be prepared as was done in *Phipps v Boardman* to authorise the payment (over and above out of pocket expenses) of an allowance for the skill and labour of the first five defendants in promoting the compositions and performances and managing the business affairs of Mr. O'Sullivan . . . Such an allowance could include a profit element in the way that solicitors' costs do.'

The Court of Appeal emphasised its jurisdiction to make such orders as were 'practically just' between the parties. On the facts, it was practically just to allow the defendant to retain some remuneration for his services, but at a rate substantially less than that provided for in the contract.

12.6 UNCONSCIONABILITY AND INEQUALITY OF BARGAINING POWER

It has been suggested that the approach of the courts to the issues of duress and undue influence simply reflect a general reluctance to enforce transactions that are so unfair as to be regarded as 'unconscionable'. This argument was famously made by Lord Denning in *Lloyd's Bank Ltd v Bundy* [1975] QB 326.

Lloyd's Bank Ltd v Bundy [1975] QB 326

'*The general rule*
Now let me say at once that in the vast majority of cases a customer who signs a bank guarantee or a charge cannot get out of it. No bargain will be upset which is the result of the ordinary interplay of forces. There are many hard cases which are caught by this rule. Take the case of a poor man who is homeless. He agrees to pay a high rent to a landlord just to get a roof over his head. The common law will not interfere. It is left to Parliament. Next take the case of a borrower in urgent need of money. He borrows it from the bank at high interest and it is guaranteed by a friend. The guarantor gives his bond and gets nothing in return. The common law will not interfere. Parliament

has intervened to prevent moneylenders charging excessive interest. But it has never interfered with banks.

Yet there are exceptions to this general rule. There are cases in our books in which the courts will set aside a contract, or a transfer of property, when the parties have not met on equal terms – when the one is so strong in bargaining power and the other so weak – that, as a matter of common fairness, it is not right that the strong should be allowed to push the weak to the wall. Hitherto those exceptional cases have been treated each as a separate category in itself. But I think the time has come when we should seek to find a principle to unite them. I put on one side contracts or transactions which are voidable for fraud or misrepresentation or mistake. All those are governed by settled principles. I go only to those where there has been inequality of bargaining power, such as to merit the intervention of the court.

The categories

The first category is that of "duress of goods". A typical case is when a man is in a strong bargaining position by being in possession of the goods of another by virtue of a legal right, such as by way of pawn or pledge or taken in distress. The owner is in a weak position because he is in urgent need of the goods. The stronger demands of the weaker more than is justly due: and he pays it in order to get the goods. Such a transaction is voidable. He can recover the excess: see *Astley v Reynolds* (1731) 2 Stra 915 and *Green v Duckett* (1883) 11 QBD 275. To which may be added the cases of "*colore officii*", where a man is in a strong bargaining position by virtue of his official position or public profession. He relies upon it so as to gain from the weaker – who is urgently in need – more than is justly due: see *Pigott's* case cited by Lord Kenyon CJ in *Cartwright v Rowley* (1799) 2 Esp 723, 723–724; *Parker v Bristol and Exeter Railway Co* (1851) 6 Exch 702 and *Steele v Williams* (1853) 8 Exch 625. In such cases the stronger may make his claim in good faith honestly believing that he is entitled to make his demand. He may not be guilty of any fraud or misrepresentation. The inequality of bargaining power – the strength of the one versus the urgent need of the other – renders the transaction voidable and the money paid to be recovered back: see *Maskell v Horner* [1915] 3 KB 106.

The second category is that of the "unconscionable transaction". A man is so placed as to be in need of special care and protection and yet his weakness is exploited by another far stronger than himself so as to get his property at a gross undervalue. The typical case is that of the "expectant heir". But it applies to all cases where a man comes into property, or is expected to come into it – and then being in urgent need – another gives him ready cash for it, greatly below its true worth, and so gets the property transferred to him: see *Evans v Llewellin* (1787) 1 Cox 333. Even though there be no evidence of fraud or misrepresentation, nevertheless the transaction will be set aside ... This second category is said to extend to all cases where an unfair advantage has been gained by an unconscientious use of power by a stronger party against a weaker: see the cases cited in *Halsbury's Laws of England,* 3rd edn, vol 17

(1956), p 682 and, in Canada, *Morrison v Coast Finance Ltd* (1965) 55 DLR (2d) 710 and *Knupp v Bell* (1968) 67 DLR (2d) 256.

The third category is that of "undue influence" usually so called. These are divided into two classes as stated by Cotton LJ in *Allcard v Skinner* (1887) 36 ChD 145, 171. The first are those where the stronger has been guilty of some fraud or wrongful act – expressly so as to gain some gift or advantage from the weaker. The second are those where the stronger has not been guilty of any wrongful act, but has, through the relationship which existed between him and the weaker, gained some gift or advantage for himself. Sometimes the relationship is such as to raise a presumption of undue influence, such as parent over child, solicitor over client, doctor over patient, spiritual adviser over follower. At other times a relationship of confidence must be proved to exist . . .

The fourth category is that of "undue pressure". The most apposite of that is *Williams v Bayley* (1866) LR 1 HL 200, where a son forged his father's name to a promissory note and, by means of it, raised money from the bank of which they were both customers. The bank said to the father, in effect: "Take your choice – give us security for your son's debt. If you do take that on yourself, then it will all go smoothly: if you do not, we shall be bound to exercise pressure". Thereupon the father charged his property to the bank with payment of the note. The House of Lords held that the charge was invalid because of undue pressure exerted by the bank . . .

Other instances of undue pressure are where one party stipulates for an unfair advantage to which the other has no option but to submit. As where an employer – the stronger party – has employed a builder – the weaker party – to do work for him. When the builder asked for payment of sums properly due (so as to pay his workmen) the employer refused to pay unless he was given some added advantage. Stuart V-C said: "Where an agreement, hard and inequitable in itself, has been exacted under circumstances of pressure on the part of the person who exacts it, this court will set it aside": see *Ormes v Beadel* (1860) 2 Giff 166, 174 (reversed on another ground, 2 De GF & J 333) and *D & C Builders v Rees* [1966] 2 QB 617, 625.

The fifth category is that of salvage agreements. When a vessel is in danger of sinking and seeks help, the rescuer is in a strong bargaining position. The vessel in distress is in urgent need. The parties cannot be truly said to be on equal terms. The Court of Admiralty have always recognised that fact. The "fundamental rule" is "if the parties have made an agreement, the court will enforce it, unless it be manifestly unfair and unjust; but if it be manifestly unfair and unjust, the court will disregard it and decree what is fair and just". See *Akerblom v Price* (1881) 7 QBD 129, 133, *per* Brett LJ, applied in a striking case *The Port Caledonia and The Anna* [1903] P 184, when the rescuer refused to help with a rope unless he was paid £1,000.

The general principles

Gathering all together, I would suggest that through all these instances there runs a single thread. They rest on "inequality of bargaining power". By virtue of it, the English law gives relief to one who, without independent advice, enters into a contract upon terms which are very unfair or transfers property for a consideration which is grossly inadequate, when his bargaining power is grievously impaired by reason of his own needs or desires, or by his own ignorance or infirmity, coupled with undue influences or pressures brought to bear on him by or for the benefit of the other. When I use the word "undue" I do not mean to suggest that the principle depends on proof of any wrongdoing. The one who stipulates for an unfair advantage may be moved solely by his own self-interest, unconscious of the distress he is bringing to the other. I have also avoided any reference to the will of the one being "dominated" or "overcome" by the other. One who is in extreme need may knowingly consent to a most improvident bargain, solely to relieve the straits in which he finds himself. Again, I do not mean to suggest that every transaction is saved by independent advice. But the absence of it may be fatal. With these explanations, I hope this principle will be found to reconcile the cases.'

Although the label 'inequality of bargaining power' suggests procedural unfairness, it is clear that Lord Denning's principle requires both procedural and substantive unfairness. There must be both a consideration that is grossly inadequate (substantive unfairness) and a bargaining power that has been grievously impaired (procedural unfairness). Lord Denning's principle has met with academic support, an example of which is provided below.

Waddams, S, 'Unconscionability in contracts' (1976) 39 MLR 369, 390–393

TOWARDS A GENERAL PRINCIPLE

The common law traditionally develops by the use of fictions. Lip service continues to be paid to an old rule, but as decisions multiply exceptions to it, it becomes an empty shell and at last can be discarded without effecting any great change in the actual practice of the courts. My argument is that this stage has now been reached in respect to a rule of unconscionability. I have attempted to show that, despite lip service to the notion of absolute freedom of contract, relief is every day given against agreements that are unfair, inequitable, unreasonable or oppressive. Unconscionability, as a word to describe such control, might not be the lexicographer's first choice, but I think it is the most acceptable general word. It has historical antecedents; it occurs consistently throughout the cases in the various branches of the law discussed; it has been accepted as a general ground of relief in modern Canadian cases, and it is recognised by statute both in Commonwealth and American jurisdictions.

An argument frequently raised against recognition of a general power of relief is that it would contribute to uncertainty. I would say that certainty, though an important value in contract law, is not an absolute one, and the cases discussed in this article show that other values cannot be suppressed. Moreover, if my argument is accepted, that is that agreements are in practice set aside quite frequently and generally, it must conduce to certainty rather than uncertainty to recognise the general principle. At present we have the worst of both worlds – what for example could be less certain than the law on exemption clauses? The effect of suppressing the true principle underlying a line of cases is to produce a rule that not only fails to relieve when relief is justified but that strikes down agreements that are perfectly fair and reasonable. Only with open recognition of the true principle can the courts begin to develop rational criteria and guidelines that will satisfactorily explain their decisions and offer a useful guide for the future. I do not underestimate the difficulty of developing such guidelines, but I do maintain that to make a start on that task would be an advance in certainty as well as in justice.

Another compelling reason for adopting a general principle of unconscionability is the need to fill the gaps between the existing islands of intervention. The clause that is not quite a penalty clause or not quite an exemption clause or just outside the provisions of the Moneylenders' Act or the Misrepresentation Act 1967 will fall under the general power to relieve and anomalous distinctions like those castigated by Lord Denning in *Bridge v Campbell Discount* will disappear.

FUTURE DEVELOPMENT

Given the open recognition of a general principle of unconscionability one would expect the courts to develop guidelines. There is every reason to think that they would be fully equal to this task. . . . Clearly inequality of values exchanged cannot in itself be enough or the courts would "throw every thing into confusion and set afloat all the contracts of mankind." But a large inequality of exchange combined with inequality of bargaining power, the twin criteria adopted by the modem Canadian cases, goes a long way to suggest a case for relief. It is not said to be conclusive, but to cast an onus on the party seeking to uphold the transaction, an onus that might possibly be discharged on a showing that the disadvantaged party was independently advised, or that he knew of the comparative values and intended a part gift. On the other hand, not every case lends itself to analysis in terms of equality of exchange and in some cases there may be grounds for relief even when the values exchanged are approximately equal. The Supply of Goods (Implied Terms) Act 1973 offers a list of criteria to guide the courts in determining what exemption clauses are fair and reasonable. The list is not exhaustive, and, no doubt, further criteria will be judicially developed. I would readily recognise that the adoption of a principle of unconscionability is a mere beginning, but I would maintain that it is a useful beginning.

There will be a need for development of bars to relief. Execution in itself should not be a bar, but execution followed by a long delay, affirmation, and intervention of third party rights might well be held to place limits on relief. The court need not choose between an all or nothing solution, but could use the power to grant relief on conditions, as the mortgage cases grant relief to the mortgagor on payment of the mortgagee's costs. A condition of relief might appropriately be the payment of the other party's reasonable expenses incurred in reliance on the agreement, thus protecting the latter's reliance interest, but not his contractual expectation.

> Contract law has been passing through a period of exceptional rigidity, but there are signs that it is capable of recovering its former flexibility, as, I think, it must if it is to meet the present needs of society.

In the above extract, Professor Waddams claims that a general doctrine of unconscionability could provide the key to understanding the pre-existing law of duress, undue influence, exemption clauses and penalty clauses. Furthermore, such a doctrine could provide the crucial basis for developing a set of criteria to determine the scope of judicial intervention in the future. Calls for such a principle have not met with judicial support, however. In *National Westminster Bank v Morgan* [1985] AC 686, Lord Scarman expressly disapproved of Lord Denning's 'inequality of bargaining power' doctrine:

'The question which the House does have to answer is: did the court in *Lloyds Bank v Bundy* accurately state the law?

Lord Denning MR believed that the doctrine of undue influence could be subsumed under a general principle that English courts will grant relief where there has been "inequality of bargaining power" (p 339). He deliberately avoided reference to the will of one party being dominated or overcome by another. The majority of the court did not follow him; they based their decision on the orthodox view of the doctrine as expounded in *Allcard v Skinner*, 36 Ch D 145. The opinion of the Master of the Rolls, therefore, was not the ground of the court's decision, which was to be found in the view of the majority, for whom Sir Eric Sachs delivered the leading judgment.

Nor has counsel for the respondent sought to rely on Lord Denning MR's general principle: and, in my view, he was right not to do so. The doctrine of undue influence has been sufficiently developed not to need the support of a principle which by its formulation in the language of the law of contract is not appropriate to cover transactions of gift where there is no bargain. The fact of an unequal bargain will, of course, be a relevant feature in some cases of undue influence. But it can never become an appropriate basis of principle of an equitable doctrine which is concerned with transactions "not to be reasonably accounted for on the ground of friendship, relationship, charity, or other ordinary motives on which ordinary men act" (Lindley LJ in *Allcard v Skinner*, at p 185), and even in the field of contract I question whether there is any need in the modern law to erect a general principle of relief against inequality of bargaining power. Parliament has undertaken the task – and it is essentially a legislative task – of enacting such restrictions upon freedom of contract as are in its judgment necessary to relieve against the mischief: for example, the hire-purchase and consumer protection legislation, of which the Supply of

Goods (Implied Terms) Act 1973, Consumer Credit Act 1974, Consumer Safety Act 1978, Supply of Goods and Services Act 1982 and Insurance Companies Act 1982 are examples. I doubt whether the courts should assume the burden of formulating further restrictions.'

Lord Scarman's criticisms of the 'inequality of bargaining power' doctrine are somewhat unfair. His Lordship focused on the label given to the doctrine rather than on its substantive content. This meant that he failed to consider whether it would be beneficial for the common law to have a ground for intervening in contracts that are substantively unfair. Had his Lordship considered this question, he may have been more reluctant to dismiss the doctrine out of hand. Lord Scarman also opined that the doctrine was unnecessary because Parliament had already intervened in this area to place legislative restrictions on freedom of contract. This is true, but, as Professor Waddams has noted, there are gaps in the legislative framework. Lord Scarman assumed that the courts should not fill these gaps because Parliament had already intervened. However, his Lordship could just as easily have concluded that Parliament's intervention evidenced a commitment to fairness, which should be reflected in the development of new gap-filling principles by the courts.

Other jurisdictions have shown a greater willingness to adopt a general doctrine of unconscionability, for example, Australia (*Commercial Bank of Australia Ltd v Amadio* (1983) 151 CLR 447; *Bridgewater v Leahy* (1998) 194 CLR 457), Canada (*Morrison v Coast Finance Ltd* (1965) 55 DLR (2d); *Harry v Kreutziger* (1978) 95 DLR (3d) 231), New Zealand (*Nicholas v Jessup (No 2)* [1986] NZLR 237; *Bowkett v Action Finance Ltd* [1992] 1 NZLR 449), the United States (s 2–302 of the United States Universal Commercial Code).

Typically it has been assumed that a doctrine of unconscionability would be economically inefficient since it inhibits freedom of contract. However, Eric Posner, a leading law and economics scholar has forcefully made the contrary argument.

Posner, E, 'Contract law in the welfare state: a defence of the unconscionability doctrine, usury laws, and related limitations on the freedom to contract' (1995) 24 J Legal Stud 283, 285–287

THE MINIMUM WELFARE THEORY

I assume that the state has two commitments. First, it is committed to maintaining a free market and accordingly enforces property rights and contracts. Second, the state is committed to reducing poverty, or, more formally, to preventing all citizens from falling below a minimum welfare level. The minimum welfare level is a standard of living, not simply a net worth, and comprises the consumption of shelter, food, medical care, and other 'basic necessities'. The state maintains the minimum welfare level by transferring cash and other benefits to anyone who falls beneath it.

The simultaneous commitment to enforcement of contracts and to maintenance of a minimum welfare level raises two basic problems of concern to us here. First, it raises the problem of 'welfare opportunism'. Because loss of income or other assets entitles an individual to payment from the state, the magnitude of the loss suffered by an investor as a result of an investment failure is smaller in a welfare regime than it would be in the case of an identical investment outside of a welfare regime. The riskier the investment, the greater is the expected value of the welfare benefits and the greater is the contribution of welfare to the present value of the investment. As a result, inside a welfare regime actors make riskier investments and more often suffer failure than they would outside a welfare regime. This distortion of behaviour in the direction of risk taking, in particular, credit risk, drives up the cost of welfare.

Second, the simultaneous commitment to a free market and to poverty reduction raises the problem of 'welfare circumvention'. Some people are willing to endure a lifestyle the state considers below the minimum welfare level because they have idiosyncratic preferences – they have different views as to what count as the 'basic necessities'. Others are willing to *risk* enduring a lifestyle below the minimum welfare level for the sake of an attractive, and chancy, investment. Because we assume a free market, people in both groups would be able to exchange their right to receive welfare benefits for cash, and the cash for the idiosyncratic goods and risky investments. Although the welfare state restricts the alienation of welfare benefits – in effect, by making them illiquid, discouraging their use for idiosyncratic purposes – a person on welfare or with a low income can, in a free market, reliquidate his benefits. By borrowing against income and assets, he can use the loans to make idiosyncratic purchases of goods that are inconsistent with the minimum welfare level and to make investments that place his at risk of falling below that level.

The welfare opportunism and welfare circumvention problems are closely related. Both arise from the commitment to poverty reduction and the provision of welfare, and both result in, among other distortions, excessive risky borrowing. However, welfare opportunism is foremost a threat to the state's fisc: it increases the number of people to whom the state must pay benefits. In contrast, welfare circumvention is foremost a threat to the commitment to a minimum welfare level: it increases the number of people who fall below the minimum welfare level. Together the problems endanger any program of reducing poverty at reasonable cost.

My argument is that a partial violation of the commitment to the free market is the appropriate response to these problems. Because welfare opportunism and welfare circumvention take the form of high-risk credit activity, the state should enact laws that restrict such activity. Restrictive contract doctrines, such as usury laws, perform this function. By allowing debtors to escape from high-interest credit contracts, they force creditors to withdraw such contracts from the market, denying the debtors the opportunity to obtain high-risk credit in the first place.

So far, English law has shied away from any general doctrine of unconscionability. Instead, the courts have focused on specific rules that govern procedural impropriety such as duress and undue influence. This is likely to remain the position of English law unless the influence of European law forces a change. It is with this in mind that we turn to consider the proposals for reform contained in the Principles of European Contract law.

12.7 UNDUE INFLUENCE UNDER THE PRINCIPLES OF EUROPEAN CONTRACT LAW

The approach to undue influence and unconscionability in the Principles of European Contract Law is found in Chapter 4 of the draft. It states the following:

Article 4.109 – Excessive benefit or unfair advantage

(1) A party may avoid a contract if, at the time of the conclusion of the contract:

    (a) it was dependent on or had a relationship of trust with the other party, was in economic distress or had urgent needs, was improvident, ignorant, inexperienced or lacking in bargaining skill, and

    (b) the other party knew or ought to have known of this and, given the circumstances and purpose of the contract, took advantage of the first party's situation in a way which was grossly unfair or took an excessive benefit.

(2) Upon the request of the party entitled to avoidance, a court may if it is appropriate adapt the contract in order to bring it into accordance with what might have been agreed had the requirements of good faith and fair dealing been followed.

(3) A court may similarly adapt the contract upon the request of a party receiving notice of avoidance for excessive benefit or unfair advantage, provided that this party informs the party who gave the notice promptly after receiving it and before that party has acted in reliance on it.

Paragraph 1 of the Article states that a contract may be set aside if two conditions are met:

(a) The first condition concerns the relationship between the parties. Most of these relationships are covered by the English law of undue influence or the rule in *Fry v Lane* (1888) 40 Ch D 312 (concerning sales at an undervalue to a 'poor and ignorant man'). By including 'economic distress' and 'urgent needs', however, the principles go further than English law. Lando and Beale (*Principles of European Contract Law Parts I and II*, 2000, p 262, The Hague: Kluwer Law International) give the following example of urgent need:

'*Illustration 3*: U and her family are on holiday are on holiday abroad when they are involved in a car crash and U's husband is badly hurt. He urgently needs medical treatment which is not locally available. V agrees to take the man by ambulance to the nearest major hospital, charging approximately five times the normal amount for such a journey. U is so worried that she agrees without getting other quotations; she does not discover until later that she has been overcharged. She may obtain relief.'

(b) The second condition relates to the knowledge and actions of the party alleged to have taken an unfair advantage. It is defendant-focused and looks to 'wrong-doing'. It must be shown that the party knew, or ought to have known, of the circumstances leading to the other party falling under the first condition, and that he took advantage of that situation in a way which was grossly unfair or took an excessive benefit. The following illustrations are given by Lando and Beale (*Principles of European Contract Law Parts I and II*, 2000, pp 262–263, The Hague: Kluwer Law International):

'Illustration 2: X, an uneducated person with no business experience, is left some property. He is contacted by Y who offers to buy it for a sum much less than it is actually worth, telling X that he must sell it quickly or he will lose the chance. X agrees without consulting anyone else. X may avoid the contract.

Illustration 5: X, a widow, lives with her many children in a large but dilapidated house which Y, a neighbour, has long wanted to buy. X has come to rely on Y's advice in business matters. Y is well aware of this and manipulates it to his advantage: he persuades her to sell it to him. He offers her the market price but without pointing out to her that she will find it impossible to live in the neighbourhood for that amount of money. X may avoid the contract.'

The approach taken in the Principles to these two conditions is broadly similar to that taken by English law. The provisions certainly do not amount to a general principle of unconscionability.

A much more expansive and flexible approach is taken in relation to remedies, however. Paragraph 2 enables the court, upon the request of the claimant, to modify the contract in accordance with the requirements of good faith and fair dealing, as an alternative to rescission. Paragraph 3 gives the court a similar power to modify the contract at the request of the defendant, provided that the claimant has not already acted on the notice of avoidance. Lando and Beale note that the court 'should adapt the contract only if this is an appropriate remedy in the circumstances'. They suggest that adaptation would not be appropriate in a case like illustration 5 above.

In addition, as with duress, Article 4:117 provides that damages can be recovered either in addition to or in lieu of rescission. These damages will be measured on the reliance basis and are limited to the amount by which the claimant is worse off compared to his position prior to the formation of the contract.

▌12.8 ADDITIONAL READING

Atiyah, PS, 'Contract and fair exchange', in Atiyah, P, *Essays on Contract*, 1986, Oxford: Clarendon.

Bamforth, N, 'Unconscionability as a vitiating factor' [1995] LMCLQ 538.

Capper, D, 'Undue influence and unconscionability: a rationalisation' (1998) 114 LQR 479.

Enman, SR, 'Doctrines of unconscionability in Canadian, English and Commonwealth contract law' (1987) 16 Anglo-Am LR 191.

O'Sullivan, D, 'Developing *O'Brien*' (2002) 118 LQR 337.

Pawlowski, M and Brown, J, *Undue Influence and the Family Home*, 2002, London: Cavendish.

Smith, SA, 'In defence of substantive unfairness' (1996) 112 LQR 138.

Thompson, MP, 'Wives, sureties and banks' [2002] Conv 174.

Wong, S, 'Revisiting *Barclays Bank v O'Brien* and independent legal advice for vulnerable sureties' [2002] JBL 439.

CHAPTER 13

ILLEGALITY

CONTENTS

▌13.1 INTRODUCTION

In English law an agreement may possess all the requisite elements of a binding contract and yet be deemed to be unenforceable due to the contravention of a legal rule or a principle of public policy. These rules or policies may be derived from statute or from the principles of the common law. In some cases the contract will be illegal in its formation, such as a contract to commit a crime. In others, the illegality will arise in the performance of an otherwise valid contract, such as a contract for the carriage of goods where the vehicle that is used to transport the goods exceeds the speed limit on the journey. It is only when the vehicle exceeds the speed limit that any issue of illegality will arise.

In this chapter we will be examining the concept of illegality in general. We will consider the underlying basis of the doctrine of illegality, the categories of illegality and the effects of illegality on the enforcement of the relevant contract. In Chapter 14, we will turn to consider a specific type of illegal contract, namely, contracts in restraint of trade.

13.2 POLICY ARGUMENTS

The courts rarely explain the reasons why the courts intervene to render 'illegal' contracts unenforceable. In an oft-quoted speech from *Holman v Johnson* (1775) 1 Cowp 341, Lord Mansfield said the following:

'No court will lend its aid to a man who founds his cause of action upon an immoral or illegal act. If from the plaintiff's own stating or otherwise, the cause of action appears to arise *ex turpi causa* (i.e. out of an evil cause), or the transgression of a positive law of this country, there the courts says he has no right to be assisted.'

The courts intervene because it would be contrary to public policy for a court to assist a party that is seeking to rely on illegality. The court has an interest in protecting its own integrity, and for this reason the judge himself can introduce the issue of illegality, even if it has not been pleaded by the parties (*Northwestern Salt v Electrolytic Alkali Co* [1914] AC 461). A number of commentators have attempted to explore the policies underlying this area of the law.

> ### Atiyah, *An Introduction to the Law of Contract*, 1995, 5th edn, pp 342–344, Oxford: Clarendon
>
> The policy considerations involved here appear to include at least the following factors, though not all will be involved in every case. First, there is the desirability of deterring parties from criminal or anti-social conduct, and the associated (though different) object of punishing them if they commit such conduct. Normally it is the criminal law that performs these functions, but there may be forms of anti-social conduct which are not criminal, and yet which it may be desirable to deter (eg prostitution), and there may also be advantages in using contract law as an additional deterrent over and above that provided by the criminal law . . .
>
> A second policy consideration which is undoubtedly involved in some cases is the undesirability of jeopardizing the dignity of the courts. Respect for the law and Courts of Justice is an important aspect of judicial policy, and this respect could be gravely impaired if courts were required to adjudicate on certain types of illegal transaction . . .
>
> A third possible policy consideration may in some cases be the desirability of bringing an illegal or undesirable state of affairs to an end. If, for instance, a woman takes a lease of a flat and then uses it for prostitution, it may be desirable that the landlord should be able to evict her by legal process, in order to terminate this state of affairs.
>
> It will be seen that some of these factors may well conflict in any given case. For example, if a landlord knowingly lets premises to a prostitute and then seeks to evict her for non-payment of rent, the first and third policy considerations would conflict . . . But apart from conflicts of this nature in the relevant policy considerations, there is

often likely to be conflict between the considerations suggesting that illegal contracts should not be enforced, and the general desirability of upholding contracts . . . [T]here is an acute conflict between the desire to do justice between the individual parties and the more general considerations . . . concerning the undesirability of enforcing illegal contracts. In this situation the traditional result has been to ignore the injustice which may be done in the individual case in the belief that this is outweighed by the public interest in refusing redress in such cases. But in recent years there has been a perceptible trend in the reverse direction . . .

Enonchong, N, *Illegal Transactions*, 1998, pp 15–17, London: LLP

The overall object of the defence of illegality and the forfeiture rule is the protection of the public through deterrence from crime and other illegal conduct. Thus in *Amicable Insurance Society v Bolland* assignees of a forger failed to recover the proceeds of a life insurance policy on the death of the forger at the hands of justice by reason of his forgery. The Lord Chancellor said that if such a contract were enforceable it would 'take away one of those restraints operating on the minds of men against the commission of crimes' . . . If indeed the policy behind the principle is deterrence then it may be argued that for the deterrent effect to have force there must be a clear rule which is applied strictly by the courts and is known, at least by lawyers who advise members of the public.

Some have expressed doubts about the deterrent effect of the illegality defence and the forfeiture rule. In *Tinsley v Milligan*, for example, Lord Lowry made it clear that he was 'not impressed' by the argument that a defence of illegality which precludes a transferor from recovering property transferred for an illegal purpose acts as a deterrent to persons in the transferor's position. One reason advanced for this view is that such persons may not be aware of the rule and are unlikely to consult a reputable solicitor. Other judges have advanced essentially the same argument. But the argument is surprising. And it is the more startling when it is put forward in a case, such as *Tribe v Tribe*, where the parties' scheme to break the law had been carefully contrived after obtaining professional advice from accountants and lawyers . . .

In any event, if deterrence is not the policy objective of the broad principles there is another policy on which they have been put. This has been identified as a policy which seeks to protect the integrity of the judicial system from the disrepute which would attach to it if the courts were seen to be encouraging conduct which they ought to denounce . . . [I]t has been argued [that] it would reflect adversely on the judicial system if the public were to perceive a fundamental inconsistency in the law, as would be the case if a civil remedy were provided to a plaintiff on the basis of his conduct which is criminal.

As Professor Atiyah and Professor Enonchong note there are two main reasons for refusing to enforce illegal contracts:

1. deterrence of wrongdoing;
2. protection of the integrity of the civil justice system.

At times the policy against enforcing illegal contracts comes into conflict with the desirability of preventing the defendant from being unjustly enriched at the claimant's expense. If restitution of benefits conferred under an illegal contract is not allowed, the defendant may be left with a substantial and undeserved windfall gain. The problems associated with a strict application of the policy against illegal contracts were recognised by Bingham LJ in *Saunders v Edwards* [1987] 2 All ER 651:

'Where issues of illegality are raised, the courts have to steer a middle course between two unacceptable positions. On the one hand it is unacceptable that any court of law should aid or lend its authority to a party seeking to pursue or enforce an object or agreement which the law prohibits. On the other hand, it is unacceptable that the court should, on the first indication of unlawfulness affecting any aspect of a transaction, draw up its skirts and refuse all assistance to the plaintiff, no matter how serious his loss or how disproportionate his loss to the unlawfulness of his conduct.'

The balance to be struck between these two competing policies will be considered in greater detail when we examine the effect of illegality later in this chapter.

13.3 CATEGORIES OF ILLEGALITY

Categorising illegal contracts is a notoriously difficulty task and there is no perfect classification. For the sake of simplicity we will consider illegal contracts under two main headings: statutory illegality and common-law illegality.

13.3.1 STATUTORY ILLEGALITY

Statute may declare a contract to be illegal, either in its formation or in its performance. The contract may be declared to be void, unenforceable, or illegal.

13.3.1.1 Contracts illegal in their formation

Section 18 of the Gaming Act 1845 provides the following:

All contracts or agreements, whether by parole or in writing, by way of gaming or wagering, shall be null and void; and no suit shall be brought or maintained in any court of law and equity for recovering any sum of money or valuable thing alleged to be won upon any wager, or which shall have been deposited in the hands of any person to abide the event on which any wager shall have been made: Provided always, that this enactment shall not be deemed to apply to any subscription or contribution, or agreement to subscribe or contribute, for or towards any plate, prize, or sum of money to be awarded to the winner or winners of any lawful game, sport, pastime, or exercise.

The Act makes gaming and wagering contracts void and unenforceable. It does not make them illegal. This means that people are still free to enter into gambling agreements; they simply cannot enforce them in the courts. Section 334 of the Gambling Act 2005 repeals s 18 of the Gaming Act 1845. This will come into effect on a date to be set by the Secretary of State (s 358(1) of the Gambling Act 2005). Gambling contracts entered into after that date will be legally enforceable.

A statute may establish a licensing system that expressly prohibits contracts made in violation of the system.

Re Mahmoud and Ispahani [1921] 2 KB 716

Facts: At the time of the case, contracts for the sale of linseed oil were governed by the regulations contained in the Seeds, Oils and Fats Order, 1919. These provided that 'a person shall not either on his own behalf or on behalf of any other person buy or sell or otherwise deal in' linseed oil 'except under and in accordance with the terms of a licence issued by or under the authority of the Food Controller.' The plaintiff seller, who had a licence, asked the defendant whether he had a licence. The defendant replied that he did even though he did not. When the plaintiff attempted to deliver the oil the defendant refused to take delivery on the ground that the contract was illegal, as he did not possess a licence under the Order. The plaintiff brought a claim for damages for non-acceptance.

Held: The Court of Appeal held that, as the defendant had no licence, the contract of sale was prohibited and no claim could be made under the contract.

Atkin LJ:
'When the Court has to deal with the question whether a particular contract or class of contract is prohibited by statute, it may find an express prohibition in the statute, or it may have to infer the prohibition from the fact that the statute imposes a penalty upon the person entering into that class of contract. In the latter case one has to examine very carefully the precise terms of the statute imposing the penalty upon the individual. One may find that the statute imposes a penalty upon an individual, and yet does not prohibit the contract if it is made with a party who is innocent of the offence which is created by the statute. I prefer not to deal with the question of contracts forbidden by

the common law as being contrary to public policy, because, despite the great authority of Parke B. (*Cope v Rowlands*, 2 M & W 157), I think a question might be raised whether or not it is right to say that those contracts are prohibited by the common law. The right view may be that the common law refuses to enforce them. I think a different set of circumstances may arise in respect of such contracts as those, but here it appears to me to be plain that this particular contract was expressly prohibited by the terms of the Order which imposes the necessity of a compliance with the licence. With great respect to the learned judge, I think the underlying fallacy in his judgment is that he has not directed his attention to the terms of the licence or to the terms of the Order which says that no sale shall be made unless it complies with the terms of the licence. When one looks at the licence one finds an express prohibition against the plaintiff selling to the defendant as the latter had not a licence. I do not think it is necessary to pursue the matter any further so far as the statutory prohibition is concerned.'

It might be thought that this decision was somewhat harsh; the claimant was innocent after all and he had proceeded with the transaction in reliance on the defendant's misrepresentation that he possessed the necessary licence. Nevertheless, the Court of Appeal held that the policy underlying the regulation was to prevent the trade of linseed oil other than between those who held licences. The innocence of the seller was irrelevant in the pursuit of this policy.

It has recently been confirmed that a contract that is prohibited by subordinate legislation is also to be regarded as an illegal contract.

Mohamed v Alaga & Co (a firm) [2000] 1 WLR 1815

Facts: The plaintiff, a leading member of the Somali community in the UK, claimed that the defendant solicitor had agreed to pay him 50 per cent of the relevant legal aid fees in return for introducing Somali asylum seekers and assisting in the preparation and presentation of their claims. The defendant accepted that the plaintiff had been engaged to work as an interpreter and translator but denied the existence of the agreement as alleged. In any event, he claimed that a contract made in the terms alleged would be unenforceable due to it being contrary to rules 3 and 7 of the Solicitor's Practice Rules 1990, made under s 31 of the Solicitors Act 1974. Lightman J held that since the agreement was in breach of the Solicitors' Rules it was void and unenforceable even though the plaintiff was unaware of the Rules. The judge also refused to allow the plaintiff's claim for a *quantum meruit* in relation to the work he had done.

Held: The Court of Appeal held that the contract was void and unenforceable for illegality but upheld the plaintiff's claim for a *quantum meruit* on the ground that the parties were not equally to blame.

Lord Bingham CJ:

'The first issue on this appeal concerns the plaintiff's right under the contract which is assumed to have been made to recover 50 per cent of the legal aid fees received by the solicitors. [Counsel for the plaintiff], in a well-constructed argument, advanced a series of propositions which I hope may be fairly summarised as involving five main planks.

(1) In the absence of any statutory or other legal restriction everyone is free to make any contract they like and such contracts are enforceable. (2) While the Solicitors Act confers power on the Law Society to make rules to regulate the conduct of solicitors, the Law Society has no power to regulate the conduct of the public at large who are not solicitors. (3) Thus, while the Law Society may lawfully forbid solicitors to make fee-sharing agreements, it has no power to forbid anyone else, nor to ordain that such agreements shall be unenforceable save by solicitors. (4) In the absence of an effective legal prohibition a non-solicitor party who makes a fee-sharing agreement with a solicitor is entitled to enforce it. (5) It would be repugnant if the party prohibited from making such an agreement (the solicitor) were free to take the benefits accruing to him under the agreement, but were then entitled to plead the illegality of the agreement when called upon to pay the consideration due to the other contracting party, particularly when (as assumed here) that party is ignorant of the prohibition binding on the solicitor.

While recognising that that argument is by no means without force, I would not for my part accept it. I reject it for these reasons.

(1) Section 31 confers power on the Law Society to make, with the concurrence of the Master of the Rolls, subordinate legislation governing the professional practice and conduct of solicitors. (2) When making such subordinate legislation the Law Society is acting in the public interest and not (should there be any conflict) in the narrower interests of the solicitor's profession: see *Swain v The Law Society* [1983] 1 AC 598. The concurrence of the Master of the Rolls is required as a guarantee that the interests of the public are fully safeguarded. (3) By rule 3 of the Practice Rules, and by the Referral Code, solicitors are permitted to accept referrals and introductions only provided that introducers are not rewarded by commission or otherwise. (4) By rule 7 solicitors are prohibited from sharing fees or agreeing to do so. (5) Thus there is a prohibition on the making by solicitors of agreements of the kind assumed to have been made in this case. (6) Although it is true that the prohibition is only imposed in terms on solicitors, and they alone are liable to imposition of a professional penalty for breach, a contract requires the concurrence of at least two parties and the effect of the prohibition, if observed, is to outlaw the making of such agreements. (7) There are substantial reasons why, in the public interest, such agreements should be outlawed, some of those reasons being described by Lightman J. (8) It follows that it would defeat the public interest, which rule 7 in particular exists to promote, if a non-solicitor party to a fee-sharing agreement could enlist the aid of the court to enforce against a solicitor an agreement which the solicitor is prohibited from making. (9) If the court were to allow its process to be used to enforce agreements of this kind, the risk would inevitably arise that such agreements would abound, outwith the knowledge of the Law Society, to the detriment of the public . . .

It seems to me that that passage is unhelpful to the plaintiff. This is in my judgment plainly a case in which the relevant legislation (rule 7) prohibits not only the act but the contract to perform it also. Despite [Counsel for the plaintiff's] argument, I have little hesitation in agreeing with Lightman J on this first point.'

The Court of Appeal concluded that the public interest, which Rule 7 existed to promote, would be defeated if a non-solicitor could enlist the aid of the court to enforce an agreement which the solicitor was prohibited from making. In particular, Lord Bingham was concerned that, were the court to enforce the contract, such agreements would abound outside the knowledge of the Law Society. The case was followed one year later by the Court of Appeal in *Awwad v Geraghty & Co* [2000] QB 570. Later in this chapter we will return to *Mohammed v Alaga* to consider the claim for a *quantum meruit*, a claim that succeeded in the Court of Appeal.

13.3.1.2 Contracts illegal in their performance

In some cases, the contract may be legal in its formation but performed in a manner that contravenes statute. The Consumer Credit Act 1974 provides the following:

Form and content of agreements

Section 60

(1) The Secretary of State shall make regulations as to the form and content of documents embodying regulated agreements, and the regulations shall contain such provisions as appear to him appropriate with a view to ensuring that the debtor or hirer is made aware of–

   (a) the rights and duties conferred or imposed on him by the agreement,
   (b) the amount and rate of the total charge for credit (in the case of a consumer credit agreement),
   (c) the protection and remedies available to him under this Act, and
   (d) any other matters which, in the opinion of the Secretary of State, it is desirable for him to know about in connection with the agreement.

(2) Regulations under subsection (1) may in particular–

   (a) require specified information to be included in the prescribed manner in documents, and other specified material to be excluded;
   (b) contain requirements to ensure that specified information is clearly brought to the attention of the debtor or hirer, and that one part of a document is not given insufficient or excessive prominence compared with another.

Signing of agreement

Section 61

(1) A regulated agreement is not properly executed unless–

  (a) a document in the prescribed form itself containing all the prescribed terms and conforming to regulations under section 60(1) is signed in the prescribed manner both by the debtor or hirer and by or on behalf of the creditor or owner, and

Consequences of improper execution

Section 65

(1) An improperly executed regulated agreement is enforceable against the debtor or hirer on an order of the court only . . .

Enforcement orders in cases of infringement

Section 127

(1) In the case of an application for an enforcement order under . . . section 65(1) (improperly executed agreements) . . . the court shall dismiss the application if, but (subject to subsections (3) and (4)) only if, it considers it just to do so having regard to–

  (i) prejudice caused to any person by the contravention in question, and the degree of culpability for it; and

  (ii) the powers conferred on the court by subsection (2) and sections 135 and 136.

(2) If it appears to the court just to do so, it may in an enforcement order reduce or discharge any sum payable by the debtor or hirer, or any surety, so as to compensate him for prejudice suffered as a result of the contravention in question . . .

If the formalities prescribed in the statute are not complied with, the credit agreement will be unenforceable against the debtor. The formalities ensure that the debtor is fully aware of the nature of the transaction that s/he is entering into. The penalty of unenforceability is used to encourage creditors to comply with the procedures set out by Parliament.

It is sometimes difficult for the courts to determine the effect of the statute on the contract concerned, as demonstrated in *St John Shipping Corp v Joseph Rank Ltd*.

St John Shipping Corp v Joseph Rank Ltd [1957] 1 QB 267

Facts: The defendants chartered a ship from the plaintiffs to carry grain from the USA to the UK. The ship was overloaded in contravention of s 44 of the Merchant Shipping (Safety and Load Line Conventions) Act 1932. When the ship arrived in the UK the master was prosecuted and fined £1,200. The defendants paid for part of the freight but withheld a sum equivalent to the value of the freight earned by overloading. The plaintiffs brought a claim for the balance of the freight owed. The defendants contended that the plaintiffs were not entitled to recover any part of the sum because they had performed the contract in an illegal manner.

Held: The court held that the plaintiffs could recover the balance of the freight due. The contravention of a statute in the performance of a contract does not render the contract illegal unless the contract, as performed, was one that the statute meant to prohibit. The Merchant Shipping (Safety and Load Line Conventions) Act 1932 did not prohibit the contract of carriage which was made in contravention of its provisions.

Devlin J:

'There are two general principles. The first is that a contract which is entered into with the object of committing an illegal act is unenforceable. The application of this principle depends upon proof of the intent, at the time the contract was made, to break the law; if the intent is mutual the contract is not enforceable at all, and, if unilateral, it is unenforceable at the suit of the party who is proved to have it. This principle is not involved here. Whether or not the overloading was deliberate when it was done, there is no proof that it was contemplated when the contract of carriage was made. The second principle is that the court will not enforce a contract which is expressly or impliedly prohibited by statute. If the contract is of this class it does not matter what the intent of the parties is; if the statute prohibits the contract, it is unenforceable whether the parties meant to break the law or not. A significant distinction between the two classes is this. In the former class you have only to look and see what acts the statute prohibits; it does not matter whether or not it prohibits a contract; if a contract is deliberately made to do a prohibited act, that contract will be unenforceable. In the latter class, you have to consider not what acts the statute prohibits, but what contracts it prohibits; but you are not concerned at all with the intent of the parties; if the parties enter into a prohibited contract, that contract is unenforceable . . .

Two questions are involved. The first – and the one which hitherto has usually settled the matter – is: does the statute mean to prohibit contracts at all? But if this be answered in the affirmative, then one must ask: does this contract belong to the class which the statute intends to prohibit? For example, a person is forbidden by statute from using an unlicensed vehicle on the highway. If one asks oneself whether there is in such an enactment an implied prohibition of all contracts for the use of unlicensed vehicles, the answer may well be that there is, and that contracts of hire would be unenforceable. But if one asks oneself whether there is an implied prohibition of contracts for the carriage of goods by unlicensed vehicles or for the repairing of unlicensed vehicles or for the garaging of unlicensed vehicles, the answer may well be different. The answer might be that collateral contracts of this sort are not within the ambit of the statute.

The relevant section of the Act of 1932, section 44, provides that the ship "shall not be so loaded as to submerge" the appropriate loadline. It may be that a contract for the loading of the ship which necessarily has this effect would be unenforceable. It might be, for example, that the contract for bunkering at Port Everglades which had the effect of submerging the loadline, if governed by English law, would have been unenforce-able. But an implied prohibition of contracts of loading does not necessarily extend to contracts for the carriage of goods by improperly loaded vessels. Of course, if the parties knowingly agree to ship goods by an overloaded vessel, such a contract would be illegal; but its illegality does not depend on whether it is impliedly prohibited by the statute, since it falls within the first of the two general heads of illegality I noted above where there is an intent to break the law. The way to test the question whether a particular class of contract is prohibited by the statute is to test it in relation to a contract made in ignorance of its effect.

In my judgment, contracts for the carriage of goods are not within the ambit of this statute at all. A court should not hold that any contract or class of contracts is pro-hibited by statute unless there is a clear implication, or "necessary inference", as Parke B put it, that the statute so intended. If a contract has as its whole object the doing of the very act which the statute prohibits, it can be argued that you can hardly make sense of a statute which forbids an act and yet permits to be made a contract to do it; that is a clear implication. But unless you get a clear implication of that sort, I think that a court ought to be very slow to hold that a statute intends to interfere with the rights and remedies given by the ordinary law of contract. Caution in this respect is, I think, especially necessary in these times when so much of commercial life is governed by regulations of one sort or another, which may easily be broken without wicked intent. Persons who deliberately set out to break the law cannot expect to be aided in a court of justice, but it is a different matter when the law is unwittingly broken. To nullify a bargain in such circumstances frequently means that in a case – perhaps of such triviality that no authority would have felt it worth while to prosecute – a seller, because he cannot enforce his civil rights, may forfeit a sum vastly in excess of any penalty that a criminal court would impose; and the sum forfeited will not go into the public purse but into the pockets of someone who is lucky enough to pick up the windfall or astute enough to have contrived to get it. It is questionable how far this contributes to public morality. In *Vita Food Products Inc v Unus Shipping Co* [1939] AC 277 Lord Wright said: "Nor must it be forgotten that the rule by which contracts not expressly forbidden by statute or declared to be void are in proper cases nullified for disobedience to a statute is a rule of public policy only, and public policy understood in a wider sense may at times be better served by refusing to nullify a bargain save on serious and sufficient grounds". It may be questionable also whether public policy is well served by driving from the seat of judgment everyone who has been guilty of a minor transgres-sion. Commercial men who have unwittingly offended against one of a multiplicity of regulations may nevertheless feel that they have not thereby forfeited all right to justice, and may go elsewhere for it if courts of law will not give it to them. In the last resort they will, if necessary, set up their own machinery for dealing with their own disputes in the way that those whom the law puts beyond the pale, such as gamblers, have done. I have said enough, and perhaps more than enough, to show how import-ant it is that the courts should be slow to imply the statutory prohibition of contracts, and should do so only when the implication is quite clear. I have felt justified in saying as much because, to any judge who sits in what is called the Commercial Court, it must be a matter of special concern. This court was instituted more than half a century ago so that it might solve the disputes of commercial men in a way which they understood and appreciated, and it is a particular misfortune for it if it has to deny that service to any except those who are clearly undeserving of it.

The Act of 1932 imposes a penalty which is itself designed to deprive the offender of the benefits of his crime. It would be a curious thing if the operation could be performed twice – once by the criminal law and then again by the civil. It would be curious, too, if in a case in which the magistrates had thought fit to impose only a nominal fine, their decision could, in effect, be overridden in a civil action. But the question whether the rule applies to statutory offences is an important one which I do not wish to decide in the present case . . .

The rights which cannot be enforced must be those "directly resulting" from the crime. That means, I think, that for a right to money or to property to be unenforceable the property or money must be identifiable as something to which, but for the crime, the plaintiff would have had no right or title. That cannot be said in this case. The amount of the profit which the plaintiffs made from the crime, that is to say, the amount of freight which, but for the overloading, they could not have earned on this voyage, was, as I have said, £2,295. The quantity of cargo consigned to the defendants was approximately 35 per cent of the whole and, therefore, even if it were permissible to treat the benefit as being divisible pro rata over the whole of the cargo, the amount embodied in the claim against the defendants would not be more than 35 per cent of £2,300. That would not justify the withholding of £2,000 . . . But in truth there is no warrant for any particular form of division. The fact is that in this type of case no claim or part of a claim for freight can be clearly identified as being the excess illegally earned.'

Devlin J said that it was necessary to ask two questions:

1. Does the statute prohibit contracts at all?
2. Does this contract belong to the class that the statute is intended to prohibit?

The 1932 Act provided a specific penalty for noncompliance in the form of a criminal fine. Devlin J was concerned that the civil courts should not inflict double punishment by refusing to enforce the contract as well (see also *Hughes v Asset Managers plc* [1995] 3 All ER 668). The judge also emphasised that the knowledge of the parties was crucial. Had the facts been different and the plaintiff been aware that the goods were to be shipped on an overloaded vessel he would have declared the contract to be unenforceable. Devlin J was also keen to draw attention to the fact that commercial illegality covers a broad spectrum of wrongdoing. He warned that the commercial courts should be reluctant to nullify a bargain when the illegality consists of a mere triviality, especially when such judicial action is likely to result in a windfall accruing to one of the parties. The conflict between these two contrasting policy objectives was noted in the introduction to this chapter. In the final paragraph of his judgment, Devlin J provided a helpful summary of the test to be applied in cases of statutory illegality. He said that 'the rights which cannot be enforced must be those "directly resulting" from the crime'. It is not sufficient that the contract merely relates to the illegal conduct. The contract itself must be 'directly resulting' from the illegal conduct. On the facts of *St John Shipping*, it could not be said that the carriage of goods contract was directly resulting from the breach of the 1932 Act.

Archbolds (Freightage) Ltd v S Spanglett Ltd [1961] 1 QB 374

Facts: The defendant furniture manufacturers owned a number of vans with 'C' licences, enabling them, under the Road and Rail Traffic Act 1933, to carry their own goods but not the goods of others. The plaintiffs, believing that the defendants possessed 'A' licences, arranged for the defendants to carry 200 cases of whisky from Leeds to London. The whisky was stolen on the journey due to the negligence of the defendants' driver. The defendants argued that they were not liable because the contract was illegal. At first instance, Slade J held for the plaintiffs.

Held: The Court of Appeal dismissed the appeal. There was no evidence that the plaintiffs knew or should have known that the defendants' van did not have an 'A' licence, and that being so, the contract was not prohibited either expressly or impliedly by the statute. Nor was the contract illegal on the ground of public policy.

Pearce LJ:
'If a contract is expressly or by necessary implication forbidden by statute, or if it is *ex facie* illegal, or if both parties know that though *ex facie* legal it can only be performed by illegality or is intended to be performed illegally, the law will not help the plaintiffs in any way that is a direct or indirect enforcement of rights under the contract and for this purpose both parties are presumed to know the law.

The first question, therefore, is whether this contract of carriage was forbidden by statute. The two cases on which the defendants mainly rely are *In re an Arbitration between Mahmoud and Isphani* [1921] 2 KB 716 and *J Dennis & Co Ltd v Munn* [1949] 2 KB 327. In both those cases the plaintiffs were unable to enforce their rights under contracts forbidden by statute . . . In neither case could the plaintiff bring his contract within the exception that alone would have made its subject-matter lawful, namely, by showing the existence of a licence. Therefore, the core of both contracts was the mischief expressly forbidden by the statutory order and the statutory regulation respectively.

In *Mahmoud's* case the object of the order was to prevent (except under licence) a person buying and a person selling, and both parties were liable to penalties. A contract of sale between those persons was therefore expressly forbidden. In *Dennis's* case the object of the regulation was to prevent (except under licence) owners from performing building operations, and builders from carrying out the work for them. Both parties were liable to penalties and a contract between these persons for carrying out an unlawful operation would be forbidden by implication.

The case before us is somewhat different. The carriage of the plaintiffs' whisky was not as such prohibited; the statute merely regulated the means by which carriers should carry goods. Therefore this contract was not expressly forbidden by the statute.

Was it then forbidden by implication? The Road and Rail Traffic Act, 1933, section 1, says: "no person shall use a goods vehicle on a road for the carriage of goods . . . except under licence", and provides that such use shall be an offence. Did the statute thereby intend to forbid by implication all contracts whose performance must on all the facts (whether known or not) result in a contravention of that section?

The plaintiffs' part of the contract could not constitute an illegal use of the vehicle by them since they were not "using" the vehicle. If they were aware of the true facts they would, of course, be guilty of aiding and abetting the defendants, but if they acted in good faith they would not be guilty of any offence under the statute . . .

The object of the Road and Rail Traffic Act, 1933, was not (in this connection) to interfere with the owner of goods or his facilities for transport, but to control those who provided the transport, with a view to promoting its efficiency. Transport of goods was not made illegal but the various licence holders were prohibited from encroaching on one another's territory, the intention of the Act being to provide an orderly and comprehensive service. Penalties were provided for those licence holders who went outside the bounds of their allotted spheres. These penalties apply to those using the vehicle but not to the goods owner. Though the latter could be convicted of aiding and abetting any breach, the restrictions were not aimed at him. Thus a contract of carriage was, in the sense used by Devlin J, "collateral", and it was not impliedly forbidden by the statute.

This view is supported by common sense and convenience. If the other view were held it would have far-reaching effects. For instance, if a carrier induces me (who am in fact ignorant of any illegality) to entrust goods to him and negligently destroys them, he would only have to show that (though unknown to me) his licence had expired, or did not properly cover the transportation, or that he was uninsured, and I should then be without a remedy against him. Or, again, if I ride in a taxicab and the driver leaves me stranded in some deserted spot, he would only have to show that he was (though unknown to me) unlicensed or uninsured, and I should be without remedy. This appears to me an undesirable extension of the implications of a statute . . .

It is for the defendants to show that contracts by the owner for the carriage of goods are within the ambit of the implied prohibition of the Road and Rail Traffic Act, 1933. In my judgment they have not done so.

The next question is whether this contract though not forbidden by statute was *ex facie* illegal. Must any reasonable person on hearing the terms of the contract (which presumed knowledge of the law) realise that it was illegal? There is nothing illegal in its terms. Further knowledge, namely, knowledge of the fact that Randall's van was not properly licensed, would show that it could only be performed by contravention of the statute, but that does not make the contract ex facie illegal.

However, if both parties had that knowledge the contract would be unenforceable as being a contract which to their knowledge could not be carried out without a violation of the law: see *per* Lord Blackburn in *Waugh v Morris* (1873) LR 8 QB 202, 208. But where one party is ignorant of the fact that will make the performance illegal, is it established that the innocent party cannot obtain relief against the guilty party? The case has been argued with skill and care on both sides, and yet no case has been cited to us establishing the proposition that where a contract is on the face of it legal and is not forbidden by statute, but must in fact produce illegality by reason of a circumstance known to one party only, it should be held illegal so as to debar the innocent party from relief. In the absence of such a case I do not feel compelled to so unsatisfactory a conclusion, which would injure the innocent, benefit the guilty, and put a premium on deceit.

Such a conclusion (in cases like this where a contract is not forbidden by statute) can only derive from public policy ... No question of moral turpitude arises here. The alleged illegality is, so far as the plaintiffs were concerned, the permitting of their goods to be carried by the wrong carrier, namely, a carrier who unknown to them was not allowed by his licence to carry that particular class of goods. The plaintiffs were never in delicto since they did not know the vital fact that would make the performance of the contract illegal.

In my view, therefore, public policy does not constrain us to refuse our aid to the plaintiffs and they are therefore entitled to succeed. I would dismiss the appeal.'

The argument of the defendants was quite outrageous. They were using their own illegal performance as a defence to a claim by the innocent plaintiffs. This was an example of illegality being used as a technical defence to wrongdoing. The argument was given short shrift by the Court of Appeal. Since the contract could have been performed in a legal manner, the illegal performance could not be used as a defence. The statute neither expressly nor impliedly prohibited contracts of carriage. The situation would have been quite different, however, had the plaintiffs known that the defendants did not hold an 'A' licence. In such a situation Pearce LJ confirmed that the law would have been unwilling to help the plaintiffs. This is not always the case, however, as was shown by the decision in *Ailion v Spiekermann* [1976] Ch 158. The case concerned a contract for the assignment of a lease with a premium. Such contracts were illegal under s 86(1) of the Rent Act 1968 and both parties were aware of this. Nevertheless, the court held that the premium requirement could be severed and the remainder of the agreement enforced by the court. We will return to consider severance later in the chapter when we examine the effects of illegality.

It seems that the courts will apply a test of remoteness when considering whether illegal performance renders a contract illegal. Such a test was applied by Field J in

21st Century Logistic Solutions Ltd (In Liquidation) v. Madysen Ltd (2004) 2 Lloyd's Rep 92. The claimants, 21st Century, commenced proceedings against the defendants for the price of 7,200 computers sold and delivered. The defendants denied liability on the ground that the claimants' operations sought to defraud Her Majesty's Customs and Excise. The claimants purchased the CPUs VAT-free from suppliers in Luxembourg and sold them on to businesses in the UK with a VAT element included in the price. Field J held that the contract was lawful and enforceable because there was insufficient proximity between the claimants' fraudulent intention and the contract. He said:

'In my opinion 21stC's fraudulent intention is too remote from the contract for it to be held that the contract is unenforceable on grounds of illegality. The VAT element in the price paid for a supply is not held on trust by the supplier for HMCE. A taxable supplier's only material obligations under the VAT legislation are to account for VAT at the end of each accounting period and to keep proper records. The use of the VAT element of sale proceeds on some purpose other than payment of VAT due to HMCE is therefore not unlawful. It follows that the fraud on HMCE intended by 21stC would only have been finally committed when 21stC failed to account to HMCE at the end of the relevant accounting period. The contract between 21stC and Madysen was a straightforward agreement for the sale of goods. In and of itself it was a lawful contract. It provided the opportunity for Darren King to profit from the intended fraud but that was all: the crucial act that had to be performed to work the fraud was a failure to account to HMCE.'

In summary, when considering whether a contract is unenforceable for statutory illegality the court will ask itself two questions. First, does the statute prohibit contracts? The remedies provided by the statute will often prove determinative on this issue. Second, is this particular contract illegal? Here, the court will consider the knowledge of the parties, the relative fault of the parties and the proximity of the illegality to the contract. These considerations will often overlap with the more general issue of the effect of illegality, which will be considered in greater detail below.

13.3.2 COMMON LAW ILLEGALITY

Common law illegality is based on considerations of public policy. If a court decides that a contract is 'contrary to public policy', it can declare it to be illegal and unenforceable.

13.3.2.1 Public policy

Public policy as a ground for invalidating an agreement is a powerful weapon in the hands of the judiciary and for this reason the courts have traditionally emphasised the need to keep it on a tight reign. In *Richardson v Mellish* (1824) 2 Bing 229, Burrough J said that 'public policy is a very unruly horse, and once you get astride it you never know where it will carry you'. Other judges have adopted a more flexible attitude. In *Enderby Town FC Ltd v The Football Association* [1971] Ch 591, Lord Denning drew on Burrough J's metaphor and said: 'I disagree. With a good man in the saddle, the unruly horse can be kept in control. It can jump over obstacles. It can leap the fences put up by fictions and come down on the side of justice.'

It has been said that the categories of common-law public policy are closed so that the courts will not apply the concept to a type of contract to which it has not been applied in the past. In *Printing and Numerical Registering Company v Sampson* (1875) LR 19 Eq 462, Jessel MR said:

'It must not be forgotten that you are not to extend arbitrarily those rules which say that a given contract is void as being against public policy, because if there is one thing which more than another public policy requires it is that men of full age and competent understanding shall have the utmost liberty of contracting, and that their contracts when entered into freely and voluntarily shall be held sacred and shall be enforced by Courts of justice. Therefore, you have this paramount public policy to consider – that you are not lightly to interfere with this freedom of contract. Now, there is no doubt public policy may say that a contract to commit a crime, or a contract to give a reward to another to commit a crime, is necessarily void. The decisions have gone further, and contracts to commit an immoral offence, or to give money or reward to another to commit an immoral offence, or to induce another to do something against the general rules of morality, though far more indefinite than the previous class, have always been held to be void. I should be sorry to extend the doctrine much further. I do not say there are no other cases to which it does apply; but I should be sorry to extend it much further.'

In *Janson v Driefontein Consolidated Mines Ltd* [1902] AC 484, Lord Halsbury LC went even further:

'In treating of various branches of the law learned persons have analysed the sources of the law, and have sometimes expressed their opinion that such and such a provision is bad because it is contrary to public policy; but I deny that any Court can invent a new head of public policy; so a contract for marriage brokerage, the creation of a perpetuity, a contract in restraint of trade, a gaming or wagering contract, or, what is relevant here, the assisting of the

King's enemies, are all undoubtedly unlawful things; and you may say that it is because they are contrary to public policy they are unlawful; but it is because these things have been either enacted or assumed to be by the common law unlawful, and not because a judge or Court have a right to declare that such and such things are in his or their view contrary to public policy.'

It is true that restricting the scope of common law illegality promotes certainty and keeps judicial discretion within reasonable bounds. However, Lord Halsbury's claim that the categories of common-law illegality are now closed is somewhat doubtful. Indeed, in *Fender v St John Mildmay* [1938] AC 1, Lord Atkin explicitly disapproved of this part of Lord Halsbury's speech:

In [*Janson v Driefontein*] Lord Halsbury indeed appeared to decide that the categories of public policy are closed, and that the principle could not be invoked anew unless the case could be brought within some principle of public policy already recognized by the law. I do not find, however, that this view received the express assent of the other members of the House; and it seems to me, with respect, too rigid.'

In practice there is little difference between creating a new category of public policy and expanding a pre-existing category to incorporate a new situation. For this reason, it does not really matter whether we speak of the categories being closed or open; either way the courts will intervene where necessary in the interests of public policy. Moreover, the recognition that a category of public policy may be closed by the courts as a result of changes in society's values (contrast *Cowan v Milbourn* (1867) LR 2 Exch 230 and *Bowman v Secular Society* [1917] AC 406), strongly suggests that new categories might also be opened up as a result of changes in social attitudes and advances in technology.

13.3.2.2 Categories

The courts have developed a number of well-established categories of public policy. We will consider each of these in turn.

13.3.2.2.1 *Contracts to commit a criminal offence*

The expression 'contract killer' is an oxymoron because contracts to commit a crime are unenforceable. In *Bigos v Bousted* [1951] 1 All ER 92, the High Court refused to enforce a contract for the supply of foreign currency because it constituted an offence under s 1(1) of the Exchange Control Act 1947. Certain contracts are made illegal by statute. For example, under the Obscene Publications Act 1959, it is illegal to sell an 'obscene article'. The criminal offence is committed by the seller alone, but neither party will be entitled to enforce the contract, due to its illegality.

13.3.2.2.2 Contracts to commit a tort

An agreement to commit a civil wrong is illegal and unenforceable. In *Allen v Rescous* (1677) 2 Lev 174; 83 ER 505, the defendant agreed to pay the plaintiff a sum of money in return for his promise to beat another person 'out of a close'. The Court held that the 'consideration and whole contract' was 'illegal and void'. A contract for the publication of a libel is also illegal and unenforceable. In *Clay v Yates* (1856) 1 H & N 73 (1856), the plaintiff agreed to publish a book written by the defendant. On delivery of the manuscript the plaintiff discovered that the dedication in the book was libellous. He refused to publish that part of the book and the defendant refused to pay him for any of the work he had done. Martin B held that although the contract was illegal, the defendant was liable 'to pay the plaintiff for that part which he has performed'.

13.3.2.2.3 Contracts to defraud the revenue

A contract that is designed to defraud the revenue is illegal and unenforceable.

Alexander v Rayson [1936] 1 KB 169

Facts: In 1929 the plaintiff agreed to let a flat in Piccadilly to the defendant at a rent of £1,200 per year. The agreement was effected by two documents. The first was a lease for £450 per year together with the benefits of certain services rendered by the plaintiff, and the second was a service agreement providing for the plaintiff to render services which were practically the same as those to be provided under the lease in consideration of an extra £750 per year. The defendant refused to pay an instalment due under the agreement, and when the plaintiff sought to recover, the defendant argued that the contract was void for illegality and that its enforcement would be contrary to public policy. The purpose of the two agreements was that only the lease would be disclosed to the Westminster City Council so that the rateable value of the flat would be reduced.

Held: The Court of Appeal held that the plaintiff could not enforce either the lease or the service agreement since he intended to use the agreements for an illegal purpose.

Judgment of the Court (Greer, Romer and Scot LJJ):
'It is settled law that an agreement to do an act that is illegal or immoral or contrary to public policy, or to do any act for a consideration that is illegal, immoral or contrary to public policy, is unlawful and therefore void. But it often happens that an agreement which in itself is not unlawful is made with the intention of one or both parties to make use of the subject matter for an unlawful purpose, that is to say a purpose that is illegal, immoral or contrary to public policy. The most common instance of this is an agreement for the sale or letting of an object, where the agreement is unobjectionable on the face of it, but where the intention of both or one of the parties is that the object shall be used by the purchaser or hirer for an unlawful purpose. In such a case any party to the

---

agreement who had the unlawful intention is precluded from suing upon it. *Ex turpi causa non oritur actio*. The action does not lie because the Court will not lend its help to such a plaintiff.'

13.3.2.2.4 Contracts to indemnify

It is generally illegal to indemnify against criminal liability. There is an exception, however, where the criminal offence is one of strict liability and the court is satisfied that the defendant is morally innocent.

Osman v J Ralph Moss Ltd [1970] 1 Lloyd's Rep 313

Facts: The plaintiff was of Turkish origin and struggled to read and understand English. The defendant brokers negligently failed to inform the plaintiff that his motor insurance policy had expired due to the collapse of the insurance company. The plaintiff was involved in a motor accident and fined £25 by Beacontree Magistrates. He sought to recover this sum from the defendants in an action for negligence.

Held: The Court of Appeal held that the plaintiff could recover the amount of the fine from the defendants in damages.

Sachs LJ:

'Having examined the authorities as to cases where the person fined was under an absolute liability, it appears that such fine can be recovered in circumstances such as the present as damages unless it is shown that there was on the part of the person fined a degree of *mens rea* or of culpable negligence in the matter which resulted in the fine. The onus in cases such as the present is on the defendants, who were the true cause of the sequence of events leading to the fine, to show that there are circumstances which make that fine irrecoverable as damages by the plaintiff.'

A contract to indemnify against civil liability will be legal and enforceable unless the wrong consists of deliberate and intentional conduct. It is therefore legal for a motorist to insure against third-party liability arising from his own negligence or recklessness. It is not, however, legal for a person to insure against the consequences of his intentional wrongful acts.

Geismar v Sun Alliance & London Insurance Ltd [1978] QB 383

Facts: The plaintiff had imported various items of jewellery into the United Kingdom without having declared them for the payment of customs and excise duty. He had thus committed an offence in relation to the non-payment of duty and the jewellery was liable to forfeiture at any time. The jewellery was subsequently stolen from the plaintiff's home and he brought a claim against the defendant insurers under his building and contents policy. The defendants refused to pay out on the claim on the grounds of public policy.

Held: The Court of Appeal held that the plaintiff could not recover under the policy for the uncustomed jewellery because this would allow him to recover in respect of items that might have been confiscated at any time. Permitting the plaintiff to benefit in such a way would have been contrary to public policy.

Talbot J:
'The plaintiff is seeking the assistance of the court to enforce contracts of insurance so that he may be indemnified against loss of articles which he deliberately and intentionally imported into this country in breach of the Customs and Excise Act 1952.

I am not concerned with cases of unintentional importation or of innocent possession of uncustomed goods. I would think that different considerations would apply in those cases. But where there is a deliberate breach of the law I do not think the court ought to assist the plaintiff to derive a profit from it, even though it is sought indirectly through an indemnity under an insurance policy.'

It is therefore clear that a person can insure against liability for non-intentional torts, but not against liability for intentional wrongdoing. A notable exception to this rule exists in the context of road traffic claims where the public interest in ensuring that victims are adequately compensated overrides the policy against allowing intentional wrongdoers to obtain an indemnity. In *Gardner v Moore* [1984] AC 548, the first defendant deliberately drove his car into the plaintiff following an altercation. This amounted to an offence of wounding with intent to cause grevious bodily harm under s 18 of the Offences against the Person Act 1861, for which the defendant was sentenced to three years' imprisonment. The defendant was uninsured at the time of the incident and therefore the plaintiff joined the Motor Insurers' Bureau (MIB) as second defendants. The question was whether it would be contrary to public policy to allow the MIB to indemnify the driver. Lord Hailsham LC (with whom the other Law Lords agreed) concluded that it would not:

'The MIB agreements impose on the appellants an obligation to underwrite this liability so far as regards uninsured or untraceable tortfeasors. The two agreements were intended precisely to protect the innocent third party either because the insurer did not choose or was not able to discharge his liability under section 149 of the Road Traffic Act 1972, or where the wrongdoer was not covered by a relevant policy of insurance at all (which is the present appeal) or was untraceable. To invoke, as the MIB now do, the well-known doctrine of public policy that a man may not profit by the consequences of his own wrongdoing seems to me to stand the principle of public policy on its head. There are no socially desirable consequences flowing from its application in the sense contended for by the appellants. On the contrary, all the pointers in sections 143 and 145 read alone, or in sections 143 and 145 as read in conjunction with sections 148 and 149, seem to me to point exactly in the opposite direction. The construction of the MIB agreement contended for by the appellants is contrary to the grammatical sense of the agreement, read, as it must be read, in the context of the statute, and the construction of the statute contended for by the appellants is contrary both to its manifest grammatical meaning and to the policy illustrated by its more mature articulation.'

13.3.2.2.5 *Contracts prejudicial to the administration of justice*

A contract that is prejudicial to the administration of justice is contrary to public policy and therefore void. Examples of such contracts include agreements to withhold information about wrongdoing and agreements to oust the jurisdiction of the courts. An example of the former is seen in *Initial Services Ltd v Putterill*.

Initial Services Ltd v Putterill [1968] 1 QB 396

Facts: The defendant was employed as the sales manager of the plaintiff launderers. He resigned his position and took with him a number of documents belonging to the plaintiff. He disclosed these documents to reporters from the Daily Mail who published articles alleging the existence of a liaison system between laundries by which they artificially inflated their prices. The plaintiff claimed damages against the defendant for breach of an implied term to the effect that he would not disclose to strangers confidential information obtained by him in the course of or as a result of his employment. The defendant claimed that there was an exception to this implied term if the employer's misconduct was of such a nature that it was in the public interest to disclose it. He alleged this to be the case on the facts because the plaintiff's conduct was contrary to section 6 of the Restrictive Trade Practices Act 1956, and should have been registered under section 9 of that Act and referred to the Monopolies Commission. Cusack J refused to strike out the defence and the plaintiffs appealed.

Held: The Court of Appeal dismissed the appeal. A term purporting to prevent an employee from disclosing misconduct which ought in the public interest to be disclosed to an appropriate person is illegal and unenforceable. It was arguable that the information disclosed by the defendant fell within this category and therefore there was no ground for striking out the defendant's defence.

Lord Denning MR:

'In support of the appeal, Mr Michael Kerr said that in the employment of every servant there is implied an obligation that he will not, before or after his service, disclose information or documents which he has received in confidence. Now I quite agree that there is such an obligation. It is imposed by law. But it is subject to exceptions. Take a simple instance. Suppose a master tells his servant: "I am going to falsify these sale notes and deceive the customers. You are not to say anything about it to anyone." If the master thereafter falsifies the sale notes, the servant is entitled to say: "I am not going to stay any longer in the service of a man who does such a thing. I will leave him and report it to the customers." It was so held in *Gartside v Outram* (1856) 26 L J Ch 113.

Mr Michael Kerr suggested that this exception was confined to cases where the master has been "guilty of a crime or fraud". But I do not think that it is so limited. It extends to any misconduct of such a nature that it ought in the public interest to be disclosed to others. Wood, VC put it in a vivid phrase: "There is no confidence as to the disclosure of iniquity."

In *Weld-Blundell v Stephens* [1919] 1 KB 520, Bankes LJ rather suggested that the exception is limited to the proposed or contemplated commission of a crime or a civil wrong. But I should have thought that was too limited. The exception should extend to crimes, frauds and misdeeds, both those actually committed as well as those in contemplation, provided always – and this is essential – that the disclosure is justified in the public interest. The reason is because "no private obligations can dispense with that universal one which lies on every member of the society to discover every design which may be formed, contrary to the laws of the society, to destroy the public welfare": see *Annesley v Anglesea (Earl)* (1743) LR 5 QB 317n; 17 State Tr 1139.

The disclosure must, I should think, be to one who has a proper interest to receive the information. Thus it would be proper to disclose a crime to the police; or a breach of the Restrictive Trade Practices Act to the registrar. There may be cases where the misdeed is of such a character that the public interest may demand, or at least excuse, publication on a broader field, even to the press.

Let me apply these principles to the particular facts of this case, because we are only concerned to see whether the defence of Mr Putterill is arguable or not. Firstly, as to the Restrictive Trade Practices Act. If the allegations of the defence are correct, there was an agreement or arrangement between these laundry firms which should have been registered. If it had been registered, particulars of it would have been entered in the register. Once on the register, any individual on paying the requisite amount, I think one shilling, could have obtained full particulars of that agreement or arrangement. Now I ask myself: Is this laundry company entitled to say that that information is confidential, seeing that they ought to have supplied it themselves to the registrar, and it would then have been made public? There is an argument at least that such information was not within the realm of confidence to which the master could hold his servant . . . I am not prepared to say that this defence is unfounded. I think this matter should go for trial. I would dismiss the appeal.'

It is clear that the courts will refuse to enforce an agreement not to disclose misconduct that is of such a nature that it ought in the public interest to be disclosed to others. This rule is not restricted to cases where the misconduct relates to the commission of a crime or fraud, and in certain cases the misconduct may be of such a character as to make it appropriate to disclose the misconduct to the press.

Agreements that purport to oust the jurisdiction of the court are also contrary to public policy and therefore void, as illustrated by the case of *Baker v Jones*.

Baker v Jones [1954] 1 WLR 1005

Facts: The rules of the British Amateur Weightlifters' Association vested the government of the association in a central council consisting of the officers and a number of the members of the association. The rules stated that the council was to be the sole interpreter of the rules of the association and was to act on behalf of the association regarding any matter not dealt with by the rules. In all circumstances the decision of the council was to be final.

Held: The High Court held that the rules were void to the extent that they purported to give the council the power to make final decisions on questions of law.

Lynskey J:

'Although parties to a contract may, in general, make any contract they like, there are certain limitations imposed by public policy, and one of those limitations may be that the parties cannot, by contract, oust the ordinary courts from their jurisdiction (Scott v Avery (1856) 5 HLC 811). The parties can, of course, make a tribunal or council the final arbiter on questions of fact. They can leave questions of law to the decision of a tribunal, but they cannot make it the final arbiter on questions of law. They cannot prevent its decisions being examined by the courts. As Denning LJ said in *Lee v Showmen's Guild of Great Britain* [1952] 2 QB 329, 342:

"If parties should seek, by agreement, to take the law out of the hands of the courts and put it into the hands of a private tribunal, without any recourse at all to the courts in case of error of law, then the agreement is to that extent contrary to public policy and void."

With this statement of the law I respectfully agree. The interpretation of the rules is a question of law which the courts will examine. In my view, therefore, the provision in the BAWLA rules, making the central council the sole interpreter of the rules and their decision in all cases final, is contrary to public policy and void.'

There are two exceptions to the general rule against agreements purporting to oust the jurisdiction of the courts. First, the parties may insert a clause into the contract stating that any dispute between the parties is to be resolved by referral to arbitration. Such a clause will be upheld as valid and enforceable. In *Scott v Avery* (1855) 5 HLC 811, the House of Lords upheld a clause stating that the award of an arbitrator was to be a condition precedent to the accrual of a cause of action. It was said that such a clause did not oust the jurisdiction of the court, but merely meant that the cause of action was not complete until the arbitration award was made. Under the Arbitration Act 1996, there is a limited right of appeal to the court on a point of law, but only with the agreement of the other side, or the leave of the court itself.

ARBITRATION ACT 1996

Appeal on point of law

Section 69

(1) Unless otherwise agreed by the parties, a party to arbitral proceedings may (upon notice to the other parties and to the tribunal) appeal to the court on a question of law arising out of an award made in the proceedings.

An agreement to dispense with reasons for the tribunal's award shall be considered an agreement to exclude the court's jurisdiction under this section.

(2) An appeal shall not be brought under this section except–

(a) with the agreement of all the other parties to the proceedings, or

(b) with the leave of the court.

The right to appeal is also subject to the restrictions in section 70(2) and (3).

(3) Leave to appeal shall be given only if the court is satisfied–

(a) that the determination of the question will substantially affect the rights of one or more of the parties,

(b) that the question is one which the tribunal was asked to determine,

(c) that, on the basis of the findings of fact in the award–

(i) the decision of the tribunal on the question is obviously wrong, or

(ii) the question is one of general public importance and the decision of the tribunal is at least open to serious doubt, and

(d) that, despite the agreement of the parties to resolve the matter by arbitration, it is just and proper in all the circumstances for the court to determine the question.

According to the conditions set out in subsection (3) the jurisdiction of the court is retained only in cases where the decision of the tribunal was clearly wrong or where the case concerns a matter of 'general public importance'. In all other situations the finality of the arbitral ruling is maintained along with its associated benefits of speed, certainty and reduction in costs.

The second exception to the general rule against contracts purporting to oust the jurisdiction of the courts concerns maintenance agreements. In *Hyman v Hyman*

[1929] AC 601, a husband, as part of a separation agreement, promised to pay his wife a lump sum of £2,200 and a weekly allowance of £20 in return for her promise not to apply to the court for maintenance. The House of Lords held that the agreement was contrary to public policy and therefore did not prevent the wife from applying to the court for maintenance. Lord Atkin said:

> 'In my view no agreement between the spouses can prevent the Court from considering the question whether in the circumstances of the particular case it shall think fit to order the husband to make some reasonable payment to the wife, "having regard to her fortune, if any, to the ability of her husband and to the conduct of the parties". The wife's right to future maintenance is a matter of public concern, which she cannot barter away.'

Although such agreements are void to the extent that the wife is free to apply to the court for maintenance, they are valid and enforceable in respect of the husband's promise to pay. This is confirmed by s 34 of the Matrimonial Causes Act 1973, which states:

> (1) If a maintenance agreement includes a provision purporting to restrict any right to apply to a court for an order containing financial arrangements, then—
>
> (a) that provision shall be void; but
> (b) any other financial arrangements contained in the agreement shall not thereby be rendered void or unenforceable and shall, unless they are void or unenforceable for any other reason . . . be binding on the parties to the agreement.

13.3.2.2.6 *Contracts prejudicial to the institution of marriage*

It is considered to be in the interests of society to preserve the status of marriage. For this reason, agreements that are regarded as threatening to the institution of marriage are illegal and unenforceable.

Brodie v Brodie [1917] P 271

Facts: Mr Brodie agreed to marry the woman who was carrying his child on condition that a written agreement to separate was drawn up prior to the marriage. The effect of this agreement was to preclude the woman from bringing legal proceedings against Mr Brodie.

Held: The Court held that the agreement was contrary to public policy and therefore could not be enforced. The woman was entitled to petition the court for restitution of conjugal rights.

Horridge J:

'I find as a fact that . . . the two documents formed part of an agreement entered into before marriage for future separation. Such an agreement is void and against public policy: see *Cocksedge v Cocksedge* (1844) 14 Sim 244, the judgment of Rigby LJ in *Marlborough v Marlborough* [1901] 1 Ch 165, 171, and the judgment of Kennedy LJ in *Wilson v Carnley* [1908] 1 KB 729, 743. I therefore hold the plea of the respondent is no answer to the petition.'

The rule set out in *Brodie v Brodie* does not apply to an agreement made in anticipation of an immediate separation. It is not contrary to public policy for separating parties to make agreements as to the distribution of their joint property or the maintenance of one of the parties. Nor does the rule affect agreements between spouses who have been separated and have subsequently been reconciled, since it is presumed that the making of such an agreement is likely to aid the reconciliation (*Harrison v Harrison* [1910] 1 KB 35).

Agreements that aim to restrict or limit the freedom of a person to marry are void for illegality (*Lowe v Peers* (1768) 4 Burr 2225). Likewise contracts for the brokerage of marriage are contrary to public policy.

Hermann v Charlesworth [1905] 2 KB 123

Facts: The plaintiff, Miss Hermann, entered into an agreement with the defendant under which she would be required to pay him £250 if he introduced her to a gentleman whom she later married. She paid a deposit of £52 which, after several unsuccessful introductions, she sought to recover. The county court judge held that the agreement was illegal. However, since the parties were not in *pari delicto*, the defendant being the more culpable as having instigated the agreement, the plaintiff was entitled to recover the deposit. The Divisional Court reversed the decision of the county court judge on the ground that the contract was not one of marriage brokerage.

Held: The Court of Appeal allowed the appeal, holding that the contract was one of marriage brokerage and the plaintiff was entitled to recover her £52 deposit.

Collins MR:

'The Divisional Court came to the conclusion that the particular arrangement in this case to procure introductions with a view to marriage, giving the lady a choice among the persons introduced to her, was not within the mischief attributed to marriage brokage contracts. As I understand, they took the view that a marriage brokage contract was confined to the case of a contract to procure marriage with one particular person. Going back to the principle on which this branch of the law as to such contracts rests, I am unable to find any ground for that distinction. It seems to me that the principle is as much violated in the class of cases to which the present one belongs as in cases where the contract relates to bringing about a marriage with a particular individual.'

It is unlikely that this case would be decided the same way today, given the popularity of 'dating' and 'introduction' agencies. Perhaps this is one example of the way in which public policy evolves in line with changing attitudes in society.

Finally, the courts will refuse to enforce contracts purporting to transfer parental duties to a third party. In *Humphreys v Polak* [1901] 2 KB 385, Stirling LJ said the following:

'What is the bargain in this case as appearing from the statement of claim? It is in substance that the child is to remain in the possession of the defendants for the purpose of enabling the defendants to treat the child as their own and relieve the mother of all responsibility in connection with the bringing up of the child; in other words, the defendants were to undertake the duties which the law imposes on the mother, and to have the rights which the law gives her in relation to the child. In my opinion, the law does not permit such a transfer of the mother's rights and liabilities.'

The obvious exception to the rule stated in *Humphreys v Polak* is legal adoption orders under the Adoption Act 1976.

13.3.2.2.7 *Contracts promoting sexual immorality*
Contracts promoting sexual immorality are deemed to be contrary to public policy. The conduct concerned need not constitute a criminal offence and the courts will generally refuse to enforce any contract that directly or indirectly promotes sexual immorality.

Pearce v Brooks (1865–66) LR 1 Ex 213

Facts: The plaintiff coach-builders supplied the defendant with an ornamental brougham (a type of carriage), which was to be paid for by instalments. After one instalment had been paid, the brougham was returned in a damaged condition. The plaintiff brought a claim to recover the 15 guineas that was owed for early return of the brougham. At trial, the jury found that the plaintiff knew that the defendant was a prostitute and supplied the brougham in the knowledge that it was to be used by her to attract men.

Held: The Court of Exchequer held that the contract was illegal and that the plaintiff could not recover the unpaid instalment from the defendant.

Pollock CB:

'. . . I have always considered it as settled law, that any person who contributes to the performance of an illegal act by supplying a thing with the knowledge that it is going to be used for that purpose, cannot recover the price of the thing so supplied. If, to create that incapacity, it was ever considered necessary that the price should be bargained or expected to be paid out of the fruits of the illegal act (which I do not stop to examine), that proposition had been overruled by the cases I have referred to, and has now ceased to be law. Nor can any distinction be made between an illegal and an immoral purpose; the rule which is applicable to the matter is, *Ex turpi causâ non oritur actio*, and whether it is an immoral or an illegal purpose in which the plaintiff has participated, it comes equally within the terms of that maxim, and the effect is the same; no cause of action can arise out of either the one or the other.'

Pigott B:

'. . . If a woman, who is known to be a prostitute, wants an ornamental brougham, there can be very little doubt for what purpose she requires it . . . It cannot be necessary that the plaintiffs should look to the proceeds of the immoral act for payment; the law would indeed be blind if it supported a contract where the parties were silent as to the mode of payment, and refused to support a similar contract in the rare case where the parties were imprudent enough to express it. The plaintiffs knew the woman's mode of life, and where the means of payment would come from, and to require the proposed addition to the rule would be to make it futile.'

Bramwell B:

'I am of the same opinion. There is no doubt that the woman was a prostitute; no doubt to my mind that the plaintiffs knew it; there was cogent evidence of the fact, and the jury have so found. The only fact really in dispute is for what purpose was the brougham hired, and if for an immoral purpose, did the plaintiffs know it? At the trial I doubted whether there was evidence of this, but, for the reasons I have already stated, I think the jury were entitled to infer, as they did, that it was hired for the purpose of display, that is, for the purpose of enabling the defendant to pursue her calling, and that the plaintiffs knew it.

That being made out, my difficulty was, whether, though the defendant hired the brougham for that purpose, it could be said that the plaintiffs let it for the same purpose. In one sense, it was not for the same purpose. If a man were to ask for duelling pistols, and to say: "I think I shall fight a duel to-morrow", might not the seller answer: "I do not want to know your purpose; I have nothing to do with it; that is your business: mine is to sell the pistols, and I look only to the profit of trade". No doubt the act would be immoral, but I have felt a doubt whether it would be illegal; and I should still feel it, but that the authority of *Cannan v Bryce* 3 B & A 179 and *M'Kinnell v Robinson* 3 M & W 434 concludes the matter. In the latter case the plea does not say that the money was lent on the terms that the borrower should game with it; but only that it was borrowed by the defendant, and lent by the plaintiff "for the purpose of the defendant's illegally playing and gaming therewith". The case was argued by Mr Justice Crompton against the plea, and by Mr Justice Wightman in support of it; and the considered judgment of the Court was delivered by Lord Abinger, who says (p 441):

"As the plea states that the money for which the action is brought was lent for the purpose of illegally playing and gaming therewith, at the illegal game of 'Hazard', this money cannot be recovered back, on the principle, not for the first time laid down, but fully settled in the case of *Cannan v Bryce*. This principle is that the repayment of money, lent for the express purpose of accomplishing an illegal object, cannot be enforced."

This Court, then, following *Cannan v Bryce*, decided that it need not be part of the bargain that the subject of the contract should be used unlawfully, but that it is enough if it is handed over for the purpose that the borrower shall so apply it. We are, then, concluded by authority on the point; and, as I have no doubt that the finding of the jury was right, the rule must be discharged.'

It was crucial to the decision in *Pearce v Brooks* that both parties knew that the brougham was to be used for the purposes of prostitution. Had this not been known to the plaintiff it is highly likely that recovery would have been allowed. Indeed, in *Appleton v Campbell* (1826) 2 C & P 347; 172 ER 157 – a case concerning the recovery of board and lodging for a room rented to a prostitute – the court held that the plaintiff would only be denied recovery if he knew that the defendant intended to use the room to entertain her clients. There are thus two factors that are necessary for the contract to be unenforceable. First, it must be shown that the plaintiff knew that the other party was a prostitute; and second, it must be shown that the plaintiff knew that what was supplied under the contract was to be used for the purposes of prostitution.

13.3.2.2.8 *Contract prejudicial to the interests of state*

Contracts that are prejudicial to the interests of state are unenforceable on the ground of common law illegality. One obvious example of such a contract is a trading agreement between a British citizen and a foreign enemy in time of war (*Potts v Bell* (1800) 8 Term R 548). This category of common law illegality has now been recognised by Parliament in the Trading with the Enemy Act 1939. Contracts that tend to injure the United Kingdom's friendly relations with another state are also unenforceable for illegality. In *De Wutz v Hendricks* (1824) 2 Bing 314, the Court of Common Pleas held that it was illegal for persons residing in England to enter into agreements to raise money by way of loan for the purpose of supporting Greek citizens in revolting against their government. Best CJ said:

'It occurred to me at the trial that it was contrary to the law of nations (which in all cases of international law is adopted into the municipal code of every civilized country), for persons in England to enter into engagements to raise money to support the subjects of a government in amity with our own, in hostilities against their government, and that no right of action could arise out of such a transaction.'

The English courts will also refuse to enforce a contract if its performance would involve doing an act in a foreign and friendly State that violates the law of that State.

Regazzoni v KC Sethia Ltd [1958] AC 301

Facts: Sethia agreed to sell and deliver to Regazzoni at Genoa in Italy a quantity of jute bags. Both parties knew that these goods would be shipped from India to Genoa for resale in South Africa. At that time the export of jute from India to South Africa was prohibited by Indian law. The jute bags were not delivered by Sethia and Regazzoni brought an action for non-delivery of the goods.

Held: The House of Lords held that the contract was unenforceable on the ground that it was contrary to public policy and international comity.

Lord Reid:
'To my mind, the question whether this contract is enforceable by English courts is not, properly speaking, a question of international law. The real question is one of public policy in English law: but in considering this question we must have in mind the background of international law and international relationships often referred to as the comity of nations. This is not a case of a contract being made in good faith but one party thereafter finding that he cannot perform his part of the contract without committing a breach of foreign law in the territory of the foreign country. If this contract is held to be unenforceable, it should, in my opinion, be because from the beginning the contract was tainted so that the courts of this country will not assist either party to enforce it.

. . . [I]t was argued that, even if there be a general rule that our courts will take notice of foreign laws so that agreements to break them are unenforceable, that rule must be subject to exceptions and this Indian law is one of which we ought not to take notice. It may be that there are exceptions. I can imagine a foreign law involving persecution of such a character that we would regard an agreement to break it as meritorious. But this Indian law is very far removed from anything of that kind. It was argued that this prohibition of exports to South Africa was a hostile act against a Commonwealth country with which we have close relations, that such a prohibition is contrary to international usage, and that we cannot recognize it without taking sides in the dispute between India and South Africa. My Lords, it is quite impossible for a court in this country to set itself up as a judge of the rights and wrongs of a controversy between two friendly countries, we cannot judge the motives or the justifications of governments of other countries in these matters and, if we tried to do so, the consequences might seriously prejudice international relations. By recognizing this Indian law so that an agreement which involves a breach of that law within Indian territory is unenforceable we express no opinion whatever, either favourable or adverse, as to the policy which caused its enactment. In my judgment this appeal should be dismissed.'

The export of jute bags to South Africa was prohibited under Indian law, due to a continuing dispute between the two countries over the treatment of Indian nationals in South Africa. The House of Lords was unwilling to adjudicate on the merits of this law. Lord Reid did emphasise, however, that in some cases the foreign law would be so abhorrent to English principles of justice and liberty that, far from enforcing the law, the courts would regard an agreement to break it as 'meritorious'.

13.3.2.2.9 Contracts promoting corruption in public life

The final category of common law illegality concerns contracts that tend to promote corruption in public life. It is contrary to public policy to sell public offices and honours.

Parkinson v College of Ambulance Ltd [1925] 2 KB 1

Facts: Mr Harrison, the secretary of the College of Ambulance, fraudulently represented to Mr Parkinson that he would receive a knighthood if he made a large donation to the charity. Mr Parkinson, relying upon that representation, made a donation of £3,000. When he failed to receive the knighthood, Parkinson brought an action against the College and Mr Harrison to recover the money he had paid as money had and received or as damages for deceit or breach of contract.

Held: It was held that a contract for the purchase of a title was contrary to public policy. Since Mr Parkinson knew that he was entering into an illegal contract he could not recover the money he had paid to the charity.

Lush J:

'The contract, in my opinion, is one that could not be sanctioned or recognized in a Court of justice. Such a contract as that which the plaintiff and Harrison made is, in my judgment, an illegal and improper contract to enter into. I do not, of course, say that it involves the same degree of moral turpitude that an actually immoral contract involves; still less a contract to commit a crime . . . The money paid by the plaintiff was not paid as the price or "wages" of immorality. It was not paid as a bribe to Harrison. It was paid to a public charity, a meritorious service in itself. But the contract which was entered into is not a contract which one can describe as innocent in itself . . .

Now the first question to consider is this. The contract being against public policy, and being of the character that I have described, can the plaintiff still rely upon the fraud of Harrison and recover damages against him; and can he, as against the college, recover the £3,000 which the college has received through that fraud, as money had and received to his use? . . . [T]he plaintiff knew that he was entering into an illegal and improper contract. He was not deceived as to the legality of the contract he was making. How then can he say that he is excused? How can he say that he has suffered a loss through being defrauded into making a contract which he knew he ought never to have made? The answer is that he ought not to have made it. Where he was deceived was that he thought he would make a profit, derive a benefit from his unlawful act. He cannot be heard to say that. He has himself to blame for the loss that he has incurred. It is no excuse to say that Harrison was more blameworthy than he, which is all that he really can say. That being the position, the plaintiff is in this difficulty. He cannot recover damages either against Harrison or the college, because he is disclosing or setting up a contract which is unlawful, and which he had no right to make. For the same reason he cannot recover the £3,000 from the college as money had and received.'

13.4 THE EFFECT OF ILLEGALITY

Traditionally the courts have adopted a strict approach to the effect of illegality, refusing to enforce illegal contracts and refusing to order restitution of benefits conferred under such contracts. Lord Mansfield explained the principle in *Holman v Johnson* (1775) 1 Cowp 341:

'The objection, that a contract is immoral or illegal as between plaintiff and defendant sounds at all times very ill in the mouth of the defendant. It is not for his sake, however, that the objection is ever allowed; but it is founded in general principles of policy, which the defendant has the advantage of, contrary to the real justice, as between him and the plaintiff, by accident, if I may so say. The principle of public policy is this; *ex dolo malo non oritur actio*. No court will lend its aid to a man who founds his cause of action upon an immoral or an illegal act. If, from the plaintiff's own stating or otherwise, the cause of action appears to arise *ex turpi causa*, or the transgression of a positive law of this country, there the Court says he has no right to be assisted. It is upon that ground the Court goes; not for the sake of the defendant, but because they will not lend their aid to such a plaintiff. So if the plaintiff and defendant were to change sides, and the defendant was to bring his action against the plaintiff, the latter would then have the advantage of it; for where both are equally in fault, *potior est conditio defendentis*.'

Lord Mansfield pronounced two Latin maxims that were applicable to illegal contracts:

1. *ex dolo malo non oritur actio* – no right of action can have its origin in fraud;
2. *in pari delicto potior est conditio defendentis* – where the parties are equally at fault, the court will favour the defendant.

13.4.1 EXCEPTIONS TO THE STRICT RULES

These maxims are by no means universally applied, not least because the seriousness of the illegality often varies. The courts have admitted a number of exceptions to the two rules.

First, the courts have often shown themselves to be willing to enforce contracts tainted by illegality. In *Archbolds (Freightage) Ltd v S Spanglett Ltd* [1961] 1 QB 374, the Court of Appeal enforced a contract in favour of an innocent plaintiff who was unaware of the fact that the defendant intended to perform the contract in an illegal manner. In *21st Century Logistic Solutions Ltd (In Liquidation) v Madysen Ltd* (2004) 2 Lloyd's Rep 92, Field J enforced a contract in favour of a plaintiff who had participated in a VAT fraud on the basis that the illegality was 'too remote' from the contract to prevent its enforcement. It also appears that a contract will be enforced if the illegality is 'one-way' and the innocent party is ignorant of the facts that constitute the illegality. In *Bloxsome v Williams* (1824) 3 B & C 232, the plaintiff agreed to purchase a horse from the defendant for 39 guineas, subject to a warranty that the horse was not more than seven years old and sound. Unknown to the plaintiff, the defendant exercised trade as a horse dealer and for that reason the sale, which took place on a Sunday, was illegal under s 2 of the Sunday Observance Act 1677. The horse proved to be unsound and was in fact more than 17 years old. The defendant claimed that the plaintiff was barred from bringing a claim for breach of warranty because the contract was void for illegality. Bayley J rejected this argument:

'[T]he defendant was the person offending within the meaning of the statute by exercising his ordinary calling on the Sunday. He might be thereby deprived of any right to sue upon a contract so illegally made, and upon the same principle any other person knowingly aiding him in the breach of the law, by becoming a party to such a contract, with the knowledge that it was illegal, could not sue upon it. But in this case the fact that the defendant was a dealer in horses was not known to the plaintiff or his son, he therefore has not knowingly concurred in aiding the defendant to offend the law, and that being so, it is not competent to the defendant to set up his own breach of the law as an answer to this action.'

Bloxsome v Williams should be distinguished from *Re Mahmoud and Ispahani* (see above) where the statute had the effect of making the contract unlawful per se. This meant that the intentions of the parties were irrelevant and the plaintiff was denied recovery even though he had been unaware of the fact that the defendant did not possess a linseed oil licence. The harsh results of this rule can be relieved if the claimant is able to establish a claim on some alternative ground independent of the illegal contract. We will consider this in further detail below.

Second, the courts have recognised a number of exceptions to the rule against restitution of money and benefits conferred under an illegal contract. Recovery will generally be allowed in three situations: first, where the parties are not equally to blame; second, where the claimant can establish a claim on some alternative ground independent of the illegal contract; and, third, where the claimant withdraws from the contract before the illegal purpose has been carried into effect.

13.4.1.1 Parties not equally to blame

First, the claimant may be entitled to recover money paid under an illegal contract where the parties are not equally to blame. Such a situation is likely to arise if the policy behind the rule rendering the contract illegal concerns the protection of a class of people of whom the claimant is a member. In such situations it is sensible to allow the 'victim' to recover money paid under the contract.

Kiriri Cotton Co Ltd v Dewani [1960] AC 192

Facts: The defendant let a flat to the plaintiff in Kampala, Uganda. The lease was for a period of seven years and in consideration of a premium and a rent. Charging a premium was illegal under section 3 (2) of the Uganda Rent Restriction Ordinance 1949, although neither party knew this at the time. When the plaintiff discovered that the charging of a premium was illegal he sought to recover the money paid. The High Court of Uganda gave judgment for the plaintiff and this decision was affirmed by the Court of Appeal for Eastern Africa. The defendant appealed to the Privy Council.

Held: The Privy Council dismissed the appeal. The duty of observing the law was firmly placed on the landlord for the protection of the tenant. Because of this, the parties were not *in pari delicto* and the plaintiff could recover the premium.

Lord Denning:
'[I]f as between the two of them the duty of observing the law is placed on the shoulders of the one rather than the other – it being imposed on him specially for

the protection of the other then they are not in *pari delicto* and the money can be recovered back ... In applying these principles to the present case, the most important thing to observe is that the Rent Restriction Ordinance was intended to protect tenants from being exploited by landlords in days of housing shortage ... This is apparent from the fact that the penalty is imposed only on the landlord or his agent and not upon the tenant ... It may be that the tenant who pays money is an accomplice or an aider and abettor (see *Johnson v Youden* [1950] 1 KB 544 and section 3 of the Rent Restriction (Amendment) Ordinance, 1954), but he can hardly be said to be *in pari delicto* with the landlord. The duty of observing the law is firmly placed by the Ordinance on the shoulders of the landlord for the protection of the tenant: and if the law is broken, the landlord must take the primary responsibility. Whether it be a rich tenant who pays a premium as a bribe in order to "jump the queue", or a poor tenant who is at his wit's end to find accommodation, neither is so much to blame as the landlord who is using his property rights so as to exploit those in need of a roof over their heads.

Seeing then that the parties are not *in pari delicto*, the tenant is entitled to recover the premium by the common law: and it is not necessary to find a remedy given by the Ordinance, either expressly or by implication.'

A claimant will also be entitled to recover money paid or property transferred under an illegal contract if he entered into the contract as a result of the other party's fraudulent misrepresentation. In *Hughes v Liverpool Victoria Legal Friendly Society* [1916] 2 KB 482, the plaintiff took up five life insurance policies on the lives of persons in which she had no insurable interest. The defendants had fraudulently told her that the policies were valid and enforceable. When the plaintiff discovered that the policies were illegal and void, she sought to recover the premiums she had paid. The Court of Appeal held that she was entitled to recover because the parties were not *in pari delicto*. Bankes LJ said:

'Given fraud, the authorities seem to me to be all one way, namely, that an innocent plaintiff is entitled to say that he is not *in pari delicto* with the defendants whose agents by a false and fraudulent representation induced him to believe that the transaction was an innocent one, and one which was enforceable in law. On these grounds, in my opinion, the appellant is entitled to succeed.'

It is clear that, had the misrepresentation not been fraudulent, the plaintiff would have been denied recovery (*Harse v Pearl Life Assurance Co* [1904] 1 KB 558).

If the claimant was in a weak bargaining position, so that there was virtually no choice as to whether to enter into the contract, he may be entitled to restitution.

***Atkinson v Denby* (1862) 7 H & N 934; 158 ER 749**

Facts: The plaintiff, who was in financial difficulty, offered his creditors a composition agreement of five shillings in the pound. The defendant, who was one of the plaintiff's creditors refused to accept the agreement unless the plaintiff paid him £50, so gaining an advantage over the other creditors. The plaintiff paid, but later brought an action to recover the £50.

Held: The Exchequer Chamber held that although the agreement was an illegal contract, the oppression meant that the parties did not stand *in pari delicto*, and the plaintiff was entitled to recover the £50 in an action for money had and received.

Cockburn CJ:
'Where a debtor offers his creditors a composition, whereby they are all to receive the same proportionate amount in respect of their debts, it is contrary to the policy of the law to allow him to purchase the consent of one creditor by payment of his debt in full. It is said that both parties are *in pari delicto*. It is true that both are *in delicto*, because the act is a fraud upon the other creditors, but it is not *par delictum*, because the one has the power to dictate, the other no alternative but to submit.'

Restitution will also be available under an illegal contract if the claimant was unaware of the facts constituting the illegality. In *Oom v Bruce* (1810) 12 East 225, the plaintiffs entered into a contract of insurance with the defendants in respect of goods to be transported from St Petersburgh to London on board the ship 'Elbe'. Unknown to the plaintiffs, hostilities broke out between Great Britain and Russia on the day before the contract was concluded. This meant that the contract was void and unenforceable. The plaintiffs sought to recover the premiums they had paid under the illegal contract. Lord Ellenborough CJ said:

'[T]he plaintiffs had no knowledge of the commencement of hostilities by Russia, when they effected this insurance; and, therefore, no fault is imputable to them for entering into the contract; and there is no reason why they should not recover back the premiums which they have paid for an insurance from which, without any fault imputable to themselves, they could never have derived any benefit.'

It is also possible to recover a *quantum meruit* for work done under an illegal contract if the parties are not equally to blame. For example, in *Mohamed v Alaga* [2000] 1 WLR 1815 (the facts of which we have already considered above), the Court of Appeal held that although the contract was void for illegality the plaintiff could recover a *quantum meruit* for the work he had done in introducing Somali asylum seekers to the defendants. Lord Bingham MR explained the award as follows:

'[T]he plaintiff is not seeking to recover any part of the consideration payable under the unlawful contract, but simply a reasonable reward for professional services rendered. I accept that as an accurate description of what on this limited basis the plaintiff is, in truth, seeking. It is furthermore in my judgment relevant that the parties are not in a situation in which their blameworthiness is equal. The defendant is a solicitor's firm and bound by the rules. It should reasonably be assumed to know what the rules are and to comply with them. If, in truth, it made the agreement as alleged, then it would seem very probable that it acted in knowing disregard of professional rules binding upon it. By contrast the plaintiff, on the assumption made (which I have no difficulty in accepting), was ignorant that there was any reason why the defendant should not make the agreement which he says was made. In other commercial fields, after all, such agreements are common.'

13.4.1.2 Claim not based on the illegal contract

It is clear that a claimant can recover property transferred under an illegal contract if he is able to assert his claim without reliance on the illegality. He may do this in a number of ways.

13.4.1.2.1 *Legal title*
First, the claimant may be able to assert a claim based on retention of legal title. This will be possible under a contract of bailment or lease.

Bowmakers Ltd v Barnet Instruments Ltd [1945] KB 65

Facts: The defendants entered into three hire purchase agreements with the plaintiffs for the acquisition of machine tools. These agreements were illegal under a government order which required those disposing of machine tools to obtain a licence from the Minister of Supply. The plaintiffs had not obtained such a licence. The defendants sold the machines which were the subject of two of the agreements, but kept the others. They refused to return them to the plaintiffs, or to pay the hire. The plaintiffs brought a claim for conversion.

Held: The Court of Appeal held that the plaintiffs could establish their rights over the machine tools without the need to rely on the illegal contracts. The defendants' rights as bailees came to an end with their actions, and so the plaintiffs could assert their basic right of ownership.

Du Parcq LJ:
'The question, then, is whether in the circumstances the plaintiffs are without a remedy. So far as their claim in conversion is concerned, they are not relying on the hiring

---

agreements at all. On the contrary, they are willing to admit for this purpose that they cannot rely on them. They simply say that the machines were their property, and this, we think, cannot be denied. We understood Mr Gallop to concede that the property had passed from Smith to the plaintiffs, and still remained in the plaintiffs at the date of the conversion . . .

Why then should not the plaintiffs have what is their own? No question of the defendants' rights arises. They do not, and cannot, pretend to have had any legal right to possession of the goods at the date of the conversion. Their counsel has to rely, not on any alleged right of theirs, but on the requirements of public policy. He was entitled, and bound, to do so, although, as Lord Mansfield long ago observed, "The objection, that a contract is immoral or illegal as between plaintiff and defendant, sounds at all times very ill in the mouth of the defendant". "No court", Lord Mansfield added, "will lend its aid to a man who founds his cause of action upon an immoral or an illegal act": *Holman v Johnson* (1775) 1 Cowp 341, 343 . . . Prima facie, a man is entitled to his own property, and it is not a general principle of our law (as was suggested) that when one man's goods have got into another's possession in consequence of some unlawful dealings between them, the true owner can never be allowed to recover those goods by an action. The necessity of such a principle to the interests and advancement of public policy is certainly not obvious. The suggestion that it exists is not, in our opinion, supported by authority. It would, indeed, be astonishing if (to take one instance) a person in the position of the defendant in *Pearce v Brooks* (1866) LR 1 Ex 213, supposing that she had converted the plaintiff's brougham to her own use, were to be permitted, in the supposed interests of public policy, to keep it or the proceeds of its sale for her own benefit . . .

In our opinion, a man's right to possess his own chattels will as a general rule be enforced against one who, without any claim of right, is detaining them, or has converted them to his own use, even though it may appear either from the pleadings, or in the course of the trial, that the chattels in question came into the defendant's possession by reason of an illegal contract between himself and the plaintiff, provided that the plaintiff does not seek, and is not forced, either to found his claim on the illegal contract or to plead its illegality in order to support his claim.

Mr Gallop sought to derive assistance from the decision of the Court of Queen's Bench in *Taylor v Chester* (1869) LR 4 QB 309. The decision there was, however, entirely consonant with the view which we have expressed. It differed from the present case in one essential respect, since in that case the defendant had prima facie a right to possession of the half-note which the plaintiff claimed. She was holding it as a pledge to secure the payment of money which remained due. The plaintiff could only defeat her plea by showing that the money due had been lent for an immoral purpose, and this could not avail him since he was *in pari delicto* with her . . .'

Du Parcq LJ's reference to *Taylor v Chester* (1869) LR 4 QB 309 serves to illustrate how difficult it can be to establish a proprietary right without reference to the illegal contract. Taylor deposited half a £50 bank note with Chester by way of pledge to guarantee payment for a night of debauchery at Chester's brothel. Taylor sought to recover the half-note, but failed on the ground that he could not establish his proprietary right without reference to the illegal contract. In practice, this will often be the case.

Some commentators have suggested that similar problems arise on the facts of *Bowmakers*. While the bailee's right to possession was clearly brought to an end in relation to the first and third agreements following the resale of the machine tools, the same cannot be said for the defendants' right to possession under the second agreement. Here, the machine tools had not been resold; the defendant had merely refused to pay the hire charge on them. It was therefore impossible for the plaintiff to establish his proprietary right to the tools without reference to the illegal contract.

Hamson, CJ, 'Illegal Contracts and Limited Interests' (1949) 10 CLJ 249, 258–9

The question in *Bowmakers' Case* is: 'when can a bailor recover from the bailee under an illegal bailment the chattel bailed or its value?' The simplest answer would no doubt have been to treat an illegal bailment as a bailment at will and to permit the bailor always to recover the chattel upon mere demand. This answer has however been rejected in *Taylor v Chester* despite Herschell's argument; and the court in *Bowmakers' Case* accepts that decision as correct. The bailee accordingly still acquires, by virtue of the illegal bailment, some interest or property in the chattel other than one defeasible merely on demand. In *Bowmakers' Case*, however, the court goes on to hold that the bailor can recover the chattel bailed under an illegal hire purchase contract even though the only wrongful act by the bailee, in one of the instances, was his mere continuance in possession after demand made for the return of the chattel upon his failure to pay some instalments of the hire reserved by the bailment. Those instalments could not, by reason of the illegality, be recovered directly by action against the bailee. The difficulty is that the court, while declaring, as indeed it was bound to, that 'no claim founded on an illegal contract will be enforced' and that 'no technical meaning must be ascribed to the words "founded on an illegal contract" ', nevertheless appears to come very close, under cover of an action in tort, to enforcing the terms of the illegal bailment against the defendants.

It is suggested that, despite the court's laudable desire to avoid technicalities, the question who is to keep a chattel which has been subject of an illegal contract will continue to be decided with the aid of very abstruse technicalities, that the established principle that delivery or conveyance under an illegal contract effects a valid transfer of property or of an interest in property is itself no mean technicality and forms the basis of rules which are therefore likely to have a technical bias; and that in *Bowmakers'*

Case perhaps the court applied the technicalities with less consideration than they merited, and with results which both to the technician and to the layman are somewhat startling.

13.4.1.2.2 *Equitable title*

The decision in *Bowmakers' Case* was certainly controversial in relation to its application to the facts of the second agreement. Nevertheless, its central premise has been followed and applied by the House of Lords in relation to a claim based upon equitable title. In *Tinsley v Milligan* [1994] 1 AC 340, the House of Lords (by a bare majority) held that an equitable interest by way of resulting trust could be enforced by the defendant because it was possible to establish the equitable interest without reference to the illegal purpose. Lord Browne-Wilkinson said:

'Neither at law nor in equity will the court enforce an illegal contract which has been partially, but not fully, performed. However, it does not follow that all acts done under a partially performed contract are of no effect. In particular it is now clearly established that at law (as opposed to in equity), property in goods or land can pass under, or pursuant to, such a contract. If so, the rights of the owner of the legal title thereby acquired will be enforced, provided that the plaintiff can establish such title without pleading or leading evidence of the illegality. It is said that the property lies where it falls, even though legal title to the property was acquired as a result of the property passing under the illegal contract itself . . .

The position at law is well illustrated by the decision in *Bowmakers v Barnet Instruments* [1945] KB 65 . . . In my judgment to draw such distinctions between property rights enforceable at law and those which require the intervention of equity would be surprising. More than 100 years has elapsed since the administration of law and equity became fused. The reality of the matter is that, in 1993, English law has one single law of property made up of legal and equitable interests. Although for historical reasons legal estates and equitable estates have differing incidents, the person owning either type of estate has a right of property, a right *in rem* not merely a right *in personam*. If the law is that a party is entitled to enforce a property right acquired under an illegal transaction, in my judgment the same rule ought to apply to any property right so acquired, whether such right is legal or equitable . . .

A party to an illegality can recover by virtue of a legal or equitable property interest if, but only if, he can establish his title without relying on his own illegality. As applied in the present case, that principle would operate as follows. Miss Milligan established a resulting trust by showing that she had contributed to the purchase price of the house and that there was common understanding between her and Miss Tinsley that they owned the house equally. She had no need to allege or prove *why* the house was conveyed into the name of Miss Tinsley alone, since that fact was irrelevant to her claim: it was enough to show that the house was in fact vested in Miss Tinsley alone. The illegality only emerged at all because Miss Tinsley sought to raise it. Having proved these facts, Miss Milligan had raised a presumption of resulting trust. There was no evidence to rebut that presumption. Therefore Miss Milligan should succeed.'

13.4.1.2.3 *Tort*

The claimant may also be able to make a claim in the law of tort if he is able to assert his right without reliance on the illegal contract.

Saunders v Edwards [1987] 1 WLR 1116

Facts: The plaintiffs agreed to purchase a London flat from the defendant for £45,000 in reliance on the defendant's fraudulent misrepresentation that the flat included a roof top terrace. During the pre-contract negotiations the parties agreed to apportion the purchase price between the chattels and the flat. A value of £5,000 was placed on the chattels even though they were worth much less than that. This was done in order to save £300 on stamp duty. When the plaintiffs discovered that they had no right to use the roof terrace they brought an action for fraudulent misrepresentation. The defendant contended that the plaintiffs were barred from bringing such a claim because the contract was tainted by illegality.

Held: The Court of Appeal held that, although the plaintiffs' performance of the contract may have been tainted by illegality, they could still bring a claim for fraudulent misrepresentation since they did not need to rely on the illegal contract.

Bingham LJ:
'Even if it be assumed that these plaintiffs deliberately inflated the value of the fixtures and fittings and reduced the value of the flat so as unlawfully to avoid payment of stamp duty properly payable, I do not think that the plaintiffs' claim can be said to arise from that unlawfulness. The action arises from the first defendant's fraud, not theirs. The loss which they have suffered as a result of the first defendant's fraudulent misrepresentation was neither greater nor smaller than it would have been however the purchase price had been apportioned. Their claim is a very simple one. They overpaid because they were deceived. Public policy does not in my view require that the defendant should be left to enjoy the fruits of his deceit simply because the plaintiffs in their turn deceived the Inland Revenue (if they did).'

It is thus clear that an independent claim in the tort of deceit can be brought so long as the claimant does not need to rely on the illegal contract.

13.4.1.2.4 A collateral contract

A final possibility is that the court may allow the claimant to assert a 'collateral contract'. This contract must be independent of the original transaction, otherwise it will also be tainted with illegality. In *Fisher v Bridges* (1854) 3 E & B 642, the plaintiff agreed to convey land to the defendant for a purpose known to be illegal (the land was to be sold by way of lottery). The defendant still owed money under the transaction and so executed a deed, promising to pay the plaintiff the outstanding sum. The Court of Exchequer held that this deed was unenforceable because it was tainted by the illegality of the original transaction. *Fisher v Bridges* can be contrasted with the facts of *Strongman v Sincock* where the Court of Appeal held that the collateral agreement was genuinely independent of the original transaction.

Strongman (1945) Ltd v Sincock [1955] 2 QB 525

Facts: The defendant architect employed the plaintiff builders to convert some of his old buildings into modern homes. He promised orally that he would obtain all the licences necessary under regulation 56A of the Defence (General) Regulations 1939. The defendant did obtain a licence but it only covered one third of the cost of the works. The defendant paid one third of the contract price for the work performed but refused to pay the remainder. The plaintiffs brought a claim for the outstanding sum. The defendant resisted the claim, insisting that the sum could not be recovered since the underlying contract was illegal.

Held: The Court of Appeal held that, although the main contract was illegal, the plaintiff's assurance that he would obtain the necessary licences amounted to a collateral contract, which was not tainted by illegality. Since the defendants had not been morally to blame for the failure to obtain the necessary licences, they could bring a claim under the collateral agreement.

Denning LJ:
'Let me say first that the builders cannot sue here on the contract to do the work, which was done in 1948 and 1949. At that time it was unlawful under defence Regulation 56A for the work to be done without a proper licence. Licences were only in force to the amount of £2,150. When work was done to the value of over £6,000 the builders and the architect were all guilty of an offence for which they might have been prosecuted. Under many decisions in this court it has been held that a builder doing work without a licence cannot recover under the contract.

The builders seek to overcome this objection by saying that there was a warranty, or (putting it more accurately) a promise by the architect that he would get supplementary licences, or that if he failed to get them he would stop the work. The builders say that on the faith of that promise they did the work, and as the promise was broken they can recover damages in respect of it.

The first question raised before us was whether there was such a promise, or warranty, as it was called. On this point the finding of the official referee was this: "I am satisfied that when the plaintiffs agreed to do work for the defendant he assured them that he would get all licences which were necessary, and that if the work exceeded the amounts of the original licences he would apply for supplementary licences. I am also satisfied that he said that if he failed to get a supplementary licence he would instruct them to stop work. Consequently I regard the plea of warranty as being well founded." . . .

The second question is whether the builders can recover in law on this collateral promise. The promise itself was not illegal, but it is said that damages cannot be recovered for the breach of it. It is said that, if damages could be recovered, it would be an easy way of getting round the law about illegality. This does not alarm me at all. It is, of course, a settled principle that a man cannot recover for the consequences of his own unlawful act, but this has always been confined to cases where the doer of the act knows it to be unlawful or is himself in some way morally culpable. It does not apply when he is an entirely innocent party . . . I think the law is that, although a man may have been guilty of an offence which is absolutely prohibited so that he is answerable in a criminal court, nevertheless if he has been led to commit that offence by the representation or by the promise of another, then in those circumstances he can recover damages for fraud if there is fraud, or for breach of promise or warranty if he prove such to have been given, provided always that he himself has not been guilty of culpable negligence on his part disabling him from that remedy.

[Counsel for the defendant] referred us to the observations of this court in *In re Mahmoud & Ispahani* [1921] 2 KB 716. On a consideration of that case it seems to me that the court only decided that no action lay upon the contract for the purchase of goods. They did not decide whether there was an action for fraud or breach of promise or warranty: and I do not think that their observations were intended to express any view on the matter.

The third question is whether the plaintiffs were guilty of negligence. I can well see that if there was culpable negligence on the part of the person seeking damages, he might not be entitled to recover . . . It was contended before us by [counsel for the defendant] that on the facts of this case there must have been negligence and that in point of law the official referee ought to have found it. I think not. The official referee found: "I do not consider that the plaintiffs in the present case have done an immoral act, nor were they negligent in not insisting on the production of supplementary licences. They had done a great deal of other work for the defendant without any question being raised with regard to the sufficiency of the licences".

As I said at the beginning of this case, it comes very ill from the mouth of the defendant to raise this point as against the plaintiffs. His attitude was well shown by an observation which he made to the solicitor, Mr. Ratcliffe. He said: "If the Nicholls can be bluffed they deserve to lose their money". In other words, he was saying: "If they were fools enough to trust in me, they ought to lose their money". That is a very wrong attitude for a professional man, an architect, to take up. It shows quite clearly that on his own admission he has misled them and now seeks to turn it to his own advantage. In my judgment, his objection fails. On the findings of the official referee, the plaintiffs were entirely innocent people who were led into this unfortunate illegality by the representation of the architect, amounting to a collateral contract, that he would get the licences. That contract not having been fulfilled, I see no objection in point of law to the plaintiffs recovering the damages, and I think that the appeal should be dismissed.'

Although the Court of Appeal reached an instinctively just result, the decision in the case raises a number of difficulties. First, what was the consideration for the architect's promise under the collateral contract? Presumably it was the fulfilment of the building obligation, but the builders were already obliged to do this under the main contract (*Stilk v Myrick* (1809) 2 Camp 317). The builders could argue, of course, that the main agreement was void for illegality and therefore they were under no obligation to do the work, but this still leaves us with the problem that it is very odd to speak of a 'collateral contract' when there was no main contract to which it was 'collateral'.

Second, the decision is difficult to reconcile with the outcome in *Re Mahmoud & Ispahani* [1921] 2 KB 716. Denning LJ sought to distinguish *Re Mahmoud* on the ground that the court in that case had not been asked to consider whether there had been a breach of a collateral warranty. Does that mean that recovery would have been possible had the plaintiff argued for the existence of a collateral warranty? Professor Treitel (*The Law of Contract*, 2003, 11th edn, p 489, London: Sweet & Maxwell) has argued that this should not follow:

'[T]o allow the innocent party to sue on a "collateral warranty" in a case like *Re Mahmoud and Ispahani* would be quite inconsistent with the rationale of the rule denying him a remedy on the contract. It would be mere sophistry to say: we will protect the public interest by denying a remedy on the contract, but we will also protect the innocent claimant by giving him as good a remedy on a collateral warranty. This remedy should be granted only where it will provide no incentive to do the illegal act and where the defendant was not careless.'

The collateral contract is a powerful weapon in the hands of the courts. In *Strongman v Sincock*, Birkett LJ expressed his view that 'it is a very good thing that in almost every case where a litigant comes without merit the court does its very best to see that justice is done.' The collateral contract is a judicial device for ensuring that justice is done. As such, its scope and application will be strictly limited.

13.4.1.3 Illegal purpose not yet carried out

Third, a claimant may be able to recover money paid or goods transferred under an illegal contract if he is able to show that he has withdrawn from the contract before it has been substantially performed. This is sometimes referred to as the *locus poenitentiae* ('the space for repentance'). There are two requirements; the withdrawal must be:

(a)   on time; and

(b)   on a voluntary basis.

13.4.1.3.1 On time

Withdrawal must be made before the illegal purpose is carried out.

Taylor v Bowers (1876) 1 QBD 291

Facts: The plaintiff was in dire financial circumstance. In order to defraud his creditors he made a fictitious assignment of his stock to a friend. Meetings of the creditors had already taken place but no compromise had been reached. In the meantime, the friend had mortgaged the stock to the defendant who was aware of the fictitious assignment. The plaintiff sought to recover the stock from the defendant.

Held: The Court of Appeal held that, because the fraudulent purpose had not been carried out, the plaintiff was not relying on the illegal transaction and was therefore entitled to recover his goods.

Mellish LJ:

'If money is paid or goods delivered for an illegal purpose, the person who had so paid the money or delivered the goods may recover them back before the illegal purpose is carried out; but if he waits till the illegal purpose is carried out, or if he seeks to enforce the illegal transaction, in neither case can he maintain an action; the law will not allow that to be done. In the present action the facts come within the first alternative; and I am of opinion that the Queen's Bench Division has properly held, that the plaintiff does not require the aid of the illegal transaction, but is really bringing the action to set it aside.'

The case was followed by the Court of Appeal in *Tribe v Tribe* [1996] Ch 107, where the plaintiff transferred shares to his son in order to keep them out of the hands of his landlords who were expected to be seeking substantial contributions towards the cost of repairs on property rented by the father. In the event, the repairs were not required, and the plaintiff sought to recover the shares from his son. The Court of Appeal, following *Taylor v Bowers* and *Tinsley v Milligan*, allowed the father to recover the shares. Millett LJ said: 'The transferor can lead evidence of the illegal purpose whenever it is necessary for him to do so provided that he has withdrawn from the transaction before the illegal purpose has been *wholly or partly* carried into effect.'

When the illegal purpose has been substantially carried into effect, recovery will not be allowed.

Kearley v Thomson (1890) 24 QBD 742

Facts: The defendant firm of solicitors was acting on behalf of a creditor against a bankrupt named Clarke. The plaintiff, a friend of Clarke's, agreed to pay the defendants their costs, in return for which they would neither appear at the public examination of Clarke, nor oppose his order for discharge. The defendants, on receiving the promised payment, did not appear at Clarke's examination, in accordance with their illegal agreement. The plaintiff subsequently changed his mind and sought to recover the money he had paid prior to the application for Clarke's discharge.

Held: The Court of Appeal held that the illegal purpose of the agreement concerned interference with the course of justice. Since this purpose had been substantially achieved, the withdrawal came too late.

Fry LJ:
'What is the condition of things if the illegal purpose has been carried into effect in a material part, but remains unperformed in another material part? As I have already pointed out in the present case, the contract was that the defendants should not appear at the public examination of the bankrupt or at the application for an order of discharge. It was performed as regards the first; but the other application has not yet been made. Can it be contended that, if the illegal contract has been partly carried into effect and partly remains unperformed, the money can still be recovered? In my judgment it cannot be so contended with success . . . I hold, therefore, that where there has been a partial carrying into effect of an illegal purpose in a substantial manner, it is impossible though there remains something not performed, that the money paid under that illegal contract can be recovered back.'

13.4.1.3.2 *On a voluntary basis*

The second requirement for a valid withdrawal is that it must be voluntary. If the purpose of the contract is simply frustrated by the intervention of the police or a third party, or by the other party's breach of contract, recovery will not be allowed.

Bigos v Bousted [1951] 1 All ER 92

Facts: The plaintiff, in contravention of s 1 of the Exchange Control Act 1947, agreed to supply the defendant with the equivalent of £150 in Italian currency. As security for

---

his promise, the defendant deposited with the plaintiff a share certificate for 140 shares in a company. The plaintiff failed to supply the Italian currency and the defendant's wife and daughter had to return to England sooner than they would have returned had they received the money. The defendant sought to recover the share certificate arguing that, although the contract was an illegal one, it was still executory and therefore he was entitled to withdraw from it and obtain restitution.

Held: The court held that the reason that the illegal transaction was not carried out was due to the plaintiff's dishonesty, not to any repentance on the part of the defendant. Therefore, the defendant was not entitled to recover the share certificate.

Pritchard J:

'I confess that there was a time when I thought it would be right to apply to the facts of this case the reasoning of the decision in *Taylor v Bowers*, but, having considered all the authorities, I do not take that view. I think that what is to be extracted from the authorities may be stated as follows. I think that they show, first, that there is a distinction between what may, for convenience, be called the repentance cases, on the one hand, and the frustration cases, on the other hand. If a particular case may be held to fall within the category of repentance cases, I think the law is that the court will help a person who repents, provided his repentance comes before the illegal purpose has been substantially performed. If I were able, in this case, to take the view that the defendant had brought himself within that sphere of the authorities, it might well be that I would have been able to help him by saying that his repentance had come before the illegal purpose had been substantially performed, but I do not take that view. I think, however, that this case falls within the category of cases which I call the frustration case . . .

On the return of the defendant's wife and daughter from Italy the whole project fell to the ground. There was no repentance which caused the contract not to be carried out. The defendant desired that it should be carried out until the plaintiff failed to do so, and, when she failed, the defendant's wife and daughter had to return to England because, as the result of the plaintiff's failure, they could no longer afford to stay in Italy. By the plaintiff's failure the whole venture was frustrated, and, in those circumstances, I do not think that the reason for this illegal contract not having come to fruition was the repentance of the defendant. The reason was that the whole object of the contract was frustrated by the failure on the part of the plaintiff to provide the lira which she had contracted to provide in Italy.'

13.4.2 SEVERANCE

In most cases, the illegality only taints part of the agreement. In such situations, the courts have the jurisdiction to sever the illegal part so long as the remainder of the agreement is left substantially intact (*Henry Pigot's Case* (1572–1616) 11

Co Rep 26; 77 ER 1177). If the entire contract is tainted by the illegality, severance will not be possible. In *Napier v National Business Agency* [1951] 2 All ER 264, the plaintiff was employed to act as the defendant's secretary and accountant at a salary of £13 a week together with £6 a week for expenses. Both parties knew that the plaintiff's expenses would never reach £6 a week, but this provision was included in order to defraud the Inland Revenue. Following his summary dismissal, the plaintiff brought a claim for payment in lieu of notice. The Court of Appeal denied the claim on the basis that the whole agreement was tainted by illegality. Sir Raymond Evershed MR said:

'[T]he further point arises whether the terms of the agreement relating to the two branches of the plaintiff's reward can be severed, ie, whether the plaintiff can reject the tainted part of the contract relating to the £6 a week for expenses, and sue only, as he has done, in respect of the £13 a week for remuneration simply so called. I think the answer to that point is in the negative. The contract is, to my mind, not severable. It cannot properly be treated as consisting of two separate and distinct bargains, and, therefore, although it is true that the plaintiff sues only in respect of £13 a week, he is really seeking to enforce a contract which is tainted to the extent I have mentioned. It being so tainted, I think that the court will not enforce it at his suit.'

By contrast, in *Carney v Herbert* [1985] AC 301, severance was permitted. The case concerned a contract for the sale of shares by instalments. The sellers asked for security for the payment of these instalments but the security given was illegal under s 67 of the Companies Act 1961. The Privy Council held that the illegal security could be severed from the contract for the purchase of shares. The defendant therefore remained liable to pay the purchase price of the shares. Lord Brightman concluded:

'The plaintiffs wanted only the purchase money. It made no difference to the plaintiffs, or to the nature of the transaction, what security was provided so long as it was satisfactory security. The mortgage did not go to the heart of the transaction, and its elimination would leave unchanged the subject matter of the contract and the primary obligations of the vendors and the purchaser. The debenture is therefore capable of being severed from the remainder of the transaction and its illegality does not taint the whole contract. There is no public policy objection to the enforcement of the contract from which the debenture has been divorced.'

The possibility of severance most commonly arises in cases concerning contracts in restraint of trade. These will be discussed in the following chapter and we will delay our discussion of severance until then.

13.5 PROPOSALS FOR REFORM

It is widely accepted that there is a need for reform of this area. In 1999, the Law Commission put out a consultation paper (Consultation Paper No 154, *Illegal Transactions: The Effect of Illegality on Contracts and Trusts*, 1999) suggesting ways in which this could be achieved. It criticised the current law in the following terms (at para 2.2):

'The rules relating to when illegality is a defence to the enforcement of contractual obligations are numerous and complex. It is difficult to extract the various principles applied by the courts and some of the decisions are hard to reconcile.'

The Commission's provisional proposal is that the current rules on illegality should be replaced by a structured discretion. This is summarised in paras 1.18–1.21 of the Consultation Paper:

1.18 Our broad provisional proposal is that the present technical and complex rules governing the effect of illegality in relation to contracts and trusts should be replaced by a discretion. Under that discretion the court could decide whether or not to enforce an illegal transaction, to recognise that property rights have been transferred or created by it, or to allow benefits conferred under it to be recovered. We do not, however, recommend that the court should have an open-ended discretion to produce whatever it considers to be the 'just' solution. That is, we provisionally propose that, generally, illegality should continue to be used only as a defence to what would otherwise be a standard claim for a contractual or restitutionary remedy or for the recognition of legal or equitable property rights. We discuss one possible exception to this general rule (withdrawal during the *locus poenitentiae*), where illegality may act as a cause of action.

1.19 We also provisionally recommend that the proposed discretion should be structured, in order to provide greater certainty and guidance. We therefore provisionally propose that, in exercising its discretion, a court should consider: (i) the seriousness of the illegality involved; (ii) the knowledge and intention of the party seeking to enforce the illegal transaction, seeking the recognition of legal or equitable rights under it, or seeking to recover benefits conferred under it; (iii) whether refusing to allow standard rights and remedies would deter illegality; (iv) whether refusing to allow standard rights and remedies would further the purpose of the rule which renders the transaction illegal; and (v) whether refusing to allow standard rights and remedies would be proportionate to the illegality involved.

1.20 Where, however, a statute has expressly provided what should be the effect of the involvement of illegality on a transaction, we provisionally recommend that our proposed discretion should not apply. That is, we do not suggest that the courts should be able to use the discretion to override the express provisions of a statute.

1.21 We consider that these provisional proposals would have two major advantages over the present law. First, a court would be able to reach its decision on the facts of a particular case using open and explicit reasoning, giving full effect to the relevance of the illegality on the transaction. Secondly, we believe that the provisional proposals would be likely to result in illegality being used less frequently to deny a plaintiff his or her usual rights or remedies. That is, under the discretion, illegality would only act as a defence where there is a clear and justifiable public interest that it should do so.

The proposals are to be welcomed, although it seems rather doubtful that legislative reform will follow. One of the main criticisms levelled at the proposed 'structured discretion' is that it will produce uncertainty and unpredictability in commercial transactions. These concerns are somewhat overstated, however, as Professor Buckley has shown.

Buckley, RA, 'Illegal transactions: chaos or discretion?'
(2000) 20 LS 155, 179–180

The difficulties surrounding the definition of an illegal transaction, and the consequent problem of ensuring that the *scope* of any proposed reform is clear and unambiguous, might be prayed in aid by those who fear that a regime based upon statutory discretion might have a wider impact than intended and infect commercial law with destabilising uncertainty. More specifically, opponents of reform might object that rescuing parties to illegal transactions from the consequences of their activities could paradoxically give preferential treatment to such parties as contrasted with those whose contracts fail for other reasons. The importance of ensuring that property rights remain clear, and that the policies underlying findings of illegality are not disregarded or compromised, might also be advanced as reasons for proceeding with caution. But these arguments represent a challenge to get the proposals right rather than overwhelming arguments against reform. The high degree of uncertainty which already characterises this area is apt to impose disproportionate penalties upon parties to commercial transactions. And the confused doctrines of 'reliance' and locus poenitentiae cause confusion in relation to the enforceability of property rights. Overall, the existing law in England relating to illegality in contract is in a chaotic state; leading the House of Lords in *Tinsley* v *Milligan* to call for an examination by the Law Commission. In all the Commonwealth countries – now including England – in which reform has been considered, an approach centred upon the conferring of an overt judicial discretion has been perceived to be the only route forward. Judicial attempts to compress the infinite variety of situations, with all their complexity and differing degrees of gravity, into fixed rules have merely resulted in artificial technicalities and in arbitrariness.

In New Zealand the Illegal Contracts Act 1970 appears to have worked well, and not to have led to the uncertainty which some commentators feared. This is so notwithstanding the inclusion of the power to apportion losses in illegality cases, which the Law Commission in England has provisionally rejected.

13.6 ADDITIONAL READING

Buckley, R, 'Illegality in contract and conceptual reasoning' (1983) Anglo-American LR 280.

Cohen, N, 'The quiet revolution in the enforcement of illegal contracts', [1994] LMCLQ 163.

Coote, B, 'Another look at *Bowmakers v Barnet Instruments*' (1972) 35 MLR 38.

Enonchong, N, 'Title claims and illegal transactions' (1995) 111 LQR 135.

Furmston, M, 'The analysis of illegal contracts' (1966) 16 U of Tor LJ 267.

Grodecki, JK, '*In pari delicto potior est conditio defendentis*' (1955) 71 LQR 254.

McLauchlan, DW, 'Contract and commercial law reform in New Zealand' (1984–1985) 11 NZULR 36.

Stewart, A, 'Contractual illegality and the recognition of proprietary interests' (1986) 1 JCL 134.

Stowe, H, 'The "unruly horse" has bolted: *Tinsley v Milligan*' (1994) 57 MLR 441.

Chapter 14

CONTRACTS IN RESTRAINT OF TRADE

14.1 INTRODUCTION

The common law has historically been opposed to agreements that seek to limit an individual's freedom to exercise his/her lawful trade or profession. This position is rather conflicting, however, because the only means by which the law is capable of protecting an individual's freedom to trade is by restricting his/her freedom to contract. This has been explained by Professor Stephen Smith ('Reconstructing Restraint of Trade' (1995) 15 OJLS 565) in the following extract:

'The doctrine of restraint of trade is a strange beast. Its role in contract law is traditionally understood to be that of denying validity to contracts that unduly restrain the freedom of one or both of the contracting parties. The doctrine appears to place non-procedural limitations on freedom of contract and, moreover, to place these limitations because of a concern for the contracting parties' freedom. A concern for freedom is being used, it appears, to limit freedom . . .

Refusing to enforce unnecessary restraints can be defended on either of two grounds. First, it can be defended on the ground that autonomy is a crucial ingredient in individual well-being and that the law should not help individuals to give up future autonomy unnecessarily. Some limitations on future freedom are an inevitable byproduct of contracting (itself defensible for the way it helps individuals achieve goals autonomously), but contracts in which freedom is unnecessarily relinquished should not be facilitated. Second, it can be defended on the ground that unnecessary restraints hinder the free flow of labour and resources crucial to the efficient functioning of a market economy. My own view is that the first explanation is preferable, but for our purposes the differences between the explanations are not material.'

The common-law's response to contracts in restraint of trade has been rather piece-meal. A number of contracts and contractual provisions that have been regarded as being 'in restraint of trade' have been treated as being illegal, for reasons of public policy, and therefore unenforceable. This approach has mainly been applied in the context of contracts of employment and contracts for the sale of a business, where limits have been placed on the economic activity which the employee or the seller is free to engage in after leaving the employment or selling the business. More recently, the approach has been applied to contracts of 'exclusive dealing', where a party commits themselves to obtain all supplies of a particular product from a single supplier. It has been left to Parliament and the European Union (EU) to deal with the broader issues of 'anti-competitive' practice, such as cartels and monopolies. There is now extensive legislation to control this area, mostly contained in the Competition Act 1998.

In this chapter we will deal first with the common law rules on 'restraint of trade'. We will consider the elements of a restraint of trade claim and the main areas in which the doctrine operates. We will then consider the doctrine of severance and the situations in which the courts might be willing to sever the offending provisions, leaving the remainder of the contract intact. Finally, we will examine the statutory provisions that operate in this area.

14.2 THE ELEMENTS OF A CLAIM

From as early as the seventeenth century, the English courts have held contracts in restraint of trade to be prima facie void.

Claygate v Batchelor (1602) Owen 143; 74 ER 961

In debt upon a bond of thirty pound, the condition was, that if Robert Batchelor, son to the defendant, did use the trade of haberdasher as journeyman servant, or apprentice, or as a master, within the county of Kent, within the Cities of Canterbury and

Rochester, within four years after the date, that then, if he pay twenty pound upon request, the obligation to be voyd. And all the justices agreed that the condition was against law, and then all is voyd, for it is against the liberty of a free-man, and against the statute of Magna Carta cap. 20 and is against the commonwealth. And Anderson said, that he might as well bind himself, that he would not go to church. And judgment was given against the plaintiff.

The current position was authoritatively stated by Lord MacNaghten in *Nordenfelt v Maxim Nordenfelt*.

Nordenfelt v Maxim Nordenfelt [1894] AC 535

Facts: Mr Thorsten Nordenfelt, a Swedish gentleman, had established in England and Sweden a valuable business in the manufacture of machine guns. His customers were few in number but truly global including most national governments. In 1886, he sold the business to a company which subsequently transferred the business to Maxim Nordenfelt in 1888. Mr Nordenfelt entered into a restrictive covenant with Maxim Nordenfelt stating that he would not for a term of twenty-five years from the date of the incorporation of the company, 'engage except on behalf of the company either directly or indirectly in the trade or business of a manufacturer of guns, gun-mountings or carriages, gunpowder explosives or ammunition'. Mr Nordenfelt broke the covenant contending that it was void in law as being a covenant in restraint of trade.

Held: The House of Lords affirmed the decision of the Court of Appeal, holding that the covenant, though unrestricted as to space, was not wider than was necessary to protect the interests of Maxim Nordenfelt. Furthermore, it was not injurious to the public interest.

Lord Macnaghten:
'In the age of Queen Elizabeth all restraints of trade, whatever they were, general or partial, were thought to be contrary to public policy, and therefore void (*Colgate v Bacheler* Cro Eliz 872). In time, however, it was found that a rule so rigid and far-reaching must seriously interfere with transactions of every-day occurrence. Traders could hardly venture to let their shops out of their own hands; the purchaser of a business was at the mercy of the seller; every apprentice was a possible rival. So the rule was relaxed . . .

The true view at the present time I think, is this: The public have an interest in every person's carrying on his trade freely: so has the individual. All interference with individual liberty of action in trading, and all restraints of trade of themselves, if there is nothing more, are contrary to public policy, and therefore void. That is the general rule. But there are exceptions: restraints of trade and interference with individual liberty of action may be justified by the special circumstances of a particular case. It is a sufficient justification, and indeed it is the only justification, if the restriction is reasonable – reasonable, that is, in reference to the interests of the parties concerned and reasonable in reference to the interests of the public, so framed and so guarded as to afford adequate protection to the party in whose favour it is imposed, while at the same time it is in no way injurious to the public. That, I think, is the fair result of all the authorities.'

The basic presumption is that contracts or provisions within a contract, which are in restraint of trade, are unenforceable. That presumption can be rebutted, however, if it is shown that the restraint is reasonable, both between the parties themselves and in relation to the public interest. There are thus three questions to be asked:

1. Does the restraint of trade doctrine apply?
2. Is the restraint reasonable between the parties?
3. Is the restraint reasonable in the public interest?

We will consider each of these questions in turn.

14.2.1 THE SCOPE OF THE RESTRAINT OF TRADE DOCTRINE

All contracts are prima facie restrictive. If I agree to sell you my house I cannot then sell it to someone else without breaking my contract with you. For this reason it has traditionally been assumed that the scope of the restraint of trade doctrine is extremely limited. For many years, it was assumed that it only applied to three categories of contractual provision: (1) post-employment covenants; (2) sale of business covenants; and (3) horizontal agreements, for example, a cartel arrangement between suppliers to fix prices. This view was overturned, however, by the Court of Appeal in the landmark case of *Petrofina (GT Britain) Ltd v Martin* [1966] Ch 146. The case concerned a solus agreement, which bound the defendant to sell only the plaintiff's products for a period of 12 years in exchange for a discount on the price of petrol. The Court of Appeal held that the agreement fell within the scope of the restraint of trade doctrine. Lord Denning MR said:

'Every member of the community is entitled to carry on any trade or business he chooses and in such manner as he thinks most desirable in his own interests, so long as he does nothing unlawful: with the consequence that any contract which interferes with the free exercise of his trade or business, by restricting him in the work he may do for others, or the arrangements which he may make with others, is a contract in restraint of trade. It is invalid unless it is reasonable as between the parties and not injurious to the public interest.

[Counsel for the plaintiff] sought to limit the width of this principle by reference to the *kind* of restraint. He quoted *Cheshire and Fifoot's The Law of*

Contract (6th edn (1964), p 324), and said that contracts in restraint of trade are of three kinds: first, by an employee who agrees that, after leaving his employment, he will not compete against his employer; second, by the vendor of a business who agrees that he will not carry on a business in competition with the purchaser; third, by a group of merchants who form a combine to restrict output or to fix prices, or the like. Those are the three kinds usually found in the books. But the law is not limited to those three. There is a fourth kind, where a tradesman agrees to limit his mode of trade, such as to execute orders for one particular person only: see *Young v Timmins* (1831) 1 Cr & J 331; *Collins v Locke* (1879) 4 App Cas 674; or to make one particular kind of machine only: see *Jones v Lees* (1856) 1 H & N 189, and there may be more kinds. The categories of restraint of trade are not closed. As methods of trading change, so do the areas of restraint expand. The law, if it is to fulfil its purpose, must keep pace with them.'

Following the decision of the Court of Appeal in *Petrofina*, there have been calls to scrap the scope test altogether. Justice Heydon ('The Frontiers of the Restraint of Trade Doctrine' (1969) 85 LQR 229, 250–251) has written:

'A limited application of the restraint of trade doctrine substantially stultifies the courts' power to deal with a wide range of evils which a sophisticated legal system should not tolerate and which English law in many instances does not tolerate. Since the evils it does tolerate and those it does not arise in substantially the same circumstances, the restraint of trade doctrine should be applied wherever trade is restrained in any way. Any limitation on the doctrine is analogous to the exclusion of relevant evidence: it may cause injustice and should only be done for some good policy reason. None exists; nor has any limitation suggested so far been satisfactory . . . The litigation that will be conducted about [the scope of the doctrine] may perhaps be slightly less in quantity than that which would result if the restraint of trade doctrine were of universal application, but it will be of a very unsatisfactory kind. It will lead to the worst kind of law – unprincipled, or based on dubious principles, full of anomalies and exceptions, and in the last resort incomprehensibly complicated.'

If the scope test were to be scrapped this would mean that all contract terms would be subjected to the reasonableness test. Since a restraint is unreasonable if it is unnecessary for achieving the contract's objective, this will radically change the face of English contract law. A large number of terms would fail this reasonableness test, particularly in commercial contracts that often contain unnecessary supplementary provisions. Professor Stephen Smith ('Reconstructing Restraint of Trade' (1995) 15 OJLS 565, 570) has contended:

'[A]ny type of contract is capable of unreasonably restraining future freedom. But it does not follow that all contracts should be scrutinized on this basis. Four general considerations, considerations that are significant whenever courts contemplate scrutinizing contractual terms, must first be taken into account. First, invalidating a contractual provision upsets the expectations of the parties. This is undesirable and must be weighed against the harm avoided by refusing to enforce a bad provision. Second, the costs of litigation of a rule allowing invalidation, both to themselves and to the parties, are important. Not every harm justifies a legal response. Third, the possibility of legal controls other than invalidation need to be considered. Remedial rules, in particular, can and do help to control 'unnecessary' contractual provisions. Breach of an unnecessary contractual provision does not attract an award of damages because the promisee has not suffered a loss. Remedial rules are an imperfect solution to the problem of unnecessary restraints, however, because, *inter alia,* parties must breach their contracts in order to establish their rights conclusively. Finally, the abilities of the contracting parties themselves to guard against the problem – here the problem of unnecessary restraints – must be taken into account. If the courts are unlikely to improve upon the parties' efforts to establish an appropriate restraint, they should not intervene. This is likely to be the case if the parties' self-interest is a strong safeguard and/or if there is a low risk of cognitive error – making a mistake – in the framing of the contract.'

Professor Smith concludes that a scope test is needed in order to ensure that the courts only scrutinise onerous restraints. He suggests that a contract should be subject to the scrutiny of the court if it satisfies one or more of the following criteria:

1.   The restraint is relatively onerous.
2.   The parties' self-interest is a weak check.
3.   There is a high risk of cognitive error in the framing of the contract.

This is broadly consistent with the courts' current practice in recognising four categories of restraint that are subject to the restraint of trade doctrine: post-employment covenants, sale of business covenants, horizontal restraints and certain (though not all) vertical restraints (such as solus agreements and exclusive service covenants). We will consider these categories of restraint in greater detail later in the chapter.

14.2.2 REASONABLE BETWEEN THE PARTIES

The next stage of a restraint of trade claim is to ask whether the restraint is reasonable between the parties. This is to be assessed at the time the contract was made, not in the light of later circumstances (*Shell UK Ltd v Lostock Garage* [1976] 1 WLR 1187). There are two elements to this question.

14.2.2.1 Legitimate interest to protect

First, the court must determine whether there is a valid interest that the party imposing the restraint is seeking to protect. In *Nordenfelt v Maxim Nordenfelt* [1894] AC 535, the House of Lords held that Maxim Nordenfelt had a legitimate interest in protecting the recognition and goodwill of the business they had just acquired. Lord MacNaghten said:

'It is a principle of law and of public policy that trading should be encouraged and that trade should be free; but a fetter is placed on trade and trading is discouraged if a man who has built up a valuable business is not to be permitted to dispose of the fruits of his labours to the best advantage . . . [I]n the present case it was hardly disputed that the restraint was reasonable, having regard to the interests of the parties at the time when the transaction was entered into. It enabled Mr Nordenfelt to obtain the full value of what he had to sell; without it the purchasers could not have been protected in the possession of what they wished to buy.'

14.2.2.2 Protection no more than adequate

Second, the protection provided by the restraint must be no more than adequate to protect the legitimate interest. In *Herbert Morris Ltd v Saxelby* [1916] 1 AC 688, Lord Parker said:

'To be reasonable in the interests of the parties the restraint must afford adequate protection to the party in whose favour it is imposed . . . I think it clear that what is meant is that for a restraint to be reasonable in the interests of the parties it must afford *no more than* adequate protection to the party in whose favour it is imposed.'

A restraint must be reasonable in terms of its geographical scope (*Mason v Provident Clothing and Supply Co* [1913] AC 724), its duration (*M & S Drapers v Reynolds* [1957] 1 WLR 9) and the type of employment/trade in issue (*British Reinforced Concrete Engineering Co Ltd v Schelff* [1921] 2 Ch 563).

14.2.3 REASONABLE IN THE PUBLIC INTEREST

The third stage of a claim, as outlined by Lord MacNaghten in *Nordenfelt*, is to ask whether the restraint is reasonable in the public interest. This stage is rather controversial, and although it has never been explicitly rejected, the courts often overlook it. In *Attorney-General of the Commonwealth of Australia v The Adelaide Steamship Company* [1913] AC 781, Lord Parker observed that:

> 'Their Lordships are not aware of any case in which a restraint though reasonable in the interests of the parties has been held unenforceable because it involved some injury to the public.'

In *Wyatt v Krelinger and Fernau* [1933] 1 KB 793, the Court of Appeal held that a term in an employment contract, making the plaintiff's pension contingent on his not working in the wool trade, was void, irrespective of whether it was reasonable between the parties, because it was contrary to public interest. This decision was followed in the later case of *Bull v Pitney Bowes* [1966] 3 All ER 384. In both these cases, however, it was clear that the offending term was also unreasonable between the parties.

Many commentators have argued that the public interest test should be retained in the context of horizontal and vertical restraints because of the obvious danger in such cases that the interests of the parties will conflict with the interests of the public. For example, a cartel agreement to fix prices between producers of oil will often result in significant benefits for the oil producers, but significant harm to the public. This argument for the retention of the public interest test is predicated on the assumption that such agreements will not also fall foul of the parties' interests test. But as Professor Smith ('Reconstructing Restraint of Trade' (1995) 15 OJLS 565, 594–5) has shown, this assumption is false:

> 'If the parties' interests were a test of subjective benefit, then the distinction between market-fixing restraints and normal restraints would justify an additional public interest test. Yet . . . the parties' interests tests is not a test of 'subjective' reasonableness or (the same thing) of adequacy of consideration. That both parties to a restraint financially benefit does not make the restraint reasonable. Reasonableness is determined by the objective need for the restraint. For this reason, a cartel arrangement can be (and almost always is) unreasonable under the parties' interests test. What distinguishes market-fixing restraints from normal restraints is the nature of the covenantee's legitimate interest. The covenantee in a market-fixing case will argue that a restraint is necessary, not because of the special relationship between the parties and the consequent need to protect a particular investment, but (broadly speaking) because it is necessary to fix the market if any business like the covenantee's is to be viable. The evidence needed to establish such a claim is of a 'public' nature, in the sense that it pertains to the conditions in the market generally and not just to the situation of the contracting parties. But this evidence is relevant under the parties' interests test.'

The close connection between the public interest test and the parties' interest test was recognised by Lord Pearce in *Esso Petroleum v Harper Garage (Stourport) Ltd* [1968] AC 269, although he seemed to think that the parties' interest test was encompassed within the public interest requirement:

> 'There is not, as some cases seem to suggest, a separation between what is reasonable on grounds of public policy and what is reasonable as between the parties. There is one broad question: is it in the interests of the community that this restraint should, as between the parties, be held to be reasonable and enforceable?'

Although the public interest test is formally retained as a separate requirement of a claim for restraint of trade, in practice the courts appear to subsume this requirement within the parties' interest test. This will be evident as we turn to look at the different categories of restraint of trade in the following section.

14.3 CATEGORIES

In this section we will consider the four main categories of restraint of trade and examine how the doctrine has been applied in each of these contexts.

14.3.1 POST-EMPLOYMENT COVENANTS

Post-employment covenants that purport to restrain the employee's freedom to work after the termination of his employment will generally be treated with scepticism by the courts. Such clauses are prima facie void and will only be treated as valid if the employer is able to demonstrate s/he has a legitimate interest that requires protection. Such interests include trade secrets, confidential information and freedom from solicitation of employees or clients. A clause will not be upheld if its sole purpose is to protect the employer from competition.

Herbert Morris Ltd v Saxelby [1916] 1 AC 688

Facts: The plaintiff company was the leading manufacturer of hoisting machinery in the United Kingdom. The defendant had been in the company's employment since leaving school. After several years service he was engaged by the company to act as an engineer. His contract of service contained a covenant which stated the following: 'The employee covenants and agrees with the company their successors and assigns that he will not at any time during a period of seven years from the date of his ceasing to be employed by the company whether under this agreement or otherwise howsoever either in the United Kingdom of Great Britain or Ireland carry on either as principal agent servant or otherwise alone or jointly or in connection with any other person firm or company or be concerned or assist directly or indirectly whether for reward or otherwise in the sale or manufacture of pulley blocks hand overhead runways electric overhead runways hand overhead travelling cranes or any part thereof or be concerned or assist as aforesaid in any business connected with such sale or manufacture.'

Held: The House of Lords held that the covenant was wider than necessary for the protection of the plaintiff and was therefore unenforceable.

Lord Parker of Waddington:

'My Lords, in the case of *Nordenfelt v Maxim Nordenfelt* [1894] AC 535 Lord Macnaghten considered most if not all of the prior cases relating to contracts in restraint of trade and came to certain conclusions . . . It will be observed that in Lord Macnaghten's opinion two conditions must be fulfilled if the restraint is to be held valid. First, it must be reasonable in the interests of the contracting parties, and, secondly, it must be reasonable in the interests of the public. In the case of each condition he lays down a test of reasonableness. To be reasonable in the interests of the parties the restraint must afford adequate protection to the party in whose favour it is imposed; to be reasonable in the interests of the public it must be in no way injurious to the public.

With regard to the former test, I think it clear that what is meant is that for a restraint to be reasonable in the interests of the parties it must afford *no more than* adequate protection to the party in whose favour it is imposed. So conceived the test appears to me to be valid both as regards the covenantor and covenantee, for though in one sense no doubt it is contrary to the interests of the covenantor to subject himself to any restraint, still it may be for his advantage to be able so to subject himself in cases where, if he could not do so, he would lose other advantages, such as the possibility of obtaining the best terms on the sale of an existing business or the possibility of obtaining employment or training under competent employers. As long as the restraint to which he subjects himself is no wider than is required for the adequate protection of the person in whose favour it is created, it is in his interest to be able to bind himself for the sake of the indirect advantages he may obtain by so doing . . .

My Lords, it appears to me that Lord Macnaghten's statement of the law requires amplification in another respect. If the restraint is to secure no more than "adequate protection" to the party in whose favour it is imposed, it becomes necessary to consider in each particular case what it is for which and what it is against which protection is required. Otherwise it would be impossible to pass any opinion on the adequacy of the protection.

In the *Nordenfelt* case that which it was required to protect was the goodwill of a business transferred by the covenantor to the covenantee, and that against which protection was sought was competition by the covenantor throughout the area in which such business was carried on. Under the particular circumstances of the case a world-wide covenant against competition was held no more than adequate for the purchaser's protection. It was argued before your Lordships that no distinction can be drawn between the position of the purchaser of the goodwill of a business taking such a covenant from his vendor and the case of the owner of a business taking such a covenant from his servant or apprentice. In both cases it was said that the property to be protected was the same and the dangers to be guarded against the same. I am of opinion that this argument cannot be accepted. The distinction between the two cases is, I think, quite clear, and is recognised both by Lord Macnaghten and Lord Herschell in the *Nordenfelt* case. The goodwill of a business is immune from the danger of the owner exercising his personal knowledge and skill to its detriment, and if the purchaser is to take over such goodwill with all its advantages it must, in his hands, remain similarly immune. Without, therefore, a covenant on the part of the vendor against competition, a purchaser would not get what he is contracting to buy, nor could the vendor give what he is intending to sell. The covenant against competition is, therefore, reasonable if confined to the area within which it would in all probability enure to the injury of the purchaser.

It is quite different in the case of an employer taking such a covenant from his employee or apprentice. The goodwill of his business is, under the conditions in which we live, necessarily subject to the competition of all persons (including the servant or apprentice) who choose to engage in a similar trade. The employer in such a case is not endeavouring to protect what he has, but to gain a special advantage which he could not otherwise secure. I cannot find any case in which a covenant against competition by a servant or apprentice has, as such, ever been upheld by the Court. Wherever such covenants have been upheld it has been on the ground, not that the servant or apprentice would, by reason of his employment or training, obtain the skill and knowledge necessary to equip him as a possible competitor in the trade, but that he might obtain such personal knowledge of and influence over the customers of his employer, or such an acquaintance with his employer's trade secrets as would enable him, if competition were allowed, to take advantage of his employer's trade connection or utilise information confidentially obtained . . .

An attempt was . . . made in argument to justify the restraint on the ground that it was no more than adequate for the protection of the plaintiffs' trade connection and trade secrets. I am of opinion that this attempt completely failed. With regard to the plaintiffs' connection, there is little or no evidence that the defendant ever came into personal contact with the plaintiffs' customers. For a period, it is true, he was manager of the London branch of the plaintiffs' business, and for another period sales manager at Loughborough. With the exception of these periods he was employed entirely in the engineering department. Had the restraint been confined to London and Loughborough and a reasonable area round each of these centres, it might possibly have been supported as reasonably necessary to protect the plaintiffs' connection, but a restraint extending over the United Kingdom was obviously too wide in this respect.

With regard to trade secrets, I am not satisfied that the defendant was entrusted with any trade secret in the proper sense of the word at all.'

An employer does not have a legitimate interest in preventing its employees from competing with it following termination of their employment. The employer will need to demonstrate that the restraint is necessary in order to prevent the divulgence of trade secrets or the solicitation of customers. A restraint clause was upheld on the former ground in *Littlewoods Organisation Ltd v Harris*.

Littlewoods Organisation Ltd v Harris [1977] 1 WLR 1472

Facts: The defendant was employed by the plaintiff, a large mail order and retail business, whose main competitor in the UK was Great Universal Stores (GUS). As executive director of Littlewoods' mail order business, the defendant was responsible for planning and compiling Littlewoods' catalogues. A clause in his contract of employment stated that, following determination of the agreement, the defendant 'shall not at any time within 12 months after such determination enter into a contract of service or other agreement of a like nature with Great Universal Stores Ltd or any company subsidiary thereto' and that clause continued to apply to the defendant on his various promotions. On January 4, 1977, the defendant tendered his resignation in a letter informing the plaintiffs that he had accepted an offer of employment from the GUS group. The plaintiff issued a writ claiming an injunction to restrain the defendant from accepting employment with the GUS group for a period of 12 months from the determination of the agreement. Caulfield J refused to grant the injunction on the ground that the plaintiff did not possess confidential information which they were entitled to protect.

Held: The Court of Appeal (Browne LJ dissenting) allowed the appeal. Although the employer could not protect itself from competition by an ex-employee, it could by means of a restraint clause protect its trade secrets and confidential information.

Lord Denning MR:
'The plaintiffs claim that . . . the defendant has acquired a great deal of confidential information about their forthcoming catalogue. It is not practicable to separate it from that which is not confidential. And he can carry it away in his head. The only practicable protection is a covenant restraining him from going to their rivals the GUS group for a period of 12 months . . .

[Confidential information] has been acquired at great expense and by great expertise by Littlewoods. No servant should be at liberty to carry it off to a rival in trade – and thus save him the expense and expertise of doing it himself – or even so as to show the rival the nature of the catalogue in advance. Although the rival catalogues come out at the same time, the information can be used by the rival for the purpose of supplemental leaflets which we are told are issued from time to time. It seems to me, looking at the evidence, and even reading between the lines of what Caulfield J said, this really was a case where Littlewoods had a great a deal of confidential information which Mr. Harris had acquired in the course of his service with them and which they were entitled to protect by a reasonable covenant against his going away and taking it to their rivals in trade, the great GUS group.

So I come back to the question: Was this clause reasonable? Is it enforceable or not? The only ground on which it is said that it is not enforceable is that it is said it is too wide . . .

It is said to be too wide in that it prevents Mr Harris being concerned or interested in the businesses of Great Universal Stores and its subsidiaries – and those businesses are infinitely varied and are worldwide: whereas Littlewoods are confined to the United Kingdom and operate in the two fields only of a mail order business and a chain of retail stores.

I would first consider the phrase 'Great Universal Stores or any company subsidiary thereto'. It appears that Great Universal Stores have 200 or more subsidiaries all over the world, carrying an all sorts of businesses. An instance given in argument was a restaurant in Alice Springs in the centre of Australia. Does that invalidate the clause? Is the introduction of 'subsidiaries' a ground for not enforcing it? This is an important point in these days when so many companies are multinational in their operations. The answer is, I think, the law to-day has regard to the realities of big business. It takes the group as being one concern under one supreme control. It does not regard each subsidiary as being a separate and independent entity . . .

[T]he phrase "Great Universal Stores or any company subsidiary thereto" denotes in reality one group in which the individual subsidiaries cannot usefully be distinguished one from the other. The group is under one unified control. Those in charge of the group are able to switch a servant from one subsidiary to another without any difficulty whatever. They can lend his services or transmit his information and knowledge, as they please, within the group. If the clause is to afford any protection to Littlewoods at all, it must cover the whole GUS group, that is, not only the parent company but also its subsidiaries.

The next point is that the business of Littlewoods is within the United Kingdom whereas the businesses of the GUS group are worldwide. In this regard the clause should, I think, be limited by relation to its object. It should be limited to such part of the business of the GUS group as operates within the United Kingdom.

Then there is this point. The only business of the plaintiffs which can reasonably require protection is their mail order business, not their retail chain stores. The clause should, I think, be limited to the mail order business of both concerns . . .

In summary I think that limiting words ought to be read into the clause so as to limit it to the part of the business for which the plaintiffs are reasonably entitled to protection. It should be construed in relation to the surrounding circumstances at the time of renewal in 1976 when the defendant was made executive director of the mail order business. The object was to protect Littlewoods in respect of the mail order business. Great Universal Stores should not be allowed to entice or induce this servant away so as to be in their mail order business for 12 months after he left the employment of Littlewoods.'

Browne LJ:

'I go therefore to the construction of clause 9 (i) of this contract. It seems to me that the question is divided into two parts. First, is it enforceable as it stands? Second, if not, can it be cut down by construction or severance so as to make it enforceable? . . .

It seems to me quite plain that if the clause is read literally it is much too wide and is void or unenforceable . . . [The clause] would prevent the defendant from entering into the service of any subsidiary of Great Universal Stores engaged in any of their manifold activities in any part of the world. For this reason I have no doubt that it is too wide. It seems to me that if, for instance, the defendant were employed by a subsidiary in Canada the application of this clause would plainly be unreasonable . . .

But it is said, and my Lords take the view, that one can cut down the literal meaning of this clause as a matter of construction to a point where it becomes reasonable . . . In the cases to which my Lords have referred the court was able to hold it right as a matter of the construction of the agreement as a whole, and having regard to the surrounding circumstances, to limit the application to what was reasonable. Some at any rate of those cases seem to me to be considerably stronger than the present case because support for the construction adopted by the court could be found within the terms of the agreement itself . . . In this case there is nothing in the agreement itself about competition and there is nothing about the mail order business. What Mr. Rankin submits one can and should do as a matter of construction is to read into clause 8 (i) after the words "any company subsidiary thereto" the words "in competition with Littlewoods", and after "trading or business of the said Great Universal Stores Ltd. or any such company aforesaid" again one should read in "in competition with Littlewoods". This of course would leave the obligation not to enter into a contract with Great Universal Stores itself unlimited. Megaw LJ takes the view that one can construe the agreement as containing the very much more elaborate limitations to which he has referred. With all deference to my Lords, I think this is re-writing the clause, and re-writing it so as to make enforceable that which would otherwise be unenforceable. With all deference and respect, I think that is something which this court cannot do.'

Their Lordships were in agreement that the plaintiff had a proprietary interest in the protection of confidential information obtained by the defendant in the course of his employment. They were also in agreement that the restraint clause, as drafted, was too wide to be reasonable between the parties. The difference of opinion came on the issue of severance. Lord Denning MR and Megaw LJ were willing to sever the offending provisions and read limiting words into the clause so as to make it reasonable. Browne LJ was unwilling to do this and for that reason dissented. We will return to the issue of severance in due course. At this stage it is important to note that an employer has a legitimate interest in protecting confidential information so long as the clause used to provide this protection is not drafted too widely.

An employer also has a legitimate interest in preventing the solicitation of its customers by former employees. A line must be drawn here between an employee who has acquired influence over his employer's customers, and one who merely has acquired knowledge of those customers.

Fitch v Dewes [1921] 2 AC 158

Facts: The defendant was employed by the plaintiff as a managing clerk of a solicitors practice in Tamworth. The defendant's contract contained the following covenant: 'The said Thomas Birch Fitch hereby expressly agrees with the said John Hunt Dewes that he will not on the expiration or sooner determination of the said term of three years or any extended term as herein provided either alone or jointly with any other person or persons directly or indirectly be engaged or manage or concerned in the office profession or business of a solicitor within a radius of seven miles of the Town Hall of Tamworth.' Following the termination of his employment the defendant intentionally committed a breach of the covenant in order to test its validity.

Held: The House of Lords held that the covenant was enforceable even though it was unlimited in duration because it did not exceed what was reasonably necessary to protect the plaintiff and it was not contrary to the public interest.

Lord Birkenhead LC:
'What then is it in respect of which on such facts the covenantee is entitled to be protected? Because it is not until we reach a conclusion upon this point that we shall be in a position to decide whether or not this particular restriction does in fact exceed that which is so required. I conceive, my Lords, that the covenantee is entitled to this. He is the founder, or at least the possessor, of the business of an attorney. Such a business depends upon the existence of goodwill; upon the association and the intimacy which exist between him who carries on that business and the clients of the firm, an intimacy founded upon many complex considerations not easily to be defined, but very easily to be understood. Such a covenantee is taking into his employment in his firm a young man in circumstances which make it certain that the latter will acquire a close personal acquaintance with the clients from whom, and from whom alone, the business of the firm arises. How intimate were the opportunities given to the appellant in this case of acquiring a close acquaintance with the clients of the firm is made abundantly plain by figures presented in evidence . . . My Lords, it is therefore clear that if you take the period between 1910 and 1914 it is not a very great exaggeration to say that half the people who came to this office, perhaps not particularly caring whom they saw but merely asking to consult somebody who represented the business, were shown in to the appellant, so that, under the aegis of the firm, he either originally made or continued their business acquaintance. And this circumstance enables me to answer without the slightest ambiguity, so far as I myself am concerned, the question

which I proposed a moment ago, What was it that in such a case the protection of the covenantee rendered reasonable? He might claim in my judgment, for his protection, that that business which was his, and to which he had admitted the appellant in the manner defined by the successive agreements, should continue to be his, and that if at any time the contract of employment between himself and his employee came to an end, on such determination the latter should not be in a position to use the intimacies and the knowledge which he had acquired in the course of his employment in order to create a practice of his own in that same place and by doing so undermine the business and the connection of the respondent. I have only to ask myself whether the restriction which is contained in clause 8 is excessive for that purpose; because I dismiss in this connection the contention which was not seriously argued by Mr Clayton that there is anything in such a clause which is in conflict with the public interest. Indeed I am of opinion that it is in the public interest that a proper restrictive agreement of this kind between an established solicitor, possibly an elderly man, and a younger man should be allowed. It is in the public interest, because otherwise solicitors carrying on their business without a partner would be extremely chary of admitting competent young men to their offices and to the confidential knowledge to be derived by frequenting those offices. There is therefore nothing in the clause which I have read which conflicts with public interest unless, of course, it exceeds what is necessary for the protection of the covenantee, in which case the excess itself would be against the public interest.

My Lords, it is not contended that there is anything which is open to attack in clause 8 except that part of the clause which for all time excludes the appellant from carrying on practice within seven miles of Tamworth. Are we then to say that such a restriction so unlimited goes farther than is permitted in relation to the standard which I have restated? I am of opinion that it does not go too far. One of your Lordships asked Mr Clayton in the course of his argument what period in his judgment would be a reasonable period, and Mr Clayton replied that he thought that ten years might be a reasonable period. My Lords, why? Why is it to be said that ten years is a reasonable period? I can quite easily understand that at the end of a period of ten years the appellant in this case, who by this very clause is not prevented from maintaining and even developing his business acquaintance with the clients of the firm so long as he does not practise within a range of seven miles, might have retained all these circum- stances of special, and as I think of illegitimate, advantage for the purpose of com- peting with the business of the respondent, and then might come forward and do that very thing against which in my judgment the covenantee is abundantly entitled to be protected. Therefore I should dismiss a period of ten years and I should even say of twenty or thirty years that it was quite impossible to be dogmatic upon the period proper to each individual case.'

Viscount Cave:

'Here the practice to be protected is that of a solicitor, to which a goodwill is no doubt attached. It is manifest that a person employed in such a practice as managing clerk must in the course of his duties acquire a knowledge of the affairs, the documents

and the disposition of the clients of the business such as to give him a special equipment which he could, if not restrained by contract, use in obtaining employment
as their legal adviser and that in this manner the goodwill of the employer's business
might be impaired and perhaps destroyed. Now the object being to protect the
employer's business against the use of that special advantage, was it unreasonable
to extend this covenant to the life of the employee? I think not. It is impossible to
say that there must in every case be some specified limit of time defined by a figure.
Nor can we say that the contract ought to be confined to the life of the covenantee,
for he might die in the next year or so and the goodwill might then be lost to his
successors.'

The restraint clause was upheld by the House of Lords on the ground that it was
necessary to protect the plaintiff from solicitation of his clients. The defendant had
acquired influence over the plaintiff's clients and this influence could have been
exploited if the defendant were allowed to set up a practice of his own in Tamworth.
Interestingly, the House of Lords also held that the restraint was reasonable in the
public interest on the ground that elderly solicitors would be unwilling to take on
young clerks if such clauses were not permissible. Again, we see the public interest
test being subsumed within the parties' interest test.

14.3.2 SALE OF BUSINESS COVENANTS

In relation to contracts for the sale of a business, the interest that the purchaser is
seeking to protect is the 'goodwill' of the business, that is the existing trade and
reputation of the business that has been built up by the seller. In general, the courts
are more willing to uphold restraints in this context than they are in respect of
post-employment covenants. Some commentators have suggested that this is
because there is less likely to be an inequality of bargaining power in contracts
for the sale of a business. This is not necessarily true, however, and in any event
it is clear that considerations of procedural and substantive fairness are irrelevant
to the operation of the restraint of trade doctrine (see commentary on *A Schroeder
Music Publishing Co Ltd v Macualay* [1974] 1 WLR 1308). The real reason why
restraints are often upheld in sale of business contracts is because the purchaser
usually has a legitimate interest in seeking to protect the 'goodwill' of the business
he is purchasing. Lord Shaw expressed it well in *Herbert Morris Ltd v Saxelby* [1916]
1 AC 688:

'When a business is sold, the vendor . . . seeks to realise this piece of property,
and obtains a purchaser upon a condition without which the whole transaction
would be valueless. He sells, he himself agreeing not to compete; and the law
upholds such a bargain, and declines to permit a vendor to derogate from his

own grant. Public interest cannot be invoked to render such a bargain nugatory; to do so would be to use public interest for the destruction of property.
Nothing could be a more sure deterrent to commercial energy and activity
than a principle that its accumulated results could not be transferred save
under conditions which would make its buyer insecure.'

Although the purchaser of a business will often be able to show a legitimate interest, he will also need to show that the scope of the restraint was reasonably necessary
for the protection of the particular business he has purchased. If the clause is drafted
too widely, it will be void and unenforceable.

British Reinforced Concrete Engineering Co Ltd v Schelff [1921] 2 Ch 563

Facts: The plaintiff company manufactured and sold 'BRC' road reinforcements
throughout the UK. The defendant, Schelff and his partners, carried on a much smaller
and more local business, selling (but not manufacturing) 'Loop' road reinforcements.
The defendant sold his business to the plaintiff, covenanting that he would not enter
into competition with them (either in business or in the employment of a rival) in the
manufacture or sale of road reinforcements. Some time later the defendant took up
employment with a road reinforcement company and the plaintiff brought an action for
breach of covenant.

Held: The High Court held that the covenant was too wide in area and subject matter.
Although the provision as to subject matter, i.e. manufacture as well as sale, could be
severed the remainder of the covenant was still too wide in area for the protection of
the goodwill of the small business sold.

Younger LJ (for Astbury J)
'In some respects the covenant is too wide to be supported. It is admittedly too wide
in scope . . . and if the legitimate purpose of the covenant is the protection of the
business sold as distinct from the purchasers' other business it is too wide in area. It is
also admittedly too wide in scope in that it extends to the manufacture of road
reinforcements as well as their sale. The Loop firm never at any time manufactured
reinforcements. Now in this last respect the covenant can, I think, quite properly be
severed. This is a severance in respect of the subject matter of the restriction which is
fully justified by the authorities. But to cut out the servant clause from the agreement is
another matter altogether . . . To my mind there is reason for not carrying the principle
so far as is here required. Its application does not authorise the making of a new
contract for the parties and the particular clause now in question is really a principal if
not the main approach to the business of the sale of road reinforcements, all access to
which it is the purport of the covenant to bar so as to prevent the covenantors from
having any part or lot whatsoever in it during the period of restriction. Like the covenant
in *Attwood v Lamont* [1920] 2 KB 146 it is merely a part of one entire covenant in

mosaic, and to permit the severance asked would, I think, be to go further than has ever yet been permitted in such a case.

I will, however, contrary to my opinion, assume that the covenant may be severed as desired . . . The question then arises whether that covenant, even after severance, was not still too wide for the reasonable protection of the plaintiffs at the time it was entered into. I am of opinion that it was. This raises the most important legal question in the case – namely, whether in an agreement for sale of a business the reasonableness of a vendor's restrictive covenant is to be judged by the extent and circumstances of the business sold or by the extent and range of any business of the purchaser of which after transfer to him it is to form a part.

The plaintiffs' claim here is based on the hypothesis that the legitimate subject of protection is the plaintiffs' business, and there can, I think, be no doubt that the restrictive covenant is framed with reference to the requirements of that business and no other. Its extravagance in range as applied to the altogether insignificant business sold hardly requires statement. . . .

In my judgment . . . this severed covenant must be judged only with reference to the goodwill of the business sold, and so judged it is far wider than is necessary for the reasonable protection of the plaintiffs.'

The problem for the plaintiff was that they had drafted the clause for the protection of their existing business interests, not for the protection of the business they were purchasing. This meant that the restraint provided more protection than was reasonably necessary and it was therefore void.

14.3.2.1 Partnerships

Restraint clauses in partnership agreements do not fit neatly into either of the categories that have been considered so far. This was recognised by Lord Fraser of Tullybelton in *Bridge v Deacons* [1984] AC 795:

'The agreement, in the present case, being one between partners, does not conform exactly to either [a sale of a business or an employment contract], although it has some resemblance to both. Their Lordships are of the opinion that a decision on whether the restrictions in this agreement are enforceable or not cannot be reached by attempting to place the agreement in any particular category, or by seeking for the category to which it is most closely analogous.'

The case concerned a restraint clause in a partnership agreement, which provided that no partner of the firm on ceasing to be a partner would, for a period of five years, act as a solicitor in Hong Kong for any person, firm or company that had in the past three years been a client of the partnership. It was held that this clause was reasonable between the parties because it was necessary for the protection of the partners' legitimate interests in the assets and the goodwill of the partnership. The partners had determined the period of the restrictions necessary to protect their goodwill and, without evidence to the contrary, it was to be assumed that the duration of the restriction was reasonable.

The Privy Council (PC) also held that the restraint was reasonable in the interests of the public. Their Lordships rejected the argument that it would be contrary to public policy for a solicitor to be precluded from acting for a client when that client wanted him to act for him. Such an argument was described as 'unsupported by authority' and directly contrary to the House of Lords' decision in *Fitch v Dewes*. Instead, their Lordships thought that such restraints were very much in the interests of the public because they facilitated the assumption by established solicitors' firms of younger men as partners. It is clear that the PC was involved in a delicate balancing of the public interest between the freedom of clients to instruct the solicitor of their choice and the freedom of solicitors to protect the goodwill of their practice.

It is maybe unsurprising that the PC found in favour of the law firm on the facts of *Bridge v Deacons*. It is rather more surprising that the decision was followed two years later by the Court of Appeal in *Kerr v Morris* [1987] Ch 90. Here a restraint clause was included in a partnership agreement between GPs stating that no partner should carry on the profession of general medical practitioner within two miles of the practice for two years after leaving the partnership. The plaintiffs sought to enforce the covenant against the defendant. He contended that the covenant was void for being contrary to public policy in preventing a medical practitioner from giving patients the care he was obliged to give them under the National Health Service. This argument was rejected by the Court of Appeal. Dillon LJ referred to the Privy Council's decision in *Bridge v Deacons* and continued:

> 'It seems to me that the same reasoning really can apply to a National Health Service doctor. The solicitor can go from the area at any time and can bind himself by contract that in certain events he will go. The doctor can go from the area at any time and I do not see why public policy should prevent him binding himself by contract that in certain events he will go.'

This decision is further evidence of the reluctance of the courts to invalidate a restraint clause, merely on the grounds of public policy.

14.3.3 HORIZONTAL RESTRAINTS

Horizontal agreements may be considered to be in restraint of trade. In practice, however, the courts have encountered two problems with bringing such agreements within the scope of the doctrine. First, it is often argued that horizontal restraints are reasonable between the parties because they are freely negotiated and entered into to avoid harmful competition. This argument rests on the assumption that the parties' interest test is subjective rather than objective. As noted above, this assumption is rather doubtful, but it nevertheless remains the position adopted by the English courts. Second, it seems that the courts are reluctant to hold that horizontal agreements are contrary to the public interest. In *Attorney-General of the Commonwealth v The Adelaide Steamship Company* [1913] AC 781, Lord Parker of Waddington famously said:

> '[N]o contract was ever an offence at common law merely because it was in restraint of trade . . . The right of the individual to carry on his trade or business in the manner he considers best in his own interests involves the right of combining with others in a common course of action, provided such common course of action is undertaken with a single view to the interests of the combining parties and not with a view to injure others.'

Due to these obstacles and the fact that horizontal agreements rarely come before the courts (unless one of the parties fails to perform and is sued for breach), the common law has been regarded as rather impotent in tackling horizontal restraints. Indeed, the perceived weaknesses of the common law have led to the intervention of Parliament and the enactment of the Competition Act 1998 (see below). That is not to say, however, that the common law has been wholly ineffective in this area, as the following cases show.

Kores Manufacturing Co Ltd v Kolok Manufacturing Co Ltd [1959] Ch 108

Facts: Two companies agreed that neither would, without the consent of the other, employ any person who had been employed by the other company within the past five years. The agreement was intended to protect trade secrets because both companies were involved in manufacturing similar products involving chemical processes. In addition, it was contemplated at the time of the agreement that their factories would be adjoining. The plaintiffs sought an injunction to restrain the defendants from employing a certain employee of the plaintiffs.

Held: The Court of Appeal held that, although the parties had a legitimate inertest to protect, the restraint was drafted too widely. It covered all employees regardless of the nature and terms of their employment and the circumstances in which that employment was terminated.

Jenkins LJ:
'We agree that where traders dealing on equal terms have become parties to (for example) a scheme for maintaining prices or for central selling, and there is nothing in its provisions which is obviously unreasonable in the interests of the parties, the court will be slow to set it aside at the instance of a party who has freely agreed to it. But

the mere fact that parties dealing on equal terms have entered into an agreement subjecting themselves to restraints of trade does not preclude the court from holding the agreement bad where the restraints are clearly unreasonable in the interests of the parties. In the present case, the restraint reciprocally imposed on the plaintiffs and the defendants by the agreement of 1934 was such as to preclude the plaintiffs from employing at any time any person who had, during the then past five years, been a servant of the defendants, and vice versa.

To put the matter from the defendants' point of view, since they are asserting the invalidity of the agreement of 1934, they placed it out of their power to take into their service any person who had during the preceding five years been in the service of the plaintiffs for any period, however short, and in any capacity, however humble. The five-year ban was equally applicable to an unskilled manual labourer who had been for a single day in the employment of the plaintiffs, and to a chief chemist with many years' service. It would also, so far as we can see, be just as much applicable to a person whom the plaintiffs had dismissed from their service as to a person who had left their service of his own accord.'

Eastham v Newcastle United Football Club Ltd [1964] Ch 413

Facts: George Eastham, a professional footballer wanted a transfer from Newcastle United. Under the rules of the Football Association and the Football League his employment with the club was governed by a 'retain and transfer' system whereby a player retained by his club at the end of a year's engagement was debarred from joining another club unless he obtained the consent of the club that had retained him. Eastham challenged these rules.

Held: The High Court held that, although some system was required to regulate football transfers, the current system was more restrictive on the player's freedom of employment than was necessary. The court granted a declaration against Newcastle United and against the FA whose rules led to the unjustifiable restraint on his freedom of employment.

Wilberforce J:

'[I]s it open to an employee to bring an action for a declaration that the contract between the employers is in restraint of trade? To my mind it would seem unjust if this were not so. The employees are just as much affected and, indeed, aimed at by the employers' agreement as the employers themselves. Their liberty of action in seeking employment is threatened just as much as the liberty of the employers to give them employment, and their liberty to seek employment is considered by the law to be an important public interest. Is the defence of that interest to be left exclusively in the hands of the employers themselves, who have set up the ring against the employees and who have (as here) shown every intention of maintaining it as long as they can; left to the chance that one day there may be a blackleg among the employers who will challenge it? In my judgment to grant a remedy by way of declaration to the persons whose interests are vitally affected would be well within the spirit and intent of the rule as to declaratory judgments.'

The decision in *Eastham* emphasised just how ineffective the common law was at dealing with horizontal agreements since, although Eastham obtained declarations against the FA and his employers, these were not actually enforceable. Fortunately for Eastham the FA and the Football League did decide to alter the transfer system in response to the decision.

14.3.4 VERTICAL RESTRAINTS

Vertical restraints are agreements by which a party agrees to deal exclusively with only one supplier. The leading case on the operation of the doctrine in this context is *Esso Petroleum v Harper's Garage (Stourport) Ltd*.

Esso Petroleum v Harper's Garage (Stourport) Ltd [1968] AC 269

Facts: The defendant company owned two petrol garages. It entered into two agreements (known as 'solus' agreements) with the defendant under which it agreed to sell only Esso petrol at its garages. Under the first agreement the defendant agreed to supply Esso petrol for four years and five months in return for a discount on the price of the petrol. Under the second agreement, the defendant agreed to supply Esso petrol for 21 years in return for a £7,000 loan, secured by a mortgage against the property. When cheaper petrol became available, the defendant stopped supplying Esso petrol. The plaintiff sought an injunction which was resisted by the defendant on the ground that the solus agreements were in restraint of trade. The plaintiff contended that the agreements fell outside the doctrine and, even if they did not, they were nevertheless reasonable between the parties.

Held: The House of Lords held that solus agreements could be regarded as being in restraint of trade and that, while the four years and five months agreement was reasonable, the 21-year agreement was not, particularly as it was linked to a mortgage.

Lord Reid:

'In my view this agreement is within the scope of the doctrine of restraint of trade as it had been developed in English law. Not only have the respondents agreed negatively not to sell other petrol but they have agreed positively to keep this garage open for the sale of the appellants' petrol at all reasonable hours throughout the period of the tie. It was argued that this was merely regulating the respondent's trading and rather promoting than restraining his trade. But regulating a person's existing trade may be a greater restraint than prohibiting him from engaging in a new trade. And a contract to take one's whole supply from one source may be much more hampering than a contract to sell one's whole output to one buyer. I would not attempt to define the dividing line between contracts which are and contracts which are not in restraint of trade, but in my view this contract must be held to be in restraint of trade. So it is necessary to consider whether its provisions can be justified.

[I]t is necessary to consider first whether the restraint went farther than to afford adequate protection to the party in whose favour it was granted, secondly whether it can be justified as being in the interests of the party restrained, and, thirdly, whether it must be held contrary to the public interest . . .

Where two experienced traders are bargaining on equal terms and one has agreed to a restraint for reasons which seem good to him the court is in grave danger of stultifying itself if it says that it knows that trader's interest better than he does himself. But there may well be cases where, although the party to be restrained has deliberately accepted the main terms of the contract, he has been at a disadvantage as regards other terms: for example where a set of conditions has been incorporated which has not been the subject of negotiation – there the court may have greater freedom to hold them unreasonable . . .

[W]hether or not a restraint is in the personal interests of the parties, it is I think well established that the court will not enforce a restraint which goes further than affording adequate protection to the legitimate interests of the party in whose favour it is granted. This must I think be because too wide a restraint is against the public interest. It has often been said that a person is not entitled to be protected against mere competition. I do not find that very helpful in a case like the present. I think it better to ascertain what were the legitimate interests of the appellants which they were entitled to protect and then to see whether these restraints were more than adequate for that purpose.

When petrol rationing came to an end in 1950 the large producers began to make agreements, now known as solus agreements, with garage owners under which the garage owner, in return for certain advantages, agreed to sell only the petrol of the producer with whom he made the agreement. Within a short time three-quarters of the filling stations in this country were tied in that way and by the dates of the agreements in this case over 90 per cent had agreed to ties. It appears that the garage owners were not at a disadvantage in bargaining with the large producing companies as there was intense competition between these companies to obtain these ties. So we can assume that both the garage owners and the companies thought that such ties were to their advantage. And it is not said in this case that all ties are either against the public interest or against the interests of the parties. The respondents' case is that the ties with which we are concerned are for too long periods.

The advantage to the garage owner is that he gets a rebate on the wholesale price of the petrol which he buys and also may get other benefits or financial assistance. The main advantages for the producing company appear to be that distribution is made easier and more economical and that it is assured of a steady outlet for its petrol over a period. As regards distribution, it appears that there were some 35,000 filling stations in this country at the relevant time, of which about a fifth were tied to the appellants. So they only have to distribute to some 7,000 filling stations instead of to a very much larger number if most filling stations sold several brands of petrol. But the main reason why the producing companies want ties for five years and more, instead of ties for one or two years only, seems to be that they can organise their business better if on the average only one-fifth or less of their ties come to an end in any one year. The appellants make a point of the fact that they have invested some £200 millions in refineries and other plant and that they could not have done that unless they could foresee a steady and assured level of sales of their petrol. Most of their ties appear to have been made for periods of between five and 20 years. But we have no evidence as to the precise additional advantage which they derive from a five-year tie as compared with a two-year tie or from a 20-year tie as compared with a five-year tie.

The Court of Appeal held that these ties were for unreasonably long periods. They thought that, if for any reason the respondents ceased to sell the appellants' petrol, the appellants could have found other suitable outlets in the neighbourhood within two or three years. I do not think that that is the right test. In the first place there was no evidence about this and I do not think that it would be practicable to apply this test in practice. It might happen that when the respondents ceased to sell their petrol, the appellants would find such an alternative outlet in a very short time. But, looking to the fact that well over 90 per cent of existing filling stations are tied and that there may be great difficulty in opening a new filling station, it might take a very long time to find an alternative. Any estimate of how long it might take to find suitable alternatives for the respondents' filling stations could be little better than guesswork.

I do not think that the appellants' interest can be regarded so narrowly. They are not so much concerned with any particular outlet as with maintaining a stable system of distribution throughout the country so as to enable their business to be run efficiently and economically. In my view there is sufficient material to justify a decision that ties of less than five years were insufficient, in the circumstances of the trade when these agreements were made, to afford adequate protection to the appellants' legitimate interests. And if that is so I cannot find anything in the details of the [five year] agreement which would indicate that it is unreasonable. It is true that if some of the provisions were operated by the appellants in a manner which would be commercially unreasonable they might put the respondents in difficulties. But I think that a court must have regard to the fact that the appellants must act in such a way that they will be able to obtain renewals of the great majority of their very numerous ties, some of which will come to an end almost every week. If in such circumstances a garage owner chooses to rely on the commercial probity and good sense of the producer, I do not think that a court should hold his agreement unreasonable because it is legally capable of some misuse. I would therefore allow the appeal as regards the [five year] agreement.

But the [21 year] agreement involves much more difficulty ... A tie for 21 years stretches far beyond any period for which developments are reasonably foreseeable. Restrictions on the garage owner which might seem tolerable and reasonable in reasonably foreseeable conditions might come to have a very different effect in quite different conditions: the public interest comes in here more strongly. And, apart from a case where he gets a loan, a garage owner appears to get no greater advantage from a 21-year tie than he gets from a five-year tie. So I would think that there must at least be some clearly established advantage to the producing company – something to show that a shorter period would not be adequate – before so long a period could be justified. But in this case there is no evidence to prove anything of the kind. And the other material which I have thought it right to consider does not appear to me to assist the appellant here. I would therefore dismiss the appeal as regards the [21 year] agreement.

I would add that the decision in this case – particularly in view of the paucity of evidence – ought not, in my view, to be regarded as laying down any general rule as to the length of tie permissible in a solus agreement ... I must not be taken as expressing any opinion as to the validity of ties for periods mid-way between the two periods with which the present case is concerned.'

Lord Reid's decision on the reasonableness of the restraint was clearly influenced by a great number of factors including: Esso's expenditure on oil refineries, the difficulty of finding alternative purchasers, the cost of transporting petrol to a large number of garages, the need to ensure a steady and assured level of sales and the general state of the industry. All these factors combined were sufficient to support the conclusion that the four-year restraint was reasonable. The 21-year restraint, on the other hand, was less easy to justify. In particular, the plaintiff had failed to demonstrate why a 21-year tie was necessary. The conclusion was that, although the plaintiff had a legitimate interest to protect, the 21-year restraint provided more protection than was needed.

Lord Reid was keen to emphasise that he was not laying down any general rule as to the length of tie permissible in a solus agreement. Indeed, in the later case of *Alec Lobb (Garages) v Total Oil* [1985] 1 WLR 173, the Court of Appeal upheld a solus agreement linked to a 21-year lease on the ground that the lease could be terminated after seven or 14 years.

Another form of vertical restraint is the exclusive service agreement. These are often entered into by songwriters, or pop musicians, with music publishers or recording companies. The artist is required to commit himself to one company for a lengthy period of time, with no guarantee that the company will promote or even publish his work. It has been decided that this type of vertical agreement is within the scope of the restraint of trade doctrine.

Schroeder Music Publishing Co Ltd v Macaulay (formerly Instone)
[1974] 1 WLR 1308

Facts: The plaintiff was a 21-year-old and unknown songwriter who entered into a standard form contract with the defendant music publishers. The agreement stated that the copyright in all the plaintiff's compositions for the next five years was assigned to the defendants, with an automatic extension of five years if the royalties during the initial term exceeded £5,000. A clause in the contract stated that the publishers could terminate the agreement at any time by one month's notice, but there was no similar provision for the plaintiff. The contract also stated the publishers had the right to assign the agreement, but there was no similar right given to the plaintiff. The defendants were under no obligation to publish any of the plaintiff's work. The plaintiff brought an action claiming a declaration that the agreement was in restraint of trade and void. At first instance, Plowman J gave the declaration sought and this was affirmed by the Court of Appeal.

Held: The House of Lords dismissed the appeal. The restriction in the agreement went beyond what was reasonably necessary to protect the defendants' legitimate interests. In particular, it was unreasonable for the plaintiff to be completely committed to the defendants while the defendants were under no obligation to publish any of his work.

Lord Reid:

'The public interest requires in the interests both of the public and of the individual that everyone should be free so far as practicable to earn a livelihood and to give to the public the fruits of his particular abilities. The main question to be considered is whether and how far the operation of the terms of this agreement is likely to conflict with this objective. The respondent is bound to assign to the appellants during a long period the fruits of his musical talent. But what are the appellants bound to do with those fruits? Under the contract nothing. If they do use the songs which the respondent composes they must pay in terms of the contract. But they need not do so. As has been said they may put them in a drawer and leave them there.

No doubt the expectation was that if the songs were of value they would be published to the advantage of both parties. But if for any reason the appellants chose not to publish them the respondent would get no remuneration and he could not do anything. Inevitably the respondent must take the risk of misjudgment of the merits of his work by the appellants. But that is not the only reason which might cause the appellants not to publish. There is no evidence about this so we must do the best we can with common knowledge. It does not seem fanciful and it was not argued that it is fanciful to suppose that purely commercial consideration might cause a publisher to refrain from publishing and promoting promising material. He might think it likely to be more profitable to promote work by other composers with whom he had agreements and unwise or too expensive to try to publish and popularise the respondent's work in addition. And there is always the possibility that less legitimate reasons might influence a decision not to publish the respondent's work . . .

[I]t appears to me to be an unreasonable restraint to tie the composer for this period of years so that his work will be sterilised and he can earn nothing from his abilities as a composer if the publisher chooses not to publish. If there had been in clause 9 any provision entitling the composer to terminate the agreement in such an event the case might have had a very different appearance. But as the agreement stands not only is the composer tied but he cannot recover the copyright of work which the publisher refuses to publish.

It was strenuously argued that the agreement is in standard form, that it has stood the test of time, and that there is no indication that it ever causes injustice. Reference was made to passages in the speeches of Lord Pearce and Lord Wilberforce in *Esso Petroleum v Harper's Garage (Stourport) Ltd* [1968] AC 269 with which I wholly agree. Lord Pearce said, at p 323:

> "It is important that the court, in weighing the question of reasonableness, should give full weight to commercial practices and to the generality of contracts made freely by parties bargaining on equal terms," . . .

But those passages refer to contracts "made freely by parties bargaining on equal terms" or "moulded under the pressures of negotiation, competition and public opinion". I do not find from any evidence in this case, nor does it seem probable, that this form of contract made between a publisher and an unknown composer has been moulded by any pressure of negotiation. Indeed, it appears that established composers who can bargain on equal terms can and do make their own contracts.

Any contract by which a person engages to give his exclusive services to another for a period necessarily involves extensive restriction during that period of the common law right to exercise any lawful activity he chooses in such manner as he thinks best. Normally the doctrine of restraint of trade has no application to such restrictions: they require no justification. But if contractual restrictions appear to be unnecessary or to be reasonably capable of enforcement in an oppressive manner, then they must be justified before they can be enforced.

In the present case the respondent assigned to the appellants "the full copyright for the whole world" in every musical composition "composed created or conceived" by him alone or in collaboration with any other person during a period of five or it might be 10 years. He received no payment (apart from an initial £50) unless his work was published and the appellants need not publish unless they chose to do so. And if they did not publish he had no right to terminate the agreement or to have copyrights re-assigned to him. I need not consider whether in any circumstances it would be possible to justify such a one-sided agreement. It is sufficient to say that such evidence as there is falls far short of justification. It must therefore follow that the agreement so far as unperformed is unenforceable.'

Lord Diplock:

'My Lords, the contract under consideration in this appeal is one whereby the respondent accepted restrictions upon the way in which he would exploit his earning power as a song writer for the next ten years. Because this can be classified as a contract in restraint of trade the restrictions that the respondent accepted fell within one of those limited categories of contractual promises in respect of which the courts still retain the power to relieve the promisor of his legal duty to fulfil them. In order to determine whether this case is one in which that power ought to be exercised, what your Lordships have in fact been doing has been to assess the relative bargaining power of the publisher and the song writer at the time the contract was made and to decide whether the publisher had used his superior bargaining power to exact from the song writer promises that were unfairly onerous to him. Your Lordships have not been concerned to inquire whether the public have in fact been deprived of the fruit of the song writer's talents by reason of the restrictions, nor to assess the likelihood that they would be so deprived in the future if the contract were permitted to run its full course.

It is, in my view, salutary to acknowledge that in refusing to enforce provisions of a contract whereby one party agrees for the benefit of the other party to exploit or to refrain from exploiting his own earning power, the public policy which the court is implementing is not some 19th-century economic theory about the benefit to the general public of freedom of trade, but the protection of those whose bargaining power is weak against being forced by those whose bargaining power is stronger to enter into bargains that are unconscionable. Under the influence of Bentham and of laissez-faire the courts in the 19th century abandoned the practice of applying the public policy against unconscionable bargains to contracts generally, as they had formerly done to any contract considered to be usurious; but the policy survived in its application to penalty clauses and to relief against forfeiture and also to the special category of contracts in restraint of trade. If one looks at the reasoning of 19th-century judges in cases about contracts in restraint of trade one finds lip service paid to current economic theories, but if one looks at what they said in the light of what they did, one finds that they struck down a bargain if they thought it was unconscionable as between the parties to it and upheld it if they thought that it was not.

So I would hold that the question to be answered as respects a contract in restraint of trade of the kind with which this appeal is concerned is: "Was the bargain fair?" The test of fairness is, no doubt, whether the restrictions are both reasonably necessary for the protection of the legitimate interests of the promisee and commensurate with the benefits secured to the promisor under the contract. For the purpose of this test all the provisions of the contract must be taken into consideration.

My Lords, the provisions of the contract have already been sufficiently stated by my noble and learned friend, Lord Reid. I agree with his analysis of them and with his conclusion that the contract is unenforceable. It does not satisfy the test of fairness as I have endeavoured to state it. I will accordingly content myself with adding some observations directed to the argument that because the contract was in a "standard form" in common use between music publishers and song writers the restraints that it imposes upon the song writer's liberty to exploit his talents must be presumed to be fair and reasonable.

Standard forms of contracts are of two binds. The first, of very ancient origin, are those which set out the terms upon which mercantile transactions of common occurrence are to be carried out. Examples are bills of lading, charterparties, policies of insurance, contracts of sale in the commodity markets. The standard clauses in these contracts have been settled over the years by negotiation by representatives of the commercial interests involved and have been widely adopted because experience has shown that they facilitate the conduct of trade. Contracts of these kinds affect not only the actual parties to them but also others who may have a commercial interest in the transactions to which they relate, as buyers or sellers, charterers or shipowners, insurers or bankers. If fairness or reasonableness were relevant to their enforceability the fact that they are widely used by parties whose bargaining power is fairly matched would raise a strong presumption that their terms are fair and reasonable.

The same presumption, however, does not apply to the other kind of standard form of contract. This is of comparatively modern origin. It is the result of the concentration of particular kinds of business in relatively few hands. The ticket cases in the 19th century provide what are probably the first examples. The terms of this kind of standard form of contract have not been the subject of negotiation between the parties to it, or approved by any organisation representing the interests of the weaker party. They have been dictated by that party whose bargaining power, either exercised alone or in conjunction with others providing similar goods or services, enables him to say: "If you want these goods or services at all, these are the only terms on which they are obtainable. Take it or leave it."

To be in a position to adopt this attitude towards a party desirous of entering into a contract to obtain goods or services provides a classic instance of superior bargaining power. It is not without significance that on the evidence in the present case music publishers in negotiating with song writers whose success has been already established do not insist upon adhering to a contract in the standard form they offered to the respondent. The fact that the appellants' bargaining power vis-à-vis the respondent was strong enough to enable them to adopt this take-it-or-leave-it attitude raises no presumption that they used it to drive an unconscionable bargain with him, but in the field of restraint of trade it calls for vigilance on the part of the court to see that they did not.'

[Viscount Dilhourne, Lord Kilbrandon and Lord Simon of Glaisdale delivered concurring judgments]

The speeches in *Schroeder* were significant because of the links their Lordships drew between the doctrine of restraint of trade and issues of substantive and procedural fairness. In the first paragraph of the printed extract, Lord Diplock claims that the court's real focus in cases of restraint of trade is on whether superior bargaining power has been used to extract the unfair terms – procedural fairness (see also *Clifford Davis Ltd v WEA Records* [1975] 1 WLR 61; *Leeds Rugby Ltd v Harris* [2005] EWHC 2290). In the next paragraph, his Lordship claims that the real issue is whether the bargain is unconscionable – substantive unfairness. But then in the third paragraph, Lord Diplock reverts to the traditional question of whether the restraint was reasonably necessary for the protection of the legitimate interests of the promisee.

Dealing with issues of substantive justice first, it is strongly arguable (see Smith, S (1995) 15 OJLS 565, 589) that the adequacy of consideration is relevant to the parties' interest test in exclusive dealing cases. This is because the legitimate interests of the covenantee (which he seeks to protect by means of the restraint) are virtually identical to the consideration received by the covenantor. For example, in *Esso v Harper*, Harper Garages accepted a restraint in return for a loan from Esso, a discount on petrol, guaranteed supply and help in setting up the petrol station. Esso required a restraint to protect its legitimate interest in that outlay. Similarly, in *Schroeder*, the consideration provided by the record company, that is, the risk assumed by the company and the payments made to the artist, were the legitimate interests that the record company sought to protect. The court could only assess the reasonableness of the restraint if it first considered the nature of the legitimate interests being protected. Thus references to the adequacy of consideration in vertical restraint cases are readily explicable without the need to import considerations of substantive justice (see, also, *Societa Esplosivi Industriali SpA v Ordnance Technologies (UK) Ltd* [2004] 1 All ER (Comm) 619).

Lord Diplock's concern with procedural fairness is far harder to explain away. Having said that, it is rather uncertain whether there actually was procedural unfairness on the facts of *Schroeder*. Professor Smith (1995) 15 OJLS 565, 584–5, has suggested that there was not:

'In the cases where bargaining power is most often raised, the vertical restraint cases, the relevant industries (music publishing and petroleum) appear to be very competitive. In addition, many of the procedural factors raised in *Schroeder* and others decisions, such as the existence of a standard form contract, how "desperately" the covenantor needed the contract, and the relative financial resources of the parties, are poor indicators of abuse of bargaining power. The well-established explanation of why standard form contracts are used in a wide variety of contexts is that they save parties the significant costs of writing individual contracts. Admittedly, standard form contracts are often not fully read or understood, but, even ignoring the competitive pressures to offer reasonable terms, it is unlikely that many potential covenantors are unaware of the existence or extent of a restraint. Most restraint of trade contracts are one-shot deals (unlike, for example, a car rental agreement) of which the restraints are not insignificant features. The two other factors are irrelevant in a competitive market. A desperate impecunious songwriter can go to another publisher if he or she does not like what is on offer. Remember also that an individual may be "desperate" for a contract precisely because he is a high-risk venture (for example, an impecunious debtor—or an unknown songwriter). Contracts with such individuals often appear to contain harsh terms. In the songwriter cases, there is undoubtedly a special danger of undue influence, but most other restraint of trade cases, including cases where covenants have been invalidated, involve mature parties dealing at arm's length.

These observations are consistent with the fact that, aside from market-fixing situations, a party who is able to dictate contractual terms is unlikely to exploit this power by demanding overly-restrictive covenants.'

It is submitted that issues of procedural fairness and inequality of bargaining power are best left to be dealt with by the distinct doctrines of duress and undue influence (see Chapters 11 and 12). It is wrong to conflate rules against restraints with rules against unfair bargains. The two issues are distinct in the law of contract and they should remain that way.

14.4 SEVERANCE

The general rule is that a covenant that is in restraint of trade will be unenforceable. In certain circumstances, however, the courts will sever the offending provisions of the restraint, leaving the remainder intact and enforceable. There have traditionally been two tests that the courts apply in this context: (1) the 'blue pencil test' and (2) the 'nature of the agreement test'.

14.4.1 THE BLUE PENCIL TEST

The court will ask whether the restraint could be made reasonable by simply striking out parts of it with a blue pencil. The court will not become involved with redrafting the contract:

Mason v Provident Clothing & Supply Co Ltd [1913] AC 724

Facts: The defendant worked in Islington, London, as a canvasser and collector for the plaintiff clothing company. A clause in his contract of employment restrained him from entering into similar employment within 25 miles of London for a period of three years after leaving the plaintiff's employment.

Held: The House of Lords held that the restraint was wider than was reasonably necessary for the plaintiffs' protection.

Lord Moulton:

'[I]t would be reasonable for the employer to protect himself against the danger of his former servant canvassing or collecting for a rival firm in the district in which he had been employed. If he were permitted to do so before the expiry of a reasonably long interval he would be in a position to give to his new employer all the advantages of that personal knowledge of the inhabitants of the locality, and more especially of his former customers, which he had acquired in the service of the respondents and at their expense. Against such a contingency the master might reasonably protect himself, but I can see no further or other protection which he could reasonably demand . . .

These, then, being the limits of the protection which the master might reasonably insist on, I turn to the covenant in order to see whether it exceeds these limits . . . [I]t prohibits the appellant from entering into a similar employment within twenty-five miles "of London in the county of Middlesex" for a period of three years after leaving the respondents' service. Such an area must include something like six million persons, that is to say, that on a moderate estimate it is an area a thousand times as great as the district assigned to him when in the respondents' service. Considering the strictly local character of the employment, I have no hesitation in saying that I should be prepared to hold that such an area is very far greater than could be reasonably required for the protection of his former employers.

It was suggested in the argument that even if the covenant was, as a whole, too wide, the Court might enforce restrictions which it might consider reasonable (even though they were not expressed in the covenant), provided they were within its ambit. My Lords, I do not doubt that the Court may, and in some cases will, enforce a part of a covenant in restraint of trade, even though taken as a whole the covenant exceeds what is reasonable. But, in my opinion, that ought only to be done in cases where the part so enforceable is clearly severable, and even so only in cases where the excess is of trivial importance, or merely technical, and not a part of the main purport and substance of the clause. It would in my opinion be *pessimi exempli* if, when an employer had exacted a covenant deliberately framed in unreasonably wide terms, the Courts were to come to his assistance and, by applying their ingenuity and knowledge of the law, carve out of this void covenant the maximum of what he might validly have required. It must be remembered that the real sanction at the back of these covenants is the terror and expense of litigation, in which the servant is usually at a great disadvantage, in view of the longer purse of his master. It is sad to think that in this present case this appellant, whose employment is a comparatively humble one, should have had to go through four Courts before he could free himself from such unreasonable restraints as this covenant imposes, and the hardship imposed by the exaction of unreasonable covenants by employers would be greatly increased if they could continue the practice with the expectation that, having exposed the servant to the anxiety and expense of litigation, the Court would in the end enable them to obtain everything which they could have obtained by acting reasonably. It is evident that those who drafted this covenant aimed at making it a penal rather than a protective covenant, and that they hoped by means of it to paralyse the earning capabilities of the man if and when he left their service, and were not thinking of what would be a reasonable protection to their business, and having so acted they must take the consequences.'

Goldsoll v Goldman [1915] 1 Ch 292

Facts: The defendant was a dealer in imitation jewellery. He sold his business to the plaintiff covenanting that for two years he would not: 'either solely or jointly with or as agent or employee for any other person or persons or company directly or indirectly carry on or be engaged concerned or interested in or render services (gratuitously or otherwise) to the business of a vendor of or dealer in real or imitation jewellery in the county of London or any part of the United Kingdom of Great Britain and Ireland and the Isle of Man or in France, the United States, Russia, or Spain, or within twenty-five miles of Potsdamerstrasse, Berlin, or St. Stefans Kirche, Vienna.' The defendant joined a rival firm of jewellers and the plaintiff sought an injunction to restrain the breach of covenant.

Held: The Court of Appeal held that the covenant was too wide in terms of subject matter because it referred to real jewellery when the defendant had not traded in real jewellery. It was also too wide in geographical area because the defendant had not traded overseas. These restrictions were severable, however, leaving a covenant that the defendant would not trade in imitation jewellery in the UK or the Isle of Man.

Lord Cozens-Hardy MR:
'It is perfectly clear that there has been a breach of the covenant; but that is not conclusive of the case, for what we have to consider is whether the covenant he has broken can be treated as good either in whole or in part, and can be enforced. On the question of the space covered by the covenant Neville J has held, and I entirely agree with him, that it is unnecessarily large in so far as it is intended to cover not merely the United Kingdom and the Isle of Man but also the foreign countries mentioned in the covenant. He has also held, and his decision is consistent with a long series of authorities, that the covenant can be severed as regards the space covered by it. It is clear that part of the covenant dealing with the area is reasonable, and the learned judge has limited the injunction he has granted to "the county of London, England, Scotland, Ireland, Wales, or any part of the United Kingdom of Great Britain and Ireland and the Isle of Man". That such a covenant is severable in this respect has been decided by authorities nearly 200 years old. No objection is taken or could be taken with regard to the limit of time, but the further difficulty has been raised that, while the business of the plaintiffs was, as I said, a business in imitation jewellery, the covenant is against carrying on or being interested in "the business of a vendor of or dealer in real or imitation jewellery". It is admitted that the business of a dealer in real jewellery is not the same as that of a dealer in imitation jewellery. There are many shopkeepers who would be insulted if they were asked whether they sold imitation

jewellery. That being so, it is difficult to support the whole of this provision, for the covenant must be limited to what is reasonably necessary for the protection of the covenantee's business. Then comes the question whether the doctrine of severability is applicable to this part of the covenant. In my opinion it is, and the covenant is good in so far as it operates to restrain the covenantor from carrying on business in imitation jewellery.'

Kennedy LJ:

'The doctrine of severability has been admitted by the Courts, and while I am far from saying that I do not see the force of the great objections brought forward by Lord Moulton in *Mason v Provident Clothing and Supply Co* and by Neville J. in this case, it is of no use going into that, because it has been held in decisions binding on this Court that, if words are used in a covenant such as admit of severability by mentioning different areas, we must sever the covenant so as to limit its operation to an area which is not too large. Moreover, if ever there was a case of severability we have it here, for countries are specified which may be treated as representing the United Kingdom as distinguished from foreign countries. There is therefore no sound objection to holding, as Neville J has, that severed in that way there is a reasonable part of the covenant which ought to be enforced in favour of the plaintiffs.'

It seems that the distinction between the two cases is one of form rather than substance. In *Goldsoll* only deletion was required; the court could use the 'blue pencil' to excise the words 'real or', and the list of countries. In *Mason*, however, both deletion and addition were required: '25 miles of London' needed to be replaced by 'Islington'. The House of Lords refused to make these changes on the ground that it would have constituted a rewriting of the agreement. In practice, however, there was little difference between what the Court of Appeal did in *Goldsoll* and what the House of Lords refused to do in *Mason*. The approach taken in *Goldsoll* is also difficult to reconcile with the policy advocated by Lord Moulton in *Mason*. There, his Lordship insisted that the courts should be slow to assist a covenantee who had deliberately framed a covenant in unreasonably wide terms. Such a person should be left to 'take the consequences' of his own actions. The Court of Appeal in *Goldsoll* expressed no such concerns. It seems that the law in this area is tied to rather arbitrary and technical rules.

14.4.2 THE NATURE OF THE AGREEMENT TEST

A second test that is applied by the courts is the requirement that the nature of the agreement must not be altered by severance.

Attwood v Lamont [1920] 3 KB 571

Facts: The plaintiff owned a general outfitters in Kidderminster. The defendant was employed in the tailoring department as a tailor and cutter. His contract stated that, following termination of his employment, he would not work as a 'tailor, dress-maker, general draper, milliner, hatter, haberdasher, gentlemen's, ladies' or children's outfitter at any place within a radius of ten miles of Kidderminster'. The defendant subsequently breached the covenant and the plaintiff applied to the court for an injunction.

Held: The Court of Appeal held that the covenant was a single entity for the protection of the plaintiff's business, which could not be severed without altering the nature of the covenant.

Younger LJ:

'[T]his was not a case in which upon any principle this severance was permissible. The learned judges of the Divisional Court, I think, took the view that such severance always was permissible when it could be effectively accomplished by the action of a blue pencil. I do not agree. The doctrine of severance has not, I think, gone further than to make it permissible in a case where the covenant is not really a single covenant but is in effect a combination of several distinct covenants. In that case and where the severance can be carried out without the addition or alteration of a word, it is permissible. But in that case only.

Now, here, I think, there is in truth but one covenant for the protection of the respondent's entire business, and not several covenants for the protection of his several businesses. The respondent is, on the evidence, not carrying on several businesses but one business, and, in my opinion, this covenant must stand or fall in its unaltered form.

But, further, I am of opinion that even if this were not so this case is not one in which any severance, even if otherwise technically permissible, ought to be made. In my view the necessary effect of the application of the principle on which *Mason's Case* [1913] AC 724 and *Morris v Saxelby* [1916] 1 AC 688 have both been decided has been to render obsolete the cases in which the Courts have severed these restrictive covenants when acting on the view that being prima facie valid it was their duty to bind the covenantee to them as far as was permissible.'

It is very difficult to reconcile this case with the earlier decision in *Goldsoll*. Nevertheless, the principle stated in *Attwood* remains good law and it must be assumed that the test represents an additional requirement for severance. Exactly how the principle will be applied, however, is very unpredictable.

14.4.3 DEVELOPMENTS IN THE INTERPRETATION OF RESTRAINTS

In recent years the courts have adopted a more flexible approach to interpreting restraint clauses in order to avoid the need for severance. The following case provides a good example of this practice.

Home Counties Dairies v Skilton [1970] 1 WLR 526

Facts: The defendant milk roundsman was employed by the plaintiffs. His contract of employment contained the following clause: 'The employee expressly agrees not at any time during the period of one year after termination of his employment . . . to serve or sell milk or dairy produce to . . . any person who at any time during the last six months of his employment shall have been a customer of the employer and served by the employee in the course of his employment.' The defendant left the plaintiffs and started work with another dairy company. At once he began to operate a milk round covering the same district as the one he had worked in for the plaintiffs. The plaintiff sought an injunction to restrain his breach of covenant. At first instance, the judge held that since the restraint covered 'dairy produce' it prevented the plaintiff from working as a grocer who sold butter and cheese and therefore went beyond the protection necessary to protect the defendant from solicitation of its customers.

Held: The Court of Appeal allowed the appeal, holding that the restraint must be read in the context of the whole agreement. As such, it only applied in circumstances where the employee left his employment and engaged in a dairy business either on his own account or in the employment of another dairy business.

Harman LJ:
'It is the first principle in construing written documents, whether wills or any other documents in writing, to consider the circumstances at the time when they were made and the position of the parties to them. Now the first thing to observe here is that this is an agreement between a dairyman and one of his roundsmen then operating a milk round on his behalf. It may therefore be supposed to be concerned with the employer's trade as a dairyman and the employee's trade as a milk roundsman, and there are indications throughout the document that it is with this subject-matter that it is concerned. For instance, in clause 9, what is to be recorded in "the rounds book" are amounts of milk, dairy and other commodities issued to the roundsman for sale to customers; that is to say, customers of the dairyman living on the milk round or near it, and being therefore such articles as are dealt with in the course of such activities. I am therefore of opinion that, on a true construction of the agreement, it has nothing to do with any commodity not such as is dealt with by the roundsman in the course of his round. The fact that butter and cheese may be described as "dairy produce and other commodities" does not seem to me to have the effect of preventing this man from entering the employment of someone other than a dairyman who happens to sell butter and cheese. If it were so, he could not be employed in a restaurant, and this

> seems to me to be outside the scope of the agreement altogether. It is in fact, on its
> true construction, an agreement not to serve an employer as a milk roundsman calling
> on the customers of the old milk round whom he has served in the last six months. This
> is precisely the area which, to my mind, the employer is entitled to protect.'

A more flexible approach to the interpretation of a restraint clause was also taken by the Court of Appeal in *Littlewoods Organisation Ltd v Harris* [1977] 1 WLR 1472. Megaw LJ referred to the decision in *Home Counties Dairies v Skilton* and said the following:

'There is no doubt, I should have thought, that on the literal meaning of the words, "dairy produce" would include butter and cheese; but the court had no difficulty in rejecting the argument that that made the covenant unenforceable. That was done, not by re-writing the covenant, but by construing the words "dairy produce" as being the limited sort of dairy produce with which the defendant had been concerned in his employment by the plaintiff.'

In reliance on *Skilton*, the majority rejected the view that the restraint on Mr Harris should be given its literal meaning. Instead, their Lordships concluded that 'limiting words ought to be read into the clause so as to limit it to the part of the business for which the plaintiffs [we]re reasonably entitled to protection'. A similar approach was taken in *Clarke v Newland* [1991] 1 All ER 397, where the plaintiff, a general medical practitioner, undertook 'not to practise in the practice area' (which was physically defined) within a period of three years following the termination of his employment. This broad restraint was construed to mean that the plaintiff would not 'practice as a general medical practitioner' (rather than practice in hospital medicine) since that was the role in which the defendant had previously been employed. Balcombe LJ said:

'In order . . . to consider what qualification should be given to the word "practice" in cl 15, one must, as I said, apply the ordinary principles of construction which require one to look at the remainder of the agreement and also at the matrix of surrounding circumstances in which it was made . . . Applying those principles, it is clear to me that, looking at the agreement of 3 October 1985 in the matrix of surrounding circumstances, "practice" in cl 15 means practice as a general medical practitioner.'

Interpreting restraint clauses in this way is likely to lead to the restraint, as redefined, being found to be reasonable. This will obviously change the way in which the courts tackle restraint clauses because it obviates the need to consider severance.

14.5 LEGISLATIVE CONTROL OF ANTI-COMPETITIVE PRACTICES

The common law rules on restraint of trade are rather limited in their effectiveness in controlling horizontal restraints. There are two reasons for this. First, the courts have historically assumed that horizontal agreements are reasonable between the parties (see *Attorney-General of the Commonwealth v The Adelaide Steamship Company* [1913] AC 781). Second, horizontal agreements very rarely come before the courts because the parties have no reason to litigate on them.

Over the years, Parliament has intervened to regulate horizontal agreements by enacting various pieces of legislation. These Acts of Parliament have now been superseded by the Competition Act 1998, which came into force on 1 March 2000. This Act replaces the previous legislation and implements various provisions based on the competition provisions to be found in the EC Treaty. In this section we will briefly examine the main provisions of the 1998 Act and consider the effect they will have on contracts in restraint of trade. We will also consider Arts 81 and 82 of the EC Treaty and their associated case law in order to better understand the provisions of the 1998 Act.

14.5.1 THE COMPETITION ACT 1998 CHAPTER I PROHIBITION

The Chapter I prohibition is contained in s 2 of the Competition Act 1998 and corresponds with Art 81 of the EC Treaty. It provides the following:

COMPETITION ACT 1998

Section 2

(1) Subject to section 3, agreements between undertakings, decisions by associations of undertakings or concerted practices which–

    (a) may affect trade within the United Kingdom, and

    (b) have as their object or effect the prevention, restriction or distortion of competition within the United Kingdom,

are prohibited unless they are exempt in accordance with the provisions of this Part.

(2) Subsection (1) applies, in particular, to agreements, decisions or practices which–

    (a) directly or indirectly fix purchase or selling prices or any other trading conditions;

    (b) limit or control production, markets, technical development or investment;

    (c) share markets or sources of supply;

    (d) apply dissimilar conditions to equivalent transactions with other trading parties, thereby placing them at a competitive disadvantage;

    (e) make the conclusion of contracts subject to acceptance by the other parties of supplementary obligations which, by their nature or according to commercial usage, have no connection with the subject of such contracts.

. . .

(4) Any agreement or decision which is prohibited by subsection (1) is void.

Section 2(1) clearly prohibits horizontal agreements to directly or indirectly fix prices (see s 2(2)), even when the agreements are an informal and nonbinding 'gentleman's agreement' (see *ACF Chemiefarma NV v Commission* (Cases 41, 44 and 45/69) [1970] ECR 661).

Certain agreements are excluded from the Chapter I prohibition by virtue of s 3 which provides the following:

COMPETITION ACT 1998

Section 3

(1) The Chapter I prohibition does not apply in any of the cases in which it is excluded by or as a result of–

(a) Schedule 1 (mergers and concentrations);

(b) Schedule 2 (competition scrutiny under other enactments);

(c) Schedule 3 (planning obligations and other general exclusions);

. . .

(6) Schedule 3 also gives the Secretary of State power to exclude agreements from the Chapter I prohibition in certain circumstances.

This section excludes agreements that are regulated by other procedures, such as mergers and concentrations (dealt with by the Enterprise Act 2002 or under the EC Merger Regulation) and investment businesses (dealt with by the Financial Services and Markets Act 2000). It also excludes undertakings that provide a service of general economic interest (such as a postal service or the provision of utilities infrastructure) and restrictions that are required to ensure compliance with other legal obligations or international law (paras 5 and 6 of Schedule 3). Para 7 of Schedule 3 also provides the following:

(1) If the Secretary of State is satisfied that there are exceptional and compelling reasons of public policy why the Chapter I prohibition ought not to apply to–

(a) a particular agreement, or

(b) any agreement of a particular description,

he may by order exclude the agreement, or agreements of that description, from the Chapter I prohibition.

The Secretary of State has not yet made use of this power. Professor Richard Whish (*Competition Law*, 5th edn, 2003, London: Lexis-Nexis, p 330) suggests that the provision will rarely be used in practice because it requires the Secretary of State to discharge the significant burden of establishing that there are 'exceptional and compelling' reasons why the power should be exercised. One situation in which the power might be exercised is in relation to the defence industry.

The effect of s 2 in respect of vertical agreements is rather complicated. Until 1 May 2005 vertical agreements were virtually all excluded from the Chapter 1 prohibition by virtue of the Competition Act (Land and Vertical Agreements) Order 2000, made pursuant to s 50 of the 1998 Act. However, in order to align the UK regime on competition with that in EC law (EC Modernisation Regulation – Council Regulation 1/2003 [2003] OJ L1/1), the Order was repealed subject to a one-year transitional period to allow companies to adapt. That transitional period expired on 1 May 2005, and since then the only remaining exemption for vertical agreements is that contained in Regulation 2790/1999/EC. This exempts most vertical agreements, but does not apply where the supplier (or buyer in an agreement for exclusive supply) has a market share of 30 per cent, or where one of the 'hardcore' restrictions listed in the Regulation apply, such as price-fixing or restrictions concerning territory into which a buyer may sell (for further information see OFT Guideline 419, *Vertical Agreements*, 2004). It is thus clear that the impact of the Chapter I prohibition on vertical restraints is rather limited.

14.5.1.1 The effect of the Chapter I prohibition

Section 2(4) provides that any agreement prohibited by subsection (1) is void. This does not mean, however, that the whole agreement will be avoided since the European Court of Justice (ECJ) has recognised the concept of 'severance' (*Société Technique Minière v Maschinebau Ulm GmbH* (Case 56/65) [1966] ECR 235, [1966] CMLR 357) and this will, by virtue of s 60 of the 1998 Act have effect in respect of the Chapter I prohibition as well.

A possible conflict exists between EC law and UK law in regard to the effect of 'voidness'. In *Gibbs Mew plc v Gemmell* [1998] Eu LR 588, the Court of Appeal held that the parties to an agreement which breached Article 81 could not bring an action for damages or restitution since they themselves were party to an illegal contract – the principle *in pari delicto potior est conditio defendentis* applied. However, this decision now seems wrong following a referral to the ECJ in a similar case.

Courage Ltd v Crehan (Case C–453/99); [2001] ECR I–6297

Facts: The defendant was the tenant of two public houses in Staines, West London. He was tied to the claimant brewery under an agreement which required him to buy beer

---

exclusively from the claimant at fixed prices. The claimant brought an action against the defendant for £15,266 for unpaid deliveries of beer. He defended the action on the ground that the tie agreement was contrary to Article 81 (Article 85 as it then was) of the EC Treaty and therefore unenforceable. The defendant also counterclaimed for damages on the ground that the claimant sold beer to other public houses at lower prices than those imposed on the tied tenants, thus reducing the profitability of the tied tenants. The Court of Appeal referred the case to the European Court of Justice.

Held: The European Court of Justice held that the national rule of law that barred a claim for damages on the ground that the claimant was a party to the contract was incompatible with Article 81. A party could recover damages provided that they did not bear significant responsibility for the distortion of competition. Factors to be taken into account in assessing the party's degree of responsibility include the respective bargaining power of the parties.

20 September 2001. The following judgment was delivered in open court in Luxembourg:

'**17.** . . . [T]he referring court is asking essentially whether a party to a contract liable to restrict or distort competition within the meaning of article 85 of the Treaty can rely on the breach of that provision before a national court to obtain relief from the other contracting party. In particular, it asks whether that party can obtain compensation for loss which he alleges to result from his being subject to a contractual clause contrary to article 85 and whether, therefore, Community law precludes a rule of national law which denies a person the right to rely on his own illegal actions to obtain damages.

18. If Community law precludes a national rule of that sort, the national court wishes to know . . . what factors must be taken into consideration in assessing the merits of such a claim for damages.

24. . . . [A]ny individual can rely on a breach of article 85(1) of the Treaty before a national court even where he is a party to a contract that is liable to restrict or distort competition within the meaning of that provision.

25. As regards the possibility of seeking compensation for loss caused by a contract or by conduct liable to restrict or distort competition, it should be remembered from the outset that, in accordance with settled case law, the national courts whose task it is to apply the provisions of Community law in areas within their jurisdiction must ensure that those rules take full effect and must protect the rights which they confer on individuals . . .

26. The full effectiveness of article 85 of the Treaty and, in particular, the practical effect of the prohibition laid down in article 85(1) would be put at risk if it were not open to any individual to claim damages for loss caused to him by a contract or by conduct liable to restrict or distort competition.

27. Indeed, the existence of such a right strengthens the working of the Community competition rules and discourages agreements or practices, which are frequently covert, which are liable to restrict or distort competition. From that point of view, actions for damages before the national courts can make a significant contribution to the maintenance of effective competition in the Community.

28. There should not therefore be any absolute bar to such an action being brought by a party to a contract which would be held to violate the competition rules.

29. However, in the absence of Community rules governing the matter, it is for the domestic legal system of each member state to designate the courts and tribunals having jurisdiction and to lay down the detailed procedural rules governing actions for safeguarding rights which individuals derive directly from Community law, provided that such rules are not less favourable than those governing similar domestic actions (principle of equivalence) and that they do not render practically impossible or excessively difficult the exercise of rights conferred by Community law . . .

33. . . . [I]t is for the national court to ascertain whether the party who claims to have suffered loss through concluding a contract that is liable to restrict or distort competition found himself in a markedly weaker position than the other party, such as seriously to compromise or even eliminate his freedom to negotiate the terms of the contract and his capacity to avoid the loss or reduce its extent, in particular by availing himself in good time of all the legal remedies available to him.

36. Having regard to all the foregoing considerations, the questions referred are to be answered as follows. A party to a contract liable to restrict or distort competition within the meaning of article 85 of the Treaty can rely on the breach of that article to obtain relief from the other contracting party. Article 85 of the Treaty precludes a rule of national law under which a party to a contract liable to restrict or distort competition within the meaning of that provision is barred from claiming damages for loss caused by performance of that contract on the sole ground that the claimant is a party to that contract. Community law does not preclude a rule of national law barring a party to a contract liable to restrict or distort competition from relying on his own unlawful actions to obtain damages where it is established that that party bears significant responsibility for the distortion of competition.'

According to the European Court, if there is inequality of bargaining power, the party that finds themselves in the weaker position should be entitled to claim damages or restitution under the void contract. Such inequality has not traditionally been viewed as an exception to the *in pari delicto* principle in English law. It therefore seems that the English courts will have to adopt a more flexible approach to the availability of remedies in relation to contracts that are void under the Chapter I prohibition than they have done in the past. As it turned out, on the facts of *Crehan*, the House of Lords eventually decided that the beer ties did not infringe

Article 81 and therefore the defendant was not entitled to damages (*Crehan v Inntrepreneur Pub Co (CPC)* [2006] 3 WLR 148).

14.5.2 THE COMPETITION ACT 1998 CHAPTER II PROHIBITION

The Chapter II prohibition is contained in s 18 of the Competition Act 1998 and corresponds with Art 82 of the EC Treaty. It provides the following:

COMPETITION ACT 1998

Section 18

(1) Subject to section 19, any conduct on the part of one or more undertakings which amounts to the abuse of a dominant position in a market is prohibited if it may affect trade within the United Kingdom.

(2) Conduct may, in particular, constitute such an abuse if it consists in–

(a) directly, or indirectly imposing unfair purchase or selling prices or other unfair trading conditions;

(b) limiting production, markets or technical development to the prejudice of consumers;

(c) applying dissimilar conditions to equivalent transactions with other trading parties, thereby placing them at a competitive disadvantage;

(d) making the conclusion of contracts subject to acceptance by the other parties of supplementary obligations which, by their nature or according to commercial usage, have no connection with the subject of the contracts.

Section 18 deals with the abuse by one or more undertakings of a dominant market position. It applies to an even wider range of behaviour than the Chapter I prohibition, although for our purposes we will only consider its impact on contracts. Subsection (2) refers to the types of conduct that might amount to an 'abuse' and this roughly corresponds to those listed in s 2(2) in relation to the Chapter I prohibiton. It is assumed that this list is a nonexhaustive list of mere examples.

The classic definition on the meaning of dominant position in EC competition law was provided by the ECJ in *Hoffmann-la Roche & Co AG v Commission of the European Communities* (Case 85/76) [1979] ECR 461:

[A] dominant position . . . relates to a position of economic strength enjoyed by an undertaking which enables it to prevent effective competition being maintained on the relevant market by affording it the power to behave to an appreciable extent independently of its competitors, its customers and ultimately of the consumers. Such a position does not preclude some competition, which it does where there is a monopoly or a quasi-monopoly, but enables the undertaking which profits by it, if not to determine, at least to have an appreciable influence on the conditions under which that competition will develop, and in any case to act largely in disregard of it so long as such conduct does not operate to its detriment. . . . The existence of a dominant position may derive from several factors which, taken separately, are not necessarily determinative but among these factors a highly important one is the existence of very large market shares.'

The ECJ has since declared that there is a rebuttable presumption that an undertaking will be in a dominant market position if it has more than a 50 per cent market share (*AKZO Chemie BV v EC Commission* (Case C–62/86) [1991] ECR I–3359). In *British Airways v Commission* [2003] ECR II–5917 [2004] 4 CMLR 19, British Airways was held to be in a dominant market position with a market share of just 39.7 per cent. This appears to be the lowest point at which the European courts have found a dominant market position. In the UK, the OFT has suggested (OFT Guideline 415, *Assessment of Market Power*, 1999) that, in relation to s 18 of the Competition Act it is unlikely that an undertaking will be dominant if its market share is less than 40 per cent.

There are a number of exceptions to the Chapter II prohibition which are contained in section 19:

COMPETITION ACT 1998

Section 19

(1) The Chapter II prohibition does not apply in any of the cases in which it is excluded by or as a result of–

    (a) Schedule 1 (mergers and concentrations); or

    (b) Schedule 3 (general exclusions).

(2) The Secretary of State may at any time by order amend Schedule 1, with respect to the Chapter II prohibition, by–

    (a) providing for one or more additional exclusions; or

    (b) amending or removing any provisions (whether or not it has been added by an order under this subsection).

These exceptions are less extensive than those for the Chapter I prohibition.

Neither s 18 nor Art 82 specify the effect of a contract falling within the Chapter II prohibition, although it has always been assumed that such contracts are void. That said, it is likely that the customer will be able to enforce the contract against the dominant undertaking since the parties are not *in pari delicto* (*GT-Link A/S v De Danske Statsbaner* (Case C 242/95) [1997] ECR I–4349). This will mean that an agreement contravening s 18 of the 1998 Act will be void against the dominant firm, but enforceable by the customer.

14.6 ADDITIONAL READING

Heydon, JD, *The Restraint of Trade Doctrine*, 2nd edn, 1999, Sydney: Butterworths.

Marsh, NS, 'The Severance of Illegality in Contract' (1948) 64 LQR 230.

Odudu, O and Edelman, J, 'Compensatory Damages for Breach of Article 81' (2002) European Law Review 327.

Slot, JS and Johnston, A, *An Introduction To Competition Law*, 2006, Oxford: Hart.

Trebilcock, MJ, *The Common Law Doctrine of Restraint of Trade: A Legal and Economic Analysis*, 1986, Toronto: Carswell.

Whish, R, *Competition Law*, 5th edn, 2003, London: Lexis-Nexis.

CHAPTER 15

FRUSTRATION

15.1 INTRODUCTION

In this chapter we will be considering the doctrine of frustration. This concerns the situation where, following formation of a contract, an event occurs that renders further performance impossible, illegal or radically different from that which was originally envisaged. If such an event occurs, the parties will be partially or wholly relieved from further obligations and may be able to recover money and goods transferred under the contract.

There are clear links between the doctrine of frustration and the doctrine of common mistake. They both involve 'impossibility': common mistake concerning 'initial impossibility' (impossibility that arises prior to the formation of the contract) and frustration concerning 'subsequent impossibility' (impossibility that arises after formation of the contract). A significant difference between the two doctrines is that while common mistake renders the contract void *ab initio* (from the beginning), frustration merely discharges the parties from their future obligations.

In this respect, there are many similarities between the doctrine of frustration and the topics of performance and breach, to be dealt with in Chapter 16.

This chapter is divided into six sections. First, we will consider the nature of the doctrine, examining the underlying basis of frustration. Second, we will look at the categories of event that have been recognised by the courts as amounting to frustration of the contract. Third, the limitations on the doctrine will be examined. Fourth, we will consider the effects of the doctrine at common law and fifth we will examine the impact of the Law Reform (Frustrated Contracts) Act 1943. Finally, we will examine the provisions of the UNIDROIT Principles and The Principles of European Contract Law, and see how these international instruments make provision for the adjustment of the contract in cases of hardship.

15.1.1 THE NATURE OF THE DOCTRINE

Initially, English law adopted a very strict approach, insisting on the literal performance of contracts. In *Paradine v Jane* (1647) Aleyn 26, a tenant of a farm was dispossessed for two years following an invasion by Prince Rupert of Germany. The tenant claimed that he was not liable to pay rent for the two-year period. The court held in favour of the landlord: 'Now the rent is a duty created by the parties upon the reservation, and had there been a covenant to pay it, there had been no question but the lessee must have made it good, notwithstanding the interruption by enemies, for the law would not protect him beyond his own agreement . . .'. The justification for refusing to discharge the parties from their obligations was that the parties could, if they wished, have included a specific term in the contract to deal with the eventuality. Such clauses (known as *force majeure* or 'hardship' clauses) are commonplace in commercial contracts and it is arguable that the *Paradine v Jane* approach is the most economically efficient since the parties are in the best position to determine the allocation of risk. Professor McKendrick ('The regulation of long term contracts in English Law', Chapter 12 in Beatson, J and Friedmann, D (eds), *Good Faith and Fault in Contract Law*, 1995, pp 326–7, Oxford: Clarendon Press) has commented:

> '[T]he diversity and sophistication of the various *force majeure* clauses which are currently in use underlines the complexity of the issues dealt with by these clauses and they are best resolved by the parties, not the courts. A *force majeure* clause can be expected to define the events which are to trigger the clause, make provision for the procedure to be followed upon the occurrence of such an event, stipulate the effect which the event is to have on the contract itself and, possibly, make provision for the adjudication of any disputes arising out of the clause . . . The diversity of *force majeure* clauses suggests that it is impossible to draft a 'boiler-plate' *force majeure* clause which will be suitable

for all occasions and that it would be equally impossible for the courts to provide a simple all-encompassing solution to all these problems via a wider doctrine of frustration.'

Force majeure clauses are rare, however, outside of commercial contracts and eventually the courts recognised that the strict approach could lead to oppressive and unjust results. Blackburn J adopted a more liberal approach in *Taylor v Caldwell*.

Taylor v Caldwell (1863) 3 B & S 826

Facts: On 27 May 1861, the plaintiffs entered into a contract by which the defendants agreed to let the plaintiffs have the use of the Surrey Gardens and music hall on 17 June, 16 July, 5 August and 17 August, for the purpose of giving a series of four concerts. After the making of the agreement, but before the first day on which a concert was to be given, the music hall was destroyed by fire. The fire was not due to the fault of either party but the damage caused was so extensive that the concerts could not go ahead as intended. The plaintiffs brought a claim against the defendants for breach of contract in failing to supply the hall.

Held: The Court of Queen's Bench held that the contract was discharged for frustration on the ground that it contained an implied condition that the parties shall be excused from performance if the subject matter of the contract is destroyed.

Blackburn J:
'There seems no doubt that, where there is a positive contract to do a thing not in itself unlawful, the contractor must perform it or pay damages for not doing it, although, in consequence of unforeseen accident, the performance of his contract has become unexpectedly burdensome, or even impossible . . . But this rule is only applicable when the contract is positive and absolute and not subject to any condition either expressed or implied; and there are authorities which, as we think, establish the principle that where, from the nature of the contract, it appears that the parties must from the beginning have known that it could not be fulfilled unless, when the time for the fulfilment of the contract arrived, some particular specified thing continued to exist, so that when entering into the contract they must have contemplated such continued existence as the foundation of what was to be done, there, in the absence of any expressed or implied warranty that the thing shall exist, the contract is not to be construed as a positive contract, but as subject to an implied condition that the parties shall be excused in case, before breach, performance becomes impossible from the perishing of the thing without default of the contractor.

There seems little doubt that this implication tends to further the great object of making the legal construction such as to fulfil the intention of those who enter into the contract, for, in the course of affairs, men, in making such contracts, in general, would, if it were brought to their minds, say that there should be such a condition.

Accordingly, in the civil law, such an exception is implied in every obligation of the class, which they call *obligatio de certo corpore* ... Although the civil law is not of itself an authority in an English court, it affords great assistance in investigating the principles on which the law is grounded, and it seems to us that the common law authorities establish that, in such a contract, the same condition of the continued existence of the thing is implied by English law ...

It may, I think, be safely asserted to be now English lain that in all contracts of loan of chattels or bailment, if the performance of the promise of the borrower or bailee to return the thing lent or borrowed becomes impossible because it has perished, this impossibility, if not arising from the fault of the bailee, or from some risk which he has taken upon himself, excuses the borrower or bailee from the performance of his promise to redeliver the chattel ... The principle seems to us to be that in contracts in which the performance depends on the continued existence of a given person or thing, a condition is implied that the impossibility of performance arising from the perishing of the person or thing shall excuse the performance. In none of these cases is the promise in words other than positive, nor is there any express stipulation that the destruction of the person or thing shall excuse the performance; that excuse is by law implied, because from the nature of the contract it is apparent that the parties contracted on the basis of the continued existence of the particular person or chattel. In the present case, looking at the whole contract, we find that the parties contracted on the basis of the continued existence of the music hall at the time when the concerts were to be given, that being essential to their performance. We think, therefore, that, the music hall having ceased to exist without fault of either party, both parties are excused, the plaintiffs from taking the gardens and paying the money, the defendants from performing their promise to give the use of the hall and gardens, and other things. The rule must be made absolute to enter the verdict for the defendants.'

The first point to note is that by restricting the implied condition to 'the impossibility of performance arising from the perishing of the person or thing', Blackburn J avoided a direct conflict with the decision in *Paradine v Jane*, since in that case the subject matter had not perished. Blackburn J purported to recognise an exception to the general rule as stated in *Paradine v Jane*. However, as Professor Treitel (Treitel, G, *Frustration and Force Majeure*, 2nd edn, 2004, Para 2–025, London: Sweet & Maxwell) has noted: 'the formulation of the exception took a form which made it possible for later judges to extend the scope of the exception, so that in the course of time what was the exception has become the general rule, and conversely'. Blackburn J's exception was based on the view that the general rule 'is only applicable when the contract is positive and absolute and not subject to any condition either expressed or implied'. The reference to implied conditions provided the flexibility necessary for later courts to apply the exception in cases where the frustrating event was something other than the perishing of the subject matter.

The implied term approach to frustration had the merit of being consistent with the prevailing notion of freedom of contract. It based the intervention of the court, not on any assumed right of the law to intervene, but on the implied intention of the parties. It was soon shown to be fictitious, however.

Davis Contractors Ltd v Fareham UDC [1956] AC 696

Facts: On 9 July 1946, Davis Contractors entered into a contract to build 78 houses for Fareham UDC within eight months for £94,425. Due to unexpected circumstances, which were not the fault of either party, adequate supplies of labour were not available and the work took 22 months to complete at a cost to Davis of £115,233. Fareham UDC paid Davis the contract price. Davis argued that the contract had been frustrated and claimed to be entitled on a *quantum meruit* to a reasonable sum for the work done (which would have exceeded the contract price).

Held: The House of Lords held that the contract had not been frustrated. The shortage of labour had rendered the contract more onerous than had been contemplated but was not sufficient to discharge the contract for frustration.

Lord Reid:
'Frustration has often been said to depend on adding a term to the contract by implication: for example, Lord Loreburn in *FA Tamplin Steamship Co Ltd v Anglo-Mexican Petroleum Products Co Ltd* [1916] 2 AC 397, 404 after quoting language of Lord Blackburn, said:

> "That seems to me another way of saying that from the nature of the contract it cannot be supposed the parties, as reasonable men, intended it to be binding on them under such altered conditions. Were the altered conditions such that, had they thought of them, they would have taken their chance of them, or such that as sensible men they would have said 'if that happens, of course, it is all over between us'? What, in fact, was the true meaning of the contract? Since the parties have not provided for the contingency, ought a court to say it is obvious they would have treated the thing as at an end?"

I find great difficulty in accepting this as the correct approach because it seems to me hard to account for certain decisions of this House in this way . . .
I may be allowed to note an example of the artificiality of the theory of an implied term given by Lord Sands in *James Scott & Sons Ltd v Del Sel* 1922 SC 592, 597:

> "A tiger has escaped from a travelling menagerie. The milkgirl fails to deliver the milk. Possibly the milkman may be exonerated from any breach of contract; but, even so, it would seem hardly reasonable to base that exoneration on the ground that 'tiger days excepted' must be held as if written into the milk contract."

I think that there is much force in Lord Wright's criticism in *Denny, Mott & Dickson Ltd v James B Fraser & Co Ltd* [1944] AC 265, 275:

"The parties did not anticipate fully and completely, if at all, or provide for what actually happened. It is not possible, to my mind, to say that, if they had thought of it, they would have said: 'Well, if that happens, all is over between us.' On the contrary, they would almost certainly on the one side or the other have sought to introduce reservations or qualifications or compensations."

It appears to me that frustration depends, at least in most cases, not on adding any implied term, but on the true construction of the terms which are in the contract read in light of the nature of the contract and of the relevant surrounding circumstances when the contract was made . . .'

Lord Radcliffe:

'The theory of frustration belongs to the law of contract and it is represented by a rule which the courts will apply in certain limited circumstances for the purpose of deciding that contractual obligations, *ex facie* binding, are no longer enforceable against the parties. The description of the circumstances that justify the application of the rule and, consequently, the decision whether in a particular case those circumstances exist are, I think, necessarily questions of law . . .

Lord Loreburn ascribes the dissolution to an implied term of the contract that was actually made. This approach is in line with the tendency of English courts to refer all the consequences of a contract to the will of those who made it. But there is something of a logical difficulty in seeing how the parties could even impliedly have provided for something which *ex hypothesi* they neither expected nor foresaw; and the ascription of frustration to an implied term of the contract has been criticised as obscuring the true action of the court which consists in applying an objective rule of the law of contract to the contractual obligations that the parties have imposed upon themselves. So long as each theory produces the same result as the other, as normally it does, it matters little which theory is avowed (see *British Movietonews Ltd v London and District Cinemas Ltd* [1952] AC 166, 184 *per* Viscount Simon). But it may still be of some importance to recall that, if the matter is to be approached by way of implied term, the solution of any particular case is not to be found by inquiring what the parties themselves would have agreed on had they been, as they were not, forewarned. It is not merely that no one can answer that hypothetical question: it is also that the decision must be given "irrespective of the individuals concerned, their temperaments and failings, their interest and circumstances" (*Hirji Mulji v Cheong Yue Steamship Co Ltd* [1926] AC 497). The legal effect of frustration "does not depend on their intention or their opinions, or even knowledge, as to the event." On the contrary, it seems that when the event occurs "the meaning of the contract must be taken to be, not what the parties did intend (for they had neither thought nor intention regarding it), but that which the parties, as fair and reasonable men, would presumably have agreed upon if, having such possibility in view, they had made express provision as to their several rights and liabilities in the event of its occurrence" (*Dahl v Nelson* (1881) 6 App Cas 38, *per* Lord Watson).

By this time it might seem that the parties themselves have become so far disembodied spirits that their actual persons should be allowed to rest in peace. In their place there rises the figure of the fair and reasonable man and the spokesman of the fair and reasonable man, who represents after all no more than the anthropomorphic conception of justice, is and must be the court itself. So perhaps it would be simpler to say at the outset that frustration occurs whenever the law recognises that without default of either party a contractual obligation has become incapable of being performed because the circumstances in which performance is called for would render it a thing radically different from that which was undertaken by the contract. *Non haec in foedera veni*. It was not this that I promised to do.

There is, however, no uncertainty as to the materials upon which the court must proceed. "The data for decision are, on the one hand, the terms and construction of the contract, read in the light of the then existing circumstances, and on the other hand the events which have occurred" (*Denny, Mott & Dickson Ltd v James B Fraser & Co Ltd* [1944] AC 265, 274–275 *per* Lord Wright). In the nature of things there is often no room for any elaborate inquiry. The court must act upon a general impression of what its rule requires. It is for that reason that special importance is necessarily attached to the occurrence of any unexpected event that, as it were, changes the face of things. But, even so, it is not hardship or inconvenience or material loss itself which calls the principle of frustration into play. There must be as well such a change in the significance of the obligation that the thing undertaken would, if performed, be a different thing from that contracted for.

I am bound to say that, if this is the law, the appellants' case seems to me a long way from a case of frustration. Here is a building contract entered into by a housing authority and a big firm of contractors in all the uncertainties of the post-war world. Work was begun shortly before the formal contract was executed and continued, with impediments and minor stoppages but without actual interruption, until the 78 houses contracted for had all been built. After the work had been in progress for a time the appellants raised the claim, which they repeated more than once, that they ought to be paid a larger sum for their work than the contract allowed; but the respondents refused to admit the claim and, so far as appears, no conclusive action was taken by either side which would make the conduct of one or the other a determining element in the case.

That is not in any obvious sense a frustrated contract . . .'

Before considering their Lordships' rejection of the implied term theory, it is important to note why the contractors' claim failed. The case is not an example of commercial impossibility at all. In fact, Davis Contractors were able to fulfil their contractual obligations at a cost of just 23 per cent over the contract price. The essence of their claim was that it had become commercially disadvantageous for them to perform the contract at the agreed price. This is not a recognised ground for discharging a contract under English law.

Turning to their Lordships' rejection of the implied term theory, Lord Radcliffe believed that there was 'a logical difficulty in seeing how the parties could . . . impliedly have provided for something which *ex hypothesi* they neither expected nor foresaw'. This objection is perhaps overstated. *Force majeure* clauses frequently contain provisions as to the effect of unforeseen events. If this can be done by an express clause, there seems to be no reason why it cannot be done by one that is implied. Nevertheless, it is true to say that the implied term theory obscures what the courts are actually doing. As the cases reveal, the courts are really seeking to determine whether the supervening event has such an effect on the contract that it is unfair to hold parties to their bargain, in the absence of fault and of any assumption of the risk by either party. The theory preferred by Lords Reid and Radcliffe is based on the construction of the contract. Both of these theories were included in a list of possible bases for the doctrine of frustration provided by Lord Hailsham LC in *National Carriers v Panalpina (Northern) Ltd*.

National Carriers v Panalpina (Northern) Ltd [1981] AC 675

Lord Hailsham LC:

'At least five theories of the basis of the doctrine of frustration have been put forward at various times, and, since the theoretical basis of the doctrine is clearly relevant to the point under discussion, I enumerate them here. The first is the "implied term" or "implied condition" theory on which Blackburn J plainly relied in *Taylor v Caldwell*, as applying to the facts of the case before him. To these it is admirably suited. The weakness, it seems to me, of the implied term theory is that it raises once more the spectral figure of the officious bystander intruding on the parties at the moment of agreement . . .

Counsel for the respondent sought to argue that *Taylor v Caldwell*, 3 B & S 826, could as easily have been decided on the basis of a total failure of consideration. This is the second of the five theories. But *Taylor v Caldwell* was clearly not so decided, and in any event many, if not most, cases of frustration which have followed *Taylor v Caldwell* have occurred during the currency of a contract partly executed on both sides, when no question of total failure of consideration can possibly arise.

In *Hirji Mulji v Cheong Yue Steamship Co Ltd* [1926] AC 497, 510 Lord Sumner seems to have formulated the doctrine as a ". . . device [sic], by which the rules as to absolute contracts are reconciled with a special exception which justice demands" and Lord Wright in *Denny, Mott & Dickson Ltd v James B Fraser & Co Ltd* [1944] AC 265, 275 seems to prefer this formulation to the implied condition view. The weakness of the formulation, however, if the implied condition theory, with which Lord Sumner coupled it, be rejected, is that, though it admirably expresses the purpose of the doctrine, it does not provide it with any theoretical basis at all.

Hirji Mulji v Cheong Yue Steamship Co Ltd is, it seems to me, really an example of the more sophisticated theory of "frustration of the adventure" or "foundation of the contract" formulation, said to have originated with *Jackson v Union Marine Insurance Co Ltd* (1874) LR 10 CP 125, compare also, for example, *per* Goddard J in *WJ Tatem Ltd v Gamboa* [1939] 1 KB 132, 138. This, of course, leaves open the question of what is, in any given case, the foundation of the contract or what is "fundamental" to it, or what is the "adventure". Another theory, of which the parent may have been Earl Loreburn in *FA Tamplin Steamship Co Ltd v Anglo-Mexican Petroleum Products Co Ltd* [1916] 2 AC 397 is that the doctrine is based on the answer to the question: "What in fact is the true meaning of the contract?": see p 404. This is the "construction theory". In *Davis Contractors Ltd v Fareham UDC* [1956] AC 696, 729 Lord Radcliffe put the matter thus, and it is the formulation I personally prefer:

". . . frustration occurs whenever the law recognises that without default of either party a contractual obligation has become incapable of being performed because the circumstances in which performance is called for would render it a thing radically different from that which was undertaken by the contract. *Non haec in foedera veni*. It was not this that I promised to do." '

Although Lord Hailsham regarded the theoretical basis of the doctrine as being 'clearly relevant to the point under discussion', several commentators have doubted its practical importance. The point is made in H Beale, (ed) *Chitty on Contracts*, 29th edn, 2004, para 23–018, London: Sweet & Maxwell:

'It is difficult to discern any practical consequence which flows from the different tests . . . The courts have regard to the construction of the contract, the effect of the changed circumstances on the parties' contractual obligations, the intention of the parties (objectively construed) and the demands of justice in deciding whether or not a contract has been frustrated. No one factor is conclusive: the court will balance these different factors in determining whether a contract has been frustrated.'

Professor Treitel agrees. He notes that in *Davis Contractors*, Lord Reid opined that the parties' intentions were relevant to the implied term theory, but not to the construction theory. Professor Treitel (Treitel, G, *Frustration and Force Majeure*, 2nd edn, 2004, Para 16–016, London: Sweet & Maxwell) doubts whether this is true:

'[I]n construing the contract, the court does not wholly disregard the intention of the parties. The court may not have to ask: what would the parties have said, had they thought of the frustrating event? But it does have to ask: in what circumstances did the parties intend the contract to operate? In answering this question, the court will no doubt apply an objective test and may refuse to admit evidence of the parties' "subjective intent"; but it is only after

913

the question has been answered that the intention of the parties becomes irrelevant: that is, it is not necessary to go on and ask whether they would (if they had considered the event) have agreed to discharge, or to some other compromise solution. But this question does not arise under the "implied term" theory either, as frustration at common law always results in total discharge of the contract.'

Although there may be little practical difference between the five bases of the doctrine, it seems that the 'construction theory' is the one that is currently favoured (it has been adopted in the context of common mistake as well: see *Great Peace Shipping Ltd v Tsavliris Salvage (International) Ltd* [2003] QB 679). The courts will ask what the original contract required of the parties and then consider whether the frustrating event has rendered performance 'radically different' from that which was originally envisaged. This approach requires the courts to decide what situations will make performance 'radically different'. It is to this that we now turn in the following section.

▌15.2 FRUSTRATING EVENTS

It is impossible to formulate an exhaustive list of frustrating events. The following are given as examples of events that have been recognised by the courts as amounting to frustration of the contract.

15.2.1 IMPOSSIBILITY

Impossibility of performance is the most obvious ground of frustration and it may arise for a number of reasons.

15.2.1.1 Destruction of the subject matter

In *Taylor v Caldwell*, the performance of the contract was rendered impossible by the destruction of the subject matter. The case is an example of partial impossibility because the contract related to the use of the hall and the gardens, but it was only the hall that was destroyed by the fire. Nevertheless, the use of the hall was deemed to be a fundamental element of the contract (the hall being required for the giving of concerts) and its destruction was sufficient to frustrate it.

It is not necessary to show complete destruction of the subject matter as long as the nature of the thing has been materially altered. In *Asfar v Blundell* [1896] 1 QB 123, a cargo of dates was being carried on a barge that sunk in the Thames. The dates were recovered and although they were still of value for the purpose of distillation into spirit, they had become contaminated with sewage and were in such a condition of fermentation that they were no longer merchantable as dates. Lord Esher MR said:

> 'The nature of a thing is not necessarily altered because the thing itself has been damaged; wheat or rice may be damaged, but may still remain the things dealt with as wheat or rice in business. But if the nature of the thing is altered, and it becomes for business purposes something else, so that it is not dealt with by business people as the thing which it originally was, the question for determination is whether the thing insured, the original article of commerce, has become a total loss. If it is so changed in its nature by the perils of the sea as to become an unmerchantable thing, which no buyer would buy and no honest seller would sell, then there is a total loss. That test was applied in the present case by the learned judge in the Court below, who decided as a fact that the dates had been so deteriorated that they had become something which was not merchantable as dates. If that was so, there was a total loss of the dates.'

15.2.1.2 Death or incapacity

A contract for personal services will be frustrated on the death of either party (*Cutter v Powell* (1795) 6 TR 320). The same principle applies where either party is permanently incapacitated from performing the contract. In *Condor v Barron Knights* [1966] 1 WLR 87, a 17-year-old drummer collapsed and was admitted to a psychiatric hospital. Medical opinion was that he would only be fit to work four nights a week. The band had engagements for seven nights a week and so the defendants decided to dismiss the drummer. The court held it was, in a business sense, impossible for the drummer to perform the contract and for that reason the contract was discharged for frustration.

15.2.1.3 Unavailability

A contract may be frustrated if the subject matter is temporarily unavailable. The court will have to determine whether the contractual performance when resumed will be fundamentally different to what the parties had agreed to.

***Jackson v Union Marine Insurance Company Ltd* (1874) LR 10 CP 125**

Facts: The plaintiff shipowner entered into a charterparty by which the ship was to 'proceed with all possible dispatch from Liverpool to Newport, and there load a cargo of iron rails for San Francisco'. The ship set sail from Liverpool on 2 January 1872 but ran aground on the following day in Carnarvon Bay. The repairs took eight months to complete. In the meantime, on 15 February, the charterers repudiated the charter and chartered another ship to carry the rails. The shipowner brought an action on his insurance policy. In order to make a claim it was necessary for him to show that he could not have brought a claim against the charterers for failing to load. A jury found that the time necessary for repairs was so long as to make it unreasonable for the charterers to supply the agreed cargo at the end of August and so long as to put an end, in a commercial sense, to the commercial speculation entered upon by the shipowner and the charterers.

Held: The Exchequer Chamber affirmed the decision of the court below, holding that the contract was frustrated and the charterers were not under an obligation to load. Accordingly, the shipowner was entitled to make a claim under his insurance policy.

Bramwell B:

'I understand that the jury have found that the voyage the parties contemplated had become impossible; that a voyage undertaken after the ship was sufficiently repaired would have been a different voyage, not, indeed, different as to the ports of loading and discharge, but different as a different adventure, – a voyage for which at the time of the charter the plaintiff had not in intention engaged the ship, nor the charterers the cargo; a voyage as different as though it had been described as intended to be a spring voyage, while the one after the repair would be an autumn voyage . . .

The question turns on the construction and effect of the charter. By it the vessel is to sail to Newport with all possible dispatch, perils of the seas excepted. It is said this constitutes the only agreement as to time, and, provided all possible dispatch is used, it matters not when she arrives at Newport. I am of a different opinion. If this charter-party be read as a charter for a definite voyage or adventure, then it follows that there is *necessarily* an implied condition that the ship shall arrive at Newport in time for it. Thus, if a ship was chartered to go from Newport to St Michael's in terms in time for the fruit season, and take coals out and bring fruit home, it would follow . . . that, if she did not get to Newport in time to get to St Michael's for the fruit season, the charterer would not be bound to load at Newport, though she had used all possible dispatch to get there, and though there was an exception of perils of the seas.'

The court concluded that performance after the delay would have been a different voyage altogether, and of no use to the charterer.

15.2.1.4 Government intervention

A contract may be frustrated by government intervention. For example, if, following a declaration of war, one of the parties to the contract has become an enemy alien, then the contract will be frustrated (*Fibrosa Spolka Ackyjna v Fairbairn Lawson Combe*

Barbour Ltd [1943] AC 32). Similarly, if property is requisitioned by the government, this may have the effect of frustrating the contract if the intervention radically alters the nature of the contract.

FA Tamplin Steamship Company Ltd v Anglo-Mexican Petroleum Products Co Ltd [1916] 2 AC 397

Facts: The defendants chartered a tank steamship for a period of five years to be used for the carriage of oil. The charterparty contained the usual exceptions, including arrests and restraints of princes, rulers, and peoples. The charterers also were permitted to sublet the ship to the Admiralty or other service. Following the outbreak of the war, when the charterparty still had three years to run, the ship was requisitioned by the Admiralty for use as a transport for troops. The owners claimed that the charterparty had been discharged by the requisition. The charterers, who wished to continue with the contract, claimed that the government's intervention was not sufficient to frustrate the contract.

Held: The House of Lords held (Viscount Haldane and Lord Atkinson dissenting), that the contract had not been frustrated.

Earl Loreburn:
'Taking into account . . . all that has happened, I cannot infer that the interruption either has been or will be in this case such as makes it unreasonable to require the parties to go on. There may be many months during which this ship will be available for commercial purposes before the five years have expired. It might be a valuable right for the charterer during those months to have the use of this ship at the stipulated freight. Why should he be deprived of it? No one can say that he will or that he will not regain the use of the ship, for it depends upon contingencies which are incalculable. The owner will continue to receive the freight he bargained for so long as the contract entitles him to it, and if, during the time for which the charterer is entitled to the use of the ship, the owner received from the Government any sums of money for the use of her, he will be accountable to the charterer . . . Loss may arise to some one whether it be decided that these people are or that they are not still bound by the charterparty. But the test for answering that question is not the loss that either may sustain. It is this: Ought we to imply a condition in the contract that an interruption such as this shall excuse the parties from further performance of it? I think not. I think they took their chance of lesser interruptions, and the condition I should imply goes no further than that they should be excused if substantially the whole contract became impossible of performance, or in other words impracticable, by some cause for which neither was responsible. Accordingly I am of opinion that this charterparty did not come to an end when the steamer was requisitioned and that the requisition did not suspend it or affect the rights of the owners or charterers under it, and that the appeal fails.

It will be noted that Earl Loreburn relied on the 'implied term' approach to frustration. There is no reason to believe, however, that a different outcome would have been reached had a 'construction' approach been applied. The contract was not deemed to have been frustrated because it was still likely that the ship would have been available for commercial purposes prior to the expiry of the contract. The owners had failed to demonstrate that 'substantially the whole contract' had become 'impossible of performance'.

The contract will not be frustrated merely because government intervention has made the contract more difficult or costly to perform.

Tsakiroglou & Co Ltd v Noble Thorl GmbH [1962] AC 93

Facts: The appellants agreed to sell Sudanese groundnuts to the respondents for shipment from Port Sudan to Hamburg. Both parties expected that the shipment would be made via the Suez Canal but there was no express term in the written contract to this effect. On 2 November 1956 the Suez Canal was closed and the only alternative route available to the appellants was to ship the goods round the Cape of Good Hope. This would have taken twice as long and doubled the cost of carriage. The appellants failed to ship the goods and the respondents sued for non-performance.

Held: The House of Lords refused to imply a term into the contract that the goods should be shipped via the Suez Canal and held that the contract had not been frustrated. Although the alternative route via the Cape of Hope involved a change in the method of performance, it did not amount to a fundamental change from that which had been agreed.

Viscount Simmonds:

'I come then to the main issue and, as usual, I find two questions interlocked: (1) What does the contract mean? In other words, is there an implied term that the goods shall be carried by a particular route? (2) Is the contract frustrated?

It is convenient to examine the first question first, though the answer may be inconclusive. For it appears to me that it does not automatically follow that, because one term of a contract, for example, that the goods shall be carried by a particular route, becomes impossible of performance, the whole contract is thereby abrogated. Nor does it follow, because as a matter of construction a term cannot be implied, that the contract may not be frustrated by events. In the instant case, for example, the impossibility of the route via Suez, if that were assumed to be the implied contractual obligation, would not necessarily spell the frustration of the contract.

It is put in the forefront of the appellants' case that the contract was a contract for the shipment of goods via Suez. This contention can only prevail if a term is implied, for the contract does not say so. To say that that is nevertheless its meaning is to say in other words that the term must be implied. For this I see no ground . . .

'I turn now to what was the main argument for the appellants: that the contract was frustrated by the closure of the Canal from November 2, 1956, till April 1957. Were it not for the decision of McNair J in Green's case [1959] 1 QB 131, I should not have thought this contention arguable and I must say with the greatest respect to that learned judge that I cannot think he has given full weight to the decisions old and new of this House upon the doctrine of frustration . . . [H]e concluded that the continued availability of the Suez route was a fundamental assumption at the time when the contract was made and that to impose upon the sellers the obligation to ship by an emergency route via the Cape would be to impose upon them a fundamentally different obligation which neither party could at the time when the contract was performed have dreamed that the sellers would be required to perform. Your Lordships will observe how similar this line of argument is to that which supports the implication of a term that the route should be via Suez and no other. I can see no justification for it. We are concerned with a cif contract for the sale of goods, not a contract of affreightment, though part of the sellers' obligation will be to procure a contract of affreightment. There is no evidence that the buyers attached any importance to the route. They were content that the nuts should be shipped at any date in November or December. There was no evidence, and I suppose could not be, that the nuts would deteriorate as the result of a longer voyage and a double crossing of the Equator, nor any evidence that the market was seasonable. In a word, there was no evidence that the buyers cared by what route or, within reasonable limits, when the nuts arrived. What, then, of the sellers? I recall the well-known passage in the speech of Lord Atkinson in *Johnson v Taylor Bros & Co Ltd* [1920] AC 144, 155, where he states the obligations of the vendor of goods under a cif contract, and ask which of these obligations is (to use McNair J's word) "fundamentally" altered by a change of route. Clearly the contract of affreightment will be different and so may be the terms of insurance. In both these respects the sellers may be put to greater cost: their profit may be reduced or even disappear. But it hardly needs reasserting that an increase of expense is not a ground of frustration: see *Larrinaga Co Ltd v Société Franco-Américaine des Phosphates de Medulla, Paris* (1922) 38 TLR 739; 28 Com Cas 1, CA.

Nothing else remains to justify the view that the nature of the contract was "fundamentally" altered . . . I venture to say what I have said myself before and others more authoritatively have said before me: that the doctrine of frustration must be applied within very narrow limits. In my opinion this case falls far short of satisfying the necessary conditions.'

The mere fact that the method of performance had become impossible was insufficient to frustrate the contract. It was necessary to show that the nature of the contract had been 'fundamentally altered' by the closure of the Suez Canal, and the appellants had failed to demonstrate this. Interestingly, it seems that the result would have been exactly the same, even if the contract had stipulated that the goods were to be shipped via the Suez Canal (see *The Washington Trader* [1972] 1 Lloyd's Rep 463).

The government intervention need not relate to international matters. In *Gamerco SA v ICM/Fair Warning (Agency) Ltd* [1995] 1 WLR 1226, the Spanish government's decision to close a stadium due to structural defects was held to frustrate a contract to hold a rock concert there. Garland J concluded: 'I am in no doubt whatsoever that this contract was frustrated when, due to the discovery of high alumina cement in the construction of the stadium, its use was banned pending further investigations and the permit for its use was revoked.'

15.2.2 SUPERVENING ILLEGALITY

The doctrine of illegality was examined in Chapter 13. We saw that the courts will not enforce a contract that is tainted by illegality at its formation. Here we are concerned with contracts that are legal when formed, but have become illegal due to a supervening prohibition.

Denny, Mott & Dickson Ltd v James B Fraser & Company Ltd
[1944] AC 265

Facts: In 1929, the respondents and appellants entered into an agreement under which the respondents leased the appellants a timber yard (with an option to purchase it) and agreed to purchase all their supplies of timber from the appellants. In 1939, further transactions in timber were made illegal by virtue of the Control of Timber (No 4) Order 1939. The appellants continued to occupy the timber yard and in July 1941 sent a letter to the respondents purporting to terminate the agreement and stating their intention to exercise the option to purchase the timber yard.

Held: The House of Lords held that the agreement was a single contract which had been discharged due to frustration of its main object. The respondents were therefore unable to exercise the option to purchase the timber yard.

In the following section we will examine a number of limitations on the doctrine of frustration. In particular, we will see that there will be no frustration if the parties foresaw the event or assumed the risk of it occurring. Neither of these limitations applies when the contract is frustrated by supervening illegality (*Ertel Bieber and Co v Rio Tinto Co Ltd* [1918] AC 260). This is because, in such cases, the public interest in seeing the law observed may trump the importance of achieving a fair distribution of losses between the parties (see Treitel, *The Law of Contract*, 11th edn, 2003, p 887, London: Sweet & Maxwell).

15.2.3 FRUSTRATION OF PURPOSE

As we have seen it is very rare for the courts to hold that a contract has been frustrated by an event that merely renders its performance more difficult or expensive than anticipated (*Davis Contractors Ltd v Fareham UDC* [1956] AC 696; *Tsakiroglou & Co Ltd v Noble Thorl GmbH* [1962] AC 93). The courts will not permit the doctrine to be used as a means of escape for a party that has simply entered into a bad bargain. Similarly, the courts are reluctant to hold that a contract has been discharged merely because its purpose has been frustrated. This is illustrated by the cases of *Krell v Henry* and *Herne Bay Steam Boat Co v Hutton*.

Krell v Henry [1903] 2 KB 740

Facts: The defendant had agreed to hire from the plaintiff some rooms at 56A Pall Mall to watch the coronation procession of King Edward VII on 26 and 27 June 1902. He paid £25 as a deposit and was to pay the balance of £50 on 24 June. The King became seriously ill and the coronation processions were postponed. The defendant refused to pay the balance and the plaintiff brought a claim for the outstanding balance. The defendant counter-claimed to recover the £25 deposit he had paid. At first instance, Darling J held that there was an implied term in the contract that the procession should take place. Accordingly, he gave judgment for the defendant on both the claim and the counterclaim.

Held: The Court of Appeal dismissed the appeal, holding that the contract had been frustrated.

Vaughan Williams LJ:
'The real question in this case is the extent of the application in English law of the principle of the Roman law which has been adopted and acted on in many English decisions, and notably in the case of *Taylor v Caldwell* 3 B & S 826 . . .

English law applies the principle not only to cases where the performance of the contract becomes impossible by the cessation of existence of the thing which is the subject-matter of the contract, but also to cases where the event which renders the contract incapable of performance is the cessation or non-existence of an express condition or state of things, going to the root of the contract, and essential to its performance. It is said, on the one side, that the specified thing, state of things, or condition the continued existence of which is necessary for the fulfilment of the contract, so that the parties entering into the contract must have contemplated the continued existence of that thing, condition, or state of things as the foundation of what was to be done under the contract, is limited to things which are either the subject-matter of the contract or a condition or state of things, present or anticipated, which is expressly mentioned in the contract. But, on the other side, it is said that the condition or state of things need not be expressly specified, but that it is sufficient if that condition or state of things clearly appears by extrinsic evidence to have been assumed by the parties to be the foundation or basis of the contract, and the event which causes the impossibility is of such a character that it cannot reasonably be supposed to have been in the contemplation of the contracting parties when the contract was made. In such a case the contracting parties will not be held bound by the general words which, though large enough to include, were not used with reference to a possibility of a particular event rendering performance of the contract impossible. I do not think that the principle of the civil law as introduced into the English law is limited to cases in which the event causing the impossibility of performance is the destruction or non-existence of some thing which is the subject-matter of the contract or of some condition or state of things expressly specified as a condition of it. I think that you first have to ascertain, not necessarily from the terms of the contract, but, if required, from necessary inferences, drawn from surrounding circumstances recognised by both contracting parties, what is the substance of the contract, and then to ask the question whether that substantial contract needs for its foundation the assumption of the existence of a particular state of things. If it does, this will limit the operation of the general words, and in such case, if the contract becomes impossible of performance by reason of the non-existence of the state of things assumed by both contracting parties as the foundation of the contract, there will be no breach of the contract thus limited. Now what are the facts of the present case? The contract is contained in two letters of June 20 which passed between the defendant and the plaintiff's agent, Mr Cecil Bisgood. These letters do not mention the coronation, but speak merely of the taking of Mr Krell's chambers, or, rather, of the use of them, in the daytime of June 26 and 27, for the sum of £75, £25 then paid, balance £50 to be paid on the 24th. But the affidavits, which by agreement between the parties are to be taken as stating the facts of the case, shew that the plaintiff exhibited on his premises, third floor, 56A, Pall Mall, an announcement to the effect that windows to view the Royal coronation procession were to be let, and that the defendant was induced by that announcement to apply to the housekeeper on the premises, who said that the owner was willing to let the suite of rooms for the purpose of seeing the Royal procession for both days, but not nights, of June 26 and 27. In my judgment the use of the rooms was let and taken for the purpose of seeing the Royal procession. It was not a demise of the rooms, or even an agreement to let and take the rooms. It is a licence to use rooms for a particular purpose and none other. And in my judgment the taking place of those processions on the days proclaimed along the proclaimed route, which passed 56A, Pall Mall, was regarded by both contracting parties as the foundation of the contract; and I think that it cannot reasonably be supposed to have been in the contemplation of the contracting parties, when the contract was made, that the coronation would not be held on the proclaimed days, or the processions not take place on those days along the proclaimed route; and I think that the words imposing on the defendant the obligation to accept and pay for the use of the rooms for the named days, although general and unconditional, were not used with reference to the possibility of the particular contingency which afterwards occurred. It was suggested in the course of the argument that if the occurrence, on the proclaimed days, of the coronation and the procession in this case were the foundation of the contract, and if the general words are thereby limited or qualified, so that in the event of the non-occurrence of the coronation and procession along the proclaimed route they would discharge both parties from further performance of the contract, it would follow that if a cabman was engaged to take some one to Epsom on Derby Day at a suitable enhanced price for such a journey, say £10, both parties to the contract would be discharged in the contingency of the race at Epsom for some reason becoming impossible; but I do not think this follows, for I do not think that in the cab case the happening of the race would be the foundation of the contract. No doubt the purpose of the engager would be to go to see the Derby, and the price would be proportionately high; but the cab had no special qualifications for the purpose which led to the selection of the cab for this particular occasion. Any other cab would have done as well. Moreover, I think that, under the cab contract, the hirer, even if the race went off, could have said, "Drive me to Epsom; I will pay you the agreed sum; you have nothing to do with the purpose for which I hired the cab," and that if the cabman refused he would have been guilty of a breach of contract, there being nothing to qualify his promise to drive the hirer to Epsom on a particular day. Whereas in the case of the coronation, there is not merely the purpose of the hirer to see the coronation procession, but it is the coronation procession and the relative position of the rooms which is the basis of the contract as much for the lessor as the hirer; and I think that if the King, before the coronation day and after the contract, had died, the hirer could not have insisted on having the rooms on the days named. It could not in the cab case be reasonably said that seeing the Derby race was the foundation of the contract, as it was of the licence in this case. Whereas in the present case, where the rooms were offered and taken, by reason of their peculiar suitability from the position of the rooms for a view of the coronation procession, surely the view of the coronation procession was the foundation of the contract, which is a very different thing from the purpose of the man who engaged the cab – namely, to see the race – being held to be the foundation of the contract. Each case must be judged by its own circumstances. In each case one must ask oneself, first, what, having regard to all the circumstances, was the foundation of the contract? Secondly, was the performance of the contract prevented? Thirdly, was the event which prevented the performance of the contract of such a character that it cannot reasonably be said to have been in the contemplation of the parties at the date of the contract? If all these questions are answered in the affirmative (as I think they should be in this case), I think both parties are discharged from further performance of the contract. I think that the coronation procession was the foundation of this contract, and that the non-happening of it prevented the performance of the contract; and, secondly, I think that the non-happening of the procession, to use the words of Sir James Hannen in *Baily v De Crespigny* LR 4 QB 185, was an event "of such a character that it cannot reasonably be supposed to have been in the contemplation of the contracting parties when the contract was made, and that they are not to be held bound by general words which, though large enough to include, were not used with reference to the possibility of the particular contingency which afterwards happened" . . .

In the present case the condition which fails and prevents the achievement of that which was, in the contemplation of both parties, the foundation of the contract, is not expressly mentioned either as a condition of the contract or the purpose of it; but I think for the reasons which I have given that the principle of *Taylor v Caldwell* ought to be applied.'

[ROMER and STIRLING JJ delivered concurring judgments]

Herne Bay Steam Boat Company v Hutton [1903] 2 KB 683

Facts: Mr Hutton agreed to hire the steamship *Cynthia* from Herne Bay for 28 and 29 June 'for the purpose of viewing the naval review and for a day's cruise round the fleet'. The hire charge was £250 and Mr Hutton paid a deposit of £50. On 25 June the review was officially cancelled because of the King's illness, but the fleet remained in place. Mr Hutton sought to repudiate the contract. Herne Bay brought a claim for the balance owing minus the profit they had made from using the *Cynthia* for their own purposes on 28 and 29 June. Mr Hutton counter-claimed for the return of his £50 deposit. At first instance, Grantham J held that neither Herne Bay nor Mr Hutton could recover.

Held: The Court of Appeal allowed the appeal, holding that the contract had not been frustrated and accordingly the plaintiffs were entitled to recover damages for breach of contract.

Vaughan Williams LJ:
'Mr Hutton, in hiring this vessel, had two objects in view: first, of taking people to see the naval review, and, secondly, of taking them round the fleet. Those, no doubt, were the purposes of Mr Hutton, but it does not seem to me that because, as it is said, those purposes became impossible, it would be a very legitimate inference that the happening of the naval review was contemplated by both parties as the basis and foundation of this contract, so as to bring the case within the doctrine of *Taylor v Caldwell* 3 B & S 826. On the contrary, when the contract is properly regarded, I think the purpose of Mr Hutton, whether of seeing the naval review or of going round the fleet with a party of paying guests, does not lay the foundation of the contract within the authorities.

Having expressed that view, I do not know that there is any advantage to be gained by going on in any way to define what are the circumstances which might or might not constitute the happening of a particular contingency as the foundation of a contract. I will content myself with saying this, that I see nothing that makes this contract differ from a case where, for instance, a person has engaged a brake to take himself and a party to Epsom to see the races there, but for some reason or other, such as the spread of an infectious disease, the races are postponed. In such a case it could not be said that he could be relieved of his bargain. So in the present case it is sufficient to say that the happening of the naval review was not the foundation of the contract.'

Romer LJ:

'In my opinion, as my Lord has said, it is a contract for the hiring of a ship by the defendant for a certain voyage, though having, no doubt, a special object, namely, to see the naval review and the fleet; but it appears to me that the object was a matter with which the defendant, as hirer of the ship, was alone concerned, and not the plaintiffs, the owners of the ship.

The case cannot, in my opinion, be distinguished in principle from many common cases in which, on the hiring of a ship, you find the objects of the hiring stated. Very often you find the details of the voyage stated with particularity, and also the nature and details of the cargo to be carried. If the voyage is intended to be one of pleasure, the object in view may also be stated, which is a matter that concerns the passengers. But this statement of the objects of the hirer of the ship would not, in my opinion, justify him in saying that the owner of the ship had those objects just as much in view as the hirer himself. The owner would say, "I have an interest in the ship as a passenger or cargo carrying machine, and I enter into the contract simply in that capacity; it is for the hirer to concern himself about the objects".

The view I have expressed with regard to the general effect of the contract before us is borne out by the following considerations. The ship (as a ship) had nothing particular to do with the review or the fleet except as a convenient carrier of passengers to see it: any other ship suitable for carrying passengers would have done equally as well. Just as in the case of the hire of a cab or other vehicle, although the object of the hirer might be stated, that statement would not make the object any the less a matter for the hirer alone, and would not directly affect the person who was letting out the vehicle for hire. In the present case I may point out that it cannot be said that by reason of the failure to hold the naval review there was a total failure of consideration. That cannot be so. Nor is there anything like a total destruction of the subject-matter of the contract. Nor can we, in my opinion, imply in this contract any condition in favour of the defendant which would enable him to escape liability. A condition ought only to be implied in order to carry out the presumed intention of the parties, and I cannot ascertain any such presumed intention here. It follows that, in my opinion, so far as the plaintiffs are concerned, the objects of the passengers on this voyage with regard to sight-seeing do not form the subject-matter or essence of this contract . . .'

Stirling LJ:

'It is said that, by reason of the reference in the contract to the "naval review", the existence of the review formed the basis of the contract, and that as the review failed to take place the parties became discharged from the further performance of the contract, in accordance with the doctrine of *Taylor v Caldwell*. I am unable to arrive at that conclusion. It seems to me that the reference in the contract to the naval review is easily explained; it was inserted in order to define more exactly the nature of the voyage, and I am unable to treat it as being such a reference as to constitute the naval review the foundation of the contract so as to entitle either party to the benefit of the doctrine in *Taylor v Caldwell*. I come to this conclusion the more readily because the object of the voyage is not limited to the naval review, but also extends to a cruise round the fleet. The fleet was there, and passengers might have been found willing to go round it. It is true that in the event which happened the object of the voyage became limited, but, in my opinion, that was the risk of the defendant whose venture the taking the passengers was.'

Much ink has been spilt on identifying the distinction between *Krell* and *Hutton*. Both cases were decided at the same time by the same panel of judges, yet they appear to be hard to reconcile. Why was a contract to let a room for the viewing of the coronation frustrated by the cancellation of the coronation, while a contract to hire a boat from which to watch the naval review was not? A number of answers have been given:

1. The purpose in *Krell* (watching the coronation) was wholly frustrated by the postponement of the coronation, whereas the purpose in *Hutton* was only partially frustrated. As Stirling LJ noted, the object of the voyage was not limited to the naval review, but also extended to a cruise round the fleet. The fleet was still in place, and so the tour could go still ahead. Professor Treitel (Treitel, G, *Frustration and Force Majeure*, 2nd edn, 2004, Para 7–014, London: Sweet & Maxwell) has commented:

    'This reflects a recurrent feature of the cases on frustration of purpose, which shows that the approach of the law to partial frustration of purpose differs from that which it adopts to partial impossibility. In cases of partial impossibility, a contract can be discharged if its *main* purpose can no longer be achieved; but in cases of frustration of purpose the courts have applied the more rigorous test of asking whether *any* part of the contractual purpose (other than a part which was wholly trivial) could still be achieved: if so, they have refused to apply the doctrine of discharge.'

2. The 'common purpose' of both parties in *Krell* was for the rooms to be used for the viewing of the procession and this purpose was frustrated when the coronation was postponed. There was no such common purpose in *Hutton*. Romer LJ considered that, '[the] statement of the objects of the hirer of the ship would not . . . justify him in saying that the owner of the ship had those objects just as much in view as the hirer himself.' This meant that, although the postponement had frustrated Hutton's purpose in entering into the contract, it had not frustrated Herne Bay's purpose, which was presumably to provide a tour of the fleet. Professor Treitel (at para 7–014) has written:

'This emphasis on the requirement that the purpose of *both* parties must be frustrated is found also in other English and American cases. It means that the supervening event must prevent one party from supplying, and the other from obtaining, what the former had contracted to provide and the latter to acquire under the contract.'

This also explains why the contract was not frustrated in Vaughan LJ's example of the taxi cab hired to go to Epsom on Derby Day. Although it was the hirer's purpose to view the Derby, this was not the taxi owner's purpose.

3. Professor Brownsword ('Towards a rational law of contract', in Willhelmson, T (ed), *Perspectives of Critical Contract Law*, 1993, Aldershot: Dartmouth, pp 246–247) has suggested that the true distinction lies in the fact Hutton was engaged in a commercial enterprise (he intended to sell tickets for the trip on the *Cynthia* at a profit), whereas Henry was in effect a 'consumer', whose only interest was in getting a good view of the procession. The Court of Appeal in *Hutton* was unwilling to allow the doctrine of frustration to be used as a means of escaping from a bad commercial bargain.

4. A further explanation of the decision in *Krell* was provided by Posner CJ in *Northern Indiana Public Service Co v Carbon County Coal Co* 799 F 2d 265. He noted that, 'Krell could always relet the room, at the premium rental, for the coronation's new date'. However, as Professor Treitel has observed (at para 7–011), this argument overlooks the fact that the procession that eventually took place in October took a different route from the one that was planned for June. Furthermore, it fails to take into account the expenditure that Mr Krell had wasted on making preparations for the June procession.

15.3 LIMITATIONS ON THE DOCTRINE

There are two specific limitations on the doctrine of frustration.

15.3.1 SELF-INDUCED FRUSTRATION

The event that renders performance of the contract 'radically different' from that which was envisaged must not be attributable to the fault of the party seeking to rely on it. As Lord Sumner said in *Bank Line Ltd v Arthur Capel & Co* [1919] AC 435, 452:

'[I]t is now well settled that the principle of frustration of an adventure assumes that the frustration arises without blame or fault on either side.

Reliance cannot be placed on a self-induced frustration; indeed, such conduct might give the other party the option to treat the contract as repudiated.'

If a party wishes to argue that a frustrating event is self-induced by the other party they must prove it on the balance of probabilities (*Joseph Constantine Steamship Line Ltd v Imperial Smelting Corpn Ltd* [1942] AC 154). The limitation on self-induced frustration is relatively straightforward but, in practice, it is often difficult to apply.

Maritime National Fish Ltd v Ocean Trawlers Ltd [1935] AC 524

Facts: The appellants chartered a steam trawler, the *St Cuthbert*, from the respondents. It was fitted with an 'otter trawl', which it was an offence to use without a licence from the Minister of Fisheries. In March 1933 the appellants applied for licences for the five trawlers which they were operating. The Minister said that he would only grant three licences and asked the appellants to name the three trawlers in respect of which the licences would apply. The three trawler names given by the appellants did not include the *St Cuthbert*. The appellants thereupon claimed that the charterparty had been frustrated by the Minister's refusal to issue a licence. The respondents brought a claim for the hire due under the charter. The trial judge, Doull J, gave judgment for the appellants. This decision was reversed by the Supreme Court of Nova Scotia.

Held: The Privy Council dismissed the appeal. The contract had not been frustrated because the appellants' own election had prevented the respondents' trawler from being used as an otter trawl.

Lord Wright (delivering the opinion of the Privy Council):
'It is clear that the appellants were free to select any three of the five trawlers they were operating and could, had they willed, have selected the *St Cuthbert* as one, in which event a licence would have been granted to her. It is immaterial to speculate why they preferred to put forward for licences the three trawlers which they actually selected. Nor is it material, as between the appellants and the respondents, that the appellants were operating other trawlers to three of which they gave the preference. What matters is that they could have got a licence for the *St Cuthbert* if they had so minded. If the case be figured as one in which the *St Cuthbert* was removed from the category of privileged trawlers, it was by the appellants' hand that she was so removed, because it was their hand that guided the hand of the Minister in placing the licences where he did and thereby excluding the *St Cuthbert*. The essence of "frustration" is that it should not be due to the act or election of the party . . .

If it be assumed that the performance of the contract was dependent on a licence being granted, it was that election which prevented performance, and on that assumption it was the appellants' own default which frustrated the adventure: the appellants cannot rely on their own default to excuse them from liability under the contract . . .

> [T]heir Lordships are of opinion that the loss of the *St Cuthbert's* licence can correctly be described, quoad the appellants, as "a self induced frustration" . . . On this ground . . . their Lordships are of opinion that the appeal should be dismissed with costs.'

Few would argue with the decision in *Maritime National Fish Ltd*. The appellants had a choice as to the allocation of the licences and decided to allocate them to their own trawlers rather than to the *St Cuthbert*. The issue would have been much more difficult had all the trawlers been chartered to the appellants, so that they had to decide which of the five chartered ships should be denied a licence. Such a situation arose in *The Super Servant Two*.

J Lauritzen AS v Wijsmuller BV (The Super Servant Two)
[1990] 1 Lloyd's Rep 1

Facts: The defendants, Wijsmuller, agreed to carry Lauritzen's drilling rig (the *Dan King*) from a shipyard in Japan to a delivery location off the coast of the Netherlands. The rig was to be delivered on a date between 20 June 1981 and 20 August 1981, using either the *Super Servant One* or the *Super Servant Two*. The contract contained a *force majeure* clause which provided the following:

'17. *Cancellation*
17.1 Wijsmuller has the right to cancel its performance under this Contract whether the loading has been completed or not, in the event of force majeur(sic), Acts of God, perils or danger and accidents of the sea, acts of war, warlike-operations, acts of public enemies, restraint of princes, rulers or people or seizure under legal process, quarantine restrictions, civil commotions, blockade, strikes, lockout, closure of the Suez or Panama Canal, congestion of harbours or any other circumstances whatsoever, causing extra-ordinary periods of delay and similar events and/or circumstances, abnormal increases in prices and wages, scarcity of fuel and similar events, which reasonably may impede, prevent or delay the performance of this contract.'

The defendants had intended to use *Super Servant Two* for the *Dan King* contract and had entered into other contracts which they intended to perform using *Super Servant One*. On 29 Jan 1981, *Super Servant Two* sank. The defendants informed the plaintiffs that they could no longer carry out the *Dan King* contract, claiming that they were permitted to cancel the contract under cl 17 and that, in any event, the contract had been frustrated by the sinking of *Super Servant Two*.

Held: The Court of Appeal held that the contract could only be cancelled under cl 17 if the loss of *Super Servant Two* had not been due to the negligence of the defendants. The doctrine of frustration did not operate on the facts of the case because the defendants could have fulfilled their contractual obligations by using *Super Servant One*. Additionally, the defendants would be precluded from relying on the doctrine of frustration if it could be shown that the loss of *Super Servant Two* had been caused by their own negligence.

Bingham LJ:

'Certain propositions, established by the highest authority, are not open to question:

1. The doctrine of frustration was evolved to mitigate the rigour of the common law's insistence on literal performance of absolute promises . . . The object of the doctrine was to give effect to the demands of justice, to achieve a just and reasonable result, to do what is reasonable and fair, as an expedient to escape from injustice where such would result from enforcement of a contract in its literal terms after a significant change in circumstances . . .

2. Since the effect of frustration is to kill the contract and discharge the parties from further liability under it, the doctrine is not to be lightly invoked, must be kept within very narrow limits and ought not to be extended . . .

3. Frustration brings the contract to an end forthwith, without more and automatically . . .

4. The essence of frustration is that it should not be due to the act or election of the party seeking to rely on it . . . A frustrating event must be some outside event or extraneous change of situation . . .

5. A frustrating event must take place without blame or fault on the side of the party seeking to rely on it . . .

Question 2(a)

Mr Clarke for Wijsmuller submitted that the extraneous supervening event necessary to found a plea of frustration occurred when *Super Servant Two* sank on Jan 29, 1981. The *Dan King* contract was not, however, thereupon frustrated but remained alive until Wijsmuller decided a fortnight later that that contract could not be, or would not be, performed. There was, he submitted, factually, no break in the chain of causation between the supervening event and the non-performance of the contract. He acknowledged that *Maritime National Fish Ltd*, contained observations on their face inimical to his argument, but distinguished that as a decision on causation confined to its own peculiar facts and laying down no general rule. For authoritative support Mr Clarke relied on cases dealing with the application of *force majeure* clauses in commodity contracts, and in particular on an unreported judgment of Mr Justice Robert Goff, as he then was, adopted with approval by the Court of Appeal in *Bremer Handelsgesellschaft mbh v Continental Grain Co* [1983] 1 Lloyd's Rep 269 at p 292:

"... the question resolves itself into a question of causation; in my judgment, at least in a case in which a seller can (as in the present case) claim the protection of a clause which protects him where fulfilment is hindered by the excepted peril,

> subsequent delivery of his available stock to other customers will not be regarded
> as an independent cause of shortage, provided that in making such delivery the
> seller acted reasonably in all the circumstances of the case. . . ."

A similar approach was reflected in other cases: see, for example, *Intertradex SA v Lesieur – Tourteaux SARL* [1977] 2 Lloyd's Rep 146 at p 115, per Mr Justice Donaldson as he then was; [1978] 2 Lloyd's Rep 509 at p 513, per Lord Denning, MR. Reliance was also placed on passages in *The Law of Contract* (7th edn) by Professor Treitel, which the Judge quoted in his judgment at p 152. Thus, Mr Clarke urged, this was a case in which Wijsmuller could not perform all their contracts once *Super Servant Two* was lost; they acted reasonably (as we must assume) in treating the *Dan King* contract as one they could not perform; so the sinking had the direct result of making that contract impossible to perform.

Mr Legh-Jones answered that since the contract provided for the carriage to be performed by one or other vessel the loss of one did not render performance radically different, still less impossible. That apart, Wijsmuller's argument fell foul of the principles summarised above since (among other things) the frustration they sought to establish did not bring the contract to an end forthwith, without more and automatically and was not independent of the act or election of Wijsmuller. The *force majeure* cases were good law so far as they went, but it was one thing to construe and apply a consensual *force majeure* clause, another to determine whether the facts were such that the law should hold the contract to be discharged.

The doctrine of frustration depends on a comparison between circumstances as they are or are assumed to be when a contract is made and circumstances as they are when a contract is, or would be, due to be performed. It is trite law that disappointed expectations do not of themselves give rise to frustrated contracts. To frustrate, an event must significantly change –

> ". . . the nature (not merely the expense or onerousness) of the outstanding contractual rights and/or obligations from what the parties could reasonably have contemplated at the time of [the contract's] execution . . . [*National Carriers Ltd*, at p 700, per Lord Simon of Glaisdale].

Had the *Dan King* contract provided for carriage by *Super Servant Two* with no alternative, and that vessel had been lost before the time for performance, then assuming no negligence by Wijsmuller (as for purposes of this question we must), I feel sure the contract would have been frustrated. The doctrine must avail a party who contracts to perform a contract of carriage with a vessel which, through no fault of his, no longer exists. But that is not this case. The *Dan King* contract did provide an alternative. When that contract was made one of the contracts eventually performed by *Super Servant One* during the period of contractual carriage of *Dan King* had been made, the other had not, at any rate finally. Wijsmuller have not alleged that when the *Dan King* contract was made either vessel was earmarked for its performance. That, no doubt, is why an option was contracted for. Had it been foreseen when the *Dan King* contract was made that *Super Servant Two* would be unavailable for performance, whether because she had been deliberately sold or accidentally sunk, Lauritzen at least would have thought it no matter since the carriage could be performed with the other. I accordingly accept Mr Legh-Jones' submission that the present case does not fall within the very limited class of cases in which the law will relieve one party from an absolute promise he has chosen to make.

But I also accept Mr Legh-Jones' submission that Wijsmuller's argument is subject to other fatal flaws. If, as was argued, the contract was frustrated when Wijsmuller made or communicated their decision on Feb 16, it deprives language of all meaning to describe the contract as coming to an end automatically. It was, indeed, because the contract did not come to an end automatically on Jan. 29, that Wijsmuller needed a fortnight to review their schedules and their commercial options. I cannot, furthermore, reconcile Wijsmuller's argument with the reasoning or the decision in *Maritime National Fish Ltd*. In that case the Privy Council declined to speculate why the charterers selected three of the five vessels to be licensed but, as I understand the case, regarded the interposition of human choice after the allegedly frustrating event as fatal to the plea of frustration. If Wijsmuller are entitled to succeed here, I cannot see why the charterers lost there. The cases on frustrating delay do not, I think, help Wijsmuller since it is actual and prospective delay (whether or not recognized as frustrating by a party at the time) which frustrates the contract, not a party's election or decision to treat the delay as frustrating.

I have no doubt that *force majeure* clauses are, where their terms permit, to be construed and applied as in the commodity cases on which Wijsmuller relied, but it is in my view inconsistent with the doctrine of frustration as previously understood on high authority that its application should depend on any decision, however reasonable and commercial, of the party seeking to rely on it.

I reach the same conclusion as the Judge for the reasons which he lucidly and persuasively gave.

Question 2(b)

The issue between the parties was short and fundamental: what is meant by saying that a frustrating event, to be relied on, must occur without the fault or default, or without blame attaching to, the party relying on it?

Mr Clarke's answer was that a party was precluded from relying on an event only when he had acted deliberately or in breach of an actionable duty in causing it. Those conditions were not met here since it was not alleged Wijsmuller sank *Super Servant Two* deliberately and at the material time Wijsmuller owed Lauritzen no duty of care if (as I have held) cl 15 did not apply when the vessel sank. Mr Clarke relied on tentative doubts expressed in *Joseph Constantine Steamship Ltd*, whether mere negligence would render an event "self induced" and on a statement of Lord Diplock in *Cheall v Association of Professional Executive and Clerical Computer Staff* [1983] 2 AC 180 at pp 188–189 . . .

Wijsmuller's test would, in my judgment, confine the law in a legalistic strait-jacket and distract attention from the real question, which is whether the frustrating event relied upon is truly an outside event or extraneous change of situation or whether it is an event which the party seeking to rely on it had the means and opportunity to prevent but nevertheless caused or permitted to come about. A fine test of legal duty is inappropriate; what is needed is a pragmatic judgment whether a party seeking to rely on an event as discharging him from a contractual promise was himself responsible for the occurrence of that event.

Lauritzen have pleaded in some detail the grounds on which they say that *Super Servant Two* was lost as a result of the carelessness of Wijsmuller, their servants or agents. If those allegations are made good to any significant extent Wijsmuller would (even if my answer to Question 2(a) is wrong) be precluded from relying on their plea of frustration.

I would answer this question also as the Judge did and would therefore dismiss the appeal.'

Dillon LJ:

'Issues 2(a) and (b) are concerned with frustration. Was the contract frustrated by the sinking of *Super Servant Two* or by that event coupled with the subsequent election by the defendants to use *Super Servant One* on other voyages and not for carrying the *Dan King*? . . .

It is the view of Professor Treitel, expressed both in his own book on the *Law of Contract* – see the 7th edn at pp 674–675 and 700–701 – and in the current editions of well-known textbooks of which he is editor or an editor, that where a party has entered into a number of contracts with other parties and an uncontemplated supervening event has the result that he is deprived of the means of satisfying all those contracts, he can, provided he acts "reasonably" in making his election, elect to use such means as remains available to him to perform some of the contracts, and claim that the others, which he does not perform, have been frustrated by the supervening event. The reasoning depends on the proposition that if it is known to those concerned that the party will have entered into commitments with others and if he acts "reasonably" in his allocation of his remaining means to his commitments, the chain of causation between the uncontemplated supervening event and the non-performance of those of his contracts which will not have been performed will not have been broken by the election to apply his remaining means in a "reasonable" way. Similar reasoning was, as my Lord has pointed out, used by Mr Justice Robert Goff in relation to an exceptions clause in the unreported case of *Westfalische Central-Genossenschaft GmbH v Seabright Chemicals Ltd*.

Such an approach is however inconsistent to my mind with the view expressed by Lord Wright in that passage in *Maritime National Fish* . . . where he said: "It is immaterial to speculate why they preferred to put forward for licences the three trawlers which they actually selected." It is also, as my Lord has pointed out, inconsistent with the long accepted view that frustration brings the contract to an end forthwith, without more ado automatically. Plainly the sinking of *Super Servant Two* did not do that, since even after that sinking the defendants could have used *Super Servant One* to perform the contract.

We in this Court should apply *Maritime National Fish* and the other authorities to which my Lord has referred. Accordingly I agree with my Lord and the learned Judge that issues 2(a) and (b) should be answered in the negative.'

The first point to note is that a party will only be entitled to rely on the doctrine of frustration if s/he can show that the frustrating event took place 'without blame or fault' on his/her part. For this reason, the Court of Appeal held that the defendants would be precluded from relying on the doctrine of frustration if it could be shown that *Super Servant Two* had been lost as a result of their own negligence.

Second, Bingham LJ held that the mere existence of a choice for one of the parties was sufficient to preclude reliance on the doctrine of frustration. He relied on the decision of the Privy Council in *Maritime National Fish Ltd*, and distinguished the authorities relied on by the defendants on the ground that they concerned the construction of *force majeure* clauses rather than the operation of frustration. The decision in *Super Servant Two* has been strongly criticised by Professor Treitel (Treitel, G, *Frustration and Force Majeure*, 2nd edn, 2004, Para 14–024, London: Sweet & Maxwell):

'Three lines of reasoning are given in the judgments but it is submitted with great respect that none of them is wholly convincing. First, it was said that the *Maritime National Fish* case had established that a party could not rely on frustration where his failure or inability was due to his "election"; and that the court in *The Super Servant Two* should follow the decision. It is, however, submitted that the two cases are readily distinguishable: in the *Maritime National Fish* case it was possible for the charterer to perform *all* the contracts which he had made with the owners of the other trawlers, even though only three licences had been allocated to him; while in *The Super Servant Two* it was no longer possible, after the loss of the ship, for the carrier to perform all the contracts which he had made to carry drilling rigs during the period in question. Secondly, it was said that, if the carrier were given a choice which of the contracts he would perform, frustration of the other or others could come about only as a result of the exercise of that choice, and such a position would be inconsistent with the rule that frustration occurs automatically, *without* any election by either party. Again, it is submitted that this line of reasoning is not conclusive since the rule that frustration operates automatically is subject to qualification precisely in cases of allegedly self-induced frustration . . . Moreover, the element of "election" could be eliminated if the question, which of the contracts was to be discharged, were left to be determined, not by the free choice of the promisor, but by a rule of law, e.g. by a rule to the effect that the various contracts should for this purpose rank in the order in which they were made. It may, from this point of view, be relevant that, in *The Super Servant Two*, some of the contracts which the carrier chose to perform (by the use of his other ship during the relevant period) had not been made "at any rate finally" until *after* the contract with the claimant . . . The third reason given for the decision is that: "It is within the promisor's own control how many contracts he enters into and the risk should be his". But this reasoning seems to undermine the whole basis of the doctrine of frustration: it has just as much force where the promisor enters into a single contract as it has where he enters into two or more, with different contracting parties. This, indeed, is the fundamental objection to the reasoning of *The Super Servant Two*, and it is submitted that the rationale of the doctrine should lead to discharge of some of the contracts where the supervening event which makes it impossible to perform them all occurs without the fault of the party claiming discharge. Consistency with the reasoning of the *Maritime National Fish* case could be preserved by holding that *which* contracts were to be discharged should depend, not on the free election of the party who can no longer perform them all, but on a rule of law. On this view, the actual decision in *The Super Servant Two* could be justified by reference to the order in which the various contracts with the carrier were made.'

Professor Treitel's criticisms are compelling. In practice, however, the effects of the rule are often mitigated by the inclusion of a specific clause in the contract to deal with the situation if it arises. Indeed, in *The Super Servant Two*, the Court of Appeal held that the defendants were entitled to rely on cl 7 of the contract (a *force majeure* clause), provided that the sinking of the vessel was not caused by their own negligence, even though the contract was not held to have been frustrated under the common law. This brings us on to our second limitation – events foreseen and provided for in the contract.

15.3.2 EVENTS FORESEEN AND PROVIDED FOR

If the contract itself makes provision for the supervening event, then the doctrine of frustration will have no role to play. It is a question of construction whether the terms of the contract are apt to cover the situation that has arisen. Historically, the courts have narrowly construed *force majeure* clauses. In *Jackson v Union Marine Insurance Co Ltd* (1874) LR 10 CP 125 (the facts of which we have already considered), the charter stated that the ship should 'proceed with all possible dispatch (dangers and accidents of navigation excepted)'. It was held by the Exchequer Chamber that the exception in the contract absolved the shipowner of liability in the event of delay, but did not give him the right to bring an action if the delay was bad enough to frustrate the contract. Bramwell B said:

'Now, what is the effect of the exception of perils of the seas, and of delay being caused thereby? . . . I think this: they excuse the shipowner, but give him no right. The charterer has no cause of action, but is released from the charter. When I say *he* is, I think *both* are. The condition precedent has not been performed, but by default of neither . . . The exception is an excuse for him who is to do the act, and operates to save him from an action and make his non-performance not a breach of contract, but does not operate to take away the right the other party would have had, if the non-performance had been a breach of contract, to retire from the engagement: and, if one party may, so may the other.'

Similarly, the House of Lords adopted a narrow construction of words defining an event in:

Metropolitan Water Board v Dick Kerr [1918] AC 119

Facts: In 1914, the defendants agreed to construct a reservoir for the plaintiff water board. The work was to be completed within six years, subject to a proviso (condition 32) that 'if by reason of . . . any difficulties, impediments, obstructions, oppositions, doubts, disputes, or differences, whatsoever and howsoever occasioned, the contractor shall, in the opinion of the engineer (whose decision shall be final), have been unduly delayed or impeded in the completion of this contract, it shall be lawful for the engineer, if he shall so think fit, to grant . . . such extension of time either prospectively or retrospectively . . . as to him may seem reasonable'. In 1916, the Ministry of Munitions ordered the contractors to cease work on the contract pursuant to their powers under the Defence of the Realm Acts and Regulations. The defendants claimed that the contract had been frustrated. The plaintiffs argued that the contract had not been frustrated on the ground that the event was provided for by the terms of the contract.

Held: The House of Lords held that the provision was only intended to deal with temporary delays and did not apply to the prohibition of the Ministry. Accordingly, the contract was discharged for frustration.

Lord Finlay LC:
'It is admitted that the prosecution of the works became illegal in consequence of the action of the Minister of Munitions. It became illegal on February 21, 1916, and remains illegal at the present time. This is not a case of a short and temporary stoppage, but of a prohibition in consequence of war, which has already been in force for the greater part of two years, and will, according to all appearances, last as long as the war itself,

> as it was the result of the necessity of preventing the diversion to civil purposes of labour and material required for purposes immediately connected with the war. Condition 32 provides for cases in which the contractor has, in the opinion of the engineer, been unduly delayed or impeded in the completion of his contract by any of the causes therein enumerated or by any other causes, so that an extension of time was reasonable. Condition 32 does not cover the case in which the interruption is of such a character and duration that it vitally and fundamentally changes the conditions of the contract, and could not possibly have been in the contemplation of the parties to the contract when it was made.'

It is clear that the parties will need to be very specific if they intend a clause to deal with an event that would otherwise amount to frustration. In modern times, however, the courts have shown an increased willingness to interpret *force majeure* clauses within their factual matrix, giving effect to the purposes that such clauses are intended to fulfil.

There is an argument that *force majeure* clauses are in effect exclusion clauses, falling within the scope of the UCTA 1977 (see Wheeler, S and Shaw, J, *Contract Law Cases, Materials and Commentary*, 1994, p 760, Oxford: Clarendon Press). To the extent that the clause provides that the contract is to remain in force, it is not a clause that excludes or restricts liability. On the contrary, it is a clause that preserves contractual liability, which would otherwise be discharged on the occurrence of the frustrating event. If, however, the clause also deals with the effects of a frustrating event, for example, by prohibiting restitution, the clause may fall within the scope of the UCTA 1977, and it will need to meet the requirements of reasonableness under ss 3 and 11 of the Act (see Chapter 8).

▌15.4 EFFECTS OF FRUSTRATION: COMMON LAW

The effects of a frustrating event are governed by the common law and the provisions of the Law Reform (Frustrated Contracts) Act (LR(FC)A) 1943. In this section we will examine the common law rules, and in the next we will consider the main provisions of the Act. We will see that the objectives of the doctrine become important in this context. The common law has historically adopted the view that the aim of the doctrine is to relieve the parties from the burden of having to perform obligations that have subsequently become impossible. This objective is achieved by the automatic termination of the contract and a limited right to restitutionary relief. A wider role for the doctrine has been envisaged by Parliament. The 1943 Act enables the courts to apportion the losses resulting from the unforeseen event by means of a more flexible form of restitutionary relief.

15.4.1 AUTOMATIC DISCHARGE

If a contract is frustrated it is automatically discharged at common law. It is not open to the parties to decide that the contract should continue.

Hirji Mulji v Cheong Yue Steamship Co Ltd [1926] AC 497

Facts: In November 1916, the respondents entered into a charterparty under which they agreed to place their ship, the *Singaporean*, at the disposal of the appellants on 1 March 1917 for 10 months. Shortly afterwards, the ship was requisitioned by the Government. The respondents thought that the ship would soon be released and asked the appellants whether they would still be willing to take up the charter when this happened. The appellants said that they would. In fact, the ship was not released until February 1919 and the appellants refused to take delivery of her at that time. The respondents argued that the appellants had affirmed the contract after the frustrating event and were therefore bound to take delivery of the ship.

Held: The Privy Council held that the contract had been automatically discharged by the frustrating event. Accordingly, affirmation of the contract was not possible.

Lord Sumner (delivering the opinion of the Privy Council):
'Throughout the line of cases, now a long one, in which it has been held that certain events frustrate the commercial adventure contemplated by the parties when they made the contract, there runs an almost continuous series of expressions to the effect that such a frustration brings the contract to an end forthwith, without more and automatically . . . [W]hatever the consequences of the frustration may be upon the conduct of the parties, its legal effect does not depend on their intention or their opinions, or even knowledge, as to the event, which has brought this about, but on its occurrence in such circumstances as show it to be inconsistent with further prosecution of the adventure. Sometimes the event is such as to speak for itself, like the outbreak of war on August 4, 1914, in *Horlock v Beal*: see per Lord Wrenbury [1916] 1 AC 486, 528. Sometimes the frustration is evident, when the gravity and the circumstances of the breakdown can be known, as in *Bensaude's* case [1897] AC 609; sometimes, as in the case of requisition, when it can be known that in all reasonable probability the delay will be prolonged and a fortiori when it has continued so long as to defeat the adventure. Frustration is then complete. It operates automatically: *Larrinaga & Co's* case (1922) 27 Com Cas 160. What the parties say and do is only evidence, and not necessarily weighty evidence, of the view to be taken of the event by informed and experienced minds.'

15.4.2 PROSPECTIVE OPERATION OF DISCHARGE

Frustration discharges the contract prospectively. This means that the parties are excused from their future obligations but not from the obligations that existed prior to the time of the frustrating event. Often this can lead to one party being unjustly enriched at the expense of the other. For example, suppose that I agree to provide you with a room from which to view the coronation of the new king of England. Under the agreement you are required to pay me in full, 10 days prior to the coronation. Tragically, the new king dies two days before his coronation and the contract is frustrated. I am no longer bound to provide you with the room, since the frustrating event has automatically discharged my future obligations. You, however, are unable to recover the money you paid in advance, since the obligation to pay the money arose prior to the frustrating event.

The traditional common law position was that money paid prior to the frustrating event could not be recovered and money payable prior to discharge remained due (*Chandler v Webster* [1904] 1 KB 493). This rule was based on the mistaken assumption that a restitutionary claim for total failure of consideration could only be made if the underlying contract had been rescinded *ab initio* (from the beginning – as in cases of common mistake). In other words, total failure of consideration requires a total failure of the contractual promise, that is, the contractual consideration. This view was rejected by the House of Lords in *Fibrosa Spolka Akcyjna v Fairbairn Lawson Combe Barbour Ltd.* [1943] AC 32 (see full extract in Chapter 18). Viscount Simon LC distinguished consideration in the formation of a contract from restitutionary failure of consideration:

> 'In English law, an enforceable contract may be formed by an exchange of a promise for a promise, or by the exchange of a promise for an act . . . and thus, in the law relating to the formation of a contract, the promise to do a thing may often be the consideration, but when one is considering the law of failure of consideration and of the quasi-contractual right to recover money on that ground, it is, generally speaking, not the promise which is referred to as the performance of the promise. The money was paid to secure performance and, if performance fails the inducement which brought about the payment is not fulfilled.'

Failure of consideration thus means failure of performance, not failure of the promise. Accordingly, a party can recover money paid under the frustrated contract as long as s/he has received no part of the performance which s/he bargained for in exchange for the payment.

Although the decision in *Fibrosa* opened the door to restitution under frustrated contracts, the 'total failure' requirement represented a significant limitation on its availability. If the other party has provided any part of the bargained-for performance, no matter how small, recovery will not be possible. In *Whincup v Hughes* (1871) LR 6 CP 78, a father paid a premium of £25 to have his son apprenticed to a watchmaker for six years. The watchmaker died after one year, frustrating the contract. It was held that the father could not recover the premium in respect of the remaining five years because the consideration for the payment had only partially failed. A second limitation on the availability of restitution at common law is that it does not take into account any expenditure that may have been incurred by the recipient in relation to the contract. This means that a recipient will be left out of pocket if s/he has spent some or all of the prepayment on materials necessary for performance. The common law also fails to provide assistance to a party who has supplied services prior to the frustration of the contract, as seen in *Appleby v Myers*.

Appleby v Myers (1867) LR 2 CP 651

Facts: The plaintiffs contracted to erect and maintain certain machinery at the defendant's factory for a period of two years. Payment was to be made on completion of the work. After some of the work had been completed, the factory and all the machinery in it were destroyed by fire.

Held: The Exchequer Chamber held that the contract was frustrated and both parties were discharged from future performance. The plaintiffs were not entitled to be paid in respect of any of the work that had been completed because the obligation to pay had not arisen at the time the contract was frustrated.

Blackburn J:

'Had the accidental fire left the defendant's premises untouched, and only injured a part of the work which the plaintiffs had already done, we apprehend that it is clear the plaintiffs under such a contract as the present must have done that part over again, in order to fulfil their contract to complete the whole and "put it to work for the sums above named respectively". As it is, they are, according to the principle laid down in *Taylor v Caldwell*, excused from completing the work; but they are not therefore entitled to any compensation for what they have done, but which has, without any fault of the defendant, perished. The case is in principle like that of a shipowner who has been excused from the performance of his contract to carry goods to their destination, because his ship has been disabled by one of the excepted perils, but who is not therefore entitled to any payment on account of the part-performance of the voyage, unless there is something to justify the conclusion that there has been a fresh contract to pay freight pro rata.'

The LR(FC)A 1943 was enacted to address some of these inadequacies in the common law.

15.5 EFFECTS OF FRUSTRATION: LAW REFORM (FRUSTRATED CONTRACTS) ACT 1943

The provisions of the LR(FC)A 1943 are set out in full below:

S 1 Adjustment of rights and liabilities of parties to frustrated contracts

(1) Where a contract governed by English law has become impossible of performance or been otherwise frustrated, and the parties thereto have for that reason been discharged from the further performance of the contract, the following provisions of this section shall, subject to the provisions of section two of this Act, have effect in relation thereto.

(2) All sums paid or payable to any party in pursuance of the contract before the time when the parties were so discharged (in this Act referred to as 'the time of discharge') shall, in the case of sums so paid, be recoverable from him as money received by him for the use of the party by whom the sums were paid, and, in the case of sums so payable, cease to be so payable:

Provided that, if the party to whom the sums were so paid or payable incurred expenses before the time of discharge in, or for the purpose of, the performance of the contract, the court may, if it considers it just to do so having regard to all the circumstances of the case, allow him to retain or, as the case may be, recover the whole or any part of the sums so paid or payable, not being an amount in excess of the expenses so incurred.

(3) Where any party to the contract has, by reason of anything done by any other party thereto in, or for the purpose of, the performance of the contract, obtained a valuable benefit (other than a payment of money to which the last foregoing subsection applies) before the time of discharge, there shall be recoverable from him by the said other party such sum (if any), not exceeding the value of the said benefit to the party obtaining it, as the court considers just, having regard to all the circumstances of the case and, in particular, –

  (a) the amount of any expenses incurred before the time of discharge by the benefited party in, or for the purpose of, the performance of the contract, including any sums paid or payable by him to any other party in pursuance of the contract and retained or recoverable by that party under the last foregoing subsection, and

  (b) the effect, in relation to the said benefit, of the circumstances giving rise to the frustration of the contract.

(4) In estimating, for the purposes of the foregoing provisions of this section, the amount of any expenses incurred by any party to the contract, the court may, without prejudice to the generality of the said provisions, include such sum as appears to be reasonable in respect of overhead expenses and in respect of any work or services performed personally by the said party.

(5) In considering whether any sum ought to be recovered or retained under the foregoing provisions of this section by any party to the contract, the court shall not take into account any sums which have, by reason of the circumstances giving rise to the

frustration of the contract, become payable to that party under any contract of insurance unless there was an obligation to insure imposed by an express term of the frustrated contract or by or under any enactment.

(6) Where any person has assumed obligations under the contract in consideration of the conferring of a benefit by any other party to the contract upon any other person, whether a party to the contract or not, the court may, if in all the circumstances of the case it considers it just to do so, treat for the purposes of subsection (3) of this section any benefit so conferred as a benefit obtained by the person who has assumed the obligations as aforesaid.

S 2 Provision as to application of this Act

(1) This Act shall apply to contracts, whether made before or after the commencement of this Act, as respects which the time of discharge is on or after the first day of July, nineteen hundred and forty-three, but not to contracts as respects which the time of discharge is before the said date.

(2) This Act shall apply to contracts to which the Crown is a party in like manner as to contracts between subjects.

(3) Where any contract to which this Act applies contains any provision which, upon the true construction of the contract, is intended to have effect in the event of circumstances arising which operate, or would but for the said provision operate, to frustrate the contract, or is intended to have effect whether such circumstances arise or not, the court shall give effect to the said provision and shall only give effect to the foregoing section of this Act to such extent, if any, as appears to the court to be consistent with the said provision.

(4) Where it appears to the court that a part of any contract to which this Act applies can properly be severed from the remainder of the contract, being a part wholly performed before the time of discharge, or so performed except for the payment in respect of that part of the contract of sums which are or can be ascertained under the contract, the court shall treat that part of the contract as if it were a separate contract and had not been frustrated and shall treat the foregoing section of this Act as only applicable to the remainder of that contract.

(5) This Act shall not apply –

   (a) to any charterparty, except a time charterparty or a charterparty by way of demise, or to any contract (other than a charterparty) for the carriage of goods by sea; or

   (b) to any contract of insurance, save as is provided by subsection (5) of the foregoing section; or

   (c) to any contract to which [section 7 of the Sale of Goods Act 1979] (which avoids contracts for the sale of specific goods which perish before the risk has passed to the buyer) applies, or to any other contract for the sale, or for the sale and delivery, of specific goods, where the contract is frustrated by reason of the fact that the goods have perished.

15.5.1 THE SCOPE OF THE ACT

Section 2 sets out some important limitations on the scope of the Act. Section 2(3) makes it clear that the parties can agree to exclude the provisions of the LR(FC)A 1943. If the parties chose to do this, such exclusion will not be subject to the UCTA 1977, since s 29(1)(a) of the 1977 Act states that the Act does not effect any contractual provision that 'is authorised . . . by the express terms . . . of an enactment'. The exclusion may, however, be affected by the UTCCR 1999 if it is contained in a standard form consumer contract. In practice, the fact that s 2(3) expressly authorises the parties to exclude the LR(FC)A 1943, is likely to support the conclusion that the term is not 'unfair'.

Section 2(4) provides that if parts of the contract that have been wholly performed can properly be severed from the remainder of the contract, they are to be treated as a separate contract, which has not been frustrated. The remainder of the contract will be subject to s 1 of the LR(FC)A 1943.

Section 2(5) contains a list of contracts that are excluded from the scope of the Act. This includes charterparties for a particular voyage and contracts of insurance. It also includes contracts falling within s 7 of the Sale of Goods Act 1979. Professor Glanville Williams has argued convincingly that there is no justification for this latter exclusion (see *Law Reform (Frustrated Contracts) Act 1943*, 1944, London: Stevens).

15.5.2 THE KEY PROVISIONS OF THE ACT

There are two key provisions in the Act. The first, s 1(2), deals with money paid or owing under the contract prior to the frustrating event and the second, s 1(3), deals with the situation where a party has obtained a non-money benefit before the time of discharge. The leading case on the operation of these provisions is *BP Exploration Co (Libya) Ltd v Hunt (No 2)*.

BP Exploration Co (Libya) Ltd v Hunt (No 2) [1979] 1 WLR 783

Facts: The defendant, Mr Hunt, was the owner of an oil concession in Libya. He entered into a 'farm-in' agreement with the plaintiff oil company under which they would explore, develop and operate the oil concession and also make 'farm-in' contributions to the defendant in cash and oil. In return, the plaintiff would receive a half share of the concession. Furthermore, if oil was found, the plaintiff would be entitled to repayment of its expenditure (both the 'farm-in' contributions and a half share of the expenditure on exploration and development) out of the defendant's share of the oil. Large quantities of oil were discovered and the field came on stream in 1967. In 1971, following a revolution in Libya, the plaintiff's interest in the oil field was expropriated by the Libyan government. The defendant continued to export oil from the field until 11

June 1973, when his interest was expropriated. By this time, the plaintiff had already received approximately one-third of the 50 million barrels of 'reimbursement oil' to which it was entitled. It also received some compensation from the Libyan government in relation to the facilities left at the field. The plaintiff claimed that the contract had been frustrated by the expropriation of its interest in the oil field and sought an award of a just sum under s 1(3) of the LR(FC)A 1943.

Held: Goff J held that the contract was frustrated and awarded the plaintiff a just sum under s 1(3) of the LR(FC)A 1943.

Goff J:

'*(1) The principle of recovery*
(a) The principle, which is common to both section 1(2) and (3), and indeed is the fundamental principle underlying the Act itself, is prevention of the unjust enrichment of either party to the contract at the other's expense. It was submitted by [counsel for the plaintiff] that the principle common to both subsections was one of restitution for net benefits received, the net benefit being the benefit less an appropriate deduction for expenses incurred by the defendant. This is broadly correct so far as section 1(2) is concerned; but under section 1 (3) the net benefit of the defendant simply provides an upper limit to the award – it does not measure the amount of the award to be made to the plaintiff. This is because in section 1 (3) a distinction is drawn between the plaintiff's performance under the contract, and the benefit which the defendant has obtained by reason of that performance – a distinction about which I shall have more to say later in this judgment: and the net benefit obtained by the defendant from the plaintiff's performance may be more than a just sum payable in respect of such performance, in which event a sum equal to the defendant's net benefit would not be an appropriate sum to award to the plaintiff. I therefore consider it better to state the principle underlying the Act as being the principle of unjust enrichment, which underlies the right of recovery in very many cases in English law, and indeed is the basic principle of the English law of restitution, of which the Act forms part.

(b) Although section 1 (2) and (3) is concerned with restitution in respect of different types of benefit, it is right to construe the two subsections as flowing from the same basic principle and therefore, so far as their different subject matters permit, to achieve consistency between them. Even so, it is always necessary to bear in mind the difference between awards of restitution in respect of money payments and awards where the benefit conferred by the plaintiff does not consist of a payment of money. Money has the peculiar character of a universal medium of exchange. By its receipt, the recipient is inevitably benefited; and (subject to problems arising from such matters as inflation, change of position and the time value of money) the loss suffered by the plaintiff is generally equal to the defendant's gain, so that no difficulty arises concerning the amount to be repaid. The same cannot be said of other benefits, such as goods or services. By their nature, services cannot be restored; nor in many cases can goods be restored, for example where they have been consumed or transferred to another.

Furthermore the identity and value of the resulting benefit to the recipient may be debatable. From the very nature of things, therefore, the problem of restitution in respect of such benefits is more complex than in cases where the benefit takes the form of a money payment; and the solution of the problem has been made no easier by the form in which the legislature has chosen to draft section 1 (3) of the Act.

(c) The Act is not designed to do certain things: (i) It is not designed to apportion the loss between the parties. There is no general power under either section 1(2) or section 1(3) to make any allowance for expenses incurred by the plaintiff (except, under the proviso to section 1 (2), to enable him to enforce *pro tanto* payment of a sum payable but unpaid before frustration); and expenses incurred by the defendant are only relevant in so far as they go to reduce the net benefit obtained by him and thereby limit any award to the plaintiff. (ii) It is not concerned to put the parties in the position in which they would have been if the contract had been performed. (iii) It is not concerned to restore the parties to the position they were in before the contract was made. A remedy designed to prevent unjust enrichment may not achieve that result; for expenditure may be incurred by either party under the contract which confers no benefit on the other, and in respect of which no remedy is available under the Act.

(d) An award under the Act may have the effect of rescuing the plaintiff from an unprofitable bargain. This may certainly be true under section 1 (2), if the plaintiff has paid the price in advance for an expected return which, if furnished, would have proved unprofitable; if the contract is frustrated before any part of that expected return is received, and before any expenditure is incurred by the defendant, the plaintiff is entitled to the return of the price he has paid, irrespective of the consideration he would have recovered had the contract been performed. Consistently with section 1 (2), there is nothing in section 1 (3) which necessarily limits an award to the contract consideration. But the contract consideration may nevertheless be highly relevant to the assessment of the just sum to be awarded under section 1 (3); this is a matter to which I will revert later in this judgment.

(2) Claims under section 1 (2)

Where an award is made under section 1 (2), it is, generally speaking, simply an award for the repayment of money which has been paid to the defendant in pursuance of the contract, subject to an allowance in respect of expenses incurred by the defendant. It is not necessary that the consideration for the payment should have wholly failed: claims under section 1 (2) are not limited to cases of total failure of consideration, and cases of partial failure of consideration can be catered for by a cross-claim by the defendant under section 1 (2) or section 1 (3) or both. There is no discretion in the court in respect of a claim under section 1 (2), except in respect of the allowance for expenses; subject to such an allowance (and, of course, a cross-claim) the plaintiff is entitled to repayment of the money he has paid. The allowance for expenses is probably best rationalised as a statutory recognition of the defence of change of position. True, the expenses need not have been incurred by reason of the plaintiff's payment; but they must have been incurred in, or for the purpose of, the performance of the contract under which the plaintiff's payment has been made, and for that reason it is just that they should be brought into account. No provision is made in the subsection for any increase in the sum recoverable by the plaintiff, or in the amount of expenses to be allowed to the defendant, to allow for the time value of money. The money may have been paid, or the expenses incurred, many years before the date of frustration; but the cause of action accrues on that date, and the sum recoverable under the Act as at that date can be no greater than the sum actually paid, though the defendant may have had the use of the money over many years, and indeed may have profited from its use. Of course, the question whether the court may award interest from the date of the accrual of the cause of action is an entirely different matter, to which I shall refer later in this judgment.

(3) Claims under section 1 (3)

(a) *General*. In contract, where an award is made under section 1 (3), the process is more complicated. First, it has to be shown that the defendant has, by reason of something done by the plaintiff in, or for the purpose of, the performance of the contract, obtained a valuable benefit (other than a payment of money) before the time of discharge. That benefit has to be identified, and valued, and such value forms the upper limit of the award. Secondly, the court may award to the plaintiff such sum, not greater than the value of such benefit, as it considers just having regard to all the circumstances of the case, including in particular the matters specified in section 1 (3) (a) and (b). In the case of an award under section 1 (3) there are, therefore, two distinct stages – the identification and valuation of the benefit, and the award of the just sum. The amount to be awarded is the just sum, unless the defendant's benefit is less, in which event the award will be limited to the amount of that benefit. The distinction between the identification and valuation of the defendant's benefit, and the assessment of the just sum, is the most controversial part of the Act. It represents the solution adopted by the legislature of the problem of restitution in cases where the benefit does not consist of a payment of money, but the solution so adopted has been criticised by some commentators as productive of injustice, and it certainly gives rise to considerable problems, to which I shall refer in due course.

(b) Identification of the defendant's benefit. In the course of the argument before me, there was much dispute whether, in the case of services, the benefit should be identified as the services themselves, or as the end product of the services. One example canvassed (because it bore some relationship to the facts of the present case) was the example of prospecting for minerals. If minerals are discovered, should the benefit be regarded (as counsel for the defendant contended) simply as the services of prospecting, or (as counsel for the plaintiff contended) as the minerals themselves being the end product of the successful exercise? Now, I am satisfied that it was the intention of the legislature, to be derived from section 1 (3) as a matter of construction, that the benefit should in an appropriate case be identified as the end product of the services. This appears, in my judgment, not only from the fact that section 1 (3) distinguishes between the plaintiff's performance and the defendant's benefit, but also from section 1 (3) (b) which clearly relates to the product of the plaintiff's performance. Let me take the example of a building contract. Suppose that a contract for work on a building is frustrated by a fire which destroys the building and which, therefore, also destroys a substantial amount of work already done by the plaintiff. Although it might be thought just to award the plaintiff a sum assessed on a *quantum meruit* basis, probably a rateable part of the contract price, in respect of the work he has done, the effect of section 1 (3) (b) will be to reduce the award to nil, because of the effect, in relation to the defendant's benefit, of the circumstances giving rise to the frustration of the contract. It is quite plain that, in section 1 (3) (b), the word "benefit" is intended to refer, in the example I have given, to the actual improvement to the building, because that is what will be affected by the frustrating event; the subsection therefore contemplates that, in such a case, the benefit is the end product of the plaintiff's services, not the services themselves. This will not be so in every case, since in some cases the services will have no end product; for example, where the services consist of doing such work as surveying, or transporting goods. In each case, it is necessary to ask the question: what benefit has the defendant obtained by reason of the plaintiff's contractual performance? But it must not be forgotten that in section 1 (3) the relevance of the value of the benefit is to fix a ceiling to the award. If, for example, in a building contract, the building is only partially completed, the value of the partially completed building (i.e. the product of the services) will fix a ceiling for the award; the stage of the work may be such that the uncompleted building may be worth less than the value of the work and materials that have gone into it, particularly as completion by another builder may cost more than completion by the original builder would have cost. In other cases, however, the actual benefit to the defendant may be considerably more than the appropriate or just sum to be awarded to the plaintiff, in which event the value of the benefit will not in fact determine the quantum of the award. I should add, however, that, in a case of prospecting, it would usually be wrong to identify the discovered mineral as the benefit. In such a case there is always (whether the prospecting is successful or not) the benefit of the prospecting itself, i.e. of knowing whether or not the land contains any deposit of the relevant minerals; if the prospecting is successful, the benefit may include also the enhanced value of the land by reason of the discovery; if the prospector's contractual task goes beyond discovery and includes development and production, the benefit will include the further enhancement of the land by reason of the installation of the facilities, and also the benefit of in part transforming a valuable mineral deposit into a marketable commodity.

I add by way of footnote that all these difficulties would have been avoided if the legislature had thought it right to treat the services themselves as the benefit. In the opinion of many commentators, it would be more just to do so; after all, the services in question have been requested by the defendant, who normally takes the risk that they may prove worthless, from whatever cause. In the example I have given of the building destroyed by fire, there is much to be said for the view that the builder should be paid for the work he has done, unless he has (for example by agreeing to insure the works) taken upon himself the risk of destruction by fire. But my task is to construe the Act as it stands. On the true construction of the Act, it is in my judgment clear that the defendant's benefit must, in an appropriate case, be identified as the end product of the plaintiff's services, despite the difficulties which this construction creates, difficulties which are met again when one comes to value the benefit . . .

(d) Valuing the benefit. Since the benefit may be identified with the product of the plaintiff's performance, great problems arise in the valuation of the benefit. First, how does one solve the problem which arises from the fact that a small service may confer an enormous benefit, and conversely, a very substantial service may confer only a very small benefit? The answer presumably is that at the stage of valuation of the benefit (as opposed to assessment of the just sum) the task of the court is simply to assess the value of the benefit to the defendant. For example, if a prospector after some very simple prospecting discovers a large and unexpected deposit of a valuable mineral, the benefit to the defendant (namely, the enhancement in the value of the land) may be enormous; it must be valued as such, always bearing in mind that the assessment of a just sum may very well lead to a much smaller amount being awarded to the plaintiff. But conversely, the plaintiff may have undertaken building work for a substantial sum which is, objectively speaking, of little or no value – for example, he may commence the redecoration, to the defendant's execrable taste, of rooms which are in good decorative order. If the contract is frustrated before the work is complete, and the work is unaffected by the frustrating event, it can be argued that the defendant has obtained no benefit, because the defendant's property has been reduced in value by the plaintiff's work; but the partial work must be treated as a benefit to the defendant, since he requested it, and valued as such. Secondly, at what point in time is the benefit to be valued? If there is a lapse of time between the date of the receipt of the benefit, and the date of frustration, there may in the meanwhile be a substantial variation in the value of the benefit. If the benefit had simply been identified as the services rendered, this problem would not arise; the court would simply award a reasonable remuneration for the services rendered at the time when they were rendered, the defendant taking the risk of any subsequent depreciation and the benefit of any subsequent appreciation in value. But that is not what the Act provides: section 1 (3) (b) makes it plain that the plaintiff is to take the risk of depreciation or destruction by the frustrating event. If the effect of the frustrating event upon the value of the benefit is to be measured, it must surely be measured upon the benefit as at the date of frustration. For example, let it be supposed that a builder does work which doubles in value by the date of frustration, and is then so severely damaged by fire that the contract is frustrated; the valuation of the residue must surely be made on the basis of the value as at the date of frustration . . .

Other problems can arise from the valuation of the defendant's benefit as the end product; I shall come to these later in the consideration of the facts of the present case. But there is a further problem which I should refer to, before leaving this topic. Section 1 (3) (a) requires the court to have regard to the amount of any expenditure incurred before the time of discharge by the benefited party in, or for the purpose of, the performance of the contract. The question arises – should this matter be taken into account at the stage of valuation of the benefit, or of assessment of the just sum? Take a simple example. Suppose that the defendant's benefit is valued at £150, and that a just sum is assessed at £100, but that there remain to be taken into account defendant's expenses of £75: is the award to be £75 or £25? The clue to this problem lies, in my judgment, in the fact that the allowance for expenses is a statutory recognition of the defence of change of position. Only to the extent that the position of the defendant has so changed that it would be unjust to award restitution, should the court make an allowance for expenses. Suppose that the plaintiff does work for the defendant which produces no valuable end product, or a benefit no greater in value than the just sum to be awarded in respect of the work; there is then no reason why the whole of the relevant expenses should not be set off against the just sum. But suppose that the defendant has reaped a large benefit from the plaintiff's work, far greater in value than the just sum to be awarded for the work. In such circumstances it would be quite wrong to set off the whole of the defendant's expenses against the just sum. The question whether the defendant has suffered a change of position has to be judged in the light of all the circumstances of the case. Accordingly, on the Act as it stands, under section 1 (3) the proper course is to deduct the expenses from the value of the benefit, with the effect that only in so far as they reduce the value of the benefit below the amount of the just sum which would otherwise be awarded will they have any practical bearing on the award . . .

(e) *Assessment of the just sum*. The principle underlying the Act is prevention of the unjust enrichment of the defendant at the plaintiff's expense. Where, as in cases under section 1 (2), the benefit conferred on the defendant consists of payment of a sum of money, the plaintiff's expense and the defendant's enrichment are generally equal; and, subject to other relevant factors, the award of restitution will consist simply of an order for repayment of a like sum of money. But where the benefit does not consist of money, then the defendant's enrichment will rarely be equal to the plaintiff's expense. In such cases, where (as in the case of a benefit conferred under a contract thereafter frustrated) the benefit has been requested by the defendant, the basic measure of recovery in restitution is the reasonable value of the plaintiff's performance – in a case of services, a *quantum meruit* or reasonable remuneration, and in a case of goods, a *quantum valebat* or reasonable price. Such cases are to be contrasted with cases where such a benefit has not been requested by the defendant. In the latter class of case, recovery is rare in restitution; but if the sole basis of recovery was that the defendant had been incontrovertibly benefited, it might be legitimate to limit recovery to the defendant's actual benefit – a limit which has (perhaps inappropriately) been imported by the legislature into section 1 (3) of the Act. However, under section 1 (3) as it stands, if the defendant's actual benefit is less than the just or reasonable sum which would otherwise be awarded to the plaintiff, the award must be reduced to a sum equal to the amount of the defendant's benefit.

A crucial question, upon which the Act is surprisingly silent, is this: what bearing do the terms of the contract, under which the plaintiff has acted, have upon the assessment of the just sum? First, the terms upon which the work was done may serve to indicate the full scope of the work done, and so be relevant to the sum awarded in respect of such work. For example, if I do work under a contract under which I am to receive a substantial prize if successful, and nothing if I fail, and the contract is frustrated before the work is complete but not before a substantial benefit has been obtained by the defendant, the element of risk taken by the plaintiff may be held to have the effect of enhancing the amount of any sum to be awarded. Secondly, the contract consideration is always relevant as providing some evidence of what will be a reasonable sum to be awarded in respect of the plaintiff's work. Thus if a prospector, employed for a fee, discovers a gold mine before the contract under which he is employed is frustrated (for example, by illegality or by his illness or disablement) at a time when his work was incomplete, the court may think it just to make an award in the nature of a reasonable fee for what he has done (though of course the benefit obtained by the defendant will be far greater), and a rateable part of the contract fee may provide useful evidence of the level of sum to be awarded. If, however, the contract had provided that he was to receive a stake in the concession, then the just sum might be enhanced on the basis that, in all the circumstances, a reasonable sum should take account of such a factor: cf *Way v Latilla* [1937] 3 All ER 759. Thirdly, however, the contract consideration, or a rateable part of it, may provide a limit to the sum to be awarded. To take a fairly extreme example, a poor householder or a small businessman may obtain a contract for building work to be done to his premises at considerably less than the market price, on the basis that he cannot afford to pay more. In such a case, the court may consider it just to limit the award to a rateable part of the contract price, on the ground that it was the understanding of the parties that in no circumstances (including the circumstances of the contract being frustrated) should the plaintiff recover more than the contract price or a rateable part of it. Such a limit may properly be said to arise by virtue of the operation of section 2 (3) of the Act. But it must not be forgotten that, unlike money, services can never be restored, nor usually can goods, since they are likely to have been either consumed or disposed of, or to have depreciated in value; and since, *ex hypothesi*, the defendant will only have been prepared to contract for the goods or services on the basis that he paid no more than the contract consideration, it may be unjust to compel him, by an award under the Act, to pay more than that consideration, or a rateable part of it, in respect of the services or goods he has received. It is unnecessary for me to decide whether this will always be so; but it is likely that in most cases this will impose an important limit upon the sum to be awarded – indeed it may well be the most relevant limit to an award under section 1 (3) of the Act. The legal basis of the limit may be section 2 (3) of the Act; but even if that subsection is inapplicable, it is open to the court, in an appropriate case, to give effect to such a limit in assessing the just sum to be awarded under section 1 (3), because in many cases it would be unjust to impose upon the defendant an obligation to make restitution under the subsection at higher than the contract rate.'

Applying this approach to the facts of the case, Goff J found that the valuable benefit obtained by the defendant, following frustration of the contract, consisted of the value of the oil he had actually obtained from the oilfield, plus the compensation received from the Libyan government. This produced a 'valuable benefit' of $85 million. In assessing the 'just sum', Goff J took into account the expenses incurred by the plaintiff and the 'farm-in' contributions received by the defendant, and then deducted from this figure the value of the reimbursement oil received by the plaintiff. This produced a total of $35 million, which being less than the 'valuable benefit', was awarded in full.

For our purposes, we do not need to focus on the complex facts of the case. Instead we will direct our attention to the comments made by Goff J about the key provisions of the Act.

15.5.2.1 The underlying purpose of the Act

Goff J considered that the purpose underlying the Act was the prevention of unjust enrichment. The Court of Appeal affirmed his decision (as did the House of Lords), although Lawton LJ doubted his analytical approach:

'Mr Rokison, on behalf of the plaintiffs, accepted that there could be more than one way of assessing a just sum. He pointed out that there was nothing in the Act to indicate that its purpose was to enable the judge to apportion losses or profits, or to put the parties in the positions which they would have been in if the contract had been fully performed or if it had never been made. This we accept. He submitted that the concept behind the Act was to prevent unjust enrichment. This is what the judge had thought. We get no help from the use of words which are not in the statute.'

It has been suggested that the assessment of a 'just sum' under s 1(3) exposes the fact that the Act is really just a mechanism for loss apportionment. Haycroft and Waksman ('Frustration and Restitution' [1984] JBL 207, 225) have written:

'Unjust enrichment cannot be regarded as the basis of the Act; to suggest otherwise simply ignores its wording and the conceptual distortion which follows from such an idea can be seen to lead to great practical difficulties.

All that can be ventured about the real basis of the Act is that it is designed to provide a flexible machinery for the adjustment of loss.

The inclusion of the word "just" merely sets a general standard for the exercise of the court's discretion as can be found in many other statutes, and should not be seen as an invocation of the principle of unjust enrichment'

With respect, this is incorrect. Although the Act does confer a discretion on the court, this does not amount to 'a flexible machinery for the adjustment of loss'. The first step for the court is to identify the benefit that the defendant has obtained at the claimant's expense. This figure operates as a ceiling for the defendant's claim and ensures that recovery is limited to the amount by which the defendant has been unjustly enriched at the claimant's expense. It is only at this stage that the judicial discretion comes into play. This discretion allows the courts to reduce recovery to take into account the losses sustained by the defendant, but it does not allow for the apportionment of losses, which are not matched by a corresponding enrichment. Thus the discretion to adjust recovery is only a very narrow discretion and it operates within the general framework of recovery for unjust enrichment.

15.5.2.2 Operation of section 1(2): restitution of money

As Goff J notes, a major change brought about by s 1(2) of the LR(FC)A 1943 is that money paid under a frustrated contract is recoverable, even where there is not a total failure of consideration. This is a significant improvement on the common-law position and it is argued elsewhere (see Chapter 18), that the same approach should be applied to all claims for failure of consideration.

Section 1(2) also introduces a proviso that permits the court to set off against the advance payment any expenses that may have been incurred by the defendant prior to the frustrating event. Goff J suggested that this proviso is 'best rationalised as a statutory recognition of the defence of change of position'. This would mean that the defendant is permitted, as of right, to set off expenses incurred in 'the performance of the contract under which the plaintiff's payment has been made'. A different view was, however, taken by Garland J in *Gamerco SA v ICM/Fair Warning (Agency) Ltd* [1995] 1 WLR 1226. The case concerned a contract to promote a 'Guns N' Roses' concert, which was frustrated by the Spanish government's decision to close the stadium in which the concert was due to take place. The plaintiff had paid the defendant $412,500 prior to the frustrating event and sought to recover this amount under s 1(2). The defendants had incurred expenditure of approximately $50,000 and argued that they should be allowed to retain this amount. Garland J held that, taking into account the plaintiff's loss (approximately $450,000), justice would be done by allowing the plaintiffs to recover the advance payment in full without any deduction for the defendant's expenses. He concluded his judgment as follows:

'The *approach to the proviso*
The following have to be established: (1) that the defendants incurred expenses paid or payable (2) before the discharge of the contract on 2 July (3) in performance of the contract (which is not applicable) or (4) for the purposes of the performance of the contract, and (5) that it is just in all the circumstances to allow them to retain the whole or any part of the sums so paid or payable.

The onus of establishing these matters must lie on the defendant. It is, in the broad sense, his case to be made out and I am assisted by the Victorian case of *Lobb v Vasey Housing Auxiliary (War Widows Guild)* [1963] VR 239 under the corresponding Victorian Act of 1959, which is in very similar terms to the Act of 1943.

I have already dealt with (1), (2) and (4) so far as the evidence allows. I turn to (5) . . . Various views have been advanced as to how the court should exercise its discretion and these can be categorised as follows.

(1) *Total retention.* This view was advanced by the Law Revision Committee in 1939 (Cmd. 6009) on the questionable ground "that it is reasonable to assume that in stipulating for prepayment the payee intended to protect himself from loss under the contract". As the editor of *Chitty on Contracts*, 27th edn. (1994), vol. 1, p 1141, para. 23–060, note 51 (Mr E G McKendrick) comments: "He probably intends to protect himself against the possibility of the other party's insolvency or default in payment". To this, one can add: "and secure his own cash flow."

In *BP Exploration Co (Libya) Ltd v Hunt (No 2)* [1979] 1 WLR 783, Robert Goff J considered the principle of recovery under subsections (2) and (3). He said . . .

> "There is no discretion in the court in respect of a claim under section 1(2), except in respect of the allowance for expenses; subject to such an allowance . . . the plaintiff is entitled to repayment of the money he has paid. The allowance for expenses is probably best rationalised as a statutory recognition of the defence of change of position. True, the expenses need not have been incurred by reason of the plaintiff's payments; but they must have been incurred in, or for the purpose of, the performance of the contract under which the plaintiff's payment has been made, and for that reason it is just that they should be brought into account."

I do not derive any specific assistance from the *BP Exploration Co* case. There was no question of any change of position as a result of the plaintiffs' advance payment.

(2) *Equal division.* This was discussed by Professor Treitel in *Frustration and Force Majeure*, pp 555–556, paras. 15–059 and 15–060. There is some attraction in splitting the loss, but what if the losses are very unequal? Professor Treitel considers statutory provisions in Canada and Australia but makes the point that unequal division is unnecessarily rigid and was rejected by the Law Revision Committee in the 1939 report to which reference has already been made. The parties may, he suggests, have had an unequal means of providing

against the loss by insurers, but he appears to overlook subsection (5). It may well be that one party's expenses are entirely thrown away while the other is left with some realisable or otherwise usable benefit or advantage. Their losses may, as in the present case, be very unequal. Professor Treitel therefore favours the third view.

(3) *Broad discretion*. It is self-evident that any rigid rule is liable to produce injustice. The words, "if it considers it just to do so having regard to all the circumstances of the case", clearly confer a very broad discretion. Obviously the court must not take into account anything which is not "a circumstance of the case" or fail to take into account anything that is and then exercise its discretion rationally. I see no indication in the Act, the authorities or the relevant literature that the court is obliged to incline towards either total retention or equal division. Its task is to do justice in a situation which the parties had neither contemplated nor provided for, and to mitigate the possible harshness of allowing all loss to lie where it has fallen.

I have not found my task easy. As I have made clear, I would have welcomed assistance on the true measure of the defendants' loss and the proper treatment of overhead and non-specific expenditure. Because the defendants have plainly suffered some loss, I have made a robust assumption. In all the circumstances, and having particular regard to the plaintiffs' loss, I consider that justice is done by making no deduction under the proviso.'

Carter and Tolhurst ('Gigs N' Restitution – Frustration and the Statutory Adjustment of Payments and Expenses' (1996) 10 JCL 264) have criticised the approach adopted by Garland J in *Gamerco*. They note that the judge gave no reason for his rejection of the 'change of position' rationalisation and question why he neglected to consider the position at common law. They conclude as follows:

'[W]hether or not one accepts change of position as the rationalisation, it ought at least to have been clear that the Band was entitled to something, because the circumstances activated the defence. In this regard it may be important that the proviso requires an award of "the whole or . . . part of the sums so paid or payable, not being an amount in excess of the expenses . . . incurred". Arguably, there was no discretion to award a nil sum. In other words, the discretion was to award a sum which was just in the circumstances. But even if that is not the correct interpretation, it can at least be said that once the Band proved some expenses, Garland J ought to have awarded something unless it was unjust to do so. Clearly, there was nothing in the evidence to indicate that a zero sum was a just sum.'

It is regrettable that Garland J refused to identify any principles upon which the discretion exercisable under s 1(2) is to be based. We are left with a discretion that is both ill-defined and difficult to apply. All we can really say is what the discretion is not. First, attractive though the theory may be, the proviso cannot be rationalised as a form of change of position defence. This is because the proviso allows the courts to take into account 'all the circumstances of the case', including the claimant's loss (*Gamerco*). Such considerations are irrelevant to change of position, which focuses solely on the loss sustained by the defendant. Second, however, the proviso cannot be rationalised as a full-blown mechanism for loss apportionment either. This is because recovery is only possible where the claimant was obliged to pay money prior to the frustrating event and recovery is limited to the value of the advance payment. In truth, what we have in s 1(2) is a severely restricted mechanism for loss apportionment, arbitrarily limited by the value of the defendant's enrichment.

15.5.2.3 Operation of section 1(3): restitution of non-money benefits

Goff J indicated that there are three stages to the operation of s 1(3). First, it has to be shown that the defendant has obtained a 'valuable benefit' from the claimant prior to the time of discharge. Second, the benefit must be valued. Third, the court must determine what would be a 'just sum' to award to the claimant, having regard to all the circumstances of the case, including in particular the matters specified in section 1 (3)(a) and (b).

In relation to the valuing of the benefit, Goff J noted that s 1(3) (b) of the Act requires the court to take into account 'the effect, in relation to the said benefit, of the circumstances giving rise to the frustration of the contract'. This led him to the conclusion that the benefit is to be identified as the end product of the claimant's services rather than the services themselves. If this is correct, then *Appleby v Myers* would be decided in the same way today. It will be remembered that in *Appleby v Myers* the plaintiff provided valuable machinery to the defendant, which was subsequently destroyed by fire. According to Goff's J's interpretation of s 1(3) (b) this would mean that the 'valuable benefit' received by the defendant was nil, and since the 'just sum' cannot exceed the 'valuable benefit', the 'just sum' must also be nil. There are reasons to believe that Goff J's approach to the interpretation of s 1(3) is incorrect.

Burrows, A, *The Law of Restitution,* 2nd edn, 2002, Oxford: OUP, at pp 370–371

With great respect, it is possible that Robert Goff J took a false step in regarding there as being a crucial difference, so far as restitution is concerned, between the end product of contracted-for services and the services (or performance of the services) themselves. *Even if there is an end product produced by the services the defendant's benefit comprises his saving of expense in paying for the services producing that end product.* And the crucial line between when services constitute mere reliance loss to the performer and when they become objectively beneficial to the other party (and hence subject to subjective devaluation, belong within restitution) is, it is submitted, when the other party receives the services. When the purpose of the services is to produce an end product (eg, building work) it is true that one regards the owner as receiving the services at the time when it receives part of the end product (eg, when the first part of the building is erected). But the same notion of receipt explains why a theatregoer is only objectively benefited when the play begins or why a home owner who engages a gardener to mow the lawn is only objectively benefited when the gardener starts to cut the lawn. On a restitutionary interpretation of s 1(3) the important distinction is therefore between services that are not received and services that are received and not between services and the end product of those services.

Once one excises the distinction between end product and services the acute problems encountered by Robert Goff J in interpreting s 1(3) disappear. For example, there is now no problem of a small service producing very substantial end products and vice versa; there is no need to carve out inconsistent 'exceptions' where there is no end product or an end product of no objective value; there is no reason to confine a true restitutionary analysis to the assessment of the just sum; and, while the same conclusion may be reached by applying 'change of position' reasoning, s 1 (3) (b) does not have to be interpreted as meaning that no valuable benefit was obtained where a building under construction is destroyed by fire.'

Treitel, G, *The Law of Contract*, 11th edn, 2003, London: Sweet & Maxwell at p 915

[A]n alternative interpretation of s 1(3) is to be preferred. This would make the destruction of the benefit relevant, not to the identification of the benefit, but to the assessment of the just sum. Two points seem to support such an interpretation. First, s 1(3) applies where a valuable benefit has been obtained *before* the time of discharge: thus to identify the benefit in a case like *Appleby v Myers* the court must look at the facts as they were before, and not after, the fire. The partly completed installation would at least prima facie be a benefit, since completion of the installation would be likely to cost less after part of the work has been done. Secondly, there is the structure of the subsection. This begins by setting out the circumstances in which the court has power to make an award (ie when a valuable benefit has been obtained) and then provides guidelines for the exercise of that power. The guideline contained in s 1(3)(b) is introduced by the words 'such sum as the court thinks just having regard to . . .'; and these words seem to link the guideline to the *exercise* rather than to the *existence* of the court's discretion. This interpretation cannot cause any injustice, for if the court thinks that very little or nothing should be awarded it can exercise its discretion to that effect; and for this purpose the court can take the destruction of the benefit into account so as to split the loss in such proportions as the court thinks just. But if such destruction necessarily led to the conclusion that no valuable benefit had been obtained before frustration, the court would have no discretion to award anything at all. It would be a pity if this useful discretion were restricted in a way that is neither clearly required by the words of the subsection nor necessary to promote justice.

It is submitted that the criticisms of Professor Burrows and Professor Treitel are compelling. Although the destruction of the end product is relevant to the assessment of the just sum under s 1(3), it should not be taken into account at the earlier stage of assessing the benefit received by the defendant. The view expressed by Goff J that s 1(3)(a) is a statutory recognition of the change of position defence should also be rejected. This is clearly too narrow a view of the provision given that s 1(3)(a) and (b) clearly allow the courts, within limits, to apportion the losses between the parties.

15.5.3 CRITICISMS OF THE LAW REFORM (FRUSTRATED CONTRACTS) Act 1943

The LR(FC)A 1943 has been criticised on a number of grounds. Professor McKendrick ('The Consequences of Frustration – The Law Reform (Frustrated Contracts) Act 1943' in *Force Majeure and Frustration of Contract*, 2nd edn, 1995, London: Lloyds of London Press at p 243) writes:

'It is now clear that the Law Reform (Frustrated Contracts) Act 1943 suffers from a number of deficiencies and that the Law Reform Commission of British Columbia was right to conclude that the Act "was not well thought out or well drafted".'

Criticisms of the Act proceed on two fronts. First, it is argued that the Act leaves too much discretion to the trial judge. Professor McKendrick (above at p 238) writes:

'Lawton LJ [in *BP v Hunt*] concluded that "[w]hat is just is what the trial judge thinks is just" and he held that an appellate court is not entitled to interfere with the assessment of the just sum by the trial judge "unless it is so plainly wrong that it cannot be just". This leaves the issue virtually to the untrammelled discretion of the trial judge and it is regrettable that the Court of Appeal did not establish guidelines to assist trial judges in the exercise of their discretion and to ensure a measure of consistency in decided cases and out of court settlement.'

McKendrick's criticisms are perhaps overstated. If the parties desire certainty, then this can be achieved by incorporating a *force majeure* clause into the contract. Indeed, this is what many commercial contractors choose to do. The rules on frustration only come into play when something unforeseen has occurred. It is pointless suggesting that contractual planning can be made more efficient in this area by the adoption of fixed guidelines, since frustration necessarily involves events that the parties have not planned for. The problem is not that the LR(FC)A 1943 confers too much discretion on the courts, but that it limits that discretion in arbitrary ways.

This leads us onto our second ground for criticising the Act, which is that it is hopelessly muddled. Graham Virgo (*The Principles of the Law of Restitution*, 2nd edn, 2006, Oxford: OUP, p 369) writes:

'Subsections 1(2) and 1(3) of the 1943 Act are somewhat schizophrenic provisions, embodying as they do both principles of restitution founded on the reversal of the defendant's unjust enrichment and the allocation of losses between the parties. But this attempt to allocate losses is half-hearted.'

Professor Campbell (*Remedies in Contract and Tort*, 2nd edn, 2002, Cambridge: CUP at p 248) agrees, arguing that the proviso under s 1(2) is a 'curious hybrid unknown to reliance or restitution' with 'no sound foundation in either principle'. Would it be better then to replace the LR(FC)A 1943 with a new scheme, which allows for the full apportionment of losses between the parties? Stewart and Carter think not.

Stewart, A and Carter, JW, 'Frustrated contracts and statutory adjustment: the case for a reappraisal' (1992) CLJ 66, 109–110

[I]t is our view that the philosophy of loss apportionment should be rejected. We have already questioned the assumptions underlying the notion that post-frustration losses should be shared. For all the incursions of equity in Australia, the common law of contract in that country, as much as in Britain, is still marked by a refusal to view ordinary commercial transactions as joint ventures. Unconscionable conduct is increasingly attracting liability, but the point has not yet been reached where contractors are expected to take positive steps to conserve the welfare of their 'partners'. And even if this admittedly harsh and individualist stance were to be rejected, the case for apportionment would still lack substance. If one looks past the slogans, it is hard to find convincing reasons, economic or otherwise, for compelling one party to act as the other's insurer.

Moreover, even if a favourable view were taken of the principle of loss apportionment, successfully putting it into practice appears to be another matter altogether. The three statutory models [in South Australia, New South Wales and British Columbia] amply demonstrate what we consider the impracticability of finding a workable formula which adequately separates out those losses to be attributed to the frustrated contract from those which are referable to the parties' general business activities, or which fairly and predictably identifies the losses of one which can reasonably be foisted on the other. Nor does there appear to be an acceptable way of respecting the strength or weakness of the original bargain. Only the British Columbian Act adopts a workable approach; but that is achieved by excluding all anticipatory or overhead expenses from the equation, a restrictive approach which becomes so arbitrary in its application as to make a mockery of the apportionment principle and which is as biased in its own way to recipients as the New South Wales and South Australian schemes are to performers.

Professor Burrows (*The Law of Restitution*, 2nd edn, 2003, London: Butterworths at pp 365–366) argues that loss splitting 'contradicts the basic individualistic tradition of contract law whereby contracting parties are viewed as pursuing their own self interest and taking their own risk'. It will also lead to uncertainty, Professor Burrows contends, not least because it will require the courts to take into account the relative fault of the parties. Goff and Jones (*The Law of Restitution*, 6th edn, 2002, London: Sweet & Maxwell at para 20–082) agree: 'Apportionment of loss suffered in consequence of an unforeseen event is superficially a seductive principle. But to direct a court to apportion loss is to initiate an inquiry of considerable complexity'.

Other commentators argue that we should adopt a scheme of full apportionment of losses.

McKendrick, E, 'Frustration, Restitution and Loss Apportionment' in Burrows, A (ed), *Essays on the Law of Restitution*, 1991, Oxford: Clarendon Press, pp 168–169

[T]here are arguments in favour of apportioning the loss between the parties. The first is that apportionment of loss is 'economically sounder' because 'each of the two parties may be able to bear half the loss without serious consequences when the whole loss might come close to ruining him'. The second argument is that a failure to take explicit account of the reliance interest may lead to the adoption of an unnatural definition of benefit. Restitution lawyers have been warned about adopting an 'over-inclusive concept of enrichment' and of 'marginalising' the 'principle of injurious reliance'. The classic example of this process is, of course, the British Columbian Frustrated Contracts Act which ... defines a benefit as 'something done in the fulfilment of contractual obligations whether or not the person for whose benefit it was done received the benefit'. To force losses incurred into the language of benefit distorts the concept of benefit and hinders the development of a principle of injurious reliance in English law.

The final argument is that the situation with which frustrated contracts legislation is concerned 'is the familiar one in which one of two parties has to suffer loss for which neither is responsible' and that in the 'normal case' the just course 'would be to order the retention or repayment of half the loss incurred'. The 'justice' involved in being required to share in the losses of the other party may not be readily apparent. But, while it may be true to say that contracting parties enter into contracts to serve their own interests, it should not be assumed that upholding the pursuit of self-interest is the basis of the doctrine of frustration . . . It must . . . be remembered that the frustrating event which has occurred is one which neither party has foreseen and neither party has assumed the risk of its occurrence. Moreover, neither party has been at fault. Justice and reasonableness surely demand that such expenditure be brought into account so that, on the frustration of a contract, the position is reached whereby both parties are discharged from their obligations to perform in the future (the expectation interest of neither party being protected), benefits conferred must be paid for (thus protecting the restitution interest), and losses suffered as a result of wasted expenditure be apportioned between the parties (thus taking account of the reliance interest).

On balance, it is submitted that a scheme that allows for the full apportionment of losses is preferable. The arguments levelled against such an approach largely ignore the fact that we are dealing with events that are unforeseen and not provided for by the contract. In such a context, arguments based on the need for certainty and the individualistic tradition of contract law carry little weight.

Should we therefore expect to see a change in the law? The answer is probably no. In the 50 years since the Act was passed, there have only been two decisions interpreting the Act. This suggests that its provisions do not present any real problems for the commercial community. Professor Campbell (*Remedies in Contract and Tort*, 2nd edn, 2002, Cambridge: CUP at p 253) explains why:

'Competent commercial parties, faced with the absurdity of the law of . . . frustration, have included modification provisions in contracts of sufficient value and complexity to make this worthwhile. These clauses provide for non-binding alternative dispute resolution or arbitration (including arbitration *ex aequo et bono*), which gives the parties far more flexibility to apportion loss than any conceivable restitutionary recasting of the frustration rules might do.'

It therefore seems that reform is unlikely for the simple reason that the law of frustration is of little practical importance in the commercial world.

15.6 RELIEF IN CASES OF HARDSHIP UNDER THE INTERNATIONAL CONTRACT LAW INSTRUMENTS

A wider doctrine of frustration exists in Australia where relief may be given on the ground that one of the party's obligations have become more onerous (see *Codelfa Construction Pty Ltd v State Rail Authority of New South Wales* (1982) 149 CLR 33). The Principles of European Contract Law and the UNIDROIT Principles of International Commercial Contracts, both of which contain provisions for hardship, adopt a similar approach.

PRINCIPLES OF EUROPEAN CONTRACT LAW

Article 6:111: Change of Circumstances

(1) A party is bound to fulfil its obligations even if performance has become more onerous, whether because the cost of performance has increased or because the value of the performance it receives has diminished.

(2) If, however, performance of the contract becomes excessively onerous because of a change of circumstances, the parties are bound to enter into negotiations with a view to adapting the contract or terminating it, provided that:

    (a) the change of circumstances occurred after the time of conclusion of the contract,

    (b) the possibility of a change of circumstances was not one which could reasonably have been taken into account at the time of conclusion of the contract, and

    (c) the risk of the change of circumstances is not one which, according to the contract, the party affected should be required to bear.

(3) If the parties fail to reach agreement within a reasonable period, the court may:

    (a) end the contract at a date and on terms to be determined by the court; or

    (b) adapt the contract in order to distribute between the parties in a just and equitable manner the losses and gains resulting from the change of circumstances.

In either case, the court may award damages for the loss suffered through a party refusing to negotiate or breaking off negotiations contrary to good faith and fair dealing.

Article 8:108: Excuse Due to an Impediment

(1) A party's non-performance is excused if it proves that it is due to an impediment beyond its control and that it could not reasonably have been expected to take the impediment into account at the time of the conclusion of the contract, or to have avoided or overcome the impediment or its consequences.

(2) Where the impediment is only temporary the excuse provided by this Article has effect for the period during which the impediment exists. However, if the delay amounts to a fundamental non-performance, the creditor may treat it as such.

(3) The non-performing party must ensure that notice of the impediment and of its effect on its ability to perform is received by the other party within a reasonable time after the non-performing party knew or ought to have known of these circumstances. The

other party is entitled to damages for any loss resulting from the non-receipt of such notice.

UNIDROIT PRINCIPLES OF INTERNATIONAL COMMERCIAL CONTRACTS

Article 6.2.1 (Contract to be observed)
Where the performance of a contract becomes more onerous for one of the parties, that party is nevertheless bound to perform its obligations subject to the following provisions on hardship.

Article 6.2.2 (Definition of hardship)
There is hardship where the occurrence of events fundamentally alters the equilibrium of the contract either because the cost of a party's performance has increased or because the value of the performance a party receives has diminished, and

(a) the events occur or become known to the disadvantaged party after the conclusion of the contract;
(b) the events could not reasonably have been taken into account by the disadvantaged party at the time of the conclusion of the contract;
(c) the events are beyond the control of the disadvantaged party; and
(d) the risk of the events was not assumed by the disadvantaged party.

Article 6.2.3 (Effects of hardship)

(1) In case of hardship the disadvantaged party is entitled to request renegotiations. The request shall be made without undue delay and shall indicate the grounds on which it is based.
(2) The request for renegotiation does not in itself entitle the disadvantaged party to withhold performance.
(3) Upon failure to reach agreement within a reasonable time either party may resort to the court.
(4) If the court finds hardship it may, if reasonable,

    (a) terminate the contract at a date and on terms to be fixed, or
    (b) adapt the contract with a view to restoring its equilibrium.

Article 7.1.7 (Force majeure)

(1) Non-performance by a party is excused if that party proves that the non-performance was due to an impediment beyond its control and that it could not reasonably be expected to have taken the impediment into account at the time of the conclusion of the contract or to have avoided or overcome it or its consequences.
(2) When the impediment is only temporary, the excuse shall have effect for such period as is reasonable having regard to the effect of the impediment on the performance of the contract.
(3) The party who fails to perform must give notice to the other party of the impediment and its effect on its ability to perform. If the notice is not received by the other party within a reasonable time after the party who fails to perform knew or ought

to have known of the impediment, it is liable for damages resulting from such non-receipt.

(4) Nothing in this article prevents a party from exercising a right to terminate the contract or to withhold performance or request interest on money due.

The international instruments draw a distinction between events that make a contract more onerous (hardship) and events that constitute an impediment to performance (frustration). If the event falls within the former category the contract is not discharged, but the parties are required to renegotiate. This is a concept that is alien to English law and although renegotiation is not unusual in commercial practice, the difference here is that it becomes mandatory. If the parties fail to reach an agreement within a reasonable time, the court can step in and terminate or modify the agreement. The court even has power under the Principles of European Contract Law to award damages against a party that has refused to negotiate or broken off negotiations contrary to good faith and fair dealing.

It is rather difficult to predict what change of circumstances will amount to hardship under the international instruments. Lando and Beale (*Principles of European Contract Law Parts I and II*, 2000, The Hague: Kluwer Law International at p 324) state that 'the change in circumstances must have brought about a major imbalance in the contract'. This may include certain types of frustrating event, but clearly it includes a much wider range of circumstances. It will, for instance, include the closure of the Suez Canal (Lando and Beale at p 325), which has been held by the English courts not to amount to frustration (see *Tsakiroglou & Co Ltd v Noble Thorl GmbH* [1962] AC 93). Uncertainty also surrounds the scope of the hardship provisions under the UNIDROIT Principles. According to the Official Comments to the 1994 edition of the Principles an 'alteration amounting to 50% or more of the cost or the value of the performance is likely to amount to a fundamental alteration'. Ten years later, however, in the 2004 edition, the comments state: 'Whether an alteration is "fundamental" in a given case will of course depend on the circumstances'. This level of uncertainty is undesirable from an English perspective.

The provisions on impediment/*force majeure* are much more familiar to English lawyers and they are generally in line with the rules that apply in English law to contracts frustrated by impossibility. One difference is that both instruments require the non-performing party to give notice of the impediment within a reasonable time. The other party will be entitled to damages for any loss resulting from failure to give such notice.

15.7 ADDITIONAL READING

Law Reform Committee of British Columbia, 'Report on the need for frustrated contracts legislation in British Columbia' (Project No 8).

Lookofsy, J, 'Impediments and hardship in international sales: a commentary on Catherine Kessedjian's "Competing approaches to force majeure and hardship" ' (2005) 25 International Review of Law and Economics 434.

Posner, RA, and Rosenfield, AM, 'Impossibility and related doctrines in contract law: an economic analysis' (1977) 6 JLS 83.

Schanze, E, 'Failure of long-term contracts and the duty to re-negotiate', in Rose, F (ed), *Failure of Contracts*, 1997, Oxford: Hart Publishing.

Smith, JC, 'Contracts: mistake, frustration and implied terms' (1994) 110 LQR 400.

Weiss, PD, 'Apportioning loss after discharge of a burdensome contract: a statutory solution', (1960) 69 YLJ 1054.

CHAPTER 16

DISCHARGE BY PERFORMANCE OR BREACH

16.1 INTRODUCTION

In this chapter we are concerned with the ways in which a contract may be discharged, thus freeing the parties from their obligations under it. There are four main ways in which a contract may be discharged:

1. **Discharge by agreement.** The parties may expressly agree to extinguish their continuing obligations under the contract. If the contract is still executory on both sides this will be unproblematic because each party will be agreeing to release their rights under the contract in exchange for the other party's agreement to do the same. The situation is much more difficult, however, where the executory obligations are all on one side, as for instance where a window cleaner has cleaned the windows of a house, but the owner has not yet paid the price. If the parties agree to discharge the contract, the window cleaner will receive nothing of value in exchange for his agreement to release his rights under the contract. This issue has already been dealt with in Chapter 3, in connection with the doctrine of consideration and the equitable concept of promissory estoppel, and there is no need to discuss it further here.

2. **Discharge by frustration.** As we saw in the previous chapter, the occurrence

of a frustrating event will automatically discharge the contract and free the parties from their continuing obligations under it.

3. **Discharge by performance.** If the parties have done all that they are bound to do under a contract it will be discharged by performance. The 'primary' obligations will cease, even though some of the 'secondary' obligations may continue, such as the obligation to pay compensation if the goods turn out to be defective after delivery.

4. **Discharge by breach.** A breach of contract may (depending on the nature of the term breached) entitle the innocent party to terminate the contract.

The focus in this chapter is on discharge by performance or breach. Some textbooks treat these topics separately, but as Professor Furmston (*Cheshire, Fifoot and Furmston's Law of Contract*, 15th edn, 2007, p 672, Oxford: OUP) notes, there are good reasons to consider the topics together:

> 'It is easy to see that if one party completely and perfectly performs what he has promised to do, his obligations are at an end. However, important and difficult questions arise as to the effect of something less than perfect performance. From the viewpoint of the performer, this is a problem in performance but to the other party it will appear as a problem in breach, since usually a less than perfect performance will be a breach.'

16.2 DISCHARGE BY PERFORMANCE

The most important question we need to ask is: What constitutes satisfactory performance? Must performance conform precisely to what is stipulated in the contract? If there is some minor defect in performance, does this entitle the other party to withhold its own performance of the contract?

16.2.1 PERFORMANCE MUST BE PRECISE AND EXACT

The general rule is that performance must be precise and exact. If there is even a slight deviation from the terms of the contract, the innocent party may be entitled to claim that the contract has not been performed, and on this ground claim damages and termination of the contract. The strict application of this rule can be seen in the following two cases, both of which were decided under s 13 of the Sale of Goods Act 1893.

Re Moore & Co Ltd and Laundauer & Co [1921] 2 KB 519

Facts: The defendants agreed to buy from the plaintiffs 3,000 tins of Australian canned fruit. The goods were stated as being in cases containing 30 tins each, payment to be per dozen tins. When the goods were delivered, a substantial part of the consignment was packaged in cases of 24 tins. The buyers refused to take delivery, and the dispute was referred to arbitration. The arbitrator held that there was no difference in the market value of the goods, and therefore the delivery of the consignment was a good delivery.

Held: The Court of Appeal held that the contract was for a sale of goods by description, and that as the goods contracted for had been mixed with goods of another description, the defendants were entitled under s 30(3) of the Sale of Goods Act 1893 to reject the whole consignment.

Bankes LJ

'If it is true to say, as I think it is, that this is a sale of goods by description, and the statement in the contract that the goods are packed thirty tins in a case is part of the description, there is, under s 13 of the Sale of Goods Act, 1893, an implied condition that the goods shall correspond with the description. The goods tendered did not as to about one-half correspond with that description. The effect of that is stated in s 30, sub-s 3, which provides that "where the seller delivers to the buyer the goods he contracted to sell mixed with goods of a different description not included in the contract, the buyer may accept the goods which are in accordance with the contract and reject the rest, or he may reject the whole".

That was the buyers' position as defined by the Act, and they rejected the whole. The question of law, as stated by the umpire, admits, as it seems to me, of only one answer – namely, that the buyers were entitled to reject the whole.'

Arcos Ltd v EA Ronaasen & Son [1933] AC 470

Facts: The English buyers had ordered a quantity of staves of Russian redwood and whitewood, for use in the making of cement barrels. The contract description allowed some variation in the length and in the breadth of the staves but stipulated that they should be ½ inch thick. Most of the staves delivered were 9/16 inch thick. They were still perfectly usable for making barrels. Six months after delivery, in a falling market, the buyers sought to reject the goods on the grounds that they did not conform to the contract description.

Held: The House of Lords affirmed the decision of the Court of Appeal, holding that the buyers were entitled to demand goods matching the description in the contract and were therefore not bound to accept the consignment.

Lord Atkin:

'It was contended that in all commercial contracts the question was whether there was a "substantial" compliance with the contract: there always must be some margin: and it is for the tribunal of fact to determine whether the margin is exceeded or not. I cannot agree. If the written contract specifies conditions of weight, measurement and the like, those conditions must be complied with. A ton does not mean about a ton, or a yard about a yard. Still less when you descend to minute measurements does 1/2 inch mean about 1/2 inch. If the seller wants a margin he must and in my experience does stipulate for it. Of course by recognized trade usage particular figures may be given a different meaning, as in a baker's dozen; or there may be even incorporated a definite margin more or less: but there is no evidence or finding of such a usage in the present case.

No doubt there may be microscopic deviations which business men and therefore lawyers will ignore. And in this respect it is necessary to remember that description and quantity are not necessarily the same: and that the legal rights in respect of them are regulated by different sections of the code, description by s 13, quantity by s 30. It will be found that most of the cases that admit any deviation from the contract are cases where there has been an excess or deficiency in quantity which the Court has considered negligible. But apart from this consideration the right view is that the conditions of the contract must be strictly performed. If a condition is not performed the buyer has a right to reject. I do not myself think that there is any difference between business men and lawyers on this matter. No doubt, in business, men often find it unnecessary or inexpedient to insist on their strict legal rights. In a normal market if they get something substantially like the specified goods they may take them with or without grumbling and a claim for an allowance. But in a falling market I find that buyers are often as eager to insist on their legal rights as courts of law are ready to maintain them. No doubt at all times sellers are prepared to take a liberal view as to the rigidity of their own obligations, and possibly buyers who in turn are sellers may also dislike too much precision. But buyers are not, as far as my experience goes, inclined to think that the rights defined in the code are in excess of business needs.

It may be desirable to add that the result in this case is in no way affected by the umpire's finding that the goods were fit for the particular purpose for which they were required. The implied condition under s 14, sub-s 1, unless of course the contract provides otherwise, is additional to the condition under s 13. A man may require goods for a particular purpose and make it known to the seller so as to secure the implied condition of fitness for that purpose: but there is no reason why he should not abandon that purpose if he pleases, and apply the goods to any purpose for which the description makes them suitable. If they do not correspond with the description there seems no business or legal reason why he should not reject them if he finds it convenient so to do.'

It seems that only if the deviation in performance is 'microscopic' will the contract be taken to have been performed. Section 13 of the Sale of Goods Act 1893 is now contained in s 13 of the Sale of Goods Act (SGA) 1979. In recent years, the courts have taken a more flexible approach to the requirement that goods must meet their description. In *Reardon Smith Line Ltd v Hansen-Tangen* [1976] 1 WLR 989, the House of Lords refused to accept that, by analogy with s 13 of the SGA 1979, delivery of a tanker could be rejected on the ground that it was constructed at a different yard to that stipulated in the contract. Lord Wilberforce said:

'I am not prepared to accept that authorities as to, "description" in sale of goods cases are to be extended, or applied, to such a contract as we have here. Some of these cases either in themselves (*Re Moore & Co and Laundauer & Co* [1921] 2 KB 519) or as they have been interpreted (eg *Behn v Burness* (1863) 3 B & S 751) I find to be excessively technical and due for fresh examination in this House. Even if a strict and technical view must be taken as regards the description of unascertained future goods (e.g., commodities) as to which each detail of the description must be assumed to be vital, it may be, and in my opinion is, right to treat other contracts of sale of goods in a similar manner to other contracts generally so as to ask whether a particular item in a description constitutes a substantial ingredient of the "identity" of the thing sold, and only if it does to treat it as a condition (see *Couchman v Hill* [1947] KB 554, 559, *per* Scott LJ).'

The inflexibility of s 13 of the SGA 1979 has been mitigated to some extent by s 15A (1), which provides:

Where in the case of a contract of sale—

(a) the buyer would, apart from this subsection, have the right to reject goods by reason of a breach on the part of the seller of a term implied by section 13, 14 or 15 above, but

(b) the breach is so slight that it would be unreasonable for him to reject them, then, if the buyer does not deal as consumer, the breach is not to be treated as a breach of condition but may be treated as a breach of warranty.

Section 15A places a significant restriction on a buyer's right to 'insist on their strict legal rights' (per Lord Wilberforce in *Arcos*). It is subject to a number of requirements, however, which significantly limit its scope. First, the breach must only be slight. Second, it must be unreasonable for the buyer to reject the goods. Third, the buyer must not be dealing as a consumer.

In sale of goods cases, the consequences for the seller of failing to meet the terms of the contract are very grave indeed. He will be judged not to have performed the contract, and the buyer will be entitled to withhold her performance by refusing to pay the contract price. To avoid this outcome the parties will need to ensure that the terms of the contract provide for flexibility in its performance.

16.2.2 PARTIAL PERFORMANCE

It follows from the rule that performance must be precise and exact that a party who only partially performs a contract will not be entitled to payment.

Cutter v Powell (1795) 6 Term Rep 320; [1775–1802] All ER Rep 159

Facts: The defendant agreed to pay Mr Cutter 30 guineas in return for him serving as second mate on a voyage from Jamaica to Liverpool. The ship 'Governor Party' set sail from Kingston on 2nd August 1793 and arrived at Liverpool on 9th October 1793. Mr Cutter died on 20 September, 19 days prior to the ship's arrival at Liverpool. Mr Cutter's widow brought an action to recover a proportion of the contract price.

Held: The Court held that Mr Cutter had undertaken an entire obligation and completion of the voyage was a condition precedent for payment. Since Mr Cutter had not completed the voyage, his widow was not entitled to recover the contract price.

Lord Kenyon CJ:

'[I]t seems to me at present that the decision of this case may proceed on the particular words of this contract and the precise facts here stated, without touching marine contracts in general. That where the parties have come to an express contract none can be implied has prevailed so long as to be reduced to an axiom in the law. Here the defendant expressly promised to pay the intestate thirty guineas, provided he proceeded, continued and did his duty as second mate in the ship from Jamaica to Liverpool; and the accompanying circumstances disclosed in the case are that the common rate of wages is four pounds per month, when the party is paid in proportion to the time he serves: and that this voyage is generally performed in two months. Therefore if there had been no contract between these parties, all that the intestate could have recovered on a *quantum meruit* for the voyage would have been eight pounds; whereas here the defendant contracted to pay thirty guineas provided the mate continued to do his duty as mate during the whole voyage, in which case the latter would have received nearly four times as much as if he were paid for the number of months he served. He stipulated to receive the larger sum if the whole duty were performed, and nothing unless the whole of that duty were performed: it was a kind of insurance. On this particular contract my opinion is formed at present; at the same time I must say that if we were assured the notes are in universal use, and that the commercial world have received and acted upon them in a different sense, I should give up my own opinion.'

Ashurst J:

'We cannot collect that there is any custom prevailing among merchants on these contracts; and therefore we have nothing to guide us but the terms of the contract itself. This is a written contract, and it speaks for itself. And as it is entire, and as the defendant's promise depends on a condition precedent to be performed by the other party, the condition must be performed before the other party is entitled to receive any thing under it. It has been argued however that the plaintiff may now recover on a *quantum meruit* but she has no right to desert the agreement; for wherever there is an express contract the parties must be guided by it; and one party cannot relinquish or abide by it as it may suit his advantage. Here the intestate was by the terms of his contract to perform a given duty before he could call upon the defendant to pay him any thing; it was a condition precedent, without performing which the defendant is not liable. And that seems to me to conclude the question: the intestate did not perform the contract on his part; he was not indeed to blame for not doing it; but still as this was a condition precedent, and as he did not perform it, his representative is not entitled to recover.'

The contract was interpreted as being an 'entire contract'. Cutter was only entitled to payment upon completion of the voyage. The court justified this result on the ground that the promised payment was vastly in excess of the market rate for such a voyage. The court viewed the contract as being something of a gamble; Cutter agreeing to take the chance of a larger sum at the end of the voyage, rather than accepting a smaller wage payable on a weekly basis. This reasoning has been doubted by Professor Dockray ('*Cutter v Powell*: a trip outside the text' (2001) 117 LQR 664, 673), who has pointed out that the court overlooked the fact that Cutter's special skill as a carpenter would have been of special value to Powell:

'Thomas Cutter had a special value to Powell as a second mate since as well as being a seaman, he was also a shipwright, a necessary skill in wooden ships on long voyages and especially valued in slave ships, in which the carpenter was responsible amongst other things for the secure construction of the "rooms" below the main deck in which slaves were confined, and for the barricade on deck that was usually erected to guard against a revolt. The normal rate of pay for the carpenter on a Liverpool slave ship in 1792 was up to £10 a month for a round trip. This and the evidence of rates on pay in Jamaica after February 1793 make the offer of 30 guineas for 10 weeks work, in war-time, on an old ship not sailing in convoy, appear less extraordinary that it seemed to the court.'

Whether or not the court was correct to construe the agreement as an 'entire contract', the case has subsequently been taken to lay down a general rule that nothing is payable under an 'entire contract' until the contract has been performed in full.

16.2.2.1 Severable obligations

The rule in *Cutter v Powell* will only apply if the contract is 'entire'. If it is severable or divisible, the party in breach will be able to recover payment for each part of the performance provided. Most contracts of employment will be treated as severable and the employee will be entitled to recover payment for the period actually served. Indeed, had the contract in *Cutter v Powell* specified a certain rate per week rather than a lump sum on completion, it is highly likely that Cutter's widow would have been able to recover. In *Taylor v Laird* (1856) 1 H & N 266 25 LJ Ex 329, the plaintiff was employed to command a steamer 'for an exploring and trading voyage up the river Niger and its tributaries . . . at the rate of £50 per month commencing from 1st December 1857'. The vessel proceeded up the Niger under the command of the plaintiff until it reached Dagbo, at which point the plaintiff refused to proceed and abandoned the command. It was held that this was not an entire contract for the whole voyage. The contract expressly provided for payment each month and the plaintiff was entitled to claim for the months served. Pollock CB said:

'We are of opinion that the plaintiff is entitled to a verdict for £500 on the first count, on the ground that the contract between the parties was for a monthly payment, that eight of those months had elapsed and only seven been paid for . . . "per month" means "each month" or "monthly", and gives a cause of action as each month accrues, which, once vested, is not subsequently lost or divested by the plaintiff's desertion or abandonment of his contract. The words are plain; and no mercantile man would doubt what was meant. But further, if this meaning is not given, the result would be, that had the plaintiff died or the voyage failed at the last moment, nothing would be payable by the defendant, because, according to his contention, the performance of the entire work contracted for was a condition precedent to the right to receive anything. This cannot have been intended.'

Statute now provides that salaries will be treated as 'accruing from day to day'.

APPORTIONMENT ACT 1870

S 2 Rents to accrue from day to day and be apportionable in respect of time

All rents, annuities, dividends, and other periodical payments in the nature of income (whether reserved or made payable under an instrument in writing or otherwise) shall, like interest on money lent, be considered as accruing from day to day, and shall be apportionable in respect of time accordingly.

S 5 Interpretation of terms

In the construction of this Act–

. . . The word 'annuities' includes salaries and pensions.

As a result of these provisions, a person who leaves a contract of employment will be entitled to be paid *pro rata* for the work s/he has completed.

Building contracts will often be construed as entire if they provide for payment in full on completion of the work. It is possible, however, for such contracts to contain concurrent, but independent, obligations. In *Bolton v Mahadeva* [1972] 1 WLR 1009, the plaintiff had agreed to install a central heating system and to supply a bathroom suite. The central heating system turned out to be defective and the defendant was not required to pay for this part of the contract. He was, however, obliged to pay for the supply of the bathroom suite, which was held to be a severable obligation.

16.2.2.2 Substantial performance

The doctrine of substantial performance provides a controversial exception to the rule that an entire contract must be performed in full. If a contract has been substantially performed, the promisee will not be discharged from the obligation to pay, but will be entitled to a set-off or a counterclaim for damages in respect of any loss caused by the partial failure to perform.

H Dakin & Co Ltd v Lee [1916] 1 KB 566

Facts: The plaintiff builders agreed to perform certain repairs on the defendant's house at a cost of £264. The defendant refused to pay for the work on the ground that it had not been completed to specification in three important respects: (1) the concrete underpinning was only half the contract depth; (2) the columns to support a bay window were of 4 inch diameter solid iron, instead of the specified 5 inch diameter hollow iron; (3) the joists over the bay window were not cleated at angles and not bolted to caps and to each other. The official referee held that the plaintiffs had not performed their contract, and were therefore not entitled to recover any part of the contract price or any sum in respect of the work completed.

Held: The Court of Appeal allowed the appeal, holding that there was a distinction between failing to perform and performing badly. The plaintiffs were entitled to recover the contract price with a set-off for the loss caused by the breach.

Pickford LJ:
'We have been told that if we affirm this judgment we shall be upsetting all the cases which have ever been decided in regard to contracts made for payment of a lump sum. To my mind our decision does not interfere with any one of them. Certainly I have not the slightest wish to differ from the view that if a man agrees to do a certain amount of work for a lump sum and only does part of it he cannot sue for the lump sum; but I cannot accept the proposition that if a man agrees to do a certain amount of work for

a lump sum every breach which he makes of that contract by doing his work badly, or by omitting some small portion of it, is an abandonment of his contract, or is only a performance of part of his contract, so that he cannot be paid his lump sum. It seems to me that there would be a performance of the contract, although some part of it was done badly, and that seems to me to be the position here.'

Dakin v Lee was followed by the Court of Appeal in *Hoenig v Isaacs* [1952] 2 All ER 176. Here the plaintiff, an interior decorator, agreed to decorate and furnish the defendant's flat at a cost of £750. The defendant refused to pay the balance of the contract price on the ground that there were a number of defects in the furniture supplied, which would cost £55 to repair. The Court of Appeal held that there had been substantial performance of the contract, and that the plaintiff could recover the contract price, subject to a set-off for the cost of making good the defects. Romer LJ said:

'[W]hen a man fully performs his contract in the sense that he supplies all that he agreed to supply but what he supplies is subject to defects of so minor a character that he can be said to have substantially performed his promise, it is, in my judgment, far more equitable to apply the *H Dakin & Co Ltd v Lee* principle than to deprive him wholly of his contractual rights and relegate him to such remedy (if any) as he may have on a *quantum meruit*, nor, in my judgment, are we compelled to a contrary view (having regard to the nature and terms of the agreement and the official referee's finding) by any of the cases in the books.'

Professor Treitel (*The Law of Contract*, 11th edn, 2003, p 787–8, London: Sweet & Maxwell) has argued that *Hoenig v Isaacs* was not decided on the ground that the plaintiff had substantially performed an 'entire contract'. He claims that such an explanation of the case is based on the error that *contracts*, as opposed to particular *obligations*, can be entire. According to Professor Treitel, the plaintiff in *Hoenig v Isaacs* (and by implication *Dakin v Lee*) undertook two independent and severable obligations: an obligation as to the *quantity* of the work and an obligation as to its *quality*. The former obligation was entire; the latter was not. Since it was only the latter obligation that was breached, the fact that the obligation was substantially performed was sufficient to preclude discharge. This analysis is appealing, but it sits uneasily with Pickford LJ's judgment in *Dakin v Lee* where his lordship recognised that there may still be 'substantial performance' of the contract, even when the contractor has breached the contract by 'omitting some small portion of it'.

It is clear that the doctrine of 'substantial performance' only has a limited role to play in mitigating the harshness of the 'entire contract' rule, since it is often difficult to establish that the contract has been substantially performed.

Bolton v Mahadeva [1972] 1 WLR 1009

Facts: The plaintiff agreed to install a central heating system in the defendant's house for a lump sum of £560. The system gave off insufficient and uneven heat, and also caused fumes in one of the rooms. The defendant refused to pay for the work. At first instance, the judge held that the plaintiff was entitled to recover the contract price (less the cost of rectifying the defects) since he had substantially performed the contract.

Held: The Court of Appeal allowed the appeal. The plaintiff was not entitled to recover as there had been no substantial performance.

Cairns LJ:

'In considering whether there was substantial performance I am of opinion that it is relevant to take into account both the nature of the defects and the proportion between the cost of rectifying them and the contract price. It would be wrong to say that the contractor is only entitled to payment if the defects are so trifling as to be covered by the *de minimis* rule.

The main matters that were complained of in this case were that when the heating system was put on, fumes were given out which made some of the living rooms (to put it at the lowest) extremely uncomfortable and inconvenient to use; secondly, that by reason of there being insufficient radiators and insufficient insulation, the heating obtained by the central heating system was far below what it should have been . . .

Now, certainly it appears to me that the nature and amount of the defects in this case were far different from those which the court had to consider in *H Dakin & Co Ltd v Lee* [1916] 1 KB 566 and *Hoenig v Isaacs* [1952] 2 All ER 176. For my part, I find it impossible to say that the judge was right in reaching the conclusion that in those circumstances the contract had been substantially performed. The con-tract was a contract to install a central heating system. If a central heating system when installed is such that it does not heat the house adequately and is such, further, that fumes are given out, so as to make living rooms uncomfortable, and if the putting right of those defects is not something which can be done by some slight amendment of the system, then I think that the contract is not substantially performed.'

Sachs LJ:

'When . . . one looks at the aggregate of the number of defects that [the trial judge] held to have been established, at the importance of some of those defects, and at the way in which some of them prevented the installation being one that did what was intended, I find myself, like Cairns LJ, quite unable to agree that there was a substantial performance by the plaintiff of this lump sum contract. It is not merely that so very much of the work was shoddy, but it is the general ineffectiveness of it for its primary purpose that leads me to that conclusion.'

It is interesting to note that the defect in *Bolton v Mahadeva* was a defect as to the quality of the plaintiff's work, not as to its quantity. The plaintiff had fitted a complete central heating system, but it was so defective that it failed to fulfil its 'primary purpose'. It is thus clear that a serious defect as to quality may be construed as constituting only partial performance of an entire contract.

The doctrine of substantial performance is rarely used in practice (for recent examples of its use see: *Williams v Roffey Bros & Nicholls (Contractors) Ltd* [1991] 1 QB 1; *Young v Thames Properties Ltd* [1999] EWCA Civ 629). This is probably because the doctrine is difficult to reconcile with the general rule that nothing is payable under an 'entire' contract until it has been fully performed. As Professor Beatson (*Anson's Law of Contract*, 28th edn, 2002, Oxford OUP, at p 514) notes, the doctrine of substantial performance effectively sets aside the contractual allocation of risks. For this reason, it is submitted that the doctrine should either be restricted or abolished. In its place, the courts should develop the rules allowing for restitution under contracts discharged for breach. It is to these rules that we now turn.

16.2.2.3 Restitution of benefits in kind

In Chapter 18 we examine the law of unjust enrichment. One of the most frequently pleaded grounds for restitution is total failure of consideration. As the label suggests this ground entitles the claimant to recover benefits transferred under a consideration that has failed. If the reason for the failure is discharge by breach, it is trite law that the non-breaching party may recover money paid (*Rowland v Divall* [1923] 2 KB 500) and benefits conferred (*De Bernardy v Harding* (1853) 8 Exch 822) under the contract. It is also clear that the party in breach may recover money paid (*Dies v British and International Mining and Finance Corpn* [1939] 1 KB 724) under the contract, but may they also claim restitution for benefits conferred? More specifically, in the situation currently under consideration, may a party who renders incomplete performance under an entire contract, claim restitution for the value of their partial performance? It seems that s/he may do so as long as the non-breaching party voluntarily accepted the benefits conferred.

Christy v Row (1808) 1 Taunt 300; 127 ER 849

Facts: The case concerned a contract of carriage in relation to seven keels of coal from Shields to Hamburg. The ship was prevented by restraints of princes from reaching Hamburg. At the defendant's request, the plaintiff delivered the cargo to Gluckstadt.

Held: The court held that the plaintiff was entitled to recover freight at the contract rate of £20 per keel.

> Mansfield CJ:
>
> 'The master then having delivered, and the consignees having accepted, this part of the cargo, is the master to receive nothing for carrying it? I can find no justice in that: it might as well be contended that if goods are sent to Exeter, and the consignee meets, and takes them at Honiton, the waggon must proceed empty to Exeter, or the carrier be entitled to nothing. But it is said, that the true meaning of the agreement and the bill of lading, taken together, is, not that the Defendant should be liable, but that the freight should be taken by Ross and Schleiden. What then is the meaning of the agreement, by which the freighter positively undertakes that the freight shall be paid for, after the rate of £20 per keel, and that, by a good bill? To say that the Defendant is not liable, would be wholly to do away this contract. I therefore think that the Plaintiff is entitled to recover £140 given him for the freight of the seven keels.'

This case did not concern a breach of contract since the parties had included an exclusion clause in the contract for 'restraints of princes and rulers'. Nevertheless, the case did establish the important principle that a person who voluntarily accepts partial or defective performance of a contract must make some payment for it. The plaintiff in *Christy v Row* recovered the full freight, but later cases have established that the claimant is only entitled to freight *pro rata* for the proportion of the voyage actually completed. Mansfield CJ said that liability was based on a fresh agreement involving an implied promise to pay for the benefits received. This implied contract analysis of restitutionary liability has since been rejected by the courts (see Chapter 18 and *Lipkin Gorman v Karpnale* [1991] 2 AC 548; *Westdeutsche Landesbank Girozentrale v Islington London Borough Council* [1996] AC 669) in favour of an analysis based on unjust enrichment.

Liability for acceptance of partial performance has been incorporated into statute by the SGA 1979:

s 30 Delivery of wrong quantity

(1) Where the seller delivers to the buyer a quantity of goods less than he contracted to sell, the buyer may reject them, but if the buyer accepts the goods so delivered he must pay for them at the contract rate.

Restitution will not be available for partial performance if the party not in breach has no option other than to accept the performance, as seen in *Sumpter v Hedges*.

Sumpter v Hedges [1898] 1 QB 673

Facts: The plaintiff, a builder, agreed to build two houses and stables on the defendant's land for £565. The plaintiff did work to the value of £333, but then abandoned the contract because he had no money left. The defendant finished the building work himself using materials that the plaintiff had left behind at the premises. The plaintiff brought a claim for the value of the materials and the value of the work he had done. At first instance, the judge allowed the claim for the value of the materials but refused to award a *quantum meruit* in respect of the work which the plaintiff had done on the buildings.

Held: The Court of Appeal dismissed the appeal and refused to award the plaintiff a *quantum meruit* for the work he had done.

Collins LJ:

'I think the case is really concluded by the finding of the learned judge to the effect that the plaintiff had abandoned the contract. If the plaintiff had merely broken his contract in some way so as not to give the defendant the right to treat him as having abandoned the contract, and the defendant had then proceeded to finish the work himself, the plaintiff might perhaps have been entitled to sue on a *quantum meruit* on the ground that the defendant had taken the benefit of the work done. But that is not the present case. There are cases in which, though the plaintiff has abandoned the performance of a contract, it is possible for him to raise the inference of a new contract to pay for the work done on a *quantum meruit* from the defendant's having taken the benefit of that work, but, in order that that may be done, the circumstances must be such as to give an option to the defendant to take or not to take the benefit of the work done. It is only where the circumstances are such as to give that option that there is any evidence on which to ground the inference of a new contract. Where, as in the case of work done on land, the circumstances are such as to give the defendant no option whether he will take the benefit of the work or not, then one must look to other facts than the mere taking the benefit of the work in order to ground the inference of a new contract. In this case I see no other facts on which such an inference can be founded. The mere fact that a defendant is in possession of what he cannot help keeping, or even has done work upon it, affords no ground for such an inference. He is not bound to keep unfinished a building which in an incomplete state would be a nuisance on his land. I am therefore of opinion that the plaintiff was not entitled to recover for the work which he had done.'

The result in *Sumpter v Hedges* appears to be rather unfair. The defendant had clearly been benefited by the plaintiff's work, having received a considerable part of what he had bargained for. Indeed, the consequence of denying restitution was that the buildings were constructed at a price considerably less than the defendant had contracted for. Given that the plaintiff had clearly been enriched and a total failure of consideration had occurred, why was the plaintiff denied restitution? Professor Burrows (Burrows, A, *The Law of Restitution*, 2nd edn, 2002, pp 355–357, Oxford: OUP) has noted that there are five arguments advanced in favour of the present law's denial of restitution:

1. Breach cancels out the injustice of the non-breaching party's enrichment.
2. In 'entire' contracts the defendant can only be said to have been benefited where he has received the full performance that he had contracted for.
3. An entire contract operates in the same way as a forfeiture clause. The promissor accepts that, in the event of breach, the work done would be forfeited. In other words, the parties contract out of restitution. This is a simplification of the position adopted by McFarlane and Stevens ('In Defence of *Sumpter v Hedges*' (2002) 118 LQR 569).
4. Refusing restitution plays an important role in deterring breach (see Brian Davenport QC's dissent from Law Commission, *Pecuniary Restitution on Breach of Contract*, Report no 121, 1983).
5. The denial of restitution makes up for the inadequacies in the assessment of damages for breach of contract.

Most of these arguments are unconvincing. We have already rejected the second argument and recognised that a defendant is presumptively benefited by receiving a part of that which he has bargained for. The first argument is also unconvincing since the injustice of a contract breaker's wrongdoing is adequately dealt with by his liability to pay damages for breach of contract. Similarly, the fourth argument underplays the role of contract damages as a deterrent to breach. The fifth argument is, in Professor Burrows' words, 'pragmatism in an extreme and untenable form'. If a problem exists in the law on contractual damages (which is questionable), the proper approach is to reform the law of damages directly and openly. It is the third argument that proves to be the most convincing. However, as Professor Burrows notes, the argument exaggerates the true position. While it is true that some contracts are entire simply because the parties intend to contract out of restitution, in other cases the reason has more to do with cash-flow problems or a fear that the payor will be unable to recover an advance payment if the other party abandons the contract.

On balance, it is submitted that a defendant ought to be able to claim restitution for part performance of an entire contract. Support for such a position can be found in two decisions of the House of Lords (*Hain Steamship Co Ltd v Tate and Lyle Ltd* (1936) 55 Lloyd's Law Rep 159; *Miles v Wakefield* [1987] AC 539) and a report issued by the Law Commission in 1983. The core proposals of the Law Commission report are set out in the following extract.

> **Law Commission, *Pecuniary Restitution on Breach of Contract*, Report no 121, 1983 at para 2.37**
>
> The party who has conferred the benefit shall be entitled as against the other party to such sum as represents the value of what he has done under the contract to the person who has the benefit of it. The remedy will not be available either where the contract is

still on foot or, subject to one exception, where the party who has failed to complete has a remedy under the present law. The party in breach can, of course, only have a remedy in respect of the work done under the contract, though the person who benefits from this work may not necessarily be the other party to the contract. The benefit obtained by the innocent party must be a benefit obtained *in terms of* the contract. The sum payable pursuant to the remedy should not exceed the sum representing the proportion that what has been done under the contract bears to what was promised to be done. The normal rules relating to remoteness of damage and mitigation of damages should continue to apply with regard to any set-off (or counterclaim) which the innocent party makes against the party in breach. It should be open to the parties to exclude the new remedy but in order to do so it will be necessary to show that the parties both adverted to the possibility of less than complete performance and provided for it.

Unfortunately, the Lord Chancellor did not accept the recommendations of the Law Commission and, as a result, the proposals were never implemented. The strong and unprecedented note of dissent prepared by Brian Davenport QC no doubt influenced Lord Hailsham's decision.

16.2.3 WITHHOLDING PERFORMANCE UNDER THE PRINCIPLES OF EUROPEAN CONTRACT LAW

The right to withhold performance is dealt with by Article 9:201:

Article 9:201: Right to Withhold Performance

(1) A party who is to perform simultaneously with or after the other party may withhold performance until the other has tendered performance or has performed. The first party may withhold the whole of its performance or a part of it as may be reasonable in the circumstances.

(2) A party may similarly withhold performance for as long as it is clear that there will be a non-performance by the other party when the other party's performance becomes due.

The notes to the article make it clear that it is intended to provide a more flexible right to withhold performance than that provided for under the common law. Lando and Beale (*Principles of European Contract Law Parts I and II*, 2000, p 324, The Hague: Kluwer Law International) note:

'In the common law countries the right to withhold performance is restricted to cases where the contract expressly or impliedly makes the obligations conditional upon one another and to cases of fundamental non-performance; in other cases the aggrieved party must perform its obligations in full (though if the non-performance is a breach it may have a claim for damages). Other systems are more flexible, permitting withholding of performance as a way of coercing the non-performing party even when the non-performance is minor, provided that the amount withheld is not wholly disproportionate and the withholding party acts in good faith. It is this approach which is adopted by this Article, which must be read together with Article 1:201 (Good Faith and Fair Dealing).'

16.2.4 TENDER OF PERFORMANCE

Tender of performance simply means attempted performance. If one party is ready and willing to perform, this will be treated as equivalent to performance, in the sense that if the tender is rejected, then the tenderer will be discharged from further liability.

16.2.4.1 Definition of tender

The essence of tender of performance is encapsulated by s 37(1) of the SGA 1979 which provides:

'When the seller is ready and willing to deliver the goods, and requests the buyer to take delivery, and the buyer does not within a reasonable time after such request take delivery of the goods, he is liable to the seller for any loss occasioned by his neglect or refusal to take delivery, and also for a reasonable charge for the care and custody of the goods.'

The operation of 'tender of performance' is illustrated by the facts and judgment in the following nineteenth-century case.

Startup v Macdonald (1843) 6 Man & G 593; 134 ER 1029

Facts: The plaintiff contracted to sell 10 tons of linseed oil to the defendant. Delivery was to be 'within the last fourteen days of March, and paid for at the expiration of that time in cash'. Delivery was in fact tendered at 8.30pm on 31 March, which was a Saturday. The defendant refused to accept or to pay for the goods, claiming that it was unreasonable and improper to deliver at that time of night.

Held: The Court of Common Please held that, on the facts, the plaintiffs had tendered the oil in good time and that they were therefore entitled to damages for non-acceptance.

Rolfe B:

'Now, it may be observed, that in every contract by which a party binds himself to deliver goods, or pay money, to another, he in fact engages to do an act which he cannot completely perform without the concurrence of the party to whom the delivery or the payment is to be made. Without acceptance on the part of him who is to receive, the act of him who is to deliver or to pay, can amount only to a tender. But the law considers a party who has entered into a contract to deliver goods or pay money to another, as having, substantially, performed it, if he has tendered the goods or money to the party to whom the delivery or payment was to be made, provided only that the tender has been made under such circumstances that the party to whom it has been made, has had a reasonable opportunity of examining the goods, or the money, tendered, in order to ascertain that the thing tendered really was what it purported to be. Indeed, without such an opportunity an offer to delivery or pay does not amount to a tender. The contract was to deliver the oil before the end of March. The plaintiffs did, in pursuance of that contract, tender the oil to the defendant at a time which, according to the express finding of the jury, left him full opportunity to examine, weigh and receive it, before the end of March. If he had then accepted it, there can be no doubt but that the contract would have been literally performed; and the neglect of the defendant to perform his part of the contract when he had the opportunity of doing so within the stipulated time, cannot, in my opinion, in any manner affect the rights of the plaintiffs. All they stipulated for was, to deliver the oil before the end of March, that is, to tender it to the defendant at such a time as should enable him to examine, weigh, and receive it before the end of March. This they did, and thereby, in my opinion, they fulfilled all they had contracted to do.

The judgment of Rolfe B sets out the requirements for a valid 'tender of performance'. The tender must meet the strict terms of the contract and it must be brought to the attention of the other party in time for the performance to be examined and any rights arising from the tender to be exercised.

16.2.4.2 Tender of money

If a party tenders payment, and this is not accepted, the obligation to pay is not thereby terminated. The debtor need not, however, attempt to pay again, but can wait until the creditor calls for payment.

Payment must be in 'legal tender'. There are statutory provisions as to the maximum amount of particular types of coin and note that can be tendered.

COINAGE ACT 1971

S 2 Legal tender

(1) Gold coins shall be legal tender for payment of any amount, but shall not be legal tender if their weight has become less than that specified in Schedule 1 to this Act, or in the proclamation under which they are made, as the least current weight.

(1A) Subject to any provision made by proclamation under section 3 of this Act, coins of cupro-nickel, silver or bronze shall be legal tender as follows–

   (a) coins of cupro-nickel or silver of denominations of more than 10 pence, for payment of any amount not exceeding £10;

   (b) coins of cupro-nickel or silver of denominations of not more than 10 pence, for payment of any amount not exceeding £5;

   (c) coins of bronze, for payment of any amount not exceeding 20 pence.

CURRENCY AND BANK NOTES ACT 1954

s 1 Issue and recall of bank notes by Bank of England

(2) All bank notes issued under this section shall be legal tender in England and Wales, and all such notes of denominations of less than five pounds shall be legal tender in Scotland and Northern Ireland.

The exact amount of money must be tendered. If the debtor overpays he has not the right to receive change (*Robinson v Cook* (1815) 6 Taunt 336; 128 ER 1064), although in practice, most creditors will be happy to provide this.

16.2.5 TIME OF PERFORMANCE

Once the contractually stipulated time for performance has passed, the party who has unjustifiably failed to perform will usually be liable to pay damages for breach if s/he does later perform the contract. In addition, the innocent party may be entitled to terminate the contract for breach if it is held that 'time was of the essence' of the contract.

The common law took the view that, unless the parties had expressed a contrary intention, time was of the essence of the contract (*Parkin v Thorold* (1852) 16 Beav 59; 51 ER 698). Equity, took the opposite view, holding that time was not of the essence of the contract unless the parties had specifically made it so. This meant that, where it could do so without injustice, equity decreed specific performance, notwithstanding the failure of the plaintiff to meet the contractually stipulated time for completion (*Stickney v Keeble* [1915] AC 386). The administration of equity and the common law was fused by the Judicature Acts 1873 and 1875 and the supremacy of equity was confirmed by s 25(11) of the 1873 Act, which provided:

'Generally in all matters not herein-before particularly mentioned, in which there is any conflict or variance between the rules of equity and the rules of the common law with reference to the same matter, the rules of equity shall prevail.'

Section 41 of the Law of Property Act 1925 re-enacts s 25 of the Judicature Act 1873 and provides:

s 41 Stipulations not of the essence of a contract

Stipulations in a contract, as to time or otherwise, which according to rules of equity are not deemed to be or to have become of the essence of the contract, are also construed and have effect at law in accordance with the same rules.

Section 10 of the SGA 1979 also confirms that time is not of the essence of a contract of sale unless the parties expressly provide otherwise:

s 10 Stipulations about time

(1) Unless a different intention appears from the terms of the contract, stipulations as to time of payment are not of the essence of a contract of sale.
(2) Whether any other stipulation as to time is or is not of the essence of the contract depends on the terms of the contract.
(3) In a contract of sale 'month' prima facie means calendar month.

The reference to the intention of the parties is of general application, outside of the context of contracts for the sale of goods:

United Scientific Holdings Ltd v Burnley Borough Council [1978] AC 904

Facts: The appellants had leased premises to the respondents for 99 years at a rent of £1,000 per year from 31 August 1962. The lease contained a rent review clause which provided that during the year preceding the second and subsequent 10-year periods of the lease the appellants could take steps to activate the machinery for a rent review if they wished to raise the rent. The appellants took no steps to implement the rent review until 12 October 1972. The respondents argued that time was of the essence and that since the appellants had not acted in time they were debarred from raising the rent for the following ten years. At first instance, the judge held that time was of the essence. This decision was upheld by the Court of Appeal.

Held: The House of Lords allowed the appeal, holding that there was nothing in the lease to displace the presumption that time was not of the essence of the contract.

Lord Simon of Glaisdale:
'My Lords, I have had the privilege of reading in draft the speech delivered by my noble and learned friend on the Woolsack. I agree with his arguments culminating in the

propositions that, in general, in modern English law time is prima facie not of the essence of a contract, and that there is nothing in the two leases the subject of the instant appeals which rebuts that presumption so as to make the stipulations as to time essential to the operation of their rent review clauses.

The respective outlooks of the old common law and equity on contractual stipulations as to time diverged owing to their different historical developments . . . [B]y 1873 the two systems [of law and equity] had evolved into a situation whereby in the courts of common law stipulations as to time were prima facie regarded as of the essence of a contract, while in the Court of Chancery stipulations as to time were prima facie regarded as not essential . . . No doubt further evolution would have taken place in each system, and they would probably have further converged. But before any such further development could take place, both systems had to be brought together (also with those applied in Doctors' Commons) in a single code to be administered in one Supreme Court of Judicature. This involved determining which system should prevail in those respects where they were at variance. Those that were in legislative contemplation were resolved in section 25 (1) to (10) of the Supreme Court of Judicature Act 1873. But it was envisaged (correctly as it proved) that there might be other respects not within the immediate contemplation of Parliament where the rules of common law and equity diverged. So subsection (11) provided:

> "Generally in all matters not hereinbefore particularly mentioned, in which there is any conflict or variance between the rules of equity and the rules of the common law with reference to the same matter, the rules of equity shall prevail."

One of the contemplated differences between the rules of common law and equity was with regard to contractual stipulations as to time. That difference was resolved in favour of equity by section 25 (7), replaced by section 41 of the consolidating Law of Property Act 1925, which is the provision that falls for construction in the instant appeals . . .

This can only be interpreted by bearing in mind that the object of section 25 of the Supreme Court of Judicature Act 1873 was to reconcile the differences between common law and equity so that the two systems (together with the admiralty, testamentary and matrimonial) could form a single coherent code. This merely reinforces the plain and ordinary sense of the words. I cannot read section 41 of the Law of Property Act as meaning other than that, whenever contractual stipulations as to time fall for consideration in any court, they shall not be construed as essential, except where equity would before 1875 have so construed them – ie, only when the strict observance of the stipulated time for performance was a matter of express agreement or of necessary implication.

In my view the modern law in the case of contracts of all types is correctly summarised in *Halsbury's Laws of England*, 4th edn, vol 9, para 481, p 338:

> "Time will not be considered to be of the essence unless: (1) the parties expressly stipulate that conditions as to time must be strictly complied with; or (2) the nature of the subject matter of the contract or the surrounding circumstances show that time should be considered to be of the essence; . . ." '

Lord Fraser of Tullybelton:

'I consider that section 41 should now be taken to mean what it appears to say and that the law is correctly summarised in the following passage from Halsbury's Laws of England, 4th edn, vol 9, para 481:

"The modern law, in the case of contracts of all types, may be summarised as follows. Time will not be considered to be of the essence unless: (1) the parties expressly stipulate that conditions as to time must be strictly complied with; or (2) the nature of the subject matter of the contract or the surrounding circumstances show that time should be considered to be of the essence; or (3) a party who has been subject to unreasonable delay gives notice to the party in default making time of the essence." . . .

Clearly neither the first nor the third of these exceptions is applicable to either of the instant appeals. The question is whether the nature of the subject matter or the surrounding circumstances of rent review clauses as a class show that all or any stipulations as to time in such clauses normally fall within the second exception . . . It was argued on behalf of the respondents . . . that tenants would be seriously prejudiced if the new rent were not ascertained before the review date because they would not know the amount of their liability for the future. This argument carried considerable weight with the Court of Appeal in the *Burnley* case. But I think, with respect, that the prejudice likely to be caused to the tenant by the rent not being ascertained until after the review date has been exaggerated and that the likely prejudice to the landlord has been understated. In time of inflation it is to be expected that the landlord will call for a review on every occasion where he is entitled to do so, especially if (as in both the instant appeals) a review cannot lead to the rent being reduced below the level that would prevail if there were no review. So far as the tenant is concerned, he will of course want to know the amount of his liability but he will normally be able with the aid of skilled advice to arrive at a reasonably close estimate of the current market rent. So far as the landlord is concerned, he may be very seriously prejudiced by delay in ascertaining the reviewed rent if, as is usual, it is higher than the former rent, because he will be unable to collect the reviewed rent until it has been ascertained, and any delay will keep him out of his money representing the difference between it and the former rent. Conversely the tenant will have the use of the money until the reviewed rent has been ascertained . . .

As the substance of a review clause is, in my opinion, to provide machinery for ascertaining the market rent from time to time, at the intervals agreed in the interests of both parties, rather than to confer a benefit on the landlord, it seems to me that stipulations as to time ought not to be strictly enforced unless there is something in a particular clause to indicate that time is of the essence in that case . . .

I am of the opinion that the equitable rule against treating time as of the essence of a contract is applicable to rent review clauses unless there is some special reason for excluding its application to a particular clause. The rule would of course be excluded if the review clause expressly stated that time was to be of the essence. It would also be excluded if the context clearly indicated that that was the intention of the parties – as for instance where the tenant had a right to break the lease by notice given by a specified date which was later than the last date for serving the landlord's trigger notice. The tenant's notice to terminate the contract would be one where the time limit was mandatory, and the necessary implication is that the time limit for giving the landlords notice of review must also be mandatory . . .'

The House of Lords refused to be bound by the common law and equitable rules prior to 1873, and preferred to look at the nature of the contract itself. Three of the Law Lords (Viscount Dilhourne, Lord Simon and Lord Fraser) approved of the statement of the law given in *Halsbury's Laws of England*, which confirms that time is not presumed to be of the essence of the contract. All three Law Lords also agreed that the presumption could be rebutted if: (1) the parties expressly stipulate that conditions as to time must be strictly complied with; or (2) the nature of the subject matter of the contract or the surrounding circumstances show that time should be considered to be of the essence. The first category is unproblematic. The second has been the cause of some debate. It has been suggested that commercial contracts should be regarded as always falling within its scope. In *Bunge Corporation v Tradax Export SA* [1981] 1 WLR 711, Lord Wilberforce said:

'I do not doubt that, in suitable cases, the courts should not be reluctant, if the intentions of the parties as shown by the contract so indicate, to hold that an obligation has the force of a condition, and that indeed they should usually do so in the case of time clauses in mercantile contracts . . . [T]he statement of the law in Halsbury's Laws of England, 4th edn, vol. 9 (1974), paras 481–482, including the footnotes to paragraph 482 (generally approved in the House in the United Scientific Holdings case), appears to me to be correct, in particular in asserting (1) that the court will require precise compliance with stipulations as to time wherever the circumstances of the case indicate that this would fulfil the intention of the parties, and (2) that broadly speaking time will be considered of the essence in "mercantile" contracts.'

This statement is problematic for two reasons. First, it suggests a prima facie rule that is contrary to the presumption in *Halsbury*. The starkness of this contradiction is increased, given that Lord Wilberforce expressly approved of the statement in *Halsbury* in the very same sentence. Second, Lord Wilberforce's statement is irreconcilable with the position adopted by Lord Diplock in *United Scientific Holdings*:

'I do not think that the question of principle . . . can be solved by classifying the contract of tenancy as being of a commercial character. In some stipulations in commercial contracts as to the time when something must be done by

987

one of the parties or some event must occur, time is of the essence; in others it is not. In commercial contracts for the sale of goods prima facie a stipulated time of delivery is of the essence, but prima facie a stipulated time of payment is not (Sale of Goods Act 1893, section 10 (1)) . . .'

Lord Wilberforce dismissed *United Scientific Holdings* as 'a case on which I do not need to comment on this occasion' (at p 716). In light of the apparent conflict between the two decisions, it is regrettable that Lord Wilberforce did not seek to elaborate further. Ultimately, Lord Wilberforce's comments are rather difficult to understand and his lordship did emphasise that he was only 'broadly speaking'. For this reason, it is probably best to view the issue as being determined on the basis of the commercial context of the contract in question rather than of the basis of any specific presumption (see Treitel, G, *The Law of Contract*, 11th edn, 2003, p 827, London: Sweet & Maxwell).

Lord Fraser also approved of the third limb of the paragraph from *Halsbury*, which states that the presumption will not operate if '(3) a party who has been subject to unreasonable delay gives notice to the party in default making time of the essence'. Normally, if time is not of the essence, late performance will only be a ground for termination if it causes a 'frustrating delay', that is, the delay deprives the party not in default of substantially the whole benefit of the contract (*Universal Cargo Carriers Corpn v Citati* [1957] 2 QB 401). If the delay does not amount to a 'frustrating delay', the party not in default can either wait until the delay becomes a 'frustrating delay', or he can give notice to the other making time of the essence. If he does this, it will only be necessary for him to give a reasonable time for further performance rather than waiting the longer period necessary for a 'frustrating delay'.

There is some uncertainty about how long the innocent party must wait after the contractual date for performance before serving notice on the other party to perform within a reasonable period of time. In *British and Commonwealth Holdings plc v Quadrex Holdings Inc* [1989] QB 842, the Court of Appeal suggested that there must be an unreasonable delay before the right to give notice making time of the essence arises. This dicta was disapproved of by the Court of Appeal in *Behzadi v Shaftesbury Hotels Ltd* [1992] Ch 1. Purchas LJ said:

'I see no reason for the imposition of any further period of delay after the breach of contract has been established by non-performance in accordance with its terms before it is open to a party to serve such a notice. The important matter is that the notice must in all the circumstances of the case give a reasonable opportunity for the other party to perform his part of the contract. However, one who elects to serve a notice immediately upon the breach of the contract will be well advised to be cautious in his selection of the period to be included in the notice before he reserves the right to repudiate.

In coming to this conclusion I am very conscious that I am differing from some statements contained in the judgment of Sir Nicolas Browne-Wilkinson V-C in *British and Commonwealth Holdings plc v Quadrex Holdings Inc* [1989] QB 842 . . . With great respect to Sir Nicolas Browne-Wilkinson V-C, he does not distinguish between the date when a right to serve a notice arises and the length of time to be allowed for performance by the contents of the notice. In one sense the earlier a notice is given to the other party that performance is to be required by an appropriate date the better. As Nourse LJ has said, the expression of opinion above cited was not part of the ratio decidendi.'

Since both of these cases are Court of Appeal decisions, the later decision in *Behzadi* should be followed, pending a decision of the House of Lords. The decision in *Behzadi* also appears to be the most acceptable statement of the law, since there is no good reason why the innocent party should be forced to wait before serving notice on the party in default.

16.3 DISCHARGE BY BREACH

A number of consequences may flow from a breach of contract. Every breach gives rise to a claim for damages (dealt with in Chapter 17), some will entitle the innocent party to seek an order of specific performance (see Chapter 17), and some will give rise to a right to terminate the contract. It is those breaches that give rise to a right to terminate that we are concerned with in this chapter since on termination the parties will be discharged from their future obligations. The innocent party will also be entitled to claim damages for losses sustained as a result of the breach of contract.

16.3.1 EFFECT OF REPUDIATORY BREACH

A breach of contract that gives rise to a right to terminate the contract is called a 'repudiatory breach'. At various times it has been suggested that a repudiatory breach will bring a contract to an end automatically, irrespective of the wishes of the parties. For example, in *Harbutt's Plasticine v Wayne Tank and Pump* [1970] 1 QB 447, the facts of which are given in Chapter 8, Lord Denning MR said:

'In considering the consequences of a fundamental breach, it is necessary to draw a distinction between a fundamental breach which still leaves the contract open to be performed, and a fundamental breach which itself brings the contract to an end.

(i) The first group
In cases where the contract is still open to be performed, the effect of a fundamental breach is this: it gives the innocent party, when he gets to know

989

of it, an option either to *affirm* the contract or to disaffirm it. If he elects to *affirm* it, then it remains in being *for the future* on both sides. Each has a right to sue for damages for *past or future* breaches. If he elects to disaffirm it (namely, accepts the fundamental breach as determining the contract), then it is at an end from that moment. It does not continue into the future. All that is left is the right to sue for past breaches or for the fundamental breach, but there is no right to sue for *future* breaches.

(ii) The second group

In cases where the fundamental breach itself brings the contract to an end, there is no room for any option in the innocent party. The present case is typical of this group. The fire was so disastrous that it destroyed the mill itself. If the fire had been accidental, it would certainly have meant that the contract was frustrated and brought to an end by a supervening event; just as in the leading case in 1863 when the Surrey Music Hall was burnt down: see *Taylor v Caldwell* (1863) 3 B & S 826. At the time of the fire at this mill, the cause of it was not known. It might have been no one's fault. In that case the contract would plainly have been frustrated. It would have been automatically at an end, so far as the future was concerned, with no option on either side. Does it make any difference because, after many years, the cause of the fire has been found? It has been found to be the fault of the defendants. I cannot think that this makes any difference. The contract came to an end when the mill was burnt down. It came to an end by a frustrating event, without either side having an election to continue it. It is not to be revived simply because it has been found to be the fault of one of the parties. All that happens is that the innocent party can sue the guilty party for the breach.

All that I have said thus far is so obvious that it needs no authority.'

The view that a repudiatory breach automatically brings a contract to an end was rejected by the House of Lords in *Photo Production Ltd v Securicor Transport Ltd* [1980] AC 827. It is now clear that the effect of a repudiatory breach is to give the innocent party a choice whether to terminate the contract or to allow it to continue. The right to terminate is a self-help remedy. It does not require the intervention of the courts, although the courts may exercise a supervisory jurisdiction (see Harris, D, Campbell, D and Halson, R, *Remedies in Contract and Tort*, 2nd edn, 2002, p 56, Cambridge: CUP).

The courts sometimes refer to termination for repudiatory breach as rescission, but rescission in this context is quite different to rescission for misrepresentation or undue influence. First, there will always be a right to claim damages for repudiatory breach, whereas in cases of innocent misrepresentation, rescission alone may be the remedy. Second, termination for repudiatory breach only discharges future obligations. It does not operate retrospectively, whereas rescission for misrepresentation requires the whole transaction to be undone. Lord Wilberforce explained the difference in *Johnson v Agnew* [1980] AC 367:

'[I]t is important to dissipate a fertile source of confusion and to make clear that although the vendor is sometimes referred to . . . as "rescinding" the contract, this so-called "rescission" is quite different from rescission ab initio, such as may arise for example in cases of mistake, fraud or lack of consent. In those cases, the contract is treated in law as never having come into existence . . . In the case of an accepted repudiatory breach the contract has come into existence but has been put an end to or discharged. Whatever contrary indications may be disinterred from old authorities, it is now quite clear, under the general law of contract, that acceptance of a repudiatory breach does not bring about "rescission *ab initio*". I need only quote one passage to establish these propositions. In *Heyman v Darwins Ltd* [1942] AC 356 Lord Porter said, at p 399:

"To say that the contract is rescinded or has come to an end or has ceased to exist may in individual cases convey the truth with sufficient accuracy, but the fuller expression that the injured party is thereby absolved from future performance of his obligations under the contract is a more exact description of the position. Strictly speaking, to say that on acceptance of the renunciation of a contract the contract is rescinded is incorrect. In such a case the injured party may accept the renunciation as a breach going to the root of the whole of the consideration. By that acceptance he is discharged from further performance and may bring an action for damages, but the contract itself is not rescinded." '

16.3.2 NATURE OF REPUDIATORY BREACH

What types of breach of contract entitle the innocent party to treat the contract as repudiated and therefore to terminate it? There are a number of different ways to approach this issue:

1. It could be left to the parties to determine what types of breach give rise to a right to terminate the contract. The problem with this approach is that often the parties do not make express provision for the consequences of breach.
2. The law could establish a set of rules, which categorise terms according to what consequences will flow from their breach. The focus is on the nature of the term broken rather than on the breach itself. The problem with this approach is that it lacks flexibility and can lead to injustice.
3. The issue could be left to the sole discretion of the courts to be determined in

light of all the circumstances of the case including the consequences of the actual breach. The problem with this approach is that it undermines certainty and makes it very difficult for the parties to predict what consequences will flow from a breach of contract.

Historically, English law has emphasised the need for certainty and classified terms as either 'conditions' of 'warranties'. At the same time, however, the courts have acknowledged the need for flexibility and recognised the existence of intermediate or innominate terms, where the right to terminate depends on the seriousness of the breach. This section is divided into three parts. First, we will consider the traditional distinction between conditions and warranties. Second, we will trace the development of intermediate terms and finally we will consider the role played by the parties in the categorisation of terms.

16.3.2.1 Conditions and warranties

Contract terms are traditionally labelled as being either conditions or warranties. This distinction was explained by Fletcher Moulton LJ in *Wallis, Son & Wells v Pratt and Haynes* [1910] 2 KB 1003:

'A party to a contract who has performed, or is ready and willing to perform, his obligations under that contract is entitled to the performance by the other contracting party of all the obligations which rest upon him. But from a very early period of our law it has been recognised that such obligations are not all of equal importance. There are some which go so directly to the substance of the contract or, in other words, are so essential to its very nature that their non-performance may fairly be considered by the other party as a substantial failure to perform the contract at all. On the other hand there are other obligations which, though they must be performed, are not so vital that a failure to perform them goes to the substance of the contract. Both classes are equally obligations under the contract, and the breach of any one of them entitles the other party to damages. But in the case of the former class he has the alternative of treating the contract as being completely broken by the non-performance and (if he takes the proper steps) he can refuse to perform any of the obligations resting upon himself and sue the other party for a total failure to perform the contract. Although the decisions are fairly consistent in recognising this distinction between the two classes of obligations under a contract there has not been a similar consistency in the nomenclature applied to them. I do not, however, propose to discuss this matter, because later usage has consecrated the term 'condition' to describe an obligation of the former class and 'warranty' to describe an obligation of the latter class. I do not think that the choice of terms is happy, especially so far as regards the word 'condition', for it is a word which is used in many other connections and has considerable variety of meaning. But its use with regard to the obligations under a contract is well known and recognised, and no confusion need arise if proper regard be had to the context.

This usage has been followed in the codification of the law of the contract of sale in the Sale of Goods Act. . . .'

As Fletcher Moulton LJ notes, the drafters of the Sale of Goods Act also adopted the terminology.

SALE OF GOODS ACT 1979

s 11 When condition to be treated as warranty

(3) Whether a stipulation in a contract of sale is a condition, the breach of which may give rise to a right to treat the contract as repudiated, or a warranty, the breach of which may give rise to a claim for damages but not to a right to reject the goods and treat the contract as repudiated, depends in each case on the construction of the contract; and a stipulation may be a condition, though called a warranty in the contract.

The Act uses the terminology of condition and warranty to distinguish between repudiatory and other breaches. If the term is a condition the breach will be repudiatory, but if the term is a warranty the breach will only give rise to a claim for damages.

At this point, it is important to note (as Fletcher Moulton LJ recognised) that the words 'condition' and 'warranty' are likely to cause confusion because they have a number of different meanings in other contexts:

Treitel, G, ' "Conditions" and "Conditions Precedent" '(1990) 106 LQR 185

One of the most notorious sources of difficulty in the law of contract is the variety of senses in which it uses the expression 'condition'. One source of confusion is the use of the expression 'condition precedent' in both a contingent and a promissory sense; and the present writer would with respect agree with the view of Sir Robin Cooke P in the recent *New Zealand case of Robertson Enterprises Ltd v Cope* (April 6, 1989), that failure to distinguish between these two senses can lead to arguments which are 'unnecessarily complicated'. One might even regret the fact that the common law uses the expression 'condition' in a promissory sense at all; but the usage is deeply embedded in the relevant legislation and case-law. Even the concept of promissory condition is used in two senses, and it is with these senses that this note is concerned. The first relates to the order of performance, while the second relates to the conformity of the performance rendered with that promised. Where a promise relates to the time of performance, it is easy to lose sight of the distinction between these two senses, but the distinction exists even in such cases, for promises may be performed at the wrong time but in the right order. One way of reducing the difficulty is to use 'condition' with different points of contrast for the two purposes just described: that is, to contrast 'conditions precedent' with 'concurrent condition' and 'independent covenant' when discussing the order of performance (e.g. Sale of Goods Act 1979, s 28; *The Odenfeld* [1978] 2 Lloyd's Rep. 357), while contrasting 'condition' with 'warranty' (and, more recently, with 'intermediate term') when discussing problems of conformity (eg Sale of Goods Act 1979, ss 11–15). Historically, this approach gives rise to problems since references to 'condition precedent' were formerly common in discussions of the condition-warranty distinction (eg in *Bentsen v Taylor Sons & Co* [1983] 2 QB 274 at p 281). But in modern discussions of this distinction, such references have become relatively less common, and they are misleading in that 'condition precedent' (when used in relation to the order of performance) refers to an event (i.e. the performance of one party's obligation) while 'condition' (when used in relation to the conformity of performance) refers to a term of the contract (or to the content of one party's obligation).

Conditions (relating to a term of the contract) must be distinguished from conditions precedent (relating to the order of performance of the contract). The word 'warranty' can also give rise to confusion because it is sometimes used in other contexts to refer to a 'promise' or a 'guarantee', that is, a precontractual representation (see Chapter 9). Care is needed, therefore, to ensure that the meaning of these words is clear when they are being used to discuss contractual terms.

A term may be classified as a condition for one of three reasons:

1. Statute provides so – see ss 13–15 SGA 1979;
2. The contract expressly states that it is – see below;
3. The court construes it as a condition.

The main factor that the courts will consider in determining whether the term should be construed as a condition will be its importance to the contract as a whole. In *L Schuler AG v Wickman Machine Tool Sales Ltd* [1974] AC 235, Lord Reid said:

'[A] condition . . . is a term the breach of which by one party gives to the other an option either to terminate the contract or to let the contract proceed and, if he so desires, sue for damages for the breach. Sometimes a breach of a term gives that option to the aggrieved party because it is of a fundamental character going to the root of the contract, sometimes it gives that option because the parties have chosen to stipulate that it shall have that effect.'

The traditional approach of the courts is well illustrated by contrasting the following two cases from the late nineteenth century.

Bettini v Gye (1875–1876) 1 QBD 183

Facts: The plaintiff singer, Mr Bettini, agreed to fill the part of prime tenor assoluto for the defendant's opera. Paragraph 7 of the contract stated: 'Mr Bettini agrees to be in London without fail at least six days before the commencement of his engagement, for the purpose of rehearsals'. Due to temporary illness, the plaintiff arrived four days late for rehearsals. The defendant purported to terminate the contract for breach of clause 7.

Held: The Divisional Court held that the term was not a condition because it did not go to the root of the contract.

Blackburn J:

'The question raised by the demurrer is, not whether the plaintiff has any excuse for failing to fulfil this part of his contract, which may prevent his being liable in damages for not doing so, but whether his failure to do so justified the defendant in refusing to proceed with the engagement, and fulfil his, the defendant's part. And the answer to that question depends on whether this part of the contract is a condition precedent to the defendant's liability, or only an independent agreement, a breach of which will not justify a repudiation of the contract, but will only be a cause of action for compensation in damages . . .

We think the answer to this question depends on the true construction of the contract taken as a whole.

Parties may think some matter, apparently of very little importance, essential; and if they sufficiently express an intention to make the literal fulfilment of such a thing a condition precedent, it will be one; or they may think that the performance of some matter, apparently of essential importance and primâ facie a condition precedent, is not really vital, and may be compensated for in damages, and if they sufficiently expressed such an intention, it will not be a condition precedent.

In this case, if to the 7th paragraph of the agreement there had been added words to this effect: "And if Mr Bettini is not there at the stipulated time Mr Gye may refuse to proceed further with the agreement"; or if, on the other hand, it had been said, "And if not there, Mr Gye may postpone the commencement of Mr Bettini's engagement for as many days as Mr Bettini makes default, and he shall forfeit twice his salary for that time", there could have been no question raised in the case. But there is no such declaration of the intention of the parties either way. And in the absence of such an express declaration, we think that we are to look to the whole contract, and applying the rule stated by Parke, B., to be acknowledged, see whether the particular stipulation goes to the root of the matter, so that a failure to perform it would render the performance of the rest of the contract by the plaintiff a thing different in substance from what the defendant has stipulated for; or whether it merely partially affects it and may be compensated for in damages. Accordingly, as it is one or the other, we think it must be taken to be or not to be intended to be a condition precedent.

If the plaintiff's engagement had been only to sing in operas at the theatre, it might very well be that previous attendance at rehearsals with the actors in company with whom he was to perform was essential. And if the engagement had been only for a few performances, or for a short time, it would afford a strong argument that attendance for the purpose of rehearsals during the six days immediately before the commencement of the engagement was a vital part of the agreement. But we find, on looking to the agreement, that the plaintiff was to sing in theatres, halls, and drawing-rooms, both public and private, from the 30th of March to the 13th of July, 1875, and that he was to sing in concerts as well as in operas, and was not to sing anywhere out of the theatre in Great Britain or Ireland from the 1st of January to the 31st of December, 1875, without the written permission of the defendant, except at a distance of more than fifty miles from London.

The plaintiff, therefore, has, in consequence of this agreement, been deprived of the power of earning anything in London from the 1st of January to the 30th of March; and though the defendant has, perhaps, not received any benefit from this, so as to preclude him from any longer treating as a condition precedent what had originally been one, we think this at least affords a strong argument for saying that subsequent stipulations are not intended to be conditions precedent, unless the nature of the thing strongly shews they must be so.

And, as far as we can see, the failure to attend at rehearsals during the six days immediately before the 30th of March could only affect the theatrical performances and, perhaps, the singing in duets or concerted pieces during the first week or fortnight of this engagement, which is to sing in theatres, halls, and drawing-rooms, and concerts for fifteen weeks.

We think, therefore, that it does not go to the root of the matter so as to require us to consider it a condition precedent.'

Poussard v Spiers and Pond (1875–1876) 1 QBD 410

Facts: The plaintiff singer agreed to play the part of Friquette in Lecocq's opera 'Les Pres Saint Gervais' commencing on or about the 14th November. The first performance was announced for 28th November, and no objection was raised by the plaintiff as to this delay. She attended several rehearsals but was then taken ill. As a result of her illness, the plaintiff missed the remaining rehearsals and the first four performances of the opera. By the time the plaintiff was well enough to return, the defendant had found a replacement for her and he purported to treat her failure to appear as a repudiatory breach.

Held: The Divisional Court held that the plaintiff's failure to perform on the opening and early performances went to the root of the contract and was a breach of condition.

Brightman J:
'We think that the question, whether the failure of a skilled and capable artiste to perform in a new piece through serious illness is so important as to go to the root of the

consideration, must to some extent depend on the evidence; and is a mixed question of law and fact. Theoretically, the facts should be left to and found separately by the jury, it being for the judge or the Court to say whether they, being so found, shew a breach of a condition precedent or not. But this course is often (if not generally) impracticable; and if we can see that the proper facts have been found, we should act on these without regard to the form of the questions.

Now, in the present case, we must consider what were the courses open to the defendants under the circumstances. They might, it was said on the argument before us (though not on the trial), have postponed the bringing out of the piece till the recovery of Madame Poussard, and if her illness had been a temporary hoarseness incapacitating her from singing on the Saturday, but sure to be removed by the Monday, that might have been a proper course to pursue. But the illness here was a serious one, of uncertain duration, and if the plaintiff had at the trial suggested that this was the proper course, it would, no doubt, have been shewn that it would have been a ruinous course; and that it would have been much better to have abandoned the piece altogether than to have postponed it from day to day for an uncertain time, during which the theatre would have been a heavy loss.

The remaining alternatives were to employ a temporary substitute until such time as the plaintiff's wife should recover; and if a temporary substitute capable of performing the part adequately could have been obtained upon such a precarious engagement on any reasonable terms, that would have been a right course to pursue; but if no substitute capable of performing the part adequately could be obtained, except on the terms that she should be permanently engaged at higher pay than the plaintiff's wife, in our opinion it follows, as a matter of law, that the failure on the plaintiff's part went to the root of the matter and discharged the defendants.'

The failure of Madame Poussard to meet the obligation to be present at the opening performances of the opera was treated as much more serious than Mr Bettini's failure to meet the obligation to be present for the rehearsals. Breach of the former term went to the root of the contract, whereas breach of the latter term did not.

The categorisation of terms as either conditions or warranties is a rather cumbersome procedure for determining the availability of remedies. It implies that the actual consequence of a particular breach is not a relevant factor. If a term is categorised as a 'condition', any breach of it will give rise to a right to terminate the contract, no matter how trivial the breach or how easily it can be remedied. Similarly, a breach of warranty will only ever give rise to a claim for damages. The innocent party will never be entitled to terminate the contract, no matter how serious the breach or how great the loss caused. This approach has the merit of certainty, in that it enables the parties to accurately predict whether a particular breach will give rise to a right to terminate the contract. But it is unduly inflexible, giving rise to anomalous and unjust results.

997

16.3.2.2 Intermediate terms

The perceived inflexibility of the traditional categorisation led the Court of Appeal to recognise an intermediate category in 1962 in the case of *Hong Kong Fir Shipping Co Ltd v Kawasaki Kisen Kaisha Ltd*.

Hong Kong Fir Shipping Co Ltd v Kawasaki Kisen Kaisha Ltd [1962] 2 QB 26

Facts: The defendant chartered a ship from the plaintiff on a 24-month time charter. The charterparty stated that the ship was 'in every way fitted for ordinary cargo service' and Clause 3 provided that the owners should 'maintain her in a thoroughly efficient state in hull and machinery during service'. The ship was delivered to the defendant on 13 February 1957, and on that date set sail from Liverpool to Newport News, Virginia, to load a cargo of coal for carriage to Osaka. At the date of delivery, the ship was unseaworthy because she had old engines. Her age was such that she needed to be maintained by an experienced, competent, careful and adequate team of engine room staff. There were insufficient numbers of staff and the chief engineer was inefficient and an alcoholic. As a result, repairs had to be carried out on the way to Osaka. In June 1957, following a fall in freight rates since the date of the charter, the defendant terminated the charterparty. The plaintiff brought a claim for damages for wrongful repudiation. At first instance, Salmon J found for the plaintiffs.

Held: The Court of Appeal dismissed the appeal, holding that the breach of contract was not sufficiently serious to entitle the defendants to terminate the contract.

Sellers LJ:

'In my judgment authority over many decades and reason support the conclusion in this case that there was no breach of a condition which entitled the charterers to accept it as a repudiation and to withdraw from the charter. It was not contended that the maintenance clause is so fundamental a matter as to amount to a condition of the contract. It is a warranty which sounds in damages.'

Upjohn LJ:

'Why is this apparently basic and underlying condition of seaworthiness not, in fact, treated as a condition? It is for the simple reason that the seaworthiness clause is breached by the slightest failure to be fitted "in every way" for service. Thus, to take examples from the judgments in some of the cases . . . if a nail is missing from one of the timbers of a wooden vessel or if proper medical supplies or two anchors are not on board at the time of sailing, the owners are in breach of the seaworthiness stipulation. It is contrary to common sense to suppose that in such circumstances the parties contemplated that the charterer should at once be entitled to treat the contract as at an end for such trifling breaches . . .

It is open to the parties to a contract to make it clear either expressly or by necessary implication that a particular stipulation is to be regarded as a condition which goes to the root of the contract, so that it is clear that the parties contemplate that any breach of it entitles the other party at once to treat the contract as at an end. That matter has to be determined as a question of the proper interpretation of the contract . . . Where, however, upon the true construction of the contract, the parties have not made a particular stipulation a condition, it would in my judgment be unsound and misleading to conclude that, being a warranty, damages is necessarily a sufficient remedy.

In my judgment the remedies open to the innocent party for breach of a stipulation which is not a condition strictly so called, depend entirely upon the nature of the breach and its foreseeable consequences. Breaches of stipulation fall, naturally, into two classes. First there is the case where the owner by his conduct indicates that he considers himself no longer bound to perform his part of the contract; in that case, of course, the charterer may accept the repudiation and treat the contract as at an end. The second class of case is, of course, the more usual one and that is where, due to misfortune such as the perils of the sea, engine failures, incompetence of the crew and so on, the owner is unable to perform a particular stipulation precisely in accordance with the terms of the contract try he never so hard to remedy it. In that case the question to be answered is, does the breach of the stipulation go so much to the root of the contract that it makes further commercial performance of the contract impossible, or in other words is the whole contract frustrated? If yea, the innocent party may treat the contract as at an end. If nay, his claim sounds in damages only.

If I have correctly stated the principles, then as the stipulation as to the seaworthiness is not a condition in the strict sense the question to be answered is, did the initial unseaworthiness as found by the judge, and from which there has been no appeal, go so much to the root of the contract that the charterers were then and there entitled to treat the charterparty as at an end? The only unseaworthiness alleged, serious though it was, was the insufficiency and incompetence of the crew, but that surely cannot be treated as going to the root of the contract for the parties must have contemplated that in such an event the crew could be changed and augmented. In my judgment, on this part of his case Mr. Roskill necessarily fails.'

Diplock LJ:
'Every synallagmatic contract contains in it the seeds of the problem: in what event will a party be relieved of his undertaking to do that which he has agreed to do but has not yet done? The contract may itself expressly define some of these events, as in the cancellation clause in a charterparty; but, human prescience being limited, it seldom does so exhaustively and often fails to do so at all. In some classes of contracts such as sale of goods, marine insurance, contracts of affreightment evidenced by bills of lading and those between parties to bills of exchange, Parliament has defined by statute some of the events not provided for expressly in individual contracts of that class; but where an event occurs the occurrence of which neither the parties nor Parliament have expressly stated will discharge one of the parties from further performance of his undertakings, it is for the court to determine whether the event has this effect or not.

The test whether an event has this effect or not has been stated in a number of metaphors all of which I think amount to the same thing: does the occurrence of the event deprive the party who has further undertakings still to perform of substantially the whole benefit which it was the intention of the parties as expressed in the contract that he should obtain as the consideration for performing those undertakings?

This test is applicable whether or not the event occurs as a result of the default of one of the parties to the contract, but the consequences of the event are different in the two cases. Where the event occurs as a result of the default of one party, the party in default cannot rely upon it as relieving himself of the performance of any further undertakings on his part, and the innocent party, although entitled to, need not treat the event as relieving him of the further performance of his own undertakings. This is only a specific application of the fundamental legal and moral rule that a man should not be allowed to take advantage of his own wrong. Where the event occurs as a result of the default of neither party, each is relieved of the further performance of his own undertakings, and their rights in respect of undertakings previously performed are now regulated by the Law Reform (Frustrated Contracts) Act, 1943.

This branch of the common law has reached its present stage by the normal process of historical growth, and the fallacy in [counsel for the defendant's] contention that a different test is applicable when the event occurs as a result of the default of one party from that applicable in cases of frustration where the event occurs as a result of the default of neither party lies, in my view, from a failure to view the cases in their historical context. The problem: in what event will a party to a contract be relieved of his undertaking to do that which he has agreed to do but has not yet done? has exercised the English courts for centuries . . .

Once it is appreciated that it is the event and not the fact that the event is a result of a breach of contract which relieves the party not in default of further performance of his obligations, two consequences follow. (1) The test whether the event relied upon has this consequence is the same whether the event is the result of the other party's breach of contract or not, as Devlin J pointed out in *Universal Cargo Carriers Corporation v Citati* [1957] 2 QB 401, 434; (2) The question whether an event which is the result of the other party's breach of contract has this consequence cannot be answered by treating all contractual undertakings as falling into one of two separate categories: "conditions" the breach of which gives rise to an event which relieves the party not in default of further performance of his obligations, and "warranties" the breach of which does not give rise to such an event.

Lawyers tend to speak of this classification as if it were comprehensive, partly for the historical reasons which I have already mentioned and partly because Parliament itself adopted it in the Sale of Goods Act, 1893, as respects a number of implied terms in contracts for the sale of goods and has in that Act used the expressions "condition" and "warranty" in that meaning. But it is by no means true of contractual undertakings in general at common law.

No doubt there are many simple contractual undertakings, sometimes express but more often because of their very simplicity ("It goes without saying") to be implied, of which it can be predicated that every breach of such an undertaking must give rise to an event which will deprive the party not in default of substantially the whole benefit which it was intended that he should obtain from the contract. And such a stipulation, unless the parties have agreed that breach of it shall not entitle the non-defaulting party to treat the contract as repudiated, is a "condition". So too there may be other simple contractual undertakings of which it can be predicated that no breach can give rise to an event which will deprive the party not in default of substantially the whole benefit which it was intended that he should obtain from the contract; and such a stipulation, unless the parties have agreed that breach of it shall entitle the non-defaulting party to treat the contract as repudiated, is a "warranty".

There are, however, many contractual undertakings of a more complex character which cannot be categorised as being "conditions" or "warranties", if the late nineteenth-century meaning adopted in the Sale of Goods Act, 1893, and used by Bowen LJ in *Bentsen v Taylor, Sons & Co* [1893] 2 QB 274, 280; 9 TLR 552, CA, be given to those terms. Of such undertakings all that can be predicated is that some breaches will and others will not give rise to an event which will deprive the party not in default of substantially the whole benefit which it was intended that he should obtain from the contract; and the legal consequences of a breach of such an undertaking, unless provided for expressly in the contract, depend upon the nature of the event to which the breach gives rise and do not follow automatically from a prior classification of the undertaking as a "condition" or a "warranty". For instance, to take Bramwell B's example in *Jackson v Union Marine Insurance Co Ltd* itself, breach of an undertaking by a shipowner to sail with all possible dispatch to a named port does not necessarily relieve the charterer of further performance of his obligation under the charterparty, but if the breach is so prolonged that the contemplated voyage is frustrated it does have this effect . . .

As my brethren have already pointed out, the shipowners' undertaking to tender a seaworthy ship has, as a result of numerous decisions as to what can amount to "unseaworthiness", become one of the most complex of contractual undertakings. It embraces obligations with respect to every part of the hull and machinery, stores and equipment and the crew itself. It can be broken by the presence of trivial defects easily and rapidly remediable as well as by defects which must inevitably result in a total loss of the vessel.

Consequently the problem in this case is, in my view, neither solved nor soluble by debating whether the shipowner's express or implied undertaking to tender a seaworthy ship is a "condition" or a "warranty". It is like so many other contractual terms an undertaking one breach of which may give rise to an event which relieves the charterer of further performance of his undertakings if he so elects and another breach of which may not give rise to such an event but entitle him only to monetary compensation in the form of damages. It is, with all deference to [counsel for the defendant's] skilful argument, by no means surprising that among the many hundreds of previous cases about the shipowner's undertaking to deliver a seaworthy ship there is none where it was found profitable to discuss in the judgments the question whether that undertaking is a "condition" or a "warranty"; for the true answer, as I have already indicated, is that it is neither, but one of that large class of contractual undertakings one breach of which may have the same effect as that ascribed to a breach of "condition" under the Sale of Goods Act, 1893, and a different breach of which may have only the same effect as that ascribed to a breach of "warranty" under that Act . . .

What the judge had to do in the present case, as in any other case where one party to a contract relies upon a breach by the other party as giving him a right to elect to rescind the contract, and the contract itself makes no express provision as to this, was to look at the events which had occurred as a result of the breach at the time at which the charterers purported to rescind the charterparty and to decide whether the occurrence of those events deprived the charterers of substantially the whole benefit which it was the intention of the parties as expressed in the charterparty that the charterers should obtain from the further performance of their own contractual undertakings . . .

The question which the judge had to ask himself was, as he rightly decided, whether or not at the date when the charterers purported to rescind the contract, namely, June 6, 1957, or when the shipowners purported to accept such rescission, namely, August 8, 1957, the delay which had already occurred as a result of the incompetence of the engine-room staff, and the delay which was likely to occur in repairing the engines of the vessel and the conduct of the shipowners by that date in taking steps to remedy these two matters, were, when taken together, such as to deprive the charterers of substantially the whole benefit which it was the intention of the parties they should obtain from further use of the vessel under the charterparty.

In my view, in his judgment – on which I would not seek to improve – the judge took into account and gave due weight to all the relevant considerations and arrived at the right answer for the right reasons.'

The term in question was the undertaking as to the 'seaworthiness' of the ship. This proved to be problematic because the term could be breached in a number of different ways. For example, the failure to supply the correct number of anchors at the time of sailing could render the ship 'unseaworthy', just as much as a major defect in the hull. Their lordships adopted three different approaches to this problem:

1. Sellers LJ adopted the most straightforward approach. He classified the term as a warranty and held that its breach only entitled the defendant to damages.

2. Diplock LJ adopted a more innovative approach. He refused to classify the term as either a condition or a warranty. Instead he classified it as an intermediate term, holding that the remedial consequences of its breach depended on the effect of the actual breach that had occurred (the third approach outlined at the start of this section). If the breach was so serious as to deprive the innocent party of substantially the whole of the performance to which he was entitled, it would be treated as repudiatory, in the same way as if it was a breach of a condition; if it was less serious it would give rise only to a remedy in damages, like a warranty.

3. Upjohn LJ adopted a third approach. He said that the crucial question to ask was whether the term was a condition. If it was, it automatically gave rise to a right to terminate the contract. If it was not, it did not inevitably follow that the defendant's only remedy was in damages. Instead the court would examine the effects of the breach and determine whether the defendant ought to be entitled to terminate the contract. Lord Denning has since restated this approach in *Cehave NV v Bremer Handelgesellschaft mbH. (The Hansa Nord)* [1976] QB 44, 66.

The remedial flexibility provided by the latter two approaches clearly makes them the more suitable. Essentially, Diplock LJ's test provides for three categories of term – conditions, warranties and intermediate terms – while Upjohn LJ's test provides for just two: conditions and intermediate terms. Further, Upjohn LJ's test has the merit of avoiding the difficulty of distinguishing between warranties and intermediate terms.

Reynolds, FMB, 'Discharge of contract by breach; (1981) 97 LQR 541, 548

The word 'warranty', with its different usages in different parts of the law (eg insurance) and in ordinary speech (the manufacturer's warranty) is productive of confusion. Its prominence seems connected with the old idea that in a sale, the warranty was separate from the sale, and actionable by a separate action: but warranty in the general context of breach of contract seems to mean a little more than a contractual promise other than the central obligation of the contract, and not always even that. It is submitted that the use of the term could well be abandoned, with the simple result that the *Hong Kong Fir* test applies to all promises which are not conditions. If this is too difficult to achieve, the use of the term warranty should be retained for all contractual promises other than conditions, without any implication that there are terms *no* breach of which can ever entitle to discharge. Either route would make the phrase 'innominate' or 'intermediate term' superfluous. The existence of *three* categories is surely unnecessary.

Yet, it is Diplock LJ's approach that has found favour with the courts and the commentators.

Treitel, G, *The Law of Contract*, 11th edn, 2003, London: Sweet & Maxwell, at pp 796–7

The general view is that there are three classes of contractual terms: conditions, the breach of which at common law invariably gives rise to a right to rescind; warranties, the breach of which gives rise only to a right to damages; and intermediate terms, the breach of which gives rise to a right to rescind if it is sufficiently serious, but otherwise sounds only in damages. There is, however, some support for the alternative view that there are only two categories: conditions and other terms. This view is based on the argument that the injured party may be entitled to rescind even for a breach of warranty, if the effect of the breach is sufficiently serious. There is . . . considerable force in this argument and if it is correct a warranty may be said to resemble an intermediate term, in that the availability of rescission as a remedy for breach of either type of term depends on the seriousness of the breach. Nevertheless, the weight of authority supports the continued existence of the threefold division of contractual terms. It is respectfully submitted that this is the preferable view since the distinction between warranties and intermediate terms remains for practical purposes an important one. Even if, in extreme cases, rescission is available for breach of warranty, there is at least a *prima facie* rule that the normal remedy for such a breach is by way of damages. In relation to intermediate terms, there is no such *prima facie* rule; so that (to put the matter at its lowest) there is a greater likelihood that rescission will be available for breach of an intermediate term than for breach of warranty.

A further point to note from the case is that Diplock LJ appeared to suggest that a term would only be classified as a condition if every breach of it would 'deprive the party not in default of substantially the whole benefit which it was intended that he should obtain from the contract'. This suggestion was based on a rather questionable analogy with the law of frustration, and it has since been rejected by the House of Lords in *Bunge Corporation v Tradax Export SA* [1981] 1 WLR 711.

The decision in *Hong Kong Fir* has been highly influential, giving the courts the remedial flexibility that they had long craved for. It has even been adopted, somewhat surprisingly, in relation to sale of goods contracts.

Cehave NV v Bremer Handelgesellschaft mbH. (The Hansa Nord) [1976] QB 44, 66

Facts: The German sellers agreed to sell to the Dutch buyers 12,000 tons of US citrus pulp pellets for use as animal feed. The contract was made on the Grain and Feed Association (GAFTA) terms. Clause 7 provided 'shipment to be made in good condition'. The buyers paid the price of £100,000 and received the shipping documents, but when the goods arrived at Rotterdam it was discovered that part of the shipment had been damaged by overheating. The buyers rejected the whole shipment, and when the sellers refused to refund the purchase price, the buyers applied to the Rotterdam county court to obtain an order for the shipment to be sold. The shipment was sold on 2 June to an importer who on the same day resold the whole cargo to the buyers for the same sum of £30,000. The buyers then used the entire cargo for their original purpose, making animal feed. Mocatta J held in the buyer's favour. Terms under the Sale of Goods Act must be either conditions or warranties and since breach of the 'shipped in good condition' term might have serious consequences, it had to be a condition. The sellers appealed.

Held: The Court of Appeal allowed the appeal. The 'shipped in good condition' term was an intermediate term. Since the whole cargo was eventually used for its intended purpose as animal feed, the breach did not go to the root of the contract and the buyers, though entitled to damages, were not entitled to reject.

Lord Denning MR:

' "Shipped in good condition". Was this a condition strictly so called, so that *any* breach of it entitled the buyer to reject the goods? Or was it an intermediate stipulation, so that the buyer cannot reject unless the breach is so serious as to go to the root of the contract? If there was any previous authority holding it to be a *condition* strictly so called, we should abide by it, just as we did with the clause "expected ready to load": see *Finnish Government (Ministry of Food) v H Ford & C Ltd* (1921) 6 L1 L Rep 188 . . . But, there is no such authority with the clause "shipped in good condition". I regard this clause as comparable to a clause as to quality, such as "fair average quality". If a small portion of the goods sold was a little below that standard, it would be met by commercial men by an allowance off the price. The buyer would have no right to reject the whole lot unless the divergence was serious and substantial: see *Biggin & Co Ltd v Permanite Ltd* [1951] 1 KB 422, 439, *per* Devlin J and *Christopher Hill Ltd v Ashington Piggeries Ltd* [1972] AC 441, 511, *per* Lord Diplock . . .

In my opinion, therefore, the term "shipped in good condition" was not a condition strictly so called: nor was it a warranty strictly so called. It was one of those intermediate stipulations which gives no right to reject unless the breach goes to the root of the contract.

On the facts stated by the board of appeal, I do not think the buyer was entitled to reject these instalments of the contract. The board only said that "not all the goods in hold no. 1 were shipped in good condition". That does not say how many were bad. In any case, their condition cannot have been very bad, seeing that all of them were in fact used for the intended purpose. The breach did not go to the root of the contract. The buyer is entitled to damages, but not to rejection.

Merchantable

The board of appeal made this finding: "The goods in hold 1 were 'merchantable' on arrival at Rotterdam in a commercial sense, though at a lower price than would be paid for sound goods; we find and hold, however, that they were not 'of merchantable quality' within the meaning of the phrase when used in the Sale of Goods Act 1893".

The board of appeal were not lawyers: but they had a legal adviser and I am afraid that in reaching that finding they were not advised correctly. The statute uses the words "merchantable quality" in a commercial sense. The board should, therefore, have applied it in the commercial sense. They should not have been persuaded to give it some other "statutory sense" .

Now we were taken through many of the definitions which have been given by judges of "merchantable quality" . . . For myself, I think the definition in the latest statute is the best that has yet been devised. It is contained in section 7(2) of the Supply of Goods (Implied Terms) Act 1973. The statute itself only applies to contracts made after May 18, 1973. But the definition seems to me appropriate for contracts made before it. It runs as follows:

> "Goods of any kind are of merchantable quality within the meaning of this Act if they are as fit for the purpose or purposes for which goods of that kind are commonly bought as it is reasonable to expect having regard to any description applied to them, the price (if relevant) and all other relevant circumstances; and any reference in this Act to unmerchantable goods shall be construed accordingly."

In applying that definition, it is as well to remember that, by the statute, we are dealing with an implied *condition*, strictly so called, and not a warranty. For any breach of it, therefore, the buyer is entitled to *reject* the goods: or, alternatively, if he chooses to accept them or has accepted them, he has a remedy in damages. In these circumstances, I should have thought a fair way of testing merchantability would be to ask a commercial man: was the breach such that the buyer should be able to reject the goods? In answering that question the commercial man would have regard to the various matters mentioned in the new statutory definition. . . . If there was a clause, express or implied, which would give the buyer an allowance off the price for the particular shortcomings, such that a commercial man would say: "The buyer is entitled to a price allowance but not to reject them" – again the goods would be of merchantable quality. The buyer would be entitled to an allowance or damages in lieu, but not entitled to reject the lot.

Our present case comes within that last illustration. These citrus pulp pellets were bought for cattle food. That was the purpose for which such pellets are commonly bought. They were as fit for that purpose as it was reasonable to expect. That is shown by the fact that they were actually used for that purpose. Some of them arrived damaged, but not to such an extent that the buyer was entitled to reject the cargo in both holds, or either of them. That damage was such as to entitle the buyer to an allowance off the price for breach of the clause "shipped in good condition": but not such as to entitle him to reject the lot on the ground that it was not of "merchantable quality" . . . Having found that in a commercial sense the goods were merchantable, there was no breach of section 14 (2).'

Roskill LJ:

'In my view, a court should not be over ready, unless required by statute or authority so to do, to construe a term in a contract as a "condition" any breach of which gives rise to a right to reject rather than as a term any breach of which sounds in damages – I deliberately avoid the use of the word "warranty" at this juncture. In principle contracts are made to be performed and not to be avoided according to the whims of market fluctuation and where there is a free choice between two possible constructions I think the court should tend to prefer that construction which will ensure performance and not encourage avoidance of contractual obligations. . . .

In principle it is not easy to see why the law relating to contracts for the sale of goods should be different from the law relating to the performance of other contractual obligations, whether charterparties or other types of contract. Sale of goods law is but one branch of the general law of contract. It is desirable that the same legal principles should apply to the law of contract as a whole and that different legal principles should not apply to different branches of that law.'

Ormrod LJ:

'If one asks oneself the question in the form, "Did the parties intend that the buyer should be entitled to reject the goods if they were not shipped in good condition?" the answer must be that it depends on the nature and effects of the breach. This is directly in line with Diplock LJ's approach in the *Hongkong Fir Shipping Co* case [1962] 2 QB 26, 69–70, not surprisingly, since there can be very little difference in principle between whether the ship is seaworthy and whether goods are in good condition. There is obviously a strong case for applying the general principle of the *Hongkong Fir Shipping Co* case to contracts for the sale of goods. The question remains, however . . . whether it is open to the court to do so. The parties themselves, of course, can do it by express agreement as, indeed, they have done in the present case in relation to quality . . . If it can be done expressly, it can be done by implication, unless it is in some way prohibited. [Counsel for the buyers] argues that section 11 (1) (b) compels the court to choose between condition and warranty. I do not think that the subsection was intended to have any prohibitory effect. It is essentially a definition section, defining "condition" and "warranty" in terms of remedies. Nor is the classification absolutely rigid, for it provides that a buyer may treat a condition as a warranty if he wishes, by accepting the goods. It does not, however, envisage the possibility that a breach of warranty might go to the root of the contract, and so, in certain circumstances, entitle the buyer to treat the contract as repudiated. But the law has developed since the Act was passed. It is now accepted as a general principle since the *Hongkong Fir Shipping Co* case [1962] 2 QB 26, that it is the events resulting from the breach, rather than the breach itself, which may destroy the consideration for the buyer's promise and so enable him to treat the contract as repudiated.

The problem is how to integrate this principle with section 11 (1)*(b)*. In practice it may not arise very often . . . The difficulty only arises if the court had already categorised the stipulation as a warranty. The present case provides an example. If the relevant part of clause 7 is construed as a warranty in this case, and later, another dispute occurs in relation to another contract in the same form, between the same parties, for the sale of similar goods, in which the breach of clause 7 has produced much more serious consequences for the buyer, is the court bound by its decision in this case to hold that the buyer is precluded from rejecting the goods under the later contract because, as a matter of construction, it has already categorised the stipulation as a warranty? . . . If the answer is in the affirmative section 11 (1)*(b)* has, by implication, excluded one of the general common law rules of contract. It was clearly not intended to have this effect and I agree with Lord Denning MR, for the reasons that he has given in his judgment, that the Act should not, if it can be avoided, be construed in this way. Section 61 (2) seems to provide an answer. If this view is correct it is bound to have important repercussions on the way in which courts in future will approach the construction of stipulations in contracts for the sale of goods. It will no longer be necessary to place so much emphasis on the potential effects of a breach on the buyer, and to feel obliged, as Mocatta J did in this case, to construe a stipulation as a condition because in other cases or in other circumstances the buyer ought to be entitled to reject. Consequently, the court will be freer to regard stipulations, as a matter of construction, as warranties, if what might be called the "back-up" rule of the common law is available to protect buyers who ought to be able to reject in proper circumstances. I doubt whether, strictly speaking, this involves the creation of a third category of stipulations; rather, it recognises another ground for holding that a buyer is entitled to reject, namely, that, de facto, the consideration for his promise has been wholly destroyed.

The result may be summarised in this way. When a breach of contract has taken place the question arises: "Is the party who is not in breach entitled in law to treat the contract as repudiated or, in the case of a buyer, to reject the goods?" The answer depends on the answers to a series of other questions. Adopting Upjohn LJ's judgment in the *Hongkong Fir Shipping Co* case [1962] 2 QB 26, 64, the first question is: "Does the contract expressly provide that in the event of the breach of the term in question the other party is entitled to terminate the contract or reject the goods?" If the answer is No, the next question is: "Does the contract when correctly construed so provide?" The relevant term, for example, may be described as a "condition". The question then arises whether this word is used as a code word for the phrase "shall be entitled to repudiate the contract or reject the goods", or in some other sense, as in *Wickman Machine Tool Sales Ltd v L Schuler AG* [1972] 1 WLR 840. The next question is whether the breach of the relevant term creates a right to repudiate or reject. This may arise either from statute or as a result of judicial decision on particular contractual terms. For example, if the requirements of section 14 (1) or (2) of the Sale of Goods Act 1893 are fulfilled, the buyer will be entitled to reject the goods, as a result of this section, read with section 11 (2). In fact, in all those sections of the Sale of Goods Act 1893 which create implied conditions the word "condition" is, by definition a code word for "breach of this term will entitle the buyer to reject the goods", subject to any other relevant provision of the Act.

In other cases, the courts have decided that breach of some specific terms, such as, for example, an "expected ready to load" stipulation, will ipso facto give rise to a right in the other party to repudiate the contract: *The Mihalis Angelos* [1971] 1 QB 164, 194, *per* Lord Denning MR. In these two classes of case the consequences of the breach are irrelevant or, more accurately, are assumed to go to the root of the contract, and to justify repudiation. There remains the non-specific class where the events produced by the breach are such that it is reasonable to describe the breach as going to the root of the contract and so justifying repudiation.

If this approach is permissible in the present case I would unhesitatingly hold that the stipulation in clause 7 that the goods were to be shipped in good condition was not a condition, and that on the facts of this case the breach did not go to the root of the contract, and that, consequently, the buyers were not entitled to reject the goods.'

There are two important points to note here. First, the Court of Appeal unanimously rejected the argument that the sellers had breached s 14(2) of the SGA 1893 by supplying goods that were not of 'merchantable quality'. This was uncontroversial, given that the goods were still fit for their original purpose, and were in fact used for that purpose by the buyers. Of more interest to us are the comments made by Lord Denning about how the issue of merchantability should be determined. He suggested that 'in these circumstances . . . a fair way of testing merchantability would be to ask a commercial man: was the breach such that the buyer should be able to reject the goods?' In other words, was the effect of the breach such that the conduct amounted to a breach of an implied *condition*? By this ingenious method, Lord Denning imported the *Hong Kong Fir* approach into the analysis of statutorily implied conditions though the back door. While ingenious, this analysis is extremely dubious and it was not supported by either of the other members of the Court of Appeal. In any event, the case has probably now been superseded by the more specific statutory definitions of quality to be found in the SGA 1979 (see Chapter 17).

The second point to note is that the court unanimously agreed that the *Hong Kong Fir* approach should apply to an express term in a sale of goods contract. The term in question, cl 7 (which provided that the goods should be 'shipped in good condition') was held to be an intermediate term and not a condition. Since the goods were still fit for their original purpose, the breach was of insufficient seriousness to justify termination. Mr Weir (Weir, T, 'Contract – the buyer's right to reject defective goods' [1976] CLJ 33) has criticised this decision, complaining that it 'rewards incompetence'. He notes that the seller had made a very good bargain; the market for pellets having fallen rapidly after the contract was made. By refusing to let the buyer terminate the contract, the Court of Appeal effectively forced the buyer to pay not only the true value of the spoilt cargo, but the seller's profit as well. Weir criticises the result and summarises the unhappy state of the law in the following way: 'The guilty party is to get all that he bargained for unless the innocent party gets no part of what he bargained for'.

Mr Weir's criticisms carry some force, but it should not be forgotten that the buyer was attempting to escape from a bad bargain. Cehave had received the goods they had bargained for (albeit in a slightly different condition), but wished to withdraw from the transaction in order to pursue a better bargain elsewhere. The Court of Appeal's decision prevented them from doing this (see Brownsword, R, 'Retrieving reasons, retrieving rationality? A new look at the right to withdraw for breach of contract' (1992) 5 JCL 83). Unfortunately, it also left us with an unacceptable degree of uncertainty in the law. Whereas in the past, commercial lawyers had been able to accurately predict when a breach of contract would give rise to a right to terminate a contract, the approach taken by the Court of Appeal in *The Hansa Nord* suggested that this was no longer possible.

Fortunately for commercial lawyers, a different approach has since been adopted in relation to common clauses in commercial contracts. The seeds for this approach were sown by the Court of Appeal in *The Mihalis Angelos*.

Maredelanto Compania Naviera SA v Bergbau-Handel GmbH (The Mihalis Angelos) [1971] 1 QB 164

Facts: A ship was chartered to transport a cargo of minerals from Haiphong. The charterparty contained a clause to the effect that the ship was 'expected ready to load under this charter about 1 July 1965'. The charterers were unable to get the cargo to the port in time and purported to cancel the charter on 17 July. The owners brought an action for wrongful repudiation. The charterers argued that they were entitled to terminate the contract on 17 July following the owner's breach of the readiness to load clause.

Held: The Court of Appeal held that the readiness to load clause was a condition, breach of which entitled the charterers to terminate the contract.

Megaw LJ:

'In my judgment, such a term in a charterparty ought to be regarded as being a condition of the contract, in the old sense of the word "condition": that is, that when it has been broken, the other party can, if he wishes, by intimation to the party in breach, elect to be released from performance of his further obligations under the contract; and he can validly do so without having to establish that on the facts of the particular case the breach has produced serious consequences which can be treated as "going to the root of the contract" or as being "fundamental", or whatever other metaphor may be thought appropriate for a frustration case ... One of the essential elements of law is some measure of uniformity. One of the important elements of the law is predictability. At any rate in commercial law, there are obvious and substantial advantages in having, where possible, a firm and definite rule for a particular class of legal relationship: for example, as here, the legal categorisation of a particular, definable type of contractual clause in common use. It is surely much better, both for shipowners and charterers (and, incidentally, for their advisers), when a contractual obligation of this nature is under consideration, and still more when they are faced with the necessity for an urgent decision as to the effects of a suspected breach of it, to be able to say categorically: "If a breach is proved, then the charterer can put an end to the contract", rather than that they should be left to ponder whether or not the courts would be likely, in the particular case, when the evidence has been heard, to decide that in the particular circumstances the breach was or was not such as "to go to the root of the contract". Where justice does not require greater flexibility, there is everything to be said for, and nothing against, a degree of rigidity in legal principle.'

As we have seen earlier in the chapter, a similar approach was taken to a time clause in a mercantile contract in *Bunge Corporation v Tradax Export SA* [1981] 1 WLR 711. Lord Wilberforce said that to treat time clauses in mercantile contracts as intermediate terms would be 'commercially most undesirable':

'It would expose the parties, after a breach of one, two, three, seven and other numbers of days to an argument whether this delay would have left time for the seller to provide the goods. It would make it, at the time, at least difficult, and sometimes impossible, for the supplier to know whether he could do so. It would fatally remove from a vital provision in the contract that certainty which is the most indispensable quality of mercantile contracts, and lead to a large increase in arbitrations. It would confine the seller – perhaps after arbitration and reference through the courts – to a remedy in damages which might be extremely difficult to quantify. These are all serious objections in practice. But I am clear that the submission is unacceptable in law. The judgment of Diplock LJ does not give any support and ought not to give any encouragement to any such proposition; for beyond doubt it recognises that it is open to the parties to agree that, as regards a particular obligation, any breach shall entitle the party not in default to treat the contract as repudiated ... It remains true, as Lord Roskill has pointed out in *Cehave NV v Bremer Handelgesellschaft mbH. (The Hansa Nord)* [1976] QB 44, 66, that the courts should not be too ready to interpret contractual clauses as conditions. And I have myself commended, and continue to commend, the greater flexibility in the law of contracts to which Hongkong Fir points the way (*Reardon Smith Line Ltd v Yngvar Hansen-Tangen (trading as HE Hansen-Tangen)* [1976] 1 WLR 989, 998). But I do not doubt that, in suitable cases, the courts should not be reluctant, if the intentions of the parties as shown by the contract so indicate, to hold that an obligation has the force of a condition, and that indeed they should usually do so in the case of time clauses in mercantile contracts.'

Applying this approach to the facts of the case, the House of Lords held that a four-day delay in giving notice of the ship's readiness to load was a breach of condition, entitling the sellers to terminate the contract. The same approach was applied by the Privy Council in *Union Eagle Ltd v Golden Achievement Ltd* [1997] AC 514, again in relation to a time clause. More recently, the approach has been applied to a clause guaranteeing the acquisition of approval of a vessel within a specified period of time: *BS & N Ltd v Micado Shipping Ltd (Malta) (The Seaflower)* [2001] 1 Lloyd's Rep 341.

This line of cases may give the impression that a term will be held to be a condition whenever the demands of commerce require it. The reality, however, is much more complex. When the parties fail to stipulate whether a term is a condition, warranty or intermediate term, the court must engage in a delicate interpretative exercise to determine the true nature of the term. Inevitably, judicial differences will mean that different results will be reached by different judges (see *Universal Bulk Carriers Pte Ltd v Andre et Cie SA* [2001] 2 Lloyd's Rep 65, where a time clause in a charterparty was held not to be a condition). Accordingly, this area of the law continues to be shrouded in uncertainty.

16.3.2.3 Categorisation by the parties

The parties are, of course, free to stipulate the nature of the terms in the contract itself. For example, the contract may expressly provide that some of the terms are conditions, while the rest are warranties. The use of such labels will not, however, be conclusive as *L Schuler AG v Wickman Machine Tools Sales Ltd* shows.

L Schuler AG v Wickman Machine Tools Sales Ltd [1974] AC 235

Facts: Wickman was appointed as the sole UK distributor of Schuler's panel presses. Clause 7(b) of the contract provided that, 'It shall be [a] condition of this agreement that [Wickman] shall send its representatives to visit' the six largest United Kingdom motor manufacturers 'at least once in every week' to solicit orders for panel presses. Wickman's representatives failed to make a number of these weekly visits and Schuler terminated the agreement under clause 11(a)(i). That clause provided that either party could terminate the agreement if the other committed a material breach of its obligations and failed to remedy it within 60 days of being required to do so. Wickman brought a claim for wrongful termination.

Held: The House of Lords (Lord Wilberforce dissenting) held that the word 'condition' in clause 7(b) did not make the clause a condition in the sense that a single breach of it, however trivial, would entitle the innocent party to terminate the whole contract.

Lord Reid:

'In the ordinary use of the English language "condition" has many meanings, some of which have nothing to do with agreements. In connection with an agreement it may mean a pre-condition: something which must happen or be done before the agreement can take effect. Or it may mean some state of affairs which must continue to exist if the agreement is to remain in force. The legal meaning on which Schuler relies is, I think, one which would not occur to a layman; a condition in that sense is not something which has an automatic effect. It is a term the breach of which by one party gives to the other an option either to terminate the contract or to let the contract proceed and, if he so desires, sue for damages for the breach.

Sometimes a breach of a term gives that option to the aggrieved party because it is of a fundamental character going to the root of the contract, sometimes it gives that option because the parties have chosen to stipulate that it shall have that effect. Blackburn J said in *Bettini v Gye* (1876) 1 QBD 183, 187: "Parties may think some matter, apparently of very little importance, essential; and if they sufficiently express an intention to make the literal fulfilment of such a thing a condition precedent, it will be one; . . ."

In the present case it is not contended that Wickman's failures to make visits amounted in themselves to fundamental breaches. What is contended is that the terms of clause 7 "sufficiently express an intention" to make any breach, however small, of the obligation to make visits a condition so that any breach shall entitle Schuler to rescind the whole contract if they so desire.

Schuler maintains that the use of the word "condition" is in itself enough to establish this intention. No doubt some words used by lawyers do have a rigid inflexible meaning. But we must remember that we are seeking to discover intention as disclosed by the contract as a whole. Use of the word "condition" is an indication – even a strong indication – of such an intention but it is by no means conclusive.

The fact that a particular construction leads to a very unreasonable result must be a relevant consideration. The more unreasonable the result the more unlikely it is that the parties can have intended it, and if they do intend it the more necessary it is that they shall make that intention abundantly clear.

Clause 7 (b) requires that over a long period each of the six firms shall be visited every week by one or other of two named representatives. It makes no provision for Wickman being entitled to substitute others even on the death or retirement of one of the named representatives. Even if one could imply some right to do this, it makes no provision for both representatives being ill during a particular week. And it makes no provision for the possibility that one or other of the firms may tell Wickman that they cannot receive Wickman's representative during a particular week. So if the parties gave any thought to the matter at all they must have realised the probability that in a few cases out of the 1,400 required visits a visit as stipulated would be impossible. But if Schuler's contention is right, failure to make even one visit entitles them to terminate the contract however blameless Wickman might be.

This is so unreasonable that it must make me search for some other possible meaning of the contract. If none can be found then Wickman must suffer the consequences. But only if that is the only possible interpretation.

If I have to construe clause 7 standing by itself then I do find difficulty in reaching any other interpretation. But if clause 7 must be read with clause 11 the difficulty disappears. The word "condition" would make any breach of clause 7 (b), however excusable, a material breach. That would then entitle Schuler to give notice under clause 11 (a) (i) requiring the breach to be remedied. There would be no point in giving such a notice if Wickman were clearly not in fault but if it were given Wickman would have no difficulty in showing that the breach had been remedied. If Wickman were at fault then on receiving such a notice they would have to amend their system so that they could show that the breach had been remedied. If they did not do that within the period of the notice then Schuler would be entitled to rescind.

In my view, that is a possible and reasonable construction of the contract and I would therefore adopt it. The contract is so obscure that I can have no confidence that this is its true meaning but for the reasons which I have given I think that it is the preferable construction. It follows that Schuler was not entitled to rescind the contract as it purported to do. So I would dismiss this appeal.'

Lord Wilberforce:

'Does clause 7 (b) amount to a "condition" or a "term"? (to call it an important or material term adds, with all respect, nothing but some intellectual assuagement). My Lords, I am clear in my own mind that it is a condition, but your Lordships take the contrary view. On a matter of construction of a particular document, to develop the reasons for a minority opinion serves no purpose. I am all the more happy to refrain from so doing because the judgments of Mocatta J, Stephenson LJ, and indeed of Edmund Davies LJ, on construction, give me complete satisfaction and I could in any case add little of value to their reasons. I would only add that, for my part, to call the clause arbitrary, capricious or fantastic, or to introduce as a test of its validity the ubiquitous reasonable man (I do not know whether he is English or German) is to assume, contrary to the evidence, that both parties to this contract adopted a standard of easygoing tolerance rather than one of aggressive, insistent punctuality and efficiency. This is not an assumption I am prepared to make, nor do I think myself entitled to impose the former standard upon the parties if their words indicate, as they plainly do, the latter. I note finally, that the result of treating the clause, so careful and specific in its requirements, as a term is, in effect, to deprive the appellants of any remedy in respect of admitted and by no means minimal breaches. The arbitrator's finding that these breaches were not "material" was not, in my opinion, justified in law in the face of the parties' own characterisation of them in their document: indeed the fact that he was able to do so, and so leave the appellants without remedy, argues strongly that the legal basis of his finding – that clause 7 (b) was merely a term – is unsound. I would allow this appeal.'

In total there were 20 clauses in the contract. Only clause 7(b) was referred to as a 'condition', which would seem to indicate that the parties intended that any breach of it would be repudiatory. This was not, however, the interpretation adopted by the majority. Lord Reid's view was that such an interpretation was so unreasonable that some other possible meaning had to be found. The other meaning advanced by his Lordship was to treat the clause as merely indicative of the type of 'material breach' that would trigger the operation of cl 11. This meaning, it is submitted, is even less satisfactory than the meaning advanced by Schuler. Clause 11 provided for termination in the event of a 'material breach' not being 'remedied' within 60 days of notice being given. In what sense could Wickman's failure to make regular weekly visits have been remedied? It was not possible for Wickman to go back in time and make the missed visits. The answer adopted by Lord Reid was that Wickman could have remedied the breach by amending its internal systems so as to ensure that the breach did not recur. But this interpretation of the word 'remedy' is surely rather generous towards Wickman.

It is hard to escape the conclusion that the majority were guilty of rewriting the parties' agreement. Judicial intervention on this scale is rather worrying. Even more concerning is the fact that the approach seems to have been repeated several years later by the Court of Appeal. This time the parties expressly stipulated the circumstances in which the right to terminate for breach would arise.

Rice v Great Yarmouth Borough Council [2001] 3 LGLR 4

Facts: The claimant contracted with the defendant council to provide leisure management and grounds maintenance services for a period of four years. Clause 23.2.1 of the contract provided: 'If the contractor commits a breach of any of its obligations under the Contract; . . . the Council may, without prejudice to any accrued rights or remedies under the Contract, terminate the Contractor's employment under the Contract by notice in writing having immediate effect.' Clause 27 also entitled the defendant to serve 'default notices' on the claimant specifying breaches and the time permitted for rectification. Approximately three months after the contract had commenced the defendant started to serve default notices on the claimant. Several months later, the defendant informed the claimant that they were terminating the contract under clause 23. The claimant sought to recover damages for wrongful repudiation. At first instance, the judge held that clause 23 should not be interpreted literally, and that there should only be a right to terminate the contract where the breach was serious enough to be repudiatory. The defendant appealed.

Held: The Court of Appeal dismissed the appeal, holding that the clause should be interpreted in a common sense way so as to limit the defendant's right to terminate to situations where the claimant's breach had been repudiatory.

Hale LJ:
'The council argued first that clause 23.2.1 should be applied literally so as to give them the right to terminate the contract for the breach of any of the obligations contained in it, other than the trivial. The judge was referred to a number of well-known authorities. On the one hand, "it is open to the parties to agree that, as regards a particular obligation, any breach shall entitle the party not in default to treat the contract as repudiated": see *Bunge Corporation v Tradax Export SA* [1981] 1 WLR 711, per Lord Wilberforce at 715E. On the other hand ". . . if detailed semantic and syntactical analysis of words in a commercial contract is going to lead to a conclusion that flouts business commonsense, it must yield to business commonsense": see *Antaios Compania SA v Sakeb Rederierna* [1985] AC 191, per Lord Diplock at p 201D. The judge pointed out

that none of these authorities ". . . dealt with commercial circumstances having many parallels to those of a local authority and a contractor who is contractually required for a period of years to provide a wide variety of services on a repetitive basis."

He continued: "There has long been a tension in the world of contract between an attachment to literal meaning that makes for certainty with all in black and white and the parties knowing exactly where they are and little room for the relative unpredictability of judicial intervention, and a desire to avoid consequences seen as unfair or seen as offending commercial commonsense." As to which line of authority should apply, he concluded: "In the context of a contract intended to last for four years, involving substantial investment or at least substantial undertaking of financial obligations by one party and involving a myriad of obligations of differing importance and varying frequency, I have no hesitation in holding that the common sense interpretation should be imposed upon the strict words of the contract and that a repudiatory breach or an accumulation of breaches that as a whole can properly be described as repudiatory are a precondition to termination pursuant to clause 23.2.1."

Another point in favour of a commercial, common sense interpretation was ". . . that ephemeral breaches, even where substantial and not trivial, are subject to substantial contractual disciplines, default notices, deductions, performance by others at the contractor's expense and so on." . . .

In my view the judge was entirely right to reach the conclusion he did on this aspect of the case and for the reasons he gave.

The council argued that, in any event, the totality of breaches found by the judge were sufficient to justify it in terminating the contract. . . . In my view, the judge was right to ask himself whether the cumulative breaches were such as to justify an inference that the contractor would continue to deliver a substandard performance. However, I would agree with [counsel for the defendant] that the inference should be that the council would thereby be deprived of a substantial part of the totality of that which it had contracted for that year, subject to the additional possibility that some aspects of the contract were so important that the parties are to be taken to have intended that depriving the council of that part of the contract would be sufficient in itself. That is not what the judge found in this case.

Once it is accepted that the proven breaches are relevant to show what will happen in the future, it is clear that the judge was entitled to take both the drought and the knock on effect of the council's own behaviour in relation to the summer bedding into account. He examined the facts of this case in great detail over a trial lasting some 13 days. He was well placed to evaluate the true importance of the proven breaches in the context of the contracts as a whole and all the circumstances of the case. He had a judgment to make. If anything, the test which he applied was somewhat more favourable to the council than the test which, in my judgment, he should have applied. He was undoubtedly entitled to reach the conclusion that he did.

I would dismiss this appeal.'

(May and Peter Gibson LJJ concurred)

The Court of Appeal refused to accept the literal meaning of cl 23.2.1. Instead, in agreement with the trial judge, their lordships insisted that a common-sense interpretation ought to be imposed upon the strict words of the contract. That meaning, according to their Lordships, was that termination under cl 23 could only operate where there was a repudiatory breach or an accumulation of breaches that could be said to be repudiatory. Such an interpretation, however, renders the clause utterly meaningless. The defendant council already had a right to terminate the contract on the occurrence of a repudiatory breach under the general law. Why would the defendant insert a clause into the contract if its only effect was to restate rights that already existed under the general law? The answer, of course, is that they would not.

The decision in *Rice* is cause for concern. It means that the parties must be absolutely explicit if they wish to provide for termination of the contract on the occurrence of a breach that is not a repudiatory breach at common law. Fortunately, the instrumental approach adopted by the courts in *Schuler* and *Rice* does not seem to be commonplace. Elsewhere the courts have emphasised the need to give effect to the parties' express categorisation of terms. In *Awilco A/S v Fulvia SpA di Navigazione (The Chikuma)* [1981] 1 WLR 314, for example, Lord Bridge emphasised the need to maintain commercial certainty by giving effect to the plain meaning of the terms of the contract:

> 'The ideal at which the courts should aim, in construing such clauses, is to produce a result, such that in any given situation both parties seeking legal advice as to their rights and obligations can expect the same clear and confident answer from their advisers and neither will be tempted to embark on long and expensive litigation in the belief that victory depends on winning the sympathy of the court. This ideal may never be fully attainable, but we shall certainly never even approximate to it unless we strive to follow clear and consistent principles and steadfastly refuse to be blown off course by the supposed merits of individual cases.'

16.3.3 ANTICIPATORY BREACH

An anticipatory breach occurs where, before the time for performance, one party informs the other that they intend to break the contract. The rule in English law is that an anticipatory breach gives rise to an immediate right to treat the contract as repudiated and to bring a claim for damages.

Hochster v De La Tour (1853) 2 El & Bl 678; 118 ER 922

Facts: On 12 April 1852, the defendant engaged the plaintiff to work as his courier for three months beginning on 1 June 1852. On 11 May, the defendant wrote to the plaintiff to inform him that his services were no longer required. On 22 May, the plaintiff commenced an action for breach of contract, and the defendant responded that there could be no breach of contract before 1 June.

Held: The Court held that the plaintiff could commence an action on 22 May and did not have to wait until 1 June.

Lord Campbell CJ:

'The defendant's counsel very powerfully contended that, if the plaintiff was not contented to dissolve the contract and to abandon all remedy upon it, he was bound to remain ready and willing to perform it till the day when the actual employment as courier in the service of the defendant was to begin, and that there could be no breach of the agreement, before that day, to give a right to action. But it cannot be laid down as a universal rule that, where by agreement an act is to be done on a future day, no action can be brought for breach of agreement till the day for doing the act has arrived. If a man promises to marry a woman on a future day and before that day marries another woman, he is instantly liable to an action for breach of promise of marriage: *Short v Stone*. If a man contracts to execute a lease on and from a future day for a certain term, and, before that day, executes a lease to another for the same term, he may be immediately sued for breaking the contract: *Ford v Tiley* (6 B & C 325). So, if a man contracts to sell and deliver specific goods on a future day, and before that day he sells and delivers them to another, he is immediately liable to an action at the suit of the person with whom he first contracted to sell and deliver them: *Bowdell v Parsons* (10 East 359). One reason alleged in support of such an action is that the defendant has, before that day, rendered it impossible for the plaintiff to perform the contract at the day, but this does not necessarily follow, for, prior to the day fixed for doing the act, the first wife may have died, a surrender of the lease executed might be obtained, and the defendant might have re-purchased the goods as to be in a situation to sell and deliver them to the plaintiff. Another reason may be that where there is a contract to do an act on a future day there is a relation constituted between the parties in the meantime by the contract, and that they impliedly promise that in the meantime neither will do any thing to the prejudice of the other inconsistent with that relation. As an example, a man and woman engaged to marry are affianced to one another during the period between the time of the engagement and the celebration of the marriage.

In the present case, of traveller and courier, from the day of hiring till the day when the employment was to begin, the parties were engaged to each other, and it seems to be a beach of an implied contract if either of them renounces the engagement . . . If the plaintiff has no remedy for breach of contract unless he treats the contract as in force, and acts upon it down to June 1, 1852, it follows that, till then, he must enter into no employment which will interfere with his promise 'to start with the defendant on such travels on the day and year', and that he must then be properly equipped in all respects as a courier for three months' tour on the continent of Europe.

But it is surely much more rational, and more for the benefit of both parties, that, after the renunciation of the agreement by the defendant, the plaintiff should be at liberty to consider himself absolved from any future performance of it, retaining his right to sue for any damage he has suffered from breach of it. Thus, instead of remaining idle and laying out money in preparations which must be useless, he is at liberty to seek service under another employer, which would go to mitigation of the damages to which he would otherwise be entitled for a breach of contract. It seems strange that the defendant, after renouncing the contract, and absolutely declaring that he will never act under it, should be permitted to object that faith is given to his assertion, and that an opportunity is not left to him of changing his mind. If the plaintiff is barred of any remedy by entering into an engagement inconsistent with starting as a courier with the defendant on June 1, he is prejudiced by putting faith in the defendant's assertion, and it would be more consonant with principle, if the defendant were precluded from saying that he had not broken the contract when he declared that he entirely renounced it . . .

   If it should be held that, upon a contract to do an act on a future day, a renunciation of the contract by one party dispenses with a condition to be performed in the meantime by the other, there seems no reason for requiring the other to wait till the day arrives before seeking his remedy by action, and the only ground on which the condition can be dispensed with seems to be that the renunciation may be treated as a breach of the contract. Upon the whole, we think that the declaration in this case is sufficient . . . [W]e must give judgment for the plaintiff.'

The reason for allowing an action on an anticipatory breach was explained by Lord Cockburn CJ in *Frost v Knight* (1872) LR 7 Exch 111. The case concerned a situation very similar to one of the examples given by Lord Campbell CJ in *Hochster*. The defendant promised to marry the plaintiff as soon as his father died (the defendant's father did not approve of the plaintiff). During the father's lifetime the defendant broke off the engagement. The plaintiff sued for breach of the promise even though the father was still alive. In explaining why the plaintiff's claim succeeded, Lord Cockburn CJ said:

'It is true . . . that there can be no actual breach of a contract by reason of non-performance so long as the time for performance has not yet arrived. But, on the other hand, there is – and the decision in *Hochster v De la Tour* proceeds on that assumption – a breach of the contract when the promisor repudiates it and declares he will no longer be bound by it. The promisee has an inchoate right to the performance of the bargain, which becomes complete when the time for performance has arrived. In the mean time he has a right to have the contract kept open as a subsisting and effective contract. Its unimpaired and unimpeached efficacy may be essential to his interests. His rights acquired under it may be dealt with by him in various ways for his benefit and advantage. Of all such advantage the repudiation of the contract by the other party, and the announcement that it never will be fulfilled, must of course deprive him. It is therefore quite right to hold that such an announcement amounts to a violation of the contract *in omnibus*, and that upon it the promisee, if so minded, may at once treat it as a breach of the entire contract, and bring his action accordingly.'

The innocent party does not, of course, have to accept the anticipatory breach as repudiating the contract. As we will see in the following section, the innocent party may elect to affirm the contract and wait for the time for performance. It has even been held that the innocent party can affirm the contract, even if this will lead to a significant increase in his loss (*White and Carter (Councils) Ltd v McGregor* [1962] AC 413). This is an important exception to the mitigation principle, which will be discussed in greater detail in Chapter 17.

If the innocent party accepts the anticipatory breach and terminates the contract, it is immediately entitled to sue for damages. These damages will be limited to the extent of the innocent party's actual loss from the breach. This was recently confirmed by the Court of Appeal in *Golden Strait Corpn v Nippon Yusen Kubishika Kaisha*.

Golden Strait Corpn v Nippon Yusen Kubishika Kaisha ('The Golden Victory') [2006] 1 WLR 533

Facts: In 1988, the defendant agreed to charter a ship from the claimant on a seven-year charterparty. Clause 33 of the charterparty provided that each party had a right to cancel the charter in the event of war between any two of a number of countries including the United States, the United Kingdom and Iraq. On 14 December 2001, the defendant committed an anticipatory breach by purporting to redeliver the vessel to the claimant. The anticipatory breach was accepted by Golden Strait three days later and the charterparty was therefore terminated by the claimant on 17 December 2001, approximately four years before the date on which the charterparty would have expired. In March 2003, the United States and the United Kingdom went to war against Iraq. In September 2003, the claimant brought an action against the defendant claiming damages for the charterer's repudiation. The defendant did not dispute its liability but did dispute the claimant's assessment of damages which was calculated by reference to the remaining four years under the charterparty rather than the 14-month period between the acceptance of the breach and the outbreak of war. Both the arbitrator and Langley J at first instance ruled in favour of the defendant, holding that the war had placed a limit on the damages recoverable.

Held: The Court of Appeal dismissed the claimant's appeal, holding that damages were to be calculated having regard to the fact that the defendant would have cancelled the charter under the war clause.

Lord Mance:
'**23.** . . . As the judge observed, this charter always had inherent in it the uncertainty involved in the War Clause. In many circumstances, this uncertainty could be dis-

regarded – e.g. if damages were being assessed after the end of the original charter period and no relevant war had occurred, or if damages were being assessed during the original charter period on the basis that there was no significant prospect of any such war. In other circumstances, if damages were being assessed during the original charter period, account might have to be taken of the contingency (to use Lord Denning's word) or chance (to use Waller LJ's) that a war might occur, and consideration would then also have to be given to whether or not charterers would in that event probably cancel.

24. Certainty, finality and ease of settlement are all of course important general considerations. But the element of uncertainty, resulting from the War Clause, meant that the owners were never entitled to absolute confidence that the charter would run for its full 7 year period. They never had an asset which they could bank or sell on that basis. There is no reason why the transmutation of their claims to performance of the charter into claims for damages for non-performance of the charter should improve their position in this respect.

25. Further, as Mr Young submitted, the assessment of damages often depends on, or is informed by, subsequent events, and the claim for loss on the spot market from 17th December 2001 until 1st April 2002, the claim based on a substitute rate as from 1st April 2002 and the claim for loss of a profit share – which as I have said would surely depend on looking at actual market rates over the balance of the original charter – are all instances applicable in this case. The additional need to take into account the now known fact of the Second Gulf War is simply another instance.

26. In any event, I consider that this is a situation where any considerations of the type mentioned in the first sentence of paragraph 24 above would have, so far as necessary, to yield to the greater importance of achieving an assessment of damages and compensation which more accurately reflects the actual loss which the owners can, at whatever is the date of assessment, now be seen to have suffered as a result of the charterers' repudiation.'

The claimant in *The Golden Victory* argued that damages ought to be calculated at or very shortly after the date of breach, and that subsequent events (such as the outbreak of the Gulf War triggering the war clause) were irrelevant to the calculation of damages unless those subsequent events could be said to have been inevitable at the date of the breach. The argument was founded on the view that the acceptance of the anticipatory breach 'crystallised' the amount of damages recoverable. Such a rule, it was argued, was essential in order to maintain business certainty. The Court of Appeal rejected this line of argument. While recognising that certainty, finality and ease of settlement were important considerations in the assessment of damages for repudiatory breach, Lord Mance noted that uncertainty was already written into the charterparty. The war clause meant that Golden Strait was never entitled to absolute confidence that the charter would run for its full seven-year period. Furthermore, in his Lordship's view, considerations of certainty needed 'to yield to the greater importance of achieving an assessment of damages and compensation that more accurately reflects the actual loss which the owners can, at whatever is the date of assessment, now be seen to have suffered as a result of the charterers' repudiation'. The Court of Appeal's decision has recently been affirmed by the House of Lords (Lord Bingham and Lord Walker dissenting): [2007] UK HL 12. It is thus clear that subsequent events can be taken into account in the assessment of damages for an anticipatory breach in order to ensure that the claimant is not overcompensated for its loss.

16.3.4 THE RIGHT OF ELECTION

On the occurrence of an anticipatory breach, the innocent party must elect either to terminate the contract, and claim for damages, or to affirm the contract, notwithstanding the breach. The general rule is that the innocent party must communicate its decision to the other party. This is not, however, always necessary.

Vitol SA v Norelf Ltd (The 'Santa Clara') [1996] AC 800

Facts: On 11 February 1991, Vitol agreed to purchase from Norelf a cargo of propane. On 8 March, while the ship was still loading, Vitol sent a telex to Norelf purporting to repudiate the contract. It was subsequently accepted that this communication amounted to an anticipatory breach. Neither party took any further step to perform the contract. On 15 March, following a slump in the market for propane, Norelf resold the cargo at a significantly reduced price. Norelf brought a claim for the difference between the contract price and the price they received for the cargo. The arbitrator found for Norelf, holding that its failure to take any further step to perform the contract constituted sufficient communication of acceptance of Vitol's anticipatory breach. Phillips J upheld the arbitrator's decision. The Court of Appeal, however, reversed the decision, holding that Norelf's failure to perform did not constitute a clear and unequivocal acceptance of the Vitol's anticipatory breach. This was because silence and inaction is as much consistent with affirmation of the contract as it is with the acceptance of a repudiation. Norelf appealed to the House of Lords.

Held: The House of Lords allowed the appeal.

Lord Steyn:
'I would accept as established law the following propositions. (1) Where a party has repudiated a contract the aggrieved party has an election to accept the repudiation or to affirm the contract: *Fercometal SARL v Mediterranean Shipping Co SA* [1989] AC 788. (2) An act of acceptance of a repudiation requires no particular form: a communication does not have to be couched in the language of acceptance. It is sufficient that the communication or conduct clearly and unequivocally conveys to the repudiating party that that aggrieved party is treating the contract as at an end. (3) It is rightly

conceded by counsel for the buyers that the aggrieved party need not personally, or by an agent, notify the repudiating party of his election to treat the contract as at an end. It is sufficient that the fact of the election comes to the repudiating party's attention, e.g. notification by an unauthorised broker or other intermediary may be sufficient: *Wood Factory Pty Ltd v Kiritos Pty Ltd* (1985) 2 NSWLR 105, 146, *per* McHugh JA; *Majik Markets Pty Ltd v S & M Motor Repairs Pty Ltd (No 1)* (1987) 10 NSWLR 49, 54, *per* Young J; *Carter and Harland, Contract Law in Australia*, 3rd edn (1996), pp 689–691, para 1970.

The arbitrator did not put forward any heterodox general theory of the law of repudiation. On the contrary he expressly stated that unless the repudiation was accepted by the sellers and the acceptance was communicated to the buyers the election was of no effect. It is plain that the arbitrator directed himself correctly in accordance with the governing general principle. The criticism of the arbitrator's reasoning centres on his conclusion that "the failure of [the sellers] to take any further step to perform the contract which was apparent to [the buyers] constituted sufficient communication of acceptance". By that statement the arbitrator was simply recording a finding that the buyers knew that the sellers were treating the contract as at an end. That interpretation is reinforced by the paragraph in his award read as a whole. The only question is whether the relevant holding of the arbitrator was wrong in law.

It is now possible to turn directly to the first issue posed, namely whether non-performance of an obligation is ever as a matter of law capable of constituting an act of acceptance. On this aspect I found the judgment of Phillips J entirely convincing. One cannot generalise on the point. It all depends on the particular contractual relationship and the particular circumstances of the case. But, like Phillips J, I am satisfied that a failure to perform may sometimes signify to a repudiating party an election by the aggrieved party to treat the contract as at an end. Postulate the case where an employer at the end of a day tells a contractor that he, the employer, is repudiating the contract and that the contractor need not return the next day. The contractor does not return the next day or at all. It seems to me that the contractor's failure to return may, in the absence of any other explanation, convey a decision to treat the contract as at an end. Another example may be an overseas sale providing for shipment on a named ship in a given month. The seller is obliged to obtain an export licence. The buyer repudiates the contract before loading starts. To the knowledge of the buyer the seller does not apply for an export licence with the result that the transaction cannot proceed. In such circumstances it may well be that an ordinary businessman, circumstanced as the parties were, would conclude that the seller was treating the contract as at an end. Taking the present case as illustrative, it is important to bear in mind that the tender of a bill of lading is the pre-condition to payment of the price. Why should an arbitrator not be able to infer that when, in the days and weeks following loading and the sailing of the vessel, the seller failed to tender a bill of lading to the buyer he clearly conveyed to a trader that he was treating the contract as at an end? . . . Turning to the observation of Nourse LJ [1996] QB 108, 116–117, that a failure to perform a contractual obligation is necessarily and always equivocal I respectfully disagree.

Sometimes in the practical world of businessmen an omission to act may be as pregnant with meaning as a positive declaration. While the analogy of offer and acceptance is imperfect, it is not without significance that while the general principle is that there can be no acceptance of an offer by silence, our law does in exceptional cases recognise acceptance of an offer by silence. Thus in *Rust v Abbey Life Assurance Co Ltd* [1979] 2 Lloyd's Rep 334 the Court of Appeal held that a failure by a proposed insured to reject a proffered insurance policy for seven months justified on its own an inference of acceptance: see also *Treitel, The Law of Contract*, 9th edn (1995), pp 30–32. Similarly, in the different field of repudiation, a failure to perform may sometimes be given a colour by special circumstances and may only be explicable to a reasonable person in the position of the repudiating party as an election to accept the repudiation.

My Lords, I would answer the question posed by this case in the same way as Phillips J. did. In truth the arbitrator inferred an election, and communication of it, from the tenor of the rejection telex and the failure, inter alia, to tender the bill of lading. That was an issue of fact within the exclusive jurisdiction of the arbitrator.

For these reasons I would allow the appeal of the sellers.'

The decision in *Vitol* opens up the possibility of acceptance by silence and inaction. It is always safer, however, for the innocent party to communicate their intention to terminate in clear and unequivocal terms. This avoids the danger of the acceptance not being effective and the innocent party taking action, which itself constitutes a repudiatory breach of obligations under the contract.

The right to terminate the contract may be lost through lapse of time if 'thereby there [i]s prejudice to the defendant' (*Allen v Robles* [1969] 1 WLR 1193, 1196 *per* Fenton Atkinson LJ). The innocent party is, of course, entitled to wait for performance of the contract, but if s/he does so s/he runs the risk of losing his/her right to terminate. This was explained by Rix LJ in *Stocznia Gdanska SA v Latvian Shipping Co* [2002] 2 Lloyd's Rep 436, 452:

'[T]here is of course a middle ground between acceptance of repudiation and affirmation of the contract, and that is the period when the innocent party is making up his mind what to do. If he does nothing for too long, there may come a time when the law will treat him as having affirmed. If he maintains the contract in being for the moment, while reserving his right to treat it as repudiated if his contract partner persists in his repudiation, then he has not yet elected. As long as the contract remains alive, the innocent party runs the risk that a merely anticipatory repudiatory breach, a thing "writ in water" until acceptance can be overtaken by another event which prejudices the innocent party's rights under the contract – such as frustration or even his own breach. He also runs the risk, if that is the right word, that the party in repudiation will resume performance of the contract and thus end any continuing right in the innocent party to elect to accept the former repudiation as terminating the contract.'

The right to terminate may also be lost by virtue of s 11(4) of the Sale of Goods Act 1979, which provides:

'Where a contract of sale is not severable and the buyer has accepted the goods or part of them, the breach of a condition to be fulfilled by the seller can only be treated as a breach of warranty, and not as a ground for rejecting the goods and treating the contract as repudiated, unless there is an express or implied term of the contract to that effect.'

16.3.4.1 Risks of acceptance

When a party treats an action by the other party as repudiatory, that party runs the risk of committing a repudiatory breach themselves if the court determines that the other party's actions did not constitute a repudiation of the contract. We have seen plenty of examples of this. In *Hong Kong Fir Shipping* [1962] 2 QB 26, the defendant was liable for wrongful repudiation because the failure of the plaintiff to provide a seaworthy ship did not constitute a repudiatory breach of the contract. Similarly, in *The Hansa Nord* [1976] QB 44, the pellets provided by the German sellers were not sufficiently damaged to provide a ground for the Dutch buyers repudiation of the contract. Accordingly, the buyers were liable for wrongful repudiation. In *Federal Commerce and Navigation Ltd v Molena Alpha Inc (The 'Nanfri')* [1979] AC 757, the charterers under three six-year charterparties deducted various amounts from the hire they paid to the owners. The owners objected to this and by a telex on 4 October 1977, informed the charterers that the masters of all three ships were being instructed 'to withdraw all direct or implied authority to the charterer or its agents to sign bills of lading'. The House of Lords held that this amounted to a repudiatory breach by the owners, entitling the charterers to terminate the charterparties.

In *Woodar Investment Development Ltd v Wimpey Construction UK Ltd* [1980] 1 WLR 277, the majority of the House of Lords took the view that a party, acting as a result of a mistake made in good faith about his rights under the contract, would not be held to have committed a repudiatory breach. Lord Scarman said:

'[T]he notice of rescission, which the defendants gave, was not, in the circumstances which existed when it was given, one which the defendants had any contractual right to give. But they honestly believed the contract did give them the right. When one examines the totality of their conduct and its impact upon Mr Cornwell it is plain . . . that the defendants, though claiming mistakenly to exercise a power given them by the contract to bring it to an end, were not evincing an intention not to be bound by the contract. On the contrary, they believed they were acting pursuant to the contract . . . It never occurred to Mr Cornwell that the defendants, if held not to have been entitled to give notice of rescission, would refuse to perform the contract. In fact, it would seem that he believed exactly the contrary. Such was the impact upon him of the defendants' conduct.

Lord Wilberforce agreed, declaring:

'[I]t would be a regrettable development of the law of contract to hold that a party who bona fide relies upon an express stipulation in a contract in order to rescind or terminate a contract should, by that fact alone, be treated as having repudiated his contractual obligations if he turns out to be mistaken as to his rights. Repudiation is a drastic conclusion which should only be held to arise in clear cases of a refusal, in a matter going to the root of the contract, to perform contractual obligations.'

The majority of commentators have doubted this aspect of the *Woodar v Wimpey* decision. The preferred view, supported by the bulk of authorities, is that an unjustified failure to meet contractual obligations is itself a repudiatory breach, even if it is based on the mistaken belief that termination is possible following a repudiatory breach by the other party.

16.3.4.2 Risks of affirmation

Once the innocent party has elected to affirm the contract their decision is final and irrevocable. The only exception to this rule is if the party in default continues with their non-performance or commits a fresh repudiatory breach, giving rise to a new right to terminate the contract (*Johnson v Agnew* [1980] AC 367). The irrevocability of the election to affirm means that it carries risks as well. For example, having affirmed the contract, the innocent party is not entitled to rely on the breach to justify their own subsequent failure to fulfil their contractual obligations (*Fercometal Sarl v Mediterranean Shipping Co SA* [1989] AC 788). Similarly, following an affirmation of the contract, the innocent party loses the right to bring an action if, prior to the time for performance, the contract is discharged for frustration.

Avery v Bowden (1855) 5 E & B 714

Facts: The defendant chartered a ship from the plaintiff to load a cargo at Odessa. The contract stated that the cargo was to be loaded within 45 days. Before that time had

---

elapsed, an agent for the defendant informed the master of the ship that the cargo would not be available in time. The master elected to affirm the contract and remained at port in Odessa. Before the 45-day period had elapsed war broke out between England and Russia. This constituted a frustration of the contract because it was no longer legally impossible to load the cargo at an enemy port. The plaintiff brought a claim for damages.

Held: The Court held that the plaintiff could not recover damages for breach of contract. The anticipatory breach had been affirmed by the master of the defendant's ship. The contract was then frustrated, discharging the defendant's future obligations.

Lord Campbell CJ:
'The war having dissolved the contract on the 1st of April, when the defendant was prevented from loading the ship without trading with the Queen's enemies, it was incumbent upon the plaintiff to prove that the cause of action on which he sues had previously accrued to him. But we think that, giving credit to what his witnesses swore, no previous cause of action is proved . . .

It thus appears that the captain of The "Lebanon", who represented the plaintiff down to the 16th day of April, and long after the declaration of war was known at Odessa, continuously insisted on the performance of the charter party by the defendant, and remained at Odessa demanding a cargo. Was there any evidence that, on or before the 1st of April, a cause of action had accrued to the plaintiff for breach of the charter party? We think not. According to our decision in *Hochster v De La Tour* (2 E & B 678), to which we adhere, if the defendant, within the running days and before the declaration of war, had positively informed the captain of The Lebanon that no cargo had been provided or would be provided for him at Odessa, and that there was no use in his remaining there any longer, the captain might have treated this as a breach and renunciation of the contract; and thereupon, sailing away from Odessa, he might have loaded a cargo at a friendly port from another person; whereupon the plaintiff would have had a right to maintain an action on the charter party to recover damages equal to the loss he had sustained from the breach of contract on the part of the defendant. The language used by the defendant's agent before the declaration of war can hardly be considered as amounting to a renunciation of the contract: but, if it had been much stronger, we conceive that it could not be considered as constituting a cause of action after the captain still continued to insist upon having a cargo in fulfilment of the charter party.

Judgment for the defendant.'

16.3.5 TERMINATION UNDER THE PRINCIPLES OF EUROPEAN CONTRACT LAW

Termination for breach is dealt with in Chapter 9, Section 3 of The Principles of European Contract Law:

Article 9.301: Right to Terminate the Contract

(1) A party may terminate the contract if the other party's non-performance is fundamental.
(2) In the case of delay the aggrieved party may also terminate the contract under Article 8:106 (3).

Article 9.302: Contract to be Performed in Parts
If the contract is to be performed in separate parts and in relation to a part to which a counter-performance can be apportioned, there is a fundamental non-performance, the aggrieved party may exercise its right to terminate under this Section in relation to the part concerned. It may terminate the contract as a whole only if the non-performance is fundamental to the contract as a whole.

. . . .

Article 9.304: Anticipatory Non-Performance
Where prior to the time for performance by a party it is clear that there will be a fundamental non-performance by it the other party may terminate the contract.

Article 9.305: Effects of Termination in General

(1) Termination of the contract releases both parties from their obligation to effect and to receive future performance, but, subject to Articles 9:306 to 9:308, does not affect the rights and liabilities that have accrued up to the time of termination.
(2) Termination does not affect any provision of the contract for the settlement of disputes or any other provision which is to operate even after termination.

The effects of termination contained in Art 9.305 are consistent with the position adopted under English law. Article 9.301 states that there is a right to terminate where 'the other party's non-performance is fundamental'. The words 'non-performance' and 'fundamental' are defined elsewhere in the Principles:

Article 1.301: Meaning of Terms

. . .

(4) 'non-performance' denotes any failure to perform an obligation under the contract, whether or not excused, and includes delayed performance, defective performance and failure to co-operate in order to give full effect to the contract.

Article 8.103: Fundamental Non-Performance
A non-performance of an obligation is fundamental to the contract if:

(a) strict compliance with the obligation is of the essence of the contract; or
(b) the non-performance substantially deprives the aggrieved party of what it was entitled to expect under the contract, unless the other party did not foresee and could not reasonably have foreseen that result; or
(c) the non-performance is intentional and gives the aggrieved party reason to believe that it cannot rely on the other party's future performance.

The inclusion of non-cooperation in Art 1.301 goes beyond the English law concept of 'breach', which requires a failure to perform a specific contractual obligation.

Two of the three categories of fundamental non-performance are likely to be familiar to English lawyers. Category (a) roughly corresponds with the English concept of a 'condition' of the contract. Category (b) is much closer to the concept of a serious breach of an intermediate term. The main difference is that the Principles include a test of reasonable foreseeability, which is only relevant in English law to the question of the recoverability of damages (see Chapter 17). Lando and Beale's commentary (Lando, O and Beale, H, *Principles of European Contract Law Parts I and II*, 2000, p 365, The Hague: Kluwer Law International) provides the following example of the operation of the reasonable forseeability test:

> 'A agrees to install central heating in B's house with a temperature control system which will enable the temperature to be maintained at a constant temperature of 20 degrees centigrade. Unknown to A, one room is required to develop and preserve certain rare species of plant which are extremely sensitive to changes in temperature and which have taken several years' intensive work to breed. As a result of a defect in one of the heating pipes in the room the temperature falls by two degrees centigrade and all the plants die, rendering abortive years of work. A's non-performance is not fundamental, as it could not reasonably have foreseen that such grave consequences would ensue from a slight temperature fluctuation in the room of a private house.'

Category (c) has no equivalent in English law, which traditionally views the motives of the parties as irrelevant. The Principles adopt a much more relational approach to the issue (see Chapter 1), emphasising the need for the parties to maintain each other's confidence in their willingness and ability to perform. Lando and Beale's Commentary (at pp 365–6) explains the category as follows: 'Even where the contractual term broken is minor and the consequences of non-performance do not substantially deprive the aggrieved party of the benefit of the bargain it may treat the non-performance as fundamental if it was intentional and gave it reason to believe that it could not rely on the other party's future performance'.

Article 9.302 deals with contracts that are to be performed in parts. It is more specific than English law in that it allows the aggrieved party to reject performance of a divisible part of the contract, rather than simply claiming damages for defective performance. Article 9.304 deals with anticipatory breach. The notes to the provision state that it is based on the common law, in particular the English decision in *Hochster v De La Tour* 2 E & B 678. It is therefore to be expected that the Principles are consistent with English law in relation to anticipatory breach.

The Principles contain some further provisions on the subject of non-performance:

Article 8:104: Cure by Non-Performing Party

A party whose tender of performance is not accepted by the other party because it does not conform to the contract may make a new and conforming tender where the time for performance has not yet arrived or the delay would not be such as to constitute a fundamental non-performance.

Article 8:105: Assurance of Performance

(1) A party who reasonably believes that there will be a fundamental non-performance by the other party may demand adequate assurance of due performance and meanwhile may withhold performance of its own obligations so long as such reasonable belief continues.

(2) Where this assurance is not provided within a reasonable time, the party demanding it may terminate the contract if it still reasonably believes that there will be a fundamental non-performance by the other party and gives notice of termination without delay.

Article 8:106: Notice Fixing Additional Period for Performance

(1) In any case of non-performance the aggrieved party may by notice to the other party allow an additional period of time for performance.

(2) During the additional period the aggrieved party may withhold performance of its own reciprocal obligations and may claim damages, but it may not resort to any other remedy. If it receives notice from the other party that the latter will not perform within that period, or if upon expiry of that period due performance has not been made, the aggrieved party may resort to any of the remedies that may be available under chapter 9.

(3) If in a case of delay in performance which is not fundamental the aggrieved party has given a notice fixing an additional period of time of reasonable length, it may terminate the contract at the end of the period of notice. The aggrieved party may in its notice provide that if the other party does not perform within the period fixed by the notice the contract shall terminate automatically. If the period stated is too short, the aggrieved party may terminate, or, as the case may be, the contract shall terminate automatically, only after a reasonable period from the time of the notice.

Article 8.104 corresponds with the current position under English law where a tender of performance is permissible up until the time for performance. The right to demand an assurance of performance under Art 8.105 currently does not exist in English law. It provides a helpful remedy, however, to a party who believes that the other party is unable or unwilling to perform, but does not have sufficient evidence to take the risk of electing to terminate the contract. Article 8.106 incorporates into the Principles a similar rule to that stated by the Court of Appeal in *Behzadi v Shaftesbury Hotels Ltd* [1992] Ch 1, allowing for the aggrieved party to give notice to the party in default that time is to become 'of the essence'.

16.4 ADDITIONAL READING

Bojczuk, W, 'When is a condition not a condition?' [1987] JBL 353.

Corbin, A, 'Conditions in the law of contract' (1919) 28 Yale LJ 739.

Girvin, SD, 'Time charter overlap: determining legitimacy and the operation of repudiatory breach of contract' [1995] JBL 200.

Liu, Q, 'Accepted anticipatory breach: duty of mitigation and damages assessment' [2006] LMCLQ 2006 17.

Opeskin, B, 'Damages for breach of contract terminated under express terms' (1990) 106 LQR 293.

Smith, JC, 'Anticipatory breach of contract', in Lomnicka, E and Morse, CJG (eds), *Contemporary Issues in Commercial Law; Essays in Honour of A G Guest*, 1994, London: Sweet & Maxwell.

Stannard, JE, 'In the contractual last chance saloon: notices making time of the essence' (2004) 120 LQR 137.

Treitel, GH, 'Affirmation after repudiatory breach' (1998) 114 LQR 22.

Treitel, GH, 'Assessment of damages for wrongful repudiation' (2007) 123 LQR 9.

CHAPTER 17

REMEDIES

<table>
<tr><td colspan="3" align="center">CONTENTS</td></tr>
</table>

▌17.1 INTRODUCTION

In this chapter we shall be considering remedies for breach of contract. In the past decade there has been considerable debate about the meaning of the word 'remedy'. Professor Birks famously argued that the word 'remedy' should be jettisoned from our legal dictionary because of its inherent 'instability' and its tendency to 'impede' the development of a classification of responses to private law actions (see, particularly, Birks, P, 'Rights, Wrongs and Remedies' (2000) 20 OJLS 1, 3–4). This drastic course of action is probably not necessary. Rafal Zakrewski has provided us with a stable core meaning of remedy in his work *Remedies Reclassified*, 2005, Oxford: OUP. He suggests that we should 'use the term "remedy" only in the sense of the rights arising from certain court orders or pronouncements'. That definition will be adopted here.

We will be considering the two main remedies for breach of contract in this chapter – the award of damages and the order of specific relief. Following a breach of contract, the courts aim to award a remedy that puts the claimant 'in a situation as beneficial to him as if the agreement were specifically performed' (*Harnett v Yielding* (1805) 2 Sch & Lef 549, 553). Usually an award of compensatory damages will be sufficient to achieve this purpose because the claimant can use the damages to purchase substitute performance from an alternative source. In some situations, however, substitute performance will be unavailable or will be insufficient to protect the claimant's interest in performance of the contract. In such cases the courts will turn to alternative remedies, such as gain-based damages or specific relief. We will see that the principle underlying the availability of each of these remedies is the protection of the parties' bargained-for interest in performance.

We will begin by considering the remedy of damages, and will then examine specific relief.

17.2 DAMAGES

Damages will be available as of right, following every breach of contract. Several legal commentators have suggested that the sole purpose of damages is compensation for loss. For example, eminent legal commentator, Dr Harvey McGregor, begins the 16th edition of his seminal treaty on the law of damages with this statement: 'Damages *are* pecuniary compensation' (McGregor, H (ed), *McGregor on Damages*, 16th edn, 1997, p 1, London: Sweet & Maxwell). But as a matter of empirical fact this claim is unsustainable as Dr McGregor acknowledges in the 17th edition of his work (McGregor, H (ed), *McGregor on Damages*, 17th edn, 2003, p 1, London: Sweet & Maxwell). While it is true that damages are usually compensatory in English law, they are not *always* compensatory. Nominal damages, compensatory damages, gain-based damages, and exemplary (or punitive) damages are also available. In his recent work on damages, Dr James Edelman gave the following definition of damages: ' "damages" means nothing more specific than a monetary award given for a wrong' (J Edelman, *Gain-Based Damages*, 2002, p 5, Oxford: Hart). This is correct and in this chapter we will examine three different measures of contract damages: compensatory, gain-based and punitive damages. We will begin by considering compensatory damages, since these are the most commonly awarded form of damages.

17.2.1 COMPENSATORY DAMAGES: THE DIFFERENT MEASURES

The purpose of compensatory damages is to compensate the claimant for the loss he has suffered as a result of the breach of contract. In a two-part article in the Yale Law Journal entitled 'The Reliance Interest in Contract Damages', Fuller and Perdue famously expounded the three different measures of compensatory damages, what they labelled the reliance, expectation and restitution interests. The article was significant both for the terminology it used and for its elevation of the reliance interest above the expectation interest.

Fuller, L, & Purdue Jr, W, 'The reliance interest in contract damages' (1936) 46 YLJ 52, 52–62

The proposition that legal rules can be understood only with reference to the purposes they serve would today scarcely be regarded as an exciting truth. The notion that law exists as a means to an end has been commonplace for at least half a century. There is, however, no justification for assuming, because this attitude has now achieved respectability, and even triteness, that it enjoys a pervasive application in practice. Certainly there are even today few legal treatises of which it may be said that the author has throughout clearly defined the purposes which his definitions and distinctions serve . . .

In no field is this more true than in that of damages. In the assessment of damages the law tends to be conceived, not as a purposive ordering of human affairs, but as a kind of juristic mensuration. The language of the decisions sounds in terms not of command but of discovery.

. . . For example, one frequently finds the 'normal' rule of contract damages (which awards to the promisee the value of the expectancy, 'the lost profit') treated as a mere corollary of a more fundamental principle, that the purpose of granting damages is to make 'compensation' for injury. Yet in this case we 'compensate' the plaintiff by giving him something he never had. This seems on the face of things a queer kind of 'compensation'. We can, to be sure, make the term 'compensation' seem appropriate by saying that the defendant's breach 'deprived' the plaintiff of the expectancy. But this is in essence only a metaphorical statement of the effect of the legal rule. In actuality the loss which the plaintiff suffers (deprivation of the expectancy) is not a datum of nature but the reflection of a normative order. It appears as a 'loss' only by reference to an unstated *ought*. Consequently, when the law gauges damages by the value of the promised performance it is not merely measuring a quantum, but is seeking an end, however vaguely conceived this end may be.

It is for this reason that it is impossible to separate the law of contract damages from the larger body of motives and policies which constitutes the general law of contracts. It is, unfortunately for the simplicity of our subject, impossible to assume that the purposive and policy-directed element of contract law has been exhausted in the rules which define contract and breach. If this were possible the law of contract damages would indeed be simple, and we would have but one measure of recovery for all contracts. Of course this is not the case . . .

THE PURPOSES PURSUED IN AWARDING CONTRACT DAMAGES

It is convenient to distinguish three principal purposes which may be pursued in awarding contract damages. These purposes, and the situations in which they become appropriate, may be stated briefly as follows:

First, the plaintiff has in reliance on the promise of the defendant conferred some value on the defendant. The defendant fails to perform his promise. The court may force the defendant to disgorge the value he received from the plaintiff. The object here may be termed the prevention of gain by the defaulting promisor at the expense of the promisee; more briefly, the prevention of unjust enrichment. The interest protected may be called the *restitution interest* . . .

Secondly, the plaintiff has in reliance on the promise of the defendant changed his position. For example, the buyer under a contract for the sale of land has incurred expense in the investigation of the seller's title, or has neglected the opportunity to enter other contracts. We may award damages to the plaintiff for the purpose of undoing the harm which his reliance on the defendant's promise has caused him. Our object is to put him in as good a position as he was in before the promise was made. The interest protected in this case may be called the *reliance interest*.

Thirdly, without insisting on reliance by the promisee or enrichment of the promisor, we may seek to give the promisee the value of the expectancy which the promise created. We may in a suit for specific performance actually compel the defendant to render the promised performance to the plaintiff, or, in a suit for damages, we may make the defendant pay the money value of this performance. Here our object is to put the plaintiff in as good a position as he would have occupied had the defendant performed his promise. The interest protected in this case we may call the *expectation interest*.

It will be observed that what we have called the restitution interest unites two elements: (1) reliance by the promisee, (2) a resultant gain to the promisor. It may for some purposes be necessary to separate these elements. In some cases a defaulting promisor may after his breach be left with an unjust gain which was not taken from the promisee (a third party furnished the consideration), or which was not the result of reliance by the promisee (the promisor violated a promise not to appropriate the promisee's goods). Even in those cases where the promisor's gain results from the promisee's reliance it may happen that damages will be assessed somewhat differently, depending on whether we take the promisor's gain or the promisee's loss as the standard of measurement. Generally, however, in the cases we shall be discussing, gain by the promisor will be accompanied by a corresponding and, so far as its legal measurement is concerned, identical loss to the promisee, so that for our purposes the most workable classification is one which presupposes in the restitution interest a correlation of promisor's gain and promisee's loss. If, as we shall assume, the gain involved in the restitution interest results from and is identical with the plaintiff's loss through reliance, then the restitution interest is merely a special case of the reliance interest; all of the cases coming under the restitution interest will be covered by the reliance interest, and the reliance interest will be broader than the restitution interest only to the extent that it includes cases where the plaintiff has relied on the defendant's promise without enriching the defendant . . .

It is obvious that the three 'interests' we have distinguished do not present equal claims to judicial intervention. It may be assumed that ordinary standards of justice would regard the need for judicial intervention as decreasing in the order in which we have listed the three interests. The "restitution interest", involving a combination of unjust impoverishment with unjust gain, presents the strongest case for relief. If, following Aristotle, we regard the purpose of justice as the maintenance of an equilibrium of goods among members of society, the restitution interest presents twice as strong a claim to judicial intervention as the reliance interest, since if A not only causes B to lose one unit but appropriates that unit to himself, the resulting discrepancy between A and B is not one unit but two.

On the other hand, the promisee who has actually relied on the promise, even though he may not thereby have enriched the promisor, certainly presents a more pressing case for relief than the promisee who merely demands satisfaction for his disappointment in not getting what was promised him. In passing from compensation for change of position to compensation for loss of expectancy we pass, to use Aristotle's terms again, from the realm of corrective justice to that of distributive justice. The law no longer seeks merely to heal a disturbed status quo, but to bring into being a new situation. It ceases to act defensively or restoratively, and assumes a more active role. With the transition, the justification for legal relief loses its self-evident quality. It is as a matter of fact no easy thing to explain why the normal rule of contract recovery should be that which measures damages by the value of the promised performance. Since this 'normal rule' throws its shadow across our whole subject it will be necessary to examine the possible reasons for its existence. It may be said parenthetically that the discussion which follows, though directed primarily to the normal measure of recovery where damages are sought, also has relevance to the more general question, why should a promise which has not been relied on ever be enforced at all, whether by a decree of specific performance or by an award of damages? . . .

WHY SHOULD THE LAW EVER PROTECT THE EXPECTATION INTEREST?

Perhaps the most obvious answer to this question is one which we may label 'psychological'. This answer would run something as follows: The breach of a promise arouses in the promisee a sense of injury. This feeling is not confined to cases where the promisee has relied on the promise. Whether or not he has actually changed his position because of the promise, the promisee has formed an attitude of expectancy such that a breach of the promise causes him to feel that he has been 'deprived' of something which was 'his'. Since this sentiment is a relatively uniform one, the law has no occasion to go back on it. It accepts it as a datum and builds its rule about it.

The difficulty with this explanation is that the law does in fact go back on the sense of injury which the breach of a promise engenders. No legal system attempts to invest with juristic sanction all promises. Some rule or combination of rules effects a sifting out for enforcement of those promises deemed important enough to society to justify the law's concern with them. Whatever the principles which control this sifting out process may be, they are not convertible into terms of the degree of resentment which the breach of a particular kind of promise arouses. Therefore, though it may be assumed that the impulse to assuage disappointment is one shared by those who make and influence the law, this impulse can hardly be regarded as the key which solves the whole problem of the protection accorded by the law to the expectation interest.

A second possible explanation for the rule protecting the expectancy may be found in the much-discussed 'will theory' of contract law. This theory views the contracting parties as exercising, so to speak, a legislative power, so that the legal enforcement of a contract becomes merely an implementing by the state of a kind of private law already established by the parties . . . It is not necessary to discuss here the contribution which the will theory is capable of making to a philosophy of contract law. Certainly some borrowings from the theory are discernible in most attempts to rationalize the bases of contract liability. It is enough to note here that while the will theory undoubtedly has some bearing on the problem of contract damages, it cannot be regarded as dictating in all cases a recovery of the expectancy. If a contract represents a kind of private law, it is a law which usually says nothing at all about what shall be done when it is violated. A contract is in this respect like an imperfect statute which provides no penalties, and which leaves it to the courts to find a way to effectuate its purposes. There would, therefore, be no necessary contradiction between the will theory and a rule which limited damages to the reliance interest. Under such a rule the penalty for violating the norm established by the contract would simply consist in being compelled to compensate the other party for detrimental reliance . . .

A third and more promising solution of our difficulty lies in an economic or institutional approach. The essence of a credit economy lies in the fact that it tends to eliminate the distinction between present and future (promised) goods. Expectations of future values become, for purposes of trade, present values. In a society in which credit has become a significant and pervasive institution, it is inevitable that the expectancy created by an enforceable promise should be regarded as a kind of property, and breach of the promise as an injury to that property. In such a society the breach of a promise works an 'actual' diminution of the promisee's assets . . .

The most obvious objection which can be made to the economic or institutional explanation is that it involves a *petitio principii*. A promise has present value, why? Because the law enforces it. 'The expectancy', regarded as a present value, is not the cause of legal intervention but the consequence of it. This objection may be reinforced by a reference to legal history. Promises were enforced long before there was anything corresponding to a general system of 'credit', and recovery was from the beginning measured by the value of the promised performance, the 'agreed price'. It may therefore be argued that the 'credit system' when it finally emerged was itself in large part built on the foundations of a juristic development which preceded it.

The view just suggested asserts the primacy of law over economics; it sees law not as the creature but as the creator of social institutions. The shift of emphasis thus implied suggests the possibility of a fourth explanation for the law's protection of the unrelied-on expectancy, which we may call *juristic*. This explanation would seek a justification for the normal rule of recovery in some policy consciously pursued by courts and other lawmakers. It would assume that courts have protected the expectation interest because they have considered it wise to do so, not through a blind acquiescence in habitual ways of thinking and feeling, or through an equally blind deference to the individual will. Approaching the problem from this point of view, we are forced to find not a mere explanation for the rule in the form of some sentimental, volitional, or institutional datum, but articulate reasons for its existence.

What reasons can be advanced? In the first place, even if our interest were confined to protecting promisees against an out-of-pocket loss, it would still be possible to justify the rule granting the value of the expectancy, both as a cure for, and as a prophylaxis against, losses of this sort.

It is a cure for these losses in the sense that it offers the measure of recovery most likely to reimburse the plaintiff for the (often very numerous and very difficult to prove) individual acts and forbearances which make up his total reliance on the contract. If we take into account 'gains prevented' by reliance, that is, losses involved in foregoing the opportunity to enter other contracts, the notion that the rule protecting the expectancy is adopted as the most effective means of compensating for detrimental reliance seems not at all far-fetched. Physicians with an extensive practice often charge their patients the full office call fee for broken appointments. Such a charge looks on the face of things like a claim to the promised fee; it seems to be based on the 'expectation interest'. Yet the physician making the charge will quite justifiably regard it as compensation for the loss of the opportunity to gain a similar fee from a different patient. This foregoing of other opportunities is involved to some extent in entering most contracts, and the impossibility of subjecting this type of reliance to any kind of measurement may justify a categorical rule granting the value of the expectancy as the most effective way of compensating for such losses.

The rule that the plaintiff must after the defendant's breach take steps to mitigate damages tends to corroborate the suspicion that there lies hidden behind the protection of the expectancy a concern to compensate the plaintiff for the loss of the opportunity to enter other contracts. Where after the defendant's breach the opportunity remains open to the plaintiff to sell his services or goods elsewhere, or to fill his needs from another source, he is bound to embrace that opportunity. Viewed in this way the rule of 'avoidable harms' is a qualification on the protection accorded the expectancy, since it means that the plaintiff, in those cases where it is applied, is protected only to the extent that he has in reliance on the contract foregone other equally advantageous opportunities for accomplishing the same end.

But, as we have suggested, the rule measuring damages by the expectancy may also be regarded as a prophylaxis against the losses resulting from detrimental reliance. Whatever tends to discourage breach of contract tends to prevent the losses occasioned through reliance. Since the expectation interest furnishes a more easily administered measure of recovery than the reliance interest, it will in practice offer a more effective sanction against contract breach. It is therefore possible to view the rule measuring damages by the expectancy in a quasi-criminal aspect, its purpose being not so much to compensate the promisee as to penalize breach of promise by the promisor. The rule enforcing the unrelied-on promise finds the same justification, on this theory, as an ordinance which fines a man for driving through a stop-light when no other vehicle is in sight.

In seeking justification for the rule granting the value of the expectancy there is no need, however, to restrict ourselves by the assumption, hitherto made, that the rule can only be intended to cure or prevent the losses caused by reliance. A justification can be developed from a less negative point of view. It may be said that there is not only a policy in favor of preventing and undoing the harms resulting from reliance, but also a policy in favor of promoting and facilitating reliance on business agreements. As in the case of the stop-light ordinance we are interested not only in preventing collisions but in speeding traffic. Agreements can accomplish little, either for their makers or for society, unless they are made the basis for action. When business agreements are not only made but are also acted on, the division of labor is facilitated, goods find their way to the places where they are most needed, and economic activity is generally stimulated. These advantages would be threatened by any rule which limited legal protection to the reliance interest. Such a rule would in practice tend to discourage reliance. The difficulties in proving reliance and subjecting it to pecuniary measurement are such that the business man knowing, or sensing, that these obstacles stood in the way of judicial relief would hesitate to rely on a promise in any case where the legal sanction was of significance to him. To encourage reliance we must therefore dispense with its proof. For this reason it has been found wise to make recovery on a promise independent of reliance, both in the sense that in some cases the promise is enforced though not relied on (as in the bilateral business agreement) and in the sense that recovery is not limited to the detriment incurred in reliance.

The juristic explanation in its final form is then twofold. It rests the protection accorded the expectancy on (1) the need for curing and preventing the harms occasioned by reliance, and (2) the need for facilitating reliance on business agreements.

Fuller and Perdue challenged the traditional assumption that expectation damages are the primary measure of relief. The authors adopt a corrective justice approach to contract damages and argue that the need for judicial intervention is much stronger where the promisee has changed his position in reliance on the promise. Thus the restitution and reliance interests are much more worthy of judicial protection than the expectation interest.

Ultimately Fuller and Perdue stop short of arguing for the abolition of expectation damages. Their real thesis is that the theoretical justification for such damages is not rooted in a commitment to protecting the expectations created by a binding promise. Rather, expectation damages serve two functions that both relate to the reliance interest: (1) they provide a cure for reliance losses where the promisee has foregone the opportunity to enter into other contracts; (2) they act as a prophylaxis (a deterrent) against reliance losses.

Fuller and Perdue's thesis has been developed by other authors, most notably Professor Atiyah, who has used it to challenge the court's willingness to enforce purely executory contracts.

Atiyah, P, 'Contracts, promises and the law of obligations' in Atiyah, P, *Essays in Contract*, 1986, Oxford: Clarendon, pp 39–40

Virtually all discussion of the source of contractual and promissory obligation, in law and in morality, has failed to draw the all important distinction between promises and contracts which rest purely on intention, and promises and contracts which depend partly on action. Surely, nobody can doubt that morally speaking promises are more strongly binding where payment has already been received, or where there is a clear and significant act in reliance which would worsen the position of the promisee if the promise were not performed . . . [I]t may be suggested that promises themselves are frequently of an evidentiary character. The purpose of a promise, far from being, as is so often assumed, to create some wholly independent source of an obligation, is frequently to bolster up an already existing duty. Promises help to clarify, to quantify, to give precision to moral obligations, many of which already exist or would arise anyhow from the performance of acts which are contemplated or invited by the promise. The promise which is given without any independent reason for it is a peculiarity, just as the wholly executory contract is a legal peculiarity. Is it pure coincidence that the phrase, a 'gratuitous promise', means both a promise without payment and a promise without reason? Could it then be that the refusal of English law to recognise the binding force of executory gratuitous promises is not the peculiarity, the idiosyncrasy it has so long been thought to be? Might it not be that the real oddity lies in the belief that a bare promise creates a moral obligation and should create a legal obligation, without any inquiry into the reason for which the promise was given, or the effect that the promise has had?

These arguments, of course, require much greater development than they can be given here; but enough has been said to show that, if they stand up to further examination, they should suffice to dethrone the executory contract from the central place which it occupies in contract theory. The consequences of this would be to require some drastic redrawing of the lines of the conceptual structure of contractual and promissory obligation. In the first place, the distinction between contract and restitution would surely come crashing to the ground . . .

This passage forms part of a larger thesis, which challenges the traditional distinction between voluntarily assumed obligations (in the law of contract) and legally imposed obligations (in the law of tort). Professor Atiyah suggests that the law of obligations could be recast around the notions of benefit and reliance. This thesis has failed to win the support of the academy or the judiciary and it has been subjected to sustained criticism by Professor Burrows in 'Contract, tort and restitution – a satisfactory distinction or not' (1983) 99 LQR 217, and Professor Birks in 'Restitution and the freedom of contract' [1983] CLP 141. More recently, Professor Friedmann has convincingly challenged Fuller and Purdue's analysis of the primacy of the reliance interest.

Friedmann, D, 'The performance interest in contract damages' (1995) 111 LQR 628, 628–638, 646–651, 654

The Reliance Interest article by Fuller and Perdue, published in 1936, lay half dormant for rather a long time. It surged into great prominence many years later, probably in the sixties, and has since enjoyed a dazzling academic success, being described as the most significant article on contract law and the most famous contract article ever written. The article introduced new, albeit inappropriate, terminology which has become the standard terminology in American legal parlance and is now rapidly spreading over the Atlantic. By contrast, its effect on substantive law has been remarkably meagre. The basic ideology, advocated in the article with regard to the performance interest (in the article's terms, 'expectation interest'), has been rejected. Indeed, the protection granted to this interest, since the publication of the article, has been greatly expanded. The irony is that while rejecting the article's basic approach, courts and scholars increasingly employ the terminology which it introduced . . .

The purpose of this paper is to point out the inappropriateness of the terminology used, the difficulties in the reliance approach and thus to offer an explanation for the fact that despite its immense reputation, The Reliance Interest failed to have a significant effect on substantive contract law.

THE PERFORMANCE INTEREST AND ITS PROTECTION

The essence of contract is performance. Contracts are made in order to be performed. This is usually the one and only ground for their formation. Ordinarily, a person enters into a contract because he is interested in getting that which the other party has to offer and because he places a higher value on the other party's performance than on the cost and trouble he will incur to obtain it. This interest in getting the promised performance (hereafter the 'performance interest') is the only pure contractual interest. The performance interest is protected by specific remedies, which aim at granting the innocent party the very performance promised to him, and by substitutional remedies. The specific remedies are:

(1) Specific performance and injunction . . .
(2) The recovery of a debt . . .

The substitutional remedies are:

(1) Compensating damages or 'loss of the bargain' damages. It is also possible to term them 'performance damages', since they are intended to put the plaintiff in as good a position as that in which he would have been, had the contract been performed. These damages, which constitute the most important substitutional remedy, are currently described by the unfortunate term 'expectation damages' introduced by Fuller and Perdue.
(2) Recovery of the 'substitute', which relates to the situation in which the promisor can no longer perform but has obtained a substitute for the promised performance.

(3)   Recovery in restitution of profits made by the other party through the breach. This
      remedy partly overlaps the right to the substitute ((2) above), but the extent of its
      availability has been much debated . . .

The performance interest is also protected against third parties by means of the tort of
inducement of breach of contract and also by equitable and restitutionary remedies.

THE RANKING OF INTERESTS AND THE NEW TERMINOLOGY

As already indicated, there is but one genuine contractual interest. Needless to say
that if it is observed, there is no room for any of the above mentioned remedies. Only if
it is infringed do they come into play. Fuller and Perdue, however, identified three
interests: the expectation interest, the reliance interest and the restitution interest.
These interests were ranked in accordance with the strength of their claim for judicial
intervention. Restitution arrived first and reliance second. The expectation interest
ended at the bottom of the list.

The expectation interest is simply an inappropriate term describing the performance
interest. The other two have acquired the title 'interest' probably under the influence of
German law. Whatever is the nature of reliance and restitution, they are certainly not
contractual interests. Thus, the interest of a person who made a payment in order to
get a house, a car or even a pizza is to get the house, the car or the pizza. Such a
person will be greatly surprised to learn that upon contracting to purchase a house, he
acquired an interest in getting his payment back (restitution interest). In all probability
he is likely to protest that this is not what he wanted. Had he preferred the money to the
house he would not have made the contract in the first place. He would need a lot of
coaching in an American course on contracts to learn that his interest in getting his
payment back ranks higher in the hierarchy than his interest in getting the house.

Indeed, the use of the term 'interest' to describe restitution or reliance is somewhat
problematic. If we understand 'interest' to reflect the purpose or the reason for entering
the contract, then performance is the only genuine contractual interest . . .

The greatest terminological innovation of Fuller and Perdue and the most inappropriate one, was the invention of 'expectation' or 'expectancy'. This term . . . was used
to describe the normal measure of contractual damages, namely, the measure based
upon the right to get the promised performance . . . In fact one can hardly conceive of a
term that is less appropriate than 'expectancy' or 'expectation'. 'Expectancy' is often
used to describe a prospect or a probability of receiving a benefit in the future, when
this possibility is not supported by a legal right. The term usually relates to a contingency which falls short of a legal right and is to be distinguished from a 'vested right'
as, e.g. in the case of an expectant heir . . . Indeed, the term 'expectation' may be more
appropriate in this context, in which the expectation is not based upon a legal right,
than in the contractual context, in which the plaintiff has a legal right to receive that
which was promised to him.

THE MARGINALISATION OF THE PERFORMANCE INTEREST

The next step in Fuller and Perdue's derogation of the right to performance comes
in the process of the ranking of interests, in which the performance interest (now

already diminished to mere 'expectancy') is outclassed by both restitution and reliance. That being accomplished, there comes a question which casts doubts upon the very legitimacy of the right to performance. The subtitle on page 57 of the article reads: 'Why Should the Law Ever Protect the Expectation Interest?' . . .

The . . . only justification which Fuller and Perdue find for what they term 'expectation' damages lies in the 'difficulties in proving reliance and subjecting it to pecuniary measurement. . . . To encourage reliance we must therefore dispense with its proof.' Performance damages, thus, receive an additional blow. They are not justified in their own right. They are merely parasitic and exist because of the difficulties in measuring the 'real' interest, namely reliance.

The argument is most unconvincing. The proof of reliance losses is by no means more difficult than proof of performance (or 'expectation') losses, even if they are to include 'loss of opportunity'. However, in order to justify the adoption of the performance measurement, Fuller and Perdue must elevate this difficulty to the level of 'impossibility' . . . In fact, reliance damages are sometimes awarded on the ground that it is impossible to appraise the performance, or 'loss of the bargain', damages. This, of course, is the very opposite of the argument made by Fuller and Perdue.

The difficulties with Fuller and Perdue's reasoning is, however, more fundamental. As already indicated, they accept the 'will theory' and the premise that a contractual promise is legally binding. They assume, however, that the question of the remedy is completely divorced from the nature of the right . . . The reasoning is, however, most unconvincing. It is, of course, legitimate to examine the grounds for recognising the binding effect of contracts . . . However, Fuller and Perdue avoided this question. They accepted the validity of the contractual obligation but erroneously assumed that it entails few consequences as to the remedy.

It is, of course, true that the mere recognition of a specific right does not provide answers to all issues regarding the remedies available for its protection. . . . It is, however, an unwarranted jump to conclude that the right tells us nothing about the remedy and that rights and remedies raise totally unrelated issues.

It is submitted that the very recognition of a legal right entails some consequences regarding the remedy, one of which relates to the initial point of inquiry. This initial point relates to the value of legal right, at least where such value can be ascertained. The right of recovery may be qualified or subject to exceptions. The initial point is, however, clear.

Thus, suppose that P acquired for $300 shares which are now worth $1,000. The shares have been misappropriated by D. In Fuller and Perdue's terminology the $300 represents 'reliance loss' whereas the $1,000 represents 'expectation damages'. After all, P never had the $1,000. He had shares which he could expect to sell. This expectation, if realised, would yield him $1,000. However, the translation of the situation into Fuller and Perdue's terminology merely confuses the issue. The historical expenditure or the reliance interest (in the above example, $300) is irrelevant, except where it serves as evidence of existing value. Recovery is based upon the present value of the shares. The recognition of P's right of property suffices to justify such recovery.

It is clearly legitimate to question the justification of private property. However, once private ownership is recognised, it follows as a matter of course that the owner whose property has been misappropriated will either recover it *in specie* or will get damages reflecting its value. In order to justify this result, there is no need to resort to the 'lost opportunity' explanation (the owner could have bought other shares that might have similarly appreciated in value) or to some other fiction.

Let us now revert to the contract situation. Suppose that in consideration of $300 D undertook to transfer to P, within 6 months, certain shares. After 5 months, when the price of the shares reaches $1,000, D reneges. If we assume that the contract was valid so that it vested in P the right to the promised performance, it follows that P would be entitled either to specific performance (the value of which is $1,000) or to the substitutionary remedy of damages, which will be based upon the value of the promised performance, namely $1,000.

This argument, as well as the analogy to property, is strengthened by the possibility of assignment. In the property example P could sell the shares for $1,000. In the contract example he could have assigned his contractual right to receive the shares for a similar amount. In both instances, the measure of recovery ought, therefore, to be similar. To claim that the contract was binding, i.e. that P was entitled to D's performance, and yet that recovery can be confined to P's expenditure ($300), is a contradiction in terms.

Fuller and Perdue feel, however, that the obvious result needs explanation. The superfluous explanation is based upon the lost opportunity theory, which forms part of the reliance loss. Because P entered into contract no. 1 with D, he gave up the possibility of another potential contract (contract no. 2) with a third party (T) which would have yielded him similar gains. The argument is doubly flawed. First, if P's gains from the actual contract (no. 1) with D are not recoverable in their own right as part of his performance (or 'expectation') interest, why do these very gains become recoverable when attributed to another potential contract (contract no. 2)? Is it because they have changed denomination and appear under the guise of reliance? Second, the whole argument is based on circular reasoning. If it is assumed that the entitlement to recover performance (expectation) damages in contract no. 1 derives solely from the lost opportunity (potential contract no. 2), we have to examine the value of this opportunity. This is obviously dependent upon the nature of the entitlement and the ensuing measure of damages in potential contract no. 2. If there is no justification for performance damages (other than lost opportunity) then the value of contract no. 2 was not $1,000, but a mere $300, unless we assume that the recovery will again be based on lost opportunity (potential contract no. 3) and so *ad infinitum*.

THE IMPACT OF FULLER AND PERDUE – TERMINOLOGY AND SUBSTANCE

(a) Terminological impact

As already pointed out, the most significant effect of Fuller and Perdue lies in the introduction of a new terminology. No student is likely to complete an American course on contracts without reciting 'expectation interest' and 'reliance interest'. In recent

years the new terminology has spread to England and to other Commonwealth jurisdictions although the traditional terms such as 'compensatory damages' or 'loss of the
bargain' are still in use . . .

(b) Substantive impact
It has been suggested that 'The Reliance Interest has influenced American law less
than we might expect, considering its prominence in casebooks and law reviews'. The
view has also been expressed that 'the reliance interest plays virtually no role in the
calculation of damages in contract cases.' I think that these views are correct . . .

Fuller and Perdue did not expressly advocate the curtailment of the protection
granted to the performance interest. However, much of the article consists of an
attempt to question its justification, to describe it as an 'expectancy' and to suggest
that its legitimacy depends on reliance. They also hinted at the possibility of limiting
recovery to reliance losses in certain cases in which a binding contract has been
concluded, notably in situations that are not within the credit system. Professor Atiyah
went a step further. He was 'troubled and uncertain about the extent to which executory contracts should be enforced, and the extent to which the expectation damages
measure is appropriate . . .'. He also considered that 'it would not be surprising if future
developments tend to show a still further whittling down of expectation damages'.

Modern law hardly reflects any traces of this approach . . . [T]he main thrust of
modern law has been in the very opposite direction. Notwithstanding The Reliance
Interest there are no signs of weakening of the performance interest. On the contrary,
one of the major trends in modern contract law is the strengthening of the protection
accorded to the performance interest. Traditional limitations upon the availability of
specific performance and upon the recovery of performance damages have either
been removed or severely curtailed . . .

The law of damages shows similar signs of expanding the protection granted to the
performance interest. The fundamental principle under which, so far as money can do
it, the injured party should be placed in the same situation as if the contract had been
performed, is constantly applied. Furthermore, legal rules that have in the past limited
the prospects of obtaining full performance damages seem to lose at least part of their
effect. Thus, the traditional English rule regarding the date for the assessment of damages has been that of the date of the breach. The rule is disadvantageous to the
plaintiff in periods of rising costs and inflation, notably if he lacks the means to make a
substitute transaction. The traditional rule has now been attenuated. It is no longer
absolute 'and the court has power to fix such other date as may be appropriate in the
circumstances' . . .

Another development which reflects the strengthening of the performance interest
relates to the measure of recovery where the defendant renders a defective performance or a performance which is not in line with the contract requirements. The cost
of curing the defect is usually higher than the difference in market value between
the performance as rendered and the value of the performance had it conformed to the
terms of the contract. In this type of situation recovery was often confined to the

difference in value, if the cost of cure was disproportionate to the difference in value. However, the present tendency is to award the plaintiff the cost of repair even where there is a large disparity between this cost and the difference in value, provided that it is reasonable for the plaintiff to insist on reinstatement. Furthermore, circumstances are conceivable in which the costs of repair are unreasonable while the difference in value is small or even nil. Under the traditional approach, in such a case, the plaintiff might have been left without a remedy. The recent decision of the House of Lords in *Ruxley Electronics Ltd* indicates that these two measures of recovery are not exhaustive, and that damages might be awarded by reference to the fact that the plaintiff's performance interest has been frustrated by the defendant's breach. The court may, thus, be required to appraise an element that has no market price in order to provide an adequate remedy. Needless to say, this development is predicated on the approach that *pacta sunt servanda* and that the plaintiff's performance interest should be respected.

The expansion of the protection accorded to the performance interest is also reflected in the rules relating to non-economic losses. Traditionally, recovery of damages for such losses, resulting from breach of contract, has not been allowed. But this rule is becoming the subject of ever-increasing exceptions . . .

The move towards expanding the protection granted to the performance interest has on occasion been checked but the general trend is clear, and it is obviously not in line with the Reliance Interest article . . .

CONCLUSION

There is a great discrepancy between The Reliance Interest's intellectual appeal and its effect on substantive law. The article made a deep impact on academic thinking, upon the language and discourse of contracts and led to the adoption of new terminology, which in the case of 'expectation' was an unhappy development. Its effect on substantive law is at best secondary. The attack upon the performance interest goes against the grain. This interest constitutes the very core of contract law. Its ample protection is likely to be maintained and possibly expanded as long as the essence of contract law as we know it remains.

As Friedman rightly notes, the terminology used by Fuller and Perdue has had a much greater impact on the development of the law than the substantive content of their thesis. The courts now regularly reason in terms of the 'expectation', 'reliance' and 'restitution' interests of a contract, but far from relegating the 'expectation' (or 'performance') interest to only peripheral significance, the major trend in modern contract law has been 'the strengthening of the protection afforded to the performance interest'. We will see this as we examine the different remedial responses to a breach of contract. First, we will consider the three different measures of compensatory damages, and notice how the protection of the performance interest of the contract has been of utmost importance to the courts in recent decisions.

17.2.1.1 The expectation measure

Damages measured on the expectation basis aim to put the claimant in the position s/he would have been in had the contract been performed. Parke B classically expounded this measure in *Robinson v Harman* (1848) 1 Ex 850, 855:

'The rule of the common law is, that where a party sustains a loss by reason of a breach of contract, he is, so far as money can do it, to be placed in the same situation, with respect to damages, as if the contract had been performed.'

This statement expresses a clear commitment to protection of the performance interest of a contract. The claimant is entitled to receive the benefits that s/he would have received had the contract been successfully completed. In addition, the claimant will also be entitled to recover any consequential losses flowing from the breach.

To illustrate, consider the following example. A engages B to provide widgets for use in the manufacture of A's cans of beer. A tells B that he needs the widgets by 1 June, because A has a contract with C, a beer wholesaler, for supply of the cans by 10 June. If B, in breach of contract, fails to supply the widgets by 1 June, A will probably be able to claim the lost profit of the contract with C. If B had performed the contract properly, A would have made the profit, and therefore it should be recoverable. Furthermore, if C brought a claim against A for breach of the contract to supply the beer, then A might be able to recover the damages he is required to pay C, as consequential losses flowing from the breach of contract by B.

Calculation of the expectation interest is simply a matter of looking at where the claimant would have ended up if the contract had been performed according to its terms. Problems do arise, however, when the profit that would have been made from the completed contract is uncertain.

Chaplin v Hicks [1911] 2 KB 786

Facts: The plaintiff, an actress, entered a competition organised by the defendant, a well-known actor and theatre manager. The prize was a three-year term of employment at the defendant's theatre. The plaintiff was successful at the first stage of the competition, being selected by readers of a newspaper as one of fifty out of 6,000 entrants to proceed to the second stage of the competition. The second stage involved an interview with the defendant, who would then select the twelve who would receive the promised engagements. The plaintiff was deprived of the opportunity to attend the interview due to a breach of contract by the defendant. She brought an action against the defendant, claiming damages for the loss of a chance of winning the competition. The jury found in favour of the plaintiff and assessed the damages at £100. The defendant appealed.

Held: The Court of Appeal dismissed the appeal and upheld the award at first instance.

Vaughan Williams LJ:

'I am of opinion that this appeal should be dismissed . . . It was said that the plaintiff's chance of winning a prize turned on such a number of contingencies that it was impossible for any one, even after arriving at the conclusion that the plaintiff had lost her opportunity by the breach, to say that there was any assessable value of that loss. It is said that in a case which involves so many contingencies it is impossible to say what was the plaintiff's pecuniary loss. I am unable to agree with that contention. I agree that the presence of all the contingencies upon which the gaining of the prize might depend makes the calculation not only difficult but incapable of being carried out with certainty or precision. The proposition is that, whenever the contingencies on which the result depends are numerous and difficult to deal with, it is impossible to recover any damages for the loss of the chance or opportunity of winning the prize . . . I do not agree with the contention that, if certainty is impossible of attainment, the damages for a breach of contract are unassessable. I agree, however, that damages might be so unassessable that the doctrine of averages would be inapplicable because the necessary figures for working upon would not be forthcoming; there are several decisions, which I need not deal with, to that effect. I only wish to deny with emphasis that, because precision cannot be arrived at, the jury has no function in the assessment of damages . . .

[F]rom first to last there were, as there are now, many cases in which it was difficult to apply definite rules. In the case of a breach of a contract for the delivery of goods the damages are usually supplied by the fact of there being a market in which similar goods can be immediately bought, and the difference between the contract price and the price given for the substituted goods in the open market is the measure of damages; that rule has been always recognized. Sometimes, however, there is no market for the particular class of goods; but no one has ever suggested that, because there is no market, there are no damages. In such a case the jury must do the best they can, and it may be that the amount of their verdict will really be a matter of guesswork. But the fact that damages cannot be assessed with certainty does not relieve the wrongdoer of the necessity of paying damages for his breach of contract. I do not wish to lay down any such rule as that a judge can in every case leave it to the jury to assess damages for a breach of contract. There are cases, no doubt, where the loss is so dependent on the mere unrestricted volition of another that it is impossible to say that there is any assessable loss resulting from the breach. In the present case there is no such difficulty . . . The jury came to the conclusion that the taking away from the plaintiff of the opportunity of competition, as one of a body of fifty, when twelve prizes were to be distributed, deprived the plaintiff of something which had a monetary value. I think that they were right and that this appeal fails.'

The case shows that the courts are committed to overcoming assessment difficulties wherever possible. It is interesting to note that the award of damages may have had the effect of putting Ms Chaplin in a better position than she would have been in had the contract not been broken. This is because it is quite possible that she would not have been selected, even if she had been able to attend the audition. The award may be explained on the ground that it contained a punitive element. This is certainly hinted at in Vaughan Williams LJ's statement: 'the fact that damages cannot be assessed with certainty does not relieve the wrong-doer of the necessity of paying damages for his breach of contract'. In other words the damages were awarded to mark the court's disapproval of the defendant's conduct.

Damages measured on the expectation measure aim to put the claimant in a position as beneficial to him or her as if the contract had been performed. In recent times there has been some discussion about how to measure the claimant's expectation interest. There are two principal methods of calculation:

1. **Diminution of value**. This is the difference in value between the performance for which the claimant contracted and the performance which s/he received. For example, if the breach of contract led to the loss of a contract or the construction of a building of lesser value than the one contracted for, the damage award would be assessed at the value of the lost contract or the difference in value between the house contracted for and the house received. This measure only protects the claimant's economic interest in performance. It fulfils his or her financial expectations but does not protect his or her interest in performance itself.

2. **Cost of cure**. This measure provides the claimant with the money s/he needs in order to purchase substitute performance from an alternative source. For example, if the defendant negligently destroyed the claimant's lorry or failed to construct a greenhouse as agreed to in a contract, the claimant will normally be entitled to the cost of a replacement lorry or of an equivalent building contract. This measure enables the claimant to obtain performance itself rather than the economic value of performance. In a real sense it is a form of substitute specific relief (see Smith, S, 'Substitute Specific Relief', in Rickett, C, *Justifying Remedies in the Law of Obligations*, 2008, Oxford: Hart).

Usually the difference in value between these two measures is insignificant. However, in some cases the difference can be very substantial indeed, and the parties may devote a considerable amount of legal argument as to which method of calculation ought to be used.

Tito v Waddell (No. 2) [1977] Ch 106

Facts: The case concerned phosphate mining operations on Ocean Island in the South Pacific. The defendant, British Phosphate Commissioners, had promised to replant the island with 'coconuts and other food-bearing trees' once it had completed its mining operations. The company failed to do this and the islanders claimed the cost of cure calculated at 73,140 Australian dollars per acre.

Held: Megarry VC refused to award damages measured on the 'cost of cure' basis because, by the time of the action, all the islanders had resettled 1,500 miles away on an island called Rabi. His Lordship awarded damages measured on the 'diminution in value' basis at a mere A$75 per acre.

Megarry VC:

'[I]t is clear that in some cases of a contract to do work to the plaintiff's land the measure of damages for breach is the reduction in value of the plaintiff's interest in the land, and in other cases it is the cost of doing the work. But which? I have been unable to find any clear statement of principle in the cases or books put before me, or in other sources that I consulted.

In the absence of any clear authority on the matter before me, I think I must consider it as a matter of principle. I do this in relation to the breach of a contract to do work on the land of another, whether to build, repair, replant or anything else: and I put it very broadly. First, it is fundamental to all questions of damages that they are to compensate the plaintiff for his loss or injury by putting him as nearly as possible in the same position as he would have been in had he not suffered the wrong . . . Second, if the plaintiff has suffered monetary loss, as by a reduction in the value of his property by reason of the wrong, that is plainly a loss that he is entitled to be recouped . . . Third, if the plaintiff can establish that his loss consists of or includes the cost of doing work which in breach of contract the defendant has failed to do, then he can recover as damages a sum equivalent to that cost. It is for the plaintiff to establish this: the essential question is what his loss is.

In the present case, the loss caused to the plaintiffs by the British Phosphate Commissioners' failure to replant is the diminution in the value of their land resulting from that failure, or, if it is established that the land would be replanted, the cost of replanting . . . Have the plaintiffs shown that the cost of replanting represents the loss to them caused by the failure to perform the replanting obligation? Only one answer to that question seems possible, and that is No. The plaintiffs own small scattered plots of land; there is nothing to establish that the owners of neighbouring plots of land, who are not parties to these proceedings, would procure the replanting of their plots rather than keep any damages for themselves or other purposes; the Banabans are now well established in Rabi, over 1,500 miles away; and there they have an island over 10 times the size and unaffected by mining, as contrasted with the much smaller Ocean Island with some five-sixths of it mined.

Tito v Waddell demonstrates that the courts' commitment to protecting the plaintiff's performance interest is not absolute. It was crucial to Megarry VC that the plaintiffs had no intention of using the damages to effect the cure, that is, to replant

Ocean Island. It is somewhat surprising that the claimant's intention was so crucial to the decision, given that the courts normally refuse to take into account the use to which a claimant puts an award of damages. Nevertheless, this approach and the general reluctance to awarding 'cost of cure' damages where it would be out of all proportion to the benefit thereby obtained was followed by the House of Lords in *Ruxley Electronics & Construction Ltd v Forsyth*.

Ruxley Electronics & Construction Ltd v Forsyth [1996] AC 344

Facts: Forsyth agreed to build a swimming pool in Ruxley's garden. The contract specified that the pool would have a diving area seven feet, six inches deep. When constructed, the diving area was only six feet deep. This was still a safe depth for diving and one which did not affect the value of the pool. Forsyth was not happy, however, and he brought an action for breach of contract claiming the cost of having the pool demolished and rebuilt (the cost of cure), a sum of £21,560.

At first instance the judge rejected the claim for 'cost of cure' damages on the ground that it was an unreasonable claim in the circumstances, but awarded Forsyth 'loss of amenity damages' of £2,500. This award was reversed by the Court of Appeal which held that damages should be awarded at the amount required to place Forsyth in the same position as he would have been in had the contract been performed, which in the circumstances was the cost of rebuilding the pool. Ruxley appealed to the House of Lords.

Held: The House of Lords allowed the appeal holding that the cost of cure of rebuilding the pool was out of all proportion to any benefit that would be obtained. Ruxley did not challenge the first instance award of £2,500 in loss of amenity damages, and so this award was reinstated.

Lord Jauncey:
'Damages are designed to compensate for an established loss and not to provide a gratuitous benefit to the aggrieved party from which it follows that the reasonableness of an award of damages is to be linked directly to the loss sustained. If it is unreasonable in a particular case to award the cost of reinstatement it must be because the loss sustained does not extend to the need to reinstate . . .

I take the example suggested during argument by my noble and learned friend, Lord Bridge of Harwich. A man contracts for the building of a house and specifies that one of the lower courses of brick should be blue. The builder uses yellow brick instead. In all other respects the house conforms to the contractual specification. To replace the yellow bricks with blue would involve extensive demolition and reconstruction at a very large cost. It would clearly be unreasonable to award to the owner the cost of reconstructing because his loss was not the necessary cost of reconstruction of his house, which was entirely adequate for its design purpose, but merely the lack of aesthetic pleasure which he might have derived from the sight of blue bricks. Thus in the present appeal the respondent has acquired a perfectly serviceable swimming pool, albeit one lacking the specified depth. His loss is thus not the lack of a useable pool with consequent need to construct a new one. Indeed were he to receive the cost of building a new one and retain the existing one he would have recovered not compensation for loss but a very substantial gratuitous benefit, something which damages are not intended to provide.

My Lords, the trial judge found that it would be unreasonable to incur the cost of demolishing the existing pool and building a new and deeper one. In so doing he implicitly recognised that the respondent's loss did not extend to the cost of reinstatement. He was, in my view, entirely justified in reaching that conclusion. It therefore follows that the appeal must be allowed.

It only remains to mention two further matters. The appellant argued that the cost of reinstatement should only be allowed as damages where there was shown to be an intention on the part of the aggrieved party to carry out the work. Having already decided that the appeal should be allowed I no longer find it necessary to reach a conclusion on this matter. However I should emphasise that in the normal case the court has no concern with the use to which a plaintiff puts an award of damages for a loss which has been established. Thus irreparable damage to an article as a result of a breach of contract will entitle the owner to recover the value of the article irrespective of whether he intends to replace it with a similar one or to spend the money on something else. Intention, or lack of it, to reinstate can have relevance only to reasonableness and hence to the extent of the loss which has been sustained. Once that loss has been established intention as to the subsequent use of the damages ceases to be relevant.

The second matter relates to the award of £2,500 for loss of amenity made by the trial judge. The respondent argued that he erred in law in making such award. However as the appellant did not challenge it, I find it unnecessary to express any opinion on the matter.'

Lord Mustill:
'I add some observations of my own on the award by the trial judge of damages in a sum intermediate between, on the one hand, the full cost of reinstatement, and on the other the amount by which the malperformance has diminished the market value of the property on which the work was done: in this particular case, nil. This is a question of everyday practical importance to householders who have engaged contractors to carry out small building works, and then find (as often happens) that performance has fallen short of what was promised. I think it proper to enter on the question here, although there is no appeal against the award, because the possibility of such a recovery in a suitable case sheds light on the employer's claim that reinstatement is the only proper measure of damage.

The proposition that these two measures of damage represent the only permissible bases of recovery lie at the heart of the employer's case. From this he reasons that there is a presumption in favour of the cost of restitution, since this is the only way in which he can be given what the contractor had promised to provide. Finally, he contends that there is nothing in the facts of the present case to rebut this presumption.

The attraction of this argument is its avoidance of the conclusion that, in a case such as the present, unless the employer can prove that the defects have depreciated the market value of the property the householder can recover nothing at all. This conclusion would be unacceptable to the average householder, and it is unacceptable to me. It is a common feature of small building works performed on residential property that the cost of the work is not fully reflected by an increase in the market value of the house, and that comparatively minor deviations from specification or sound workmanship may have no direct financial effect at all. Yet the householder must surely be entitled to say that he chose to obtain from the builder a promise to produce a particular result because he wanted to make his house more comfortable, more convenient and more conformable to his own particular tastes; not because he had in mind that the work might increase the amount which he would receive if, contrary to expectation, he thought it expedient in the future to exchange his home for cash. To say that in order to escape unscathed the builder has only to show that to the mind of the average onlooker, or the average potential buyer, the results which he has produced seem just as good as those which he had promised would make a part of the promise illusory, and unbalance the bargain. In the valuable analysis contained in *Radford v De Froberville* [1977] 1 WLR 1252, Oliver J emphasised, at p 1270, that it was for the plaintiff to judge what performance he required in exchange for the price. The court should honour that choice. *Pacta sunt servanda*. If the appellant's argument leads to the conclusion that in all cases like the present the employer is entitled to no more than nominal damages, the average householder would say that there must be something wrong with the law.

In my opinion there would indeed be something wrong if, on the hypothesis that cost of reinstatement and the depreciation in value were the only available measures of recovery, the rejection of the former necessarily entailed the adoption of the latter; and the court might be driven to opt for the cost of reinstatement, absurd as the consequence might often be, simply to escape from the conclusion that the promisor can please himself whether or not to comply with the wishes of the promise which, as embodied in the contract, formed part of the consideration for the price. Having taken on the job the contractor is morally as well as legally obliged to give the employer what he stipulated to obtain, and this obligation ought not to be devalued. In my opinion however the hypothesis is not correct. There are not two alternative measures of damage, at opposite poles, but only one; namely, the loss truly suffered by the promisee. In some cases the loss cannot be fairly measured except by reference to the full cost of repairing the deficiency in performance. In others, and in particular those where the contract is designed to fulfil a purely commercial purpose, the loss will very often consist only of the monetary detriment brought about by the breach of contract. But these remedies are not exhaustive, for the law must cater for those occasions where the value of the promise to the promisee exceeds the financial enhancement of his position which full performance will secure. This excess, often referred to in the literature as the 'consumer surplus' (see for example the valuable discussion by Harris, Ogus and Philips (1979) 95 LQR 581) is usually incapable of precise valuation in terms of money, exactly because it represents a personal, subjective and non-monetary gain. Nevertheless where it exists the law should recognise it and compensate the promisee if the misperformance takes it away. The lurid bathroom tiles, or the grotesque folly instanced in argument by my noble and learned friend, Lord Keith of Kinkel, may be so discordant with general taste that in purely economic terms the builder may be said to do the employer a favour by failing to install them. But this is too narrow and material-istic a view of the transaction. Neither the contractor nor the court has the right to substitute for the employer's individual expectation of performance a criterion derived from what ordinary people would regard as sensible. As my Lords have shown, the test of reasonableness plays a central part in determining the basis of recovery, and will indeed be decisive in a case such as the present when the cost of reinstatement would be wholly disproportionate to the non-monetary loss suffered by the employer. But it would be equally unreasonable to deny all recovery for such a loss. The amount may be small, and since it cannot be quantified directly there may be room for difference of opinion about what it should be. But in several fields the judges are well accustomed to putting figures to intangibles, and I see no reason why the imprecision of the exercise should be a barrier, if that is what fairness demands.

My Lords, once this is recognised the puzzling and paradoxical feature of this case, that it seems to involve a contest of absurdities, simply falls away. There is no need to remedy the injustice of awarding too little, by unjustly awarding far too much. The judgment of the trial judge acknowledges that the employer has suffered a true loss and expresses it in terms of money. Since there is no longer any issue about the amount of the award, as distinct from the principle, I would simply restore his judgment by allowing the appeal.'

Lord Lloyd:

'*Reasonableness*
The starting point is *Robinson v Harman* 1 Exch 850, where Parke B said:

> "The rule of the common law is, that where a party sustains a loss by reason of a breach of contract, he is, so far as money can do it, to be placed in the same situation, with respect to damages, as if the contract had been performed."

This does not mean that in every case of breach of contract the plaintiff can obtain the monetary equivalent of specific performance. It is first necessary to ascertain the loss the plaintiff has in fact suffered by reason of the breach . . . In building cases, the pecuniary loss is almost always measured in one of two ways; either the difference in value of the work done or the cost of reinstatement. Where the cost of reinstatement is less than the difference in value, the measure of damages will invariably be the cost of reinstatement. By claiming the difference in value the plaintiff would be failing to take reasonable steps to mitigate his loss. In many ordinary cases, too, where reinstatement presents no special problem, the cost of reinstatement will be the obvious measure of damages, even where there is little or no difference in value, or where the difference in value is hard to assess. This is why it is often said that the cost of reinstatement is the ordinary measure of damages for defective performance under a building contract.

But it is not the only measure of damages . . . If the court takes the view that it would be unreasonable for the plaintiff to insist on reinstatement, as where, for example, the expense of the work involved would be out of all proportion to the benefit to be obtained, then the plaintiff will be confined to the difference in value. If the judge had assessed the difference in value in the present case at, say, £5,000, I have little doubt that the Court of Appeal would have taken that figure rather than £21,560. The difficulty arises because the judge has, in the light of the expert evidence, assessed the difference in value as nil. But that cannot make reasonable what he has found to be unreasonable.

So I cannot accept that reasonableness is confined to the doctrine of mitigation. It has a wider impact . . . How then does [counsel for the defendant] seek to support the majority judgment? It can only be, I think, by attacking the judge's finding of fact that the cost of rebuilding the pool would have been out of all proportion to the benefit to be obtained. [Counsel for the defendant] argues that this was not an ordinary commercial contract but a contract for a personal preference . . . I am far from saying that personal preferences are irrelevant when choosing the appropriate measure of damages ('predilections' was the word used by Ackner LJ in *GW Atkins Ltd v Scott* 7 Const LJ 215, 221, adopting the language of Oliver J in *Radford v De Froberville* [1977] 1 WLR 1262). But such cases should not be elevated into a separate category with special rules. If, to take an example mentioned in the course of argument, a landowner wishes to build a folly in his grounds, it is no answer to a claim for defective workmanship that many people might regard the presence of a well built folly as reducing the value of the estate. The eccentric landowner is entitled to his whim, provided the cost of reinstatement is not unreasonable. But the difficulty of that line of argument in the present case is that the judge, as is clear from his judgment, took Mr. Forsyth's personal preferences and predilections into account. Nevertheless, he found as a fact that the cost of reinstatement was unreasonable in the circumstances. The Court of Appeal ought not to have disturbed that finding . . .

Intention

I fully accept that the courts are not normally concerned with what a plaintiff does with his damages. But it does not follow that intention is not relevant to reasonableness, at least in those cases where the plaintiff does not intend to reinstate. Suppose in the present case Mr Forsyth had died, and the action had been continued by his executors. Is it to be supposed that they would be able to recover the cost of reinstatement, even though they intended to put the property on the market without delay?

There is, as Staughton LJ observed, a good deal of authority to the effect that intention may be relevant to a claim for damages based on cost of reinstatement. The clearest decisions on the point are those of Sir Robert Megarry V-C in *Tito v Waddell (No 2)* [1977] Ch 106, and Oliver J in *Radford v De Froberville* [1977] 1 WLR 1262 . . . In the present case the judge found as a fact that Mr Forsyth's stated intention of rebuilding the pool would not persist for long after the litigation had been concluded. In these circumstances it would be "mere pretence" to say that the cost of rebuilding the pool is the loss which he has in fact suffered.

Loss of amenity

I turn last to the head of damages under which the judge awarded £2,500 . . .

Addis v Gramophone Co Ltd [1909] AC 488 established the general rule that in claims for breach of contract, the plaintiff cannot recover damages for his injured feelings. But the rule, like most rules, is subject to exceptions. One of the well established exceptions is when the object of the contract is to afford pleasure, as, for example, where the plaintiff has booked a holiday with a tour operator. If the tour operator is in breach of contract by failing to provide what the contract called for, the plaintiff may recover damages for his disappointment: see *Jarvis v Swan Tours Ltd* [1973] QB 233 and *Jackson v Horizon Holidays Ltd* [1975] 1 WLR 1468.

This was, as I understand it, the principle which Judge Diamond applied in the present case. He took the view that the contract was one 'for the provision of a pleasurable amenity'. In the event, Mr. Forsyth's pleasure was not so great as it would have been if the swimming pool had been 7 feet 6 inches deep. This was a view which the judge was entitled to take. If it involves a further inroad on the rule in *Addis v Gramophone Co Ltd* [1909] AC 488, then so be it. But I prefer to regard it as a logical application or adaptation of the existing exception to a new situation. I should, however, add this note of warning. Mr Forsyth was, I think, lucky to have obtained so large an award for his disappointed expectations. But as there was no criticism from any quarter as to the quantum of the award as distinct from the underlying principle, it would not be right for your Lordships to interfere with the judge's figure. That leaves one last question for consideration. I have expressed agreement with the judge's approach to damages based on loss of amenity on the facts of the present case. But in most cases such an approach would not be available. What is then to be the position where, in the case of a new house, the building does not conform in some minor respect to the contract, as, for example, where there is a difference in level between two rooms, necessitating a step. Suppose there is no measurable difference in value of the complete house, and the cost of reinstatement would be prohibitive. Is there any reason why the court should not award by way of damages for breach of contract some modest sum, not based on difference in value, but solely to compensate the buyer for his disappointed expectations? Is the law of damages so inflexible, as I asked earlier, that it cannot find some middle ground in such a case? I do not give a final answer to that question in the present case. But it may be that it would have afforded an alternative ground for justifying the judge's award of damages and if the judge had wanted a precedent, he could have found it in Sir David Cairns's judgment in *GW Atkins Ltd v Scott* 7 Const LJ 215, where, it will be remembered, the Court of Appeal upheld the judge's award of £250 for defective tiling. Sir David Cairns said, at p 221:

"There are many circumstances where a judge has nothing but his common sense to guide him in fixing the quantum of damages, for instance, for pain and suffering, for loss of pleasurable activities or for inconvenience of one kind or another."

If it is accepted that the award of £2,500 should be upheld, then that at once disposes of [counsel for the defendant's] argument that Mr Forsyth is entitled to the cost of reinstatement, because he must be entitled to something. But even if he were entitled to nothing for loss of amenity, or for difference in value, it would not follow as [counsel for the defendant] argued that he was entitled to the cost of reinstatement. There is no escape from the judge's finding of fact that to insist on the cost of reinstatement in the circumstances of the present case was unreasonable.

I would therefore allow the appeal and restore the judgment of Judge Diamond.'

In *Ruxley*, their Lordships were faced with a dilemma. Should they award damages on the diminution of value basis, which would be nominal on the ground that Mr Forsyth's economic expectations had not been affected? Or should they award cost of cure damages to protect Mr Forsyth's expectation of performance, even though this would result in a windfall for Mr Forsyth because, despite his protestations to the contrary, he was unlikely to use the money to rebuild the pool.

It had been held that the standard measure of damages for breach of a building contract was the cost of repairing the defect or completing the building work (*Mertens v Home Freeholds* [1921] 2 KB 526). However, this measure was subject to the reasonableness requirement – 'cost of cure' damages would not be awarded if the cost of cure was out of all proportion to the benefit conferred on the claimant by performance of the contract (*Watts v Morrow* [1991] 4 All ER 937). This limitation did not, however, normally apply to the situation where the 'cure' relates to the provision of something that the defendant expressly promised to provide in the contract (see *Radford v De Froberville* [1977] 1 WLR 1262).

On the facts of *Ruxley*, a unanimous House of Lords held that it would be unreasonable to award the cost of rebuilding the swimming pool. Two reasons were given for this. First, the cost of rebuilding the pool would have been out of all proportion to the benefit to be obtained by Mr Forsyth. He had a perfectly safe and useable swimming pool. As Lord Jauncey put it, 'were he to receive the cost of building a new one and retain the existing one he would have recovered not compensation for loss but a very substantial gratuitous benefit, something which damages are not intended to provide'. Their Lordships were not only concerned with the risk of over-compensating Mr Forsyth, but also with the danger of causing unnecessary hardship to Ruxley.

Second, the House of Lords found that cost of cure damages would be unreasonable because Forsyth had no real intention of effecting the cure (see also the more recent case of *Birse Construction Ltd v Eastern Telegraph Company Ltd* [2004] EWHC 2512 (TCC); [2004] All ER (D) 92 (Nov)). Both Lords Jauncey and Lloyd noted that the courts are usually unconcerned about how the plaintiff uses an award of damages once loss has been established. Intention was relevant, however, to the issue of whether a cost of cure award would be reasonable. A claimant's intention to cure a particular breach is crucial evidence of the extent of his non-pecuniary loss flowing from the breach. The fact that Mr Forsyth's stated intention of rebuilding the pool was unlikely to persist for long after the litigation meant that 'it would be "mere pretence" to say that the cost of rebuilding the pool is the loss which he has in fact suffered' (per Lord Lloyd).

The decision to refuse 'cost of cure' damages appears to be sensible on the facts of the case, but it may establish a dangerous precedent for the future. The decision opens the door for unscrupulous builders to render performance substantially different from that which they had agreed to supply, and then to deny liability on the ground that the performance they have provided is of the same financial value as the performance stipulated in the contract. The innocent party is effectively left without a remedy, even though he has not received the performance he requested. A comparison can be made with sale of goods contracts, where the claimant may still have a remedy, even though the goods are 'fit for purpose', if the goods fail to correspond to their contractual description (s 13 of the Sale of Goods Act 1979). It now seems that a person who contracts for the construction of a building is in a weaker position than a purchaser of goods. Ultimately, we must wait for further decisions to see just how far down this line the courts will go.

The House of Lords rejected the 'cost of cure' measure for overcompensating Forsyth, but also rejected the 'diminution of value' measure for undercompensating him. Their Lordships preferred to reinstate the award made by the judge at first instance of £2,500 in 'loss of amenity' damages. But what is the precise nature of this award? There are two possibilities. First, it could be based on the concept of the 'consumer surplus' as suggested by Lord Mustill. Such an award compensates the claimant for loss of his non-pecuniary interest in performance, that is, something he had contracted for, which went beyond the market value of performance. Second, the award could be an example of damages awarded to compensate Forsyth for Ruxley's failure to provide him with the pleasure that he had contracted to receive (see *Jarvis v Swan Tours Ltd* [1973] QB 233), as suggested by Lord Lloyd. Subsequent cases (such as *Alfred McAlpine Construction Ltd v Panatown Ltd* [2001] 1 AC 518, 588 per Lord Millett; *Farley v Skinner* [2002] 2 AC 732, 767 per Lord Scott) have suggested that the award was of the former type. This will be discussed in greater detail below. It is clear that the award of £2,500 was at the upper end of the permissible scale, but due to the fact that Ruxley did not contest the award, the House of Lords were happy to uphold it.

The last issue for us to consider is whether the damages awarded in *Ruxley* provided adequate protection to Mr Forsyth's performance interest. Opinion is divided on the issue. It is clear that the award provided better protection than diminution of value damages would have. However, the award failed to provide Forsyth with the means of obtaining substitute performance. It was insufficient to pay for another builder to come to his house and construct a pool 7 feet, 6 inches deep. Did this mean that the court was unwilling to protect Forsyth's interest in performance? It is submitted that the answer to this question should be no. Cost of cure damages are a form of monetised specific performance. Their aim is to allow the claimant to cure the breach. If the claimant has no intention of doing this, the rationale for the award disappears. This is why cost of cure damages were refused on the facts of *Ruxley*. The award would not have accurately represented the value of the bargained-for performance.

The extent to which the law provides protection to the claimant's interest in performance is also very much at issue in cases concerning loss of performance to a third party. To illustrate, if I contract with you to retile the roof of my mother's house and you fail to perform, do I have a claim against you for damages even though your breach had caused me no financial loss? If the answer to that question is no, does that mean that you can wilfully refuse to perform in the full knowledge that you will not be required to pay more than nominal damages. These issues arose for consideration in *Alfred McAlpine Constructions Ltd v Panatown Ltd*. The issues at stake in the case were very complex and the law report very long. The claim for damages was made on two grounds. For reasons of simplicity, we will only consider one ground here (the other ground is considered in Chapter 5): what the House of Lords described as the 'broad ground'.

Alfred McAlpine Constructions Ltd v Panatown Ltd [2001] 1 AC 518

Facts: McAlpine entered into a contract with Panatown to design and build an office block and multi-storey car park on a site in Cambridge. Panatown alleged that the building was seriously defective and might even have to be demolished, thus raising the possibility of a £40 million claim arising from breach of a £10 million contract. However, at no stage had Panatown owned the construction site, which at all times belonged to their associated company Unex Investment Properties Ltd ('UIPL'). The reason for this arrangement was that it (legitimately) avoided the payment of VAT. On the day the construction contract was signed, McAlpine entered into a separate Duty of Care Deed (the 'DCD') with UIPL under which McAlpine accepted limited liability for negligence.

Panatown claimed damages for breach of contract on two grounds. The 'broad ground' was a claim for the loss that they, as promisee, had sustained as a result of McAlpine's failure to perform the contract. In other words, they claimed damages for loss of performance of the contract, even though that loss of performance had not caused them any financial loss. The Court of Appeal held that Panatown was entitled to recover substantial damages.

Held: The House of Lords allowed the appeal. In relation to the broad ground, four Law Lords: Lords Goff, Millett, Jauncey and Browne-Wilkinson acknowledged that, in principle, there was a claim for loss of performance even if that loss of performance had caused no financial loss to the claimant. However, two of those Law Lords, Lords Jauncey and Brown-Wilkinson, were of the view that Panatown's claim on this ground was excluded by the existence of the DCD with UIPL. Lord Clyde denied the existence of a claim for loss of performance altogether.

Lord Clyde:

'I turn accordingly to what was referred to in the argument as the broader ground . . . What it proposes is that the innocent party to the contract should recover damages for himself as a compensation for what is seen to be his own loss . . . This approach however seems to me to have been developed into two formulations.

The first formulation, and the seeds of the second, are found in the speech of Lord Griffiths in the *St Martins case* [1994] 1 AC 85, 96. At the outset his Lordship expressed the opinion that the Corporation, faced with a breach by McAlpine of their contractual duty to perform the contract with sound materials and with all reasonable skill and care, would be entitled to recover from McAlpine the cost of remedying the defect in the work as the normal measure of damages. He then dealt with two possible objections. First, it should not matter that the work was not being done on property owned by Corporation. Where a husband instructs repairs to the roof of the matrimonial home it cannot be said that he has not suffered damage because he did not own the property. He suffers the damage measured by the cost of a proper completion of the repair:

> "In cases such as the present the person who places the contract has suffered financial loss because he has to spend money to give him the benefit of the bargain which the defendant had promised but failed to deliver." (See p 97.)

The second objection, that the Corporation had in fact been reimbursed for the cost of the repairs was answered by the consideration that the person who actually pays for the repairs is of no concern to the party who broke the contract. But Lord Griffiths added, at p 97:

> "The court will of course wish to be satisfied that the repairs have been or are likely to be carried out but if they are carried out the cost of doing them must fall upon the defendant who broke his contract."

In the first formulation this approach can be seen as identifying a loss upon the innocent party who requires to instruct the remedial work. That loss is, or may be, measured by the cost of the repair. The essential for this formulation appears to be that the repair work is to be, or at least is likely to be, carried out. This consideration does not appear to be simply relevant to the reasonableness of allowing the damages to be measured by the cost of repair. It is an essential condition for the application of the approach, so as to establish a loss on the part of the plaintiff. Thus far the approach appears to be consistent with principle, and in particular with the principle of privity. It can cover the case where A contracts with B to pay a sum of money to C and B fails to do so. The loss to A is in the necessity to find other funds to pay to C and provided that he is going to pay C, or indeed has done so, he should be able to recover the sum by way of damages for breach of contract from B. If it was evident that A had no intention to pay C, having perhaps changed his mind, then he would not be able to recover the amount from B because he would have sustained no loss, and his damages would at best be nominal.

But there can also be found in Lord Griffiths's speech the idea that the loss is not just constituted by the failure in performance but indeed consists in that failure. This is the "second formulation". In relation to the suggestion that the husband who instructs repair work to the roof of his wife's house and has to pay for another builder to make good the faulty repair work has sustained no damage Lord Griffiths observed, at p 97:

> "Such a result would in my view be absurd and the answer is that the husband
> has suffered loss because he did not receive the bargain for which he had con-
> tracted with the first builder and the measure of damages is the cost of securing
> the performance of that bargain by completing the roof repairs properly by the
> second builder."

That is to say that the fact that the innocent party did not receive the bargain for which he contracted is itself a loss. As Steyn LJ put it in *Darlington Borough Council v Wiltshier Northern Ltd* [1995] 1 WLR 68, 80: "He suffers a loss of bargain or of expectation interest." . . .

I find some difficulty in adopting the second formulation as a sound way forward . . . The loss of an expectation which is here referred to seems to me to be coming very close to a way of describing a breach of contract. A breach of contract may cause a loss, but is not in itself a loss in any meaningful sense. When one refers to a loss in the context of a breach of contract, one is in my view referring to the incidence of some personal or patrimonial damage. A loss of expectation might be a loss in the proper sense if damages were awarded for the distress or inconvenience caused by the disappointment. Professor Coote ("Contract Damages, *Ruxley* and the Performance Interest" [1997] CLJ 537) draws a distinction between benefits in law, that is bargained-for contractual rights, and benefits in fact, that is the enjoyment of the fruits of performance. Certainly the former may constitute an asset with a commercial value. But while frustration may destroy the rights altogether so that the contract is no longer enforceable, a failure in the obligation to perform does not destroy the asset. On the contrary it remains as the necessary legal basis for a remedy. A failure in performance of a contractual obligation does not entail a loss of the bargained-for contractual rights. Those rights remain so as to enable performance of the contract to be enforced, as by an order for specific performance. If one party to a contract repudiates it and that repudiation is accepted, then, to quote Lord Porter in *Heyman v Darwins Ltd* [1942] AC 356, 399, "By that acceptance he is discharged from further performance and may bring an action for damages, but the contract itself is not rescinded." The primary obligations under the contract may come to an end, but secondary obligations then arise, among them being the obligation to compensate the innocent party. The original rights may not then be enforced. But a consequential right arises in the innocent party to obtain a remedy from the party who repudiated the contract for his failure in performance.'

Lord Goff:

'I wish to state that I find persuasive the reasoning and conclusion expressed by Lord Griffiths in his opinion in the *St Martins case* [1994] 1 AC 85, that the employer under a building contract may in principle recover substantial damages from the building contractor, because he has not received the performance which he was entitled to receive from the contractor under the contract, notwithstanding that the property in the building site was vested in a third party. The example given by Lord Griffiths of a husband contracting for repairs to the matrimonial home which is owned by his wife is most telling. It is not difficult to imagine other examples, not only within the family, but also, for example, where work is done for charitable purposes – as where a wealthy man who lives in a village decides to carry out at his own expense major repairs to, or renovation or even reconstruction of, the village hall, and himself enters into a contract with a local builder to carry out the work to the existing building which belongs to another, for example to trustees, or to the parish council. Nobody in such circumstances would imagine that there could be any legal obstacle in the way of the charitable donor enforcing the contract against the builder by recovering damages from him if he failed to perform his obligations under the building contract, for example because his work failed to comply with the contract specification . . .

I do not regard Lord Griffiths's broader ground as a departure from existing authority, but as a reaffirmation of existing legal principle. Indeed, I know of no authority which stands in its way. On the contrary, there have been statements in the cases which provide support for his view. Thus in *Darlington Borough Council v Wiltshier Northern Ltd* [1995] 1 WLR 68, 80, Steyn LJ described Lord Griffiths's broader ground as based on classic contractual theory, a statement with which I respectfully agree. Moreover, Lord Griffiths's reasoning was foreshadowed in the opinions of members of the Appellate Committee in *Woodar Investment Development Ltd v Wimpey Construction UK Ltd* [1980] 1 WLR 277; see especially the opinion of Lord Keith of Kinkel, at pp 297–298, and in addition the more tentative statements of Lord Salmon, at p 291, and Lord Scarman, at pp 300–301. . . Even if it is not thought, as I think, that the solution which I prefer is in accordance with existing principle, nevertheless it is surely within the scope of the type of development of the common law which, especially in the law of obligations, is habitually undertaken by appellate judges as part of their ordinary judicial function . . .

The present case provides, in my opinion, a classic example of a case which falls properly within the judicial province. I, for my part, have therefore no doubt that it is desirable, indeed essential, that the problem in the present case should be the subject of judicial solution by providing proper recognition of the plaintiff's interest in the performance of the contractual obligations which are owed to him . . .

The DCD

I now turn to the second issue in the case, which relates to the possible impact of the DCD on Panatown's remedy against McAlpine in damages.

It was the submission of McAlpine that the existence of the building owner's remedy under the DCD had the effect of precluding Panatown from recovering damages from McAlpine under the building contract . . .

This reasoning has, however, no application to Lord Griffiths' broader ground, under which the employer is seeking to recover damages for his own account in respect of his own loss, ie the damage to his interest in the performance of the building contract to which he, as employer, is party and under which he has contracted to pay for the building. The mere fact that the building contractor, McAlpine, has entered into a separate contract in different terms with another party with regard to possible defects in the building which is the subject of the building contract cannot of itself detract from its obligations to the employer under the building contract itself.

For the reasons I have given, I would dismiss McAlpine's appeal from the decision of the Court of Appeal, and I would order that McAlpine pay the costs of the appeal to your Lordships' House.'

Lord Jauncey:

'Since writing this speech, I have had the advantage of reading in draft the speech of my noble and learned friend, Lord Goff of Chieveley. I respectfully agree with his rejection of the proposition that the employer under a building contract is unable to recover substantial damages for breach of the contract if the work in question is to be performed on land or buildings which are not his property. In such a case the employer's right to substantial damages will, in my view, depend upon whether he has made good or intends to make good the effects of the breach . . . This produces a sensible result and avoids the recovery of an "uncovenanted" profit by an employer who does not intend to take steps to remedy the breach.

However, there is a further matter to be considered in this case, namely the DCD in favour of UIPL. This, in my view, is equally relevant to the broader as to the narrow ground. The former as does the latter seeks to find a rational way of avoiding the "black hole". What is the justification for allowing A to recover from B as his own a loss which is truly that of C when C has his own remedy against B? I would submit none . . . I therefore consider that Panatown is not entitled to recover under Mr Friedman's broader ground not only because they have suffered no financial loss but also because UIPL have a direct right of action against McAlpine under the DCD.'

Lord Browne-Wilkinson:

'I will assume that the broader ground is sound in law and that in the ordinary case where the third party (C) has no direct cause of action against the building contractor (B) A can recover damages from B on the broader ground. Even on that assumption, in my judgment Panatown has no right to substantial damages in this case because UIPL (the owner of the land) has a direct cause of action under the DCD.

The essential feature of the broader ground is that the contracting party A, although not himself suffering the physical or pecuniary damage sustained by the third party C, has suffered his own damage being the loss of his performance interest, ie the failure to provide C with the benefit that B had contracted for C to receive. In my judgment it follows that the critical factor is to determine what interest A had in the provision of the service for the third party C. If, as in the present case, the whole contractual scheme was designed, inter alia, to give UPIL and its successors a legal remedy against McAlpine for failure to perform the building contract with due care, I cannot see that Panatown has suffered any damage to its performance interests: subject to any defence based on limitation of actions, the physical and pecuniary damage suffered by UPIL can be redressed by UPIL exercising its own cause of action against McAlpine. It is not clear to me why this has not occurred in the present case: but, subject to questions of limitation which were not explored, there is no reason even now why UPIL should not be bringing the proceedings against McAlpine. The fact that the DCD may have been primarily directed to ensuring that UPIL's successors in title should enjoy a remedy in tort against McAlpine is nothing to the point: the contractual provisions were directed to ensuring that UPIL and its successors in title did have the legal right to sue McAlpine direct. So long as UPIL enjoys this right Panatown has suffered no failure to satisfy its performance interest . . .

For these reasons I would allow the appeal.'

Lord Millett:

'To my mind the most significant feature of the academic literature is that no one has suggested that the adoption of the broad ground would have any adverse consequences on commercial arrangements. Nor, despite every incentive to do so, has McAlpine been able to suggest a situation in which it would cause difficulties or defeat the commercial expectations of the parties. In my view it would help to rationalise the law and provide a sound basis for decisions like *Ruxley Electronics and Construction Ltd v Forsyth* [1996] AC 344 and *Jackson v Horizon Holidays* [1975] 1 WLR 1468. If it is adopted, it will be for future consideration whether it would provide the better solution in cases such as *St Martins* also.

In the *Ruxley* case your Lordships' House refused to allow the full costs of reinstatement on the well-recognised ground that reinstatement would be an unreasonable course to take. But it was not constrained to withhold substantial damages on the ground that the value of the property was unaffected by the breach. It expressly rejected the view that these were the only two possible measures of damage in a building case. It awarded an intermediate sum for "loss of amenity". The evidence, however, showed that, viewed objectively, there was no loss of amenity either. The amenity in question was entirely subjective to the plaintiff; and its loss could equally well, and perhaps more accurately, be described as defeated expectation . . .

It must be wrong to adopt a Procrustean approach which leaves parties without a remedy for breach of contract because their arrangements do not fit neatly into some precast contractual formula. When such arrangements have been freely entered into and are of an everyday character or are commercially advantageous to the parties, it is surely time to re-examine the position.

This is the product of the narrow accountants' balance sheet quantification of loss which measures the loss suffered by the promisee by the diminution in his overall financial position resulting from the breach. One of the consequences of this approach is to produce an artificial distinction between a contract for the supply of goods to a third party and a contract for the supply of services to a third party. A man who buys a car for his wife is entitled to substantial damages if an inferior car is supplied, on the assumption (not necessarily true) that the property in the car is intended to vest momentarily in him before being transferred to his wife, whereas a man who orders his wife's car to be repaired is entitled to nominal damages only if the work is imperfectly carried out. This is surely indefensible; the reality of the matter is that in both cases the man is willing to undertake a contractual liability in order to be able to provide a benefit to his wife.

The idea that a contracting party is entitled to damages measured by the value of his own defeated interest in having the contract performed was not new in 1994. A strong case for its adoption in the case of consumer contracts was made in an important article "Contract Remedies and the Consumer Surplus" (1979) 95 LQR 581, in which the authors explained that this would make a significant difference only in a minority of cases . . .

[His Lordship discussed the decisions in *Woodar Investment Development Ltd v Wimpey Construction UK Ltd* [1980] 1 WLR 277 and *Radford v De Froberville* [1977] 1 WLR 1262.]

The seed was planted more than 20 years ago. It has been long in germination, but it has been watered and nurtured by favourable judicial and academic commentators in the meantime. I think the time has come to give it the imprimatur of your Lordships' House. I am not impressed by the argument that such a radical change, with the attendant risk of opening the floodgates to capricious and complex claims to damages in unforeseen situations of every kind, should be left to Parliament. In the first place, I do not think that it is a radical change. I respectfully agree with Steyn LJ in *Darlington Borough Council v Wiltshier Northern Ltd* [1995] 1 WLR 68, that it is based on orthodox contractual principles. And in the second place, the development of the remedial response to civil wrongs and the appropriate measure of damages are matters which have traditionally been the province of the judiciary. For the present I would restrict the broad ground to building contracts and other contracts for the supply of work and materials where the claim is in respect of defective or incomplete work or delay in completing it. I would not exclude the claim for damages for delay, since the performance interest extends to having the work done timeously as well as properly. There is no difficulty in quantifying the loss due to delay, at least in the family or group context. In the case of building contracts the broad ground is in line with the principle that the prima facie measure of damages is the cost of repair rather than the reduction in the market value of the property or any loss of amenity, even where the cost of repair is substantially greater, subject only to the qualification that the carrying out of the repairs must be a reasonable course to adopt . . .

Does the existence of the DCD bar recovery?

I am unable to accept McAlpine's submission that the parties were well aware of the problem caused by the fact that Panatown was not the owner of the site, and that the DCD was intended to cater for this. It is much more likely that the parties, being businessmen and more sensible than lawyers, assumed that it made no difference which company in the group owned the land. If the present problem had been foreseen, Panatown would surely have insisted on taking the benefit of an unqualified warranty such as was proposed to be given to a future tenant. It would make no commercial sense for a future tenant to have a more effective remedy than either the building employer or the building owner.

I agree with the Court of Appeal that the existence of the DCD does not demonstrate an intention that any damages caused by defective or incomplete performance of McAlpine's obligations under the building contract should be recoverable by UIPL under the DCD and not by Panatown under the building contract. I do not, however, agree with their formulation of the question: whether the parties contemplated that the DCD would "replace" the more detailed provisions of the building contract. It is not correct to ask whether Panatown would have had a claim under the building contract if there had been no DCD and then ask whether the parties intended to replace that claim by a claim by UIPL under the DCD. If it be relevant to impute intention to the parties, the correct approach is to examine the whole complex of contracts and ask whether they contemplated that the building contract could be enforced by Panatown.

But the broad ground does not rest on imputed intention . . . [It] is based on ordinary contractual principles. It has nothing to do with the privity rule. The plaintiff is a contracting party who recovers for his own loss, not that of a third party. Whatever arrangements the third party may have entered into, these do not concern the plaintiff and cannot deprive him of his contractual rights . . .

The real significance of the DCD is different. By giving the third party a cause of action, it raises the spectre of double recovery. Even though the plaintiff recovers for his own loss, this obviously reflects the loss sustained by the third party. The case is, therefore, an example, not unknown in other contexts, where breach of a single obligation creates a liability to two different parties. Since performance of the primary obligation to do the work would have discharged the liability to both parties, so must performance of the secondary obligation to pay damages. Payment of damages to either must *pro tanto* discharge the liability to both. The problem, in my view, is not one of double recovery, but of ensuring that the damages are paid to the right party.

There can be no complaint by the building employer if the damages are recovered by the building owner, since he was the intended beneficiary of the arrangements in the first place. The building employer's performance interest will be satisfied by carrying out the remedial work or by providing the building owner with the means to pay for it to be done. This provides the key to the proper approach in the converse case like the present where the action is brought by the building employer despite the existence of a cause of action in the building owner. Since the building employer's expectation loss reflects and cannot exceed the loss suffered by the building owner, and would be

> satisfied by any award of damages to the latter, his claim should normally be subordinated to any claim made by the building owner. While, therefore, I do not accept that Panatown's claim to substantial damages is excluded by the existence of the DCD, I think that an action like the present should normally be stayed in order to allow the building owner to bring his own proceedings. The court will need to be satisfied that the building owner is not proposing to make his own claim and is content to allow his claim to be discharged by payment to the building employer before allowing the building employer's action to proceed.
>
> In the present case UIPL is fully aware of the present proceedings and supports Panatown's claim to substantial damages. It has no wish to be forced to invoke its own subsidiary and inferior remedy under the DCD. There is no need to join it in the proceedings or require it to enter into a formal waiver of its claim under the DCD. Any claim it may have under the DCD will be satisfied by the payment of damages to Panatown.
>
> I would dismiss the appeal.'

Ultimately the issue that decided the case was the existence of the DCD. The majority of their Lordships (Lords Goff and Millett dissenting) held that because UIPL had a claim against McAlpine under the DCD there was no 'legal black hole'. It is respectfully submitted that this conclusion is wrong. The DCD conferred significantly fewer rights on UIPL than the main contract conferred on McAlpine. The purpose of the DCD was to provide the means for future purchasers of the land to sue McAlpine for negligent building defects (it appears that the lawyers accurately predicted the decision in *Murphy v Brentwood CC* [1991] 1 AC 398). The main contract conferred more substantial rights on Panatown including strict liability for the building work and an arbitration clause. By deciding that the DCD superseded the main contract, the majority of the House of Lords effectively cast these additional rights into the legal 'black hole'. Even more worrying was that their Lordships allowed the performance interest of a non-party, UIPL, to trump the performance interest of an actual party, Panatown, who had provided the consideration for the promise from McAlpine.

The most interesting feature of the case was the sharp disagreement between their Lordships on the status of the 'broad ground' – the claim that Panatown were entitled to compensation for loss of their performance interest. Lord Clyde was clearly of the view that no such claim existed: 'A breach of contract may cause a loss, but is not in itself a loss in any meaningful sense.' Lords Goff and Millett disagreed, the latter referring to Lord Clyde's approach as being founded on a 'narrow accountants' balance sheet quantification of loss'. It appears that Lord Jauncey sided with Lord Clyde. Thus it was left to Lord Browne-Wilkinson to decide the issue. Ultimately he decided that the claim should fail because of the existence of the DCD, which meant that his comments on the broad ground were strictly obiter. However, his Lordship did say that he would 'assume that the broader ground was sound in law'. This is extremely significant. Effectively it meant that the majority of the House of Lords were of the view that a promisee's interest in performance ought to be protected even if he had suffered no pecuniary loss.

McKendrick, E, 'The common law at work: the saga of *Alfred McAlpine Construction Ltd v Panatown Ltd*' (2003) OUCLJ 145, 167–168

[T]he central question of principle that is, in my view posed by the fact pattern in *Panatown* [is]: what rights are conferred on a promisee by an enforceable promise? . . .

In many ways, it is surprising that, at this stage in the development of our law of contract, such a fundamental question remains without a definitive answer. Yet the cases do not speak with one voice. It is probably fair to say that the courts have traditionally awarded damages to claimants in order to compensate them for the financial losses they have suffered as a result of the breach. In many ways this is not surprising. Many, if not most, contracting parties enter into a contract in order to make a profit and the law reflects that reality in the approach which it adopts in the assessment of damages payable in the event of a breach. But not all contracting parties enter into contracts with a view to making money. This is particularly true in the case of consumers. The consumer who orders a new bathroom suite does not enter into the contract in order to make a profit but to obtain a particular suite of his or her choice. Local authorities who enter into contracts for the provision of services or amenities for residents do not do so with a view to enhancing their own financial position but rather to provide a service for their constituents. Similarly, Panatown did not enter into a contract with McAlpine in order to make a profit itself but rather to benefit the corporate group as a whole. Against this background, it is suggested that the conception of loss adopted by the law of contract should extend beyond physical damage and financial loss in order to reflect the fact that, increasingly, we enter into contracts with a view other than to make money. Thus we enter into contract in pursuit of our leisure interests or to obtain services which promote the quality of our lives but do not directly enhance our financial position. These are interests which our society values and they should be reflected in the law of contract . . . There is more to life than money and there is more to the law of contract than the protection of financial interests. This should be reflected in the conception of loss adopted by the law of contract and in the rules applicable to the assessment of damages.

Professor McKendrick is surely correct. Fuller and Perdue's legacy left us with an unduly economic driven conception of the law of contract. Instead of speaking of a promisee's interest in 'performance', we have been encouraged to refer to the promisee's 'expectation' interest. This conceals the fact that the parties' real expectation is an expectation of performance, not merely the economic value of performance.

Whether this will be recognised in the future is still a matter of doubt. Although Lord Millett argued that the damages awarded in *Ruxley* were really awarded on this basis, this is somewhat doubtful. Furthermore, the speeches in *Panatown* are inconclusive because of their obiter nature. Ultimately, we must wait for further cases before this issue is finally resolved.

17.2.1.2 The reliance measure

Where it proves difficult for the claimant to calculate the profits that would have been made had the contract not been broken, he may instead seek recovery of the expenditure that he incurred in anticipation of the contract. This measure is referred to as the 'reliance measure'. The result of this type of award is that the claimant is put back into the position he was in prior to the contract being made. Reliance damages are backwards looking and to this extent they are like damages in the law of tort. The Court of Appeal awarded reliance damages in *Anglia Television Ltd v Reed*.

Anglia Television Ltd v Reed [1972] 1 QB 60

Facts: Robert Reed was an actor who was under a contract to play a leading role in a film for television entitled 'The Man in the Wood'. The film was about an American man married to an English woman who had an adventure in an English wood! At a late stage Reed withdrew from the film and the project was unable to go ahead. Anglia Television sued Reed for breach of contract. Due to the uncertainties of the entertainment industry Anglia Television were unable to accurately estimate the profits they would have made from the film. Therefore Anglia sought to recover the expenses they had incurred in setting up the film. At first instance, the master awarded Anglia Television damages of £2,750, a sum that included expenditure incurred by Anglia Television prior to the contract with Reed.

Held: The Court of Appeal dismissed the appeal.

Lord Denning MR:
'It seems to me that a plaintiff in such a case as this has an election: he can either claim for loss of profits; or for his wasted expenditure. But he must elect between them. He cannot claim both. If he has not suffered any loss of profits – or if he cannot prove what his profits would have been – he can claim in the alternative the expenditure which has been thrown away, that is, wasted, by reason of the breach . . .

If the plaintiff claims the wasted expenditure, he is not limited to the expenditure incurred *after* the contract was concluded. He can claim also the expenditure incurred *before* the contract, provided that it was such as would reasonably be in the contemplation of the parties as likely to be wasted if the contract was broken. Applying that principle here, it is plain that, when Mr. Reed entered into this contract, he must have known perfectly well that much expenditure had already been incurred on director's fees and the like. He must have contemplated – or, at any rate, it is reasonably to be imputed to him – that if he broke his contract, all that expenditure would be wasted, whether or not it was incurred before or after the contract. He must pay damages for all the expenditure so wasted and thrown away. This view is supported by the recent decision of Brightman J in *Lloyd v Stanbury* [1971] 1 WLR 535. There was a contract for the sale of land. In anticipation of the contract – and before it was concluded – the purchaser went to much expense in moving a caravan to the site and in getting his furniture there. The seller afterwards entered into a contract to sell the land to the purchaser, but afterwards broke his contract. The land had not increased in value, so the purchaser could not claim for any loss of profit. But Brightman J. held, at p 547, that he could recover the cost of moving the caravan and furniture, because it was "within the contemplation of the parties when the contract was signed". That decision is in accord with the correct principle, namely, that wasted expenditure can be recovered when it is wasted by reason of the defendant's breach of contract. It is true that, if the defendant had never entered into the contract, he would not be liable, and the expenditure would have been incurred by the plaintiff without redress; but, the defendant having made his contract and broken it, it does not lie in his mouth to say he is not liable, when it was because of his breach that the expenditure has been wasted.'

The decision in *Reed* was controversial because the Court of Appeal allowed Anglia to recover damages in respect of precontractual expenditure. Lord Denning justified this on the ground that, at the time the contract was entered into, Reed must have been aware of the expenditure that had already taken place. Professor Anthony Ogus has doubted that this is a sound basis for allowing recovery of precontractual expenditure under the heading of reliance losses.

Ogus, A, 'Damages for pre-contract expenditure' (1972) 35 MLR 423, 424

The measure of damages so envisaged would not put the plaintiffs in the position they would have been in if the contract had not been made, for the expenses would still have been incurred. The expenses were incurred not in reliance on the defendant's promise to perform – they were incurred merely in the hope that agreement with the defendant would be secured. There was indeed no causal connection between the loss (the wasted expenses) and either the making of the contract or its breach. In the United States of America these theoretical objections have proved decisive: all attempts to recover pre-contract expenditure (where there was no special agreement binding the defaulting party to pay) have failed.

Now it may be conceded that dogmatically to insist that there may be recovery of expenditure incurred only from the moment that the contract was complete may lead to artificial results. If the parties have clearly reached agreement on the substance of the contract and all that remains is for their legal advisers to draft and execute the contract, it would be unfair to the plaintiff to disallow a claim for expenses incurred at this stage. On the other hand, the doctrine of *restitutio in integrum* which lies at the heart of the reliance interest award surely dictates that while a contract is still being negotiated a party who incurs expenditure does so at his own risk. Perhaps the best solution would be for the reliance interest award to comprise those expenses incurred as from the time when there was substantial agreement between the parties.

Professor Ogus seems to be correct, assuming that the damages awarded in the case were really awarded to compensate for reliance losses. However, it is quite possible that the award could be recharacterised as an award of expectation damages, in which case the decision is more readily explicable. This will be considered in further detail below.

The decision as to whether to seek expectation or reliance damages will normally lie with the claimant, as Lord Denning confirmed in *Anglia Television v Reed*. In some circumstances, however, the court may decide that reliance is the appropriate measure.

McRae v Commonwealth Disposals Commission (1951) 84 CLR 377

Facts: The defendants invited tenders for the purchase of a shipwrecked oil tanker stated to be lying on Jourmand Reef in the Pacific. McRae made an offer, which was accepted. They were unable to locate Jourmaund Reef on a map and, on inquiry, were supplied by the defendants with the latitude and longitude at which the tanker was alleged to be lying. At considerable expense the McRae fitted out a salvage expedition. When they arrived at the stated site they found that the tanker was not there and proved that it did not exist and never had existed.

Held: The High Court of Australia held that McRae was entitled to recover from the defendant damages for breach of contract. The amount McRae was entitled to recover as damages was the agreed purchase price of the shipwreck together with the expenditure wasted in reliance on the promise that there was an oil tanker at the locality given. The court refused to award damages measured on the expectation basis because the lost profits were too speculative.

Dixon and Fullagar JJ:
'[I]f we approach this case as an ordinary case of wrongful non-delivery of goods sold, and attempt to apply the ordinary rules for arriving at the sum to be awarded as damages, we seem to find ourselves at once in insuperable difficulties. There was obviously no market into which the buyers could go to mitigate their loss, and the rule normally applied would require us to arrive at the value of the goods to the buyer at the place where they ought to have been delivered and at the time when they ought to

have been delivered. But it is quite impossible to place any value on what the Commission purported to sell . . .

It was strongly argued for the plaintiffs that mere difficulty in estimating damages did not relieve a tribunal from the responsibility of assessing them as best it could. This is undoubtedly true. In the well-known case of *Chaplin v Hicks* [1911] 2 KB 786 Vaughan Williams LJ said: "The fact that damages cannot be assessed with certainty does not relieve the wrongdoer of the necessity of paying damages for his breach of contract". . . . The present case seems to be more like *Sapwell v Bass* (1910) 2 KB 486 than *Chaplin v Hicks* . . . It does not seem possible to say that "any assessable loss has resulted from" non-delivery as such . . . Here we seem to have something which cannot be assessed. If there were nothing more in this case than a promise to deliver a stranded tanker and a failure to deliver a stranded tanker, the plaintiffs would, of course, be entitled to recover the price paid by them, but beyond that, in our opinion, only nominal damages.

There is, however, more in this case than that, and the truth is that to regard this case as a simple case of breach of contract by non-delivery of goods would be to take an unreal and misleading view of it. The practical substance of the case lies in these three factors – (1) the Commission promised that there was a tanker at or near to the specified place; (2) in reliance on that promise the plaintiffs expended considerable sums, of money; (3) there was in fact no tanker at or anywhere near to the specified place. In the waste of their considerable expenditure seems to lie the real and understandable grievance of the plaintiffs . . .'

The decision in *McRae* demonstrates that the court itself might refuse to award damages measured on the expectation basis where it is difficult to prove loss. In other situations the court might refuse to award reliance damages. The most common situation in which reliance damages are refused is when they would enable a claimant to escape from a bad bargain.

C & P Haulage v Middleton [1983] 1 WLR 1461

Facts: Middleton permitted C & P Haulage to use their premises for a car repair business. The licence expressly provided for the use to be reviewed every six months and for any fixtures put in by the defendant to be left on the premises following termination of the licence. Despite this clause, C & P Haulage undertook extensive building works on the premises. Several weeks before the end of the six-month period, Middleton summarily ejected C & P haulage from its premises. The owner of C & P Haulage was forced to run the business out of the garage at his home. C & P Haulage claimed damages calculated by reference to its expenditure on improving Middleton's premises.

Held: The Court of Appeal rejected C & P Haulage's claim on the ground that the cost of the improvements would have been lost in any event when the licence was lawfully terminated after six months.

Ackner LJ:

'It is not the function of the courts where there is a breach of contract knowingly, as this would be the case, to put a plaintiff in a better financial position than if the contract had been properly performed. In this case the plaintiff would indeed be in a better position because, as I have already indicated, had the contract been lawfully determined as it could have been in the middle of December, there would have been no question of his recovering these expenses.'

Fox LJ:

'The present case seems to me to be quite different both from *Anglia Television Ltd v Reed* [1972] 1 QB 60 and from *Lloyd v Stanbury* [1971] 1 WLR 535 in that while it is true that the expenditure could in a sense be said to be wasted in consequence of the breach of contract, it was equally likely to be wasted if there had been no breach, because the plaintiffs wanted to get the defendant out and could terminate the licence at quite short notice. A high risk of waste was from the very first inherent in the nature of the contract itself, breach or no breach. The reality of the matter is that the waste resulted from what was, on the defendant's side, a very unsatisfactory and dangerous bargain.'

C & P Haulage were unable to recover their reliance losses because they would have incurred the loss in any event when the licence was lawfully terminated after six months. The loss flowed from C & P Haulage's poor judgment in entering into a bad bargain, not from Middleton's breach of contract. For this reason, the expenditure was not really a loss incurred in reliance on the contract. Allowing recovery in such circumstances would have enabled C & P Haulage to avoid the contractual allocation of risk.

The same approach has been adopted in Canada. In *Bowlay Logging Ltd v Domtar Ltd* (1978) 135 DLR (3d) 179, a timber owner breached a logging contract. The logger claimed damages for the expenses that he had incurred in reliance on the contract. The Court of Appeal of British Columbia held that these losses were not recoverable because they would have been incurred even if the contract had not been terminated. Seaton JA said:

'On the evidence it seems clear that the appellant was losing heavily; not because of the respondent's breach, but because of an improvident contract and grossly inefficient work practices. The appellant claim that it expended $232,905 partially completing a project that was to yield $150,000 demonstrates the extent to which it was losing money. The result of the breach was to

1073

release the appellant from further losses. In short, no damage was sustained by the appellant as a consequence of the respondent's breach'.

The burden of proving that the bargain was 'bad' falls on the defendant (*CCC Films (London) Ltd v Impact Quadrant Films Ltd* [1985] QB 16). This is only fair because it was the defendant's breach that occasioned the need to assess damages. Therefore it should be the defendant who bears the burden of proving loss. This will be a difficult burden to discharge in most cases.

It is often assumed that a claimant cannot recover both reliance damages and expectation damages. The remedies are said to be alternative, not cumulative. Thus Professor Beatson writes: 'A claimant who recovers for the loss of a bargain cannot, as a general rule, combine a claim for reliance loss with one for loss of expectation so as to recover twice in respect of the same loss' (Beatson, J, *Anson's Law of Contract*, 28th edn, 2002, p 599, Oxford: OUP). The case usually cited for this proposition is *Cullinane v British Rema Manufacturing Co Ltd*.

Cullinane v British Rema Manufacturing Co Ltd [1954] 1 QB 292

Facts: The claimant purchased a clay pulverizing machine from the defendants who warranted that the plant would be able to process the plaintiff's clay at the rate of six tons per hour. When it failed to do so the claimant sought damages under two heads:

(1) the expenditure incurred on installing the machine, with interest, making allowance for the unpaid balance of the purchase price and the residual value of the machine at the time of the claim.

(2) the loss of profit for the three years up to the hearing of the case, deducting from this sum interest on capital, depreciation, maintenance and other expenses.

The official referee awarded £7,370 damages for capital thrown away, plus interest and £8,913 loss of profit.

Held: The majority of the Court of Appeal (Morris LJ dissenting) allowed the appeal, holding that the damages awarded were excessive and should be reduced. The claimant could not recover both his capital loss and his loss of gross profits because this would result in double recovery. He must elect between the two claims.

The decision in *Cullinane* has been subjected to searching academic criticism.

Harris, D, Campbell, D, Halson, R, *Remedies in Contract and Tort*, 2nd edn, 2002, Cambridge: CUP, p 131

It is submitted that the position taken by the majority in this case is confused: their concern to avoid double recovery led them to overlook the fact that a *net* loss of profit can be calculated in such a way as to avoid overlapping with the wasted capital expenditure. They were correct in holding that *gross* profit expected to be earned by the machine during its useful life would include the expected return of the capital expenditure by C. But, as Morris LJ pointed out in his dissent, C was not claiming his expected profits, but his net profit calculated after a deduction of depreciation, which represented the return to him of the capital element; therefore his claim for his net capital outlay did not overlap with his claim for loss of net profits. It is submitted that the view of Morris LJ is to be preferred, and that a split claim should be permitted so long as the calculations show that no overlapping occurs in the different heads of claim.

It is submitted that the criticisms of Harris, Campbell and Halson are correct. Indeed their position is supported by the recent case of *Naughton v O'Callaghan* [1990] 3 All ER 94, where the claimant was permitted to recover both his net loss of profit and the expenses he had incurred in reliance on the contract.

Finally, it was noted above that, in the cases in which the courts have purported to award reliance damages, the damages could be recharacterised as examples of expectation damages. This recharacterisation helps to explain the decision in *Anglia Television v Reed* and provides a more convincing rationale for the bad bargain rule in *C & P Haulage v Middleton*.

McLauchlan, D, 'Reliance Damages for Breach of Contract' [2007] NZ L Rev (forthcomimng)

THE RELIANCE INTEREST

It is undoubtedly the law, indeed it almost seems too trite to observe, that 'where a party sustains a loss by reason of a breach of contract, he is, so far as money can do it, to be placed in the same situation, with respect to damages, as if the contract had been performed'. Thus, subject to the rules on remoteness and mitigation of damage, plaintiffs are entitled to recover in respect of their loss of bargain or, as we say nowadays, their expectation or performance interest. This principle, commonly referred to as the *Robinson v Harman* principle, is invariably reaffirmed whenever an issue concerning contract damages comes before the highest appellate courts.

Nevertheless, it is regularly asserted that victims of breach of contract also have a reliance interest. There is an 'alternative principle . . . of general application' under which they can claim reliance damages, the object being to restore them to the position they would have occupied if they had not entered into the contract. It is a curiously limited reliance interest, however, because reliance loss is equated with wasted expenditure and no account is taken of the possibility of claiming in respect of lost opportunities for gain under alternative contracts. Curiouser still, recovery is denied to the extent that it is proved that a bad bargain was made and hence all or part of the expenditure claimed would not have been recovered if the contract had been performed. This reflects an important value judgment that the promisor should only be responsible for losses caused by the breach. It is essentially an expectation measure of recovery because the focus of the inquiry is the situation if the breach had not occurred.

In any event, even if we disregard this ramification of the expectation ceiling, it is difficult to see how a plaintiff can have both a reliance interest and a performance interest. How can it be that, as from the moment of formation, the promisee is, in effect, entitled to say to the promisor: 'If you breach this contract, I can claim compensation for either the consequences of my entering into this contract or the consequences of your breach'? The choice is conceptually unsustainable. Let us assume, as of course we must when we are talking about damages for breach of contract, that a binding contract has been formed that creates mutual rights and obligations to perform according to the agreed terms. In that event, there can be no question of a return to the status quo when the promisor later breaches. The promisee cannot say: 'But for your breach I would not have entered into the contract'. Formation must occur before there can be a breach, even if the gap may only be a *scintilla temporis* in the case of a broken warranty. The right infringed is the promisee's right to the promised performance, and compensatory damages must necessarily seek to provide a monetary substitute for that performance. The promisee must, so far as money can do so, be put in the position he or she would have occupied if the wrong (the breach of an admitted contract) had not been committed. It is therefore difficult to envisage any circumstances in which a plaintiff whose sole cause of action is breach of contract could justify an entitlement to be placed in the same position as if the contract had not been entered into. The obligation on the defendant is to perform the contract. The *wrong* is the breach of contract—the failure, without legal excuse, to provide the promised performance. Making a promise that you do not keep is not a wrong. On this view, there is no such thing as a 'reliance interest' in the context of damages for breach of contract . . .

. . . [R]eliance terminology is at least 'understandable' in the latter context, it is entirely inappropriate and misleading when, as in the usual case of breach of contract, the expenditure is not a consequence of the wrong. The plaintiff incurs the expenditure in reliance on the making of the contract but that of course is not a wrong. As I have said, there is no wrong until there is a breach of the contract, and damages inevitably involve compensating the plaintiff for whatever loss is caused by that breach.

This is not to say, of course, that contract damages awards cannot be made in respect of wasted expenditure. To the contrary, as we shall see, where a breach causes expenditure to be wasted and such loss was within the reasonable contemplation of the parties at the time of the contract, it is prima facie recoverable. To describe it as a reliance loss is simply unnecessary and confusing.

DAMAGES FOR WASTED EXPENDITURE

It is well established that where, in an action for breach of contract, it is impossible or too difficult to establish the value of the promised performance the courts will allow the plaintiff to recover in respect of expenditure wasted as a result of the breach (plus, of course, any further expenses caused by the breach), and in doing so will, sometimes implicitly, give the plaintiff the benefit of a presumption or inference that full performance by the defendant would at least have resulted in recoupment of the expenditure. However, where it is established that a bad bargain was made so that full performance would have resulted in a net loss, the plaintiff will only recover to the extent that the expenditure exceeds that loss, and if there is no such excess only nominal damages will be recovered.

It does not follow, however, that the making of an award for wasted expenditure involves the making of an exception to the normal object of awarding damages for breach of contract. As Barnes usefully points out:

> 'The law's interest in placing the injured party in the position she would have occupied had the other not breached does not suddenly change. Rather, the injured party simply has failed to prove the full amount of her loss. The law's goal is to get as close as possible to the award of net expectancy consistent with its standards of proof. The award [of wasted expenditure] . . . is simply the closest provable approximation of the net expectancy amount.'

As suggested earlier, the very fact that the plaintiff cannot recover in respect of wasted expenditure to the extent that it is established that she entered into a losing bargain is proof in itself that there is no such thing as a distinct reliance interest. Moreover, the acceptance in the authorities of variously expressed presumptions or inferences that expenditure would have been recouped also serves to reinforce that the goal is to award the best approximation of expectation recovery in the circumstances. If there were truly a reliance interest to be protected, such presumptions or inferences would be otiose and it would be immaterial that the contract was a losing one: the breach would entitle the plaintiffs to elect to be restored to the position they would have been in if the contract had not been formed. But, as Ackner LJ pointed out in *C & P Haulage v Middleton*, there is simply no such entitlement.

Of course, in the ordinary case where the plaintiff *is* able to establish that performance by the defendant would have resulted in a profit or improvement in her position, expenditure wasted as a result of the breach will simply be one component in the damages calculation. The task of the court is to put the plaintiff in the position she would have been if the contract had been performed. Expenditure incurred will be accounted for differently depending on the calculation method chosen. The long way is to compare the plaintiff's 'promised' position with her actual position, and then award the difference between the two. The former involves a determination of the total revenue or benefits that would have resulted from full performance less the expenditure that would have to be incurred to earn that revenue or benefits. The latter will be (a) the sum of pre-breach expenditure already incurred (whether that be expenditure in performing or preparing to perform obligations assumed under the contract or in exploiting the anticipated benefits of the contract) and additional costs caused by the breach, but reduced by (b) off-setting benefits derived from, for example, the defendant's part performance and any salvage values or mitigation efforts.

Alternatively, and sometimes more simply, the damages prima facie recoverable may be calculated in one or other of the following ways: first, as the difference between the total revenue or benefits that would have resulted from full performance and the expenditure that remained to be incurred; or secondly, as the amount of wasted expenditure plus the *net* profit that would have resulted from full performance. In each instance there may have to be a deduction for the value of any part performance by the defendant and an addition of costs caused by the breach.

THE PROBLEM OF PRE-CONTRACT EXPENDITURE

The classification of damages for wasted expenditure as protecting the plaintiff's reliance interest, and hence restoring the plaintiff to the position he or she would have been in if the contract had not been entered into, means that logically no award can be made in respect of wasted pre-contract expenditure. Such expenditure, by definition, is not incurred in reliance on the contract, and to allow recovery would put the plaintiff in a better position than if the contract had not been entered into.

As is well known, however, the English Court of Appeal in *Anglia Television Ltd v Reed* took a different view . . . This conclusion was immediately criticised in an often cited and influential note by Ogus in the Modern Law Review . . . The author concluded his note by observing:

'The award in *Anglia Television v Reed* is unsatisfactory in that it is consistent neither with reliance interest compensation nor with expectation interest compensation but reveals an unhappy confusion between the two.'

In my view, this criticism is misconceived. If we discard the 'reliance interest' and 'expectation interest' jargon and return to first principles of damages law we will see that the real issue is quite straightforward. That issue is whether the basic rule of contract damages that a plaintiff is entitled to recover in respect of losses caused by the breach which are within the reasonable contemplation of the parties at the time of the contract can be satisfied in the case of a claim for pre-contract expenditure. In *Anglia Television* Lord Denning had no doubt on the matter. The defendant could reasonably be taken to have contemplated that if he repudiated the contract pre-contract expenditure would be wasted. The opposing view, of course, is that, even if the loss was reasonably foreseeable, it was not caused by the breach. Lord Denning's reliance on the usual remoteness of damage test in *Anglia Television* was misconceived because that test is only relevant when the loss arises after and is caused by the breach.

Is the causation requirement satisfied on the facts of *Anglia Television*? I suggest that it is. Of course, a plaintiff takes a risk of loss where expenditure is incurred in anticipation of a particular contract with the defendant and that expenditure will be unsalvageable if the contract does not materialise. But it is only a risk. From the plaintiff's point of view the expenditure is an investment. He expects that, once the contract is formed and later duty performed, the expenditure will be reimbursed. Thus, at the time of the expenditure, there is no question of a *loss* having been suffered. An expenditure may have been incurred but it is certainly not wasted or thrown away at this stage. There is only a potential loss in the event that the anticipated contract does not eventuate. When the contract is concluded the risk is removed and the plaintiff can be regarded as, in a manner of speaking, appropriating the expenditure to the contract. The expenditure has been put to its intended use and the plaintiff now has the immediate opportunity of reimbursing it from the fruits of the contract which he had earlier anticipated. Once the contract is breached, this opportunity is lost and the expenditure is wasted, at least to the extent that it is not salvageable. It is at this stage that the loss arises. That loss is plainly caused by the breach. In this respect there can be no justification for treating pre-contract expenditure any differently from post-contract expenditure.

Thus, while it is true to say that in a case such as *Anglia Television* the *expenditure* was not caused by the making of the contract or its breach, that is beside the point. The real question is whether the loss, *the wasting of the expenditure*, was caused by the breach. Clearly it was, since the plaintiffs lost their opportunity to reimburse the expenditure as a result of the defendant's repudiation and, given that it was reasonably foreseeable at the time of the contract that such expenditure had been incurred and would be wasted on breach, there can be no objection in principle or policy to its recovery . . .

There may, of course, be situations where the nature of the expenditure and the circumstances of the case make it unreasonable to saddle the defendant with all of the plaintiff's pre-contract expenditure. However, it will be a rare case where the appropriate limitation on the damages award cannot be accomplished through application of the ordinary rules as to remoteness of damage.

17.2.1.3 The restitution measure

Fuller and Perdue describe the restitution interest in the following terms: 'the plaintiff has in reliance on the promise of the defendant conferred some value on the defendant. The defendant fails to perform his promise. The court may force the defendant to disgorge the value he received from the plaintiff.' The authors note that the object of restitutionary damages is the prevention of unjust enrichment. In the contractual context, an actionable unjust enrichment may occur in a number of different situations. These will be discussed in Chapter 18.

The particular example that Fuller and Perdue give is a claim for restitution, based on a total failure of consideration following a repudiatory breach (see Chapter 16). If such a breach is accepted, and the claimant agrees to return any benefits received, then s/he will be entitled to claim restitution of any goods or money which have been transferred to the defendant. The claim is based on unjust enrichment by subtraction, not on the wrong of breach of contract. This is important because it enables a claimant, following a breach of contract, to claim both restitution for unjust enrichment and compensatory damages for the breach of contract. This is precisely what occurred on the facts of *Millar Machinery Co Ltd v David Way & Son* (1935) 40 Com Cas 204. The case concerned a contract for the sale of a machine, which was defective on delivery and rejected by the purchaser. The disappointed purchaser was able to recover the price paid (restitution for unjust enrichment), the installation costs (reliance damages) and the profits he had lost from use of the machine (expectation damages).

So restitution is available for unjust enrichment following termination of a contract, but such a remedy is not accurately described as restitutionary damages since it is based on an unjust enrichment, not the breach of contract (see Birks, P, 'The concept of a civil wrong', in Owen, D (ed), *Philosophical Foundations of Tort Law*, 1995, p 51, Oxford: Clarendon). As we will see, however, restitutionary damages *are* available for breach of contract in certain situations. This will be discussed in further detail later in the chapter when we consider gain-based remedies for breach of contract, including both restitutionary damages (requiring the defendant to 'give back' a gain) and disgorgement damages (requiring the defendant to 'give up' a gain).

17.2.2 COMPENSATORY DAMAGES FOR NON-PECUNIARY LOSSES

An award of compensatory damages, whether calculated by reference to the expectation measure or the reliance measure, is primarily concerned with economic loss of one kind or another, and as such is pecuniary. In some situations, however, non-pecuniary losses will be caused by a breach of contract. For example, if I purchase a defective car, which catches fire and causes serious injury to me, there is no reason why I should not be able to recover damages for the pain and suffering caused to me.

Grant v Australian Knitting Mills Ltd [1936] AC 85

Facts: The claimant, Grant, bought a pair of underpants manufactured by the defendants. After wearing the underpants, Grant contracted dermatitis. The dermatitis got so bad that Grant was confined to bed for seventeen weeks and the attendant physician believed for some time that he was going to die. Grant claimed that the dermatitis had been caused by the presence of free sulphite in the cuffs and ankle ends of the underpants and sued the defendant for breach of an implied warranty in the contract of sale. At first instance, the judge awarded Grant A$2,450 of damages in respect of the physical injury caused by the breach of contract.

Held: The House of Lords dismissed the defendant's appeal and upheld the first instance award.

It is clear that compensatory damages can be recovered in respect of personal injury caused by a breach of contract. It is less clear, however, whether damages can be recovered in relation to mental distress, anguish or annoyance caused by a breach of contract. The courts have generally been wary of awarding damages in such circumstances, due to concerns about opening the floodgates to claims.

17.2.2.1 The traditional rule

The traditional rule is that a person has no right to compensation for the upset caused by the manner of the breach of contract.

Addis v Gramophone Co Ltd [1909] AC 488

Facts: Addis was employed as the manager of Gramophone's business in Calcutta at a salary together with commission on trade done. His contract entitled him to six months' notice. The defendants gave him notice and immediately replaced him with another employee. This action deprived the plaintiff of his right to act as manager during the notice period, and thus deprived him of the commission he would have earned. The plaintiff sued for breach of contract.

Held: The House of Lords held that, although the plaintiff could recover a sum representing his salary for the period of notice and the commission he would have earned during that period, he could not recover damages to compensate him for the harsh manner in which he was dismissed.

Lord Loreburn LC:
'I cannot agree that the manner of dismissal affects these damages. Such considerations have never been allowed to influence damages in this kind of case . . . If there be a dismissal without notice the employer must pay an indemnity; but that indemnity cannot include compensation either for the injured feelings of the servant, or for the loss he may sustain from the fact that his having been dismissed of itself makes it more difficult for him to obtain fresh employment.'

Addis was followed in a more recent dismissal case.

Bliss v South East Thames RHA [1985] IRLR 308

Facts: Bliss was a consultant orthopaedic surgeon. His relationship with one of his colleagues deteriorated and as a result the health authority required the surgeon to undergo a psychiatric examination. He refused and was suspended. Bliss sued the health authority for breach of contract and, at first instance, was awarded £2,000 for mental distress.

Held: The Court of Appeal allowed the Health Authority's appeal, holding that it was bound by *Addis v Gramophone*, and that damages could not be awarded for mental distress in an action for wrongful dismissal.

The decisions in *Addis* and *Bliss* must now be considered in light of the speeches delivered by the House of Lords in *Malik v BCCI* [1998] AC 20. The facts of that case were given in Chapter 7. The House of Lords held that where the employer had breached an implied term of trust and confidence in an employment contract, damages could be recovered for loss of reputation, or difficulty in obtaining future employment. The House did not, however, consider the question of whether damages could be recovered for mental distress caused by the manner of dismissal. Therefore *Malik* should not be considered as having overruled *Addis* (see *Johnson v Unisys* [2003] 1 AC 518). Damages for mental anguish and injury to feelings resulting from the manner of dismissal remain unavailable in an action for breach of contract.

17.2.2.2 Exceptions to the traditional rule

A number of exceptions have developed over the years since *Addis*. It has been held that damages for distress and disappointment can be recovered where one of the purposes of the contract is the provision of pleasure and enjoyment.

Jarvis v Swan Tours Ltd [1973] QB 233

Facts: James Jarvis, a solicitor, paid £63.45 for a 15-day Christmas winter sports holiday with Swan Tours. Swan Tours' brochures promised a 'house-party' with a variety of activities, entertainment (including a yodelling evening) and food and drink. The holiday was a great disappointment and the provisions fell far short of the brochure descriptions. There were only thirteen people at the hotel in the first week and Jarvis was on his own in the second week. The county court judge found that for the first week he got a holiday which was to some extent inferior and, for the second week, a holiday which was very largely inferior to what he had been led to expect and awarded him £31.72 damages. Jarvis appealed against the amount of damages.

Held: The Court of Appeal allowed the appeal, holding that Jarvis was entitled to be compensated for his disappointment and distress at the loss of the entertainment and facilities for enjoyment which he had been promised in the defendants' brochure. The court held that his damages should be increased to £125.

Lord Denning MR:

'In a proper case damages for mental distress can be recovered in contract, just as damages for shock can be recovered in tort. One such case is a contract for a holiday, or any other contract to provide entertainment and enjoyment. If the contracting party breaks his contract, damages can be given for the disappointment, the distress, the upset and frustration caused by the breach. I know that it is difficult to assess in terms of money, but it is no more difficult than the assessment which the courts have to make every day in personal injury cases for loss of amenities.'

It seems, however, that this exception to the general rule does not extend to commercial contracts.

Hayes v James and Charles Dodd (a firm) [1990] 2 All ER 815

Facts: Hayes ran a motor repair business. He instructed a solicitor to represent him in the purchase of a new workshop. The solicitors gave Hayes an assurance that a right of way existed in relation to access to the property which Hayes was interested in purchasing. This turned out to be untrue, and Hayes' business failed. He sued the solicitors for breach of contract. At first instance, the judge awarded damages on the basis of capital expenditure thrown away, plus expenses (including interest) and damages for anguish and vexation.

Held: The Court of Appeal allowed the appeal in part, holding that the damages for anguish and vexation were not recoverable, as they arose out of a purely commercial contract.

Staughton LJ:
'. . . [D]amages for mental distress in contract are, as a matter of policy, limited to certain classes of case. I would broadly follow the classification of Dillon LJ in *Bliss v South East Thames RHA*: ". . . where the contract which has been broken was itself a contract to provide peace of mind or freedom from distress." It may be that the class is somewhat larger than that. But it should not, in my judgment, include any case where the object of the contract was not comfort or pleasure, or the relief of discomfort, but simply carrying on a commercial activity with a view to profit.'

The general rule and its exceptions were restated by Bingham LJ in *Watts v Morrow* [1991] 1 WLR 1421:

'A contract-breaker is not in general liable for any distress, frustration, anxiety, displeasure, vexation, tension or aggravation which his breach of contract may cause to the innocent party. This rule is not, I think, founded on the assumption that such reactions are not foreseeable, which they surely are or may be, but on considerations of policy.

But the rule is not absolute. Where the very object of a contract is to provide pleasure, relaxation, peace of mind or freedom from molestation, damages will be awarded if the fruit of the contract is not provided or if the contrary result is procured instead ... In cases not falling within this exceptional category, damages are in my view recoverable for *physical inconvenience* and discomfort caused by the breach and mental suffering directly related to that inconvenience and discomfort.'

Bingham LJ's summary of the law permitted recovery of damages for non-pecuniary loss in two categories of case:

1. Cases where the 'very object' of the contract is the provision of pleasure, relaxation, peace of mind or freedom from molestation, for example, contracts for a holiday (*Jarvis v Swan Tours* [1973] QB 233), a holiday rental car (*Jackson v Chrysler Acceptances Ltd* [1978] RTR 474), wedding photographs (*Diesen v Sampson* 1971 SLT (Sh Ct) 49), or burial rights (*Reed v Madon* [1989] Ch 408).
2. Cases where the breach of contract has caused 'physical inconvenience and discomfort'.

For some time *Watts* was the leading case on recovery for non-pecuniary loss. It has now been superseded by the decision of the House of Lords in *Farley v Skinner*.

Farley v Skinner [2002] 2 AC 732

Facts: Mr Farley employed Mr Skinner to survey a house that he was considering purchasing as a country residence. The house was situated close to Gatwick Airport so Farley asked Skinner to investigate, in addition to the usual matters, whether the property would be affected by aircraft noise, telling him that he did not want to be on a flight path. Skinner reported: 'You have also asked whether we felt the property might be affected by aircraft noise, but we were not conscious of this during the time of our inspection, and think it unlikely that the property will suffer greatly from such noise, although some planes will inevitably cross the area, depending on the direction of the wind and the positioning of the flight paths.' After moving in, Farley discovered that the house was close to a navigation beacon which is used by aircraft waiting to land at Gatwick and, as a result, the property was substantially affected by noise. Farley brought an action for damages, alleging that Skinner had been negligent in carrying out his obligations under the contract. At first instance, the judge held that Skinner was liable for breach of contract. The judge found that the value of the house was not affected by the breach, but awarded Farley damages of £10,000 for the distress and inconvenience caused to him by the aircraft noise. The Court of Appeal reversed this award of non-pecuniary damages on the ground that, applying the *Watts v Morrow* tests, Farley had not experienced any physical discomfort and inconvenience as a result of the breach of contract, and that the object of the contract was not the provision of pleasure or peace of mind.

Held: The House of Lords allowed Farley's appeal and restored the judgment at first instance. Damages for non-pecuniary loss were available under both of Millett LJ's categories from *Watts v Morrow*.

Lord Steyn said:

'*The very object of the contract: the framework*
. . . An important development for this branch of the law was *Ruxley Electronics & Construction Ltd v Forsyth* [1996] AC 344 . . . [Lord Steyn set out the facts and continued] Lord Mustill and Lord Lloyd of Berwick justified the award in carefully reasoned judgments which carried the approval of four of the Law Lords. It is sufficient for present purposes to mention that for Lord Mustill, at p 360, the principle of *pacta sunt servanda* would be eroded if the law did not take account of the fact that the consumer often demands specifications which, although not of economic value, have value to him. This is sometimes called the "consumer surplus": see Harris, Ogus and Phillips, "Contract Remedies and the Consumer Surplus" (1979) 95 LQR 581. Lord Mustill rejected the idea that "the promisor can please himself whether or not to comply with the wishes of the promise which, as embodied in the contract, formed part of the consideration for the price". Lords Keith of Kinkel and Bridge of Harwich agreed with Lord Mustill's judgment and with Lord Lloyd of Berwick's similar reasoning. Labels sometimes obscure rather than illuminate. I do not therefore set much store by the description "consumer surplus". But the controlling principles stated by Lord Mustill and Lord Lloyd are important. It is difficult to reconcile this decision of the House with the decision of the Court of Appeal [2000] Lloyd's Rep PN 516 in the present case. I will in due course return to the way in which the majority attempted to distinguish *Ruxley Electronics & Construction Ltd v Forsyth* [1996] AC 344. At this stage, however, I draw attention to the fact that the majority in the Court of Appeal, at p 521, regarded the relevant observations of Lord Mustill and Lord Lloyd as *obiter dicta*. I am satisfied that the principles enunciated in Ruxley's case in support of the award of £2,500 for a breach of respect of the provision of a pleasurable amenity have been authoritatively established.

The very object of the contract: the arguments against the plaintiff's claim
Counsel for the surveyor advanced three separate arguments each of which he said was sufficient to defeat the plaintiff's claim. First, he submitted that even if a major or important part of the contract was to give pleasure, relaxation and peace of mind, that was not enough. It is an indispensable requirement that the object of the entire contract must be of this type. Secondly, he submitted that the exceptional category does not extend to a breach of a contractual duty of care, even if imposed to secure pleasure, relaxation and peace of mind. It only covers cases where the promisor guarantees achievement of such an object. Thirdly, he submitted that by not moving out of Riverside House the plaintiff forfeited any right to recover non-pecuniary damages.
    The first argument fastened onto a narrow reading of the words "the very object of [the] contract" as employed by Bingham LJ in *Watts v Morrow* [1991] 1 WLR 1421, 1445. Cases where a major or important part of the contract was to secure pleasure,

relaxation and peace of mind were not under consideration in *Watts v Morrow*. It is difficult to see what the principled justification for such a limitation might be . . . Counsel was, however, assisted by the decision of the Court of Appeal in *Knott v Bolton* (1995) 11 Const LJ 375, which in the present case the Court of Appeal treated as binding on it. In *Knott v Bolton* an architect was asked to design a wide staircase for a gallery and impressive entrance hall. He failed to do so. The plaintiff spent money in improving the staircase to some extent and he recovered the cost of the changes. The plaintiff also claimed damages for disappointment and distress at the lack of an impressive staircase. In agreement with the trial judge the Court of Appeal disallowed this part of his claim. Reliance was placed on the dicta of Bingham LJ in *Watts v Morrow* [1991] 1 WLR 1421, 1445.

Interpreting the dicta of Bingham LJ in *Watts v Morrow* narrowly the Court of Appeal in *Knott v Bolton* ruled that the central object of the contract was to design a house, not to provide pleasure to the occupiers of the house. It is important, however, to note that *Knott v Bolton* was decided a few months before the decision of the House in *Ruxley Electronics & Construction Ltd v Forsyth* [1996] AC 344. In any event, the technicality of the reasoning in *Knott v Bolton*, and therefore in the Court of Appeal judgments in the present case, is apparent. It is obvious, and conceded, that if an architect is employed only to design a staircase, or a surveyor is employed only to investigate aircraft noise, the breach of such a distinct obligation may result in an award of non-pecuniary damages. Logically the same must be the case if the architect or surveyor, apart from entering into a general retainer, concludes a separate contract, separately remunerated, in respect of the design of a staircase or the investigation of aircraft noise. If this is so the distinction drawn in *Knott v Bolton* and in the present case is a matter of form and not substance . . .

There is no reason in principle or policy why the scope of recovery in the exceptional category should depend on the object of the contract as ascertained from all its constituent parts. It is sufficient if a major or important object of the contract is to give pleasure, relaxation or peace of mind . . .

That brings me to the second issue, namely whether the plaintiff's claim is barred by reason of the fact that the surveyor undertook an obligation to exercise reasonable care and did not guarantee the achievement of a result. This was the basis upon which Hale LJ after the first hearing in the Court of Appeal thought that the claim should be disallowed. This reasoning was adopted by the second Court of Appeal and formed an essential part of the reasoning of the majority. This was the basis on which they distinguished *Ruxley Electronics & Construction Ltd v Forsyth* [1996] AC 344. Against the broad sweep of differently framed contractual undertakings, and the central purpose of contract law in promoting the observance of contractual promises, I am satisfied that this distinction ought not to prevail. It is certainly not rooted in precedent . . . I fully accept, of course, that contractual guarantees of performance and promises to exercise reasonable care are fundamentally different. The former may sometimes give greater protection than the latter. Proving breach of an obligation of reasonable care may be more difficult than proving breach of a guarantee. On the other hand, a party may in practice be willing to settle for the relative reassurance offered by the obligation of reasonable care undertaken by a professional man. But why should this difference between an absolute and relative contractual promise require a distinction in respect of the recovery of non-pecuniary damages? Take the example of a travel agent who is consulted by a couple who are looking for a golfing holiday in France. Why should it make a difference in respect of the recoverability of non-pecuniary damages for a spoiled holiday whether the travel agent gives a guarantee that there is a golf course very near the hotel, represents that to be the case, or negligently advises that all hotels of the particular chain of hotels are situated next to golf courses? If the nearest golf course is in fact 50 miles away a breach may be established. It may spoil the holiday of the couple. It is difficult to see why in principle only those plaintiffs who negotiate guarantees may recover non-pecuniary damages for a breach of contract. It is a singularly unattractive result that a professional man, who undertakes a specific obligation to exercise reasonable care to investigate a matter judged and communicated to be important by his customer, can in Lord Mustill's words in *Ruxley Electronics & Construction Ltd v Forsyth* [1996] AC 344, 360 "please himself whether or not to comply with the wishes of the promise which, as embodied in the contract, formed part of the consideration for the price". If that were the law it would be seriously deficient. I am satisfied that it is not the law. In my view the distinction drawn by Hale LJ and by the majority in the Court of Appeal between contractual guarantees and obligations of reasonable care is unsound . . .

Quantum

In the surveyor's written case it was submitted that the award of £10,000 was excessive. It was certainly high. Given that the plaintiff is stuck indefinitely with a position which he sought to avoid by the terms of his contract with the surveyor I am not prepared to interfere with the judge's evaluation on the special facts of the case. On the other hand, I have to say that the size of the award appears to be at the very top end of what could possibly be regarded as appropriate damages. Like Bingham LJ in *Watts v Morrow* [1991] 1 WLR 1421, 1445h I consider that awards in this area should be restrained and modest. It is important that logical and beneficial developments in this corner of the law should not contribute to the creation of a society bent on litigation . . .'

Lord Clyde:

'The judge found that the plaintiff was not a man of excessive susceptibility and he refers to the inconvenience he was suffering as "real discomfort". I do not consider it appropriate to explore the detail of the inconvenience as being "physical", either because it impacts upon his eardrums, or because it has some geographical element, such as the relative locations of the aircraft and the property, or the obviously greater audibility of their movements when the plaintiff is seeking to enjoy the amenity of the terrace and the gardens than when he is inside the house. In my view the real discomfort which the judge found to exist constituted an inconvenience to the plaintiff which is not a mere matter of disappointment or sentiment. It is unnecessary that the noise should be so great as to make it impossible for the plaintiff to sit at all on his terrace. Plainly it significantly interferes with his enjoyment of the property and in my view that inconvenience is something for which damages can and should be awarded.

. . . In my view the appeal can be allowed on the foregoing basis.

But it is possible to approach the case as one of the exceptional kind in which the claim would be for damages for disappointment. If that approach was adopted so as to seek damages for disappointment, I consider that it should also succeed.

It should be observed at the outset that damages should not be awarded, unless perhaps nominally, for the fact of a breach of contract as distinct from the consequences of the breach. That was a point which I sought to stress in *Alfred McAlpine Constructions v Panatown Ltd* [2001] 1 AC 518. For an award to be made a loss or injury has to be identified which is a consequence of the breach but not too remote from it, and which somehow or other can be expressed and quantified in terms of a sum of money. So disappointment merely at the fact that the contract has been breached is not a proper ground for an award. The mere fact of the loss of a bargain should not be the subject of compensation. But that is not the kind of claim which the plaintiff is making here. What he is seeking is damages for the inconvenience of the noise, the invasion of the peace and quiet which he expected the property to possess and the diminution in his use and enjoyment of the property on account of the aircraft noise.

The critical factor on this approach, as it seems to me, is that the plaintiff made the specific request of the defendant to discover whether the property might be affected by aircraft noise. It is suggested that because this point was wrapped up together with a number of other matters in the instructions given by the plaintiff it cannot be regarded as constituting the "very object" of the contract. But that approach seems to me simply to be playing with words. What is referred to as a breach of contract is often a breach of a particular provision in a contract. The effect of that breach may affect the continued existence of the other terms of the contract, so as to bring the whole to an end. But the point which is the focus of concern is a particular provision in the whole agreement. I can see no reason for distinguishing the present case from a situation where the plaintiff had instructed the defendant simply to advise on the matter of aircraft noise, having already obtained a survey report covering all the other matters . . .

The request for the report on aircraft noise was additional to the usual matters expected of a surveyor in the survey of a property and could properly have attracted an extra fee if he had spent extra time researching that issue. It is the specific provision relating to the peacefulness of the property in respect of aircraft noise which makes the present case out of the ordinary. The criterion is not some general characteristic of the contract, as, for example, that it is or is not a "commercial" contract. The critical factor is the object of the particular agreement.

The present case can in my view qualify as one of the exceptional cases where a contract for peace or pleasure has been made and breached, thereby entitling the injured party to claim damages for the disappointment occasioned by the breach.'

Lord Hutton:
'I . . . consider that there is no valid distinction between a case where a party promises to achieve a result and a case where a party is under a contractual obligation to take reasonable care to achieve a result. Suppose a case where a householder's enjoyment of his garden is spoilt by an unpleasant smell from a septic tank at the bottom of the garden and he employs a company to clean out the tank. If the contract constituted a promise by the company to clean out the tank and it failed to do so, with the result that the smell continued, I think that in accordance with the principle stated by Lord Mustill in *Ruxley v Forsyth* [1996] AC 344, 360–361 the householder would be entitled to recover a modest sum of damages for the annoyance caused by the continuation of the smell. But if the contract provided that the company would exercise reasonable care and skill to clean out the tank and due to its negligence the tank was not cleaned out, I consider that the householder would also be entitled to damages . . .

It will be for the courts, in the differing circumstances of individual cases, to apply the principles stated in your Lordships' speeches in this case, and the matter is not one where any precise test or verbal formula can be applied, but . . . I consider that as a general approach it would be appropriate to treat as cases falling within the exception and calling for an award of damages those where: (1) the matter in respect of which the individual claimant seeks damages is of importance to him, and (2) the individual claimant has made clear to the other party that the matter is of importance to him, and (3) the action to be taken in relation to the matter is made a specific term of the contract. If these three conditions are satisfied, as they are in the present case, then I consider that the claim for damages should not be rejected on the ground that the fulfilment of that obligation is not the principal object of the contract or on the ground that the other party does not receive special and specific remuneration in respect of the performance of that obligation . . .

Physical inconvenience and discomfort
. . . The aircraft noise was something which affected the plaintiff through his hearing and can be regarded as having a physical effect upon him, and on the evidence which was before him I consider that it was open to the judge to find that the plaintiff suffered physical inconvenience and discomfort.

I agree with Judge and Clarke LJJ that on first impression the award of £10,000 damages appears to be a very high one, but I also agree with them that this is a very unusual case where the inconvenience and discomfort caused to the plaintiff will continue, and on further consideration I do not consider that it would be right for an appellate court to set aside the award as being excessive. Therefore I would allow the appeal and restore the order of the judge.'

Lord Scott:
'Ruxley's case establishes, in my opinion, that if a party's contractual performance has failed to provide to the other contracting party something to which that other was,

under the contract, entitled, and which, if provided, would have been of value to that party, then, if there is no other way of compensating the injured party, the injured party should be compensated in damages to the extent of that value. Quantification of that value will in many cases be difficult and may often seem arbitrary. In Ruxley's case the value placed on the amenity value of which the pool owner had been deprived was £2,500. By that award, the pool owner was placed, so far as money could do it, in the position he would have been in if the diving area of the pool had been constructed to the specified depth.

In Ruxley's case the breach of contract by the builders had not caused any consequential loss to the pool owner. He had simply been deprived of the benefit of a pool built to the depth specified in the contract. It was not a case where the recovery of damages for consequential loss consisting of vexation, anxiety or other species of mental distress had to be considered.

In *Watts v Morrow* [1991] 1 WLR 1421, however, that matter did have to be considered. As in the present case, the litigation in *Watts v Morrow* resulted from a surveyor's report. The report had negligently failed to disclose a number of defects in the property. The clients, who had purchased the property in reliance on the report, remedied the defects and sued for damages. The judge awarded them the costs of the repairs and also general damages of £4,000 each for "distress and inconvenience" (p 1424). As to the cost of repairs, the Court of Appeal substituted an award of damages based on the difference between the value of the property as the surveyor's report had represented it to be and the value as it actually was. Nothing, for present purposes, turns on that. As to the damages for "distress and inconvenience" the Court of Appeal upheld the award in principle but held that the damages should be limited to a modest sum for the physical discomfort endured and reduced the award to £750 for each plaintiff. Bingham LJ, at p 1445, in an important passage, set out the principles to be applied where contractual damages for distress and inconvenience are claimed:

"A contract-breaker is not in general liable for any distress, frustration, anxiety, displeasure, vexation, tension or aggravation which his breach of contract may cause to the innocent party. This rule is not, I think, founded on the assumption that such reactions are not foreseeable, which they surely are or may be, but on considerations of policy.

But the rule is not absolute. Where the very object of a contract is to provide pleasure, relaxation, peace of mind or freedom from molestation, damages will be awarded if the fruit of the contract is not provided or if the contrary result is procured instead. If the law did not cater for this exceptional category of case it would be defective. A contract to survey the condition of a house for a prospective purchaser does not, however, fall within this exceptional category.

In cases not falling within this exceptional category, damages are in my view recoverable for physical inconvenience and discomfort caused by the breach and mental suffering directly related to that inconvenience and discomfort."

In the passage I have cited, Bingham LJ was dealing with claims for consequential damage consisting of the intangible mental states and sensory experiences to which he refers. Save for the matters referred to in the first paragraph, all of which reflect or are brought about by the injured party's disappointment at the contract breaker's failure to carry out his contractual obligations, and recovery for which, if there is nothing more, is ruled out on policy grounds, Bingham LJ's approach is, in my view, wholly consistent with established principles for the recovery of contractual damages.

There are, however, two qualifications that I would respectfully make to the proposition in the final paragraph of the cited passage that damages "for physical inconvenience and discomfort caused by the breach" are recoverable.

First, there will, in many cases, be an additional remoteness hurdle for the injured party to clear. Consequential damage, including damage consisting of inconvenience or discomfort, must, in order to be recoverable, be such as, at the time of the contract, was reasonably foreseeable as liable to result from the breach: see *McGregor on Damages*, 16th edn, pp 159–160, para 250.

Second, the adjective "physical", in the phrase "physical inconvenience and discomfort", requires, I think, some explanation or definition. The distinction between the "physical" and the "non-physical" is not always clear and may depend on the context. Is being awoken at night by aircraft noise "physical"? If it is, is being unable to sleep because of worry and anxiety "physical"? What about a reduction in light caused by the erection of a building under a planning permission that an errant surveyor ought to have warned his purchaser-client about but had failed to do so? In my opinion, the critical distinction to be drawn is not a distinction between the different types of inconvenience or discomfort of which complaint may be made but a distinction based on the cause of the inconvenience or discomfort. If the cause is no more than disappointment that the contractual obligation has been broken, damages are not recoverable even if the disappointment has led to a complete mental breakdown. But, if the cause of the inconvenience or discomfort is a sensory (sight, touch, hearing, smell etc) experience, damages can, subject to the remoteness rules, be recovered.

In summary, the principle expressed in *Ruxley Electronics and Construction Ltd v Forsyth* [1996] AC 344 should be used to provide damages for deprivation of a contractual benefit where it is apparent that the injured party has been deprived of something of value but the ordinary means of measuring the recoverable damages are inapplicable. The principle expressed in *Watts v Morrow* [1991] 1 WLR 1421 should be used to determine whether and when contractual damages for inconvenience or discomfort can be recovered . . .

It is time for me to turn to the present case and apply the principles expressed in *Ruxley Electronics and Construction Ltd v Forsyth* [1996] AC 344 and *Watts v Morrow* [1991] 1 WLR 1421. In my judgment, Mr Farley is entitled to be compensated for the "real discomfort" that the judge found he suffered. He is so entitled on either of two alternative bases.

First, he was deprived of the contractual benefit to which he was entitled. He was entitled to information about the aircraft noise from Gatwick-bound aircraft that Mr Skinner, through negligence, had failed to supply him with. If Mr Farley had, in the event, decided not to purchase Riverside House, the value to him of the contractual benefit of which he had been deprived would have been nil. But he did buy the property. And he took his decision to do so without the advantage of being able to take into account the information to which he was contractually entitled. If he had had that information he would not have bought. So the information clearly would have had a value to him. Prima facie, in my opinion, he is entitled to be compensated accordingly.

In these circumstances, it seems to me, it is open to the court to adopt a *Ruxley Electronics and Construction Ltd v Forsyth* [1996] AC 344 approach and place a value on the contractual benefit of which Mr Farley has been deprived. In deciding on the amount, the discomfort experienced by Mr Farley can, in my view, properly be taken into account. If he had had the aircraft noise information he would not have bought Riverside House and would not have had that discomfort.

Alternatively, Mr Farley can, in my opinion, claim compensation for the discomfort as consequential loss. Had it not been for the breach of contract, he would not have suffered the discomfort. It was caused by the breach of contract in a *causa sine qua non* sense. Was the discomfort a consequence that should reasonably have been contemplated by the parties at the time of contract as liable to result from the breach? In my opinion, it was. It was obviously within the reasonable contemplation of the parties that, deprived of the information about aircraft noise that he ought to have had, Mr Farley would make a decision to purchase that he would not otherwise have made. Having purchased, he would, having become aware of the noise, either sell in which case at least the expenses of the resale would have been recoverable as damages or he would keep the property and put up with the noise. In the latter event, it was within the reasonable contemplation of the parties that he would experience discomfort from the noise of the aircraft. And the discomfort was "physical" in the sense that Bingham LJ in *Watts v Morrow* [1991] 1 WLR 1421, 1445 had in mind. In my opinion, the application of *Watts v Morrow* principles entitles Mr Farley to damages for discomfort caused by the aircraft noise.

I would add that if there had been an appreciable reduction in the market value of the property caused by the aircraft noise, Mr Farley could not have recovered both that difference in value and damages for discomfort. To allow both would allow double recovery for the same item.'

A number of observations can be made:

17.2.2.2.1 *The very object of the contract category*

First, it is clear that Bingham LJ's first category from *Watts v Morrow* should not be too narrowly confined. The contract does not have to be solely concerned with the provision of pleasure. According to Lord Steyn, 'it is sufficient if a major or important object of the contract is to give pleasure, relaxation or peace of mind'. This is entirely sensible and avoids the injustice of cases like *Knott v Bolton* (1995) 11

Const LJ 375, where the claimants were denied a remedy for an architect's breach in designing their house because the contract also had an economic purpose. As Lord Clyde noted, it would be ludicrous to distinguish between the facts of *Farley* and a situation where the plaintiff had instructed the defendant simply to advise on the matter of aircraft noise, having already obtained a survey report covering all the other matters.

Lord Hutton attempted to provide specific guidance as to when the provision of pleasure would be a sufficiently major and important object of the contract. He set out three requirements: '(1) the matter in respect of which the individual claimant seeks damages is of importance to him, and (2) the individual claimant has made clear to the other party that the matter is of importance to him, and (3) the action to be taken in relation to the matter is made a specific term of the contract.' Lord Scott appeared to go even further. Relying on *Ruxley* he concluded that, 'if a party's contractual performance has failed to provide to the other contracting party something to which that other was, under the contract, entitled, and which, if provided, would have been of value to that party, then, if there is no other way of compensating the injured party, the injured party should be compensated in damages to the extent of that value.' The question for Lord Scott is therefore simply whether there is an obligation of the relevant type in the contract. It does not have to be a major part of the contract. At the heart of Lord Scott's analysis is a commitment to protecting the performance interest of the contract (but see Lord Clyde's restatement of the position he adopted in *Alfred McAlpine*).

Their Lordships also emphasised that non-pecuniary damages could be recovered for breach of negative obligations as well as breach of positive obligations. Lord Hutton gave the following example:

'Suppose a case where a householder's enjoyment of his garden is spoilt by an unpleasant smell from a septic tank at the bottom of the garden and he employs a company to clean out the tank. If the contract constituted a promise by the company to clean out the tank and it failed to do so, with the result that the smell continued, I think that . . . the householder would be entitled to recover a modest sum of damages for the annoyance caused by the continuation of the smell. But if the contract provided that the company would exercise reasonable care and skill to clean out the tank and due to its negligence the tank was not cleaned out, I consider that the householder would also be entitled to damages.'

The obligation breached in *Farley* was a negative obligation. Skinner did not undertake to guarantee that the property was unaffected by aircraft noise, but to exercise reasonable care in checking whether the house was so affected. This did not make any difference, however, and Farley was entitled to recover damages for his non-pecuniary loss flowing from Skinner's breach of a negative obligation.

17.2.2.2.2 *Physical inconvenience and discomfort*

Their Lordships were also of the view that Mr Farley could have recovered damages for his non-pecuniary loss under Bingham LJ's second category – non-pecuniary loss flowing out of physical inconvenience and discomfort. In fact this was Lord Clyde's primary ground for his decision. The Court of Appeal had held that Mr Farley could not recover under this category because the aircraft noise did not constitute 'physical inconvenience'. The House of Lords disagreed. Their Lordships opined that the distinction between physical and nonphysical was unhelpful. Lord Scott asked: 'Is being awoken at night by aircraft noise "physical"? If it is, is being unable to sleep because of worry and anxiety "physical"? What about a reduction in light caused by the erection of a building under a planning permission that an errant surveyor ought to have warned his purchaser-client about, but had failed to do so?'

For Lord Clyde the true distinction exists between real discomfort for which non-pecuniary damages are recoverable and mere disappointment for which they are not. On the facts, the aircraft noise constituted real discomfort and inconvenience to Mr Farley, which went beyond mere disappointment or sentiment. Lord Scott came to a similar conclusion, but for him, the crucial fact was that the inconvenience of the aircraft noise was a sensory experience. He said: 'If the cause is no more than disappointment that the contractual obligation has been broken, damages are not recoverable even if the disappointment has led to a complete mental breakdown. But, if the cause of the inconvenience or discomfort is a sensory (sight, touch, hearing, smell, etc.) experience, damages can, subject to the remoteness rules, be recovered.' Of the two definitions Lord Scott's is probably the most workable.

17.2.2.2.3 *Quantum*

On the issue of quantification, their Lordships were of the view that the judge's award of £10,000 was at the top end of the scale. However, they were not prepared to deem it excessive because of the continuing impact of the discomfort and inconvenience. Lord Steyn noted that awards of non-pecuniary damages should be restrained and modest in order to prevent the creation of a 'society bent on litigation', but he declined to give any specific guidance on how judges should approach the issue of quantification in the future. One limiting factor that was introduced, however, was Lord Scott's insistence that a claimant could not recover damages for both discomfort and diminution of value. In his view, to allow both would allow double recovery for the same loss.

The principles set out in *Farley v Skinner* were applied more recently in *Hamilton-Jones v David & Snape (a firm)*.

Hamilton-Jones v David & Snape (a firm) [2004] 1 WLR 924

Facts: The claimant approached the defendant solicitors after the breakdown of her marriage. She was extremely concerned that her husband would attempt to abduct her children and take them back to his native country, Tunisia. The defendant obtained 'residence' and 'prohibited steps' orders for the claimant and notified the passport agency, asking it not to issue passports in respect of her children. The passport agency confirmed that the childrens' names would remain on its register for a year. After a year the registration lapsed. The claimant's husband succeeded in becoming a British citizen and had the childrens' names added to the passport. He used this passport to remove the children from the UK. The claimant sued the defendant for breach of contract and claimed damages for the mental distress sustained as a result of the breach.

Held: The High Court held that the claimant was entitled to recover damages of £20,000 in respect of the distress which she had suffered.

Neuberger J:

'I return . . . to what I regard as the centrally relevant, and difficult, question, namely, whether it can fairly be said that the contract between the claimant and the defendants in the present case can be said to have had as its object the provision of "pleasure, relaxation, peace of mind or freedom from molestation", or something akin thereto. There is obviously room for argument, whether one judges the matter from the perception of the claimant or of the defendants, as to the primary purpose of the claimant's instruction to the defendants from February 1994 until July 1996. For a relatively altruistic parent, the claimant's primary concern could be said to have been the children; a more selfish parent would have had her own interests in the forefront. However, on any view, it appears to me that both the claimant and the defendants would have had in mind that a significant reason for the claimant instructing the defendants was with a view to ensuring, so far as possible, that the claimant retained custody of her children for her own pleasure and peace of mind. It would, I think, be a relatively unusual parent who, in the position of the claimant in the present case, would not have had, and would not be perceived by her solicitors to have had, her own peace of mind and pleasure in the company of her children as an important factor. In these circumstances, subject to any further argument which the defendants might raise, I consider that the principles as developed in *Watts v Morrow* [1991] 1 WLR 1421 and in *Farley v Skinner* [2002] 2 AC 732 indicate that the claimant should be entitled to recover damages for mental distress . . .

The measure of damages to be awarded to the claimant for mental distress raises a very difficult problem, albeit that it is the sort of problem with which the court is not infrequently faced. As was said by Mummery LJ in *Vento v Constable of West Yorkshire Police* [2003] ICR 318, 331, para 50, "translating hurt feelings into hard currency is bound to be an artificial exercise". In that case, the Court of Appeal said, at p 335, para 65, that general damages for injured feelings where "there had been a lengthy campaign of discriminatory harassment on the ground of sex or race" should normally be between £15,000 and £25,000 . . .'

[Neuberger J outlined the details of the case and continued]

'Describing the grief, anxiety and hurt she must have suffered, and the mitigating factors, does not make it any easier to translate her mental distress into monetary consideration. I have not been referred to any authority which gives convincingly help-ful guidance as to the right figure. In my view, bearing in mind the serious distress which, as I find, was caused to the claimant, both by the initial shock of the twins being kidnapped by Mr Bougossa and taken to Tunisia, and by the continuing loss of having the company of, and the ability to bring up, the twins, albeit subject to the mitigating factors I have mentioned, I think that the correct measure of damages is £20,000. . .'

The fairly substantial award suggests that the courts may be willing to move beyond the cautious approach to quantification advocated by the House of Lords in *Farley v Skinner*. Of course the award in *Hamilton Jones* may be explicable on the exceptional facts of the case. Nevertheless, if such large sums continue to be awarded and the courts embrace the expansive definition of the categories advocated by Lord Scott in *Farley*, the floodgates for claims will open. More and more the courts will need to rely on the rules limiting recovery of damages, which will be discussed in the following section.

17.2.3 LIMITATIONS ON THE RECOVERY OF DAMAGES

We have already considered restrictions on the type and measure of loss that can be compensated for in an award of damages. In addition, there are a number of rules that limit the claimant's ability to obtain full protection of his performance interest. These rules mean that the claimant can only recover for losses which are: (i) causally linked to the breach of contract; (ii) reasonably foreseeable; and (iii) unavoidable. We will consider each of these limitations in turn.

17.2.3.1 Causation

A claimant must demonstrate that his loss has been caused by the breach of con-tract. He cannot recover damages for loss caused by a supervening event and his award may be reduced if it is proven that his own negligence contributed to the loss.

17.2.3.1.1 Supervening events

The claimant must prove that the breach of contract was the 'dominant' or 'effect-ive' cause of the loss. The courts often need to resort to common sense principles in ascertaining whether the breach was the cause of the loss. In *Galoo Ltd v Bright Grahame Murray* [1994] 1 WLR 1360, 1374–5, Glidewell LJ said:

'If a breach of contract by a defendant is to be held to entitle the plaintiff to claim damages, it must first be held to have been an "effective" or "dominant" cause of his loss. The test in *Quinn v Burch Bros (Builders) Ltd* [1966] 2 QB 370, that it is necessary to distinguish between a breach of contract which causes a loss to the plaintiff and one which merely gives the opportunity for him to sustain the loss, is helpful but still leaves the question to be answered "How does the court decide whether the breach of duty was the cause of the loss or merely the occasion for the loss?" . . . The answer in the end is "By the application of the court's common sense." '

Where another event has occurred after the breach of contract and affected the loss, that other event will not be taken to have broken the chain of causation unless such an event would be deemed 'unlikely' to happen following the breach of contract.

Monarch Steamship Co Ltd v Karlshamns Oljefabriker (A/B) [1949] AC 196

Facts: A British ship was chartered in April 1939 to transport soya beans from Manchuria to Karlsgamn, Sweden. The voyage was delayed by the unseaworthiness of the ship so that it arrived in European water after the outbreak of World War II and was diverted by the British Admiralty to Glasgow. The charter contained a war risks clause exempting the owners of the ship from liability flowing from any orders given by the British government.

Held: The House of Lords held that the outbreak of war and the Admiralty's orders did not break the chain of causation. The defendants were liable for the loss caused due to their failure to provide a seaworthy ship.

Lord Porter:
'I take into account the distinction drawn . . . between [the present] case and that of a vessel struck by lightning or running into a typhoon which she would have avoided had she sailed with reasonable dispatch. Either may happen as much at one place or time as another, whereas delay, at a time when war is likely to occur, gives more opportunity for its incidence than a speedy and proper dispatch would give. Where, however, the basis of liability is delay, it is, as I think, the reasonable anticipation which matters and, but for the finding that the appellants ought to have foreseen the likelihood of war breaking out, I should have thought that your Lordships' decision would rightly have been given in favour of the appellants.'

Lord Du Parcq:

'Damage arises "according to the usual course of things" if, in the circumstances existing at the date of the contract, both parties to it, supposing them to have considered the probable effects of a breach of the contract, with due regard to events which might reasonably be expected to occur, must be assumed as reasonable men to have foreseen such damage as at least a serious possibility. Unseaworthiness in itself may, if fortune is kind, occasion no damage to anybody, but, apart from other obvious dangers, it is very likely to cause delay. Delay may produce damage of many kinds, some of it predictable. If it be once granted that there was a real, and known, danger of war at the date of the contract, I understand that all your Lordships who heard the argument are agreed that the diversion of the ship which caused such grave loss to the respondents followed in the usual course of things from the delay and the unseaworthiness which caused it.

In order that the respondents might succeed in establishing their case, it was not necessary, in my opinion, that the parties to the contract should be shown to have contemplated the outbreak of war as something certain and unavoidable. They are not to be supposed to have had the gift of prophecy. It is enough if they may reasonably be assumed to have contemplated a war, and the likelihood that it would lead to such an embargo as was in fact imposed, as a real danger which must be taken into account. I agree with my noble and learned friend Lord Wright that Mr. Sheriff's evidence, and the addition to the charter of the war risks clause, support the view that this assumption may fairly be made. I also agree that there was at the material date a general fear of war. . .'

The outbreak of war and the Admiralty's orders that the ship should divert to Glasgow did not break the chain of causation because these events were deemed to be 'likely' to happen at the time of the breach of contract. Reference to the likelihood of the supervening event occurring means that there is significant overlap between *causation* of loss and *remoteness* of loss (see below).

Sometimes the supervening event will be an act of the claimant. If so, he will be unable to recover damages if the act was unreasonable and likely to cause the loss sustained.

Quinn v Burch Bros (Builders) Ltd [1966] 2 QB 370

Facts: Quinn worked for Burch as an independent sub-contractor carrying out plastering and other work to make good holes in the walls and ceilings of a building. Burch sub-contracted work to Quinn on the basis that he would charge for his labour at the rate of six shillings per hour and that they would supply any equipment reasonably necessary for the carrying out of his work. Quinn requested a step-ladder for the work but Burch failed to supply him with one. In the absence of the step-ladder, Quinn propped a folded trestle against the wall and used it as a ladder. The trestle was not footed, and while Quinn was standing on one of the rungs, the trestle slipped and Quinn fell and suffered personal injuries, fracturing his *os calcis*. He sued Burch for breach of contract in failing to supply him with a step-ladder. At first instance, Paull J held that the defendants were in breach of contract in failing to supply the plaintiff with a step-ladder, but that that breach did not cause the accident.

Held: The Court of Appeal dismissed the appeal holding that the defendant's breach did not cause the accident but merely gave Quinn the opportunity to injure himself by the use of unsuitable equipment.

Sellers LJ:
'One only has to state the facts in that way, it seems to me, to reveal that this cannot be said to be an accident which was caused by the defendants' breach of contract. No doubt that circumstance was the occasion which brought about this conduct of the plaintiff but it in no way caused it. It was in no way something flowing probably and naturally from the breach of contract.'

Danckwerts LJ:
'The argument in this case seemed to me to go round and round; but I can express my judgment in four propositions which I believe to be established by the facts and the law relating to the matter: (1) Assuming that the defendants were in breach of contract by not providing the equipment reasonably necessary for the work, there was no obligation on the plaintiff to do the work without suitable equipment. (2) The plaintiff voluntarily and without the defendants' knowledge chose to use the trestle, which was unsuitable and subject to the risk of slipping. (3) The cause of the plaintiff's accident was the choice by the plaintiff to use the unsuitable equipment. (4) The failure of the defendants to provide the equipment required may have been the occasion of the accident but was not the cause of the accident.'

The Court of Appeal drew a distinction between a breach that caused the loss and a breach that merely brought about the occasion for the loss. Damages could be recovered in the former situation but not in the latter. When the supervening event is an act of the claimant, the line between causation and contributory negligence is blurred.

17.2.3.2 Contributory negligence

Since 1945, it has been possible for the courts to reduce the amount of damages recoverable in tort on the ground that the claimant's own negligence contributed to his loss.

LAW REFORM (CONTRIBUTORY NEGLIGENCE) ACT 1945

Section 1. Apportionment of liability in case of contributory negligence

(1) Where any person suffers damage as the result partly of his own fault and partly of the fault of any other person or persons, a claim in respect of that damage shall not be defeated by reason of the fault of the person suffering the damage, but the damages recoverable in respect thereof shall be reduced to such extent as the court thinks just and equitable having regard to the claimant's share in the responsibility for the damage . . .

Section 4. Interpretation

The following expressions have the meanings hereby respectively assigned to them, that is to say–

'fault' means negligence, breach of statutory duty or other act or omission which gives rise to a liability in tort or would, apart from this Act, give rise to the defence of contributory negligence.

The current law on contributory negligence in contract was stated by the Court of Appeal in *Forsikringsaktieselskapet Vesta v Butcher* [1989] AC 852. The court distinguished three different types of situation:

'(1) Where the defendant's liability arises from some contractual provision which does not depend on negligence on the part of the defendant.
(2) Where the defendant's liability arises from a contractual obligation which is expressed in terms of taking care (or its equivalent) but does not correspond to a common law duty to take care which would exist in the given case independently of contract.
(3) Where the defendant's liability in contract is the same as his liability in the tort of negligence independently of the existence of any contract.'

In *Vesta* it was held that the Act applies to the third situation and accordingly damages can be reduced for contributory negligence where the contractual duty of care coexists with the tortious duty of care (recently affirmed by the House of Lords in *Platform Home Loans Ltd v Oyston Shipways* [2000] 2 AC 190). The Act does not apply in the first category, however.

Barclays Bank plc v Fairclough Building Ltd [1995] QB 214

Facts: Fairclough agreed to carry out work for Barclays Bank at Millbrook Industrial Estate, Wythenshawe. The work included the cleaning of roofs made of corrugated asbestos sheets. Fairclough failed to take any of the recommended precautions when using the high pressure hose method of cleaning the asbestos roofs, with the result that the premises became contaminated by asbestos and required extensive remedial works. Barclays brought an action to recover the costs of the works, claiming that Fairclough had breached two of the main obligations under the contract. Fairclough accepted liability but contended that Barclays Bank had been contributorily negligent, in that it had failed to supervise the work through its architectural services department. Barclays Bank countered that its claim lay only in contract and thus the defence of contributory negligence was not available. At first instance, the judge held that the breach of contract was co-existent with a breach of a duty of care in tort. As such, the defence of contributory negligence was available and damages could be reduced by 40 per cent.

Held: The Court of Appeal allowed the appeal holding that, where the defendant had breached a strict contractual obligation, damages could not be reduced on the grounds of contributory negligence.

Beldam LJ:
'[The courts have classified] contractual duties under three headings: (i) where a party's liability arises from breach of a contractual provision which does not depend on a failure to take reasonable care; (ii) where the liability arises from an express contractual obligation to take care which does not correspond to any duty which would exist independently of the contract; (iii) where the liability for breach of contract is the same as, and coextensive with, a liability in tort independently of the existence of a contract. This analysis was adopted by Hobhouse J in *Forsikringsaktieselskapet Vesta v Butcher* [1986] 2 All ER 488 and by the Court of Appeal in the same case [1989] AC 852, 860, 862, 866–867. The judgments in the Court of Appeal in that case assert that in category (iii) cases the Court of Appeal is bound by the decision in *Sayers v Harlow Urban District Council* [1958] 1 WLR 623 to admit the availability of the defence.

. . . [I]n category (i) cases there is no decision in which contributory negligence has been held to be a partial defence. There are powerful dicta to the effect that it cannot be: see the judgment of the court in *Tennant Radiant Heat Ltd v Warrington Development Corporation* [1988] 1 EGLR 41, in *Bank of Nova Scotia v Hellenic Mutual War Risks Association (Bermuda) Ltd* [1990] 1 QB 818, 904, and the observations of Nolan LJ in *Schering Agrochemicals Ltd v Resibel NV SA* (unreported), 26 November 1992; Court of Appeal (Civil Division) Transcript No 1298 of 1992, noted in (1993) 109 LQR 175, 177 . . .

I have already stated my conclusion that in the present case the defendant was in breach of two conditions which required strict performance and did not depend on a mere failure to take reasonable care . . . In my judgment . . . in the present state of the law contributory negligence is not a defence to a claim for damages founded on breach of a strict contractual obligation. I do not believe the wording of the Law Reform (Contributory Negligence) Act 1945 can reasonably sustain an argument to the contrary. Even if it did, in the present case the nature of the contract and the obligation undertaken by the skilled contractor did not impose on the plaintiff any duty in its own interest to prevent the defendant from committing the breaches of contract. To hold otherwise would, I consider, be equivalent to implying into the contract an obligation on the part of the plaintiff inconsistent with the express terms agreed by the parties. The contract clearly laid down the extent of the obligations of the plaintiff as architect and of the defendant. It was the defendant who was to provide appropriate supervision on site, not the architect . . .'

Simon Brown LJ:

'The very imposition of a strict liability on the defendant is to my mind inconsistent with an apportionment of the loss. And not least because of the absurdities that the contrary approach carries in its wake. Assume a defendant, clearly liable under a strict contractual duty. Is his position to be improved by demonstrating that besides breaching that duty he was in addition negligent? Take this very case. Is this contract really to be construed so that the defendant is advantaged by an assertion of its own liability in nuisance or trespass as well as in contract? Are we to have trials at which the defendant calls an expert to implicate him in tortious liability, whilst the plaintiff's expert seeks paradoxically to exonerate him? The answer to all these questions is surely "No". Whatever arguments exist for apportionment in other categories of case – and these are persuasively deployed in the 1993 Law Commission Report (Law Com. No 219) – to my mind there are none in the present type of case and I for my part would construe the contract accordingly.'

The decision in *Fairclough* leads to some surprising results. It is now in a defendant's interests to argue that he is concurrently liable in tort as well as in contract so that he can take advantage of the 1945 Act to reduce his liability. Likewise, it is in a claimant's interests to deny that he has a claim in tort so that he can recover full damages from the defendant in a claim for breach of contract (see *Barclays Bank plc v Fairclough Building Ltd (No 2)* [1995] IRLR 605). This bizarre state of affairs is difficult to justify. Two solutions present themselves. Either contributory negligence should be allowed as a defence to all claims for breach of contract (see Burrows, 'Contributory Negligence in Contract: Ammunition for the Law Commission (1993) 109 LQR 175) or it should be denied any role in the law of contract (this is the approach adopted in Australia: *Astley v Austrust Ltd* (1999) 197 CLR 1). Either solution is better than the present state of affairs.

It seems that the defence of contributory negligence is also unavailable for a claim in category ii – cases where the contractual liability is based on 'negligence', but there is no concurrent duty in tort. In practice, category ii cases are very rare, but the few cases that have come to the court suggest that the defence is not available (see *De Meza v Apple* [1975] 1 Lloyd's Rep 498; *Raflatac Ltd v Eade* [1999] 1 Lloyd's Rep 506). The Law Commission, however, has recommended that contributory negligence should be available in category ii cases by analogy to category iii cases.

> **Law Commission, *Contributory Negligence as a Defence in Contract*, Law Com No 219 (1993)**
>
> *Liability for breach of a contractual duty of reasonable care*
>
> 4.7 Where the plaintiff has suffered damage partly as the result of his own failure to take reasonable care for the protection of himself or his interests and partly as the result of the defendant's breach of a contractual duty to take reasonable care or exercise reasonable skill, we believe that it is correct in principle for his damages to be apportioned. As we stated in the consultation paper, there is a clear similarity in substance between an action for breach of a contractual duty of care and an action for a breach of a tortious duty of reasonable care. Whether a duty of reasonable care is classified as tortious or contractual does not affect the content of that duty, and it is not, in our view, desirable that the availability of apportionment should depend upon how the duty is classified. Furthermore, where the defendant undertakes only a contractual duty of reasonable care, he has not (in contrast to the case where he has accepted a strict contractual obligation) guaranteed to produce a particular outcome. Thus it is unfair to assume that he has undertaken to compensate the plaintiff even where the plaintiff has contributed to his own loss . . . [T]he rules on causation, remoteness and mitigation do not provide an adequate substitute for apportionment and can be unfair to either defendant or plaintiff. This is because they either produce 'all or nothing' results, or do not have the flexibility of apportionment on the basis of what the court thinks just and equitable, given the agreed allocation of risks.

17.2.3.3 Remoteness

The rule of remoteness prevents consequential losses extending too far, and placing unreasonable burdens on the defendant. An example of such a burden was given by Willes J in *British Columbia & Vancouver Island Spar, Lumber and Saw Mill Co v Nettleship* (1868) LR CP 499, 508: '. . . where a man going to be married to an heiress, his horse having cast a shoe on the journey, employed a blacksmith to replace it, who did the work so unskilfully that the horse was lamed, and, the ride not arriving in time, the lady married another; and the blacksmith was held liable for the loss of the marriage.'

Francis Dawson has written that the remoteness rule determines 'the extent of the secondary obligation undertaken by the promisor. It does so by assessing the extent of the liability to which the promisor may be presumed to have assented when undertaking his primary obligation' (Dawson, F, 'Reflections on Certain Aspects of the Law of Damages for Breach of Contract' (1995) 9 JCL 125, 125). This is correct; the rule of remoteness is a rule that the parties are assumed to have assented to in order to limit the scope of their potential liability.

The leading case on remoteness in the law of contract is *Hadley v Baxendale*.

Hadley v Baxendale (1854) 9 Exch 341; 156 ER 145

Facts: The plaintiff, the owner of a flour mill contracted with the defendant, a common carrier, for the transport of a broken crank shaft from the plaintiff's mill to an engineer, who was going to use the broken shaft as a pattern by which to make a new shaft. In breach of contract, the defendant delayed in delivering the crank shaft to the engineer. As a result, the plaintiffs did not receive the new shaft until five days after the date agreed with the carrier. The plaintiff claimed damages for the loss of profit for the five days that the mill was shut as a consequence of the defendant's breach of contract.

Held: The Exchequer Court held that the loss of profits could not be recovered because the loss was too remote.

Alderson B:

'Now we think the proper rule in such a case as the present is this: Where two parties have made a contract which one of them has broken, the damages which the other party ought to receive in respect of such breach of contract should be such as may fairly and reasonably be considered either arising naturally, i.e., according to the usual course of things, from such breach of contract itself, or such as may reasonably be supposed to have been in the contemplation of both parties, at the time they made the contract, as the probable result of the breach of it. Now, if the special circumstances under which the contract was actually made were communicated by the plaintiffs to the defendants, and thus known to both parties, the damages resulting from the breach of such a contract, which they would reasonably contemplate, would be the amount of injury which would ordinarily follow from a breach of contract under these special circumstances so known and communicated. But, on the other hand, if these special circumstances were wholly unknown to the party breaking the contract, he, at the most, could only be supposed to have had in his contemplation the amount of injury which would arise generally, and in the great multitude of cases not affected by any special circumstances, from such a breach of contract. For, had the special circumstances been known, the parties might have specially provided for the breach of contract by special terms as to the damages in that case; and of this advantage it would be very unjust to deprive them . . . Now, in the present case, if we are to apply the principles above laid down, we find that the only circumstances here communicated by the plaintiffs to the defendants at the time the contract was made, were, that the article to be carried was the broken shaft of a mill, and that the plaintiffs were the millers of that mill. But how do these circumstances shew reasonably that the profits of the mill must be stopped by an unreasonable delay in the delivery of the broken shaft by the carrier to the third person? Suppose the plaintiffs had another shaft in their possession put up or putting up at the time, and that they only wished to send back the broken shaft to the engineer who made it; it is clear that this would be quite consistent with the above circumstances, and yet the unreasonable delay in the delivery would have no effect upon the intermediate profits of the mill. Or, again, suppose that, at the time of the delivery to the carrier, the machinery of the mill had been in other respects defective, then, also, the same results would follow. Here it is true that the shaft was actually sent back to serve as a model for a new one, and that the want of a new one was the only cause of the stoppage of the mill, and that the loss of profits really arose from not sending down the new shaft in proper time, and that this arose from the delay in delivering the broken one to serve as a model. But it is obvious that, in the great multitude of cases of millers sending off broken shafts to third persons by a carrier under ordinary circumstances, such consequences would not, in all probability, have occurred; and these special circumstances were here never communicated by the plaintiffs to the defendants. It follows, therefore, that the loss of profits here cannot reasonably be considered such a consequence of the breach of contract as could have been fairly and reasonably contemplated by both the parties when they made this contract. For such loss would neither have flowed naturally from the breach of this contract in the great multitude of such cases occurring under ordinary circumstances, nor were the special circumstances, which, perhaps, would have made it a reasonable and natural consequence of such breach of contract, communicated to or known by the defendants.'

There are two aspects of the *Hadley v Baxendale* test that should be noted. First, it is clear that the focus of the test is on the knowledge of the parties at the time the contract is made. The reason for this is that, if the parties are aware of the risk, they can make changes to the terms of the contract to allocate the risk. In the example given above by Willes J, had the blacksmith been aware of the marriage he could have decided to: (a) charge a higher price; (b) incorporate a limitation or exclusion clause; (c) take out insurance to cover the risk; (d) refuse to enter the contract at all. It is assumed that the parties have agreed to the rule at the time the contract was entered into on the basis of their knowledge at that time. Thus knowledge acquired after the formation of the contract is irrelevant to the rule of remoteness.

There is some uncertainty about the degree of knowledge that is required to hold the defendant liable for the losses sustained. It is clear that 'knowledge' means more than mere 'awareness'. The relevant information must be communicated to the defendant in a context where it is clear that the defendant is expected to assume the risk. Thus in *Kemp v Intasun Holidays* [1987] BTLC 353, communication of the claimant's medical condition at the time a holiday was booked was insufficient to make the defendant liable for losses resulting from it. If communication takes place as part of precontractual negotiations, however, it will normally be assumed that the defendant has accepted liability (see *Simpson v London and North Western Railway Co* (1876) 1 QBD 274). Professor Danzig has noted the inflexibility of the notice requirement and its inappropriateness in the modern industrial world.

> **Danzig, R, 'Hadley v Baxendale: a study in the industrialization of the law'
> (1975) 4 JLS 249, 279–280**
>
> Whether viewed as a simple 'notice' or a more exacting 'contemplation' requirement,
> however, this portion of the rule in *Hadley v Baxendale* runs counter to the tide of an
> industrializing economy. It was already somewhat out of date when expressed in the
> Exchequer opinion. For in *Hadley v Baxendale*, the court spoke as though entre-
> preneurs were universally flexible enough and enterprises small enough for individuals
> to be able to serve 'notice' over the counter of specialized needs calling for unusual
> arrangements. But in mass-transition situations a seller cannot plausibly engage in an
> individualized 'contemplation' of the consequences of breach and a subsequent tailor-
> ing of a transaction. In the course of his conversion of a family business into a modern
> industrial enterprise, Baxendale made Pickfords itself into an operation where the
> contemplation branch of the rule in *Hadley v Baxendale* was no longer viable. Even in
> the 1820's the Pickfords' operations were 'highly complex' . . .
>
> By 1865 the business . . . was 'an enormous mercantile establishment with a huge
> staff of busy clerks, messengers and porters . . . It is divided into innumerable depart-
> ments, the employees in each of which find it as much as they can comfortably do to
> master its details without troubling themselves about any other'.
>
> A century later most enterprises fragment and standardize operations in just this
> way. This development – and the law's recognition of it – makes it self-evidently
> impossible to serve legally cognizable notice on, for example, an airline that a sched-
> uled flight is of special importance or on the telephone company that uninterrupted
> service is particularly vital at a particular point in a firm's business cycle.

The second important aspect of the rule in *Hadley v Baxendale* is that it appears to
have two parts:

1. losses that may fairly and reasonably be considered to arise *naturally* from the
   breach;
2. losses that may reasonably be supposed to have been in the *contemplation* of both
   parties, at the time they made the contract.

Later decisions (*Victoria Laundry (Windsor) Ltd v Newman Industries* [1949] 2 KB
528; *Koufos v C Czarnikow Ltd, The Heron II* [1969] 1 AC 350) have treated these
two parts as aspects of the same general principle. In the recent case of *Jackson v
Royal Bank of Scotland* [2005] 1 WLR 377, 390–1, Lord Walker said:

'In my opinion the familiar passage from the judgment of Alderson B . . .
cannot be construed and applied as if it were a statutory text, nor are its two
limbs mutually exclusive. The first limb . . . tends to beg the question, since it
makes the damages recoverable under the first limb depend on how the breach

of contract is characterised. If for instance (by reference to the facts of *Hadley v Baxendale* itself) the breach is described simply as a carrier's failure to convey goods from Gloucester and deliver them to Greenwich within two days as promised, it is a matter of speculation what damages would arise naturally and in the ordinary course. If on the other hand the breach is described as a delay in delivering to the manufacturer at Greenwich a broken crankshaft to serve as a model for a new crankshaft urgently required for the only steam engine at a busy flour mill at Gloucester (which was standing idle until the new crankshaft arrived) then loss of business profits is seen to be an entirely natural consequence. The appropriate characterisation of the breach depends on the terms of the contract, its business context, and the reasonable contemplation of the parties (although Baron Alderson used the latter expression in relation to the second limb).'

Both limbs of the test are concerned with the same question: Did the defendant know, or ought he reasonably to have known, that such a loss was likely to result from the breach of contract? The first limb deals with normal types of loss, which the reasonable defendant is deemed to know about because they arise naturally from a breach of contract. The second limb deals with the more unusual types of loss, which the defendant will only be liable for if he had sufficient actual knowledge of the risk. The application of this two-limbed test can be seen in the case of:

Victoria Laundry (Windsor) v Newman Industries [1949] 2 KB 528

Facts: The plaintiffs, launders and dyers, entered into a contract with the defendants for the purchase of a large boiler. At the time the contract was concluded, the boiler was installed at the defendants' premises. The defendants hired a third party to dismantle the boiler. During the dismantling, the boiler rolled over and sustained serious damage. This meant that delivery of the boiler was delayed by five months. The defendants were aware of the nature of the plaintiffs' business, and had been informed by a letter from the plaintiffs that they intended to put the boiler in use in the shortest possible space of time. In an action for breach of contract, the plaintiffs claimed damages for the loss of profits they had sustained as a result of the delay.

Held: The Court of Appeal held that the plaintiffs were entitled to recover damages for lost profits at a level reasonably to be anticipated from a business of its kind. However, the plaintiffs could not recover damages for lost profits on some particularly lucrative dyeing contracts with the Ministry of Defence, of which the defendants were unaware.

Asquith LJ:
'What propositions applicable to the present case emerge from the authorities as a whole . . .? We think they include the following:

(1) It is well settled that the governing purpose of damages is to put the party whose rights have been violated in the same position, so far as money can do so, as if his rights had been observed: *Sally Wertheim v Chicoutimi Pulp Company* [1911] AC 301. This purpose, if relentlessly pursued, would provide him with a complete indemnity for all loss de facto resulting from a particular breach, however improbable, however unpredictable. This, in contract at least, is recognised as too harsh a rule. Hence,

(2) In cases of breach of contract the aggrieved party is only entitled to recover such part of the loss actually resulting as was at the time of the contract reasonably foreseeable as liable to result from the breach.

(3) What was at that time reasonably so foreseeable depends on the knowledge then possessed by the parties or, at all events, by the party who later commits the breach.

(4) For this purpose, knowledge "possessed" is of two kinds; one imputed, the other actual. Everyone, as a reasonable person, is taken to know the "ordinary course of things" and consequently what loss is liable to result from a breach of contract in that ordinary course. This is the subject matter of the "first rule" in *Hadley v. Baxendale* 9 Exch. 341. But to this knowledge, which a contract-breaker is assumed to possess whether he actually possesses it or not, there may have to be added in a particular case knowledge which he actually possesses, of special circumstances outside the "ordinary course of things", of such a kind that a breach in those special circumstances would be liable to cause more loss. Such a case attracts the operation of the "second rule" so as to make additional loss also recoverable.

(5) In order to make the contract-breaker liable under either rule it is not necessary that he should actually have asked himself what loss is liable to result from a breach. As has often been pointed out, parties at the time of contracting contemplate not the breach of the contract, but its performance. It suffices that, if he had considered the question, he would as a reasonable man have concluded that the loss in question was liable to result (see certain observations of Lord du Parcq in the recent case of *A/B Karlshamns Oliefabriker v Monarch Steamship Company Limited* [1949] AC 196.

(6) Nor, finally, to make a particular loss recoverable, need it be proved that upon a given state of knowledge the defendant could, as a reasonable man, foresee that a breach must necessarily result in that loss. It is enough if he could foresee it was likely so to result. It is indeed enough, to borrow from the language of Lord du Parcq in the same case, at page 158, if the loss (or some factor without which it would not have occurred) is a "serious possibility" or a "real danger". For short, we have used the word "liable" to result. Possibly the colloquialism "on the cards" indicates the shade of meaning with some approach to accuracy.

If these, indeed, are the principles applicable, what is the effect of their application to the facts of this case? . . . No commercial concern commonly purchases for the purposes of its business a very large and expensive structure like this – a boiler 19 feet high and costing over £2,000 – with any other motive, and no supplier, let alone an engineering company, which has promised delivery of such an article by a particular date, with knowledge that it was to be put into use immediately on delivery, can reasonably contend that it could not foresee that loss of business (in the sense indicated above) would be liable to result to the purchaser from a long delay in the delivery thereof. The suggestion that, for all the supplier knew, the boiler might have been needed simply as a "standby," to be used in a possibly distant future, is gratuitous and was plainly negatived by the terms of the letter of April 26, 1946 . . .'

[In respect of losses flowing from the contract with the Ministry of Defence he continued]

'Here, no doubt, the learned judge had in mind the particularly lucrative dyeing contracts to which the plaintiffs looked forward and which they mention in para 10 of the statement of claim. We agree that in order that the plaintiffs should recover specifically and as such the profits expected on these contracts, the defendants would have had to know, at the time of their agreement with the plaintiffs, of the prospect and terms of such contracts. We also agree that they did not in fact know these things. It does not, however, follow that the plaintiffs are precluded from recovering some general (and perhaps conjectural) sum for loss of business in respect of dyeing contracts to be reasonably expected, any more than in respect of laundering contracts to be reasonably expected.'

The plaintiffs' claim did not succeed in relation to the loss of profits on the contracts with the Ministry of Defence because the defendant did not have actual knowledge of these contracts. The Court of Appeal drew a distinction between ordinary business profits and exceptional profits. This is a distinction of degree rather than kind and in the following case the Court of Appeal held that only the type of loss (and not the extent of the loss) needed to be foreseeable.

Parsons (Livestock) Ltd v Uttley Ingham & Co Ltd [1978] QB 791

Facts: The plaintiffs ordered a bulk food storage hopper from the defendants. They informed the defendants that they intended to use the hopper to store pignuts for feeding their top grade pigherd. When they installed the hopper, the defendants failed to notice that the ventilator at the top of the hopper was closed. As a result, the pignuts dispensed by the hopper were mouldy and a large number of pigs contracted E. coli. The plaintiffs brought an action for breach of contract claiming substantial damages including loss of profit. The defendants denied that they were liable for the loss of profits on the ground that the loss was too remote a consequence of the breach of contract.

Held: The Court of Appeal held that the defendants were liable for the loss of profits because some harm to the pigs was within the reasonable contemplation of the parties as something which would result from supplying a hopper that was unfit for the purpose of storing food for pigs.

Scarman LJ:

'The judge put it this way:

> "The natural result of feeding toxic food to animals is damage to their health and may be death, which is what occurred, albeit from a hitherto unknown disease and to particularly susceptible animals. There was therefore no need to invoke the question of reasonable contemplation in order to make the defendant liable".

The judge in this critical passage is contrasting a natural result, i.e. one which people placed as these parties were would consider as a serious possibility, with a special, specific result, i.e. E. coli disease, which, as he later found, the parties could not at the time of contract reasonably have contemplated as a consequence. He distinguished between "presumed contemplation" based on a special knowledge from ordinary understanding based upon general knowledge and concludes that the case falls within the latter category. He does so because he has held that the assumption, or hypothesis, to be made is that the parties had in mind at the time of contract not a breach of warranty limited to the delivery of mouldy nuts but a warranty as to the fitness of the hopper for its purpose. The assumption is of the parties asking themselves not what is likely to happen if the nuts are mouldy but what is likely to happen to the pigs if the hopper is unfit for storing nuts suitable to be fed to them. While, on his finding, nobody at the time of contract could have expected E. coli to ensue from eating mouldy nuts, he is clearly – and, as a matter of common sense, rightly – saying that people would contemplate, upon the second assumption, the serious possibility of injury and even death among the pigs.

And so the question becomes: was he right to make the assumption he did? In my judgment, he was: see *Grant v Australian Knitting Mills Ltd* [1936] AC 85, and particularly the well-known passage in the speech of Lord Wright at pp 97–100.

I would agree with *McGregor on Damages*, 13th edn (1972), pp 131–132 that

> ". . . in contract as in tort, it should suffice that, if physical injury or damage is within the contemplation of the parties, recovery is not to be limited because the degree of physical injury or damage could not have been anticipated."

This is so, in my judgment, not because there is, or ought to be, a specific rule of law governing cases of physical injury but because it would be absurd to regulate damages in such cases upon the necessity of supposing the parties had a prophetic foresight as to the exact nature of the injury that does in fact arise. It is enough if upon the hypothesis predicated physical injury must have been a serious possibility. Though in loss of market or loss of profit cases the factual analysis will be very different from cases of physical injury, the same principles, in my judgment, apply. Given the situation of the parties at the time of contract, was the loss of profit, or market, a serious possibility, something that would have been in their minds had they contemplated breach?'

The difficulty of reconciling *Parsons* with *Victoria Laundry* has been noted by Professor Burrows.

Burrows, A, *Remedies for Torts and Breach of Contract*, 3rd edn, 2004, Oxford: OUP, p 90

One could argue, for example, that since illness and death of pigs were regarded as the same type of loss, and merely differed in extent, the majority's approach is irreconcilable with *Victoria Laundry*; for one could argue that the type of loss in issue there was loss of profits, and that the exceptional profits were merely a greater extent of that same type of loss. Presumably, the majority's answer to this would be that its test allows the courts a discretion as to how to divide up the loss, and that *Victoria Laundry* is reconcilable by regarding the ordinary loss of profits as a different type of loss from the exceptional loss of profits. But such discretion and flexibility in the test is only achieved at the expense of certainty. However, some support for the majority's approach does derive from Megarry J's earlier holding in *Wroth v Tyler*, that the extraordinary and uncontemplated rise in the market price of houses was not too remote because the type of loss – a difference between the market and contract prices – had been contemplated. But it can be argued that the case is better regarded as turning on the fact that the claimants were 'consumers', who wanted the house to live in, rather than businessmen. As such their loss was most accurately described as the loss of a home of a certain standard rather than a loss of profit. Viewed in this way, the loss was clearly contemplated, and remoteness and the type/extent distinction were not in issue.

By permitting the courts to draw the line between type of loss and extent of loss the law has imported a significant degree of judicial discretion into the rule of remoteness. But is it really possible to maintain that illness and death are the same type of loss while ordinary loss of profits and exceptional loss of profits are not? Recently, the House of Lords confirmed the latter distinction in the case of *Balfour Beatty Construction (Scotland) Ltd v Scottish Power plc* 1994 SLT 807. The defendants agreed to supply electricity to the plaintiffs who were the main construction company working on the Edinburgh bypass. The supply of electricity failed while the plaintiff was in the middle of the construction of an aqueduct. This work required a 'continuous pour' of concrete and, as a result of the failure, the work which had been done was worthless and had to be demolished. The House of Lords refused to award damages for the full losses suffered by the plaintiff because there was no evidence that the defendants were aware of the need for a continuous pour. Nor was it possible to presume that the defendants were aware of the plaintiffs' business activities.

Ultimately, the judicial discretion inherent in the distinction between type of loss and extent of loss enables the courts to allocate the responsibility for the consequences of breach in a way that corresponds to the implied assumption of responsibility between the parties. This is surely desirable. Had *Balfour Beatty* been decided the other way, Scottish Power would have been forced to recoup the cost of meeting the damages claim by raising prices for consumers. This would have been unfair on society as a whole. Balfour Beatty had voluntarily engaged in a high-risk construction project that required a constant supply of electricity. They had failed to inform Scottish Power of this exceptional use and had not negotiated express terms as to the allocation of risk. In such circumstances, it is surely fair to presume that Balfour Beatty had accepted the risk and assumed responsibility for any exceptional loss flowing from the breach of contract by Scottish Power.

Finally, it is necessary to consider the degree of risk that must be proven in order to recover damages for breach of contract. In the law of tort the test is one of 'reasonable forseeability'. In the law of contract, the test appears to be stricter.

Koufos v C Czarnikow Ltd, The Heron II [1969] 1 AC 350

Facts: The plaintiff chartered a ship to carry a cargo of sugar from Constanza to Basrah. In breach of contract, the ship deviated from its route and reached Basrah nine days late. The sugar was sold immediately but the market price for sugar had fallen significantly. The plaintiff sought to recover the difference in price as damages. The defendant argued that they were unaware of the charters' intention to sell the sugar.

Held: The House of Lords held that the defendants were liable for the loss.

Lord Reid:
'I am satisfied that the court did not intend that every type of damage which was reasonably foreseeable by the parties when the contract was made should either be considered as arising naturally, i.e., in the usual course of things, or be supposed to have been in the contemplation of the parties. Indeed the decision makes it clear that a type of damage which was plainly foreseeable as a real possibility but which would only occur in a small minority of cases cannot be regarded as arising in the usual course of things or be supposed to have been in the contemplation of the parties: the parties are not supposed to contemplate as grounds for the recovery of damage any type of loss or damage which on the knowledge available to the defendant would appear to him as only likely to occur in a small minority of cases. In cases like *Hadley v Baxendale* 9 Exch 341, or the present case it is not enough that in fact the plaintiff's loss was directly caused by the defendant's breach of contract. It clearly was so

caused in both. The crucial question is whether, on the information available to the defendant when the contract was made, he should, or the reasonable man in his position would, have realised that such loss was sufficiently likely to result from the breach of contract to make it proper to hold that the loss flowed naturally from the breach or that loss of that kind should have been within his contemplation.

The modern rule of tort is quite different and it imposes a much wider liability. The defendant will be liable for any type of damage which is reasonably foreseeable as liable to happen even in the most unusual case, unless the risk is so small that a reasonable man would in the whole circumstances feel justified in neglecting it and there is good reason for the difference. In contract, if one party wishes to protect himself against a risk which to the other party would appear unusual, he can direct the other party's attention to it before the contract is made, and I need not stop to consider in what circumstances the other party will then be held to have accepted responsibility in that event. But in tort there is no opportunity for the injured party to protect himself in that way, and the tortfeasor cannot reasonably complain if he has to pay for some very unusual but nevertheless foreseeable damage which results from his wrongdoing. I have no doubt that today a tortfeasor would be held liable for a type of damage as unlikely as was the stoppage of Hadley's Mill for lack of a crankshaft: to anyone with the knowledge the carrier had that may have seemed unlikely but the chance of it happening would have been seen to be far from negligible. But it does not at all follow that *Hadley v Baxendale* 9 Exch. 341 would today be differently decided.'

Lord Morris:

[Referring to *R & H Hall Ltd v W H Pim (Junior) & Co Ltd* 33 Com Cas 324 he continued]

'Though that case was one in which the parties had made express provisions in regard to sub-sales with the result that they must have "recognised" that a purchaser might have to pay damages to his sub-purchaser if the vendor failed to deliver, the expressions used in the speeches illustrate that damages could be recoverable in respect of a loss which might occur or which the parties could contemplate as not unlikely to occur. The present case is one in which no special information was given to the carrier as to what the respondents intended to do with the goods after they arrived at Basrah. In those circumstances in deciding what damages would fairly and reasonably be regarded as arising if the delivery of the goods was delayed I think that the reasonable contemplation of a reasonable ship owner at the time of the making of the charter party must be considered. I think that such a ship owner must reasonably have contemplated that if he delivered the sugar at Basrah some nine or ten days later than he could and should have delivered it then a loss by reason of a fall in the market price of sugar at Basrah was one that was liable to result or at least was not unlikely to result.'

Lord Pearce:

'In 1948 in *Monarch Steamship Co Ltd v Karlshamns Oljefabriker (A/B)* [1949] AC 196, a case of damages for delay in carriage by sea, Lord du Parcq used the words "at least a serious possibility" and "a real danger which must be taken into account". Lord

Uthwatt spoke of "the chance of war, not as a possibility of academic interest . . . but as furnishing matter which commercially ought to be taken into account" and Lord Morton of Henryton spoke of "a grave risk."

Accordingly in my opinion the expressions used in the *Victoria Laundry* case were right. I do not however accept the colloquialism "on the cards" as being a useful test because I am not sure just what nuance it has either in my own personal vocabulary or in that of others. I suspect that it owes its attraction, like many other colloquialisms, to the fact that one may utter it without having the trouble of really thinking out with precision what one means oneself or what others will understand by it, a spurious attraction which in general makes colloquialism unsuitable for definition, though it is often useful as shorthand for a collection of definable ideas. It was in this latter convenient sense that the judgment uses the ambiguous words "liable to result". They were not intended as a further or different test from "serious possibility" or "real danger". . . .'

Lord Upjohn:

'It is clear that on the one hand the test of foreseeability as laid down in the case of tort is not the test for breach of contract; nor on the other hand must the loser establish that the loss was a near certainty or an odds-on probability. I am content to adopt as the test a "real danger" or a "serious possibility". There may be a shade of difference between these two phrases but the assessment of damages is not an exact science and what to one judge or jury will appear a real danger may appear to another judge or jury to be a serious possibility . . .

Applying this test to the facts of this case . . . the *Heron II* took very nearly 50 per cent more than the reasonably predicted time and for no other reason than her owner's breaches of contract. It is perfectly true that at the time of the contract nothing was said as to the purpose for which the charterer wanted the sugar delivered at Basrah; he might have wanted to do so to stock up his supply of sugar or to carry out a contract already entered into which had nothing to do with the market at Basrah; or he might sell it during the voyage, but all that is pure speculation. It seems to me that on the facts of this case the parties must be assumed to have contemplated that there would be a punctual delivery to the port of discharge and that port having a market in sugar there was a real danger that as a result of a delay in breach of contract the charterer would miss the market and would suffer loss accordingly. It being established that the goods were in fact destined for the market the ship owner is liable for that loss.'

It is somewhat difficult to ascertain the precise test to be used in future cases. Lord Reid spoke in terms of the loss being 'sufficiently likely to result' from the breach of contract. Lord Morris used the phrases 'not unlikely to occur' and 'liable to result'. Lords Pearce and Upjohn preferred the words 'a real danger' or 'a serious possibility'. The Law Lords did agree that a higher degree of likelihood of the loss occurring was required in contract than in the law of tort. Professor Burrows (*Remedies for Torts and Breach of Contract*, 3rd edn, 2004, p 88, Oxford: OUP) has provided the following summary of the case:

> 'Perhaps the clearest way of expressing the essence of their Lordships' reasoning is that, while a slight possibility of the loss occurring is required in tort, a serious possibility of the loss occurring is required in contract. So, on the facts, the loss of profit from the market fall was not too remote because the defendant should have reasonably contemplated that loss as a serious possibility had it thought about the breach at the time the contract was made.'

17.2.3.4 Mitigation

Following a breach of contract, a claimant is not entitled to sit back and watch his losses accumulate. He is under an obligation to take reasonable steps to 'mitigate' his loss. The principle of mitigation is described by Professor Bridge in the following extract.

Bridge, M, 'Mitigation of damages in contract and the meaning of avoidable loss' (1989) 105 LQR 398, 398–9

The principle of mitigation breaks down into three basic rules. First, a party injured upon the occurrence of a breach of contract may not hold the contract-breaker responsible in respect of losses which he could reasonably have avoided. Secondly, expenses reasonably incurred in avoiding or minimising a loss resulting from breach of contract may be charged to the contract-breaker. Thirdly, regardless of whether an injured party in the circumstances had to mitigate, any action he does take after the breach of contract, which in fact avoids or minimises the loss, will serve correspondingly to diminish the contract-breaker's liability in damages . . .

. . . [A] few preliminary observations have to be made. First of all, it is quite inaccurate to speak of the plaintiff having a "duty" to mitigate, for it is not met by any corresponding right of the defendant that mitigation take place. Rather, the principle of mitigation operates *pro tanto* as a conditional bar to the recovery of damages. Since, however, the language of duty is so well entrenched and difficult to substitute, it will be used throughout this article.

Secondly, the burden of proof that mitigation should have taken place rests on the defendant, though the plaintiff has to show that loss incurred was in fact caused by the defendant's breach of contract. Since the rule is commonly explained in the language of factual causation, a degree of tension plainly exists between these two propositions. This tension, however, may be abated in practice by the use of tactical or evidentiary presumptions. As the plaintiff points to the apparent link between his loss and the defendant's breach, the defendant is driven to show why the loss should more properly be attributed to the plaintiff's failure to mitigate.

The final preliminary observation is that the plaintiff who ought to mitigate will not be held to an extraordinary standard of behaviour. The extent to which there should have been mitigation is a question of fact and the plaintiff must take steps consistent with the demands of reasonable and prudent action. The plaintiff will not have to embark upon a difficult and hazardous course of action, nor to act in such a way as to impair his commercial reputation. Subjective circumstances are taken into account to the extent of relieving an impecunious plaintiff from incurring expenditure, provided such impecuniosity does not betoken a reprehensible abdication of commercial responsibility on entering into the contractual adventure.

The obligation to mitigate was laid down by the House of Lords in *British Westinghouse Electric and Manufacturing Co v Underground Electric Railways Co of London* [1912] AC 673. Viscount Haldane explained that the obligation:

'imposes on a plaintiff the duty of taking all reasonable steps to mitigate the loss consequent on the breach, and debars him from claiming any part of the damage which is due to his neglect to take such steps. In the words of James LJ in *Dunkirk Colliery Co v Lever* (1878) 9 Ch D 20, at p 25, "The person who has broken the contract is not to be exposed to additional cost by reason of the plaintiffs not doing what they ought to have done as reasonable men, and the plaintiffs not being under any obligation to do anything otherwise than in the ordinary course of business."

As James LJ indicates, this second principle does not impose on the plaintiff an obligation to take any step which a reasonable and prudent man would not ordinarily take in the course of his business. But when in the course of his business he has taken action arising out of the transaction, which action has diminished his loss, the effect in actual diminution of the loss he has suffered may be taken into account even though there was no duty on him to act.'

The principle of mitigation has both a positive and a negative limb:

1. If the claimant takes steps to mitigate his loss, he will only be entitled to recover his actual losses. He will not be permitted to recover the hypothetical sum that he would have obtained had he failed to take steps to mitigate his loss, even though those steps might have gone beyond what could reasonably have been expected. For example, if a seller fails to deliver on a contract for the sale of 100 widgets and the buyer manages to find an alternative widget supplier on eBay who will sell at the same price, the buyer will only be entitled to nominal damages.

2. The claimant is required to act and must take reasonable steps to minimise his loss. He will be debarred from recovering damages in respect of loss attributable to his failure to mitigate. For example, if an employer wrongfully

dismisses an employee and the employee fails to seek alternative employment, he will be debarred from recovering damages for the loss of wages attributable to his failure to mitigate.

The principle of mitigation imposes a significant burden on the claimant. As Professor Bridge notes, mitigation is not a duty in the legal sense, because the defendant cannot sue the claimant for failure to mitigate. However, the fact that the claimant is barred from recovering damages in respect of losses attributable to his failure to mitigate gives the claimant a substantial incentive to mitigate his losses. In practice, the doctrine of mitigation amounts to a significant qualification of the law's commitment to protection of the claimant's interest in performance.

Mitigation may require the claimant to go to significant lengths to reduce his losses. It may even require him to accept an offer of alternative performance from the party in breach.

Payzu Ltd v Saunders [1919] 2 KB 581

Facts: The plaintiff entered into a contract with the defendants for the sale of a quantity of silk, to be delivered in instalments. The contract provided for payment within one month of delivery of each instalment. The plaintiffs failed to make punctual payment for the first instalment. The defendant, in breach of contract, refused to deliver any further instalments unless the plaintiff agreed to pay in cash with each order. The plaintiffs refused to accept this offer, and, the market price of the goods having risen, brought an action against the defendant for breach of contract, claiming as damages the difference between the market price and the contract price.

Held: The Court of Appeal held that the defendant was liable for damages but that the plaintiffs should have mitigated their loss by accepting the defendant's offer. As a result the plaintiff was only entitled to damages for such loss as they would have suffered if they had accepted that offer.

Scrutton LJ:
'The plaintiff must take "all reasonable steps to mitigate the loss consequent on the breach", and this principle "debars him from claiming any part of the damage which is due to his neglect to take such steps": *British Westinghouse Electric and Manufacturing Co v Underground Electric Railways Co of London* [1912] AC 673, per Lord Haldane LC. [Counsel for the plaintiffs] has contended that in considering what steps should be taken to mitigate the damage all contractual relations with the party in default must be excluded. That is contrary to my experience. In certain cases of personal service it may be unreasonable to expect a plaintiff to consider an offer from the other party who has grossly injured him; but in commercial contracts it is generally reasonable to accept an offer from the party in default.'

The decision in Payzu has been criticised by Professor Bridge.

> ### Bridge, M, 'Mitigation of damages in contract and the meaning of avoidable loss' (1989) 105 LQR 398, 413–414
>
> The decision in *Payzu* seems thoroughly sensible and pragmatical. Indeed, it appears not to have troubled or even intrigued commentators. Yet, it is worth examining in some detail the trial judge's assertion that 'extraordinary results would follow if the plaintiffs were entitled to reject the defendant's offer and incur a substantial measure of loss which would have been avoided by their acceptance of the offer'.
>
> The contract concerned raw silk fabric used in the manufacture of formal ladies' attire. On the basis of the meagre information contained in the report, there was evidently an available market in which the value of the commodity could be measured from time to time. It is not possible, however, to quantify the volume of trading. On the plaintiff's own evidence, the market was rising and there was a shortage of crêpe de chine. Putting aside the small difficulty of the date of reference to the market, the following problem presents itself. Any loss suffered by the plaintiff in not taking the goods at the below-market price offered by the defendant was exactly matched by the defendant's gain when, liberated by the plaintiff's refusal to take up the goods, she was enabled to dispose of those same goods at the higher market rate. Another way of putting the matter is to say that the defendant was enriched by the plaintiff's failure to mitigate. She was permitted to recover the market rise she had lost after contracting at the lower rate, a rise moreover that she would still have lost had the plaintiff accepted her offer of mitigation. This must be wrong. The doctrine of mitigation should not be applied where it serves only to reverse the roles of contract-breaker and injured party. There was nothing in the case to show a loss of trading volume when the defendant declined to take the goods and, furthermore, it is most unlikely that such a loss could have occurred, given the rising value of crêpe de chine and the shortage of available stocks on the market at the relevant time. If the rules of mitigation exist to prevent an unfair imposition of loss on the defendant, it is impossible to see such a policy at work in the present case, which appears rather to punish the plaintiff for its tactical mistake in not accepting the defendant's offer.

Despite the criticisms of *Payzu*, the principle was applied and extended in *Sotiros Shipping Inc v Sameiet Solholt (The Soholt)* [1983] 1 Lloyd's Rep 605. The Court of Appeal held that the buyers of a ship who lawfully repudiated the contract for late delivery could not claim damages for the difference in value between the contract price ($5 million) and the market price ($5.5 million) because they had failed to offer to buy the ship at the contract price minus the costs of delay to them. This decision has been roundly criticised by commentators. It had the effect of allowing the defendants to benefit from the rising market. They eventually sold the ship to a third party for $5.8 million. This meant that, despite their breach of contract, they made a gain of $800,000. Meanwhile, the innocent plaintiffs were left uncompensated and were forced to pay more to purchase a substitute ship in a rising market.

While mitigation can sometimes have harsh results, it is important to note that it only requires the claimant to act 'reasonably' in the circumstances. The particular circumstances of the claimant might mean that it is impossible for him or her to mitigate his or her loss in the way that a reasonable person would. In *Lagden v O'Connor* [2004] 1 AC 1067, the claimant was involved in a road traffic accident that was not his fault. He was unemployed and could not afford to pay for a hire car so he obtained a car on credit, which was more expensive. The House of Lords held that he could recover his full loss. Lord Nicholls said: 'in measuring the loss suffered by an impecunious plaintiff by loss of use of his own car the law will recognise that, because of his lack of financial means, the timely provision of a replacement vehicle for him costs more than it does in the case of his more affluent neighbour'.

Mitigation presents a number of problems in the context of anticipatory breach. Normally a claimant has the option either to accept the breach or to reject it. Is the claimant entitled to accept the breach and affirm the contract even though this will lead to a significant increase in his or her loss if the defendant fails to perform?

White and Carter (Councils) Ltd v McGregor [1962] AC 413

Facts: The defendants contracted to purchase advertising space on litter bins belonging to the plaintiffs. This contract was wrongfully cancelled by the defendants. The plaintiffs refused to accept the anticipatory breach and they went ahead with the production and display of the advertisements over the full three-year term of the contract. The defendants refused to pay any sums due under the contract and the plaintiffs sued for the whole amount.

Held: The House of Lords held, by a majority of 3:2, that there is no obligation on the plaintiffs in such a situation to mitigate its losses. The plaintiffs were not obliged to accept the repudiation and claim damages for the full sum due under the contract.

Lord Reid:
'The general rule cannot be in doubt. It was settled in Scotland at least as early as 1848 and it has been authoritatively stated time and again in both Scotland and England. If one party to a contract repudiates it in the sense of making it clear to the other party that he refuses or will refuse to carry out his part of the contract, the other party, the innocent party, has an option. He may accept that repudiation and sue for damages for breach of contract, whether or not the time for performance has come; or he may if he chooses disregard or refuse to accept it and then the contract remains in full effect . . .

I need not refer to the numerous authorities. They are not disputed by the respondent but he points out that in all of them the party who refused to accept the repudiation had no active duties under the contract. The innocent party's option is generally said to be to *wait* until the date of performance and then to claim damages estimated as at that date. There is no case in which it is said that he may, in face of the repudiation, go on and incur useless expense in performing the contract and then claim the contract price. The option, it is argued, is merely as to the date as at which damages are to be assessed.

Developing this argument, the respondent points out that in most cases the innocent party cannot complete the contract himself without the other party doing, allowing or accepting something, and that it is purely fortuitous that the appellants can do so in this case. In most cases by refusing co-operation the party in breach can compel the innocent party to restrict his claim to damages. Then it was said that, even where the innocent party can complete the contract without such co-operation, it is against the public interest that he should be allowed to do so. An example was developed in argument. A company might engage an expert to go abroad and prepare an elaborate report and then repudiate the contract before anything was done. To allow such an expert then to waste thousands of pounds in preparing the report cannot be right if a much smaller sum of damages would give him full compensation for his loss. It would merely enable the expert to extort a settlement giving him far more than reasonable compensation.

The respondent founds on the decision of the First Division in *Langford & Co Ltd v Dutch*. There an advertising contractor agreed to exhibit a film for a year. Four days after this agreement was made the advertiser repudiated it but, as in the present case, the contractor refused to accept the repudiation and proceeded to exhibit the film and sue for the contract price. The Sheriff-Substitute dismissed the action as irrelevant and his decision was affirmed on appeal. In the course of a short opinion Lord President Cooper said: "It appears to me that, apart from wholly exceptional circumstances of which there is no trace in the averments on this record, the law of Scotland does not afford to a person in the position of the pursuers the remedy which is here sought. The pursuers could not force the defender to accept a year's advertisement which she did not want, though they could of course claim damages for her breach of contract. On the averments the only reasonable and proper course, which the pursuers should have adopted, would have been to treat the defender as having repudiated the contract and as being on that account liable in damages, the measure of which we are, of course, not in a position to discuss."

The Lord President cited no authority and I am in doubt as to what principle he had in mind . . .

. . . We must now decide whether that case was rightly decided. In my judgment it was not. It could only be supported on one or other of two grounds. It might be said that, because in most cases the circumstances are such that an innocent party is unable to complete the contract and earn the contract price without the assent or co-operation of the other party, therefore in cases where he can do so he should not be allowed to do so. I can see no justification for that.

The other ground would be that there is some general equitable principle or element of public policy which requires this limitation of the contractual rights of the innocent party. It may well be that, if it can be shown that a person has no legitimate interest, financial or otherwise, in performing the contract rather than claiming damages, he ought not to be allowed to saddle the other party with an additional burden with no benefit to himself. If a party has no interest to enforce a stipulation, he cannot in general enforce it: so it might be said that, if a party has no interest to insist on a particular remedy, he ought not to be allowed to insist on it. And, just as a party is not allowed to enforce a penalty, so he ought not to be allowed to penalise the other party by taking one course when another is equally advantageous to him. If I may revert to the example which I gave of a company engaging an expert to prepare an elaborate report and then repudiating before anything was done, it might be that the company could show that the expert had no substantial or legitimate interest in carrying out the work rather than accepting damages: I would think that the *de minimis* principle would apply in determining whether his interest was substantial, and that he might have a legitimate interest other than an immediate financial interest. But if the expert had no such interest then that might be regarded as a proper case for the exercise of the general equitable jurisdiction of the court. But that is not this case. Here the respondent did not set out to prove that the appellants had no legitimate interest in completing the contract and claiming the contract price rather than claiming damages; there is nothing in the findings of fact to support such a case, and it seems improbable that any such case could have been proved. It is, in my judgment, impossible to say that the appellants should be deprived of their right to claim the contract price merely because the benefit to them, as against claiming damages and re-letting their advertising space, might be small in comparison with the loss to the respondent: that is the most that could be said in favour of the respondent. Parliament has on many occasions relieved parties from certain kinds of improvident or oppressive contracts, but the common law can only do that in very limited circumstances. Accordingly, I am unable to avoid the conclusion that this appeal must be allowed and the case remitted so that decree can be pronounced as craved in the initial writ.'

Lord Morton of Henryton [dissenting]:
'It is well established that repudiation by one party does not put an end to a contract. The other party can say "I hold you to your contract, which still remains in force." What then is his remedy if the repudiating party persists in his repudiation and refuses to carry out his part of the contract? The contract has been broken. The innocent party is entitled to be compensated by damages for any loss which he has suffered by reason of the breach, and in a limited class of cases the court will decree specific implement. The law of Scotland provides no other remedy for a breach of contract and there is no reported case which decides that the innocent party may act as the appellants have acted. The present case is one in which specific implement could not be decreed, since the only obligation of the respondent under the contract was to pay a sum of money for services to be rendered by the appellants. Yet the appellants are claiming a kind of inverted specific implement of the contract. They first insist on performing their

part of the contract, against the will of the other party, and then claim that he must perform his part and pay the contract price for unwanted services. In my opinion, my Lords, the appellants' only remedy was damages, and they were bound to take steps to minimise their loss, according to a well-established rule of law. Far from doing this, having incurred no expense at the date of the repudiation, they made no attempt to procure another advertiser, but deliberately went on to incur expense and perform unwanted services with the intention of creating a money debt which did not exist at the date of the repudiation . . .'

Lord Hodson:

'It is settled as a fundamental rule of the law of contract that repudiation by one of the parties to a contract does not itself discharge it. See Viscount Simon's speech in *Heyman v Darwins Ltd* [1942] AC 356, 361, citing with approval the following sentence from a judgment of Scrutton LJ in *Golding v London and Edinburgh Insurance Co Ltd* (1932) 43 Lloyd's Law Rep 487, 488: "I have never been able to understand what effect the repudiation of one party has unless the other party accepts the repudiation."

In *Howard v Pickford Tool Co Ltd* [1951] 1 KB 417, 421, Asquith LJ said: "An unaccepted repudiation is a thing writ in water and of no value to anybody: it confers no legal rights of any sort or kind." These are English cases but that the law of Scotland is the same is, I think, clear from the authorities, of which I need only refer to one, namely, *Howie v Anderson* 10 D 355, where language to the same effect is to be found in the opinions of the Lord President and Lord Moncrieff.

It follows that, if, as here, there was no acceptance, the contract remains alive for the benefit of both parties and the party who has repudiated can change his mind but it does not follow that the party at the receiving end of the proffered repudiation is bound to accept it before the time for performance and is left to his remedy in damages for breach.

[Counsel for the respondent] did not seek to dispute the general proposition of law to which I have referred but sought to argue that if at the date of performance by the innocent party the guilty party maintains his refusal to accept performance and the innocent party does not accept the repudiation, although the contract still survives, it does not survive so far as the right of the innocent party to perform it is concerned but survives only for the purpose of enforcing remedies open to him by way of damages or specific implement. This produces an impossible result; if the innocent party is deprived of some of his rights it involves putting an end to the contract except in cases, unlike this, where, in the exercise of the court's discretion, the remedy of specific implement is available.

The true position is that the contract survives and does so not only where specific implement is available. When the assistance of the court is not required the innocent party can choose whether he will accept repudiation and sue for damages for anticipatory breach or await the date of performance by the guilty party. Then, if there is failure in performance, his rights are preserved.

It may be unfortunate that the appellants have saddled themselves with an unwanted contract causing an apparent waste of time and money. No doubt this 'aspect impressed the Court of Session but there is no equity which can assist the respondent. It is trite that equity will not rewrite an improvident contract where there is no disability on either side. There is no duty laid upon a party to a subsisting contract to vary it at the behest of the other party so as to deprive himself of the benefit given to him by the contract. To hold otherwise would be to introduce a novel equitable doctrine that a party was not to be held to his contract unless the court in a given instance thought it reasonable so to do. In this case it would make an action for debt a claim for a discretionary remedy. This would introduce an uncertainty into the field of contract which appears to be unsupported by authority either in English or Scottish law save for the one case upon which the Court of Session founded its opinion and which must, in my judgment, be taken to have been wrongly decided.'

The decision in *White & Carter* has been criticised for encouraging wasteful performance and causing undue hardship to the contract breaker (see Furmston, M, 'The Case of the Insistent Performer' (1962) 25 MLR 364; Goodhart, W, 'Measure of Damages when a Contract is Repudiated' (1962) 78 LQR 263). Lord Reid's speech did admit of two restrictions on the innocent party's right to affirm a contract following an anticipatory breach:

1. **Need for co-operation.** This is a practical limitation on the right to affirm. In most cases, the innocent party will be forced to repudiate the contract because he will not be able to complete his own performance without the co-operation of the defendant. In *Ministry of Sound (Ireland) Ltd v World Online Ltd* [2003] 2 All ER (Comm) 823, Nicholas Strauss QC explained this limitation in the following terms: 'In essence, the principle is that the breach of contract does not convert a dependent obligation into an independent one; if the right to the payment claimed is dependent upon the performance of contractual obligations, the prevention of performance by the other party's breach of contract does not alter the position.'

2. **Legitimate interest.** This is a legal limitation on the right to affirm. The innocent party cannot affirm the contract unless he can prove that he has a legitimate interest, financial or otherwise, in performing the contract. As Lord Reid noted, the defendants in *White & Carter* did not attempt to do this, but that is fairly unsurprising given that they were not aware of the need to do so until Lord Reid told them! In *Ocean Marine Navigation Ltd v Koch Carbon Inc ('The Dynamic')* [2003] 2 Lloyd's Rep 693, 698, Simon J summarised the law on the legitimate interest requirement as follows: '(i) The burden is on the *contract-breaker* to show that the innocent party has no legitimate interest in performing the contract rather than claiming damages. (ii) This burden is not discharged merely by showing that the benefit to the other party is small in comparison to the loss to the contract breaker. (iii) The exception to the

general rule applies only in extreme cases: where damages would be an adequate remedy and where an election to keep the contract alive would be unreasonable.'

Lord Reid did not specify what might constitute a legitimate interest, but subsequent cases have provided some guidance on the issue. In *Gator Shipping Corp v Trans-Asiatic Oil Ltd SA ('The Odenfeld')* [1978] 2 Lloyd's Rep 357, Kerr J held that the owners of a ship under a time charter had a legitimate interest in continuing with the contract because it would have been difficult to find other employment for the ship and damages would have been difficult to quantify.

In other cases, the courts have been more receptive to the argument that the contract should be terminated because the innocent party has no legitimate interest in performance. For example, in *Attica Sea Carriers Corp v Ferrostaal Poseidon Bulk Reederei GmbH ('The Puerto Buitrago')* [1976] 1 Lloyd's Rep 250, a charterer attempted to return a ship early and unrepaired in breach of the terms of the contract. This was because the repairs would have cost £2 million when the value of the ship fully repaired was only £1 million. The ship owner refused to accept the return of the ship, insisting that the charterers were liable to continue to pay the charter hire until the ship was repaired. The Court of Appeal rejected this argument for a number of reasons, including the fact that the shipowners had no legitimate interest in continuing the charter. A similar outcome was reached in *Clea Shipping Corp v Bulk Oil International Ltd ('The Alaskan Trader')* [1984] 1 All ER 129. The plaintiff charterers attempted to return a ship one year into a two-year charterparty, due to the ship having developed a serious engine defect that would have required extensive repairs over a period of several months. The owners proceeded to repair the ship and kept it fully manned and ready for the plaintiff's use for the remaining nine months of the charterparty. The arbitrator, Lloyd J, held that the owners did not have a legitimate interest in continuing with the charterparty. Furthermore, even though it might have been difficult to rehire the ship, Lloyd J was of the opinion that damages would not have been too difficult to assess.

17.2.4 GAIN-BASED DAMAGES

Historically, it has been assumed that damages for breach of contract are always compensatory – assessed by reference to the claimant's loss. Gain-based damages – measured by reference to the defendant's gain – were not thought to be available. In more recent years, however, the courts have come to recognise that gain-based damages have a vital role to play in the protection of the claimant's performance interest.

There are four distinct parts to this section. The first part considers the historical development of gain-based damages, the second part examines the landmark case of

A-G v Blake, the third considers how the *A-G v Blake* test has been applied in later cases, and the fourth traces the development of two separate measures of gain-based damages.

17.2.4.1 The history of gain-based damages for breach of contract

As recently as 1993, the Court of Appeal insisted that gain-based damages were unavailable for breach of contract.

Surrey County Council v Bredero Homes Ltd [1993] 1 WLR 1361

Facts: The plaintiff council sold a piece of land to Bredero Homes at a price of £1.5 million. Bredero covenanted to develop the land in accordance with a scheme which the council had agreed to. However, in breach of covenant, Bredero built five extra homes on the site. The plaintiff sued Bredero for breach of covenant. The judge found Bredero liable for breach of contract but awarded merely nominal damages because the council had suffered no pecuniary loss. The plaintiff appealed, claiming that it was entitled to damages measured by reference to the profit acquired by Bredero as a result of its breach.

Held: The Court of Appeal dismissed the appeal, holding that since damages for breach of contract were awarded as compensation for loss, the damages awarded to the plaintiffs had to be merely nominal.

Dillon LJ:
'The plaintiffs have suffered no damage. Therefore on basic principles, as damages are awarded to compensate loss, the damages must be merely nominal'.

Steyn LJ:
'The introduction of restitutionary remedies to deprive cynical contract breakers of the fruits of their breaches of contract will lead to greater uncertainty in the assessment of damages in commercial and consumer disputes. It is of paramount importance that the way in which disputes are likely to be resolved by the courts must be readily predictable. Given the premise that the aggrieved party has suffered no loss, is such a dramatic extension of restitutionary remedies justified in order to confer a windfall in each case on the aggrieved party? I think not. In any event such a widespread availability of restitutionary remedies will have a tendency to discourage economic activity in relevant situations . . . In a range of cases such liability would fall on underwriters who have insured relevant liability risks. Inevitably underwriters would have to be compensated for the new species of potential claims. Insurance premiums would have to go up. That, too, is a consequence which mitigates against the proposed extension. The recognition of the proposed extension will in my view not serve the public interest. It is sound policy to guard against extending the protection of the law of obligations too widely. For these substantive and policy reasons I regard it as undesirable that the

---

range of restitutionary remedies should be extended in the way in which we have been invited to do so.'

The Court of Appeal rejected Surrey County Council's claim on the grounds that an award of gain-based damages lacked historical precedent and was likely to lead to commercial uncertainty. There may be some weight in the latter objection, but the former was not strictly true. There was at least one case where gain-based damages had been awarded for breach of contract, a case that would later be referred to as a 'solitary beacon, showing that in contract as well as tort damages are not always narrowly confined to recoupment of financial loss' (*A-G v Blake* [2001] 1 AC 268, 283 per Lord Nicholls).

Wrotham Park Estate Co Ltd v Parkside Homes Ltd [1974] 1 WLR 798

Facts: The defendant, Parkside Homes, erected homes on their land in breach of a covenant with Wrotham Park. The homes did not affect the value of Wrotham Park's land and thus compensatory damages would have been merely nominal. Wrotham Park sought a mandatory injunction requiring the demolition of the homes.

Held: Brightman J refused to grant a mandatory injunction on the grounds that it would have constituted an unpardonable waste of much needed houses. He awarded damages in lieu of an injunction calculated at 5% of Parkside's anticipated profit.

Brightman J:
'In the present case I am faced with the problem of what damages ought to be awarded to the plaintiffs in the place of mandatory injunctions which would have restored the plaintiffs' rights. If the plaintiffs are merely given a nominal sum, or no sum, in substitution for injunctions, it seems to me that justice will manifestly not have been done.

As I have said, the general rule would be to measure damages by reference to that sum which would place the plaintiffs in the same position as if the covenant had not been broken. Parkside and the individual purchasers could have avoided breaking the covenant in two ways. One course would have been not to develop the allotment site. The other course would have been for Parkside to have sought from the plaintiffs a relaxation of the covenant. On the facts of this particular case the plaintiffs, rightly conscious of their obligations towards existing residents, would clearly not have granted any relaxation, but for present purposes I must assume that it could have been induced to do so. In my judgment a just substitute for a mandatory injunction would be such a sum of money as might reasonably have been demanded by the plaintiffs from Parkside as a quid pro quo for relaxing the covenant . . .

I think that damages must be assessed in such a case on a basis which is fair and, in all the circumstances, in my judgment a sum equal to five per cent of Parkside's

> anticipated profit is the most that is fair. I accordingly award the sum of £2,500 in substitution for mandatory injunctions.'

17.2.4.2 The landmark case

The conflict between *Wrotham Park* and *Bredero Homes* was eventually resolved in favour of the availability of gain-based damages in the landmark case of *A-G v Blake*.

Attorney-General v Blake [2001] 1 AC 268

Facts: Blake was a Soviet informant who was working as a member of the British Secret Intelligence Service. On discovery of his treason he was tried and imprisoned in the UK but in 1966 he escaped custody and fled to Moscow. Whilst in Moscow, he wrote his autobiography outlining details of his work with the British Secret Services. This book was published in 1990 and Blake was set to receive significant royalties from the book. At the time that Blake joined the secret service he had signed a lifelong contract stating that he would never disclose anything about his work, either in the press or in book form. The publication of his autobiography clearly breached this undertaking. The Attorney General brought an action against Blake to recover the profits that Blake had made as a result of his breach of contract.

Held: The House of Lords (Lord Hobhouse dissenting) upheld the Crown's claim for gain-based damages.

Lord Nicholls of Birkenhead:

'*Breach of contract*
I turn to consider the remedies available for breaches of contract. The basic remedy is an award of damages. In the much quoted words of Baron Parke, the rule of the common law is that where a party sustains a loss by reason of a breach of contract, he is, so far as money can do it, to be placed in the same position as if the contract had been performed: *Robinson v Harman* (1848) 1 Exch 850, 855. Leaving aside the anomalous exception of punitive damages, damages are compensatory. That is axiomatic. It is equally well established that an award of damages, assessed by reference to financial loss, is not always "adequate" as a remedy for a breach of contract. The law recognises that a party to a contract may have an interest in performance which is not readily measurable in terms of money. On breach the innocent party suffers a loss. He fails to obtain the benefit promised by the other party to the contract. To him the loss may be as important as financially measurable loss, or more so. An award of damages, assessed by reference to financial loss, will not recompense him properly. For him a financially assessed measure of damages is inadequate.

The classic example of this type of case, as every law student knows, is a contract for the sale of land. The buyer of a house may be attracted by features which have little

1127

or no impact on the value of the house. An award of damages, based on strictly financial criteria, would fail to recompense a disappointed buyer for this head of loss. The primary response of the law to this type of case is to ensure, if possible, that the contract is performed in accordance with its terms. The court may make orders compelling the party who has committed a breach of contract, or is threatening to do so, to carry out his contractual obligations. To this end the court has wide powers to grant injunctive relief. The court will, for instance, readily make orders for the specific performance of contracts for the sale of land, and sometimes it will do so in respect of contracts for the sale of goods . . .

All this is trite law. In practice, these specific remedies go a long way towards providing suitable protection for innocent parties who will suffer loss from breaches of contract which are not adequately remediable by an award of damages. But these remedies are not always available. For instance, confidential information may be published in breach of a non-disclosure agreement before the innocent party has time to apply to the court for urgent relief. Then the breach is irreversible. Further, these specific remedies are discretionary. Contractual obligations vary infinitely. So do the circumstances in which breaches occur, and the circumstances in which remedies are sought. The court may, for instance, decline to grant specific relief on the ground that this would be oppressive.

An instance of this nature occurred in *Wrotham Park v Parkside Homes* [1974] 1 WLR 798. For social and economic reasons the court refused to make a mandatory order for the demolition of houses built on land burdened with a restrictive covenant. Instead, Brightman J made an award of damages under the jurisdiction which originated with Lord Cairns's Act. The existence of the new houses did not diminish the value of the benefited land by one farthing. The judge considered that if the plaintiffs were given a nominal sum, or no sum, justice would manifestly not have been done. He assessed the damages at 5% of the developer's anticipated profit, this being the amount of money which could reasonably have been demanded for a relaxation of the covenant . . .

I turn to the decision of the Court of Appeal in *Surrey County Council v Bredero Homes* [1993] 1 WLR 1361 . . . This is a difficult decision. It has attracted criticism from academic commentators and also in judgments of Sir Thomas Bingham MR and Millett LJ in *Jaggard v Sawyer* [1995] 1 WLR 269. I need not pursue the detailed criticisms. In the *Bredero* case Dillon LJ himself noted, at p 1364, that had the covenant been worded differently, there could have been provision for payment of an increased price if a further planning permission were forthcoming. That would have been enforceable. But, according to the *Bredero* decision, a covenant not to erect any further houses without permission, intended to achieve the same result, may be breached with impunity. That would be a sorry reflection on the law. Suffice to say, in so far as the *Bredero* decision is inconsistent with the approach adopted in the *Wrotham Park* case, the latter approach is to be preferred.

The *Wrotham Park* case, therefore, still shines, rather as a solitary beacon, showing that in contract as well as tort damages are not always narrowly confined to recoupment of financial loss. In a suitable case damages for breach of contract may be measured by the benefit gained by the wrongdoer from the breach. The defendant must make a reasonable payment in respect of the benefit he has gained. In the present case the Crown seeks to go further. The claim is for all the profits of Blake's book which the publisher has not yet paid him. This raises the question whether an account of profits can ever be given as a remedy for breach of contract. The researches of counsel have been unable to discover any case where the court has made such an order on a claim for breach of contract . . .

There is a light sprinkling of cases where courts have made orders having the same effect as an order for an account of profits, but the courts seem always to have attached a different label. A person who, in breach of contract, sells land twice over must surrender his profits on the second sale to the original buyer. Since courts regularly make orders for the specific performance of contracts for the sale of land, a seller of land is, to an extent, regarded as holding the land on trust for the buyer: *Lake v Bayliss* [1974] 1 WLR 1073. In *Reid-Newfoundland Co v Anglo-American Telegraph Co Ltd* [1912] AC 555 a railway company agreed not to transmit any commercial messages over a particular telegraph wire except for the benefit and account of the telegraph company. The Privy Council held that the railway company was liable to account as a trustee for the profits it wrongfully made from its use of the wire for commercial purposes. In *British Motor Trade Association v Gilbert* [1951] 2 All ER 641 the plaintiff suffered no financial loss but the award of damages for breach of contract effectively stripped the wrongdoer of the profit he had made from his wrongful venture into the black market for new cars.

These cases illustrate that circumstances do arise when the just response to a breach of contract is that the wrongdoer should not be permitted to retain any profit from the breach. In these cases the courts have reached the desired result by straining existing concepts. Professor Peter Birks has deplored the "failure of jurisprudence when the law is forced into this kind of abusive instrumentalism"; see 'Profits of Breach of Contract' (1993) 109 LQR 518, 520 . . .

My conclusion is that there seems to be no reason, in principle, why the court must in all circumstances rule out an account of profits as a remedy for breach of contract. I prefer to avoid the unhappy expression "restitutionary damages". Remedies are the law's response to a wrong (or, more precisely, to a cause of action). When, exceptionally, a just response to a breach of contract so requires, the court should be able to grant the discretionary remedy of requiring a defendant to account to the plaintiff for the benefits he has received from his breach of contract. In the same way as a plaintiff's interest in performance of a contract may render it just and equitable for the court to make an order for specific performance or grant an injunction, so the plaintiff's interest in performance may make it just and equitable that the defendant should retain no benefit from his breach of contract.

The state of the authorities encourages me to reach this conclusion, rather than the reverse. The law recognises that damages are not always a sufficient remedy for breach of contract. This is the foundation of the court's jurisdiction to grant the remedies of specific performance and injunction. Even when awarding damages, the law does not adhere slavishly to the concept of compensation for financially measurable loss. When the circumstances require, damages are measured by reference to the benefit obtained by the wrongdoer. This applies to interference with property rights. Recently, the like approach has been adopted to breach of contract. Further, in certain circumstances an account of profits is ordered in preference to an award of damages. Sometimes the injured party is given the choice: either compensatory damages or an account of the wrongdoer's profits. Breach of confidence is an instance of this. If confidential information is wrongfully divulged in breach of a non-disclosure agreement, it would be nothing short of sophistry to say that an account of profits may be ordered in respect of the equitable wrong but not in respect of the breach of contract which governs the relationship between the parties. With the established authorities going thus far, I consider it would be only a modest step for the law to recognise openly that, exceptionally, an account of profits may be the most appropriate remedy for breach of contract. It is not as though this step would contradict some recognised principle applied consistently throughout the law to the grant or withholding of the remedy of an account of profits. No such principle is discernible.

The main argument against the availability of an account of profits as a remedy for breach of contract is that the circumstances where this remedy may be granted will be uncertain. This will have an unsettling effect on commercial contracts where certainty is important. I do not think these fears are well founded. I see no reason why, in practice, the availability of the remedy of an account of profits need disturb settled expectations in the commercial or consumer world. An account of profits will be appropriate only in exceptional circumstances. Normally the remedies of damages, specific performance and injunction, coupled with the characterisation of some contractual obligations as fiduciary, will provide an adequate response to a breach of contract. It will be only in exceptional cases, where those remedies are inadequate, that any question of accounting for profits will arise. No fixed rules can be prescribed. The court will have regard to all the circumstances, including the subject matter of the contract, the purpose of the contractual provision which has been breached, the circumstances in which the breach occurred, the consequences of the breach and the circumstances in which relief is being sought. A useful general guide, although not exhaustive, is whether the plaintiff had a legitimate interest in preventing the defendant's profit-making activity and, hence, in depriving him of his profit.

It would be difficult, and unwise, to attempt to be more specific. In the Court of Appeal [1998] Ch 439 Lord Woolf MR suggested there are at least two situations in which justice requires the award of restitutionary damages where compensatory damages would be inadequate: see p 458. Lord Woolf MR was not there addressing the question of when an account of profits, in the conventional sense, should be available. But I should add that, so far as an account of profits is concerned, the suggested categorisation would not assist. The first suggested category was the case of "skimped" performance, where the defendant fails to provide the full extent of services he has contracted to provide. He should be liable to pay back the amount of expenditure he saved by the breach. This is a much discussed problem. But a part refund of the price agreed for services would not fall within the scope of an account of profits as ordinarily understood. Nor does an account of profits seem to be needed in this context. The resolution of the problem of cases of skimped performance, where the plaintiff does not get what was agreed, may best be found elsewhere. If a shop-keeper supplies inferior and cheaper goods than those ordered and paid for, he has to refund the difference in price. That would be the outcome of a claim for damages for breach of contract. That would be so, irrespective of whether the goods in fact served the intended purpose. There must be scope for a similar approach, without any strain-ing of principle, in cases where the defendant provided inferior and cheaper services than those contracted for.

The second suggested category was where the defendant has obtained his profit by doing the very thing he contracted not to do. This category is defined too widely to assist. The category is apt to embrace all express negative obligations. But something more is required than mere breach of such an obligation before an account of profits will be the appropriate remedy.

Lord Woolf MR [1998] Ch 439, 457, 458, also suggested three facts which should not be a sufficient ground for departing from the normal basis on which damages are awarded: the fact that the breach was cynical and deliberate; the fact that the breach enabled the defendant to enter into a more profitable contract elsewhere; and the fact that by entering into a new and more profitable contract the defendant put it out of his power to perform his contract with the plaintiff. I agree that none of these facts would be, by itself, a good reason for ordering an account of profits.

The present case

The present case is exceptional. The context is employment as a member of the security and intelligence services. Secret information is the lifeblood of these services. In the 1950s Blake deliberately committed repeated breaches of his undertaking not to divulge official information gained as a result of his employment. He caused untold and immeasurable damage to the public interest he had committed himself to serve. When he joined the Secret Intelligence Service Blake expressly agreed in writing that he would not disclose official information, during or after his service, in book form or otherwise. He was employed on that basis. That was the basis on which he acquired official information. The Crown had and has a legitimate interest in preventing Blake profiting from the disclosure of official information, whether classified or not, while a member of the service and thereafter. Neither he, nor any other member of the service, should have a financial incentive to break his undertaking. It is of paramount import-ance that members of the service should have complete confidence in all their dealings with each other, and that those recruited as informers should have the like confidence. Undermining the willingness of prospective informers to co-operate with the services, or undermining the morale and trust between members of the services when engaged on secret and dangerous operations, would jeopardise the effectiveness of the service. An absolute rule against disclosure, visible to all, makes good sense.

In considering what would be a just response to a breach of Blake's undertaking the court has to take these considerations into account. The undertaking, if not a fiduciary obligation, was closely akin to a fiduciary obligation, where an account of profits is a standard remedy in the event of breach. Had the information which Blake has now disclosed still been confidential, an account of profits would have been ordered, almost as a matter of course. In the special circumstances of the intelligence services, the same conclusion should follow even though the information is no longer confidential. That would be a just response to the breach. I am reinforced in this view by noting that most of the profits from the book derive indirectly from the extremely serious and damaging breaches of the same undertaking committed by Blake in the 1950s. As already mentioned, but for his notoriety as an infamous spy his autobiography would not have commanded royalties of the magnitude Jonathan Cape agreed to pay.'

Lord Steyn:

'In the Court of Appeal in *Surrey County Council v Bredero Homes Ltd* [1993] 1 WLR 1361, I discussed some of the difficulties inherent in creating a general remedy for the recovery of restitutionary damages for breach of contract. On that occasion I remarked that it is not traditional to describe a claim for restitution following a breach of contract as damages. The terminology is however less important than the substance: under consideration are claims for the disgorgement of profits against a contract breaker. There has been a substantial academic debate on the merits of the actual decision in the *Bredero* case. Since this issue has not been directly debated in the present case I propose to express no view on it. But it is right to acknowledge that the academic comment has been critical of the decision in the *Bredero* case I would, however, respectfully offer a comment on the valuable academic debate. On the one hand, there is no or virtually no support for a general action for disgorgement of profits made by a contract breaker by reason of his breach. On the other hand, there is significantly absent from the post-*Bredero* academic comment a reasoned statement of the particular circumstances when such a remedy should be available. That is not surprising because it is a notoriously difficult subject. But the Court of Appeal has been bold. It is said that the remedy should be available in two situations, viz (1) in cases of "skimped" performance (where the "gain" would take the form of expense saved) and (2) "where the defendant has obtained his profit by doing the very thing which he contracted not to do". The second would cover the present case. But it potentially has wide application. Sir Guenter Treitel QC in *The Law of Contract*, 10th edn (1999), pp 868–869, has questioned the soundness of the observations of the Court of Appeal: see also the valuable comment by Janet O'Sullivan, "Reflections on the role of restitutionary damages to protect contractual expectations" (to be published) and Hanoch Dagan, "Restitutionary Damages for Breach of Contract: An Exercise in Private Law Theory" [2000] 1 Theoretical Inquiries in Law 115. I am not at present willing to endorse the broad observations of the Court of Appeal. Exceptions to the general principle that there is no remedy for disgorgement of profits against a contract breaker are best hammered out on the anvil of concrete cases.'

Lord Hobhouse:

'My Lords, when he opened this appeal, Mr Clayton, to whose pro bono services on behalf of the appellant George Blake I, too, would wish to pay tribute, warned your Lordships against being drawn into making bad law in order to enable an intuitively just decision to be given against a traitor.

Your Lordships have concluded that this claim should be allowed. I cannot join your Lordships in that conclusion. I have two primary difficulties. The first is the facts of the present case. The speech of my noble and learned friend explores what is the "just response" to the defendant's conduct. The "just response" visualised in the present case is, however it is formulated, that Blake should be punished and deprived of any fruits of conduct connected with his former criminal and reprehensible conduct. The Crown have made no secret of this. It is not a commercial claim in support of any commercial interest. It is a claim relating to past criminal conduct. The way it was put by the Court of Appeal [1998] Ch 439, 464 was:

"The ordinary member of the public would be shocked if the position was that the courts were powerless to prevent [Blake] profiting from his criminal conduct."

The answer given by my noble and learned friend does not reflect the essentially punitive nature of the claim and seeks to apply principles of law which are only appropriate where commercial or proprietary interests are involved. Blake has made a financial gain but he has not done so at the expense of the Crown or making use of any property of or commercial interest of the Crown either in law or equity.

My second difficulty is that the reasoning of my noble and learned friend depends upon the conclusion that there is some gap in the existing state of the law which requires to be filled by a new remedy. He accepts that the term "restitutionary damages" is unsatisfactory but, with respect, does not fully examine why this is so, drawing the necessary conclusions.'

In his speech, Lord Nicholls acknowledged that a common fear associated with the availability of gain-based damages was that their availability would be uncertain and would lead to commercial instability. His Lordship dismissed such fears as being unfounded, but a closer examination of his speech reveals much fuel for such fears.

Lord Nicholls began his exposition of the test to be applied by declaring that no fixed rules could be prescribed. Such a statement necessarily strikes fear into all those pursuing clarity and certainty in the commercial law. His Lordship continued by recommending that the courts should have regard 'to all the circumstances, including the subject matter of the contract, the purpose of the contractual provision which has been breached, the circumstances in which the breach occurred, the consequences of the breach and the circumstances in which relief is being sought'. This statement tells us little, if anything, about how the courts should go about deciding whether to award gain-based damages. It merely declares that the award of such damages is at the discretion of the court. This is hardly conducive to certain and consistent court practice.

Fortunately, Lord Nicholls did provide what he referred to as a 'useful guide' for the courts. Gain-based damages should be available whenever compensatory damages are inadequate and the 'plaintiff has a legitimate interest in preventing the defendant's profit making activity'. The problem with this test is that it is ambiguous in the extreme. When does a plaintiff have a legitimate interest in preventing the defendant's profit making activity? Or perhaps, it is more appropriate to ask: When does a plaintiff *not* have a legitimate interest in preventing the defendant's profit-making activity? Surely the innocent party in every case of breach of contract has a legitimate interest in preventing the defendant from profiting by his breach.

Lord Nicholls did provide some guidance as to what amounts to a 'legitimate interest' by reference to the facts of *Blake* itself. He said, 'the Crown had and has a legitimate interest in preventing Blake profiting from the disclosure of official information, whether classified or not, while a member of the service and thereafter'. While it is undoubtedly true that the Crown had a legitimate interest in preventing Blake's profit-making breach while he was a member of the secret service, it is far less obvious that such an interest subsisted Blake's treachery and escape to the Soviet Union. Why did such a legitimate interest still exist? Blake was no longer in the employment of the Secret Service and the information was no longer confidential since it had been published in a national newspaper. What 'legitimate interest' remained except the interest that the contract should be performed according to its terms? If this is sufficient, then gain-based damages will be available for every breach of contract whenever the contract breaker makes a profit and alternative remedies are inadequate. This may of course be a welcome outcome, but it certainly was not Lord Nicholls' intention, since earlier in his speech he insisted that gain-based damages should only be 'exceptionally' available. Thus Lord Nicholls' 'useful general guide' must be narrower in application than it at first appears. But how much narrower? Ultimately, this is a question that can only be answered by later courts as they seek to interpret and apply Lord Nicholls' criteria. As Lord Steyn said in *Blake*:

> 'Exceptions to the general principle that there is no remedy for disgorgement of profits [gain-based damages] against a contract breaker are best hammered out on the anvil of concrete cases.'

The 'anvil of concrete cases' that have applied *Blake* are considered in the next part of this section. Before moving on to consider those, it is important to note the warning issued by Lord Hobhouse in his dissent. He cautioned his fellow Law Lords, 'against being drawn into making bad law in order to enable an intuitively just decision to be given against a traitor'. It is arguable that this is precisely what the majority did in formulating the vague and unworkable 'legitimate interest' test. Professor Steve Hedley has suggested that the facts of *Blake* were so exceptional that it is of little value as a precedent.

Hedley, S, ' "Very much the wrong people": the House of Lords and publication of spy memoirs' *Web JCLI* 2000

The reasoning of their lordships . . . cannot, I think, be severed from its Cold War roots, and is of little value as a precedent, except of course in relation to the publication of spy memoirs. The hope that their lordships might make a serious contribution to the difficult problems of restitution was not an unreasonable one . . . But in the event, that hope has been dashed. Despite a veneer of restitutionary reasoning, the case quickly departs from the doctrinal and commercial concerns that would have to be at the forefront of any real solution to those problems. It is to be hoped that the Lords will someday soon return to them, undistracted by past battles, and alert to the real dangers we confront.

Undoubtedly, Professor Hedley's criticisms of the case are well founded since the 'legitimate interest' test is riddled with problems. Later cases, however, have relied on *Blake* as a precedent (contrary to Hedley's assertions) and refined Lord Nicholls' criteria into a workable test.

17.2.4.3 Application of Lord Nicholls' 'useful guide'

The first case to follow and apply the decision in *Blake* was *Esso Petroleum Co Ltd v Niad Ltd*.

Esso Petroleum Co Ltd v Niad Ltd [2001] EWHL Ch 458 (unreported)

Facts: The case concerned the operation of a petrol marketing scheme called 'Pricewatch'. Petrol dealers agreed to report competitors' prices and to abide by prices set daily by Esso in return for financial support from Esso to assist them to do this. Niad broke the agreement by failing to maintain prices as agreed on four occasions. Esso sued Niad for breach of contract. Since Esso was unable to establish the loss it had sustained it claimed gain-based damages for the breach of contract.

Held: Morritt VC held that Niad was liable and Esso was entitled to either an account of profits or a restitutionary remedy, requiring Niad to pay to Esso the amount by which the actual prices charged to customers had exceeded the recommended prices.

Morritt VC:

'If [a claim for expectation damages] is pursued Esso will have to establish that it has lost sales of motor fuels by reason of the failure of Niad to charge at or below the Pricewatch recommended price. This may not be easy. In any event the amount is unlikely to be commensurate with the amount of additional price support derived by Niad from Pricewatch which it should have passed on to its customers.

For this reason Esso seeks an account of the profits derived by Niad from its breaches of contract. It relies on the recent decision of the House of Lords in *AG v Blake* [2001] 1 AC 268. But this too is unlikely to yield by way of recompense the amount of additional price support obtained by Niad from Pricewatch which it did not pass on. No doubt it is for this reason that Esso also seeks a restitutionary remedy whereby it recovers the amount by which the charges made at the Leyburn Service Station exceeded the recommended prices on the basis of unjust enrichment. It is accepted that these remedies are alternative not cumulative; but Esso contends that it is entitled to the judgment of the court on which of them is available before electing which to pursue . . .

In my judgment the remedy of an account of profits should be available for breaches of contract such as these. First, damages is an inadequate remedy. It is almost impossible to attribute lost sales to a breach by one out of several hundred dealers who operated Pricewatch. Second, the obligation to implement and maintain the recommended pump prices was fundamental to Pricewatch. Failure to observe it gives the lie to the advertising campaign by which it was publicised and therefore undermines the effectiveness of Pricewatch in achieving the benefits intended for both Esso and all its dealers within Pricewatch. Third, complaint was made of Niad on four occasions. On all of them Niad appeared to comply without demur. It now appears that the breaches of its obligation were much more extensive than Esso at first thought. Fourth, Esso undoubtedly has a legitimate interest in preventing Niad from profiting from its breach of obligation.

I turn then to the restitutionary remedy. It is undoubted that Niad obtained a benefit, in the form of the price support, to which it was only entitled if it complied with its obligation to implement and maintain the recommended pump prices to be supported. In these circumstances it can hardly be denied that Niad was enriched to the extent that it charged pump prices in excess of the recommended prices. The enrichment was unjust because it was obtained in breach of contract. It was obtained at the expense of Esso because Esso was providing price support for a lower price than that charged by Niad. I can see no reason why this remedy should be unavailable to Esso if it wishes to pursue it. Indeed it appears to me to be the most appropriate remedy in that it matches most closely the reality of the case, namely that Niad took an extra benefit to which it was not entitled. It is just that it should be made to restore it to its effective source.'

The decision in *Niad* was significant because it demonstrated that gain-based damages are available outside of the exceptional circumstances of *Blake*. Indeed, despite the warnings of Lord Hobhouse and Professor Hedley, gain-based damages were awarded for breach of a commercial contract.

Morritt VC acknowledged at the outset that gain-based damages remain an exceptional remedy. Nevertheless, he thought that they were appropriate on the facts of the case for four reasons: (i) compensatory damages were an inadequate remedy; (ii) the obligation to implement and maintain the recommended pump prices was fundamental to the contract; (iii) complaint was made of the defendant on four occasions and the defendant gave the appearance of complying with Esso's request; and (iv) Esso had a legitimate interest in preventing the defendant from profiting from its breach of obligation.

At first sight, Morritt VC appeared to be applying more stringent criteria than those set out by Lord Nicholls in *Blake*. However, on a closer examination it can be seen that the Vice Chancellor's four reasons were really just an elaboration of Lord Nicholls' two criteria: (1) compensatory damages must be inadequate; (2) the claimant must have a legitimate interest in preventing the defendant's profit-making breach. Reasons (i) and (iii) concerned the inadequacy of damages requirement. Compensatory damages were inadequate because of the difficulty of determining loss and the fact that the breach was calculated, extensive and deliberate. Reasons (ii) and (iv) concerned the legitimate interest requirement. This is obvious in relation to reason (iv) since it really just restates Lord Nicholls' test. Reason (ii) provides a more stringent requirement for establishing a legitimate interest. It requires the claimant to prove that the breach went to the root of the contract and gave lie to its integrity. Thus the judgment delivered in *Niad* goes some way to clarifying and developing the 'legitimate interest' test established in *Blake*.

The final point to note about the case is that Morritt VC identified two alternative gain-based remedies: an account of profits and a restitutionary remedy.

17.2.4.4 Two measures of gain-based damages

The Court of Appeal considered the difference between these two remedies in *Experience Hendrix LLC v PPX Enterprises Inc*.

Experience Hendrix LLC v PPX Enterprises Inc, Edward Chalpin [2003] EWCA Civ 323; [2003] EMLR 25

Facts: The claimant was the estate of Jimi Hendrix, the rock legend of the 1960s, who died in 1970 from a drug overdose. The respondents, PPX Enterprises Inc were Jimi Hendrix's former recording company. In 1967 PPX brought proceedings against Jimi

Hendrix for alleged breaches of a recording contract that required Hendrix to record exclusively for PPX. These proceedings were eventually settled in 1973, three years after Hendrix's death, and the contract of settlement was incorporated into an order of the court. Since 1973, however, PPX had exploited various master recordings in breach of the settlement agreement. Experience Hendrix brought an action for breach of the settlement agreement. At first instance, Buckley J granted an injunction to restrain PPX from future unauthorised use of the master recordings, but held that Experience Hendrix was only entitled to nominal damages in respect of the past breaches. The claimant appealed.

Held: The Court of Appeal allowed the appeal and awarded damages measured on the *Wrotham Park* basis. The court declined to award a full account of profits because the facts of *Hendrix* were not sufficiently exceptional to justify such an order.

Mance LJ:

'I turn to apply these principles to the present facts. As in *Blake*, we are concerned with a breach of a negative obligation, and PPX did do the very thing it had contracted not to do ... On the other hand, there are also obvious distinctions from *Blake's* case. First, we are not concerned with a subject anything like as special or sensitive as national security. The State's special interest in preventing a spy benefiting by breaches of his contractual duty of secrecy, and so removing at least part of the financial attraction of such breaches, has no parallel in this case. Second, the notoriety which accounted for the magnitude of Blake's royalty earning capacity derived from his prior breaches of secrecy, and that too has no present parallel. Third, there is no direct analogy between PPX's position and that of a fiduciary.

The case of *Niad* presents a similar feature to the present, in so far as damages may be said to be an inadequate remedy, because of the practical impossibility in each case of demonstrating the effect of a defendant's undoubted breaches on the appellant's general programme of promoting their product. But, despite [counsel for the appellants'] evidence, it is not shown that the present defendant's breaches went to the root of the appellant's programme or gave the lie to its integrity. Nor is the present a case where the defendant can be said to have profited directly, by receipt under the agreement which it broke of monies that it ought in fairness to restore ...

I consider that any reasonable observer of the situation would conclude that, as a matter of practical justice, PPX should make (at the least) reasonable payment for its use of masters in breach of the settlement agreement ... It would in these circumstances be anomalous and unjust, if PPX could, by simply breaching the agreement, avoid paying royalties or any sum, when they have to pay royalties in respect of Schedule A masters and they would have expected that, even if consent to the extension or renewal of existing licences of non-Schedule A masters was forthcoming at all, it would only be on terms as to payment of further royalties ...

However, I do not regard this case as exceptional to the point where the Court should order a full account of all profits which have been or may be made by PPX by its breaches. I have already drawn attention to significant features of *Blake* which have no counterpart in this case ... Here, the breaches, though deliberate, took place in a commercial context. PPX, though knowingly and deliberately breaching its contract, acted as it did in the course of a business, to which it no doubt gave some expenditure of time and effort and probably the use of connections and some skill (although how much is evidently in issue, and is not a matter on which we can at this stage reach any view). An account of profits would involve a detailed assessment of such matters, which, as is very clear from *Blake*, should not lightly be ordered.

For the past, in the absence of any proven loss, I would confine any financial remedy to an order that PPX pay a reasonable sum for its use of material in breach of the settlement agreement. That sum can properly be described as being "such sum as might reasonably have been demanded" by Jimi Hendrix's estate "as a quid pro quo for agreeing to permit the two licences into which PPX entered in breach of the settlement agreement", which was the approach adopted by Brightman J in *Wrotham Park* ... This involves an element of artificiality, if, as in *Wrotham Park*, no permission would ever have been given on any terms. And, where no injunction is possible, even the value of a bargaining opportunity depends on the value which the court puts on the right infringed (cf paragraph 19 above, citing Lord Nicholls in *Blake*). That said, the approach adopted by Brightman J has the merit of directing the court's attention to the commercial value of the right infringed and of enabling it to assess the sum payable by reference to the fees that might in other contexts be demanded and paid between willing parties. It points in the present case towards orders that PPX pay over, by way of damages, a proportion of each of the advances received to date and (subject to deduction of such proportion) an appropriate royalty rate on retail selling prices. I would therefore allow the appeal against the judge's decision on the first point and declare accordingly.

The decision of the Court of Appeal in this case was significant because it distinguished between two different measures of gain-based damages.

Cunnington, R, 'Rock, restitution and disgorgement' (2004) JO & R 46, 47–50

In *Hendrix* the Court of Appeal was of the view that there are essentially two different types of gain-based damages, measured on two different bases. Such a distinction had already been drawn by Morritt VC two years earlier in the case of *Esso Petroleum* v *Niad* ...

The *Blake* measure
In *Blake*, the Crown's claim was 'for all the profits of Blake's book which the publisher had not yet paid him'. Commentators have drawn a distinction between gain-based awards that require a defendant to 'give up' a gain and gain-based awards that require a defendant to 'give back' a gain. The measure of damages awarded in *Blake* was of the

former category. Blake was required to give a full account of his gross profit without any allowance being made for the time, effort and skill which he put into writing the book.

Blake was not compelled to 'give back' the profits to the Crown, he was compelled to 'give up' or disgorge the profits. It was unnecessary for the Crown to show that the profits received by Blake had been derived directly from the Crown. Indeed, the Attorney General would still have been entitled to claim an account of profits even if Blake had been able to demonstrate that all of his profits had been generated by his own work and skill. In the words of Dr Edelman: 'Whether a transfer of value occurs or not is irrelevant.'

The *Blake* measure is a blunt tool which requires the defendant to give up all of the profits he has made from the breach. This was affirmed by Mance LJ in *Hendrix*, who said that to apply the *Blake* measure would be to 'order a full account of all profits which have been made or may be made by PPX by its breaches.' The *Blake* measure of damages is calculated by reference to the actual profit accruing to the defendant from the wrong. Whether the profits are derived from the claimant or not is irrelevant. There need be no transfer of value and there need be no loss sustained by the claimant.

The *Wrotham Park* measure

The measure of damages applied by the House of Lords in *Blake* was very different to the measure applied in the cases relied upon by the Crown . . . The primary authority for the Crown was *Wrotham Park Estate Ltd* v *Parkside Homes Ltd* . . . It is clear that the damages awarded in *Wrotham Park* were not compensatory in the ordinary sense . . . Nor were they an account of profits. Lord Nicholls has suggested, extra-judicially, that the *Wrotham Park* case is an example of partial disgorgement of profits . . . These comments have been used to support the thesis that gain-based damages for breach of contract are awarded, 'on a "sliding scale" extending from various levels of partial disgorgement (hypothetical release damages) to total disgorgement (account of profits).' It is respectfully submitted that there is no such sliding scale. Lord Nicholls was mistaken in his comments because the damages awarded in *Wrotham Park* were calculated by reference to Parkside's *anticipated* profit, not by reference to Parkside's *actual* profit. The *Wrotham Park* damages were not a partial account of profits. They had nothing to do with Parkside's actual profits. They were calculated by reference to, 'such sum as might reasonably have been demanded by the plaintiffs from Parkside as a *quid pro quo* for relaxing the covenant'. Brightman J held such a sum was roughly equivalent to five per cent of their *anticipated* profit.

The *Blake* measure of damages is a real assessment of the actual profits received by the defendant as a consequence of his breach. The *Wrotham Park* measure is a judicial assessment of the objective value received by the defendant as a consequence of his breach. Dr Edelman has described the *Wrotham Park* measure of damages as, 'a monetary award which reverses a transfer of value. It is an award which gives back value transferred from a claimant to a defendant as a result of a defendant's wrong and is almost always measured by the objective gain received by the defendant.' This understanding of the *Wrotham Park* measure of damages is affirmed by the decision of the Court of Appeal in *Hendrix*. Mance LJ said that, if the measure was to be applied to the facts of *Hendrix*, the court would award damages equivalent to what would be a 'reasonable payment for the use of masters in breach of the settlement agreement'. This is a judicially determined value placed on the objective benefit transferred from Experience Hendrix to PPX. It is not tied to the actual profit made by the defendant. This was confirmed by Mance LJ who said: 'In such a context it is natural to pay regard to any profit made by the wrongdoer (although a wrongdoer surely cannot always rely on avoiding having to make reasonable recompense by showing that despite his wrong he failed, perhaps simply due to his own incompetence, to make any profit).' Thus the *Wrotham Park* measure of damages is different to the *Blake* measure; it is a judicially assessed measure that can exceed the *Blake* measure where the defendant, by his own incompetence, has failed to make any profit.

The next important issue to address is the juridical basis of the *Wrotham Park* measure of damages. Were they restitutionary, i.e. gain-based, or were they compensatory? . . . [I]n his dissenting speech in *Blake* Lord Hobhouse described *Wrotham Park* as a case decided on compensatory principles – the claimant's loss being, 'the sum which he could have extracted from the defendant as the price of his consent to the development'. In *Hendrix*, Mance LJ noted Lord Hobhouse's comments and said: 'Whether the adoption of a standard measure of damages represents a departure from a compensatory approach depends upon what one understands by compensation and whether the term is only apt in circumstances where an injured party's financial position, viewed subjectively, is being precisely restored.'

Pey – Woan Lee has argued that this statement in *Hendrix* supports the view that the damages awarded in *Wrotham Park* were compensatory damages for a lost opportunity to bargain. It is respectfully submitted that such an analysis of *Wrotham Park* is fallacious.

The 'Damages for Lost Opportunity to Bargain' thesis was originally articulated by Sharpe and Waddams in their seminal 1982 article of the same name. They contended that, in circumstances where the defendant has profited from his violation of the claimant's property right, damages can be awarded based upon the defendant's gain to compensate the claimant for his lost opportunity to bargain.

A number of commentators have rightly rejected this approach as being fictitious. The main objection to the approach is that gain-based damages have been awarded in cases where either: (a) the claimant would never have agreed to release the defendant from his obligations; or (b) there never had been an opportunity to bargain release from the defendant's obligations. Indeed, both these objections arise on the facts of *Wrotham Park* itself. Brightman J made it clear that the claimants 'rightly conscious of their obligations towards existing residents', would clearly not have granted any relaxation of the restrictive covenant. Furthermore, there was never an opportunity to bargain release with the second defendants who were the purchasers of the properties from Parkside Homes. They did not purchase the properties until after the building work was complete. By this time the covenant was unenforceable because a mandatory injunction would, in the words of Brightman J, constitute 'an unpardonable waste of much needed houses'. Therefore, there was no historical point at which the claimant would have been able to enforce the covenant against the second defendants. The damages awarded against the second defendants cannot be considered to be compensation for a lost opportunity to bargain since no such opportunity ever existed with the second defendants.

Fortunately it seems that, contrary to Lee's assertions, the Court of Appeal in *Hendrix* did not adopt the Lost Opportunity to Bargain theory to explain the *Wrotham Park* measure of damages. Peter Gibson LJ referred to the theory as wholly fictional in the context of cases where the claimant would never have agreed to release the defendant from his obligations. Mance LJ also noted the artificiality of the approach, and described the award as 'the value which the court puts on the right infringed'. This value is not compensatory and it is not based on the actual profit made by the defendant. It is a judicially determined assessment of the objective value received by the defendant as a consequence of his breach – it is restitutionary.

As this article explains, the Court of Appeal identified two different measures of gain-based damages:

1. The *Blake* measure – requiring the defendant to 'give up' his gain – a real assessment of the actual profits received by the defendant as a consequence of the breach of contract.
2. The *Wrotham Park* measure – requiring the defendant to 'give back' his gain – a judicial assessment of the objective value received by the defendant, at the expense of the claimant, as a consequence of the breach of contract.

In two recent cases (*Lane v O'Brien Homes* [2004] EWHC 303 (QB); *WWF v World Wrestling Federation Entertainment Inc* [2006] EWHC 184 (Ch)) the High Court has explained the *Wrotham Park* measure as compensation for a 'lost opportunity to bargain'. It is submitted that, for the reasons set out in the extract, this approach is fictitious and should be rejected in favour of a gain-based rationale for the award.

On the facts of *Hendrix*, *Blake* damages were not awarded. The reason for this is unclear. Mance LJ identified and applied the criteria expounded by Lord Nicholls in *Blake*:

1. Compensatory damages were *inadequate* 'because of the practical impossibility in each case of demonstrating the effect of a defendant's undoubted breaches on the appellant's general programme of promoting their product.'
2. Experience Hendrix had a *legitimate interest* in preventing the PPX's profit-making activity, which was evidenced by the availability of an injunction to prevent PPX from breaching the settlement agreement again in the future.

Despite the fact that these two criteria were fulfilled, Mance LJ refused to award the

Blake measure on the ground that two further criteria (taken from the judgment in *Niad*) had not been fulfilled:

(1) PPX's breach had not gone to the root of the contract and given lie to its integrity.
(2) The profits received by PPX were not derived directly from the breach of contract.

With respect, these two conclusions are questionable. First, it is surely arguable that PPX's breaches did go to the root of the settlement agreement. The purpose of the agreement was to prevent PPX exploiting Hendrix's songs without fair compensation. This purpose was achieved by providing that only some of the songs could be exploited. PPX violated the very basis of this agreement by licensing many of the songs that they were not entitled to exploit. Thus it appears that Experience Hendrix did have a legitimate interest in preventing PPX's profit-making breach. The breach went to the very root of the contract and 'gave lie to its integrity'. Second, it is difficult to understand why Mance LJ concluded that the profits received by PPX were not derived directly from the breach of contract. The use of the masters' recordings was the breach of the settlement agreement of 1973. Therefore, the profits derived from the use of the masters' recordings were directly derived from the breach of contract.

It is hard to comprehend why the Court of Appeal held that these criteria were not met on the facts of *Hendrix*. The only points of distinction between *Hendrix* and *Blake* were ones of historical particularity, such as the notoriety of Blake's breach. There was no obvious point of substance that distinguished *Hendrix* from *Blake*. Perhaps the Court determined that, in light of Jimi Hendrix's own breach of his 1965 contract with PPX, the need for deterrence was not so great as to justify a full disgorgement of PPX's profit. If so, the crucial criterion for the availability of such damages is the need to deter the defendant's profit-making breach.

Although the Court of Appeal refused to award *Blake* damages the court did award damages measured on the *Wrotham Park* basis. It seems that the crucial fact influencing this decision was the inadequacy of compensatory damages. This inadequacy necessitated the award of gain-based damages. As Mance LJ observed in relation to the facts of *Hendrix*: 'any reasonable observer of the situation would conclude that, as a matter of practical justice, PPX should make (at the least) reasonable payment for its use of masters in breach of the settlement agreement'.

In summary, following *Hendrix* there are two alternative measures of gain-based damages. The *Wrotham Park* measure, requiring the defendant to 'give back' his gain, appears to be available whenever compensatory damages are inadequate to protect the claimant's interest in performance of the contract. The *Blake* measure, requiring the defendant to 'give up' his gain, is subject to more stringent criteria. It will only be awarded when the claimant has a legitimate interest in preventing the defendant's profit-making activity and the breach goes to the root of the contract.

17.2.5 PUNITIVE DAMAGES

Punitive damages (also known as exemplary damages) are awarded to punish the defendant. They focus on the defendant's wrongdoing and seek to punish the defendant for his conduct and to deter similar behaviour by him or by others in the future.

17.2.5.1 The traditional position

Traditionally, it has been assumed that punitive damages are unavailable for breach of contract. In *Ruxley v Forsyth*, Lord Bridge said, 'damages for breach of contract must reflect, as accurately as the circumstances allow, the loss which the claimant has sustained because he did not get what he bargained for. There is no question of punishing the contract breaker.' The leading textbook writers agree. In his seminal text, Professor Treitel writes (*The Law of Contract*, 11th edn, 2003, p 935, London: Sweet & Maxwell): 'Punitive damages cannot be awarded in a purely contractual action, since the object of such an action is not to punish the defendant but to compensate the claimant'. Professor Beatson concurs (*Anson's Law of Contract*, 28th edn, 2002, p 592, Oxford: OUP):

> 'Damages for breach of contract are given by way of compensation for loss suffered, and not by way of punishment for wrong inflicted. The measure of damages is therefore not affected by the motive of the breach. 'Vindictive' or 'exemplary' damages have no place in the law of contract. Contractual damages cannot be used to punish, however outrageous the defendant's conduct.'

In reaching this conclusion, Professor Beatson and others have relied on the case of *Addis v Gramophone Co* [1909] AC 488. We have already considered this case in the section on damages for non-pecuniary loss. The House of Lords held that the unfairly dismissed plaintiff could recover a sum of money representing his salary and commission for the period of notice, but could not recover damages to compensate him for the harsh manner in which he was dismissed. The damages claimed by the plaintiff were compensatory damages for mental distress. Lord James of Hereford described them as being based on 'aggravation of the injury in consequence of the manner of dismissal'. Such damages are compensatory, not punitive. Only two of the Law Lords directly considered whether the plaintiff in *Addis* could recover punitive damages and their decision was split. Lord Collins thought that such damages were available and Lord Atkinson thought that they were not.

Ultimately, the decision was inconclusive on the point, but it is clear that the case is not an incontrovertible authority for the denial of punitive damages in English contract law.

17.2.5.1.1 *The 'cause of action' restriction*

Nevertheless, until very recently the questionable status of *Addis* was of little significance because of a further restriction on the availability of punitive damages for breach of contract – the 'cause of action' test. This restriction was imposed by the Court of Appeal in *AB v South West Water Services Ltd* [1993] QB 507. It meant that punitive damages were only available for causes of action in which punitive damages had been awarded prior to the decision of the House of Lords in *Rookes v Barnard* [1964] AC 1129. This arbitrary restriction was condemned by the Law Commission as 'rationally indefensible' (*Aggravated, Exemplary and Restitutionary Damages* (London: HMSO, 1997) para 5.49) and eventually rejected by the House of Lords in *Kuddus v Chief Constable of Leicestershire Constabulary* [2002] 2 AC 122. With the 'cause of action' bar removed and the authority of *Addis* doubted, the door is now open for the courts to consider afresh whether punitive damages should be available for breach of contract.

17.2.5.1.2 *The efficient breach theory*

A common objection to punitive damages is the efficient breach theory, which has its roots in Oliver Wendell Holmes' famous claim that contracts carry no obligation to perform. In the twentieth century, Chief Judge Posner and other legal economists developed Holmes' views into a fully formed theory of 'efficient breach'. Central to the theory is the view that it is uneconomical to induce completion of performance of a contract after it has been broken. To illustrate, suppose A has entered into a contract with B for the sale of 1,000 widgets, which only A can supply. B agrees to pay £1,000 for the widgets and will suffer £100 loss if they are not supplied. Subsequently, C offers to pay A £1,500 for the widgets. The efficient breach theory suggests that it is socially desirable for A to break his contract with B in these circumstances and supply the widgets to C instead. This is because A will be able to compensate B for his loss while still making an additional £400 profit for himself from the sale of the widgets to C. This is said to be 'Pareto efficient', because it causes a net increase in wealth and no person is made worse off by the transaction.

The efficient breach theory seeks to provide an economic justification for the idea that a party has the right to break a contract and choose to pay compensatory damages instead of rendering performance. If the argument were to be accepted – specific performance, gain-based damages and punitive damages – all of which seek to protect the performance interest of the contract by deterring breaches, would never be appropriate. Although the theory has exerted considerable influence both in the US (see *Restatement (Second) of Contracts* reporter's note at 101) and in this country (see Campbell, D and Harris, D, 'In defence of breach: a critique of restitution and the performance interest' (2002) 22 LS 208), several convincing arguments can be made as to why it should be rejected.

Cunnington, R, 'Should Punitive Damages be part of the judicial arsenal in contract cases?' (2006) 26 LS 369, 385–389

In recent times the efficient breach theory has come under sustained criticism. There are a number of compelling reasons why it should be rejected.

(i) The Theory is Economically Inefficient

First, the theory is not as economically efficient as its name might suggest. This is because it fails to distinguish between opportunistic and efficient breaches of contract. A breach is opportunistic if the breaching party attempts to get more than he bargained for at the expense of the nonbreaching party. For example, if you supply me with 1,000 widgets and I withhold payment in bad faith in the hope that you will reduce the contract price then I am breaching the contract opportunistically. Such breaches are neither 'Pareto' efficient nor 'Kaldor-Hicks' efficient since they do not increase the net wealth of society; the breaching party merely gains at the expense of the nonbreaching party.

Opportunistic behaviour does not create wealth; it simply redistributes wealth from one party to another. And this redistribution actually consumes wealth because, 'potential opportunists and victims expend resources perpetrating and protecting against opportunism'. None of these expenditures increase the net wealth of society. Therefore, even Chief Judge Posner has recognised that, when a promissor breaches opportunistically, 'we might as well throw the book at the promissor . . . Such conduct has no economic justification and ought simply to be deterred'. Thus, it is clear that the doctrine of efficient breach does not apply to all types of breach as Holmes and others would suggest. Opportunistic behaviour is economically inefficient and should be deterred.

Second, it is not even clear that the efficient breach doctrine applies to so-called 'efficient breaches'. This is because the theory fails to take into account transaction costs. This point was made many years ago by Ronald Coase, who argued that efficient breach was actually unnecessary since where resources would be more efficiently employed elsewhere, parties to a contract will compromise for release. This, it is argued is more economically efficient, since the costs associated with release are less than those associated with breach.

The proponents of the efficient breach theory disagree. Posner recognises that the parties are free to negotiate release from their obligations but he argues that 'the additional negotiation will not be costless'. Specifically, he asserts that negotiating release will be more costly because it requires an additional transaction to achieve efficiency. If the widget manufacturer from the above example (A) is required to negotiate release from B before selling to C, then two transactions are required. If A can breach and pay damages to B, there is only one transaction between A and C. However, as Professor Friedmann has shown, this all depends on what transactions you count. He argues that, if A is allowed to break his contract with B, there will be two transactions: one between A and C for the sale of the widgets and the other a dispute between A and B regarding the assessment of the damages. Friedmann continues:

> 'The implied assumption in Posner's analysis is that the payment of damages by A to B entails no transaction costs. This, however, is totally unrealistic. The payment of damages is hardly ever a standard transaction of the type the parties are routinely engaged in. It is likely to follow protracted negotiations, or even litigation, over difficult questions of fact and law. Finally, the breach may lead to an expensive tort action for inducement of breach of contract by the promisee (B) against the third party (C). The claim may breed another transaction between C and A regarding A's liability for losses suffered by C.'

Posner also argues that the costs of negotiation will be high because of the existence of a 'bilateral monopoly', that is, neither party has a good alternative to dealing with the other. This will encourage the parties to behave strategically, attempting to obtain as much as possible from each other. Posner even suggests that the parties 'may be so determined to engross the greater part of the potential profits from the transaction that they never succeed in coming to terms'. This point is undoubtedly over-stated. Although strategic behaviour may increase the costs of negotiation, it is generally agreed that it will not prevent parties from coming to terms. Furthermore, it is wrong to assume that the costs of breach and subsequent litigation will be any less. Litigation carries its own costs which arise from the difficulty in coming to agreement about the compensation to be paid to the disappointed promisee. It is important to remember that litigation over damages, like negotiation for a release, occurs in a bilateral monopoly. Indeed, it has been said that litigation is the ultimate bilateral monopoly. It is therefore unsurprising to see that litigation over damages is also affected by strategic behaviour. In addition there are further costs associated with litigation such as: the cost of lawyers, the costs of going to court and the error costs of misdetermining damages. These costs outweigh the transaction costs associated with negotiation. This in turn decreases the net wealth of society and provides a compelling objection to the efficient breach theory.

(ii) The theory does not correspond to the present law
The second major criticism of the efficient breach theory is that it fails to correspond to the existing law. Holmes himself once said that, 'the first call of a theory of law is that it should fit the facts'. The efficient breach theory manifestly fails to do this. For example, the right to specific performance is incompatible with the efficient breach theory since it compels the contract breaker to perform his primary obligations. Holmes concedes that 'it is true that in some instances equity does what is called compelling specific performance'. However, he argues that he is speaking only about the common law and not equity. Furthermore, he argues that equity never wholly compels specific

performance. This reasoning is not really satisfactory since a rigid bifurcation between law and equity is no longer accepted today. Furthermore, whenever equity intervenes to enforce a contract, there is clearly an implied duty to perform the contract.

In addition to the right to specific performance there are a number of other contract rules which presuppose the existence of a duty to perform a contract, for example, the tort of inducing a breach of contract. In the leading case of *Lumley v Gye*, Erle J declared: 'He who maliciously procures a damage to another by violation of his right ought to be made to indemnify, and that whether he procures an actionable wrong or a breach of contract'. It is clear from this extract that Erle J viewed performance of the contract as a right belonging to the plaintiff. If he didn't then his comments make no sense because the plaintiff had not been deprived of anything other than performance of the contract. Mr Lumley still had recourse against Miss Wagner on the contract and indeed he brought a separate action for this. Thus, the only right that required indemnification from a third party was the right to performance, a right which the doctrine of efficient breach rejects.

English law also protects the performance of contracts by the right to repudiate a contract for breach of an essential term and, in the case of entire contracts, to refuse to pay anything for less than substantial performance. Similarly, where a claimant has contracted for a special service but an inferior service has been delivered, the claimant will only have to pay the value of the inferior service, even if he has not suffered any loss. The efficient breach theory is irreconcilable with these legal doctrines.

Finally, the efficient breach theory is inconsistent with what the courts claim to be doing in contract cases. As Atiyah has noted: 'If judges constantly describe the duty to perform a contract in moral terms and if they constantly devise rules which they justify by praying in aid the principle that a contract does impose a duty of performance, then the realist will not really understand how the law works if he ignores what the judges have to say'.

(iii) The theory is anomalously applied

The third criticism of the efficient breach theory is that its proponents only ever seek to apply it to the law of contract. Since the theory is not predicated on the nature of a contractual right, the theory should be equally applicable to property rights. However no one has ever made a serious argument for the adoption of a theory of 'efficient conversion' or 'efficient theft' even though the economic justification for these theories would be exactly the same.

(iv) The theory fails to correspond to the expectations of contracting parties

The final line of criticism against the efficient breach theory is that it fails to correspond to the reasonable expectations of contracting parties. As Buckland once noted: 'One does not buy a right to damages, one buys a horse'. Similarly Pollock has observed: 'A man who bespeaks a coat of his tailor will scarcely be persuaded that he is only betting with the tailor that such a coat will not be made and delivered within a certain time. What he wants and means to have is the coat, not an insurance against not having a coat'.

17.2.5.2 When should punitive damages be available for breach of contract?

On the assumption that there is no principled objection to punitive damages, it is necessary to consider *when* such damages ought to be awarded. In *Kuddus*, Lord Nicholls gave the following advice:

'Stated in its broadest form, the relevant principle is tolerably clear: the availability of exemplary damages should be co-extensive with its rationale. As already indicated, the underlying rationale lies in the sense of outrage which a defendant's conduct sometimes evokes, a sense not always assuaged fully by a compensatory award of damages, even when the damages are increased to reflect emotional distress.'

According to Lord Nicholls, punitive damages should be awarded in cases where compensatory damages would be inadequate to provide redress for the wrong. In the context of a claim for breach of contract, this may occur in exceptional cases where compensatory damages are inadequate to protect the claimant's interest in performance and gain-based damages are unavailable (because the defendant has failed to make a profit from the breach). In such cases, punitive damages may have a vital role to play in deterring outrageous breaches of contract.

Punitive damages have been awarded in contract cases in Canada for well over a decade. One example of a recent case will provide a helpful insight into the role that punitive damages might play in this country.

Whiten v Pilot Insurance Company (2002) 209 DLR (4th) 257

Facts: Mrs Whiten's home and its entire contents were destroyed by an overnight fire in mid-January when the temperature outside was minus 18 degrees Celsius. The family were forced to flee the house wearing only their nightclothes. Mr Whiten gave his slippers to his daughter to go for help and he suffered serious frostbite to his feet for which he was hospitalised and thereafter confined to a wheelchair. Pilot made a single $5,000 payment for living expenses and covered the family's rent for a couple of months, but then ceased payment without giving notice to the Whitens. The insurer claimed that the Whitens had burned their home and persisted in this allegation in a hostile and confrontational manner for over two years despite the fact that the local fire chief, Pilot's own expert investigator and its initial investigator all concluded that there was no evidence of arson. Pilot's action required Mrs Whiten to spend $320,000 in legal costs to collect the $345,000 that was owed to her. At trial, the jury awarded compensatory damages of $345,000 and punitive damages of $1,000,000. In the Ontario Court of Appeal, the punitive award was reduced to $100,000 on the ground that the lesser sum would be sufficient to deter insurers from repeating such unacceptable behaviour in settling claims.

Held: The Supreme Court of Canada restored the jury's award of $1,000,000 in punitive damages.

Binnie J:

'The jury followed the "if but only if" model, i.e., punitive damages should be awarded "if but only if" the compensatory award is insufficient. The form and order of the questions put to the jury required them first of all to deal with compensation for the loss of the plaintiff's house (replacement or cash value), its contents, and any increase in her living and moving expenses. Only after those matters had been dealt with was the jury instructed to turn their minds to a final question on punitive damages. They were clearly aware that compensatory damages might well be sufficient punishment to avoid a repetition of the offence and a deterrent to others. In this case, the jury obviously concluded that the compensatory damages ($345,000) were not sufficient for those purposes. It was no more than the respondent had contractually obligated itself to pay under the insurance policy. In this case, the power imbalance was highly relevant. Pilot holds itself out to the public as a sure guide to a "safe harbour" . . .

Insurance contracts, as Pilot's self-description shows, are sold by the insurance industry and purchased by members of the public for peace of mind. The more devastating the loss, the more the insured may be at the financial mercy of the insurer, and the more difficult it may be to challenge a wrongful refusal to pay the claim. Deterrence is required. The obligation of good faith dealing means that the appellant's peace of mind should have been Pilot's objective, and her vulnerability ought not to have been aggravated as a negotiating tactic. It is this relationship of reliance and vulnerability that was outrageously exploited by Pilot in this case. The jury, it appears, decided a powerful message of retribution, deterrence and denunciation had to be sent to the respondent and they sent it.'

The Supreme Court of Canada has recently confirmed the availability of punitive damages to punish insurers who fail to pay insurance benefits: *Fidler v Sun Life Assurance Co of Canada* [2006] 2 SCR 3.

17.2.6 LIQUIDATED DAMAGES AND PENALTY CLAUSES

The parties to a contract may specifically agree on the compensation to be paid in the event of a breach. Such a term is referred to as a liquidated damages clause, because it liquidates the sum payable on the occurrence of a breach. At the time of writing, the owners of Wembley Stadium are making a claim for £35 million in liquidated damages against Multiplex, the constructors of Wembley Stadium, for late completion of the stadium. As a rule, the courts are inclined to uphold liquidated damages clauses because they enable the parties to allocate between themselves the extent of the risks assumed.

Harris, D, Campbell, D, Halson, R, *Remedies in Contract and Tort*, 2nd edn, 2002, London: Butterworths, p 139–142

In comparison with unliquidated damages assessed under the ordinary rules (causation, remoteness, mitigation, etc) an agreed provision has the following advantages:

(1) Reduction in post-breach transaction costs. This is the orthodox argument: C can avoid the cost and difficulty of proving the actual loss which he suffers; he 'derives an advantage from having the figure fixed and so being assured of payment without the expense and difficulty of proof. The more difficult the proof, the more likely it is that an agreed sum will be enforced; and the higher the probability of enforcement, the greater the incentive on D to settle C's claim out of court. Although there will be a saving in post-breach transaction costs in these relatively rare situations of breach, this saving may be outweighed by certain pre-breach costs. Most obviously these include the extra costs of negotiating the agreed damages clause . . .

(2) Avoiding the risk of under-compensation. At the time of contracting, the promisee C may fear that a damages award assessed under the ordinary principles would be inadequate compensation. Consequential or indirect losses may not be covered, nor may loss of reputation or idiosyncratic losses. An agreed damages clause may be the best way of dealing with the unusual risks – better even than C's informing D of the risks in the hope that damages would be awarded under the second rule in *Hadley v Baxendale* . . .

(3) An assurance of reliability. If D the promissor is able to accept an obvious disincentive to breach he can give C an assurance that his promise to perform can be relied upon . . .

(4) Limitation of liability. An agreed damages clause may perform the same function as an exemption clause: an agreed sum may place a *ceiling* on the financial risk which D is willing to accept . . . These clauses may often be designed as the basis for insurance arrangements to be made by the parties. C may obtain insurance against the risk of loss beyond the agreed ceiling, but D may not be able to obtain insurance against a potentially unlimited risk, or against the consequences of his own failure to perform, and he may be unwilling to accept an uninsurable responsibility for unpredictable loss.

(5) Flexibility. The final advantage is the ability to combine the relevant factors. An agreed damages clause permits the parties to take account of all the factors in any combination. The agreed sum will be a 'trade-off' of the various factors in the foregoing list of advantages, plus any other factors, so as to produce the correct 'mix' of factors to suit the particular case. Among the other factors will be:

(a) The different attitudes of the parties to the risk of the particular breach occurring . . .

(b) The extent of insurance protection desired by C. If C obtains the consent of

D to an enforceable agreed damages clause, he has purchased a form of lump-sum insurance against the consequences of non-performance . . .

(c)   C may wish (to the extent permitted by the 'genuine pre-estimate' test) to give D the desired level of incentive actually to perform . . .

In view of the advantages of agreed damages clauses, it is not surprising that generally economic analysis supports their enforcement (except in cases of initial 'unfairness or other bargaining abnormalities').

As Harris *et al* note, liquidated damages clauses are generally enforced by the courts because they promote economic efficiency and facilitate freedom of contract. The one restriction placed on such clauses is that they must represent a 'genuine' or 'bona fide' pre-estimate of the actual loss likely to be caused by the breach. If the clause exceeds this amount it will be struck out as a penalty and damages will be awarded on the usual principles. This rule was established in *Dunlop Pneumatic Tyre Co Ltd v New Garage and Motor Co Ltd*.

Dunlop Pneumatic Tyre Co Ltd v New Garage and Motor Co Ltd [1915] AC 79

Facts: A contract was agreed for the supply of car tyres and inner tubes to the respondents who would in turn sell the goods on to their customers. The contract contained a clause stating that a sum of £5 would be payable 'by way of liquidated damages and not as a penalty' if the respondents sold the tyres at a price lower than the list price. The respondents committed a breach of contract by selling the tyres to Motorists Mutual Co-operative Society at a price less than the current list price. The appellants brought an action for payment of the agreed sum. At first instance, the judge held that the clause was a valid liquidated damages clause but on appeal this decision was overturned and the clause was held to be an unenforceable penalty clause.

Held: The House of Lords allowed the appeal and held that the clause was not a penalty clause with the result that the appellants were entitled to enforce the clause.

Lord Dunedin:

'I shall content myself with stating succinctly the various propositions which I think are deducible from the decisions which rank as authoritative:

1. Though the parties to a contract who use the words "penalty" or "liquidated damages" may prima facie be supposed to mean what they say, yet the expression used is not conclusive. The Court must find out whether the payment stipulated is in truth a penalty or liquidated damages. This doctrine may be said to be found *passim* in nearly every case.

2. The essence of a penalty is a payment of money stipulated as *in terrorem* of the

offending party; the essence of liquidated damages is a genuine covenanted pre-estimate of damage (*Clydebank Engineering and Shipbuilding Co v Don Jose Ramos Yzquierdo y Castaneda*).

4. The question whether a sum stipulated is penalty or liquidated damages is a question of construction to be decided upon the terms and inherent circumstances of each particular contract, judged of as at the time of the making of the contract, not as at the time of the breach (*Public Works Commissioner v Hills* and *Webster v Bosanquet*).

5. To assist this task of construction various tests have been suggested, which if applicable to the case under consideration may prove helpful, or even conclusive. Such are:

a) It will be held to be penalty if the sum stipulated for is extravagant and unconscionable in amount in comparison with the greatest loss that could conceivably be proved to have followed from the breach. (Illustration given by Lord Halsbury in *Clydebank Case*.)

b) It will be held to be a penalty if the breach consists only in not paying a sum of money, and the sum stipulated is a sum greater than the sum which ought to have been paid (*Kemble v Farren*). This, though one of the most ancient instances, is truly a corollary to the last test. Whether it had its historical origin in the doctrine of the common law that when A promised to pay B a sum of money on a certain day and did not do so, B could only recover the sum with, in certain cases, interest, but could never recover further damages for non-timeous payment, or whether it was a survival of the time when equity reformed unconscionable bargains merely because they were unconscionable – a subject which much exercised Jessel MR in *Wallis v Smith* – is probably more interesting than material.

c) There is a presumption (but no more) that it is penalty when "a single lump sum is made payable by way of compensation, on the occurrence of one or more or all of several events, some of which may occasion serious and others but trifling damage" (Lord Watson in *Lord Elphinstone v Monkland Iron and Coal Co*).

On the other hand:

d) It is no obstacle to the sum stipulated being a genuine pre-estimate of damage, that the consequences of the breach are such as to make precise pre-estimation almost an impossibility. On the contrary, that is just the situation when it is probable that pre-estimated damage was the true bargain between the parties (*Clydebank Case*, Lord Halsbury; *Webster v Bosanquet Lord Mersey*).

Turning now to the facts of the case, it is evident that the damage apprehended by the appellants owing to the breaking of the agreement was an indirect and not a direct damage. So long as they got their price from the respondents for each article sold, it could not matter to them directly what the respondents did with it. Indirectly it did. Accordingly, the agreement is headed "Price Maintenance Agreement", and the way in which the appellants would be damaged if prices were cut is clearly explained in evidence by Mr Baisley, and no successful attempt is made to controvert that evidence. But though damage as a whole from such a practice would be certain, yet damage from any one sale would be impossible to forecast. It is just, therefore, one of those cases where it seems quite reasonable for parties to contract that they should estimate that damage at a certain figure, and provided that figure is not extravagant there would seem no reason to suspect that it is not truly a bargain to assess damages, but rather a penalty to be held *in terrorem*.

The argument of the respondents ... overpressed, in my judgment, the dictum of Lord Watson in *Lord Elphinstone's Case*, reading it as if he had said that the matter was conclusive, instead of saying, as he did, that it raised a presumption ...

... I have considerable doubt whether the stipulated payment here can fairly be said to deal with breaches, "some of which" – I am quoting Lord Watson's words – "may occasion serious and others but trifling damage". As a mere matter of construction, I doubt whether clause 5 applies to anything but sales below price. But I will assume that it does. None the less the mischief, as I have already pointed out, is an indirect mischief, and I see no data on which, as a matter of construction, I could settle in my own mind that the indirect damage from selling a cover would differ in magnitude from the indirect damage from selling a tube; or that the indirect damage from a cutting-price sale would differ from the indirect damage from supply at a full price to a hostile, because prohibited, agent. You cannot weigh such things in a chemical balance. The character of the agricultural land which was ruined by slag heaps in *Elphinstone's Case* was not all the same, but no objection was raised by Lord Watson to applying an overhead rate per acre, the sum not being in itself unconscionable.

I think *Elphinstone's Case*, or rather the dicta in it, do go this length, that if there are various breaches to which one indiscriminate sum to be paid in breach is applied, then the strength of the chain must be taken at its weakest link. If you can clearly see that the loss on one particular breach could never amount to the stipulated sum, then you may come to the conclusion that the sum is penalty. But further than this it does not go; so, for the reasons already stated, I do not think the present case forms an instance of what I have just expressed.'

The House of Lords held that the parties' own statement as to the nature of the clause was not conclusive of the issue. The court still had to determine whether the clause was a 'genuine pre-estimate of damage' or an 'extravagant and unconscionable' sum in comparison with the loss likely to be sustained following a breach. The situation in *Dunlop* was complicated, due to the fact that the liquidated sum was payable on the occurrence of a range of events, each of which could have led to a range of different losses. The argument was that this universal application of the clause showed that it was not a genuine pre-estimate of loss. Their Lordships rejected this argument. The losses flowing from each event were indirect and difficult to predict ('you cannot weigh such things in a chemical balance'). Because of this, it was acceptable to use a liquidated damages clause to 'average' the likely losses resulting from a range of breaches.

The House of Lords emphasised that the time for assessing the clause was the time of the contract, not the time of breach. Nevertheless, it is clear that what happened subsequently can provide helpful evidence of what loss might reasonably have been expected at the time the contract was entered into.

Philips Hong Kong Ltd v Attorney General of Hong Kong (1993) 61 BLR 41

Facts: The plaintiffs agreed to design, supply, test and install a computerised supervisory system for the approach roads and twin tube tunnels which were to be constructed under Smuggler's Ridge and Needle Hill Mountains in Hong Kong. The contract stipulated liquidated damages that would be payable if the plaintiff failed to meet 'Key Dates' by which certain items had to be completed so as to enable other contractors to continue with their work unimpeded. The contract also contained a separate liquidated damages clause for failure to complete the whole project on time. Philips successfully claimed that the clauses were unenforceable as penalties. The Court of Appeal of Hong Kong reversed this decision and Philips appealed to the Privy Council.

Held: The Privy Council dismissed the appeal.

Lord Woolf:

'[T]he court should not adopt an approach to provisions as to liquidated damages which could, as indicated earlier, defeat their purpose.

Except possibly in the case of situations where one of the parties to the contract is able to dominate the other as to the choice of the terms of a contract, it will normally be insufficient to establish that a provision is objectionably penal to identify situations where the application of the provision could result in a larger sum being recovered by the injured party than his actual loss. Even in such situations so long as the sum payable in the event of non-compliance with the contract is not extravagant, having regard to the range of losses that it could reasonably be anticipated it would have to cover at the time the contract was made, it can still be a genuine pre-estimate of the loss that would be suffered and so a perfectly valid liquidated damage provision. The use in argument of unlikely illustrations should therefore not assist a party to defeat a provision as to liquidated damages . . .

A difficulty can arise where the range of possible loss is broad. Where it should be obvious that, in relation to part of the range, the liquidated damages are totally out of proportion to certain of the losses which may be incurred, the failure to make special provision for those losses may result in the "liquidated damages" not being recoverable . . . However the court has to be careful not to set too stringent a standard and bear in mind that what the parties have agreed should normally be upheld. Any other approach will lead to undesirable uncertainty especially in commercial contracts.

> In seeking to establish that the sum described in the Philips contract as liquidated damages was in fact a penalty, Philips has to surmount the strong inference to the contrary resulting from its agreement to make the payments as liquidated damages and the fact that it is not suggested in these proceedings that the sum claimed is excessive in relation to the actual loss suffered by the Government. The fact that the issue has to be determined objectively, judged at the date the contract was made, does not mean what actually happens subsequently is irrelevant. On the contrary it can provide valuable evidence as to what could reasonably be expected to be the loss at the time the contract was made. Likewise the fact that two parties who should be well capable of protecting their respective commercial interests agreed the allegedly penal provision suggests that the formula for calculating liquidated damages is unlikely to be oppressive . . .'

The Privy Council adopted a flexible (and some might say unpredictable) approach to assessing liquidated damages clauses. The court will consider all the circumstances of the case. On the facts of *Philips*, their Lordships were clearly influenced by the fact that this was a commercial contract, entered into by two parties who were well capable of protecting their respective commercial interests. To establish that the clause was a penalty, the plaintiffs would have had to have shown that the stipulated sum was extravagant and out-of-all proportion to the loss likely to be sustained. It was not enough merely to show that the clause could result in a larger sum being recovered than the loss actually suffered by the defendant. The court was unimpressed by such hypothetical illustrations. It was, however, willing to consider subsequent events as evidence of what could reasonably be expected to be the loss at the time the contract was agreed.

The distinction between liquidated damages and penalties was considered recently by the High Court in *Alfred McAlpine Capital Projects Ltd v Tilebox Ltd*.

Alfred McAlpine Capital Projects Ltd v Tilebox Ltd [2005] EWHC 281

Facts: Tilebox, a property developer, entered into a building contract with McAlpine. The contract contained a clause which provided that £45,000 per week would be payable if completion of the project was delayed. In fact, completion was delayed by many months and McAlpine claimed that the clause was a penalty and therefore invalid.

Held: It was held that the clause was a valid liquidated damages clause.

Jackson J:

'Let me . . . make four general observations, which are pertinent to the issues in the present case.

1. There seem to be two strands in the authorities. In some cases judges consider whether there is an unconscionable or extravagant disproportion between the damages stipulated in the contract and the true amount of damages likely to be suffered. In other cases the courts consider whether the level of damages stipulated was reasonable. Mr Darling submits, and I accept, that these two strands can be reconciled. In my view, a pre-estimate of damages does not have to be right in order to be reasonable. There must be a substantial discrepancy between the level of damages stipulated in the contract and the level of damages which is likely to be suffered before it can be said that the agreed pre-estimate is unreasonable.

2. Although many authorities use or echo the phrase "genuine pre-estimate", the test does not turn upon the genuineness or honesty of the party or parties who made the pre-estimate. The test is primarily an objective one, even though the court has some regard to the thought processes of the parties at the time of contracting.

3. Because the rule about penalties is an anomaly within the law of contract, the courts are predisposed, where possible, to uphold contractual terms which fix the level of damages for breach. This predisposition is even stronger in the case of commercial contracts freely entered into between parties of comparable bargaining power.

4. Looking at the bundle of authorities provided in this case, I note only four cases where the relevant clause has been struck down as a penalty. These are *Commissioner of Public Works v Hills* [1906] AC 368, *Bridge v Campbell Discount Co Ltd* [1962] AC 600, *Workers Trust and Merchant Bank Ltd v Dojap Investments Ltd* [1993] AC 573, and *Ariston SRL v Charly Records* (Court of Appeal 13th March 1990). In each of these four cases there was, in fact, a very wide gulf between (a) the level of damages likely to be suffered, and (b) the level of damages stipulated in the contract.'

Once again the court emphasised that it was committed to upholding liquidated damages clauses, especially when the clause was agreed at arm's-length between commercial parties. Jackson J held that the sum of £45,000 was 'at or slightly above the top of the range of possible weekly losses', but that the difference was not nearly wide enough to make the clause a penalty. A substantial disparity would have been required.

One slight concern is the distinction that the judge drew between the 'genuineness' of the pre-estimate and its 'reasonableness'. There are not two separate tests for validity; there is just one – the genuineness of the pre-estimate (see Lord Dunedin in *Dunlop Pneumatic Tyre Co Ltd v New Garage and Motor Co Ltd* [1915] AC 79). Reasonableness is only relevant in so far as it provides evidence of the parties' objective intentions. The more unreasonable the sum the less likely it is to be a genuine and bona fide pre-estimate of loss.

There have also been recent indications from the Court of Appeal that subjective factors, such as the intention of the parties, may be relevant to the question of whether the clause amounts to a genuine pre-estimate of loss.

Murray v Leisureplay [2005] EWCA Civ 963; [2005] IRLR 946

Facts: The appellant, Mr Murray, set up Murray Financial Corporation (later to become Leisureplay plc) in June 1988. He was appointed Chief Executive Director of the company on a service agreement which contained a 'golden parachute' clause (clause 17). This stated that Mr Murray was entitled to the payment of a year's gross salary in the event of his employment being terminated without one year's notice. On 7 May 2003, Mr Murray received a letter from Leisureplay purporting to terminate his employment with effect from 30 June 2003. The letter did not contain an offer of payment in accordance with the terms of the agreement. Mr Murray brought a claim for liquidated damages under the 'golden parachute' clause. At first instance, Bunton J held that the clause was unenforceable as a penalty. It exceeded the amount available under the common law, and was not a genuine pre-estimate of loss. Mr Murray appealed this decision.

Held: The Court of Appeal allowed Murray's appeal, holding that the clause was a genuine pre-estimate of loss.

Arden LJ:

'**54.** . . . [I]n my judgment, the following (with the explanation given below) constitutes a practical step by step guide as to the questions which the court should ask in a case like this:

i)   To what breaches of contract does the contractual damages provision apply?

ii)   What amount is payable on breach under that clause in the parties' agreement?

iii)   What amount would be payable if a claim for damages for breach of contract was brought under common law?

iv)   What were the parties' reasons for agreeing for the relevant clause?

v)   Has the party who seeks to establish that the clause is a penalty shown that the amount payable under the clause was imposed *in terrorem*, or that it does not constitute a genuine pre-estimate of loss for the purposes of the *Dunlop* case, and, if he has shown the latter, is there some other reason which justifies the discrepancy between i) and ii) above? . . .

69. The burden of showing that a clause for the payment of damages on breach is a penalty clause is on the party who seeks to escape liability under it, not on the party who seeks to enforce it . . .

70. The judge considered that the deciding issue was the absence of an allowance for the failure to mitigate. Any allowance, however, which the parties could have made would of necessity have been rough and ready. The judge was also concerned by the lack of any evidence as to any independent review of the clause by the other directors. As against that, however, there was no concealment of the terms from the board, who did indeed approve them and MFC was advised by solicitors. Furthermore, and perhaps of more significance for the type of review that the court makes on a penalty issue, the term agreed was not out of line with market expectations. Particulars of the directors' service agreements had been included in the pathfinder prospectus issued by MFC's financial advisers, Peel Hunt. The particulars related to Mr Murray's agreement before the reduction of the period under clause 17 to one year, with three years only if there was an agreement to acquire (for example) an insurance company. The reaction of at least one investor was that the provision for three years was excessive. No objection was taken to the provisions disclosed for other directors, providing for one year's gross salary alone. The clause in the agreement was then amended, and the offering of shares and admission to trading on the Alternative Investment Market, was successfully achieved. The inference to be drawn from this sequence of events in my judgment is that the clause as finally agreed did not cut across market expectations. . . .

71. The next point is that the agreement contains some fierce restrictions on competition. During the period of the agreement, Mr Murray was only due to work for MFC for three days a week. Nonetheless, as clause 12 of the agreement set out above shows, Mr Murray could not after termination of his agreement engage for one year in any business which competed with MFC. The type of business was restricted to the business of acquiring building societies and other financial institutions etc "being activities of a kind with which [Mr Murray] was concerned to a material extent during the period of one year prior to termination of his contract" . . . [T]he restrictions which Mr Murray undertook to observe on termination of his contract were important and significant. He had set out to make his name in business through the acquisition of building societies and so the restriction could result in his not being able to pursue his business plans during the year following termination, leading to diminished earnings after that year was up. If MFC wanted a restriction of this kind, it would not be unreasonable for Mr Murray to demand some recompense . . .

74. There are other relevant points. Clause 17 gave MFC the advantage that if it wanted to dismiss Mr Murray it could effect a clean break and know the measure of its financial exposure without what might well be damaging publicity and lengthy litigation. If MFC wanted to terminate the agreement, it would no doubt be because Mr Murray's continued connection with MFC was damaging to MFC. In those circumstances as a commercial matter it might well want to end the relationship swiftly and without the glare of publicity. Damages for breach of an employment contract can be difficult to determine in advance because of the difficulty of knowing what alternative employment might be available. The negotiation of clause 17 achieves the further advantage of avoiding spending management time and money on lawyers' fees to work such damages out . . .

76. In the circumstances, I have come to a different conclusion from the judge. On the facts of this case, it is not shown that the parties could not reasonably have come to the view that clause 17 was a genuine pre-estimate of damage or that it was not otherwise justifiable. MFC was of course the contract-breaker. In the considerations referred to above, I have taken into account the disadvantages to it of wrongful termination without a pre-determined damages clause. I do not consider that the court is precluded from taking such matters into account. To do so is consistent with freedom of contract, which the doctrine of penalties has so far as possible to respect. Such considerations may help explain why a party may wish to take on an obligation which (without that explanation) might be considered to be sufficiently onerous to be a penalty within paragraph a) of Lord Dunedin's guidance. Such considerations may indeed be best described as justification for the clause said to be a penalty, rather than elements of a genuine pre-estimate of the damage. In my formulation of the steps above, I do not intend to exclude such considerations or the possibility that a clause could be justified on this sort of ground alone.'

Clarke LJ:
'105. I have had the benefit of reading the judgments of Arden LJ and Buxton LJJ in draft. I agree with them that the appeal on the penalty issue should be allowed. In so far as there is a difference of approach between them, I prefer the broader approach of Buxton LJ.'

Buxton LJ:
'113. The approach that should be applied at trial would be in more general terms than that suggested by my Lady . . . that always requires a comparison between the liquidated and the common law damages to see if the comparison discloses a discrepancy; and then requires that discrepancy to be justified as a genuine pre-estimate of damages, or by some other form of justification.

114. I venture to disagree with that approach because it introduces a rigid and inflexible element into what should be a broad and general question. It is also inconsistent with warnings by judges of high authority that, at least in connexion with commercial contracts, great caution should be exercised before striking down a clause as penal; and with the tests that they have postulated to that end. My Lady has cited in her paragraph 66 the observations of Diplock LJ in *Robophone v Blank* [1966] 1 WLR 1428 at p 1447. I would add the well-known passage of Lord Woolf in *Philips Hong Kong v A-G of Hong Kong* (1993) 61 BLR 49 at pp 58–59:

> "Except possibly in the case of situations where one of the parties to the contract is able to dominate the other as to the choice of the terms of a contract, it will normally be insufficient to establish that a provision is objectionably penal to identify situations where the application of the provision could result in a larger sum being recovered by the injured party than his actual loss. Even in such situations so long as the sum payable in the event of non-compliance with the contract is not extravagant, having regard to the range of losses that it could reasonably be anticipated it would have to cover at the time the contract was made, it can still be a genuine pre-estimate of the loss that would be suffered and so a perfectly valid liquidated damages provision"

And exclusive concentration on the factual difference between the liquidated and the contractual damages overlooks a principal test formulated by Lord Dunedin to identify a penalty, [1915] AC at p 87, that

> "It will be held to be a penalty if the sum stipulated for is extravagant and unconscionable in amount in comparison with the greatest loss that could conceivably be proved to have followed from the breach."

115. Neither the literal wording of that test nor the spirit of it applies here. Mr Murray's terms were generous, but they were not unconscionable. As to the absence of any requirement of mitigation in clause 17.1, to which as we have seen the judge attached determinative importance, two comments have to be made. First, it must have been difficult to say with confidence at the time of entering into the contract what might happen to Mr Murray were he to be dismissed: provisions protecting an employee in the case of wrongful termination may take the form that they do because such an event can damage his future employability, at least in the short term. Second, in order to meet this criticism a pre-estimate of damages clause would have to be drafted to encompass not only the fact of mitigation in terms of income from other sources but also the duty to seek such mitigation. Such a clause would directly invite disputes about the reasonableness of Mr Murray's behaviour after termination, of the kind that clauses stipulating the amount of compensation are precisely designed to avoid . . .

116. It is therefore necessary to stand back and look at the reality of this agreement. Although I agree that evidence about it is sparse, I am prepared to take judicial notice of the fact that an entrepreneurial company such as MFC, promoting a product conceived by one man, will often place a high value upon retaining the services, and the loyalty and attention, of that one man as its chief executive: to the extent of including in his "package" generous reassurance against the eventuality of dismissal. That such reassurance exceeds the likely amount of contractual damages on dismissal does not render the terms penal unless the party seeking to avoid the terms can demonstrate that they meet the test of extravagance posited by Lord Dunedin and by Lord Woolf. I regard that as a comparatively broad and simple question, that will not normally call for detailed analysis of the contractual background. Applying that test, which I accept differs from that adopted by my Lady, I would accordingly allow the appeal on the penalty issue.'

The majority in the Court of Appeal (Buxton and Clarke LJJ) rejected Arden LJ's step-by-step analysis. In their view, her emphasis on the comparison between the liquidated sum and the amount payable as common law damages introduced a 'rigid and inflexible element into what should be a broad and general question' (at [114]). They preferred the test set out by Lord Dunedin in *Dunlop*: 'It will be held to be a penalty if the sum stipulated for is extravagant and unconscionable in amount in comparison with the greatest loss that could conceivably be proved to have followed from the breach'.

The decision in *Murray* is of particular interest because of the emphasis placed by their Lordships on various subjective factors, most notably the intentions of the parties. Arden LJ thought that the discrepancy between the amount payable under the clause and the amount payable in a claim for damages was justifiable on the ground that the clause was part of an agreement that placed onerous restrictions on Mr Murray and enabled Leisureplay to dismiss him without the damaging publicity and cost of lengthy litigation (at [71] and [74]). Buxton LJ also alluded to subjective factors including the benefit of such clauses to companies seeking to attract key employees (at [116]). This is all in stark contract to the traditional emphasis on the objective nature of the *Dunlop Pneumatic Tyre* test. We must wait to see whether the courts continue to make use of such subjective considerations in the future.

A final point to note on liquidated damages clauses is that if they impose an obligation on a consumer to pay a 'disproportionately high sum', they may be unenforceable under Sched 3, para 1(e) of the Unfair Terms in Consumer Contracts Regulations (see Chapter 8).

17.3 SPECIFIC RELIEF

As noted at the beginning of this chapter, an award of damages is usually sufficient to put the claimant 'in a situation as beneficial to him as if the agreement were specifically performed' (*Harnett v Yielding* (1805) 2 Sch & Lef 549, 553). However, in certain situations damages will be inadequate for this purpose and the courts will need to consider whether an order of specific relief ought to be made.

In this section we will be examining two different forms of specific relief: specific performance and injunctions. An order of specific performance compels the defendant to perform his positive contractual obligations. An injunction restrains the defendant from acting in breach of his negative obligations. The sanction for failure to comply with either is that the person concerned will be in contempt of court and will face either a fine or possibly even imprisonment.

17.3.1 SPECIFIC PERFORMANCE

Specific performance has its roots in the courts' equitable jurisdiction to grant remedies to supplement the common law. As a result, the remedy is awarded at the discretion of the court and will only be available instead of damages when the court 'can by that means do more and complete justice' (*Wilson v Northampton and Banbury Junction Rly Co* (1874) 9 Ch App 279, 284 per Lord Selbourne). The discretionary element in specific performance inevitably means that its availability is subject to a degree of uncertainty. Over the years, however, the courts have developed a number of rules about its use, and these mean that in most cases it will be fairly easy to predict whether or not an order is likely to be granted.

17.3.1.1 Adequacy of damages

The first rule is that specific performance will only be available in situations where compensatory damages are inadequate to do justice between the parties. This adequacy-of-damages test is long established and controversial. Professor Dawson once described it as, 'an unnecessary and irksome restriction of specific perform-ance', which is applied in an 'arbitrary and irrational' way (Dawson, J, 'Specific Performance in France and Germany' (1959) 57 Mich LR 495, 532). This criticism may be true, but the test is generally considered to perform an invaluable role in restraining the use of coercive remedies that carry the threat of contempt proceed-ings. Over the years, the courts have established a number of well-recognised situations in which damages are deemed to be inadequate.

17.3.1.1.1 No market substitute

If no market substitute for performance is available, damages are deemed to be inadequate. This is the reason why contracts concerning land are specifically enforceable. The courts assume that land is unique and that no market substitute is available (*Adderley v Dixon* (1824) 1 Sim & St 607, 610 per Leach VC). On this basis, specific performance is available in respect of contracts for the sale of land, for the grant of an interest in land and even for the grant of a licence to occupy land (*Verall v Great Yarmouth Borough Council* [1981] QB 202).

Contracts for the sale of goods are generally not specifically enforceable because damages can be used to purchase substitute performance. There are two situations, however, where specific performance may be available. First, where the subject matter of the contract is unique – such as a rare book, a sculpture or a painting – substitute performance will be prima facie unavailable, and the court may be will-ing to order specific performance. In *Falcke v Gray* (1859) 4 Drew 651, this was the ground for ordering specific performance of a contract for the sale of two oriental jars. In the words of Kindersley VC, the jars were of such 'unusual beauty, rarity and distinction' that damages would provide an inadequate remedy for nonperformance since substitutes were not available.

Second, specific performance may be ordered of contracts for the sale of non-unique goods if circumstances exist that mean that substitutes are *practically* unavailable.

Sky Petroleum Ltd v VIP Petroleum Ltd [1974] 1 WLR 576

Facts: The plaintiffs entered into a contract with the defendants for the supply of petrol and diesel for a period of ten years. At a time when the supply of petrol was restricted and the plaintiffs had no prospect of finding an alternative source of supply, the defendants purported to terminate the contract. The plaintiffs sought an injunction to restrain the defendants from withholding supplies.

Held: Goulding J granted the injunction even though he acknowledged that it amounted to specific performance of a contract to buy and sell personal property.

Goulding J:

'Now I come to the most serious hurdle in the way of the plaintiffs which is the well known doctrine that the court refuses specific performance of a contract to sell and purchase chattels not specific or ascertained ... [T]he ratio behind the rule is, as I believe, that under the ordinary contract for the sale of non-specific goods, damages are a sufficient remedy. That, to my mind, is lacking in the circumstances of the present case. The evidence suggests, and indeed it is common knowledge that the petroleum market is in an unusual state in which a would-be buyer cannot go out into the market and contract with another seller, possibly at some sacrifice as to price. Here, the defendants appear for practical purposes to be the plaintiffs' sole means of keeping their business going, and I am prepared so far to depart from the general rule as to try to preserve the position under the contract until a later date. I therefore propose to grant an injunction.'

17.3.1.1.2 *Damages would be difficult to quantify*

The second situation in which damages are deemed to be inadequate will sometimes arise in connection with the first. If supply of alternative performance is restricted it may be extremely difficult for the court to quantify compensatory damages because it is unclear how much it will cost the claimant to obtain alternative performance. In such circumstances damages will be found to be inadequate and specific performance will be ordered (*Adderley v Dixon* (1824) 1 Sim & St 607, 611 per Leach VC). It is for this reason that specific performance has been ordered of contracts to sell or pay annuities (*Clifford v Turrell* (1841) 1 Y & C Ch Cas 138), and of contracts to indemnify (*Ranelaugh Earl v Hayes* (1683) 1 Vern 189). Damages are inadequate because they would be calculated by conjecture and would leave the claimant with something less than what he bargained for.

17.3.1.1.3 *Only nominal damages available*

The final situation in which damages are held to be inadequate is where damages are merely nominal because the claimant has suffered no pecuniary loss.

Beswick v Beswick [1968] AC 58

Facts: Mr Beswick made a contract with his nephew whereby the nephew promised to make payments to Mr Beswick's widow during his lifetime in return for Mr Beswick's promise to transfer his business to the nephew. When Mr Beswick died, the nephew refused to pay and Mrs Beswick brought an action for breach of contract in her capacity as Mr Beswick's personal representative. The nephew argued that, since Mr Beswick had died, his estate had suffered no loss as a result of the breach of contract, and thus nominal damages were adequate.

Held: The House of Lords rejected the nephew's argument and ordered specific performance of the agreement.

Lord Pearce:
'It is argued that the estate can only recover nominal damages and that no other remedy is open, either to the estate or to the personal plaintiff. Such a result would be wholly repugnant to justice and commonsense and if the argument were right it would show a very serious defect in the law.

In the first place, I do not accept the view that damages must be nominal . . . It is not necessary, however, to consider the amount of damages more closely since this is a case in which, as the Court of Appeal rightly decided, the more appropriate remedy is that of specific performance.

The administratrix is entitled, if she so prefers, to enforce the agreement rather than accept its repudiation, and specific performance is more convenient than an action for arrears of payment followed by separate actions as each sum falls due. Moreover, damages for breach would be a less appropriate remedy since the parties to the agreement were intending an annuity for a widow; and a lump sum of damages does not accord with this. If (contrary to my view) the argument that a derisory sum of damages is all that can be obtained be right, the remedy of damages in this case is manifestly useless.

The present case presents all the features which led the equity courts to apply their remedy of specific performance. The contract was for the sale of a business. The defendant could on his part clearly have obtained specific performance of it if Beswick senior or his administratrix had defaulted. Mutuality is a ground in favour of specific performance. Moreover, the defendant on his side has received the whole benefit of the contract and it is a matter of conscience for the court to see that he now performs his part of it . . .'

Lord Hodson:
'[I]t is said nominal damages are adequate and the remedy of specific performance ought not to be granted. That is, with all respect, wholly to misunderstand that principle. Equity will grant specific performance when damages are inadequate to meet the justice of the case.

But in any event quantum of damages seldom affects the right to specific performance. If X contracts with Y to buy Blackacre or a rare chattel for a fancy price because the property or chattel has caught his fancy he is entitled to enforce his bargain and it matters not that he could not prove any damage.

In this case the court ought to grant a specific performance order all the more

> because damages *are* nominal. C has received all the property; justice demands that he pay the price and this can only be done in the circumstances by equitable relief . . .'

A number of comments can be made about this decision. First, it will not always be the case that specific performance will be ordered whenever compensatory damages are merely nominal. If that were so, specific performance would be available in all cases where the contract has been breached and substitute performance is available at a lower price than the contractually agreed one. The claimant must demonstrate that s/he has a non-pecuniary interest in performance, which would not be protected by an award of nominal damages. In *Beswick*, the uncle had a non-pecuniary interest in seeing his wife provided for after his death. Such an interest would not have received adequate protection from an award of nominal damages.

Second, Lord Pearce indicated in his speech that the inadequacy of compensatory damages is not a 'necessary' requirement of a claim for specific performance. Instead, he emphasised that specific performance will be awarded whenever it is deemed to be the most 'appropriate' remedy. Jones and Goodhart (Jones, G and Goodhart, W, *Specific Performance*, 2nd edn, 1996, p 37, London: Butterworths) have written:

> 'The alternative test, "which is the more effective remedy in serving the ends of justice?", has the merit of greater clarity and directs the court to the real question which should be answered. It may encourage the courts to grant specific performance more freely. It is unlikely, however, that there will be a significant extension of equitable jurisdiction for the simple reason that most innocent parties will still be anxious immediately to mitigate their loss and will therefore sue for damages. Moreover, in most cases damages will remain the most effective remedy in serving the ends of justice.'

The shift from language of 'inadequacy' to that of 'appropriateness' or 'effectiveness' does not mean that the inadequacy of damages is no longer important; it is simply no longer decisive. Whether the shift is merely one of terminology instead of substance remains to be seen.

17.3.1.2 Factors affecting the availability of specific performance

Once the claimant has demonstrated that compensatory damages would be inadequate the court has jurisdiction to order specific performance, but it may, of course, refuse to make such an order on discretionary grounds. The rest of this section looks at these grounds.

17.3.1.2.1 *The need for constant supervision*

Specific performance will not be ordered if it is likely to require constant supervision by the court. In *Ryan v Mutual Tontine Westminster Chambers Association* [1893] 1 Ch 116, the Court of Appeal refused to order specific performance of a covenant to provide a porter for the tenants of a block of residential flats. The reason given by Lord Esher MR was that such an order 'would require constant superintendence by the Court, which the Court in such cases has always declined to give'. The constant supervision restriction must now be understood in the light of the House of Lords' decision in *Co-operative Insurance Society Ltd v Argyll Stores (Holdings) Ltd*.

Co-operative Insurance Society Ltd v Argyll Stores (Holdings) Ltd [1998] AC 1

Facts: Argyll leased a unit for use as a supermarket in a new shopping centre owned by Co-operative Insurance Society. The lease contained the following covenant: 'To keep the demised premises open for retail trade during the usual hours of business in the locality and the display windows properly dressed in a suitable manner in keeping with a good class parade of shops'. Competition in the supermarket business was fierce and Argyll decided to scale down its operations. The supermarket in Co-operative's shopping centre had made a loss of £70,000 in the previous year, so Argyll announced its intention to close the store. Co-operative Insurance sought specific performance of the covenant in the lease. At first instance the trial judge refused specific performance. The Court of Appeal reversed this decision.

Held: The House of Lords allowed Argyll's appeal and held that it was not normally appropriate to give an order of specific performance requiring someone to carry on a business.

Lord Hoffman:
'The most frequent reason given in the cases for declining to order someone to carry on a business is that it would require constant supervision by the court . . . There has, I think, been some misunderstanding about what is meant by continued superintendence. It may at first sight suggest that the judge (or some other officer of the court) would literally have to supervise the execution of the order. In *CH Giles & Co Ltd v Morris* [1972] 1 WLR 307, 318 Megarry J said that "difficulties of constant superintendence" were a "narrow consideration" because:

"there is normally no question of the court having to send its officers to supervise the performance of the order . . . Performance . . . is normally secured by the realisation of the person enjoined that he is liable to be punished for contempt if evidence of his disobedience to the order is put before the court; . . ."

This is, of course, true but does not really meet the point. The judges who have said that the need for constant supervision was an objection to such orders were no doubt well aware that supervision would in practice take the form of rulings by the court, on applications made by the parties, as to whether there had been a breach of the order. It is the possibility of the court having to give an indefinite series of such rulings in order to ensure the execution of the order which has been regarded as undesirable.

Why should this be so? A principal reason is that, as Megarry J pointed out in the passage to which I have referred, the only means available to the court to enforce its order is the quasi-criminal procedure of punishment for contempt. This is a powerful weapon; so powerful, in fact, as often to be unsuitable as an instrument for adjudicating upon the disputes which may arise over whether a business is being run in accordance with the terms of the court's order. The heavy-handed nature of the enforcement mechanism is a consideration which may go to the exercise of the court's discretion in other cases as well, but its use to compel the running of a business is perhaps the paradigm case of its disadvantages and it is in this context that I shall discuss them.

The prospect of committal or even a fine, with the damage to commercial reputation which will be caused by a finding of contempt of court, is likely to have at least two undesirable consequences. First, the defendant, who *ex hypothesi* did not think that it was in his economic interest to run the business at all, now has to make decisions under a sword of Damocles which may descend if the way the business is run does not conform to the terms of the order. This is, as one might say, no way to run a business . . .

Secondly, the seriousness of a finding of contempt for the defendant means that any application to enforce the order is likely to be a heavy and expensive piece of litigation. The possibility of repeated applications over a period of time means that, in comparison with a once-and-for-all inquiry as to damages, the enforcement of the remedy is likely to be expensive in terms of cost to the parties and the resources of the judicial system.

This is a convenient point at which to distinguish between orders which require a defendant to carry on an activity, such as running a business over a more or less extended period of time, and orders which require him to achieve a result. The possibility of repeated applications for rulings on compliance with the order which arises in the former case does not exist to anything like the same extent in the latter. Even if the achievement of the result is a complicated matter which will take some time, the court, if called upon to rule, only has to examine the finished work and say whether it complies with the order . . .

This distinction between orders to carry on activities and orders to achieve results explains why the courts have in appropriate circumstances ordered specific performance of building contracts and repairing covenants: see *Wolverhampton Corporation v. Emmons* [1901] 1 KB 515 (building contract) and *Jeune v Queens Cross Properties* [1974] Ch 97 (repairing covenant) . . .'

Lord Hoffman attempted to explain the rationale behind the constant supervision restriction. It did not envisage that the court would literally have to supervise the execution of the order. Rather, it was concerned to prevent the possibility of the court being required to give an indefinite series of rulings over a period of time to ensure compliance with the order. This would be an utterly inappropriate way to run a business, not least because such rulings would be backed up with the heavy-handed remedy of contempt of court, thus draining the resources of the judicial system. A one-off award of damages would be much more satisfactory.

Lord Hoffman also took the opportunity to distinguish between orders that require a defendant to carry on an activity – such as running a business – and orders that require a defendant to achieve a result. The potential for repeated orders on compliance in the former category of case does not exist to anything like the same extent in the latter. This distinction helps to explain the decision in *Wolverhampton Corp v Emmons* [1901] 1 KB 515, where the Court of Appeal ordered specific performance of a contract for the construction of eight new houses. AL Smith MR said that the building plans 'define the work to be done sufficiently to enable the Court to make an order for specific performance'.

17.3.1.2.2 *Personal services*

It is a well-established rule that equity will not enforce a contract for personal service at the suit of either party. This is for both moral and practical reasons. First, forcing a defendant to work for the claimant by fear of imprisonment would constitute a serious infringement of his or her personal liberty. Second, it would be undesirable for the state to enforce the continuance of a 'personal relationship' between two unwilling parties.

In more recent times the traditional rule against the enforcement of contracts for personal service has been questioned. This is due to the fact that the modern relationship of employer and employee is much less personal than the traditional relationship of master and servant, which subsisted at the time that the general rule was recognised. Where it can be established that mutual trust and respect remains between the parties, specific performance may be available. In *Hill v CA Parsons & Co Ltd* [1972] 1 Ch 305, for example, an order was made because the dismissal had resulted from union pressure, rather than a dispute between the employer and employee. Nowadays, employment disputes such as that in *Hill* would normally be dealt with under unfair dismissal legislation. Sections 113–117 of the Employment Rights Act 1996 provide for the remedies of reinstatement and re-engagement as well as compensation, but the level of reinstatement in practice appears to be very low (see Davies, P and Freedland, M, *Labour Legislation and Public Policy: A Contemporary History*, 1993, p 210, Oxford: Clarendon).

17.3.1.2.3 *The need for mutuality*

The court will not order specific performance in favour of a claimant unless it could also have ordered specific performance in favour of the defendant. For this reason, a party who undertakes to render personal service cannot specifically enforce the contract, because it is not enforceable against him or her (*Blackett v Bates* (1865) LR 1 Ch App 117.) Likewise, a minor is unable to obtain specific performance of a contract for non-necessary goods (*Flight v Bolland* (1828) 4 Russ 298). The leading case on the mutuality rule is *Price v Strange*.

Price v Strange [1978] Ch 337

Facts: The defendant granted the plaintiff a continuation of the underlease of a maisonette in return for an increase in rent and an agreement to carry out certain works of repair. When the plaintiff had completed half the work the defendant refused to allow him to continue and purported to terminate the agreement. The plaintiff brought an action for specific performance of the agreement. The judge dismissed the action on the grounds that the plaintiff's obligations to carry out the repairs would not have been specifically enforceable, so that there was a lack of mutuality.

Held: The Court of Appeal allowed the appeal. The date for assessing mutuality was the time of trial and by this time all the repairs had been carried out and there was no risk of the defendant being required to grant the underlease whilst not being able to enforce the obligation to carry out the repairs.

Goff LJ:

'The true principle is that one judges the defence of want of mutuality on the facts and circumstances as they exist at the hearing, albeit in the light of the whole conduct of the parties in relation to the subject matter, and in the absence of any other disqualifying circumstances the court will grant specific performance if it can be done without injustice or unfairness to the defendant.'

Buckley LJ:

'The time at which the mutual availability of specific performance and its importance must be considered is, in my opinion, the time of judgment, and the principle to be applied can I think be stated simply as follows: the court will not compel a defendant to perform his obligations specifically if it cannot at the same time ensure that any unperformed obligations of the plaintiff will be specifically performed, unless, perhaps, damages would be an adequate remedy to the defendant for any default on the plaintiff's part.'

The decision in *Price v Strange* confirms that the time of trial is the correct point at which to assess mutuality. Furthermore, the Court of Appeal advocated a more flexible approach to the mutuality requirement, confirming that lack of mutuality is not an absolute bar to an order of specific performance. This was followed in the more recent case of *Rainbow Estates Ltd v Tokenhold Ltd* [1999] Ch 64, 69, where Lawrence Collins QC said:

'[A]s regards the requirement of mutuality, it is now clear that it does not follow from the fact that specific performance is not available to one party that it is not available to the other: want of mutuality is a discretionary, and not an absolute, bar to specific performance. The court will grant specific performance if it can be done without injustice or unfairness to the defendant: *Price v Strange* [1978] Ch 337, 357, *per* Goff LJ.'

17.3.1.2.4 *Hardship to the defendant*

Specific performance may be refused on the ground that the order will cause severe hardship to the defendant. In *Denne v Light* (1857) 8 DM & G 774, the court refused to grant specific performance of a contract for the sale of land. This was because it would have left the buyer with a plot wholly surrounded by land owned by others, all of whom were unwilling to grant him a right of way.

Severe hardship may be a ground for refusing specific performance even when the hardship does not arise directly from the contract.

Patel v Ali [1984] Ch 283

Facts: The defendant, Mrs Ali, and a Mr Ahmed agreed to sell Mrs Ali's home to Mr and Mrs Patel. Contracts were exchanged in July 1979 but completion of the sale was delayed for various reasons. In 1980 it was discovered that the defendant had bone cancer in her right thigh and she became heavily dependent on her neighbours for support and care. This support network would have been lost if she had been forced to move house and it would have been very expensive for her to pay for alternative help. The plaintiffs eventually sought specific performance of the contract for sale.

Held: Goulding J refused to order specific performance on the grounds that it would cause undue hardship to the defendant. The plaintiffs were left to their remedy in damages.

Goulding J:
'Another limitation suggested by [counsel for the plaintiffs] was that, in the reported cases, as he said, hardship successfully relied on has always related to the subject matter of the contract and has not been just a personal hardship of the defendant. Certainly, mere pecuniary difficulties, whether of purchaser or of vendor, afford no excuse from performance of a contract. In a wider sense than that, I do not think the suggested universal proposition can be sustained . . .

The important and true principle, in my view, is that only in extraordinary and persuasive circumstances can hardship supply an excuse for resisting performance of a contract for the sale of immovable property. A person of full capacity who sells or buys a house takes the risk of hardship to himself and his dependants, whether arising from existing facts or unexpectedly supervening in the interval before completion. This is where, to my mind, great importance attaches to the immense delay in the present case, not attributable to the defendant's conduct. Even after issue of the writ, she could not complete, if she had wanted to, without the concurrence of the absent Mr. Ahmed. Thus, in a sense, she can say she is being asked to do what she never bargained for, namely to complete the sale after more than four years, after all the unforeseeable changes that such a period entails.'

Goulding J made clear that the defence of severe hardship is only available in 'extraordinary and persuasive circumstances'. Mere pecuniary difficulties are not sufficient. Hardship must be combined with some additional factor. On the facts of *Patel v Ali* the plaintiff's delay in seeking specific performance provided that additional factor.

17.3.1.2.5 *Conduct of the claimant*

Specific performance is an equitable remedy and as such the claimant is required to come to the court with 'clean hands'. Specific performance will be refused if the contract has been procured by means that are unfair, even if those means do not amount to grounds that will void the contract. In *Mountford v Scott* [1975] Ch 258, the plaintiff was denied specific performance on the grounds that he had taken advantage of the illiteracy of a defendant who had not been independently advised. Similarly, in *Walters v Morgan* (1861) 3 DF & J 718, the court refused to order specific performance of a lease over land because the seller had been 'surprised and was induced to sign the agreement in ignorance of the value of his property.'

17.3.2 INJUNCTIONS

An injunction restrains the defendant from acting in breach of his negative contractual obligations.

17.3.2.1 Types of injunction

There are several different types of injunction that the court can order. Injunctions can be either mandatory or prohibitory. Prohibitory injunctions apply to future breaches and order a person to refrain from, or to discontinue from, a breach. Mandatory injunctions are ordered against past breaches and require the defendant to undo his wrong. For example, if a person plans to build a house on his land in breach of a restrictive covenant, a prohibitory injunction can be requested to prevent him from proceeding with this course of action. If, however, the house has already been completed the claimant can obtain a mandatory injunction for the demolition of the house.

Injunctions may be either perpetual or interlocutory. A perpetual injunction is granted as a final remedy to protect the claimant's rights after a full hearing of the issue. An interlocutory injunction, on the other hand, is procedural and granted, pending a full hearing to protect the parties' interests from being further prejudiced.

Since injunctions are an equitable remedy they are granted at the discretion of the court. As a rule, the courts will be more willing to grant a prohibitory injunction than a mandatory injunction. This is for a number of reasons. First, a prohibitory injunction normally protects rights that cannot be adequately protected by an award of damages. For example, in *AG v Blake* [2001] 1 AC 268, damages provided inadequate protection to the Crown's right to restrain Blake from divulging information about his work. Second, mandatory injunctions require positive action and are therefore more of an infringement of the defendant's personal liberty. Finally, mandatory injunctions often require constant supervision by the court. For all of these reasons, prohibitory injunctions are generally granted as of course (*Doherty v Allman* (1878) 3 App Cas 709, 720), while mandatory injunctions are entirely at the discretion of the court (*Redland Bricks Ltd v Morris* [1970] AC 652).

17.3.2.2 Injunctions and indirect specific performance

An injunction will generally be refused if its effect is to either directly or indirectly order specific performance of the contract. The reason for this is the judicial concern that injunctions should not be used to compel a party to perform contractual obligations in circumstances where specific performance would not be available. The classic example of such a circumstance is in contracts of employment.

Page One Records Ltd v Britton [1968] 1 WLR 157

Facts: The pop group known as 'The Troggs' employed Page One Records to be their managers. Over time, the group fell out with Page One and sought to appoint new managers. Page One sought an injunction to restrain the group from appointing a new manager.

Held: Stamp J refused to grant the injunction because it would have forced the group to employ Page One as their manager and would have amounted to an indirect enforcement of a contract for personal services.

Stamp J:
'[H]ere the obligations of the first plaintiff, involving personal services, were obligations of trust and confidence and were obligations which, plainly, could not be enforced at the suit of the Troggs. Here, indeed, so it seems to me, the totality of the obligations between the parties are more a joint venture, almost approaching the relationship of

partners than anything else, involving mutual confidence and reciprocal obligations on all sides . . .

[T]he proposition, correctly stated, is, I think, this, that where a contract of personal service contains negative covenants the enforcement of which will amount either to a decree of specific performance of the positive covenants of the contract or to the giving of a decree under which the defendant must either remain idle or perform those positive covenants, the court will not enforce those negative covenants.'

Earlier decisions, however, have shown that the court will grant an injunction to prevent breach of a negative stipulation if it would not amount to compelling the employee to work.

Warner Bros Pictures Inc v Nelson [1937] 1 KB 209

Facts: Bette Davis entered into a contract with Warner Bros which restrained her from working in film or theatre for any other company. In breach of this agreement, Bette Davis agreed to work for another film company in the UK. Warner Bros sought an injunction to prevent her from undertaking this work.

Held: The court granted an injunction on the ground that she was not being compelled to work for Warner Bros because she could have sought other work.

Branson J:

'The case before me is . . . one in which it would be proper to grant an injunction unless to do so would in the circumstances be tantamount to ordering the defendant to perform her contract or remain idle or unless damages would be the more appropriate remedy.

With regard to the first of these considerations, it would, of course, be impossible to grant an injunction covering all the negative covenants in the contract. That would, indeed, force the defendant to perform her contract or remain idle; but this objection is removed by the restricted form in which the injunction is sought. It is confined to forbidding the defendant, without the consent of the plaintiffs, to render any services for or in any motion picture or stage production for any one other than the plaintiffs.

It was also urged that the difference between what the defendant can earn as a film artiste and what she might expect to earn by any other form of activity is so great that she will in effect be driven to perform her contract. That is not the criterion adopted in any of the decided cases. The defendant is stated to be a person of intelligence, capacity and means, and no evidence was adduced to show that, if enjoined from doing the specified acts otherwise than for the plaintiffs, she will not be able to employ herself both usefully and remuneratively in other spheres of activity, though not as remuneratively as in her special line. She will not be driven, although she may be 'tempted, to perform the contract, and the fact that she may be so tempted is no objection to the grant of an injunction . . .'

The decision in *Warner Bros* was technically correct, but practically unrealistic. It would be thoroughly unreasonable to expect Bette Davis to have earned her living through other work. In reality, the practical effect of the injunction was to compel Davis to work for Warner Bros. It is to be hoped that, following *Page One Records*, a more flexible approach will be adopted in the future.

17.4 REMEDIES UNDER THE PRINCIPLES OF EUROPEAN CONTRACT LAW

The approach to contract remedies in the Principles of European Contract Law is found in Chapter 9 of the draft. It states the following:

Section 1: Right to Performance

Article 9:101: Monetary Obligations

(1) The creditor is entitled to recover money which is due.
(2) Where the creditor has not yet performed its obligation and it is clear that the debtor will be unwilling to receive performance, the creditor may nonetheless proceed with its performance and may recover any sum due under the contract unless:
   (a) it could have made a reasonable substitute transaction without significant effort or expense; or
   (b) performance would be unreasonable in the circumstances.

Article 9:102: Non-monetary Obligations

(1) The aggrieved party is entitled to specific performance of an obligation other than one to pay money, including the remedying of a defective performance.
(2) Specific performance cannot, however, be obtained where:
   (a) performance would be unlawful or impossible; or
   (b) performance would cause the debtor unreasonable effort or expense; or
   (c) the performance consists in the provision of services or work of a personal character or depends upon a personal relationship, or
   (d) the aggrieved party may reasonably obtain performance from another source.
(3) The aggrieved party will lose the right to specific performance if it fails to seek it within a reasonable time after it has or ought to have become aware of the non-performance.

Article 9:103: Damages Not Precluded

The fact that a right to performance is excluded under this Section does not preclude a claim for damages.

Section 5: Damages and Interest

Article 9:501: Right to Damages

(1) The aggrieved party is entitled to damages for loss caused by the other party's non-performance which is not excused under Article 8:108.

(2) The loss for which damages are recoverable includes:

(a) non-pecuniary loss; and

(b) future loss which is reasonably likely to occur.

Article 9:502: General Measure of Damages

The general measure of damages is such sum as will put the aggrieved party as nearly as possible into the position in which it would have been if the contract had been duly performed. Such damages cover the loss which the aggrieved party has suffered and the gain of which it has been deprived.

Article 9:503: Foreseeability

The non-performing party is liable only for loss which it foresaw or could reasonably have foreseen at the time of conclusion of the contract as a likely result of its non-performance, unless the non-performance was intentional or grossly negligent.

Article 9:504: Loss Attributable to Aggrieved Party

The non-performing party is not liable for loss suffered by the aggrieved party to the extent that the aggrieved party contributed to the non-performance or its effects.

Article 9:505: Reduction of Loss

(1) The non-performing party is not liable for loss suffered by the aggrieved party to the extent that the aggrieved party could have reduced the loss by taking reasonable steps.

(2) The aggrieved party is entitled to recover any expenses reasonably incurred in attempting to reduce the loss.

Article 9:509: Agreed Payment for Non-performance

(1) Where the contract provides that a party who fails to perform is to pay a specified sum to the aggrieved party for such non-performance, the aggrieved party shall be awarded that sum irrespective of its actual loss.

(2) However, despite any agreement to the contrary the specified sum may be reduced to a reasonable amount where it is grossly excessive in relation to the loss resulting from the non-performance and the other circumstances.

17.4.1 DAMAGES

The right to damages for breach of contract is recognised by Art 9.501, and sub-s 2 specifically states that damages can be recovered for non-pecuniary losses and 'loss of a chance'. Article 9.502 states that the general measure of damages is 'such sum as will put the aggrieved party as nearly as possible into the position in which it would have been if the contract had been duly performed'; this is the 'expectation' measure of 'performance' measure of damages. There is no reference to the 'reliance' measure which suggests that it might not be available under the Principles. Alternatively, as suggested above, the reliance measure may in fact be a form of expectation damages.

Article 9.503 provides a rule of remoteness under the heading 'foreseeability'. The use of 'reasonable foreseeability' rather than 'reasonable contemplation' suggests that the rule may cover a wider range of losses than the English rule. Furthermore, the Principles state that the rule does not apply when the breach was intentional or grossly negligent. These rules import into the general law of contract, rules that usually only apply in the law of tort (see Chapter 9 on misrepresentations). This means that, in a substantial number of cases, no remoteness rule will apply and the defendant will be liable for all the losses directly flowing from the breach of contract.

Contributory negligence is dealt with by Art 9.504. This article provides for a more general principle of contributory negligence than currently available in English law. The claimant's conduct can be taken into account even when it does not amount to actionable negligence. Article 9.505 deals with mitigation and the rules are substantially the same as those in English law. Liquidated damages and penalty clauses are dealt with by Art 9.506. The Principles adopt a much more flexible approach than English law. Instead of striking out clauses that do not represent a 'genuine pre-estimate of loss', the Principles provide that the sum 'may be reduced to a reasonable amount'. The notes to the Article (Lando, O and Beale, H, *The Principles of European Contract Law*, 2000, p 454, Kluwer) suggest that the 'reasonable amount' may exceed the loss sustained, in order to reflect the fact that the parties inserted the clause in order to deter breach.

17.4.2 SPECIFIC PERFORMANCE

In civilian law, specific performance is available as of right as the primary remedy for breach of contract. Some commentators have suggested that English law should follow the same approach.

Schwartz, A, 'The Case for Specific Performance' (1979) 89 YLJ 271, 305–306

The compensation goal of contract law can be achieved by requiring the promisor to pay damages or by requiring the promisor to render the promised performance. Under the current law, a promisee is entitled to a damage award as of right but the court retains discretion to decide whether specific performance should be granted. Because specific performance is a superior method for achieving the compensation goal, promisees should be able to obtain specific performance on request. An expanded specific performance remedy would not generate greater transaction costs than the damage remedy involves, nor would its increased use interfere unduly with the liberty interests of promisors. Making specific performance freely available also would eliminate uncertainty costs of planning and litigation created by the difficulty of predicting whether the remedy will be available. In addition, this reform would reduce the negotiation costs incurred by parties in attempting to create forms of contractual specific performance such as liquidated damage clauses. Further defenses to requests for specific performance that rest on unfairness of contract terms or prices and that differ from the defenses in actions at law should be eliminated; the grounds for denial of specific performance should be the same as those that now will bar a damage suit. Finally, the defense based on difficulty of supervision should be greatly restricted. If the law is committed to putting disappointed promisees in as good a position as they would have been had their promisors performed, specific performance should be available as a matter of course to those promisees who request it.

Professor Schwartz's argument has been criticised by a number of commentators including Professors Kronman ('Specific Performance (1978) 45 Uni Chicago LR 351) and Muris ('The Costs of Freely Granting Specific Performance' [1982] Duke LJ 1053). English law continues to recognise specific performance as the secondary remedy for breach of contract.

Article 9.102 of the Principles attempts to reach a compromise position between the common law and the civil law. Specific performance is dealt with prior to damages in Chapter 9, reflecting the civil law position, and paragraph (1) recognises the existence of a general entitlement to specific performance. This is limited, however, by the list of considerations in paragraphs (2) and (3) which are broadly similar to those limiting the exercise of the discretion to order specific performance in English law. How similar the Principles are to English law really depends on how terms such as 'unreasonable effort or expense' and 'reasonable time' will be interpreted. It is clear that the Principles do not go as far as English law, in that they do not require damages to be inadequate as a prerequisite to an order of specific performance.

▌ADDITIONAL READING

Burrows, A, 'Limitations on compensation', in Burrows, A and Peel, E, (eds), *Commercial Remedies: Current Issues and Problems*, 2003, Oxford: OUP.

Cartwright, J, 'Remoteness of damage in contract and tort: a reconsideration' [1996] CLJ 488.

Chandler, A, and Devenney, J, 'Breach of contract and the expectation deficit: inconvenience and disappointment' (2007) 27 LS 126.

Coote, B, 'The performance interest, *Panatown*, and the problem of loss' (2001) 117 LQR 81.

Cunnington, R, 'A lost opportunity to clarify' (2007) 123 LQR 48.

J Edelman, *Gain-Based Damages*, 2002, Oxford: Hart.

Goetz, R and Scott, R, 'Liquidated damages, penalties and the just compensation principle' (1977) 77 Col LR 554.

Harris, D, 'Specific performance – a regular remedy for consumers' (2003) 119 LQR 541.

Kramer, A, 'An agreement-centred approach to remoteness and contract damages', in Cohen, N, and McKendrick, E (eds), *Comparative Remedies for Breach of Contract*, 2004, Oxford: Hart.

McKendrick, E and Graham, M, 'The sky's the limit: contractual damages for non-pecuniary loss' [2002] LMCLQ 161.

CHAPTER 18

UNJUST ENRICHMENT

CONTENTS	

18.1 INTRODUCTION

The law of unjust enrichment is independent of the law of contract, but nevertheless closely related to it. Indeed, the links between the two sources of obligation are so close that commentators once referred to unjust enrichment as the law of implied contract (*Chitty on Contract*, 20th edn, 1947, London: Sweet & Maxwell) or the law of quasi-contract (Gaius, *Aurea*, Bk 3 D 44.7.5 pr–3). More recently, those labels have been shown to be unhelpful because unjust enrichment is entirely independent of the law of a contract and a claim for unjust enrichment can often arise in the absence of a valid contract.

We have already seen a number of examples of claims for the reversal of an unjust enrichment:

- Chapter 13, a *quantum meruit* claim for work done under an illegal contract (*Mohammed v Alaga* [1999] 3 All ER 699);
- Chapter 15, a claim for the recovery of money paid under a frustrated contract (*Fibrosa Spolka Ackyjna v Fairbairn Lawson Combe Barbour Ltd* [1943] AC 32);
- Chapter 16, a *quantum meruit* claim for work done under a contract discharged by breach (*Sumpter v Hedges* [1898] 1 QB 673).

The need for a body of law structured around the concept of unjust enrichment was recognised by Lord Wright in *Fibrosa Spolka Ackyjna* [1943] AC 32:

'It is clear that any civilised system of law is bound to provide remedies for cases of what has been called unjust enrichment or unjust benefit, that is to prevent a man from retaining the money of or some benefit derived from another which it is against conscience that he should keep. Such remedies in English law are generically different from remedies in contract or in tort, and are now recognized to fall within a third category of the common law which has been called quasi-contract or restitution.'

Lord Wright used the phrase 'unjust enrichment' in a descriptive sense to describe the common situations in which the law requires a defendant to give back a benefit received from the claimant. It was not until 1991 that unjust enrichment was recognised as a substantive principle, giving rise to a claim for restitution (*Lipkin Gorman v Karpnale* [1991] 2 AC 548).

To establish a claim for unjust enrichment, four questions must be answered:

(1) Has the defendant been enriched?
(2) Was the enrichment received at the claimant's expense?
(3) Was the enrichment unjust, that is, does the claim fall within one of the recognised grounds for restitution?
(4) Are there any defences that reduce or deny the claim?

The standard measure of response to a claim for unjust enrichment is an order of restitution – the defendant is required to 'give back' the money, goods or services received. In many cases, restitution of goods or services will take the form of a monetary substitute, a *quantum meruit* in relation to a claim for services or a *quantum valebat* in relation to a claim for the use of goods.

It is important to remember that both the law of unjust enrichment and the law of contract have a role to play in respect of remedying unjust enrichment. This has been helpfully explained by Professor Waddams in the following extract from his book, *Dimensions of Private Law*.

Waddams, S, *Dimensions of Private Law*, 2003, Cambridge: CUP, pp 165–166

To assign unjust enrichment and contracts to separate 'areas' of a conceptual map is to introduce the possibility – indeed the certainty – of conflict between them, and to make it necessary to determine if and when one of them is supplemental, subordinate, secondary or subsidiary to the other, or when they may be combined ... The contractual view of the matter and the unjust enrichment view are aspects of the same question. Another way of putting it is that *prevention* of unjust enrichment cannot be separated from *reversal* of it ...

> ... [T]he concept of unjust enrichment has played an important part – often the principal part – in the resolution of many legal issues that cannot, however, be assigned exclusively to unjust enrichment as a distinct branch or area of law. Prevention of unjust enrichment has been as important as the reversal of it, and the principle has often operated as a defence, rather than as a source of obligations.

As Professor Waddams succinctly notes, the law of contract often acts to *prevent* an unjust enrichment before it takes place, while the law of unjust enrichment operates to *reverse* an unjust enrichment once it has already occurred. It is to this we now turn.

18.2 UNJUST FACTORS

The law has recognised a number of grounds for restitution, which are commonly referred to as unjust factors. These are roughly analogous to the different torts in the law of torts. Here we will examine the two main unjust factors that impact on the law of contract.

18.2.1 FAILURE OF CONSIDERATION

As the label suggests, this ground for restitution entitles the claimant to recover benefits transferred under a consideration that has failed.

The language of consideration is rather misleading, however, since 'consideration' does not mean the same thing in this context as it means in the law of contract. Contractual consideration includes the exchange of promises whereas consideration in the law of unjust enrichment refers to the *performance* of the promise (see *Fibrosa Spolka Akcyjna v Fairbairn Lawson Combe Barbour Ltd* [1943] AC 32). Furthermore, it need not be a contractual performance that has failed. A claimant will be able to recover benefits transferred, subject to a non-contractual condition that has not been fulfilled, or a contemplated state of affairs that has failed to materialise. The label 'failure of consideration' is inapt to cover such situations and therefore the phrase 'failure of basis' is preferable. In the words of Gummow J, this simply means 'the failure to sustain itself of the state of affairs contemplated as a basis for the payment' (*Roxborough v Rothmans* (2001) 185 ALR 335). Despite its misleading emphasis the phrase 'failure of consideration' will continue to be used in this chapter because it is the language adopted by the courts in the majority of the cases.

In the contractual context, there are a number of reasons why the consideration for the payment may fail. We will examine four: frustration, breach, void contracts and contracts that fail to materialise.

18.2.1.1 Contracts discharged by frustration

Prior to the enactment of the Law Reform (Frustrated Contracts) Act 1943, the leading case on restitution following the frustration of a contract was *Fibrosa Spolka Akcyjna v Fairbairn Lawson Combe Barbour Ltd*.

Fibrosa Spolka Akcyjna v Fairbairn Lawson Combe Barbour Ltd [1943] AC 32

Facts: The respondents, an English company, agreed to sell to the appellants, a Polish company, a number of 'flax-hackling machines' for £4,800. The appellants paid £1,000 in advance in accordance with a clause requiring advance payment of one third of the contract price. Prior to delivery of the machines, war broke out between Great Britain and Germany. The appellants claimed that the contract had been frustrated and sought to recover the advance payment of £1,000.

Held: The House of Lords held that the contract had been discharged under the doctrine of frustration. The appellants were entitled to restitution of the £1,000 because there had been a total failure of consideration.

Viscount Simon LC:
'The *locus classicus* for the view which has hitherto prevailed [in the law of frustration] is to be found in the judgment of Collins MR in *Chandler v Wesbter* [1904] 1 KB 493. It was not a considered judgment, but it is hardly necessary to say that I approach this pronouncement of the then Master of the Rolls with all the respect due to so distinguished a common lawyer. When his judgment is studied, however, one cannot but be impressed by the circumstance that he regarded the proposition that money in such cases could not be recovered back as flowing from the decision in *Taylor v Caldwell* 3 B & S 826. *Taylor v Caldwell*, however, was not a case in which any question arose whether money could be recovered back, for there had been no payment in advance, and there is nothing in the judgment of Blackburn J, which, at any rate in terms, affirms the general proposition that "the loss lies where it falls". The application by Collins MR of *Taylor v Caldwell* to the actual problem with which he had to deal in *Chandler v Webster* deserves close examination. He said: "The plaintiff contends that he is entitled to recover the money which he has paid on the ground that there has been a total failure of consideration. He says that the condition on which he paid the money was that the procession should take place, and that, as it did not take place, there has been a total failure of consideration. That contention does no doubt raise a question of some difficulty, and one which has perplexed the courts to a considerable extent in several cases. The principle on which it has been dealt with is that which was applied in *Taylor v Caldwell* – namely, that where, from causes outside the volition of the parties, something which was the basis of, or essential to the fulfilment of, the contract has become impossible, so that, from the time when the fact of that impossibility has been ascertained, the contract can no further be performed by either party, it remains a

perfectly good contract up to that point, and everything previously done in pursuance of it must be treated as rightly done, but the parties are both discharged from further performance of it. If the effect were that the contract were wiped out altogether, no doubt the result would be that money paid under it would have to be repaid as on a failure of consideration. But that is not the effect of the doctrine; it only releases the parties from further performance of the contract. Therefore the doctrine of failure of consideration does not apply."

It appears to me that the reasoning in this crucial passage is open to two criticisms: (a) The claim of a party, who has paid money under a contract, to get the money back, on the ground that the consideration for which he paid it has totally failed, is not based on any provision contained in the contract, but arises because, in the circumstances that have happened, the law gives a remedy in quasi-contract to the party who has not got that for which he bargained. It is a claim to recover money to which the defendant has no further right because in the circumstances that have happened the money must be regarded as received to the plaintiff's use. It is true that the effect of frustration is that, while the contract can no further be performed, "it remains a perfectly good contract up to that point, and everything previously done in pursuance of it must be treated as rightly done", but it by no means follows that the situation existing at the moment of frustration is one which leaves the party that has paid money and has not received the stipulated consideration without any remedy. To claim the return of money paid on the ground of total failure of consideration is not to vary the terms of the contract in any way. The claim arises not because the right to be repaid is one of the stipulated conditions of the contract, but because, in the circumstances that have happened, the law gives the remedy. It is the failure to distinguish between (1) the action of *assumpsit* for money had and received in a case where the consideration has wholly failed, and (2) an action on the contract itself, which explains the mistake which I think has been made in applying English law to this subject-matter ... Once it is realized that the action to recover money for a consideration that has wholly failed rests, not on a contractual bargain between the parties, but, as Lord Sumner said in *Sinclair v Brougham* [1914] AC 398, 452, "upon a notional or imputed promise to repay", or (if it is preferred to omit reference to a fictitious promise) upon an obligation to repay arising from the circumstances, the difficulty in the way of holding that a prepayment made under a contract which has been frustrated can be recovered back appears to me to disappear. (b) There is, no doubt, a distinction between cases in which a contract is "wiped out altogether", eg, because it is void as being illegal from the start or as being due to fraud which the innocent party has elected to treat as avoiding the contract, and cases in which intervening impossibility "only releases the parties from further performance of the contract". But does the distinction between these two classes of case justify the deduction of Collins MR that "the doctrine of failure of consideration does not apply" where the contract remains a perfectly good contract up to the date of frustration? This conclusion seems to be derived from the view that, if the contract remains good and valid up to the moment of frustration, money which has already been paid under it cannot be regarded as having been paid for a consideration which has wholly failed. The party that has paid the money has had the advantage, whatever it may be worth, of the promise of the other party. That is true, but it is necessary to draw a distinction. In English law, an enforceable contract may be formed by an exchange of a promise for a promise, or by the exchange of a promise for an act – I am excluding contracts under seal – and thus, in the law relating to the formation of contract, the promise to do a thing may often be the consideration, but when one is considering the law of failure of consideration and of the quasi-contractual right to recover money on that ground, it is, generally speaking, not the promise which is referred to as the consideration, but the performance of the promise. The money was paid to secure performance and, if performance fails the inducement which brought about the payment is not fulfilled.

If this were not so, there could never be any recovery of money, for failure of consideration, by the payer of the money in return for a promise of future performance, yet there are endless examples which show that money can be recovered, as for a complete failure of consideration, in cases where the promise was given but could not be fulfilled . . .

While this result obviates the harshness with which the previous view in some instances treated the party who had made a prepayment, it cannot be regarded as dealing fairly between the parties in all cases, and must sometimes have the result of leaving the recipient who has to return the money at a grave disadvantage. He may have incurred expenses in connexion with the partial carrying out of the contract which are equivalent, or more than equivalent, to the money which he prudently stipulated should be prepaid, but which he now has to return for reasons which are no fault of his. He may have to repay the money, though he has executed almost the whole of the contractual work, which will be left on his hands. These results follow from the fact that the English common law does not undertake to apportion a prepaid sum in such circumstances . . . It must be for the legislature to decide whether provision should be made for an equitable apportionment of prepaid moneys which have to be returned by the recipient in view of the frustration of the contract in respect of which they were paid. I move that the appeal be allowed, and that judgment be entered for the appellants.'

There are two points to note. First, the House of Lords held that the failure of consideration must be total. If there had been partial performance, that is, the respondent had delivered one of the flax-hackling machines, restitution would have been unavailable. This 'total failure' requirement will be considered in greater detail later in the chapter.

Second, restitution was only available for the money transferred, not for the work done or the benefits conferred. Viscount Simon noted that this could lead to significant hardship where the defendant has used the money to make preparations for performance. For example, had the respondents spent £2,000 on raw materials to be used in the manufacture of the machines, it would have been very harsh to have required them to make restitution of the £1,000 paid in advance by the appellants. Their Lordships recognised the potential for injustice in such situations but said that it was for the legislature to remedy the defect. This remedy was provided one year later when Parliament enacted the Law Reform (Frustrated Contracts) Act 1943 (see Chapter 15).

18.2.1.2 Contracts discharged by breach

An innocent party is entitled to recover restitution of money paid under a consideration that has totally failed following the discharge of a contract by breach. A classic example of this is the case of *Rowland v Divall*.

Rowland v Divall [1923] 2 KB 500

Facts: The plaintiff purchased a motor car from the defendant in May 1992 and resold it in July 1992. Two months later the police seized the car as stolen property. The plaintiff refunded the purchase price to the person who had purchased the car from him and then sought to recover the price he had paid to the defendant on the ground of total failure of consideration.

Held: The Court of Appeal held that the plaintiff was entitled to recover the money.

Bankes LJ:

'Whatever doubt there may have been in former times as to the legal rights of a purchaser in the position of the present plaintiff was settled by the Sale of Goods Act, 1893, by s 12 of which it was provided that: "In a contract of sale, unless the circumstances of the contract are such as to show a different intention, there is (1.) An implied condition on the part of the seller that. . . . he has a right to sell the goods." [Counsel for the defendants] contends that this is a case in which the buyer is compelled to treat the condition as a warranty within the meaning of that section, because, having had the use of the car for four months, he cannot put the seller in status quo and therefore cannot now rescind, and he has referred to several authorities in support of that contention. But when those authorities are looked at I think it will be found that in all of them the buyer got some part of what he contracted for. In *Taylor v Hare* 1 B & P (NR) 260, 262, the question was as to the right of the plaintiff to recover back money which he had paid for the use of a patent which turned out to be void. But there the Court treated the parties, who had made a common mistake about the validity of the patent, as being in the nature of joint adventurers in the benefit of the patent; and Chambre J expressly pointed out that "The plaintiff has had the enjoyment of what he stipulated for." The language there used by Heath J, though it may have been correct as applied to the facts of that case, is much too wide to be applied to such a case as the present. In *Hunt v Silk* 5 East, 449, 452, Lord Ellenborough went upon the ground that the plaintiff had received part of what he bargained for. He said: "Where a contract is to be rescinded at all, it must be rescinded *in toto*, and the parties put in status quo. But here was an intermediate occupation, a part execution of the agreement, which was incapable of being rescinded." And *Lawes v Purser* 6 E & B 930, proceeded on the same ground, that the defendant had derived benefit from the execution of the contract. But in the present case it cannot possibly be said that the plaintiff received any portion of what he had agreed to buy. It is true that a motor car was delivered to him, but the person who sold it to him had no right to sell it, and therefore he did not get what he paid for – namely, a car to which he would have title; and under those circumstances the user of the car by the purchaser seems to me quite immaterial for the purpose of considering whether the condition had been converted into a warranty. In my opinion the plaintiff was entitled to recover the whole of the purchase money, and was not limited to his remedy in damages as the judge below held.'

The Court of Appeal held that the consideration had totally failed because the plaintiff had not received 'any portion of what he had agreed to buy'. In other words, the essence of the contract was the conferral of title and the right to possession, and the plaintiff did not receive this. The same approach was adopted in *Butterworth v Kingsway Motors* [1954] 1 WLR 1286, where a hire-purchaser had use of a car for 11 months.

A different approach is adopted, however, where the innocent party receives good title to the car, but it is so defective as to be unroadworthy.

Yeoman Credit Ltd v Apps [1962] 2 QB 508

Facts: The defendant acquired a car under a hire-purchase agreement with the plaintiffs. Before signing the agreement the defendant had pointed out a number of minor defects to the dealer who promised to have them remedied prior to delivery. The repairs were not carried out and the car was delivered in an unroadworthy and unsafe condition. The defendant made some complaints about the car's condition to the hire-purchase company, but he kept the car and paid the instalments due under the hire-purchase agreement for three months. He then defaulted on payments and the plaintiffs determined the agreement and recovered the car. The plaintiffs brought an action to recover the arrears of rental instalments and damages. The defendant counter-claimed for the £170 he had paid under the hire-purchase agreement on the ground that it was paid under a consideration which had totally failed.

Held: The Court of Appeal held that the defendant could claim damages for breach of the plaintiffs' obligations under the hire-purchase agreement but could not recover any of the instalments he had paid because he could not show that there had been a total failure of consideration.

Holroyd Pearce LJ:

'. . . I accept the finding of the judge on the facts "that the plaintiffs were in breach of a fundamental term of the contract to hire a motor-car suitable for use on the highway and cannot rely on the exemption clause". There was, to use the words of Lord Dunedin, "such a congeries of defects as to destroy the workable character of the machine". I cannot, however, with all respect, agree with the judge that there was a total failure of consideration. The defendant was plainly entitled to reject the car, to accept the plaintiff's repudiation of the contract by their delivery of such a car, and to rescind the contract. Had he done so, there would have been a total failure of consideration, and he would have recovered the sums paid. But, as the judge found, he made no serious effort to return the car. He kept it for five or six months, and approbated the contract by paying three instalments. He intended (to quote his evidence) "to keep the car, and hoped Goodbody would pay half the cost". He tried to find out from the plaintiffs what he could do to make Goodbody carry out the work. In those circumstances he was at that stage continuing with the agreement while protesting against the state of the car which was due to a breach of condition by the plaintiffs. This is not a case like *Rowland v Divall* [1923] 2 KB 500 where title was lacking, and the defendant never had lawful possession. Here the defendant had the possession of the car and its use, such as it was. In evidence he said: "That month I got copy of agreement. I had had the car by that time. I had been able to drive it – very poor". Admittedly the use was of little (if any) value, but in my view that use, coupled with possession, and his continuance of the hiring agreement with the intention of keeping the car and getting Goodbody to pay half the repairs, debars the defendant from saying that there was a total failure of consideration . . .'

The cases are hard to reconcile. Why should a defect of title be treated differently to serious defects of quality? It seems that *Rowland v Divall* was wrongly decided: the Court of Appeal adopted an artificially broad interpretation of the total failure requirement in order to reach an intuitively just result. Perhaps the better approach would have been to recognise the availability of restitution for partial failure of consideration (see below).

An innocent party may also be able to recover restitution for benefits in kind conferred under a contract that has subsequently been discharged by breach.

De Bernardy v Harding (1853) 8 Exch 822

Facts: Following the death of the Duke of Wellington, the defendant undertook to erect seats for the purpose of letting them to people who wished to watch the Duke's funeral procession. He entered into a contract with the plaintiff who agreed to advertise the funeral overseas and to sell tickets for the seats. The plaintiff would receive a 10 per cent commission on all the tickets which he sold. After the plaintiff had spent significant time and money on advertising the funeral, the defendant sought to withdraw from the contract in order to sell the tickets himself. The plaintiff brought a claim for a *quantum meruit* for the work he had done.

Held: The court held that the plaintiff was entitled to bring a claim for a *quantum meruit* and the issue should have been left open to the jury.

Alderson B:
'I also think that it ought to have been left to the jury to say whether the special contract was abandoned. Where one party has absolutely refused to perform, or had rendered himself incapable of performing, his part of the contract, he puts it in the power of the other party either to sue for breach of it, or to rescind the contract and sue on a *quantum meruit* for the work actually done.'

The claim for restitution is founded on an action for unjust enrichment, independent of the contract itself. Because of this, a claim for unjust enrichment can be used to escape the consequences of the innocent party having entered into a 'bad bargain'.

Ebrahim Dawood Ltd v Heath Ltd [1961] 2 Lloyd's Rep 512

Facts: The defendants contracted to supply the plaintiffs with 50 tons of steel sheets of five different sizes. The defendants delivered 50 tons of one size only and the plaintiffs, who had paid in advance, claimed to accept one-fifth of the sheets and reject the remainder. They sought recovery of the money paid in respect of the goods validly rejected.

Held: The High Court held that the plaintiffs could reject four-fifths of the steel supplied and, in respect of the amount rejected, recover their advance payment as money paid for a consideration that had wholly failed.

McNair J:
'The next point is whether the plaintiffs' right to recover the money which they have paid in advance under the letter of credit in respect of four-fifths of the contract weight, which was, in my judgment so far, not delivered in accordance with the contract, stands as a claim to recover the money as money paid to the use of the plaintiffs, or paid for a consideration which has wholly failed. The contrary view is that the remedy only stands in damages, so that if . . . the market price at the time of the delivery conformed to £70 against the contract price of £73 10s, there would be recovered on this argument only £70 per ton and not £73 10s per ton, leaving a profit of £3 10s in the pockets of the seller . . . The buyers' right to recover that part of the purchase price which relates to the goods so properly rejected, is clearly a right . . . to recover money for a consideration which has wholly failed . . .'

McNair J made it clear that the claim for unjust enrichment might entitle the buyer to a higher sum than would have been available in a claim for damages for breach of contract. This is entirely correct. The claim for restitution of money paid under a consideration that has failed is a separate cause of action from breach of contract and there is no reason why recovery should be limited by the contract price. It also seems that an innocent party can escape a bad bargain by making a claim for benefits in kind rendered under a consideration that has subsequently failed, due to breach (see *Lodder v Slowey* [1904] AC 442; *Renard Constructions (ME) Pty Ltd v Minister for Public Works* (1992) 26 NSWLR 234).

A further consequence of the independence of the action for unjust enrichment is that it can entitle a contract breaker to obtain restitution of money paid under a consideration that has totally failed for breach.

Dies v British and International Mining and Finance Corpn [1939] 1 KB 724

Facts: The defendants agreed to sell rifles and ammunition to the plaintiff for £270,000. The plaintiff paid £100,000 in advance, but thereafter, in breach of contract, failed to take delivery of any of the rifles or ammunition and sought restitution of the £100,000.

Held: Stable J allowed the plaintiff's claim.

The approach taken in *Dies* was followed by the Court of Appeal in *Rover International Ltd v Cannon Film Sales Ltd (No 3)* [1989] 1 WLR 912. Of course, the innocent party is still entitled to bring a claim for breach of contract, which will often exceed the amount that can be recovered by the contract breaker under an unjust enrichment claim for total failure of consideration.

In principle, a contract breaker should be entitled to recover restitution for benefits in kind conferred under a contract that has been discharged by breach. In practice, however, a claim will often be denied because the agreement will be construed as an entire contract (see Chapter 16). As a result, the innocent party will not be considered to have been enriched by the contract breaker's goods or services (see *Sumpter v Hedges* [1898] 1 QB 673; *Bolton v Mahadeva* [1972] 1 WLR 1009).

18.2.1.3 Void contracts

Parties to a void contract may recover restitution on the ground of total failure of consideration.

Canons Ltd was enriched because it recei[...] defendant may have been incontrovertibly had not performed those services the co[...] the claimant's expense' in the subtractive other person to carry them out. Comme[...] sis would be equally applicable to where unjust factor was in the case. Some comm[...] ontract although, in accordance with the G, *The Principles of the Law of Restitution*[...] s would probably insist that the failure of The problem with this analysis is that th[...] utionary analysis is an acceptance that the authority to appoint him, appears to h[...] bility should not rule out the independent mistake of fact, and prior to the decision[...] traction. *Ltd v Lincoln City Council* [1999] 2 AC 3[...] for mistake of law. The better analysis is t[...] time to examining the ground of restitu- a total failure of consideration. The plain[...] to materialise. In most cases, however, it been promised by the company in return[...] on the ground of failure of consideration

In most cases where a contract is void[...] re in the expectation that s/he would be on total failure of consideration will fail,[...] ed. illegal transaction. This will not be the c[...] blameworthy as the defendant. In Chapte[...] *Alaga* [2000] 1 WLR 181. Mohammed[...] under an illegal fee-sharing arrangeme[...] ...td v Davis* [1957] 1 WLR 932 Mohammed, he brought a claim for brea[...] claim on the contract failed because t[...] premises rebuilt due to damage inflicted in Mohammed succeeded in a claim based[...] ers, submitted a tender for the work and *tum meruit* for the work actually done. o believe that they would be awarded the of the defendant, the plaintiffs submitted k so that the defendants could make a war

18.2.1.4 Contracts which fail to m[...]

It was noted in Chapter 9 that English la[...] sion. After the plaintiffs had completed this negotiating a contract and therefore a pa[...] ead of proceeding with the reconstruction. tual negotiations without incurring any l[...] ontract. however, a party may incur liability to[...] obtained from the other party during[...] for breach of contract failed because no Burrows suggests that such liability is[...] arties. However, the plaintiffs were entitled consideration. t at the request of the defendant.

Canons Ltd* [1936] 2 KB 403 and continued] etween work done which was to be paid for believed to be in existence, and work done

Burrows, A, *The Law of Restitution*[...] s of a contract which both parties errone- [T]he leading cases can be straightforwar[...] ither case was the work to be done gratuit- ation within unjust enrichment by subtrac[...] m payment was sought requested the work its bargained-for promise (partially or totall[...] se did the parties actually intend to pay for ing the benefit to the defendant. The defe[...] sed contract, or as part of the total price tively established where it has received [...] pected contract was made. In both cases, , the law implied an obligation – and, in this case, I think the law should imply an obligation – to pay a reasonable price for the services which had been obtained. I am, of course, fully aware that in different circumstances it might be held that work was done gratuitously merely in the hope that the building scheme would be carried out and that the person who did the work would obtain the contract. That, I am satisfied, is not the position here. In my judgment, the proper inference from the facts proved in this case is not that this work was done in the hope that this building might possibly be reconstructed and that the plaintiff company might obtain the contract, but that it was done under a mutual belief and understanding that this building was being reconstructed and that the plaintiff company was obtaining the contract.'

The judgment indicates that the case falls squarely within the failure of consideration analysis. The plaintiffs undertook the work on the assumption that they would be able to recover their costs from the profit they would make under the contract, once it was made. This basis for the work failed when the contract failed to materialise. A similar line was taken in *British Steel Corp v Cleveland Bridge & Engineering Co Ltd*.

British Steel Corp v Cleveland Bridge & Engineering Co Ltd [1984] 1 All ER 504

Facts: The plaintiffs tendered for the construction and delivery of a set of cast steel nodes. The defendants sent the plaintiffs a 'letter of intent' in which they indicated that they intended to enter into the contract with the plaintiffs. The defendants then asked the plaintiffs to start work on construction of the nodes. Further negotiations took place over a period of time during which the plaintiff continued to manufacture the nodes. Eventually negotiations broke down because the parties could not agree on a number of major terms, including the price. The defendant refused to make any payment for the nodes that they had received. The plaintiffs brought an action against the defendant for a *quantum valebat* for the value of the nodes.

Held: The High Court held that the plaintiffs were able to recover upon a *quantum valebat*.

Robert Goff J:
'In my judgment, the true analysis of the situation is simply this. Both parties confidently expected a formal contract to eventuate. In these circumstances, to expedite performance under that anticipated contract, one requested the other to commence the contract work, and the other complied with the request. If thereafter, as anticipated, a contract was entered into, the work done as requested will be treated as having been performed under that contract; if, contrary to their expectation, no contract was entered into, then the performance of the work is not referable to any contract the terms of which can be ascertained, and the law simply imposes an obligation

on the party who made the request to pay a reasonable sum for such work as has been done pursuant to that request, such an obligation sounding in quasi contract or, as we now say, in restitution. Consistently with that solution, the party making the request may find himself liable to pay for work which he would not have had to pay for as such if the anticipated contract had come into existence, eg preparatory work which will, if the contract is made, be allowed for in the price of the finished work (cf *William Lacey (Hounslow) Ltd v Davis* [1957] 1 WLR 932).'

A restitutionary claim for work done in anticipation of a contract that fails to materialise will be denied if the work has not enriched the defendant. In *Regalian Properties Ltd v London Docklands Development Corporation* [1995] 1 WLR 212, the plaintiff property developer entered into an agreement with the defendant for the development of part of the docklands area of London. This agreement was expressly made subject to contract. The plaintiff incurred considerable expense in obtaining architect's designs and site investigations. The defendants eventually withdrew from the project because of a fall in property prices. Because no contract had been concluded the plaintiff sought reimbursement of its expenditure in an action for unjust enrichment. The claim failed for two reasons. First, the work had been carried out on a 'subject to contract' basis. Both parties knew that they were entitled to withdraw from the negotiations at any time and therefore the plaintiff had incurred the expenditure at its own risk. Second, the trial judge was not satisfied that the defendant had been enriched by the defendant's work. Ratee J said:

'Regalian contended that the production of designs and obtaining of detailed planning permission for the proposed development did benefit LDDC in that it enhanced the value of the Hermitage sites and also other adjacent land belonging to LDDC. Despite the evidence of Mr Warner, a surveyor called to give expert evidence on behalf of Regalian, I am not satisfied that any such or any other ascertainable benefit accrued to LDDC. LDDC did not own the copyright in the designs. It could not have used them itself or enabled any other developer to do so. More important was the fact that by the time the negotiations between the parties fell through the fall in the residential property market had been such that Regalian was not, and no-one else would have been, interested in buying the land concerned to carry out the sort of development for which designs had been produced.'

18.2.1.5 The total failure requirement

It has frequently been noted that the failure of consideration must be total. This means that a claim will be denied whenever the claimant has received any part of the performance that he bargained for (*Rover International Ltd v Cannon Film Ltd.* [1989] 1 WLR 912, 923 per Kerr LJ). In contracts for the supply of work and materials there will generally be no total failure once work has begun because the courts will view detrimental performance as constituting the consideration bargained for in such contracts (*Stocznia Gdanska SA v Latvia Shipping* [1998] 1 WLR 574, 588 per Lord Goff). The total failure requirement is often justified on the ground that it prevents the subversion of the law of contract by unjust enrichment. However, this argument is unconvincing as explained in the following extract.

Cunnington, R, 'Failure of basis' [2004] LMCLQ 234, 244–247

[T]he case for the total failure requirement is weak and the argument for retention of the requirement due to the primacy of contract is unconvincing. As Professor Birks has pointed out 'total failure' provides a very blunt instrument for protecting the primacy of contract. Its effect is to reduce the number of cases in which a claimant can have restitution for failure of consideration. However, if we are to take the argument for primacy of contract seriously a more drastic response is required. Either there should be an absolute bar to the claim in unjust enrichment whenever the claimant has an alternative cause of action in contract, or, slightly less drastically, there should be a cap placed on the action in unjust enrichment preventing the recovery exceeding the amount which would have been available had the claimant recovered for breach of contract. If we are to take the argument for primacy of contract seriously the 'total failure' requirement provides inadequate protection. Furthermore, the 'total failure' requirement is indefensibly blunt affecting causes of action where there is no action for breach of contract. . . . [F]ailure of basis incorporates both contractual and non-contractual failures of performance. The problem of competition between different measures of recovery does not arise when the action is for non-contractual failure of basis. Thus, as Birks concludes, the core justification for the 'total failure' requirement is unsound – 'it cannot be explained as a vehicle for ensuring the subsidiarity of [unjust enrichment]'.

A second argument advanced in favour of the 'total failure' requirement is the danger of opening the restitution floodgates. It is submitted that this fear is unfounded given the broad array of defences currently available for an action in unjust enrichment, most notably change of position. The floodgates are adequately guarded by these defences and the principled availability of unjust enrichment should not be inhibited. A third argument used to support retaining total failure of consideration is the difficulty that the courts would face with valuing non-monetary benefits. This argument is again unconvincing. Although it is true that claims based on partial failure of consideration would give rise to difficult questions of valuation, the courts have overcome these difficulties in other contexts. For example, the courts have been prepared to engage in the valuation of non-monetary benefits when payment is being assessed on a *quantum meruit* basis for a total failure of consideration. Equity has also shown itself willing to put a value on non-monetary benefits for the purpose of counter-restitution. Finally, in the context of frustrated contracts where the 'total failure' requirement has been abandoned the courts have been forced to value non-monetary benefits.

It is clear that the traditional arguments advanced in favour of the 'total failure' requirement are unsound. However, are there convincing arguments in favour of restitution for partial failure of consideration? It is submitted that there are. Firstly, the unjust factor, failure of basis, applies regardless of whether the failure of consideration is total or partial. The extent of the injustice differs but the fact remains that the defendant has been unjustly enriched at the expense of the claimant.

Secondly, partial failure of consideration provides the best explanation of previously decided cases. There are numerous cases where the 'total failure' requirement has been contorted to achieve a just outcome. For example in *Rowland v Divall* and *Rover International Ltd v Cannon Film Sales Ltd (No 3)* the Court of Appeal held that there had been a total failure of consideration even though goods had passed under the contracts. In the former case Atkin LJ declared that there had been a total failure, despite the buyer having had use of the car for two months, because he had not been given good title to the car. In the latter case, the Court of Appeal held that there had been a total failure even though Rover had received the films from Cannon because Rover had bargained for the 'opportunity to earn a substantial share of the gross receipts'. It is submitted that in both cases the Court of Appeal adopted a strained interpretation of the meaning of total failure. The cases would be better rationalised as examples of partial failure of consideration.

The courts have also manipulated the tool of apportionment to allow the award of restitution on facts that would best be explained as examples of partial failure of consideration . . . Perhaps the most extraordinary example of this was the Court of Appeal's decision in *DO Ferguson & Associates v Sohl*. The defendant contracted with the plaintiff to perform building work. The contract price was £32,194.25. Disputes arose between the parties and the builders left the site having been paid £26,738.75 for work done that was actually worth £22,065. The builders brought proceedings for the balance of the sum owing under the contract. Sohl counter-claimed for damages for the builders' repudiatory breach of contract, and for repayment of any overpayment made to the builders. The Court of Appeal held that Sohl was entitled to be repaid the amount of the overpayment to Ferguson on the basis that the consideration for it had failed. Hirst LJ concluded: '[For] the £4,673 there was indeed a total failure of consideration because £4,673 was paid by the defendant for work that was never done at all.' This use of apportionment to establish a total failure of consideration was extraordinary. The Court of Appeal effectively broke up the consideration pound by pound to enable them to find a total failure of the severed part. Such analysis removes any real distinction between partial and total failure of consideration. Perhaps the judgment of Nourse LJ provides an explanation for this instrumental approach:

'I think that it would be a sorry state of affairs if the defendant was unable to recover that amount. I am quite satisfied that he can. If it is necessary, out of respect for well-established principles in the law of contract and restitution, to base our decision on the proposition that there was a total failure of consideration in regard to the £4,673, so be it. For myself, I would have held that simple common sense was every bit as sure a foundation.'

Although the result achieved appears just it is submitted that the reasoning applied was faulty and can only lead to uncertainty and inconsistency in the future. The courts have clung to the use of apportionment because it enables the court, somewhat fictitiously, to find a total failure of consideration. However, the courts can only make apportionment when the consideration can be clearly broken up . . . On the facts of *DO Ferguson*, the consideration could not be clearly 'broken up'. Building contracts are normally agreed to on the basis of a price for entire performance. If the contract is only half completed it is nonsense to say that the builders deserve half the contract price. Entire contracts cannot be broken up with such ease. Some parts of the contract may be more complex than others, requiring more expensive materials and labour. Thus the first half of the building contract may not be worth more than one quarter of the contract price. Such valuations of part performance are virtually impossible to determine. As such, apportionment of consideration should only be permitted in building contracts if the parties themselves have broken up the contract price. This did not happen on the facts of *DO Ferguson*, and the imposition of a valuation by the Court of Appeal was manifestly wrong.

In practice, apportionment of consideration should be relatively rare because most contracts cannot be clearly 'broken up'.

It is submitted that the law ought to recognise partial failure of consideration (or better still partial failure of basis) as a ground for restitution. Such a proposal received significant judicial support from Lord Goff in *Westdeutsche Landesbank Girozentrale v Islington London Borough Council* [1996] AC 669:

'There has long been a desire among restitution lawyers to escape from the unfortunate effects of the so-called rule that money is only recoverable at common law on the ground of failure of consideration where the failure is total, by reformulating the rule upon a more principled basis; and signs that this will in due course be done are appearing in judgments throughout the common law world, as appropriate cases arise for decision.'

18.2.2 MISTAKE

The claim for money paid under a mistaken belief is a paradigm example of unjust enrichment. All three elements of a claim are present:

1. The unjust factor is the mistake of the payor. The payor's intention to make the payment can be regarded as vitiated by the mistake.

2. The enrichment is the sum of money received by the payee.
3. The enrichment is at the payor's expense because it is subtracted from the payor's assets.

Traditionally, English law distinguished between mistakes of fact and mistakes of law, denying restitution for the latter. As we will see, that restriction no longer applies.

18.2.2.1 Mistake of fact

The traditional rule was that money paid under a mistake of fact would only be recoverable if the mistake was as to liability to make the payment.

Aiken v Short (1856) 1 H & N 210

Facts: The plaintiff bank believed that it had purchased certain mortgaged property from George Carter, subject to a £200 charge in favour of the defendant. The bank paid the defendant £200 to obtain release from the charge. It transpired that George Carter had no title to the property and Short therefore had no charge over the property securing the debt owed to him by Carter. The plaintiff sought to recover back the money as having been paid under a mistake of fact.

Held: The court refused the claim.

Pollock CB:
'The bank had paid the money in one sense without any consideration, but the defendant had a perfect right to receive the money from Carter, and the bankers paid for him. They should have taken care not to have paid over the money to get a valueless security; but the defendant has nothing to do with their mistake. Suppose it was announced that there was to be a dividend on the estate of a trader, and persons to whom he was indebted went to an office and received instalments of the debts due to them, could the party paying recover back the money if it turned out that he was wrong in supposing that he had fund in hand? The money was, in fact, paid by the Bank, as agents for Carter.'

Bramwell B:
'In order to entitle a person to recover back money paid under a mistake of fact, the mistake must be as to a fact which, if true, would make the person liable to pay the money; not where, if true, it would merely make it desirable that he should pay the money. Here if the fact was true, the bankers were at liberty to pay or not, as they pleased. But relying on the belief that the defendant had a valid security, they, having a subsequent legal mortgage, chose to pay off the defendant's charge. It is impossible to say that this case falls within the rule. The mistake of fact was that the Bank thought that they could sell the estate for a better price. It is true that if the plaintiff could

---

recover back this money from the defendant, there would be no difficulty in the way of the defendant suing Carter . . . But that does not shew that plaintiffs can maintain this action, and I am of the opinion they cannot, having voluntarily parted with their money to purchase that which the defendant had to sell, though no doubt it turned out to be different to, and of less value than, what they expected.'

The majority view, expressed by Pollock CB, was that the claim should fail because the plaintiff's payment was made under a valid contract for the discharge of Carter's debt. On this reasoning, the unjust enrichment claim should have been made against Carter, not the defendant. Bramwell B's reasoning was slightly different. He adopted the 'supposed liability' test, holding that the claim should fail because the mistake of fact was not one of supposed liability. This 'supposed liability' restriction was subsequently applied by the courts in *Baylis v Bishop of London* [1913] 1 Ch 127 and *Holt v Markham* [1923] 1 KB 504. In *Larner v LCC* [1949] 2 KB 683, it was extended to include supposed 'moral' liability. Ultimately, however, the test has been rejected in favour of a prima facie test of whether the mistake caused the payment.

Barclays Bank Ltd v WJ Simms, Son and Cooke (Southern) Ltd [1980] QB 677

Facts: A housing association gave a cheque for £24,000 to the defendant building company. On the following day, the association discovered that a receiver had been appointed to call in the defendant's assets. The association telephoned the plaintiff bank and asked them to stop the cheque. The bank's computer was programmed accordingly. On the following day the defendant sought to cash the cheque. The bank clerk overlooked the stop instruction and mistakenly allowed the cheque to be cashed. The bank sought restitution of the £24,000 as money paid under a mistake of fact.

Held: The court held that the money was recoverable because it was caused by the plaintiff's mistake of fact.

Robert Goff J:

'*The principles upon which money is recoverable on the ground that it has been paid under a mistake of fact*
Nearly 40 years ago, Asquith J stated that "it is notoriously difficult to harmonise all the cases dealing with payment of money under a mistake of fact": see *Weld-Blundell v Synott* [1940] 2 KB 107, 112. This is indeed true, and it does not make easy the task of the trial judge, whose duty it is both to search for guiding principles among the authorities, and to pay due regard to those authorities by which he is bound. I have however come to the conclusion that it is possible for me, even in this field, to achieve

both these apparently irreconcilable objectives. The key to the problem lies, in my judgment, in a careful reading of the earliest and most fundamental authorities, and in giving full effect to certain decisions of the House of Lords. It is necessary therefore for me to review the leading authorities.

I shall go straight to [the] early cases, the first of which provided the basis of the modern law on this topic. That is *Kelly v Solari* (1841) 9 M & W 54 ... The case was concerned with a payment made with the intention of discharging a supposed liability of the plaintiff to the defendant. It is no doubt for that reason that the first part of Parke B's statement of principle was directed to such a case; though it is to be observed that, in the context of such a case, Parke B did not place any restriction on the nature of the mistake which would ground recovery. But it would not, in my judgment, be right to infer that Parke B was stating that money paid under a mistake of fact was only recoverable in cases where the plaintiff's mistake led him to believe that he was under a liability to the defendant to pay the money to him. There is nothing to indicate that the first part of his statement of principle was intended so to restrict the right of recovery; indeed later in his judgment he stated the principle of recovery in broader terms, as did Rolfe B, which appears to indicate that it is sufficient to ground recovery that the plaintiff's mistake has caused him to make the payment.

The second of these three cases is *Aiken v Short* (1856) 1 H & N 210 ... It is a crucial fact in the case that, the payment having been authorised by Carter, it was effective to discharge the debt which was in fact owed by Carter to the defendant; the defendant therefore gave consideration for the payment which was, for that reason, irrecoverable. This was the basis of the decision of both Pollock CB and Platt B; it seems likely, from interventions in the argument, that Martin B. (who was absent when judgment was given) would have decided the case on the same basis ...

The case is however remembered principally for an obiter dictum of Bramwell B. He said, at p 215:

> "In order to entitle a person to recover back money paid under a mistake of fact, the mistake must be as to a fact which, if true, would make the person paying liable to pay the money; not where, if true, it would merely make it desirable that he should pay the money."

He recognised that the bankers were under no antecedent obligation to pay the money: they "were at liberty to pay or not, as they pleased": and, "having voluntarily parted with their money to purchase that which the defendant had to sell", they were unable to recover. It appears from the rather fuller report in 25 LJ Ex 321, 324 that Bramwell B did not necessarily regard his statement of principle as comprehensive. But, strictly construed, it appears to restrict the right of recovery more narrowly than did Parke B in *Kelly v Solari*, 9 M & W 54. It purports to exclude recovery in cases where the plaintiff's mistake did not lead him to believe that he was liable to pay the money to the defendant; and it appears in particular to exclude recovery in a case where the plaintiff had paid the money to the defendant in the mistaken belief, not that he was liable to the defendant to pay it, but that he was under an obligation to a third party to pay it to the defendant, even when the payment did not discharge a debt owing to the defendant who therefore gave no consideration for it. Subsequent decisions of the House of Lords show that so restricted a statement of the principle of recovery does not represent the law.

Such are the early cases most frequently cited on this topic. I propose to go next to three cases in the House of Lords, in which the law on this subject was authoritatively established ... The first is *Kleinwort, Sons & Co v Dunlop Rubber Co* (1907) 97 LT 263 ... The main question in the case was whether the appellants could rely upon the defence of change of position; but that plea was conclusively negatived by the answers of the jury at the trial. For present purposes, the interest of the case lies in two matters. First, there was no question of the respondents mistakenly believing that they were under any liability to the appellants to pay the money to them. Second, Lord Loreburn LC stated the principle of recovery in very broad terms. He said, at p 264:

"... it is indisputable that, if money is paid under a mistake of fact and is re-demanded from the person who received it before his position has been altered to his disadvantage, the money must be repaid in whatever character it was received."

The second of these cases is *Kerrison v Glyn, Mills, Currie & Co* (1911) 81 LJKB 465 ... It ... appears that, provided the plaintiff's mistake is "vital" or "material", which I understand to mean that the mistake caused the plaintiff to pay the money, the money is prima facie recoverable; but that if the payment discharged an existing debt owing to the payee (or to a principal on whose behalf the payee is authorised to receive the payment), it is irrecoverable. Such a conclusion is, if I may say so with respect, entirely consistent with the decision in Aiken v Short, 1 H & N 210, though not with the dictum of Bramwell B in that case.

The third decision of the House of Lords to which I must refer is *RE Jones Ltd v Waring and Gillow Ltd* [1926] AC 670 ... I wish to make three comments on the decision of the House of Lords ... First, the House of Lords must have rejected the view, expressed by Pollock MR, that to ground recovery the mistake must have been "as between" payer and payee, in the sense of having been a mistake shared by both parties. Second, it is implicit in the speeches of all their Lordships that it is not a prerequisite of recovery that the plaintiff must have mistakenly believed that he was liable to the defendant to pay the money to him. Third, as I understand their Lordships' speeches, in particular the speech of Viscount Cave L.C. (with which Lord Atkinson agreed) and the speeches of Lord Shaw and Lord Carson, it is sufficient to ground recovery that the plaintiff's mistake should have caused him to pay the money to the payee ...

From this formidable line of authority certain simple principles can, in my judgment, be deduced: (1) If a person pays money to another under a mistake of fact which causes him to make the payment, he is prima facie entitled to recover it as money paid under a mistake of fact. (2) His claim may however fail if (a) the payer intends that the payee shall have the money at all events, whether the fact be true or false, or is deemed in law so to intend; or (b) the payment is made for good consideration, in particular if the money is paid to discharge, and does discharge, a debt owed to the payee (or a principal on whose behalf he is authorised to receive the payment) by the payer or by a third party by whom he is authorised to discharge the debt; or (c) the payee has changed his position in good faith, or is deemed in law to have done so.

Where a bank pays a cheque drawn upon it by a customer of the bank, in what circumstances may the bank recover the payment from the payee on the ground that it was paid under a mistake of fact?

In [some] cases . . . a bank which pays a cheque drawn or purported to be drawn by its customer pays without mandate. A bank does so if, for example, it overlooks or ignores notice of its customer's death, or if it pays a cheque bearing, the forged signature of its customer as drawer, but, more important for present purposes, a bank will pay without mandate if it overlooks or ignores notice of countermand of the customer who has drawn the cheque. In such cases the bank, if it pays the cheque, pays without mandate from its customer; and unless the customer is able to and does ratify the payment, the bank cannot debit the customer's account, nor will its payment be effective to discharge the obligation (if any) of the customer on the cheque, because the bank had no authority to discharge such obligation.

It is against the background of these principles, which were not in dispute before me, that I have to consider the position of a bank which pays a cheque under a mistake of fact. In such a case, the crucial question is, in my judgment, whether the payment was with or without mandate. The two typical situations, which exemplify payment with or without mandate, arise first where the bank pays in the mistaken belief that there are sufficient funds or overdraft facilities to meet the cheque, and second where the bank overlooks notice of countermand given by the customer. In each case, there is a mistake by the bank which causes the bank to make the payment. But in the first case, the effect of the bank's payment is to accept the customer's request for overdraft facilities; the payment is therefore within the bank's mandate, with the result that not only is the bank entitled to have recourse to its customer, but the customer's obligation to the payee is discharged. It follows that the payee has given consideration for the payment; with the consequence that, although the payment has been caused by the bank's mistake, the money is irrecoverable from the payee unless the transaction of payment is itself set aside. Although the bank is unable to recover the money, it has a right of recourse to its customer. In the second case, however, the bank's payment is without mandate. The bank has no recourse to its customer; and the debt of the customer to the payee on the cheque is not discharged. Prima facie, the bank is entitled to recover the money from the payee, unless the payee has changed his position in good faith, or is deemed in law to have done so . . .

Application of the foregoing principles to the present case

In the light of the above principles, it is plain that in the present case the plaintiff bank is entitled to succeed in its claim. First, it is clear that the mistake of the bank, in overlooking the drawer's instruction to stop payment of the cheque, caused the bank to pay the cheque. Second, since the drawer had in fact countermanded payment, the bank was acting without mandate and so the payment was not effective to discharge the drawer's obligation on the cheque; from this it follows that the payee gave no consideration for the payment, and the claim cannot be defeated on that ground. Third, there is no evidence of any actual change of position on the part of either of the defendants or on the part of the National Westminster Bank; and, since notice of dishonour is not required in a case such as this, the payee is not deemed to have changed his position by reason of lapse of time in notifying them of the plaintiff's error and claiming repayment.

I must confess that I am happy to be able to reach the conclusion that the money is recoverable by the plaintiff bank. If the bank had not failed to overlook its customer's instructions, the cheque would have been returned by it marked "Orders not to pay", and there would have followed a perfectly bona fide dispute between the association and the receiver on the question, arising on the terms of the building contract, whether the association was entitled to stop the cheque – which ought to be the real dispute in the case. If the plaintiff bank had been unable to recover the money, not only would that dispute not have been ventilated and resolved on its merits but, in the absence of ratification by the association, the plaintiff bank would have had no recourse to the association. Indeed, if under the terms of the building contract the money had not been due to the defendant company, non-recovery by the plaintiff bank would have meant quite simply a windfall for the preferred creditors of the defendant company at the plaintiff bank's expense. As however I have held that the money is recoverable, the situation is as it should have been; nobody is harmed, and the true dispute between the association and the receiver can be resolved on its merits . . .'

Strictly speaking, it was not necessary for Robert Goff J to reject the 'supposed liability' test because the case could have been decided by simply extending the meaning of supposed liability. On the facts, as it believed them to be, the plaintiff bank thought that it was under a legal obligation to its client to make the payment of £24,000 to the defendant. Robert Goff J did not adopt this rationalisation of the case, however, and preferred to reject the 'supposed liability' test in favour of a 'causation' test. His Lordship found support for such an approach in three decisions of the House of Lords (*Kleinwort, Sons & Co v Dunlop Rubber Co* (1907) 97 LT 263; *Kerrison v Glyn, Mills, Currie & Co* (1911) 81 LJKB 465; *RE Jones Ltd v Waring and Gillow Ltd* [1926] AC 670). Robert Goff J dismissed Bramwell B's judgment in *Aiken v Short* as obiter dicta and no longer binding on the court. The decision in *Barclays Bank v WJ Sims* has since been approved of by the Court of Appeal in *Lloyd's Bank plc v Independent Insurance Co Ltd* [2000] QB 110. The House of Lords accepted a 'causation' test for mistaken payments in *Banque Financière de la Cité v Parc (Battersea) Ltd* [1999] 1 AC 221 and *Kleinwort Benson Ltd v Lincoln City Council* [1999] 2 AC 349.

Robert Goff J was right to reject the 'supposed' liability test because it placed an unprincipled limitation on the availability of restitution for payments made under a mistake of fact. Fears about opening the floodgates to restitutionary claims should have been assuaged by the three qualifications that his Lordship established:

1. Restitution will be denied if the payor intended the payee to benefit in any event.
2. Restitution will be denied if the payment is made for good consideration, for example, for the discharge of a debt.
3. Restitution will be denied if the payee has changed his position in good faith in reliance on the payment.

The judgment in *WJ Simms* both expanded the scope of restitution for mistaken payments and increased the protection available to recipients by introducing three defences to a claim. As we will see, the third defence, change of position, is far and away the most significant. Indeed, it is quite possible that the good consideration defence will be subsumed within the wider defence of change of position (in *Lloyd's Bank plc v Independent Insurance Co Ltd* [2000] QB 110, Waller LJ assumed that the good consideration defence was a form of change of position).

None of the defences applied on the facts of the case. Professor Burrows has suggested that the good consideration defence should have applied because the payment was made to discharge a debt (see Burrows, A, *The Law of Restitution*, 2nd edn, 2003, pp 140–1, Oxford: OUP). However, on the facts of the case, the payment did not discharge the debt because the Association had countermanded the payment, thus withdrawing authority from the bank. This meant that the debt was still outstanding and the defendant could still sue the Association on the debt. On those facts, it was appropriate to allow restitution.

18.2.2.2 Mistake of law

Historically, restitution has not been available for payments made under a mistake of law. In *Bilbie v Lumley* (1802) 2 East 469, Lord Ellenborough CJ said:

'Every man must be taken to be cognisant of the law; otherwise there is no saying to what extent the excuse of ignorance might not be carried. It would be urged in almost every case. In *Lowrie v Bourdieu* Dougl 467, money paid under a mere mistake of law (was endeavoured to be recovered back), and there Buller J observed that *ignorantia juris non excusat.*'

'Ignorance of the law is no excuse'. The mistake of law bar created insuperable difficulties for judges who were faced with the unenviable task of distinguishing between mistakes of fact and mistakes of law. Eventually the mistake of law bar was abolished.

Kleinwort Benson Ltd v Lincoln City Council [1999] 2 AC 349

Facts: The case concerned interest rate swap agreements entered into between the defendant councils and the claimant bank. These were basically financial gambling arrangements whereby one party agreed to pay a fixed rate of interest on a notional sum whilst the other agreed to pay the market rate of interest. In *Hazell v Hammersmith and Fulham London Borough Council* [1992] 2 AC 1, the House of Lords declared that such transactions were *ultra vires* as regards the local authorities and so were null and void. The claimant bank sought restitution of the money it had paid to the defendant and, because of the law relating to limitation periods, it was forced to rely on a claim for mistake.

Held: The House of Lords allowed restitution of the money paid and removed the mistake of law bar.

Lord Goff:

'Issue (1): Whether the present rule, under which in general money is not recoverable in restitution on the ground that it was paid under a mistake of law, should be maintained as part of English law

. . . The main criticisms of the rule are now widely perceived as threefold (see the Law Commission's Consultation Paper No. 120 on Restitution of Payments Made Under a Mistake of Law (1991), paras 2.24–2.26). First, the rule allows the payee to retain a payment which would not have been made to him but for the payer's mistake, whereas justice appears to demand that money so paid should be repaid unless there are special circumstances justifying its retention. Second, the distinction drawn between mistakes of fact (which can ground recovery) and mistakes of law (which cannot) produces results which appear to be capricious. It is usual here to compare the results in *Bilbie v Lumley*, 2 East 469 and *Kelly v Solari*, 9 M & W 54, each concerned with an action by an underwriter to recover back money paid under an insurance policy under a mistake. In the former case, where he did not appreciate that the law enabled him to repudiate a policy for non-disclosure, his action failed; but in the latter, where he forgot that the premium had not been paid and so the policy had lapsed, his action was successful. The same comment can be made of the exceptions and qualifications to which the rule became subject. These are usefully listed in paras 2.5–2.15 of the Law Commission's Report, "Restitution: Mistakes of Law and Ultra Vires Public Authority Receipts and Payments" (1994) (Law Com No 227). They are well-known, and it is unnecessary for me to rehearse them in this opinion. It is however legitimate to comment that, apart from limits such as the recently recognised defence of change of position and an as yet undefined limit in cases in which the payment has been made in settlement of an honest claim, these exceptions and qualifications are heterogeneous and in truth betray an anxiety to escape from the confines of a rule perceived to be capable of injustice; and that, as a result, the law appeared to be arbitrary in its effect. Third, as a result of the difficulty in some cases of drawing the distinction between mistakes of fact and law, and the temptation for judges to manipulate that distinction in order to achieve practical justice in particular cases, the rule became uncertain and unpredictable in its application . . .

For all these reasons, I am satisfied that your Lordships should, if you decide to consider the point yourselves rather than leave it to the Law Commission, hold that the mistake of law rule no longer forms part of English law. I am very conscious that the Law Commission has recommended legislation. But the principal reasons given for this were that it might be some time before the matter came before the House, and that one of the dissentients in the *Woolwich* case (Lord Keith of Kinkel) had expressed the opinion that the mistake of law rule was too deeply embedded to be uprooted judicially: [1993] AC 70, 154. Of these two reasons, the former has not proved to be justified, and the latter does not trouble your Lordships because a more robust view of judicial development of the law is, I understand, taken by members of the appellate committee hearing the present appeals. Moreover, especially in the light of developments in other major common law jurisdictions, not to mention South Africa and Scotland, the case for abrogation is now so strong that the respondents in these appeals have not argued for its retention. In these circumstances I can see no good reason for postponing the matter for legislation, especially when we do not know whether or, if so, when Parliament may legislate. Finally I believe that it would, in all the circumstances, be unjust to deprive the appellant bank of the benefit of the decision of the House on this point. I would therefore conclude on issue (1) that the mistake of law rule should no longer be maintained as part of English law, and that English law should now recognise that there is a general right to recover money paid under a mistake, whether of fact or law, subject to the defences available in the law of restitution.

Issue (1A): Payments made under a settled understanding of the law
I turn now to a central question in these appeals. This relates to the fact that the payments of which recovery is sought in these cases were made under contracts which at the time were understood by all concerned to be valid and binding, so that the payments themselves were believed to be lawfully due under those contracts. This misunderstanding was, of course, removed by the decision of this House in *Hazell's case* [1992] 2 AC 1 that the contracts were beyond the powers of the local authorities involved and so void. The argument now advanced by the authorities is that payments so made on the basis of a settled understanding of the law which is later changed by a judicial decision should not be recoverable on the ground of mistake of law . . .

Historically speaking, the declaratory theory of judicial decisions is to be found in a statement by Sir Matthew Hale over 300 years ago, viz. that the decisions of the courts do not constitute the law properly so called, but are evidence of the law and as such "have a great weight and authority in expounding, declaring, and publishing what the law of this Kingdom is": see *Hale's Common Law of England,* 6th edn (1820), p 90 . . . To the like effect, *Blackstone Commentaries*, 6th edn (1774), pp 88–89, stated that "the decisions of courts are the evidence of what is the common law." In recent times, however, a more realistic approach has been adopted, as in Sir George Jessel MR's celebrated statement that rules of equity, unlike rules of the common law, are not supposed to have been established since time immemorial, but have been invented, altered, improved and refined from time to time: see *In re Hallett's Estate; Knatchbull v Hallett* (1880) 13 Ch D 696, 710 . . . When a judge decides a case which comes before him, he does so on the basis of what he understands the law to be. This he discovers from the applicable statutes, if any, and from precedents drawn from reports of previous judicial decisions . . . It is in this context that we have to reinterpret the declaratory theory of judicial decision. We can see that, in fact, it does not presume the existence of an ideal system of the common law, which the judges from time to time reveal in their decisions. The historical theory of judicial decision, though it may in the past have served its purpose, was indeed a fiction. But it does mean that, when the judges state what the law is, their decisions do, in the sense I have described, have a retrospective effect. That is, I believe, inevitable . . .

It is in the light of the foregoing that I have to ask myself whether the Law Commission's "settled understanding of the law" proposal forms part of the common law. This, as I understand the position, requires that I should consider whether parties in the position of the appellant bank were mistaken when they paid money to local authorities under interest swap agreements which they, like others, understood to be valid but have later been held to be void. To me, it is plain that the money was indeed paid over under a mistake, the mistake being a mistake of law. The payer believed, when he paid the money, that he was bound in law to pay it. He is now told that, on the law as held to be applicable at the date of the payment, he was not bound to pay it. Plainly, therefore, he paid the money under a mistake of law, and accordingly, subject to any applicable defences, he is entitled to recover it . . .

Issue (1B): Honest receipt

This issue arises from a principle proposed by Brennan CJ (then Brennan J) in *David Securities Pty Ltd v Commonwealth Bank of Australia* (1992) 175 CLR 353, 399. It reads:

> "It is a defence to a claim for restitution of money paid or property transferred under a mistake of law that the defendant honestly believed, when he learnt of the payment or transfer, that he was entitled to receive and retain the money or property."

In my opinion, it would be most unwise for the common law, having recognised the right to recover money paid under a mistake of law on the ground of unjust enrichment, immediately to proceed to the recognition of so wide a defence as this which would exclude the right of recovery in a very large proportion of cases. The proper course is surely to identify particular sets of circumstances which, as a matter of principle or policy, may lead to the conclusion that recovery should not be allowed; and in so doing to draw on the experience of the past, looking for guidance in particular from the analogous case of money paid under a mistake of fact, and also drawing upon the accumulated wisdom to be found in the writings of scholars on the law of restitution. However, before so novel and far-reaching defence as the one now proposed can be recognised, a very strong case for it has to be made out; and I can discover no evidence of a need for so wide a defence as this. In particular, experience since the recognition of the right of recovery of money paid under a mistake of law in the common law world does not appear to have revealed any such need.

For these reasons, with all respect to Brennan J, I am unable to accept that the defence proposed by him forms part of the common law.'

The decision in *Kleinwort Benson* followed the removal of the mistake of law bar in Canada (*Air Canada v British Columbia* (1989) 59 DLR (4th) 161) and Australia (*David Securities Pty Ltd v Commonwealth Bank of Australia* (1992) 175 CLR 353), and recommendations for a similar change in this country from the Law Commission (Law Commission, Report No 22, *Restitution: Mistakes of Law and Ultra Vires Public Receipts and Payments*, 1994). Thus the decision came as little surprise.

The House of Lords confirmed that retention of the mistake of law bar would lead to significant injustice and capricious distinctions between mistakes of fact and mistakes of law. On the facts, there had been a mistake of law because the parties had entered into the agreements in the belief that they were *intra vires*. Due to the declaratory and retrospective effect of judicial decisions, that view of the law was never correct (even though the parties could not have discovered this at the time of entering into the agreements).

Their Lordships held that the recipient's honest belief in its entitlement to the money would not in itself constitute a defence to restitution. Lord Goff said that, 'immediately to proceed to the recognition of so wide a defence as this which would exclude the right of recovery in a very large proportion of cases'. Instead, the defence of change of position was sufficient to ensure that the recipient was not unfairly deprived of the money he had received. The House also confirmed that restitution would not be denied merely because the relevant transaction had already been fully performed.

Although *Kleinwort Benson* has opened the door to restitutionary claims for mistake of law, difficulties still exist in relation to how the claims will operate in practice. This is illustrated by the facts of *Nurdin and Peacock plc v DB Ramsden & Co Ltd* [1999] 1 WLR 1249. The defendant landlord leased business premises to the claimant. The defendant increased the rent on the premises even though they were not entitled to do so without undertaking a rent review. The claimant paid the first five instalments at this increased rent under a mistake of fact. It then discovered that the landlord was not permitted to increase the rent without first undertaking a rent review. Nevertheless, the claimant paid five more instalments on the basis of incorrect legal advice to the effect that they could automatically recover the payments if proceedings being taken against the defendant were successful.

Neuberger J held that all 10 overpayments were recoverable. The first five payments were straightforward because they were made under a mistake of fact or law. The latter five payments were much more complicated, however, because the mistake of law (that the payments could be recovered if the proceedings against the defendant were successful) would no longer be a mistake of law if the proceedings were indeed successful, which would be the consequence of finding a mistake of law. The argument is clearly circular and for this reason Neuberger J purported to 'cut the vicious circle' by holding that restitution was available for a mistake of law as to the recoverability of a payment. He said:

> 'It may also be said that my conclusion involves wrong advice turning out to be right, a logical paradox of the type illustrated by the fictional Cretan who said that all Cretans were liars. That is on the basis that the advice to Nurdin was that the overpayments were recoverable, the advice was wrong, Nurdin followed that advice, therefore Nurdin paid under a mistake of law, therefore the advice was right; therefore, no mistake was made . . . The trouble with this argument is that it appears to me to amount to a classic vicious circle, because, if one follows the last step in the argument, the overpayment is not repayable, in which case the advice given to Nurdin, upon which it relied, was wrong, in which case the overpayment was made pursuant to a mistake. In my judgment, at least following the decision in the *Kleinwort Benson* case, and in light of the factors I have already discussed, it seems to me that the right point at which to cut the vicious circle is at the point where one concludes that Nurdin made the . . . overpayment under a mistake of law. In other words, while I accept that the particular nature of the mistake in the present case does present an unusual logical problem in relation to the payer's claim for repayment, I do not think that it should stand in the way of the conclusion I have reached.'

In summary, over the past three decades, English law has adopted an increasingly expansive approach towards restitutionary liability for mistaken payments. Restitution is now available whenever a person pays money to another under a mistake of fact or law that causes him to make the payment. This expansive view of liability has been counterbalanced by an increasing emphasis on the availability of defences, in particular the defence of change of position. It is to this that we now turn.

18.3 DEFENCES

In the introduction to this chapter we noted that there are four questions that need to be answered in order to establish whether a claim for unjust enrichment has been made out. The fourth question is: 'Are there any defences that reduce or deny the claim?' As the grounds for restitution have been expanded the need for effective defences to maintain security of receipt and deter excessive restitution has grown. The most important defence to a claim for unjust enrichment is the defence of change of position.

18.3.1 CHANGE OF POSITION

If you mistakenly paid me £5,000, believing me to be your father, would it be just to require me to make restitution of the £5,000? Undoubtedly, the answer is 'yes'. The money was paid under a mistake of fact. Suppose I received the £5,000 in good faith, believing it to be a birthday present from you. Because I have enough money I decide to give it away to charity. Would it be just to require me to make restitution now, even though the money is no longer in my possession? Such a situation is an example of change of position. The defence was recognised by the House of Lords in *Lipkin Gorman v Karpnale Ltd*.

Lipkin Gorman v Karpnale Ltd [1991] 2 AC 548

Facts: Cass was a partner in the plaintiff firm of solicitors and was one of the signatorys on the firm's client account at Lloyds Bank. He was a compulsive gambler, and unbeknown to the other partners he used money from the firm's client account to pay for his gambling debts at the Playboy Club. In total, Cass spent £220,000 from the firm's client account on gambling at the Playboy Club. The Playboy Club only retained £150,000 of this sum because the rest had been paid out to Cass in winnings on the bets he had placed. The plaintiff sought restitution of the money that had been transferred to the club from the firm's client account.

Held: The House of Lords held that the defendants were liable to make restitution of £150,000. Restitution of the full £220,000 was not required because the defendants had a defence of change of position in respect of the money paid out in winnings.

Lord Goff:
'Whether change of position is, or should be, recognised as a defence to claims in restitution is a subject which has been much debated in the books. It is however a matter on which there is a remarkable unanimity of view, the consensus being to the effect that such a defence should be recognised in English law. I myself am under no doubt that this is right.

Historically, despite broad statements of Lord Mansfield to the effect that an action for money had and received will only lie where it is inequitable for the defendant to retain the money (see in particular *Moses v Macferlan* (1760) 2 Burr. 1005), the defence has received at most only partial recognition in English law. I refer to two groups of cases which can arguably be said to rest upon change of position: (1) where an agent can defeat a claim to restitution on the ground that, before learning of the plaintiff's claim, he has paid the money over to his principal or otherwise altered his position in relation to his principal on the faith of the payment; and (2) certain cases concerned with bills of exchange, in which money paid under forged bills has been held irrecoverable on grounds which may, on one possible view, be rationalised in terms of change of position: see, e g *Price v Neal* (1762) 3 Burr 1355, and *London and River Plate Bank Ltd v Bank of Liverpool* [1896] 1 QB 7. There has however been no general recognition of any defence of change of position as such; indeed any such defence is inconsistent with the decisions of the Exchequer Division in *Durrant v Ecclesiastical Commissioners for England and Wales* (1880) 6 QBD 234, and of the Court of Appeal in *Baylis v Bishop of London* [1913] 1 Ch 127. Instead, where change of position has been relied upon by the defendant, it has been usual to approach the problem as one of estoppel: see, e.g. *RE Jones Ltd v Waring and Gillow Ltd* [1926] AC 670 and *Avon County Council v Howlett* [1983] 1 WLR 605 . . .

In these circumstances, it is right that we should ask ourselves: why do we feel that it would be unjust to allow restitution in cases such as these? The answer must be that, where an innocent defendant's position is so changed that he will suffer an injustice if called upon to repay or to repay in full, the injustice of requiring him so to repay outweighs the injustice of denying the plaintiff restitution. If the plaintiff pays money to the defendant under a mistake of fact, and the defendant then, acting in good faith, pays the money or part of it to charity, it is unjust to require the defendant to make restitution to the extent that he has so changed his position. Likewise, on facts such as those in the present case, if a thief steals my money and pays it to a third party who gives it away to charity, that third party should have a good defence to an action for money had and received. In other words, bona fide change of position should of itself be a good defence in such cases as these. The principle is widely recognised throughout the common law world. It is recognised in the United States of America (see American Law Institute, Restatement of the Law, Restitution (1937), section 142, pp 567–578 and *Palmer, The Law of Restitution* (1978), vol III, para 16.8); it has been judicially recognised by the Supreme Court of Canada (see *Rural Municipality of Storthoaks v Mobil Oil Canada Ltd* (1975) 55 DLR(3d) 1); it has been introduced by statute in New Zealand (Judicature Act 1908, section 94B (as amended)), and in Western Australia (see Western Australia Law Reform (Property, Perpetuities and Succession) Act 1962, section 24, and Western Australia Trustee Act 1962, section 65(8)), and it has been judicially recognised by the Supreme Court of Victoria: see *Bank of New South Walkes v Murphett* [1983] 1 VR 489. In the important case of *Australia and New Zealand Banking Group Ltd v Westpac Banking Corporation* (1988) 78 ALR 157, there are strong indications that the High Court of Australia may be moving towards the same destination (see especially at pp 162 and 168, *per curiam*). The time for its recognition in this country is, in my opinion, long overdue.

I am most anxious that, in recognising this defence to actions of restitution, nothing should be said at this stage to inhibit the development of the defence on a case by case basis, in the usual way. It is, of course, plain that the defence is not open to one who has changed his position in bad faith, as where the defendant has paid away the money with knowledge of the facts entitling the plaintiff to restitution; and it is commonly accepted that the defence should not be open to a wrongdoer. These are matters which can, in due course, be considered in depth in cases where they arise for consideration. They do not arise in the present case. Here there is no doubt that the respondents have acted in good faith throughout, and the action is not founded upon any wrongdoing of the respondents. It is not however appropriate in the present case to attempt to identify all those actions in restitution to which change of position may be a defence. A prominent example will, no doubt, be found in those cases where the plaintiff is seeking repayment of money paid under a mistake of fact; but I can see no reason why the defence should not also be available in principle in a case such as the present, where the plaintiff's money has been paid by a thief to an innocent donee, and the plaintiff then seeks repayment from the donee in an action for money had and received. At present I do not wish to state the principle any less broadly than this: that the defence is available to a person whose position has so changed that it would be inequitable in all the circumstances to require him to make restitution, or alternatively to make restitution in full. I wish to stress however that the mere fact that the defendant has spent the money, in whole or in part, does not of itself render it inequitable that he should be called upon to repay, because the expenditure might in any event have been incurred by him in the ordinary course of things. I fear that the mistaken assumption that mere expenditure of money may be regarded as amounting to a change of position for present purposes has led in the past to opposition by some to recognition of a defence which in fact is likely to be available only on comparatively rare occasions. In this connection I have particularly in mind the speech of Lord Simonds in *Ministry of Health v Simpson* [1951] AC 251, 276.'

Lipkin Gorman v Karpnale is a difficult case because it is rather doubtful that it actually involved an unjust enrichment claim. The House of Lords failed to identify the unjust factor (most commentators speculatively suggest 'ignorance') and the benefit was conferred on the defendant by a third party (Cass) rather than by the plaintiffs (the solicitors). Thus two of the four factors ('unjust factor' and 'at the expense of') required for an unjust enrichment claim were not present. Nevertheless, the case is generally regarded as the landmark decision in which the House of Lords first recognised unjust enrichment as a claim and change of position as a defence.

Lord Goff was reluctant to be too specific about the circumstances in which the defence could be established. This was because he did not wish to inhibit its development. His Lordship did confirm that the defence would not be available where the defendant has changed his position in bad faith. Thus, if the defendant spent a mistaken payment on champagne and caviar in the hope of pleading change of position as a defence, he would be unsuccessful. Lord Goff acknowledged that the defence would most frequently arise in cases of mistaken payments, but said that there was no reason to limit the defence to just those cases. This has been followed in *Goss v Chilcott* [1996] AC 788, where the Privy Council accepted that change of position could be available in a claim for total failure of consideration. Lord Goff also noted that the expenses incurred by the defendant must be extraordinary. By this he meant that the defendant would not otherwise have incurred those expenses. Thus if the mistaken payment was spent on necessary groceries, the defence would not be available.

In the years since *Lipkin Gorman* was decided, two main versions of the defence have been suggested. The narrow version insists that change of position is only available where the expenditure has been incurred in reliance on the receipt. Thus the defence is available where the defendant spends the money on a round-the-world trip, but not where he has it stolen by a pickpocket. The broad version of the defence does not require detrimental reliance. Instead it allows the defence whenever the defendant has changed his position, consequent on receipt of the money, in such a way that it would be inequitable to require him to make restitution. Although this version of the defence does not require detrimental reliance, it does require causation. Thus the fact that the recipient has suffered some misfortune is not a defence unless the misfortune is causally linked to the mistaken receipt. The broad view of the defence has received significant judicial support from the Court of Appeal in *Scottish Equitable v Derby* [2001] 3 All ER 818 and the New Zealand Court of Appeal in *National Bank of New Zealand Ltd v Waitaki International Processing (NI) Ltd* [1999] 2 NZLR 211. It is submitted that acceptance of the broad defence is to be welcomed because it provides much needed protection to the security of receipt in an age of expanding liability for unjust enrichment. The defence of change of position has played a key role in the development of liability for unjust enrichment and it is certain to play a key role in its future.

18.4 ADDITIONAL READING

Birks, P, *Introduction to the Law of Restitution*, 1989, Oxford: Clarendon Press.

Birks, P, *Unjust Enrichment*, 2nd edn, 2005, Oxford: Clarendon Press.

Birks, P, 'Failure of consideration', in Rose, F (ed), *Consenus Ad Idem*, 1996, London: Sweet & Maxwell.

Burrows, A, *The Law of Restitution*, 2nd edn, 2003, Oxford: OUP.

Burrows, A, McKendrick, E and Edelman, J, *Cases and Materials on the Law of Restitution*, 2007, Oxford: OUP.

Goff, R and Jones, G, *The Law of Restitution*, 6th edn, 2002, London: Sweet & Maxwell.

McKendrick, E, 'Total failure of consideration and counter-restitution: two issues or one?', in Birks, P (ed), *Laundering and Tracing*, 1995, Oxford: OUP.

Virgo, G, *The Principles of the Law of Restitution*, 2nd edn, 2006, Oxford: OUP.

INDEX